# The Best Books for
# Academic Libraries

# The Best Books for Academic Libraries
## 10 Volumes (ISBN 0-7222-0010-2)

**Volume 1 — Science, Technology, and Agriculture**
**(ISBN 0-7222-0011-0)**
Q        Science
S        Agriculture
T        Technology, Engineering

**Volume 2 — Medicine**
**(ISBN 0-7222-0012-9)**
BF       Psychology
R        Medicine
RM-RS    Therapeutics
RT       Nursing

**Volume 3 — Language and Literature**
**(ISBN 0-7222-0013-7)**
P        Language and Literature
PA       Classical Language and Literature
PB-PH    Modern European Languages and Slavic
         Languages and Literature
PJ-PL    Oriental Language and Literature
PN       Literature: General and Comparative
PQ       Romance Literatures
PR       English Literature
PS       American Literature
PT       German, Dutch and Scandinavian Literature
PZ       Juvenile Literature

**Volume 4 — History of the Americas**
**(ISBN 0-7222-0014-5)**
E          America
E151-E970  United States
F1-975     US Local History
F1001-3799 Canada, Latin America

**Volume 5 — World History**
**(ISBN 0-7222-0015-3)**
C        Auxiliary Sciences of History
D        History

**Volume 6 — Social Sciences**
**(ISBN 0-7222-0016-1)**
G-GF     Geography, Oceanography, Human Ecology
GN       Anthropology, Ethnology, Archaeology
GR-GT    Folklore, Customs, Costumes
GV       Recreation, Physical Training, Sports
H-HA     Social Sciences. General Statistics
HB-HJ    Economics, Population
HM-HV    Sociology, Social History, Social Pathology
HX       Socialism, Communism, Anarchism

**Volume 7 — Political Science, Law, Education**
**(ISBN 0-7222-0017-X)**
J        Political Science
L        Education
K        Law

**Volume 8 — Religion and Philosophy**
**(ISBN 0-7222-0018-8)**
B-BJ     Philosophy
BL-BX    Religion

**Volume 9 — Music & Fine Arts**
**(ISBN 0-7222-0019-6)**
ML, MT   Music
N-NX     Fine Arts

**Volume 10 — General Works, Military & Naval,**
**Library Science Author Index, Title Index,**
**Subject Guide**
**(ISBN 0-7222-0020-X)**
A        General Works
U        Military Science
V        Naval Science
Z        Bibliography, Library Science Author and
         Title Indexes Subject Guide

# The Best Books for Academic Libraries

## Science, Technology & Agriculture

### Volume 1

First Edition

**The Best Books, Inc.**
P. O. Box 893520
Temecula, CA. 92589-3520

```
        Library of Congress Cataloging-in-Publication Data


The best books for academic libraries.-- 1st ed.
        v. cm.
Includes indexes.
Contents: v. 1. Science, technology, and agriculture -- v. 2. Medicine
-- v. 3. Language and literature -- v. 4. History of the Americas -- v.
5. World history -- v. 6. Social sciences -- v. 7. Political science,
law, education -- v. 8. Religion and philosophy -- v. 9. Music & fine
arts -- v. 10. General works, military & naval, library science.
   ISBN 0-7222-0010-2 (set : alk. paper) -- ISBN 0-7222-0011-0 (v. 1 :
alk. paper) -- ISBN 0-7222-0012-9 (v. 2 : alk. paper) -- ISBN 0-7222-
0013-7 (v. 3 : alk. paper) -- ISBN 0-7222-0014-5 (v. 4 : alk.
paper) -- ISBN 0-7222-0015-3 (v. 5 : alk. paper) -- ISBN 0-7222-0016-1
(v. 6 : alk. paper) -- ISBN 0-7222-0017-X (v. 7 : alk. paper) -- ISBN
0-7222-0018-8 (v. 8 : alk. paper) -- ISBN 0-7222-0019-6 (v. 9 : alk.
paper) -- ISBN 0-7222-0020-X (v. 10 : alk. paper)
   1. Academic libraries--United States--Book lists.  I. Best Books,
Inc.

Z1035 .B545 2002
011'.67--dc21   2002013790
```

For further information, contact:

**The Best Books, Inc.**
P.O. Box 893520
Temecula, CA 92589-3520
(Voice) 888-265-3531
(Fax) 888-265-3540

For product information/customer service, e-mail: customerservice@thebbooks.net

Visit our Web site: www.bestbooksfor.com

# Table of Contents

# Introduction

**ABOUT THE PROJECT:**

*The Best Books for Academic Libraries* was created to fill a need that has been growing in collection development for College and Academic Libraries since the late 1980s. Our editorial department organized *The Best Books* database (designed as a resource for University Libraries) by consulting the leading book review journals, bibliographies, and reference books with subject bibliographies.

**PROCESSES FOR SUBJECT SELECTION AND COMPILATION:**

To create *The Best Books for Academic Libraries*, the Editor conducted a comprehensive search of prominent Subject Librarians, experts in their area(s), to recommend the best books for undergraduate institutions. The editorial processes utilized by The Best Books editorial staff are as follows:

1. Subject Librarians and Subject Specialists were invited to participate in selecting the best books to recommend for Undergraduate libraries. Those who volunteered selected approximately one-third from over 170,000 books in our cumulative *The Best Books* database. These advisors made their recommendations from a complete list, organized by Library of Congress (LC) Classification Number. They identified approximately one-third of the books that they felt were essential to undergraduate work in their area(s) of expertise. They added their choices of titles that they felt were omitted from the surveys, and updated titles to the newest editions.

2. The Best Books' editorial staff tabulated the returned surveys and added the omissions into the database to arrive at a consensus of approximately the best 60,000 books to include in the cumulative surveys.

3. Senior Subject Advisors conducted a final review from the surveys and determined which books to add or delete from those lists. Senior Subject Advisors added any omitted titles they felt were essential to undergraduate work in their area(s) of expertise, and returned them to The Best Books editorial staff.

4. The final surveys were then tabulated and final omissions were added to create this First Edition of the 10 Volume set – *The Best Books for Academic Libraries*.

*The Best Books* database was compiled based upon the LC MARC records, which were used as the bibliographic standard for this work. Each section was organized based upon LC Classification, and their selected areas were given to the Subject Advisor(s) for their review. The actual title selection was left to the Subject Advisors. Each advisor used the bibliographic resources available to them in their subject areas to make the best possible recommendations for undergraduate institutions. Any titles that were deemed "omitted" from *The Best Books* database were added to the database, following the LC MARC record standard. When there was a discrepancy in the LC sorting and/or the description of the "omitted" titles by the Advisors, The Best Books editorial staff defaulted to the information available on the LC MARC records.

The intention of The Best Books editorial staff was to include only books in this listing. However, other titles were included, based on recommendations by Subject Advisors and Senior Subject Advisors. In some cases, Advisors did select annual reviews and multi-volume sets for inclusion in this work.

The editorial department has made every attempt to list the most recent publications in this work. In the interest of maintaining a current core-collection list, wherever possible, our Advisors were asked to note the most recent publications available, especially with regards to series and publishers that regularly produce new editions. Books were listed as the original edition (or latest reprint) when no information of a recent publication was available.

## ERRORS, LACUNAE, AND OMISSIONS:

The Subject Advisors and Senior Subject Advisors were the sole source for recommending titles in the completed work, and no titles were intentionally added or omitted other than those that the Subject Advisors and Senior Subject Advisors recommended. There is no expressed or implied warranty or guarantee on this product.

The Best Books' editorial department requests that any suggestions or errors be sent, via e-mail or regular mail, to be corrected in future editions of this project.


## BEST BOOKS EDITORIAL STAFF:

This work is the product of the group effort of a number of enthusiastic individuals: The Best Books editorial staff includes: Annette Wiles, Lee Anne Kawaguchi; Database Administrator, Richelle Tague; and Editor, Ashley Ludwig.

## CONTRIBUTING ADVISORS:

This volume would not be possible without the dedicated work of our Subject Advisors and Senior Subject Advisors who donated their time, resources and knowledge towards creating this Best Books list. To them, we are truly grateful.

## SUBJECT ADVISORS:

**Robert Behlke,** *Librarian, Ella McIntire Library, SiTanka/Huron University*
    QB - Astronomy

**Simone E. Blake,** *Technical Services Librarian, Fitchburg State College*
    QE – Geology; TR – Photography

**Kelly Blessinger,** *Reference Librarian, Louisiana State University*
    QE – Geology

**Marianne Bracke,** *Reference Librarian, University of Arizona*
    S – Agriculture; TX – Home Economics

**Kathleen M. H. Brady,** *Director, Tampa Technical Institute Library*
    Q – Science (General); QA – Mathematics; QC – Physics; TC – Hydraulic Engineering; TK – Electrical
    Engineering, Electronics, Nuclear Engineering; TT – Handicrafts, Arts and Crafts; TX – Home Economics

**Lori Bronars,** *Science Reference Librarian, Kline Science Library, Yale University*
    QH – Natural History, Biology (General); QK – Botany; QL – Zoology

**Angela Camack,** *Assistant Professor / Librarian, Sussex County Community College*
    QM – Human Anatomy; TT – Handicrafts, Arts and Crafts

**Nancy F. Carter,** *Head, Oliver C. Lester Library of Mathematics and Physics, University of Colorado*
    QA – Mathematics; QB – Astronomy; QC – Physics

**Kathryn Cline,** *Reference Librarian, Embry, Riddle Aeronautical University - Library*
    QK – Botany; TA – Engineering, Civil, Engineering (General); TL – Motor Vehicles, Aeronautics, Astronautics

**Wendy Culotta,** *Biological Sciences/Chemistry Librarian, California State University, Long Beach,*
    QD – Chemistry; QK – Botany; QL – Zoology; QM – Human Anatomy; QP – Physiology; QR - Microbiology

**Aimee de Chambeau,** *Subject Bibliographer, Science & Technology Library, University of Akron*
    Q – Science (General); QA – Mathematics; QE - Geology

**Betty Galbraith,** *Head of Collection Development, Owen Science & Engineering Library, Washington State University
    Library*
    QE – Geology

**Jeremy Garritano,** *Science Reference/Liaison Librarian, George Mason University*
    QD – Chemistry; QH – Natural History, Biology (General); QK – Botany; TP – Chemical Technology

**Kebede Gessesse,** *Head, Biological & Environmental Sciences Library, Duke University*
    QE – Geology, QK – Botany

**Cindy A. Gillham,** *Reference Department, University of Detroit Mercy*
    QH – Natural History, Biology (General); QK - Botany

**Elizabeth A. Ginno,** *Librarian, California State University – Hayward*
    T – Technology (General)

**Katalin Harkanyi,** *Technical Librarian, Science Library, San Diego State University*
     QD – Chemistry; TA – Engineering, Civil Engineering (General); TC – Hydraulic Engineering;
     TD – Environmental Technology, Sanitary Engineering; TE – Highway Engineering, Roads and Pavements;
     TF – Railroad Engineering and Operation; TG – Bridge Engineering; TH – Building Construction;
     TJ – Mechanical Engineering and Machinery; TK – Electrical Engineering, Electronics, Nuclear Engineering

**Robert Heyer-Gray,** *Engineering Librarian, Physical Sciences & Engineering Library, University of California, Davis*
     T – Technology (General); TA – Engineering, Civil Engineering (General); TE – Highway Engineering, Roads
     and Pavements; TF – Railroad Engineering and Operation; TG – Bridge Engineering; TH – Building
     Construction; TJ – Mechanical Engineering and Machinery; TK – Electrical Engineering, Electronics, Nuclear
     Engineering; TL – Motor Vehicles, Aeronautics, Astronautics; TN – Mining Engineering, Metallurgy;
     TP – Chemical Technology; TS - Manufactures

**Deborah Huerta,** *Science Librarian, Colgate University*
     SF – Animal Culture

**Elaine F. Jurries,** *Bibliographer for Science and Engineering, University of Colorado – Denver*
     QH – Natural History, Biology (General); QK – Botany; QL – Zoology; QM – Human Anatomy;
     QP – Physiology; QR – Microbiology

**Paul Kelsey,** *Reference Librarian, The LSU Libraries, Louisiana State University*
     SD – Forestry

**Pat Lacourse,** *Engineering and Science Librarian, Scholes Library, Alfred University*
     TP – Chemical Technology

**Mary L. Larsgaard,** *Assistant Head, Map and Imagery Laboratory, Davidson Library, University of California, Santa Barbara*
     QE – Geology; TN – Mining Engineering, Metallurgy

**Deborah Lee,** *Associate Professor, Reference Librarian, Mississippi State University, Mitchell Memorial Library*
     Q – Science (General); QA – Mathematics; QB – Astronomy; QC – Physics; TR – Photography;
     TS – Manufactures; TT – Handicrafts, Arts and Crafts; TX – Home Economics

**Liz Lucke,** *Librarian, United States Geological Survey*
     SD – Forestry

**Theodore Mack,** *Reference Librarian, Paul Smith's College, Joan Weill Library*
     QH – Natural History, Biology (General); SD – Forestry

**Barbara M. Macke,** *Reference Librarian, Swedenborg Memorial Library, Urbana University*
     TT – Handicrafts, Arts and Crafts

**Marlene Metzgar,** *Librarian, Kaplan College*
     QM – Human Anatomy

**Joan Omoruyi,** *Librarian, Northern University*
     Q – Science (General); T – Technology (General)

**Joan G. Packer,** *Head, Reference Department, Central Connecticut State University*
     Q – Science (General); QH – Natural History, Biology (General); QK – Botany; SB – Plant Culture

**Lorraine J. Pellack**, *Head, Science and Technology Dept., Iowa State University of Science and Technology*
QD – Chemistry; QE – Geology; QH – Natural History, Biology (General); QK – Botany; QL – Zoology; QR – Microbiology; S – Agriculture; SD – Forestry; TA – Engineering, Civil Engineering (General); TC – Hydraulic Engineering; TD – Environmental Technology, Sanitary Engineering; TE – Highway Engineering, Roads and Pavements; TF – Railroad Engineering and Operation; TG – Bridge Engineering; TH – Building Construction; TJ – Mechanical Engineering and Machinery; TK – Electrical Engineering, Electronics, Nuclear Engineering; TL – Motor Vehicles, Aeronautics, Astronautics; TN – Mining Engineering, Metallurgy; TP – Chemical Technology; TS – Manufactures; TX – Home Economics

**Charles Rhine**, *Reference Librarian, University of Northern Colorado*
Q – Science (General); QA – Mathematics; QB – Astronomy; QC – Physics; QD – Chemistry; TR - Photography

**Arlieda Ries**, *Science Librarian and Bibliographer, Miami University*
Q – Science (General); QB – Astronomy; QD – Chemistry; TS – Manufactures

**Elyse Rukkila**, *Librarian, AMEC Earth & Environmental Technical Library*
QE – Geology; TA – Engineering, Civil Engineering (General); TC – Hydraulic Engineering; TD – Environmental Technology, Sanitary Engineering; TE – Highway Engineering, Roads and Pavements; TG – Bridge Engineering

**Mark E. Shelton**, *Reference/Collection Development Librarian, Brown University*
QA – Mathematics; QB – Astronomy; QC – Physics; TA - Engineering, Civil Engineering (General)

**Martha Stephenson**, *Reference Librarian, University of Wisconsin – Whitewater,*
QB – Astronomy; QC – Physics; QD – Chemistry

**Frederick W. Stoss**, *Reference, Science Reference, Environmental Reference Librarian, University at Buffalo – State University New York*
QH – Natural History, Biology (General); QK – Botany; QL – Zoology; QP – Physiology; SH – Agriculture, Fisheries, Angling

**Annie Szuch,** *Reference Librarian & Cataloging Technician, University of Michigan – Flint*
QH – Natural History, Biology (General); QK – Botany; QL – Zoology

**Tom Volkening,** *Engineering Librarian, Engineering Library, Michigan State University*
QA (QA 76 only) – Mathematics (Computer Science only); T – Technology (General); TA – Engineering, Civil Engineering (General); TD – Environmental Technology, Sanitary Engineering; TE – Highway Engineering, Roads and Pavements; TG – Bridge Engineering; TH – Building Construction; TJ – Mechanical Engineering and Machinery; TK – Electrical Engineering, Electronics, Nuclear Engineering; TL – Motor Vehicles, Aeronautics, Astronautics; TP – Chemical Technology; TS – Manufactures

**Mary Anne Waltz**, *Coordinator of Reference/Instructional Services, Renesselaer Polytechnic Institute*
Q – Science (General); T – Technology (General); TT – Handicrafts, Arts and Crafts

**Paul Wermager**, *Head, Science-Technology Reference, Hamilton Library, University of Hawaii*
QM – Human Anatomy; QP – Physiology

## SENIOR SUBJECT ADVISORS:

**Dr. Nancy F. Carter** — *Head, Oliver C. Lester Library of Mathematics, and Physics, University Libraries, University of Colorado, Boulder*. Dr. Nancy Carter earned her Ph.D. at the University of Colorado, Boulder in 1974. She subsequently earned her Masters of Library Science from the University of Denver in 1980. Dr. Carter's undergraduate and graduate education was achieved at the University of North Carolina, Greensboro, focusing on Mathematics. She has served as editor and co-editor for both "Mathematics News" and the "Colorado Libraries" magazines. Dr. Carter has also authored several papers and delivered presentations for the ALA. She served as Chair of the ALA Chapter Relations Division, Journal and Newsletter Editors Subcommittee from 1996-1999. She currently is serving on the Colorado Library Association's Bulgarian Library Project Committee, and numerous other CLA committees. Her honors and awards include earning the Literary Award from the Colorado Library Association in October, 1999.

Senior Subject Advisor for the following sections: QA – Mathematics; QB – Astronomy; QC – Physics.

**Jean E. Crampon** — *Librarian, Science Center, Information Services Division, University of Southern California*. Jean Crampon earned her Masters of Library Science from the University of North Carolina, Chapel Hill in 1971. Her undergraduate work was conducted at San Diego State University. She has certifications by the Academy of Health Information Professionals and the Medical Library Association. Crampon's professional experience has included serving as the Curator of the Hancock Memorial Museum, and acting as the Head of the Hancock Library of Biology and Oceanography. She is a registered trainer for the *Basics of Searching MEDLINE for the Health Professional* at the Pacific Southwest Regional Medical Library and at the Southern Illinois University School of Medicine. Crampon has written multiple articles for conferences such as the Annual IAMSLIC and 17th Polar Libraries Colloquy Conference. She is a book reviewer for *Library Journal* magazine, as well as *Science and Technology Annual Reference Review*. Jean is active at the University of Southern California, involved in the Information Services Division's Ad Hoc Instruction Task Force, and Remuneration Committee. She continues to serve on the USC Faculty Women's Club. Crampon is affiliated with the International Association of Aquatic and Marine Science Libraries and Information Centers, the Biosciences Information Service, the Special Libraries Association, the Library Management Division, and the Biological and Life Sciences Division.

Senior Subject Advisor for the following sections:  QE – Geology; QH – Natural History, Biology (General); QK – Botany; QL – Zoology; QP – Physiology; QR – Microbiology.

**Erik Ennerberg** — *Bibliographer, College of Agriculture, Cal Poly Pomona*. Erik Ennerberg received his MPA from the University of Southern California, where he also received his Masters of Library Science. He earned his Bachelor of Arts degree from the University of California, Riverside. Mr. Ennerberg has spent his career working as Librarian at Cal Poly Pomona. He works as Bibliographer for Agriculture, Food and Nutrition, Kinesiology – Physical Education, and Geography.

Senior Subject Advisor for the following sections:  S  – Agriculture; SB – Plant culture; SD – Forestry; SF – Animal Culture; SH – Agriculture, Fisheries, Angling; SK – Hunting.

**Julia Gelfand** – *Applied Sciences and Engineering Librarian, University of California, Irvine*. Julia Gelfand received her Masters of Science in Library Science, and a Masters in History from Case Western Reserve University. She is a PhD candidate at the University of Denver in the area of Higher Education/Administration. Ms. Gelfand is the Applied Sciences and Engineering Librarian at the University of California, Irvine Library. She was granted the rank of Librarian III with distinction in July of 2001, and serves as the senior Bibliographer for the School of Social Ecology, School of Engineering and the Department of Information and Computer Science. Ms. Gefand has worked at the University of Irvine Libraries as the Applied Sciences Librarian, Acting Engineering Librarian, Acting Head of the Research and Instruction department, and Assistant to the AUL for Collections. Previously, she was the Assistant Head of Reference and Reference Librarian at the Penrose Library, University of Denver. Of her many publications, Gelfand has served as co-editor for the *Library Hi-Tech News*, has written essays for *Encyclopedia of Library, Information Science, Global Librarianship, Choice*, as well as numerous papers at professional conferences. She is currently the Chair of the IFLA's Science and Technology Standing Committee, IFLA Science and Technology Section Delegate, the ASEE – Engineering Librarians Division, and the Liaison to IFLA SciTech Section. Julia has long been a member of many professional organizations, including the ACRL President's Program Committee, the ACRL KG Saur Award Committee, the IRRT Continuing Education Committee, and many others. Other professional associations include the ALA, the SSP, the ACM, CARL, and the AAAS. Ms. Gelfand's awards include being recognized for outstanding achievement in Grey Literature with a Literati Award for Excellence by MCB University Press in London, England. She has been awarded by the University of California, Irvine for Faculty Career Development, and received a Fulbright U.K. Professional Librarian Research Award.

Senior Subject Advisor for the following sections: Q – Science (General); T – Technology (General); TA – Engineering, Civil Engineering (General); TD – Environmental Technology, Sanitary Engineering; TE – Highway Engineering, Roads and Pavements; TH – Building Construction; TJ – Mechanical Engineering and Machinery; TK – Electrical Engineering, Electronics, Nuclear Engineering; TL – Motor Vehicles, Aeronautics, Astronautics.

**Katalin Harkányi** – *Reference Librarian, San Diego State University, Malcolm A. Love Library*. Katalin Harkányi is the Subject Specialist for Biotechnology, Chemistry, Energy Studies, and Engineering (Environmental Chemistry and Engineering, Mechanical Engineering, and Civil Engineering) at the Malcolm A. Love Library. Her other areas of Subject Specialty include: patent finding, Hungarian Language and Literature, and Russian Language and Literature for San Diego State University Libraries.

Senior Subject Advisor for the following sections: TA – Engineering, Civil Engineering (General); TC – Hydraulic Engineering; TD – Environmental Technology, Sanitary Engineering; TE – Highway Engineering, Roads and Pavements; TF – Railroad Engineering and Operation; TG – Bridge Engineering; TH – Building Construction; TJ – Mechanical Engineering and Machinery; TK – Electrical engineering, Electronics, Nuclear Engineering.

**Robert Heyer-Gray** – *Engineering Librarian, Physical Sciences & Engineering Library, University of California, Davis*. Robert Heyer-Gray earned his Masters of Library Science from the University of California, Berkeley. He began serving as the Engineering Librarian at UC Davis in 1999. There, he oversees engineering reference, collection development, instruction and liaison activities in the areas of Chemical Engineering & Materials Science, Civil Engineering, Transportation Studies, Electrical & Computer Engineering, and Mechanical and Aerospace Engineering. Prior to coming to UC Davis, Heyer-Gray had over six years of professional library experience at the University of Missouri-Rolla, where he acted as Head of the Reference Department for the last two years of his employ. Robert has his membership in several professional organizations, including the Engineering Libraries Division (ELD) of the American Society of Engineering Educators, and the California Chapter of the Association of College and Research Libraries (CARL).

Senior Subject Advisor for the following sections: TE – Highway Engineering, Roads and Pavements; TF – Railroad Engineering and Operation; TG – Bridge Engineering; TL – Motor Vehicles, Aeronautics, Astronautics; TN – Mining Engineering, Metallurgy; TP – Chemical Technology.

**Deborah Lee** – *Reference Librarian, Mississippi State University*. Deborah Lee received her Ph.D. in Business Administration from Mississippi State University, with focus on Economics. She received her Masters of Science in Business Administration from Mississippi State University, and her Masters in Library and Information Science from the University of North Carolina, Chapel Hill. She has also earned credits towards her Masters degree in Political Science, and earned her Bachelor of Arts with honors from the University of North Carolina, Chapel Hill in Political Science, and Latin American Studies. Deborah has served at Mississippi State University Libraries as Associate Professor, Assistant Professor, and Lecturer. Her professional experience includes working as the Reference Services Librarian, Coordinator of Serials, and as Acquisitions Librarian for Mississippi State University Library. Prior to that, she served as the Collections Development Librarian for Milsaps College Library. Deborah's research activities have included writing for the *Atlantic Economic Journal, Mississippi Libraries*, and reviewing for *Behavioral and Social Sciences Librarian, Choice, Journal of Business and Finance Librarianship*, as well as having refereed research for ACRL/MLA proceedings. She is a member of the Library Administration and Management Association/American Library Association, the American Economic Association, the Southern Economic Association, and the Mississippi Library Association.

Senior Subject Advisor for the following sections: TR – Photography; TS – Manufactures; TT – Handicrafts, Arts and Crafts; TX – Home Economics.

**Marlene Metzgar** – *Director, Science & Technology Librarian, Kaplan College.* Marlene Metzgar received her Master of Arts in Library and Information studies from the School of Library and Information Studies, Northern Illinois University. Her undergraduate education was conducted at Marycrest College. Currently, she is serving as the Director of Library Services at Kaplan College, where she has overseen the Medical and Nursing library for over 20 years. Kaplan College, Davenport is a member of the River Bend Library System, a networked consortium of public, academic, medical, and "special libraries." Ms. Metzgar has most recently taken the responsibility of overseeing the Kaplan College Virtual Library for associate and bachelor students at the University. Marlene has dedicated her career to working in academic libraries for over 20 years, on both the community college and university level. She is a member of the Iowa Library Association, and of the Association of College and Research Librarians.

Senior Subject Advisor for the following section: QM – Human Anatomy.


**Lorraine J. Pellack (Knox)** – *Head, Science and Technology Department, Associate Professor, Parks Library, Iowa State University.* Lorraine J. Pellack received her Masters of Library Science from Emporia State University. She conducted her undergraduate education at the Upper Iowa University, majoring in Biology. Her duties as Head of the Science and Technology Department at the Parks Library include collection development, reference and instruction in regards to chemistry, general science, geology, materials science, and reference tools in science and technology. Prior to serving at Iowa State University, Pellack served as Assistant Science Librarian at the Anshutz Science Library at the University of Kansas, and as Physical Science Bibliographer, Life Science Bibliographer, and Reference Librarian at the University of North Dakota. Lorraine has reviewed books for *Science and Technology Annual Reference Review.* Her publications include writing for *Issues in Science & Technology Librarianship.*

Senior Subject Advisor for the following sections: QD – Chemistry; QL – Zoology.


**Charles Rhine** – *Reference Librarian, University of Northern Colorado.* Charles Rhine has thirty years experience as a Science Librarian at the University of Northern Colorado, James A. Michener Library. Mr. Rhine has degrees in Physics, Chemistry, and Library science. He is also a Professor of University Libraries.

Senior Subject Advisor for the following sections: QA – Mathematics; QB – Astronomy; QC – Physics; QD – Chemistry.


**Mark E. Shelton** – *Reference/Collection Development Librarian, Brown University.* Mark E. Shelton received his Masters in Library science from the University of Missouri-Columbia, where he was a National Library of Medicine, Medical Informatics Pre-Doctoral Fellow. He earned his Ph.D. in the Ceramics Engineering Ph.D. Program from the University of Missouri-Rolla. His undergraduate work was conducted at Lyon College, where he received his Bachelor of Science in Applied Mathematics. Shelton's duties as Reference/Collection Development Librarian at Brown University include acting as Subject Specialist in Engineering, Math, Physics, and Computer Science. He is also the Sciences Library Reference SLAS Supervisor. Prior to his work at Brown, Mark Shelton worked at the University of Nebraska-Lincoln, where he was Subject Specialist in Engineering, Math, Physics and Computer Science, as well as the Head of the Math and Physics Branch Libraries. Shelton has prepared multiple presentations for such conferences as the Special Libraries Association of Rhode Island, the American Society for Engineering Education, the Health Sciences Consortium, and the American Medical Informatics Association. He has written papers for the American Society for Engineering Education, and the ASIS Annual Meeting. He is an active book reviewer for *Collection Building,* MCB University Press.

Senior Subject Advisor for the following sections: QA – Mathematics; QB – Astronomy; QC – Physics; QD – Chemistry.


**Robert Sickles** – *Agricultural Subject Librarian, Iowa State University.* Bob Sickles earned his Masters of Science from Syracuse University, and his Bachelor of Science from Sterling College. He currently is Iowa State University Library's Reference/Collections Specialist for Agriculture/Life Sciences: Plant and Soil Sciences. Previously, he served as the Agriculture/Biological Sciences Bibliographer and Public Services/Reference Librarian at Iowa State University's Parks-University Library. He currently is the Reference/Collections/Academic Department Liaison in the departments of Agronomy, Botany, Forestry, Horticulture, and Plant Pathology.

Senior Subject Advisor for the following sections: S – Agriculture; SB – Plant Culture; SD – Forestry; SF – Animal Culture; SH – Agriculture, Fisheries, Angling; SK – Hunting.

# Q Science (General)

## Q10 Societies — International

**Q10.M38 1985**
**McClellan, James E.**
   Science reorganized : scientific societies in the eighteenth century / James E. McClellan III. New York : Columbia University Press, 1985. xxix, 413 p.
84-022993          506          0231059965
   *Science -- Societies, etc. -- History -- 18th century.  Learned institutions and societies -- History -- 18th century.*

**Q10.W67 1982**
   World guide to scientific associations = Internationales Verzeichnis wissenschaftlicher Verbande und Gesellschaften / [edited by Michael Zils and Willi Gorzny]. Munchen ; Saur ; 1982. 619 p. ;
82-199881          506          3598205171
   *Science -- Societies, etc. -- Directories.  Learned institutions and societies -- Directories.*

## Q11-40 Societies — America — United States

**Q11.C9 vol. 49, p. 1-339**
**Trimpi, Helen P.,**
   Melville's confidence men and American politics in the 1850s / Helen P. Trimpi. Hamden, Conn. : Published for The Academy by Archon Books, 1987. xviii, 339 p.
86-032158          813/.3          0208021302
   *Melville, Herman, -- 1819-1891. -- Confidence-man.    Political satire, American -- History and criticism.  Swindlers and swindling in literature.    United States -- Politics and government -- 1849-1861.*

**Q11.K66 1999**
**Kohlstedt, Sally Gregory,**
   The establishment of science in America : 150 years of the American Association for the Advancement of Science / Sally Gregory Kohlstedt, Michael M. Sokal, Bruce V. Lewenstein. New Brunswick, N.J. : Rutgers University Press, c1999. xiv, 236 p. :
99-014096          506/.073          0813527058

**Q11.N5**
   Medical ethics at the dawn of the 21st century / edited by Raphael Cohen-Almagor. New York : New York Academy of Sciences, 2000. vii, 265 p. ;
00-040186          500 s          1573312991
   *Davy, Humphry, -- Sir, -- 1778-1829.    Chemists -- England -- Biography.*

**Q11.N5 vol. 360**
   Victorian science and Victorian values : literary perspectives / edited by James Paradis and Thomas Postlewait. New York, N.Y. : New York Academy of Sciences, 1981. xiii, 362 p.
80-029513          500 s          0897661095
   *English literature -- 19th century -- History and criticism. Literature and science -- Great Britain -- History -- 19th century. Science -- Social aspects -- Great Britain -- History -- 19th century. Great Britain -- Intellectual life -- 19th century.*

**Q11.N5 vol. 869**
   Women in science and engineering : choices for success / edited by Cecily Cannan Selby. New York : New York Academy of Sciences, 1999. xix, 263 p. :
99-020357          500 s          1573311669
   *Women scientists -- Congresses.  Women engineers -- Congresses.*

**Q11.P612 vol. 181**
**Schmidt, Albert J.**
   The architecture and planning of classical Moscow : a cultural history / Albert J. Schmidt. Philadelphia : American Philosophical Society, 1989. xiii, 218 p.
88-071549          081 s          0871691817
   *Neoclassicism (Architecture) -- Russia (Federation) -- Moscow. Architecture -- Russia (Federation) -- Moscow.  City planning -- Russia (Federation) -- Moscow.  Moscow (Russia) -- Buildings, structures, etc.*

**Q11.P612 vol. 184, etc.**
**Clagett, Marshall,**
   Ancient Egyptian science : a source book / by Marshall Clagett. Philadelphia : American Philosophical Society, 1989-1999 v. 1-3; in 4
89-084668          081 s          0871691841
   *Science -- Egypt -- History.  Science -- Egypt -- History – Sources.*

**Q11.P612 vol. 186**
**Zupko, Ronald Edward.**
   Revolution in measurement : Western European weights and measures since the age of science / Ronald Edward Zupko. Philadelphia : American Philosophical Society, 1990. xiii, 548 p.
89-084666          081 s          0871691868
   *Weights and measures -- Europe -- History.*

**Q11.P612 vol. 216**
**Balas, Edith.**
   Michelangelo's Medici Chapel : a new interpretation / Edith Balas. Philadelphia : American Philosophical Society, 1995. x, 196 p. :
94-078511          0871692163
   *Michelangelo Buonarroti, -- 1475-1564 -- Criticism and interpretation. Medici, House of -- Tombs.    Sculpture, Italian – Italy -- Florence. Mannerism (Art) -- Italy -- Florence.*

**Q11.P612 vol. 220**
**Jungnickel, Christa.**
   Cavendish / by Christa Jungnickel and Russell McCormmach. Philadelphia, Pa. : American Philosophical Society, 1996. 414 p. :
95-079391          0871692201
   *Cavendish, Henry, -- 1731-1810.  Cavendish, Charles, – Lord, – 1692 or 3-1783.    Chemists -- Great Britain -- Biography.  Politicians – Great Britain -- Biography.  Fathers and sons -- Great Britain.*

**Q11.P6 n.s., vol.41, pt.1**
**Briggs, Lawrence Palmer.**
   The ancient Khmer Empire.    Philadelphia, American Philosophical Society, 1951. 295 p.
51-002328          959.6
   *Khmers -- Antiquities.  Archaeology, Medieval -- Cambodia. Khmer Empire -- History -- 800-1444.*

**Q11.P6 n.s., vol. 41, pt. 3 1969**
**Allen, Elsa Guerdrum.**
   The history of American ornithology before Audubon. New York, Russell & Russell [1969] 387-591 p.
68-027045          598.297
   *Birds -- North America.  Ornithologists -- United States.*

**Q11.S79 1989**
**Smithsonian Institution.**
   Guide to photographic collections at the Smithsonian Institution / Diane Vogt O'Connor. Washington : Smithsonian Institution Press, c1989-c1995 v. 1-4   :
89-600116          026/.779/074753          0874749271

**Q11.S7 vol. 114**
**Smithsonian Institution.**
   Smithsonian meteorological tables. Washington, 1951. xi, 527 p.
51-061623          551.50835
   *Meteorology -- Tables.*

**Q11.S8.O4**
**Oehser, Paul Henry,**
   Sons of science; the story of the Smithsonian Institution and its leaders. New York, H. Schuman [1949] xvii, 220 p.
49000526          506
   *Research -- history -- United States  Science -- history -- United States*

**Q16 .N55**
   The foundations of Newtonian scholarship / editors, Richard H. Dalitz, Michael Nauenberg. River Edge, NJ : World Scientific Pub., 2000. p. cm.
99-088303          530/.092          9810239203
*Newton, Isaac, -- Sir, -- 1642-1727 -- Congresses.     Physics -- History -- Congresses.*

**Q40.H35 2000**
**Hall, Carl W.**
   Laws and models : science, engineering, and technology / Carl W. Hall. Boca Raton, FL : CRC Press, c2000. xxxi, 524 p.
99-029327          500          0849320186
   *Science -- Handbooks, manuals, etc. Technology --Handbooks, manuals, etc.*

### Q41 Societies — Europe — Great Britain

**Q41.L85.H35 1984**
**Hall, Marie Boas,**
   All scientists now : the Royal Society in the nineteenth century / Marie Boas Hall. Cambridge [Cambridgeshire] ; Cambridge University Press, 1984. xii, 261 p. :
84-007705          506/.041          0521267463
   *Science -- Great Britain -- History.*

**Q41.L85.H95 1982**
**Hunter, Michael Cyril William.**
   The Royal Society and its fellows, 1660-1700 : the morphology of an early scientific institution / Michael Hunter. Chalfont St. Giles, Bucks, England : British Society for the History of Science, 1982. 270 p. ;
83-209776          506/.041          0906450039
   *Scientists -- Great Britain -- Registers.*

**Q41.L85.W66 1997**
   Women, science and medicine 1500-1700 : mothers and sisters of the Royal Society / edited by Lynette Hunter & Sarah Hutton. Thrupp, Stroud, Gloucestershire : Sutton Pub., 1997. xx, 292 p. :
98-100834          500/.82/0941          0750913347
   *Women in science -- Great Britain. Science, Renaissance. Women scientists -- Great Britain.*

**Q41.L86.P86 1967a**
**Purver, Margery.**
   The Royal Society: concept and creation. With an introd. by H. R. Trevor-Roper. Cambridge, M.I.T. Press [1967] xvii, 246 p.
66-025631          506/.2/421

### Q46 Societies — Europe — France

**Q46.A15.H33**
**Hahn, Roger,**
   The anatomy of a scientific institution: the Paris Academy of Sciences, 1666-1803.   Berkeley, University of California Press, 1971. xiv, 433 p.
70-130795          506/.2/44          0520018184

**Q46.L89 1989**
**Lux, David Stephan.**
   Patronage and royal science in seventeenth-century France : the Academie de physique in Caen / David S. Lux. Ithaca : Cornell University Press, 1989. xiii, 199 p.
89-001002          506/.044          0801423341
   *Science -- France -- Societies, etc. -- History -- 17th century. Science -- France -- History -- 17th century. Benefactors --France -- History -- 17th century.*

### Q105 Societies — Museums. Exhibitions — By region or country, A-Z

**Q105.U5.A64 1998**
**Cohen, Paul S.,**
   America's scientific treasures : a travel companion / Paul S. Cohen and Brenda H. Cohen. Washington, D.C. : American Chemical Society, c1998. xviii, 446 p.
97-051948          507/.473          0841234442
   *Science museums -- United States -- Guidebooks. Historic sites -- United States -- Guidebooks. National parks and reserves -- United States -- Guidebooks. United States -- Guidebooks.*

**Q105.U5.D36 1990**
**Danilov, Victor J.**
America's science museums / Victor J. Danilov. New York : Greenwood Press, 1990. x, 483 p. ;
90-033627          507.4/73          0313258651
*Science museums -- United States -- Handbooks, manuals, etc. Industrial museums -- United States -- Handbooks, manuals, etc. Museums -- United States -- Handbooks, manuals, etc.*

**Q105.U5.G66 1991**
**Goode, G. Brown**
The origins of natural science in America : the essays of George Brown Goode / edited and with an introduction by Sally Gregory Kohlstedt. Washington : Smithsonian Institution Press, c1991. xi, 411 p. :
91-010266          507.4/73          1560980982
*Goode, G. Brown -- (George Brown), -- 1851-1896.    Science museums -- Educational aspects -- United States. Science museums – Philosophy.    Science museums -- United States -- History.*

## Q111 Societies — Collected works — Series of monographs. Serial collections (nonperiodical)

**Q111.J58**
**Jones, Howard Mumford,**
A treasury of scientific prose, a nineteenth-century anthology. Edited by Howard Mumford Jones and I. Bernard Cohen with the assistance of Everett Mendelsohn. Boston, Little, Brown [1963] 372 p.
62010533          508.2
*Science.*

**Q111.J6**
Roots of scientific thought, a cultural perspective. Edited by Philip P. Wiener, and Aaron Noland. New York, Basic Books [1957] 677 p. ;
57012414          508
*Science.*

**Q111.S48 1965**
**Shapley, Harlow,**
The new treasury of science. Edited by Harlow Shapley, Samuel Rapport and Helen Wright. New York, Harper & Row [1965] xv, 762 p.
65-020439          508
*Science.*

## Q121 Encyclopedias.

**Q121.E53 2001**
Encyclopedia of science and technology / James Trefil, general editor ; contributing editors, Harold Morowitz, Paul Ceruzzi. New York : Routledge, c2001. 554 p. :
503 21     0415937248
*Science -- Encyclopedias. Technology -- Encyclopedias.*

**Q121.I48 1999**
The international encyclopedia of science and technology / [editor, Steve Luck]. New York : Oxford University Press, 1999. 471 p. :
01-266342          503          0195216830
*Science -- Encyclopedias. Technology -- Encyclopedias.*

**Q121.M3 2002**
McGraw-Hill encyclopedia of science & technology 9th ed. New York : McGraw-Hill, 2002. p. cm.
503 21
*Science -- Encyclopedias. Technology -- Encyclopedias.*

**Q121.S34 2000**
Science & technology encyclopedia.   Chicago : University of Chicago Press, 2000. 572 p. :
00-025292          503          0226742679
*Science -- Encyclopedias. Technology -- Encyclopedias.*

**Q121.V65 1999**
**Volti, Rudi.**
The Facts On File encyclopedia of science, technology, and society / Rudi Volti. New York, NY : Facts on File, c1999. 3 v. (ix, 115
98-039014          503          0816031231
*Science -- Encyclopedias. Technology -- Encyclopedias. Science -- Social aspects -- Encyclopedias.*

**Q121.W676**
World of scientific discovery.   Detroit : Gale Research Inc., c1994. v. :
503 20     1071-0981
*Science -- Encyclopedias.   Scientists -- Biography -- Encyclopedias. Discoveries in science -- Encyclopedias.*

**Q121.B86 2000**
**Bunch, Bryan H.**
The Penguin desk encyclopedia of science and mathematics / Bryan Bunch and Jenny Tesar. New York : Penguin Reference, 2000. viii, 696 p. :
503 21     0670885282
*Science -- Encyclopedias. Mathematics -- Encyclopedias.*

## Q123 Dictionaries

**Q123.B3 1961a**
**Ballentyne, D. W. G.**
A dictionary of named effects and laws in chemistry, physics, and mathematics [by] D. W. G. Ballentyne and L. E. Q. Walker. London, Chapman & Hall, 1961. v, 234 p.
62-006314
*Chemistry -- Dictionaries. Physics -- Dictionaries. Mathematics -- Dictionaries.*

**Q123.C4817 1996**
**Chakalov, G.**
  Elsevier's dictionary of science and technology, English-Russian / Compiled by G. Chakalov. Amsterdam ; New York : Elsevier's Science, 1996. 1134 p. ;
          503 20      044481955X
  *Science -- Dictionaries. Technology -- Dictionaries. English language -- Dictionaries -- Russian.*

**Q123.C482 1995**
  Larousse dictionary of science and technology / general editor, Peter M.B. Walker. New York : Larousse, c1995. xii, 1236 p.
  94-073123          503      0752300105
  *Science -- Dictionaries. Technology -- Dictionaries.*

**Q123.D673 1981**
**Dorian, A. F.**
  Dictionary of science and technology : German-English / compiled and arranged by A.F. Dorian. Amsterdam ; Elsevier Scientific, 1981. 1119 p. ;
  81-208536          503/.31          0444419977
  *Science -- Dictionaries -- German. Technology -- Dictionaries -- German. German language -- Dictionaries -- English.*

**Q123.E497 2002**
  Encyclopedia of physical science and technology / editor-in-chief, Robert A. Meyers. 3rd ed. San Diego : Academic Press, c2002. 18 v. :
          503 21      0122274105
  *Physical sciences -- Encyclopedias. Technology -- Encyclopedias.*

**Q123.F334 1999**
  The Facts on File encyclopedia of science. New York, NY : Facts on File, c1999. 2 v. (840 p.)
  98-053201          503      0816040087
  *Science -- Dictionaries.*

**Q123.M182 1999**
**Macura, Paul.**
  Elsevier's Russian-English dictionary / compiled by Paul Macura. Amsterdam ; Elsevier, 1999. 4 v. (xiv, 35
  99-031050          491.73/21          0444824839
  *Science -- Dictionaries -- Russian. Humanities -- Dictionaries -- Russian. Social sciences -- Dictionaries -- Russian.*

**Q123.M34 1994**
  McGraw-Hill dictionary of scientific and technical terms / Sybil P. Parker, editor in chief.. New York : McGraw-Hill, c1994. xvii, 2194, 4
  93-034772          503      0070423334
  *Science -- Dictionaries. Technology -- Dictionaries.*

**Q123.T844 1993**
**Tung, Louise Watanabe.**
  Japanese/English English/Japanese glossary of scientific and technical terms / Louise Watanabe Tung = [Wa-Ei Ei-Wa kagaku kogaku yogo jiten / Watanabe Hisako]. New York : Wiley, c1993. xxi, 1146 p.
  92-028867          503      0471574635
  *Science -- Dictionaries -- Japanese. Engineering -- Dictionaries -- Japanese. Science -- Dictionaries.*

**Q123.U43 1998**
  Ultimate visual dictionary of science. 1st American ed. New York : DK Pub., 1998. 448 p. :
          503 21      0789435128
  *Science -- Dictionaries. Picture dictionaries, English.*

**Q123.Z55 1992**
**Zimmerman, Milhail.**
  Russian-English translator's dictionary : a guide to scientific and technical usage / Mikhail Zimmerman, Claudia Vedeneeva. 3rd ed. Chichester [West Sussex] ; New York : Nauka Publishers ; Wiley, c1991. 735 p. :
          503 20      0471933163
  *Science -- Dictionaries -- Russian. Engineering -- Dictionaries -- Russian. Russian language -- Dictionaries -- English.*

# Q124 Translating services

**Q124.M66 2000**
**Montgomery, Scott L.**
  Science in translation : movements of knowledge through cultures and time / Scott L. Montgomery. Chicago : University of Chicago Press, 2000. xi, 325 p. :
  99-053389          500      0226534804
  *Science -- Translating -- History. Science -- Language.*

## Q124.8 History — Dictionaries and encyclopedias

**Q124.8.S43 2001**
**Sebastian, Anton.**
  A dictionary of the history of science / Anton Sebastian. New York : Parthenon Pub. Group, c2001. vi, 373 p. :
  00-057428          503      185070418X
  *Science -- History -- Dictionaries. Technology -- History -- Dictionaries.*

## Q124.95 History — Ancient

**Q124.95.L55 1992**
**Lindberg, David C.**
  The beginnings of Western science : the European scientific tradition in philosophical, religious, and institutional context, 600 B.C. to A.D. 1450 / David C. Lindberg. Chicago : University of Chicago Press, 1992. xviii, 455 p.
  91-037741          509.4          0226482308
  *Science, Ancient -- History. Science, Medieval -- History.*

**Q124.95.S35 1985**
**Schlagel, Richard H.,**
  From myth to the modern mind : a study of the origins and growth of scientific thought / Richard H. Schlagel. New York : P. Lang, c1985- v. 1   ;
  84-023361          509/.3          0820402192
  *Science, Ancient. Science -- Philosophy -- History.*

## Q124.97 History — Medieval

**Q124.97.S35**
Science in the Middle Ages / edited by David C. Lindberg. Chicago : University of Chicago Press, 1978. xv, 549 p. :
78-005367          509/.02          0226482324
*Science, Medieval.*

## Q125 History — Modern — General works

**Q125.A765 1994**
**Asimov, Isaac,**
Asimov's chronology of science and discovery / Isaac Asimov. 1st ed., updated and illustrated. New York, N.Y. : HarperCollins, c1994. 790 p. :
          509 20          0062701134
*Science -- History. Science -- Social aspects. Inventions -- History.*

**Q125.B88 1988**
**Brush, Stephen G.**
The history of modern science : a guide to the second scientific revolution, 1800-1950 / Stephen G. Brush. Ames : Iowa State University Press, 1988. xv, 544 p. ;
87-026177          509/.034          0813808839
*Science -- History. Anthropology -- History. Psychology -- History.*

**Q125.B97 1957a**
**Butterfield, Herbert,**
The origins of modern science: 1300-1800. New York, Macmillan, 1957. 242 p.
57-014603          509
*Science -- History. Science -- Philosophy.*

**Q125.C538 1994**
**Cohen, H. F.**
The scientific revolution : a historiographical inquiry / H. Floris Cohen. Chicago : University of Chicago Press, c1994. xviii, 662 p.
93-041784          509.4/09032          0226112799
*Science -- History. Science -- Europe -- History. Science -- Historiography.*

**Q125.C54**
**Cohen, I. Bernard,**
From Leonardo to Lavoisier, 1450-1800 / I. Bernard Cohen. New York : Scribner, c1980. xiii, 298 p.
80-015542          509/.03          0684153777
*Science -- History.*

**Q125.C542 1985**
**Cohen, I. Bernard,**
Revolution in science / I. Bernard Cohen. Cambridge, Mass. : Belknap Press of Harvard University Press, 1985. xx, 711 p., [
84-012916          509          0674767772
*Science -- History.*

**Q125.C68 1961**
**Crombie, A. C.**
Augustine to Galileo. A.C. Crombie. Cambridge, Mass., Harvard University Press, 1961. 2 v. in 1
61016151          0674052730
*Science  Science -- history*

**Q125.D17 1966**
**Dampier, William Cecil Dampier,**
A history of science and its relations with philosophy & religion. London, Cambridge U.P., 1966. xxvii, 544 p.
66-070313          509
*Science -- History. Philosophy.*

**Q125.D34**
**De Santillana, Giorgio,**
The origins of scientific thought; from Anaximander to Proclus, 600 B.C. to 300 A.D.   [Chicago] University of Chicago Press [1961] 320 p.
61-017073          509.3
*Science, Ancient.*

**Q125.D45**
Dictionary of the history of science / edited by W.F. Bynum, E.J. Browne, Roy Porter. Princeton, N.J. : Princeton University Press, c1981. 494 p. :
81-047116          509          0691082871
*Science -- History.*

**Q125.D65 1991**
**Dorn, Harold,**
The geography of science / Harold Dorn. Baltimore : Johns Hopkins University Press, c1991. xx, 219 p. :
90-025149          509          0801841518
*Science -- History.*

**Q125.D814**
**Dubos, Rene J.**
Reason awake: science for man [by] Rene Dubos. New York, Columbia University Press, 1970. xviii, 280 p.
70-111327          500          0231031815
*Science and civilization.*

**Q125.E34 1994**
**Eamon, William.**
Science and the secrets of nature : books of secrets in medieval and early modern culture / William Eamon. Princeton, N.J. : Princeton University Press, c1994. xv, 490 p. :
93-031794          509/.4/0902          0691034028
*Science -- History. Science, Medieval. Science -- Experiments -- History.*

**Q125.E362 1999**
**Ebert, John David,**
Twilight of the clockwork God : conversations on science and spirituality at the end of an age / John David Ebert. Tulsa, Okla. : Council Oak Books, 1999. p. cm.
98-032417          501          1571780793
*Science -- History. Religion and science -- History. Philosophy, European -- History.*

**Q125.E36313 1990**
Eckert, Michael,
Crystals, electrons, transistors : from scholar's study to industrial research / Michael Eckert, Helmut Schubert ; translated by Thomas Hughes. New York : American Institute of Physics, c1990. xxii, 241 p.
89-014941            530/.09            0883186225
*Science -- History. Physics -- Research -- History. Research, Industrial -- History.*

**Q125.E45 1996**
Elliott, Clark A.
History of science in the United States : a chronology and research guide / Clark A. Elliott. New York : Garland, 1996. x, 543 p. ;
95-043891            509.73            0815313098
*Science -- United States -- History -- Chronology. Science -- United States -- History -- Handbooks, manuals, etc.*

**Q125.E53 2000**
Encyclopedia of the scientific revolution : from Copernicus to Newton / editor Wilbur Applebaum. New York : Garland Pub., 2000. xxxv, 758 p. :
            509.4/03 21            0815315031
*Science -- Europe -- History -- 16th century -- Encyclopedias. Science -- Europe -- History -- 17th century -- Encyclopedias.*

**Q125.F425 1988**
Ferris, Timothy.
Coming of age in the Milky Way / Timothy Ferris. New York : Morrow, c1988. 495 p. :
88-005153            509            0688058892
*Science -- History. Space and time. Cosmology.*

**Q125.F43 1991**
Feuer, Lewis Samuel,
The scientific intellectual : the psychological & sociological origins of modern science / Lewis S. Feuer ; with a new introduction by the author. New Brunswick, U.S.A. : Transaction Publishers, c1992. xlix, 441 p.
91-004205            509            1560005718
*Science -- History. Science -- Philosophy -- History. Science -- Social aspects -- History.*

**Q125.F592 1998**
Flowers, Charles.
A science odyssey : 100 years of discovery / Charles Flowers ; foreword by Charles Osgood ; introduction by Charles Kuralt. 1st ed. New York : Morrow, c1998. xvi, 316 p. :
            509/.04 21            0688151965
*Science -- History -- 20th century. Discoveries in science -- History -- 20th century. Technology -- History -- 20th century.*

**Q125.G38**
Garrett, Alfred Benjamin,
The flash of genius. Princeton, N.J., Van Nostrand [1963] 249 p.
63-003921            608.7
*Science -- History -- Addresses, essays, lectures. Inventions -- Addresses, essays, lectures.*

**Q125.G49**
Gillispie, Charles Coulston.
The edge of objectivity; an essay in the history of scientific ideas. Princeton, N.J., Princeton University Press, 1960. 562 p.
60-005748            509
*Science -- History. Science -- Philosophy.*

**Q125.G495 1989**
Gingerich, Owen.
The physical sciences in the twentieth century / Owen Gingerich. New York : Scribner, c1989. xiv, 306 p. :
88-024007            500.2/09/04            0684154978
*Physical sciences -- History -- 20th century.*

**Q125.G54 1984**
Gjertsen, Derek.
The classics of science : a study of twelve enduring scientific works / Derek Gjertsen. New York : Lilian Barber Press, 1984. iii, 374 p. :
83-027539            509            0936508094
*Science -- History -- Sources.*

**Q125.H28 1983**
Hall, A. Rupert
The revolution in science, 1500-1750 / A. Rupert Hall. London ; Longman, 1983. viii, 373 p.
82-008978            509/.03            0582491339
*Science -- History. Science -- Methodology. Science -- Philosophy.*

**Q125.H355 1985**
Hankins, Thomas L.
Science and the Enlightenment / Thomas L. Hankins. Cambridge ; Cambridge University Press, 1985. viii, 216 p.
84-016988            509            0521243491
*Science -- History.*

**Q125.H5574 1998**
Hellman, Hal,
Great feuds in science : ten of the liveliest disputes ever / Hal Hellman. New York : Wiley, c1998. xv, 240 p. ;
97-039824            509/.2/2            0471169803
*Science -- History. Scientists -- Social aspects -- History. Vendetta -- Case studies.*

**Q125.H5587 2001**
Henry, John.
The scientific revolution and the origins of modern science / John Henry. 2nd ed. New York : Palgrave, 2001. ix, 160 p. :
            509.4/09/032 21
*Science -- History. Science -- Methodology. Science -- Philosophy.*

**Q125.K42**
Kearney, Hugh F.
Science and change, 1500-1700 [by] Hugh Kearney. New York, McGraw-Hill [1971] 255 p.
76-096433            509/.031
*Science -- History.*

**Q125.L25 1998**
**Laidler, Keith James,**
   To light such a candle : chapters in the history of science and technology / by Keith J. Laidler. Oxford ; Oxford University Press, 1998. xii, 384 p. :
97-024690          609          0198500564
   *Science -- History. Technology -- History. Discoveries in science -- History.*

**Q125.N17**
**Nasr, Seyyed Hossein.**
   Science and civilization in Islam. With a pref. by Giorgio de Santillana. Cambridge, Mass., Harvard University Press, 1968. xiv, 384 p.
68-025616          509/.176/7
   *Science, Medieval. Civilization, Islamic.*

**Q125.O24 1995**
**Ochoa, George.**
   The timeline book of science / George Ochoa and Melinda Corey. 1st ed. New York : Ballantine, c1995. xi, 434 p. :
          509 20          034538265X
*Science -- History -- Chronology.*

**Q125.P595 2001**
**Pickstone, John V.**
   Ways of knowing : a new history of science, technology, and medicine / John V. Pickstone. Chicago : University of Chicago Press, 2001. xii, 271 p. ;
00-053248          509          0226667944
   *Science -- History. Technology -- History. Medicine -- History.*

**Q125.P928 2000**
   Prediction : science, decision making, and the future of nature / edited by Daniel Sarewitz, Roger A. Pielke, Jr., and Radford Byerly, Jr. Washington, D.C. : Island Press, c2000. xv, 405 p. :
00-008179          363.1/07          1559637757
   *Science and state. Decision making. Forecasting.*

**Q125.R335 2000**
   Reader's guide to the history of science / edited by Arne Hessenbruch. London ; Chicago : Fitzroy Dearborn, 2000. xxix, 934 p. ;
          509/.03 21          188496429X
*Science -- History Encyclopedias.*

**Q125.R34 1990**
   Reappraisals of the scientific revolution / edited by David C. Lindberg and Robert S. Westman. Cambridge [England] ; Cambridge University Press, 1990. xxvii, 551 p.
89-070859          509/.031          0521342627
   *Science -- History -- 16th century. Science -- History -- 17th century.*

**Q125.R7426 1982**
**Ronan, Colin A.**
   Science : its history and development among the world's cultures / by Colin A. Ronan. New York, N.Y. : Facts on File, c1982. 543 p. :
82-012176          509          0871967456
   *Science -- History.*

**Q125.S246**
**Sarton, George,**
   A history of science. Cambridge, Harvard University Press, 1952-59. 2 v.
52-005041          509/.01
   *Science -- History. Science, Ancient. Civilization, Ancient.*

**Q125.S25 1956**
**Sarton, George,**
   The history of science and the new humanism. New York, G. Braziller, 1956. xix, 196 p.
56000791          509
   *Science -- History Civilization -- History. Humanism -- 20th century.*

**Q125.S323 1960**
**Sarton, George,**
   The life of science; essays in the history of civilization. Introd. by Conway Zirkle. Bloomington, Indiana University Press [1960] 197 p.
60-050082          504
   *Science -- History. Civilization.*

**Q125.S326**
**Sarton, George,**
   Six wings: men of science in the Renaissance. Bloomington, Indiana University Press, 1957. xiv, 318 p.
56-011998          509.03
   *Scientists -- Biography. Science -- History. Renaissance.*

**Q125.S434337 1997**
   Science in the twentieth century / edited by John Krige & Dominique Pestre. Amsterdam : Harwood Academic Publishers, c1997. xxxv, 941 p. :
          9057021722
*Science -- History -- 20th century.*

**Q125.S43713 1988**
   The History of science and techology : a narrative chronology. New York : Facts on File, c1988. 2 v. (889 p.)
88-026052          509          0871964775
   *Science -- History. Technology -- History.*

**Q125.S5166 1996**
**Shapin, Steven.**
   The scientific revolution / Steven Shapin. Chicago, IL : University of Chicago Press, 1996. xiv, 218 p. ;
96-013196          509          0226750205
   *Science -- History.*

**Q125.T52**
**Thorndike, Lynn,**
   A history of magic and experimental science. New York, Macmillan, 1923-58. 8 v.
23-002984          509
   *Science -- History. Magic -- History.*

**Q125.W59 1999**
**Whitfield, Peter.**
   Landmarks in western science : from prehistory to the atomic age / Peter Whitfield. New York : Routledge, c1999. 256 p. :
99-024976          509          0415925339
   *Science -- History.*

**Q125.Z56 1994**
**Ziman, J. M.**
   Prometheus bound : science in a dynamic steady state / John Ziman. Cambridge [England] ; Cambridge University Press, 1994. ix, 289 p. ;
93-005922          338.9/26          0521434300
   *Science and state. Science -- Social aspects. Research -- Management.*

### Q125.2 History — Modern — Renaissance through 1700

**Q125.2.B53 1997**
**Blair, Ann,**
   The theater of nature : Jean Bodin and Renaissance science / by Ann Blair. Princeton, NJ : Princeton University Press, 1997. xiv, 382 p. :
96-040164          113/.092          0691056757
*Bodin, Jean, -- 1530-1596.   Physics -- History. Philosophy of nature -- History. Science, Renaissance.*

**Q125.2.D4**
**Debus, Allen G.**
   Man and nature in the Renaissance / Allen G. Debus. Cambridge ; Cambridge University Press, 1978. x, 159 p. ;
77-091085          509/.024          0521219728
   *Science, Renaissance. Science -- Philosophy. Human beings.*

**Q125.2.J33 1998**
**Jacob, James R.**
   The scientific revolution : aspirations and achievements, 1500-1700 / James R. Jacob. Atlantic Highlands, NJ : Humanities Press, 1998. xviii, 148 p.
97-017851          509/.4/0903          0391039776
   *Science, Renaissance. Science -- France -- History – 17th century. Science -- England -- History -- 17th century.*

**Q125.2.R45 1993**
   Renaissance and revolution : humanists, scholars, craftsmen, and natural philosophers in early modern Europe / edited and introduced by J.V. Field and Frank A.J.L. James. Cambridge [England] ; Cambridge University Press, 1993. xv, 291 p. :
93-006624          509.4/0903          0521434270
   *Science, Renaissance. Science -- Europe -- History – 18th century. Technology -- Europe -- History -- 18th century.*

### Q126.8 History — Addresses, essays, lectures

**Q126.8.L58 1991**
   The Literary structure of scientific argument : historical studies / edited by Peter Dear. Philadelphia : University of Pennsylvania Press, c1991. vi, 211 p. :
90-045803          509          0812281853
   *Science -- History. Science -- Study and teaching -- History. Technical writing -- History.*

### Q126.9 History — Study and teaching. Research

**Q126.9.S58 1999**
   Situating the history of science : dialogues with Joseph Needham / edited by S. Irfan Habib and Dhruv Raina. New Delhi ; Oxford University Press, c1999. x, 358 p. ;
99-935798          507/.22          0195646398
*Needham, Joseph, -- 1900- -- Congresses.   Science -- Historiography -- Congresses.*

### Q127 History — By region or country, A-Z

**Q127.A5.H84 1993**
**Huff, Toby E.,**
   The rise of early modern science : Islam, China, and the West / Toby E. Huff. Cambridge [England] ; Cambridge University Press, 1993. xiv, 409 p. :
92-036531          509          0521434963
   *Science -- Arab countries -- History. Science --Islamic countries -- History. Science -- China -- History.*

**Q127.C5.B63 1991**
**Bodde, Derk,**
   Chinese thought, society, and science : the intellectual and social background of science and technology in pre-modern China / Derk Bodde. Honolulu : University of Hawaii Press, c1991. p. cm.
91-004437          509.51          0824813340
   *Science -- China -- History. Science -- Social aspects –China– History. Technology -- China -- History. China -- Civilization.*

**Q127.C5.S333 1989**
   Science and technology in post-Mao China / edited by Denis Fred Simon and Merle Goldman. Cambridge, Mass. : Council on East Asian Studies, Harvard Universit 1989. xv, 461 p. :
88-028456          338.95106          0674794753
   *Science -- China -- History -- 20th century. Technology –China– History -- 20th century.   China -- History -- 1976-*

**Q127.E8**
**Dear, Peter Robert.**
   Revolutionizing the sciences : European knowledge and its ambitions, 1500-1700 / Peter Dear. Princeton, N.J. : Princeton University Press, 2001. viii, 208 p.
00-109720          509.4/09/031          0691088594
   *Science -- Europe -- History.*

**Q127.E8.C76 1994**
**Crombie, A. C.**
   Styles of scientific thinking in the European tradition : the history of argument and explanation especially in the mathematical and biomedical sciences and arts / A.C. Crombie. London : Duckworth, c1994. 3 v. (xxxi, 2
95-107982      501      0715624393
   *Science -- history -- Europe. Science -- methods -- Europe. Science -- Europe -- History.*

**Q127.G3.W35 1995**
**Walker, Mark,**
   Nazi science : myth, truth, and the German atomic bomb / Mark Walker. New York : Plenum Press, c1995. viii, 325 p.
95-006102      509.43/09/044      0306449412
   *Science -- Germany -- History. National socialism and science. Atomic bomb -- Germany -- History.*

**Q127.I4.H58 1999**
   History of Indian science, technology, and culture, A.D. 1000-1800 / edited by A. Rahman. New Delhi : Oxford University Press, 1999. xx, 445 p. :
99-935800      509.54      0195646525
   *Science -- India -- History. Science, Medieval. Technology -- India -- History.*

**Q127.I4.K86 1995**
**Kumar, Deepak,**
   Science and the Raj, 1857-1905 / Deepak Kumar. Delhi ; Oxford University Press, 1995. xiv, 273 p. :
95-904408      0195635620
   *Science -- India -- History -- British occupation, 1765-1947. Science and state -- India -- History -- British occupation, 1765-1947.*

**Q127.I742.T78 1997**
**Turner, Howard R.,**
   Science in medieval Islam : an illustrated introduction / by Howard R. Turner. Austin : University of Texas Press, 1997. xviii, 262 p.
97-007733      509/.17/671      0292781474
   *Science -- Islamic countries -- History. Science, Medieval. Civilization, Medieval.*

**Q127.I8.S44 1991**
**Segre, Michael,**
   In the wake of Galileo / Michael Segre. New Brunswick, N.J. : Rutgers University Press, c1991. xix, 192 p. :
90-024573      509.45      0813517001
   *Galilei, Galileo, -- 1564-1642. Science -- Italy --History. Science -- Historiography Italy -- Intellectual life -- 1789-1900.*

**Q127.J3.B37 1989**
**Bartholomew, James R.,**
   The formation of science in Japan : building a research tradition / James R. Bartholomew. New Haven : Yale University Press, c1989. xvii, 371 p.,
88-036817      509.52      0300042612
   *Science -- Japan -- History. Research -- Japan -- History.*

**Q127.R9.S65 1994**
**Soifer, Valeriaei.**
   Lysenko and the tragedy of Soviet science / Valery N Soyfer ; translated from the Russian by Leo Gruliow and Rebecca Gruliow. New Brunswick, N.J. : Rutgers University Press, c1994. xxiv, 379 p.
93-039566      575.1/0947      0813520878
   *Lysenko, Trofim Denisovich, -- 1898-1976. Political purges -- Russia (Federation) -- History. Genetics -- Russia (Federation) -- History. Science and state -- Russia (Federation) -- History.*

**Q127.S696.G729 1993**
**Graham, Loren R.**
   Science in Russia and the Soviet Union : a short history / Loren R. Graham. Cambridge ; Cambridge University Press, 1993. x, 321 p. :
92-005087      509.47      0521245664
   *Science -- Soviet Union -- History.*

**Q127.U5**
**Mann, Alfred K.**
   For better or for worse : the marriage of science and government in the United States / Alfred K. Mann. New York : Columbia University Press, c2000. xvi, 240 p. :
00-060120      509.73      023111706X
   *Science and state -- United States -- History -- 20th century.*

**Q127.U6**
   The history of science in the United States : an encyclopedia / edited by Marc Rothenberg. New York : Garland, 2000. p. cm.
99-043757      509.73      0815307624
   *Science -- United States -- History -- Encyclopedias.*

**Q127.U6.D33**
**Daniels, George H.**
   Science in American society; a social history [by] George H. Daniels. New York, Knopf, 1971. xii, 390, x p
79-118708      301.2/43/0973      0394443861
   *Science -- United States -- History. Science and civilization.*

**Q127.U6.G43 1997**
**Gibbons, John H.,**
   This gifted age : science and technology at the millennium / John H. Gibbons ; foreword by Vice President Al Gore. Woodbury, N.Y. : AIP Press, c1997. xvii, 346 p.
96-051110      333.79      1563961296
   *Science and state -- United States -- History. Technology and state -- United States -- History.*

**Q127.U6.R397 1991**
**Reingold, Nathan,**
   Science, American style / Nathan Reingold. New Brunswick : Rutgers University Press, c1991. 429 p. ;
90-009068      509.73      0813516609
   *Science -- United States -- History. Science -- United States -- History -- 19th century.*

**Q127.U6.S25 1996**
**Sarewitz, Daniel R.**
   Frontiers of illusion : science, technology, and the politics of progress / Daniel Sarewitz. Philadelphia : Temple University Press, 1996. xi, 235 p. ;
95-031840          338.97306          1566394155
   *Science and state -- United States. Technology and state – United States. Research -- Philosophy.*

**Q127.U6.T384 1994**
**Teitelman, Robert.**
   Profits of science : the American marriage of business and technology / Robert Teitelman. New York, NY : BasicBooks, c1994. xi, 258 p. ;
93-033277          303.48/3/0973          0465039839
   *Science -- United States. Science -- Economic aspects – United States. Science -- Political aspects -- United States.*

**Q127.U6.W36 1999**
**Wang, Jessica.**
   American science in an age of anxiety : scientists, anticommunism, and the cold war / Jessica Wang. Chapel Hill, NC : University of North Carolina Press, c1999. xii, 375p. :
98-014441          509.73          080782447X
   *Science -- United States -- History -- 20th century. Science and state -- United States -- History -- 20th century.*

**Q127.U6.W48 1994**
   Who will do science? : educating the next generation / edited by Willie Pearson, Jr., and Alan Fechter. Baltimore : Johns Hopkins University Press, 1994. xxii, 169 p.
94-009005          338.97306          0801848571
   *Science and state -- United States. Engineering and state – United States. Education and state -- United States.*

# Q130 Women in science

**Q130.E85 2000**
**Etzkowitz, Henry,**
   Athena unbound : the advancement of women in science and technology / Henry Etzkowitz, Carol Kemelgor, Brian Uzzi, with Michael Neushatz ... [et al.]. Cambridge ; Cambridge University Press, 2000. 282 p. ;
00-020997          500/.82          0521563801
   *Women in science. Women in technology. Feminism and science.*

**Q130.G43 2000**
   The gender and science reader / edited by Muriel Lederman and Ingrid Bartsch. New York : Routledge, 2000. p. cm.
00-044646          500/.82          0415213576
   *Women in science. Women in technology. Feminism and science.*

**Q130.H365 1996**
**Hanson, Sandra L.**
   Lost talent : women in the sciences / Sandra L. Hanson. Philadelphia : Temple University Press, 1996. xii, 220 p. :
96-000219          500/.82          1566394465
   *Women in science -- United States. Women science students -- United States.*

**Q130.M47 1980**
**Merchant, Carolyn.**
   The death of nature : women, ecology, and the scientific revolution / Carolyn Merchant. San Francisco : Harper & Row, c1980. xx, 348 p. :
79-001766          304.2          0062505718
   *Women in science -- Social aspects. Philosophy of nature. Human ecology.*

**Q130.P53 1990**
**Phillips, Patricia,**
   The scientific lady : a social history of women's scientific interests, 1520-1918 / Patricia Phillips. New York : St. Martin's Press, 1990. xiii, 279 p.,
90-048085          305.43/5          0312056850
   *Women in science -- Great Britain -- History. Women -- Great Britain -- Intellectual life -- History.*

**Q130.R68 1982**
**Rossiter, Margaret W.**
   Women scientists in America : struggles and strategies to 1940 / Margaret W. Rossiter. Baltimore : Johns Hopkins University Press, c1982. xviii, 439 p.
81-020902          331.4/815/0973          0801824435
   *Women scientists -- United States. Women in science -- United States.*

**Q130.S32 1989**
**Schiebinger, Londa L.**
   The mind has no sex? : women in the origins of modern science / Londa Schiebinger. Cambridge, Mass. : Harvard University Press, 1989. xi, 355 p. :
88-034945          500/.82          0674576233
   *Women in science -- History. Sex discrimination in science -- History. Sex discrimination against women -- History.*

**Q130.S327 1991**
   Science and sensibility : gender and scientific enquiry, 1780-1945 / edited by Marina Benjamin. Oxford, UK ; B. Blackwell, 1991. x, 295 p. :
90-039668          500/.82          0631166491
   *Women in science.*

**Q130.S66 1995**
**Sonnert, Gerhard,**
   Who succeeds in science? : the gender dimension / Gerhard Sonnert with the assistance of Gerald Holton. New Brunswick, N.J. : Rutgers University Press, c1995. xvi, 215 p. ;
95-008598          305.43/5          0813522196
   *Women in science -- United States. Science – Vocational guidance -- United States -- Sex differences. Science -- Study and teaching – United States -- Sex differences.*

**Q130.W655 1998**
   Women in science : meeting career challenges / edited by Angela M. Pattatucci. Thousand Oaks, Calif. : Sage Publications, c1998. xiv, 304 p. ;
98-009052          508.2          0761900489
   *Women in science.*

**Q130.W672 2001**

Women, science, and technology : a reader in feminist science studies / edited by Mary Wyer ... [et al.]. New York : Routledge, 2001. xxviii, 376 p

00-046452          500/.82          0415926076

*Women in science. Science -- Study and teaching. Women -- Education.*

**Q130.W676 2000**

Women succeeding in the sciences : theories and practices across disciplines / edited by Jody Bart. West Lafayette, Ind. : Purdue University Press, c2000. x, 277 p. ;

99-026055          507.1          1557531218

*Women in science. Feminism.*

## Q141 Biography — Collective

**Q141.A74 1982**
**Asimov, Isaac,**

Asimov's biographical encyclopedia of science and technology : the lives and achievements of 1510 great scientists from ancient times to the present chronologically arranged / by Isaac Asimov. Garden City, N.Y. : Doubleday, 1982. xxxv, 941 p.,

81-047861          509/.2/2          0385177712

*Scientists -- Biography -- Chronology. Scientists -- Biography -- Dictionaries.*

**Q141.B25 1994**
**Bailey, Martha J.**

American women in science : a biographical dictionary / Martha J. Bailey. Santa Barbara, Calif. : ABC-CLIO, c1994. xxi, 463 p. :

94-010096          509.2/273          0874367409

*Women scientists -- United States -- Biography -- Dictionaries.*

**Q141.B254 1998**
**Bailey, Martha J.**

American women in science : 1950 to the present : a biographical dictionary / Martha J. Bailey. Santa Barbara, CA : ABC-CLIO, c1998. xxxiii, 455 p

98-022433          500/.82/092273          0874369215

*Women scientists -- United States -- Biography -- Dictionaries. Women in science -- United States -- Biography -- Dictionaries.*

**Q141.B32 1994**
**Bass, Thomas A.**

Reinventing the future : conversations with the world's leading scientists / Thomas A. Bass. Reading, Mass. : Addison-Wesley Pub., c1994. vi, 249 p. :

93-014576          574/.092/2          020162642X

*Scientists -- Interviews. Research -- History.*

**Q141.B42 1993**
**McGrayne, Sharon Bertsch.**

Nobel Prize women in science : their lives, struggles, and momentous discoveries / Sharon Bertsch McGrayne. Secaucus, N.J. : Carol Pub. Group, c1993. xi, 419 p. :

92-021131          509/.2/2          1559721464

*Women scientists -- Biography. Science -- Awards. Nobel Prizes.*

**Q141.B528 2000**

The biographical dictionary of scientists. 3rd ed. / consultant editors, Roy Porter, Marilyn Ogilvie. New York : Oxford University Press, 2000. 2 v. (1196p.) :

          509.2/2 B 21          0195216636

*Scientists -- Biography -- Dictionaries.*

**Q141.B5285 2000**

The biographical dictionary of women in science : pioneering lives from ancient times to the mid-20th century / Marilyn Ogilvie and Joy Harvey, editors. New York : Routledge, 2000. 2 v. (xxxviii

99-017668          509/.2/2          0415920388

*Scientists -- Biography -- Dictionaries.*

**Q141.B58 1990**
**Sammons, Vivian O.**

Blacks in science and medicine / Vivian Ovelton Sammons. New York : Hemisphere Pub. Corp., c1990. xii, 293 p. ;

89-032934          509.2/2          0891166653

*Afro-American scientists -- Biography. Afro-American physicians -- Biography.*

**Q141.B777 1998**
**Bragg, Melvyn,**

On giants' shoulders : great scientists and their discoveries : from Archimedes to DNA / Melvyn Bragg, with Ruth Gardiner. New York : Wiley, 1998. xiii, 365 p.

99-029005          509.2/2          0471357324

*Scientists -- Biography. Science -- History.*

**Q141.C128 1996**

The Cambridge dictionary of scientists / David Millar ... [et al.]. Cambridge ; Cambridge University Press, 1996. xii, 387 p. :

95-038471          509.2/2          052156185X

*Scientists -- Biography -- Dictionaries. Science -- History.*

**Q141.C69 1998**
**Creese, Mary R. S.,**

Ladies in the laboratory? : American and British women in science, 1800-1900 : a survey of their contributions to research / Mary R.S. Creese, with contributions by Thomas M. Creese. Lanham, Md. : Scarecrow Press, 1998. xii, 452 p. :

97-001125          500/.82/094109034
0810832879

*Women in science -- United States -- History -- 19th century. Women in science -- Great Britain -- History -- 19th century. Women scientists -- United States -- Biography.*

**Q141.D5 1981**

Dictionary of scientific biography / Charles Coulston Gillispie, editor in chief. New York : Scribner, 1981, c1980-c v. 1-18; in 1

80-027830          509/.2/2          0684169622

*Scientists -- Biography -- Dictionaries.*

**Q141.D535 1996**

Distinguished African American scientists of the 20th century / James H. Kessler ... [et al.] ; with Sigrid Berge, portrait artist, and Alyce Neukirk, computer graphics artist. Phoenix, Ariz. : Oryx Press, 1996. ix, 382 p. :
95-043880          509.2/273          0897749553
   *Scientists -- United States -- Biography. Afro-American scientists -- Biography.*

**Q141.H2167 2001**
**Haines, Catharine M.C.**

International women in science : a biographical dictionary to 1950 / Catharine M.C. Haines ; with Helen M. Stevens. Santa Barbara, Calif. : ABC-CLIO, c2001. xix, 383 p. :
          509.2/2 B 21          1576070905
*Women scientists -- Biography.*

**Q141.J46 1996**
**Jenkins, Edward Sidney.**

To fathom more : African American scientists and inventors / Edward Sidney Jenkins ; with contributions by Patricia Stohr-Hunt, Exyie C. Ryder, S. Maxwell Hines. Lanham, Md. : University Press of America, c1996. 399 p. ;
95-045159          509.2/273          0761802142
   *Scientists -- United States -- Biography. Afro-American scientists -- Biography. Afro-American inventors -- Biography.*

**Q141.L36 1994**

Larousse dictionary of scientists / editor, Hazel Muir. Edinburgh [Scotland] ; Larousse, 1994. ix, 595 p. ;
94-075739          509/.2/2          0752300024
   *Scientists -- Biography.*

**Q141.M358 1998b**
**McGrayne, Sharon Bertsch.**

Nobel Prize women in science : their lives, struggles, and momentous discoveries / Sharon Bertsch McGrayne. 2nd ed. Washington, D.C. : Joseph Henry Press, c1998. xi, 451 p. :
          509.2/2 B 21          0309072700
*Women scientists -- Awards. Science -- Awards. Nobel Prizes.*

**Q141.N726 1999**

Notable Black American scientists / Kristine Krapp, editor. Detroit : Gale Research, c1999. xxvi, 349 p.
94005263          509.2/273          0787627895
   *Afro-Americans -- Biography. Afro-American scientists -- United States -- Biography. Scientists -- United States -- Biography.*

**Q141.N73 1995 Suppl.**

Notable twentieth century scientists. Kristine M. Krapp, editor. Detroit : Gale, c1998. xxv, 617 p. :
98-014016          509.2/2          0787627666
   *Scientists -- Biography -- Dictionaries. Engineers -- Biography -- Dictionaries.*

**Q141.N734 1997**

Notable women in the physical sciences : a biographical dictionary / edited by Benjamin F. Shearer and Barbara S. Shearer. Westport, Conn. : Greenwood Press, 1997. xi, 479 p. :
96-009024          500.2/092/2          0313293031
   *Women physical scientists -- Biography.*

**Q141.N736 1999**

Notable women scientists / Pamela Proffitt, editor. Detroit : Gale Group, c1999. xxvi, 668 p.
99-035741          500/.82/092          0787639001
   *Women scientists -- Biography -- Juvenile literature. Scientists. Women -- Biography.*

**Q141.O25 2001**
**Oakes, Elizabeth H.,**

Encyclopedia of world scientists / Elizabeth H. Oakes. New York : Facts on File, c2001. xii, 450 p. :
00-029419          509.2/2          081604130X
   *Scientists -- Biography -- Dictionaries.*

**Q141.O25 2001**
**Oakes, Elizabeth H.,**

Encyclopedia of world scientists / Elizabeth H. Oakes. New York : Facts on File, c2001. xii, 450 p. :
          509.2/2 B 21          081604130X
*Scientists -- Biography -- Encyclopedias.*

**Q141.O34 1986**
**Ogilvie, Marilyn Bailey.**

Women in science : antiquity through the nineteenth century : a biographical dictionary with annotated bibliography / Marilyn Bailey Ogilvie. Cambridge, Mass. : MIT Press, c1986. xi, 254 p. ;
86-007507          509.2/2          026215031X
   *Women scientists -- Biography -- Dictionaries. Women in science -- Bibliography. Scientists -- Biography -- Dictionaries.*

**Q141.S3717 1996**

Scientists : the lives and works of 150 scientists / Peggy Saari and Stephen Allison, editors. [Detroit, MI] : U*X*L, c1996- v. :
          509/.2/2 B 20          0787609595
*Physical scientists -- Biography. Social scientists -- Biography.*

**Q141.S54 1999**

Scientists, mathematicians, and inventors : lives and legacies : an encyclopedia of people who changed the world / edited by Doris Simonis ; writers, Caroline Hertzenberg . . . [et al.] Phoenix, Ariz. : Oryx Press, 1999. x, 244 p. :
          509.2/2 B 21          1573561517
*Scientists -- Biography -- Encyclopedias. Mathematicians -- Biography -- Encyclopedias. Inventors -- Biography -- Encyclopedias.*

**Q141.S65 1998**

Spiritual evolution : scientists discuss their beliefs / edited by John Marks Templeton and Kenneth Seeman Giniger. Philadelphia, Pa. : Templeton Foundation Press, 1998. p. cm.
          200/.88/5 21          1890151165
*Scientists -- Biography. Scientists -- Religious life. Spiritual biography. Faith.*

**Q141.V25 1999**
**Van der Does, Louise Q.**

Renaissance women in science / Louise Q. van der Does, Rita J. Simon. Lanham, Md. : University Press of America, c1999. iii, 192 p. :
99-038106          500/.82/0922          0761814809
   *Women scientists -- Biography.*

**Q141.W367 1999**
**Warren, Wini.**
   Black women scientists in the United States / Wini Warren.
Bloomington : Indiana University Press, c1999. xx, 366 p. :
99-040264          500/.82/0973          0253336031
   *African American women scientists -- Biography.*

**Q141.W43 1999**
**Webster, Raymond B.**
   African American firsts in science and technology /
Raymond B. Webster ; guest foreword by Wesley L. Harris.
Detroit, MI : Gale Group, c1999. xiii, 461 p. :
            508.996/073 21          0787638765
*Afro-American scientists -- Biography -- Juvenile literature. Afro-
American inventors -- Biography -- Juvenile literature. Scientists.
Inventors. Afro-Americans -- Biography.*

**Q141.W7**
   World who's who in science: a biographical dictionary of
notable scientists from antiquity to the present. Editor: Allen
G. Debus. Associate editors: Ronald S. Calinger [and] Edward
J. Collins. Managing editor: Stephen J. Kennedy. Chicago,
Marquis-Who's Who, inc. [1968] xvi, 1855 p.
68-056149          509/.22          0837910013
   *Scientists -- Biography -- Dictionaries.*

**Q141.Y675 1999**
**Yount, Lisa.**
   A to Z of women in science and math / Lisa Yount. New
York, NY : Facts on File, c1999. xvii, 254 p.
98-046093          509.2/2          0816037973
   *Women scientists -- Biography -- Encyclopedias. Women
mathematicians -- Biography -- Encyclopedias.*

**Q141.B528 2000**
   The biographical dictionary of scientists.   New York :
Oxford University Press, 2000. 2 v. (1196 p.
00-036752          509.2/2          0195216636
   *Scientists -- Biography -- Encyclopedias.*

## Q143 Biography — Individual

**Q143.B77.S27 1995**
**Sargent, Rose-Mary.**
   The diffident naturalist : Robert Boyle and the philosophy of
experiment / Rose-Mary Sargent. Chicago : University of
Chicago Press, 1995. xi, 355 p. ;
94-019205          530/.092          0226734951
*Boyle, Robert, -- 1627-1691.     Scientists -- GreatBritain --
Biography.*

**Q143.F8.T36 1989**
**Tanford, Charles,**
   Ben Franklin stilled the waves : an informal history of
pouring oil on water with reflections on the ups and downs of
scientific life in general / by Charles Tanford. Durham : Duke
University Press, 1989. viii, 227 p.
88-029344          539/.6/09          0822308762
*Franklin, Benjamin, -- 1706-1790 -- Knowledge -- Science.
Molecules. Scientists -- United States -- Biography.*

**Q143.G53.F56 1991**
**Fink, Karl J.,**
   Goethe's history of science / Karl J. Fink. Cambridge
[England] ; Cambridge University Press, 1991. xii, 242 p. :
91-008631          509          0521402115
*Goethe, Johann Wolfgang von, -- 1749-1832 -- Knowledge – Science.
Science -- History. Science -- Philosophy -- History. Science --
Historiography.*

**Q143.H956.D47 1997**
**Desmond, Adrian J.,**
   Huxley : from devil's dsciple to evolution's high priest /
Adrian Desmond. Reading, Mass : Addison-Wesley, c1997.
xx, 820 p. :
97-022480          509.2          0201959879
*Huxley, Thomas Henry, -- 1825-1895.     Scientists – GreatBritain –
Biography.*

**Q143.L5.A3 1989**
**Leonardo,**
   Leonardo da Vinci.   New Haven : Yale University Press in
association with the So c1989. 246 p. :
88-037855          709.2          0300045085
*Leonardo, -- da Vinci, -- 1452-1519 -- Exhibitions.     Research –
Exhibitions. Inventions -- Exhibitions.*

**Q143.P17.A33 1995**
**Adamson, Donald.**
   Blaise Pascal : mathematician, physicist, and thinker about
God / Donald Adamson. New York : St. Martin's, 1995. xii,
297 p. :
94-031137          194          031212502X
*Pascal, Blaise, -- 1623-1662.     Science -- History. Philosophy –
History. Scientists -- France -- Biography.*

**Q143.P2.D3313 1998**
**Debre, P.**
   Louis Pasteur / Patrice Debre ; translated by Elborg Forster.
Baltimore : Johns Hopkins University Press, 1998. xxv, 552 p.
:
97043686          509/.2          0801858089
*Pasteur, Louis, -- 1822-1895.     Science -- History -- 19th century.
Scientists -- France -- Biography.*

**Q143.P2.R49 1994**
**Reynolds, Moira Davison.**
   How Pasteur changed history : the story of Louis Pasteur
and the Pasteur Institute / Moira Davison Reynolds. Bradenton,
Fla. : McGuinn & McGuire Pub., c1994. 151 p. :
94-002757          509.2          1881117057
*Pasteur, Louis, -- 1822-1895.     Science -- History. Medical sciences
-- France -- History. Scientist -- France -- Biography.*

**Q143.P25**
**Pauling, Linus,**
   Linus Pauling : scientist and peacemaker / edited by
Clifford Mead, Thomas Hager. Corvallis : Oregon State
University Press, 2001. 272 p. :
00-011894          540/.92          0870714899
*Pauling, Linus, -- 1901-     Science -- History. Scientists -- United
States -- Biography.*

## Q143.P25.A3 1995
**Pauling, Linus,**

Linus Pauling : in his own words : selected writings, speeches, and interviews / edited by Barbara Marinacci ; introduction by Linus Pauling. New York : Simon & Schuster, c1995. 320 p. ;
95-031123      081      0684813874
*Pauling, Linus, -- 1901-   Science -- History. Scientists -- United States -- Biography.*

## Q143.P25.G64 1995
**Goertzel, Ted George.**

Linus Pauling : a life in science and politics / Ted Goertzel and Ben Goertzel, with the assistance of Mildred Goertzel, Victor Goertzel, with original drawings by Gwen Goertzel. New York : Basic Books, c1995. xvii, 300 p.,
95-009005      540/.92      0465006728
*Pauling, Linus, -- 1901-   Scientists -- United States -- Biography.*

## Q143.P8.S8
**Stegner, Wallace Earle,**

Beyond the hundredth meridian: John Wesley Powell and the second opening of the West. With an introd. by Bernard De Voto. Boston, Houghton, Mifflin, 1954. xxiii, 438 p.
53-009245      925
*Powell, John Wesley, -- 1834-1902.      West (U.S.) -- History.*

## Q143.S56.B76 1989
**Brown, Chandos Michael,**

Benjamin Silliman : a life in the young republic / Chandos Michael Brown. Princeton, N.J. : Princeton University Press, c1989. xvi, 377 p. :
88-032086      509.2/4      0691085331
*Silliman, Benjamin, -- 1779-1864.      Scientists -- United States -- Biography.*

# Q147-149 Science as a profession

## Q147.H47 1998
**Hermanowicz, Joseph C.**

The stars are not enough : scientists--their passions and professions / Joseph C. Hermanowicz. Chicago : University of Chicago Press, 1998. xv, 268 p. :
98-003141      306.4/5      0226327663
*Scientists -- Social aspects. Science -- Vocational guidance.*

## Q147.P53 1998
**Pickover, Clifford A.**

Strange brains and genius : the secret lives of eccentric scientists and madmen / Clifford A. Pickover. New York : Plenum Trade, c1998. xiv, 332 p. :
98-010232      509.2      0306457849
*Scientists -- Psychology. Genius. Eccentrics and eccentricities.*

## Q148.S55 1996
**Simmons, John G.,**

The scientific 100 : a ranking of the most influential scientists, past and present / John Simmons. Secaucus, N.J. : Carol Pub. Group, c1996. xix, 504 p. :
95-049911      509.2/2      0806517492
*Scientists -- Rating of. Scientists -- Biography -- Chronology. Science -- History.*

## Q149.U5.B57 1989
Blacks, science, and American education / edited by Willie Pearson, Jr., and H. Kenneth Bechtel. New Brunswick : Rutgers University Press, c1989. xx, 174 p. :
88-030606      508/.996/073      0813513979
*Afro-American scientists -- United States. Afro-Americans -- Education -- United States -- Science. Science – Study and teaching – United States.*

## Q149.U5.R45 1997
**Reis, Richard M.,**

Tomorrow's professor : preparing for academic careers in science and engineering / Richard M. Reis ; IEEE Education Society, sponsor. New York : IEEE Press, c1997. xix, 416 p. :
96-037355      507/.1/1      0780311361
*Scientists -- Vocational guidance -- United States -- Handbooks, manuals, etc. Scientists -- Vocational guidance -- Canada -- Handbooks, manuals, etc. Engineers -- Vocational guidance – United States -- Handbooks, manuals, etc.*

# Q151-157 Early works through 1800

## Q151.A7.H6
**Aristotle.**

Physics. Newly translated by Richard Hope, with an analytical index of technical terms. [Lincoln] University of Nebraska Press, 1961. xiii, 241 p.
61005498      530.938
*Science, Ancient. Physics -- Early works to 1800.*

## Q151.A72 1970
**Aristotle.**

Aristotle's Physics. Books 1 & 2; translated [from the Greek] with introduction and notes by W. Charlton. Oxford, Clarendon P., 1970. xvii, 151 p.
70-503838      501      0198720254
*Science, Ancient. Physics -- Early works to 1800.*

## Q151.A8.A75 1991
Aristotle's Physics : a collection of essays / edited by Lindsay Judson. Oxford [England] : Clarendon Press ; 1991. 286 p. ;
91-019303      530      019824844X
*Aristotle. -- Physics.*

**Q151.A8.L36 1992**
**Lang, Helen S.,**
  Aristotle's Physics and its medieval varieties / Helen S. Lang. Albany : State University of New York Press, c1992. ix, 322 p. ;
91-035652          500          0791410838
*Aristotle. -- Physics.     Learning and scholarship -- History -- Medieval, 500-1500. Science, Ancient. Physics -- Early works to 1800.*

**Q151.A8.S23 1995**
**Sachs, Joe.**
  Aristotle's physics : a guided study / Joe Sachs. New Brunswick, N.J. : Rutgers University Press, c1995. xi, 260 p. ;
94-046477          530          0813521912
*Aristotle. -- Physics.     Physics -- Early works to 1800.*

**Q151.A8.W35 1996**
**Wallace, William A.**
  The modeling of nature : philosophy of science and philosophy of nature in synthesis / William A. Wallace. Washington, D.C. : The Catholic University of America Press, c1996. xx, 450 p. :
96-005378          501          0813208599
*Aristotle -- Views on science.     Science -- Philosophy. Science -- Methodology. Philosophy of nature.*

**Q155.D433**
**Descartes, Rene,**
  Discourse on method, Optics, Geometry, and Meteorology. Translated, with an introd. by Paul J. Olscamp. Indianapolis, Bobbs-Merrill [1965] xxxvi, 361 p.
65026521          509.24
  *Science -- Methodology. Refraction. Meteorology.*

**Q157.B24 2001**
**Bauer, Henry H.**
  Science or pseudoscience : magnetic healing, psychic phenomena, and other heterodoxies / Henry H. Bauer. Urbana : University of Illinois Press, c2001. xi, 275 p. ;
00-008332          133          0252026012
  *Pseudoscience -- Encyclopedias.*

**Q157.E57 2000**
  Encyclopedia of pseudoscience / William F. Williams, general editor. New York, NY : Facts On File, c2000. xxvi, 416 p.
98-047141          001.9          081603351X
  *Pseudoscience -- Encyclopedias.*

**Q157.S48 1997**
**Shermer, Michael.**
  Why people believe weird things : pseudoscience, superstition, and other confusions of our time / Michael Shermer ; foreword by Stephen Jay Gould. New York : W.H. Freeman, 1997. xii, 306 p. :
97-003387          133          0716730901
  *Science -- Miscellanea. Belief and doubt. Parapsychology and science.*

## Q158 General works and treatises — 1801-1969

**Q158.R8**
**Russell, Bertrand Russell**
  The scientific outlook, by Bertrand Russell. New York, W. W. Norton & company, inc. [c1931] x p., 1 l., 1
31025032          500
  *Civilization, Modern. Science.*

## Q158.5 General works and treatises — 1970-

**Q158.5.D47 1999**
**Derry, Gregory Neil,**
  What science is and how it works / Gregory N. Derry. Princeton, N.J. : Princeton University Press, c1999. xi, 311 p. :
99-017186          500          0691058776
  *Science.*

**Q158.5.D97 1992**
**Dyson, Freeman J.**
  From Eros to Gaia / Freeman Dyson. New York : Pantheon Books, c1992. xi, 371 p. ;
91-050889          500
  *Science. Scientists. Physics.*

**Q158.5.K74 2001**
**Krebs, Robert E.,**
  Scientific laws, principles, and theories : a reference guide / Robert E. Krebs ; illustrations by Rae Dejur. Westport, Conn. : Greenwood Press, 2001. 402 p. :
00-023297          509          0313309574
  *Science. Science -- History.*

**Q158.5.M34 1992**
  Magill's survey of science. edited by Frank N. Magill ; consulting editor, Thomas A. Tombrello. Pasadena, Calif. : Salem Press, c1992-c1998. 7 v. (lxiv, 3
91-032962          500.2          0893566187
  *Physical sciences. Computer science.*

**Q158.5.S73 1992**
**Strahler, Arthur Newell,**
  Understanding science : an introduction to concepts and issues / Arthur N. Strahler. Buffalo, N.Y. : Prometheus Books, 1992. xiv, 409 p. :
92-006704          501          0879757248
  *Science.*

**Q158.5.W44 1994**
**Wheeler, John Archibald,**
  At home in the universe / John Archibald Wheeler. New York : American Institute of Physics, c1994. vi, 371 p. :
91-043425          500          0883188627
  *Science. Physics.*

## Q162 Popular works

**Q162.A8 1984**
**Asimov, Isaac,**
  Asimov's New guide to science / Isaac Asimov. New York : Basic Books, c1984. xvi, 940 p. :
          500 19
  *Science -- Popular works.*

**Q162.G23 1988**
**Gamow, George,**
  One, two, three-- infinity : facts and speculations of science / George Gamow, illustrated by the author. New York : Dover publications. 1988. xii, 340 p. :
          500 19
  *Science -- Popular works.*

**Q162.G67 1983**
**Goswami, Amit.**
  The cosmic dancers : exploring the physics of science fiction / by Amit Goswami, with Maggie Goswami. New York : Harper & Row, c1983. xi, 292 p. :
  82-048118          809.3/876          0060150831
   *Science -- Popular works. Physics -- Popular works. Science fiction -- History and criticism.*

**Q162.Z48 1995**
**Zimmerman, Michael,**
  Science, nonscience, and nonsense : approaching environmental literacy / Michael Zimmerman. Baltimore : Johns Hopkins University Press, 1995. xvi, 220 p. ;
  95-005006          303.48/3          0801850908
   *Science -- Popular works. Science -- Social aspects -- Popular works. Environmental education -- Popular works.*

## Q171 Addresses, essays, lectures

**Q171.B5375 2001**
**Bernstein, Jeremy,**
  The merely personal : observations on science and scientists / Jeremy Bernstein. Chicago : Ivan R. Dee, 2001. 245 p. ;
  00-063917          500          1566633443
   *Science. Hypothesis.*

**Q171.C76225 1952**
**Conant, James Bryant,**
  Modern science and modern man. New York, Columbia University Press, 1952. 111 p.
  52-014147          504
   *Science. Science -- Philosophy.*

**Q171.E374 2001**
**Ehrlich, Robert,**
  Nine crazy ideas in science : a few might even be true / Robert Ehrlich. Princeton, N.J. : Princeton University Press, c2001. 244 p. :
  00-065210          500          0691070016
   *Science. Scientists.*

**Q171.H902**
**Huxley, Thomas Henry,**
  Collected essays. New York, Greenwood Press [1968] 9 v.
  68-057614
   *Science -- Addresses, essays, lectures.*

**Q171.O6**
**Oppenheimer, J. Robert,**
  Science and the common understanding. New York, Simon and Schuster [1954] 120 p.
  54008650          504
   *Science. Science -- essays.*

**Q171.P7**
**Planck, Max,**
  Scientific autobiography, and other papers; with a memorial address on Max Planck, by Max von Laue. Tr. from German by Frank Gaynor. New York, Philosophical Library [1949] 192 p.
  49011086          504
   *Science. Science -- Philosophy. Philosophy -- essays*

## Q172 Special aspects of the subject as a whole

**Q172.T44**
**Teller, Edward,**
  The pursuit of simplicity / Edward Teller. Malibu, Calif. : Pepperdine University Press, c1980. 173 p. :
  80-082499          500          0932612024
   *Science.*

## Q172.5 Special Topics, A-Z

**Q172.5.C45.B75 1989**
**Briggs, John,**
  Turbulent mirror : an illustrated guide to chaos theory and the science of wholeness / John Briggs and F. David Peat ; illustrations by Cindy Tavernise. New York : Harper & Row, c1989. 222 p. :
  88-045567          003          0060160616
   *Chaotic behavior in systems.*

**Q172.5.C45.C36 1993**
**Cambel, Ali Bulent,**
  Applied chaos theory : a paradigm for complexity / A.B. Cambel. Boston : Academic Press, c1993. xviii, 246 p.
  92-027983          003/.7          0121559408
   *Science -- Philosophy. Complexity (Philosophy) Chaotic behavior in systems.*

**Q172.5.C45.C713 1993**
**Cramer, Friedrich,**
  Chaos and order : the complex structure of living systems / F. Cramer ; foreword by I. Prigogine ; translated by D.I. Loewus. Weinheim ; VCH, c1993. xiv, 249 p. :
  93-032939          003/.7          1560818123
   *Chaotic behavior in systems. Evolution (Biology) Scientists -- Interviews.*

**Q172.5.C45.D87 1993**
**Dupre, John.**
   The disorder of things : metaphysical foundations of the disunity of science / John Dupre. Cambridge, Mass. : Harvard University Press, 1993. viii, 308 p.
92012930          501          0674212606
   *Determinism (Philosophy) Chaotic behavior in systems. Reductionism.*

**Q172.5.C45.N3413 1999**
**Nagashima, Hiroyuki.**
   Introduction to chaos : physics and mathematics of chaotic phenomena / Hiroyuki Nagashima and Yoshikazu Baba ; translated from Japanese by Mikio Nakahara. Bristol, PA : Institute of Physics Pub., c1999. viii, 168 p.
98-039253          003/.857          075030507X
   *Chaotic behavior in systems -- Mathematics.*

**Q172.5.C45.S55 1998**
**Smith, Peter,**
   Explaining chaos / Peter Smith. Cambridge ; Cambridge University Press, 1998. viii, 193 p.
98-021477          003/.857          0521471710 hb
   *Chaotic behavior in systems.*

**Q172.5.E77.B48 1997**
**Dewdney, A. K.**
   Yes, we have no neutrons : an eye-opening tour through the twists and turns of bad science / A.K. Dewdney. New York : Wiley, c1997. 180 p. :
96-035312          500          0471108065
   *Errors, Scientific -- Popular works.*

**Q172.5.E77.K74 1999**
**Krebs, Robert E.,**
   Scientific development and misconceptions through the ages : a reference guide / Robert E. Krebs. Westport, Conn. : Greenwood Press, 1999. vii, 286 p. :
98-005173          509          031330226X
   *Errors, Scientific -- History. Science -- History.*

**Q172.5.P77P37 2002**
**Park, Robert L.**
   Voodoo science : the road from foolishness to fraud / Robert L. Park. New York : Oxford University Press, 2002. p. cm.
          500 21     0198604432
*Pseudoscience -- Popular works.*

**Q172.5.P77W96 2001**
**Wynn, Charles M.**
   Quantum leaps in the wrong direction : where real science ends -- and pseudoscience begins / Charles M. Wynn and Arthur W. Wiggins ; with cartoons by Sidney Harris. Washington, D.C. : Joseph Henry Press, c2001. x, 226 p. :
          501 21     030907309X
*Pseudoscience -- Popular works. Science -- Methodology – Popular works.*

**Q172.5.S95.R67**
**Rosen, Joe,**
   Symmetry discovered : concepts and applications in nature and science / Joe Rosen. Cambridge ; Cambridge University Press, 1975. xi, 138 p. :
75-006006          500          0521206952
   *Symmetry.*

**Q172.5.S95.R673 1995**
**Rosen, Joe,**
   Symmetry in science : an introduction to the general theory / Joe Rosen. New York : Springer-Verlag, c1995. xv, 213 p. :
94-030622          501/.51164          0387943757
   *Symmetry. Group theory.*

# Q173 Miscellany and curiosa

**Q173.G34 2000**
**Gardner, Martin,**
   Did Adam and Eve have navels? : discourses on reflexology, numerology, urine therapy, and other dubious subjects / Martin Gardner. New York : W.W. Norton, 2000. xi, 333 p. ;
00-034870          500          0393049639
   *Science -- Miscellanea.*

**Q173.S24 1997**
**Sagan, Carl,**
   Billions and billions : thoughts on life and death at the brink of the millennium / Carl Sagan. New York : Random House, c1997. xii, 241 p. :
96-052730          500          0679411607
   *Science -- Miscellanea -- Popular works.*

**Q173.S395**
   Science & technology almanac.   Phoenix, Ariz. : Oryx Press, 1999- v. :
99-008373
   *Science -- Handbooks, manuals, etc. Science -- Miscellanea – Periodicals. Technology -- Handbooks, manuals, etc.*

**Q173.S397 1993**
   Science and technology desk reference : 1,500 answers to frequently-asked or difficult-to-answer questions / the Carnegie Library of Pittsburgh Science and Technology Department. Washington, D.C. : Gale Research, c1993. xviii, 741 p.
92-075423          500          0810388847
   *Science -- Miscellanea. Technology -- Miscellanea.*

**Q173.S427 1999**
   The Scientific American science desk reference. New York : John Wiley, c1999. xi, 690 p. :
          500 21     0471356751
*Science -- Miscellanea. Science -- Handbooks, manuals, etc.*

**Q173.S428 2000**
Scientifically speaking : a dictionary of quotations / selected and arranged by Carl C. Gaither and Alma E. Cavazos-Gaither ; illustrated by Andrew Slocombe. Philadelphia, PA : Institute of Physics Pub., c2000. xiv, 482 p. :
99-059800          500          075030636X
*Science -- Quotations, maxims, etc.*

## Q174 Miscellany and curiosa — Societies, congresses, serial collections, yearbooks

**Q174.B67 vol. 127**
**Bechler, Z.**
Newton's physics and the conceptual structure of the scientific revolution / Zev Bechler. Dordrecht ; Kluwer Academic Publishers, c1991. xviii, 588 p.
90-020715          501          0792310543
*Science -- Philosophy -- History. Science -- Philosophy -- Historiography.*

## Q174.8 Miscellany and curiosa — History

**Q174.8.A24 1991**
**Achinstein, Peter.**
Particles and waves : historical essays in the philosophy of science / Peter Achinstein. New York : Oxford University Press, 1991. 337 p. :
90-007188          501          0195065476
*Science -- Philosophy -- History. Physics -- Methodology -- History. Wave-particle duality -- History.*

**Q174.8.G55 1993**
**Gillies, Donald,**
Philosophy of science in the twentieth century : four central themes / Donald Gillies. Oxford, UK ; Blackwell, c1993. xv, 251 p. ;
92-036318          501          0631158642
*Science -- Philosophy -- History -- 20th century.*

**Q174.8.H45 1995**
**Helmholtz, Hermann von,**
Science and culture : popular and philosophical essays / Hermann von Helmholtz ; edited, and with an introduction by David Cahan. Chicago : University of Chicago Press, 1995. xviii, 418 p.
95-012217          500          0226326586
*Helmholtz, Hermann von, -- 1821-1894 -- Knowledge – Philosophy. Science -- Social aspects -- History -- 19th century. Science -- Philosophy -- History -- 19th century.*

**Q174.8.S335 1995**
**Schlagel, Richard H.,**
From myth to modern mind : a study of the origins and growth of scientific thought / Richard H. Schlagel. New York : P. Lang, c1995-c1996. 2 v. :
94-047030          509          0820426725
*Science -- Philosophy -- History. Science -- History.*

## Q175 Miscellany and curiosa — General works, treatises, and advanced textbooks

**Q175.B225 1991**
**Barrow, John D.,**
Theories of everything : the quest for ultimate explanation / John D. Barrow. Oxford [England] : Clarendon Press ; 1991. xi, 223 p. :
90-047394          501          0198539282
*Science -- Philosophy. Cosmology. Physics.*

**Q175.B25 1992**
**Bauer, Henry H.**
Scientific literacy and the myth of the scientific method / Henry H. Bauer. Urbana : University of Illinois Press, c1992. ix, 180 p. :
91-018627          502.8          0252018567
*Science -- Methodology. Science -- Philosophy. Science – Study and teaching.*

**Q175.B415 1988**
**Bechtel, William.**
Philosophy of science : an overview for cognitive science / William Bechtel. Hillsdale, N.J. : L. Erlbaum, c1988. p. cm.
87-030463          153/.01          0898596955
*Science -- Philosophy. Logical positivism. Cognition.*

**Q175.B7918 1974**
**Bronowski, Jacob,**
The ascent of man [by] J. Bronowski. Boston, Little, Brown [1974, c1973] 448 p.
73-020446          501          0316109304
*Science -- Philosophy. Science -- History. Human beings.*

**Q175.C613 1994**
**Cohen, Jack.**
The collapse of chaos : discovering simplicity in a complex world / Jack Cohen & Ian Stewart. New York : Viking, 1994. 495 p. :
93-033511          501          0670849839
*Science -- Philosophy. Science -- Methodology. Complexity (Philosophy)*

**Q175.D33 1998**
**Dawkins, Richard,**
Unweaving the rainbow : science, delusion, and the appetite for wonder / Richard Dawkins. Boston : Houghton Mifflin, 1998. xiv, 336 p. ;
98-040879          501          0395883822
*Science -- Philosophy. Science news.*

**Q175.F58 1997**
The flight from science and reason / edited by Paul R. Gross, Norman Levitt, and Martin W. Lewis. New York : New York Academy of Sciences ; 1997. xi, 593 p. :
96-053491          500          0801856760
*Science -- Philosophy -- Congresses. Science -- Social aspects – Congresses. Women in science -- Congresses.*

**Q175.F782**
**Frank, Philipp,**
Philosophy of science; the link between science and philosophy. Englewood Cliffs, N.J., Prentice-Hall 1957. xxii, 394 p.
57006980          501
*Science -- Philosophy. Philosophy -- essays. Science -- essays.*

**Q175.F927 2000**
**Fuller, Steve,**
Thomas Kuhn : a philosophical history for our times / Steve Fuller. Chicago : University of Chicago Press, c2000. xvii, 472 p.
99-056974          501          0226268942
*Kuhn, Thomas S. -- Structure of scientific revolutions. Science -- History. Science -- Philosophy.*

**Q175.H7748 1993**
**Holton, Gerald James.**
Science and anti-science / Gerald Holton. Cambridge, Mass. : Harvard University Press, 1993. x, 203 p. ;
93-000272          501          067479298X
*Science -- Philosophy. Science -- History.*

**Q175.H794 1996**
**Horgan, John,**
The end of science : facing the limits of knowledge in the twilight of the scientific age / John Horgan. Reading, Mass. : Addison-Wesley Pub., c1996. x, 308 p. ;
96-004374          501          0201626799
*Science -- Philosophy. Science -- History.*

**Q175.H87 1993**
**Howson, Colin.**
Scientific reasoning : the Bayesian approach / Colin Howson and Peter Urbach. Chicago : Open Court, 1993. xix, 470 p. :
93-033935          501          0812692349
*Science -- Philosophy. Reasoning. Bayesian statistical decision theory.*

**Q175.K179 2001**
Kant and the sciences / edited by Eric Watkins. Oxford ; Oxford University Press, 2001. p. cm.
99-087207          501          0195133056
*Science -- Philosophy.*

**Q175.K548 1997**
**Klee, Robert,**
Introduction to the philosophy of science : cutting nature at its seams / Robert Klee. New York : Oxford University Press, 1997. xi, 258 p. :
96-018851          501          0195106105
*Science -- Philosophy. Immunology.*

**Q175.K8648 1992**
**Kosso, Peter.**
Reading the book of nature : an introduction to the philosophy of science / Peter Kosso. Cambridge [England] ; Cambridge University Press, 1992. vii, 198 p. :
91-034429          501          0521416752
*Science -- Philosophy.*

**Q175.K95**
**Kuhn, Thomas S.**
The structure of scientific revolutions. [Chicago] University of Chicago Press [1962] xv, 172 p.
62-019621          501
*Science -- Philosophy. Science -- History.*

**Q175.M4116 1998**
**Maxwell, Nicholas,**
The comprehensibility of the universe : a new conception of science / Nicholas Maxwell. Oxford : Clarendon Press ; 1998. xiii, 316 p.
98-007550          501          0198237766
*Science -- Philosophy. Metaphysics. Science -- Methodology.*

**Q175.M433 1984**
**Medawar, P. B.**
The limits of science / P.B. Medawar. New York : Harper & Row, c1984. xiii, 108 p.
83-048841          501          0060390360
*Science -- Philosophy.*

**Q175.P33**
**Palter, Robert.**
Whitehead's philosophy of science. [Chicago] University of Chicago Press [1960] 248 p.
60007241          501
*Whitehead, Alfred North, -- 1861-1947. Science -- Philosophy.*

**Q175.P384 1991**
Persuading science : the art of scientific rhetoric / Marcello Pera and William R. Shea, editors. Canton, MA : Science History Publications, USA, 1991. xi, 212 p. :
91-010554          501          0881350710
*Science -- Philosophy. Persuasion (Rhetoric)*

**Q175.P3865 2000**
**Pesic, Peter.**
Labyrinth : a search for the hidden meaning of science / Peter Pesic. Cambridge, Mass. : MIT Press, c2000. 186 p. :
99-058366          501          0262161907
*Science -- Philosophy. Science -- Methodology.*

**Q175.P523 1997**
**Pickover, Clifford A.**
The loom of God : mathematical tapestries at the edge of time / Clifford A. Pickover. New York : Plenum Press, c1997. 292 p. :
96-045675          119          0306454114
*Science -- Philosophy. Religion and science. Mathematics -- Philosophy.*

**Q175.P57**
**Planck, Max,**
Where is science going? By Max Planck ... prologue by Albert Einstein; translation and biographical note by James Murphy. New York, W.W. Norton & Company, inc. [c1932] 221 p.
33027009          501
*Science -- Philosophy. Physics -- Philosophy. Causation.*

**Q175.P8 1946**
**Poincare, Henri,**
    The foundations of science: Science and hypothesis, The value of science, Science and method, by H. Poincare. Authorized translation by George Bruce Halsted, with a special preface by Poincare and an introduction by Josiah Royce. Lancaster, Pa., The Science Press, 1946. xi, 553 p.
47001921          501
    *Science -- Philosophy. Science -- Methodology. Mathematics – Philosophy.*

**Q175.P863**
**Popper, Karl Raimund,**
    The logic of scientific discovery.   New York, Basic Books [1959] 479 p.
59-008371          501.8
    *Science -- Methodology.*

**Q175.P8822 1984**
**Prigogine, I.**
    Order out of chaos : man's new dialogue with nature / by Ilya Prigogine and Isabelle Stengers ; foreword by Alvin Toffler. Boulder, CO : New Science Library : 1984. xxxi, 349 p.
84-008415          501          0877733023
    *Science -- Philosophy. Physics -- Philosophy.*

**Q175.R393327 1999**
**Rescher, Nicholas.**
    The limits of science / Nicholas Rescher. Pittsburgh, Pa. : University of Pittsburgh Press, c1999. xii, 282 p. :
99-006975          501          0822957132
    *Science -- Philosophy.*

**Q175.R5475 2001**
**Rosenberg, Alexander,**
    Philosophy of science : a contemporary introduction / Alex Rosenberg. New York : Routledge, Inc., 2001. p. cm.
00-026960          501          0415152801
*Kuhn, Thomas S.     Science -- Philosophy. Science -- History.*

**Q175.R86 1952a**
**Russell, Bertrand,**
    The impact of science on society.   New York, Simon and Schuster, 1953 [i.e. 19 114 p.
52014878          504
    *Science -- Philosophy.*

**Q175.S215 1995**
**Sagan, Carl,**
    The demon-haunted world : science as a candle in the dark / Carl Sagan. New York : Random House, c1995. xviii, 457 p.
95-034076          001.9          039453512X
    *Science -- Methodology -- Popular works. Science -- Study and teaching -- Popular works. Literacy -- Popular works.*

**Q175.S2326 1983**
**Salk, Jonas,**
    Anatomy of reality : merging of intuition and reason / Jonas Salk. New York : Columbia University Press, 1983. xxvii, 127 p.
82-017828          128          0231053282
    *Science -- Philosophy. Reality. Intuition.*

**Q175.S23415 1984**
**Salmon, Wesley C.**
    Scientific explanation and the causal structure of the world / Wesley C. Salmon. Princeton, N.J. : Princeton University Press, c1984. xiv, 305 p. ;
84-042562          501          0691072930
    *Science -- Philosophy. Science -- Methodology.*

**Q175.S42323 2000**
    Scientific controversies : philosophical and historical perspectives / edited by Peter Machamer, Marcello Pera, and Aristedes Baltas. New York : Oxford University Press, 2000. x, 278 p. :
98-038234          501          0195119878
    *Science -- Philosophy.*

**Q175.S564 1981**
**Simon, Herbert Alexander,**
    The sciences of the artificial / Herbert A. Simon. Cambridge, Mass. : MIT Press, c1981. xiii, 247 p.
80-028273          501          0262191938
    *Science -- Philosophy.*

**Q175.T74 1993**
**Trigg, Roger.**
    Rationality and science : can science explain everything? / Roger Trigg. Oxford, UK ; Blackwell, 1993. vii, 248 p. ;
93-017136          501          0631190368
    *Science -- Philosophy.*

**Q175.W62 1968**
**Whitehead, Alfred North,**
    Essays in science and philosophy. New York, Greenwood Press, 1968 [c1947] vi, 348 p.
68-021332          082
    *Science -- Addresses, essays, lectures. Philosophy -- Addresses, essays, lectures. Education -- Addresses, essays, lectures.*

**Q175.W6516 1961**
**Wiener, Norbert,**
    Cybernetics; or, Control and communication in the animal and the machine. New York, M.I.T. Press, 1961. 212 p.
61-013034          006
    *Cybernetics.*

### Q175.3 Miscellany and curiosa — Addresses, essays, lectures

**Q175.3.C65 2000**
A companion to the philosophy of science / edited by W.H. Newton-Smith. Malden, Mass. : Blackwell Publishers, 2000. xvi, 576 p. :
99-047598          501          0631170243
*Science -- Philosophy.*

**Q175.3.W67 1993**
World changes : Thomas Kuhn and the nature of science / edited by Paul Horwich. Cambridge, Mass. : MIT Press, c1993. vi, 356 p. :
92-000518          501          0262082160
*Kuhn, Thomas S.     Science -- History. Science -- Philosophy.*

### Q175.32 Miscellany and curiosa — Special topics, A-Z

**Q175.32.R45.K67 1996**
**Koslowski, Barbara.**
Theory and evidence : the development of scientific reasoning / Barbara Koslowski. Cambridge, Mass. : MIT Press, c1996. xii, 298 p. :
95-017409          501/.9          0262112094
*Reasoning. Science -- Philosophy.*

## Q175.37 Scientific ethics

**Q175.37.B45 1992**
**Bell, Robert,**
Impure science : fraud, compromise, and political influence in scientific research / Robert Bell. New York : Wiley, c1992. xvi, 301 p. ;
91-043148          507.2073          0471529133
*Fraud in science -- United States. Research -- Moral and ethical aspects -- United States.*

**Q175.37.S65 2000**
The Sokal hoax : the sham that shook the academy / edited by the editors of Lingua franca. Lincoln : University of Nebraska Press, c2000. ix, 271 p. ;
00-026113          501          0803279957
*Sokal, Alan D., -- 1955-     Science -- Philosophy. Science – Social aspects. Humanities.*

## Q175.5-175.55 Social Aspects

**Q175.5.C62 1994**
**Cohen, I. Bernard,**
Interactions : some contacts between the natural sciences and the social sciences / I. Bernard Cohen. Cambridge, Mass. : MIT Press, c1994. xx, 204 p. ;
94-011074          303.48/3          0262032236
*Science -- Social aspects -- History. Science -- History. Sociology -- Methodology -- History.*

**Q175.5.F52 1998**
**Feynman, Richard Phillips.**
The meaning of it all : thoughts of a citizen scientist / Richard P. Feynman. Reading, Mass. : Perseus Books, c1998. 133 p. ;
97-048250          500          0201360802
*Science -- Social aspects -- Miscellanea. Religion and science.*

**Q175.5.F845 2000**
**Fuller, Steve,**
The governance of science : ideology and the future of the open society / Steve Fuller. Philadelphia, PA : Open University Press, 2000. p. cm.
99-039402          303.48/3          0335202357
*Science -- Social aspects. Science and state. Science -- Philosophy.*

**Q175.5.G73 1998**
**Graham, Loren R.**
What have we learned about science and technology from the Russian experience? / Loren R. Graham. Stanford, Calif. : Stanford University Press, c1998. xiii, 177 p.
97-041635          306.4/5/0974          0804729859
*Science -- Social aspects. Technology -- Social aspects. Science – History -- 20th century.*

**Q175.5.G744 1998**
**Gregory, Jane,**
Science in public : communication, culture, and credibility / Jane Gregory and Steve Miller. New York : Plenum Trade, c1998. x, 294 p. :
                306.4/5 21          0306458608
*Science -- Public opinion. Science -- Social aspects.*

**Q175.5.N49 1999**
**Newton, David E.**
Social issues in science and technology : an encyclopedia / David E, Newton. Santa Barbara, Calif. : ABC-CLIO, c1999. x, 303 p. :
99-030274          303.48/3/03          0874369207
*Science -- Social aspects -- Encyclopedias. Technology – Social aspects -- Encyclopedias.*

**Q175.5.P67 1995**
**Porter, Theodore M.,**
Trust in numbers : the pursuit of objectivity in science and public life / Theodore M. Porter. Princeton, N.J. : Princeton University Press, c1995. xiv, 310 p. ;
94-021440          306.4/5          0691037760
*Science -- Social aspects. Objectivity.*

**Q175.52.G7.S48 1994**
**Shapin, Steven.**
A social history of truth : civility and science in seventeenth-century England / Steven Shapin. Chicago : University of Chicago Press, c1994. xxxi, 483 p.
93-041950          306.4/5/094109032
0226750183
*Science -- Social aspects -- England -- History -- 17th century. Science -- Moral and ethical aspects -- England -- History -- 17th century.*

**Q175.52.U5.P37 2000**
**Park, Robert L.**
Voodoo science : the road from foolishness to fraud / Robert L. Park. New York : Oxford University Press, 2000. x, 230 p. ;
99-040911          509/.73          0195135156
*Science -- Social aspects -- United States. Fraud in science -- United States.*

**Q175.55.B49 2000**
Beyond the science wars : the missing discourse about science and society / edited by Ullica Segerstrale. Albany : State University of New York Press, c2000. x, 238 p. ;
99-053390          303.48/3          0791446174
*Science -- Social aspects. Science and state.*

**Q175.55.S294 1996**
Science wars / Andrew Ross, editor. Durham : Duke University Press, 1996. vi, 333 p. ;
96-022506          303.48/3          0822318814
*Science -- Social aspects. Science and state.*

## Q179 Nomenclature, terminology, notation, abbreviation

**Q179.E64 2001**
**Erb, Uwe.**
Scientific and technical acronyms, symbols, and abbreviations / Uwe Erb, Harald Keller. New York : Wiley-Interscience, c2001. xiii, 2100 p.
01-017598          501/.48          0471388025
*Science -- Abbreviations. Technology -- Abbreviations. Science – Acronyms.*

## Q179.97 Research — Computer network resources

**Q179.97.T48 1998**
**Thomas, Brian J.**
The World Wide Web for scientists & engineers : a complete reference for navigating, researching & publishing online / Brian J. Thomas. Bellingham, Wash. : SPIE Press ; c1998. xv, 357 p. ;
97-043434          004.67/8/0245          0819427756
*Science -- Computer network resources. Engineering – Computer network resources. Online data processing.*

## Q179.98 Research — Directories

**Q179.98.G68**
Government research directory. Detroit, Mich. : Gale Research Co., c1985- v. ;
85-647549          001.4/025/73
*Research -- United States -- Directories. Research institutes -- United States -- Directories. Government Agencies -- United States – directories.*

## Q180.A1 Research — General works, treatises, and advanced textbooks

**Q180.A1**
**Valiela, Ivan.**
Doing science : design, analysis, and communication of scientific research / by Ivan Valiela. New York : Oxford University Press, 1999. p. cm.
99-021693          507.2          0195079620
*Science -- Research. Communication in science. Technical writing.*

**Q180.A1.W4**
**Weinberg, Alvin Martin,**
Reflections on big science [by] Alvin M. Weinberg. Cambridge, M.I.T. Press [1967] ix, 182 p.
67014205          507.2
*Research Research -- essays Science -- essays*

## Q180.G4-U5 Research — History — By region or country, A-Z

**Q180.G4.M3 1993**
**Macrakis, Kristie.**
Surviving the swastika : scientific research in Nazi Germany / Kristie Macrakis. New York : Oxford University Press, 1993. xii, 280 p.,
93-019919          506/.043/09043          0195070100
*Research -- Germany -- History. Science and state – Germany – History. Germany -- Politics and government -- 1933-1945.*

**Q180.U5.M326 1992**
**Martino, Joseph Paul,**
Science funding : politics and porkbarrel / Joseph P. Martino. New Brunswick, N.J., U.S.A. : Transaction Publishers, c1992. xiii, 392 p.
91-029638          507/.2/073          1560000333
*Research -- United States -- Finance. Waste in government spending -- United States. Science and state -- United States.*

**Q180.U5.S28 1999**
**Savage, James D.,**
Funding science in America : congress, universities, and the politics of the academic pork barrel / James D. Savage. Cambridge, U.K. ; Cambridge University Press, 1999. xiii, 219 p.
98-011654          338.97306          0521643155
*Research -- Government policy -- United States. Federal aid to research -- United States. Peer review -- Government policy – United States.*

## Q180.5 Research — Addresses, essays, lectures

**Q180.5.M67M33 2000**
**Macrina, Francis L.**
   Scientific integrity : an introductory text with cases / Francis L. Macrina. 2nd ed. Washington, D.C. ASM Press, 2000. xxi, 338 p. :
           174/.95072 21      1555811523
*Research -- Moral and ethical aspects. Medical sciences – Research -- Moral and ethical aspects. Integrity.*

**Q180.5.M67S74 1997**
**Stern, Judy E.**
   The ethics of scientific research : a guidebook for course development / Judy E. Stern, Deni Elliott. Hanover, NH : University Press of New England, c1997. x, 116 p. :
           174/.95072 20      0874517982
*Research -- Moral and ethical aspects -- Handbooks, manuals, etc.*

## Q180.55 Research — Special Topics, A-Z

**Q180.55.D57**
**Klahr, David.**
   Exploring science : the cognition and development of discovery processes / David Klahr with Kevin Dunbar ... [et al.] ; foreword by Herbert A. Simon. Cambridge, Mass. : MIT Press, c2000. xvi, 239 p. :
99-031045         509        0262112485
   *Discoveries in science.*

**Q180.55.D57.M33 1998**
**Maddox, John Royden,**
   What remains to be discovered : mapping the secrets of the universe, the origins of life, and the future of the human race / John Maddox. New York : Martin Kessler Books, c1998. xiv, 434 p. ;
98-029137         500        068482292X
   *Discoveries in science. Science -- History. Research -- Miscellanea.*

**Q180.55.D57.W34 2000**
**Wagman, Morton.**
   Scientific discovery processes in humans and computers : theory and research in psychology and artificial intelligence / Morton Wagman. Westport, CT : Praeger, 2000. xiii, 199 p.
99-032026         001.4/2        0275966542
   *Discoveries in science. Cognitive science. Artificial intelligence.*

**Q180.55.M4.B38 1994**
**Bausell, R. Barker,**
   Conducting meaningful experiments : 40 steps to becoming a scientist / R. Barker Bausell. Thousand Oaks, CA : Sage Publications, c1994. 146 p. :
93-042140         001.4/34        0803955308
   *Research -- Methodology. Scientists -- Vocational guidance.*

**Q180.55.M4.K63 1994**
**Kohler, Robert E.**
   Lords of the fly : Drosophila genetics and the experimental life / Robert E. Kohler. Chicago : University of Chicago Press, 1994. xv, 321 p. :
93-029436         502.8        0226450627
   *Research -- Methodology. Scientists. Drosophila -- Research.*

**Q180.55.M4.S35 1999**
**Schloss, Patrick J.**
   Conducting research / Patrick J. Schloss, Maureen A. Smith. Upper Saddle River, NJ : Prentice Hall, c1999. xix, 236 p. :
98-011113         001.4/2        0024073709
   *Research -- Methodology.*

**Q180.55.M4L43 2001**
**Leedy, Paul D.**
   Practical research : planning and design / Paul D. Leedy, Jeanne Ellis Ormrod. 7th ed. Upper Saddle River, NJ : Merrill Prentice Hall, 2001. xx, 318 p. :
           001.4 21
*Research -- Methodology.*

**Q180.55.M4S67 1995**
**Sproull, Natalie L.,**
   Handbook of research methods : a guide for practitioners and students in the social sciences / by Natalie L. Sproull. 2nd ed. Metuchen, N.J. : Scarecrow Press, 1995. xiii, 430 p. :
           001.4/2 20
*Research -- Methodology -- Handbooks, manuals, etc. Social sciences -- Research -- Methodology -- Handbooks, manuals, etc.*

**Q180.55.M67.E83 1994**
   Ethical issues in scientific research : an anthology / by Edward Erwin, Sidney Gendin, and Lowell Kleiman. New York : Garland, 1994. xii, 413 p. ;
93-037482         174/.95072        0815306415
   *Research -- Moral and ethical aspects. Fraud in science.*

**Q180.55.M67.S48 1994**
**Shrader-Frechette, K. S.**
   Ethics of scientific research / Kristin Shrader-Frechette. Lanham, Md. : Rowman & Littlefield, c1994. x, 243 p. ;
94-019148         174/.95        0847679810
   *Research -- Moral and ethical aspects. Scientists -- Professional ethics.*

**Q180.55.P75.S78 1996**
**Stuster, Jack,**
   Bold endeavors : lessons from polar and space exploration / Jack Stuster. Annapolis, Md. : Naval Institute Press, c1996. xxii, 377 p.
96-008131         155.9/6        155750749X
   *Research -- Psychological aspects. Space flight -- Psychological aspects. Social isolation -- Psychological aspects. Antarctica -- Research -- Psychological aspects.*

## Q181-183.3 Study and teaching

**Q181.A1E3**
Educators guide to free science materials / compiled and edited by Mary H. Saterstrom. Randolph, Wisconsin : Educators Progress Service, [1960- v. :
507      0070-9425
*Science -- Study and teaching -- United States -- Periodicals. Free material -- Directories. Science -- Study and teaching -- Audio-visual aids -- Catalogs.*

**Q181.C56 1951**
**Conant, James Bryant,**
On understanding science : an historical approach / by James B. Conant. With a new foreword by the author. [New York] New American Library [1951] xv, 144 p.
51008972      507
*Science -- Study and teaching. Science -- History. Science -- Philosophy.*

**Q181.I654 1999**
Innovations in science and mathematics education : advanced designs for technologies of learning / edited by Michael J. Jacobson, Robert B. Kozma. Mahwah, N.J. : L. Erlbaum, 2000. xiv, 430 p. :
99-029076      507/.12      080582846X
*Science -- Study and teaching. Science -- Philosophy. Science -- Methodology.*

**Q181.S694 2000**
**Stavy, Ruth.**
How students (mis-) understand science and mathematics : intuitive rules / Ruth Stavy and Dina Tirosh. New York : Teachers College Press, 2000. viii, 127 p.
00-032560      507/.1      0807739596
*Science -- Study and teaching. Science -- Philosophy. Science -- Methodology.*

**Q181.T3538 1995**
Teaching the majority : breaking the gender barrier in science, mathematics, and engineering / edited by Sue V. Rosser. New York : Teachers College Press, c1995. vii, 264 p. :
94-044738      507.1      0807762776
*Science -- Study and teaching -- Sex differences. Mathematics -- Study and teaching -- Sex differences. Engineering -- Study and teaching -- Sex differences.*

**Q181.W4416 2000**
**Wellington, J. J.**
Teaching and learning secondary science : contemporary issues and practical approaches / Jerry Wellington. London ; Routledge, 2000. xv, 276, p. :
99-016842      507/.1/2      0415214033
*Science -- Study and teaching (Secondary)*

**Q181.W75 1990**
Windows into science classrooms : problems associated with higher-level cognitive learning / edited by Kenneth Tobin, Jane Butler Kahle, Barry J. Fraser. London ; Falmer Press, 1990. xv, 246 p. :
90-032248      507/.1      1850005427
*Science -- Study and teaching. Cognitive learning.*

**Q181.5.P76 1998**
Problems of meaning in science curriculum / edited by Douglas A. Roberts and Leif Ostman ; foreword by F. James Rutherford. New York : Teachers College Press, c1998. xii, 228 p. :
97-046462      507/.1      0807737089
*Science -- Study and teaching -- Curricula. Meaning (Philosophy) Science -- Study and teaching (Secondary) -- North America.*

**Q182.3.P55 1996**
**Pilger, Mary Anne,**
Science experiments index for young people / Mary Anne Pilger. 2nd ed. Englewood, Colo. : Libraries Unlimited, 1996. xxxii, 504 p. :
016.507/8 20      1563083418
*Science -- Experiments -- Juvenile literature -- Indexes. Science -- Experiments -- Indexes. Experiments -- Indexes.*

**Q183.3.A1.A788 2001**
Atlas of science literacy / Project 2061. Washington, DC : National Science Teachers Association, 2001. ix, 165 p. :
507/.1073 21      0871686686
*Science -- Study and teaching -- United States -- Charts, diagrams, etc. Mathematics -- Study and teaching -- United States -- Charts, diagrams, etc. Engineering -- Study and teaching -- United States -- Charts, diagrams, etc.*

**Q183.3.A1.B46 1993**
Benchmarks for science literacy. New York : Oxford University Press, 1993. xv, 418 p. :
93-039107      507/.1/273      0195089863
*Science -- Study and teaching -- United States. Mathematics -- Study and teaching -- United States. Engineering -- Study and teaching -- United States.*

**Q183.3.A1.D4 1991**
**DeBoer, George E.**
A history of ideas in science education : implications for practice / George E. DeBoer. New York : Teachers College Press, c1991. xiv, 269 p. ;
90-046958      507/.073      0807730548
*Science -- Study and teaching -- United States -- History -- 19th century. Science -- Study and teaching -- United States -- History -- 20th century.*

**Q183.3.A1.N364 1996**
National Science Education Standards : observe, interact, change, learn. Washington, DC : National Academy Press, c1996. ix, 262 p. :
95-045778      507.1/0973      0309053269
*Science -- Study and teaching -- Standards -- United States.*

**Q183.3.A1.P425**
Peterson's top colleges for science. Princeton, N.J. : Peterson's, c1996- v. ;
96-660627          507.1/173
*Science -- Study and teaching (Higher) -- Directories.*

**Q183.3.A1.S45 1995**
**Shamos, Morris H.**
The myth of scientific literacy / Morris H. Shamos. New Brunswick, N.J. : Rutgers University Press, c1995. xviii, 261 p.
94-041057          507.1/073          0813521963
*Science -- Study and teaching -- United States. Literacy – United States.*

**Q183.3.A1D48 2000**
Designs for science literacy. New York : Oxford University Press, 2000. xi, 300 p.
507/.1/073 21          0195132785
*Science -- Study and teaching -- United States. Mathematics – Study and teaching -- United States. Engineering -- Study and teaching – United States.*

## Q184.5-185 Instruments and apparatus

**Q184.5.I57 1998**
Instruments of science : an historical encyclopedia / editors, Robert Bud, Deborah Jean Warner ; associate editor, Stephen Johnston ; managing editor, Betsy Bahr Peterson ; picture editor, Simon Chaplin. New York : Science Museum, London, and National Museum of A 1998. xxv, 709 p. :
97-015296          502.8/4          0815315619
*Scientific apparatus and instruments -- History -- Encyclopedias.*

**Q185.B563 2001**
**Blackburn, James A.**
Modern instrumentation for scientists and engineers / James A. Blackburn. New York : Springer, 2001. xv, 319 p. :
00-040040          502/.8          0387950567
*Beckman, Arnold O.      Scientific apparatus and instruments – United States -- History -- 20th century. Instrument manufacture -- United States -- History -- 20th century. Instrument manufacture -- United States -- Biography.*

## Q199 Handbooks, tables, formulas, etc.

**Q199.F57 1991**
Rules of thumb for engineers and scientists / David Fisher, editor. Houston, Tex. : Gulf Pub. Co., 1991. xiv, 242 p. :
90038439          500          0872017869
*Engineering -- Handbooks, manuals, etc. Science – Handbooks, manuals, etc.*

## Q222 Scientific illustration

**Q222.F67 1993**
**Ford, Brian J.**
Images of science : a history of scientific illustration / Brian J. Ford. New York : Oxford University Press, 1993. viii, 208 p.
92-027290          502.2/2          0195209834
*Scientific illustration -- History.*

## Q223 Communication in science — General works

**Q223.P33 1997**
**Paradis, James G.,**
The MIT guide to science and engineering communication / James G. Paradis and Muriel L. Zimmerman. Cambridge, Mass. : MIT Press, c1997. x, 290 p. :
96-034048          808/.0665          0262161427
*Communication in science. Communication in engineering. Technical writing.*

**Q223.S2385 2001**
Science communication in theory and practice / edited by Susan M. Stocklmayer, Michael M. Gore, and Chris Bryant. Dordrecht ; Boston : Kluwer Academic Publishers, c2001. xv, 284 p. :
501/.4 21          1402001304
*Communication in science.*

**Q223.S248 1997**
Scientific and technical communication : theory, practice, and policy / editor, James H. Collier, with David M. Toomey. Thousand Oaks, CA : Sage Publications, c1997. xvi, 415 p. :
501.4 20          0761903208
*Communication in science. Communication of technical information.*

### Q224 Communications in science — Information Services — General works

**Q224.Z56 1995**
**Zimmerman, Donald E.**
The elements of information gathering : a guide for technical communicators, scientists, and engineers / by Donald E. Zimmerman and Michel Lynn Muraski. Phoenix, Ariz. : Oryx Press, 1995. xiii, 242 p.
94-036806          001.4/33/0245          089774800X
*Science -- Information services -- Methodology -- Handbooks, manuals, etc.. Technology -- Information services -- Methodology – Handbooks, manuals, etc. Information storage and retrieval systems – Science -- Methodology -- Handbooks, manuals, etc.*

## Q225.5 Scientific Literature

**Q225.5.L63 1992**
**Locke, David M.**
Science as writing / David Locke. New Haven : Yale University Press, c1992. x, 237 p. ;
92-007824      808/.0665      0300054521
*Scientific literature. Communication in science. Technical writing.*

### Q325 Cybernetics — Self-organizing systems. Conscious automata — General works

**Q325.J65 2001**
**Johnson, Steven.**
Emergence : the connected lives of ants, brains, cities, and software / Steven Johnson. New York : Scribner, c2001. 288 p. :
003/.7 21      068486875X
*Self-organizing systems. Swarm intelligence. Systems engineering.*

### Q325.5 Cybernetics — Self-organizing systems. Conscious automata — Machine learning

**Q325.5.B76 1994**
**Brown, Robert Alan,**
Machines that learn : based on the principles of empirical control / Robert Alan Brown. New York : Oxford University Press, 1994. viii, 891 p.
93-023985      006.3/1      0195069668
*Machine learning. Artificial intelligence. Neural computers – Design and construction.*

**Q325.5.M36 2001**
**Mandic, Danilo P.**
Recurrent neural networks for prediction : learning algorithms, architectures, and stability / Danilo p. Mandic, Jonathon A. Chambers. Chichester ; New York : John Wiley, c2001. xxi, 285 p. :
006.3/2 21      0471495174
*Machine learning. Neural networks (Computer science)*

## Q334.2 Artificial intelligence — Dictionaries and encyclopedias

**Q334.2.R39 1999**
**Raynor, William J.**
The international dictionary of artificial intelligence / William J. Raynor, Jr. Chicago : Glenlake Pub. Co. ; c1999. viii, 318 p.
00-269803      006.3/03      0814404448
*Artificial intelligence -- Dictionaries.*

## Q335 Artificial intelligence — General works, treatises, and textbooks

**Q335.A3 1998**
**Adami, Christoph.**
Introduction to artificial life / Christoph Adami. New York : Springer, c1998. xviii, 374 p.
97-037605      570/.13      0387946462
*Artificial intelligence. Artificial life. Neural networks (Computer science)*

**Q335.A78714 1990**
Artificial intelligence : concepts and applications in engineering / edited by A.R. Mirzai. Cambridge, Mass. : MIT Press, 1990. xix, 304 p. :
89-013911      006.3      0262132567
*Artificial intelligence.*

**Q335.C66 1993**
**Crevier, Daniel,**
AI : the tumultuous history of the search for artificial intelligence / Daniel Crevier. New York, NY : Basic Books, c1993. xiv, 386 p. :
91-055461      006.3/09      0465029973
*Artificial intelligence -- History.*

**Q335.D97 1997**
**Dyson, George,**
Darwin among the machines : the evolution of global intelligence / George B. Dyson. Reading, Mass. : Addison-Wesley Pub. Co., c1997. xii, 286 p. :
97-000858      006.3      0201406497
*Artificial intelligence. Artificial life. Neural networks (Computer science)*

**Q335.E53 1992**
Encyclopedia of artificialk intelligence / Stuart C. Shapiro, editor-in-chief. 2nd ed. New York : Wiley, c1992. 2 v. :
006.3/03 20      047150307X
*Artificial intelligence -- Encyclopedias.*

**Q335.G358 2000**
**Gardenfors, Peter.**
Conceptual spaces : the geometry of thought / Peter Gardenfors. Cambridge, Mass. : MIT Press, c2000. x, 307 p. :
99-046109      006.3      0262071991
*Artificial intelligence. Cognitive science.*

**Q335.G54 1996**
**Gillies, Donald,**
Artificial intelligence and scientific method / Donald Gillies. Oxford [England] ; Oxford University Press, c1996. xii, 176 p. :
95-026846      006.3      0198751583
*Artificial intelligence. Science -- Philosophy.*

**Q335.K87 1990**
**Kurzweil, Ray.**
 The age of intelligent machines / Raymond Kurzweil. Cambridge, Mass. : MIT Press, c1990. xiii, 565 p.
 89-013606          006.3          0262111217
  *Artificial intelligence.*

**Q335.K88 1999**
**Kurzweil, Ray.**
 The age of spiritual machines : when computers exceed human intelligence / Ray Kurzweil. New York : Viking, 1999. xii, 388 p. :
          006.3 21          0670882178
*Artificial intelligence. Computers.*

**Q335.P415 1989**
**Penrose, Roger.**
 The emperor's new mind : concerning computers, minds, and the laws of physics / Roger Penrose ; foreword by Martin Gardner. Oxford ; Oxford University Press, 1989. xiii, 466 p.
 89-008548          006.3          0198519737
  *Artificial intelligence. Thought and thinking. Physics -- Philosophy.*

**Q335.P46 1999**
**Pfeifer, Rolf,**
 Understanding intelligence / Rolf Pfeifer and Christian Scheier ; with figures by Alex Riegler and cartoons by Isabelle Follath. Cambridge, Mass. : MIT Press, c1999. xx, 697 p. :
 98-049138          006.3          0262161818
  *Artificial intelligence. Cognitive science. Expert systems (Computer science)*

**Q335.P657 1997**
**Poole, David L.**
 Computational intelligence : a logical approach / David Poole, Alan Mackworth, Randy Goebel. New York : Oxford University Press, 1998. xvi, 558 p. :
 97-009075          006.3          0195102703
  *Artificial intelligence.*

**Q335.T9 1998**
**Tveter, Donald R.,**
 The pattern recognition basis of artificial intelligence / Donald R. Tveter. Los Alamitos, Calif. : IEEE Computer Society, c1998. xiv, 369 p. :
 97-032259          006.3          0818677961
  *Artificial intelligence. Pattern perception.*

**Q335.W342 1999**
**Wagman, Morton.**
 The human mind according to artificial intelligence : theory, research, and implications / Morton Wagman. Westport, Conn. : Praeger, 1999. p. cm.
 98-033627          006.3          0275962857
  *Artificial intelligence. Brain. Philosophy of mind.*

## Q335.5 Artificial intelligence — Addresses, essays, lectures

**Q335.5.L44 1996**
 The legacy of Alan Turing / edited by P.J.R. Millican and A. Clark. Oxford : Clarendon Press ; 1996. 2 v. :
 96-025418          006.3          0198235933
  *Artificial intelligence.*

## Q336 Artificial intelligence — Data processing

**Q336.T36 1987**
**Tanimoto, S.**
 The elements of artificial intelligence : an introduction using LISP / Steven L. Tanimoto. Rockville, MD : Computer Science Press, c1987. xxii, 530 p.
 86-031044          006.3          0881751138
  *Artificial intelligence -- Data processing. LISP (Computer program language)*

## Q337.3 Artificial intelligence — Distributed artificial intelligence

**Q337.3.K45 2001**
**Kennedy, James F.**
 Swarm intelligence / James Kennedy, Russell C. Eberhart, with Yuhui Shi. San Francisco : Morgan Kaufmann Publishers, c2001. xxvii, 512 p.
 00-069641          006.3          1558605959
  *Swarm intelligence. Systems engineering. Distributed artificial intelligence.*

## Q360 Cybernetics — Information theory — General works, treatises, and textbooks

**Q360.J68 2000**
**Jones, Gareth A.**
 Information and coding theory / Gareth A. Jones and J. Mary Jones. London ; Springer, c2000. xiii, 210 p.
 00-030074          003/.54          1852336226
  *Information theory. Coding theory.*

**Q360.L84 1989**
**Lucky, R.W.**
 Silicon dreams : information, man, and machine / Robert W. Lucky. 1st ed. New York : St. Martin's Press, c1989. xiii, 411 p. :
          003/.54/ 20          0312029608
*Information theory.*

**Q360.P5**
**Pierce, John Robinson,**
 Symbols, signals, and noise: the nature and process of communication. New York, Harper [1961] 305 p.
 61-010215          006
  *Information theory.*

# QA Mathematics

## QA1 Societies, congresses, serial collections, yearbooks

**QA1.A19**
Advances in mathematics. New York, Academic Press, 1965- v.
61-018295
*Mathematics.*

**QA1.A647 vol. 115-117**
**Taylor, Michael Eugene,**
Partial differential equations / Michael E. Taylor. New York : Springer, c1996. 3 v. :
95-054104          510 s          0387946535
*Differential equations, Partial.*

**QA1.J978**
Journal of the American Mathematical Society [Providence, R.I.] : The Society,
96-030023          510
*Mathematics -- Periodicals.*

**QA1.M4233.M37**
The Mathematical Association of America: its first fifty years. Kenneth O. May, editor. [Washington] Mathematical Association of America [c1972] vii, 172 p.
73-158045          510/.6/273

**QA1.M76**
Mathematical reviews. Lancaster, Pa. : American Mathematical Society, [1940- v. ; 30 cm.
          510/.5     0025-5629
*Mathematics -- Periodicals.*

**QA1.N3 26**
**National Council of Teachers of Mathematics.**
Evaluation in mathematics. Washington, 1961. iii, 216 p.
61011906          510.7
*Mathematics -- Study and teaching. Mathematics – Examinations, questions, etc.*

## QA3 Collected works (nonserial)

**QA3.B18 1989 vol. 1**
**Babbage, Charles,**
Mathematical papers. New York : New York University Press, 1989. 51, 456 p. :
88-032926          510 s          0814711138
*Mathematics.*

**QA3.F732513 1984**
**Frege, Gottlob,**
Collected papers on mathematics, logic, and philosophy / Gottlob Frege ; edited by Brian McGuinness ; translated by Max Black ... [et al.]. Oxford, UK ; B. Blackwell, 1984. viii, 412 p.
84-012490          510          0631127283
*Mathematics.*

**QA3.N48**
**Newman, James Roy,**
The world of mathematics; a small library of the literature of mathematics from Ah-mose the scribe to Albert Einstein, presented with commentaries and notes by James R. Newman. New York, Simon and Schuster, 1956. 4 v. (xviii,
55-010060          510.82
*Mathematics.*

**QA3.P7 3 1940**
**Eisenhart, Luther Pfahler,**
An introduction to differential geometry, with use of the tensor calculus, by Luther Pfahler Eisenhart ... Princeton, Princeton University Press; 1940. x, 304 p.
41003507          513.7
*Geometry, Differential. Calculus of tensors.*

**QA3.P8 vol. 60**
**Hirsch, Morris W.,**
Differential equations, dynamical systems, and linear algebra [by] Morris W. Hirsch and Stephen Smale. New York, Academic Press [1974] xi, 358 p.
73-018951          510/.8 s          0123495504
*Differential equations. Algebras, Linear.*

**QA3.P8 vol. 63**
**Boothby, William M.**
An introduction to differentiable manifolds and Riemannian geometry / William M. Boothby. New York : Academic Press, 1975. xiv, 424 p. :
73-018967          516/.36          0121160505
*Differentiable manifolds. Riemannian manifolds.*

**QA3.P8 vol. 72**
**Stroyan, K. D.**
Introduction to the theory of infinitesimals / K. D. Stroyan in collaboration with W. A. J. Luxemburg. New York : Academic Press, 1976. xiii, 326 p.
76-014344          510/.8 s          0126741506
*Nonstandard mathematical analysis.*

**QA3.P8 vol. 79**
**Jech, Thomas J.**
Set theory / Thomas Jech. New York : Academic Press, 1978. xi, 621 p. :
77-011214          510/.8 s          0123819504
*Set theory.*

**QA3.P8 vol. 85**
**Rotman, Joseph J.,**
An introduction to homological algebra / Joseph J. Rotman. New York : Academic Press, 1979. xi, 376 p. :
78-020001          512/.55          0125992505
*Algebra, Homological.*

**QA3.R33 1985**
**Ramanujan Aiyangar, Srinivasa,**
Ramanujan's notebooks / [edited by] Bruce C. Berndt. New York : Springer-Verlag, c1985-c1998 v. 1, 3-5
84-020201          510          0387961100
*Mathematics.*

## QA5 Dictionaries and encyclopedias

**QA5.D4983 2001**
Dictionary of algebra, arithmetic, and trigonometry / edited by Steven G. Krantz. Boca Raton : CRC Press, c2001. 331 p.
          510/.3 21          158488052X
*Algebra -- Dictionaries. Arithmetic -- Dictionaries. Trigonometry – Dictionaries.*

**QA5.D53 2000**
Dictionary of analysis, calculus, and differential equations / [edited by] Douglas N. Clark. Boca Raton : CRC Press, c2000. 273 p. ;
99-087759          515/.03          0849303206
*Mathematical analysis -- Dictionaries. Calculus -- Dictionaries. Differential equations -- Dictionaries.*

**QA5.F35 1999**
The Facts on File dictionary of mathematics / edited by John Daintith, John Clark. New York : Facts On File, c1999. 241 p. :
99-017789          510/.3          0816039135
*Mathematics -- Dictionaries.*

**QA5.H42**
**Herland, Leo**
Dictionary of mathematical sciences [by] Leo Herland. New York, F. Ungar Pub. Co. [1965] 2 v.
65-016622          510/.3
*Mathematics -- Dictionaries -- German. German language -- Dictionaries -- English. Mathematics -- Dictionaries.*

**QA5.I8313 1987**
Encyclopedic dictionary of mathematics / by the Mathematical Society of Japan ; edited by Kiyosi Ito. Cambridge, Mass. : MIT Press, c1987. 4 v. (xvii, 2
86-021092          510/.3/21          0262090260
*Mathematics -- Dictionaries.*

**QA5.J32 1976**
**James, Glenn,**
Mathematics dictionary / James [and] James ; contributors, Armen A. Alchian ... [et al.] ; translators, J. George Adashko ... [et al.]. New York : Van Nostrand Reinhold Co., c1976. vii, 509 p. :
76-000233          510/.3          0442240910
*Mathematics -- Dictionaries -- Polyglot. Dictionaries, Polyglot.*

**QA5.K692 1999**
**Kornegay, Chris.**
Math dictionary with solutions, 2nd : a math review / by Chris Kornegay. Thousand Oaks, CA : Sage Publications, 1999. p. cm.
98-055316          510/.3
*Mathematics -- Dictionaries. Mathematics -- Problems, exercises, etc.*

**QA5.S375 1994**
**Schwartzman, Steven.**
The words of mathematics : an etymological dictionary of mathematical terms used in English / Steven Schwartzman. Washington, DC : Mathematical Association of America, c1994. vii, 261 p. :
93-080612          510/.3          0883855119
*Mathematics -- Dictionaries.*

**QA5.W45 1999**
**Weisstein, Eric W.**
CRC concise encyclopedia of mathematics / Eric W. Weisstein. Boca Raton, Fla. : CRC Press, c1999. 1969 p. :
98-022385          510/.3          0849396409
*Mathematics -- Encyclopedias.*

## QA7-7.2 Addresses, essays, lectures

**QA7.C38 1994**
A century of mathematics : through the eyes of the Monthly / edited by John Ewing. [Washington, D.C.] : Mathematical Association of America, c1994. xi, 323 p. :
93-081168          510/.973/0904          0883854597
*Mathematics -- History -- 20th century. Mathematics.*

**QA7.H3 1967**
**Hardy, G. H.**
A mathematician's apology, by G. H. Hardy. London, Cambridge U.P., 1967. 153 p.
67-021958          510
*Mathematics.*

**QA7.H72 1988**
**Hoffman, Paul,**
Archimedes' revenge : the joys and perils of mathematics / Paul Hoffman. New York : Norton, c1988. viii, 285 p.
88-001754          510          0393025225
*Mathematics.*

**QA7.H773 1991**
**Honsberger, Ross,**
More mathematical morsels / Ross Honsberger. [Washington, D.C.] : Mathematical Association of America, c1991. xii, 322 p. :
90-070792          510          0883853132
*Mathematics.*

**QA7.L28 1985**
**Lang, Serge,**
The beauty of doing mathematics : three public dialogues / Serge Lang. New York : Springer-Verlag, c1985. vii, 127 p. :
85-013838          510          0387961496
*Mathematics.*

**QA7.L286 1999**
**Lang, Serge,**
Math talks for undergraduates / Serge Lang. New York : Springer, 1999. p. cm.
98-055410          510          0387987495
*Mathematics.*

**QA7.M3235 2001**
Mathematical conversations : selections from The mathematical intelligencer / compiled by Robin Wilson, Jeremy Gray. New York : Springer, c2001. vii, 488 p. :
98-043867          510          0387986863
*Mathematics.*

**QA7.M34457 2000**
Mathematics : frontiers and perspectives / V. Arnold ... [et al.], editors. Providence, R.I. : American Mathematical Society, c2000. xi, 459 p. :
99-047980          510          0821820702
*Mathematics.*

**QA7.S2**
**Saaty, Thomas L.**
Lectures on modern mathematics. New York, Wiley [1963-65] 3 v.
63-020639          510.8
*Mathematics -- Addresses, essays, lectures.*

**QA7.2.T36 1999**
**Tan, Soo Tang.**
College mathematics / S.T. Tan. Pacific Grove, CA : Brooks/Cole Pub. Co., c1999. xviii, 1230 p
98-015592          510          0534361218
*Mathematics. Management -- Mathematics. Social sciences – Mathematics.*

## QA8.4 Philosophy — General works, treatises, and textbooks

**QA8.4.H47 1997**
**Hersh, Reuben,**
What is mathematics, really? / Reuben Hersh. New York : Oxford University Press, 1997. xxiv, 343 p.
96-038483          510/.1          0195113683
*Mathematics -- Philosophy.*

**QA8.4.H56 1996**
**Hintikka, Jaakko,**
The principles of mathematics revisited / Jaakko Hintikka. Cambridge ; Cambridge University Press, 1996. xii, 288 p. :
95-023111          511.3          0521496926
*Mathematics -- Philosophy. First-order logic.*

**QA8.4.L38 1994**
**Lavine, Shaughan.**
Understanding the infinite / Shaughan Lavine. Cambridge, Mass. : Harvard University Press, 1994. ix, 372 p. :
93-049697          511.3/22          0674920961
*Mathematics -- Philosophy.*

**QA8.4.L47 2000**
**Liebeck, M. W.**
A concise introduction to pure mathematics / Martin Liebeck. Boca Raton : Chapman & Hall/CRC, c2000. xiv, 162 p. ;
99-462376          510          1584881933
*Mathematics.*

**QA8.4.R473 1997**
**Resnik, Michael D.**
Mathematics as a science of patterns / Michael D. Resnik. Oxford : Clarendon Press ; 1997. xiii, 285 p.
96-051610          510/.1          0198236085
*Mathematics -- Philosophy.*

**QA8.4.W5613 1978b**
**Wittgenstein, Ludwig,**
Remarks on the foundations of mathematics / by Ludwig Wittgenstein ; edited by G. H. von Wright, R. Rhees, G. E. M. Anscombe ; translated by G. E. M. Anscombe. Cambridge, Mass. : MIT Press, 1978. 444 p. :
78-059781          510/.1          0262230801
*Mathematics -- Philosophy.*

## QA8.6 Philosophy — Addresses, essays, lectures

**QA8.6.D39 1986**
**Davis, Philip J.,**
Descartes' dream : the world according to mathematics / Philip J. Davis, Reuben Hersh. San Diego : Harcourt Brace Jovanovich, c1986. xvii, 321 p.
86-011967          510/.1          0151252602
*Mathematics -- Philosophy. Mathematics -- Social aspects. Computers and civilization.*

## QA9-9.8 Philosophy — Mathematical logic

**QA9.A236 2000**
**Aczel, Amir D.**
Mystery of the aleph : mathematics, the kabbalah, and the search for infinity / by Amir D. Aczel. New York : Four Walls Eight Windows, 2000. p. cm.
00-041705          511.3          156858105X
*Cantor, Georg, -- 1845-1918.     Cabala. Infinite.*

**QA9.F7514 1968**
**Frege, Gottlob,**
The foundations of arithmetic; a logico-mathematical enquiry into the concept of number. English translation by J. L. Austin. Evanston, Ill., Northwestern University Press, 1968 [c1959] xii, xii [sup
68-008996       512/.81
*Number concept. Arithmetic -- Foundations.*

**QA9.G698**
**Greenstein, Carol Horn.**
Dictionary of logical terms and symbols / Carol Horn Greenstein. New York : Van Nostrand Reinhold, c1978. xiii, 188 p.
77-017513       511/.3/03       0442228341.
*Logic, Symbolic and mathematical -- Dictionaries.*

**QA9.H293 1998**
**Halmos, Paul R.**
Logic as algebra / Paul Halmos, Steven Givant. [Washington, D.C.] : Mathematical Association of America, c1998. ix, 141 p. :
97-080864       511.3       0883853272
*Logic, Symbolic and mathematical.*

**QA9.M316 1991**
**Maor, Eli.**
To infinity and beyond : a cultural history of the infinite / Eli Maor. Princeton, N.J. : Princeton University Press, [1991], c1987 xvi, 284 p. :
91-004396       511.3       0691025118
*Infinite.*

**QA9.M4 1979**
**Mendelson, Elliott.**
Introduction to mathematical logic / Elliott Mendelson. New York : Van Nostrand, c1979. viii, 328 p.
78-065959       511/.3       0442253079
*Logic, Symbolic and mathematical.*

**QA9.N3**
**Nagel, Ernest,**
Godel's proof, by Ernest Nagel and James R. Newman. [New York] New York University Press, 1958. 118 p.
58-005610       510.1
*Godel's theorem.*

**QA9.P515 1995**
**Pickover, Clifford A.**
Keys to infinity / Clifford A. Pickover. New York : Wiley & Sons, c1995. xviii, 332 p.
94-045541       793.7/4       0471118575
*Infinite.*

**QA9.P57**
**Polya, George,**
Mathematics and plausible reasoning. Princeton, N.J., Princeton University Press, 1954. 2 v.
53-006388       510.1
*Mathematics -- Philosophy. Logic, Symbolic and mathematical.*

**QA9.R7264 2000**
**Rodgers, Nancy,**
Learning to reason : an introduction to logic, sets and relations / Nancy Rodgers. New York : Wiley, 2000. xv, 437 p. :
00-023492       511.3       047137122X
*Logic, Symbolic and mathematical. Proof theory. Set theory.*

**QA9.R8 1970**
**Russell, Bertrand,**
Introduction to mathematical philosophy. London, G. Allen and Unwin [1970] xii, 208 p.
79-025179       510/.1       0045100209
*Mathematics -- Philosophy.*

**QA9.R88 1938**
**Russell, Bertrand,**
Principles of mathematics [by] Bertrand Russell, F.R.S. New York, W.W. Norton, [1938] xxxix, 534 p.
38027192       510.1
*Mathematics -- Philosophy.*

**QA9.T28 1965**
**Tarski, Alfred.**
Introduction to logic and to the methodology of deductive sciences / Alfred Tarski ; [translated by Olaf Helmer]. New York : Oxford University Press, c1965. xviii, 252 p.
65003257       510.1       0195010760
*Mathematics -- Philosophy. Arithmetic -- Foundations.*

**QA9.V38 1994**
**Velleman, Daniel J.**
How to prove it : a structured approach / Daniel J. Velleman. Cambridge [England] ; Cambridge University, 1994. ix, 309 p. :
93-014567       511.3       0521441161
*Logic, Symbolic and mathematical. Mathematics.*

**QA9.W5 1925**
**Whitehead, Alfred North,**
Principia mathematica, by Alfred North Whitehead ... and Bertrand Russell ... Cambridge [Eng.] The University Press, 1925- v.
25015133
*Mathematics. Logic, Symbolic and mathematical. Mathematics -- Philosophy.*

**QA9.54.E23 1997**
**Eccles, Peter J.,**
An introduction to mathematical reasoning : lectures on numbers, sets, and functions / Peter J. Eccles. New York : Cambridge University Press, 1997. p. cm.
97-011977       511.3       0521592690
*Proof theory.*

**QA9.54.G367 1996**
**Garnier, Rowan.**
100% mathematical proof / Rowan Garnier, John Taylor. Chichester ; Wiley, c1996. viii, 317 p.
96-194203       511.3       0471961981
*Proof theory. Logic, Symbolic and mathematical.*

**QA9.58.B47 2000**
**Berlinski, David,**
  The advent of the algorithm : the idea that rules the world / David Berlinski. New York : Harcourt, c2000. xviii, 345 p.
98-043755          511/.8          0151003386
  *Algorithms.*

**QA9.6.S67 1994**
**Smullyan, Raymond M.**
  Diagonalization and self-reference / Raymond M. Smullyan. Oxford ; Clarendon Press, 1994. xv, 396 p. :
94-003400          511.3          0198534507
  *Recursion theory. Fixed point theory.*

**QA9.615.D38 1982**
**Davis, Martin, 1928-**
  Computability & unsolvability / Martin Davis. Dover ed. New York : Dover, 1982. xxv, 248 p. ;
          511.3 19          0486614719
  *Recursive functions. Unsolvability (Mathematical logic) Computable functions.*

**QA9.64.M86 2001**
**Mukaidono, Masao,**
  Fuzzy logic for beginners / Masao Mukaidono. Singapore ; World Scientific, c2001. x, 105 p. :
01-273590          9810245343
  *Fuzzy logic.*

**QA9.65.S53 1994**
**Shankar, N.**
  Metamathematics, machines, and Godel's proof / N. Shankar. Cambridge ; Cambridge University Press, 1994. xv, 202 p. ;
94-222366          511.3/0285/53          052142027X
  *Godel's theorem -- Data processing. Automatic theorem proving.*

**QA9.65.S68 1987**
**Smullyan, Raymond M.**
  Forever undecided : a puzzle guide to Godel / by Raymond Smullyan. New York, N.Y. : Knopf, 1987. xii, 257 p. ;
86-045297          511.3          0394549430
  *Godel's theorem. Mathematical recreations.*

**QA9.65.S69 1992**
**Smullyan, Raymond M.**
  Godel's incompleteness theorems / Raymond M. Smullyan. New York : Oxford University Press, 1992. xiii, 139 p.
92-016377          511.3          0195046722
  *Godel's theorem.*

**QA9.7.P65 2000**
**Poizat, Bruno.**
  A course in model theory : an introduction to contemporary mathematical logic / Bruno Poizat ; translated by Moses Klein. New York : Springer, c2000. xxxi, 443 p.
99-053572          511/.8          0387986553
  *Model theory.*

**QA9.8.H63**
**Hofstadter, Douglas R.,**
  Godel, Escher, Bach : an eternal golden braid / Douglas R. Hofstadter. New York : Basic Books, c1979. xxi, 777 p. :
78-019943          510/.1          0465026850
*Bach, Johann Sebastian, -- 1685-1750. Escher, M. C. -- (Maurits Cornelis), -- 1898-1972. Godel, Kurt. Metamathematics. Symmetry. Artificial intelligence.*

## QA10.4 Philosophy — Information theory in mathematics

**QA10.4.R83 1987**
**Rucker, Rudy v. B.**
  Mind tools : the five levels of mathematical reality / Rudy Rucker. Boston : Houghton Mifflin, 1987. viii, 328 p.
86-027790          510/.1          0395383153
  *Information theory in mathematics. Mathematics -- Philosophy.*

## QA10.5 Mathematics as a profession

**QA10.5.A15 1996**
  101 careers in mathematics / edited by Andrew Sterrett. [Washington, DC] : Mathematical Association of America, c1996. x, 260 p. :
96-075575          510/.2373          0883857049
  *Mathematics -- Vocational guidance. Mathematicians – United States*

## QA11 Study and teaching. Research

**QA11.C673**
**Copeland, Richard W.**
  How children learn mathematics; teaching implications of Piaget's research [by] Richard W. Copeland. [New York] Macmillan [1970] viii, 310 p.
76-103689          372.7
*Piaget, Jean, -- 1896- Mathematical ability. Mathematics – Study and teaching (Elementary)*

**QA11.E665 2001**
  Encyclopedia of mathematics education / editors-in-chief, Louise S. Grinstein, Sally I. Lipsey. New York : Routledge, 2001. p. cm.
01-016599          510/.71          081531647X
  *Mathematics -- Study and teaching -- Encyclopedias.*

**QA11.H256 1999**
  Handbook of research design in mathematics and science education / edited by Anthony E. Kelly, Richard A. Lesh. Mahwah, N.J. : L. Erlbaum, 2000. 993 p. :
99-028610          507.1          0805832815
  *Mathematics -- Study and teaching -- Research. Science – Study and teaching -- Research.*

**QA11.H26 1992**
Handbook of research on mathematics teaching and learning / Douglas A. Grouws, editor. New York : Macmillan ; c1992. p. cm.
91-037820          510/.71          0029223814
*Mathematics -- Study and teaching -- Research.*

**QA11.M79 2000**
Multiple perspectives on mathematics teaching and learning / edited by Jo Boaler. Westport, CT : Ablex Pub., 2000. ix, 278 p. :
00-035567          510/.71          1567505341
*Mathematics -- Study and teaching.*

**QA11.P586 1995**
**Pimm, David.**
Symbols and meanings in school mathematics / David Pimm. London ; Routledge, 1995. xiv, 220 p. :
94-039323          510 s          0415113849
*Mathematics -- Study and teaching. Mathematical notation.*

**QA11.P6 1957**
**Polya, George,**
How to solve it; a new aspect of mathematical method Garden City, N.Y., Doubleday, 1957. 253 p.
57005794
*Mathematics -- Problems, exercises, etc Mathematics – Study and teaching*

**QA11.R47**
**Resnick, Lauren B.**
The psychology of mathematics for instruction / Lauren B. Resnick, Wendy W. Ford. Hillsdale, N.J. : L. Erlbaum Associates, 1981. vi, 266 p. :
80-029106          370.15/6          0898590299
*Mathematics -- Study and teaching -- Psychological aspects.*

**QA11.S83 1998**
**Stueben, Michael.**
Twenty years before the blackboard : the lessons and humor of a mathematics teacher / Michael Stueben with Diane Sandford. [Washington, DC] : Mathematical Association of America c1998. xi, 155 p. :
97-074343          510/.71/2          0883855259
*Mathematics -- Study and teaching -- Miscellanea. Mathematics – Humor.*

**QA11.T67 1978**
**Tobias, Sheila.**
Overcoming math anxiety / Sheila Tobias. New York : Norton, c1978. 278 p. :
78-017583          510/.7          0393064395
*Mathematics -- Study and teaching -- Psychological aspects.*

**QA11.Z37 1994**
**Zaslavsky, Claudia.**
Fear of math : how to get over it and get on with your life / Claudia Zaslavsky. New Brunswick, N.J. : Rutgers University Press, c1994. x, 264 p. :
93-043904          370.15/651          0813520908
*Math anxiety. Mathematics -- Study and teaching. Self-help techniques.*

### QA13 Study and teaching. Research — By region or country — United States

**QA13.C538 1992**
**Clewell, Beatriz C.**
Breaking the barriers : helping female and minority students succeed in mathematics and science / Beatriz Chu Clewell, Bernice Taylor Anderson, Margaret E. Thorpe. San Francisco : Jossey-Bass, 1992. xviii, 333 p.
92-021619          510/.71/273          1555424821
*Mathematics -- Study and teaching (Secondary) -- United States. Science -- Study and teaching (Secondary) -- United States. Minorities -- Education (Secondary) -- United States.*

**QA13.C6525 1998**
Confronting the core curriculum : considering change in the undergraduate mathematics major : conference proceedings / edited by John A. Dossey. [Washington, DC] : Mathematical Association of America, c1998. xii, 136 p. :
97-074332          510/.71/173          0883851555
*Mathematics -- Study and teaching (Higher) -- United States – Congresses. Curriculum change -- United States -- Congresses.*

**QA13.D74 1996**
**Drew, David E.**
Aptitude revisited : rethinking math and science education for America's next century / David E. Drew. Baltimore : The Johns Hopkins University Press, c1996. xii, 254 p. ;
95-035256          510/.71/073          0801851432
*Mathematics -- Study and teaching -- United States. Science – Study and teaching -- United States.*

**QA13.H43 2000**
**Heaton, Ruth M.**
Teaching mathematics to the new standards : relearning the dance / Ruth M. Heaton ; foreword by Magdalene Lampert. New York : Teachers College Press, c2000. xiii, 177 p.
00-030237          510.71/073          0807739693
*Mathematics -- Study and teaching -- United States.*

### QA21 History — General

**QA21.A54 1994**
**Anglin, W. S.**
Mathematics, a concise history and philosophy / W.S. Anglin. New York : Springer-Verlag, c1994. xi, 261 p. :
94-008075          510/.9          0387942807
*Mathematics -- History. Mathematics -- Philosophy.*

**QA21.B4 1945**
**Bell, Eric Temple,**
The development of mathematics, by E. T. Bell. New York, McGraw-Hill book company, inc., 1945. xiii, 637 p.
45-010599          510.9
*Mathematics -- History.*

**QA21.B42**
**Bell, Eric Temple,**
Mathematics, queen and servant of science. New York, McGraw-Hill [1951] xx, 437 p.
51-009241      510.9
*Mathematics -- History.*

**QA21.C13 1917**
**Cajori, Florian,**
A history of elementary mathematics, with hints on methods of teaching, by Florian Cajori. New York, The Macmillan Company; 1917. viii, 324 p.
17006771
*Mathematics -- Study and teaching. Mathematics -- History.*

**QA21.C15 1919**
**Cajori, Florian,**
A history of mathematics, by Florian Cajori. New York, The Macmillan company; 1919. viii p., 1.,
19012334
*Mathematics -- History.*

**QA21.C645 1994**
Companion encyclopedia of the history and philosophy of the mathematical sciences / edited by I. Grattan-Guinness. London ; Routledge, 1994. 2 v. (xiii, 1
92-013707      510/.9      0415037859
*Mathematics -- History. Mathematics -- Philosophy.*

**QA21.F76 1994**
From five fingers to infinity : a journey through the history of mathematics / edited by Frank J. Swetz. Chicago : Open Court, c1994. xx, 770 p. :
94-020802      510/.9      0812691938
*Mathematics -- History.*

**QA21.G695 1998**
**Grattan-Guinness, I.**
The Norton history of the mathematical sciences : the rainbow of mathematics / Ivor Grattan-Guinness. New York : W.W. Norton, 1998. 817 p. :
98-007876      510/.9      0393046508
*Mathematics -- History.*

**QA21.H729 1961**
**Hogben, Lancelot Thomas,**
Mathematics in the making. Garden City, N.Y., Doubleday [1961, c1960] 320 p.
61-005067      510.9
*Mathematics -- History.*

**QA21.K52**
**Kline, Morris,**
Mathematics in Western culture. New York, Oxford University Press, 1953. 484 p.
53-009187      510.9
*Mathematics -- History.*

**QA21.M3612 2000**
Mathematics across cultures : the history of nonwestern mathematics / Helaine Selin, editor, Ubiratan D'Ambrosio, advisory editor. Boston, MA : Kluwer Academic, 2000. p. cm.
00-056016      510/.9      0792364813
*Mathematics -- History. Ethnomathematics. Mathematics, Ancient.*

**QA21.M846 1993**
**Motz, Lloyd,**
The story of mathematics / Lloyd Motz and Jefferson Hane Weaver. New York : Plenum Press, c1993. x, 356 p. :
93-026527      510/.9      0306445085
*Mathematics -- History.*

**QA21.S87 1967**
**Struik, Dirk Jan,**
A concise history of mathematics, by Dirk J. Struik. New York, Dover Publications [1967] x, 195 p.
66-028622      510/.09
*Mathematics -- History.*

## QA22 History — Ancient

**QA22.C86 2000**
**Cuomo, S.**
Pappus of Alexandria and the mathematics of late antiquity / S. Cuomo. Cambridge ; Cambridge University Press, 2000. ix, 234 p. :
99-012317      510/.938      0521642116
*Pappus, -- of Alexandria. -- Mathematical collections. Mathematics, Greek.*

**QA22.H4**
**Heath, Thomas Little,**
A history of Greek mathematics, by Sir Thomas Heath... Oxford, The Clarendon press, 1921. 2 v.
22005925
*Mathematics -- History. Mathematics, Greek.*

**QA22.S85 1999**
**Stein, Sherman K.**
Archimedes : what did he do besides cry eureka? / Sherman Stein. Washington, DC : Mathematical Association of America, c1999. x, 155 p. :
99-062795      510      0883857189
*Archimedes. Mathematics, Greek.*

## QA23 History — Medieval

**QA23.D33 1977**
**Daffa`, `Ali `Abd Allah.**
The Muslim contribution to mathematics / Ali Abdullah Al-Daffa. Atlantic Highlands, N.J. : Humanities Press, c1977. 121 p. :
77003521      510/.917/4927      0391007149
*Mathematics, Arab.*

## QA27 History — By region or country, A-Z

**QA27.C5.L4713 1987**
**Li, Yen,**
Chinese mathematics : a concise history / by Li Yan and Du Shiran ; translated by John N. Crossley and Anthony W.-C. Lun. Oxford [England] : Clarendon Press, 1987. xiii, 290 p.
86-017955          510/.951          0198581815
*Mathematics -- China -- History. Mathematics, Chinese.*

**QA27.G7.D8**
**Dubbey, J. M.**
The mathematical work of Charles Babbage / J. M. Dubbey. Cambridge, [Eng.] : Cambridge University Press, 1978. viii, 235 p.
77-071409          519.4/092/4          0521216494
*Babbage, Charles, -- 1791-1871.     Mathematics -- Great Britain -- History. Computers -- History.*

# QA27.5 Women in mathematics. Women mathematicians

**QA27.5.H46 1997**
**Henrion, Claudia,**
Women in mathematics : the addition of difference / Claudia Henrion. Bloomington : Indiana University Press, c1997. xxxi, 293 p.
97-002546          305.43/51          0253332796
*Women in mathematics -- United States. Women mathematicians -- United States -- Interviews.*

**QA27.5.S53 1995**
She does math! : real-life problems from women on the job / Marla Parker, editor. [Washington, DC] : Mathematical Association of America, c1995. xv, 253 p. :
95-076294          510/.23          0883857022
*Women in mathematics -- United States Mathematics -- Problems, exercises, etc.*

**QA27.5.W68 1997**
Women in mathematics : scaling the heights / Deborah Nolan, editor. [Washington, DC] : Mathematical Association of America, c1997. x, 121 p. :
97-074346          510/.82/0973          0883851563
*Women in mathematics -- United States -- Congresses. Mathematics -- Study and teaching (Graduate) -- United States -- Congresses.*

## QA28 Biography — Collective

**QA28.B4**
**Bell, Eric Temple,**
Men of mathematics, by E. T. Bell. New York, Simon and Schuster, 1937. xxi, 592 p.,
37-027177          925.1
*Mathematicians. Mathematics -- History.*

**QA28.B58**
Black mathematicians and their works / edited by Virginia K. Newell ... [et al.]. Ardmore, Pa. : Dorrance, c1980. xvi, 327 p. :
78-072929          510          0805925562
*Afro-American mathematicians. Mathematics -- Addresses, essays, lectures.*

**QA28.B78 1999**
**Bruno, Leonard C.**
Math and mathematicians : the history of math discoveries around the world / Leonard C. Bruno ; Lawrence W. Baker, editor. Detroit, MI : U X L, 1999. p. cm.
99-032424          510/.92/2          0787638129
*Mathematicians -- Biography -- Juvenile literature. Mathematics -- History -- Encyclopedias, Juvenile. Mathematicians -- Encyclopedias.*

**QA28.H44**
**Heims, Steve J.**
John Von Neumann and Norbert Wiener : from mathematics to the technologies of life and death / Steve J. Heims. Cambridge, Mass. : MIT Press, c1980. xviii, 547 p.
80-016185          510/.92/2          0262081059
*Von Neumann, John, -- 1903-1957. Wiener, Norbert, -- 1894-1964. Mathematicians -- United States -- Biography.*

**QA28.N66 1998**
Notable mathematicians : from ancient times to the present / Robyn V. Young, editor ; Zoran Minderovic, associate editor. Detroit : Gale, c1998. xxi, 612 p. :
97-033662          510/.92/2          0787630713
*Mathematicians -- Biography.*

**QA28.N68 1998**
Notable women in mathematics : a biographical dictionary / edited by Charlene Morrow and Teri Perl. Westport, Conn. : Greenwood Press, 1998. xv, 302 p. :
97-018598          510/.92/2          0313291314
*Women mathematicians -- Biography.*

## QA29 Biography — Individual, A-Z

**QA29.B2.A3 1994**
**Babbage, Charles,**
Passages from the life of a philosopher / Charles Babbage ; edited, with a new introduction, by Martin Campbell-Kelly. New Brunswick, N.J. : Rutgers University Press ; 1994. 383 p. :
93-043903          510/.92          0813520665
*Babbage, Charles, -- 1791-1871. Mathematicians -- England -- Biography.*

**QA29.B37.B44 1990**
Before Newton : the life and times of Isaac Barrow / edited by Mordechai Feingold. Cambridge [England] ; Cambridge University Press, 1990. xi, 380 p. :
89-038508          510/.92          0521306949
*Barrow, Isaac, -- 1630-1677. Mathematicians -- England -- Biography. Clergy -- England -- Biography.*

**QA29.B447.R45 1993**
**Reid, Constance.**

The search for E.T. Bell : also known as John Taine / Constance Reid. Washington, DC : Mathematical Association of America, c1993. x, 372 p. :
93-078369          510/.92          0883855089
*Bell, Eric Temple, -- 1883-1960.     Mathematicians – United States – Biography. Authors, American -- 20th century -- Biography.*

**QA29.E68.H64 1998**
**Hoffman, Paul,**

The man who loved only numbers : the story of Paul Erdos and the search for mathematical truth / by Paul Hoffman. New York : Hyperion, c1998. 301 p. :
98-014027          510/.92          0786863625
*Erdos, Paul, -- 1913-    Mathematicians -- Hungary -- Biography.*

**QA29.E8.D86 1999**
**Dunham, William,**

Euler : the master of us all / William Dunham. [Washington, D.C.] : Mathematical Association of America, c1999. xxviii, 185 p
98-088271          510/.92          0883853280
*Euler, Leonhard, -- 1707-1783.     Mathematics -- History -- 18th century. Mathematicians -- Switzerland -- Biography.*

**QA29.G3.B83**
**Buhler, W. K.**

Gauss : a biographical study / W.K. Buhler. Berlin ; Springer-Verlag, c1981. viii, 208 p.
80029515          510/.92/4
*Gauss, Carl Friedrich, -- 1777-1855. -- cn     Mathematicians -- Germany -- Biography.*

**QA29.G58**
**Casti, J. L.**

Godel : a life of logic / John L. Casti and Werner DePauli. Cambridge, Mass. : Perseus Pub., c2000. 210 p. :
00-105215          0738202746
*Godel, Kurt.     Logicians -- United States -- Biography. Logicians – Austria -- Biography.*

**QA29.G58.W357 1996**
**Wang, Hao,**

A logical journey : from Godel to philosophy / Hao Wang. Cambridge, Mass. : MIT Press, c1996. xiv, 391 p. ;
96-032568          193     0262231891
*Godel, Kurt.     Logicians -- United States -- Biography. Logicians – Austria -- Biography.*

**QA29.K67.K6 1983**
**Koblitz, Ann Hibner.**

A convergence of lives : Sofia Kovalevskaia, scientist, writer, revolutionary / Ann Hibner Koblitz. Boston : Birkhauser, c1983. xx, 305 p., [
83-017233          510/.92/4          0817631623
*Kovalevskaia, S. V. -- (Sofia Vasilevna), -- 1850-1891. Mathematicians -- Soviet Union -- Biography.*

**QA29.L72**
**Woolley, Benjamin.**

The bride of science : romance, reason, and Byron's daughter / Benjamin Woolley. New York : McGraw-Hill, c1999. viii, 416 p.
01-274424          510/.92          0071373292
*Lovelace, Ada King, -- Countess of, -- 1815-1852.     Women mathematicians -- Great Britain -- Biography. Computers and women -- History -- 19th century. Aristocracy (Social class) -- England – Biography.*

**QA29.L72A4**
**Lovelace, Ada King, Countess of,**

Ada, the enchantress of numbers : a selection from the letters of Lord Byron's daughter and her description of the first computer / narrated and edited by Betty A. Toole. 1st ed. Mill Valley, Calif. ; Sausalito, CA : Strawberry Press ; Orders to Critical Connection, c1992. xv, 439 p. :
510/.92 B 20          0912647094
*Lovelace, Ada King, Countess of, 1815-1852 -- Correspondence. Mathematicians -- Great Britain -- Correspondence. Calculators. Computers.*

**QA29.M5234.M63 1993**

Mobius and his band : mathematics and astronomy in nineteenth-century Germany / edited by John Fauvel, Raymond Flood, and Robin Wilson. Oxford ; Oxford University Press, 1993. 172 p. :
92-046692          510/.943/09034          019853969X
*Mobius, August Ferdinand, -- 1790-1868.     Mathematics – Germany -- History -- 19th century. Astronomy -- Germany -- History – 19th century. Mathematicians -- Germany -- Biography.*

**QA29.R3.K36 1991**
**Kanigel, Robert.**

The man who knew infinity : a life of the genius, Ramanujan / Robert Kanigel. New York : C. Scribner's ; c1991. ix, 438 p. :
90-049788          510/.92          0684192594
*Ramanujan Aiyangar, Srinivasa, -- 1887-1920. Hardy, G. H. -- (Godfrey Harold), -- 1877-1947.     Mathematicians -- India -- Biography. Mathematicians -- England -- Biography.*

**QA29.R575.R45 1996**
**Reid, Constance.**

Julia, a life in mathematics / Constance Reid. [Washington, DC] : Mathematical Association of America, c1996. xi, 123 p. :
96-077366          510/.92          0883855208
*Robinson, Julia, -- d. 1985.     Mathematicians -- United States – Biography. Women mathematicians -- United States -- Biography.*

**QA29.T8H63 2000**
**Hodges, Andrew.**

Alan Turing : the enigma / Andrew Hodges ; foreword by Douglas Hofstadter. New York : Walker, 2000. xvii, 587 p.
510/.92 B 21
*Turing, Alan Mathison, 1912-1954. Mathematicians – Great Britain -- Biography.*

**QA29.W497.A3**
**Wiener, Norbert,**
   Ex-prodigy: my childhood and youth. New York, Simon and Schuster, 1953. 309 p.
53007583          925.1
*Wiener, Norbert, -- 1894-1964.*

**QA29.W497.A35**
**Wiener, Norbert,**
   I am a mathematician, the later life of a prodigy; an autobiographical account of the mature years and career of Norbert Wiener and a continuation of the account of his childhood in Ex-prodigy.   Garden City, N.Y., Doubleday, 1956. 380 p.
56-005598          925.1
*Wiener, Norbert, -- 1894-1964.  Wiener, Norbert, -- 1894-1964. Mathematicians -- United States -- Biography.*

## QA31 Early works through 1800 — Greek

**QA31.A692**
**Archimedes.**
   Works. Edited in modern notation, with introductory chapters by T. L. Heath. With a supplement, The method of Archimedes, recently discovered by Heiberg. New York, Dover Publications [195-?] clxxxvi, 326,
53003224
   *Mathematics, Greek.  Geometry -- Early works to 1800 Mechanics -- Early works to 1800.*

**QA31.E9.A78 1999**
**Artmann, Benno.**
   Euclid : the creation of mathematics / Benno Artmann. New York : Springer, c1999. xvi, 343 p. :
98-031042          510          0387984232
*Euclid. -- Elements.   Mathematics, Greek.*

## QA32 Early works through 1800 — Medieval

**QA32.F4813 1987**
**Fibonacci, Leonardo,**
   The book of squares / Leonardo Pisano Fibonacci ; an annotated translation into modern English by L.E. Sigler. Boston : Academic Press, 1987. xx, 124 p. :
86-017336          510          0126431302
*Fibonacci, Leonardo, -- ca. 1170-ca. 1240.   Number theory – Early works to 1800. Mathematics -- Early works to 1800. Mathematics, Medieval -- Sources.*

## QA35 Early works through 1800 — 1701-1800

**QA35.N5647**
**Newton, Isaac,**
   The mathematical papers of Isaac Newton, edited by D. T. Whiteside with the assistance in publication of M. A. Hoskin. Cambridge, Cambridge U.P., 1967-1981. 8 v.
65-011203          510/.8   0521071194
   *Mathematics -- Early works to 1800. Mathematics.*

## QA36 General works — Comprehensive treatises

**QA36.B37 1992**
**Barrow, John D.,**
   Pi in the sky : counting, thinking, and being / John D. Barrow. Oxford : Clarendon Press ; 1992. ix, 317 p. :
92-020217          510          0198539568
   *Mathematics.*

**QA36.G86 1997**
**Gullberg, Jan.**
   Mathematics : from the birth of numbers / Jan Gullberg ; technical illustrations, Par Gullberg. New York : W.W. Norton, c1997. xxii, 1093 p.
96-013428          510/.9          039304002X
   *Mathematics.*

**QA36.H6 1951**
**Hogben, Lancelot Thomas,**
   Mathematics for the million; illustrated by J. F. Horrabin. New York, Norton [1951] 697 p.
51008025          510
   *Mathematics.  Mathematics -- History.  Civilization.*

### QA37-37.2 General works — Textbooks — Advanced

**QA37.B29**
**Bartle, Robert Gardner,**
   The elements of real analysis [by] Robert G. Bartle. New York, Wiley [1964] xiv, 447 p.
64-020061          517
   *Mathematical analysis.*

**QA37.C675**
**Courant, Richard,**
   What is Mathematics? An elementary approach to ideas and methods, by Richard Courant and Herbert Robbins. London, Oxford university press [c1941] 3 p. l., v-xi
41-025632          510
   *Mathematics.*

**QA37.K62**
**Kline, Morris,**
   Mathematics for liberal arts.   Reading, Mass., Addison-Wesley Pub. Co. [1967] xiii, 577 p.
67-012831          510
   *Mathematics.*

**QA37.K74**
**Korn, Granino Arthur,**
   Mathematical handbook for scientists and engineers; definitions, theorems, and formulas for reference and review [by] Granino A. Korn [and] Theresa M. Korn. New York, McGraw-Hill, 1961. 943 p.
59-014456          510
   *Mathematics -- Handbooks, manuals, etc.*

**QA37.M33 1956**
**Margenau, Henry,**
    The mathematics of physics and chemistry, by Henry Margenau and George Moseley Murphy. Princeton, Van Nostrand [1956-64] 2 v.
55-010911        530.151
    *Mathematics. Mathematical physics. Chemistry, Physical and theoretical -- Mathematics.*

**QA37.2.F35 1997**
**Fanchi, John R.**
    Math refresher for scientists and engineers / John R. Fanchi. New York : Wiley, c1997. xii, 259 p. :
97-018910        512/.1        0471191019
    *Mathematics.*

**QA37.2.M43 1994**
**McGregor, C. M.**
    Fundamentals of university mathematics / C.M. McGregor, J.J.C. Nimmo, and W.W. Strothers. Chichester : Albion ; 1994. 540 p. :
99-474270        510        1898563101
    *Mathematics.*

### QA39-39.2 General works — Textbooks — Intermediate (without calculus)

**QA39.K35 1966**
**Kemeny, John G.**
    Introduction to finite mathematics [by] John G. Kemeny, J. Laurie Snell [and] Gerald L. Thompson. Englewood Cliffs, N.J., Prentice-Hall [1966] xiv, 465 p.
66-019894        510
    *Mathematics. Social sciences -- Mathematics.*

**QA39.2.B42 2000**
**Beck, Anatole.**
    Excursions into mathematics / Anatole Beck, Michael N. Bleicher, Donald W. Crowe. Natick, Mass. : A.K. Peters, c2000. xxv, 499 p. :
99-058794        510        1568811152
    *Mathematics.*

**QA39.2.G733 1994**
**Graham, Ronald L.,**
    Concrete mathematics : a foundation for computer science / Ronald L. Graham, Donald E. Knuth, Oren Patashnik. 2nd ed. Reading, Mass. : Addison-Wesley, c1994. xiii, 657 p. :
        510 20    0201558025
*Mathematics. Computer science -- Mathematics.*

**QA39.2.G7473 1993**
**Gries, David.**
    A logical approach to discrete math / David Gries, Fred B. Schneider. New York : Springer-Verlag, c1993. xvi, 497 p. :
93-027848        510        0387941150
    *Mathematics.*

**QA39.2.L97 1995**
**Lyons, Louis.**
    All you wanted to know about mathematics but were afraid to ask : mathematics for science students / Louis Lyons. Cambridge ; Cambridge University Press, 1995-1998. 2 v. :
94-028451        510        0521434653
    *Mathematics.*

**QA39.2.S525 1988**
**Sirovich, L.,**
    Introduction to applied mathematics / L. Sirovich. New York : Springer-Verlag, c1988. xii, 370 p. :
88-027821        515        0387968849
    *Mathematics.*

**QA39.2.S745 1990**
**Stephenson, G.**
    Advanced mathematical methods for engineering and science students / G. Stephenson and P.M. Radmore. Cambridge ; Cambridge University Press, 1990. xi, 255 p. :
89-036870        510        0521363128
    *Mathematics.*

**QA39.2.S755 1998**
**Stillwell, John.**
    Numbers and geometry / John Stillwell. New York: Springer, c1998. xiv, 339 p. :
97-022858        510        0387982892
    *Mathematics.*

**QA39.2.T413 1999**
**Taylor, Paul,**
    Practical foundations of mathematics / Paul Taylor. Cambridge ; Cambridge University Press, 1999. xi, 572 p. ;
98-039472        510        0521631076
    *Mathematics.*

### QA39.3 General works — Textbooks — Elementary

**QA39.3.L47 2001**
**Lerner, Marcia.**
    Math smart / by Marcia Lerner. Rev. and updated 2nd ed. New York : Random House, c2001 xii, 302 p. :
        510 21    0375762167
*Mathematics.*

## QA40 Handbooks, manuals, etc.

**QA40.H34 1983**
    Handbook of applied mathematics : selected results and methods / edited by Carl E. Pearson. New York : Van Nostrand Reinhold Co., c1983. xiii, 1307 p.
82-020223        510/.2/02        0442238665
    *Mathematics -- Handbooks, manuals, etc.*

**QA40.S76 1998**
Harris, J.
Handbook of mathematics and computational science / John W. Harris, Horst Stocker. New York : Springer, 1998. xxviii, 1028
98-020290          510          0387947469
*Mathematics -- Handbooks, manuals, etc. Computer science -- Handbooks, manuals, etc.*

## QA41 Formulas, notation, abbreviations

**QA41.L58 1999**
Liu, John.
Mathematical handbook of formulas and tables. 2nd ed. / Murray R. Spiegel, John Liu. New York : McGraw-Hill, c1999. viii, 278 p. :
          510/.2/12 21          0070382034
*Mathematics -- Formulae. Mathematics -- Tables.*

**QA41.R34 1995**
Rade, Lennart.
Mathematics handbook for science and engineering / Lennart Rade, Bertil Westergren. Cambridge, MA : Birkhauser Boston, c1995. 539 p. :
96-124564          510/.212          081763858X
*Mathematics -- Formulae. Mathematics -- Tables. Mathematics -- Handbooks, manuals, etc.*

## QA42 Communication of mathematical information

**QA42.K73 1997**
Krantz, Steven G.
A primer of mathematical writing : being a disquisition on having your ideas recorded, typeset, published, read and appreciated / Steven G. Krantz. Providence, R.I. : American Mathematical Society, c1997. xv, 223 p. ;
96-045732          808/.0665          0821806351
*Mathematics -- Authorship.*

## QA43 Problems, exercises, examinations

**QA43.A52 2000**
Andreescu, Titu,
Mathematical Olympiad challenges / Titu Andreescu, Razvan Gelca ; foreword by Mark Saul. Boston : Birkhauser, c2000. xv, 260 p. :
99-086229          510/.76          0817641904
*Mathematics -- Problems, exercises, etc.*

**QA43.G345 1997**
Gardiner, A.
The Mathematical Olympiad handbook : an introduction to problem solving based on the first 32 British mathematical olympiads 1965-1996 / A. Gardiner. Oxford ; Oxford University Press, 1997. xii, 229 p. :
97-017647          510/.76          0198501056
*Mathematics -- Problems, exercises, etc.*

**QA43.G346 1997**
Gardiner, A.
More mathematical challenges / Tony Gardiner. Cambridge, U.K. ; Cambridge University Press, 1997. 140 p. :
97-184218          510/.76          0521585686
*Mathematics -- Problems, exercises, etc.*

**QA43.G54 1993**
Gilbert, George Thomas.
The Wohascum County problem book / Gilbert, Krusemeyer, Larson. [Washington, D.C.] : Mathematical Association of America, c1993. ix, 233 p. :
91-061586          510/.76          0883853000
*Mathematics -- Problems, exercises, etc.*

**QA43.H63 1996**
Honsberger, Ross,
From Erdos to Kiev : problems of Olympiad caliber / Ross Honsberger. [Washington, DC] : Mathematical Association of America, c1996. xii, 257 p. :
95-076288          510/.76          0883853248
*Mathematics -- Problems, exercises, etc.*

**QA43.H633 1997**
Honsberger, Ross,
In Polya's footsteps : miscellaneous problems and essays / Ross Honsberger. [Washington, D.C.] : Mathematical Association of America, c1997. x, 315 p. :
97-070506          510/.76          0883853264
*Mathematics -- Problems, exercises, etc.*

**QA43.S695 1998**
Souza, Paulo Ney de.
Berkeley problems in mathematics / Paulo Ney de Souza, Jorge-Nuno Silva. New York : Springer, c1998. xiv, 443 p. :
97-034135          515/.076          038794933X
*Mathematics -- Examinations, questions, etc.*

## QA47 Tables — General tables

**QA47.M315**
CRC standard mathematical tables and formulae. Boca Raton : CRC Press, c1991- v. :
91-659327          510/.212
*Mathematics -- Tables -- Periodicals.*

## QA55 Tables — Logarithms. Tables of mathematical functions — General works

**QA55.J3 1960**
**Jahnke, E.**
  Tables of higher functions [by] Jahnke, Emde [and] Losch. New York, McGraw-Hill [1960] 318 p.
60-013611          517.5
  *Mathematics -- Tables. Functions.*

QA63 Tables — Logarithms. Tables of mathematical functions — Theory and use of logarithms

**QA63.C64 1990**
**Cofman, Judita.**
  What to solve? : problems and suggestions for young mathematicians / Judita Cofman. Oxford : Clarendon Press ; 1990. xiii, 250 p.
89-022150          510/.76          0198532962
  *Problem solving. Mathematics -- Problems, exercises, etc.*

**QA63.K73 1997**
**Krantz, Steven G.**
  Techniques of problem solving / Steven G. Krantz. Providence, R.I. : American Mathematical Society, c1997. xiii, 465 p.
96-023878          510/.76          082180619X
  *Problem solving.*

**QA63.M53 2000**
**Michalewicz, Zbigniew.**
  How to solve it : modern heuristics / Zbigniew Michaelewicz, David B. Fogel. Berlin ; New York : Springer, c2000. xv, 467 p. :
                  153.4/3 21          3540660615
*Problem solving. Heuristic.*

## QA75 Instruments and machines — Calculating machines — Electronic computers. Computer science

**QA75.B28**
**Babbage, Charles,**
  Charles Babbage and his calculating engines; selected writings by Charles Babbage and others. Edited with an introd. by Philip Morrison and Emily Morrison. New York, Dover Publications [1961] 400 p.
61-019855          510.78
  *Calculators. Scientists -- Correspondence.*

## QA76 Instruments and machines — Calculating machines — Electronic computers. Computer science — General works, treatises, and textbooks

**QA76.A28**
**Adler, Irving.**
  Thinking machines, a layman's introduction to logic, Boolean algebra, and computers. With diagrs. by Ruth Adler. New York, John Day Co. [1961] 189 p.
61-005924          510.78
  *Computers -- Popular works.*

**QA76.B445 1999**
**Bernstein, Ira H.**
  Computer literacy : getting the most from your PC / Ira H. Bernstein, Paul Havig. Thousand Oaks, Calif. : Sage Publications, [1988], c1999 xxi, 426 p. :
98-025450          004          0761911383
  *Computer literacy.*

**QA76.B495 1997**
**Biermann, Alan W.,**
  Great ideas in computer science : a gentle introduction / Alan W. Biermann. Cambridge, Mass. : MIT Press, c1997. xxiv, 539 p.
96-041198          004          0262522233
  *Computer science.*

**QA76.C57315 1997**
  The computer science and engineering handbook / editer-in-chief, Allen B. Tucker, Jr. Boca Raton, FL : CRC Press, c1997. xxxix, 2611 p
96-020442          004          0849329094
  *Computer science -- Handbooks, manuals, etc. Engineering – Handbooks, manuals, etc.*

**QA76.C5834 1990**
  Computing before computers / edited by William Aspray ; contributors W. Aspray ... [et al.]. Ames : Iowa State University Press, 1990. ix, [x] 266 p
89-026745          681/.14          0813800471
  *Calculators -- History. Computers -- History.*

**QA76.D45 1989**
**Dewdney, A. K.**
  The Turing omnibus : 61 excursions in computer science / A.K. Dewdney. Rockville, MD : Computer Science Press, c1989. xiv, 415 p. :
87-037501          004          0716781549
  *Electronic data processing. Computers.*

**QA76.F54 1995**
**Fiume, Eugene L.**
  An introduction to scientific, symbolic, and graphical computation / Eugene Fiume. Wellesley, Mass. : A K Peters, c1995. xv, 306 p. :
94-046591          510/.285/51          1568810512
  *Electronic data processing.*

**QA76.F895 2001**
  Fuzzy learning and applications / [edited by] Marco Russo, Lakhmi C. Jain. Boca Raton : CRC Press, c2001. xii, 391 p. :
00-048560          006.3/2          0849322693
  *Computer science. Programmable controllers. Fuzzy systems.*

**QA76.H265 1997**
  HAL's legacy : 2001s computer as dream and reality / edited by David G. Stork. Cambridge, Mass. : MIT Press, c1997. xxi, 384 p. :
96-031375          791.43/72          0262193787
  *Computer science. Supercomputers.*

**QA76.H279 1990**
Handbook of theoretical computer science / edited by Jan van Leeuwen. Amsterdam ; Elsevier ; 1990. 2 v. :
90-003485       004       0444880755
*Computer science.*

**QA76.H3475 1994**
**Harvey, Brian,**
Simply scheme : introducing computer science / Brian Harvey, Matthew Wright ; foreword by Harold Abelson. Cambridge, Mass. : MIT Press, c1994. xxxii, 583 p.
93-034469       005.13/3       0262082268
*Computer science. Scheme (Computer program language)*

**QA76.I63 1989**
Introduction to computer systems : analysis, design, and applications / John A. Aseltine ... [et al.]. New York : Wiley, c1989. xvii, 375 p.
89-005683       004       0471637041
*Computers. System analysis. System design.*

**QA76.L79 1994**
**Luo, Zhaohui.**
Computation and reasoning : a type theory for computer science / Zhaohui Luo. Oxford : Clarendon Press ; c1994. xi, 228 p. :
93-046644       004       0198538359
*Computer science.*

**QA76.P465 1991**
**Pickover, Clifford A.**
Computers and the imagination : visual adventures beyond the edge / Clifford A. Pickover. New York : St. Martin's Press, 1991. xix, 419 p. :
91-012058       004       0312061315
*Computers. Computer simulation. Computer graphics.*

**QA76.S5159 2000**
**Siegfried, Tom.**
The bit and the pendulum : from quantum computing to M theory-- the new physics of information / Tom Siegfried. New York : Wiley, c2000. vi, 281 p. :
99-022275       004       0471321745
*Computer science. Physics. Information technology.*

**QA76.V6**
**Von Neumann, John,**
The computer and the brain. New Haven, Yale University Press, 1958. 82 p.
58-006542       005.3
*Computers. Cybernetics. Nervous system.*

**QA76.W24313 1986**
**Warnier, Jean Dominique.**
Computers and human intelligence / Jean-Dominique Warnier. Englewood Cliffs, N.J. : Prentice-Hall, c1986. xv, 141 p. ;
85-021483       006.3       0835909654
*Computers. Computers and civilization. Artificial intelligence.*

**QA76.W24513**
**Warnier, Jean Dominique.**
Logical construction of systems / Jean Dominique Warnier. New York : Van Nostrand Reinhold, c1981. xi, 179 p. ;
80-019363       001.64       0442225563
*Electronic data processing. Database management.*

**QA76.W38 1986**
**Webster, Frank.**
Information technology : a luddite analysis / Frank Webster, Kevin Robins. Norwood, N.J. : Ablex Pub. Corp., c1986. x, 387 p. ;
85-046065       004       089391343X
*Electronic data processing. Information storage and retrieval systems. Information technology.*

## QA76.15 Instruments and machines — Calculating machines — Electronic computers. Computer science — Dictionaries and encyclopedias

**QA76.15.C93 1996**
Cyber dictionary : your guide to the wired world / edited and introduced by David Morse. Santa Monica, CA : Knowledge Exchange, c1996. xiv, 313 p. :
      004/.03 21       1888232048
*Computers -- Dictionaries. Computer networks -- Dictionaries.*

**QA76.15.D5255 2001**
Dictionary of computer and internet words : an A to Z guide to hardware, software, and cyberspace. Boston : Houghton Mifflin Co., 2001. p. cm.
01-016890       004/.03       0618101373
*Computer science -- Encyclopedias.*

**QA76.15.D5258 2001**
Dictionary of computer science, engineering, and technology / editor-in-chief, Phillip A. Laplante. Boca Raton, FL : CRC Press, c2001. 543 p. :
00-052882       004/.03       0849326915
*Computers -- Dictionaries. Internet -- Dictionaries.*

**QA76.15.D5259 1995**
Dictionary of computer words. Boston : Houghton Mifflin, c1995. xv, 332 p. :
95-001175       004/.03       0395728347
*Computers -- Dictionaries.*

**QA76.15.E52 2001**
Encyclopedia of computers and computer history / Raul Rojas, editor in chief. Chicago : Fitzroy Dearborn, c2001. 2 v. :
      1579582354
*Computers -- Dictionaries. Internet -- Dictionaries.*

**QA76.15.F732 1996**
**Freedman, Alan,**
The computer desktop encyclopedia / Alan Freedman. New York : American Management Association, c1996. xv, 1005 p. :
96-000724       004/.03       0814400124
*Computers -- Dictionaries.*

**QA76.15.S64 1993**
**Spencer, Donald D.**
   Computer dictionary / Donald D. Spencer. Ormond Beach, Fla. : Camelot Pub. Co., c1993. ix, 459 p. :
92-034432        004/.03        0892182393
   *Computers -- Dictionaries. Electronic data processing -- Dictionaries.*

### QA76.17 Instruments and machines — Calculating machines — Electronic computers. Computer science — History

**QA76.17.B37 2000**
**Bardini, Thierry.**
   Bootstrapping : Douglas Engelbart, coevolution, and the origins of personal computing / Thierry Bardini. Stanford, Calif. : Stanford University Press, 2000. xvi, 284, [1]
00-056360        004.16/09        0804737231
   *Microcomputers -- History. Human-computer interaction. User interfaces (Computer systems)*

**QA76.17.C47 1998**
**Ceruzzi, Paul E.**
   A history of modern computing / Paul E. Ceruzzi. Cambridge, Mass. : MIT Press, 1998. x, 398 p. :
98-022856        004/.09/045        0262032554
   *Computers -- History. Electronic data processing -- History.*

**QA76.17.C67 1996**
**Cortada, James W.**
   Second bibliographic guide to the history of computing, computers, and the information processing industry / compiled by James W. Cortada. Westport, Conn. : Greenwood Press, 1996. viii, 416 p.
95-020889        016.004/09        0313295425
   *Computers -- History. Electronic data processing -- History.*

**QA76.17.D38 2000**
**Davis, Martin,**
   The universal computer : the road from Leibniz to Turing / Martin Davis. New York : Norton, 2000. xii, 257 p. :
00-040200        004/.09        0393047857
   *Electronic digital computers -- History.*

**QA76.17.D38 2000**
**Davis, Martin,**
   The universal computer : the road from Leibniz to Turing / Martin Davis. New York : Norton, 2000. xii, 257 p. :
        004/.09 21        0393047857
*Electronic digital computers -- History.*

**QA76.17.H59 1990**
   A History of scientific computing / edited by Stephen G. Nash. Reading, Mass. : Addison-Wesley Pub. Co., 1990. xix, 359 p. :
90-000006        004/.09        0201508141
   *Electronic data processing -- History. Science -- Data processing -- History.*

**QA76.17.I2713 2000**
**Ifrah, Georges.**
   The universal history of computing : from the abacus to the quantum computer / Georges Ifrah ; translated from the French, and with notes by E.F. Harding, assisted by Sophie Wood ... [et al.]. New York : John Wiley, c2001. 410 p. :
00-047771        004/.09        0471396710
   *Electronic data processing -- History. Computers -- History.*

**QA76.17.O45 1996**
**Oldfield, Homer R.**
   King of the Seven Dwarfs : general electric's ambiguous challenge to the computer industry / Homer R. Oldfield. Los Alamitos, Calif. : IEEE Computer Society Press, c1996. xiv, 252 p. :
95-051341        338.7/61004/0973
0818673834
   *Computers -- United States -- History. Computer industry -- United States -- History.*

**QA76.17.W35 2001**
**Waldrop, M. Mitchell.**
   The dream machine : J. C. Licklider and the revolution that made computing personal / M. Mitchell Waldrop. New York : Viking, 2001. 502 p. :
        004.16/092 B 21        0670899763
*Licklider, J. C. R. Microcomputers -- History.*

### QA76.2.A2 Instruments and machines — Calculating machines — Electronic computers. Computer science — Biography — Collective

**QA76.2.A2.L44 1995**
   International biographical dictionary of computer pioneers / editor, J.A.N. Lee. Los Alamitos, Calif. : IEEE Computer Society Press, 1995. p. cm.
94040232        004/.092/2        081866357X
   *Computers -- Biography.*

**QA76.2.A2.S53 1995**
**Shasha, Dennis Elliott.**
   Out of their minds : the lives and discoveries of 15 great computer scientists / Dennis Shasha, Cathy Lazere. New York : Copernicus, c1995. xi, 291 p. :
95-008360        004/.092/2        0387979921
   *Computer scientists -- Biography. Computers -- History.*

### QA76.2.A35-M37 Instruments and machines — Calculating machines — Electronic computers. Computer science — Biography — Individual, A-Z

**QA76.2.A35.C65 1999**
**Cohen, I. Bernard,**
   Howard Aiken : portrait of a computer pioneer / I. Bernard Cohen. Cambridge, MA : MIT Press, 1999. xx, 329 p. :
98-043965        004/.092        0262032627
*Aiken, Howard H. -- (Howard Hathaway), -- 1900-1973. Computer engineers -- United States -- Biography. Computers -- History.*

**QA76.2.A35.M35 1999**

Makin' numbers : Howard Aiken and the computer / edited by I. Bernard Cohen and Gregory W. Welch with the cooperation of Robert V.D. Campbell. Cambridge, Mass. : MIT Press, c1999. xvii, 279 p.
98-043964        004/.092        0262032635
*Aiken, Howard H. -- (Howard Hathaway), -- 1900-1973.    Computer engineers -- United States -- Biography. Computers -- History.*

**QA76.2.A75.M65 1988**
**Mollenhoff, Clark R.**
Atanasoff : forgotten father of the computer / Clark R. Mollenhoff. Ames : Iowa State University Press, 1988. xv, 274 p. :
87-035261        621.39/092/4        0813800323
*Atanasoff, John V. -- (John Vincent)    Electronic data processing – Biography.*

**QA76.2.M37.S68 1999**
**Southwick, Karen.**
High noon : the inside story of Scott McNealy and the rise of Sun Microsystems / Karen Southwick. New York : John Wiley, 1999. xiii, 242 p.
99-016031        338.7/61004/092        0471297135
*McNealy, Scott.    Computer scientists -- Biography.*

## QA76.27 Instruments and machines — Calculating machines — Electronic computers. Computer science — Study and teaching. Research

**QA76.27.C69 1996**
Computing tomorrow : future research directions in computer science / edited by Ian Wand and Robin Milner. Cambridge ; Cambridge University Press, 1996. x, 373 p. :
95-049616        004/.072        0521460859
*Computer science -- Research.*

## QA76.4 Instruments and machines — Calculating machines — Electronic computers. Computer science — Analog Computers

**QA76.4.F76 1991**
From Memex to hypertext : Vannevar Bush and the mind's machine / [edited by] James M. Nyce, Paul Kahn. Boston : Academic Press, c1991. xi, 367 p. :
91-076751        004.1/9        0125232705
*Bush, Vannevar, -- 1890-1974.    Electronic analog computers – History.*

## QA76.5 Instruments and machines — Calculating machines — Electronic computers. Computer science — Digital computers — General works

**QA76.5.A338 1987**
Advanced microprocessors, II / edited by Amar Gupta. New York : IEEE Press, c1987. vii, 335 p. :
004.165 19
*Microprocessors.*

**QA76.5.A369 1984**
**Alexandridis, Nikitas A.,**
Microprocessor system design concepts / Nikitas A. Alexandridis. Rockville, MD : Computer Science Press, c1984. xvi, 623 p. :
82-018189        621.3819/58        0914894668
*Microprocessors. Computer architecture. Computer engineering.*

**QA76.5.B297 1971**
**Bartee, Thomas C.**
Digital computer fundamentals [by] Thomas C. Bartee. New York, McGraw-Hill [1971, c1972] xii, 467 p.
75-172254        001.6/4        0070038910
*Electronic digital computers.*

**QA76.5.B598 1996**
**Boniface, Douglas M.**
Micro-electronics : structure and operation of microprocessor-based systems / Douglas M. Boniface. Chichester : Albion Pub., 1996. 195 p. :
97-153703        621.39/16        1898563322
*Microprocessors. Microcomputers.*

**QA76.5.C387 1990**
**Caudill, Maureen.**
Naturally intelligent systems / Maureen Caudhill and Charles Butler. Cambridge, Mass. : MIT Press, c1990. 304 p. :
89-013218        006.3        0262031566
*Neural computers.*

**QA76.5.E566 1996**
**Englander, Irv.**
The architecture of computer hardware and systems software : an information technology approach / Irv Englander. New York : Wiley, c1996. xvii, 750 p.
95-050560        004.2/2        0471310379
*Computers. Systems software.*

**QA76.5.H442 1972**
**Hawkes, Nigel.**
The computer revolution. New York, Dutton [1972, c1971] 216 p.
70-166165        001.6/4        0525084053
*Electronic data processing. Electronic digital computers.*

**QA76.5.H4442 1990**
**Hecht-Nielsen, Robert.**
Neurocomputing / Robert Hecht-Nielsen. Reading, Mass. : Addison-Wesley Pub. Co., c1990. xiii, 433 p.
89-018261        006.3        0201093553
*Neural computers.*

**QA76.5.H4817 1995**
High performance computing : problem solving with parallel and vector architectures / editor, Gary W. Sabot. Reading, Mass. : Addison-Wesley Pub. Co., c1995. xvi, 246 p. :
94-019262        502/.85/5133        0201598302
*Computer programming. FORTRAN (Computer program language)*

**QA76.5.H4918 1998**
**Hillis, W. Daniel.**
The pattern on the stone : the simple ideas that make computers work / W. Daniel Hillis. New York : Basic Books, c1998. xi, 164 p. :
98-038888          004          0465025951
*Computers.*

**QA76.5.J83 1990**
**Judd, J. Stephen.**
Neural network design and the complexity of learning / J. Stephen Judd. Cambridge, Mass. : MIT Press, c1990. 150 p. :
89-013418          006.3          0262100452
*Neural computers. Computational complexity. Artificial intelligence.*

**QA76.5.K374 1975**
**Katzan, Harry.**
Introduction to computer science / Harry Katzan, Jr. New York : Petrocelli/Charter Publishers, 1975. xii, 500 p. :
75-005751          001.6/4          0884053091
*Computer science.*

**QA76.5.K47 1994**
**Kidwell, Peggy Aldrich.**
Landmarks in digital computing : a Smithsonian pictorial history / Peggy A. Kidwell, Paul E. Ceruzzi. Washington : Smithsonian Institution Press, c1994. 148 p. :
93-025428          681/.14/0973          1560983116
*Electronic digital computers -- History.*

**QA76.5.K57**
**Knuth, Donald Ervin,**
The art of computer programming [by] Donald E. Knuth. Reading, Mass., Addison-Wesley Pub. Co. 1968- v.
67-026020          651.8
*Computer programming.*

**QA76.5.K77**
**Krutz, Ronald L.,**
Microprocessors and logic design / Ronald L. Krutz. New York : Wiley, c1980. xvi, 467 p. :
79-017874          001.6/4/04          0471020834
*Microprocessors. Logic design.*

**QA76.5.L3226 1995**
**Landauer, Thomas K.**
The trouble with computers : usefulness, usability, and productivity / Thomas K. Landauer. Cambridge, Mass. : MIT Press, c1995. xiii, 425 p.
94-048745          659/.0285          0262121867
*Computers. Technological innovations.*

**QA76.5.N426 1989**
Neural computing architectures : the design of brain-like machines / edited by Igor Aleksander. Cambridge, Mass. : MIT Press, 1989. 401 p. :
88-038352          006.3          0262011107
*Neural computers. Computer architecture.*

**QA76.5.P3145 1987**
Papers of John von Neumann on computing and computer theory / edited by William Aspray and Arthur Burks. Cambridge, Mass. : MIT Press ; c1987. xviii, 624 p.
86-008588          004          026222030X
*Von Neumann, John, -- 1903-1957.     Electronic digital computers – History.*

**QA76.5.R467 2000**
**Rheingold, Howard.**
Tools for thought : the history and future of mind-expanding technology / Howard Rheingold. 1st MIT Press ed. Cambridge, Mass. : MIT Press, 2000. 359 p. :
          303.48/34 21          0262681153
*Microcomputers -- History. Technological innovations -- History.*

**QA76.5.S213**
**Sammet, Jean E.,**
Programming languages: history and fundamentals [by] Jean E. Sammet. Englewood Cliffs, N.J., Prentice-Hall [1969] xxx, 785 p.
68-028110          651.8
*Programming languages (Electronic computers)*

**QA76.5.S86 1988**
**Su, Stanley Y. W.**
Database computers : principles, architectures, and techniques / Stanley Y.W. Su. New York : McGraw-Hill, c1988. xiv, 497 p. :
87-032475          005.74          0070622957
*Electronic digital computers. Database management.*

**QA76.5.S8984 1990**
Supercomputing systems : architectures, design, and performance / [compiled by] Svetlana P. Kartashev and Steven I. Kartashev. New York : Van Nostrand Reinhold, c1990. xxxiii, 622 p
89-005267          004.1/1          0442256159
*Supercomputers.*

**QA76.5.W287 2001**
**Walters, E. Garrison.**
The essential guide to computing / E. Garrison Walters. Upper Saddle River, NJ : Prentice Hall, 2001. xxv, 499 p. :
00-062343          004          0130194697
*Computers. Electronic data processing. Computer networks.*

**QA76.5.W353 1989**
**Wasserman, Philip D.,**
Neural computing : theory and practice / Philip D. Wasserman. New York : Van Nostrand Reinhold, c1989. viii, 230 p.
88-034842          006.3          0442207433
*Neural computers.*

## QA76.54 Instruments and machines — Calculating machines — Electronic computers. Computer science — Digital computers — Real-time data processing

**QA76.54.E52 1993**
**Edwards, Keith,**
  Real-time structured methods : systems analysis / Keith Edwards. Chichester ; John Wiley, c1993 xxii, 554 p.
93-008775          005.2          0471934151
  *Real-time data processing. Electronic data processing -- Structured techniques.*

**QA76.54.S295 1994**
**Selic, Bran.**
  Real-time object-oriented modeling / Bran Selic, Garth Gullekson, Paul T. Ward. New York : Wiley & Sons, c1994. xxxii, 525 p.
93-020757          005.1          0471599174
  *Real-time programming. Object-oriented programming (Computer science)*

## QA76.55 Instruments and machines — Calculating machines — Electronic computers. Computer science — Digital computers — Online data processing

**QA76.55.K63 1996**
**Koch, Tom,**
  The message is the medium : online all the time for everyone / Tom Koch. Westport, Conn. : Praeger, 1996. 228 p. ;
95-053001          302.23          0275955494
  *Online information services.*

## QA76.575 Instruments and machines — Calculating machines — Electronic computers. Computer science — Digital computers — Multimedia systems

**QA76.575.D548 1998**
**Dillon, Patrick M.**
  Multimedia and the Web from A to Z / by Patrick M. Dillon and David C. Leonard. Phoenix, AZ : Oryx Press, 1998. xxvii, 355 p.
98-034083          006.7          1573561320
  *Multimedia systems. World Wide Web (Information retrieval systems)*

**QA76.575.M34 1994**
  The McGraw-Hill multimedia handbook / Jessica Keyes, editor. New York : McGraw-Hill, c1994. 1 v. (various
94-010682          006.6          0070344752
  *Multimedia systems.*

## QA76.58 Instruments and machines — Calculating machines — Electronic computers. Computer science — Digital computers — Parallel processing. Parallel computers

**QA76.58.C43 1991**
**Chaudhuri, Pranay,**
  Parallel algorithms : design and analysis / Pranay Chaudhuri. New York : Prentice Hall, c1992. xiv, 314 p. :
91-045016          004/.35          0133519821
  *Parallel algorithms. Parallel processing (Electronic computers)*

**QA76.58.G64 1993**
**Golub, Gene H.**
  Scientific computing : an introduction with parallel computing / Gene Golub, James M. Ortega. Boston : Academic Press, c1993. x, 442 p. :
93-009408          004/.01/51          0122892534
  *Parallel processing (Electronic computers) Vector processing (Computer science)*

**QA76.58.I58 1994**
  Introduction to parallel computing : design and analysis of algorithms / Vipin Kumar . . . [et al.] Redwood City, Calif. : Benjamin/Cummings Pub. c1994. xv, 597 p. :
          005.2 20          0805331700
  *Parallel processing (Electronic computers) Parallel algorithms.*

**QA76.58.R47 1994**
**Resnick, Mitchel.**
  Turtles, termites, and traffic jams : explorations in massively parallel microworlds / Mitchel Resnick. Cambridge, Mass. : MIT Press, c1994. xviii, 163 p.
94-010956          003/.7          0262181622
  *Parallel processing (Electronic computers) Artificial intelligence. StarLogo (Computer program language)*

**QA76.58.S59 1994**
**Skillicorn, David B.**
  Foundations of parallel programming / David Skillicorn. Cambridge ; Cambridge University Press, 1994. xii, 197 p. :
94-014979          005.2          0521455111
  *Parallel processing (Electronic computers)*

## QA76.6-76.642 Instruments and machines — Calculating machines — Electronic computers. Computer science — Digital computers — Programming

**QA76.6.A255 1996**
**Abelson, Harold.**
  Structure and interpretation of computer programs / Harold Abelson and Gerald Jay Sussman, with Julie Sussman ; foreword by Alan J. Perlis. Cambridge, Mass. : MIT Press ; c1996. xxiii, 657 p.
96-017756          005.13/3          0262011530
  *Computer programming. LISP (Computer program language)*

**QA76.6.B66 1987**
**Bornat, Richard,**
Programming from first principles / Richard Bornat. Englewood Cliffs, NJ : Prentice-Hall International, c1987. xviii, 538 p.
86-018706          005.1          0137291043
*Computer programming.*

**QA76.6.C36 1996**
**Canton, Maria P.**
The McGraw-Hill programmer's desk reference / Maria P. Canton, Julio Sanchez. New York : McGraw-Hill, c1996. vi, 470 p. :
96-033756          005.265          0079121764
*Computer programming.*

**QA76.6.F557 1998**
**Flake, Gary William.**
The computational beauty of nature : computer explorations of fractals, chaos, complex systems, and adaptation / Gary William Flake. Cambridge, Mass : MIT Press, c1998. xviii, 493 p.
97-052394          003/.3          0262062003
*Computer programming. System analysis.*

**QA76.6.H79 1989**
**Hu, David.**
Object-oriented environment in C++ : a user-friendly interface. / David Hu. Portland, Or. : Management Information Source, Inc., 1990. x, 557 p. ;
89030804          005.1          1558280146
*Object-oriented programming (Computer science)*

**QA76.6I5858 2001**
Introduction to algorithms / Thomas H. Cormen . . . [et al.]. 2nd ed. Cambridge, Mass. : MIT Press, c2001. xxi, 1180 p.
          005.1 21          0262032937
*Computer programming. Computer algorithms.*

**QA76.6.K735 1990**
**Kreutzer, Wolfgang.**
Programming for artificial intelligence : methods, tools, and applications / Wolfgang Kreutzer & Bruce McKenzie. Sydney ; Addison-Wesley Pub. Co., [1989], c1990 xiv, 682 p. :
89-014896          006.3          0201416212
*Computer programming. Artificial intelligence.*

**QA76.6.K77 1984**
**Kruse, Robert Leroy,**
Data structures and program design / Robert L. Kruse. Englewood Cliffs, N.J. : Prentice-Hall, c1984. xxi, 486 p. :
83-013839          001.64/2          0131962531
*Computer programming. Data structures (Computer science) Pascal (Computer program language)*

**QA76.6.L469 2001**
**Levy, Steven.**
Hackers : heroes of the computer revolution / Steven Levy. [Updated afterword] New York, N.Y. : Penguin Books, 2001. xv, 455 p. :
          0141000511
*Computer programming. Computer hackers.*

**QA76.6.L639**
**Lorin, Harold.**
Operating systems / Harold Lorin, Harvey M. Deitel. Reading, Mass. : Addison Wesley, c1981. xxi, 378 p. :
80-010625          001.64/25          0201144646
*Operating systems (Computers)*

**QA76.6.M336 1999**
**Maeda, John.**
Design by numbers / John Maeda. Cambridge, Mass. : MIT Press, 1999. 255 p. :
98-037583          005.1          0262133547
*Computer programming. Computer graphics.*

**QA76.6.R42 1988**
**Reed, Thomas A.,**
An introduction to algorithm design and structured programming / Thomas A. Reed. New York : Prentice Hall, 1988. xxiv, 277 p.
87-007173          005.1          0134777794
*Computer programming. Algorithms. Structured programming.*

**QA76.6.S435 1988**
**Sedgewick, Robert,**
Algorithms / Robert Sedgewick. 2nd ed. Reading, Mass. : Addison-Wesley, c1988. xii, 657 p. :
          519.4 19
*Computer algorithms.*

**QA76.6.S543**
**Shneiderman, Ben.**
Software psychology : human factors in computer and information systems / Ben Shneiderman. Cambridge, Mass. : Winthrop Publishers, c1980. xv, 320 p. :
79-017627          001.6/4/019          0876268165
*Computer programming -- Psychological aspects.*

**QA76.6.S6163 1993**
**Van de Snepscheut, Jan L. A.,**
What computing is all about / Jan L. van de Snepscheut. New York : Springer-Verlag, c1993. xii, 478 p. ;
93-012238          005.1          0387940219
*Computer programming.*

**QA76.6.Z32 1996**
**Zachary, Joseph L.**
Introduction to scientific programming : computational problem solving using Maple and C / Joseph L. Zachary. New York : TELOS, c1996. xxiv, 380 p.
96-009378          510/.1/135133          0387946306
*Computer programming. C (Computer program language)*

**QA76.62.C68 1998**
**Cousineau, Guy.**
The functional approach to programming / Guy Cousineau and Michel Mauny. English ed. Cambridge, U.K. ; New York, N.Y. : Cambridge University Press, 1998. xiv, 445 p. :
          005.13/3 21          0521571839
*Functional programming (Computer science)*

**QA76.63.B47 1996**
**Bergadano, Francesco,**
Inductive logic programming : from machine learning to software engineering / Francesco Bergadano and Daniele Gunetti. Cambridge, Mass. : MIT Press, c1996. vii, 240 p. :
95-014956          005.1/1          0262023938
*Logic programming.*

**QA76.63.D64 1994**
**Doets, Kees.**
From logic to logic programming / Kees Doets. Cambridge, Mass. : MIT Press, c1994. xii, 214 p. :
93-006196          005.1          0262041421
*Logic programming.*

**QA76.63.H36 1993**
Handbook of logic in artificial intelligence and logic programming / edited by Dov M. Gabbay, and C.J. Hogger and J.A. Robinson. Oxford : Clarendon Press ; 1993-1998. 5 v. :
92-023358          006.3/3          019853745X
*Logic programming. Artificial intelligence. Logic, Symbolic and mathematical.*

**QA76.63.M37 1998**
**Marriott, Kim.**
Programming with constraints : an introduction / Kim Marriott and Peter J. Stuckey. Cambridge, Mass. : MIT Press, c1998. xiv, 467 p. :
97-040549          005.13          0262133415
*Logic programming. Constraint programming (Computer science)*

**QA76.64.A494 2001**
**Ambler, Scott W.,**
The object primer : the application developer's guide to object orientation / Scott W. Ambler. 2nd ed. Cambridge, England ; New York : Cambridge University Press, 2001. xxiii, 523 p. :
          005.1/17 21          0521785197
*Object-oriented methods (Computer science)*

**QA76.64.E428 1995**
**Eliens, Anton.**
Principles of object-oriented software development / Anton Eliens. Wokingham, England : Addison-Wesley Pub. Co., c1995. xvii, 513 p.
95-108526          005.1/1          0201624443
*Object-oriented programming (Computer science) Computer software -- Development.*

**QA76.64.S73 1994**
**Stevens, Roger T.,**
Object-oriented graphics programming in C++ / Roger T. Stevens. Boston : AP Professional, c1994. xi, 498 p. :
94-193985          006.6/765          0126683182
*Object-oriented programming (Computer science) Computer graphics. C++ (Computer program language)*

**QA76.64.T49 1994**
Theoretical aspects of object-oriented programming : types, semantics, and language design / edited by Carl A. Gunter and John C. Mitchell. Cambridge, Mass. : MIT Press, c1994. 548 p. :
93-028984          005.1          026207155X
*Object-oriented programming (Computer science) Programming languages (Electronic computers)*

**QA76.642.C37 1990**
**Carriero, Nicholas.**
How to write parallel programs : a first course / Nicholas Carriero, David Gelernter. Cambridge, Mass. : MIT Press, c1990. 232 p. :
90-044443          005.2          026203171X
*Parallel programming (Computer science)*

**QA76.642.C47 1992**
**Chandy, K. Mani.**
An introduction to parallel programming / K. Mani Chandy and Stephen Taylor. Boston : Jones and Bartlett, c1992. p. cm.
91-029918          004/.35          0867202084
*Parallel programming (Computer science)*

**QA76.642.W553 1995**
**Wilson, Greg,**
Practical parallel programming / Gregory V. Wilson. Cambridge, Mass. : MIT Press, c1995. viii, 564 p.
95-009800          005.2          0262231867
*Parallel programming (Computer science)*

### QA76.7-76.73 Instruments and machines — Calculating machines — Electronic computers. Computer science — Digital computers — Programming languages

**QA76.7.G86 1992**
**Gunter, Carl A.**
Semantics of programming languages : structures and techniques / Carl A. Gunter. Cambridge, Mass. : MIT Press, c1992. xviii, 419 p.
92-010172          005.13          0262071436
*Programming languages (Electronic computers) -- Semantics.*

**QA76.7.H558 1996**
History of programming languages II / edited by Thomas J. Bergin, Jr. and Richard G. Gibson, Jr. New York : ACM Press ; c1996. xvi, 864 p. :
95-033539          005.13/09          0201895021
*Programming languages (Electronic computers) -- History.*

**QA76.7.M57 1996**
**Mitchell, John C.**
Foundations for programming languages / John C. Mitchell. Cambridge, Mass. : MIT Press, c1996. xix, 846 p. :
95-045243          005.13/1          0262133210
*Programming languages (Electronic computers)*

**QA76.7.S345 1994**
**Schmidt, David A.,**
The structure of typed programming languages / David A. Schmidt. Cambridge, Mass. : MIT Press, c1994. xiv, 367 p. :
93-039912          005.13/1          0262193493
*Programming languages (Electronic computers)*

**QA76.7.W555 1993**
**Winskel, G.**
The formal semantics of programming languages : an introduction / Glynn Winskel. Cambridge, Mass. : MIT Press, c1993. xviii, 361 p.
92-036718          005.13/1          0262231697
*Programming languages (Electronic computers) -- Semantics.*

**QA76.73.A35.B85 1995**
**Burns, Alan,**
Concurrency in ADA / Alan Burns and Andy Wellings. Cambridge ; Cambridge University Press, c1995. xvi, 396 p. :
94-023789          005.2          0521414717
*Ada (Computer program language) Parallel programming (Computer science)*

**QA76.73.A35.R38 1991**
Rationale for the design of the Ada programming language / J. Ichbiah ... [et al.]. Cambridge [Cambridgeshire] ; Cambridge University Press, 1991. ix, 393 p. ;
91-193840          005.13/3          0521392675
*Ada (Computer program language)*

**QA76.73.B3.K46 1987**
**Kemeny, John G.**
Structured BASIC programming / John G. Kemeny, Thomas E. Kurtz. New York : Wiley, c1987. xv, 388 p. :
86-028275          005.13/3          0471810878
*BASIC (Computer program language) Structured programming.*

**QA76.73.C15.E96 1993**
The evolution of C++ : language design in the marketplace of ideas / edited by Jim Waldo. Cambridge, Mass. : MIT Press, c1993. x, 279 p. :
93-009588          005.13/3          026273107X
*C++ (Computer program language)*

**QA76.73.C15.G57 1993**
**Glassey, Robert,**
Numerical computation using C / Robert Glassey. Boston : Academic Press, c1993. vii, 283 p. :
92-033037          519.4/0285/5133          0122861558
*C (Computer program language) Numerical analysis -- Data processing.*

**QA76.73.C15.J38 1994**
**Jarvis, Paul.**
A practical introduction to C / Paul Jarvis. Oxford ; Oxford University Press, 1994. viii, 366 p.
93-045532          005.13/3          0198538464
*C (Computer program language)*

**QA76.73.C15.J655 1997**
**Johnsonbaugh, Richard,**
C for scientists and engineers / Richard Johnsonbaugh, Martin Kalin. Upper Saddle River, N.J. : Prentice Hall, c1997. xviii, 793 p.
95-022669          005.13/3          0023611367
*C (Computer program language)*

**QA76.73.C15.K35 1994**
**Kalicharan, Noel.**
C by example / Noel Kalicharan. Cambridge ; Cambridge University Press, 1994. xviii, 362 p.
93-027877          005.13/3          0521450233
*C (Computer program language)*

**QA76.73.C15.K49 1996**
**King, K. N.**
C programming : a modern approach / K.N. King. New York : Norton, c1996. xxv, 661 p. :
96-001484          005.13/3          0393969452
*C (Computer program language)*

**QA76.73.C15.P56 1996**
**Plauger, P. J.,**
Standard C : a reference / P.J. Plauger, Jim Brodie. Upper Saddle River,N.J. : Prentice Hall PTR, c1996. viii, 248 p.
95-015055          005.13/3          0134364112
*C (Computer program language)*

**QA76.73.C153.A32 1998**
**Aberth, Oliver.**
Precise numerical methods using C++ / Oliver Aberth. San Diego, CA : Academic Press, c1998. xiv, 238 p. ;
98-117803          519.4/0285/5133          0120417502
*C++ (Computer program language) Numerical analysis – Data processing.*

**QA76.73.C153.A43 1998**
**Alger, Jeff.**
C++ for real programmers / Jeff Alger. Boston : AP Professional, c1998. xii, 388 p. ;
97-035352          005.13/3          0120499428
*C++ (Computer program language)*

**QA76.73.C153A45 1996**
**Ammeraal, L. (Leendert)**
Algorithms and data structures in C++ / Leendert Ammeraal. Chichester ; New York : Wiley, c1996. x, 352 p. :
          005.13/3 20          0471963550
*C++ (Computer program language) Computer algorithms. Data structures (Computer science)*

**QA76.73.C153D76 2001**
**Drozdek, Adam.**
Data structures and algorithms in C++ / Adam Drozdek. 2nd ed. Pacific Grove, CA : Brooks/Cole, c2001. xviii, 650 p. :
          005.13/3 21          0534375970
*C++ (Computer program language) Data structures (Computer science) Computer algorithms.*

**QA76.73.C153J69**
**Josuttis, Nicolai M.**
 The C++ standard library : a tutorial and handbook / Nicolai M. Josuttis. Reading, Mass. : Addison-Wesley, c1999. xx, 799 p. :
 005.13/3 21          0201379260
*C++ (Computer program language)*

**QA76.73.C153L577 2000**
**Lippman, Stanley B.**
 Essential C++ / Stanley B. Lippman. Reading, MA : Addison-Wesley, 2000. xiii, 276 p. ;
 005.13/3 21          0201485184
*C++ (Computer program language)*

**QA76.73.C153N83 2002**
 Numerical recipes example book (C++) / William T. Vetterling . . . [et al.]. 2nd ed. Cambridge, [England] ; New York : Cambridge University Press, 2002. viii, 318 p. ;
 519.4/0285/5133 21          0521750342
*QA76.73.C153N83 2002*

**QA76.73.C153N85 2002**
 Numerical recipes in C++ : the art of scientific computing / William H. Press . . . [et al.] 2nd ed. New York : Cambridge University Press, 2002. p. cm.
 519.4/0285/5133 21          0521750334
*C++ (Computer program language) Numerical analysis.*

**QA76.73.C154**
**Albahari, Ben.**
 C# essentials / Ben Albahari, Peter Drayton, and Brad Merrill. Cambridge, Mass. : O'Reilly, 2001. p. cm.
 01-021106          005.13/3          0596000790
 *C# (Computer program language)*

**QA76.73.C154C17 2002**
 C# : how to program / H.M. Deitel . . . [et al.]. Upper Saddle River, N.J. : Prentice Hall, c2002. lvi, 1568 p. :
 005.13/3 21          0130622214
*C# (Computer program language)*

**QA76.73.C15N865 1992**
 Numerical recipes in C : the art of scientific computing / William H. Press . . . [et al.] 2nd ed. Cambridge ; New York : Cambridge University Press, 1992. xxvi, 994 p. :
 519.4/0285/53 20          0521431085
*C (Computer program language)*

**QA76.73.F16.M47 1996**
**Metcalf, Michael.**
 The F programming language / Michael Metcalf, John Reid. Oxford ; Oxford University Press, 1996. xiv, 240 p. ;
 97-110469          005.13/3
 *F (Computer program language). FORTRAN (Computer program language).*

**QA76.73.F25.F6 1997**
 Fortran 95 handbook : complete ISO/ANSI reference / Jeanne C. Adams ... [et al.]. Cambridge, Mass : MIT Press, c1997. xii, 711 p. :
 97-022057          005.13/3          0262510960
 *FORTRAN 95 (Computer program language)*

**QA76.73.F25.H53 1994**
 The High performance Fortran handbook / Charles H. Koelbel ... [et al.]. Cambridge, Mass. : MIT Press, c1994. xiv, 329 p. :
 93-006204          005.13/3          0262111853
 *FORTRAN (Computer program language)*

**QA76.73.F25F64 1996**
 FORTRAN numerical recipes / William H. Press . . . [et al.]. 2nd ed. Cambridge [England] ; New York : Cambridge University Press, c1996. 2 v.(xxxi,1486)
 519.4/0285/52 20          052143064X
*FORTRAN (Computer program language) Numerical analysis -- Computer programs. Science -- Mathematics -- Computer programs.*

**QA76.73.F25F643**
 FORTRAN numerical recipes / William H. Press. . . . [et al.]. 2nd ed. Cambridge [England] ; New York : Cambridge University Press, 1999- v. :
 0521574390
*FORTRAN (Computer program language) Numerical analysis -- Computer programs. Science -- Mathematics -- Computer programs.*

**QA76.73.J38**
**King, K. N.**
 Java programming from the beginning / K.N. King. New York : W.W. Norton, c2000. xxiii, 788 p.
 99-059403          005.13/3          0393974375
 *Java (Computer program language)*

**QA76.73.J38.H375 1998**
**Hartley, Stephen J.**
 Concurrent programming : the Java programming language / Stephen J. Hartley. New York : Oxford University Press, 1998. xii, 260 p. :
 97-042037          005.2/752          0195113152
 *Java (Computer program language) Parallel programming (Computer science)*

**QA76.73.J38.W53 2000**
**Wiener, Richard,**
 Fundamentals of OOP and data structures in Java / Richard Wiener, Lewis Pinson. Cambridge, [England] ; Cambridge University Press, 2000. xv, 463 p. :
 99-087328          005.13/3          0521662206
 *Java (Computer program language) Object-oriented programming (Computer science) Data structures (Computer science)*

**QA76.73.J38A76 2000**
**Arnold, Ken,**
 The Java programming language / Ken Arnold, James Gosling, David Holmes. 3rd ed. Boston : Addison-Wesley, c2000. xxiv, 595 p. ;
 005.13 / 21          0201704331
*Java (Computer program language)*

**QA76.73.J38E43 2000**
The elements of Java style / Al Vermeulen . . . [et al.]. Cambridge ; New York : Cambridge University Press : SIGS Books, 2000. xiii, 128 p. ;
005.13/3 21    0521777682
*Java (Computer program language)*

**QA76.73.L23.C65 1988**
COMMON LISP : the reference / Franz Inc. Reading, Mass. : Addison-Wesley Pub. Co., c1988. xx, 899 p. ;
88-026279    005.13/3    0201114585
*COMMON LISP (Computer program language)*

**QA76.73.L23.J66 1990**
Jones, Robin.
The art of Lisp programming / Robin Jones, Clive Maynard, Ian Stewart. London ; Springer-Verlag, c1990. 169 p. :
89-021706    005.13/3    0387195688
*LISP (Computer program language)*

**QA76.73.L23.Q4613 1996**
Queinnec, Christian.
LISP in small pieces / Christian Queinnec ; translated by Kathleen Callaway. Cambridge [England] ; Cambridge University Press, 1996. xx, 514 p. :
96-019430    005.13/3    0521562473
*LISP (Computer program language)*

**QA76.73.P2.B54 1989**
Biggs, Norman.
Introduction to computing with Pascal / Norman L. Biggs. Oxford [England] : Clarendon Press ; 1989. x, 219 p. ;
88-038882    005.13/3    0198537557
*Pascal (Computer program language) Computer programming.*

**QA76.73.P2.F55 1996**
Flanders, Harley.
Scientific Pascal / Harley Flanders. Boston : Birkhauser, 1996. xii, 590 p. ;
95-035243    005.13/3    0817637605
*Pascal (Computer program language)*

**QA76.73.P2.N87 1989**
Numerical recipes in Pascal : the art of scientific computing / William H. Press ... [et al.]. Cambridge ; Cambridge University Press, 1989. xxii, 759 p.
89-015841    005.13/3    0521375169
*Pascal (Computer program language)*

**QA76.73.P22S37 2001**
Schwartz, Randal L.
Learning Perl / Randal L. Schwartz and Tom Phoenix. 3rd ed. Sebastopol, CA : O'Reilly, c2001. xvi, 316 p. :
005.13/3 21    0596001320
*Perl (Computer program language)*

**QA76.73.P22W35 2000**
Wall, Larry.
Programming Perl / Larry Wall, Tom Christiansen & Jon Orwant. 3rd ed. Beijing, ; Cambridge, Mass. : O'Reilly, 2000. xxxiii, 1067 p:
005.13/3 21    0596000278
*Perl (Computer program language)*

**QA76.73.P76.K46 1991**
Kim, Steven H.
Knowledge systems through Prolog : an introduction / Steven H. Kim. New York : Oxford University Press, 1991. xvi, 341 p. :
91-018699    006.3    0195072413
*Prolog (Computer program language) Expert systems (Computer science) Computer software -- Development.*

**QA76.73.P76.P73 1990**
The Practice of Prolog / edited by Leon S. Sterling. Cambridge, Mass. : MIT Press, c1990. 312 p. :
90-042397    005.13/3    0262193019
*Prolog (Computer program language)*

**QA76.73.S58.H45 1988**
Hendrix, James E.
A Small C compiler : language, usage, theory, and design / James E. Hendrix. Redwood City, Calif. : M&T Pub., 1988. 586 p. :
88-009291    005.265    0934375887
*Small-C (Computer program language) Compilers (Computer programs)*

### QA76.754 Instruments and machines — Calculating machines — Electronic computers. Computer science — Computer software — General works

**QA76.754.F86 1995**
The Future of software / edited by Derek Leebaert. Cambridge, Mass. : MIT Press, c1995. xi, 300 p. ;
94-028458    005.3    0262121840
*Computer software.*

**QA76.754.H35 1996**
The handbook of software for engineers and scientists / editor-in-chief, Paul W. Ross. Boca Raton, Fla. : CRC Press ; c1996. xix, 1557 p.
95-006378    005.3/0245    0849325307
*Computer software. Engineering -- Data processing. Science – Data processing.*

**QA76.754.W377 2000**
Waterfields guide to computer software / edited by Arthur L. Delcher. Ellicott City, Md. : Waterfields Press, c2000. vii, 682 p. :
95-061674    005.3    1886271054
*Computer software.*

## QA76.758 Instruments and machines — Calculating machines — Electronic computers. Computer science — Computer software — Software engineering

**QA76.758.B75 1995**
**Brooks, Frederick P.**
The mythical man-month : essays on software engineering / Frederick P. Brooks, Jr. Reading, Mass. : Addison-Wesley Pub. Co., 1995. xiii, 322 p.
94-036653          005.1/068          0201835959
*Software engineering.*

**QA76.758.B78 1992**
**Blum, Bruce I.**
Software engineering : a holistic view / Bruce I. Blum. New York : Oxford University Press, 1992. xiii, 588 p.
91-031490          005.1          019507159X
*Software engineering.*

**QA76.758.E53 1994**
Encyclopedia of software engineering / John J. Marciniak, editor-in-chief. New York : Wiley, c1994. 2 v. (xvii, 1
93-017387          005.1/03          0471540048
*Software engineering -- Encyclopedias.*

**QA76.758.H36 2001**
Handbook of software engineering & knowledge engineering / edited by S.K. Chang. River Edge, NJ : World Scientific, c2001- 2 v. :
                    981024973X
*Software engineering -- Handbooks, manuals, etc. Knowledge representation -- Information theory.*

**QA76.758.S647 1993**
Software engineer's reference book / edited by John A. McDermid. Boca Raton : CRC Press, 1993. 1 v.
          005.1 20
*Software engineering -- Handbooks, manuals, etc.*

**QA76.758.S657 2000**
**Sommerville, Ian,**
Software engineering / Ian Sommerville. 6th ed. Harlow, England ; New York : Addison-Wesley, 2000. xx, 693 p. :
          005.1 21          020139815X
*Software engineering.*

## QA76.76 Instruments and machines — Calculating machines — Electronic computers. Computer science — Computer software — Special topics, A-Z

**QA76.76.C68.L68 1992**
**Louw, Eric.**
Managing computer viruses / Eric Louw and Neil Duffy. Oxford ; Oxford University Press, 1992. ix, 171 p. :
91-047732          005.8          0198539738
*Computer viruses.*

**QA76.76.D47.I555 1996**
The international computer software industry : a comparative study of industry evolution and structure / edited by David C. Mowery. New York : Oxford University Press, 1996. viii, 324 p.
95-006887          338.4/70053/09          0195094107
*Computer software -- Development. Computer software industry.*

**QA76.76.D47.M63 1997**
Modern software tools for scientific computing / Erlend Arge, Are Magnus Bruaset, Hans Petter Langtangen, editors. Boston : Birkhauser, 1997. 380 p. :
97-006613          502.85/5          0817639748
*Computer software -- Development. Object-oriented programming (Computer science) Science -- Data processing.*

**QA76.76.D47.S25 1994**
**Salzman, Harold.**
Software by design : shaping technology and the workplace / Harold Salzman, Stephen R. Rosenthal. New York : Oxford University Press, 1994. 348 p. :
93-020812          005.1/2          0195083407
*Computer software -- Development. User interfaces.*

**QA76.76.E95.B57 1990**
**Biondo, Samuel J.**
Fundamentals of expert systems technology : principles and concepts / Samuel J. Biondo. Norwood, N.J. : Ablex Pub. Corp., c1990. vi, 145 p. :
90-021859          006.3/3          089391701X
*Expert systems (Computer science)*

**QA76.76.E95.K375 1996**
**Kasabov, Nikola K.**
Foundations of neural networks, fuzzy systems, and knowledge engineering / Nikola K. Kasabov. Cambridge, Mass. : MIT Press, c1996. xvi, 550 p. :
95-050054          006.3          0262112124
*Expert systems (Computer science) Neural networks (Computer science) Fuzzy systems.*

**QA76.76.E95.R65 1988**
**Rolston, David W.**
Principles of artificial intelligence and expert systems development / David W. Rolston. New York : McGraw-Hill, c1988. xii, 257 p. :
87-022645          006.3          0070536147
*Expert systems (Computer science) Artificial intelligence. Computer software -- Development.*

**QA76.76.H94.N54 1990**
**Nielsen, Jakob,**
Hypertext and hypermedia / Jakob Nielsen. Boston : Academic Press, c1990. xii, 263 p. :
90-000092          005.75/4          0125184107
*Hypertext systems. Interactive multimedia.*

**QA76.76.H94.N543 1995**
**Nielsen, Jakob,**
   Multimedia and Hypertext : the Internet and beyond / Jakob Nielsen. Boston : AP Professional, c1995. xiii, 480 p.
94-044429          005.75          0125184085
   *Hypertext systems.*


**QA76.76.H94M875 2000**
**Musciano, Chuck.**
   HTML and XHTML, the definitive guide / Chuck Musciano and Bill Kennedy. 4th ed. Beijing ; Sebastopol, CA : O'Reilly, 2000. xvi, 655 p. :
                  005.7/2 21          059600026X
*HTML (Document markup language) XHTML (Document markup language)*


**QA76.76.O63.F37 1988**
**Farkas, Daniel,**
   UNIX for programmers : an introduction / Daniel Farkas. New York : Wiley, c1988. xiii, 381 p.
87-029824          005.4/2          0471838128


**QA76.76.O63.K7313 1988**
**Krakowiak, Sacha.**
   Principles of operating systems / Sacha Krakowiak ; translated by David Beeson. Cambridge, Mass. : MIT Press, c1988. x, 469 p. :
87-005676          005.4/3          0262111225
   *Operating systems (Computers)*


**QA76.76.O63S55825 2000**
**Silberschatz, Abraham.**
   Applied operating system concepts / Abraham Silberschatz, Peter Galvin, Greg Gagne. 1st ed. New York : John Wiley, c2000. xviii, 840 p. :
                  005.4/3 21          0471365084
*Operating systems (Computers)*


**QA76.76.O63S5583 2002**
**Silberschatz, Abraham.**
   Operating system concepts / Abraham Silberschatz, Peter Baer Galvin, Greg Gagne. 6th ed. New York : John Wiley & Sons, c2002. xxi, 887 p. :
                  005.4/3 21          0471417432
*Operating systems (Computers)*


**QA76.76.O63S734 1998**
**Stallings, William.**
   Operating systems: internals and design principles / William Stallings. 3rd ed. Upper Saddle River, N.J. : Prentice Hall, c1998. xvii, 781 p. :
                  005.4/3 21          0138874077
*Operating.*


**QA76.76.S46O64 1999**
   Open sources : voices from the open source revolution / edited by Chris DiBona, Sam Ockman & Mark Stone. 1st ed. Beijing ; Sebastopol, CA : O'Reilly, c1999. viii, 272 p. :
                  1565925823
*Open source software. Linux.*


**QA76.8 Instruments and machines — Calculating machines — Electronic computers. Computer science — Special computers, computer systems, and microprocessors. By name, A-Z**


**QA76.8.I93.G76 1998**
**Gross, Thomas,**
   iWarp : anatomy of a parallel computing system / Thomas Gross and David R. O'Hallaron. Cambridge, Mass. : MIT Press, c1998. xxiv, 488 p.
97-041577          004/.357          0262071835
   *iWarp (Computer)*


**QA76.8.M3.L487 1994**
**Levy, Steven.**
   Insanely great : the life and times of Macintosh, the computer that changed everything / Steven Levy. New York : Viking, 1994. x, 292 p. ;
93-030495          338.7/61004165          0670852449
   *Macintosh (Computer)*


**QA76.87 Instruments and machines — Calculating machines — Electronic computers. Computer science — Neural computers. Neural networks**


**QA76.87.B53 1994**
**Bharath, Ramachandran.**
   Neural network computing / Ramachandran Bharath, James Drosen. New York : Windcrest/McGraw-Hill, c1994. xx, 188 p. :
94-001199          006.3          0070051453
   *Neural networks (Computer science)*


**QA76.87.B574 1995**
**Bishop, Christopher M.**
   Neural networks for patter recognition / Christopher M. Bishop. Oxford ; New York : Oxford University Press ; Clarendon Press, 1995. xvii, 482 p. :
                  006.4 20          0198538499
*Neural networks (Computer science) Pattern recognition systems.*


**QA76.87.C685 1998**
**Cotterill, Rodney,**
   Enchanted looms : conscious networks in brains and computers / Rodney Cotterill. Cambridge, UK ; Cambridge University Press, 1998. xiv, 508 p. :
98-020548          006.3/2          0521624355
   *Neural networks (Computer science) Neural networks (Neurobiology)*


**QA76.87.G35 1993**
**Gallant, Stephen I.**
   Neural network learning and expert systems / Stephen I. Gallant. Cambridge, Mass. : MIT Press, c1993. xvi, 365 p. :
92-020864          006.3          0262071452
   *Neural networks (Computer science) Expert systems (Computer science)*

**QA76.87.G87 1997**
**Gurney, Kevin**
An introduction to neural networks / Kevin Gurney. London : UCL Press, 1997. xi, 234 p. :
97-221231          006.3/2          1857286731
*Neural networks (Computer science)*

**QA76.87.N4845 1994**
Neural networks for knowledge representation and inference / edited by Daniel S. Levine, Manuel Aparicio IV. Hillsdale, N.J. : Lawrence Erlbaum Associates, 1994. xv, 503 p. :
93-025277          006.3          0805811583
*Neural networks (Computer science)  Knowledge representation (Information theory)*

**QA76.87.N497 2000**
**Nguyen, Hung T.,**
A first course in fuzzy logic / Hung T. Nguyen, Elbert A. Walker. 2nd ed. Boca Raton, FL : Chapman & Hall, c2000. 373 p. :
511.3 21
*Neural networks (Computer science)  Fuzzy logic.*

**QA76.87.N5 1993**
**Nigrin, Albert.**
Neural networks for pattern recognition / Albert Nigrin. Cambridge, Mass. : MIT Press, c1993. xvii, 413 p.
93-010027          006.4/2          0262140543
*Neural networks (Computer science)  Pattern recognition systems. Self-organizing systems.*

**QA76.87.S3 1997**
**Schalkoff, Robert J.**
Artificial neural networks / Robert J. Schalkoff. New York : McGraw-Hill, c1997. xxi, 422 p. :
96-049477          006.3/2          007057118X
*Neural networks (Computer science)*

**QA76.87.T37 1998**
Talking nets : an oral history of neural networks / edited by James A. Anderson and Edward Rosenfeld. Cambridge, Mass. : MIT Press, c1998. xi, 434 p. :
97-023868          006.3/2/0922          0262011670
*Neural computers.  Neural networks (Computer science) Scientists -- Interviews.*

### QA76.88-76.889 Instruments and machines — Calculating machines — Electronic computers. Computer science — Supercomputers. High performance computing

**QA76.88.K38 1993**
**Kaufmann, William J.**
Supercomputing and the transformation of science / William J. Kaufmann III, Larry L. Smarr. New York : Scientific American Library : c1993. xi, 238 p. :
92-032418          502/.85/411          0716750384
*Supercomputers.  Science -- Data processing.*

**QA76.889.M55 1998**
**Milburn, G. J.**
The Feynman processor : quantum entanglement and the computing revolution / Gerard J. Milburn ; foreword by Paul Davies. Reading, Mass. : Perseus Books, 1998. xiv, 213 p. :
98-086417          004.1          0738200166
*Feynman, Richard Phillips.     Quantum computers.*

**QA76.889.N54 2000**
**Nielsen, Michael A.**
Quantum computation and quantum information / Michael A. Nielsen and Isaac L. Chuang. Cambridge ; New York : Cambridge University Press, 2000. xxv, 676 p. :
004.1 21          0521632358
*Quantum computers.*

**QA76.889.W55 2000**
**Williams, Colin P.**
Ultimate zero and one : computing at the quantum frontier / Colin P. Williams, Scott H. Clearwater. New York : Copernicus, c2000. xiv, 250 p. :
98-042595          004.1          0387947698
*Quantum computers.*

### QA76.9 Instruments and machines — Calculating machines — Electronic computers. Computer science — Other topics, A-Z

**QA76.9.A25**
**Schneier, Bruce,**
Secrets and lies : digital security in a networked world / Bruce Schneier. New York : John Wiley, 2000. xv, 412 p. ;
00-042252          005.8          0471253111
*Computer security.  Computer networks -- Security measures.*

**QA76.9.A25.C667 1990**
Computers under attack : intruders, worms, and viruses / edited by Peter J. Denning. New York, N.Y. : ACM Press ; c1990. xx, 554, 13 p
89-018537          005.8          0201530678
*Computer security.  Computer viruses.*

**QA76.9.A25.L83 1998**
**Lubbe, J. C. A. van der**
Basic methods of cryptography / Jan C.A. van der Lubbe ; translated by Steve Gee. Cambridge ; Cambridge University Press, 1998. xiv, 229 p. :
97002668          005.8/2          0521554802
*Computer security.  Data encryption (Computer science)*

**QA76.9.A25.M463 1997**
**Menezes, A. J.**
Handbook of applied cryptography / Alfred J. Menezes, Paul C. van Oorschot, Scott A. Vanstone. Boca Raton : CRC Press, c1997. xxviii, 780 p
96-027609          005.8/2          0849385237
*Computers -- Access control -- Handbooks, manuals, etc. Cryptography -- Handbooks, manuals, etc.*

## QA76.9.A25.P56 1997
**Pipkin, Donald L.**
Halting the hacker : a practical guide to computer security / Donald L. Pipkin. Upper Saddle River, N.J. : Prentice Hall PTR, c1997. xviii, 193 p.
96-046381          005.8          013243718X
*Computer security.*

## QA76.9.A25.S35 1996
**Simonds, Fred.**
Network security : data and voice communications / Fred Simonds. New York : McGraw-Hill, c1996. p. cm.
95-030723          005.8          0070576394
*Computer security. Computer networks -- Security measures. Telephone systems -- Security measures.*

## QA76.9.A25.T43 1997
Technology and privacy : the new landscape / edited by Philip E. Agre and Marc Rotenberg. Cambridge, Mass. : MIT Press, c1997. vi, 325 p. :
97-007989          323.44/83          026201162X
*Computer security. Data protection. Privacy, Right of.*

## QA76.9.A25L49 2001
**Levy, Steven.**
Crypto : how the code rebels beat the government, saving privacy in the digital age / Steven Levy. New York : Viking, 2001. viii, 356 p. :
          005.8 21          0670859508
*Computer security. Cryptography.*

## QA76.9.A43.A43 1999
Algorithms and theory of computation handbook / edited by Mikhail J. Atallah. Boca Raton : CRC Press, c1999. 1 v. (various
98-038016          511.3          0849326494
*Computer algorithms. Computer science. Computational complexity.*

## QA76.9.A43.P38 1997
Pattern matching algorithms / edited by Alberto Apostolico, Zvi Galil. New York : Oxford University Press, 1997. 377 p. :
96-049602          006.4          0195113675
*Computer algorithms. Combinatorial analysis.*

## QA76.9.A43.S55 1998
**Skiena, Steven S.**
The algorithm design manual / Steven S. Skiena. Santa Clara, CA : TELOS--the Electronic Library of Science, c1998. xvi, 486 p. :
97-020712          005.1          0387948600
*Computer algorithms.*

## QA76.9.A43L96 1997
**Lynch, Nancy A. (Nancy Ann.),**
Distributed algorithms / Nancy A. Lynch. San Francisco, CA. : Morgan Kaufman, 1997. xxiii, 872 p. :
          005.2/76 21          1558603484
*Computer algorithms. Electronic data processing -- Distributed processing.*

## QA76.9.A73.F58 1995
**Flynn, Michael J.,**
Computer architecture : pipelined and parallel processor design / Michael J. Flynn. Boston, MA : Jones and Bartlett, c1995. xix, 788 p. :
94-041225          004.2/2          0867202041
*Computer architecture. Microprocessors -- Design and construction.*

## QA76.9.A73.T65
**Tomek, Ivan.**
Introduction to computer organization / Ivan Tomek. Rockville, Md. : Computer Science Press, c1981. xii, 456 p. :
80-024238          621.3819/52          0914894080
*Computer organization.*

## QA76.9.C65
**Odum, Howard T.,**
Modeling for all scales : an introduction to system simulation / Howard T. Odum, Elisabeth C. Odum. San Diego : Academic Press, c2000. xx, 458 p. :
99-064627          0125241704
*Computer simulation. System analysis.*

## QA76.9.C65.H35 1994
**Hannon, Bruce M.**
Dynamic modeling / Bruce Hannon, Matthias Ruth ; with a foreword by Donella H. Meadows. New York : Springer-Verlag, c1994. xiii, 248 p.
94-010015          003.3          0387942874
*Digital computer simulation. Dynamics -- Computer simulation.*

## QA76.9.C65.M393 1996
**McCullough, Malcolm.**
Abstracting craft : the practiced digital hand / Malcolm McCullough. Cambridge, Mass. : MIT Press, c1996. xvii, 309 p.
96-028356          004/.01/9          0262133261
*Digital computer simulation. Virtual reality.*

## QA76.9.C66.B3 1997
**Baase, Sara.**
A gift of fire : social, legal, and ethical issues in computing / Sara Baase. Upper Saddle River, N.J. : Prentice Hall, 1997. xvii, 382 p.
96-045254          303.48/34          0134587790
*Computers -- Social aspects. Computers -- Moral and ethical aspects.*

## QA76.9.C66.B375 1991
**Barry, John A.**
Technobabble / John A. Barry. Cambridge, Mass. : MIT Press, c1991. xv, 268 p. ;
91-012488          004/.014          0262023334
*Computers and civilization. Technology -- Philosophy.*

**QA76.9.C66.C6575 1990**

Computers, ethics, and society / [edited by] M. David Ermann, Mary B. Williams, Claudio Gutierrez. New York : Oxford University Press, 1990. ix, 376 p. ;
89-003410       303.48/34       019505850X
*Computers and civilization. Computer security. Human-computer interaction.*

**QA76.9.C66.H63 1998**
**Hobart, Michael E.,**

Information ages : literacy, numeracy, and the computer revolution / Michael E. Hobart and Zachary S. Schiffman. Baltimore : Johns Hopkins University Press, c1998. xiii, 301 p.
98-012764       303.48/34       080185881X
*Computers and civilization. Information technology.*

**QA76.9.C66.L84 1996**
**Ludlow, Peter,**

High noon on the electronic frontier : conceptual issues in cyberspace / Peter Ludlow. Cambridge, Mass. : MIT Press, c1996. xxii, 536 p.
96-003987       302.23       0262121964
*Computers -- social aspects. Information superhighway – Social aspects. Computer networks -- Security measures.*

**QA76.9.C66.R39 1996**
**Rawlins, Gregory J. E.**

Moths to the flame : the seductions of computer technology / Gregory J. E. Rawlins. Cambridge, Mass. : MIT Press, c1996. x, 184 p. ;
96-004729       303.48/34       0262181762
*Computers and civilization.*

**QA76.9.C66.R395 1997**
**Rawlins, Gregory J. E.**

Slaves of the machine : the quickening of computer technology / Gregory J.E. Rawlins. Cambridge, Mass. : MIT Press, c1997. x, 135 p. ;
97-004013       004       0262181835
*Computers and civilization. Computers -- History.*

**QA76.9.C66.R618 1998**
**Robertson, Douglas S.**

The new renaissance : computers and the next level of civilization / Douglas S. Robertson. New York : Oxford University Press, 1998. 200 p. ;
97-031239       303.48/34       0195121899
*Computers and civilization.*

**QA76.9.C66.R62 1997**
**Rochlin, Gene I.**

Trapped in the net : the unanticipated consequences of computerization / Gene I. Rochlin. Princeton, N.J. : Princeton University Press, c1997. xvi, 293 p. ;
96-041003       303.48/34       0691010803
*Computers and civilization. Electronic data processing – Social aspects. Computer networks.*

**QA76.9.C66.S88 1995**
**Stoll, Clifford.**

Silicon snake oil : second thoughts on the information highway / Clifford Stoll. New York : Doubleday, 1995. 247 p. ;
95-002537       303.48/33       0385419937
*Computers and civilization. Internet (Computer network) Information technology.*

**QA76.9.C66.T26 1995**
**Talbott, Steve.**

The future does not compute : transcending the machines in our midst / Stephen L. Talbott. Sebastopol, CA : O'Reilly & Associates, c1995. xix, 481 p. ;
96-133379       303.48/34       1565920856
*Barfield, Owen, -- 1898-    Computers -- Social aspects. Computers -- Psychological aspects. Internet (Computer network) -- Social aspects.*

**QA76.9.C66.T34 1991**

Technology 2001 : the future of computing and communications / edited by Derek Leebaert. Cambridge, Mass. : MIT Press, c1991. xvi, 392 p. :
90-040022       303.48/34       0262121506
*Computers and civilization. Telecommunication.*

**QA76.9.C66.W48 1999**
**Wertheim, Margaret.**

The pearly gates of cyberspace : a history of space from Dante to the Internet / Margaret Wertheim New York : W.W. Norton, c1999. 336 p. :
98-038200       303.48/34       039304694X
*Computers and civilization. Cyberspace. Internet (Computer network)*

**QA76.9.C66T87 1995**
**Turkle, Sherry.**

Life on the screen : identity in the age of the Internet / Sherry Turkle. New York : Simon & Schuster, c1995. 347 p. :
155.9 20       068403534
*Computers and civilization. Computer networks -- Psychological aspects.*

**QA76.9.D26.H64 1990**
**Hogan, Rex,**

A practical guide to data base design / Rex Hogan. Englewood Cliffs, N.J. : Prentice Hall, c1990. xiii, 194 p.
89-008786       005.74       0136909671
*Database design.*

**QA76.9.D26S54 2001**
**Simsion, Graeme C.**

Data modeling essentials / Graeme Simsion ; revised & updated by Graham C. Witt, Graeme C. Simsion. 2nd ed. Scottsdale, AZ : Coriolis Group Books, c2001. xx, 459 p. :
005.74 21       1576108724
*Database design. Data structures (Computer science)*

QA76.9.D3.A26 1995
**Abiteboul, S.**
Foundations of databases / Serge Abiteboul, Richard Hull, Victor Vianu. Reading, Mass. : Addison-Wesley, c1995. xviii, 685 p.
94-019295          005.74/01          0201537710
*Database management.*

QA76.9.D3.H844 1988
**Hughes, John G.,**
Database technology : a software engineering approach / John G. Hughes. New York : Prentice-Hall, 1988. xii, 273 p. :
88-006000          005.74     0131979140
*Database management. Software engineering.*

QA76.9.D3.K54 1990
**Kim, Won.**
Introduction to object-oriented databases / Won Kim. Cambridge, Mass. : MIT Press, c1990. xviii, 234 p.
90-005779          005.75     0262111241
*Object-oriented databases.*

QA76.9.D3.M649 1994
**Montgomery, Stephen L.**
Object-oriented information engineering : analysis, design, and implementation / Stephen Montgomery. Cambridge, MA : AP Professional, c1994. xiv, 324 p. :
93-043044          658.4/038/0285421
0125050402
*Object-oriented databases. Systems engineering.*

QA76.9.D3.U443 1988
**Ullman, Jeffrey D.,**
Principles of database and knowledge-base systems / Jeffrey D. Ullman. Rockville, Md. : Computer Science Press, c1988-c1989. 2 v. (xi, 113
87-038197          005.74     088175188X
*Database management. Expert systems (Computer science)*

QA76.9.D3.Y36 1988
**Yannakoudakis, E. J.,**
The architectural logic of database systems / E.J. Yannakoudakis. London ; Springer-Verlag, c1988. xiv, 318 p. :
88-003248          005.74     3540195130
*Database management. Computer architecture.*

QA76.9.D35.A38 1983
**Aho, Alfred V.**
Data structures and algorithms / Alfred V. Aho, John E. Hopcroft, Jeffrey D. Ullman. Reading, Mass. : Addison-Wesley, c1983. xi, 427 p. :
82-011596          001.64     0201000237
*Data structures (Computer science) Computer algorithms.*

QA76.9.D5.B36 1996
**Barbosa, Valmir C.**
An introduction to distributed algorithms / Valmir C. Barbosa. Cambridge, Mass. : MIT Press, c1996. xiii, 365 p.
96-013747          005.2     0262024128
*Electronic data processing -- Distributed processing. Computer algorithms.*

QA76.9.D5.R3913 1988
**Raynal, M.**
Networks and distributed computation : concepts, tools, and algorithms / Michel Raynal ; translated by Meg Sanders. Cambridge, Mass. : MIT Press, 1988, c1987. x, 166 p. ;
87-022842          004/.36     0262181304
*Electronic data processing -- Distributed processing. Computer networks.*

QA76.9.D5.T44 1994
**Tel, Gerard.**
Introduction to distributed algorithms / Gerard Tel. Cambridge ; Cambridge University Press, 1994. xii, 534 p. :
94-016147          005.2     0521470692
*Electronic data processing -- Distributed processing. Computer algorithms.*

QA76.9.D6.T48 1988
Text, ConText, and HyperText : writing with and for the computer / edited by Edward Barrett. Cambridge, Mass. : MIT Press, c1988. xxv, 368 p. :
87-036157          808/.066004          0262022753
*Electronic data processing documentation. Electronic data processing -- Authorship. Text processing (Computer science)*

QA76.9.E53.N37 1993
**Nardi, Bonnie A.**
A small matter of programming : perspectives on end user computing / Bonnie A. Nardi. Cambridge, MA : MIT Press, c1993. xvi, 162 p. :
93-009124          005.1     0262140535
*End-user computing. Computer programming.*

QA76.9.E94.J32 1991
**Jain, Raj.**
The art of computer systems performance analysis : techniques for experimental design, measurement, simulation, and modeling / Raj Jain. New York : Wiley, c1991. xxvii, 685 p.
90-045479          004.2/4     0471503363
*Electronic digital computers -- Evaluation.*

QA76.9.E94L54 2000
**Lilja, David J.**
Measuring computer performance : a practitioner's guide / David J. Lilja. Cambridge, UK ; New York : Cambridge University Press, 2000. xiv, 261 p. :
          004.2/4 21          0521641055
*Electronic digital computers -- Evaluation -- Congresses.*

QA76.9.H73H55 2000
**Hill, Mark D. (Mark Donald)**
Reading in computer architecture / Mark D. Hill, Norman P. Jouppi, Gurindar Sohi. San Francisco : Morgan Kaufman, 2000. xviii, 717 p. :
          004.2/2 21          1558605398
*Computer architecture.*

**QA76.9.H85**
**Hawkes, Lory.**

The theory and criticism of virtual texts : an annotated bibliography, 1988-1999 / Lory Hawkes, Christina Murphy, and Joe Law. Westport, Conn. : Greenwood Press, c2001. xiii, 334 p.

00-063659        016.006        0313312249

*Human-computer interaction -- Bibliography. Virtual reality – Bibliography.*

**QA76.9.H85.C68 1996**

Context and consciousness : activity theory and human-computer interaction / edited by Bonnie A. Nardi. Cambridge, Mass. : MIT Press, c1996. xiii, 400 p.

95-010974        004/.01/9        0262140586

*Human-computer interaction. Computers -- Psychological aspects.*

**QA76.9.H85.L49 1998**
**Levy, Pierre,**

Becoming virtual : reality in the Digital Age / Pierre Levy ; translated from the French by Robert Bononno. New York : Plenum Trade, c1998. 207 p. :

98-005698        004/.01/9        0306457881

*Human-computer interaction. Virtual reality.*

**QA76.9.H85.M38 1995**
**Marchionini, Gary.**

Information seeking in electronic environments / Gary Marchionini. Cambridge ; Cambridge University Press, 1995. xi, 224 p. :

94-044629        025.04        0521443725

*Human-computer interaction.*

**QA76.9.H85.M67 1999**
**Moody, Fred.**

The visionary position : the inside story of the digital dreamers who are making virtual reality a reality / Fred Moody. New York : Times Business, c1999. xxvi, 353 p.

98-022335        004/.01/9        0812928520

*Furness, Thomas A.      Virtual reality -- Research – History. Human-computer interaction -- Research -- History.*

**QA76.9.H85.O73 1996**
**Oravec, Jo Ann.**

Virtual individuals, virtual groups : human dimensions of groupware and computer networking / Jo Ann Oravec. Cambridge ; Cambridge University Press, 1996. ix, 389 p. ;

95-031984        302.3        052145493X

*Human-computer interaction. Virtual reality. Computer networks.*

**QA76.9.H85.P53 1997**
**Picard, Rosalind W.**

Affective computing / Rosalind W. Picard. Cambridge, Mass. : MIT Press, c1997. xii, 292 p. :

97-033285        004/.01/9        0262161702

*Human-computer interaction. User interfaces (Computer systems)*

**QA76.9.H85.R47 1990**

Resources in human-computer interaction / with an introduction by Wendy E. Mackay. New York, NY : ACM Press, c1990. xii, 1197 p.

90-001108        004/.01/9        0897913736

*Human-computer interaction.*

**QA76.9.H85.S63 1995**

The social and interactional dimensions of human-computer interfaces / edited by Peter J. Thomas. Cambridge ; Cambridge University Press, 1995. ix, 268 p. :

94-036921        302.2        052145302X

*Human-computer interaction.*

**QA76.9.H85.V59 1993**

Virtual reality in engineering / edited by Kevin Warwick, John Gray and David Roberts. London : Institution of Electrical Engineers, c1993. x, 196 p. :

94-134651        620/.001/13        0852968035

*Human-computer interaction. Virtual reality.*

**QA76.9.H85C673 1999**
**Cooper, Alan,**

The inmates are running the asylum / Alan Cooper. Indianapolis, IN : Sams, c1999. 261 p. :
                        0672316498

*Human-computer interaction. User interfaces (Computer systems) Consumers -- Effect of technological innovations on.*

**QA76.9.I58C37 1983**
**Card, Stuart K.**

The psychology of human-computer interaction / Stuart K. Card, Thomas P. Moran, Allen Newell. Hillsdale, N.J. : L. Erlbaum Associates, 1983. xiii, 469 p. :
                001.64/01/9 19        0898592437

*Human-computer interaction -- Psychological aspects.*

**QA76.9.L63.H88 2000**
**Huth, Michael,**

Logic in computer science : modelling and reasoning about systems / Michael Huth, Mark Ryan. Cambridge, [England] ; Cambridge University Press, 2000. xviii, 387 p.

99-015233        0521652006

*Computer logic.*

**QA76.9.M35.C66 1984**
**Cooke, D. J.**

Computer mathematics / D.J. Cooke and H.E. Bez. Cambridge [Cambridgeshire] ; Cambridge University Press, 1984. xii, 394 p. :

83-007588        519.4        0521253411

*Computer science -- Mathematics.*

**QA76.9.M35.P54 1991**
**Pierce, Benjamin C.**

Basic category theory for computer scientists / Benjamin C. Pierce. Cambridge, Mass. : MIT Press, c1991. xiii, 100 p.

91-008489        511.3        0262660717

*Computer science -- Mathematics. Categories (Mathematics)*

**QA76.9.M35.P55 1991**
**Piff, Mike.**
Discrete mathematics : an introduction for software engineers / Mike Piff. Cambridge ; Cambridge University Press, 1991. xi, 317 p. :
92-191408          004/.01/511          0521384753
*Computer science -- Mathematics.*

**QA76.9.M65**
**Himanen, Pekka.**
The hacker ethic, and the spirit of the information age / Pekka Himanen. New York : Random House, 2001. xvii, 232 p.
00-053354          174/.90904          0375505660
*Computer programming -- Moral and ethical aspects. Computer hackers. Open source software.*

**QA76.9.M65.E34 1997**
**Edgar, Stacey L.**
Morality and machines : perspectives on computer ethics / Stacey L. Edgar. Boston : Jones and Bartlett Publishers, c1997. xvi, 448 p. :
96-022261          174/.90904          076370184X
*Electronic data processing -- Moral and ethical aspects.*

**QA76.9.M65.F67 1994**
**Forester, Tom.**
Computer ethics : cautionary tales and ethical dilemmas in computing / Tom Forester and Perry Morrison. Cambridge, Mass. : MIT Press, c1994. x, 347 p. :
93-022874          174/.90904          0262061643
*Electronic data processing -- Moral and ethical aspects.*

**QA76.9.M65.W43 1997**
**Weckert, John.**
Computer and information ethics / John Weckert and Douglas Adeney. Westport, Conn. : Greenwood Press, 1997. xiii, 175 p.
96-036528          174/.90904          0313293627
*Computers -- Moral and ethical aspects.*

**QA76.9.N38.H36 1997**
Handbook of logic and language / edited by Johan van Benthem, Alice ter Meulen. Amsterdam ; Elsevier ; 1997. xxiii, 1247 p
96-027559          401/.5113          044481714X
*Natural language processing (Computer science) Logic, Symbolic and mathematical. Semantics.*

**QA76.9.O35.R93 1997**
**Ryan, Timothy W.,**
Distributed object technology : concepts and applications / Timothy W. Ryan. Upper Saddle River, N.J. : Prentice Hall PTR, c1997. xxii, 194 p.
96-032744          005.2          0133489965
*Object-oriented methods (Computer science) Distributed databases.*

**QA76.9.S63**
**Chen, G.**
Introduction to fuzzy sets, fuzzy logic, and fuzzy control systems / Guanrong Chen, Trung Tat Pham. Boca Raton, FL : CRC Press, 2001. 316 p. :
00-045431          0063          0849316588
*Soft computing. Fuzzy systems.*

**QA76.9.S63.S26 1998**
**Sangalli, Arturo,**
The importance of being fuzzy : and other insights from the border between math and computers / Arturo Sangalli. Princeton, N.J. : Princeton University Press, c1998. xvi, 173 p. :
98-003818          006.3          0691001448
*Soft computing. Fuzzy systems.*

**QA76.9.S88.E43 1994**
The Elements of system design / Amer A. Hassan ... [et al.]. Boston : Academic Press, c1994. x, 280 p. :
93-038585          620/.001/171          0123430607
*System design.*

**QA76.9.S88.S29 1994**
**Scheurer, Thierry.**
Foundations of computing : system development with set theory and logic / Thierry Scheurer. Wokingham, England ; Addison-Wesley, c1994. xxiv, 668 p.
94-016315          004.2/1          0201544296
*System design. Set theory. Logic, Symbolic and mathematical.*

**QA76.9.S88C72 1999**
**Cox, Earl.**
The fuzzy systems handbook : a practioner's guide to building using, and maintaining fuzzy systems / Earl Cox ; [foreword by Lotfi A. Zadeh]. 2nd ed. San Diego : AP Professional, c1999. xlviii, 716 p.
          003/.7 21          0121944
*System design. Adaptive control systems. Fuzzy systems.*

**QA76.9.T48.C76 1994**
**Crochemore, Maxime,**
Text algorithms / Maxime Crochemore, Wojciech Rytter. New York : Oxford University Press, c1994. xii, 412 p. :
94-020649          005.1          0195086090
*Text processing (Computer science) Computer algorithms.*

**QA76.9.U83.M67 1997**
More than screen deep : toward every-citizen interfaces to the nation's information infrastructure / Toward an Every-Citizen Interface to the Nation's Information Infrastructure Steering Committee, Computer Science and Telecommunications Board, Commission on Physical Sciences, Mathematics, and Applications, National Research Council. Washington, D.C. : National Academy Press, 1997. xiv, 433 p. :
97-021211          303.48/3          0309063574
*User interfaces (Computer systems) -- Congresses. Human-computer interaction -- Congresses. Information superhighway -- United States -- Congresses.*

## QA76.95 Instruments and machines — Calculating machines — Electronic computers. Computer science — Use of electronic computer systems

**QA76.95.A214 1997**
**Abell, Martha L.,**
Mathematica by example / Martha L. Abell, James P. Braselton. San Diego, CA : Academic Press, c1997. xii, 603 p. :
96-043815          510/.285/5369          0120415526
*Mathematics -- Data processing.*

**QA76.95.A22 1992**
**Abell, Martha L.,**
The Mathematica handbook / Martha L. Abell, James P. Braselton. Boston : Academic Press, c1992. xvi, 789 p. :
92-013599          510/.285/5369          0120415356
*Mathematics -- Data processing.*

**QA76.95.C44 1999**
**Chen, Ke,**
Mathematical explorations with MATLAB / Ke Chen, Peter Giblin, Alan Irving. Cambridge [England] ; Cambridge University Press, 1999. xiv, 306 p. :
99-019617          519.4/0285/53042          0521630789
*Mathematics -- Data processing.*

**QA76.95.E54 1993**
**Engel, Arthur.**
Exploring mathematics with your computer / by Arthur Engel. [Washington, D.C.] : Mathematical Association of America, [c1993] ix, 301 p. :
92-064177          510/.285/5133          088385600X
*Mathematics -- Data processing.*

**QA76.95.G552 2000**
**Glynn, Jerry.**
The beginner's guide to Mathematica, version 4 / Jerry Glynn, Theodore Gray. Cambridge, U.K. ; Cambridge University Press, 2000. viii, 434 p.
99-050341          510/.285/5369          0521771536
*Mathematics -- Data processing.*

**QA76.95.H35 2000**
**Hall, Cordelia,**
Discrete mathematics using a computer / Cordelia Hall and John O'Donnell. London ; Springer, c2000. xviii, 339 p.
99-026380          510/.285          1852330899
*Mathematics -- Data processing.*

**QA76.95.M3884 1998**
The Mathematica primer / Kevin R. Coombes ... [et al.]. Cambridge, UK ; Cambridge University Press, 1998. xvii, 214 p.
97-051989          510/.285/53042          0521631300
*Mathematics -- Data processing.*

**QA76.95.N53 1996**
**Nicolaides, Roy A.**
Maple : a comprehensive introduction / Roy Nicolaides, Noel Walkington. Cambridge [England] ; Cambridge University Press, 1996. xix, 466 p. :
95-047895          510/.285/53          0521562309

**QA76.95.T67 1999**
**Torrence, Bruce F.**
The student's introduction to Mathematica : a handbook for precalculus, calculus, and linear algebra / Bruce F. Torrence, Eve A. Torrence. New York : Cambridge University Press, 1999. p. cm.
98-027788          510/.285/5369          0521594456
*Mathematics -- Data processing.*

**QA76.95.W65 1999**
**Wolfram, Stephen.**
The mathematica book / Stephen Wolfram. 4th ed. Champaign, IL ; New York : Wolfram Media ; Cambridge University Press, c1999. xxvi, 1470 p. :
          510/.285/5369 21          1579550045
*Mathematica (Computer file) Mathematics -- Data processing.*

## QA93 Popular works

**QA93.B358 1999**
**Banks, Robert.**
Slicing pizzas, racing turtles, and further adventures in applied mathematics / Robert B. Banks. Princeton, N.J. : Princeton University Press, c1999. xi, 286 p. :
98-053513          510          0691059470
*Mathematics -- Popular works.*

**QA93.B36 1998**
**Banks, Robert.**
Towing icebergs, falling dominoes, and other adventures in applied mathematics / Robert B. Banks. Princeton, N.J. : Princeton University Press, c1998. xi, 328 p. :
98-004557          510          0691059489
*Mathematics -- Popular works.*

**QA93.D457 1994**
**Devlin, Keith J.**
All the math that's fit to print : articles from the Manchester guardian / Keith Devlin. Washington, DC : Mathematical Association of America, c1994. xvii, 330 p.
94-077346          510          0883855151
*Mathematics -- Popular works.*

**QA93.D4578 1998**
**Devlin, Keith J.**
The language of mathematics : making the invisible visible / Keith Devlin. New York : W.H. Freeman, c1998. viii, 344 p.,
98-038019          510          071673379X
*Mathematics -- Popular works.*

**QA93.D458 1998**
**Devlin, Keith J.**
Life by the numbers / Keith Devlin. New York : Wiley, c1998. ix, 214 p. :
97-041059        510        0471240443
*Mathematics -- Popular works.*

**QA93.D49 1993**
**Dewdney, A. K.**
200% of nothing : : an eye-opening tour through the twists and turns of math abuse and innumeracy / A.K. Dewdney. New York : Wiley, c1993. ix, 182 p. :
92-042173        510        0471577766
*Mathematics -- Popular works.*

**QA93.L553 1994**
**Lines, Malcolm E.**
On the shoulders of giants / Malcolm E. Lines. Bristol ; Institute of Physics Pub., c1994. 288 p. :
94-030118        530.1/5        075030104X
*Mathematics -- Popular works.*

**QA93.S684 1996**
**Stein, Sherman K.**
Strength in numbers : discovering the joy and power of mathematics in everyday life / Sherman K. Stein. New York : John Wiley, c1996. xiii, 272 p.
95-048056        510        0471152528
*Mathematics -- Popular works.*

**QA93.S736 1997**
**Stewart, Ian,**
The magical maze : seeing the world through mathematical eyes / Ian Stewart. New York : John Wiley & Sons, Inc., 1998. 268 p. :
98-013185        510        047119297X
*Mathematics -- Popular works. Mathematics. Mathematical recreations.*

**QA93.S737 1995**
**Stewart, Ian,**
Nature's numbers : the unreal reality of mathematical imagination / Ian Stewart. New York : BasicBooks, c1995. x, 164 p. :
95-010238        510        0465072739
*Mathematics -- Popular works.*

**QA93.W385 1995**
**Wells, D. G.**
You are a mathematician : a wise and witty introduction to the joy of numbers / David Wells. New York : Wiley, 1995. viii, 424 p.
96-053548        510        0471180777
*Mathematics -- Popular works.*

## QA95 Instruments and machines — Calculating machines — Mathematical recreations

**QA95.D6**
**Carroll, Lewis,**
Mathematical recreations of Lewis Carroll [pseud.] New York, Dover Publications [1958] 2 v.
58-014299        793.74
*Mathematical recreations. Logic, Symbolic and mathematical.*

**QA95.G24**
**Gardner, Martin,**
Aha! gotcha : paradoxes to puzzle and delight / Martin Gardner. San Francisco : W.H. Freeman, c1982. vii, 164 p. :
81-019543        793.7/4        0716714140
*Mathematical recreations. Paradox.*

**QA95.G255 1997**
**Gardner, Martin,**
The last recreations : hydras, eggs, and other mathematical mystifications / Martin Gardner. New York : Copernicus, c1997. x, 392 p. :
96-051641        793.7/4        0387949291
*Mathematical recreations.*

**QA95.G3**
**Gardner, Martin,**
The Scientific American book of mathematical puzzles & diversions, by Martin Gardner ... together with mathematical commentaries by Mr. Gardner and addenda from readers of Scientific American, plus bibliographies and, of course, solutions. New York, Simon and Schuster, 1959-61. 2 v.
61-012845        793.74
*Mathematical recreations.*

**QA95.G32**
**Gardner, Martin,**
Sixth book of mathematical games from Scientific American. San Francisco, W. H. Freeman [1971] 262 p.
75-157436        793.7/4/08        0716709449
*Mathematical recreations.*

**QA95.G3325 1996**
**Gardner, Martin,**
The universe in a handkerchief : Lewis Carroll's mathematical recreations, games, puzzles, and word plays / Martin Gardner. New York : Copernicus, c1996. x, 158 p. :
95-051303        793.73        038794673X
*Mathematical recreations. Literary recreations.*

**QA95.M366 1999**
The mathemagician and pied puzzler : a collection in tribute to Martin Gardner / edited by Elwyn Berklekamp and Tom Rodgers. Natick, Mass. : A K Peters, c1999. x, 266 p. :
98-051744        793.7/4        156881075X
*Mathematical recreations.*

## QA95.M58 2000
**Morgan, Frank.**
The math chat book / Frank Morgan ; illustrated by James F. Bredt. [Washington, DC] : Mathematical Association of America, c2000. xiv, 113 p. :
99-067970          0883855305
*Mathematical recreations.*

## QA95.O34 1972
**Ogilvy, C. Stanley**
Tomorrow's math; unsolved problems for the amateur [by] C. Stanley Ogilvy. New York, Oxford University Press, 1972. 198 p.
77-173328     510/.76     0195015088
*Mathematical recreations. Mathematics -- Problems, exercises, etc.*

## QA95.P53 2001
**Pickover, Clifford A.**
Wonders of numbers : adventures in math, mind, and meaning / by Clifford A. Pickover. New York : Oxford University, 2000. p. cm.
99-027044     793.7/4     0195133420
*Mathematical recreations. Number theory.*

# QA99 Miscellany and curiosa

## QA99.B17 2000
**Barbeau, Edward,**
Mathematical fallacies, flaws, and flimflam / Edward J. Barbeau. Washington, DC : Mathematical Association of America, c2000. xvi, 167 p. :
99-067971     510     0883855291
*Mathematics -- Miscellanea.*

## QA99.D83 1992
**Dudley, Underwood.**
Mathematical cranks / Underwood Dudley. Washington, DC : The Mathematical Association of America, 1992. x, 372 p. :
92-064179     510     0883855070
*Mathematics -- Miscellanea.*

## QA99.M363 1998
Mathematically speaking : a dictionary of quotations / selected and arranged by Carl C. Gaither and Alma E. Cavazos-Gaither ; illustrated by Andrew Slocombe. Bristol ; Institute of Physics Pub., c1998. xiii, 484 p.
98-006351     510     0750305037
*Mathematics -- Quotations, maxims, etc.*

## QA99.P48 2000
**Phillips, G. M.**
Two millennia of mathematics : from Archimedes to Gauss / George M. Phillips. New York : Springer, c2000. xii, 223 p. :
00-023807     510     0387950222
*Mathematics -- Miscellanea. Mathematics -- History.*

## QA99.S33 1993
**Schmalz, Rosemary,**
"Out of the mouths of mathematicians" : a quotation book for philomaths / Rosemary Schmalz. Washington, D.C. : Mathematical Association of America, c1993. x, 294 p. ;
93-079040     510     0883855097
*Mathematicians -- Quotations. Mathematics -- Quotations, maxims, etc.*

# QA135.5 Elementary mathematics. Arithmetic — Study and teaching

## QA135.5.B533 1991
**Bird, Marion H.,**
Mathematics for young children : an active thinking approach / Marion H. Bird. London ; Routledge, 1991. xii, 183 p. :
90-023425     372.7     0415064791
*Mathematics -- Study and teaching (Elementary)*

## QA135.5.T694 1990
Transforming children's mathematics education : international perspectives / edited by Leslie P. Steffe, Terry Wood. Hillsdale, N.J. : L. Erlbaum, 1990. xiv, 498 p. :
90-030922     372.7     0805806040
*Mathematics -- Study and teaching (Elementary) -- Congresses.*

# QA141 Elementary mathematics. Arithmetic — Numeration, number concept, numeration systems — General works, treatises, and textbooks

## QA141.D44 1997
**Dehaene, Stanislas.**
The number sense : how the mind creates mathematics / Stanislas Dehaene. New York : Oxford University Press, 1997. xi, 274 p. :
96-053840     510/.1/9     0195110048
*Number concept. Mathematics -- Study and teaching -- Psychological aspects. Mathematical ability.*

## QA141.I3713 2000
**Ifrah, Georges.**
The universal history of numbers : from prehistory to the invention of the computer / Georges Ifrah ; translated from the French by David Bellos ... [et al.]. New York : J. Wiley, 2000- v. 1 :
99-045531     513.2     0471375683
*Numeration -- History.*

## QA141.K36 2000
**Kaplan, Robert,**
The nothing that is : a natural history of zero / Robert Kaplan ; illustrations by Ellen Kaplan. Oxford ; Oxford University Press, 2000. xii, 225 p. :
99-029000     513     0195128427
*Zero (The number) Vacuum. Nothing (Philosophy)*

**QA141.R63 1992**
**Roberts, Joe.**
  Lure of the integers / Joe Roberts. [Washington, D.C.] : Mathematical Association of America, c1992. xvii, 310 p.
91-062053          512/.72          088385502X
  *Numbers, Natural.*

## QA141.3 Elementary mathematics. Arithmetic — Numeration, number concept, numeration systems — Juvenile works

**QA141.3.A85**
**Asimov, Isaac,**
  Realm of numbers. Diagrs. by Robert Belmore. Boston, Houghton Mifflin, 1959. 200 p.
59-007480          513
  *Numeration -- Juvenile literature. Number systems. Mathematics.*

## QA141.5 Elementary mathematics. Arithmetic — Numeration, number concept, numeration systems — Deodecimal system

**QA141.5.B786 1999**
**Butterworth, Brian.**
  What counts : how every brain is hardwired for math / Brian Butterworth. New York : Free Press, c1999. xv, 416 p. :
99-017314          510/.19          0684854171
  *Number concept. Mathematical ability. Mathematics -- Psychological aspects.*

## QA151 Algebra — History

**QA151.V37 1998**
**Varadarajan, V. S.**
  Algebra in ancient and modern times / V.S. Varadarajan. Providence, RI : American Mathematical Society, c1998. xii, 142 p. :
98-015355          512/.009          082180989X
  *Algebra -- History.*

## QA152-154.2 Algebra — Textbooks

**QA152.A75**
**Asimov, Isaac,**
  Realm of algebra. Diagrams by Robert Belmore. Boston, Houghton Mifflin, 1961. 230 p.
61-010637          512
  *Algebra. Algebra.*

**QA152.2.B384 1998**
**Bauer, Cameron.**
  Algebra for athletes / Cameron Bauer. Commack, NY : Nova Science Publishers, 1998. p. cm.
98-035903          512          1560725281
  *Algebra.*

**QA152.2.L36 1987**
**Lang, Serge,**
  Undergraduate algebra / Serge Lang. New York : Springer-Verlag, c1987. ix, 256 p. ;
86-020334          512.9          0387964045
  *Algebra.*

**QA152.2.R68 1994**
**Rowen, Louis Halle.**
  Algebra : groups, rings, and fields / Louis Rowen. Wellesley, Mass. : A K Peters, c1994. xxii, 239 p.
93-039371          512.9          1568810288
  *Algebra.*

**QA154.2.S28 2000**
**Scherk, John.**
  Algebra : a computational introduction/ John Scherk. Boca Raton : Chapman & Hall/CRC, c2000. x, 319 p. :
00-031432          512          1584880643
  *Algebra.*

**QA154.2.T68 1998**
**Toth, Gabor,**
  Glimpses of algebra and geometry / Gabor Toth. New York : Springer, c1998. xviii, 308 p.
97-010094          512/.12          0387982132
  *Algebra. Geometry.*

## QA155 Algebra — General works

**QA155.F65 1994**
**Foldes, Stephan,**
  Fundamental structures of algebra and discrete mathematics / Stephan Foldes. New York : Wiley, c1994. xv, 344 p. :
93-008787          512/.02          0471571806
  *Algebra.*

**QA155.S75 1994**
**Stillwell, John.**
  Elements of algebra : geometry, numbers, equations / John Stillwell. New York : Springer-Verlag, c1994. xi, 181 p. :
94-010085          512/.02          0387942904
  *Algebra.*

## QA155.5 Algebra — Special aspects of subject as a whole

**QA155.5.K**
**Kirtland, Joseph.**
  Identification numbers and check digit schemes / Joseph Kirtland. -- Washington, D.C. : Mathematical Association of America, 2001. xi, 174 p. :
00-108052          0883857200
  *Identification -- Mathematiques. Numero international normalise du livre -- Mathematiques. Produits commerciaux -- Codification – Mathematiques.*

### QA155.7.E4 Algebra — Special topics, A-Z — Electronic data processing

**QA155.7.E4.G43 1992**
**Geddes, K. O.**
   Algorithms for computer algebra / K.O. Geddes, S.R. Czapor, G. Labahn. Boston : Kluwer Academic, c1992. xviii, 585 p.
92-025697          512/.00285          0792392590
   *Algebra -- Data processing. Algorithms.*

**QA155.7.E4.H43 1993**
**Heck, A.**
   Introduction to Maple / Andre Heck. New York : Springer-Verlag, c1993. xiii, 497 p.
93-008631          510/.285/53          0387976620
   *Algebra -- Data processing.*

**QA155.7.E4.Y36 2000**
**Yap, Chee-Keng.**
   Fundamental problems of algorithmic algebra / Chee Keng Yap. New York : Oxford University Press, C2000. xv, 511 p. :
98-053667          512/.0285          0195125169
   *Algebra -- Data processing.*

**QA155.7.E4.Z87 1999**
**Zur Gathen, Joachim von.**
   Modern computer algebra / Joachim von zur Gathen and Jurgen Gerhard. Cambridge ; Cambridge University Press, 1999. xiii, 753 p.
99-232072          512.00285          0521641764
   *Algebra -- Data processing. Computer algorithms. Computer science -- Mathematics.*

### QA159 Algebra — Study and teaching. Research.

**QA159.C48 2000**
**Chazan, Daniel.**
   Beyond formulas in mathematics and teaching : dynamics of the high school algebra classroom / Daniel Chazan ; foreword by Penelope Peterson. New York : Teachers College Press, c2000. xvi, 200 p. :
99-053646          512/.071/2          0807739189
   *Algebra -- Study and teaching (Secondary)*

### QA162 Algebra — Abstract algebra

**QA162.A84 1998**
**Ash, Robert B.**
   A primer of abstract mathematics / Robert B. Ash. Washington, DC : Mathematical Association of America, c1998. x, 181 p. ;
98-085593          512/.02          0883857081
   *Algebra, Abstract.*

**QA162.C36 1998**
**Cameron, Peter J.**
   Introduction to algebra / Peter J. Cameron. Oxford ; Oxford University Press, 1998. x, 295 p. :
98-002555          512/.02          0198501951
   *Algebra, Abstract.*

**QA162.S73 1997**
**Stahl, Saul.**
   Introductory modern algebra : a historical approach / Saul Stahl. New York : Wiley, c1997. xii, 322 p. :
96-019469          512/.2          0471162884
   *Algebra, Abstract.*

### QA164-164.8 Algebra — Combinatorics. Combinatorial analysis

**QA164.B82 1993**
**Bryant, Victor.**
   Aspects of combinatorics : a wide-ranging introduction / Victor Bryant. Cambridge [England] ; Cambridge University Press, 1993. viii, 266 p.
92-006827          511/.6          0521419743
   *Combinatorial analysis.*

**QA164.C346 1994**
**Cameron, Peter J.**
   Combinatorics : topics, techniques, algorithms / Peter J. Cameron. Cambridge ; Cambridge University Press, 1994. viii, 355 p.
94-004680          511/.6          0521451337
   *Combinatorial analysis.*

**QA164.E74 1996**
**Erickson, Martin J.,**
   Introduction to combinatorics / Martin J. Erickson. New York : Wiley, c1996. xii, 195 p. :
96-028174          511/.6          0471154083
   *Combinatorial analysis.*

**QA164.H36 2000**
   Handbook of discrete and combinatorial mathematics / Kenneth H. Rosen, editor-in-chief, John G. Michaels, project editor ... [et al.]. Boca Raton : CRC Press, c2000. 1232 p. :
99-048378          511/.6          0849301491
   *Combinatorial analysis -- Handbooks, manuals, etc. Computer science -- Mathematics -- Handbooks, manuals, etc.*

**QA164.K57 1998**
**Kisacanin, Branislav,**
   Mathematical problems and proofs : combinatorics, number theory, and geometry / Branislav Kisacanin. New York : Plenum Press, c1998. xiv, 220 p. :
98-037206          511/.6          0306459671
   *Combinatorial analysis. Set theory. Number theory.*

**QA164.K73 1999**
**Kreher, Donald L.**
Combinatorial algorithms : generation, enumeration, and search / Donald L. Kreher, Douglas R. Stinson. Boca Raton, Fla. : CRC Press, c1999. 329 p. :
98-041243          511/.6          084933988X
*Combinatorial analysis. Algorithms.*

**QA164.M345 1998**
**Marcus, Daniel A.,**
Combinatorics : a problem oriented approach / Daniel A. Marcus. Washington, DC : Mathematical Association of America, c1998. x, 136 p. :
98-085594          511/.6          0883857103
*Combinatorial analysis.*

**QA164.N54 1978**
**Nijenhuis, Albert.**
Combinatorial algorithms for computers and calculators / Albert Nijenhuis and Herbert S. Wilf. New York : Academic Press, 1978. xv, 302 p. :
78-000213          511/.6/0285425          0125192606
*Combinatorial analysis -- Computer programs. Computer algorithms.*

**QA164.8.P6513 1987**
**Polya, George,**
Combinatorial enumeration of groups, graphs, and chemical compounds / G. Polya, R.C. Read. New York : Springer-Verlag, c1987. vi, 148 p. :
86-031634          511/.62          0387964134
*Combinatorial enumeration problems.*

### QA165 Algebra — Combinatorics. Combinatorial analysis — Permutations. Combinations. Partitions

**QA165.H37 2000**
**Harris, John M.**
Combinatorics and graph theory / John M. Harris, Jeffry L. Hirst, Michael J. Mossinghoff. New York : Springer, c2000. xiii, 225 p.
99-049806          511/.6          0387987363
*Combinatorial analysis. Graph theory.*

**QA165.M594 1998**
**Morris, S. Brent.**
Magic tricks, card shuffling, and dynamic computer memories / S. Brent Morris. [Washington, D.C.] : Mathematical Association of America, c1998. xviii, 148 p.
97-074358          511/.64          0883855275
*Permutations. Memory management (Computer science) Card tricks.*

### QA166 Algebra — Combinatorics. Combinatorial analysis — Graph Theory

**QA166.A425 2000**
**Aldous, Joan M.,**
Graphs and applications : an introductory approach / Joan M. Aldous and Robin J. Wilson. London ; Springer, 2000. xi, 444 p. :
99-056960          511/.5          185233259X
*Graph theory.*

**QA166.B25 2000**
**Balakrishnan, R.**
A textbook of graph theory / R. Balakrishnan, K. Ranganathan. New York : Springer, c2000. xi, 227 p. :
99-015016          511/.5          0387988599
*Graph theory.*

**QA166.D51413 1997**
**Diestel, Reinhard.**
Graph theory / Reinhard Diestel. New York : Springer, c1997. xiv, 286 p. :
97-006932          511/.5          0387982108
*Graph theory.*

**QA166.W314 2000**
**Wallis, W. D.**
A beginner's guide to graph theory / W.D. Wallis. Boston : Birkhauser, c2000. xviii, 230 p.
00-031172          511/.5          0817641769
*Graph theory.*

### QA166.7-166.75 Algebra — Combinatorics. Combinatorial analysis — Design and configurations

**QA166.7.A78 2000**
**Aste, Tomaso.**
The pursuit of perfect packing / Tomaso Aste and Denis Weaire. Bristol, PA : Institute of Physics Pub., c2000. xi, 136 p. :
00-040773          511/.6          0750306483
*Combinatorial packing and covering.*

**QA166.75.G65 1994**
**Golomb, Solomon W.**
Polyominoes : puzzles, patterns, problems, and packings / Solomon W. Golomb ; with more than 190 diagrams by Warren Lusgbaugh. Princeton, N.J. : Princeton University Press, c1994. xii, 184 p. :
93-041756          511/.6          0691085730
*Polyominoes.*

## QA167 Algebra — Combinatorics. Combinatorial analysis — Combinatorial geometry

**QA167.P33 1995**
**Pach, Janos.**
  Combinatorial geometry / Janos Pach, Pankaj K. Agarwal. New York : Wiley, c1995. xiii, 354 p.
94-048203          516/.13          0471588903
  *Combinatorial geometry.*

## QA171 Algebra — Group therapy

**QA171.R668 1990**
**Rotman, Joseph J.,**
  Galois theory / Joseph Rotman. New York : Springer-Verlag, c1990. xii, 108 p. :
90-009740          512/.3          0387973052
  *Galois theory.*

## QA171.5 Algebra — Lattice theory

**QA171.5.D38 1990**
**Davey, B. A.**
  Introduction to lattices and order / B.A. Davey, H.A. Priestley. Cambridge [England] ; Cambridge University Press, 1990. viii, 248 p.
89-009753          511.3/3          0521365848
  *Lattice theory.*

**QA171.5.E73 1989**
**Erdos, Paul,**
  Lattice points / P. Erdos, P.M. Gruber & J. Hammer. Harlow, Essex, England : Longman Scientific & Technical ; c1989. vii, 184 p. :
88-013276          511.3/3          0470211547
  *Lattice theory. Geometry of numbers.*

## QA174.2 Algebra — Group theory — General works

**QA174.2.S65 2000**
**Smith, Geoff,**
  Topics in group theory / Geoff Smith and Olga Tabachnikova. London ; Springer, c2000. xiii, 255 p :
00-037333          512/.2          1852332352
  *Group theory.*

## QA177 Algebra — Group theory — Finite groups

**QA177.H85 1996**
**Humphreys, J. F.**
  A course in group theory / John F. Humphreys. Oxford ; Oxford University Press, 1996. xii, 279 p. ;
97-108432          512/.2          0198534531
  *Finite groups. Group theory.*

## QA183 Algebra — Group theory — Geometric group theory

**QA183.N48 1994**
**Neumann, P. M.**
  Groups and geometry / Peter M. Neumann, Gabrielle A. Stoy, and Edward C. Thompson. Oxford ; Oxford University Press, 1994. vi, 254 p. ;
93-000270          512/.2          0198534523
  *Geometric group theory.*

## QA184 Algebra — Linear and multilinear algebra. Matrices — General works, treatises, and textbooks

**QA184.A96 1996**
**Axler, Sheldon Jay.**
  Linear algebra done right / Sheldon Axler. New York : Springer, c1996. xvii, 238 p.
95-044889          512/.5          0387945954
  *Algebras, Linear.*

**QA184.B34 1990**
**Baker, A. C.**
  Linear algebra and differential equations / A.C. Baker, H.L. Porteous. New York : Ellis Horwood, 1990. 424 p. :
90-004759          512/.5          0135384710
  *Algebras, Linear. Differential equations.*

**QA184.G6313 1995**
**Golan, Jonathan S.**
  Foundations of linear algebra / by Jonathan S. Golan. Dordrecht ; Kluwer Academic Publishers, c1995. viii, 236 p.
95-030190          512/.5          0792336143
  *ALgebras, Linear.*

**QA184.H36 1987**
**Hamilton, A. G.,**
  A first course in linear algebra, with concurrent examples / A.G. Hamilton. Cambridge [Cabridgeshire] ; Cambridge University Press, 1987. vi, 148 p. :
86-024426          512/.55          0521325161
  *Algebras, Linear.*

**QA184.J333 1995**
**Jacob, Bill.**
  Linear functions and matrix theory / Bill Jacob. New York : Springer-Verlag, c1995. x, 330 p. :
95-003756          512/.5          0387944516
  *Algebras, Linear. Matrices.*

**QA184.K585 1996**
**Kleinfeld, Margaret.**
  Elementary linear algebra / by Margaret and Erwin Kleinfeld. Commack, N.Y. : Nova Science Publishers, 1996. p. cm.
95-049100          512/.5          1560722924
  *Algebras, Linear.*

**QA184.N34 1998**
**Nakos, George,**
Linear algebra with applications / George Nakos, David Joyner. Pacific Grove, CA : Brooks/Cole Pub. Co., c1998. xviii, 666 p.
97-047341          512/.5          0534955266
*Algebras, Linear.*

**QA184.S645 1998**
**Solow, Daniel.**
The keys to linear algebra : applications, theory, and reasoning / by Daniel Solow. Cleveland, Ohio : D. Solow ; c1998. ix, 548 p. :
97-073562          512/.55          0964451921
*Algebras, Linear.*

**QA184.T74 1997**
**Trefethen, Lloyd N.**
Numerical linear algebra / Lloyd N. Trefethen, David Bau. Philadelphia : Society for Industrial and Applied Mathematics,r 1997. xii, 361 p. :
96-052458          512/.5          0898713617
*Algebras, Linear.  Numerical calculations.*

## QA184.5 Algebra — Linear and multilinear algebra. Matrices — Problems, exercises, examinations

**QA184.5.H35 1995**
**Halmos, Paul R.**
Linear algebra problem book / Paul R. Halmos. [Washington, DC] : Mathematical Association of America, c1995. xiii, 336 p.
94-079588          512/.5/076          0883853221
*Algebras, Linear -- Problems, exercises, etc.*

## QA188 Algebra — Linear and multilinear algebra. Matrices — Vector and tensor algebra

**QA188.B36 1990**
**Barnett, S.**
Matrices : methods and applications / Stephen Barnett. Oxford [England] : Clarendon Press ; 1990. xvi, 450 p. :
89-023942          512.9/434          0198596650
*Matrices.*

**QA188.B73 1999**
**Bressoud, David M.,**
Proofs and confirmations : the story of the alternating sign matrix conjecture / David M. Bressoud. Cambridge ; Cambridge University Press, 1999. xv, 274 p. :
99-020232          512.9/434          0521661706
*Matrices. Combinatorial analysis. Statistical mechanics.*

**QA188.K58 1997**
**Kleinfeld, Erwin.**
A short course in matrix theory / Erwin and Margaret Kleinfeld. Commack, N.Y. : Nova Science Publishers, c1997. vi, 158 p. ;
97-009516          512.9/434          1560724226
*Matrices.*

**QA188.M495 2000**
**Meyer, C. D.**
Matrix analysis and applied linear algebra / Carl Meyer. Philadelphia : Society for Industrial and Applied Mathematics,s c2000. xii, 718 p. :
00-029725          512/.5          0898714540
*Algebras, Linear.  Matrices.*

## QA191 Algebra — Linear and multilinear algebra. Matrices — Matrices

**QA191.A5 1956**
**Aitken, A. C.**
Determinants and matrices.  Edinburgh, Oliver and Boyd; 1956. 144 p.
57-002557          512.83
*Determinants.  Matrices.*

## QA201 Algebra — Linear and multilinear algebra. Matrices — Vector and tensor algebra

**QA201.H716 1993**
**Hilbert, David,**
Theory of algebraic invariants / David Hilbert ; translated by Reinhard C. Laubenbacher ; edited by Reinhard C. Laubenbacher ; with an introduction by Bernd Sturmfels. Cambridge [England] ; Cambridge University Press, 1993. xiv, 191 p. :
93-015650          512/.5          0521449030
*Invariants.*

## QA214 Algebra — Theory of equations — General resolution of equations

**QA214.B56 1996**
**Bjorck, Ake,**
Numerical methods for least squares problems / Ake Bjorck. Philadelphia : SIAM, c1996. xvii, 408 p.
96-003908          512.9/42          0898713609
*Equations, Simultaneous -- Numerical solutions.  Least squares.*

## QA218 Algebra — Theory of equations — Numeral solutions

**QA218.H4713 2000**
**Herman, Jiri.**
Equations and inequalities : elementary problems and theorems in algebra and number theory / Jiri Herman, Radan Kucera, Jaromir Simsa ; translated by Karl Dilcher. New York : Springer, c2000. x, 344 p. :
99-047384          512.9/4          0387989420
*Equations -- Numerical solutions.  Inequalities.  Problem solving.*

## QA231 Algebra — Approximation theory

**QA231.V57 2001**
**Virchenko, N. O.**
Graphs of elementary and special functions : handbook / N.O. Virchenko, I.I. Lyashko. New York : Begell House, 2001. p. cm.
01-025293        515        1567001564
*Functions -- Graphic methods. Functions, Special -- Graphic methods.*

## QA241 Algebra — Number theory — General works, treatises, and yearbooks

**QA241.A53 1995**
**Anglin, W. S.**
The queen of mathematics : an introduction to number theory / W.S. Anglin. Dordrecht ; Kluwer Academic Publishers, c1995. x, 389 p. :
94-042070        512/.7        0792332873
*Number theory.*

**QA241.B1085 1996**
**Bach, Eric.**
Algorithmic number theory / Eric Bach and Jeffrey Shallit. Cambridge, Mass. : MIT Press, c1996- v. 1   :
95-025458        512/.72/015118        0262024055
*Number theory -- Data processing. Algorithms.*

**QA241.B788 2000**
**Bressoud, David M.,**
A course in computational number theory / David Bressoud, Stan Wagon. New York : Springer, c2000. xii, 367 p. :
99-016037        512/.7        1930190107
*Number theory. Algorithms.*

**QA241.C664 1996**
**Clawson, Calvin C.**
Mathematical mysteries : the beauty and magic of numbers / Calvin C. Clawson. New York : Plenum Press, c1996. x, 313 p. :
96-031715        512/.7        0306454041
*Number theory.*

**QA241.C69513 1999**
**Coutinho, S. C.**
The mathematics of ciphers : number theory and RSA cryptography / S.C. Coutinho. Natick, Mass. : A K Peters, c1999. xv, 196 p. :
98-049611        512/.7        1568810822
*Number theory. Cryptography.*

**QA241.E37 1987**
**Edwards, A. W. F.**
Pascal's arithmetical triangle / A.W.F. Edwards. London : C. Griffin ; 1987. xii, 174 p. :
86-019264        512/.7        0852642830
*Pascal's triangle.*

**QA241.H63**
**Honsberger, Ross,**
Mathematical gems / by Ross Honsberger. [Washington] : Mathematical Association of America, c1976 v. 2   :
76-015927        512/.7        0883853000
*Number theory. Combinatorial analysis. Geometry.*

**QA241.L56 2000**
**Lemmermeyer, Franz,**
Reciprocity laws : from Euler to Eisenstein / Franz Lemmermeyer. Berlin ; Springer, c2000. xix, 487 p. ;
00-026905        512/.74        3540669574
*Reciprocity theorems.*

**QA241.M598 1998**
**Mollin, Richard A.,**
Fundamental number theory with applications / Richard A. Mollin. Boca Raton : CRC Press, c1998. xii, 439 p. :
97-033279        512/.72        0849339871
*Number theory.*

**QA241.R467 2000**
**Ribenboim, Paulo.**
My numbers, my friends : popular lectures on number theory / Paulo Ribenboim. New York : Springer, c2000. ix, 375 p. :
99-042458        512/.7        0387989110
*Number theory.*

**QA241.S318 1997**
**Schroeder, M. R.**
Number theory in science and communication : with applications in cryptography, physics, digital information, computing, and self-similarity / M.R. Schroeder. Berlin ; Springer, c1997. xxii, 362 p.
96-053994        512/.7        3540620060
*Number theory.*

**QA241.T35 1999**
**Tattersall, James J.**
Elementary number theory in nine chapters / James J. Tattersall. Cambridge ; Cambridge University Press, 1999. viii, 407 p.
98-004541        512/.72        0521585031
*Number theory.*

**QA241.V24 1989**
**Vajda, S.**
Fibonacci & Lucas numbers, and the golden section : theory and applications / S. Vajda. Chichester [England] : E. Horwood Ltd. ; 1989. 189 p. :
89-033526        512/.72        0745807151
*Fibonacci numbers. Golden section.*

**QA241.W3418 1984**
**Weil, Andre,**
Number theory : an approach through history from Hammurapi to Legendre / Andre Weil. Boston : Birkhauser, c1984. xxi, 375 p. :
83-011857        512/.7/09        0817631410
*Number theory -- History.*

### QA242 Algebra — Number theory — Divisibility. Linear congruences. Factorization. Quadratic residues. Diophantine analysis

**QA242.B4397 1997**
**Bashmakova, I. G.**
Diophantus and diophantine equations / I.G. Bashmakova; updated by Joseph Silverman ; translated from the Russian by Abe Shenitzer with the editorial assistance of Hardy Grant. [Washington, DC] : Mathematical Association of America, c1997. xiv, 90 p. :
97-074342           0883855267
*Diophantine analysis.*

**QA242.M4213 1993**
**Matiiasevich, IU. V.**
Hilbert's tenth problem / Yuri V. Matiyasevich ; with a foreword by Martin Davis. Cambridge, Mass. : MIT Press, c1993. xxii, 264 p.
93-028107     512/.7     0262132958
*Hilbert's tenth problem. Computable functions.*

### QA244 Algebra — Number theory — Higher congruences, residues. Fermat's theorem

**QA244.A29 1996**
**Aczel, Amir D.**
Fermat's last theorem : unlocking the secret of an ancient mathematical problem / by Amir D. Aczel. New York : Four Walls Eight Windows, c1996. xi, 147 p. :
96-009029     512/.74     1568580770
*Fermat's last theorem.*

**QA244.R53 1999**
**Ribenboim, Paulo.**
Fermat's last theorem for amateurs / Paulo Ribenboim. New York : Springer, c1999. xii, 407 p. :
98-041246     512/.74     0387985085
*Fermat's last theorem.*

**QA244.S55 1997**
**Singh, Simon.**
Fermat's enigma : the epic quest to solve the world's greatest mathematical problem / Simon Singh ; foreward by John Lynch. New York : Walker, 1997. xviii, 315 p.
97-020748     512/.74     0802713319
*Wiles, Andrew.    Fermat's last theorem.*

### QA246 Algebra — Number theory — Distribution of primes. Special numeric functions, etc.

**QA246.I6 1990**
**Ingham, A. E.**
The distribution of prime numbers / A.E. Ingham. Cambridge ; Cambridge University Press, 1990. xvii, 114 p.
91-105968     512/.72     0521397898
*Numbers, Prime. Functions, Zeta.*

**QA246.R47 1988**
**Ribenboim, Paulo.**
The book of prime number records / Paulo Ribenboim. New York : Springer-Verlag, c1988. xiii, 476 p.
87-014811     512/.72     0387965734
*Numbers, Prime.*

### QA247-247.5 Algebra — Number theory — Algebraic fields. Algebraic numbers

**QA247.C63**
**Cohn, Harvey.**
A classical invitation to algebraic numbers and class fields / Harvey Cohn. New York : Springer-Verlag, c1978. xiii, 328 p.
78-013785     512/.74     0387903453
*Algebraic number theory. Class field theory.*

**QA247.M63 1999**
**Mollin, Richard A.,**
Algebraic number theory / Richard A. Mollin. Boca Raton, Fla : CRC Press, c1999. xiv, 483 p. :
99-017157     512/.74     0849339898
*Algebraic number theory.*

**QA247.M65 1995**
**Mollin, Richard A.,**
Quadratics / Richard A. Mollin. Boca Raton, Fla. : CRC Press, c1996. 387 p. :
95-023311     512/.7     0849339839
*Quadratic fields.*

**QA247.5.M33 1994**
**Maor, Eli.**
e : the story of a number / Eli Maor. Princeton, N.J. : Princeton University Press, c1994. xiv, 223 p. :
93-039003     512/.73     0691033900
*e (The number)*

### QA248 Algebra — Foundations of arithmetic. Set theory. Transfinite numbers — General works

**QA248.C2**
**Cantor, Georg,**
Contributions to the founding of the theory of transfinite numbers, by Georg Cantor; tr., and provided with an introduction and notes, by Philip E.B. Jourdain. Chicago and London, The Open court publishing company, 1952 [c1915] ix, 211, [1]
15019614
*Set theory.*

**QA248.D27**
**Dauben, Joseph Warren,**
Georg Cantor : his mathematics and philosophy of the infinite / Joseph Warren Dauben. Cambridge, Mass. : Harvard University Press, 1979. ix, 404 p. ;
77-023435     512/.7     0674348710
*Cantor, Georg, -- 1845-1918.    Transfinite numbers -- History. Set theory -- History. Infinite.*

## QA248.F46 1991
**Fenrick, Maureen H.,**
Introduction to the Galois correspondence / Maureen H. Fenrick. Boston : Birkhauser, c1992. x, 189 p. :
91-031021    512    081763522X
*Galois correspondences.*

## QA248.G684 2000
**Grattan-Guinness, I.**
The search for mathematical roots, 1870-1940 : logics, set theories and the foundations of mathematics from Cantor through Russell to Godel / I. Grattan-Guinness. Princeton, N.J. : Princeton University Press, c2000. xiv, 690 p. :
00-036694    510    0691058571
*Arithmetic -- Foundations -- History -- 19th century. Arithmetic -- Foundations -- History -- 20th century. Set theory -- History -- 19th century.*

## QA248.K487 1995
**Klir, George J.,**
Fuzzy sets and fuzzy logic : theory and applications / George J. Klir and Bo Yuan. Upper Saddle River, N.J. : Prentice Hall PTR, c1995. xv, 574 p. :
94-036398    511.3    0131011715
*Fuzzy sets. Fuzzy logic.*

## QA248.P68 1990
**Potter, Michael D.**
Sets : an introduction / Michael D. Potter. Oxford ; Clarendon Press, 1990. x, 241 p. :
90-040303    511.3/2    0198533888
*Set theory.*

## QA248.S245 1996
**Sanchis, Luis E.**
Set theory, an operational approach / Luis E. Sanchis. Amsterdam, The Netherlands : Gordon and Breach, c1996. xvi, 279 p. ;
99-458373    9056995073
*Set theory.*

## QA248.S798
**Stoll, Robert Roth.**
Sets, logic, and axiomatic theories. Drawings by Evan Gillespie. San Francisco, W. H. Freeman [1961] 206 p.
61-006784    512.817
*Set theory. Logic, Symbolic and mathematical.*

## QA248.5 Algebra — Foundations of arithmetic. Set theory. Transfinite numbers — Elementary textbooks

## QA248.5.P38 1998
**Pedrycz, Witold,**
An introduction to fuzzy sets : analysis and design / Witold Pedrycz and Fernando Gomide. Cambridge, Mass. : MIT Press, c1998. xxiv, 465 p.
97-034598    006.3/01/51132    0262161710
*Fuzzy sets.*

## QA251 Algebra — Universal algebra

## QA251.S4713 1987
**Serre, Jean Pierre.**
Complex semisimple Lie algebras / Jean-Pierre Serre ; translated from the French by G.A. Jones. New York : Springer-Verlag, c1987. ix, 74 p. :
87-013037    512/.55    0387965696
*Lie algebras.*

## QA251.3 Algebra — Commutative rings and algebras

## QA251.3.C53 1998
**Chatters, A. W.**
An introductory course in commutative algebra / A.W. Chatters and C.R. Hajarnavis. Oxford ; Oxford University Press, 1998. vi, 144 p. :
97-049207    512/.24    019853423X
*Commutative algebra.*

## QA251.3.E38 1995
**Eisenbud, David.**
Commutative algebra with a view toward algebraic geometry / David Eisenbud. New York : Springer-Verlag, c1995. xvi, 785 p. :
94-017351    512/.24    0387942688
*Commutative algebra. Geometry, Algebraic.*

## QA255-266 Algebra — Complex numbers — Machine theory — General works

## QA255.H34 1994
**Hahn, Liang-shin.**
Complex numbers and geometry / Liang-shin Hahn. Washington, D.C. : Mathematical Association of America, c1994. x, 192 p. :
93-079038    516/.04    0883855100
*Numbers, Complex. Geometry, Modern.*

## QA255.N34 1998
**Nahin, Paul J.**
An imaginary tale : the story of [the square root of minus one] / Paul J. Nahin. Princeton, N.J. : Princeton University Press, c1998. xvi, 257 p. :
97-052082    515/.9    0691027951
*Numbers, Complex.*

## QA261.H33 1958
**Halmos, Paul R.**
Finite-dimensional vector spaces. Princeton, N.J., Van Nostrand [1958] 200 p.
58-008446    512.86
*Vector spaces. Transformations (Mathematics)*

**QA263.B36**
**Bellman, Richard Ernest,**
 Introduction to matrix analysis. New York, McGraw-Hill, 1960. 328 p.
59-009983          512.896
 *Matrices. Mathematical analysis.*

**QA263.P4**
**Perlis, Sam,**
 Theory of matrices. Cambridge, Mass., Addison-Wesley Press, 1952. 237 p.
51-012754          512.8
 *Matrices.*

**QA265.G55**
**Glicksman, Abraham M.**
 An introduction to linear programming and the theory of games. New York, Wiley [1963] 131 p.
63-011433          512.8
 *Linear programming. Game theory.*

**QA266.A7**
**Arnold, B. H.**
 Logic and Boolean algebra. Englewood Cliffs, N.J., Prentice-Hall, 1962. 144 p.
62-019100          512.89
 *Algebra, Boolean.*

**QA266.M254**
**Mac Lane, Saunders,**
 Algebra [by] Saunders MacLane [and] Garrett Birkhoff. New York, Macmillan [1967] xix, 598 p.
67-012338          512/.8
 *Algebra, Abstract.*

**QA266.W45**
**Whitesitt, J. Eldon**
 Boolean algebra and its applications. Reading, Mass., Addison-Wesley Pub. Co. [1961] 182 p.
61-005027          512.89
 *Algebra, Boolean.*

**QA267 Algebra — Machine theory. Abstract machines. Abstract automata — General works, treatises, and textbooks**

**QA267.C48 1987**
**Chaitin, Gregory J.**
 Algorithmic information theory / Gregory J. Chaitin. Cambridge [Cambridgeshire] ; Cambridge University Press, 1987. x, 175 p. ;
87-015876          004     0521343062
 *Machine theory. Computational complexity. LISP (Computer program language)*

**QA267.L49**
**Lewis, Harry R.**
 Elements of the theory of computation / Harry R. Lewis, Christos H. Papadimitriou. Englewood Cliffs, N.J. : Prentice-Hall, c1981. xiv, 466 p. :
80-021293          511
 *Machine theory. Formal languages. Computational complexity.*

**QA267.5 Algebra — Machine theory. Abstract machines. Abstract automata — Special types of machines, A-Z**

**QA267.5.C45.T64 1987**
**Toffoli, Tommaso.**
 Cellular automata machines : a new environment for modeling / Tommaso Toffoli, Norman Margolus. Cambridge, Mass. : MIT Press, c1987. ix, 259 p. :
86-033804          511.3     0262200600
 *Cellular automata.*

**QA267.7 Algebra — Machine theory. Abstract machines. Abstract automata — Computational complexity. Kolmogorov complexity**

**QA267.7.D8 2000**
**Du, Dingzhu.**
 Theory of computational complexity / Ding-Zhu Du, Ker-I Ko. New York : Wiley, c2000. xiii, 491 p.
99-053576          511.3     0471345067
 *Computational complexity.*

**QA267.7.P36 1994**
**Papadimitriou, Christos H.**
 Computational complexity / Christos H. Papadimitriou. Reading, Mass. : Addison-Wesley, c1994. xv, 523 p. :
          511.3 20     0201530821
 *Computational complexity.*

**QA267.7.T7 1998**
**Traub, J. F.**
 Complexity and information / J.F. Traub, A.G. Werschulz. New York : Cambridge University Press, 1998. p. cm.
98-029464          511.3     0521480051
 *Computational complexity.*

**QA268 Algebra — Machine theory. Abstract machines. Abstract automata — Coding theory**

**QA268.K585 1998**
**Koblitz, Neal,**
 Algebraic aspects of cryptography / Neal Koblitz. Berlin ; Springer, c1998. ix, 206 p. :
97-048779          005.8/2/01512     3540634460
 *Coding theory. Curves, Elliptic.*

**QA268.M65 2000**
**Mollin, Richard A.,**
An introduction to cryptography / Richard A. Mollin. Boca Raton : Chapman & Hall/CRC, c2001. xiii, 373 p.
00-055482      003/.54      1584881275
*Coding theory.*

**QA268.P74 1992**
**Pretzel, Oliver.**
Error-correcting codes and finite fields / Oliver Pretzel. Oxford : Clarendon Press ; 1992. xiii, 398 p.
92-004088      003/.54      0198596782
*Error-correcting codes (Information theory)*

**QA268.R66 1997**
**Roman, Steven.**
Introduction to coding and information theory / Steven Roman. New York : Springer, c1997. xiii, 323 p.
96-011738      005.7/2      0387947043
*Coding theory. Information theory.*

## QA269 Algebra — Game theory — General works

**QA269.B33 1989**
**Beasley, John D.**
The mathematics of games / John D. Beasley. Oxford ; Oxford University Press, 1989. viii, 169 p.
88-032453      519.3      0198532067
*Game theory.*

**QA269.B39 2000**
**Berlekamp, Elwyn R.**
The dots-and-boxes game : sophisticated child's play / Elwyn Berlekamp. Natick, Mass. : A.K. Peters, c2000. xii, 131 p. :
00-033185      519.3      1568811292
*Game theory.*

**QA269.G35 1995**
Game theory and applications / L.A. Petrosjan, V.V. Mazalov [eds.]. Commack, N.Y. : Nova Science Publishers, 1995. p. cm.
95-042812      519.3      1560722665
*Game theory.*

**QA269.M457 1998**
**Mero, Laszlo.**
Moral calculations : game theory, logic, and human frailty / Laszlo Mero. New York : Springer, 1998. p. cm.
98-017443      519.3      0387984194
*Game theory. Thought and thinking.*

**QA269.M66 1994**
**Morris, Peter,**
Introduction to game theory / Peter Morris. New York : Springer-Verlag, c1994. xvi, 230 p. :
94-006515      519.3      038794284X
*Game theory.*

**QA269.S695 1999**
**Stahl, Saul.**
A gentle introduction to game theory / Saul Stahl. Providence, R.I. : American Mathematical Society, 1999. xii, 176 p. :
98-037248      519.3      0821813390
*Game theory.*

**QA269.S77 1993**
**Straffin, Philip D.**
Game theory and strategy / by Philip D. Straffin. Washington : Mathematical Association of America, c1993. x, 244 p. :
92-064176      519.3      0883856379
*Game theory.*

**QA269.V28 1992**
**Vajda, S.**
Mathematical games and how to play them / Steven Vajda. New York : Ellis Horwood, 1992. x, 128 p. :
92-030467      519.3      0130092754
*Game theory.*

**QA269.V65 1953**
**Von Neumann, John,**
Theory of games and economic behavior, by John Von Neumann and Oskar Morgenstern. Princeton, Princeton University Press, 1953 [c1944] 641 p.
53-004426      330.182
*Game theory. Economics, Mathematical.*

## QA273.B258-273.S75343 Probabilities — General works, treatises, and textbooks

**QA273.B258 1966**
**Bartlett, M. S.**
An introduction to stochastic processes, with special reference to methods and applications, by M.S. Bartlett. Cambridge, Cambridge U.P., 1966. xvi, 362 p.
65-012497      519
*Stochastic processes.*

**QA273.B2584 1996**
**Bartoszynski, Robert.**
Probability and statistical inference / Robert Bartoszynski and Magdalena Niewiadomska-Bugaj. New York : Wiley, c1996. xvi, 826 p. :
96-004105      519.5/4      0471310735
*Probabilities. Mathematical statistics.*

**QA273.D29 1962**
**David, F. N.**
Games, gods and gambling; the origins and history of probability and statistical ideas from the earliest times to the Newtonian era. New York, Hafner Pub. Co., 1962. 275 p.
63-001601      519.1
*Probabilities -- History. Games of chance (Mathematics) -- History. Statistics -- History.*

**QA273.E4313 1993**
**Ekeland, I.**
The broken dice, and other mathematical tales of chance / Ivar Ekeland ; translated by Carol Volk. Chicago : University of Chicago Press, c1993. 183 p. ;
93-019341          519.2          0226199916
*Probabilities. Mathematical statistics.*

**QA273.E84 1999**
**Everitt, Brian.**
Chance rules : an informal guide to probability, risk, and statistics / Brian S. Everitt. New York : Springer, c1999. xiv, 202 p. :
99-011988          519.2          0387987762
*Probabilities. Chance. Mathematical statistics.*

**QA273.G3124 1996**
**Gaither, Carl C.,**
Statistically speaking : a dictionary of quotations / selected and arranged by Carl C. Gaither and Alma E. Cavazos-Gaither. Philadelphia, PA : Institute of Physics Pub., 1996. 420 p. :
96044176          519.5          0750304014
*Probabilities -- Quotations, maxims, etc. Mathematical statistics -- Quotations, maxims, etc.*

**QA273.H3544 1991**
**Hamming, R. W.**
The art of probability for scientists and engineers / Richard W. Hamming. Redwood City, Calif. : Addison-Wesley, c1991. xvii, 344 p.
90-042240          519.2          0201510588
*Probabilities.*

**QA273.I822513 1984**
**Ito, Kiyosi,**
Introduction to probability theory / Kiyosi Ito. Cambridge [Cambridgeshire] ; Cambridge University Press, 1984. ix, 213 p. ;
83-023187          519.2          0521264189
*Probabilities.*

**QA273.L685 1989**
**Lowry, Richard,**
The architecture of chance : an introduction to the logic and arithmetic of probability / Richard Lowry. New York : Oxford University Press, 1989. viii, 175 p.
88-015143          519.2          0195056078
*Probabilities. Mathematical statistics.*

**QA273.M46 1986**
**McGervey, John D.,**
Probabilities in everyday life / John D. McGervey. Chicago : Nelson-Hall, c1986. x, 269 p. :
86-002406          519.2          0830410457
*Probabilities.*

**QA273.M75**
**Moran, P. A. P.**
An introduction to probability theory [by] P. A. P. Moran. Oxford, Clarendon P., 1968. [7], 542 p.
68-092203          519/.1          0198531354
*Probabilities.*

**QA273.N29 2000**
**Nahin, Paul J.**
Duelling idiots and other probability puzzlers / Paul J. Nahin. Princeton, N.J. : Princeton University Press, c2000. xviii, 269 p.
99-087353          519.2          0691009791
*Probabilities -- Problems, exercises, etc.*

**QA273.P423 1990**
**Pfeiffer, Paul E.**
Probability for applications / Paul E. Pfeiffer. New York : Springer-Verlag, c1990. xix, 679 p. :
89-021924          519.2          0387971386
*Probabilities.*

**QA273.S7534 1994**
**Stirzaker, David.**
Elementary probability / David Stirzaker. Cambridge [England] ; Cambridge University Press, 1994. x, 406 p. :
93-012917          519.2          0521420288
*Probabilities.*

**QA273.S75343 1999**
**Stirzaker, David.**
Probability and random variables : a beginner's guide / David Stirzaker. Cambridge ; Cambridge University Press, 1999. xii, 368 p. :
98-029586          519.2          0521642973
*Probabilities. Random variables.*

## QA273.15 Probabilities — Popular works

**QA273.15.B46 1998**
**Bennett, Deborah J.,**
Randomness / Deborah J. Bennett. Cambridge, Mass. : Harvard University Press, 1998. 238 p. :
97-035054          519.2          0674107454
*Probabilities -- Popular works. Probabilities -- History. Chance -- Popular works.*

**QA273.15.H35 1999**
**Haigh, John,**
Taking chances : winning with probability / John Haigh. Oxford ; Oxford University Press, c1999. xiv, 330 p. :
98-039018          519.2          0198502923
*Probabilities -- Popular works.*

**QA273.15.O75 1999**
**Orkin, Michael.**
What are the odds? : chance in everyday life / Mike Orkin. New York : W.H. Freeman, 1999. v, 154 p. ;
99-051731          519.2          0716735601
*Probabilities -- Popular works. Chance -- Popular works.*

**QA273.15.P48 1998**
**Peterson, Ivars.**
The jungles of randomness : a mathematical safari / Ivars Peterson. New York : John Wiley & Sons, c1998. xiii, 239 p.
97-001275          519.2          0471164496
*Probabilities -- Popular works.*

### QA273.25 Probabilities — Study and teaching. Research — Problems, exercises, examinations

**QA273.25.A54 2001**
**Andel, Jiri.**
Mathematics of chance / Jiri Andel New York : Wiley, c2001. xxiii, 233 p.
00-053408          519.2          0471410896
*Probabilities -- Problems, exercises, etc.*

### QA273.4 Probabilities — Study and teaching. Research — Axioms and foundations

**QA273.4.C37**
**Carnap, Rudolf,**
Studies in inductive logic and probability. Rudolf Carnap and Richard C. Jeffrey, editors. Berkeley, University of California Press, 1971-80. 2 v.
77-136025          519.2          0520018664
*Probabilities. Induction (Mathematics)*

## QA273.5 Probabilities — Geometric probability. Stochastic geometry

**QA273.5.K47 1997**
**Klain, Daniel A.**
Introduction to geometric probability / Daniel A. Klain, Gian-Carlo Rota. Cambridge, UK ; Cambridge University Press, 1997. xiv, 178 p. ;
98-118504          519.2          052159362X
*Geometric probabilities.*

## QA273.6 Probabilties — Distributions. Characteristic functions

**QA273.6.T67 1990**
**Tong, Y. L.**
The multivariate normal distribution / Y.L. Tong. New York : Springer-Verlag, c1990. xii, 271 p. ;
89-021929          519.2/4          0387970622
*Distribution (Probability theory) Multivariate analysis.*

### QA274.D87-R46 Probabilties — Stochastic processes — General works, treatises, and textbooks

**QA274.D87 1999**
**Durrett, Richard,**
Essentials of stochastic processes / Rick Durrett. New York : Springer, c1999. vi, 281 p. :
99-014733          519.2          038798836X
*Stochastic processes.*

**QA274.R46 1992**
**Resnick, Sidney I.**
Adventures in stochastic processes / Sidney Resnick. Boston : Birkhauser, c1992. xii, 626 p. :
92-004431          519.2          0817635912
*Stochastic processes.*

### QA274.42 Probabilties — Stochastic processes — Point processes

**QA274.42.K56 1993**
**Kingman, J. F. C.**
Poisson processes / J.F.C. Kingman. Oxford : Clarendon Press ; 1993. viii, 104 p.
92-025532          519.2/3          0198536933
*Poisson processes.*

### QA274.7 Probabilties — Stochastic processes — Markov processes. Markov chains

**QA274.7.N67 1997**
**Norris, J. R.**
Markov chains / J.R. Norris. New York : Cambridge University Press, 1997. p. cm.
96-031570          519.2/33          0521481813
*Markov processes.*

## QA275 Theory of errors. Least squares

**QA275.D86 1989**
**Dunn, G.**
Design and analysis of reliability studies : the statistical evaluation of measurement errors / Graham Dunn. New York : Oxford University Press ; 1989. viii, 198 p.
89-037696          511/.43          0195207041
*Error analysis (Mathematics)*

## QA276.H22-276.W523 Mathematical statistics — General works

**QA276.H22 1991**
**Hahn, Gerald J.**
Statistical intervals : a guide for practitioners / Gerald J. Hahn, William Q. Meeker. New York : Wiley, c1991. xvii, 392 p.
91-008728          519.5          0471887692
*Mathematical statistics.*

**QA276.H57 1984**
**Hoel, Paul Gerhard,**
Introduction to mathematical statistics / Paul G. Hoel. New York : Wiley, c1984. x, 435 p. :
83-019818          519.5          0471890456
*Mathematical statistics.*

**QA276.K254 1999**
**Kelley, D. Lynn.**
Measurement made accessible : a research approach using qualitative, quantitative, and quality improvement methods / by D. Lynn Kelley. Thousand Oaks, Calif. : Sage Publications, c1999. xi, 211 p. :
99-006316          001.4/22          0761910239
*Statistics -- Methodology.*

**QA276.K565 2000**
**Knight, Keith.**
  Mathematical statistics / Keith Knight. Boca Raton : Chapman & Hall/CRC Press, c2000. 481 p. :
99-056997          519.5          158488178X
  *Mathematical statistics.*

**QA276.M375 2000**
**May, William D.**
  So much data so little math : how to predict data trends, 5 easy profitable methods / William D. May. Lanham : University Press of America, c2000. 171 p. :
99-462020          658.4/033          0761816402
  *Mathematical statistics.*

**QA276.P285 1998**
**Paulos, John Allen.**
  Once upon a number : the hidden mathematical logic of stories / John Allen Paulos. New York : Basic Books, 1998. p. cm.
98-039252          519.5          0465051588
  *Mathematical statistics.  Logic, Symbolic and mathematical.*

**QA276.R375 1991**
**Rasmussen, Shelley,**
  An introduction to statistics with data analysis / Shelley Rasmussen. Pacific Grove, Calif. : Brooks/Cole Pub. Co., c1992. xix, 707 p. :
91-009035          519.5          0534135781
  *Mathematical statistics.*

**QA276.R425 2000**
**Rencher, Alvin C.,**
  Linear models in statistics / Alvin C. Rencher. New York : Wiley, 2000. xviii, 578 p.
99-030176          519.5/35          0471315648
  *Linear models (Statistics)*

**QA276.W4 1961**
**Weatherburn, Charles Ernest,**
  A first course in mathematical statistics. Cambridge [Eng.] University Press, 1961. 277 p.
61-019163          519.9
  *Mathematical statistics.*

**QA276.W523 1996**
**Williams, John Delane,**
  Statistical methods / John Delane Williams. Lanham, Md. : University Press of America, c1996. xv, 365 p. :
95-044362          519.5          0761801731
  *Mathematical statistics.*

## QA276.12 Mathematical statistics — Elementary texts

**QA276.12.C69 1987**
**Cox, C. Philip**
  A handbook of introductory statistical methods / C. Philip Cox. New York : Wiley, 1987. xxi, 272 p. :
86-013137          001.4/22          0471819719
  *Statistics.*

**QA276.12.L66 1998**
**Lomax, Richard G.**
  Statistical concepts : a second course for education and the behavioral sciences / Richard G. Lomax. Mahwah, N.J. : L. Erlbaum Associates, c1998. xxi, 362 p. ;
97-046865          519.5          0805830510
  *Statistics.*

**QA276.12.L67 2001**
**Lomax, Richard G.**
  An introduction to statistical concepts for education and behavioral sciences / Richard G. Lomax. Mahwah, N.J. : Lawrence Erlbaum Associates, c2001. xv, 520 p. :
99-055432          519.5          0805827498
  *Statistics.  Environmental sciences -- Statistical methods.*

**QA276.12.U75 2001**
**Urdan, Timothy C.**
  Statistics in plain English / by Timothy C. Urdan. Mahwah, N.J. : Lawrence Erlbaum Association, Publishers, 2001. xi, 149 p. :
00-061755          519.5          0805834427
  *Statistics.*

**QA276.12.W52 2000**
**Wheater, C. Philip,**
  Using statistics to understand the environment / C. Philip Wheater and Penny A. Cook ; illustrated by Jo Wright. London ; Routledge, 2000. p. cm.
99-040009          519.5          0415198879
  *Statistics.  Environmental sciences -- Statistical methods.*

## QA276.15 Mathematical statistics — History

**QA276.15.D39 2000**
**David, H. A.**
  Annotated readings in the history of statistics / H.A. David, A.W.F. Edwards. New York : Springer, c2000. xiv, 252 p. ;
00-041977          519.5/09          0387988440
  *Mathematical statistics -- History.*

**QA276.15.E84 1998**
**Everitt, Brian.**
  The Cambridge dictionary of statistics / B.S. Everitt. Cambridge, UK ; Cambridge University Press, 1998. viii, 360 p.
98-036045          519.5/03          0521593468
  *Mathematical statistics -- Dictionaries.*

**QA276.15.H35 1998**
**Hald, Anders,**
  A history of mathematical statistics from 1750 to 1930 / Anders Hald. New York : Wiley, c1998. xvii, 795 p.
97-019513          519.5/09          0471179124
  *Mathematical statistics -- History.*

**QA276.15.P47 1987**
**Peters, William Stanley,**
 Counting for something : statistical principles and personalities / William S. Peters. New York : Springer-Verlag, c1987. xviii, 275 p.
86-011866          519.5/09          0387963642
 *Statistics -- History.*

**QA276.15.S755 1999**
**Stigler, Stephen M.**
 Statistics on the table : the history of statistical concepts and methods / Stephen M. Stigler. Cambridge, Mass. : Harvard University Press, 1999. ix, 488 p. :
99-013719          519.5/09          0674836014
 *Mathematical statistics -- History.*

## QA276.156 Mathematical statistics — Biography — Collective

**QA276.156.L43 1997**
 Leading personalities in statistical sciences : from the 17th century to the present / [edited by] Norman L. Johnson and Samuel Kotz. New York : Wiley, c1997. xxiii, 399 p.
97-009152          510/.92/2          0471163813
 *Statisticians -- Biography.*

## QA276.25 Mathematical statistics — Handbooks, tables, formulas, etc.

**QA276.25.B48 1968**
**Beyer, William H.,**
 CRC handbook of tables for probability and statistics. Editor: William H. Beyer. Cleveland, Chemical Rubber Co. [1968] xiv, 642 p.
68-005038          519/.0212
 *Mathematical statistics -- Tables. Probabilities -- Tables.*

**QA276.25.L56 1995**
**Lindley, D. V.**
 New Cambridge statistical tables / D.V. Lindley & W.F. Scott. Cambridge ; Cambridge University Press, 1995. 96 p. :
94-039991          519.5/0212          0521484855
 *Mathematical statistics -- Tables.*

## QA276.4 Mathematical statistics — Data processing

**QA276.4.A24 1999**
**Abell, Martha L.,**
 Statistics with Mathematica / Martha L. Abell, James P. Braselton, John A. Rafter. San Diego : Academic Press, c1999. xiv, 632 p. :
98-027879          519.5/0285/53          0120415542
 *Mathematical statistics -- Data processing.*

**QA276.4.M65 2001**
**Monahan, John F.**
 Numerical methods of statistics / John F. Monahan. Cambridge ; Cambridge University Press, 2001. xiv, 428 p. :
00-031269          519.5          0521791685
 *Mathematical statistics -- Data processing.*

**QA276.4.R33 1999**
**Rabe-Hesketh, S.**
 Handbook of statistical analysis using Stata / Sophia Rabe-Hesketh, Brian Everitt. Boca Raton, FL : Chapman & Hall/CRC, c1999. xi, 215 p. :
98-044800          519.5/0285/5369
 *Mathematical statistics -- Data processing.*

## QA276.6 Mathematical statistics — Sampling theory

**QA276.6.C6 1977**
**Cochran, William Gemmell,**
 Sampling techniques / William G. Cochran. New York : Wiley, c1977. xvi, 428 p. :
77-000728          001.4/222          047116240X
 *Sampling (Statistics)*

**QA276.6.T58 1992**
**Thompson, Steven K.,**
 Sampling / Steven K. Thompson. New York : Wiley, c1992. xv, 343 p. :
92-007099          519.5/2          0471540455
 *Sampling (Statistics)*

## QA277 Mathematical statistics — Testing of hypotheses — General works

**QA277.R395 1989**
**Rayner, J. C. W.**
 Smooth tests of goodness of fit / J.C.W. Rayner, D.J. Best. New York : Oxford University Press, 1989. xiv, 162 p. :
88-034489          519.5/6          0195056108
 *Goodness-of-fit tests.*

## QA278 Mathematical statistics — Multivariate analysis — General works

**QA278.B55 1999**
**Bilodeau, Martin,**
 Theory of multivariate statistics / Martin Bilodeau, David Brenner. New York : Springer, c1999. xiv, 288 p. :
99-026378          519.5/35          0387987398
 *Multivariate analysis.*

**QA278.D545 1994**
**Diggle, Peter.**
 Analysis of longitudinal data / Peter J. Diggle, Kung-Yee Liang, and Scott L. Zeger. Oxford : Clarendon Press ; 1994. xi, 253 p. :
94-001859          519.5/35          0198522843
 *Multivariate analysis. Time-series analysis. Longitudinal method.*

**QA278.G433 1993**
**Geer, J. P. van de**
Multivariate analysis of categorical data / John P. van de Geer. Newbury Park, CA : Sage, c1993 v. 2 :
93-003706          519.5/35          0803945647
*Multivariate analysis.*

**QA278.K73 1988**
**Krzanowski, W. J.**
Principles of multivariate analysis : a user's perspective / W.J. Krzanowski. Oxford [Oxfordshire] : Clarendon Press ; 1988. xxi, 563 p. :
87-031363          519.5/35          0198522118
*Multivariate analysis.*

**QA278.R32 2000**
Reading and understanding more multivariate statistics / edited by Laurence G. Grimm and Paul R. Yarnold. Washington, DC : American Psychological Association, c2000. xiii, 437 p.
00-035556          519.5/35          1557986983
*Multivariate analysis.  Psychometrics.*

**QA278.R45 1995**
**Rencher, Alvin C.,**
Methods of multivariate analysis / Alvin C. Rencher. New York : Wiley, c1995. xvi, 627 p. :
94-023567          519.5/35          0471571520
*Multivariate analysis.*

## QA278.2 Mathematical statistics — Multivariate analysis — Regression analysis.  Correlation analysis

**QA278.2.K34 2001**
**Kahane, Leo H.**
Regression basics / by Leo H. Kahane. Thousand Oaks, [Calif.] : Sage Publications, c2001. xi, 202 p. :
00-013066          519.5/36          0761919589
*Regression analysis.*

**QA278.2.A434 1997**
**Allen, Michael Patrick.**
Understanding regression analysis / Michael Patrick Allen. New York : Plenum Press, c1997. ix, 216 p. :
97-020373          519.5/36          0306456486
*Regression analysis.*

## QA278.7 Mathematical statistics — Order statistics

**QA278.7.A74 1993**
**Arnold, Barry C.**
A first course in order statistics / Barry C. Arnold, N. Balakrishnan, H.N. Nagaraja. New York : Wiley, c1992. xvii, 279 p.
92-013253          519.5          0471574163
*Order statistics.*

**QA278.7.H36 1996**
**Harter, H. Leon**
CRC handbook of tables for the use of order statistics in estimation / H. Leon Harter, N. Balakrishnan. Boca Raton, Fla. : CRC Press, c1996. xvii, 669 p.
96-000103          519.5/44          084939452X
*Order statistics -- Tables.*

## QA279 Mathematical statistics — Nonparametric methods — General works

**QA279.C56 1997**
**Clarke, G. M.**
Introduction to the design and analysis of experiments / Geoffrey M. Clarke, Robert E. Kempson. London : Arnold ; 1997. viii, 344 p.
97-119753          001.4/34          0340645555
*Experimental design.*

**QA279.C625 1998**
**Cobb, George W.**
Introduction to design and analysis of experiments / George W. Cobb. New York : Springer, c1998. xxx, 795 p. :
97-000996          001.4/34          0387946071
*Experimental design.  Analysis of variance.*

**QA279.K83 1992**
**Kubackova, Ludmila.**
Foundations of experimental data analysis / Ludmila Kubackova. Boca Raton : CRC Press, c1992. 368 p. :
92-033001          519.5          0849377366
*Experimental design.*

**QA279.M373 1989**
**Mason, Robert L.,**
Statistical design and analysis of experiments : with applications to engineering and science / Robert L. Mason, Richard F. Gunst, James L. Hess. New York : Wiley, c1989. xvi, 692 p. :
88-020893          519.5          047185364X
*Experimental design.  Mathematical statistics.*

**QA279.T494 1999**
**Thompson, James R.**
Simulation : a modeler's approach / James R. Thompson. New York : Wiley, c2000. xx, 297 p. :
99-033022          003          0471251844
*Experimental design.  Mathematical models.  Mathematical statistics.*

**QA279.T86 2001**
**Turner, J. Rick.**
Introduction to analysis of variance : design, analysis, & interpretation / J. Rick Turner, Julian F. Thayer. Thousand Oaks, Calif. : Sage Publications, c2001. xii, 180 p. :
00-013065          519.5/38          0803970749
*Experimental design.  Mathematical models.  Mathematical statistics.*

## QA280 Mathematical statistics — Time series analysis

**QA280.N34 1996**
**Naidu, Prabhakar S.**
Modern spectrum analysis of time series / Prabhakar S. Naidu. Boca Raton : CRC Press, c1996. 399 p. :
95-032335          519.5/5          0849324645
*Time-series analysis. Spectral theory (Mathematics)*

**QA280.P47 2000**
**Percival, Donald B.**
Wavelet methods for time series analysis / Donald B. Percival, Andrew T. Walden. Cambridge ; Cambridge University Press, 2000. xxv, 594 p. :
00-029246          519.5/5          0521640687
*Time-series analysis. Wavelets (Mathematics)*

## QA295 Mathematical statistics — Series

**QA295.E8413 1988**
**Euler, Leonhard,**
Introduction to analysis of the infinite / Leonhard Euler ; translated by John D. Blanton. New York : Springer-Verlag, c1988-c1990. 2 v. :
88-018475          515/.243          0387968245
*Series, Infinite -- Early works to 1800. Products, Infinite – Early works to 1800. Continued fractions -- Early works to 1800.*

**QA295.K72**
**Knopp, Konrad,**
Infinite sequences and series; translated by Frederick Bagemihl. New York, Dover Publications [1956] 186 p.
56-003667          512.4
*Series, Infinite. Processes, Infinite.*

## QA297 Numerical analysis — General works, treatises, and textbooks

**QA297.A52 1997**
**Shampine, Lawrence F.**
Fundamentals of numerical computing / L.F. Shampine, R.C. Allen, Jr., S. Pruess. New York : John Wiley, 1997. x, 268 p. :
96-022074          519.4/0285/51          0471163635
*Numerical analysis -- Data processing.*

**QA297.A53 1998**
**Allen, Myron B.,**
Numerical analysis for applied science / Myron B. Allen III, Eli L. Isaacson. New York : Wiley, c1998. xi, 492 p. :
97-016688          519.4          0471552666
*Numerical analysis.*

**QA297.A84**
**Atkinson, Kendall E.**
An introduction to numerical analysis / Kendall E. Atkinson. New York : Wiley, c1978. xiii, 587 p.
78-006706          519.4          0471029859
*Numerical analysis.*

**QA297.E56213 1996**
**Engeln-Mullges, Gisela.**
Numerical algorithms with C / Gisela Engeln-Mullges, Frank Uhlig ; [translated by Maria Schon and Frank Uhlig ; CD-ROM with ANSI-C programs by Albert Becker, Jurgen Dietel, and Uli Eggermann]. Berlin ; Springer, c1996. xxii, 596 p.
96-023158          519.4/0285/5133          3540605304
*Numerical analysis. Numerical analysis -- Computer programs. C (Computer program language)*

**QA297.I8 1994**
**Isaacson, Eugene.**
Analysis of numerical methods / Eugene Isaacson, Herbert Bishop Keller. New York : Dover Publications, 1994. xv, 541 p. :
          519.4 20
*Numerical analysis.*

**QA297.N866 1992**
Numerical recipes in FORTRAN : the art of scientific computing / William H. Press ... [et al.]. Cambridge [England] ; Cambridge University Press, 1992. xxvi, 963 p.
92-008876          519.4/0285/53          052143064X
*Numerical analysis -- Computer programs. Science -- Mathematics -- Computer programs. FORTRAN (Computer program language)*

**QA297.O778 1999**
**Ortega, James M.,**
An introduction to C++ and numerical methods / James M. Ortega, Andrew S. Grimshaw. New York : Oxford University Press, 1999. x, 273 p. ;
97-036115          519.4/0285/5133          0195117670
*Numerical analysis -- Data processing. C++ (Computer program language)*

**QA297.P69 1998**
**Pozrikidis, C.**
Numerical computation in science and engineering / C. Pozrikidis. New York : Oxford University Press, 1998. xi, 627 p. :
97-038185          519.4          0195112539
*Numerical analysis.*

**QA297.T5 1992**
**Thompson, William J.**
Computing for scientists and engineers : a workbook of analysis, numerics, and applications / William J. Thompson. New York : Wiley, c1992. xiii, 444 p.
92-016744          519.4          0471547182
*Numerical analysis -- Data processing. Science -- Data processing. Engineering -- Data processing.*

**QA297.T58 1977**
**Todd, John,**
  Basic numerical mathematics / by John Todd. Basel : Birkhauser Verlag, 1977-1979. 2 v. :
78-312462          519.4      3764307293
  *Numerical analysis. Numerical analysis -- Data processing.*

**QA297.T88 2001**
**Turner, Peter R.,**
  Guide to scientific computing / Peter R. Turner. 2nd ed. Boca Raton, FL : CRC Press, c2001. ix, 301 p. :
              519.4 21          0849312426
  *Numerical anaylsis.*

**QA297.U2413 1997**
**Ueberhuber, Christoph W.,**
  Numerical computation : methods, software, and analysis / Christoph W. Ueberhuber. Berlin ; Springer, c1997. 2 v. :
96-046772          519.4/0285/53      3540620583
  *Numerical analysis -- Data processing.*

## QA297.6 Numerical analysis — Smoothing — Curve fitting

**QA297.6.D54 1993**
**Dierckx, Paul.**
  Curve and surface fitting with splines / Paul Dierckx. Oxford ; Clarendon, 1993. xvii, 285 p.
92-021545          519.4      0198534418
  *Curve fitting. Spline theory.*

# QA300 Analysis — General works, treatises, and textbooks

**QA300.A573**
**Apostol, Tom M.**
  Mathematical analysis; a modern approach to advanced calculus. Reading, Mass., Addison-Wesley Pub. Co. [1957] 553 p.
57-008707          517
  *Mathematical analysis.*

**QA300.B457 1994**
**Berberian, Sterling K.,**
  A first course in real analysis / Sterling K. Berberian. New York : Springer-Verlag, c1994. xi, 237 p. :
93-046020          515      0387942173
  *Mathematical analysis. Numbers, Real.*

**QA300.B69 1998**
**Bridges, D. S.**
  Foundations of real and abstract analysis / Douglas S. Bridges. New York : Springer, c1998. xiv, 322 p. ;
97-010649          515      0387982396
  *Mathematical analysis.*

**QA300.B727 1996**
**Browder, Andrew.**
  Mathematical analysis : an introduction / Andrew Browder. New York : Springer, c1996. xiv, 333 p. :
95-044877          515      0387946144
  *Mathematical analysis.*

**QA300.C32 2000**
**Carothers, N. L.,**
  Real analysis / N.L. Carothers. Cambridge [UK] ; Cambridge University Press, 2000. xiii, 401 p.
98-031982          515      0521497493
  *Mathematical analysis.*

**QA300.D74 2001**
**Dshalalow, Jewgeni H.**
  Real analysis : an introduction to the theory of real functions and integration / Jewgeni H. Dshalalow. Boca Raton : Chapman & Hall/CRC, c2001. xiii, 567 p.
00-058593          515      1584880732
  *Mathematical analysis.*

**QA300.G42 1995**
**Gelbaum, Bernard R.**
  Modern real and complex analysis / Bernard R. Gelbaum. New York : Wiley, c1995. xi, 489 p. :
94-023715          515      0471107158
  *Mathematical analysis.*

**QA300.H352 1996**
**Hairer, E.**
  Analysis by its history / E. Hairer, G. Wanner. New York : Springer-Verlag, c1996. x, 377 p. :
95-004589          515      0387945512
  *Mathematical analysis.*

**QA300.J82 1997**
**Jordan, D. W.**
  Mathematical techniques : an introduction for the engineering, physical, and mathematical sciences / D.W. Jordan and P. Smith. Oxford ; Oxford University Press, 1997. xviii, 788 p.
97-222942          515      0198564627
  *Mathematical analysis.*

**QA300.L27**
**Lang, Serge,**
  Analysis I. Reading, Mass., Addison-Wesley Pub. Co. [1968] xi, 460 p.
68-017565          517
  *Mathematical analysis.*

**QA300.L273**
**Lang, Serge,**
  Analysis II. Reading, Mass., Addison-Wesley Pub. Co. [1969] xi, 476 p.
69-016750          517
  *Mathematical analysis.*

**QA300.L54 1997**
Lieb, Elliott H.
 Analysis / Elliott H. Lieb, Michael Loss. Providence, R.I. : American Mathematical Society, c1997. xviii, 278 p.
96-031605  515  0821806327
*Mathematical analysis.*

**QA300.M275 2000**
McGehee, O. Carruth.
 An introduction to complex analysis / O. Carruth McGehee. New York : John Wiley, c2000. xxiii, 425 p.
00-042256  515  047133233X
*Mathematical analysis.*

**QA300.R312 2000**
Rahman, M.
 Mathematical methods with applications / M. Rahman. Southampton, UK ; WIT Press, c2000. 436, [2] p. :
99-068742  515  1853128473
*Mathematical analysis.*

**QA300.R8 1964**
Rudin, Walter,
 Principles of mathematical analysis. New York, McGraw-Hill [1964] ix, 270 p.
63-021479  517
*Mathematical analysis.*

**QA300.S4315 1995**
Shankar, Ramamurti.
 Basic training in mathematics : a fitness program for science students / R. Shankar. New York : Plenum Press, c1995. xv, 365 p. :
95-013532  515  0306450356
*Mathematical analysis.*

**QA300.S882 1999**
Stahl, Saul.
 Real analysis : a historical approach / Saul Stahl. New York : J. Wiley, c1999. xiii, 269 p.
99-021917  515  0471318523
*Mathematical analysis. Functions of real variables.*

**QA300.T48 1988**
Thurston, H. A.
 Intermediate mathematical analysis / Hugh Thurston. Oxford : Clarendon Press ; 1988. vii, 164 p. ;
88-006973  515  0198532911
*Mathematical analysis.*

## QA302 Analysis — Early works through 1800

**QA302.E8513 2000**
Euler, Leonhard,
 Foundations of differential calculus / Leonhard Euler ; translated by John D. Blanton. New York : Springer, 2000. xiv, 194 p. ;
99-043386  515/.3  0387985344
*Differential calculus -- Early works to 1800.*

## QA303 Analysis — Calculus — General works, treatises, and textbooks

**QA303.A325 1997**
Acheson, David.
 From calculus to chaos : an introduction to dynamics / David Acheson. Oxford : Oxford University Press, c1997. ix, 269 :
98-121000  515  0198500777
*Calculus. Mathematics.*

**QA303.A62 1993**
 Applications of calculus / Philip Straffin, editor ; writers for this volume, Clark Benson ... [et al.]. [Washington, D.C.] : Mathematical Association of America, [c1993] xiv, 262 p. :
92-062281  515  0883850850
*Calculus.*

**QA303.B38 2001**
Bear, H. S.
 Understanding calculus : a user's guide / H.S. Bear. New York : IEEE Press, c2001. xv, 207 p. :
00-033522  515  0780360184
*Calculus.*

**QA303.B488 1995**
Berlinski, David.
 A tour of the calculus / David Berlinski. New York : Pantheon Books, c1995. xvii, 331 p.
95-004042  515  0679426450
*Calculus -- Popular works.*

**QA303.B69**
Boyer, Carl B.
 The history of the calculus and its conceptual development. (The concepts of the calculus) with a foreword by Richard Courant. [New York] Dover [1959] 346 p.
60003661
 *Mathematics -- Philosophy. Mathematics -- History. Calculus.*

**QA303.C578 1989**
Cipra, Barry.
 Misteaks [sic] and how to find them before the teacher does / Barry Cipra. Boston : Academic Press, c1989. 65 p. :
88-046167  515  012174695X
*Calculus. Calculus -- Problems, exercises, etc.*

**QA303.C838**
Courant, Richard,
 Introduction to calculus and analysis [by] Richard Courant and Fritz John. New York, Interscience Publishers [1965-74] 2 v.
65-016403  515  0471178624
*Calculus. Mathematical analysis.*

**QA303.D77 1982**
Downing, Douglas.
 Calculus the easy way / Douglas Downing. Woodbury, N.Y. : Barron's Educational Series, Inc., c1982. xii, 273 p. :
82-001609  515  0812025881
*Calculus.*

**QA303.G94 1989**
**Guicciardini, Niccolo.**
The development of Newtonian calculus in Britain, 1700-1800 / Niccolo Guicciardini. Cambridge [England] ; Cambridge University Press, 1989. xii, 228 p. ;
89-007085          515/.0941/09033          0521364663
*Calculus -- Great Britain -- History -- 18th century.*

**QA303.H154 1998**
**Hahn, Alexander,**
Basic calculus : from Archimedes to Newton to its role in science / Alexander J. Hahn. New York : Springer, c1998. xiv, 545 p. :
97-000997          515/.09          0387946063
*Calculus -- History.*

**QA303.H747 1995**
**Hsiang, Wu Yi,**
A concise introduction to calculus / W.Y. Hsiang. Singapore ; World Scientific, c1995. vii, 157 p. :
95-015402          515          9810219008
*Calculus.*

**QA303.H79 1999**
**Hubbard, John H.**
Vector calculus, linear algebra, and differential forms : a unified approach / John H. Hubbard and Barbara B. Hubbard. Upper Saddle River, N.J. : Prentice Hall, 1999. p. cm.
98-035966          515          0136574467
*Calculus. Algebras, Linear.*

**QA303.M826 1997**
Multivariable calculus / William G. McCallum ... [et al.] ; with the assistance of Paul M.N. Feehan, Adrian Iovita. New York : Wiley, c1997. xv, 503 p. :
97-133524          515/.84          0471311510
*Calculus.*

**QA303.R34 1993**
Readings for calculus / Underwood Dudley, editor. [Washington, DC] : Mathematical Association of America, c1993. xiv, 196 p. :
92-062283          515/.09          0883850877
*Calculus -- History -- Sources.*

**QA303.S845**
**Courant, Richard,**
Differential and integral calculus, by R. Courant ... translated by E.J. McShane ... New York, Nordemann Publishing Company, inc., 1938 ['36] 2 v.
39030516          517.1
*Calculus.*

**QA303.T205 1989**
**Taylor, Claudia,**
Calculus with applications / Claudia Dunham Taylor, Lawrence Gilligan. Pacific Grove, Calif. : Brooks/Cole Pub. Co., c1989. xiv, 700 p. :
88-032122          515          0534102727
*Calculus.*

**QA303.W66 1998**
**Woods, R. Grant.**
Calculus mysteries and thrillers / R. Grant Woods. Washington, DC : Mathematical Association of America, c1998. xix, 131 p. :
98-085638          515          0883857111
*Calculus -- Problems, exercises, etc. Project method in teaching.*

**QA303.Y724 1992**
**Young, Robert M.**
Excursions in calculus : an interplay of the continuous and the discrete / Robert M. Young. [Washington, D.C.] : Mathematical Association of America, c1992. xiv, 417 p. :
91-067385          515          0883853175
*Calculus.*

## QA303.5.A-Z Analysis — Calculus — Special topics, A-Z

**QA303.5.C65.C66 1998**
**Coombes, Kevin Robert,**
Multivariable calculus and Mathematica : with applications to geometry and physics / Kevin R. Coombes, Ronald L. Lipsman, Jonathan M. Rosenberg. New York, NY : Springer, c1998. xiii, 283 p.
97-044764          515/.84/078553042
0387983600
*Calculus -- Computer-assisted instruction.*

**QA303.5.D37.S77 1993**
**Stroyan, K. D.**
Calculus using Mathematica / K.D. Stroyan. Boston : Academic Press, c1993. xxv, 532 p. :
93-011835          514/.0285/5369          0126729719
*Calculus -- Data processing. Macintosh (Computer) -- Programming.*

## QA308-312 Analysis — Calculus — Integral calculus

**QA308.P75 1997**
**Priestley, H. A.**
Introduction to integration / H.A. Priestley. Oxford : Clarendon Press ; 1997. x, 306 :
98-113423          515/.43          0198501242
*Integrals.*

**QA312.L43 1966**
**Lebesgue, Henri Leon,**
Measure and the integral. Edited with a biographical essay by Kenneth O. May. San Francisco, Holden-Day, 1966. xii, 194 p.
66-026682          517.3
*Measure theory. Integrals, Generalized. Lebesgue integral.*

## QA315 Analysis — Calculus — Calculus of variations

**QA315.B5**
**Bliss, Gilbert Ames,**
   Calculus of variations, by Gilbert Ames Bliss. Chicago, Ill., Pub. for the Mathematical Association of America [c1925] xiii, 189 p.
25010087
   *Calculus of variations.*

## QA320 Analysis — Functional analysis — General works

**QA320.B63 1990**
**Boccara, Nino.**
   Functional analysis : an introduction for physicists / Nino Boccara. Boston : Academic Press, c1990. xiii, 327 p.
90-036210          515/.7     0121088103
   *Functional analysis.*

**QA320.B64 1990**
**Bollobas, Bela.**
   Linear analysis : an introductory course / Bela Bollobas. Cambridge [England] ; Cambridge University Press, c1990. xi, 240 p. ;
90026882          515/.7     0521387299
   *Functional analysis.*

**QA320.R433 1998**
**Reddy, B. Dayanand,**
   Introductory functional analysis : with applications to boundary value problems and finite elements / B. Daya Reddy. New York : Springer, c1998. xiv, 471 p. :
97-024052          515/.7     0387983074
   *Functional analysis.*

## QA322.4 Analysis — Functional analysis — Inner product spaces. Banach spaces

**QA322.4.C64 1989**
**Cohen, David W.**
   An introduction to Hilbert space and quantum logic / David W. Cohen. New York : Springer-Verlag, c1989. xii, 149 p. :
88-024989          515.7/33     0387968709
   *Hilbert space. Quantum logic.*

**QA322.4.D43 1990**
**Debnath, Lokenath.**
   Introduction to Hilbert spaces with applications / Lokenath Debnath, Piotr Mikusinski. Boston : Academic Press, c1990. xiv, 509 p. :
89-018245          515/.733     0122084357
   *Hilbert space.*

**QA322.4.Y68 1988**
**Young, Nicholas.**
   An introduction to Hilbert space / Nicholas Young. Cambridge [England] ; Cambridge University Press, 1988. 239 p. ;
87-024903          515.7/33     0521330718
   *Hilbert space.*

## QA326 Analysis — Functional analysis — Topological algebras. Banach algebras

**QA326.F55 1996**
**Fillmore, Peter A.,**
   A user's guide to operator algebras / Peter A. Fillmore. New York : Wiley, c1996. xii, 223 p. :
95-038340          512/.55     0471311359
   *Operator algebras.*

**QA326.W47 1976**
**Wermer, John.**
   Banach algebras and several complex variables / John Wermer. New York : Springer-Verlag, 1976. ix, 161 p. ;
75-034306          512/.55     0387901604
   *Banach algebras. Functions of several complex variables.*

## QA331 Analysis — Theory of functions — General works, treatises, and advanced textbooks

**QA331.A45 1979**
**Ahlfors, Lars Valerian,**
   Complex analysis : an introduction to the theory of analytic functions of one complex variable / Lars V. Ahlfors. New York : McGraw-Hill, c1979. xiv, 331 p. :
78-017078          515/.93     0070006571
   *Analytic functions.*

**QA331.B797 1997**
**Bump, Daniel,**
   Automorphic forms and representations / Daniel Bump. Cambridge ; Cambridge University Press, 1997. xiv, 574 p. ;
96-001128          515/.9     052155098X
   *Automorphic forms. Representations of groups. Lie groups.*

**QA331.J66 1987**
**Jones, Gareth A.**
   Complex functions : an algebraic and geometric viewpoint / Gareth A. Jones and David Singerman. Cambridge [Cambridgeshire] ; Cambridge University Press, 1987. xiv, 342 p. ;
85-019031          515.9     0521308933
   *Functions of complex variables.*

**QA331.L7913 1988**
**Lojasiewicz, Stanislaw.**
   An introduction to the theory of real functions / Stanislaw Lojasiewicz ; translated by G.H. Lawden ; edited by A.V. Ferreira. Chichester [West Sussex] ; Wiley, c1988. ix, 230 p. ;
87-030432          515     0471914142
   *Functions.*

**QA331.L818 1984**
**Luecking, D. H.**
 Complex analysis : a functional analysis approach / D.H. Luecking, L.A. Rubel. New York : Springer-Verlag, c1984. vi, 176 p. :
84-005354         515.9         0387909931
 *Functions of complex variables. Functional analysis.*


**QA331.M866 1997**
**Muller, J. M.**
 Elementary functions : algorithms and implementation / J.M. Muller. Boston : Birkhauser, c1997. xv, 204 p. :
97-020183         512.9/22/0285         081763990X
 *Functions -- Data processing. Algorithms.*


**QA331.T385 1997**
**Thompson, William J.**
 Atlas for computing mathematical functions : an illustrated guide for practitioners, with programs in C and Mathematica / William J. Thompson. New York : Wiley, c1997. xiv, 903 p. :
96-032557         511.3/3         0471002607
 *Functions -- Computer programs. Science -- Mathematics -- Computer programs. C (Computer program language)*


### QA331.3 Analysis — Theory of functions — Elementary textbooks

**QA331.3.D38 1998**
**Davis, Marsha Jane,**
 Precalculus in context : projects for the real world / Marsha J. Davis, Judith Flagg Moran, Mary E. Murphy. Pacific Grove, CA : Brooks/Cole Pub. Co., c1998. xvii, 311 p.
97-043190         512.9/6/078         0534352324
 *Functions.*


### QA331.5 Analysis — Theory of functions — Functions of real variables

**QA331.5.K713 1991**
**Krantz, Steven G.**
 Real analysis and foundations / Steven G. Krantz. Boca Raton, Fla. : CRC Press, c1991. xiv, 295 p. ;
91-026891         515/.8         0849371562
 *Functions of real variables. Mathematical analysis.*


**QA331.5.M413 1991**
**Medvedev, F. A.**
 Scenes from the history of real functions / Fyodor A. Medvedev ; translated from the Russian by Roger Cooke. Basel ; Birkhauser Verlag, 1991. 265 p. ;
91-039148         515/.8/09         0817625720
 *Functions of real variables -- History.*


**QA331.5.S68**
**Sprecher, David A.,**
 Elements of real analysis [by] David A. Sprecher. New York, Academic Press [1970] 341 p.
77-107550         517/.52         0126584508
 *Functions of real variables. Mathematical analysis.*


### QA331.7 Analysis — Theory of functions — Functions of complex variables

**QA331.7.A25 1997**
**Ablowitz, Mark J.**
 Complex variables : introduction and applications / Mark J. Ablowitz, Athanassios S. Fokas. Cambridge ; Cambridge University Press, 1997. xii, 647 p. :
96-048902         515/.9         0521480582
 *Functions of complex variables.*


**QA331.7.G75 1997**
**Greene, Robert Everist,**
 Function theory of one complex variable / Robert E. Greene, Steven G. Krantz. New York : Wiley, c1997. xiii, 496 p.
96-025133         515/.93         0471804681
 *Functions of complex variables.*


**QA331.7.K744 1999**
**Krantz, Steven G.**
 Handbook of complex variables / Steven G. Krantz. Boston, Mass. : Birkhauser, c1999. xxiv, 290 p.
99-020156         515/.9         0817640118
 *Functions of complex variables. Mathematical analysis.*


**QA331.7.S63 1997**
**Smithies, F.**
 Cauchy and the creation of complex function theory / Frank Smithies. Cambridge, U.K. ; Cambridge University Press, 1997. 216 p. ;
97-003028         515/.9/092         052159278X
*Cauchy, Augustin Louis, -- Baron, -- 1789-1857.    Functions of complex variables -- History -- 19th century.*


### QA333 Analysis — Theory of functions — Riemann surfaces

**QA333.A43**
**Ahlfors, Lars Valerian,**
 Riemann surfaces, by Lars V. Ahlfors and Leo Sario. Princeton, N.J., Princeton University Press, 1960. 382 p.
59-011074         517.81
 *Riemann surfaces. Topology.*


**QA333.B43 1984**
**Beardon, Alan F.**
 A primer on Riemann surfaces / A.F. Beardon. Cambridge [Cambridgeshire] ; Cambridge University Press, 1984. x, 188 p. :
82-004439         515/.223         0521271045
 *Riemann surfaces.*


**QA333.J8513 1997**
**Jost, Jurgen,**
 Compact Riemann surfaces : an introduction to contemporary mathematics / Jurgen Jost ; translated by R.R. Simha. Berlin ; Springer, c1997. xiv, 291 p. :
96-037590         515/.93         3540533346
 *Riemann surfaces.*

## QA343 Analysis — Theory of functions — Elliptic functions. Elliptic integrals. Modular functions

**QA343.L68 2001**
**Lomont, John S.,**
Elliptic polynomials / J.S. Lomont, John Brillhart. Boca Raton : Chapman & Hall/CRC, c2001. xxiii, 289 p.
00-055483     515/.983     1584882107
*Elliptic functions. Polynomials.*

## QA351 Analysis — Theory of functions — Special functions

**QA351.A75 1992**
**Andrews, Larry C.**
Special functions of mathematics for engineers / Larry C. Andrews. New York : McGraw-Hill, c1992. xix, 479 p. :
91016093     515.5     0070018480
*Functions, Special.*

## QA355 Analysis — Theory of functions — Miscellaneous special topics

**QA355.T77 1975**
**Tsuji, Masatsugu,**
Potential theory in modern function theory. New York, Chelsea Pub. Co. [c1975] x, 590 p.
74-004297     515/.7     0828402817
*Potential theory (Mathematics) Harmonic functions. Conformal mapping.*

## QA360 Analysis — Theory of functions — Geometric principles of analysis. Mapping of regions. Conformal presentation

**QA360.C3 1952**
**Caratheodory, Constantin,**
Conformal representation.    Cambridge [Eng.] University Press, 1952. 115 p.
52009985     517.5
*Surfaces, Representation of. Functions. Geometry, Non-Euclidean.*

## QA371 Analysis — Differential equations — General works, treatises, and textbooks

**QA371.B74 1987**
**Borrelli, Robert L.,**
Differential equations : a modeling approach / Robert L. Borrelli, Courtney S. Coleman. Englewood Cliffs, N.J. : Prentice-Hall, c1987. xvii, 607, 77
86-022601     515.3/5     0132115336
*Differential equations.*

**QA371.B773 1986**
**Boyce, William E.**
Elementary differential equations and boundary value problems / William E. Boyce, Richard C. DiPrima. New York : Wiley, c1986. xvi, 654, [49
85-020244     515.3/5     0471078956
*Differential equations. Boundary value problems.*

**QA371.C68213 1986**
**Collatz, L.**
Differential equations : an introduction with applications / Lothar Collatz ; translated by E.R. Dawson. Chichester [West Sussex] ; Wiley, c1986. xv, 372 p. :
85-026555     515.3/5     0471909556
*Differential equations.*

**QA371.F72**
**Forsyth, Andrew Russell,**
Theory of differential equations.    New York, Dover Publications [1959] 6 v. in 3.
60-000747     517.38
*Differential equations.*

**QA371.G644 1991**
**Goode, Stephen W.,**
An introduction to differential equations and linear algebra / Stephen W. Goode. Englewood Cliffs, N.J. : Prentice Hall, c1991. xv, 640 p. :
90-021804     512/.5     0134856570
*Algebras, Linear. Differential equations.*

**QA371.G73 1999**
**Groetsch, C. W.**
Inverse problems : activites for undergraduates / C.W. Groetsch. Washington, DC : Mathematical Association of America, c1999. xii, 222 p. :
99-062793     515/.35     0883857162
*Inverse problems (Differential equations) -- Problems, exercises, etc.*

**QA371.L36 1977**
**Lefschetz, Solomon,**
Differential equations : geometric theory / Solomon Lefschetz. New York : Dover Publications, 1977. x, 390 p. :
76-053978     515/.35     0486634639
*Differential equations. Topology.*

**QA371.M57 1970**
**Milne, William Edmund,**
Numerical solution of differential equations.    New York, Dover Publications [1970] xi, 359 p.
75-100546     517/.6     0486624374
*Differential equations -- Numerical solutions.*

**QA371.N32**
**Nayfeh, Ali Hasan,**
Introduction to perturbation techniques / Ali Hasan Nayfeh. New York : Wiley, c1981. xiv, 519 p. :
80-015233     515.3/5     0471080330
*Differential equations -- Numerical solutions. Equations -- Numerical solutions. Perturbation (Mathematics)*

**QA371.R28 1991**
**Rahman, M.**
Applied differential equations for scientists and engineers / by M. Rahman. Southampton, UK ; Computational Mechanics Publications, c1991. 2 v. :
91-076270          515/.35          185312124X
*Differential equations.  Differential equations, Partial.*

**QA371.R29 1981**
**Rainville, Earl David,**
Elementary differential equations / Earl D. Rainville, Phillip E. Bedient. New York : Macmillan ; c1981. xiv, 529 p. :
80-012849          515.3/5          0023977701
*Differential equations.*

**QA371.R34413 1986**
**Reinhard, Herve.**
Differential equations : foundations and applications / by Herve Reinhard ; translated by A. Howie. [London] : North Oxford Academic, 1986. xi, 541 p. :
86-208044          515.3/5          0946536708
*Differential equations.*

**QA371.R37 1995**
**Rice, Richard G.**
Applied mathematics and modeling for chemical engineers / Richard G. Rice, Duong D. Do. New York : Wiley, c1995. xiv, 706 p. ;
94-005245          660/.284/015118          0471303771
*Differential equations.  Chemical processes -- Mathematical models.  Chemical engineering -- Mathematics.*

**QA371.W29 1991**
**Walas, Stanley M.**
Modeling with differential equations in chemical engineering / Stanley M. Walas. Boston : Butterworth-Heinemann, c1991. xiii, 450 p.
90-049924          515/.35          0750690127
*Differential equations.  Chemical engineering -- Mathematics.*

**QA371.Z88 1989**
**Zwillinger, Daniel,**
Handbook of differential equations / Daniel Zwillinger. Boston : Academic Press, c1989. xx, 673 p. :
87-037350          515.3/5          0127843906
*Differential equations -- Handbooks, manuals, etc.*

### QA371.5.D37 Analysis — Differential equations — Special topics, A-Z

**QA371.5.D37.A23 1994**
**Abell, Martha L.,**
Differential equations with Maple V / Martha L. Abell, James P. Braselton. Boston : AP Professional, c1994. xiv, 684 p. :
94-019965          515/.35/028553          0120415488
*Differential equations -- Data processing.*

**QA371.5.D37.A24 1997**
**Abell, Martha L.,**
Differential equations with Mathematica / Martha L. Abell, James P. Braselton. San Diego, CA : Academic Press, c1997. xii, 807 p. :
96-043813          515/.35/02855369
012041550X
*Differential equations -- Data proessing.*

**QA371.5.D37.C66 1996**
Computational differential equations / K. Eriksson ... [et al.]. Cambridge ; Cambridge University Press, 1996. xvi, 538 p. :
96-226100          515/.35          0521567386
*Differential equations -- Data processing.*

**QA371.5.D37.G74 1997**
**Gray, Alfred,**
Introduction to ordinary differential equations with Mathematica : an integrated multimedia approach / Alfred Gray, Michael Mezzino, Mark A. Pinsky. Santa Clara, Calif. : TELOS, c1997. xxii, 890 p.
96-054732          515/.352/078553042
0387944818
*Differential equations -- Data processing.*

### QA371-372 Analysis — Differential equations — Ordinary differential equations (linear and nonlinear)

**QA371.W39**
**Webster, Arthur Gordon,**
Partial differential equations of mathematical physics. Edited by Samuel J. Plimpton. [New York] Dover Publications [1955] 440 p.
55013937          517.38
*Differential equations, Partial.  Mathematical physics.*

**QA372.A6913 1983**
**Arnold, V. I.**
Geometrical methods in the theory of ordinary differential equations / V.I. Arnold ; translated by Joseph Szucs ; English translation edited by Mark Levi. New York : Springer-Verlag, c1983. x, 334 p. :
82-005464          515.3/52          0387906819
*Differential equations.*

**QA372.F69 1987**
**Fox, L.**
Numerical solution of ordinary differential equations / L. Fox and D.F. Mayers. London ; Chapman and Hall, 1987. xi, 249 p. :
87-005191          515.3/5          0412226502
*Differential equations -- Numerical solutions.*

**QA372.G4**
**Gear, C. William**
Numerical initial value problems in ordinary differential equations [by] C. William Gear. Englewood Cliffs, N.J., Prentice-Hall [1971] xvii, 253 p.
75-152448        515/.352        0136266061
*Differential equations -- Data processing. Numerical integration -- Data processing.*

**QA372.I6 1956**
**Ince, E. L.**
Ordinary differential equations.        [New York] Dover Publications [1956] 558 p.
58-012618        517.382
*Differential equations.*

**QA372.M388 1996**
**Mattheij, Robert M. M.**
Ordinary differential equations in theory and practice / R.M.M. Mattheij and J. Molenaar. Chichester ; Wiley, c1996. xi, 407 p. :
96-194195        515/.352        0471956740
*Differential equations.*

**QA372.P47 1991**
**Perko, Lawrence.**
Differential equations and dynamical systems / Lawrence Perko. New York : Springer-Verlag, c1991. xii, 403 p. :
91-150070        515/.355        0387974431
*Differential equations, Nonlinear. Differentiable dynamical systems.*

**QA372.P725 1995**
**Polyanin, A. D.**
Handbook of exact solutions for ordinary differential equations / Andrei D. Polyanin, Valentin F. Zaitsev. Boca Raton : CRC Press, c1995. 707 p. :
95010217        515/.352        0849394384
*Differential equations -- Numerical solutions.*

**QA372.V47 1990**
**Verhulst, F.**
Nonlinear differential equations and dynamical systems / Ferdinand Verhulst. Berlin ; Springer-Verlag, c1990. ix, 277 p. :
89-021770        515/.355        0387506284
*Differential equations, Nonlinear. Differentiable dynamical systems.*

**QA372.W224 1998**
**Walter, Wolfgang,**
Ordinary differential equations / Wolfgang Walter ; translated by Russell Thompson. New York : Springer, c1998. xi, 380 p. :
98-004754        515/.352        0387984593
*Differential equations.*

## QA374 Analysis — Differential equations — Partial differential equations (first order)

**QA374.K97 1997**
**Kythe, Prem K.**
Partial differential equations and Mathematica / Prem K. Kythe, Pratap Puri, Michael R. Schaferkotter. Boca Raton, Fla. : CRC Press, c1997. xx, 378 p. :
96-036946        515/.353        0849378532
*Differential equations, Partial.*

**QA374.L32 1995**
**Lamb, G. L.**
Introductory applications of partial differential equations with emphasis on wave propagation and diffusion / G.L. Lamb, Jr. New York : Wiley, c1995. xii, 471 p. :
94-033111        531/.1133/01515353
0471311235
*Differential equations, Partial.*

**QA374.R424 1993**
**Renardy, Michael.**
An introduction to partial differential equations / Michael Renardy, Robert C. Rogers. New York : Springer-Verlag, c1993. xiii, 428 p.
92-037449        515/.353        0387979522
*Differential equations, Partial.*

## QA377 Analysis — Differential equations — Partial differential equations (second and higher order)

**QA377.B295 1997**
**Bassanini, Piero.**
Theory and applications of partial differential equations / Piero Bassanini and Alan R. Elcrat. New York : Plenum Press, c1997. ix, 439 p. :
97-038643        515/.353        0306456400
*Differential equations, Partial.*

**QA377.B53 1998**
**Betounes, David.**
Partial differential equations for computational science : with Maple and vector analysis / David Betounes. New York : TELOS, c1998. xix, 517 p. :
97-026381        515/.353        0387983007
*Vector analysis. Differential equations, Partial -- Numerical Solutions.*

**QA377.T9 1998**
**Tveito, Aslak,**
Introduction to partial differential equations : a computational approach / Aslak Tveito, Ragnar Winther. New York : Springer, c1998. xv, 392 p. :
98-004699        515/.353        0387983279
*Differential equations, Partial.*

### QA379 Analysis — Differential equations — Boundary value problems

**QA379.H36**
**Hanna, J. Ray.**
Fourier series and integrals of boundary value problems / J. Ray Hanna. New York : Wiley, c1982. xi, 271 p. :
81-016063      515.3/5      0471081299
*Boundary value problems. Fourier series.*

**QA379.S72**
**Stakgold, Ivar.**
Green's functions and boundary value problems / Ivar Stakgold. New York : Wiley, c1979. xv, 638 p. :
78-027259      515/.35      0471819670
*Boundary value problems. Green's functions. Mathematical physics.*

## QA381 Analysis — Differential forms and invariants. Pfaffians

**QA381.C2813 1994**
**Carmo, Manfredo Perdigao do.**
Differential forms and applications / Manfredo P. do Carmo. Berlin ; Springer-Verlag, c1994. viii, 118 p.
94-021965      515/.37      3540576185
*Differential forms.*

## QA387 Analysis — Topological groups. Lie groups

**QA387.G54**
**Gilmore, Robert,**
Lie groups, Lie algebras, and some of their applications. New York, Wiley [1974] xx, 587 p.
73-010030      512/.55      0471301795
*Lie groups. Lie algebras.*

**QA387.H636 1998**
**Hofmann, Karl Heinrich.**
The structure of compact groups : a primer for the student, a handbook for the expert / Karl H. Hofmann, Sidney A. Morris. Berlin ; W. de Gruyter, 1998. xvii, 835 p.
98-029380      512/.55      3110152681
*Compact groups.*

**QA387.K58 1986**
**Knapp, Anthony W.**
Representation theory of semisimple groups, an overview based on examples / Anthony W. Knapp. Princeton, N.J. : Princeton University Press, 1986. xvii, 773 p.
85-043295      512/.55      0691084017
*Semisimple Lie groups. Representations of groups.*

### QA401 Analysis — Analytical methods used in the solution of physical problems — General works, treatises, and textbooks

**QA401.C358 1989**
**Casti, J. L.**
Alternate realities : mathematical models of nature and man / John L. Casti. New York : Wiley, [c1989] xvii, 493 p.
88-022337      001.4/34      047161842X
*Mathematical models. System analysis.*

**QA401.F68 1994**
**Fowkes, Neville D.**
An introduction to mathematical modelling / Neville D. Fowkes and John J. Mahony. Chichester ; Wiley, c1994. xvi, 447 p. :
94-200441      620/.001/1      0471934224
*Mathematical models.*

**QA401.F94 1997**
**Fulford, Glenn.**
Modelling with differential and difference equations / Glenn Fulford, Peter Forrester, and Arthur Jones. Cambridge ; Cambridge University Press, 1997. x, 405 p. :
97-180614      511.3      0521440696
*Mathematical models. Differential equations. Difference equations.*

**QA401.G47 1999**
**Gershenfeld, Neil A.**
The nature of mathematical modeling / Neil Gershenfeld. Cambridge ; Cambridge University Press, 1999. xii, 344 p. :
98-022029      511/.8      0521570956
*Mathematical models.*

**QA401.H527 1998**
**Holland, John H.**
Emergence : from chaos to order / John H. Holland. Reading, Mass. : Addison-Wesley, c1998. xiii, 258 p.
97-021350      003/.85      0201149435
*Mathematical models. Game theory. Artificial intelligence.*

**QA401.K24 1997**
**Kalman, Dan.**
Elementary mathematical models : order aplenty and a glimpse of chaos / Dan Kalman. [Washington, DC] : Mathematical Association of America, c1997. xvi, 345 p. :
97-074331      511/.8      0883857073
*Mathematical models. Mathematical analysis.*

**QA401.M48 1993**
**Meerschaert, Mark M.,**
Mathematical modeling / Mark M. Meerschaert. Boston : Academic Press, c1993. xiv, 287 p. :
92-038059      511/.8      0124876501
*Mathematical models.*

**QA401.M63 1998**
**Mooney, Douglas D.**
A course in mathematical modeling / Douglas D. Mooney, Randall J. Swift. [Washington, DC] : Mathematical Association of America, c1999. xx 431 p. :
98-085688          511/.8          088385712X
*Mathematical models.*

**QA401.R537 1997**
**Riley, K. F.**
Mathematical methods for physics and engineering : a comprehensive guide / K.F. Riley, M.P. Hobson, and S.J. Bence. Cambridge, U.K. ; Cambridge University Press, 1997. xix, 1008 p.
96-052942          515/.1          052155506X
*Mathematical analysis.*

**QA401.S465 2000**
**Shier, Douglas R.**
Applied mathematical modeling : a multidisciplinary approach / D.R. Shier, K.T. Wallenius. Boca Raton, Fla. : Chapman & Hall/CRC, c2000. xxiv, 443 p.
99-050198          511/.8          1584880481
*Mathematical models.*

## QA402-402.3 Analysis — Analytical methods used in the solution of physical problems — System analysis

**QA402.C432 1986**
Chaos / edited by Arun V. Holden. Princeton, N.J. : Princeton University Press, c1986. vi, 324 p. :
86-004952          003          0691084238
*Chaotic behavior in systems.*

**QA402.3.J29 1993**
**Jacobs, O. L. R.**
Introduction to control theory / O.L.R. Jacobs. Oxford ; Oxford University Press, c1993. xii, 390 p. :
93-012784          629.8/312          0198562489
*Control theory.*

## QA402.5 Analysis — Mathematical optimization. Programming

**QA402.5.C476 1996**
**Chong, Edwin Kah Pin.**
An introduction to optimization / Edwin K.P. Chong and Stanislaw H. Zak. New York : Wiley, c1996. xiii, 409 p.
95-006111          519.3          0471089494
*Mathematical optimization.*

**QA402.5.C54523 1998**
Combinatorial optimization / William J. Cook ... [et al.]. New York : Wiley, c1998. x, 355 p. :
97-035774          519.7/6          047155894X
*Combinatorial optimization.*

**QA402.5.G54 1981**
**Gill, Philip E.**
Practical optimization / Philip E. Gill, Walter Murray, Margaret H. Wright. London ; Academic Press, 1981. xvi, 401 p. :
81-066366          515          0122839528
*Mathematical optimization.*

**QA402.5.H387 1998**
**Haupt, Randy L.**
Practical genetic algorithms / Randy L. Haupt & Sue Ellen Haupt. New York : Wiley, c1998. xiv, 177 p. :
97-013172          519.7          0471188735
*Genetic algorithms.*

**QA402.5.M553 1999**
**Miller, Ronald E.**
Optimization : foundations and applications / Ronald E. Miller. New York : Wiley, 2000. xvvii, 653 p.
99-021921          519.3          0471322423
*Mathematical optimization.*

**QA402.5.M5613 1986**
**Minoux, Michel.**
Mathematical programming : theory and algorithms / M. Minoux ; translated by Steven Vajda. Chichester [W. Sussex] ; Wiley, c1986. xxviii, 489 p
85-016718          519.7          0471901709
*Programming (Mathematics)*

**QA402.5.P42 1988**
**Peressini, Anthony L.**
The mathematics of nonlinear programming / Anthony L. Peressini, Francis E. Sullivan, J.J. Uhl, Jr. New York : Springer-Verlag, c1988. x, 273 p. :
87-023411          519.7/6          0387966145
*Mathematical optimization. Nonlinear programming.*

**QA402.5.P72 2001**
The practical handbook of genetic algorithms : applications / edited by Lance Chambers. 2nd ed. Boca Raton, Fla. : Chapman & Hall/CRC, c2001. xl, 501 p. :
          519.7 21          1584882409
*Genetic algorithms.*

**QA402.5.S25 1993**
**Sakawa, Masatoshi,**
Fuzzy sets and interactive multiobjective optimization / Masatoshi Sakawa. New York : Plenum, c1993. xii, 308 p. :
92-044263          658.4/033          0306443376
*Mathematical optimization. Fuzzy sets. Programming (Mathematics)*

**QA402.5.W52 1993**
**Williams, H. P.**
Model solving in mathematical programming / H.P. Williams. Chichester ; J. Wiley, c1993. xiii, 359 p.
92-001648          519.7          0471935816
*Programming (Mathematics)*

## QA403-403.3 Analysis — Mathematical optimization. Programming — Harmonic analysis (General)

**QA403.B377 1997**
**Benedetto, John.**
Harmonic analysis and applications / John J. Benedetto. Boca Raton : CRC Press, c1997. xix, 336 p. :
96-020445          515/.2433          0849378796
*Harmonic analysis.*

**QA403.B75 1988**
**Brigham, E. Oran,**
The fast Fourier transform and its applications / E. Oran Brigham. Englewood Cliffs, N.J. : Prentice Hall, c1988. xvi, 448 p. :
88-001029          515.7/23          0133075052
*Fourier transformations.*

**QA403.3.A34 1999**
**Aboufadel, Edward,**
Discovering wavelets / Edward Aboufadel and Steven Schlicker. New York : Wiley, c1999. xii, 125 p. :
99-031029          515/.2433          0471331937
*Wavelets (Mathematics)*

**QA403.3.B5713 1998**
**Blatter, Christian,**
Wavelets : a primer / Christian Blatter. Natick, Mass. : A.K. Peters, c1998. x, 202 p. :
98-029959          515/.2433          1568810954
*Wavelets (Mathematics)*

**QA403.3.C48 1992**
**Chui, C. K.**
An introduction to wavelets / Charles K. Chui. Boston : Academic Press, c1992. x, 264 p. :
91-058831          515/.2433          0121745848
*Wavelets (Mathematics)*

**QA403.3.H47 1996**
**Hernandez, Eugenio,**
A first course on wavelets / Eugenio Hernandez, Guido Weiss. Boca Raton : CRC Press, c1996. 489 p. :
96027111          515/.2433          0849382742
*Wavelets (Mathematics)*

**QA403.3.H83 1998**
**Hubbard, Barbara Burke,**
The world according to wavelets : the story of a mathematical technique in the making / Barbara Burke Hubbard. Wellesley, Mass : A.K. Peters, c1998. xx, 330 p. :
97-048738          515/.2433          1568810725
*Wavelets (Mathematics)*

**QA403.3.K35 1994**
**Kaiser, Gerald.**
A friendly guide to wavelets / Gerald Kaiser. Boston : Birkhauser, 1994. xiv, 300 p. :
94-029118          515/.2433          0817637117
*Wavelets (Mathematics)*

## QA403.5-404 Analysis — Mathematical optimization. Programming — Fourier analysis

**QA403.5.B28 2000**
**Bachman, George,**
Fourier and wavelet analysis / George Bachman, Lawrence Narici, Edward Beckenstein. New York : Springer, c2000. ix, 505 p. ;
99-036217          515/.2433          0387988998
*Fourier analysis. Wavelets (Mathematics)*

**QA403.5.C37 1990**
**Cartwright, Mark,**
Fourier methods for mathematicians, scientists and engineers / Mark Cartwright. New York : Ellis Horwood, 1990. 326 p. :
89-071633          515/.2433          0133270165
*Fourier analysis.*

**QA403.5.C47 1987**
**Champeney, D. C.**
A handbook of Fourier theorems / D.C. Champeney. Cambridge [Cambridgeshire] ; Cambridge University Press, 1987. ix, 185 p. :
86-032694          515/.2433          0521265037
*Fourier analysis.*

**QA403.5.C48 1989**
**Chandrasekharan, K.**
Classical Fourier transforms / Komaravolu Chandrasekharan. Berlin ; Springer-Verlag, c1989. 172 p. ;
88-038192          515.7/23          0387502483
*Fourier transformations.*

**QA403.5.K67 1988**
**Korner, T. W.**
Fourier analysis / T.W. Korner. Cambridge [Cambridgeshire] ; Cambridge University Press, 1988. xii, 591 p. :
85-017410          515/.2433          0521251206
*Fourier analysis.*

**QA403.5.R327 1999**
**Ramakrishnan, Dinakar.**
Fourier analysis on number fields / Dinakar Ramakrishnan, Robert J. Valenza. New York : Springer, c1999. xxi, 350 p. ;
98-016715          515/.2433          0387984364
*Fourier analysis. Topological groups. Number theory.*

**QA404.E25 1979**
**Edwards, R. E.**
Fourier series, a modern introduction / R. E. Edwards. New York : Springer-Verlag, 1979- v. ;
79-011932          515/.2433          0387904123
*Fourier series.*

## QA404.O213 1990
**Oberhettinger, Fritz.**
   Tables of Fourier transforms and Fourier transforms of distributions / Fritz Oberhettinger. Berlin ; Springer-Verlag, c1990. viii, 259 p.
90-009507          515/.723          0387506306
   *Fourier transformations. Mathematics -- Tables.*

## QA404.P56 1997
**Pinkus, Allan,**
   Fourier series and integral transforms / Allan Pinkus & Samy Zafrany. Cambridge ; Cambridge University Press, 1997. vii, 189 p. :
96-051769          515/.723          0521592097
   *Fourier series. Integral transforms.*

## QA431 Analysis — Difference equations and functional equations

### QA431.E43 1996
**Elaydi, Saber,**
   An introduction to difference equations / Saber N. Elaydi. New York : Springer, c1996. xiii, 389 p.
95-037485          515/.625          0387945822
   *Difference equations.*

### QA431.M426 1987
**Mickens, Ronald E.,**
   Difference equations / Ronald E. Mickens. New York : Van Nostrand Reinhold, c1987. xii, 243 p. :
86-010990          515/.625          0442260768
   *Difference equations.*

### QA431.P67 1990
**Porter, David,**
   Integral equations : a practical treatment, from spectral theory to applications / David Porter, David S.G. Stirling. Cambridge [England] ; Cambridge University Press, 1990. xi, 372 p. :
89-037313          515/.45          052133151X
   *Integral equations.*

## QA432 Analysis — Operational calculus. Laplace transformation

### QA432.S33 1999
**Schiff, Joel L.**
   The Laplace transform : theory and applications / Joel L. Schiff. New York : Springer, c1999. xiv, 233 p. :
99-014037          515/.723          0387986987
   *Laplace transformation.*

## QA433 Analysis — Vector and tensor analysis. Spinor analysis. Scalar field theory

### QA433.S64 1964
**Sokolnikoff, Ivan Stephen,**
   Tensor analysis, theory and applications to geometry and mechanics of continua. New York, Wiley [1964] xii, 361 p.
64-013223          515/.63
   *Calculus of tensors.*

### QA433.S9 1969
**Synge, J. L.**
   Tensor calculus / by J. L. Synge and A. Schild. Toronto : University of Toronto Press, c1949, 1969 ix, 324 p. :
75-323720          515/.63          0802010318
   *Calculus of tensors.*

## QA445 Geometry — General works, treatises, and textbooks

### QA445.B312
**Baker, H. F.**
   Principles of geometry. New York, Frederick Ungar [c1959] v.
59014676
   *Geometry.*

### QA445.S55 1997
**Singer, David A.**
   Geometry : plane and fancy / David A. Singer. New York : Springer, 1997. ix, 159 p. :
97-026383          516          0387983066
   *Geometry.*

## QA447 Geometry — Special aspects of the subject as a whole

### QA447.K37 1990
**Kappraff, Jay.**
   Connections : the geometric bridge between art and science / Jay Kappraff. New York : McGraw-Hill Pub. Co., c1990. xxi, 471 :
89-078206          516          0070342504
   *Geometry. Mathematics. Design.*

### QA447.M3613
**Mandelbrot, Benoit B.**
   Fractals : form, chance, and dimension / Benoit B. Mandelbrot. San Francisco : W. H. Freeman, c1977. xvi, 365 p. :
76-057947          516/.15          0716704730.
   *Geometry. Mathematical models. Stochastic processes.*

**QA447.P45 1986**
**Peitgen, Heinz-Otto,**
   The beauty of fractals : images of complex dynamical systems / H.-O. Peitgen, P.H. Richter. Berlin ; Springer-Verlag, c1986. xii, 199 p. :
86-003917          516          0387158510
   *Fractals.*

### QA448.D38 Geometry — Specials topics, A-Z — Data processing

**QA448.D38.O76 1998**
**O'Rourke, Joseph.**
   Computational geometry in C / Joseph O'Rourke. Cambridge, UK, ; Cambridge University Press, 1998. xiii, 376 p.
98-015363          516/.0285/5133          0521640105
   *Geometry -- Data processing.  C (Computer program language)*

### QA451 Geometry — Elementary geometry — Euclid's elements as textbooks

**QA451.H37 2000**
**Hartshorne, Robin.**
   Geometry : Euclid and beyond / Robin Hartshorne. New York : Springer, c2000. xi, 526 p., [
99-044789          516          0387986502
   *Geometry.*

### QA453 Geometry — Elementary geometry — Other textbooks, (Plane and solid)

**QA453.R66 1993**
**Roe, John,**
   Elementary geometry / John Roe. Oxford [England] ; Oxford University Press, c1993. ix, 307 p. :
92-041660          516.2          0198534574
   *Geometry.*

### QA462 Geometry — Elementary geometry — Study and teaching. Research

**QA462.F26 1998**
**Farin, Gerald E.**
   The geometry toolbox for graphics and modeling / Gerald Farin, Dianne Hansford. Natick, Mass. : A.K. Peters, c1998. xv, 288 p. :
97-041259          516.3/5          1568810741
   *Geometry -- Study and teaching.  Computer graphics.*

### QA466 Geometry — Elementary geometry — Famous problems

**QA466.K63 1991**
**Klee, Victor.**
   Old and new unsolved problems in plane geometry and number theory / Victor Klee, Stan Wagon. [Washington, D.C.] : Mathematical Association of America, c1991. xv, 333 p. :
91-061591          516.22          0883853159
   *Geometry, Plane.  Number theory.*

**QA466.K64 1956**
**Klein, Felix,**
   Famous problems of elementary geometry: the duplication of the cube, the trisection of an angle, the quadrature of the circle. Translation by Wooster Woodruff Beman and David Eugene Smith. New York, Dover Publications [1956] xi, 92 p.
63-006120          513.92
   *Geometry -- Problems, Famous.*

## QA471 Geometry — Projective geometry

**QA471.B5613 1998**
**Beutelspacher, Albrecht.**
   Projective geometry : from foundations to applications / Albrecht Beutelspacher and Ute Rosenbaum. Cambridge ; Cambridge University Press, 1998. x, 258 p. :
97-018012          516/.5          0521482771
   *Geometry, Projective.*

**QA471.H76 1995**
**Honsberger, Ross,**
   Episodes in nineteenth and twentieth century Euclidean geometry / by Ross Honsberger. Washington : Mathematical Association of America, c1995. x, 174 p. :
94-079528          516.3/72          0883856395
   *Geometry, Projective.*

**QA471.K224 1996**
**Kadison, Lars.**
   Projective geometry and modern algebra / Lars Kadison, Matthias T. Kromann. Boston : Birkhauser, c1996. xvi, 208 p. :
95-047840          516/.5          0817639004
   *Geometry, Projective.*

### QA473 Geometry — Modern geometry. Inversions — General works

**QA473.A15**
**Adler, Claire Fisher,**
   Modern geometry; an integrated first course. New York, McGraw-Hill, 1958. 215 p.
57007992          513.01
   *Geometry, Modern.  Geometry -- Foundations.*

QA473.H46 1997
Henle, Michael.
Modern geometries : the analytic approach / Michael Henle. Upper Saddle River, N.J. : Prentice Hall, c1997. xi, 372 p. :
96-015557          516/.04          013193418X
*Geometry, Modern.*

## QA483-484 Geometry — Special topics in plane geometry

QA483.L62
Lockwood, E. H.
A book of curves.   Cambridge [Eng.] University Press, 1961. xi, 198 p.
61-065797          513.1
*Curves, Plane.*

QA484.B55 1997
Blatner, David.
The joy of [pi] / David Blatner. New York : Walker and Co., 1997. xiii, 129 p.
97-023705          516.22     0802713327
*Pi.*

## QA491 Geometry — Special topics in solid geometry

QA491.C76 1997
Cromwell, Peter R.,
Polyhedra / Peter R. Cromwell. Cambridge, U.K. ; Cambridge University Press, 1997. xiii, 451 p.
96-009420          516/.15          0521554322
*Polyhedra.*

### QA533 Geometry — Trigonometry — Plane

QA533.G45 2001
Gelfand, I. M.
Trigonometry / I.M. Gelfand, Mark Saul. Boston : Birkhauser, c2001. x, 229 p. :
99-032245          516.24/2          0817639144
*Plane trigonometry.*

### QA556 Geometry — Analytic geometry — Coordinates

QA556.M15
Maxwell, E. A.
Coordinate geometry with vectors and tensors. Oxford, Clarendon Press, 1958. 194 p.
59-000176          516.5
*Coordinates. Vector analysis. Calculus of tensors.*

## QA564 Geometry — Algebraic geometry — General works, treatises, and textbooks

QA564.C688 1992
Cox, David A.
Ideals, varieties, and algorithms : an introduction to computational algebraic geometry and commutative algebra / David Cox, John Little, Donal O'Shea. New York : Springer-Verlag, c1992. xi, 513 p. :
92-013290          516.3/5          038797847X
*Geometry, Algebraic -- Data processing. Commutative algebra – Data processing.*

QA564.C6883 1998
Cox, David A.
Using algebraic geometry / David Cox, John Little, Donal O'Shea. New York : Springer, c1998. xii, 499 p. :
98-011964          516.3/5          0387984879
*Geometry, Algebraic.*

QA564.H24 1992
Harris, Joe.
Algebraic geometry : a first course / Joe Harris. New York : Springer-Verlag, c1992. xix, 328 p. :
91-033973          516.3/5          0387977163
*Geometry, Algebraic.*

QA564.I62 2000
An invitation to algebraic geometry / Karen E. Smith ... [et al.]. New York : Springer, 2000. xii, 155 p. :
00-026595          516.3/5          0387989803
*Geometry, Algebraic.*

QA564.P47 1996
Peskine, Christian.
An algebraic introduction to complex projective geometry / Christian Peskine. Cambridge ; Cambridge University Press, 1996- v. 1   ;
94-046980          516/.5          0521480728
*Geometry, Algebraic. Functions of complex variables.*

QA564.R45 1988
Reid, Miles
Undergraduate algebraic geometry / Miles Reid. Cambridge ; Cambridge University Press, 1988. viii, 129 p.
88-023793          516.3/5          0521355591
*Geometry, Algebraic.*

QA564.S4
Semple, J. G.
Introduction to algebraic geometry, by J.G. Semple and L. Roth. Oxford, Clarendon Press, 1949. xv, [1], 446
50-000028          516
*Geometry, Algebraic.*

## QA565-567.2 Geometry — Algebraic geometry — Higher algebraic curves

**QA565.G5 1998**
**Gibson, Christopher G.,**
 Elementary geometry of algebraic curves : an undergraduate introduction / C.G. Gibson. Cambridge ; Cambridge University Press, c1998. xvi, 250 p. :
98-036910          516.3/52          0521641403
 *Curves, Algebraic.*

**QA565.K57 1992**
**Kirwan, Frances Clare,**
 Complex algebraic curves / Frances Kirwan. Cambridge ; Cambridge University Press, 1992. viii, 264 p.
92-192303          516.3/52          052141251X
 *Curves, Algebraic.*

**QA567.D38 1993**
**Davis, Philip J.,**
 Spirals : from Theodorus to chaos / Philip J. Davis ; with contributions by Walter Gautschi and Arieh Iserles. Wellesley, Mass. : A.K. Peters, c1993. p. cm.
93-016735          516/.15          1568810105
 *Spirals.*

**QA567.R78 2000**
**Rutter, John W.,**
 Geometry of curves / John W. Rutter. Boca Raton, Fla. : Chapman & Hall/CRC, c2000. xvii, 361 p.
99-088667          516.3/52          1584881666
 *Curves, Plane.*

**QA567.2.E44.M38 1997**
**McKean, Henry P.**
 Elliptic curves : function theory, geometry, arithmetic / Henry McKean, Victor Moll. Cambridge, U.K ; Cambridge University Press, 1997. xiii, 280 p.
96-036605          516.3/52          0521582288
 *Curves, Elliptic.*

**QA567.2.E44.M63 1997**
 Modular forms and Fermat's last theorem / Gary Cornell, Joseph H. Silverman, Glenn Stevens, editors. New York : Springer, c1997. xix, 582 p. :
97-010930          512/.74          0387946098
 *Curves, Elliptic -- Congresses. Forms, Modular -- Congresses. Fermat's last theorem -- Congresses.*

## QA601 Geometry — Algebraic geometry — Transformations, correspondences, and general methods for algebraic configurations

**QA601.T73 1996**
 The transforms and applications handbook / editor-in-chief, Alexander D. Poularikas. Boca Raton Fla. : CRC Press, c1996. vii, 1103 p.
95-002513          515/.723          0849383420
 *Transformations (Mathematics) -- Handbooks, manuals, etc.*

## QA611.A3 Geometry — Topology — History

**QA611.A3.H57 1999**
 History of topology / edited by I.M. James. Amsterdam ; Elsevier Science B.V., 1999. ix, 1056 p. :
99-025564          514/.09          0444823751
 *Topology -- History.*

## QA611.B65813-S84 Geometry — Topology — General works, treatises, and textbooks

**QA611.B65813**
**Bourbaki, Nicolas.**
 General topology. Paris, Hermann; [1966] 2 v.
66-025377          513.83
 *Topology.*

**QA611.J33 1984**
**James, I. M.**
 General topology and homotopy theory / I.M. James. New York : Springer-Verlag, c1984. 248 p. :
84-005435          514          0387909702
 *Topology.*

**QA611.K47 1993**
**Kinsey, L. Christine.**
 Topology of surfaces / L. Christine Kinsey. New York : Springer-Verlag, c1993. viii, 262 p.
93-002605          514          0387941029
 *Topology.*

**QA611.M674 1992**
**Morgan, Frank.**
 Riemannian geometry : a beginner's guide / Frank Morgan ; illustrated by James F. Bredt. Boston : Jones and Bartlett Publishers, c1993. 119 p. :
92-013261          516.3/73          0867202424
 *Geometry, Riemannian.*

**QA611.N65**
**Northcott, D. G.**
 An introduction to homological algebra.     Cambridge, University Press, 1960. 282 p.
60-016353          512.8
 *Algebra, Homological.*

**QA611.S84**
**Stillwell, John.**
 Classical topology and combinatorial group theory / John Stillwell. New York : Springer-Verlag, c1980. xii, 301 p. :
80-016326          514          0387905162
 *Topology. Combinatorial group theory.*

## QA612-612.2 Geometry — Topology — Algebraic Topology

**QA612.B74 1993**
**Bredon, Glen E.**
Topology and geometry / Glen E. Bredon. New York : Springer-Verlag, c1993. xiv, 557 p. :
92-031618        514/.2        0387979263
*Algebraic topology.*

**QA612.F85 1995**
**Fulton, William,**
Algebraic topology : a first course / William Fulton. New York : Springer-Verlag, c1995. xviii, 430 p.
94-021786        514/.2        0387943269
*Algebraic topology.*

**QA612.M37 1977**
**Massey, William S.**
Algebraic topology, an introduction / William S. Massey. New York : Springer-Verlag, [1977] c1967. xxi, 261 p. :
77-022206        514/.2        0387902716
*Algebraic topology.*

**QA612.2.A33 1994**
**Adams, Colin Conrad.**
The knot book : an elementary introduction to the mathematical theory of knots / Colin C. Adams. New York : W.H. Freeman, c1994. xiii, 306 p.
93-049412        514/.224        071672393X
*Knot theory.*

**QA612.2.L53 1997**
**Lickorish, W. B. Raymond.**
An introduction to knot theory / W.B. Raymond Lickorish. New York : Springer, c1997. x, 201 p. :
97-016660        514/.224        038798254X
*Knot theory.*

**QA612.2.W44 1985**
**Weeks, Jeffrey R.,**
The shape of space : how to visualize surfaces and three-dimensional manifolds / Jeffrey R. Weeks. New York : M. Dekker, c1985. x, 324 p. :
85-010394        514.3        082477437X
*Three-manifolds (Topology) Surfaces.*

## QA613.6 Geometry — Topology — Manifolds and cell complexes

**QA613.6.B67 1982**
**Bott, Raoul,**
Differential forms in algebraic topology / Raoul Bott, Loring W. Tu. New York : Springer-Verlag, c1982. xiv, 331 p. :
81-009172        514/.72        0387906134
*Differential topology. Algebraic topology. Differential forms.*

## QA614.3-614.86 Geometry — Topology — Global analysis. Analysis on manifolds

**QA614.3.C66 1993**
**Conlon, Lawrence,**
Differentiable manifolds : a first course / Lawrence Conlon. Boston : Birkhauser, 1993. xii, 395 p. :
92-031098        516.3/6        0817636269
*Differentiable manifolds.*

**QA614.58.E3413 1988**
**Ekeland, I.**
Mathematics and the unexpected / Ivar Ekeland ; with a foreword by Felix E. Browder. Chicago : University of Chicago Press, 1988. xiii, 146 p.
87-030230        514/.7        0226199894
*Catastrophes (Mathematics)*

**QA614.8.A44 1997**
**Alligood, Kathleen T.**
Chaos : an introduction to dynamical systems / Kathleen T. Alligood, Tim D. Sauer, James A. Yorke. New York : Springer, c1997. xvii, 603 p.
95-051304        003/.85
*Differentiable dynamical systems. Chaotic behavior in systems.*

**QA614.8.D38 1999**
**Davies, B.**
Exploring chaos : theory and experiment / Brian Davies. Reading, Mass. : Perseus Books, c1999. xiii, 237 p.
99-062550        003/.857        0738200905
*Chaotic behavior in systems. Differentiable dynamical systems.*

**QA614.8.H65 1994**
**Holmgren, Richard A.**
A first course in discrete dynamical systems / Richard A. Holmgren. New York : Springer-Verlag, c1994. xi, 214 p. :
93-043894        514/.74        0387942084
*Differentiable dynamical systems.*

**QA614.8.K38 1995**
**Katok, A. B.**
Introduction to the modern theory of dynamical systems / Anatole Katok, Boris Hasselblatt ; with a supplement by Anatole Katok and Leonardo Mendoza. Cambridge ; Cambridge University Press, 1995. xviii, 802 p.
94-026547        515/.352        0521341876
*Differentiable dynamical systems.*

**QA614.8.P47 1982**
**Percival, Ian,**
Introduction to dynamics / Ian Percival, Derek Richards. Cambridge ; Cambridge University Press, 1982. 228 p. :
81-015514        515.3/5        0521236800
*Differentiable dynamical systems. Hamiltonian systems.*

**QA614.86.A23 1997**
**Addison, Paul S.**
Fractals and chaos : an illustrated course / Paul S. Addison. Bristol, UK ; Institute of Physics Pub., 1997. xii, 256 p. :
97-018158          514/.742          0750303999
*Fractals. Chaotic behavior in systems.*

**QA614.86.D38 1997**
**David, Guy,**
Fractured fractals and broken dreams : self-similar geometry through metric and measure / Guy David and Stephen Semmes. Oxford : Clarendon Press ; 1997. ix, 212 p. :
98-137453          514/.742          0198501668
*Fractals. Metric spaces. Measure theory.*

**QA614.86.L3813 1991**
**Lauwerier, H. A.**
Fractals : endlessly repeated geometrical figures / Hans Lauwerier ; translated by Sophia Gill-Hoffstadt. Princeton, N.J. : Princeton University Press, c1991. xiv, 209 p. :
90-040842          514/.74          069108551X
*Fractals.*

**QA614.86.P43 1992**
**Peitgen, Heinz-Otto,**
Chaos and fractals : new frontiers of science / Heinz-Otto Peitgen, Hartmut Jurgens, Dietmar Saupe. New York : Springer-Verlag, c1992. xvi, 984 p.,
92-023277          514/.74          0387979034
*Fractals. Chaotic behavior in systems.*

**QA614.86.P45 1991**
Fractals for the classroom / by Heinz-Otto Peitgen ... [et al.]. New York : Springer-Verlag, c1991-c1999. 3 v. :
91-011998          514/.74          038797346X
*Fractals.*

**QA614.86.S35 1988**
The Science of fractal images / Heinz-Otto Peitgen, Dietmar Saupe, editors ; Michael F. Barnsley ... [et al.] ; with contributions by Yuval Fisher, Michael McGuire. New York : Springer-Verlag, c1988. xiii, 312 p.
88-012683          516          0387966080
*Fractals.*

### QA641 Geometry — Differential geometry — General works, treatises, and textbooks

**QA641.C33**
**Carmo, Manfredo Perdigao do.**
Differential geometry of curves and surfaces / Manfredo P. do Carmo. Englewood Cliffs, N.J. : Prentice-Hall, c1976. viii, 503 p.
75-022094          516/.36          0132125897
*Geometry, Differential. Curves. Surfaces.*

**QA641.D23 1994**
**Darling, R. W. R.,**
Differential forms and connections / R.W.R. Darling. Cambridge ; Cambridge University Press, 1994. x, 256 p. :
93-046634          526.3/62          0521462592
*Geometry, Differential.*

**QA641.K6**
**Kobayashi, Shoshichi,**
Foundations of differential geometry [by] Shoshichi Kobayashi and Katsumi Nomizu. New York, Interscience Publishers, 1963-69. 2 v.
63-019209          516.7
*Geometry, Differential. Topology.*

**QA641.M35 1997**
**Maurin, Krzysztof.**
The Riemann legacy : Riemannian ideas in mathematics and physics / by Krzysztof Maurin. Dordrecht ; Kluwer Academic Publishers, c1997. xxii, 717 p.
97-017741          516.3/73          079234636X
*Riemann, Bernhard, -- 1826-1866.     Mathematical physics. Geometry, Riemannian.*

**QA641.M38 1994**
**McCleary, John,**
Geometry from a differentiable viewpoint / John McCleary. Cambridge [England] ; Cambridge University Press, 1994. xii, 308 p. :
93-046525          516.3/6          052141430X
*Geometry, Differential.*

### QA643 Geometry — Differential geometry — Curves on surfaces

**QA643.A52**
**Aminov, Yu A.**
Differential geometry and topology of curves / Yu. Amimov. Amsterdam, the Netherlands : Gordon and Breach Science Publishers, c2000. ix, 205 p. :
                    9056990918
*Curves on surfaces. Geometry, Differential.*

**QA643.V67 1993**
**Von Seggern, David H.**
CRC standard curves and surfaces / David von Seggern. Boca Raton : CRC Press, c1993. 388 p. :
92-033596          516.3/52          0849301963
*Curves on surfaces -- Handbooks, manuals, etc.*

### QA645 Geometry — Differential geometry — Surfaces determined by relations of curvature, etc.

**QA645.S75 1992**
**Stillwell, John.**
Geometry of surfaces / John Stillwell. New York : Springer-Verlag, c1992. xi, 216 p. :
91-036341          516.3/62          0387977430
*Surfaces of constant curvature.*

## QA681 Geometry — Foundations of geometry

**QA681.L4**
**Levi, Howard,**
Foundations of geometry and trigonometry. Englewood Cliffs, N.J., Prentice-Hall, 1960. 347 p.
60-015017          513.01
*Geometry -- Foundations.  Trigonometry.*

**QA681.R96 1956**
**Russell, Bertrand,**
An essay on the foundations of geometry; with a new foreword by Morris Kline. N[ew] Y[ork] Dover Publications [1956] 201 p.
56003665          513.01
*Geometry -- Foundations.*

## QA685 Geometry — Non-Euclidean geometry

**QA685.H515**
**Hilbert, David,**
Geometry and the imagination, by D. Hilbert and S. Cohn-Vossen; translated by P. Nemenyi. New York, Chelsea Pub. Co., 1952. 357 p.
52-002894          513
*Geometry, Non-Euclidean.*

**QA685.R6713 1988**
**Rozenfeld, B. A.**
A history of non-Euclidean geometry : evolution of the concept of a geometric space / B.A. Rosenfeld ; translated by Abe Shenitzer with the editorial assistance of Hardy Grant. New York : Springer-Verlag, c1988. ix, 471 p. :
87-009455          516/.9/09          0387964584
*Geometry, Non-Euclidean -- History.*

**QA685.S79 1993**
**Stahl, Saul.**
The Poincare half-plane : a gateway to modern geometry / Saul Stahl. Boston : Jones and Bartlett Publishers, c1993. xiii, 298 p.
92-035850          516.9          086720298X
*Geometry, Non-Euclidean.*

## QA691 Geometry — Hyperspace — General works

**QA691.B26 1990**
**Banchoff, Thomas.**
Beyond the third dimension : geometry, computer graphics, and higher dimensions / Thomas F. Banchoff. New York : Scientific American Library : c1990. ix, 210 p. :
90-008522          516.3/6          0716750252
*Hyperspace. Dimensions. Computer graphics.*

## QA699 Geometry — Hyperspace — Popular works. Fiction

**QA699.A13 1963**
**Abbott, Edwin Abbott,**
Flatland; a romance of many dimensions, with illus. by the author, a square (Edwin A. Abbott) With introd. by William Garnett. New York, Barnes & Noble [1963] 108 p.
63-012454          530.1/1          0064800059
*Fourth dimension.*

## QA803 Analytic mechanics — Newton's principia and commentaries

**QA803.A45 1969**
**Newton, Isaac,**
Mathematical principles of natural philosophy ... Translated into English by Andrew Motte in 1729. The translations rev. and supplied with an historical and explanatory appendix, by Florian Cajori. New York, Greenwood Press [1969, c1962] 2 v. (xxxiii,
73-088916          531          0837123003
*Mechanics -- Early works to 1800.  Celestial mechanics – Early works to 1800.*

**QA803.C48 1995**
**Chandrasekhar, S. (Subrahmanyan),**
Newton's Principia for the common reader / S. Chandrasekhar. Oxford ; New York : Oxford University Press ; Clarendon Press, 1995 xix, 593 p. :
          531 20          0198517440
*Newton, Isaac, Sir, 1642-1727. Principia.*

## QA805-807 Analytic mechanics — General works, treatises, and textbooks

**QA805.S45 2000**
**Selvadurai, A. P. S.**
Partial differential equations in mechanics / A.P.S. Selvadurai. Berlin ; Springer, c2000. 2 v. :
00-044024          531/.01/515353          3540672834
*Mechanics, Analytic. Differential equations, Partial.*

**QA805.T67 2000**
**Torok, Josef S.**
Analytical mechanics : with an introduction to dynamical systems / by Joseph S. Torok. New York : Wiley, 2000. p. cm.
99-022021          531          0471332070
*Mechanics, Analytic. Differentiable dynamical systems.*

**QA807.L95 1991**
**Lunn, Mary.**
A first course in mechanics / Mary Lunn. Oxford [England] ; Oxford University Press, 1991. x, 192 p. :
90-043228          531          0198534302
*Mechanics, Analytic.*

**QA807.S9 1959**
**Synge, J. L.**
Principles of mechanics [by] John L. Synge [and] Byron A. Griffith. New York, McGraw-Hill, 1959. 552 p.
58-013018         531
*Mechanics.*

## QA808 Analytic mechanics — Special aspects of the subject as a whole

**QA808.M49 1994**
**Middleton, Gerard V.**
Mechanics in the earth and environmental sciences / Gerard V. Middleton, Peter R. Wilcock. Cambridge ; Cambridge University Press, 1994. xvi, 459 p. :
93-049455         550/.1/531         0521441242
*Mechanics, Analytic. Geodynamics.*

## QA841 Analytic mechanics — Kinematics — General works

**QA841.M33 1990**
**McCarthy, J. M.**
An introduction to theoretical kinematics / J. Michael McCarthy. Cambridge, Mass. : MIT Press, c1990. 130 p. :
89-013505         531/.112         0262132524
*Kinematics.*

## QA845 Analytic mechanics — Dynamics — General works, treatises, and advanced textbooks

**QA845.A26 1982**
**Abraham, Ralph.**
Dynamics--the geometry of behavior / by Ralph H. Abraham and Christopher D. Shaw. Santa Cruz, Calif. : Aerial Press, [1982]-[1988] 4 v. :
81-071616         531/.11         0942344014
*Dynamics.*

**QA845.K36 1995**
**Kaplan, Daniel.**
Understanding nonlinear dynamics / Daniel Kaplan, Leon Glass. New York : Springer-Verlag, c1995. xix, 420 p. :
94-043113         515/.352         0387944400
*Dynamics. Nonlinear theories.*

**QA845.N39 1994**
**Nayfeh, Ali Hasan,**
Applied nonlinear dynamics : analytical, computational, and experimental methods / Ali H. Nayfeh, Balakumar Balachandran. New York : Wiley, c1995. xv, 685 p. :
94-003659         515/.352         0471593486
*Dynamics. Nonlinear theories.*

**QA845.V57 2000**
**Virgin, Lawrence N.,**
Introduction to experimental nonlinear dynamics : a case study in mechanical vibration / Lawrence N. Virgin. Cambridge, U.K. ; Cambridge University Press, c2000. xvi, 256 p. :
99-026994         003/.85         0521662869
*Dynamics. Nonlinear theories.*

## QA846 Analytic mechanics — Dynamics — Elementary textbooks

**QA846.M39**
**Maxwell, James Clerk,**
Matter and motion. Reprinted with notes and appendices by Sir Joseph Larmor. New York, Dover [1952] 163 p.
52009824
*Motion. Force and energy.*

**QA846.M39 2002**
**Maxwell, James Clerk,**
Matter and motion / by James Clerk Maxwell ; with notes and appendices by Joseph Larmor. Amherst, NY : Prometheus Books, 2002. p. cm.
         531/.11 21
*Dynamics.*

## QA852 Analytic mechanics — Dynamics — Dynamics of a particle

**QA852.M36**
**Mann, Ronald A.**
The classical dynamics of particles: Galilean and Lorentz relativity [by] Ronald A. Mann. New York, Academic Press, 1974. x, 299 p.
73-018937         531/.163         0124692508
*Dynamics of a particle. Relativity (Physics) Group theory.*

## QA862 Analytic mechanics — Rigid dynamics

**QA862.P4.B35 1990**
**Baker, Gregory L.**
Chaotic dynamics : an introduction / Gregory L. Baker and Jerry P. Gollub. Cambridge [England] ; Cambridge University Press, 1990. x, 182 p. :
89-022311         003         0521382580
*Pendulum. Chaotic behavior in systems.*

**QA862.T7.A93 1996**
**Audin, Michele.**
Spinning tops : a course on integrable systems / Michele Audin. Cambridge ; Cambridge University Press, 1996. vi, 139 p. :
96-011648         531/.34/0151474         0521561299
*Tops.*

## QA865 Analytic mechanics — Theory of vibrations. Oscillations — General works

**QA865.S49 1990**
**Shabana, Ahmed A.,**
  Theory of vibration / A.A. Shabana. New York : Springer-Verlag, c1991. 2 v. :
90-009582          531/.32          0387972765
  *Vibration.*

## QA871 Analytic mechanics — General methods of dynamics

**QA871.T33 1989**
**Tabor, Michael,**
  Chaos and integrability in nonlinear dynamics : an introduction / Michael Tabor. New York : Wiley, c1989. xiii, 364 p.
88-015516          531/.11          0471827282
  *Dynamics. Nonlinear theories. Chaotic behavior in systems.*

## QA911-929 Mechanics of deformable bodies — Fluid mechanics

**QA911.B33**
**Batchelor, G. K.**
  An introduction to fluid dynamics, by G.K. Batchelor. Cambridge, U.P., 1967. xviii, 615 p.
67-021953          532/.05
  *Fluid dynamics.*

**QA911.F434 1996**
**Ferziger, Joel H.**
  Computational methods for fluid dynamics / J.H. Ferziger, M. Peric. Berlin ; Springer, c1996. xiv,364p. :
96-000643          532/.05/015194          3540594345
  *Fluid dynamics -- Data processing.*

**QA911.K57 1997**
**Kleinstreuer, C.**
  Engineering fluid dynamics : an interdisciplinary systems approach / Clement Kleinstreuer. Cambridge, United Kingdom ; Cambridge University Press, 1997. xxi, 534 p. :
97-007689          620.1/064          0521496705
  *Fluid dynamics.*

**QA913.M39 2000**
**Mathieu, Jean,**
  An introduction to turbulent flow / Jean Mathieu, Julian Scott. Cambridge ; Cambridge University Press, 2000. ix, 374 p. :
99-016742          532/.0527          0521570662
  *Turbulence.*

**QA913.M43 1990**
**McComb, W. D.**
  The physics of fluid turbulence / W.D. McComb. Oxford : Clarendon Press ; 1990. xxiv, 572 p.
89-028440          532/.0527          0198561601
  *Turbulence. Fluid mechanics. Perturbation (Mathematics)*

**QA922.C56**
**Clift, R.**
  Bubbles, drops, and particles / R. Clift, J. R. Grace, and M. E. Weber. New York : Academic Press, 1978. xiii, 380 p.
77-006592          532/.052          012176950X
  *Multiphase flow. Particles. Drops.*

**QA927.D32 2000**
**Davis, Julian L.**
  Mathematics of wave propagation / Julian L. Davis. Princeton, NJ : Princeton University Press, 2000. xv, 395 p. :
99-044938          530.12/4          0691026432
  *Wave-motion, Theory of.*

**QA927.B25 2000**
**Billingham, J.**
  Wave motion / J. Billingham, A.C. King. Cambridge ; Cambridge University Press, 2000. ix, 468 p. :
01-270652                    0521632579
  *Wave-motion, Theory of.*

**QA927.K693 2000**
**Knobel, Roger,**
  An introduction to the mathematical theory of waves / Roger Knobel. Providence, R.I. : American Mathematical Society : c2000. xiv, 196 p. :
99-039055          531/.1133          0821820397
  *Wave motion, Theory of.*

**QA929.O25 1995**
**Ockendon, Hilary.**
  Viscous flow / H. Ockendon & J.R. Ockendon. Cambridge ; Cambridge University Press, 1995. viii, 113 p.
94-017066          532/.0533          0521452449
  *Viscous flow.*

## QA931-935 Elasticity. Plasticity — General works, treatises and textbooks

**QA931.L283 1986**
**Landau, L. D.**
  Theory of elasticity / by L.D. Landau and E.M. Lifshitz ; translated from the Russian by J.B. Sykes and W.H. Reid. Oxford [Oxfordshire] ; Pergamon Press, 1986. viii, 187 p.
86-002450          531/.38          0080339174
  *Elasticity. Elastic solids.*

**QA931.S6 1956**
**Sokolnikoff, Ivan Stephen,**
  Mathematical theory of elasticity. New York, McGraw-Hill, 1956. 476 p.
55-009554          620.1123
  *Elasticity.*

**QA931.T55 1970**
**Timoshenko, Stephen,**
Theory of elasticity [by] S. P. Timoshenko [and] J. N. Goodier. New York, McGraw-Hill [1969, c1970] xxiv, 567 p.
69-013617          531/.3823
*Elasticity. Strains and stresses. Strength of materials.*

**QA935.K38 1993**
**Kelly, S. Graham.**
Fundamentals of mechanical vibrations / S. Graham Kelly. New York : McGraw-Hill, c1993. xviii, 643 p.
92-035797          531/.32          0079115330
*Vibration.*

# QB Astronomy

## QB1 Societies, congresses, serial collections, yearbooks

**QB1.A2884**
Annual review of astronomy and astrophysics. Palo Alto, Calif., U.S.A. : Annual Reviews, c1963- v. :
63-008846          520
*Astronomy -- Periodicals. Astrophysics -- Periodicals.*

**QB1.S775 2001**
StarGuides 2001 : a world-wide directory of organizations in astronomy, related space sciences, and other related fields / compiled by Andre Heck. Dordrecht ; Kluwer Academic Publishers, c2001. xxiii, 1220 p
00-060911          520/.25          0792365097
*Astronomy -- Societies, etc. -- Directories. Astronomy -- Directories. Astronomical observatories -- Directories.*

## QB3 Collected works (nonserial)

**QB3.K3313 1992**
**Kepler, Johannes,**
New astronomy / Johannes Kepler ; translated by William H. Donahue. Cambridge [England] ; Cambridge University Press, 1992. xvi, 665 p. :
90-025494          520          0521301319
*Astronomy.*

**QB3.S52**
**Shapley, Harlow,**
Source book in astronomy, 1900-1950. Cambridge, Harvard University Press, 1960. xv, 423 p.
60-013294          520.82
*Astronomy.*

## QB6 Star catalogs

**QB6.S54 1991**
Sky catalogue 2000.0 / [edited] by Alan Hirshfeld, Roger W. Sinnott, and Francois Ochsenbein. Cambridge [England] ; Cambridge University Press ; 1991- v. 1   :
91-026764          523.8/0212          0521417430
*Stars -- Catalogs.*

**QB8 Ephemerides — 1801- — Nautical and air (or aeronautical) almanacs. By country, A-Z**

**QB8.U6A77**
The astronomical almanac for the year . . . Washington ; London : G.P.O. ; H.M.S.O., c1980- v. :
          528          0737-6421
*Nautical almanacs -- Periodicals.*

## QB14 Dictionaries and encyclopedias

**QB14.A873 1991**
The Astronomy and astrophysics encyclopedia / edited by Stephen P. Maran ; foreword by Carl Sagan. New York : Van Nostrand Reinhold, c1992. xxix, 1002 p.
91-023241          520/.3          0442263643
*Astronomy -- Encyclopedias. Astrophysics -- Encyclopedias.*

**QB14.C34 1996**
Cambridge astronomy dictionary / [editorial consultants, Ian Ridpath and John Woodruff]. Cambridge, [England] ; Cambridge University Press, 1996. 240 p. :
96-229055          520          0521580072
*Astronomy -- Dictionaries.*

**QB14.F3 2000**
The Facts on File dictionary of astronomy / edited by Valerie Illingworth, John O.E. Clark. New York : Facts on File, c2000. 490 p. :
00-055553          520/.3          0816042837
*Astronomy -- Encyclopedias. Astrophysics -- Encyclopedias.*

**QB14.I588 2001**
The illustrated encyclopedia of the universe / foreword by Martin Rees ; general editor, Ian Ridpath. New York : Watson-Guptill Publications, 2001. 384 p. :
01-087745          520/.3          0823025128
*Astronomy -- Dictionaries.*

**QB14.M3725 1993**
McGraw-Hill encyclopedia of astronomy / editors in chief, Sybil P. Parker, Jay M. Pasachoff. New York : McGraw-Hill, c1993. 531 p., [16]
92-040523          520/.3          0070453144
*Astronomy -- Encyclopedias.*

# QB14.5 Philosophy

**QB14.5.T74 1988**
**Trefil, James S.,**
The dark side of the universe : a scientist explores the mysteries of the cosmos / by James Trefil ; illustrations by Judith Peatross. New York : Scribner's, c1988. v, 197 p. :
88-001061          523.1/01          0684187957
*Astronomy -- Philosophy. Cosmology.*

# QB15 History — General works

**QB15.B67 2001**
**Brashear, Ronald,**
Star struck : one thousand years of the art and science of astronomy / Ronald Brashear, Daniel Lewis ; historical perspective, Owen Gingerich. San Marino, CA : Huntington Library, 2000. p. cm.
00-053975          520/.9          0873281861
*Astronomy -- History.*

**QB15.C36 1997**
The Cambridge illustrated history of astronomy / edited by Michael Hoskin. Cambridge ; Cambridge University Press, 1997. ix, 392 p. :
95-040923          520/.9          0521411580
*Astronomy -- History.*

**QB15.D77 1953**
**Dreyer, J. L. E.**
A history of astronomy from Thales to Kepler, formerly titled History of the planetary systems from Thales to Kepler; rev. with a foreword by W.H. Stahl. [New York] Dover Publications [1953] 438 p.
53-012387          520.9
*Astronomy -- History.     Solar system.*

**QB15.G38 1984 vol. 2**
Planetary astronomy from the Renaissance to the rise of astrophysics / edited by Rene Taton and Curtis Wilson. Cambridge [England] ; Cambridge University Press, 1989-1995. 2 v. :
88-025817          520/.9 s          0521242541
*Astronomy -- History. Astrophysics -- History.*

**QB15.G563 1993**
**Gingerich, Owen.**
The eye of heaven : Ptolemy, Copernicus, Kepler / Owen Gingerich. New York, NY : American Institute of Physics, c1993. viii, 442 p.
91-026227          520/.9          0883188635
*Ptolemy, -- 2nd cent. Copernicus, Nicolaus, -- 1473-1543. Kepler, Johannes, -- 1571-1630. Astronomy -- History.*

**QB15.H624 1997**
History of astronomy : an encyclopedia / edited by John Lankford. New York : Garland Pub., 1997. xix, 594 p. :
96-028558          520/.3          081530322X
*Astronomy -- History -- Encyclopedias.*

**QB15.L4**
**Ley, Willy,**
Watchers of the skies: an informal history of astronomy from Babylon to the space age.  New York, Viking Press [1963] xiii, 528 p.
61-007386          523.09
*Astronomy -- History.*

**QB15.L54 1992**
**Lightman, Alan P.,**
Time for the stars : astronomy in the 1990s / Alan Lightman ; with a foreword by John Bahcall. New York, N.Y., U.S.A. : Viking, 1992. xviii, 124 p.
91-018091          520/.9/049          0670839760
*Astronomy -- History.  Astronomy and state -- United States.*

**QB15.P38 2001**
**Pecker, Jean Claude.**
Understanding the heavens : thirty centuries of astronomical ideas from ancient thinking to modern cosmology / Jean-Claude Pecker ; edited by Susan Kaufman. Berlin ; Springer, c2001. xiii, 597 p.
00-024396          520/.9          3540631984
*Astronomy -- History.*

# QB16 History — Ancient — General works

**QB16.A73 1984**
Archaeoastronomy and the roots of science / edited by E.C. Krupp. Boulder, Colo. : Published by Westview Press for the American Ass 1984. xii, 336 p. :
83-050763          520/.93          0865314063
*Astronomy, Prehistoric.*

**QB16.A75 2000**
Astronomy across cultures : the history of non-Western astronomy / Helaine Selin, editor. Boston : Kluwer Academic Publishers, 2000. p. cm.
00-033053          520/.93          0792363639
*Astronomy, Ancient. Astronomy -- Asia -- History. Astronomy–Africa -- History.*

**QB16.A88 1997**
**Aveni, Anthony F.**
Stairways to the stars : skywatching in three great ancient cultures / Anthony Aveni. New York : J. Wiley, 1997. ix, 230 p. :
96-036517          520/.93          0471159425
*Astronomy, Ancient. Astronomy, Prehistoric.*

**QB16.E93 1998**
**Evans, James,**
The history and practice of ancient astronomy / James Evans. New York : Oxford University Press, 1998. xiii, 480 p.
97-016539          520/.938          0195095391
*Astronomy, Ancient.*

## QB29 History — Modern — Renaissance through 1700

**QB29.H33 1999**
**Heilbron, J. L.**
The sun in the Church : cathedrals as solar observatories / J.L. Heilbron. Cambridge, Mass. : Harvard University Press, 1999. ix, 366 p. :
99-023123        520/.94        0674854330
*Astronomy, Renaissance. Religion and science – Italy – History – 17th century. Astronomical observatories -- Italy.*

**QB29.S6 1963**
**Small, Robert,**
An account of the astronomical discoveries of Kepler. A reprinting of the 1804 text, with a foreword by William D. Stahlman. Madison, University of Wisconsin Press, 1963. 386 p.
63-010536        520.9
*Kepler, Johannes, -- 1571-1630.      Astronomy -- History.*

## QB32 History — Modern — 19th-20th centuries

**QB32.T92 1963**
**Turner, Herbert Hall,**
Astronomical discovery. Foreword by Dirk Brouwer. Berkeley, University of California Press, 1963. 225 p.
63008661        523
*Astronomy -- History.*

## QB35 Biography — Collective

**QB35.L48 2001**
**Levy, David H.,**
Cosmic discoveries : the wonders of astronomy / David H. Levy with Wendee Wallach-Levy. Amherst, N.Y. : Prometheus Books, 2001. 232 p. :
        520/.92/2 B 21        157392931X
*Astronomers -- Biography. Astronomy -- History.*

## QB36 Biography — Individual, A-Z

**QB36.A2**
**Standage, Tom.**
The Neptune file : a story of astronomical rivalry and the pioneers of planet hunting / Tom Standage. New York : Walker, c2000. x, 240 p. :
00-043486        523.48/1        0802713637
*Adams, John Couch, -- 1819-1892.    Planetology.    Neptune (Planet)*

**QB36.B63.L48 1993**
**Levy, David H.,**
The man who sold the Milky Way : a biography of Bart Bok / David H. Levy. Tucson : University of Arizona Press, c1993. xiii, 246 p.
93-004039        520/.92        0816511497
*Bok, Bart Jan, -- 1906-    Astronomers -- United States – Biography.*

**QB36.B8.T49 1990**
**Thoren, Victor E.**
The Lord of Uraniborg : a biography of Tycho Brahe / Victor E. Thoren ; with contributions by John R. Christianson. Cambridge [England] ; Cambridge University Press, 1990. xi, 523 p. :
90-001477        520/.92        0521351588
*Brahe, Tycho, -- 1546-1601.    Astronomers – Denmark – Biography. Astronomy -- History -- 16th century.*

**QB36.C46.W35 1991**
**Wali, K. C.**
Chandra : a biography of S. Chandrasekhar / Kameshwar C. Wali. Chicago : University of Chicago Press, 1991. x, 341 p., [3
90-010845        523.01/092        0226870545
*Chandrasekhar, S. -- (Subrahmanyan), -- 1910-    Astrophysicists – United States -- Biography.*

**QB36.C76.A3 2000**
**Consolmagno, Guy,**
Brother astronomer : adventures of a Vatican scientist / Guy Consolmagno. New York : McGraw-Hill, c2000. vi, 229 p. :
99-086237        520/.92        007135428X
*Consolmagno, Guy, -- 1952-    Astronomers -- Italy -- Biography.*

**QB36.G2.A233**
**Galilei, Galileo,**
The achievement of Galileo. Edited with notes by James Brophy and Henry Paolucci. With an introd. by Henry Paolucci. New York, Twayne Publishers [1962] 256 p.
61-015673        925.2
*Galilei, Galileo, -- 1564-1642.*

**QB36.G2.A25 1957**
**Galilei, Galileo,**
Discoveries and opinions of Galileo. Translated with an introd. and notes by Stillman Drake. Garden City, N.Y., Doubleday, 1957. viii, 302 p.
57-006305        520
*Astronomy – Early works to 1800.*

**QB36.G2.C27 1998**
The Cambridge companion to Galileo / edited by Peter Machamer. Cambridge ; Cambridge University Press, 1998. xii, 462 p. :
98-013357        520/.92        0521581788
*Galilei, Galileo, -- 1564-1642.    Science -- Philosophy -- History.*

**QB36.G2.D4 1955**
**De Santillana, Giorgio,**
The crime of Galileo.    [Chicago] University of Chicago Press [1955] xx, 338 p.
55-007400        925.2
*Galilei, Galileo, -- 1564-1642.*

**QB36.G2.D688**
**Drake, Stillman.**
Galileo / Stillman Drake. Oxford : Oxford University Press, 1980. vii, 100 p. ;
81-179072        520/.92/4        0192875272
*Galilei, Galileo, -- 1564-1642.    Astronomers -- Italy – Biography.*

**QB36.G2.S65 1999**
Sobel, Dava.

Galileo's daughter : a historical memoir of science, faith, and love / Dava Sobel. New York : Walker & Co., 1999. ix, 420 p. :
99-023885          520/.92          0802713432
*Galilei, Galileo, -- 1564-1642 -- Correspondence. Galilei, Maria Celeste, -- 1600-1634 -- Correspondence.   Astronomers -- Italy – Biography.*

**QB36.K4.C33**
Caspar, Max,

Kepler. Translated and edited by C. Doris Hellman. London, Abelard-Schuman [c1959] 401 p.
59-005797          925.2
*Kepler, Johannes, -- 1571-1630.   Astronomers -- Germany -- Biography.*

**QB36.L849**
Strauss, David,

Percival Lowell : the culture and science of a Boston Brahmin / David Strauss. Cambridge, Mass. : Harvard University Press, 2001. xi, 333 p. :
00-058080          520/.92          0674002911
*Lowell, Percival, -- 1855-1916.   Astronomers -- United States – Biography.*

**QB36.M378.H69 1989**
Howse, Derek.

Nevil Maskelyne, the seaman's astronomer / Derek Howse ; with a foreword by Sir Francis Graham-Smith. Cambridge [England] ; Cambridge University Press, 1989. xiv, 280 p. :
88-015967          520/.92/4          052136261X
*Maskelyne, Nevil, -- 1732-1811.   Astronomers -- Great Britain – Biography.*

**QB36.S15.D38 1999**
Davidson, Keay.

Carl Sagan : a life / Keay Davidson. New York : J.Wiley, c1999. xx, 540 p. ;
99-036206          520/.92          0471252867
*Sagan, Carl, -- 1934-   Astronomers -- United States –Biography.*

# QB41 Early works through 1700

**QB41.C815.K8**
Kuhn, Thomas S.

The Copernican revolution; planetary astronomy in the development of Western thought.   Cambridge, Harvard University Press, 1957. xviii, 297 p.
57-007612          523.2
*Copernicus, Nicolaus, -- 1473-1543. -- De revolutionibus orbium coelestis.   Cosmology.*

**QB41.C84 1939a**
Copernicus, Nicolaus,

Three Copernican treatises: the Commentariolus of Copernicus, the Letter against Werner, the Narratio prima of Rheticus; translated with introduction and notes by Edward Rosen ... New York, Columbia university press, 1939. x p., 2 l., [
40-014280
*Werner, Johannes, -- 1468-1528. -- De motu octavae sphaerae. Astronomy -- Early works to 1800.*

**QB41.G1356**
Galilei, Galileo,

Dialogue concerning the two chief world systems, Ptolemaic & Copernican; translated by Stillman Drake. Foreword by Albert Einstein. Berkeley, University of California Press, 1953. xxvii, 496 p.
53-011238          520
*Astronomy -- Early works to 1800.   Solar system – Early works to 1800.*

**QB41.G136 1953**
Galilei, Galileo,

Dialogue on the great world systems, in the Salusbury translation. [Chicago] University of Chicago Press [1953] lviii, 505 p.
53011771          520
*Astronomy -- Early works to 1800.   Solar system.*

**QB41.G173 1997**
Galilei, Galileo,

Galileo on the world systems : a new abridged translation and guide / Maurice A. Finocchiaro. Berleley : University of California Press, c1997. xi, 425 p. :
96-004256          520          0520205480
*Galilei, Galileo, -- 1564-1642. -- Dialogo dei massimi sistemi. Astronomy -- Early works to 1800.   Solar system -- Early works to 1800.*

# QB43 General works, treatises, and advanced textbooks — 1801-1969

**QB43.M55**
Motz, Lloyd,

Essentials of astronomy [by] Lloyd Motz and Anneta Duveen. Belmont, Calif., Wadsworth Pub. Co. [1966] viii, 711 p.
65-010031          523
*Astronomy.*

**QB43.U47 1997**

The universe at large : key issues in astronomy and cosmology / edited by Guido Munch, Antonio Mampaso, and Francisco Sanchez. Cambridge, U.K. ; Cambridge University Press, 1997. xi, 447 p. :
96-028580          523          0521553679
*Astronomy. Cosmology.*

## QB43.2 General works, treatises, and advanced textbooks — 1970-

**QB43.2.B45 2001**
**Bennett, Jeffrey O.**
  On the cosmic horizon : ten great mysteries for third millennium astronomy / Jeff Bennett. San Francisco, CA : Addison Wesley Longman, c2001. viii, 209 p.
00-044182        520/.9/05        0321029712
   *Astronomy. Astrophysics. Cosmology.*

**QB43.2.C35**
  The Cambridge encyclopaedia of astronomy / editor-in-chief, Simon Mitton ; foreword by Sir Martin Ryle. New York : Crown Publishers, 1977. 481 p. :
77-002766        520        0517528061
   *Astronomy.*

**QB43.2.G72 1988**
**Graham-Smith, Francis,**
  Pathways to the universe / Francis Graham-Smith, Bernard Lovell. Cambridge ; Cambridge University Press, 1988. 239 p. :
86-024517        520        0521320046
   *Astronomy.*

**QB43.2.H65 1999**
**Holliday, Keith.**
  Introductory astronomy / Keith Holliday. Chichester ; Wiley, c1999. xii, 314 p. :
98-018192        520        0471983314
   *Astronomy.*

**QB43.2.H69**
**Hoyle, Fred,**
  Astronomy and cosmology : a modern course / Fred Hoyle. San Francisco : W. H. Freeman, [1975] xiv, 711 p.,
74-028441        520        0716703513
   *Astronomy. Cosmology.*

**QB43.2.L43 1989**
**Lederman, Leon M.**
  From quarks to the cosmos : tools of discovery / Leon M. Lederman, David N. Schramm. New York : Scientific American Library : c1989. x, 242 p. :
89-010207        520        071675052X
   *Astronomy. Particles (Nuclear physics) Science -- Philosophy.*

**QB43.2.M674 1989**
**Motz, Lloyd,**
  The unfolding universe : a stellar journey / Lloyd Motz and Jefferson Hane Weaver. New York : Plenum Press, c1989. xii, 389 p. ;
89-008782        520        0306432641
   *Astronomy.*

**QB43.2.N53 1999**
**Nicolson, Iain.**
  Unfolding our universe / Iain Nicolson ; original illustrations by Mark McLellan. Cambridge ; Cambridge University Press, 1999. ix, 294 p. :
99-017151        520        0521592704
   *Astronomy.*

**QB43.2.P33 1996**
**Parker, Barry R.**
  Chaos in the cosmos : the stunning complexity of the universe / Barry Parker. New York : Plenum Press, c1996. viii, 307 p.
96-001482        520/.151474        0306452618
   *Astrophysics. Chaotic behavior in systems.*

**QB43.2.W96 1991**
**Wynn-Williams, C. G.**
  The fullness of space : nebulae, stardust, and the interstellar medium / Gareth Wynn-Williams. Cambridge [England] ; Cambridge University Press, 1992. xv, 202 p. :
91-027956        523.1/125        0521426383
   *Astronomy. Interstellar matter. Cosmic dust.*

## QB44 Popular works — Through 1969

**QB44.H86 1955a**
**Hoyle, Fred,**
  Frontiers of astronomy. New York, Harper [1955] 360 p.
55-006582        520
   *Astronomy.*

**QB44.M5425**
**Moore, Patrick.**
  The atlas of the universe. Foreword by Bernard Lovell. Epilogue by Thomas O. Paine. New York, Rand McNally [1970] 272 p.
77-653619        523
   *Astronomy -- Popular works.*

**QB44.S5734**
  Wanderers in the sky; the motions of planets and space probes. Edited by Thornton Page & Lou Williams Page. New York, Macmillan Co. [1965] xiv, 338 p.
65-012722        523
   *Astronomy -- Popular works. Astronautics in astronomy.*

## QB44.2-44.3 Popular works — 1970-

**QB44.2.A84 1980**
**Asimov, Isaac,**
  The universe : from flat earth to black holes--and beyond / Isaac Asimov. New York : Walker, c1980. 321 p., [8] 1
79-048052        523        080270655X
   *Astronomy -- Popular works.*

**QB44.2.C65 2001**
**Comins, Neil F.,**
   Heavenly errors : misconceptions about the real nature of the universe / Neil F. Comins. New York : Columbia University Press, c2001. xi, 244 p. :
00-050853          520          0231116446
   *Astronomy. Errors, Popular.*

**QB44.2.G752 1998**
**Gribbin, John R.**
   The case of the missing neutrinos : and other curious phenomena of the universe / John Gribbin. New York : Fromm International, 1998. vi, 234 p. ;
98-027948          520          0880641991
   *Astronomy -- Popular works.*

**QB44.2.G753**
**Gribbin, John R.**
   Genesis : the origins of man and the universe / John Gribbin. New York : Delacorte Press/Eleanor Friede, c1981. xvi, 360 p. :
80-024267          577          0440028329
   *Astronomy. Life -- Origin.*

**QB44.2.G758 1997**
**Gribbin, John R.**
   Origins : our place in Hubble's universe / John Gribbin, Simon Goodwin. Woodstock, N.Y. : Overlook Press, 1997. p. cm.
97-021833          520          0879518138
*Hubble, Edwin Powell, -- 1889-1953.     Astronomy. Astronomy – Pictorial works. Astronomers -- United States -- Biography.*

**QB44.2.K35 1999**
**Kanipe, Jeff,**
   A skywatcher's year / Jeff Kanipe. Cambridge, UK ; Cambridge University Press, 1999. xiv, 189 p. :
98-041631          520          0521634059
   *Astronomy -- Popular works. Astronomy -- Observers' manuals. Stars -- Observers' manuals.*

**QB44.2.P74 1996**
**Preston, Richard,**
   First light : the search for the edge of the universe / Richard Preston. New York : Random House, c1996. xvii, 275 p.
96-013065          520          0679449698
   *Astronomy -- Research -- California -- Popular works. Astronomy -- Popular works.*

**QB44.2.S235 1995**
**Sagan, Carl,**
   Cosmos / Carl Sagan. Avenel, N.J. : Wings Books : 1995. p .cm.
          520 20     051712355X
*Astronomy -- Popular works.*

**QB44.2.U554 1998**
**Upgren, Arthur R.**
   Night has a thousand eyes : a naked-eye guide to the sky, its science, and lore / Arthur Upgren. New York : Plenum Trade, c1998. ix, 301 p. :
98-013412          520          0306457903
   *Astronomy -- Popular works.*

**QB44.3.P58 2002**
**Plait, Philip C.**
   Bad astronomy : misconceptions and misuses revealed, from astrology to the moon landing 'hoax' / Philip C. Plait ; [illustrations by Tina Cash Walch]. New York : Wiley, c2002. vii, 277 p. :
                  0471409766
*Astronomy -- Popular works. Astronomy -- Miscellanea. Errors, Scientific.*

## QB45 Elementary textbooks

**QB45.A16 1987**
**Abell, George O.**
   Exploration of the universe / George O. Abell, David Morrison, Sidney C. Wolff. Philadelphia : Saunders College Pub., c1987. x, 748, [7] p
86-026045          520          0030051436
   *Astronomy.*

**QB45.B15 1971**
**Baker, Robert Horace,**
   Astronomy [by] Robert H. Baker [and] Laurence W. Fredrick. New York, Van Nostrand Reinhold Co. [1971] xiv, 631 p.
74-127649          520
   *Astronomy.*

## QB51 Addresses, essays, lectures

**QB51.A77 1984**
**Ashbrook, Joseph,**
   The astronomical scrapbook : skywatchers, pioneers, and seekers in astronomy / by Joseph Ashbrook ; edited by Leif J. Robinson ; introduction by Owen Gingerich. Cambridge [Cambridgeshire] ; Cambridge University Press ; 1984. xii, 468 p. :
84-012036          520          0521300452
   *Astronomy.*

**QB51.H8 1960**
**Hoyle, Fred,**
   The nature of the universe. New York, Harper [1960] 141 p.
60-013436          523
   *Astronomy.*

**QB51.L6**
**Lovell, Bernard,**
   The exploration of outer space. New York, Harper & Row [c1962] 87 p.
62014566          520.81
   *Astronautics and ethics. Cosmology. Astronomy.*

**QB51.T75 1992**
**Trimble, Virginia.**
Visit to a small universe / Virginia Trimble. New York, NY : American Institute of Physics, c1992. xiv, 336 p. :
91-042614          520          0883187922
*Astronomy.*

## QB51.3 Special topics, A-Z

**QB51.3.E43**
**Montenbruck, Oliver,**
Astronomy on the personal computer / Oliver Montenbruck, Thomas Pfleger ; translated by Storm Dunlop ; with a foreword by Richard M. West. Berlin ; Springer, c2000. xv, 310 p. :
00-029654          522/.85/5362          3540672214
*Astronomy -- Data processing. Microcopmuters.*

## QB52 Miscellany and curiosa

**QB52.A74 1991**
**Asimov, Isaac,**
Isaac Asimov's guide to earth and space / Isaac Asimov. New York : Random House, c1991. xiii, 285 p.
91-011097          520          0679404376
*Astronomy -- Miscellanea.     Earth -- Miscellanea.*

**QB52.O34 1998**
**Odenwald, Sten F.**
The astronomy cafe : 365 questions and answers from "Ask the Astronomer" / Sten F. Odenwald. New York : W.H. Freeman, c1998. xii, 252 p. :
98-002696          520          0716733560
*Astronomy -- Miscellanea.*

## QB54 Extraterrestrial life

**QB54.B38 1985**
**Baugher, Joseph F.**
On civilized stars : the search for intelligent life in outer space / Joseph F. Baugher. Englewood Cliffs, N.J. : Prentice-Hall, c1985. xi, 260 p. :
84-018374          574.999          0136344119
*Life on other planets.*

**QB54.C37 1997**
Carl Sagan's universe / edited by Yervant Terzian, Elizabeth Bilson. Cambridge, U.K. ; Cambridge University Press, 1997. xiii, 282 p.
96-040511          500          052157286X
*Sagan, Carl, -- 1934-     Science news. Science -- Social aspects. Life on other planets.*

**QB54.C566 2000**
**Clark, Stuart**
Life on other worlds and how to find it / Stuart Clark. London ; Springer published in association with Praxis Pu c2000. xvi, 179 p. :
99-058201          576.8/39          185233097X
*Life on other planets.*

**QB54.C76 1986**
**Crowe, Michael J.**
The extraterrestrial life debate, 1750-1900 : the idea of a plurality of worlds from Kant to Lowell / Michael J. Crowe. Cambridge [Cambridgeshire] ; Cambridge University Press, 1986. xix, 680 p. :
85-007842          574.999          0521263050
*Plurality of worlds -- History. Life on other planets -- History.*

**QB54.D38 1995**
**Davies, P. C. W.**
Are we alone? : philosophical implications of the discovery of extraterrestrial life / Paul Davies. New York : BasicBooks, 1995. xiii, 160 p.
95-002499          574.999          0465004180
*Life on other planets. Life -- Origin. Cosmology.*

**QB54.D3913 1991**
**Davoust, Emmanuel.**
The cosmic water hole / Emmanuel Davoust ; translated by Barbara Jachowicz. Cambridge, Mass. : MIT Press, 1991. xv, 206 p. :
90-042961          574.999          0262041146
*Life on other planets. Extraterrestrial anthropology.*

**QB54.D475 1998**
**Dick, Steven J.**
Life on other worlds : the 20th-century extraterrestrial life debate / Steven J. Dick. Cambridge ; Cambridge University Press, 1998. xiii, 290 p.
98-020465          576.8/39          0521620120
*Life on other planets. Exobiology.*

**QB54.D72 1992**
**Drake, Frank D.**
Is anyone out there? : the scientific search for extraterrestrial intelligence / Frank Drake and Dava Sobel. New York, N.Y. : Delacorte Press, 1992. xv, 272 p. :
92-003884          591.9099          038530532X
*Drake, Frank D.     Life on other planets. Astronomers -- United States -- Biography.*

**QB54.K54 2000**
**Koerner, David.**
Here be dragons : the scientific quest for extraterrestrial life / David Koerner, Simon LeVay. New York : Oxford University Press, 2000. 264 p. :
99-038170          576.8/39          0195128524
*Life on other planets. Life -- Origin.*

**QB54.M23 2001**
**McConnell, Brian.**
Beyond contact : a guide to SETI and communicating with alien civilizations / Brian McConnell. Beijing ; O'Reilly, c2001. vi, 417 p. :
01-273629          576.8/39          0596000375
*Life on other planets. Interstellar communication. EXTRATERRESTRIAL INTELLIGENCE. -- nasat*

**QB54.S44 1990**

SETI pioneers : scientists talk about their search for extraterrestrial intelligence / David W. Swift. Tucson : University of Arizona Press, c1990. xi, 434 p. :
89-020214      574.999      0816511195
*Life on other planets. Interstellar communication. Scientists – Interviews.*

**QB54.W336 2000**
**Ward, Peter Douglas,**

Rare earth : why complex life is uncommon in the universe / Peter Ward, Donald Brownlee. New York : Copernicus, c2000. xxviii, 333 p
99-020532      576.8/39      0387987010
*Life on other planets. Exobiology.*

## QB61 Study and teaching. Research

**QB61.L47 1997**
**Levy, David H.,**

Sharing the sky : a parent's and teacher's guide to astronomy / David H. Levy, Larry A. Lebofsky, Nancy R. Lebofsky. New York : Plenum Press, 1997. p. cm.
97-035720      372.3/5      0306456389
*Astronomy -- Study and teaching (Elementary)*

### QB62.7 Study and teaching. Research — Laboratory manuals

**QB62.7.S3713 1991**
**Schlosser, W.**

Challenges of astronomy : hands-on experiments for the sky and laboratory / W. Schlosser, T. Schmidt-Kaler, E.F. Milone. New York : Springer-Verlag, c1991. vii, 236 p.,
90-043848      522/.078      0387974083
*Astronomy -- Experiments.*

## QB63 Stargazers' guides

**QB63.A7813 1994**

The observer's guide to astronomy / edited by Patrick Martinez ; translator Storm Dunlop. Cambridge ; Cambridge University Press, 1994. 2 v. (xvi, 11
93-029830      520      052137068X
*Astronomy -- Amateurs' manuals. Astronomy -- Observers' manuals.*

**QB63.C69 2000**
**Consolmagno, Guy,**

Turn left at Orion : a hundred night sky objects to see in a small telescope -- and how to find them / Guy Consolmagno and Dan M. Davis ; illustrations by Karen Kotash Sepp, Anne Drogin, and Mary Lynn Skirvin. 3rd ed. Cambridge ; New York : Cambridge University Press, 2000. 224 p. :
      523 21      0521781906
*Astronomy -- Amateurs' manuals.*

**QB63.E39 1993**
**Ellyard, David,**

The southern sky guide / David Ellyard and Wil Tirion. Cambridge [England] ; Cambrideg University Press, 1993. vi, 82 p. :
92-039556      523.8/022/3      0521428394
*Southern sky (Astronomy) -- Observers' manuals. Southern sky (Astronomy) -- Amateurs' manuals.*

**QB63.L55 1985**
**Liller, William,**

The Cambridge astronomy guide : a practical introduction to astronomy / William Liller and Ben Mayer. Cambridge [Cambridgeshire] ; Cambridge University Press, 1985. 176 p. :
85-016582      523      0521257786
*Astronomy -- Amateurs' manuals.*

**QB63.M63 2000**
**Moore, Patrick.**

Exploring the night sky with binoculars / Patrick Moore. 4th ed. New York ; Cambridge : Cambridge University Press, 2000. vi, 213 p. :
      520/.22/3 21      0521790530
*Astronomy -- Observers' manuals.*

**QB63.M66 2001**
**Moore, Patrick.**

Stargazing : astronomy without a telescope / Patrick Moore. Cambridge ; Cambridge University Press, c2001. vi, 209 p. :
00-037884      523      0521794455
*Astronomy -- Observers' manuals.*

**QB63.R527 1998**
**Ridpath, Ian.**

Stars and planets / Ian Ridpath ; editorial consultant, Amie Gallagher ; star charts by Royal Greenwich Observatory. New York : DK Pub., c1998. 224 p. :
98-011961      520      0789435608
*Astronomy -- Observers' manuals. Stars -- Observers' manuals. Planets -- Observers' manuals.*

**QB63.S575 1993**

Sky watcher's handbook : the expert reference source for the amateur astronomer / edited by James Muirden. Oxford, Eng. : W.H. Freeman, c1993. viii, 408 p.
92-032996      520      071674502X
*Astronomy -- Amateurs' manuals. Astronomy -- Observers' manuals.*

## QB64 Observers' handbooks

**QB64.B85 1978**
**Burnham, Robert.**

Burnham's celestial handbook : an observer's guide to the Universe beyond the solar system / Robert Burnham, Jr. New York : Dover Publications, 1978. 3 v. (2138 p.
77-082888      523.8/9      048623567X
*Astronomy -- Observers' manuals.*

QB64.C58 1988
Clark, Roger N.
Visual astronomy of the deep sky / Roger N. Clark. Cambridge ; Cambridge University Press ; 1990. xiii, 355 p.
88-010290          523          0521361559
*Astronomy -- Amateurs' manuals. Telescopes -- Amateurs' manuals. Galaxies -- Atlases -- Amateurs' manuals.*

QB64.L55 1992
Liller, William,
The Cambridge guide to astronomical discovery / William Liller. Cambridge ; Cambridge University Press, 1992. xi, 257 p. :
92-002705          520          0521418399
*Astronomy -- Observers' manuals. Astronomy -- Amateurs' manuals.*

QB64.L84 1990
Luginbuhl, Christian B.
Observing handbook and catalogue of deep-sky objects / Christian B. Luginbuhl, Brian A. Skiff. Cambridge ; Cambridge University Press, 1990. xi, 352 p. :
89-007318          522          0521256658
*Astronomy -- Handbooks, manuals, etc. Astronomy – Observers' manuals.*

QB64.M623 2000
Moore, Patrick.
The data book of astronomy / Patrick Moore. Philadelphia, PA : Institute of Physics Pub. 2000. p. cm.
00-059799          520          0750306203
*Astronomy -- Observers' manuals.*

QB64.N49 1988
Newton, Jack,
The guide to amateur astronomy / Jack Newton and Philip Teece. Cambridge [Cambridgeshire] ; Cambridge University Press, 1988. viii, 327 p.,
87-007998          522          0521340284
*Astronomy -- Amateurs' manuals.*

QB64.P37 2000
Pasachoff, Jay M.
A field guide to the stars and planets. 4th ed. / Jay M. Pasachoff ; with monthly star maps and atlas charts by Wil Tirion. Boston : Houghton Mifflin, 2000. x, 578 p. :
          523 21     039593432X
*Astronomy -- Observers' manuals.*

## QB65 Atlases and charts

QB65.G37 1994
Garfinkle, Robert A.
Star-hopping : your visa to viewing the universe / Robert A. Garfinkle ; foreword by Richard Berry. Cambridge [England] ; Cambridge University Press, 1994. xxvi, 329 p.
93-008204          523.8/02/2          052141590X
*Stars -- Charts, diagrams, etc. Stars -- Observers' manuals. Stars -- Amateur's manuals.*

QB65.G6813 1994
The Cambridge atlas of astronomy / edited by Jean Audouze and Guy Israel. Cambridge ; Cambridge University Press, c1994. 470 p. :
95-112181          520          0521434386
*Astronomy -- Charts, diagrams, etc.*

QB65.N7 1989
Norton, Arthur P.
Norton's 2000.0 : star atlas and reference handbook (epoch 2000.0) / edited by Arthur P. Norton. Harlow, England : Longman Scientific & Technical ; 1989. x, 179 p. :
89-012226          523          0470214600
*Astronomy -- Observers' manuals.*

QB65.S62 1997
Sinnott, Roger W.
Millennium star atlas : an all-sky atlas comprising one million stars to visual magnitude 11 and forty thousand nonstellar objects / Roger W. Sinnott, Michael A.C. Perryman. Cambridge, MA : Sky, 1997. p. cm.
97-002552                    0933346840
*Stars -- Atlases. Astronomy -- Charts, diagrams, etc.*

QB65.T54 1998
Tirion, Wil.
Sky atlas 2000.0 : twenty-six star charts, covering both hemispheres, and seven detailed charts of selected regions / Wil Tirion and Roger W. Sinnott. Cambridge, Mass : Sky Pub., 1998. p. cm.
98-036749          523.8/022/3          0933346875
*Stars -- Atlases.*

QB65.T56 1996
Tirion, Wil.
The Cambridge star atlas / Wil Tirion. Cambridge ; Cambridge University Press, 1996. vi, 90 p. :
95-048882          523.8/0223          0521560985
*Stars -- Atlases.*

## QB82 Observatories — By region or country, A-Z

QB82.U62.F537 1994
Putnam, William Lowell.
The explorers of Mars Hill : a centennial history of Lowell Observatory, 1894-1994 / William Lowell Putnam and others. West Kennebunk, Me. : Published for Lowell Observatory by Phoenix Pub. c1994. xix, 289 p. :
93-049057          522/.19791/33          0914659693

QB82.U62.M387 1994
Parker, Barry R.
Stairway to the stars : the story of the world's largest observatory / Barry Parker ; drawings by Lori Scoffield. New York : Plenum Press, c1994. x, 350 p. :
94-021016          522/.19969/1          0306447630
*Parker, Barry R.    Astronomical observatories -- Hawaii – Mauna Kea -- History. Astronomers -- United States -- Biography.*

## QB84.5 Astronomical instruments — Societies, congresses, serial collections, yearbooks

**QB84.5.M63 1990**
Modern technology and its influence on astronomy / edited by J.V. Wall & A. Boksenberg. Cambridge [England] ; Cambridge University Press, 1990. xi, 323 p. :
88-025828          522.2          0521343135
*Brown, R. Hanbury -- (Robert Hanbury) -- Congresses.*
*Astronomical instruments -- Congresses.*

## QB88 Astronomical instruments — Modern — Telescopes. Objectives. Mirrors

**QB88.B47 2001**
**Berry, Richard,**
Build your own telescope / Richard Berry. 3rd ed. Richmond, VA : Willmann-Bell, 2001. p. cm.
                681/.4123 21          0943396697
*Telescopes.*

**QB88.K5 1979**
**King, Henry C.**
The history of the telescope / by Henry C. King ; with a foreword by Sir Harold Spencer Jones. New York : Dover Publications, 1979, c1955. xvi, 456 p. :
79-087811          681/.412          0486238938
*Telescopes -- History.*

**QB88.M85 1985**
**Muirden, James.**
How to use an astronomical telescope : a beginner's guide to observing the cosmos / by James Muirden. New York : Linden Press/Simon & Schuster, 1985. 397 p. :
84-021777          522/.2          0671477447
*Telescopes -- Amateurs' manuals.*

## QB107 Astronomical instruments — Modern — Clocks. Chronometers. Chronographs

**QB107.J66 2000**
**Jones, A. W.**
Splitting the second : the story of atomic timekeeping / A.W. Jones. Philadelphia, PA : Institute of Physics Pub., 2000. p. cm.
00-040710          529/.7          0750306408
*Atomic clocks -- History. Time measurements.*

**QB107.M35 1998**
**Major, F. G.**
The quantum beat : the physical principles of atomic clocks / F.G. Major. New York : Springer, c1998. xiv, 475 p. :
97-024027          522/.5          0387983015
*Atomic clocks.*

## QB121 Astronomical photography — General works

**QB121.M34 1993**
**Malin, David.**
A view of the universe / David Malin. Cambridge, Mass. : Sky Pub. Corp. ; 1993. xviii, 266 p.
92-046469          522/.63          0933346662
*Astronomical photography.  Color photography.*

**QB121.M39**
**Mayall, R. Newton**
Skyshooting; hunting the stars with your camera, by R. Newton Mayall and Margaret L. Mayall. New York, Ronald Press Co. [1949] xi, 174 p.
49010863          522.63
*Astronomical photography.*

## QB127.4 Electronics in astronomy — Equipment and supplies — Charge coupled devices

**QB127.4.H69 2000**
**Howell, Steve B.**
Handbook of CCD astronomy / Steve B. Howell. Cambridge, U.K. ; Cambridge University Press, 2000. xi, 164 p. :
99-040077          522/.2          052164058X
*Astronomy -- Technique.  Charge coupled devices.*

# QB135 Astronomical photometry

**QB135.B78 1993**
**Budding, E.,**
Introduction to astronomical photometry / Edwin Budding. Cambridge ; Cambridge University Press, 1993. xiii, 272 p.
92-033321          522/.62          0521418674
*Astronomical photometry.  Astrometry.*

# QB136 Space astronomy

**QB136.A79 1983**
Astronomy from space : Sputnik to space telescope / edited by James Cornell and Paul Gorenstein. Cambridge, Mass. : MIT Press, c1983. viii, 248 p.
83-009349          522          0262030977
*Space astronomy.*

**QB136.L48 2000**
**Leverington, David,**
New cosmic horizons : space astronomy from the V2 to the Hubble Space Telescope / David Leverington. Cambridge, UK ; New York : Cambridge University Press, 2000. xii, 507 p. :
                520/.9 21          0521651379
*Space astronomy -- History.*

**QB136.Z65 1990**
**Zombeck, Martin V.**
  Handbook of space astronomy and astrophysics / Martin V. Zombeck. Cambridge [Cambridgeshire] ; Cambridge University Press, 1990. 440 p. :
87-035318          520          0521345502
  *Space astronomy -- Handbooks, manuals, etc. Astrophysics – Handbooks, manuals, etc.*

## QB145 Practical and spherical astronomy — General works, treatises, and textbooks

**QB145.B52 1990**
**Birney, D. Scott,**
  Observational astronomy / D. Scott Birney. Cambridge [England] ; Cambridge University Press, 1991. ix, 328 p. :
90-031052          522          0521381991
  *Astronomy -- Observations. Astronomy -- Technique.*

**QB145.K33 1996**
**Kaler, James B.**
  The ever-changing sky : a guide to the celestial sphere / James B. Kaler. New York : Cambridge University Press, 1996. xix, 495 p. :
95-008507          522/.7          0521380537
  *Spherical astronomy. Celestial sphere.*

**QB145.N3 1948**
**Nassau, Jason John,**
  Practical astronomy / Jason John Nassau. New York : McGraw-Hill Book Co., 1948. xii, 311 p. :
48007632          522
  *Spherical astronomy.*

## QB175 Practical and spherical astronomy — Prediction of eclipses, occulations, and transits — General works

**QB175.S83 2000**
**Steele, John M.**
  Observations and predictions of eclipse times by early astronomers / by John M. Steele. Dordrecht ; Kluwer Academic Publishers, c2000. xi, 321 p. :
00-037058          523.9/9          0792362985
  *Eclipses. Astronomy, Ancient.*

## QB209 Practical and spherical astronomy — Time — General works

**QB209.E52 1994**
  Encyclopedia of time / edited by Samuel L. Macey. New York : Garland Pub., 1994. xxiv, 699 p.
93-043355          529/.03          0815306156
  *Time -- Encyclopedias.*

**QB209.F7 1982**
**Fraser, J. T.**
  The genesis and evolution of time : a critique of interpretation in physics / J.T. Fraser. Amherst : University of Massachusetts Press, 1982. 205 p. ;
82-008622          529          087023370X
  *Time. Relativity (Physics) Thermodynamics.*

**QB209.G56**
**Gold, Thomas.**
  The nature of time, edited by T. Gold, with the assistance of D. L. Schumacher. Ithaca, N.Y., Cornell University Press [1967] xiv, 248 p.
67-023761          530/.01
  *Time -- Congresses.*

**QB209.H57 1999**
**Holland, C.H. (Charles Hepworth)**
  The idea of time / Charles Hepworth Holland. Chichester ; New York : Wiley, c1999. xii, 150 p. :
          529 21          0471985457
*Time.*

**QB209.P35 1991**
**Parker, Barry R.**
  Cosmic time travel : a scientific odyssey / Barry Parker ; drawings by Lori Scoffield. New York : Plenum Press, c1991. xi, 308 p. :
91-018098          529          0306439662
  *Time. Time travel.*

## QB210 Practical and spherical astronomy — Time — Time service

**QB210.U5**
**Bartky, Ian R.**
  Selling the true time : nineteenth-century timekeeping in America / Ian R. Bartky. Stanford, Calif. : Stanford University Press, c2000. xvi, 310 p. :
99-086739          389/.17/09          0804738742
  *Time -- Systems and standards -- United States.*

## QB223 Practical and spherical astronomy — Time — Systems and standards

**QB223.B58 2000**
**Blaise, Clark.**
  Time lord : Sir Sandford Fleming and the creation of standard time / Clark Blaise. New York : Pantheon Books 2000. xv, 256 p. ;
00-058893          389/.17/09          0375401768
*Fleming, Sandford, -- Sir, -- 1827-1915.     Time -- Systems and standards -- History.*

**QB223.H75**
**Howse, Derek.**
  Greenwich time and the discovery of the longitude / Derek Howse. Oxford ; Oxford University Press, 1980. xviii, 254 p.
79-040052          529/.7          0192159488
  *Time -- Systems and standards. Longitude.*

## QB225 Practical and spherical astronomy — Longitude and latitude — Methods of determination

**QB225.S64 1995**
**Sobel, Dava.**
  Longitude : the true story of a lone genius who solved the greatest scientific problem of his time / Dava Sobel. New York : Walker, 1995. viii, 184 p.
95-017402        526/.62/09        0802713122
*Harrison, John, -- 1693-1776.    Chronometers – History. Longitude -- Measurement -- History. Clock and watch makers – Great Britain -- Biography.*

## QB281 Geodesy — General works, treatises, and textbooks

**QB281.S55 1996**
**Smith, James R.**
  Introduction to geodesy : the history and concepts of modern geodesy / J.R. Smith. New York : Wiley, 1996. p. cm.
96-033301        526/.1        047116660X
*Geodesy.*

## QB283 Geodesy — Mathematical theory of the the figure of the earth

**QB283.T63 1962**
**Todhunter, I.**
  A history of the mathematical theories of attraction and the figure of the earth from the time of Newton to that of Laplace. New York, Dover Publications [1962] 476, 508 p.
63-000321        526.1
*Attractions of ellipsoids. Rotating masses of fluid.    Earth -- Figure.*

## QB331 Gravity determinations — Societies, congresses, serial collections, yearbooks

**QB331.N37 1982**
**Narlikar, Jayant Vishnu,**
  The lighter side of gravity / Jayant V. Narlikar. San Francisco : W.H. Freeman, c1982. viii, 194 p.
81-019496        521/.1        0716713446
*Gravity.*

## QB334 Gravity determinations — General works, treatises, and textbooks

**QB334.W49 1990**
**Wheeler, John Archibald,**
  A journey into gravity and spacetime / John Archibald Wheeler. New York : Scientific American Library : c1990. xii, 257 p. :
89-024256        531/.14        0716750163
*Gravity. Space and time.*

## QB351 Theoretical astronomy and celestial mechanics — General works, treatises, and textbooks

**QB351.B7 1961**
**Brouwer, Dirk,**
  Methods of celestial mechanics [by] Dirk Brouwer [and] Gerald M. Clemence. New York, Academic Press, 1961. 598 p.
60-016909        521.1
*Celestial mechanics.*

**QB351.G69 1996**
**Grossman, Nathaniel,**
  The sheer joy of celestial mechanics / Nathaniel Grossman. Boston : Birkhauser, c1996. xvii, 181 p.
95-034467        521        0817638326
*Celestial mechanics.*

**QB351.P48 1993**
**Peterson, Ivars.**
  Newton's clock : chaos in the solar system / Ivars Peterson. New York : W.H. Freeman and Co., c1993. xiii, 317 p.
93-007176        521        0716723964
*Celestial mechanics. Chaotic behavior in systems. Ephemerides.*

**QB351.P7513 1993**
**Poincare, Henri,**
  New methods of celestial mechanics / Henri Poincare ; edited and introduced by Daniel L. Goroff. [Woodbury, NY] : American Institute of Physics, c1993. 3 v. (xxv, 10
89-014884        521        1563961148
*Celestial mechanics.*

## QB355 Theoretical astronomy and celestial mechanics — Calculation of orbits — General works, treatises, and textbooks

**QB355.B694 1995**
**Brackenridge, J. Bruce,**
  The key to Newton's dynamics : the Kepler problem and the Principia : containing an English translation of sections 1, 2, and 3 of book one from the first (1687) edition of Newton's Mathematical pri J. Bruce Brackenridge ; with English translations from the Latin by Mary Ann Rossi. Berkeley : University of California Press, c1995. xiii, 299 p.
95-032978        521/.3        0520200659
*Kepler's laws. Celestial mechanics.*

## QB355.3 Theoretical astronomy and celestial mechanics — Calculation of orbits — Kepler's laws

**QB355.3.K69 1994**
**Kozhamthadam, Job,**
  The Discovery of Kepler's laws : the interaction of science, philosophy, and religion / Job Kozhamthadam. Notre Dame, Ind. : University of Notre Dame Press, c1994. xi, 315 p. :
92-056863        521/.1        026800868X
*Kepler, Johannes, -- 1571-1630.    Science -- Philosophy. Religion and science. Kepler's laws.*

## QB361 Theoretical astronomy and celestial mechanics — Perturbations — Planetary theory

**QB361.S74 1994**
**Stephenson, Bruce.**
  The music of the heavens : Kepler's harmonic astronomy / Bruce Stephenson. Princeton, N.J. : Princeton University Press, c1994. xi, 260 p. :
93-044916          521/.3          0691034397
*Kepler, Johannes, -- 1571-1630 -- Harmonices mundi.     Planetary theory.*

## QB401-404 Theoretical astronomy and celestial mechanics — Perturbations — Satellites

**QB401.R67 1992**
**Rothery, David A.**
  Satellites of the outer planets : worlds in their own right / David A. Rothery. Oxford [England] : Clarendon Press ; 1992. 208 p. :
91-027437          523.9/8          0198542895
*Outer planets -- Satellites.*

**QB401.S74 1991**
**Stewart, John,**
  Moons of the solar system : an illustrated encyclopedia / by John Stewart. Jefferson, N.C. : McFarland, c1991. xvi, 244 p. :
91-052641          523.9/8          0899505686
*Satellites -- Handbooks, manuals, etc.     Moon -- Handbooks, manuals, etc.*

**QB404.S34 1982**
  Satellites of Jupiter / edited by David Morrison, with the assistance of Mildred Shapley Matthews ; with 47 collaborating authors. Tucson, Ariz. : University of Arizona Press, c1982. x, 972 p. :
81-013050          523.9/85          0816507627
*Satellites -- Jupiter.*

## QB450 Cosmochemistry — General works

**QB450.G75 2000**
**Gribbin, John R.**
  Stardust : supernovae and life-- the cosmic connection / John Gribbin with Mary Gribbin. New Haven : Yale University Press, c2000. xviii, 238 p.
00-035944          523/.02          0300084196
*Cosmochemistry. Supernovae.*

## QB454.2 Theoretical astronomy — Astrogeology

**QB454.2.S48**
**Levy, David H.,**
  Shoemaker by Levy : the man who made an impact / David H. Levy. Princeton : Princeton University Press, c2000. xvi, 303 p. :
00-038523          559.9/092          0691002258
*Shoemaker, Eugene Merle, -- 1928-     Astrogeologists -- United States -- Biography.*

## QB460.72 Astrophysics (General) — Biography — Individual, A-Z

**QB460.72.H69.A3 1994**
**Hoyle, Fred,**
  Home is where the wind blows : chapters from a cosmologist's life / Fred Hoyle. Mill Valley, Calif. : University Science Books, c1994. xi, 443 p., [
93-048080          520/.92          093570227X
*Hoyle, Fred, -- Sir.     Astrophysics -- History. Astrophysicists -- Great Britain -- Biography.*

## QB461 Astrophysics (General) — General works, treatises, and textbooks

**QB461.A568 1991**
**Aller, Lawrence H.**
  Atoms, stars, and nebulae / Lawrence H. Aller. Cambridge ; Cambridge University Press, 1991. xiii, 366 p.
90-043349          523.01          0521325129
*Astrophysics.*

**QB461.F79**
  Frontiers of astrophysics / Eugene H. Avrett, editor. Cambridge : Harvard University Press, 1976. vi, 554 p. :
76-010135          523.01          0674326598.
*Astrophysics.*

**QB461.H24 1992**
**Halpern, Paul,**
  Cosmic wormholes : the search for interstellar shortcuts / Paul Halpern. New York, N.Y., U.S.A. : Dutton, c1992. x, 236 p. ;
92-052868          523.01          0525934774
*Astrophysics. Space flight.*

**QB461.L52**
**Liller, William,**
  Space astrophysics. New York, McGraw-Hill, 1961. 272 p.
61-008657          523.01
*Astrophysics.*

**QB461.N4**
  Nebulae and interstellar matter. Edited by Barbara M. Middlehurst and Lawrence H. Aller. Chicago, University of Chicago Press [1968] xxii, 835 p.
66-013879          523.1/135
*Astrophysics. Interstellar matter. Nebulae.*

**QB461.S448 1991**
**Shu, Frank H.**
  The physics of astrophysics / Frank H. Shu. Mill Valley, Calif. : University Science Books, c1991. 2 v. ;
91-065168          523.01          0935702644
*Astrophysics. Radiation. Gas dynamics.*

**QB461.T5613 2001**
**Thuan, Trinh Xuan.**
Chaos and harmony : perspectives on scientific revolutions of the twentieth century / Trinh Xuan Thuan ; translated by Axel Reisinger. Oxford ; Oxford University Press, 2001. xii, 366 p. :
99-038174       523.01       0195129172
*Astrophysics -- Philosophy. Chaotic behavior in systems.*

**QB461.U58 1997**
Unsolved problems in astrophysics / John N. Bahcall and Jeremiah P. Ostriker, editors. Princeton, N.J. : Princeton University Press, c1997. xiv, 377 p. :
96-045581       523.01       0691016070
*Astrophysics. Cosmology.*

## QB462.65 Astrophysics (General) — Relativistic astrophysics

**QB462.65.H4613 1997**
**Hentschel, Klaus.**
The Einstein Tower : an intertexture of dynamic construction, relativity theory, and astronomy / Klaus Hentschel ; translated by Ann M. Hentschel. Stanford, Calif. : Stanford University Press, 1997. xiv, 226 p. :
96-048509       530.11/0943/09042
0804728240
*Astronomical observatories -- Germany -- Potsdam -- History. Astrophysics -- Research -- Germany -- Potsdam -- History. General relativity (Physics) -- Research -- Germany -- Potsdam -- History.*

## QB472 Non-optical methods of astronomy — X-ray astronomy — Societies, congresses, serial collections, yearbooks

**QB472.C46 1995**
**Charles, Philip A.**
Exploring the X-ray universe / Philip A. Charles, Frederick D. Seward. Cambridge ; Cambridge University Press, 1995. xvi, 398 p. :
92-034641       522/.6863       0521261821
*X-ray astronomy.*

**QB472.T82 2001**
**Tucker, Wallace H.**
Revealing the universe : the making of the Chandra X-ray Observatory / Wallace Tucker and Karen Tucker. Cambridge, Mass. : Harvard University Press, 2001. vi, 295 p. :
00-053862       522/.6863       0674004973
*X-ray astronomy -- United States -- History.*

## QB475 Non-optical methods of astronomy — X-ray astronomy — Radio astronomy

**QB475.A25.E37 1984**
The Early years of radio astronomy : reflections fifty years after Jansky's discovery / edited by W.T. Sullivan III. Cambridge [Cambridgeshire] ; Cambridge University Press, 1984. ix, 421 p. :
83-023227       522/.682       052125485X
*Radio astronomy -- History.*

**QB475.A25.M35 1996**
**Malphrus, Benjamin K.**
The history of radio astronomy and the National Radio Astronomy Observatory : evolution toward big science / Benjamin K. Malphrus. Malabar, Fla. : Krieger Pub., 1996. v, 199 p. :
93-003031       522/.682       0894648411
*Radio astronomy -- History.*

**QB475.R63 1996**
**Rohlfs, K.**
Tools of radio astronomy / K. Rohlfs, T.L. Wilson. Berlin ; Springer, c1996. xvi, 423 p. :
96-005678       522/.682       3540609814
*Radio astronomy. Radio astronomy -- Instruments.*

## QB476.5 Non-optical methods of astronomy — Radio astronomy — General works, treatises, and advanced textbooks

**QB476.5.B87 1997**
**Burke, Bernard F.,**
An introduction to radio astronomy / Bernard F. Burke and Francis Graham-Smith. New York : Cambridge University Press, 1997. xii, 297 p. :
96-013176       522/.682       0521554543
*Radio astronomy -- Observations. Radio astronomy -- Methodology.*

## QB500 Descriptive astronomy — University. Space. Space sciences — General works, treatises, and textbooks

**QB500.J4 1944**
**Jeans, James Hopwood,**
The universe around us, by Sir James Jeans. Cambridge [Eng.] The University Press, 1944. x, 297 p.
44006506
*Astronomy. Cosmogony.*

**QB500.K64 1997**
**Krauss, Lawrence Maxwell.**
Beyond Star Trek : physics from alien invasions to the end of time / Lawrence M. Krauss. New York, NY : Basic Books, c1997. xii, 190 p. ;
97-031127       001.9/01/53       046500637X
*Space sciences. Life on other planets. Space flight.*

**QB500.K65 1995**
**Krauss, Lawrence Maxwell.**
    The physics of Star Trek / Lawrence M. Krauss ; with a foreword by Stephen Hawking. New York : Basic Books, c1995. xvi, 188 p. :
95-033266        791.45/72        0465005594
    *Video games. Space sciences.*

**QB500.S36**
**Schrodinger, Erwin,**
    Expanding universes. Cambridge [Eng.] University Press, 1956. 93 p.
56-013868        523.1
    *Cosmology.*

### QB500.22 Descriptive astronomy — University. Space. Space sciences — Juvenile works

**QB500.22.M66 1992**
**Moore, Patrick.**
    The universe for the beginner / Patrick Moore. New York, NY : Press Syndicate of the University of Cambridge,o 1992. 48 p. :
92-187093        523.1    0521418348
    *Astronomy -- Juvenile literature. Universe. Astronomy. Outer space -- Juvenile literature.*

### QB500.25 Descriptive astronomy — University. Space. Space sciences — Special aspects of the subject as a whole

**QB500.25.T75 2000**
**Tribble, Alan C.,**
    A Tribble's guide to space / Alan C. Tribble. Princeton, N.J. : Princeton University Press, c2000. ix, 174 p., [
00-036691        500.5    0691050597
    *Space sciences -- Popular works.*

### QB500.262 Descriptive astronomy — University. Space. Space sciences — Study and teaching. Research

**QB500.262.A54 2000**
**Angelo, Joseph A.**
    Encyclopedia of space exploration / Joseph A. Angelo, Jr. New York : Facts on File, c2000. xiii, 305 p.
99-059659        919.9/04        0816039429
    *Outer space -- Exploration -- Encyclopedias.*

**QB500.262.B87 1998**
**Burrows, William E.,**
    This new ocean : the story of the space age / William E. Burrows. New York : Random House, 1998. p. cm.
98-003252        629.4    0679445218
    *Astronautics. Outer space -- Exploration.*

**QB500.262.L38 1998**
**Launius, Roger D.**
    Frontiers of space exploration / Roger D. Launius. Westport, Conn. : Greenwood Press, 1998. xxxi, 204 p.
97-034788        629.45    0313299684
    *Astronautics -- International cooperation. Outer space -- Exploration.*

**QB500.262.P7313 2000**
**Prantzos, Nikos.**
    Our cosmic future : humanity's fate in the universe / Nikos Prantzos ; translated by Stephen Lyle. Cambridge, U.K. ; Cambridge University Press, 2000. xii, 288 p. :
99-053248        919.9/04    052177098X
    *Outer space -- Exploration. Interplanetary voyages.*

**QB500.262.Z56 2000**
**Zimmerman, Robert,**
    The chronological encyclopedia of discoveries in space / by Robert Zimmerman. Phoeniz, AZ : Oryx Press, 2000. xix, 410 p. :
99-056080        500.5/09    1573561967
    *Outer space -- Exploration -- History -- Chronology.*

### QB500.267-500.268 Descriptive astronomy — University. Space. Space sciences — Orbiting astronomical observations

**QB500.267.S55 1989**
**Smith, Robert W.**
    The space telescope : a study of NASA, science, technology, and politics / Robert W. Smith with contributions by Paul A. Hanle, Robert H. Kargon, Joseph N. Tatarewicz. Cambridge [England] ; Cambridge University Press, 1989. xviii, 478 p.
89-000707        522/.29    0521266343

**QB500.268.C48 1994**
**Chaisson, Eric.**
    The Hubble wars : astrophysics meets astropolitics in the two-billion-dollar struggle over the Hubble Space Telescope / Eric J. Chaisson. New York : HarperCollins Publishers, c1994. xi, 386 p. :
93-037468        522/.2919    0060171146

**QB500.268.F5813 1996**
**Fischer, Daniel.**
    Hubble : a new window to the universe / Daniel Fischer, Hilmar Duerbeck ; translated by Helmut Jenkner and Douglas Duncan ; foreword by Robert Williams. New York : Copernicus, 1996. 175 p. :
96-004818        522/.2919    0387946721
    *Space astronomy. Astronomy -- Pictorial works.*

**QB500.268.P48 1995**
**Petersen, Carolyn Collins.**
    Hubble vision : astronomy with the Hubble Space Telescope / Carolyn Collins Petersen and John C. Brandt. Cambridge ; Cambridge University Press, 1995. xx, 252 p. :
95-032568        522/.2919    0521496438
    *Space astronomy.*

**QB500.268.W55 1998**
**Wilkie, Tom.**
 Visions of heaven : the mysteries of the universe revealed by the Hubble Space Telescope / Tom Wilkie and Mark Rosselli. London : Hodder & Stoughton, c1998. 205 p. :
 522.2919          0340717343
  *Space photography.  Astronomy -- Pictorial works.  Outer space -- Exploration.*

## QB501 Descriptive astronomy — Solar system — General works, treatises, and textbooks

**QB501.B74 1996**
**Booth, Nicholas.**
 Exploring the solar system / Nicholas Booth. Cambridge ; Cambridge University Press, 1996. 176 p. :
 96-014066          523.2          0521580056
  *Solar system.*

**QB501.E53 1999**
 Encyclopedia of the solar system / edited by Paul R. Weissman, Lucy-Ann McFadden, Torrence V. Johnson. San Diego : Academic Press, c1999. xviii, 992 p.
 98-084429          523.2/03          0122268059
  *Solar system -- Encyclopedias.*

**QB501.J65 1999**
**Jones, Barrie William.**
 Discovering the solar system / Barrie W. Jones. New York : Wiley, 1999. p. cm.
 98-039573          523.2          0471982431
  *Solar system.*

**QB501.L497 1995**
**Lewis, John S.**
 Physics and chemistry of the solar system / John S. Lewis. San Diego : Academic Press, c1995. x, 556 p. :
 94-031854          523.2          0124467407
  *Planetology. Astrophysics. Cosmochemistry. Solar system.*

**QB501.M687 1983**
**Moore, Patrick.**
 Atlas of the solar system / Patrick Moore & Garry Hunt. Chicago : Rand McNally, 1983. 464 p. :
 83-061018          523.2          0528811223
  *Solar system -- Handbooks, manuals, etc.*

**QB501.S625 1998**
 The solar system / edited by Roger Smith. Pasadena, Calif. : Salem Press, c1998. 3 v. (x, 1151
 97-051552          523.2          0893569607
  *Space astronomy.   Solar system.*

**QB501.T25 1992**
**Taylor, Stuart Ross,**
 Solar system evolution : a new perspective : an inquiry into the chemical composition, origin, and evolution of the solar system / Stuart Ross Taylor. Cambridge [England] ; Cambridge University Press, 1992. xvi, 307 p. :
 92-025784          523.2          0521372127
  *Cosmochemistry.    Solar system -- Origin. Solar system.*

## QB521-541 Descriptive astronomy — Solar system — Sun

**QB521.G26**
**Gamow, George,**
 A star called the sun. New York, Viking Press [1964] xiii, 208 p.
 64-013594          523.7
  *Sun.*

**QB521.G65 2001**
**Golub, L.**
 Nearest star : the surprising science of our sun / Leon Golub & Jay M. Pasachoff. Cambridge, Mass. : Harvard University Press, 2001. xii, 267 p. :
 00-063213          523.7          0674004671
  *Sun.*

**QB521.K6313 1994**
**Kippenhahn, Rudolf,**
 Discovering the secrets of the sun / Rudolf Kippenhahn ; translated by Storm Dunlop. Chichester ; Wiley, c1994. xvii, 262 p.
 93-006095          523.7          0471941603
  *Sun.*

**QB521.M4 1959**
**Menzel, Donald Howard,**
 Our sun. Cambridge, Harvard University Press, 1959. 350 p.
 59-012975          523.7
  *Sun.*

**QB521.P45 1992**
**Phillips, Kenneth J. H.**
 Guide to the sun / Kenneth J.H. Phillips. Cambridge [England] ; Cambridge University Press, 1992. xiv, 386 p. :
 91-035910          523.7          052139483X
  *Sun.*

**QB521.W46 1989**
**Wentzel, Donat G.,**
 The restless sun / Donat G. Wentzel. Washington : Smithsonian Institution Press, 1989. xiii, 279 p.,
 88-018491          523.7          0874749824
  *Astrophysics.   Sun.*

**QB521.4.L36 1995**
**Lang, Kenneth R.**
 Sun, earth, and sky / Kenneth R. Lang. Berlin ; Springer, c1995. xv, 282 p. :
 95-006109          523.7          3540587780
  *Astronomy -- Popular works.    Earth -- Popular works. Sun -- Popular works.*

**QB521.4.T39 1991**
**Taylor, Peter O.**
 Observing the sun / Peter O. Taylor. Cambridge [England] ; Cambridge University Press, 1991. xiii, 159 p.
 91-027809          523.7          0521401100
  *Sun -- Amateurs' manuals.*

**QB526.C9.W55 1994**
**Wilson, Peter R.**
  Solar and stellar activity cycles / Peter R. Wilson. Cambridge ; Cambridge University Press, 1994. xviii, 274 p.
93-029835          523.7          052143081X
  *Solar cycle. Stars. Astrophysics.*

**QB529.C7 1997**
**Cravens, Thomas E.,**
  Physics of solar system plasmas / Thomas E. Cravens. Cambridge ; Cambridge University Press, 1997. xvi, 477 p. :
96-048929          523.5/8          0521352800
  *Solar wind. Magnetosphere. Astrophysics.*

**QB541.H35 1997**
**Harrington, Philip S.**
  Eclipse! : the what, where, when, why, and how guide to watching solar and lunar eclipses / Philip S. Harrington. New York : J. Wiley, c1997. viii, 280 p.
96-029777          523.7/8          0471127957
  *Solar eclipses -- Observers' manuals. Lunar eclipses –Observers' manuals.*

**QB541.L69 1991**
**Littmann, Mark,**
  Totality : eclipses of the sun / Mark Littmann and Ken Willcox ; foreword by Donald N.B. Hall. Honolulu : University of Hawaii Press, c1991. xvi, 224 p. :
90-023823          523.7/8          0824813715
  *Solar eclipses.*

### QB579 Descriptive astronomy — Solar system — Lunar eclipses

**QB579.L58 1992**
**Liu, Bao-Lin.**
  Canon of lunar eclipses, 1500 B.C.-A.D. 3000 / Bao-Lin Liu, Alan D. Fiala ; illustrations by Wil Tirion unless otherwise credited. Richmond, Va. : Willmann-Bell, c1992. vi, 215 p. :
92-000429          523.3/8          0943396379
  *Lunar eclipses -- Catalogs.*

### QB581 Descriptive astronomy — Solar system — Moon

**QB581.B87 1993**
**Burgess, Eric.**
  Outpost on Apollo's moon / Eric Burgess. New York : Columbia University Press, c1993. xiii, 274 p.
92-026662          919.9/104          0231076665(ac
  *Outer space -- Exploration. Moon -- Exploration.*

**QB581.C44**
**Cherrington, Ernest H.**
  Exploring the moon through binoculars [by] Ernest H. Cherrington, Jr. New York, McGraw-Hill [1968, c1969] 211 p.
68-013624          523.3
  *Moon. Astronomy -- Observers' manuals.*

**QB581.L766 1991**
  Lunar sourcebook : a user's guide to the moon / [edited by] Grant Heiken, David Vaniman, Bevan M. French ; [foreword by Harrison H. Schmitt]. Cambridge [England] ; Cambridge University Press, 1991. xix, 736 p.,
91-010461          523.3          0521334446
  *Moon -- Handbooks, manuals, etc.*

**QB581.M6475 1999**
**Montgomery, Scott L.**
  The moon and the western imagination / Scott L. Montgomery. Tucson : University of Arizona Press, c1999. xiii, 265 p.
99006090          523.3          0816517118
  *Moon -- In literature. Moon -- Maps. Moon.*

**QB581.W63 2000**
**Wlasuk, Peter,**
  Observing the moon : a practical guide for amateur astronomers / Peter T. Wlasuk. London ; Springer, 2000. x, 181 p. :
00-033820          523.3          1852331933
  *Moon. Moon -- Observations.*

### QB601-691 Descriptive astronomy — Solar system — Planets

**QB601.B36 2000**
**Bakich, Michael E.**
  The Cambridge planetary handbook / Michael E. Bakich. Cambridge, U.K. ; Cambridge University Press, 2000. ix, 336 p. :
99-010171          523.4          0521632803
  *Planets -- Handbooks, manuals, etc.*

**QB601.M68 1962a**
**Moore, Patrick.**
  The planets. New York, Norton [1962] 189 p.
62-020547          523.4
  *Planets.*

**QB601.P67 2000**
**Price, Fred W.**
  The planet observer's handbook / Fred W. Price. Cambridge ; Cambridge University Press, 2000. xvii, 429 p.
00-028910          523.4          0521789818
  *Planets -- Observers' manuals. Planets -- Amateurs' manuals. Astronomy -- Amateurs' manuals.*

**QB601.S54 1988**
**Sheehan, William,**
  Planets & perception : telescopic views and interpretations, 1609-1909 / William Sheehan. Tucson : University of Arizona Press, c1988. xii, 324 p. :
88-020501          522/.2/0903          0816510598
  *Planets -- Observations. Perception.*

**QB601.S543 1992**
**Sheehan, William,**
Worlds in the sky : planetary discovery from earliest times through Voyager and Magellan / William Sheehan. Tucson : University of Arizona Press, c1992. xv, 243 p. :
91-039398          523.2          0816513082
*Planets. Astronomy -- History. Planets -- Exploration.*

**QB601.S76 1999**
**Stern, Alan,**
Our worlds : the magnetism and thrill of planetary exploration : as descibed by leading planetary scientists / S. Alan Stern. New York : Cambridge Unversity Press, 1999. xi, 172 p. :
98-022012          919.9/04          0521631645
*Planets -- Exploration.*

**QB601.W6 1968**
**Whipple, Fred Lawrence,**
Earth, moon, and planets [by] Fred L. Whipple. Cambridge, Mass., Harvard University Press, 1968. viii, 297 p.
68-021987          523.4
*Planets. Earth. Moon.*

**QB601.W6 1981**
**Whipple, Fred Lawrence,**
Orbiting the sun : planets and satellites of the solar system / Fred L. Whipple. Cambridge, Mass. : Harvard University Press, 1981. x, 338 p., [4
80-019581          523.2          0674641256
*Planets. Earth. Moon.*

**QB603.A85.C48 1987**
**Chamberlain, Joseph W.**
Theory of planetary atmospheres : an introduction to their physics and chemistry / Joseph W. Chamberlain ; in collaboration with Donald M. Hunten. Orlando : Academic Press, 1987. xiv, 481 p. :
86-010850          551.5/0999/2          0121672514
*Planets -- Atmospheres.*

**QB603.A85.Y86 1999**
**Yung, Y. L.**
Photochemistry of planetary atmospheres / Yuk L. Yung, William B. DeMore. New York : Oxford University Press, 1999. xiii, 456 p.
97-023575          551.51/1/09992          019510501X
*Planets -- Atmospheres. Atmosphere. Photochemistry. Earth – Environmental aspects.*

**QB603.G46.F73 1996**
**Frankel, Charles.**
Volcanoes of the solar system / Charles Frankel. Cambridge ; Cambridge University Press, 1996. xiii, 232 p.
95-036876          551.2/1/0999          0521472016
*Planets -- Geology. Lunar geology. Volcanism. Solar system.*

**QB603.M6.G66 1996**
**Goodstein, David L.,**
Feynman's lost lecture : the motion of planets around the sun / David L. Goodstein and Judith R. Goodstein. New York : Norton, c1996. 191 p. :
95-038719          521/.3          0393039188
*Feynman, Richard Phillips. Celestial mechanics. Conic sections. Planets -- Orbits.*

**QB603.R55.E44 1984**
**Elliot, James,**
Rings : discoveries from Galileo to Voyager / James Elliot and Richard Kerr. Cambridge, Mass. : MIT Press, c1984. xi, 209 p. :
84-009721          523.4          0262050315
*Planetary rings. Aeronautics in astronomy. Astronautics in astronomy.*

**QB605.B74 1982**
**Briggs, Geoffrey,**
The Cambridge photographic atlas of the planets / Geoffrey Briggs, Fredric Taylor. Cambridge [Cambridgeshire] ; Cambridge University Press, 1982. 255 p. :
81-038529          523.4/9          0521239761
*Planets -- Pictorial works.*

**QB605.2.B38 1997**
**Baum, Richard,**
In search of planet Vulcan : the ghost in Newton's clockwork universe / Richard Baum and William Sheehan. New York : Plenum Press, c1997. xvi, 310 p. :
96-045674          523.4          0306455676
*Vulcan (Hypothetical planet) Planets -- Miscellanea. Planets – Research.*

**QB621.G75 1997**
**Grinspoon, David Harry.**
Venus revealed : a new look below the clouds of our mysterious twin planet / David Harry Grinspoon. Reading, Mass. : Addison-Wesley Pub., c1997. xix, 355 p. :
          523.4/2 20          0201406551
*Venus (Planet)*

**QB621.M37 1998**
**Marov, Mikhail IAkovlevich.**
The planet Venus / Mikhail Ya. Marov and David H. Grinspoon ; with translations by Tobias Owen, Natasha Levchenko, and Ronald Mastaler. New Haven : Yale University Press, c1998. xi, 442 p. :
98-010158          523.42          0300049757
*Venus (Planet)*

**QB621.M6**
**Moore, Patrick.**
The planet Venus. London, Faber and Faber [1956] 132 p.
56-004842          523.42
*Venus (Planet)*

**QB631.E55 1992**
**Emiliani, Cesare.**
  Planet earth : cosmology, geology, and the evolution of life and environment / Cesare Emiliani. Cambridge [England] ; Cambridge University Press, 1992. xiii, 718 p.
92-005757          550          0521401232
  *Geology. Cosmology.   Earth.*

**QB631.O34 1993**
**Officer, Charles B.**
  Tales of the earth : paroxysms and perturbations of the blue planet / Charles Officer & Jake Page. New York : Oxford University Press, 1993. xiii, 226 p.
92-028320          550          0195077857
  *Earth.*

**QB631.R38 1986**
**Raup, David M.**
  The nemesis affair : a story of the death of dinosaurs and the ways of science / David M. Raup. New York, N.Y. : Norton, c1986. 220 p. :
86-000761          560          0393023427
  *Science -- History. Dinosaurs.   Earth -- Origin.*

**QB632.D78 1999**
**Drury, S. A.**
  Stepping stones : the making of our home world / Stephen Drury. New York : Oxford University Press, 1999. xviii, 409 p.
98-045284          525          0198502710
  *Life -- Origin.   Earth -- Origin.*

**QB641.B819 1990**
**Burgess, Eric.**
  Return to the red planet / Eric Burgess. New York : Columbia University Press, c1990. xi, 222 p. :
90-001653          919.9/23/04          0231069421
  *Mars probes.   Mars (Planet) -- Exploration. Outer space -- Exploration -- United States.*

**QB641.M35 1992**
  Mars / Hugh H. Kieffer ... [et al.], editors ; with 114 collaborating authors. Tucson : University of Arizona Press, c1992. xv, 1498 p. :
92-010951          522.4/3          0816512574
  *Mars (Planet)*

**QB641.S4838 2001**
**Sheehan, William,**
  Mars : the lure of the red planet / William Sheehan & Stephen James O'Meara. Amherst, N.Y. : Prometheus Books, 2001. 406 p. :
00-067358          523.43          157392900X
  *Mars (Planet)*

**QB641.S484 1996**
**Sheehan, William,**
  The planet Mars : a history of observation & discovery / William Sheehan. Tucson : University of Arizona Press, c1996. x, 270 p. :
96-004485          523.4/3          0816516405
  *Mars.*

**QB651.P44 2000**
**Peebles, Curtis.**
  Asteroids : a history / Curtis Peebles. Washington, DC : Smithsonian Institution Press, c2000. vii 280 p. :
00-020733          523.44          1560983892
  *Asteroids.*

**QB651.S35 1999**
**Schmadel, Lutz D.**
  Dictionary of minor planet names / Lutz D. Schmadel. New York : Springer-Verlag, 1999. p. cm.
99-044339          523.44/03          3540662928
  *Asteroids. Asteroids -- Dictionaries.*

**QB661.H37 2000**
**Harland, David M.**
  Jupiter odyssey : the story of NASA's Galileo mission / David M. Harland. London ; Springer ; c2000. xxvi, 448 p.
00-055636          629.45/55          1852333014
  *Jupiter (Planet) -- Exploration.*

**QB661.R64 1995**
**Rogers, John H.**
  The giant planet Jupiter / John H. Rogers. Cambridge ; Cambridge University Press, 1995. x, 418 p., 24
94-015303          523.4/5          0521410088
  *Jupiter (Planet)*

**QB671.S23 1984**
  Saturn / edited by Tom Gehrels, Mildred Shapley Matthews. Tucson, Ariz. : University of Arizona Press, c1984. xi, 968 p. :
84-002517          523.4/6          0816508291
  *Saturn (Planet)*

**QB681.H86 1989**
**Hunt, Garry E.**
  Atlas of Uranus / Garry Hunt and Patrick Moore. Cambridge [England] ; Cambridge University Press, 1989, c1988. 96 p. :
87-011643          523.4/7          0521343232
  *Uranus (Planet) -- Atlases.*

**QB691.B87 1991**
**Burgess, Eric.**
  Far encounter : the Neptune system / Eric Burgess. New York : Columbia University Press, c1991. xii, 151 p. :
91-017148          523.4/5          0231074123
  *Neptune (Planet) -- Exploration.*

**QB691.G7**
**Grosser, Morton.**
  The discovery of Neptune. Cambridge, Harvard University Press, 1962. 172 p.
62-017218          523.48
  *Neptune (Planet)*

## QB721-723 Descriptive astronomy — Solar system — Comets

**QB721.B79 2000**
**Burnham, Robert,**
Great comets / Robert Burnham ; foreword by David H. Levy. Cambridge, U.K. ; Cambridge University Press, 2000. ix, 228 p. :
98-050546      523.6      0521646006
*Comets.*

**QB721.C648 1982**
Comets / edited by Laurel L. Wilkening, with the assistance of Mildred Shapley Matthews ; with 48 collaborating authors. Tucson, Ariz. : University of Arizona Press, c1982. x, 766 p. :
81-021814      523.6      0816507694
*Comets.*

**QB721.H25 1990**
**Hall, Louis Brewer.**
Searching for comets : deciphering the secrets of our cosmic past / Louis Brewer Hall. New York : McGraw-Hill, c1990. x, 214, [16]
89-014525      523.6      0070256330
*Comets.*

**QB721.H29 1994**
Hazards due to comets and asteroids / Tom Gehrels, editor ; with the editorial assistance of M.S. Matthews and A.M. Schumann ; with 120 collaborating authors. Tucson : University of Arizona Press, c1994. xiii, 1300 p.
94-018759      363.3/49      0816515050
*Comets. Near-earth asteroids. Astrogeology.*

**QB721.L419 2000**
**Lewis, John S.**
Comet and asteroid impact hazards on a populated earth : computer modeling / John S. Lewis. San Diego : Academic Press, c2000. xv, 200 p. :
99-062311      523.5/1/0113      0124467601
*Comets -- Collisions with Earth -- Computer simulation. Asteroids -- Collisions with Earth -- Computer simulation.*

**QB721.S34 1985**
**Sagan, Carl,**
Comet / Carl Sagan and Ann Druyan. 1st ed. New York : Random House, c1985. xiv, 398 p. :
      523.6 19      0394549082
*Comets. Halley's comet.*

**QB721.S365 1997**
**Schaaf, Fred.**
Comet of the century : from Halley to Hale-Bopp / Fred Schaaf ; with illustrations by Guy Ottewell. New York : Copernicus, c1997. xv, 384 p. :
96-026567      523.6      0387947930
*Comets.*

**QB721.S367 1997**
**Schechner Genuth, Sara,**
Comets, popular culture, and the birth of modern cosmology / Sara Schechner Genuth. Princeton, N.J. : Princeton University Press, c1997. xvi, 365 p. :
96-052186      523.6      0691011508
*Comets. Cosmology. Religion and science.*

**QB721.S85 2000**
**Sumners, Carolyn.**
Cosmic pinball : the science of comets, meteors, and asteroids / by Carolyn Sumners and Carlton Allen. New York : McGraw Hill, c2000. ix, 190 p., [
99-054042      523.6      0071354603
*Comets. Meteors. Asteroids.*

**QB721.V48 1996**
**Verschuur, Gerrit L.,**
Impact! : the threat of comets and asteroids / Gerrit L. Verschuur. New York : Oxford University Press, 1996. xii, 237 p. :
95-045030      551.3/97      0195101057
*Comets. Asteroids. Impact. Earth.*

**QB721.4.L48 1994**
**Levy, David H.,**
The quest for comets : an explosive trail of beauty and danger / David H. Levy. New York : Plenum Press, c1994. xvii, 280 p.
94-002741      523.6      0306446510
*Comets -- Popular works. Comets -- Research -- Popular works.*

**QB721.4.W47 1985**
**Whipple, Fred Lawrence,**
The mystery of comets / by Fred L. Whipple assisted by Daniel W.E. Green. Washington, D.C. : Smithsonian Institution Press, 1985. xii, 276 p.,
85-008343      523.6      0874749689
*Comets -- Popular works.*

**QB723.S56.G74 1995**
The great comet crash : the impact of comet Shoemaker-Levy 9 on Jupiter / edited by John R. Spencer and Jacqueline Mitton. Cambridge ; Cambridge University Press, 1995. ix, 118 p. :
95-042372      523.6/4      0521482747
*Shoemaker-Levy 9 comet -- Collision with Jupiter.*

**QB723.S56.L48 1995**
**Levy, David H.,**
Impact Jupiter : the crash of comet Shoemaker-Levy 9 / David H. Levy, co-discoverer of the comet. New York : Plenum Press, c1995. xiv, 290 p. :
95-033339      523.6/4      0306450887
*Shoemaker-Levy 9 comet -- Collision with Jupiter.*

## QB755 Descriptive astronomy — Solar system — Meteorites

**QB755.B24 1991**
**Bagnall, Philip M.**
The Meteorite & tektite collector's handbook : a practical guide to their acquisition, preservation and display / Philip M. Bagnall. Richmond, Va. : Willmann-Bell, c1991. x, 160 p. :
90025854        523.5/1/075        094339631X
*Meteorites -- Catalogs and collections. Tektite -- Catalogs and collections. Astronomy -- Amateurs' manuals.*

**QB755.D63 1986**
**Dodd, Robert T.,**
Thunderstones and shooting stars : the meaning of meteorites / Robert T. Dodd. Cambridge, Mass. : Harvard University Press, 1986. viii, 196 p.
86-007563        523.5/1        0674891376
*Meteorites.*

**QB755.H43**
**Heide, Fritz,**
Meteorites. Translated by Edward Anders in collaboration with Eugene R. DuFresne. Chicago, University of Chicago Press [1964] x, 144 p.
63-020906        523.51
*Meteorites.*

**QB755.H63 1994**
**Hodge, Paul W.**
Meteorite craters and impact structures of the earth / Paul Hodge. New York, NY, USA : Cambridge University Press, 1994. viii, 124 p.
93-021350        551.3/97        0521360927
*Meteorite craters -- Handbooks, manuals, etc.*

**QB755.M465 1999**
**McSween, Harry Y.**
Meteorites and their parent planets / Harry Y. McSween. Cambridge ; Cambridge University Press, 1999. xii, 310 p. :
98-026494        523.5/1        0521583039
*Meteorites.*

**QB755.N52**
**Nininger, Harvey Harlow,**
Out of the sky; an introduction to meteoritics. [Denver] University of Denver Press [1952] 336 p.
52-009127        523.51
*Meteorites.*

## QB791.3 Descriptive astronomy — Interstellar matter — Dark matter

**QB791.3.B36 1993**
**Bartusiak, Marcia,**
Through a universe darkly : a cosmic tale of ancient ethers, dark matter, and the fate of the universe / Marcia Bartusiak. New York : HarperCollins, c1993. xvi, 383 p. :
92-054731        523.1/125        0060183101
*Dark matter (Astronomy) Astronomy. Cosmology.*

**QB791.3.K73 1989**
**Krauss, Lawrence Maxwell.**
The fifth essence : the search for dark matter in the universe / Lawrence M. Krauss. New York : Basic Books, c1989. xvii, 342 p.
89-042530        523.1/12        0465023754
*Dark matter (Astronomy)*

## QB791.35 Descriptive astronomy — Interstellar matter — Missing mass

**QB791.35.T38 1991**
**Tayler, R. J.**
The hidden universe / Roger J. Tayler. New York : E. Horwood, 1991. 213 p. :
91-029488        523.1        0133887111
*Missing mass (Astronomy) Cosmology. Nuclear astrophysics.*

## QB801 Descriptive astronomy — Stars — General works, treatises, and textbooks

**QB801.B29**
**Baade, Walter,**
Evolution of stars and galaxies. Edited by Cecilia Payne-Gaposchkin. Cambridge, Harvard University Press, 1963. xiii, 321 p.
63-009547        523.8
*Stars -- Evolution -- Addresses, essays, lectures. Galaxies -- Evolution -- Addresses, essays, lectures.*

**QB801.G24**
**Gaposchkin, Cecilia Helena Payne,**
Stars and clusters / Cecilia Payne-Gaposchkin. Cambridge, Mass. : Harvard University Press, 1979. 262 p. :
79-004472        523.8        0674834402
*Stars. Stars -- Clusters.*

**QB801.G25**
**Gaposchkin, Cecilia Helena Payne,**
Stars in the making. Cambridge, Harvard University Press, 1952. xii, 160 p.
52-009378        523.8
*Stars.*

**QB801.K25 1992**
**Kaler, James B.**
Stars / James B. Kaler. New York : Scientific American Library : c1992. vii, 273 p. :
91-033125        523.8        0716750333
*Stars.*

**QB801.K2813 1983**
**Kaplan, S. A.**
The physics of stars / by S.A. Kaplan ; translated by Renata Feldman. Chichester [Sussex] ; Wiley, [1983] c1982. viii, 158 p.
82-002651        523.8        0471103276
*Stars.*

**QB801.M64 1989**
**Moore, Patrick.**
    Astronomers' stars / Patrick Moore. New York : Norton, 1989, c1987. ix, 164 p. :
88-022376       523.8       0393026639
    *Stars.*

**QB801.N29 1995**
**Narlikar, Jayant Vishnu,**
    From black clouds to black holes / Jayant V. Narlikar. Singapore ; World Scientific, c1995. x, 159 p. :
95-042710       523.8       9810220324
    *Stars. Black holes (Astronomy) Astrophysics.*

## QB801.6 Descriptive astronomy — Stars — Popular works

**QB801.6.A85 1985**
**Asimov, Isaac,**
    The exploding suns : the secrets of the supernovas / Isaac Asimov ; illustrated by D.F. Bach. New York : Dutton, c1985. x, 276 p. :
84-021077       523.1       0525243232
    *Stars -- Popular works. Supernovae -- Popular works. Cosmology -- Popular works.*

## QB802 Descriptive astronomy — Stars — Constellation figures. Star names

**QB802.A4 1963**
**Allen, Richard Hinckley,**
    Star names, their lore and meaning. New York, Dover Publications [1963] xiv, 563 p.
63-021808       523.89
    *Constellations.*

**QB802.B35 1995**
**Bakich, Michael E.**
    The Cambridge guide to the constellations / Michael E. Bakich. Cambridge ; Cambridge University Press, 1995. xiii, 320 p.
94-004678       523.8/022/3       0521465206
    *Constellations -- Observers' manuals. Astronomy -- Observers' manuals.*

**QB802.S4713 1991**
**Sesti, Giuseppe Maria.**
    The glorious constellations : history and mythology / Giuseppe Maria Sesti ; introduction by Elemire Zolla ; translated from the Italian by Karin H. Ford. New York : Abrams, 1991. 495 p. :
90-001141       523.8       0810933551
    *Constellations.*

## QB805 Descriptive astronomy — Stars — Particular stars

**QB805.K525 1999**
**Kidger, Mark R.,**
    The star of Bethlehem : an astronomer's view / Mark Kidger. Princeton, N.J. : Princeton University Press, 1999. xi 306 p. :
99-029635       523.8/446       0691058237
    *Astronomy in the Bible. Astronomy, Ancient. Star of Bethlehem.*

## QB806 Descriptive astronomy — Stars — Stellar evolution

**QB806.C64 1988**
**Cohen, Martin,**
    In darkness born : the story of star formation / Martin Cohen. Cambridge [England] ; Cambridge University Press, 1988. 196 p. :
85-022424       523.8       0521262704
    *Stars -- Formation.*

**QB806.K5313 1983**
**Kippenhahn, Rudolf,**
    100 billion suns : the birth, life, and death of the stars / Rudolf Kippenhahn ; translated by Jean Steinberg. New York : Basic Books, c1983. viii, 264 p.,
82-072398       521/.58       0465052630
    *Stars -- Evolution.*

## QB808 Descriptive astronomy — Stars — Structure

**QB808.T37 1994**
**Tayler, R. J.**
    The stars : their structure and evolution / Roger J. Tayler. Cambridge [England] ; Cambridge University Press, 1994. xiii, 241 p.
93-044924       523.8       0521460638
    *Stars -- Structure. Stars -- Evolution.*

## QB815 Descriptive astronomy — Stars — Magnitudes. Photometric catalogs

**QB815.H43 1996**
**Hearnshaw, J. B.**
    The measurement of starlight : two centuries of astronomical photometry / J.B. Hearnshaw. Cambridge [England] ; Cambridge University Press, 1996. xiv, 511 p. :
95-034046       522/.62/09       0521403936
    *Astronomical photometry -- History. Stars -- Photographic measurements -- History.*

## QB816 Descriptive astronomy — Stars — Color

**QB816.M34 1984**
**Malin, David.**
    Colours of the stars / by David Malin and Paul Murdin. Cambridge ; Cambridge University Press, 1984. ix, 198 p. :
83-020928       523.8/2       052125714X
    *Stars -- Color.*

## QB819 Descriptive astronomy — Stars — Distribution

**QB819.B735 1957**
**Bok, Bart Jan,**
The Milky Way [by] Bart J. Bok and Priscilla F. Bok. Cambridge, Harvard University Press, 1957. 269 p.
56-011279          523.85
*Milky Way.*

## QB820 Descriptive astronomy — Stars — Double and multiple stars. Binary systems

**QB820.C76 1997**
**Croswell, Ken.**
Planet quest : the epic discovery of alien solar systems / Ken Croswell. New York : Free Press, 1997. xi, 324 p., [
97-009473          523          0684832526
*Extrasolar planets.*

**QB820.G65 1997**
**Goldsmith, Donald.**
Worlds unnumbered : the search for extrasolar planets / Donald Goldsmith ; illustrations by Jon Lomberg. Sausalito, Calif. : University Science Books, c1997. xii, 237 p.,
96-051826          523          0935702970
*Extrasolar planets.*

## QB843 Descriptive astronomy — Stars — Other particular types of stars, A-Z

**QB843.B55.B44 1996**
**Begelman, Mitchell C.**
Gravity's fatal attraction : black holes in the universe / Mitchell Begelman, Martin Rees. New York : Scientific American Library : c1996. vii, 246 p. :
95-042959          523.8/875          0716750740
*Black holes (Astronomy) Quasars.*

**QB843.B55.G75 1992**
**Gribbin, John R.**
Unveiling the edge of time : black holes, white holes, wormholes / John Gribbin. New York : Harmony Books, c1992. viii, 248 p.
92-010485          523.8/875          051758591X
*Black holes (Astronomy) -- History.*

**QB843.B55.S5 1983**
**Shapiro, Stuart L.**
Black holes, white dwarfs, and neutron stars : the physics of compact objects / Stuart L. Shapiro, Saul A. Teukolsky. New York : Wiley, c1983. xvii, 645 p.
82-020112          521/.5          0471873179
*Black holes (Astronomy) White dwarfs. Neutron stars.*

**QB843.B55.S54 1980**
**Shipman, Harry L.**
Black holes, quasars, and the universe / Harry L. Shipman. Boston : Houghton Mifflin, c1980. viii, 344 p.
79-049834          523          0395284996
*Black holes (Astronomy) Quasars. Cosmology.*

**QB843.B55A84 1977**
**Asimov, Isaac,**
The collapsing universe / by Isaac Asimov. New York : Walker, 1977. 204 p. :
          523          0802704867
*Black holes (Astronomy) Astronomy.*

**QB843.S95**
**Wheeler, J. Craig.**
Cosmic catastrophes : supernovae, gamma-ray bursts, and adventures in hyperspace / J. Craig Wheeler. Cambridge ; Cambridge University Press, 2000. xv, 288 p. :
99-053321          523.8/4465          0521651956
*Supernovae. Stars. Hyperspace.*

**QB843.S95.M87 1985**
**Murdin, Paul.**
Supernovae / Paul Murdin, Lesley Murdin. Cambridge [Cambridgeshire] ; Cambridge University Press, 1985. 185 p. :
84-023833          523          052130038X
*Supernovae.*

## QB851 Descriptive astronomy — Stars — Clusters and nebulae

**QB851.J6 1990**
**Glyn Jones, Kenneth.**
Messier's nebulae and star clusters / Kenneth Glyn Jones. Cambridge [England] ; Cambridge University Press, 1991. xvii, 427 p.
89-022199          523.1/125          0521370795
*Nebulae -- Catalogs. Stars -- Clusters -- Catalogs.*

**QB851.S25**
**Sandage, Allan.**
The Hubble atlas of galaxies.  Washington, Carnegie Institution of Washington, 1961. viii, 32, 50
60016568          523.11
*Nebulae. Stars -- Clusters. Stars -- Atlases.*

**QB851.S47 1972**
**Shapley, Harlow,**
Galaxies.  Cambridge, Mass., Harvard University Press, 1972. x, 232 p.
77-169859          523.1/12          0674340515
*Galaxies.*

## QB857-858.42 Descriptive astronomy — Stars — Galaxies

**QB857.K35 1997**
**Kaler, James B.**
 Cosmic clouds : birth, death, and recycling in the galaxy / James B. Kaler. New York : Scientific American Library : c1997. xii, 253 p. :
96-046769        523.1/135        0716750759
 *Galaxies. Stars. Astrophysics.*

**QB857.S63 2000**
**Sparke, Linda Siobhan.**
 Galaxies in the universe : an introduction / Linda S. Sparke, John S. Gallagher. New York : Cambridge University Press, c2000. viii, 379 p.
99-044950        523.1/12        0521592410
 *Galaxies.*

**QB857.W73 1988**
**Wray, James D.**
 The color atlas of galaxies / James D. Wray. Cambridge ; Cambridge University Press, 1988. xi, 189 p. :
86-013715        523.1/12/0222        0521322367
 *Galaxies -- Atlases.*

**QB857.7.B44 2000**
**Begelman, Mitchell C.**
 Turn right at Orion / Mitchell Begelman. Cambridge, Mass. : Perseus Pub., 2000. viii, 264 p.
                    073820207X
 *Astronomy.   Milky Way.*

**QB857.7.B64 1981**
**Bok, Bart Jan,**
 The Milky Way / Bart J. Bok and Priscilla F. Bok. Cambridge, Mass. : Harvard University Press, 1981. viii, 356 p.
80-022544        523.1/13        0674575032
 *Milky Way.*

**QB857.7.H46 1994**
**Henbest, Nigel.**
 The guide to the galaxy / Nigel Henbest and Heather Couper. Cambridge [England] ; Cambridge University Press, c1994. 265 p. :
93-008859        523.1/13        0521306221
 *Milky Way.*

**QB858.42.B47 1996**
**Bertin, G.**
 Spiral structure in galaxies : a density wave theory / G. Bertin and C.C. Lin. Cambridge, Mass. : MIT Press, c1996. x, 271 p. :
95-011635        523.1/12        0262023962
 *Spiral galaxies. Density wave theory.*

## QB871 Descriptive astronomy — Stars — Stellar spectroscopy

**QB871.K33 1989**
**Kaler, James B.**
 Stars and their spectra : an introduction to the spectral sequence / James B. Kaler. Cambridge [Cambridgeshire] ; Cambridge University Press, 1989. xvi, 300 p. :
88-009533        523.8/7        0521304946
 *Stars -- Spectra.*

# QB980.5-991 Cosmogony. Cosmology

**QB980.5.E53 1993**
 Encyclopedia of cosmology : historical, philosophical, and scientific foundations of modern cosmology / edited by Norriss S. Hetherington. New York : Garland Pub., 1993. xv, 686 p. :
92-043456        523.1/03        0824072138
 *Cosmology -- Encyclopedias.*

**QB981.A35 1999**
**Aczel, Amir D.**
 God's equation : Einstein, relativity, and the expanding universe / Amir D. Aczel. New York : Four Walls Eight Windows, c1999. xvii, 236 p.
99-036319        523.1        1568581394
 *Einstein, Albert, -- 1879-1955.     Relativity (Physics) Cosmology.*

**QB981.A96 1992**
**Atkins, P. W.**
 Creation revisited / P.W. Atkins. Oxford ; W.H. Freeman, c1992. viii, 163 p.
92-024848        523.1        0716745003
 *Cosmology.*

**QB981.B2798 1994**
**Barrow, John D.,**
 The origin of the universe / John D. Barrow. New York : BasicBooks, c1994. xv, 150 p. :
94-006343        523.1        0465053548
 *Cosmology. Astrophysics.*

**QB981.B7274 1998**
**Bothun, Greg.**
 Modern cosmological observations and problems / by Greg Bothun. London ; Taylor & Francis, c1998. xi, 300 p., [
98-176133        523.1        0748403329
 *Cosmology. Dark matter (Astronomy)*

**QB981.C596 1997**
**Clark, Stuart**
 Towards the edge of the universe : a review of modern cosmology / Stuart Clark. Chichester ; Wiley, 1997. xxi, 209 p. :
95-048036        523.1        0471962481
 *Cosmology.*

**QB981.D4313 1998**
**Delsemme, A. H.**
Our cosmic origins : from the big bang to the emergence of life and intelligence / Armand Delsemme. Cambridge, UK ; Cambridge University Press, 1998. xviii, 322 p.
97-033010          576.8/3          0521620384
*Cosmology. Astronomy -- History.*

**QB981.E3**
**Eddington, Arthur Stanley,**
The expanding universe, by Sir Arthur Eddington ... New York, The Macmillan Company; 1933. viii, [2], 18
33005593          523.1
*Nebulae. Cosmology.*

**QB981.G594 1995**
**Goldsmith, Donald.**
Einstein's greatest blunder? : the cosmological constant and other fudge factors in the physics of the Universe / Donald Goldsmith. Cambridge, Mass. : Harvard University Press, 1995. vi, 216 p., [
95-014762          523.1          0674242416
*Cosmology.*

**QB981.H32 2000**
**Harrison, Edward Robert.**
Cosmology : the science of the universe / Edward Harrison. Cambridge [England] ; Cambridge University Press, 2000. x, 567 p. :
99-010172          523.1          052166148X
*Cosmology.*

**QB981.H377 1988**
**Hawking, S. W.**
A brief history of time : from the big bang to black holes / Stephen W. Hawking ; introduction by Carl Sagan ; illustrations by Ron Miller. Toronto ; Bantam Books, 1988. x, 198 p. :
87-033333          523.1          0553052438
*Cosmology.*

**QB981.H3775 1997**
**Hawkins, Michael,**
Hunting down the universe : the missing mass, primordial black holes, and other dark matters / Michael Hawkins. Reading, Mass. : Addison-Wesley, c1997. x, 240 p. ;
97-017307          523.1          0201156989
*Cosmology. Black holes (Astronomy) Dark matter (Astronomy)*

**QB981.H754 2000**
**Hoyle, Fred,**
A different approach to cosmology : from a static universe through the big bang towards reality / F. Hoyle, G. Burbidge, and J.V. Narlikar. Cambridge [England] ; Cambridge University Press, 2000. xi, 357 p. :
99-015821          523.1          0521662230
*Cosmology.*

**QB981.K689 1996**
**Kolb, Edward W.**
Blind watchers of the sky : the people and ideas that shaped our view of the universe / Rocky Kolb. Reading, Mass. : Addison-Wesley, c1996. xii, 338 p. :
95-041438          523.1          0201489929
*Cosmology.     Solar system.*

**QB981.K73 1996**
**Kragh, Helge,**
Cosmology and controversy : the historical development of two theories of the universe / Helge Kragh. Princeton, NJ : Princeton University Press, c1996. xiii, 500 p.
96-005612          523.1          0691026238
*Cosmology -- History.*

**QB981.L36 1993**
**Lemonick, Michael D.,**
The light at the edge of the universe : leading cosmologists on the brink of a scientific revolution / Michael D. Lemonick. New York : Villard Books, 1993. viii, 325 p.
92-035058          523.1          0679413049
*Cosmology. Astrophysics. Astronomers.*

**QB981.L534 1999**
**Liddle, Andrew R.**
An introduction ot modern cosmology / Andrew Liddle. Chichester ; Wiley, c1999. xiii, 129 p.,
98-049130          523.1          0471987573
*Cosmology.*

**QB981.L54 1990**
**Lightman, Alan P.,**
Origins : the lives and worlds of modern cosmologists / Alan Lightman and Roberta Brawer. Cambridge, Mass. : Harvard University Press, 1990. xi, 563 p. :
90-004623          523.1          0674644700
*Cosmology -- Miscellanea. Astronomers -- Biography.*

**QB981.L57 2000**
**Livio, Mario,**
The accelerating universe : infinite expansion, the cosmological constant, and the beauty of the cosmos / Mario Livio. New York : Wiley, c2000. xiv, 274 p. :
99-022278          523.1          047132969X
*Cosmology.*

**QB981.M865 1982**
**Morrison, Philip.**
Powers of ten : a book about the relative size of things in the universe and the effect of adding another zero / by Philip and Phylis Morrison and the Office of Charles and Ray Eames. Redding, Conn. ; San Francisco : Scientific American Library ; c1982. 150 p. :
          500 19          0716714094
*Cosmology -- Miscellanea. Powers of ten--a film dealing with the relative size of things in the universe and the effect of adding another zero (Motion Picture)*

**QB981.M9**
**Munitz, Milton Karl,**
Theories of the universe; from Babylonian myth to modern science. Glencoe, Ill., Free Press [1957] 437 p.
57-006746          523.1
*Cosmogony. Cosmology.*

**QB981.P243 1998**
**Padmanabhan, T.**
After the first three minutes : the story of our universe / T. Padmanabhan. Cambridge ; Cambridge University Press, 1998. xi, 215 p. :
97-011060          523.1          0521620392
*Cosmology.*

**QB981.P44 1983**
**Pellegrino, Charles R.**
Darwin's universe : origins and crises in the history of life / Charles R. Pellegrino, Jesse A. Stoff. New York : Van Nostrand Reinhold, c1983. xi, 208 p. :
82-008352          577          0442275269
*Darwin, Charles, -- 1809-1882.   Cosmology. Life -- Origin.*

**QB981.R367 2000**
**Rees, Martin J.,**
Just six numbers : the deep forces that shape the universe / Martin Rees. New York : Basic Books, c2000. x, 173 p. :
00-268248          523.1/8          0465036724
*Cosmology. Big bang theory.*

**QB981.S55 2001**
**Silk, Joseph,**
The big bang / Joseph Silk. 3rd ed. New York : W.H. Freeman, c2001. xv, 496 p. :
          523.1/8 21          0716738783
*Cosmology. Big band theory.*

**QB981.S553 1994**
**Silk, Joseph,**
Cosmic enigmas / Joseph Silk. Woodbury, NY : AIP Press, c1994. xi, 213 p. :
93-040693          523.1          1563962756
*Cosmology. Astrophysics.*

**QB981.S554 1994**
**Silk, Joseph,**
A short history of the universe / Joseph Silk. New York : Scientific American Library : c1994. viii, 246 p.
94-021771          523.1          0716750481
*Cosmology. Astrophysics.*

**QB981.W48**
**Weinberg, Steven,**
The first three minutes : a modern view of the origin of the universe / Steven Weinberg. New York : Basic Books, c1977. x, 188 p., [5
76-007682          523.1/2          0465024351
*Cosmology.*

**QB982.B7813 1999**
**Brunier, Serge.**
Majestic universe : views from here to infinity / Serge Brunier ; translated by Storm Dunlop. Cambridge, U.K. ; Cambridge University Press, 1999. 216 p. :
00-266912          523.1          0521663075
*Cosmology. Cosmology -- Pictorial works. Astronomy.*

**QB982.D38 1994**
**Davies, P. C. W.**
The last three minutes : conjectures about the ultimate fate of the universe / Paul Davies. New York : BasicBooks, c1994. xiii, 162 p.
94-006345          523.1/9          0465048927
*Cosmology -- Popular works.*

**QB982.T97 1994**
**Tyson, Neil De Grasse.**
Universe down to Earth / Neil De Grasse Tyson. New York : Columbia University Press, c1994. xiv, 277 p. :
93-032259          523.1          023107560X
*Cosmology -- Popular works.*

**QB991.B54.L47 1991**
**Lerner, Eric J.**
The big bang never happened / Eric J. Lerner. New York : Times Books/Random House, c1991. xiii, 466 p.
89-040789          523.1/8          0812918533
*Big bang theory.*

**QB991.B54.S45 1995**
**Fraser, Gordon,**
The search for infinity : solving the mysteries of the universe / Gordon Fraser, Egil Lillestol, Inge Sellevag ; introduction by Stephen Hawking New York : Facts on File, c1995. 144 p. :
94-029113          523.1/8          0816032505
*Big bang theory. Cosmology. Nuclear astrophysics.*

**QB991.B54.T7 1983**
**Trefil, James S.,**
The moment of creation : big bang physics from before the first millisecond to the present universe / James S. Trefil ; illustrations by Gloria Walters. New York : Scribner, c1983. vi, 234 p. :
83-009011          523.1/8          0684179636
*Big bang theory. Cosmology -- History. Nuclear astrophysics.*

**QB991.E94.B37 1994**
**Barrow, John D.,**
The left hand of creation : the origin and evolution of the expanding universe / John D. Barrow, Joseph Silk. New York : Oxford University Press, 1994. p. cm.
93-011046          523.1/8          0195086759
*Expanding universe.*

**QB991.G73.D74 1994**
**Dressler, Alan Michael.**
Voyage to the Great Attractor : exploring intergalactic space / Alan Dressler. New York : A.A. Knopf, 1994. xi, 355 p. :
93-048580          523.1          0394588991
*Great Attractor (Astronomy)*

**QB991.I54.G88 1997**
**Guth, Alan H.**
The inflationary universe : the quest for a new theory of cosmic origins / Alan H. Guth ; with a foreword by Alan Lightman. Reading, Mass. : Addison-Wesley Publishing, 1997. xv, 358 p. :
96-046117          523.1/8          0201149427
*Inflationary universe.*

# QC Physics

## QC3 Collected works (nonserial)

**QC3.B4**
**Beiser, Arthur.**
The world of physics; readings in the nature, history, and challenge of physics. With a foreword by Edward U. Condon. New York, McGraw-Hill, 1960. 286 p.
60013759          530.82
*Physics.*

**QC3.B584**
**Bohr, Niels Henrik David,**
Collected works. General editor: L. Rosenfeld. Amsterdam, North-Holland Pub. Co., 1972-1999 v. 1, 3-8, 10
70-126498          0720418003
*Physics.*

**QC3.F4513 2000**
**Feynman, Richard Phillips.**
Selected papers of Richard Feynman : with commentary / editor, Laurie M. Brown. River Edge, NJ : World Scientific, c2000. xii, 999 p. :
00-049425          530          9810241305
*Physics.*

**QC3.M26**
**Magie, William Francis,**
A source book in physics, by William Francis Magie ... New York, McGraw-Hill Book Company, inc., 1935. xiv, 620 p.
35008094          530
*Physics. Physics -- History. Physics -- history*

**QC3.N52**
**Newton, Isaac,**
Papers & letters on natural philosophy and related documents. Edited, with general introd., by I. Bernard Cohen, assisted by Robert E. Schofield. With explanatory prefaces by Marie Boas [and others]. Cambridge, Harvard University Press, 1958. xiii, 501 p.
58-005607          508
*Physics. Science -- History.*

## QC5 Dictionaries and encyclopedias

**QC5.D485 2001**
Dictionary of pure and applied physics / edited by Dipak Basu. Boca Raton : CRC Press, c2001. 389 p. :
00-052884          530/.03          084932890X
*Physics -- Dictionaries.*

**QC5.E544 1990**
Encyclopedia of modern physics / Robert A. Meyers, editor ; Steven N. Shore, scientific consultant. San Diego : Academic Press, c1990. xii, 773 p. :
89-017886          530/.03          0122266927
*Physics -- Dictionaries.*

**QC5.F34 1999**
The Facts on File dictionary of physics. New York : Facts On File, c1999. 250 p. :
99-017780          530/.03          0816039119
*Physics -- Dictionaries.*

**QC5.M15 1996**
Macmillan encyclopedia of physics / John S. Rigden, editor in chief. New York : Simon & Schuster Macmillan, 1996. 4 v. (lxxx, 1
96-030977          530/.03          0028973593
*Physics -- Encyclopedias.*

**QC5.M424 1997**
McGraw-Hill dictionary of physics / Sybil P. Parker, editor in chief. New York : McGraw-Hill, c1997. xiii, 498 p.
96-046186          530/.03          0070524297
*Physics -- Dictionaries.*

## QC5.3 Communication in physics — General works

**QC5.3.B53 2001**
**Blakeslee, Ann M.**
Interacting with audiences : social influences on the production of scientific writing / Ann M. Blakeslee. Mahwah, NJ : Lawrence Erlbaum Associates, 2001. xvii, 141 p. :
530/.01/4 21          0805822992
*Communication in physics -- Social aspects. Technical writing.*

## QC5.52 Communication in physics — Language. Authorship

**QC5.52.A54 1989**
American Institute of Physics editorial handbook. Woodbury, NY : American Institute of Physics, 1989. 225 p. ;
89-083308          808/.06653          0883186381
*Physics -- Authorship -- Handbooks, manuals, etc.*

## QC6 Philosophy. Methadology — General works, treatises, and textbooks

**QC6.A3 1950**
**Abro, A. d'.**
 The evolution of scientific thought from Newton to Einstein. [New York] Dover Publications [1950] 481 p.
50-009480          530.1
 *Relativity (Physics) Science -- Methodology.*

**QC6.A713 1966**
**Arzelies, Henri,**
 Relativistic kinematics. Translated from an enl. and thoroughly rev. text, and brought up to date to include the latest publications. Oxford, Pergamon Press [1966] xi, 298 p.
65-014780          530.1
 *Relativistic kinematics.*

**QC6.B33 1957**
**Barnett, Lincoln Kinnear,**
 The universe and Dr. Einstein. With a foreword by Albert Einstein. New York, W. Sloane Associates, 1957] 127 p.
57-005851          530.1
*Einstein, Albert, -- 1879-1955.    Relativity (Physics)*

**QC6.B453**
**Bergmann, Peter Gabriel.**
 Introduction to the theory of relativity, by Peter Gabriel Bergmann ... with a foreword by Albert Einstein. New York, Prentice-Hall, inc., 1942. xvi, 287 p.
42014846          530.1
 *Relativity (Physics)*

**QC6.B454**
**Bergmann, Peter Gabriel.**
 The riddle of gravitation [by] Peter G. Bergmann. New York, Scribner [1968] xvi, 270 p.
68-011537          530.11
 *Relativity (Physics) Gravitation.*

**QC6.B597 1957a**
**Bohm, David.**
 Causality and chance in modern physics. Foreword by Louis de Broglie. Princeton, N.J., Van Nostrand [c1957] 170 p.
58-001489          530.1
 *Causality (Physics) Chance. Quantum theory.*

**QC6.B598**
**Bohr, Niels Henrik David,**
 Atomic physics and human knowledge.  New York, Wiley [1958] viii, 101 p.
58-009002          530.1
 *Atoms. Physics -- Philosophy. Knowledge, Theory of.*

**QC6.B599 1963**
**Bohr, Niels Henrik David,**
 Essays, 1958-1962, on atomic physics and human knowledge. [New York, Interscience Publishers, 1963] x, 100 p.
63-021771          530.1
 *Quantum theory. Atoms. Physics -- Philosophy.*

**QC6.B66 1962**
**Born, Max,**
 Einstein's theory of relativity.    New York, Dover Publications [1962] vii, 376 p.
62-005801          530.11
*Einstein, Albert, -- 1879-1955.    Relativity (Physics)*

**QC6.B72**
**Brillouin, Leon,**
 Relativity reexamined.  New York, Academic Press, 1970. xi, 111 p.
74-107560          530.11      0121349454
 *Relativity (Physics)*

**QC6.B727 1993**
**Brody, T. A.**
 The philosophy behind physics / Thomas Brody ; edited by Luis de la Pena and Peter E. Hodgson. Berlin ; Springer-Verlag, c1993. xii, 355 p. :
93-017950          530/.01          3540559140
 *Physics -- Philosophy. Quantum theory.*

**QC6.C33**
**Carnap, Rudolf,**
 Philosophical foundations of physics; an introduction to the philosophy of science. Edited by Martin Gardner. New York, Basic Books, inc. [1966] x, 300 p.
66-016499          530.01
 *Physics -- Philosophy.*

**QC6.D85 1960**
**Durell, Clement V.**
 Readable relativity. Foreword by Freeman J. Dyson. New York, Harper [1960] 146 p.
62002252
 *Relativity (Physics)*

**QC6.E33**
**Eddington, Arthur Stanley,**
 Fundamental theory, by Sir A.S. Eddington ... Cambridge [Eng.] The University Press, 1946. viii, 292 p.
47002790          530.1
 *Physics -- Philosophy. Relativity (Physics) Cosmology.*

**QC6.E35**
**Eddington, Arthur Stanley,**
 The mathematical theory of relativity, by A.S. Eddington ... Cambridge [Eng.] The University Press, 1930. ix, 270 p.
31032716          530.1
 *Relativity (Physics)*

**QC6.E37 1958**
**Eddington, Arthur Stanley,**
 The philosophy of physical science. [Ann Arbor] University of Michigan Press [1958] ix, 230 p.
58014940          530.1
 *Science -- Philosophy. Physics -- Philosophy. Knowledge,Theory of.*

**QC6.E4 1929**
**Eddington, Arthur Stanley,**
 Space, time and gravitation; an outline of the general relativity theory, by A. S. Eddington. Cambridge [Eng.] The University Press, 1929 [1920] vi p., 218 p
32017569                    530.1
 *Space and time. Gravitation. Relativity (Physics)*

**QC6.E43 1956**
**Einstein, Albert,**
 The meaning of relativity. Princeton, Princeton University Press, 1955 [c1956] 166 p.
56-001198                    530.1
 *Relativity (Physics)*

**QC6.F673 1993**
**Franklin, Allan,**
 The rise and fall of the "Fifth Force" : discovery, pursuit, and justification in modern physics / Allan Franklin. New York : American Institute of Physics, c1993. 141 p. :
92-043551          530          1563961199
 *Physics -- Methodology. Gravitation. Physics -- Philosophy.*

**QC6.F76 1986**
 From quarks to quasars : philosophical problems of modern physics / editor, Robert G. Colodny ; Alberto Coffa ... [et al.]. Pittsburgh, Pa. : University of Pittsburgh Press, c1986. xvi, 395 p. :
84-029456          530/.01          0822935155
 *Physics -- Philosophy. Quantum theory.*

**QC6.G35913 1999**
**Genz, Henning,**
 Nothingness : the science of empty space / Henning Genz ; translated by Karin Heusch. Reading, Mass. : Perseus Books, c1999. xi, 340 p. :
98-087966          530/.01          0738200611
 *Physics -- Philosophy. Nothing (Philosophy) Metaphysics.*

**QC6.H34613 1974**
**Heisenberg, Werner,**
 Across the frontiers. Translated from the German by Peter Heath. New York, Harper & Row [1974] xxii, 229 p.
73-004087          530.1          0060118245
 *Physics -- Philosophy. Science -- Philosophy.*

**QC6.J3 1969**
**Jammer, Max.**
 Concepts of space; the history of theories of space in physics. Foreword by Albert Einstein. Cambridge, Mass., Harvard University Press, 1969. xv, 221 p.
69-018034                    530.1
 *Space and time -- History. Physics -- Philosophy -- History. Science -- Philosophy -- History.*

**QC6.J383**
**Jeans, James Hopwood,**
 Physics & philosophy, by Sir James Jeans. Cambridge [Eng.] The University Press, 1942. 4 p. ., 222 p
43001642                    530.1
 *Physics -- Philosophy. Philosophy.*

**QC6.L42 1957**
**Lindsay, Robert Bruce,**
 Foundations of physics [by] Robert Bruce Lindsay [and] Henry Margenau. New York, Dover Publications [1957] 542 p.
57-014416                    530.1
 *Physics -- Philosophy.*

**QC6.L425**
**Lindsay, Robert Bruce,**
 The nature of physics; a physicist's views on the history and philosophy of his science.   Providence, Brown University Press, 1968. vi, 212 p.
68-010642                    530/.01
 *Physics.*

**QC6.M3514**
**Margenau, Henry,**
 The nature of physical reality; a philosophy of modern physics. New York, McGraw-Hill, 1950. xiii, 479 p.
50007392                    530.1
 *Physics -- Philosophy.*

**QC6.M52**
**Moller, C.**
 The theory of relativity.  Oxford, Clarendon Press, 1952. xxi, 386 p.
52010897                    530.1
 *Relativity (Physics)*

**QC6.N485 2000**
**Newton, Roger G.**
 Thinking about physics / Roger G. Newton. Princeton, N.J. : Princeton University Press, c2000. x, 198 p. :
99-035807          530/.01          0691009201
 *Physics -- Philosophy.*

**QC6.P625**
**Planck, Max,**
 The philosophy of physics, by Dr. Max Planck ... translated by H.W. Johnston. New York, W.W. Norton & Company, inc. [c1936] 128 p.
36008178                    530.1
 *Physics -- Philosophy.*

**QC6.R382**
**Reichenbach, Hans,**
 The direction of time, edited by Maria Reichenbach. Berkeley, University of California Press, 1956. xi, 280 p.
55-009883                    530.1
 *Causality (Physics) Space and time. Science -- Philosophy.*

**QC6.R477**
**Rindler, Wolfgang,**
 Essential relativity; special, general, and cosmological. New York, Van Nostrand Reinhold Co. [1969] xi, 319 p.
77-087786                    530.11
 *Relativity (Physics).*

**QC6.R48**
**Rindler, Wolfgang,**
  Special relativity. Edinburgh, Oliver and Boyd; [1960] 186 p.
60-050861          530.11
  *Relativity (Physics)*

**QC6.R8 1958**
**Russell, Bertrand,**
  The ABC of relativity. London, G. Allen & Unwin [1958] 139 p.
58-042601          530.1
  *Relativity (Physics)*

**QC6.R83 1954**
**Russell, Bertrand,**
  The analysis of matter. With a new introd. by Lester E. Denonn. New York, Dover Publications [c1954] 408 p.
55001084          530.1
  *Matter. Physics -- Philosophy.*

**QC6.S93 1965**
**Synge, J. L.**
  Relativity: the special theory, by J.L. Synge. Amsterdam, North-Holland Pub. Co.; [sole distributors for U 1965. xiv, 459 p.
65-003255          530.11
  *Relativity (Physics)*

**QC6.T526 1994**
**Thorne, Kip S.**
  Black holes and time warps : Einstein's outrageous legacy / Kip S. Thorne. New York : W.W. Norton, c1994. 619 p. :
93-002014          530.1/1          0393035050
  *Physics -- Philosophy. Relativity (Physics) Astrophysics.*

**QC6.T653 1990**
**Torretti, Roberto,**
  Creative understanding : philosophical reflections on physics / Roberto Torretti. Chicago : University of Chicago Press, 1990. xvi, 369 p. ;
90-011007          530/.01          0226808343
  *Physics -- Philosophy. Physics -- Methodology.*

## QC6.4 Philosophy. Methadology — Special topics, A-Z

**QC6.4.C3.C37 1989**
**Cartwright, Nancy.**
  Nature's capacities and their measurement / Nancy Cartwright. Oxford : Clarendon Press ; 1989. x, 268 p. :
88-033015          530/.01          0198244770
  *Causality (Physics) Probabilities. Physics -- Philosophy.*

**QC6.4.R42.E8713 1989**
**Espagnat, Bernard d'.**
  Reality and the physicist : knowledge, duration, and the quantum world / Bernard d'Espagnat ; translated by J.C. Whitehouse and Bernard d'Espagnat. Cambridge [Cambridgeshire] ; Cambridge University Press, 1989. 280 p. ;
88-003658          530/.01          052132940X
  *Reality. Physics -- Philosophy.*

**QC6.4.R42.N49 1997**
**Newton, Roger G.**
  The truth of science : physical theories and reality / Roger G. Newton. Cambridge, Mass. : Harvard University Press, 1997. viii, 260 p.
97-009079          530          0674910923
  *Physics -- Methodology. Reality. Science -- Methodology.*

## QC7 History — General works

**QC7.A26 2000**
**Adams, Steve,**
  Frontiers : twentieth century physics / Steve Adams. New York : Taylor & Francis, 2000. p. cm.
99-034590          539          0748408401
  *Physics -- History -- 20th century.*

**QC7.C13 1962**
**Cajori, Florian,**
  A history of physics in its elementary branches (through 1925): including the evolution of physical laboratories. New York, Dover Publications [1962] 424 p.
62003998          530.9
  *Physical laboratories. Physics -- History.*

**QC7.C65**
**Cohen, I. Bernard,**
  Franklin and Newton; an inquiry into speculative Newtonian experimental science and Franklin's work in electricity as an example thereof. Philadelphia, American Philosophical Society, 1956. xxvi, 657 p.
56-013224          530.903
  *Franklin, Benjamin, -- 1706-1790. Newton, Isaac, -- Sir, -- 1642-1727. Physics -- History.*

**QC7.C66**
**Cohen, I. Bernard,**
  The Newtonian revolution : with illustrations of the transformation of scientific ideas / I. Bernard Cohen. Cambridge [Eng.] ; Cambridge University Press, 1980. xv, 404 p. ;
79-018637          509          0521229642
  *Newton, Isaac, -- Sir, -- 1642-1727. -- Principia. Physics – History. Science -- History.*

**QC7.E5 1961**
**Einstein, Albert,**
  The evolution of physics; the growth of ideas from early concepts to relativity and quanta, by Albert Einstein and Leopold Infeld. New York, Simon and Schuster, 1961 [c1938] xvi, 302 p.
61000307          530.9
  *Physics -- History. Relativity (Physics) Quantum theory.*

## QC7.E52 1998

Einstein's miraculous year : five papers that changed the face of physics / edited and introduced by John Stachel ; with the assistance of Trevor Lipscombe, Alice Calaprice, and Sam Elworthy ; and with a foreword by Roger Penrose. Princeton, NJ : Princeton University Press, c1998. xv, 198 p. :
97-048441          530.1          0691059381
*Einstein, Albert, -- 1879-1955.     Physics -- History -- 20th century.*

## QC7.G26
**Gamow, George,**
Biography of physics. New York, Harper [1961] 338 p.
61-006433          530.9
*Physics -- History.*

## QC7.G5613 1988
**Gindikin, S. G.**
Tales of physicists and mathematicians / Semyon Grigorevich Gindikin ; translated by Alan Shuchat. Boston : Birkhauser, c1988. x, 157 p. :
87-024971          530/.09          0817633170
*Physics -- History. Mathematics -- History. Science -- History.*

## QC7.J86 1986
**Jungnickel, Christa.**
Intellectual mastery of nature : theoretical physics from Ohm to Einstein / Christa Jungnickel and Russell McCormmach. Chicago : University of Chicago Press, c1986. 2 v. :
85-016507          530/.09/034          0226415813
*Physics -- History. Mathematical physics -- History.*

## QC7.K7 1999
**Kragh, Helge,**
Quantum generations : a history of physics in the twentieth century / Helge Kragh. Princeton, N.J. : Princeton University Press, c1999. xiv, 494 p. :
99-017903          530/.09/04          0691012067
*Physics -- History -- 20th century.*

## QC7.L47 1992
The Life and times of modern physics : history of physics II / edited by Melba Phillips. New York, N.Y. : American Institute of Physics, 1992. xii, 366 p. :
92-012669          530/.09          0883188465
*Physics -- History. Physics -- History -- Sources.*

## QC7.M35
**McCormmach, Russell.**
Night thoughts of a classical physicist / Russell McCormmach. Cambridge, Mass. : Harvard University Press, 1982. 217 p., [2] l
81-006674          813/.54          0674624602
*Physics -- History -- Fiction.*

## QC7.S435 1984
**Segre', Emilio.**
From falling bodies to radio waves : classical physicists and their discoveries / Emilio Segre. New York : W.H. Freeman, c1984. x, 298 p. :
83016584          530/.09          0716714825
*Physics -- History. Physicists -- Biography.*

## QC7.S47
**Shamos, Morris H.**
Great experiments in physics. New York, Holt [1959] 370 p.
59-005751          530.9
*Physics -- History.*

## QC7.S78 1994
**Stehle, Philip.**
Order, chaos, order : the transition from classical to quantum physics / Philip Stehle. New York : Oxford University Press, 1994. xiv, 322 p. :
92-041506          530.1/2/09          0195075137
*Physics -- History. Quantum theory -- History.*

## QC7.T84 1995
Twentieth century physics / edited by Laurie M. Brown, Abraham Pais, Sir Brian Pippard. Bristol ; Institute of Physics Pub. ; c1995. 3 v. :
95-041186          530/.09/04          1563963140
*Physics -- History.*

# QC7.5 History — Addresses, essays, lectures

## QC7.5.S65 1990
Some truer method : reflections on the heritage of Newton / edited by Frank Durham and Robert D. Purrington. New York : Columbia University Press, c1990. vii, 257 p. :
90-001832          530/.09          0231068964
*Newton, Isaac, -- Sir, -- 1642-1727. -- Principia.     Science -- Philosophy.  Physics -- History.*

# QC9 History — By region or country, A-Z

## QC9.G8.S67 1988
**Sorabji, Richard.**
Matter, space, and motion : theories in antiquity and their sequel / Richard Sorabji. Ithaca, N.Y. : Cornell University Press, 1988. x, 377 p. ;
87-047984          530/.0938          0801421942
*Physics -- Greece -- History. Philosophy, Ancient.  Greece -- Antiquities.*

# QC15 Biography — Collective

## QC15.B74 1997
**Brennan, Richard P.**
Heisenberg probably slept here : the lives, times, and ideas of the great physicists of the 20th century / Richard P. Brennan. New York : Wiley, c1997. xi, 274 p. :
96-042935          530/.092/2          0471157090
*Physicists -- Biography. Physics -- History -- 20th century.*

## QC15.P67 1998
**Porter, Neil A.**
Physicists in conflict / Neil A. Porter. Bristol ; Institute of Physics Pub., c1998. xv, 275 p. :
98-008669          530/.092/2          0750305096
*Physicists. Conflict (Psychology) Communication in science.*

**QC15.S437 1993**
**Serafini, Anthony.**
  Legends in their own time : a century of American physical scientists / Anthony Serafini. New York : Plenum Press, c1993. xv, 361 p. ;
92-043949        500.2/092/2        0306444607
  *Physical scientists -- United States -- Biography. Physicists -- United States -- Biography. Astronomers -- United States -- Biography.*

**QC15.W4**
**Weber, Robert L.,**
  Pioneers of science : nobel prize winners in physics / Robert L. Weber ; edited by J.M.A. Lenihan. Bristol : Institute of Physics, c1980. xviii, 272 p.
81-108183        530/.92/2        0854980369
  *Physicists -- Biography. Nobel Prizes.*

## QC16 Biography — Individual, A-Z

**QC16.A342**
**Alpert, IA. L.**
  Making waves : stories from my life / Yakov Alpert. New Haven : Yale University Press, c2000. xvii, 260 p.
00-035918        530/.092        0300078218
  *Alpert, IA. L. -- (IAkov Lvovich)    Physicists -- Russia (Federation) – Biography.*

**QC16.B46.B47**
**Bernstein, Jeremy,**
  Hans Bethe, prophet of energy / Jeremy Bernstein. New York : Basic Books, c1980. xii, 212 p. ;
80-050555        539/.092/4        0465029035
  *Bethe, Hans Albrecht, -- 1906-    Physicists -- Biography. Nuclear energy -- History.*

**QC16.B63.B5713 1988**
**Blaedel, Niels.**
  Harmony and unity : the life of Niels Bohr / by Niels Blaedel. Madison, Wis. : Science Tech, 1988. xi, 323 p. :
88001928        530/.092/4        0910239142
  *Bohr, Niels Henrik David, -- 1885-1962.    Physicists – Denmark – Biography. Physics -- History.*

**QC16.B63.M87 1987**
**Murdoch, Dugald,**
  Niels Bohr's philosophy of physics / Dugald Murdoch. Cambridge [Cambridgeshire] ; Cambridge University Press, 1987. x, 294 p. ;
87-011717        530/.092/4        0521333202
  *Bohr, Niels Henrik David, -- 1885-1962.    Complementarity (Physics) Wave-particle duality. Physics -- Philosophy.*

**QC16.B79.R39 1992**
**Rayner-Canham, Marelene F.**
  Harriet Brooks : pioneer nuclear scientist / Marelene F. Rayner-Canham, Geoffrey W. Rayner-Canham. Montreal ; McGill-Queen's University Press, c1992. ix, 168 p. :
92-173880        539.7/092        0773508813
  *Brooks, Harriet, -- 1876-1933.    Women physicists -- Canada -- Biography.*

**QC16.D57.K73 1990**
**Kragh, Helge,**
  Dirac : a scientific biography / Helge Kragh. Cambridge [England] ; Cambridge University Press, 1990. x, 389 p. :
89-017257        530/.092        0521380898
  *Dirac, P. A. M. -- (Paul Adrien Maurice), -- 1902-    Physicists – Great Britain -- Biography.*

**QC16.E5.A3 1970**
**Einstein, Albert,**
  Out of my later years.  Westport, Conn., Greenwood Press [1970, c1950] 282 p.
70-089016        081        0837120861
  *Einstein, Albert, -- 1879-1955.*

**QC16.E5.A33**
**Einstein, Albert,**
  Albert Einstein, the human side : new glimpses from his archives / selected and edited by Helen Dukas and Banesh Hoffmann. Princeton, N.J. : Princeton University Press, c1979. viii, 167 p.
78-070289        530/.092/4        0691082316
  *Einstein, Albert, -- 1879-1955.    Physicists -- Biography. Physicists -- Correspondence.*

**QC16.E5.A4 1992**
**Einstein, Albert,**
  Albert Einstein/Mileva Maric--the love letters / edited and with an introduction by Jurgen Renn and Robert Schulmann ; translated by Shawn Smith. Princeton, N.J. : Princeton University Press, c1992. xxix, 107 p.,
91-040183        530/.092        0691087601
  *Einstein, Albert, -- 1879-1955 -- Correspondence. Einstein-Maric, Mileva, -- 1875-1948 -- Correspondence.    Physicists -- Correspondence.*

**QC16.E5.A4513**
**Einstein, Albert,**
  The Born-Einstein letters; correspondence between Albert Einstein and Max and Hedwig Born from 1916 to 1955. With commentaries by Max Born. Translated by Irene Born. New York, Walker [1971] x, 240 p.
76-126107        530        0802703267
  *Einstein, Albert, -- 1879-1955.    Physicists -- Correspondence.*

**QC16.E5.B737 1996**
**Brian, Denis.**
  Einstein : a life / Denis Brian. New York, N.Y. : J. Wiley, c1996. xiv, 509 p. :
95-012075        530/.092        0471114596
  *Einstein, Albert, -- 1879-1955.    Physicists -- United States -- Biography.*

**QC16.E5.J36 1999**
**Jammer, Max.**
  Einstein and religion : physics and theology / Max Jammer. Princeton, NJ : Princeton University Press, 1999. 279 p. ;
99-024124        215        0691006997
  *Einstein, Albert, -- 1879-1955 -- Religion.    Religion and science.*

**QC16.E5.K36 1996**
**Kantha, Sachi Sri.**
   An Einstein dictionary / Sachi Sri Kantha ; foreword by Kenichi Fukui. Westport, Conn. : Greenwood Press, 1996. xxvi, 298 p.
95-006485          530/.092          0313283508
*Einstein, Albert, -- 1879-1955 -- Dictionaries. Einstein, Albert, -- 1879-1955 -- Bibliography. Physicists -- Biography – Dictionaries. Physics -- Dictionaries. Science -- History -- Dictionaries.*

**QC16.E5B3513 2001**
**Balibar, Francoise.**
   Einstein : decoding the Universe / Francois Balibar ; [translated from the French by David J. Baker and Dorie B. Baker]. New York : Harry N. Abrams, 2001. 143 p. :
          530/.092 B 21          0810929805
*Einstein, Albert, 1879-1955. Physicists -- United States – Biography.*

**QC16.F2.C37 1996**
**Cantor, G. N.,**
   Michael Faraday / Geoffrey Cantor, David Gooding, and Frank A.J.L. James. Atlantic Highlands, NJ : Humanities Press, c1996. xiii, 111 p.
96-012811          530/.092          0391039814
*Faraday, Michael, -- 1791-1867. Physicists -- Great Britain -- Biography.*

**QC16.F46.S4**
**Segre, Emilio.**
   Enrico Fermi, physicist. Chicago, University of Chicago Press [1970] x, 276 p.
71107424          539.7/0924          0226744728
*Fermi, Enrico, -- 1901-1954. Physicists -- Italy -- Biography.*

**QC16.F49.A3 1988**
**Feynman, Richard Phillips.**
   What do YOU care what other people think? : further adventures of a curious character / Richard P. Feynman, as told to Ralph Leighton. New York : Norton, c1988. 255 p. :
88-022390          530/.092          0393026590
*Feynman, Richard Phillips. Physicists -- United States -- Biography. Science -- Anecdotes.*

**QC16.F49.A3 1993**
   Most of the good stuff : memories of Richard Feynman / editors, Laurie M. Brown, John S. Rigden. New York : American Institute of Physics, c1993. 181 p., [16]
92-046471          530/.092          0883188708
*Feynman, Richard Phillips. Physics -- History. Physicists – United States -- Biography.*

**QC16.F49.A3 1994**
   No ordinary genius : the illustrated Richard Feynman / edited by Christopher Sykes. New York : W.W. Norton, c1994. 272 p. :
93032449          530/.092          0393036219
*Feynman, Richard Phillips. Physicists -- United States -- Biography.*

**QC16.F49.A37 1985**
**Feynman, Richard Phillips.**
   "Surely you're joking, Mr. Feynman!" : adventures of a curious character / Richard P. Feynman as told to Ralph Leighton ; edited by Edward Hutchings. New York : W.W. Norton, c1985. 350 p. ;
84-014703          530/.092/4          0393019217
*Feynman, Richard Phillips. Physicists -- United States -- Biography. Science -- Humor.*

**QC16.F49.G54 1992**
**Gleick, James.**
   Genius : the life and science of Richard Feynman / James Gleick. New York : Pantheon Books, c1992. x, 532 p. :
92-006577          530/.092          0679408363
*Feynman, Richard Phillips. Physics -- History -- 20th century. Physicists -- United States -- Biography.*

**QC16.F49.M45 1994**
**Mehra, Jagdish.**
   The beat of a different drum : the life and science of Richard Feynman / Jagdish Mehra. Oxford [England] : Clarendon Press ; 1994. xxxii, 630 p.
93-028295          530/.092          0198539487
*Feynman, Richard Phillips. Physicists -- United States -- Biography.*

**QC16.F68.C64 1990**
**Cohen, I. Bernard,**
   Benjamin Franklin's science / I. Bernard Cohen. Cambridge, Mass. : Harvard University Press, 1990. xii, 273 p. :
89-035290          509.2          0674066588
*Franklin, Benjamin, -- 1706-1790 -- Knowledge -- Physics. Electricity -- Experiments -- History. Lightning -- Experiments -- History. Physicists -- United States -- Biography.*

**QC16.F713.A3 1991**
**Freeman, Joan,**
   A passion for physics : the story of a woman physicist / Joan Freeman. Bristol, England ; A. Hilger, 1991. x, 229 p. :
90019560          530/.092          0750300981
*Freeman, Joan, -- 1918- Physicists -- Australia -- Biography. Women scientists.*

**QC16.G5.W45 1962**
**Wheeler, Lynde Phelps.**
   Josiah Willard Gibbs, the history of a great mind. With a foreword by A. Whitney Griswold. New Haven, Yale University Press [1962] 270 p.
62006570          925
*Gibbs, J. Willard -- (Josiah Willard), -- 1839-1903.*

**QC16.G63**
**Taylor, Nick,**
   Laser : the inventor, the Nobel laureate, the thirty-year patent war / Nick Taylor. New York : Simon & Schuster, c2000. 304 p. :
00-058803          621.36/6/092          0684835150
*Gould, Gordon, -- 1920- Lasers -- History. Physicists -- United States -- Biography.*

**QC16.H33.W45 1992**
**White, Michael,**
Stephen Hawking : a life in science / Michael White and John Gribbin. New York, N.Y., U.S.A. : Dutton, c1992. ix, 304 p. ;
92-000699          530/.092          0525934472
*Hawking, S. W. -- (Stephen W.)    Astrophysics. Physicists -- Great Britain -- Biography.*

**QC16.H35.P69 1993**
**Powers, Thomas,**
Heisenberg's war : the secret history of the German bomb / Thomas Powers. New York : Knopf : 1993. xi, 607 p. :
92-014910          355.8/25119/094309044
0394514114
*Heisenberg, Werner, -- 1901-1976 -- Views on atomic bomb. Physicists -- Political activity. Atomic bomb -- Germany -- History. World War, 1939-1945 -- Technology.*

**QC16.H35.R67 1998**
**Rose, Paul Lawrence.**
Heisenberg and the Nazi atomic bomb project : a study in German culture / Paul Lawrence Rose. Berkeley, Calif. : University of California Press, c1998. xx, 352 p. :
97-018143          355.8/25119/092          0520210778
*Heisenberg, Werner, -- 1901-1976 -- Views on atomic bomb. Physicists -- Political activity. Atomic bomb -- Germany -- History. Germany -- Politics and government -- 1933-1945.*

**QC16.H37.M69 1997**
**Moyer, Albert E.,**
Joseph Henry : the rise of an American scientist / Albert E. Moyer. Washington : Smithsonian Institution Press, c1997. xii, 348 p. :
97-020686          530/.092          1560987766
*Henry, Joseph, -- 1797-1878.    Physicists -- United States -- Biography.*

**QC16.K3.S65 1989**
**Smith, Crosbie.**
Energy and empire : a biographical study of Lord Kelvin / Crosbie Smith and M. Norton Wise. Cambridge [Cambridgeshire] ; Cambridge University Press, 1989. xxvi, 866 p.
88-025685          530/.092/4          0521261732
*Kelvin, William Thomson, -- Baron, -- 1824-1907.    Physics -- History. Physicists -- Great Britain -- Biography.*

**QC16.M4.G65 1983**
**Goldman, Martin.**
The demon in the aether : the story of James Clerk Maxwell / Martin Goldman. Edinburgh : P. Harris ; 1983. 224 p., [12]
83-200363          530/.092/4          0862280265
*Maxwell, James Clerk, -- 1831-1879.    Physicists -- Great Britain -- Biography.*

**QC16.M56.J3**
**Jaffe, Bernard,**
Michelson and the speed of light.    Garden City, N.Y., Anchor Books, 1960. 197 p.
60-013533          925.3
*Michelson, Albert Abraham, -- 1852-1931.*

**QC16.M66.A34**
**Morse, Philip McCord,**
In at the beginnings : a physicist's life / Philip M. Morse. Cambridge, Mass. : MIT Press, c1977. vii, 375 p.,
76-040010          530/.092/4          0262131242
*Morse, Philip McCord, -- 1903-    Physicists -- United States -- Biography.*

**QC16.N7.C49 1984**
**Christianson, Gale E.**
In the presence of the Creator : Isaac Newton and his times / Gale E. Christianson. New York : Free Press ; c1984. xv, 623 p., [
83-049211          509/.24          0029051908
*Newton, Isaac, -- Sir, -- 1642-1727.    Physicists -- Great Britain – Biography. Mathematicians -- Great Britain -- Biography.*

**QC16.N7.H35 1992**
**Hall, A. Rupert**
Isaac Newton, adventurer in thought / A. Rupert Hall. Oxford, UK ; Blackwell, 1992. xv, 468 p. :
92-015600          509/.2          0631179062
*Newton, Isaac, -- Sir, -- 1642-1727.    Physicists -- Great Britain – Biography.*

**QC16.N7.S73 1990**
Standing on the shoulders of giants : a longer view of Newton and Halley / edited by Norman J.W. Thrower. Berkeley : University of California Press, c1990. xxvi, 429 p.
90-010715          509.2/2          0520065891
*Newton, Isaac, -- Sir, -- 1642-1727. Halley, Edmond, – 1656-1742. Newton, Isaac, -- Sir, -- 1642-1727. -- Principia. Physicists – Great Britain -- Biography. Astronomers -- Great Britain -- Biography.*

**QC16.N7.W34 1993**
**Westfall, Richard S.**
The life of Isaac Newton / Richard S. Westfall. Cambridge [England] ; Cambridge University Press, 1993. xv, 328 p., 6
92-033777          530/.092          0521432529
*Newton, Isaac, -- Sir, -- 1642-1727.    Physics -- History. Science – History. Physicists -- Great Britain -- Biography.*

**QC16.N7.W35**
**Westfall, Richard S.**
Never at rest : a biography of Isaac Newton / Richard S. Westfall. Cambridge [Eng]. ; Cambridge University Press, 1980. xviii, 908 p.
79-026294          509/.2/4          0521231434
*Newton, Isaac, -- Sir, -- 1642-1727.    Physicists -- Great Britain – Biography.*

**QC16.N7.W45 1997**
**White, Michael,**
Isaac Newton : the last sorcerer / Michael White. Reading, Mass. : Addison-Wesley, c1997. 402 p. :
97-031909          509/.2          0201483017
*Newton, Isaac, -- Sir, -- 1642-1727. Newton, Isaac, -- Sir, – 1642-1727 -- Influence.    Alchemy -- Influence. Physics – History. Science -- History.*

## QC16.O62.G66 1981
**Goodchild, Peter.**
  J. Robert Oppenheimer : shatterer of worlds / Peter Goodchild. Boston : Houghton Mifflin, 1981, c1980. 301 p. :
81-001331          530/.092/4          0395305306
*Oppenheimer, J. Robert, -- 1904-1967.     Physicists – United States – Biography.*

## QC16.P24.A3 1997
**Pais, Abraham,**
  A tale of two continents : a physicist's life in a turbulent world / Abraham Pais. Princeton, N.J. : Princeton University Press, c1997. xvi, 511 p. :
96-039313          530/.092          0691012431
*Pais, Abraham, -- 1918-    Physics -- History. Physicists -- United States -- Biography.*

## QC16.P6.H45 1986
**Heilbron, J. L.**
  The dilemmas of an upright man : Max Planck as spokesman for German science / J.L. Heilbron. Berkeley : University of California Press, c1986. xiii, 238 p.,
85-024609          530/.092/4          0520057104
*Planck, Max, -- 1858-1947.    Physics -- Germany -- History. Physicists -- Germany -- Biography.*

## QC16.S24.A3 1994
**Sagdeev, R. Z.**
  The making of a Soviet scientist : my adventures in nuclear fusion and space from Stalin to Star Wars / Roald Z. Sagdeev ; edited by Susan Eisenhower. New York : Wiley, c1994. xi, 339 p. ;
93-040709          530/.092          0471020311
*Sagdeev, R. Z.    Physicists -- Russia (Federation) -- Biography.*

## QC16.S255.S25 1991
  Sakharov remembered : a tribute by friends and colleagues / edited by Sidney D. Drell, Sergei P. Kapitza. New York, NY : American Institute of Physics, c1991. x, 303 p. :
91-011396          530/.092          0883188538
*Sakharov, Andrei, -- 1921- Congresses.    Physicists – Soviet Union -- Biography -- Congresses.*

## QC16.S265.M66 1989
**Moore, Walter John,**
  Schrodinger, life and thought / Walter Moore. Cambridge ; Cambridge University Press, 1989. xi, 513 p. :
88-025807          530/.092/4          052135434X
*Schrodinger, Erwin, -- 1887-1961.    Physicists -- Austria -- Biography.*

## QC16.S35.A3 1993
**Segre, Emilio.**
  A mind always in motion : the autobiography of Emilio Segre / Emilio Segre. Berkeley : University of California Press, c1993. xii, 332 p. :
92-010722          530/.092          0520076273
*Segre, Emilio.    Physicists -- United States -- Biography. Physicists -- Italy -- Biography.*

## QC16.T37.B57 1990
**Blumberg, Stanley A.**
  Edward Teller : giant of the golden age of physics : a biography / by Stanley A. Blumberg and Louis G. Panos. New York : Scribner's, c1990. xiv, 306 p.,
89-006262          530/.092          0684190427
*Teller, Edward, -- 1908-    Science and state -- United States -- History. Physicists -- United States -- Biography.*

## QC16.W52.A3 1992
**Wigner, Eugene Paul,**
  The recollections of Eugene P. Wigner as told to Andrew Szanton. New York : Plenum Press, c1992. xxiv, 335 p.
92-017040          530/.92          0306443260
*Wigner, Eugene Paul, -- 1902-    Physicists -- United States -- Biography.*

## QC16.W56.H54 1982
**Hilts, Philip J.**
  Scientific temperaments : three lives in contemporary science / Philip J. Hilts. New York : Simon and Schuster, c1982. 302 p. ;
82-010694          509/.2/2          0671225332
*Wilson, Robert R., -- 1914- Ptashne, Mark. McCarthy, John, – 1927- Scientists -- United States -- Biography. Biology -- Research -- History. Artificial intelligence -- History.*

## QC16.Y67.A3 1995
**York, Herbert F.**
  Arms and the physicist / Herbert F. York. Woodbury, NY : American Institute of Physics, c1995. xiii, 294 p.
94-013099          327.1/74          1563960990
*York, Herbert F. -- (Herbert Frank)    Arms race -- United States – History. National security -- United States -- History. Physicists -- United States -- Biography.*

## QC16.Z56.A3 1995
**Ziman, J. M.**
  Of one mind : the collectivization of science / John Ziman. Woodbury, NY : American Institute of Physics, c1995. xvii, 406 p.
94-034902          306.4/5          1563960656
*Ziman, J. M. -- (John M.), -- 1925-    Physics -- History. Physics – Philosophy. Physicists -- Biography.*

### QC19.6 Mathematical physics — History — General works

## QC19.6.W47 1995
**Wertheim, Margaret.**
  Pythagoras' trousers : God, physics, and the gender wars / Margaret Wertheim. New York : Times Books/Random House, c1995. viii, 279 p.
94-040095          306.4/5          081292200X
*Mathematical physics -- History. Women in science -- History. Sex discrimination in physics.*

## QC20 Mathematical physics — General works, treatises, and textbooks

**QC20.H392 2000**
**Hassani, Sadri.**
  Mathematical methods : for students of physics and related fields / Sadri Hassani. New York : Springer, c2000. xv, 659 p. :
99-052788          530.15          0387989587
  *Mathematical physics.*

**QC20.K66**
**Konopinski, Emil Jan,**
  Classical descriptions of motion; the dynamics of particle trajectories, rigid rotations, and elastic waves. San Francisco, W. H. Freeman [1969] xiii, 504 p.
71-075626          531/.1          0716703238
  *Mathematical physics. Motion.*

**QC20.K82 1998**
**Kusse, Bruce,**
  Mathematical physics : applied mathematics for scientists and engineers  / Bruce Kusse, Erik Westwig. New York : Wiley, c1998. xi, 668 p. :
98-013436          530.15          0471154318
  *Mathematical physics.*

**QC20.L66 1984**
**Longair, M. S.,**
  Theoretical concepts in physics : an alternative view of theoretical reasoning in physics for final-year undergraduates / M.S. Longair. Cambridge ; Cambridge University Press, 1984. xiii, 366 p.
83-018928          530.1          0521255503
  *Mathematical physics.*

**QC20.M6**
**Morse, Philip McCord,**
  Methods of theoretical physics [by] Philip M. Morse [and] Herman Feshbach. New York, McGraw-Hill, 1953. 2 v.
52-011515          530.151
  *Mathematical physics.*

**QC20.R37 1972**
**Reed, Michael,**
  Methods of modern mathematical physics [by] Michael Reed [and] Barry Simon. New York, Academic Press [1972- v.
75-182650          530.1/5          0125850018
  *Mathematical physics.*

**QC20.S66**
**Sommerfeld, Arnold,**
  Lectures on theoretical physics.  New York, Academic Press, 1950- v.
50-008749          530.151
  *Mathematical physics.*

**QC20.S7413 1990**
**Stauffer, Dietrich.**
  From Newton to Mandelbrot : a primer in theoretical physics / Dietrich Stauffer, H. Eugene Stanley. Berlin ; Springer-Verlag, c1990. ix, 191 p., 1
90-039591          530.1          0387526617
  *Mathematical physics.*

**QC20.T4513**
**Thirring, Walter E.,**
  A course in mathematical physics / Walter Thirring ; translated by Evans M. Harrell. New York : Springer-Verlag, c1978-c1983. 4 v. :
78-016172          530.1/5          0387814752
  *Mathematical physics.*

**QC20.T543 1963a**
**Tikhonov, A. N.**
  Equations of mathematical physics [by] A.N. Tikhonov and A.A. Samarskii. Translated by A.R.M. Robson and P. Basu; translation edited by D.M. Brink. Oxford, Pergamon Press; [distributed in the Western Hemi 1963. xvi, 765 p.
64005194          530.15
  *Mathematical physics. Differential equations*

**QC20.W66 1991**
**Wong, Chun Wa.**
  Introduction to mathematical physics : methods and concepts / Chun Wa Wong. New York : Oxford University Press, 1991. x, 386 p. :
90-045235          530.1/5          0195044738
  *Mathematical physics.*

## QC20.7 Mathematical physics — Special topics, A-Z

**QC20.7.C3.L46 1997**
**Lemons, Don S.**
  Perfect form : variational principles, methods, and applications in elementary physics / Don S. Lemons. Princeton, N.J. : Princeton University Press, 1997. xi, 117 p. :
96-009639          530.1/5564          0691026645
  *Calculus of variations. Mathematical physics.*

**QC20.7.E4.B3813 1996**
**Baumann, Gerd.**
  Mathematica in theoretical physics : selected examples from classical mechanics to fractals / Gerd Baumann. New York : Springer ; c1996. xi, 348 p. :
96-143800          530/.0285/53          0387944249
  *Mathematical physics -- Data processing.*

**QC20.7.E4.P36 1997**
**Pang, Tao,**
  An introduction to computational physics / Tao Pang. Cambridge ; Cambridge University Press, 1997. xvii, 374 p.
96-045574          530/.0285          0521481430
  *Physics -- Data processing. Physics -- Methodology. Numerical calculations.*

**QC20.7.F67.J36 1995**
**James, J. F.**
  A student's guide to Fourier transforms : with applications in physics and engineering / J.F. James. Cambridge ; Cambridge University Press, 1995. x, 131 p. :
94-022453          515/.723          0521462983
  *Fourier transformations. Mathematical physics. Engineering mathematics.*

**QC20.7.F73.G6813 1996**
**Gouyet, Jean-Francois.**
  Physics and fractal structures / Jean-Francois Gouyet ; foreword by Benoit Mandelbrot. Paris : Masson ; c1996. xiv, 234 p. :
96-160809                    0387941533
  *Fractals. Mathematical physics.*

**QC20.7.F84.R43 1980**
**Reed, Michael,**
  Methods of modern mathematical physics / Michael Reed, Barry Simon. New York : Academic Press, c1980-1 v. 1 :
80-039580          530.1/5          0125850506
  *Functional analysis. Mathematical physics.*

**QC20.7.N6.I67 1997**
  Introduction to nonlinear physics / Lui Lam, editor. New York : Springer, c1997. xiv, 417 p. :
96-014764          530.1/55252          0387947582
  *Nonlinear theories. Mathematical physics.*

**QC20.7.T65.N33 1997**
**Naber, Gregory L.,**
  Topology, geometry, and gauge fields : foundations / Gregory L. Naber. New York : Springer, c1997. xviii, 396 p.
96-049166          516.3/62          0387949461
  *Topology. Geometry. Gauge fields (Physics)*

### QC20.82 Mathematical physics — Study and teaching. Research — Problems, exercises, examinations

**QC20.82.L36 1997**
**Landau, Rubin H.**
  Computational physics : problem solving with computers / Rubin H. Landau, Manuel Jose Paez Mejia ; contributors, Hans Kowallik and Henri Jansen. New York : Wiley, c1997. xxviii, 520 p
96-051776          530/.078/5          0471115908
  *Physics -- Problems, exercises, etc. -- Data processing. Physics — Computer simulation. Mathematical physics.*

### QC21 General works, treatises, and textbooks — 1801-1969

**QC21.B4445**
  Berkeley physics course. New York, McGraw-Hill [1965-71, v. 5 v.
64-066016          530          0070048614
  *Physics.*

**QC21.C7 1967**
**Condon, Edward Uhler,**
  Handbook of physics, edited by E. U. Condon [and] Hugh Odishaw. New York, McGraw-Hill [1967] 1 v. (various
66-020002          530
  *Physics.*

**QC21.L2713 1967**
**Landau, L. D.**
  General physics; mechanics and molecular physics [by] L.D. Landau, A.I. Akhiezer [and] E.M. Lifshitz. Translated by J.B. Sykes, A.D. Petford [and] C.L. Petford. Oxford, Pergamon Press [1967] x, 372 p.
67-030260          530
  *Physics.*

### QC21.2 General works, treatises, and textbooks — 1970-

**QC21.2.A28 1987**
**Adair, Robert Kemp.**
  The great design : particles, fields, and creation / Robert K. Adair. New York : Oxford University Press, 1987. vi, 376 p. :
87-005729          539          0195043804
  *Physics. Particles (Nuclear physics) Field theory (Physics)*

**QC21.2.B59 1997**
**Bloomfield, Louis.**
  How things work : the physics of everyday life / Louis A. Bloomfield. New York : J. Wiley, c1997. xiii, 706 p.
96-014288          530          0471594733
  *Physics.*

**QC21.2.D57 1995**
**Dirac, P. A. M.**
  The collected works of P.A.M. Dirac, 1924-1948 / edited by R.H. Dalitz. Cambridge ; Cambridge University Press, 1995. xxiii, 1310 p
95-001010          530          0521362318
  *Physics.*

**QC21.2.F49 1989**
**Feynman, Richard Phillips.**
  The Feynman lectures on physics / Feynman, Leighton, Sands. Redwood City, Calif. : Addison-Wesley, c1989. 3 v. :
89-000433          530
  *Physics.*

**QC21.2.F52 1995**
**Feynman, Richard Phillips.**
  Six easy pieces : essentials of physics, explained by its most brilliant teacher / Richard P. Feynman ; originally prepared for publication by Robert B. Leighton and Matthew Sands; new introduction by Paul Davies. Reading, Mass. : Addison-Wesley, c1995. xxix, 145 p.
94-030894          530          0201409550
  *Physics.*

**QC21.2.H355 1986**
**Halliday, David,**
Physics. David Halliday, Robert Resnick. New York : Wiley, c1986. xiv, 565-1335
86-005606          530          0471832022
*Physics.*

**QC21.2.K3 1995**
**Kaku, Michio.**
Hyperspace : a scientific odyssey through parallel universes, time warps, and the tenth dimension / Michio Kaku ; illustrations by Robert O'Keefe. New York : Anchor Books, c1995. xvi, 359 p. :
530.1/42 20          0385477058
*Physics. Astrophysics. Mathematical physics.*

**QC21.2.K73 1993**
**Krauss, Lawrence Maxwell.**
Fear of physics : a guide for the perplexed / Lawrence M. Krauss. New York, NY : BasicBooks, c1993. xv, 206 p. ;
92-054523          530/.01          0465057454
*Physics.*

**QC21.2.M65 1989**
**Motz, Lloyd,**
The story of physics / Lloyd Motz and Jefferson Hane Weaver. New York : Plenum Press, c1989. xiii, 412 p.
88-033655          530          0306430762
*Physics.*

**QC21.2.N49 1989**
The New physics / edited by Paul Davies. Cambridge [Cambridgeshire] ; Cambridge University Press, 1989. 516 p. :
87-024624          530          0521304202
*Physics.*

**QC21.2.N53 1993**
**Newton, Roger G.**
What makes nature tick? / Roger G. Newton. Cambridge, Mass. : Harvard University Press, c1993. 257 p. :
93-009507          530          0674950852
*Physics.*

**QC21.2.S36 1987**
**Sears, Francis Weston,**
University physics / Francis W. Sears, Mark W. Zemansky, Hugh D. Young. Reading, Mass. : Addison-Wesley Pub. Co., c1987. v. 1-  :
85-028801          530          0201066823
*Physics.*

**QC21.2.S47 1993**
**Silverman, Mark P.**
And yet it moves : strange systems and subtle questions in physics / Mark P. Silverman. Cambridge [England] ; Cambridge University Press, 1993. xvii, 266 p.
92-038729          530          0521391733
*Physics. Quantum theory.*

**QC21.2.S647 1994**
**Speyer, Edward,**
Six roads from Newton : great discoveries in physics / Edward Speyer. New York : Wiley, c1994. xi, 196 p. :
93-045342          530          0471305030
*Physics. Physics -- History.*

**QC21.2.S688 1995**
**Stevens, Charles F.,**
The six core theories of modern physics / Charles F. Stevens. Cambridge, Mass. : MIT Press, c1995. x, 233 p. ;
94-028453          530.1          0262193590
*Physics. Mathematical physics.*

## QC23 Elementary Textbooks

**QC23.A8**
**Asimov, Isaac,**
Understanding physics. New York, Walker [1966] 3 v.
66-017227          530
*Physics.*

**QC23.F47**
**Feynman, Richard Phillips.**
The Feynman lectures on physics [by] Richard P. Feynman, Robert B. Leighton [and] Matthew Sands. Reading, Mass., Addison-Wesley Pub. Co. [1963-65] 3 v.
63-020717          530
*Physics.*

**QC23.L324 2000**
**Landsberg, Peter Theodore.**
Seeking ultimates : an intuitive guide to physics / Peter T. Landsberg. Bristol ; Institute of Physics Pub., c2000. xi, 314 p. :
99-055029          530          0750306564
*Physics.*

**QC23.L4 1946**
**Lemon, Harvey Brace,**
From Galileo to the nuclear age; an introduction to physics, by Harvey Brace Lemon ... Chicago, Ill., The University of Chicago Press [1946] xviii, 451 p.
46006075          530
*Physics.*

**QC23.R68**
**Rogers, Eric M.**
Physics for the inquiring mind; the methods, nature, and philosophy of physical science. Princeton, N.J., Princeton University Press, 1960. 778 p.
59-005603          530
*Physics.*

**QC23.S3745**
**Sears, Francis Weston,**
University physics [by] Francis Weston Sears [and] Mark W. Zemansky. Reading, Mass., Addison-Wesley Pub. Co. [1970] 1 v. (various
70-093991          530
*Physics.*

## QC24.5 Popular works

**QC24.5.G85 1995**
**Guillen, Michael.**
Five equations that changed the world : the power and poetry of mathematics / Michael Guillen. New York : Hyperion, c1995. viii, 277 p.
95-015199          530.1/5          0786861037
*Physics -- Popular works. Equations.*

## QC25 Juvenile works

**QC25.N63 1989**
The Nobel Prize winners. edited by Frank N. Magill. Pasadena, Calif. : Salem Press, c1989. 3 v. (xl, 136
89-006409          530/.079          0893565571
*Physics -- Awards -- Juvenile literature. Nobel Prizes --Juvenile literature. Physics -- Awards.*

## QC26 Recreations, home experiments, etc.

**QC26.A23 1990**
**Adair, Robert Kemp.**
The physics of baseball / Robert Kemp Adair. New York : Harper & Row, c1990. xiv, 110 p. :
89-045623          796.357/01/53          0060551887
*Physics. Baseball. Force and energy.*

**QC26.J67 1993**
**Jorgensen, Theodore P.**
The physics of golf / Theodore P. Jorgensen. New York, NY : AIP Press, c1993. p. cm.
93030146          796.352          0883189550
*Force and energy. Physics. Golf.*

**QC26.L56 1997**
**Lind, David.**
The physics of skiing : skiing at the Triple Point / David Lind, Scott P. Sanders. Woodbury, N.Y. : American Institute of Physics, c1997. xvi, 268 p. :
96-026220          796.93/01/531          1563963191
*Physics. Skis and skiing. Force and energy.*

## QC28 Special aspects of the subject as whole

**QC28.F4 1965**
**Feynman, Richard Phillips.**
The character of physical law [by] Richard Feynman. Cambridge, M.I.T. Press [1965] 173 p.
67-014527
*Physics -- Addresses, essays, lectures.*

## QC29 Physics as a professions. Vocational guidance

**QC29.K75 1992**
**Krieger, Martin H.**
Doing physics : how physicists take hold of the world / Martin H. Krieger. Bloomington : Indiana University Press, c1992. xx, 168 p. :
91-020305          530/.092/2          0253331234
*Physicists. Physics -- Methodology. Physics -- Philosophy.*

## QC30 Study and teaching. Research — General works

**QC30.A78 1997**
**Arons, A. B.**
Teaching introductory physics / Arnold B. Arons. New York : Wiley, c1997. 1 v. (various
96-016838          530/.071/1          0471137073
*Physics -- Study and teaching.*

**QC30.T5 1995**
Thinking physics for teaching / edited by Carlo Bernardini, Carlo Tarsitani, and Matilde Vincentini. New York : Plenum Press, c1995. ix, 454 p. :
95-045220          530/.071          0306451921
*Physics -- Study and teaching -- Congresses. Physics – Study and teaching -- Research -- Congresses.*

## QC32 Study and teaching. Research — Problems, exercises, examinations

**QC32.R383 1994**
**Rees, Gareth**
Physics by example : 200 problems and solutions / W.G. Rees. Cambridge ; Cambridge University Press, 1994. xiii, 374 p.
93-034300          530/.076          0521445140
*Physics -- Problems, exercises, etc.*

**QC32.T46 2000**
**Thomas, E. G.**
Physics to a degree / E.G. Thomas and D.J. Raine. Amsterdam : Gordon & Breach, c2000. xx, 228 p. :
          530          9056992767
*Physics -- Problems, exercises, etc. Physics -- Examinations – Study guides.*

**QC32.W2**
**Walker, Jearl,**
The flying circus of physics / Jearl Walker. New York : Wiley, [1975] 224 p. :
75-005670          530          0471918083
*Physics -- Problems, exercises, etc.*

## QC33 Study and teaching. Research — Experiments

**QC33.E54 1990**
**Ehrlich, Robert,**
  Turning the world inside out and 174 other simple physics demonstrations / Robert Ehrlich. Princeton, N.J. : Princeton University Press, c1990. xxvi, 216 p.
89-036976      530/.078      069108534X
  *Physics -- Experiments.*

**QC33.E55 1997**
**Ehrlich, Robert,**
  Why toast lands jelly-side down : zen and the art of physics demonstrations / Robert Ehrlich. Princeton, N.J. : Princeton University Press, c1997. x, 196 p. :
96-042053      530/.078      0691028915
  *Physics -- Experiments.*

## QC39 Study and teaching. Research — Physical measurements (General)

**QC39.A4 1992**
**Albert, David Z**
  Quantum mechanics and experience / David Z Albert. Cambridge, Mass. : Harvard University Press, 1992. x, 206 p. :
92-030585      530.1/6      0674741129
  *Physical measurements. Quantum theory.*

**QC39.B57 1984**
**Bishop, O. N.**
  Yardsticks of the universe / Owen Bishop. New York : P. Bedrick Books : 1984. 125 p. :
83-015782      530.8      0911745173
  *Physical measurements.*

**QC39.T38**
**Taylor, B. N.**
  The fundamental constants and quantum electrodynamics [by] B. N. Taylor, W. H. Parker [and] D. N. Langenberg. New York, Academic Press, 1969. xiii, 353 p.
76-101416      537.6/4
  *Physical measurements. Quantum electrodynamics. Least squares.*

**QC39.T4 1997**
**Taylor, John R.**
  An introduction to error analysis : the study of uncertainties in physical measurements / John R. Taylor. Sausalito, Calif. : University Science Books, c1997. xvii, 327 p.
96-000953      530.1/6      0935702423
  *Physical measurements. Error analysis (Mathematics) Mathematical physics.*

## QC41 Study and teaching. Research — Laboratory technique

**QC41.B7 1963**
**Braddick, H. J. J.**
  The physics of experimental method. With a foreword by P.M.S. Blackett. New York, Reinhold, 1963. 480 p.
63-004480      530.72
  *Physics -- Research. Physical instruments.*

## QC47 Study and teaching. Research — By region or country, A-Z

**QC47.G3.O43 1991**
**Olesko, Kathryn Mary.**
  Physics as a calling : discipline and practice in the Konigsberg seminar for physics / Kathryn M. Olesko. Ithaca : Cornell University Press, 1991. xviii, 488 p.
90-055717      530/.71147/47      0801422485
  *Physics -- Study and teaching (Higher) -- Germany -- History – 19th century. Physics -- Germany -- History -- 19th century.*

## QC53 Instruments and apparatus (General) — General works

**QC53.I574 1995**
  Instrumentation reference book / edited by B.E. Noltingk, with specialist contributors. Oxford, [England] ; Butterworth-Heinemann, 1995. 1 v. (various
95-001813      530/.7      0750620560
  *Physical instruments -- Handbooks, manuals, etc. Engineering instruments -- Handbooks, manuals, etc.*

## QC61 Museums. Exhibitions — Handbooks, tables, formulas, etc.

**QC61.A5 1963**
**American Institute of Physics.**
  American Institute of Physics handbook. Section editors: Bruce H. Billings [and others] Coordinating editor: Dwight E. Gray. New York, McGraw-Hill [1963] 1 v. (various
61-016965      530.83
  *Physics -- Handbooks, manuals, etc.*

**QC61.F58 1982**
**Fischbeck, Helmut J.,**
  Formulas, facts, and constants for students and professionals in engineering, chemistry, and physics / Helmut J. Fischbeck, Kurt H. Fischbeck. Berlin ; Springer-Verlag, 1982. xii, 251 p. :
82-000721      530/.0212      0387113150
  *Physics -- Handbooks, manuals, etc. Chemistry, Physical and theoretical -- Handbooks, manuals, etc. Engineering --Handbooks, manuals, etc.*

**QC61.H36 1997**
Handbook of physical quantities / edited by Igor S. Grigoriev and Evgenii Z. Meilikhov. Boca Raton : CRC Press, c1997. 1548 p. :
95-016928        530/.0212        0849328616
*Physics -- Handbooks, manuals, etc.*

**QC61.S6 1920**
**Smithsonian Institution.**
Smithsonian physical tables.    Washington, Smithsonian institution, 1920. xlvi, 450 p.
20-026804
*Physics -- Tables.*

## QC71 Museums. Exhibitions — Addresses, essays, lectures

**QC71.B63**
**Bondi, Hermann.**
Assumption and myth in physical theory, by H. Bondi. London, Cambridge U.P., 1967. vii, 88 p.
67-021954        530.1    0521042828
*Physics.*

**QC71.B6653**
**Born, Max,**
Physics and politics. Foreword by Kathleen Lonsdale. New York, Basic Books Pub. Co. [1962] vii, 86 p.
62014735        530.81
*Physics.*

**QC71.B67**
**Born, Max,**
Experiment and theory in physics.    [New York] Dover Publications [1956] 43 p.
56058690        530.4
*Physics. Physics -- essays.*

**QC71.D55**
**Dirac, P. A. M.**
Directions in physics : lectures delivered during a visit to Australia and New Zealand August/September 1975 / P. A. M. Dirac ; edited by H. Hora and J. R. Shepanski ; with a foreword by Sir Mark Oliphant. New York : Wiley, c1978. ix, 95 p. :
77-024892        530        0471029971
*Physics -- Addresses, essays, lectures.*

**QC71.F3 1960**
**Faraday, Michael,**
On the various forces of nature and their relations to each other; a course of lectures delivered before a juvenile audience at the Royal Institution. Edited, and with a pref. and notes, by William Crookes. With a new introd. by Keith Gordon Irwin. New York, Viking Press [1960] xxiv, 106 p.
60051243        530.81
*Physics.*

**QC71.P38 1997**
**Peierls, Rudolf Ernst,**
Atomic histories / Rudolf E. Peierls. Woodbury, N.Y. : AIP Press, c1997. xvii, 378 p.
96-022298        530/.09/04        1563962438
*Physics. Nuclear physics.*

**QC71.W443 1989**
**Weisskopf, Victor Frederick,**
The privilege of being a physicist / Victor F. Weisskopf. New York : W.H. Freeman, c1989. x, 235 p. :
88-024532        530        0716719827
*Physics.*

## QC73 Force and energy (General) — General works, treatises, and textbooks

**QC73.H55**
**Hiebert, Erwin N.,**
Historical roots of the principle of conservation of energy. Madison, State Historical Society of Wisconsin for the De 1962. 118 p.
62-063146        531.6
*Force and energy.*

**QC73.P54 2001**
**Pielou, E. C.,**
The energy of nature / E.C. Pielou. Chicago : University of Chicago Press, 2001. x, 244 p. :
00-048841        530        0226668061
*Force and energy.*

## QC73.8 Force and energy (General) — Study and teaching. Research — Special topics, A-Z

**QC73.8.C6**
**Bodanis, David.**
E=mc2 : a biography of the world's most famous equation / David Bodanis. New York : Walker, c2000. ix, 337 p. :
00-040857        530.11    0802713521
*Einstein, Albert, -- 1879-1955.    Mass (Physics) Mathematical physics. Force and energy.*

**QC73.8.C6.C36 1993**
**Caneva, Kenneth L.**
Robert Mayer and the conservation of energy / Kenneth L. Caneva. Princeton, N.J. : Princeton University Press, c1993. xxiii, 439 p.
92-025400        531/.6/092        069108758X
*Mayer, Julius Robert von, -- 1814-1878.    Force and energy -- History. Physicists -- Germany -- Biography.*

## QC75 Miscellany and curiosa

**QC75.E37 1994**
**Ehrlich, Robert,**
  The cosmological milk shake : a semi-serious look at the size of things / Robert Ehrlich ; illustrated by Gary Ehrlich. New Brunswick, N.J. : Rutgers University Press, c1994. xvii, 259 p.
93-028135          530          0813520452
  *Physics -- Miscellanea. Physics -- Study and teaching. Astrophysics -- Miscellanea.*

## QC82 Weights and measures — Dictionaries and encyclopedias

**QC82.F43 1998**
**Fenna, Donald,**
  Elsevier's encyclopedic dictionary of measures / Donald Fenna. Amsterdam ; Elsevier, 1998. xxiii, 582 p.
98-039007          530.8/03          0444500464
  *Weights and measures -- Encyclopedias.*

## QC83 Weights and measures — History — General works

**QC83.K813 1986**
**Kula, Witold.**
  Measures and men / Witold Kula ; translated by R. Szreter. Princeton, N.J. : Princeton University Press, c1986. x, 386 p. ;
85-042690          530.8/09          0691054460
  *Weights and measures -- History.*

## QC88 Weights and measures — General works, treatises, and textbooks

**QC88.K58**
**Klein, H. Arthur.**
  The world of measurements : masterpieces, mysteries and muddles of metrology / H. Arthur Klein. New York : Simon and Schuster, [1974] 736 p. :
74-007656          530/.8          0671215655
  *Weights and measures. Weights and measures -- History.*

## QC94 Special systems — Metric system. International system (SI)

**QC94.C67 1990**
**Cook, James L.**
  Conversion factors / James L. Cook. Oxford [England] ; Oxford University Press, 1991. xvi, 160 p. :
90-024853          502.12          0198563493
  *Metric system -- Conversion tables. Science -- Tables. Engineering -- Tables.*

## QC122 Descriptive and experimental mechanics — History — General works

**QC122.C6 1985**
**Cohen, I. Bernard,**
  The birth of a new physics / by I. Bernard Cohen. New York : W.W. Norton, c1985. xiv, 258 p. :
84-025582          530/.09          0393019942
  *Mechanics. Celestial mechanics.*

## QC123 Descriptive and experimental mechanics — Early works through 1800

**QC123.G1153**
**Galilei, Galileo,**
  On motion, and On mechanics; comprising De motu (ca. 1590) translated with introduction and notes by I.E. Drabkin, and Le meccaniche (ca. 1600) translated with introduction and notes by Stillman Drake. Madison, University of Wisconsin Press, 1960. viii, 193 p.
60-005658          531
  *Mechanics. Physics -- Early works to 1800. Science, Medieval.*

**QC123.G13 1991**
**Galilei, Galileo,**
  Dialogues concerning two new sciences / Galileo Galilei ; translated by Henry Crew and Alfonso de Salvio. Buffalo, N.Y. : Prometheus Books, 1991. ix, 294 p. :
91-061910          531          0879757078
  *Galilei, Galileo, -- 1564-1642 -- Discirsi e dimonstrazione matematiche. -- English. Mechanics -- Early works to 1800. Physics -- Early works to 1800.*

## QC133 Descriptive and experimental mechanics — Dynamics. Motion — General works, treatises, and textbooks

**QC133.B37 1989**
**Barbour, Julian B.**
  Absolute or relative motion? : a study from Machian point of view of the discovery and the structure of dynamical theories / Julian B. Barbour. Cambridge [England] ; Cambridge University Press, 1989- v. 1  :
88-011886          531/.11          052132467X
  *Motion. Dynamics. Astronomy.*

**QC133.B5313 1998**
**Blay, Michel,**
  Reasoning with the infinite : from the closed world to the mathematical universe / Michel Blay ; translated by M.B. DeBevoise. Chicago : University of Chicago Press, 1998. x, 216 p. :
97-049423          530.15          0226058344
  *Motion. Infinite. Mathematics -- Philosophy.*

## QC136 Descriptive and experimental mechanics — Dynamics. Motion — Vibrations

**QC136.M34 1984**
**Main, Iain G.,**
Vibrations and waves in physics / Iain G. Main. Cambridge [Cambridgeshire] ; Cambridge University Press, 1984. xiii, 356 p.
83-023999          531/.32          0521261244
*Vibration. Waves.*

## QC143-145.2 Descriptive and experimental mechanics — Fluids. Fluid mechanics — General works, treatises, and textbooks

**QC143.P33 1937**
**Pascal, Blaise,**
The physical treatises of Pascal: the equilibrium of liquids and the weight of the mass of the air, translated by I.H.B. and A.G.H. Spiers, with an introduction and notes by Frederick Barry. New York, Columbia University Press, 1937. xxviii, 181 p
38000410          532
*Hydrostatics. Air. Atmospheric pressure.*

**QC145.2.D3913 1995**
Chaos and determinism : turbulence as a paradigm for complex systems converging toward final states / by Alexandre Favre ... [et al.] ; foreword by Julian C.R. Hunt ; translated by Bertram Eugene Schwarzbach. Baltimore : Johns Hopkins University Press, 1995. xxvi, 176 p.
94-012691          003/.85          080184911X
*Turbulence. Fluid mechanics.*

**QC145.2.D42 1991**
**De Nevers, Noel,**
Fluid mechanics for chemical engineers / Noel de Nevers. New York : McGraw-Hill, c1991. xxi, 558 p. :
90-043155          532          0070163758
*Fluid mechanics. Chemical engineering.*

## QC151-157 Descriptive and experimental mechanics — Fluids. Fluid mechanics — Fluid dynamics. Hydrodynamics

**QC151.F33 1995**
**Faber, T. E.**
Fluid dynamics for physicists / T.E. Faber. Cambridge ; New York : 1995. xxvi, 440 p.
94-019245          532/.05          0521419433
*Fluid dynamics.*

**QC157.I54 1988**
**Ingard, K. Uno.**
Fundamentals of waves & oscillations / K.U. Ingard. Cambridge ; Cambridge University Press, 1988. xiv, 595 p. :
86-017116          531/.1133          0521327342
*Waves. Oscillations.*

**QC157.N48 1995**
**Nettel, Stephen, 1938-**
Wave physics : oscillations--solitons--chaos / Stephen Nettel. Berlin ; Springer-Verlag, c1995. viii, 252 p.
94-038373          531/.1133          0387585044
*Waves. Wave mechanics.*

## QC171-171.2 Atomic physics. Constitution and properties of matter — General works

**QC171.A3 1952**
**Abro, A. d'.**
The rise of the new physics; its mathematical and physical theories. New York] Dover Publications [1952, c1951] 2 v. (ix, 982
52-008895          530.1
*Quantum theory. Mathematical physics.*

**QC171.B63 1951**
**Born, Max,**
The restless universe. Figures by Otto Koenigsberger; authorized translation by Winifred M. Deans. New York, Dover Publications, 1951. 315 p.
51-013192          530.1
*Matter -- Constitution. Physics.*

**QC171.G29**
**Gamow, George,**
The atom and its nucleus.     [Englewood Cliffs, N.J.] Prentice-Hall [1961] 153 p.
61-006360          539
*Matter. Atoms. Nuclear physics.*

**QC171.G3**
**Gamow, George,**
Matter, earth, and sky. Englewood Cliffs, N.J., Prentice-Hall, 1958. 593 p.
58-009147          500
*Matter -- Properties. Physics. Cosmogony.*

**QC171.H75**
**Houwink, R.**
Elasticity, plasticity, and structure of matter. With a chapter on the plasticity of crystals by W. G. Burgers. New York, Dover Publications [1958] 368 p.
58014486          539.1
*Elasticity. Crystals. Plasticity.*

**QC171.K5 1962**
**Kittel, Charles.**
Elementary solid state physics; a short course. New York, Wiley [1962] 339 p.
62-017462          531
*Solid state physics.*

**QC171.2.G4613 1996**
**Gennes, Pierre-Gilles de.**
   Fragile objects : soft matter, hard science, and the thrill of discovery / Pierre-Gilles de Gennes, Jacques Badoz ; translated by Axel Reisinger. New York : Copernicus, c1996. xvi, 189 p. :
96-017039          530          0387947744
   *Matter -- Miscellanea. Surfaces (Physics) -- Miscellanea. Research -- Miscellanea.*

**QC171.2.N38 1994**
**Navrotsky, Alexandra.**
   Physics and chemistry of earth materials / Alexandra Navrotsky. Cambridge ; Cambridge University Press, 1994. xiii, 417 p.
93-043135          549/.13          0521353785
   *Matter. Materials. Minerals.*

**QC171.2.S84 1997**
**Sternglass, Ernest J.**
   Before the big bang : the origins of the universe / by Ernest J. Sternglass. New York : Four Walls Eight Windows, c1997. ix, 294 p. :
97-026395          523.1/2          1568580878
   *Matter -- History. Matter -- Mathematical models. Cosmology.*

**QC173 Atomic physics. Constitution and properties of matter — Constitution of matter and antimatter (General) — General works, treatises, and textbooks**

**QC173.B48 1956**
**Bethe, Hans Albrecht,**
   Elementary nuclear theory [by] Hans A. Bethe and Philip Morrison. New York, Wiley [1956] 274 p.
56-007152          539.1
   *Nuclear physics.*

**QC173.B535**
**Bohr, Niels Hendrik David,**
   Atomic theory and the description of nature ... by Niels Bohr. New York, The Macmillan Company; 1934-1961. v.
34032898          530.1
   *Atoms. Quantum theory.*

**QC173.E358**
**Eisberg, Robert Martin.**
   Fundamentals of modern physics. New York, Wiley [1961] 729 p.
61-006770          530.1
   *Matter -- Constitution. Quantum theory. Relativity (Physics)*

**QC173.F397**
**Fermi, Enrico,**
   Elementary particles. New Haven, Yale University Press, 1951. xii, 110 p.
51004995          539.1
   *Particles (Nuclear physics) Matter -- Constitution.*

**QC173.G34 1979**
**Gardner, Martin,**
   The ambidextrous universe : mirror asymmetry and time-reversed worlds / Martin Gardner ; illustrated by John Mackey. New York : Scribner, c1979. 293 p. :
78-016984          501          0684157896
   *Parity nonconservation. Symmetry (Physics) Particles(Nuclear physics)*

**QC173.H3854**
**Heisenberg, Werner,**
   Nuclear physics. New York, Philosophical Library [1953] 225 p.
53013280          541.2
   *Nuclear energy Nuclear physics. Nuclear Energy*

**QC173.H38613 1971**
**Heisenberg, Werner,**
   Physics and beyond; encounters and conversations. Translated from the German by Arnold J. Pomerans. New York, Harper & Row [c1971] xviii, 247 p.
78-095963          539.7
   *Nuclear physics. Physics -- Philosophy.*

**QC173.I73**
**Irvine, J. M.**
   Nuclear structure theory, by J. M. Irvine. Oxford, Pergamon Press [1972] xiii, 478 p.
72-080303          539.7          0080164013
   *Nuclear structure. Many-body problem.*

**QC173.J28**
**Jammer, Max.**
   Concepts of mass, in classical and modern physics. Cambridge, Harvard University Press, 1961. 230 p.
61-013737          531.54
   *Mass (Physics)*

**QC173.L2463 1959**
**Landau, L. D.**
   Lectures on nuclear theory, by L.D. Landau and Ya. Smorodinsky. Translated from the Russian. New York, Plenum Press, 1959. 108 p.
59-008865          539.7
   *Nuclear physics.*

**QC173.S315 1962**
**Semat, Henry,**
   Introduction to atomic and nuclear physics. New York, Holt, Rinehart and Winston [1962] 628 p.
62-012989          539
   *Physics. Atoms. Nuclear physics.*

**QC173.W66 1980**
**Woodgate, G. K.**
   Elementary atomic structure / G. K. Woodgate. Oxford : Clarendon Press ; 1980. ix, 228 p. :
79-041673          539/.14          0198511469
   *Atomic structure.*

## QC173.3 Atomic physics. Constitution and properties of matter — Properties of matter and antimatter (General) — General works, treatises, and textbooks

**QC173.3.C66 1985**
**Cotterill, Rodney,**
The Cambridge guide to the material world / Rodney Cotterill. Cambridge [Cambridgeshire] ; Cambridge University Press, 1985. 352 p. :
84-007686  500  0521246407
*Matter -- Properties.*

**QC173.3.F73 2000**
**Fraser, Gordon,**
Antimatter--the ultimate mirror / Gordon Fraser. Cambridge ; Cambridge University Press, 2000. 213 p. :
99-043749  530  0521652529
*Antimatter.*

## QC173.4 Atomic physics. Constitution and properties of matter — Properties of matter and antimatter (General) — Special topics, A-Z

**QC173.4.A87.S55 2000**
**Silverman, Mark P.**
Probing the atom : interactions of coupled states, fast beams, and loose electrons / Mark P. Silverman. Princeton, N.J. : Princeton University Press, 2000. p. cm.
99-031032  539/.14  0691009627
*Atomic structure.*

**QC173.4.C65.B37 1989**
**Barber, D. J.**
An introduction to the properties of condensed matter / D.J. Barber and R. Loudon. Cambridge [England] ; Cambridge University Press, 1989. p. cm.
88-025909  530.4/1  0521262771
*Condensed matter.*

**QC173.4.S94**
**Chung, Yip-wah,**
Practical guide to surface science and spectroscopy / Yip-Wah Chung. San Diego : Academic Press, c2001. xiii, 186 p.
00-111108  530.4/17  0121746100
*Surfaces (Physics) Spectrum analysis.*

**QC173.4.S94.F73 1997**
**Frankel, Felice.**
On the surface of things : images of the extraordinary in science / Felice Frankel and George M. Whitesides. San Francisco : Chronicle Books, c1997. 160 p. :
97-000852  530.4/17  0811813711
*Surfaces (Physics) Optical images. Surfaces (Physics) – Pictorial works.*

**QC173.4.S94.H84 1991**
**Hudson, John B.**
Surface science : an introduction / John B. Hudson. Boston : Butterworth-Heinemann, c1992. xii, 321 p. :
91-021912  530.4/27  075069159X
*Surfaces (Physics) Surface chemistry. Surfaces (Technology)*

## QC173.454 Atomic physics. Constitution and properties of matter — Properties of matter and antimatter (General) — Condensed matter physics

**QC173.454.N53 1995**
**Nichols, Carol Susan.**
Structure and bonding in condensed matter / Carol S. Nichols. Cambridge ; Cambridge University Press, 1995. xvi, 307 p. :
94-032183  530.4/11  0521462835
*Condensed matter. Electronic structure. Chemistry, Physical and theoretical.*

## QC173.55 Atomic physics. Constitution and properties of matter — Relativity physics — General works, treatises, and textbooks

**QC173.55.B49 1987**
**Bergmann, Peter Gabriel.**
The riddle of gravitation / Peter G. Bergmann. New York : Scribner, c1987. xix, 233 p. :
86-022090  530.1/1  0684184605
*Relativity (Physics) Gravitation.*

**QC173.55.C36 2000**
**Callahan, James.**
The geometry of spacetime : an introduction to special and general relativity / James J. Callahan. New York : Springer, c2000. xvi, 451 p. :
98-048083  530.11  0387986413
*Relativity (Physics) Space and time. Algebras, Linear.*

**QC173.55.C46 1988**
**Chaisson, Eric.**
Relatively speaking : relativity, black holes, and the fate of the universe / Eric Chaisson ; illustrated by Lola Judith Chaisson. New York : Norton, c1988. 254 p. :
87-011134  530.1/1  0393025365
*Relativity (Physics) Cosmology. Black holes (Astronomy)*

**QC173.55.E384513 2001**
**Einstein, Albert,**
Relativity : the special and general theory / by Albert Einstein ; translated by Robert W. Lawson. Mineola, NY : Dover Publications, 2001. p. cm.
00-052367  530.11  048641714X
*Relativity (Physics)*

**QC173.55.M66 1987**
**Mook, Delo E.,**
Inside relativity / by Delo E. Mook and Thomas Vargish. Princeton, N.J. : Princeton University Press, c1987. xiv, 306 p. :
87-045528  530.1/1  0691084726
*Relativity (Physics)*

## QC173.59 Atomic physics. Constitution and properties of matter — Relativity physics — Special topics, A-Z

**QC173.59.G44.C58 1995**
**Ciufolini, Ignazio,**
  Gravitation and inertia / Ignazio Ciufolini and John Archibald Wheeler. Princeton, N.J. : Princeton University Press, c1995. xi, 498 p. :
94-029874          530.1/1          0691033234
  *Geometrodynamics. General relativity (Physics) Gravitation.*

**QC173.59.S65**
**Gott, J. Richard.**
  Time travel in Einstein's universe : the physical possibilities of travel through time / J. Richard Gott, III. Boston : Houghton Mifflin, c2001. xii, 291 p. :
00-054243          530.11          0395955637
  *Space and time. Time travel.*

**QC173.59.S65.A4 1999**
**Al-Khalili, Jim,**
  Black holes, wormholes & time machines / Jim Al-Khalili. Bristol, UK ; Institute of Physics Pub., c1999. xxii, 265 p.
99-046327          530.11          0750305606
  *Space and time.*

**QC173.59.S65.B374 2000**
**Barbour, Julian B.**
  The end of time : the next revolution in physics / Julian Barbour. Oxford ; Oxford University Press, 2000. x, 371 p.
99-044319          530.11          0195117298
  *Space and time. Relativity (Physics) Quantum theory.*

**QC173.59.S65.E17 1989**
**Earman, John.**
  World enough and space-time : absolute versus relational theories of space and time / John Earman. Cambridge, Mass. : MIT Press, c1989. xiv, 233 p. :
88-036404          530.1/1          0262050404
  *Space and time. Absolute, The. Relationism.*

**QC173.59.S65.H4 1996**
**Hawking, S. W.**
  The nature of space and time / Stephen Hawking and Roger Penrose. Princeton, N.J. : Princeton University Press, c1996. viii, 141 p.
95-035582          530.1/1          0691037914
  *Space and time. Quantum theory. Astrophysics.*

**QC173.59.S65.S39 1986**
**Schwinger, Julian Seymour,**
  Einstein's legacy : the unity of space and time / Julian Schwinger. New York : Scientific American Library : c1986. xii, 250 p. :
85-019665          530.1/1          0716750112
  *Space and time.*

**QC173.59.T53.S23 1987**
**Sachs, Robert Green,**
  The physics of time reversal / Robert G. Sachs. Chicago : University of Chicago Press, 1987. xvi, 309 p. :
87-005826          530.1          0226733300
  *Time reversal. Symmetry (Physics)*

## QC173.6-173.65 Atomic physics. Constitution and properties of matter — Relativity physics — Special types of relativity theories

**QC173.6.A34 1975**
**Adler, Ronald.**
  Introduction to general relativity [by] Ronald Adler, Maurice Bazin [and] Menahem Schiffer. New York, McGraw-Hill [1975] xiv, 549 p.
74-018459          530.1/1          0070004234
  *General relativity (Physics)*

**QC173.6.G47**
**Geroch, Robert.**
  General relativity from A to B / Robert Geroch. Chicago : University of Chicago Press, 1978. xi, 225 p. :
77-018908          530.1/1          0226288633
  *General relativity (Physics)*

**QC173.6.H37 1992**
**Harpaz, Amos.**
  Relativity theory : concepts and basic principles / Amos Harpaz. Boston : Jones and Bartlett, c1992. viii, 224 p.
91-033056          530.1/1          0867202203
  *General relativity (Physics)*

**QC173.6.S38 1985**
**Schutz, Bernard F.**
  A first course in general relativity / Bernard F. Schutz. Cambridge [Cambridgeshire] ; Cambridge University Press, 1985. xiv, 376 p. :
83-023205          530.1/1          0521257700
  *General relativity (Physics) Astrophysics.*

**QC173.6.V57 1995**
**Visser, Matt.**
  Lorentzian wormholes : from Einstein to Hawking / Matt Visser. Woodbury, N.Y. : American Institute of Physics, c1995. xxv, 412 p. :
95-017876          530.1/1          1563963949
  *General relativity (Physics) Quantum field theory. Quantum gravity.*

**QC173.6.W55 1986**
**Will, Clifford M.,**
  Was Einstein right? : putting general relativity to the test / Clifford M. Will. New York : Basic Books, c1986. xii, 274 p.,
85-073877          530.1/1          0465090885
  *General relativity (Physics) Astrophysics.*

**QC173.65.E45 1988**
**Ellis, George Francis Rayner.**
Flat and curved space-times / George F.R. Ellis and Ruth M. Williams ; diagrams by Mauro Carfora. Oxford [England] : Clarendon Press ; 1988. x, 351 p. :
87-026340          530.1/1          0198511698
*Special relativity (Physics)  Space and time.*

**QC173.65.S35 1990**
**Schroder, Ulrich E.**
Special relativity / U.E. Schroder. Singapore ; World Scientific, 1990. xi, 214 p. :
89-048134          530.1/1          9810200684
*Special relativity (Physics)*

## QC173.7 Atomic physics. Constitution and properties of matter — Field theories. Unified field theories — General works, treatises, and textbooks

**QC173.7.P36 1986**
**Parker, Barry R.**
Einstein's dream : the search for a unified theory of the universe / Barry Parker. New York : Plenum Press, c1986. ix, 287 p. :
86-015139          530.1/42          030642343X
*Einstein, Albert, -- 1879-1955.    Unified field theories. Cosmology.*

## QC173.98  Atomic physics. Constitution and properties of matter — Quantum theory. Quantum mechanics

**QC173.98.G75 1984**
**Gribbin, John R.**
In search of Schrodinger's cat : quantum physics and reality / John Gribbin. Toronto ; Bantam Books, 1984. xvi, 302 p. :
84-002975          530.1/2/09          0553341030
*Schrodinger, Erwin, -- 1887-1961.    Quantum theory -- History. Reality.*

**QC173.98.J35**
**Jammer, Max.**
The philosophy of quantum mechanics; the interpretations of quantum mechanics in historical perspective.  New York, Wiley [1974] xi, 536 p.
74-013030          530.1/2          0471439584
*Quantum theory -- History.  Physics -- Philosophy.*

**QC173.98.W53 1995**
**Wick, David,**
The infamous boundary : seven decades of controversy in quantum physics / David Wick ; with a mathematical appendix by William Farris. Boston : Birkhauser, 1995. xii, 244 p. :
95-034320          530.1/2/09          0817637850
*Quantum theory -- History.*

## QC174-174.1  Atomic physics. Constitution and properties of matter — Quantum theory. Quantum mechanics — Early works through 1926

**QC174.D5**
**Dicke, Robert H.**
Introduction to quantum mechanics, by Robert H. Dicke and James P. Wittke. Reading, Mass., Addison-Wesley Pub. Co. [1960] 369 p.
60-011852          530.12
*Quantum theory.*

**QC174.F44**
**Fermi, Enrico,**
Notes on quantum mechanics; a course given at the University of Chicago. [Chicago] University of Chicago Press [1961] 171 p.
61-009447          530.12
*Quantum theory.*

**QC174.1.B52**
**Bjorken, James D.**
Relativistic quantum mechanics [by] James D. Bjorken [and] Sidney D. Drell. New York, McGraw-Hill [1964] x, 300 p.
63-021778          530.12
*Relativistic quantum theory.*

**QC174.1.B64 1960**
**Born, Max,**
Problems of atomic dynamics; two series of lectures on: I. The structure of the atom (20 lectures) II. The lattice theory of rigid bodies (10 lectures) With a new pref. by the author. New York, F. Ungar Pub. Co. [1960] 200 p.
60053099          539
*Quantum theory. Lattice theory.*

**QC174.1.C7**
**Cropper, William H.**
The quantum physicists and an introduction to their physics [by] William H. Cropper. New York, Oxford University Press, 1970. ix, 257 p.
73-083037          530.12
*Quantum theory.*

**QC174.1.H4 1950**
**Heisenberg, Werner,**
The physical principles of the quantum theory. Translated into English by Carl Eckart and Frank C. Hoyt. [New York] Dover Publications [1950? c1930] 183 p.
49011952          530.1          0486601137
*Quantum theory.*

**QC174.1.J26**
**Jammer, Max.**
The conceptual development of quantum mechanics. New York, McGraw-Hill [1966] xii, 399 p.
66-017914          530.123
*Quantum theory.*

QC174.1.J27 1973
**Jauch, Josef M.**
Are quanta real? A Galilean dialogue [by] J. M. Jauch. Bloomington, Indiana University Press [1973] xii, 106 p.
72-079907          530.1/2          0253308607
*Quantum theory.*

QC174.1.K45 1958
**Kemble, Edwin C.**
The fundamental principles of quantum mechanics, with elementary applications. New York, Dover [1958] 611 p.
58012613          530.1
*Quantum theory.*

QC174.1.M36 1970
**Merzbacher, Eugen.**
Quantum mechanics [by] Eugen Merzbacher. New York, J. Wiley [1970] x, 621 p.
74-088316          530.12          0471596701
*Quantum theory.*

QC174.1.P38
**Pauling, Linus,**
Introduction to quantum mechanics, with applications to chemistry, by Linus Pauling and E. Bright Wilson, jr. New York, McGraw-Hill book company, 1935. xiii, 468 p.
35-016760          530.1
*Quantum theory. Wave mechanics.*

QC174.1.S55 1968
**Slater, John Clarke,**
Quantum theory of matter [by] John C. Slater. New York, McGraw-Hill [1968] 763 p.
68-011620          530.12
*Quantum theory.*

QC174.1.W3 1968
**Waerden, B. L. van der**
Sources of quantum mechanics, edited with a historical introd. by B. L. van der Waerden. New York, Dover Publications [1968, c1967] xi, 430 p.
68-012916          530.12/3/08
*Quantum theory -- History -- Sources.*

QC174.1.Z49
**Ziman, J. M.**
Elements of advanced quantum theory, by J. M. Ziman. London, Cambridge U.P., 1969. xii, 269 p.
69-016290          530.12          0521074584
*Quantum theory.*

## QC174.12  Atomic physics. Constitution and properties of matter — Quantum theory. Quantum mechanics — General works, treatises, and textbooks

QC174.12.B34 1992
**Baggott, J. E.**
The meaning of quantum theory : a guide for students of chemistry and physics / Jim Baggott. Oxford ; Oxford University Press, 1992. xi, 230 p. :
91-034937          530.1/2          019855575X
*Quantum theory. Quantum chemistry.*

QC174.12.B364 1999
**Barrett, Jeffrey Alan.**
The quantum mechanics of minds and worlds / Jeffrey Alan Barrett. Oxford ; Oxford University Press, 1999. xiii, 267 p.
99-028680          530.12          019823838X
*Quantum theory. Physical measurements.*

QC174.12.D365 1986
**Davies, P. C. W.**
The ghost in the atom : a discussion of the mysteries of quantum physics / P.C.W. Davies and J.R. Brown. Cambridge [Cambridgeshire] ; Cambridge University Press, 1986. ix, 157 p. :
85-025478          530.1/2          0521307902
*Quantum theory. Physicists -- Interviews.*

QC174.12.G52 1987
**Gibbins, Peter.**
Particles and paradoxes : the limits of quantum logic / Peter Gibbins. Cambridge [Cambridgeshire] ; Cambridge University Press, 1987. xi, 181 p. ;
86-031758          530.1/2          0521334985
*Quantum logic. Physics -- Philosophy.*

QC174.12.H364 1997
**Hannabuss, Keith.**
An introduction to quantum theory / Keith Hannabuss. Oxford : Clarendon Press ; c1997. xiv, 380 p. :
96-030095          530.12          0198537948
*Quantum theory.*

QC174.12.H48 1987
**Hey, Anthony J. G.**
The quantum universe / Tony Hey, Patrick Walters. Cambridge [Cambridgeshire] ; Cambridge University Press, 1987. vii, 180 p. :
86-006830          530.1/2          0521267447
*Quantum theory.*

QC174.12.H67 1998
**House, J. E.**
Fundamentals of quantum mechanics / J.E. House. San Diego : Academic Press, c1998. xv, 279 p. :
98-084495          530.12          0123567750
*Quantum theory.*

**QC174.12.J67 1986**
**Jordan, Thomas F.,**
  Quantum mechanics in simple matrix form / Thomas F. Jordan. New York : Wiley, c1986. xi, 259 p. :
85-012121          530.1/2          0471817511
  *Quantum theory. Matrices.*

**QC174.12.L3513 1977**
**Landau, L. D.**
  Quantum mechanics : non-relativistic theory / by L.D. Landau and E.M. Lifshitz ; translated from the Russian by J.B. Sykes and J.S. Bell. Oxford ; Pergamon Press, 1977. xiv, 673 p. :
76-018223          530.1/2          0080209408.
  *Nonrelativistic quantum mechanics.*

**QC174.12.M34 2001**
**Malin, Shimon,**
  Nature loves to hide : quantum physics and reality, a western perspective / Shimon Malin. Oxford ; New York : Oxford University Press, 2001. xv, 288 p. :
          530.12 21          0195138945
*Quantum theory -- Philosophy.*

**QC174.12.M378 1995**
**McGervey, John D.,**
  Quantum mechanics : concepts and applications / John D. McGervey. San Diego : Academic Press, c1995. xiii, 408 p.
94-033103          530.1/2          0124835457
  *Quantum theory.*

**QC174.12.N32 1999**
**Nadeau, Robert,**
  The non-local universe : the new physics and matters of the mind / Robert Nadeau and Menas Kafatos. New York : Oxford University Press, 1999. xvi, 240 p. :
99-017062          530/.01          0195132564
  *Quantum theory. Physics -- Philosophy.*

**QC174.12.P4 1992**
**Peebles, P. J. E.**
  Quantum Mechanics / P.J.E. Peebles. Princeton, N.J. : Princeton University Press, c1992. xiv, 419 p. ;
91-039340          530.1/2          0691087555
  *Quantum theory.*

**QC174.12.S38713 1995**
**Schwabl, Franz,**
  Quantum mechanics / Franz Schwabl ; translated by Ronald Kates. Berlin ; Springer, c1995. xvi, 416 p. :
95-022048          530.1/2          3540591877
  *Quantum theory.*

**QC174.12.S525 1995**
**Silverman, Mark P.**
  More than one mystery : explorations in quantum interference / Mark P. Silverman. New York : Springer-Verlag, c1995. xiv, 212 p. :
94-021442          530.1/2          0387943404
  *Quantum theory.*

**QC174.12.S55**
**Slater, John Clarke,**
  Quantum theory of molecules and solids [by] John C. Slater. New York, McGraw-Hill [1963-74] 4 v.
62-017647          530.1/2          0070580383
  *Quantum theory. Solids. Molecules.*

**QC174.12.S8 1993**
**Stapp, Henry P.**
  Mind, matter, and quantum mechanics /Henry P. Stapp. Berlin ; Springer-Verlag, c1993. xii, 248 p. :
93-008407          128/.2          0387562893
  *Quantum theory. Physics -- Philosophy. Mind and body.*

**QC174.12.T73 1999**
**Treiman, Sam B.**
  The odd quantum / Sam Treiman. Princeton, N.J. : Princeton University Press, c1999. viii, 262 p.
99-024123          530.12          0691009260
  *Quantum theory.*

**QC174.12.Z64 1990**
**Zohar, Danah,**
  The quantum self : human nature and consciousness defined by the new physics / by Danah Zohar in collaboration with I.N. Marshall. New York : Morrow, c1990. 268 p. :
89-013194          530.1/2          0688087809
  *Quantum theory. Physics -- Philosophy. Philosophical anthropology.*

### QC174.15 Atomic physics. Constitution and properties of matter — Quantum theory. Quantum mechanics — Study and teaching. Research

**QC174.15.S66 1995**
**Squires, G. L.**
  Problems in quantum mechanics with solutions / G.L. Squires. Cambridge ; Cambridge University Press, 1995. ix, 254 p. :
93-043931          530.1/2          0521372453(ha
  *Quantum theory -- Problems, exercises, etc.*

### QC174.17 Atomic physics. Constitution and properties of matter — Quantum theory. Quantum mechanics — Special topics, A-Z

**QC174.17.G7.J67 1982**
**Joshi, A. W.**
  Elements of group theory for physicists / A.W. Joshi. New York : J. Wiley, c1982. xiii, 334 p.
82-200639          512/.2/02453
  *Group theory.*

**QC174.17.S9.B86 1989**
**Bunch, Bryan H.**
  Reality's mirror : exploring the mathematics of symmetry / Bryan Bunch. New York : Wiley, c1989. ix, 286 p. :
89-033271          539.7/25          0471501271
  *Symmetry (Physics)*

QC174.17.S9.C56 2000
**Close, F. E.**
Lucifer's legacy : the meaning of asymmetry / Frank Close. Oxford ; Oxford University Press, 2000. 259 p. :
99-052842          530          0198503806
*Symmetry (Physics)*

QC174.17.S9.S38 1990
**Schroeder, M. R.**
Fractals, chaos, power laws : minutes from an infinite paradise / Manfred Schroeder. New York : W.H. Freeman, c1991. xviii, 429 p.
90-036763          530.1          0716721368
*Symmetry (Physics)*

QC174.17.S9.W47 1983
**Wess, Julius.**
Supersymmetry and supergravity / by Julius Wess and Jonathan Bagger. Princeton, N.J. : Princeton University Press, c1983. viii, 180 p.
82-061394          530.1/43          0691083274
*Supersymmetry. Supergravity.*

## QC174.2-174.26 Atomic physics. Constitution and properties of matter — Quantum theory. Quantum mechanics — Wave mechanics

QC174.2.C6
**Condon, Edward Uhler,**
Quantum mechanics, by Edward U. Condon ... and Philip M. Morse ... New York [etc.] McGraw-Hill book company, inc., 1929. xiii, 250 p.
29-029416          530.1
*Wave mechanics. Quantum theory.*

QC174.2.H4 1956
**Heitler, Walter,**
Elementary wave mechanics, with applications to quantum chemistry. Oxford, Clarendon Press, 1956. 193 p.
56-059037          530.1
*Wave mechanics.*

QC174.2.M6 1952
**Mott, N. F.**
Elements of wave mechanics. Cambridge [Eng.] University Press, 1952. 156 p.
52-010250          530.1
*Wave mechanics.*

QC174.2.T7
**Tralli, Nunzio,**
Atomic theory; an introduction to wave mechanics [by] Nunzio Tralli [and] Frank R. Pomilla. New York, McGraw-Hill [1969] 374 p.
79-075163          530.12/4
*Wave mechanics. Atomic theory.*

QC174.26.W28.C657 1988
**Cook, David B.**
Schrodinger's mechanics / by David B. Cook. Singapore ; World Scientific, c1988. xii, 150 p. :
88-033779          530.1/24          9971507609
*Wave mechanics. Schrodinger equation.*

## QC174.3 Atomic physics. Constitution and properties of matter — Quantum theory. Quantum mechanics — Matrix mechanics

QC174.3.D5 1958
**Dirac, P. A. M.**
The principles of quantum mechanics. Oxford, Clarendon Press, 1958. 312 p.
58-000907          530.1
*Matrix mechanics. Quantum theory.*

QC174.3.V613
**Von Neumann, John,**
Mathematical foundations of quantum mechanics. Translated from the German ed. by Robert T. Beyer. Princeton [N.J.] Princeton University Press, 1955. 445 p.
53010143          530.1
*Matrix mechanics.*

## QC174.4 Atomic physics. Constitution and properties of matter — Quantum theory. Quantum mechanics — Quantum statistics

QC174.4.B3
**Band, William,**
An introduction to quantum statistics / William Band. Princeton, N.J. : D. Van Nostrand, c1955. xiii, 342 p.
55009900          530.1
*Quantum statistics.*

## QC174.45-174.5 Atomic physics. Constitution and properties of matter — Quantum theory. Quantum mechanics — Quantum field theory

QC174.45.B3
**Barut, A. O.**
Electrodynamics and classical theory of fields and particles. New York, Macmillan [1964] xv, 235 p.
64-010966          530.1
*Quantum field theory. Particles (Nuclear physics)*

QC174.45.H82 1998
**Huang, Kerson,**
Quantum field theory : from operators to path integrals / Kerson Huang. New York : Wiley, c1998. xvii, 426 p.
98-013437          530.14/3          0471141208
*Quantum field theory.*

**QC174.45.N57**
**Nishijima, K.**
Fields and particles; field theory and dispersion relations [by] K. Nishijima. New York, W. A. Benjamin, 1969. ix, 465 p.
69-012567          530.14/3
*Quantum field theory.*

**QC174.45.T53 1999**
**Ticciati, Robin.**
Quantum field theory for mathematicians / Robin Ticciati. New York : Cambridge University Press, 1999. xii, 699 p. :
98-039473          530.14/3          052163265X
*Quantum field theory.*

**QC174.5.F6**
**Fonda, Luciano.**
Symmetry principles in quantum physics [by] L. Fonda and G. C. Ghirardi. New York, M. Dekker, 1970. xiii, 515 p.
75-121045          530.12     0824712137
*Quantum theory. Symmetry (Physics)*

**QC174.5.H35**
**Hartree, Douglas R.**
The calculation of atomic structures. New York, J. Wiley, 1957. 181 p.
57-005916          530.1
*Atomic structure. Numerical analysis.*

## QC174.8 Atomic physics. Constitution and properties of matter — Statistical physics — General works, treatises, and textbooks

**QC174.8.A43 1996**
**Ambegaokar, Vinay.**
Reasoning about luck : probability and its uses in physics / Vinay Ambegaokar. Cambridge ; Cambridge University Press, 1996. xv, 231 p. :
95-047481          530.1/592          0521442176
*Statistical physics. Probability measures.*

**QC174.8.B59 1989**
**Bloch, Felix,**
Fundamentals of statistical mechanics : manuscript and notes of Felix Bloch / prepared by John Dirk Walecka. Stanford, Calif. : Stanford University Press, 1989. x, 302 p. :
88-012285          530.1/3          0804715017
*Statistical mechanics.*

**QC174.8.L3613 1979**
**Landau, L. D.**
Statistical physics / L.D. Landau and E.M. Lifshitz ; translated from the Russian by J.R. Sykes and M.J. Kearsley. Oxford ; Pergamon Press, c1980. x, 387 p. ;
78041328          530.1/33          0080230725
*Statistical physics.*

**QC174.8.M37 1977**
**Mayer, Joseph Edward,**
Statistical mechanics / Joseph Edward Mayer and Maria Goeppert Mayer. New York : Wiley, c1977. xv, 491 p. ;
76-020668          530.1/32          0471579858
*Statistical mechanics.*

**QC174.8.S55 1993**
**Sklar, Lawrence.**
Physics and chance : philosophical issues in the foundations of statistical mechanics / Lawrence Sklar. Cambridge [England] ; Cambridge University Press, 1993. xiii, 437 p.
92-046215          530.1/3          0521440556
*Statistical mechanics. Physics -- Philosophy.*

## QC175 Atomic physics. Constitution and properties of matter — Statistical physics — Kinetic theory of gases

**QC175.B7213 1995**
**Boltzmann, Ludwig,**
Lectures on gas theory / Ludwig Boltzmann ; translated by Stephen G. Brush. New York : Dover Publications, 1995. ix, 490 p. :
94-041221          533/.7          0486684555
*Kinetic theory of gases.*

**QC175.J43 1925**
**Jeans, James Hopwood,**
The dynamical theory of gases, by J. H. Jeans. Cambridge [Eng.] University Press, 1925. 4 p. l., 444
26014895
*Kinetic theory of gases.*

**QC175.K45**
**Kennard, E. H.**
Kinetic theory of gases, with an introduction to statistical mechanics, by Earle H. Kennard. New York, McGraw-Hill Book Company, inc., 1938. xiii, 483 p.
38006323          533.7
*Kinetic theory of gases. Statistical mechanics.*

**QC175.K52**
**Khinchin, Aleksandr IAkovlevich,**
Mathematical foundations of statistical mechanics; tr. from the Russian by G. Gamow. New York, Dover Publications [1949] vii, 179 p.
49009707          541.39
*Statistical mechanics.*

**QC175.K58**
**Kittel, Charles.**
Elementary statistical physics. New York, Wiley [1958] 228 p.
58-012495          541.39
*Statistical physics. Statistical mechanics.*

**QC175.L32 1969**
**Landau, L. D.**
  Statistical physics, by L. D. Landau and E. M. Lifshitz. Translated from the Russian by J. B. Sykes and M. J. Kearsley. Oxford, Pergamon Press [1969] xii, 484 p.
68-018526          530.13/2          0080091032
  *Statistical physics.*

**QC175.R43**
**Reif, F.**
  Fundamentals of statistical and thermal physics [by] F. Reif. New York, McGraw-Hill [1965] x, 651 p.
63-022730          530.13
  *Statistical mechanics. Statistical thermodynamics.*

**QC175.S77 vol.6**
**Brush, Stephen G.**
  The kind of motion we call heat : a history of the kinetic theory of gases in the 19th century / Stephen G. Brush. Amsterdam ; North-Holland Pub. Co. ; 1976. 2 v. (769, xx
75-031624          530.1/3/08 s          0444110119
  *Kinetic theory of gases -- History. Statistical mechanics – History. Physics -- History.*

## QC176 Atomic physics. Constitution and properties of matter — Solids. Solid state physics — Societies, congresses, serial collections, yearbooks

**QC176.B63 1985**
**Blakemore, J. S.**
  Solid state physics / J.S. Blakemore. Cambridge [Cambridgeshire] ; Cambridge University Press, 1985. x, 506 p. :
85-047879          530.4/1          0521309328
  *Solid state physics.*

**QC176.C47 1988**
**Christman, J. Richard.**
  Fundamentals of solid state physics / J. Richard Christman. New York : Wiley, c1988. ix, 518 p. :
87-021651          530.4/1          0471810959
  *Solid state physics.*

**QC176.D24**
**Dalven, Richard.**
  Introduction to applied solid state physics : topics in the applications of semiconductors, superconductors, and the nonlinear optical properties of solids / Richard Dalven. New York : Plenum Press, c1980. xiv, 330 p. :
79-021902          621.3/028          0306403854
  *Solid state physics. Semiconductors.*

**QC176.G8513 1989**
**Guinier, Andre.**
  The solid state : from superconductors to superalloys / Andre Guinier, Remi Jullien ; translated from the French by W.J. Duffin. [Chester? England] : International Union of Crystallography ; 1989. viii, 271 p.
89-031661          530.4/1          0198552904
  *Solid state physics.*

**QC176.I2313 1990**
**Ibach, H.,**
  Solid-state physics : an introduction to theory and experiment / Harald Ibach, Hans Luth. Berlin ; Springer-Verlag, c1991. x, 341 p. :
90-009902          530.4/1          0387522077
  *Solid state physics.*

**QC176.K5 1986**
**Kittel, Charles.**
  Introduction to solid state physics / Charles Kittel. New York : Wiley, c1986. x, 646 p. :
85-017812          530.4/1          0471874744
  *Solid state physics.*

**QC176.O98 1992**
  Out of the crystal maze : chapters from the history of solid state physics / edited by Lillian Hoddeson ... [et al.]. New York : Oxford University Press, 1992. xx, 697 p. :
89-033498          530.4/1/09          019505329X
  *Solid state physics -- History.*

**QC176.R67 1978**
**Rosenberg, H. M.**
  The solid state : an introduction to the physics of crystals for students of physics, materials science, and engineering / H. M. Rosenberg. Oxford : Clarendon Press, 1978. 274 p. :
78-040482          530.4/1          0198518447
  *Solid state physics. Crystals.*

**QC176.T32 1995**
**Tanner, B. K.**
  Introduction to the physics of electrons in solids / Brian K. Tanner. Cambridge [England] ; Cambridge University Press, 1995. xvii, 246 p.
94-011666          530.4/11          0521239419
  *Solid state physics. Energy-band theory of solids. Semiconductors.*

**QC176.W45 1970**
**Wert, Charles Allen.**
  Physics of solids [by] Charles A. Wert [and] Robb M. Thomson. New York, McGraw-Hill [1970] xi, 522 p.
77-098055          530.4/1
  *Solid state physics.*

**QC176.Z53 1972**
**Ziman, J. M.**
  Principles of the theory of solids, by J. M. Ziman. Cambridge [Eng.] University Press, 1972. xiii, 435 p.
72-080250          530.4/1          0521083826
  *Solid state physics.*

### QC176.8 Atomic physics. Constitution and properties of matter — Solids. Solid state physics — Special topics, A-Z

**QC176.8.A3.B45 1988**
**Beltzer, A. I.**
   Acoustics of solids / A.I. Beltzer. Berlin ; Springer-Verlag, c1988. xi, 235 p. :
88-004611          530.4/1          0387188886
   *Acoustic surface waves.  Solids -- Acoustic properties.  Wave guides.*

**QC176.8.E4.C43 1990**
**Chambers, R. G.**
   Electrons in metals and semiconductors / R.G. Chambers. London ; Chapman and Hall, 1990. vii, 230 p. :
          530.41    0412368404
   *Free electron theory of metals.  Semiconductors.  Metals.*

## QC178 Atomic physics. Constitution and properties of matter — Theories of gravitation

**QC178.S66 1993**
**Spolter, Pari.**
   Gravitational force of the sun / Pari Spolter. Granada Hills, Calif. : Orb Pub. Co., c1993. x, 260 p. :
93-085943          0963810758
   *Gravitation.  General relativity (Physics)*

**QC178.S8213 1982**
**Stephani, Hans.**
   General relativity : an introduction to the theory of the gravitational field / Hans Stephani ; edited by John Stewart ; translated by Martin Pollock and John Stewart. Cambridge [Cambridgeshire] ; Cambridge University Press, 1982. xvi, 298 p. :
81-010115          530.1/1          0521240085
   *Gravitational fields.  General relativity (Physics)*

**QC178.T47 1987**
   Three hundred years of gravitation / edited by S.W. Hawking, W. Israel. Cambridge [Cambridgeshire] ; Cambridge University Press, 1987. xiii, 684 p.
87-010364          531/.14          0521343127
   *Gravitation.  Cosmology.  Astrophysics.*

**QC178.Z44 1989**
**Zee, A.**
   An old man's toy : gravity at work and play in Einstein's universe / A. Zee. New York : Macmillan, c1989. xxxii, 272 p.
88-019013          531/.14          0026334402
   *Gravitation -- Popular works.  Gravity -- Popular works. Cosmology -- Popular works.*

### QC183 Atomic physics. Constitution and properties of matter — Special properties of matter and antimatter — Capillarity

**QC183.E53 1956**
**Einstein, Albert,**
   Investigations on the theory of the Brownian movement. Edited with notes by R. Furth. Translated by A. D. Cowper. [New York] Dover Publications [1956] 119 p.
57000625          539.6
   *Brownian movements.*

### QC189.5 Atomic physics. Constitution and properties of matter — Special properties of matter and antimatter — Rheology

**QC189.5.C55 1993**
**Chhabra, R. P.**
   Bubbles, drops, and particles in non-Newtonian fluids / R.P. Chhabra. Boca Raton, Fla. : CRC Press, c1993. 417 p. :
92-013131          531/.11          0849367182
   *Non-Newtonian fluids.  Fluid mechanics.*

## QC225-225.15 Acoustics. Sound — General works, treatises, and advanced textbooks

**QC225.M67 1968**
**Morse, Philip McCord,**
   Theoretical acoustics [by] Philip M. Morse [and] K. Uno Ingard. New York, McGraw-Hill, [c1968] xix, 927 p.
67-015428          534
   *Sound.*

**QC225.15.B47**
**Berg, Richard E.**
   The physics of sound / Richard E. Berg, David G. Stork. Englewood Cliffs, N.J. : Prentice-Hall, c1982. xiv, 370 p. :
81-013840          781/.22          0136742831
   *Sound.  Music -- Acoustics and physics.*

**QC225.15.S46 1989**
**Sen, S. N.,**
   Acoustics, waves and oscillations / S.N. Sen. New York : Wiley, c1990. xi, 234 p. :
88-033825          534          0470213647
   *Sound.*

## QC225.6 Acoustics. Sound — Addresses, essays, lectures

**QC225.6.S68 2000**
   Sound / edited by Patricia Kruth and Henry Stobart. Cambridge ; Cambridge University Press, 2000. v, 235 p. :
99-015819          534          0521572096
   *Sound.*

## QC225.7 Acoustics. Sound — Special aspects of the subject as whole

**QC225.7.L56**
**Lindsay, Robert Bruce,**
Physical acoustics. Edited by R. Bruce Lindsay. Stroudsburg, Pa., Dowden, Hutchinson & Ross [1974] xiii, 480 p.
73-012619          534          0879330406
*Sound. Sound-waves.*

## QC227 Acoustics. Sound — Study and teaching. Research — Laboratory manuals

**QC227.B4**
**Beranek, Leo Leroy,**
Acoustic measurements. New York, J. Wiley [1949] vii, 914 p.
49048299          534
*Sound -- Measurement. Electro-acoustics.*

## QC243 Acoustics. Sound — Special topics — Sound waves

**QC243.F86 1982**
Fundamentals of acoustics / Lawrence E. Kinsler ... [et al.]. New York : Wiley, c1982. xvi, 480 p. :
81-007463          534          0471097438
*Sound-waves. Sound -- Equipment and supplies. Architectural acoustics.*

**QC243.T46**
**Temkin, Samuel,**
Elements of acoustics / Samuel Temkin. New York : Wiley, c1981. xii, 515 p. :
80-024416          534          0471059900
*Sound-waves.*

## QC252 Heat — History and philosophy

**QC252.R6**
**Roller, Duane Emerson,**
The early development of the concepts of temperature and heat; the rise and decline of the caloric theory. Cambridge, Harvard University Press, 1950. iv, 106 p.
50008653          536
*Heat.*

## QC254 Heat — General works, treatises, and advanced textbooks

**QC254.B3713 1967**
**Becker, Richard,**
Theory of heat. Berlin, Springer-Verlag, 1967. xii, 380 p.
67-013536          536/.1
*Heat.*

**QC254.2.Z45 1981**
**Zemansky, Mark Waldo,**
Heat and thermodynamics : an intermediate textbook / Mark W. Zemansky, Richard H. Dittman. New York : McGraw-Hill, c1981. xv, 543 p. :
80-018253          536          0070728089
*Heat. Thermodynamics.*

## QC271 Heat — Thermometers. Thermometry — General works, treatises, and textbooks

**QC271.M384 1988**
**McGee, Thomas D.**
Principles and methods of temperature measurement / Thomas D. McGee. New York : Wiley, c1988. xvii, 581 p.
87-022926          536/.5/028          0471627674
*Temperature measurements.*

**QC271.M483 1991**
**Michalski, L.**
Temperature measurement / L. Michalski, K. Eckersdorf, and J. McGhee. Chichester, West Sussex, England ; J. Wiley, c1991. xiv, 514 p. :
90-025320          536/.5/0287          0471922293
*Temperature measurements.*

**QC271.M5**
**Middleton, W. E. Knowles**
A history of the thermometer and its use in meteorology, by W. E. Knowles Middleton. Baltimore, Johns Hopkins Press [1966] xiii, 249 p.
66-023978          536.5
*Thermometers -- History. Atmospheric temperature -- Measurement.*

## QC278 Heat — Low temperatures — General works, treatises, and textbooks

**QC278.C3**
**Casimir, H. B. G.**
Magnetism and very low temperatures, by H. B. G. Casimir. Cambridge [Eng.] : University Press, 1940. 93 p. :
41007627          536.5
*Magnetism. Low temperature research.*

**QC278.J3 1962**
**Jackson, Leonard Cecil,**
Low temperature physics. London, Methuen; [1962] 158 p.
62-006837          536.56
*Low temperatures.*

**QC278.K46 1993**
**Kent, Anthony.**
Experimental low temperature physics / Anthony Kent. New York : American Institute of Physics, c1993. x, 212 p. :
92-010419          536/.56          1563960303
*Low temperatures.*

**QC278.M43 1966a**
**Mendelssohn, Kurt.**
  The quest for absolute zero; the meaning of low temperature physics [by] K. Mendelssohn. New York : McGraw-Hill, [1966] 256 p. :
          536.56
*Low temperature research.*

**QC278.R6**
**Rosenberg, H. M.**
  Low temperature solid state physics; some selected topics. Oxford, Clarendon Press, 1963. xvi, 420 p.
64-000025          536.56
  *Low temperatures. Solid state physics.*

**QC278.S48 1999**
**Shachtman, Tom,**
  Absolute zero and the conquest of cold / Tom Shachtman. Boston : Houghton Mifflin Co., 1999. 261 p. ;
99-033305          536/.56          0395938880
  *Low temperature research.*

**QC307 Heat — Change of state — Continuity of state. Critical state. Critical point. Equations of state**

**QC307.S7 1971b**
**Stanley, H. Eugene**
  Introduction to phase transitions and critical phenomena, by H. Eugene Stanley. New York, Oxford University Press, 1971. xx, 308 p.
71-172087          536/.401
  *Critical phenomena (Physics) Phase rule and equilibrium.*

**QC310.2 Heat — Thermodynamics — Collected works (nonserial)**

**QC310.2.M39 1995**
**Maxwell, James Clerk,**
  Maxwell on heat and statistical mechanics : on "avoiding all personal enquiries" of molecules / edited by Elizabeth Garber, Stephen G. Brush and C.W.F. Everitt. Bethlehem : Lehigh University Press ; c1995. 550 p. :
94-025234          530.4/3/092          0934223343
*Maxwell, James Clerk, -- 1831-1879 -- Correspondence. Thermodynamics. Virial theorem. Equations of state.*

**QC310.3 Heat — Thermodynamics — Dictionaries and encyclopedias**

**QC310.3.P4713 1998**
**Perrot, Pierre.**
  A to Z of thermodynamics / Pierre Perrot. Oxford ; Oxford University Press, 1998. vi, 329 p. :
97-051538          621.402/1/03          0198565569
  *Thermodynamics -- Dictionaries.*

**QC311 Heat — Thermodynamics — General works, treatises, and advanced textbooks**

**QC311.K57 2000**
**Kirwan, A. D., Jr.**
  Mother nature's two laws : ringmasters for circus earth : lessons on entropy, energy, critical thinking, and the practice of science / A.D. Kirwan, Jr. Singapore : World Scientific , 2000. xxv, 173 p. :
          9810243146
  *Thermodynamics.*

**QC311.A3 1975**
**Adkins, C. J.**
  Equilibrium thermodynamics / C. J. Adkins. London ; McGraw-Hill, [1975] xiii, 284 p.
74-034392          536/.7          0070840571
  *Thermodynamic equilibrium.*

**QC311.B293 1999**
**Baierlein, Ralph.**
  Thermal physics / Ralph Baierlein. Cambridge, U.K. ; Cambridge University Press, 1999. xiii, 442 p.
98-038617          536/.7          0521590825
  *Thermodynamics. Entropy. Statistical mechanics.*

**QC311.B295 1994**
**Bailyn, Martin.**
  A survey of thermodynamics / Martin Bailyn. Woodbury, NY : AIP Press, c1994. xiv, 657 p. :
93-028712          536/.7          0883187973
  *Thermodynamics.*

**QC311.B95 1996**
**Burshtein, A. I.**
  Introduction to thermodynamics and kinetic theory of matter / A.I. Burshtein. New York : Wiley, c1996. xiii, 336 p.
95-011655          536/.7          0471047554
  *Thermodynamics. Kinetic theory of matter.*

**QC311.C2813 1986**
**Carnot, Sadi,**
  Reflexions on the motive power of fire : a critical edition with the surviving scientific manuscripts / Sadi Carnot ; translated and edited by Robert Fox. [Manchester] : Manchester University Press ; 1986. viii, 230 p.
86-007911          536.7          0936508167
  *Thermodynamics.*

**QC311.D86 1996**
**Dunning-Davies, J.,**
  Concise thermodynamics : principles and applications in physical science and engineering / Jeremy Dunning-Davies. Chichester : Albion, 1996. v, 126 p. :
97-153734          536/.7          1898563152
  *Thermodynamics.*

**QC311.F83 1996**
**Fuchs, Hans U.**
The dynamics of heat / Hans U. Fuchs. New York : Springer, c1996. xii, 713 p. :
95-044883          536/.7          0387946039
*Thermodynamics.*

**QC311.G55**
**Glasstone, Samuel,**
Thermodynamics for chemists, by Samuel Glasstone ... New York, D. Van Nostrand Company, inc., 1947. viii, 522 p.
47001607          536.7
*Chemistry, Physical Thermodynamics.*

**QC311.K66 1998**
**Kondepudi, D. K.**
Modern thermodynamics : from heat engines to dissipative structures / Dilip Kondepudi, Ilya Prigogine. Chichester ; John Wiley & Sons, c1998. xvii, 486 p.
97-048745          536/.7          0471973939
*Thermodynamics.*

**QC311.L4 1961**
**Lewis, Gilbert Newton,**
Thermodynamics [by] Gilbert Newton Lewis [and] Merle Randall. Rev. by Kenneth S. Pitzer [and] Leo Brewer. New York, McGraw-Hill, 1961. 723 p.
60-010604          541.369
*Thermodynamics. Chemistry, Physical and theoretical.*

**QC311.P72 1945**
**Planck, Max,**
Treatise on thermodynamics, by Dr. Max Planck, translated with the author's sanction by Alexander Ogg. New York, Dover publications, 1945. xiv p., 1 l.,
45-009816          536.7
*Thermodynamics.*

**QC311.R675 1995**
**Roy, Bimalendu Narayan.**
Principles of modern thermodynamics / B.N. Roy. Bristol, [U.K.] ; Institute of Physics Pub., c1995. xxii, 569 p.
94-023492          536/.7          0750300191
*Thermodynamics.*

**QC311.S38 1952**
**Schrodinger, Erwin,**
Statistical thermodynamics; a course of seminar lectures delivered in January-March 1944, at the School of Theoretical Physics, Dublin Institute for Advanced Studies. Cambridge [Eng.] University Press, 1962, c1952. 95 p.
52014738          536.7
*Thermodynamics. Statistical mechanics.*

**QC311.S513 1995**
**Shavit, Arthur.**
Thermodynamics : from concepts to applications / Arthur Shavit and Chaim Gutfinger. New York : Prentice Hall, 1995. xiii, 487 p.
94-029081          536/.7          0132882671
*Thermodynamics.*

**QC311.19 Heat — Thermodynamics — Addresses, essays, lectures**

**QC311.19.S4**
The Second law of thermodynamics / edited by Joseph Kestin. Stroudsburg, Pa. : Dowden, Hutchinson & Ross ; c1976. xiii, 329 p.
76-019059          536/.71          0879332425
*Thermodynamics.*

**QC311.5 Heat — Thermodynamics — Special types of thermodynamics**

**QC311.5.L4**
**Lee, John F.**
Statistical thermodynamics, by John F. Lee, Francis W. Sears [and] Donald L. Turcotte. Reading, Mass., Addison-Wesley Pub. Co. [1963] 374 p.
63-008390          536.7
*Statistical thermodynamics.*

**QC318 Heat — Thermodynamics — Other special topics, A-Z**

**QC318.E57.G65 1993**
**Goldstein, Martin,**
The refrigerator and the universe : understanding the laws of energy / Martin Goldstein, Inge F. Goldstein. Cambridge, Mass. : Harvard University Press, 1993. viii, 433 p.
93-002084          530/.7          0674753240
*Entropy. Force and energy. Entropy (Information theory)*

**QC318.M35.V66 1998**
**Von Baeyer, Hans Christian.**
Maxwell's demon : why warmth disperses and time passes / Hans Christian von Baeyer. New York : Random House, c1998. xxi, 207 p. ;
97-041543          536/.71          0679433422
*Maxwell's demon.*

**QC320 Heat — Heat transfer — General works, treatises, and textbooks**

**QC320.B44 1993**
**Bejan, Adrian,**
Heat transfer / Adrian Bejan. New York : John Wiley & Sons, Inc., c1993. xxiii, 675 p.
92-025535          621.402/2          0471502901
*Heat -- Transmission.*

**QC320.H235 1988**
Handbook of numerical heat transfer / [edited by] W.J. Minkowycz ... [et al.]. New York : Wiley, c1988. xiv, 1024 p.
87-023100          536/.2/001515          0471830933
*Heat -- Transmission -- Measurement -- Handbooks, manuals, etc. Numerical analysis -- Handbooks, manuals, etc.*

**QC320.J55 1998**
**Jiji, Latif Menashi.**
   Heat transfer essentials : a textbook / Latif Menashi Jiji.
New York : Begell House, 1998. p. cm.
98-016085          536/.2          1567001149
   *Heat -- Transmission. Heat -- Transmission -- Problems,*
*exercises, etc.*

**QC320.M63 1993**
**Modest, M. F.**
   Radiative heat transfer / Michael F. Modest. New York :
McGraw-Hill, c1993. xxv, 832 p. :
92-024671          621.402/2          0070426759
   *Heat -- Transmission. Heat -- Radiation and absorption.*

**QC320.W46 1977**
**Whitaker, Stephen.**
   Fundamental principles of heat transfer / Stephen Whitaker.
New York : Pergamon Press, c1977. xv, 556 p. :
75-041701          536/.2          0080178669.
   *Heat -- Transmission.*

## QC320.4 Heat — Heat transfer — Handbooks, tables, formulas, etc.

**QC320.4.H36 1998**
   Handbook of heat transfer / Warren M. Rohsenow, editor ;
J.P. Hartnett, editor ; Young I. Cho, editor. New York :
McGraw-Hill, c1998. 1 v. (various
97-051381          621.402/2          0070535558
   *Heat -- Transmission -- Handbooks, manuals, etc. Mass transfer --*
*Handbooks, manuals, etc.*

## QC321 Heat — Heat transfer — Conduction

**QC321.C28 1959**
**Carslaw, H. S.**
   Conduction of heat in solids, by H. S. Carslaw and J. C.
Jaeger. Oxford, Clarendon Press, 1959. 510 p.
59-001127          536.23
   *Heat -- Conduction. Laplace transformation.*

## QC331 Heat — Heat transfer — Radiation and absorption. Laws of cooling

**QC331.P73 1959**
**Planck, Max,**
   The theory of heat radiation. Authorised translation by
Morton Masius. New York, Dover Publications [1959] 224 p.
59-014225          536.33
   *Heat -- Radiation and absorption. Electromagnetic waves.*

## QC351 Optics. Light — Collected works (nonserial)

**QC351.L35**
   Lasers and light; readings from Scientific American. With
introductions by Arthur L. Schawlow. San Francisco, W. H.
Freeman [1969] vi, 376 p.
77-080079          535          0716709856
   *Light. Lasers.*

## QC352 Optics. Light — History

**QC352.P34 1997**
**Park, David Allen,**
   The fire within the eye : a historical essay on the nature and
meaning of light / David Park. Princeton, N.J. : Princeton
University Press, c1997. xiii, 377 p.,
96-045573          535          0691043329
   *Light -- History. Optics -- History.*

## QC353 Optics. Light — Early works through 1800

**QC353.H35 1993**
**Hall, A. Rupert**
   All was light : an introduction to Newton's Opticks / A.
Rupert Hall. Oxford : Clarendon Press ; 1993. vi, 252 p. :
92-043731          535          0198539851
   *Newton, Isaac, -- Sir, -- 1642-1727. -- Opticks.   Optics -- Early*
*works to 1800. Optics -- Europe -- History.*

**QC353.N52 1984**
**Newton, Isaac,**
   The optical papers of Isaac Newton / edited by Alan E.
Shapiro. Cambridge [Cambridgeshire] ; Cambridge University
Press, 1984- v. 1   :
82-014751          535          0521252482
   *Optics -- Early works to 1800. Optics -- History -- Sources.*

**QC353.N57 1952**
**Newton, Isaac,**
   Opticks; or, A treatise of the reflections, refractions,
inflections & colours of light. Based on the 4th ed., London,
1730; with a foreword by Albert Einstein, an introd. by Sir
Edmund Whittaker, a pref. by I. Bernard Cohen, and an
analytical table of contents prepared by Duane H. D. Roller.
New York, Dover Publications [1952] cxv, 406 p.
52-012165          535
   *Optics -- Early works to 1800.*

## QC355 Optics. Light — General works, treatises, and textbooks — 1801-1969

**QC355.B63 1969**
**Born, Max,**
   Principles of optics; electromagnetic theory of propagation, interference and diffraction of light, by Max Born and Emil Wolf. With contributions by A. B. Bhatia [and others] Oxford, Pergamon Press, 1969. xxviii, 808 p
77-079463       535       0080139876
   *Optics. Electromagnetic theory.*

**QC355.H533 1968**
**Heel, A. C. S. van**
   What is light? [By] A. C. S. van Heel and C. H. F. Velzel. Translated from the Dutch by J. L. J. Rosenfeld. New York, McGraw-Hill [1968] 255 p.
67-024448       535
   *Optics.*

**QC355.J4 1957**
**Jenkins, Francis A.**
   Fundamentals of optics [by] Francis A. Jenkins [and] Harvey E. White. New York, McGraw-Hill, 1957. 637 p.
56-012535       535
   *Optics.*

## QC355.2-357.2 Optics. Light — General works, treatises, and textbooks — 1970-

**QC355.2.H33**
**Haken, H.**
   Light / H. Haken. Amsterdam ; North-Holland Pub. Co. ; c1981-1985. 2 v. :
80-022397       535       0444860207
   *Light. Lasers. Nonlinear optics.*

**QC355.2.J46 1976**
**Jenkins, Francis A.**
   Fundamentals of optics /Francis A. Jenkins, Harvey E. White. New York : McGraw-Hill, c1976. xx, 746 p. :
75-026989       535       0070323305
   *Optics.*

**QC355.2.L96 1995**
**Lynch, David K.,**
   Color and light in nature / David K. Lynch, William Livingston. Cambridge ; Cambridge University Press, 1995. xi, 254 p. :
93-046711       551.5/65       0521434319(ha
   *Light. Optics. Color.*

**QC355.2.P48 1996**
**Perkowitz, S.**
   Empire of light : a history of discovery in science and art / Sidney Perkowitz. New York : Henry Holt, 1996. xi, 227 p. ;
95-050778       535       0805032118
   *Light.*

**QC355.2.W44 1981**
**Welford, W. T.**
   Optics / W.T. Welford. Oxford ; Oxford University Press, 1981. vii, 150 p. :
80-041847       535       0198518471
   *Optics.*

**QC355.2.W45 1991**
**Welford, W. T.**
   Useful optics / Walter T. Welford. Chicago : University of Chicago Press, 1991. ix, 140 p. :
91-008355       535       0226893057
   *Optics. Optical instruments.*

**QC355.2.Y68 1986**
**Young, Matt,**
   Optics and lasers : including fibers and optical waveguides / Matt Young. Berlin ; Springer-Verlag, c1986. xvi, 279 p. :
85-027795       621.36       0387161279
   *Optics. Lasers.*

**QC357.2.M48**
**Meyer-Arendt, Jurgen R.**
   Introduction to classical and modern optics [by] Jurgen R. Meyer-Arendt. Englewood Cliffs, N.J., Prentice-Hall [1972] xi, 558 p.
71-157723       535       0134794362
   *Optics.*

## QC358 Optics. Light — Elementary textbooks

**QC358.H43 1991**
**Heavens, O. S.**
   Insight into optics / O.S. Heavens and the late R.W. Ditchburn. Chichester ; Wiley, c1991. xviii, 309 p.
90-043729       535       0471927694
   *Optics.*

## QC358.5 Optics. Light — Popular works

**QC358.5.B68 1988**
**Bova, Ben,**
   The beauty of light / Ben Bova. New York : Wiley, c1988. xvi, 350 p.,
88-012228       535       0471625809
   *Light -- Popular works.*

**QC358.5.M5613 1993**
**Minnaert, M. G. J.**
   Light and color in the outdoors / Marcel Minnaert ; translated and revised by Len Seymour. New York : Springer-Verlag, c1993. xvi, 417 p.,
92-033748       535       0387979352
   *Light -- Popular works. Color -- Popular works.*

## QC369 Optics. Light — Handbooks, tables, formulas, etc.

**QC369.H35 1995**
Handbook of optics / sponsored by the Optical Society of America ; Michael Bass, editor in chief ... [et al.]. New York : McGraw-Hill, c1995. 2 v. :
94-019339          535          0070479747
*Optics -- Handbooks, manuals, etc. Optical instruments -- Handbooks, manuals, etc.*

## QC371 Optics. Light — General works, treatises, and textbooks

**QC371.L48**
**Levi, Leo,**
Applied optics; a guide to optical system design. New York, Wiley [1968]-c1980. 2 v.
67-029942          535/.33          0471050547
*Optics. Optical instruments.*

## QC373 Optics. Light — Special instruments, A-Z

**QC373.E4.H3 1966**
**Hall, Cecil Edwin,**
Introduction to electron microscopy [by] Cecil E. Hall. New York, McGraw-Hill [1966] ix, 397 p.
65027676          578.15
*Electron microscopy. Microscopy, Electron*

**QC373.E4.W5**
**Wischnitzer, Saul.**
Introduction to electron microscopy. New York, Pergamon Press, 1962. 132 p.
62-012626          578.15
*Electron microscopy.*

## QC381 Optics. Light — Geometrical optics — General works, treatises, and advanced textbooks

**QC381.M68 1997**
**Mouroulis, Pantazis.**
Geometrical optics and optical design / Pantazis Mouroulis, John Macdonald. New York ; Oxford University Press, 1997. xiv, 354 p. :
95-038009          535/.32          0195089316
*Geometrical optics. Optical instruments -- Design and construction.*

## QC383 Optics. Light — Geometrical optics — Mathematical theory

**QC383.K67 1991**
**Korsch, Dietrich.**
Reflective optics / Dietrich Korsch. Boston : Academic Press, c1991. xv, 358 p. :
90-047164          535/.323          0124211704
*Reflection (Physics) -- Mathematics. Imaging systems -- Mathematics. Mirrors -- Design and construction -- Mathematics.*

**QC383.O5**
**O'Neill, Edward L.**
Introduction to statistical optics. Reading, Mass., Addison-Wesley Pub. Co. [1963] 179 p.
63-010436          535.1
*Geometrical optics. Information theory.*

## QC385.2 Optics. Light — Geometrical optics — Lens and mirror systems

**QC385.2.D47.S53 1997**
**Shannon, Robert Rennie,**
The art and science of optical design / Robert R. Shannon. Cambridge, U.K. ; Cambridge University Press, 1997. xiv, 614 p. :
96-002867          681/.423          052145414X
*Lenses -- Design and construction.*

## QC395.2 Optics. Light — Physical optics — General works, treatises, and advanced textbooks

**QC395.2.S36 1998**
**Scott, Craig.**
Introduction to optics and optical imaging / Craig Scott. New York : IEEE Press, c1998. xiv, 386 p. :
97-023257          535/.2          078033440X
*Physical optics. Imaging systems.*

## QC401-403 Optics. Light — Physical optics — Theories of light

**QC401.G36**
**Garbuny, Max,**
Optical physics. New York, Academic Press, 1965. xiii, 466 p.
65-019999          535
*Physical optics.*

**QC401.S3**
**Sabra, A. I.**
Theories of light: from Descartes to Newton [by] A. I. Sabra. London, Oldbourne [1967] 363 p.
67-093509          535/.1
*Light.*

**QC403.B83 1989**
**Buchwald, Jed Z.**
  The rise of the wave theory of light : optical theory and experiment in the early nineteenth century / Jed Z. Buchwald. Chicago : University of Chicago Press, 1989. xxiv, 474 p.
88-018647            535/.13/09            0226078868
  *Light, Wave theory of -- History -- 19th century.*

## QC411 Optics. Light — Physical optics — Interference

**QC411.H35 1992**
**Hariharan, P.**
  Basics of interferometry / P. Hariharan. Boston : Academic Press, c1992. xvii, 213 p.
91-015685            681/.2            0123252180
  *Interferometry.*

## QC437 Optics. Light — Physical optics — Incidence

**QC437.B36**
**Bauman, R. P.**
  Absorption spectroscopy. New York, Wiley [1962] 611 p.
61-017353            535.84
  *Absorption spectra.*

## QC441 Optics. Light — Physical optics — Polarization

**QC441.P94 2001**
**Pye, J. D.**
  Polarised light in science and nature / J.D. Pye. Philadelphia, PA : Institute of Physics, 2001. p. cm.
00-054144            535.5/2            0750306734
  *Polarization (Light)*

**QC441.K55 1990**
**Kliger, David S.**
  Polarized light in optics and spectroscopy / David S. Kliger, James W. Lewis, Cora Einterz Randall. Boston : Academic Press, c1990. x, 304 p. :
89-017776            535.5/2            0124149758
  *Polarization (Light) Spectrum analysis.*

**QC441.S5 1964**
**Shurcliff, William A.**
  Polarized light [by] William A. Shurcliff and Stanley S. Ballard. Princeton, N.J., Published for the Commission on College Physics [1964] 144 p.
64-057904            535.5
  *Polarization (Light)*

## QC446.2 Optics. Light — Physical optics — Nonlinear optics. Quantum optics

**QC446.2.M34**
**Maitland, A.**
  Laser physics. By A. Maitland and M. H. Dunn. Amsterdam, North-Holland Pub. Co., 1969 [1970] xii, 413 p.
76-097205            535.5/8            0720401534
  *Lasers.*

## QC447 Optics. Light — Physical optics — Electronic optics

**QC447.C63 1950**
**Cosslett, V. E.**
  Introduction to electron optics; the production, propagation and focusing of electron beams / by V.E. Cosslett. Oxford, Clarendon Press, 1950. xiii, 293 p.
50012896            535
  *Electron optics.*

## QC450.3 Optics. Light — Spectroscopy — Dictionaries and encyclopedias

**QC450.3.E53 2000**
  Encyclopedia of spectroscopy and spectrometry / editor-in-chief, John C. Lindon ; editors, George E. Tranter, John L. Holmes. San Diego : Academic Press, c2000. 3 v. (lv, 258
98-087952            543/.0858/03            0122266811
  *Spectrum analysis -- Encyclopedias.*

## QC450.5 Optics. Light — Spectroscopy — Dictionaries and encyclopedias

**QC450.5.J33 2000**
**Jackson, Myles W.**
  Spectrum of belief : Joseph von Fraunhofer and the craft of precision optics / Myles W. Jackson. Cambridge, Mass. : MIT Press, 2000. x, 284 p. :
98-015177            509.43/09/034            0262100843
  *Fraunhofer, Joseph von, -- 1787-1826 -- Knowledge -- Optics. Spectrum analysis -- History. Physicists -- Germany -- Biography.*

## QC451 Optics. Light — Spectroscopy — General works, treatises, and textbooks

**QC451.A2**
  Advances in spectroscopy. New York, N.Y. : Interscience Publishers, 1959- 2 v. :
59-013796            535.8/4/05
  *Spectrum analysis.*

**QC451.E5**
  The Encyclopedia of spectroscopy. Edited by George L. Clark. New York, Reinhold Pub. Corp. [1960] xvi, 787 p.
60-053028            535.84082
  *Spectrum analysis -- Encyclopedias.*

## QC454 Optics. Light — Spectroscopy — Special types of spectra and spectroscopy, A-Z

**QC454.A25.G68 1999**
**Gove, H. E.**
From Hiroshima to the iceman : the development and applications of accelerator mass spectrometry / Harry E. Gove. Bristol, [England] ; Institute of Physics, c1999. xiv, 226 p. :
98-042786          543/.0873          0750305576
*Accelerator mass spectrometry -- History. Accelerator mass spectrometry -- Industrial applications.*

**QC454.A8.S85 1990**
**Svanberg, S.**
Atomic and molecular spectroscopy : basic aspects and practical applications / Sune Svanberg ; [guest editors, Arthur L. Schawlow, Koichi Shimoda]. Berlin ; Springer-Verlag, c1991. xi, 405 p. :
90-010207          539/.6          3540525947
*Atomic spectroscopy. Molecular spectroscopy.*

**QC454.C64**
**Condon, Edward Uhler,**
The theory of atomic spectra, by E.U. Condon ... and G.H. Shortley ... Cambridge [Eng.] The University Press, 1935. xiv, 441, [1]
35022624          535.84
*Spectrum analysis. Quantum theory.*

**QC454.M3.M39 1993**
**McLafferty, Fred W.**
Interpretation of mass spectra / F.W. McLafferty, Frantisek Turecek. Mill Valley, Calif. : University Science Books, c1993. xviii, 371 p.
92-082536          543/.0873          0935702253
*Mass spectrometry.*

## QC457 Optics. Light — Spectroscopy — Infrared spectrum

**QC457.B743**
**Brugel, Werner**
An introduction to infrared spectroscopy. Translated from the German original by A.R. Katritzky and A.J.D. Katritzky London, Methuen; [1962] 419 p.
62004995
*Infrared spectroscopy*

**QC457.N927 1997**
**Nyquist, Richard A.**
The handbook of infrared and Raman spectra of inorganic compounds and organic salts / Richard A. Nyquist, Curtis L. Putzig, and M. Anne Leugers. San Diego : Academic Press, c1997. 4 v. :
96-022175          543/.08583          0125234449
*Infrared spectra -- Tables. Raman effect -- Tables. Inorganic compounds -- Spectra -- Tables.*

## QC462.5 Optics. Light — Spectroscopy — Spectra of special substances

**QC462.5.H343 1991**
The Handbook of infrared and raman characteristic frequencies of organic molecules / Daimay Lin-Vien ... [et al.]. Boston : Academic Press, c1991. xvi, 503 p. :
91-008611          547.3/08583          0124511600
*Organic compounds -- Spectra. Molecular spectroscopy. Infrared spectroscopy.*

## QC475 Radiation physics — General works, treatises, and textbooks

**QC475.H43 1954**
**Heitler, Walter,**
The quantum theory of radiation. Oxford, Clarendon Press, 1954. 430 p.
55000535          535
*Radiation. Quantum theory.*

**QC475.H59 1993**
**Holmes-Siedle, A. G.**
Handbook of radiation effects / Andrew Holmes-Siedle and Len Adams. Oxford ; Oxford University Press, 1993. xxii, 479 p.
92-022567          620.1/1228          0198563477
*Radiation -- Handbooks, manuals, etc.*

## QC476 Radiation physics — Special topics, A-Z

**QC476.W38.B35 1992**
**Baierlein, Ralph.**
Newton to Einstein : the trail of light : an excursion to the wave-particle duality and the special theory of relativity / Ralph Baierlein. Cambridge [England] ; Cambridge University Press, 1992. xvi, 329 p. :
91-025083          535/.1          0521411718
*Wave-particle duality. Special relativity (Physics)*

## QC481 Radiation physics — X-rays. Roentgen rays — General works, treatises, and textbooks

**QC481.C475**
**Clark, George L.**
The encyclopedia of X-rays and gamma rays. New York, Reinhold Pub. Corp. [1963] xxvii, 1149 p
63-013449          537.535203
*X-rays -- Encyclopedias. Gamma rays -- Encyclopedias. Radiology -- Encyclopedias.*

**QC481.X24 1996**
X-rays : the first hundred years / edited by Alan Michette and Slawka Pfauntsch. Chichester ; John Wiley & Sons, c1996. xi, 262 p. :
96-027880          539.7/222          0471965022
*X-rays -- History.*

## QC482 Radiation physics — X-rays. Roentgen rays — Special topics, A-Z

**QC482.S6.A34**
**Agarwal, B. K.**
X-ray spectroscopy : an introduction / B. K. Agarwal. Berlin ; Springer-Verlag, 1979. xiii, 418 p.
79-000415          537.5/352          0387092684
*X-ray spectroscopy.*

## QC485 Radiation physics — Cosmic ray physics — General works, treatises, and textbooks

**QC485.F75 2000**
**Friedlander, Michael W.**
A thin cosmic rain : particles from outer space / Michael W. Friedlander. Cambridge, Mass. : Harvard University Press, c2000. 241 p. :
00-039594          539.7/223          0674002881
*Cosmic rays.*

**QC485.F75 1989**
**Friedlander, Michael W.**
Cosmic rays / Michael W. Friedlander. Cambridge, Mass. : Harvard University Press, 1989. 160 p. :
88-024371          539.7/223          0674174585
*Cosmic rays.*

## QC485.8 Radiation physics — Cosmic ray physics — Special topics, A-Z

**QC485.8.O7.L66**
**Longair, M. S.,**
High energy astrophysics : an informal introduction for students of physics and astronomy / M.S. Longair. Cambridge [England] ; Cambridge University Press, 1981. viii, 412 p.
81-007702          523.01/9          0521235138
*Cosmic rays. Nuclear astrophysics.*

# QC490-491 Radiation physics — Other radiations

**QC490.W4 1964**
**Wertheim, Gunther K.**
Mossbauer effect: principles and applications, by Gunther K. Wertheim. New York, Academic Press [1964] viii, 116 p.
64-024667          535.35
*Mossbauer effect.*

**QC491.G52**
**Gibb, T. C.**
Principles of Mossbauer spectroscopy / T. C. Gibb. London : Chapman and Hall ; 1976. 254 p. :
75025878          537.5/352          0470297433
*Mossbauer spectroscopy.*

## QC494.2 Radiation physics — Color — Dictionaries and encyclopedias

**QC494.2.H67 1990**
**Hope, Augustine.**
The color compendium / Augustine Hope, Margaret Walch ; introduction by Michel Pastoureau. New York : Van Nostrand Reinhold, c1990. xvi, 360 p. :
88-034339          701/.8          0442318456
*Color -- Encyclopedias.*

## QC495 Radiation physics — Color — General works, treatises, and advanced textbooks

**QC495.J79 1975**
**Judd, Deane Brewster,**
Color in business, science, and industry / Deane B. Judd and Gunter Wyszecki. New York : Wiley, [1975] xiii, 553 p.
75-006590          535.6          0471452122
*Color.*

**QC495.N35 1983**
**Nassau, Kurt.**
The physics and chemistry of color : the fifteen causes of color / Kurt Nassau. New York : Wiley, c1983. xx, 454 p., [
83-010580          535.6          0471867764
*Color. Chemistry, Physical and theoretical.*

**QC495.O6**
**Optical Society of America.**
The science of color. New York, Crowell [1953] xiii, 385 p.
52007039          535.6
*Color.*

**QC495.Z65 1999**
**Zollinger, Heinrich,**
Color : a multidisciplinary approach / Heinrich Zollinger. Zurich : Verlag Helvetica Chimica Acta ; c1999. x, 258 p. :
00-269806          3906390187
*Colors -- Analysis. Color vision. Colorimetry.*

## QC503 Electricity and magnetism — Electricity — Collected works (nonserial)

**QC503.F21 1965**
**Faraday, Michael,**
Experimental researches in electricity. New York, Dover Publications [1965] 3 v. in 2.
63-019490          537
*Electricity. Electricity -- Early works to 1850.*

## QC507 Electricity and magnetism — Electricity — History

**QC507.B73 1982**
**Bordeau, Sanford P.**
Volts to Hertz-- the rise of electricity : from the compass to the radio through the works of sixteen great men of science whose names are used in measuring electricity and magnetism / Sanford P. Bordeau. Minneapolis, Minn. : Burgess Pub. Co., c1982. ix, 308 p. :
82-017702      537/.09      0808749080
*Electricity -- History. Magnetism -- History. Physicists -- Biography.*

**QC507.R7**
**Roller, Duane Emerson,**
The development of the concept of electric charge; electricity from the Greeks to Coulomb, by Duane Roller and Duane H. D. Roller. Cambridge, Harvard University Press, 1954. iv, 97 p.
54011737      537.09
*Electric charge and distribution. Electricity -- History.*

## QC516 Electricity and magnetism — Electricity — Early works

**QC516.F85 1941**
**Franklin, Benjamin,**
Benjamin Franklin's Experiments; a new edition of Franklin's Experiments and observations on electricity. Edited, with a critical and historical introduction, by I. Bernard Cohen. Cambridge, Mass., Harvard University Press, 1941. xxviii, 453 p
41-4483      537
*Electricity -- Early works to 1850. Electricity -- History.*

## QC518-521 Electricity and magnetism — Electricity — General works, treatises, and advanced textbooks

**QC518.H27 1949**
**Harnwell, G. P.**
Principles of electricity and electromagnetism. New York, McGraw-Hill Book Co., 1949. xvi, 670 p.
49008683      537
*Electricity. Electromagnetism.*

**QC518.J43 1925**
**Jeans, James Hopwood,**
The mathematical theory of electricity and magnetism, by J.H. Jeans ... Cambridge [Eng.] The University Press, [1966, c1925] vii, [1], 652
27009321      537.1
*Electricity. Magnetism.*

**QC518.L313**
**Landau, L. D.**
Electrodynamics of continuous media, by L. D. Landau and E. M. Lifshitz. Translated from the Russian by J. B. Sykes and J. S. Bell. Oxford, Pergamon Press, 1960. 417 p.
60-014731      537.6
*Electromagnetic waves. Electrodynamics. Continuum mechanics.*

**QC518.S425**
**Scott, William T.**
The physics of electricity and magnetism. New York, Wiley [1959] 635 p.
59-005885      537
*Electricity. Magnetism.*

**QC521.L25**
**Langmuir, Robert V.**
Electromagnetic fields and waves. New York, McGraw-Hill, 1961. 227 p.
60-012774      537.12
*Electricity. Electromagnetism.*

## QC523 Electricity and magnetism — Electricity — Elementary textbooks

**QC523.K5**
**Kip, Arthur F.**
Fundamentals of electricity and magnetism. New York, McGraw-Hill, 1962. 406 p.
61-018259      537.2
*Electricity. Magnetism.*

## QC527 Electricity and magnetism — Electricity — Popular works

**QC527.A58 1991**
**Amdahl, Kenn.**
There are no electrons / by Kenn Amdahl. Arvada, Colo. : Clearwater Pub. Co., c1991. 322 p. :
91-203772      537      0962781592
*Electricity -- Popular works. Electricity -- Miscellanea. Electronics -- Popular works.*

## QC527.5 Electricity and magnetism — Electricity — Special aspects of the subject as whole

**QC527.5.M67 1998**
**Morus, Iwan Rhys,**
Frankenstein's children : electricity, exhibition, and experiment in early-nineteenth-century London / Iwan Rhys Morus. Princeton, N.J. : Princeton University Press, c1998. xiv, 324 p. :
98-009451      303.48/3      0691059527
*Electricity -- History -- 19th century. Electricity – Social aspects -- England -- London -- History -- 19th century. Electrification -- England -- London -- History -- 19th century.*

## QC535 Electricity and magnetism — Electricity — Electric measurements

**QC535.H35**
**Harris, Forest Klaire,**
Electrical measurements [by] Forest K. Harris. New York, Wiley [1952] 784 p.
51013122      621.37
*Electric measurements.*

## QC535.K45 1999
**Keithley, Joseph F.**
The story of electrical and magnetic measurements : from 500 B.C. to the 1940s / Joseph F. Keithley. New York : IEEE Press, c1999. xv, 240 p. :
98-039577        537/.028/7        0780311930
*Electric measurements -- History. Electric measurements -- Instruments -- History. Magnetic measurements -- History.*

### QC571 Electricity and magnetism — Electricity — Electrostatics. Frictional electricity

## QC571.C76 1986
**Crowley, Joseph M.**
Fundamentals of applied electrostatics / Joseph M. Crowley. New York : Wiley, c1986. xvi, 255 p. :
85-017793        537/.2        0471803189
*Electrostatics.*

## QC571.J65 1998
**Jonassen, Niels,**
Electrostatics / Niels Jonassen. New York : Chapman & Hall, 1998. p. cm.
96-029932        537/.2        0412128616
*Electrostatics.*

### QC601-612 Electricity and magnetism — Electricity — Electric current (General)

## QC601.C5
**Chance, Britton.**
Waveforms, edited by Britton Chance [and others, under the supervision of the] Office of Scientific Research and Development, National Defense Research Committee. New York, McGraw-Hill Book Co., 1949. xxii, 785 p.
49007723        537.5
*Electric circuits. Vacuum-tube circuits. Electric waves.*

## QC611.B64 1990
**Boer, K. W.**
Survey of semiconductor physics / Karl W. Boer. New York : Van Nostrand Reinhold, c1990-c1992. 2 v. :
89-021473        537.6/22        0442237936
*Semiconductors.*

## QC611.D85
**Dunlap, W. Crawford**
An introduction to semiconductors. New York, Wiley [1957] 417 p.
56-008961        537.22
*Semiconductors.*

## QC611.F72 1986
**Fraser, D. A.**
The physics of semiconductor devices / D.A. Fraser. Oxford [Oxfordshire] : Clarendon Press ; 1986. x, 196 p. :
86-005325        537.6/22        0198518668
*Semiconductors.*

## QC611.R86 1999
**Roulston, David J.**
An introduction to the physics of semiconductor devices / David J. Roulston. New York : Oxford University Press, 1999. xviii, 290 p.
97-052396        621.3815/2        0195114779
*Semiconductors.*

## QC611.S59 1978
**Smith, R. A.**
Semiconductors / R. A. Smith. Cambridge ; Cambridge University Press, 1978. xvii, 523 p.
77-028181        537.6/22        0521218241.
*Semiconductors.*

## QC611.Y88 1996
**Yu, Peter Y.,**
Fundamentals of semiconductors : physics and materials properties / Peter Y. Yu, Manuel Cardona. Berlin ; Springer, c1996. xiv, 617 p. :
95-044981        537.6/22        3540583076
*Semiconductors. Semiconductors -- Materials.*

## QC611.92.D34 1992
**Dahl, Per F.,**
Superconductivity : its historical roots and development from mercury to the ceramic oxides / Per Fridtjof Dahl. New York : American Institute of Physics, c1992. xiii, 406 p.
91-036487        537.6/23        0883188481
*Superconductivity.*

## QC611.92.H86 1989
**Hunt, V. Daniel.**
Superconductivity sourcebook / V. Daniel Hunt. New York : Wiley, c1989. x, 308 p. :
88-027676        621.3        0471617067
*Superconductivity.*

## QC611.92.V53 1993
**Vidali, Gianfranco.**
Superconductivity : the next revolution? / Gianfranco Vidali. Cambridge [England] ; Cambridge University Press, 1993. xii, 165 p. :
92-023185        537.6/23        0521373786
*Superconductivity.*

## QC611.98.H54.B87 1992
**Burns, Gerald,**
High-temperature superconductivity : an introduction / Gerald Burns. Boston : Academic Press, c1992. xiii, 199 p.
91-032808        537.6/23        0121460908
*High temperature superconductivity.*

## QC611.98.H54.N69 1997
**Nowotny, Helga.**
After the breakthrough : the emergence of high-temperature superconductivity as a research field / Helga Nowotny, Ulrike Felt. Cambridge ; Cambridge University Press, 1997. x, 210 p. :
96-012444        537.6/23/072        0521561248
*High temperature superconductivity -- Research -- History.*

**QC612.S8.L9 1969**
**Lynton, E. A.**
  Superconductivity [by] E. A. Lynton. London, Methuen, 1969. x, 219 p.
73-404530        537.6/23        0416117902
  *Superconductivity.*

**QC612.S8.R6 1969**
**Rose-Innes, Alistair Christopher.**
  Introduction to superconductivity, by A. C. Rose-Innes and E. H. Rhoderick. Oxford, Pergamon Press [1969] xvi, 228 p.
79-078591        537.6/23        0080134696
  *Superconductivity.*

### QC631 Electricity and magnetism — Electricity — Electrodynamics

**QC631.H72**
**Holt, Charles A.**
  Introduction to electromagnetic fields and waves. New York, Wiley [1963] 583 p.
63-011435        537.12
  *Electrodynamics. Electromagnetism.*

**QC631.W47 1997**
**Westgard, James B.**
  Electrodynamics : a concise introduction / James Blake Westgard. New York : Springer, c1997. ix, 435 p. ;
95-037687        530.1/41        0387945857
  *Electrodynamics.*

### QC661-673 Electricity and magnetism — Electricity — Electric oscillations. Electric waves

**QC661.C76 1995**
**Cronin, Nigel J.**
  Microwave and optical waveguides / Nigel J. Cronin. Bristol ; Institute of Physics Pub., c1995. xii, 119 p. :
95-134817        621.381/331        0750302151
  *Wave guides. Optical wave guides.*

**QC661.S74 1994**
**Staelin, David H.**
  Electromagnetic waves / David H. Staelin, Ann W. Morgenthaler, Jin Au Kong. Englewood Cliffs, N.J. : Prentice Hall, c1994. xi, 562 p. :
93-015705        539.2        0132258714
  *Electromagnetic waves. Electrodynamics.*

**QC665.E4.L3713 1975**
**Landau, L. D.**
  The classical theory of fields / L. D. Landau and E. M. Lifshitz ; translated from the Russian by Morton Hamermesh. Oxford ; Pergamon Press, 1975. xi, 402 p. :
75-004737        530.1/4        0080181767
  *Electromagnetic fields. Field theory (Physics)*

**QC665.E4.M38 1982**
**Maxwell, James Clerk,**
  A dynamical theory of the electromagnetic field / James Clerk Maxwell ; with an appreciation by Albert Einstein ; edited and introduced by Thomas F. Torrance. Edinburgh : Scottish Academic Press, c1982. xiii, 103 p.
83-140288        530.1/41        0707303249
  *Electromagnetic fields.*

**QC665.E4.S554 1997**
**Simpson, Thomas K.,**
  Maxwell on the electromagnetic field : a guided study / Thomas K. Simpson ; illustrations by Anne Farrell. New Brunswick, N.J. : Rutgers University Press, c1997. xxi, 440 p. :
96-008341        530.1/41        0813523621
  *Maxwell, James Clerk, -- 1831-1879. Mathematical physics. Electromagnetic fields.*

**QC670.B42**
**Becker, Richard,**
  Electromagnetic fields and interactions. Edited by Fritz Sauter. New York, Blaisdell Pub. Co. [1964- v.
64-007001        537.1
  *Electromagnetic fields. Electricity. Magnetism.*

**QC670.J63 1964**
**Jones, D. S.**
  The theory of electromagnetism. New York, Macmillan, 1964. xvi, 807 p.
62019277        537.12
  *Electromagnetic theory.*

**QC670.K694 1990**
**Kovetz, Attay.**
  The principles of electromagnetic theory / Attay Kovetz. Cambridge [England] ; Cambridge University Press, 1990. xvii, 221 p.
90-001375        530.1/41        0521391067
  *Electromagnetic theory.*

**QC670.L313 1962**
**Landau, L. D.**
  The classical theory of fields, by L. D. Landau and E. M. Lifshitz. Translated from the Russian by Morton Hamermesh. Oxford, Pergamon Press; 1962. 404 p.
62-009181        538.3
  *Electromagnetic theory. Field theory (Physics)*

**QC670.R4 1979**
**Reitz, John R.**
  Foundations of electromagnetic theory / John R. Reitz, Frederick J. Milford, Robert W. Christy. Reading, Mass. : Addison-Wesley, c1979. x, 534 p. :
78-018649        530.1/41        0201063328
  *Electromagnetic theory.*

**QC670.S48 1991**
**Siegel, Daniel M.**
  Innovation in Maxwell's electromagnetic theory : molecular vortices, displacement current, and light / Daniel M. Siegel. Cambridge [England] ; New York : 1991. x, 225 p. :
90-042511          530.1/41          0521353653
  *Electromagnetic theory. Physics -- History.*

**QC671.M36 1998**
**Mahajan, Virendra N.**
  Optical imaging aberrations / Virendra N. Mahajan. Bellingham, Wa. : SPIE Optical Engineering Press, 1998- v. 1 :
97-007721          621.36          081942515X
  *Aberration. Imaging systems. Geometrical optics.*

**QC673.W54 1983**
**Wilson, J.**
  Optoelectronics, an introduction / J. Wilson, J.F.B. Hawkes. Englewood Cliffs, N.J. : Prentice-Hall, c1983. xv, 445 p. :
82-016546          621.36          0136383955
  *Optoelectronics.*

## QC680 Electricity and magnetism — Electricity — Quantum electrodynamics

**QC680.C6413 1989**
**Cohen-Tannoudji, Claude,**
  Photons and atoms : introduction to quantum electrodynamics / Claude Cohen-Tannoudji, Jacques Dupont-Roc, Gilbert Grynberg. New York : Wiley, c1989. xviii, 468 p.
88-037845          537.6          0471845264
  *Quantum electrodynamics.*

**QC680.F313 1969**
**Fain, Benjamin,**
  Quantum electronics [by] V.M. Fain and Ya. I. Khanin. Translated by H.S.H. Massey. Edited by J.H. Sanders. Cambridge, Mass., M.I.T. Press [1969] 2 v.
68-023126          537.5          0080118208
  *Quantum electronics.*

**QC680.M55 1994**
**Miller, Arthur I.**
  Early quantum electrodynamics : a source book / Arthur I. Miller ; translations from the German by Walter Grant. Cambridge [England] ; Cambridge, 1994. xix, 265 p. ;
93-012774          537.6          0521431697
  *Quantum electrodynamics -- History.*

## QC688 Electricity and magnetism — Electricity — Quantum electronics

**QC688.H37 1998**
**Harbison, James P.**
  Lasers : harnessing the atom's light / James P. Harbison, Robert E. Nahory. New York : Scientific American Library : c1998. viii, 214 p.
97-040517          621.36/6          0716750813
  *Lasers.*

**QC688.M55 1988**
**Milonni, Peter W.**
  Lasers / Peter W. Milonni, Joseph H. Eberly. New York : Wiley, c1988. xvi, 731 p. :
87-026347          621.36/6          0471627313
  *Lasers.*

## QC711 Electricity and magnetism — Electricity — Electric discharge

**QC711.C5**
**Chandrasekhar, S.**
  Plasma physics; a course given at the University of Chicago. Notes compiled by S.K. Trehan. [Chicago] University of Chicago Press [1960] 217 p.
60-007234          537.532
  *Plasma (Ionized gases)*

**QC711.T5 1969**
**Thomson, J. J.**
  Conduction of electricity through gases, by J. J. Thomson and G. P. Thomson. New York, Dover Publications [1969] 2 v.
68-008881          537.5/32
  *Electric discharges through gases. Ionization of gases.*

## QC718 Electricity and magnetism — Electricity — Plasma physics. Ionized gases

**QC718.A713 1965**
**Artsimovich, L. A.**
  Elementary plasma physics [by] Lev A. Arzimovich. New York, Blaisdell Pub. Co. [1965] 188 p.
65-014569          537.532
  *Plasma (Ionized gases)*

**QC718.B45 1986**
**Bittencourt, J. A.**
  Fundamentals of plasma physics / by IA. Bittencourt. Oxford [Oxfordshire] ; Pergamon Press, 1986. xviii, 711 p.
86-003069          530.4/4          0080339247
  *Plasma (Ionized gases)*

**QC718.F713**
**Frank-Kamenetskii, D. A.**
  Plasma--the fourth state of matter [by] D. A. Frank-Kamenetskii. Translated from the Russian by Joseph Norwood, Jr. New York, Plenum Press, 1972. viii, 159 p.
71-165695          530.4/4          0306305232
  *Plasma (Ionized gases).*

**QC718.G63 1995**
**Goldston, R. J.**
  Introduction to plasma physics / Robert J. Goldston and Paul H. Rutherford. Bristol, UK ; Institute of Physics Pub., c1995. xvii, 491 p.
95-037117          530.4/4          0750303255
  *Plasma (Ionized gases)*

**QC718.S6 1962**
**Spitzer, Lyman,**
Physics of fully ionized gases. New York, Interscience Publishers, 1962. 170 p.
62-018100          537.532
*Plasma (Ionized gases)*

### QC721 Electricity and magnetism — Electricity — Physics of electrons, protons, and other particles

**QC721.A52**
**Anderson, David L.**
The discovery of the electron; the development of the atomic concept of electricity. Princeton, N.J., Published for the Commission on College Physics [1964] vi, 138 p.
64-000372
*Electrons. Electricity. X-rays.*

**QC721.F66**
**Foderaro, Anthony Harolde.**
The elements of neutron interaction theory. Cambridge, MIT Press [1971] xiv, 585 p.
79-103896          539.7/213          0262060337
*Neutrons -- Scattering.*

**QC721.G353**
**Gasiorowicz, Stephen.**
Elementary particle physics. New York, Wiley [1966] xx, 613 p.
66-017637
*Particles (Nuclear physics)*

**QC721.L64**
**Levi-Setti, Riccardo.**
Elementary particles. Chicago, University of Chicago Press [1963] 49, 103, 19 p
63022713          539.721
*Particles (Nuclear physics)*

**QC721.L725**
**Livingston, M. Stanley**
Particle physics; the high-energy frontier [by] M. Stanley Livingston. New York, McGraw-Hill [1968] ix, 230 p.
68-011615          539.7/21
*Particles (Nuclear physics)*

**QC721.L88**
**Lorentz, H. A.**
The theory of electrons and its applications to the phenomena of light and radiant heat; a course of lectures delivered in Columbia university, New York, in March and April 1906, by H.A. Lorentz ... Leipzig, B.G. Teubner; 1909. 2 p.l., 332 p
09-022739
*Electrons. Electromagnetic theory. Radiation.*

**QC721.M68 1963**
**Millikan, Robert Andrews,**
The electron, its isolation and measurement and the determination of some of its properties. Edited with an introd. by Jesse W.M. DuMond. Chicago, University of Chicago Press [1963, c1924] lxii, 268 p.
63-020910          539.7211
*Electrons.*

**QC721.M88 1965**
**Mott, N. F.**
The theory of atomic collisions, by N.F. Mott and H.S.W. Massey. Oxford, Clarendon Press, 1965. xxii, 858 p.
66-001351          539.7/54
*Collisions (Nuclear physics)*

**QC721.N4755**
**Newton, Roger G.**
Scattering theory of waves and particles [by] Roger G. Newton. New York, McGraw-Hill [1966] xviii, 681 p.
65-026485          539.72
*Scattering (Physics)*

**QC721.R94 1951**
**Rutherford, Ernest,**
Radiations from radioactive substances, by Sir Ernest Rutherford, James Chadwick, and C. D. Ellis. [Reprinted with corrections] Cambridge [Eng.] University Press, 1951. xi, 588 p.
51014724          539.7
*Radioactivity.*

**QC721.S4475**
**Segre, Emilio.**
Nuclei and particles; an introduction to nuclear and subnuclear physics. New York, W.A. Benjamin, 1964. xvi, 741 p.
64-021231          539.7
*Nuclear physics. Particles (Nuclear physics)*

### QC753-753.2 Electricity and magnetism — Magnetism — General works, treatises, and textbooks

**QC753.B32 1961**
**Bates, L. F.**
Modern magnetism. Cambridge [Eng.] University Press, 1961. 514 p.
61-065276          538
*Magnetism.*

**QC753.G36**
**Garrett, Charles Geoffrey Blythe,**
Magnetic cooling. Cambridge, Harvard University Press, 1954. 110 p.
53010474          536.56*
*Magnetism. Low temperature research.*

## QC753.M34
**Mattis, Daniel Charles,**

The theory of magnetism; an introduction to the study of cooperative phenomena [by] Daniel C. Mattis. New York, Harper & Row [1965] xvi, 303 p.
65-011138      537.1
*Magnetism.*

## QC753.2.B85 1986
**Burke, Harry E.**

Handbook of magnetic phenomena / Harry E. Burke. New York : Van Nostrand Reinhold, c1986. xix, 423 p. :
85-002409     538     0442211848
*Magnetism. Electronics.*

## QC753.2.C73 1995
**Craik, D. J.**

Magnetism : principles and applications / Derek Craik. Chichester ; Wiley, c1995. viii, 459 p.
93-038155     538     047192959X
*Magnetism.*

## QC753.2.J55 1990
**Jiles, David.**

Introduction to magnetism and magnetic materials / David Jiles. London ; Chapman and Hall, 1991. xxv, 440 p. :
90-041506     538     0412386402
*Magnetism. Magnetic materials.*

## QC753.5 Electricity and magnetism — Magnetism — Popular works

## QC753.5.V47 1993
**Verschuur, Gerrit L.,**

Hidden attraction : the history and mystery of magnetism / Gerrit L. Verschuur. New York : Oxford University Press, 1993. vii, 256 p. :
92-037690     538     0195064887
*Magnetism -- Popular works. Magnetism -- History -- Popular works. Physicists -- Popular works.*

## QC754.2 Electricity and magnetism — Magnetism — Special topics, A-Z

## QC754.2.M34.O32 1981
**O'Dell, T. H.**

Ferromagnetodynamics : the dynamics of magnetic bubbles, domains, and domain walls / T. H. O'Dell. New York : Wiley, c1981. vii, 230 p. :
80-025331     538/.44     0470270845
*Magnetic bubbles. Domain structure. Ferromagnetism.*

## QC757-757.9 Electricity and magnetism — Magnetism — Magnets

## QC757.L58 1996
**Livingston, James D.,**

Driving force : the natural magic of magnets / James D. Livingston. Cambridge, Mass. : Harvard University Press, 1996. xiv, 311 p. :
95-039595     538/.4     067421644X
*Magnets. Magnets -- Industrial applications.*

## QC757.9.C36 1994
**Campbell, Peter,**

Permanent magnet materials and their application / Peter Campbell. Cambridge [England] ; Cambridge University Press, 1994. x, 207 p. :
93-043324     621.34     0521249961
*Permanent magnets -- Design and construction. Magnetic materials.*

## QC760 Electricity and magnetism — Magnetism — Electro magnetism. Electromagnetics

## QC760.D33 2001
**De Wolf, David A.**

Essentials of electromagnetics for engineering / David A. de Wolf. Cambridge ; Cambridge University Press, 2001. xiv, 509 p. :
99-016730     537     0521662818
*Electromagnetism. Electronics. Electric engineering.*

## QC760.S24 2000
**Sadiku, Matthew N. O.**

Numerical techniques in electromagnetics / Matthew N.O. Sadiku. Boca Raton : CRC Press, 2000. xiv, 743 p. :
00-026823     537/.01/515     0849313953
*Electromagnetism. Electronics. Electric engineering.*

## QC760.S55 1969
**Slater, John Clarke,**

Electromagnetism, by John C. Slater and Nathaniel H. Frank. New York, Dover Publications [1969, c1947] xiii, 240 p.
69-017476     537     0486622630
*Electromagnetism.*

## QC762 Electricity and magnetism — Magnetism — Nuclear magnetism

## QC762.E53 1996
Encyclopedia of nuclear magnetic resonance / editors-in-chief, David M. Grant, Robin K. Harris. Chichester ; John Wiley, c1996. 8 v. (xii, 86
95-023825     538/.362     0471938718
*Nuclear magnetic resonance -- Encyclopedias.*

**QC762.H39 1993**
**Hennel, Jacek W.**
Fundamentals of nuclear magnetic resonance / Jacek W. Hennel and Jacek Klinowski. Harlow, Essex, England : Longman Scientific & Technical ; 1993. xi, 288 p. :
92-038043        538/.362        0582067030
*Nuclear magnetic resonance.*

### QC763 Electricity and magnetism — Magnetism — Paramagnetism

**QC763.W45 1994**
**Weil, John A.**
Electron paramagnetic resonance : elementary theory and practical applications / John A. Weil, James R. Bolton, John E. Wertz. New York : Wiley, c1994. xxi, 568 p. :
93-008498        543/.0877        0471572349
*Electron paramagnetic resonance spectroscopy.*

### QC770 Nuclear and particle physics. Atomic energy. Radioactivity — Societies, congresses, serial collections, yearbooks

**QC770.A5**
Annual review of nuclear science.  Palo Alto, Calif. [etc.] Annual Reviews. 27 v.
53-000995        539.1
*Nuclear physics -- Periodicals.  Nuclear energy -- Periodicals. Nuclear chemistry -- Periodicals.*

### QC772 Nuclear and particle physics. Atomic energy. Radioactivity — Dictionaries and encyclopedias

**QC772.D57 2001**
Dictionary of material science and high energy physics / edited by Dipak Basu. Boca Raton, Fla. : CRC Press, c2001. 346 p. :
00-051950        539/.03        0849328896
*Particles (Nuclear physics) -- Dictionaries.  Quantum theory – Dictionaries.  Materials -- Dictionaries.*

**QC772.A87 2000**
**Atkins, Stephen E.**
Historical encyclopedia of atomic energy / Stephen E. Atkins. Westport, Conn. : Greenwood Press, 2000. xii, 491 p. :
99-029618        333.792/4/03        0313304009
*Nuclear energy -- History -- Encyclopedias.*

### QC773-773.3 Nuclear and particle physics. Atomic energy. Radioactivity — History

**QC773.A1.C65**
**Compton, Arthur Holly,**
Atomic quest, a personal narrative.  New York, Oxford University Press, 1956. 370 p.
56-011114        623.451*
*Nuclear energy -- History. Atomic bomb.*

**QC773.A1.G7**
**Groves, Leslie R.,**
Now it can be told; the story of the Manhattan project. New York, Harper [1962] xiv, 464 p.
61-010208        623.45119
*Atomic bomb -- United States -- History.*

**QC773.A1.S47 1992**
**Serber, R.**
The Los Alamos primer : the first lectures on how to build an atomic bomb / Robert Serber ; annotated by Robert Serber ; edited with an introduction by Richard Rhodes. Berkeley : University of California Press, c1992. xxxiii, 98 p.
91-014068        623.4/5119        0520075765
*Atomic bomb -- United States -- History.  Physicists – Biography.*

**QC773.B66 1989**
**Boorse, Henry A.**
The atomic scientists : a biographical history / Henry A. Boorse, Lloyd Motz, and Jefferson Hane Weaver. New York : Wiley, c1989. vii, 472 p. :
88-035181        539/.09        0471504556
*Nuclear physics -- History.  Atomic theory -- History.*

**QC773.G6413 1990**
**Goldschmidt, Bertrand.**
Atomic rivals / Bertrand Goldschmidt ; translated by Georges M. Temmer. New Brunswick : Rutgers University Press, c1990. xvii, 372 p.,
89-010814        623.4/5119/09        0813515181
*Goldschmidt, Bertrand.    Atomic bomb -- History. Atomic bomb – France -- History.  Nuclear energy -- History.*

**QC773.J813**
**Jungk, Robert,**
Brighter than a thousand suns; a personal history of the atomic scientists. Translated by James Cleugh. New York, Harcourt Brace [1958] 369 p.
58-008581        539.76*
*Nuclear energy -- History. Atomic bomb -- History.*

**QC773.M54 1998**
**Mladenovic, Milorad,**
The defining years in nuclear physics, 1932-1960s / M. Mladjenivic. Bristol ; Institute of Physics Pub., c1998. xx, 441 p. :
98-023132        539.7/09        0750304723
*Nuclear physics -- History. Nuclear physics -- Instruments -- History. Nuclear models -- History.*

**QC773.P35 1991**
**Pais, Abraham,**
Niels Bohr's times : in physics, philosophy, and polity / Abraham Pais. Oxford : Clarendon Press ; 1991. xvii, 565 p.
90-027248        530/.092        0198520492
*Bohr, Niels Henrik David, -- 1885-1962.    Nuclear physics -- History.*

**QC773.R6**
**Romer, Alfred,**
The restless atom; [the awakening of nuclear physics. Garden City, N.Y., Anchor Books; available through Wesleyan Univers 1960. 198 p.
60-010681          539.7
*Nuclear physics. Atoms. Radiation.*

**QC773.3.U5.P53 2000**
**Palevsky, Mary,**
Atomic fragments : a daughter's questions / Mary Palevsky. Berkeley, Calif. : University of California Press, c2000. xiv, 289 p. :
99-087422          355.8/25119/0973
0520220552

**QC773.3.U5.A85 1998**
The atomic West / edited by Bruce Hevly and John M. Findlay. Seattle, Wash. : University of Washington Press, c1998. x, 286 p. ;
98-039504          363.17/99/0978          0295977493
*Atomic bomb -- West (U.S.) -- History. Nuclear energy – United States -- History. Nuclear energy -- United States -- Industrial applications -- History.*

**QC773.3.U5.C75 1993**
Critical assembly : a technical history of Los Alamos during the Oppenheimer years, 1943-1945 / Lillian Hoddeson ... [et al.] ; with contributions from Gordon Baym ... [et al.]. Cambridge [England] ; Cambridge University Press, c1993. xv, 509 p. :
92-036611          623.4/5119/0973          0521441323
*Atomic bomb -- New Mexico -- Los Alamos -- History.     Los Alamos (N. M.) -- History.*

**QC773.3.U5.D74 1993**
**Drell, Sidney D.**
In the shadow of the bomb : physics and arms control / Sidney D. Drell. New York, NY : American Institute of Physics, c1993. xx, 358 p. :
92-046573          327.1/74          1563960583
*Atomic bomb -- United States -- History. Nuclear arms control. National security -- United States. United States -- Military policy.*

**QC773.3.U5.H35 1997**
**Hales, Peter B.**
Atomic spaces : living on the Manhattan Project / Peter Bacon Hales. Urbana : University of Illinois Press, c1997. 447 p. :
97-004614          304.2          0252022963
*Atomic bomb -- United States -- History.*

**QC773.3.U5.M29 1995**
**Mason, Katrina R.**
Children of Los Alamos : an oral history of the town where the atomic age began / Katrina R. Mason. New York : Twayne Publishers ; c1995. xiv, 204 p.,
95-013825          623.4/5119          0805791388
*Atomic bomb -- New Mexico -- Los Alamos -- History. Children – New Mexico -- Los Alamos -- Biography.   Los Alamos (N.M.) -- Description and travel.*

## QC774 Nuclear and particle physics. Atomic energy. Radioactivity — Biography

**QC774.C43.B76 1997**
**Brown, Andrew P.**
The neutron and the bomb : a biography of Sir James Chadwick / Andrew Brown. Oxford ; Oxford University Press, 1997. xiv, 384 p.,
97-200691          530/.092          0198539924
*Chadwick, James, -- Sir, -- 1891-    Neutrons -- Research -- Great Britain -- History. Atomic bomb -- History. Nuclear physicists -- Great Britain -- Biography.*

**QC774.F4.F4**
**Fermi, Laura.**
Atoms in the family; my life with Enrico Fermi. [Chicago] University of Chicago Press [1954] 267 p.
54-012114          925.3
*Fermi, Enrico, -- 1901-1954.    Physicists -- Italy -- Biography.*

**QC774.G45.A3 1994**
**Gell-Mann, Murray.**
The quark and the jaguar : adventures in the simple and the complex / Murray Gell-Mann. New York : W.H. Freeman, c1994. xviii, 392 p.
94-001642          530          0716725819
*Gell-Mann, Murray -- Journeys -- Ecuador.    Particles (Nuclear physics) Nuclear physicists -- United States -- Biography.  Ecuador - - Description and travel.*

**QC774.M4.S56 1996**
**Sime, Ruth Lewin,**
Lise Meitner : a life in physics / Ruth Lewin Sime. Berkeley : University of California Press, c1996. xiii, 526 p.
95-035246          530/.092          0520089065
*Meitner, Lise, -- 1878-1968.    Women physicists -- Austria -- Biography.*

**QC774.O56.S32 2000**
**Schweber, S. S.**
In the shadow of the bomb : Bethe, Oppenheimer, and the moral responsibility of the scientist / S.S. Schweber. Princeton, NJ Princeton University Press, 2000. p. cm.
99-052225          172/.422          0691049890
*Oppenheimer, J. Robert, -- 1904-1967.  Bethe, Hans Albrecht, – 1906- Atomic bomb -- Moral and ethical aspects -- United States. Nuclear physicists -- United States -- Biography.*

## QC776 Nuclear and particle physics. Atomic energy. Radioactivity — General works, treatises, and advanced textbooks

**QC776.D37 1994**
**Das, Ashok,**
Introduction to nuclear and particle physics / Ashok Das, Thomas Ferbel. New York : J. Wiley, c1994. xvi, 327 p. :
93-019307          539.7          0471571326
*Nuclear physics. Particles (Nuclear physics)*

**QC776.G59 1991**
**Glashow, Sheldon L.**
The charm of physics / Sheldon L. Glashow. New York, NY : American Institute of Physics, c1991. xii, 306 p. :
90-024518      530      0883187086
*Nuclear physics. Astrophysics. Big bang theory.*

**QC776.G6 1967**
**Glasstone, Samuel,**
Sourcebook on atomic energy. Princeton, N.J., Van Nostrand [1967] vii, 883 p.
67-029947      539.7
*Nuclear energy.*

**QC776.M3**
**Marmier, Pierre,**
Physics of nuclei and particles [by] Pierre Marmier [and] Eric Sheldon. New York, Academic Press [1969- v.
68-014644      539.7
*Nuclear physics.*

## QC778 Nuclear and particle physics. Atomic energy. Radioactivity — Popular works

**QC778.A85 1980**
**Asimov, Isaac,**
Worlds within worlds : the story of nuclear energy / Isaac Asimov ; foreword by James Holahan. Seattle, Wash. : University Press of the Pacific ; c1980. 156 p. :
84-167298      539.7      0898750016
*Nuclear energy -- Popular works.*

**QC778.H5**
**Hill, Robert Dickson,**
Tracking down particles. New York, W. A. Benjamin, 1963. 196 p.
63011723      539.721
*Particles (Nuclear physics) Nuclear physics -- Popular works.*

## QC780 Nuclear and particle physics. Atomic energy. Radioactivity — Addresses, essays, lectures

**QC780.O6**
**Oppenheimer, J. Robert,**
The open mind; [lectures] New York, Simon and Schuster, 1955. 146 p.
55-010043      504
*Nuclear energy. Science.*

## QC782 Nuclear and particle physics. Atomic energy. Radioactivity — Special aspects of the subject as whole

**QC782.L3**
**Lang, Daniel.**
From Hiroshima to the moon; chronicles of life in the atomic age. New York, Simon and Schuster, 1959. 496 p.
59-013877      901.94
*Technology and civilization. Nuclear warfare – Moral and ethical aspects. Nuclear energy.*

## QC783 Nuclear and particle physics. Atomic energy. Radioactivity — Handbooks, tables, formulas, etc.

**QC783.F7**
**Frisch, Otto Robert,**
The nuclear handbook. With 22 specialist contributors. Princeton, N.J., Van Nostrand [1958] 1 v. (various
58-004687      539.702
*Nuclear physics -- Handbooks, manuals, etc. Nuclear engineering -- Handbooks, manuals, etc.*

## QC784 Nuclear and particle physics. Atomic energy. Radioactivity — Study and teaching. Research

**QC784.B4**
**Bederson, Benjamin.**
Atomic and electron physics: atomic interactions, edited by Benjamin Bederson [and] Wade L. Fite. New York, Academic Press, 1968. 2 v.
68-056970      539.7
*Nuclear physics -- Experiments.*

## QC786 Nuclear and particle physics. Atomic energy. Radioactivity — Instruments and apparatus — General works, treatises, and textbooks

**QC786.E54**
**England, J. B. A.**
Techniques in nuclear structure physics [by] J. B. A. England. New York, Wiley [1974- v.
74-008171      539.7/028      0470241616
*Nuclear physics -- Instruments.*

## QC787 Nuclear and particle physics. Atomic energy. Radioactivity — Instruments and apparatus — Other instruments, A-Z

**QC787.C6.G78 1996**
**Grupen, Claus.**
Particle detectors / Claus Grupen with the cooperation of Armin Bohrer and Ludek Smolik. Cambridge [England] ; Cambridge University Press, 1996. xiv, 455 p. :
95-018455          539.7/7          0521552168
*Nuclear counters.*

**QC787.S34.H36 1998**
Handbook of radioactivity analysis / Michael F. L'Annunziata ; with a foreword by Mohamed M. ElBaradei. San Diego : Academic Press, c1998. xxxviii, 771
98-084367          539.7/7          0124362559
*Liquid scintillation counting. Radioactivity -- Measurement.*

## QC789.2 Nuclear and particle physics. Atomic energy. Radioactivity — Nuclear fission

**QC789.2.D4.A27 1990**
**Aaserud, Finn.**
Redirecting science : Niels Bohr, philanthropy, and the rise of nuclear physics / Finn Aaserud. Cambridge ; Cambridge University Press, 1990. xiii, 356 p.
89-048317          539.7/0720489          0521353661
*Bohr, Niels Henrik David, -- 1885-1962.     Nuclear physics -- Research -- Denmark -- History.  Science and state -- Denmark -- History.  Research -- Denmark -- Finance -- History.*

**QC789.2.U62.A754 1997**
**Holl, Jack M.**
Argonne National Laboratory, 1946-96 / Jack M. Holl ; with the assistance of Richard G. Hewlett and Ruth R. Harris ; foreword by Alan Schriesheim. Urbana : University of Illinois Press, c1997. xxii, 644 p.
96-050031          621.042/07/277324          0252023412
*Argonne National Laboratory – History.*

**QC789.2.U62.B763 1999**
**Crease, Robert P.**
Making physics : a biography of Brookhaven National Laboratory, 1946-1972 / Robert P. Crease. Chicago : University of Chicago Press, 1999. xii, 434 p. :
98-030327          539.7/0720747/25
0226120171
*Nuclear physics -- Research -- New York (State) -- Upton -- History.*

**QC789.2.U62.L384 1989**
**Heilbron, J. L.**
Lawrence and his laboratory : a history of the Lawrence Berkeley Laboratory / J.L. Heilbron and Robert W. Seidel. Berkeley : University of California Press, c1989- v. 1   :
89-004820          539.7/0720794/67
0520064267
*Lawrence, Ernest Orlando, -- 1901-1958.     Physicists -- United States -- Biography.*

**QC789.2.U62.O257 1994**
**Johnson, Leland,**
Oak Ridge National Laboratory : the first fifty years / Leland Johnson, Daniel Schaffer. Knoxville : University of Tennessee Press, c1994. xv, 270 p. :
94-007667          621.042/0720768/73
0870498533
*Research institutes -- Tennessee -- Oak Ridge -- History. Physical laboratories -- Tennessee -- Oak Ridge -- History.*

**QC789.2.U62L677 1998**
**Shroyer, Jo Ann.**
Secret mesa : inside Los Alamos National Laboratory / Jo Ann Shroyer. New York : John Wiley & Sons, c1998. 230 p. :
620/.00720789/58 21          0471040630
*Los Alamos National Laboratory -- History.  Engineering laboratories -- New Mexico -- Los Alamos -- History.  Nuclear weapons – Research -- New Mexico -- Los Alamos -- History.*

## QC791.73-791.775 Nuclear and particle physics. Atomic energy. Radioactivity — Nuclear fusion — Controlled fusion

**QC791.73.B76 1982**
**Bromberg, Joan Lisa.**
Fusion : science, politics, and the invention of a new energy source / Joan Lisa Bromberg. Cambridge, Mass. : MIT Press, c1982. xxvi, 344 p.
82-010039          333.79/24          0262021803
*Controlled fusion.*

**QC791.73.F69 1997**
**Fowler, T. Kenneth.**
The fusion quest / T. Kenneth Fowler. Baltimore : Johns Hopkins University Press, 1997. xii, 250 p.,
96-034254          621.48/4          0801854563
*Controlled fusion.  Nuclear fusion.  Fusion reactors.*

**QC791.775.C64.C56 1991**
**Close, F. E.**
Too hot to handle : the race for cold fusion / Frank Close. Princeton, N.J. : Princeton University Press, c1991. 376 p. :
91-011727          539.7/64          0691085919
*Fleischman, Martin.  Pons, Stanley.   Cold fusion.  Cold fusion -- Research -- Utah.*

**QC791.775.C64.H85 1992**
**Huizenga, John R.**
Cold fusion : the scientific fiasco of the century / John R. Huizenga. Rochester, N.Y., U.S.A. : University of Rochester Press, 1992. xv, 259 p. :
91-047072          539.7/64          1878822071
*Cold fusion.*

## QC791.96 Nuclear and particle physics. Atomic energy. Radioactivity — Atomic energy — History

**QC791.96.C36 2000**
**Canaday, John,**
The nuclear muse : literature, physics, and the first atomic bombs / by John Canaday. Madison : University of Wisconsin Press, c2000. xviii, 310 p.
99-052229          355.8/25119          0299168506
*Nuclear energy -- History. Atomic bomb. Nuclear physics in literature.*

## QC792.4 Nuclear and particle physics. Atomic energy. Radioactivity — Atomic energy — Popular works

**QC792.4.G55 2001**
**Gilmore, Robert,**
The wizard of quarks : a fantasy of particle physics / Robert Gilmore. New York : Copernicus Books, c2001. xiii, 202 p.
00-059029          539.7/2          0387950710
*Particles (Nuclear physics) -- Popular works.*

## QC792.8 Nuclear and particle physics. Atomic energy. Radioactivity — Atomic energy — Laboratories

**QC792.8.U6.S264 1990**
**Furman, Necah Stewart.**
Sandia National Laboratories : the postwar decade / Necah Stewart Furman. Albuquerque : University of New Mexico Press, 1990. xxv, 858 p. :
89-016726          623.4/5119/072073
0826311733

## QC793 Nuclear and particle physics. Atomic energy. Radioactivity — Elementary particle physics — Societies, congresses, serial collections, yearbooks

**QC793.P358 1988**
Particle physics : a Los Alamos primer / edited by Necia Grant Cooper and Geoffrey B. West. Cambridge [Cambridgeshire] ; Cambridge University Press, 1988. xi, 199 p. :
87-010858          539.7/21          0521345421
*Particles (Nuclear physics)*

## QC793.16 Nuclear and particle physics. Atomic energy. Radioactivity — Elementary particle physics — History

**QC793.16.P53 1984**
**Pickering, Andrew.**
Constructing quarks : a sociological history of particle physics / Andrew Pickering. Chicago : University of Chicago Press, 1984. xi, 468 p. :
84-000235          539.7/21/09          0226667987
*Particles (Nuclear physics) -- History. Quarks -- History.*

## QC793.2 Nuclear and particle physics. Atomic energy. Radioactivity — Elementary particle physics — General works, treatises, and advanced textbooks

**QC793.2.C34 1989**
**Cahn, Robert N.**
The experimental foundations of particle physics / Robert N. Cahn and Gerson Goldhaber. Cambridge ; Cambridge University Press, 1989. x, 428 p. :
87-036751          539.7/21          0521332559
*Particles (Nuclear physics)*

**QC793.2.C56 1987**
**Close, F. E.**
The particle explosion / Frank Close, Michael Marten & Christine Sutton. New York : Oxford University Press, c1987. 239 p. :
86-012473          539.7/21          0198519656
*Particles (Nuclear physics)*

**QC793.2.G68 1984**
**Gottfried, Kurt.**
Concepts of particle physics / Kurt Gottfried, Victor F. Weisskopf. Oxford [Oxfordshire] : Clarendon Press ; 1984-1986. 2 v. :
83-017275          539.7/21          0195033922
*Particles (Nuclear physics)*

**QC793.2.G747 1998**
**Gribbin, John R.**
Q is for quantum : an encyclopedia of particle physics / John Gribbin ; edited by Mary Gribbin ; illustrations by Jonathan Gribbin ; timelines by Benjamin Gribbin. New York, NY : Free Press, c1998. 545 p. :
98-009918          539.7/03          068485578X
*Particles (Nuclear physics) -- Dictionaries. Particles (Nuclear physics) -- Popular works.*

**QC793.2.N3313 1990**
**Nachtmann, Otto.**
Elementary particle physics : concepts and phenomena / Otto Nachtmann ; translated by A. Lahee and W. Wetzel. Berlin ; Springer-Verlag, c1990. xix, 559 p. :
88-027328          539.7/21          0387516476
*Particles (Nuclear physics)*

**QC793.2.R64 1996**
**Roe, Byron P.**
Particle physics at the new millennium / Byron P. Roe. New York : Springer, c1996. xiii, 406 p.,
95-044879          539.7/2          0387946152
*Particles (Nuclear physics) Nuclear physics.*

**QC793.2.W44 1983**
**Weinberg, Steven,**
The discovery of subatomic particles / Steven Weinberg. New York : Scientific American Library, c1983. xiii, 206 p.
82-023157          539.7/21          0716714884
*Particles (Nuclear physics)*

## QC793.24 Nuclear and particle physics. Atomic energy. Radioactivity — Elementary particle physics — Elementary textbooks

**QC793.24.S34 1992**
**Schwarz, Cindy.**
A tour of the subatomic zoo : a guide to particle physics / Cindy Schwarz ; introduction by Sheldon Glashow. New York : American Institute of Physics, c1992. xiv, 112 p. :
92-012366        539.7        0883189542
*Particles (Nuclear physics)*

## QC793.27 Nuclear and particle physics. Atomic energy. Radioactivity — Elementary particle physics — Juvenile works

**QC793.27.F7 1997**
**Fraser, Gordon,**
The quark machines : how Europe fought the particle physics war / Gordon Fraser. Bristol ; Institute of Physics Pub., c1997. viii, 210 p.
97-014853        539.7/2        0750304472
*Particles (Nuclear physics)  Particles (Nuclear physics) -- Research.*

## QC793.28 Nuclear and particle physics. Atomic energy. Radioactivity — Elementary particle physics — Addresses, essays, lectures

**QC793.28.F49 1987**
**Feynman, Richard Phillips.**
Elementary particles and the laws of physics : the 1986 Dirac memorial lectures / Richard P. Feynman and Steven Weinberg ; lecture notes compiled by Richard MacKenzie and Paul Doust. Cambridge ; Cambridge University Press, 1987. x, 110 p. :
87-026362        539.7/21        0521340004
*Dirac, P. A. M. -- (Paul Adrien Maurice), -- 1902-  Quantum theory. Relativity (Physics)  Particles (Nuclear physics)*

## QC793.3 Nuclear and particle physics. Atomic energy. Radioactivity — Elementary particle physics — Special topics, A-Z

**QC793.3.B5.D38**
**Davies, P. C. W.**
The forces of nature / P. C. W. Davies. Cambridge ; Cambridge University Press, 1979. viii, 246 p.
78-072084        539.7        052122523X
*Nuclear forces (Physics)  Nuclear physics.*

**QC793.3.F5.M67 1983**
**Moriyasu, K.**
An elementary primer for gauge theory / K. Moriyasu. Singapore : World Scientific, c1983. xi, 177 p. :
84-147918        530.1/43        9971950944
*Gauge fields (Physics)*

**QC793.3.S9.F49 1997**
**Feynman, Richard Phillips.**
Six not-so-easy pieces : Einstein's relativity, symmetry, and space-time / Richard P. Feynman ; originally prepared for publication by Robert B. Leighton and Matthew Sands ; new introduction by Roger Penrose. Reading, Mass. : Addison-Wesley Pub., c1997. xxvii, 152 p.
96-047811        530.11        0201150255
*Symmetry (Physics)  Special relativity (Physics)  Space and time.*

## QC793.5 Nuclear and particle physics. Atomic energy. Radioactivity — Elementary particle physics — Special nuclear and subnuclear particles, antiparticles, and families of particles, A-Z

**QC793.5.B62.L43 1993**
**Lederman, Leon M.**
The God particle : if the universe is the answer, what is the question? / Leon Lederman with Dick Teresi. Boston : Houghton Mifflin, 1993. 434 p. :
92-043583        539.7/2        0395558492
*Higgs bosons.  Particles (Nuclear physics) -- Philosophy.  Matter - - Constitution.*

**QC793.5.B62.W37 1986**
**Watkins, Peter,**
Story of the W and Z / Peter Watkins. Cambridge [Cambridgeshire] ; Cambridge University Press, 1986. x, 240 p. :
85-017472        539.7/21        052126801X
*W bosons.  Z bosons.  Intermediate bosons.*

**QC793.5.E62.D34 1997**
**Dahl, Per F.,**
Flash of the cathode rays : a history of J.J. Thomson's electron / Per F. Dahl. Bristol ; Institute of Physics Pub., c1997. xvii, 526 p.
97-013642        539.7/2112/09        0750304537
*Thomson, J. J. -- (Joseph John), -- Sir, -- 1856-1940.  Cathode rays -- History.  Electrons -- History.*

**QC793.5.N42.S658 1997**
**Solomey, Nickolas.**
The elusive neutrino : a subatomic detective story / Nickolas Solomey. New York : Scientific American Library : c1997. viii, 206 p.
96-054844        539.7/215        0716750805
*Neutrinos -- History.  Particles (Nuclear physics)  Cosmology.*

**QC793.5.Q2522.H34 1984**
**Halzen, F.**
Quarks and leptons : an introductory course in modern particle physics / Francis Halzen, Alan D. Martin. New York : Wiley, c1984. xvi, 396 p. :
83-014649        539.7/21        0471887412
*Quarks.  Leptons (Nuclear physics)*

## QC794.6 Nuclear and particle physics. Atomic energy. Radioactivity — Nuclear interactions — Special topics, A-Z

**QC794.6.G7.L55 1993**
**Lindley, David,**
The end of physics : the myth of a unified theory / David Lindley. New York : BasicBooks, c1993. 275 p. ;
92-054524        539.7/2        0465015484
*Grand unified theories (Nuclear physics) Physics -- Philosophy.*

**QC794.6.S85.B75 1988**
**Brink, Lars,**
Principles of string theory / Lars Brink and Marc Henneaux. New York : Plenum Press, c1988. xiii, 297 p.
87-029815        530.1    0306426579
*String models.*

**QC794.6.S85.G75 1999**
**Greene, B.**
The elegant universe : superstrings, hidden dimensions, and the quest for the ultimate theory / Brian Greene. New York : W. W. Norton, c1999. xiii, 448 p.
98-025695        539.7/258        0393046885
*Superstring theories. Cosmology.*

## QC795 Nuclear and particle physics. Atomic energy. Radioactivity — Radioactivity and radioactive substances — General works, treatises, and textbooks

**QC795.T3 1957**
**Taylor, Denis.**
The measurement of radio isotopes.  London, Methuen; [1957] 132 p.
57004235        539.752*
*Radioactivity -- Measurement. Radioisotopes.*

**QC795.W24 1989**
**Wagner, Henry N.,**
Living with radiation : the risk, the promise / Henry N. Wagner, Jr. and Linda E. Ketchum. Baltimore : Johns Hopkins University Press, c1989. ix, 193 p. :
88-046063        363.1/79        0801837871
*Ionizing radiation. Nuclear energy.*

## QC795.5 Nuclear and particle physics. Atomic energy. Radioactivity — Radioactivity and radioactive substances — Instruments and apparatus (General)

**QC795.5.D45 1992**
**Delaney, C. F. G.**
Radiation detectors : physical principles and applications / C.F.G. Delaney and E.C. Finch. Oxford : Clarendon Press ; 1992. xii, 358 p. ;
92-249261        539.7/7        0198539231
*Radiation -- Instruments. Nuclear counters.*

## QC798 Nuclear and particle physics. Atomic energy. Radioactivity — Radioactivity and radioactive substances — Applications

**QC798.D3.L5 1955**
**Libby, Willard F.**
Radiocarbon dating.  [Chicago] University of Chicago Press, 1955. 175 p.
55-010246        539.752*
*Radiocarbon dating.*

## QC801 Geophysics. Cosmic physics — Societies, congresses, serial collections, yearbooks

**QC801.A283**
Advances in geophysics. New York, Academic Press, 1952- v.
52-012266        551.08
*Geophysics.*

## QC801.3 Geophysics. Cosmic physics — International Geophysical Committee. International Geophysical Year

**QC801.3.C45**
**Chapman, Sydney,**
IGY: year of discovery; the story of the International Geophysical Year.  Ann Arbor, University of Michigan Press [1959] 111 p.
59-009733        551.0621
*International Geophysical Year, 1957-1958.*

## QC801.9 Geophysics. Cosmic physics — Dictionaries and encyclopedias

**QC801.9.I5 1967**
International dictionary of geophysics; seismology, geomagnetism, aeronomy, oceanography, geodesy, gravity, marine geophysics, meteorology, the earth as a planet and its evolution. Editors: S. K. Runcorn [and others] With the editorial assistance of D. B. Stone. Oxford, Pergamon Press [1967] 2 v.
66-016369        551
*Geophysics -- Dictionaries.*

## QC806 Geophysics. Cosmic physics — General works, treatises, and textbooks

**QC806.B34 1958**
**Bates, David R.**
The earth and its atmosphere.  New York, Basic Books [1958] 324 p.
57-014982        551.082
*Geophysics. Meteorology.*

**QC806.S65 1977**
**Stacey, F. D.**
Physics of the earth / Frank D. Stacey. New York : Wiley, c1977. ix, 414 p. :
76-041891          551          0471819565
*Geophysics.*

# QC808.8 Geophysics. Cosmic physics — Handbooks, tables, formulas, etc.

**QC808.8.G56 1995**
Global earth physics : a handbook of physical constants / Thomas J. Ahrens, editor. Washington, D.C. : American Geophysical Union, c1995. vii, 376 p. :
94-044745          550          0875908519
*Geophysics -- Handbooks, manuals, etc. Physical constants -- Handbooks, manuals, etc.*

# QC809 Geophysics. Cosmic physics — Special topics, A-Z

**QC809.E2.M48 1983**
**Melchior, Paul J.**
The tides of the planet earth / by Paul Melchior. Oxford [Oxfordshire] ; Pergamon Press, 1983. xii, 641 p. :
82-016567          551.1/4          0080262481
*Earth tides.*

**QC809.E6.G55 1999**
Global energy and water cycles / edited by K.A. Browning and R.J. Gurney. Cambridge ; Cambridge University Press, 1999. xii, 292 p. :
98-004546          551.48          0521560578
*Hydrologic cycle. Energy budget (Geophysics)*

**QC809.M3.C65**
**Cowling, T. G.**
Magnetohydrodynamics.          New York,          Interscience Publishers, 1957. 115 p.
56-013149          537.5
*Magnetohydrodynamics.*

# QC815 Geomagnetism — General works, treatises, and textbooks — 1801-1969

**QC815.H4**
**Heiskanen, Weikko A.**
The earth and its gravity field [by] W.A. Heiskanen [and] F.A. Vening Meinesz. New York, McGraw-Hill, 1958. x, 470 p.
57-009439          538.7
*Geomagnetism.     Earth.*

# QC816 Geomagnetism — Special aspects of the subject as whole

**QC816.M47 1996**
**Merrill, Ronald T.**
The magnetic field of the earth : paleomagnetism, the core, and the deep mantle / Ronald T. Merrill, Michael W. McElhinny, Phillip L. McFadden. San Diego, Calif. : Academic Press, c1996. xiv, 531 p. :
96-028566          538/.72          0124912451
*Geomagnetism. Paleomagnetism. Dynamo theory (Cosmic physics)*

# QC852 Meteorology. Climatology — Collected works (nonserial)

**QC852.B65**
**Bolin, Bert,**
The atmosphere and the sea in motion; scientific contributions to the Rossby memorial volume. New York, Rockefeller Institute Press, 1959. 509 p.
59-014858          551.5082
*Rossby, Carl-Gustaf.     Meteorology. Oceanography.*

# QC854 Meteorology. Climatology — Dictionaries and encyclopedias

**QC854.E523 1996**
Encyclopedia of climate and weather / Stephen H. Schneider, editor in chief. New York : Oxford University Press, 1996. 2 v. (xvi, 92
95-031019          551.5/03          0195094859
*Climatology -- Encyclopedias. Weather -- Encyclopedias.*

# QC855 Meteorology. Climatology — History — General works

**QC855.H5**
**Heninger, S. K.**
A handbook of Renaissance meteorology, with particular reference to Elizabethan and Jacobean literature. Durham, N.C., Duke University Press, 1960. xii, 269 p.
59-014863          551.50942
*Meteorology -- History. Weather -- Folklore. English literature -- Early modern, 1500-1700 -- History and criticism.*

**QC855.W55 1998**
**Williams, James Thaxter.**
The history of weather / by James Thaxter Williams. Commack, N.Y. : Nova Science Publishers, 1998. p. cm.
98-040853          551.5/09          1560726229
*Meteorology -- History. Weather -- History.*

## QC857 Meteorology. Climatology — History — By region or country, A-Z

**QC857.G77**
**Jankovic, Vladimir,**
Reading the skies : a cultural history of English weather, 1650-1820 / Vladimir Jankovic. Chicago : University of Chicago Press, c2000. xiv, 272 p. :
00-053250          551.6942          0226392155
*Meteorology -- England -- History.   England -- Climate -- History.*

**QC857.U6.F54 1990**
**Fleming, James Rodger.**
Meteorology in America, 1800-1870 / James Rodger Fleming. Baltimore : Johns Hopkins University Press, c1990. xxii, 264 p.
90-030816          551.5/0973          0801839580
*Meteorology -- United States -- History.*

**QC857.U6.H56 no.1**
**Ludlum, David McWilliams,**
Early American hurricanes, 1492-1870. Boston, American Meteorological Society [c1963] xii, 198 p.
64000188          551.5520973
*Storms -- United States.   Meterology -- United States.   Weather.*

**QC857.U6.H56 no. 2**
**Ludlum, David McWilliams,**
Early American winters [by] David M. Ludlum. Boston, American Meteorological Society, 1966- v.
67-007551          551.6
*Winter -- United States.   Meteorology -- United States.*

**QC857.U6.H56 no. 4**
**Ludlum, David McWilliams,**
Early American tornadoes, 1586-1870 [by] David M. Ludlum. Boston, American Meteorological Society, 1970. 219 p.
72-023901          551.5/53/0973
*Tornadoes -- United States.*

## QC858 Meteorology. Climatology — Biography

**QC858.T48M38 1996**
**Mather, John Russell,**
The genius of C. Warren Thornthwaite, climatologist-geographer / by John R. Mather and Marie Sanderson. Norman : University of Oklahoma Press, c1996. xiv, 226 p. :
          551.6/092 B 20          0806127872
*Thornthwaite, C.W. (Charles Warren), 1899-1963.   Climatologists -- United States -- Biography.   Geographers -- United States -- Biography.*

## QC861 Meteorology. Climatology — General works, treatises, and advanced textbooks — 1801-1969

**QC861.B43**
**Berry, F. A.**
Handbook of meteorology, edited by F.A. Berry, jr. ... E. Bollay ... [and] Norman R. Beers ... New York, McGraw-Hill book company, inc., 1945. ix, 1068 p. i
45-010426          551.5
*Meteorology.*

**QC861.B9 1959**
**Byers, Horace Robert,**
General meteorology. New York, McGraw-Hill, 1959. 540 p.
58-059658          551.5
*Meteorology.   Meteorology in aeronautics.   Weather forecasting.*

**QC861.H8 1964**
**Humphreys, W. J.**
Physics of the air. With a new pref. by Julius London. New York, Dover Publications [1964] xvi, 676 p.
63-019493          551.5
*Meteorology.   Atmosphere.   Climatology.*

**QC861.P4 1969**
**Petterssen, Sverre,**
Introduction to meteorology. New York, McGraw-Hill [1968, c1969] xi, 333 p.
68-015476          551.5
*Meteorology.*

## QC861.2 Meteorology. Climatology — General works, treatises, and advanced textbooks — 1970-

**QC861.2.B465 1998**
**Beniston, Martin.**
From turbulence to climate : numerical investigations of the atmosphere with a hierarchy of models / Martin Beniston. Berlin ; Springer, c1998. x, 328 p. :
97-031666          551.55          3540634959
*Atmosphere -- Mathematical models.   Atmospheric turbulence -- Mathematical models.   Mesometeorology.*

**QC861.2.F57 1990**
**Firor, John.**
The changing atmosphere : a global challenge / John Firor. New Haven : Yale University Press, c1990. xii, 145 p. :
90-034518          363.73/92          0300033818
*Atmosphere.   Acid rain -- Environmental aspects.   Ozone layer depletion.*

**QC861.2.G64 1998**
**Gombosi, Tamas I.**
Physics of the space environment / Tamas I. Gombosi. Cambridge ; Cambridge University Press, 1998. xviii, 339 p.
97-051318          551.51/4          052159264X
*Atmospheric physics.   Space environment.   Atmosphere, Upper.*

**QC861.2.H63 1995**
**Hobbs, Peter Victor,**
   Basic physical chemistry for the atmospheric sciences / Peter V. Hobbs. Cambridge ; Cambridge University Press, 1995. x, 206 p. :
94-019216          551.5/11          0521479339
   *Atmospheric physics. Atmospheric chemistry. Chemistry, Physical and theoretical.*

**QC861.2.H68 1985**
**Houghton, Henry G.**
   Physical meteorology / Henry G. Houghton. Cambridge, Mass. : MIT Press, c1985. viii, 442 p.
84-012225          551.5          0262081466
   *Atmospheric physics.*

**QC861.2.T87 1996**
**Turekian, Karl K.**
   Global environmental change : past, present, and future / Karl K. Turekian. Upper Saddle River, NJ : Prentice Hall, c1996. viii, 200 p.
95-047832          363.7          013303447X
   *Atmospheric physics. Atmospheric chemistry. Global warming -- Environmental aspects. Earth (Planet) -- Environmental aspects.*

## QC863 Meteorology. Climatology — Elementary textbooks

**QC863.A596 2000**
**Andrews, David G.**
   An introduction to atmospheric physics / David G. Andrews. Cambridge, UK ; Cambridge University Press, 2000. x, 229 p. :
99-020191          551.51          0521620511
   *Climatology.*

**QC863.B55**
**Blumenstock, David I.**
   The ocean of air. New Brunswick, N.J., Rutgers University Press, 1959. 457 p.
59-007509          551.5
   *Meteorology. Weather.*

**QC863.D285**
**Day, John A.**
   The science of weather [by] John A. Day. Reading, Mass., Addison-Wesley Pub. Co. [1966] x, 214 p.
66-022573          551.5
   *Meteorology.*

**QC863.O7**
**Orr, Clyde.**
   Between earth and space. New York, Macmillan, 1959. 253 p.
59-005640          551.51
   *Atmosphere.*

**QC863.S346**
**Schaefer, Vincent J.**
   A field guide to the atmosphere / text and photos. by Vincent J. Schaefer and John A. Day ; drawings by Christy E. Day ; sponsored by the National Audubon Society and National Wildlife Federation. Boston : Houghton Mifflin, 1981. xx, 359 p., [
80-025473          551.5          0395240808
   *Atmosphere. Meteorology. Weather.*

## QC866.5 Meteorology. Climatology — Special topics, A-Z

**QC866.5.C65.U85 1990**
   Using meteorological information and products / edited by Avril Price-Budgen on behalf of World Meteorological Organization. New York : E. Horwood, 1990. 491 p. :
90-030886          551.5          0139469141
   *Meteorology -- Information services. Meteorological services.*

## QC875 Meteorology. Climatology — Meteorological stations and observatories. Weather services — General works

**QC875.U72.P557 1993**
**Smith, Phyllis,**
   Weather pioneers : the Signal Corps station at Pikes Peak / by Phyllis Smith. Athens, Ohio : Swallow Press, Ohio University Press, c1993. ix, 117 p. :
92-039291          551.65788/56          0804009694
   *Meteorological stations -- Colorado -- Pikes Peak -- History.*

## QC878 Meteorology. Climatology — Construction of weather maps, charts, etc.

**QC878.M59 1999**
**Monmonier, Mark S.**
   Air apparent : how meteorologists learned to map, predict, and dramatize weather / Mark Monmonier. Chicago, Ill. : University of Chicago Press, c1999. xiv, 309 p. :
98-025797          551.63/022/3          0226534227
   *Meteorology -- Charts, diagrams, etc. Weather forecasting -- Technique.*

## QC879 Meteorology. Climatology — Aeronomy. Upper atmosphere — General works, treatises, and textbooks

**QC879.H278 1992**
**Hargreaves, J. K.**
   The solar-terrestrial environment : an introduction to geospace--the science of the terrestrial upper atmosphere, ionosphere, and magnetosphere / J.K. Hargreaves. Cambridge [England] ; Cambridge University Press, 1992. xiv, 420 p. :
91-027182          551.5/14          0521327482
   *Atmosphere, Upper. Atmospheric physics. Magnetosphere.*

**QC879.R44 1989**
**Rees, M. H.**
Physics and chemistry of the upper atmosphere / M.H. Rees. Cambridge [Cambridgeshire] ; Cambridge University Press, 1989. ix, 289 p. :
88-009499          551.5/14          0521323053
*Atmosphere, Upper. Atmospheric physics. Atmospheric chemistry.*

## QC879.5 Meteorology. Climatology — Aeronomy. Upper atmosphere — Astronautics in meteorology

**QC879.5.B87 1990**
**Burroughs, William James.**
Watching the world's weather / William James Burroughs. Cambridge [England] ; Cambridge University Press, 1991. xi, 196 p. :
90-043348          551.6/3          0521343429
*Astronautics in meteorology. Meteorological satellites.*

## QC879.6 Meteorology. Climatology — Atmospheric chemistry — General works

**QC879.6.A85 1999**
Atmospheric chemistry and global change / edited by Guy P. Brasseur, John J. Orlando, Geoffrey S. Tyndall. New York : Oxford University Press, 1999. xviii, 654 p.
98-033483          551.51/1          0195105214
*Atmospheric chemistry.*

**QC879.6.F56 1986**
**Finlayson-Pitts, Barbara J.,**
Atmospheric chemistry : fundamentals and experimental techniques / Barbara J. Finlayson-Pitts, James N. Pitts, Jr. New York : Wiley, c1986. xxviii, 1098
85-022743          551.5/01/54          0471882275
*Atmospheric chemistry. Environmental chemistry.*

**QC879.6.F57 2000**
**Finlayson-Pitts, Barbara J.,**
Chemistry of the upper and lower atmosphere : theory, experiments, and applications / Barbara J. Finlayson-Pitts, James N. Pitts, Jr. San Diego : Academic Press, c2000. xxii, 969 p.
99-063218          551.51/1          012257060X
*Atmospheric chemistry.*

**QC879.6.H63 1984**
**Holland, Heinrich D.**
The chemical evolution of the atmosphere and oceans / Heinrich D. Holland. Princeton, N.J. : Princeton University Press, c1984. xii, 582 p. :
83-043077          551.5          0691083487
*Atmospheric chemistry. Chemical oceanography. Molecular evolution.*

**QC879.6.I55 1991**
The chemistry of the atmosphere : its impact on global change : perspectives and recommendations / John W. Birks, Jack G. Calvert, Robert E. Sievers, editors. Washington, DC : American Chemical Society, 1993. vi, 170 p. :
92-041499          551.5/11          084122532X
*Atmospheric chemistry -- Environmental aspects -- Congresses. Climatic changes -- Environmental aspects -- Congresses.*

**QC879.6.J33 1999**
**Jacob, Daniel J.,**
Introduction to atmospheric chemistry / Daniel J. Jacob. Princeton, N.J. : Princeton University Press, c1999. xii, 266 p. :
99-022318          551.51/1          0691001855
*Atmospheric chemistry.*

**QC879.6.S45 1998**
**Seinfeld, John H.**
Atmospheric chemistry and physics : from air pollution to climate change / John H. Seinfeld, Spyros N. Pandis. New York : Wiley, c1998. xxvii, 1326 p
97-007638          551.5/11          0471178152
*Atmospheric chemistry. Air -- Pollution -- Environmental aspects. Environmental chemistry.*

**QC879.6.W37 1988**
**Warneck, Peter.**
Chemistry of the natural atmosphere / Peter Warneck. San Diego : Academic Press, c1988. xiii, 757 p.
87-013337          551.5          0127356304
*Atmospheric chemistry.*

**QC879.6.W39 1990**
**Wayne, Richard P.**
Chemistry of atmospheres : an introduction to the chemistry of the atmospheres of earth, the planets, and their satellites / Richard P. Wayne. Oxford [England] : Clarendon Press ; 1991. xvi, 447 p. :
90-007858          551.5/11          0198555741
*Atmospheric chemistry. Planets -- Atmospheres.*

## QC879.7 Meteorology. Climatology — Atmospheric chemistry — Atmospheric ozone (General)

**QC879.7.D47 2000**
**Dessler, Andrew Emory.**
The chemistry and physics of stratospheric ozone / Andrew E. Dessler. San Diego : Academic Press, c2000. ix, 214 p. :
          0122120515
*Ozone layer depletion. Ozone layer. Atmospheric ozone.*

**QC879.7.L58 1994**
**Litfin, Karen.**
Ozone discourses : science and politics in global environmental cooperation / Karen T. Litfin. New York : Columbia University Press, c1994. 257 p. :
94-008867          363.73/84          0231081367
*Ozone layer depletion -- International cooperation. Environmental policy -- International cooperation. Science and state – International cooperation.*

**QC879.7.M34 1995**
**Makhijani, Arjun.**
    Mending the ozone hole : science, technology, and policy / Arjun Makhijani, Kevin R. Gurney. Cambridge, Mass. : MIT Press, c1995. xii, 355 p. :
95-011630            363.73/84            0262133083
    *Ozone layer depletion.*

**QC879.7.N55 1996**
**Nilsson, Annika.**
    Ultraviolet reflections : life under a thinning ozone layer / Annika Nilsson. Chichester ; Wiley, c1996. xii, 152 p. :
96-011463            363.73/84            0471958433
    *Ozone layer depletion. Ultraviolet radiation.*

**QC879.7.R684 1995**
**Rowlands, Ian H.**
    The politics of global atmospheric change / Ian H. Rowlands. Manchester ; Manchester University Press ; c1995. xxiv, 276 p.
94-031959            363.73/87            0719040949
    *Ozone layer depletion -- International cooperation. Climatic changes -- International cooperation. Nature -- Effect of human beings on -- International cooperation.*

**QC879.7.S66 1996**
**Somerville, Richard.**
    The forgiving air : understanding environmental change / Richard C.J. Somerville. Berkeley : University of California Press, c1996. xiv, 195 p. ;
95-018974            363.73/92            0520088905
    *Ozone layer depletion -- Environmental aspects. Climatic changes -- Environmental aspects. Greenhouse effect, Atmospheric -- Environmental aspects.*

## QC879.8 Meteorology. Climatology — Atmospheric chemistry — Atmospheric carbon dioxide

**QC879.8.C32 2000**
    The carbon cycle / edited by T.M.L. Wigley, D.S. Schimel. Cambridge ; Cambridge University Press, 2000. xvii, 292 p.
00-023735            551.51/12            0521583373
    *Atmospheric carbon dioxide -- Congresses. Carbon cycle (Biogeochemistry) -- Congresses.*

## QC880 Meteorology. Climatology — Dynamic meteorology — General works

**QC880.H65 1979**
**Holton, James R.**
    An introduction to dynamic meteorology / James R. Holton. New York : Academic Press, c1979. xii, 391 p. :
79-012918            551.5/153            0122543606
    *Dynamic meteorology.*

## QC880.4 Meteorology. Climatology — Dynamic meteorology — Special topics, A-Z

**QC880.4.A8.B47 1996**
**Berner, Elizabeth Kay,**
    Global environment : water, air, and geochemical cycles / Elizabeth Kay Berner, Robert A. Berner. Upper Saddle River, N.J. : Prentice Hall, c1996. xiv, 376 p. :
95-025174            551.5            0133011690
    *Atmospheric circulation. Atmospheric chemistry. Hydrologic cycle.*

**QC880.4.T5.B63 1998**
**Bohren, Craig F.,**
    Atmospheric thermodynamics / Craig F. Bohren, Bruce A. Albrecht. New York : Oxford University Press, 1998. xiv, 402 p. :
97-019688            551.5/22            0195099044
    *Atmospheric thermodynamics.*

## QC881.2 Meteorology. Climatology — Atmospheric shells (General) — Specific shells, A-Z

**QC881.2.O9.C48 2001**
**Christie, Maureen,**
    Ozone layer : a philosophy of science perspective / Maureen Christie. Cambridge, UK ; Cambridge University Press, 2001. xii, 215 p. :
00-036295            551.51/42            0521650720
    *Ozone layer. Science -- Philosophy.*

## QC883.2 Meteorology. Climatology — Cosmic relations — Special topics, A-Z

**QC883.2.C5.B87 1992**
**Burroughs, William James.**
    Weather cycles : real or imaginary / William James Burroughs. Cambridge ; Cambridge University Press, 1992. xiii, 201 p.
92-005296            551.5            0521381789
    *Meteorology -- Periodicity. Climatology.*

## QC884 Meteorology. Climatology — Paleoclimatology — General works

**QC884.A55 2000**
**Alley, Richard B.**
    The two-mile time machine : ice cores, abrupt climate change, and our future / Richard B. Alley. Princeton, N.J. : Princeton University Press, c2000. vii, 229 p. :
00-036730            551.6/09/01            0691004935
    *Paleoclimatology. Climatic changes. Ice – Greenland – Analysis.*

**QC884.B52 2000**
    Biotic response to global change : the last 145 million years / edited by Stephen J. Culver and Peter F. Rawson. New York : Cambridge University Press, 2000. xiii, 501 p.
99-016232            577.2/2            0521663040
    *Paleoclimatology. Climatic changes -- Environmental aspects.*

**QC884.B614 1999**
**Bradley, Raymond S.,**
Paleoclimatology : reconstructing climates of the quaternary / Raymond S. Bradley. San Diego, CA : Academic Press, 1999. xv, 613 p. :
98-083154          551.6/09/01          012124010X
*Paleoclimatology -- Quaternary. Geology, Stratigraphic -- Quaternary.*

**QC884.F69 1992**
**Frakes, Lawrence A.**
Climate modes of the phanerozoic : the history of the earth's climate over the past 600 million years / Lawrence A. Frakes, Jane E. Francis, Jozef I. Syktus. Cambridge ; Cambridge University Press, 1992. xi, 274 p. :
92-004727          551.6      0521366275
*Paleoclimatology. Paleontology. Historical geology.*

**QC884.N3**
**Nairn, A. E. M.,**
Descriptive palaeoclimatology.    New York, Interscience Publishers, 1961. xi, 380 p.
61-009063          551.50901
*Paleoclimatology.*

**QC884.W37 2000**
Warm climates in earth history / edited by Brian T. Huber, Kenneth G. MacLeod, Scott L. Wing. Cambridge [England] ; Cambridge University Press, 2000. xviii, 462 p.
98-051724          551.6/09/01          052164142X
*Paleoclimatology. Earth sciences.*

### QC912.3 Meteorology. Climatology — Temperature and radiation — Atmospheric radiation

**QC912.3.G75 1990**
**Gribbin, John R.**
Hothouse earth : the greenhouse effect and gaia / John Gribbin. New York : Grove Weidenfeld, 1990. 272 p. :
90-030871          363.73/87          0802113745
*Greenhouse effect, Atmospheric. Global warming. Atmospheric carbon dioxide -- Environmental aspects.*

**QC912.3.N55 1992**
**Nilsson, Annika.**
Greenhouse earth / Annika Nilsson. Chichester, West Sussex, England ; J. Wiley, 1992. xvi, 219 p. :
92-008327          574.5/222          0471935476
*Greenhouse effect, Atmospheric. Environmental protection.*

**QC912.3.O66 1990**
**Oppenheimer, Michael.**
Dead heat : the race against the greenhouse effect / Michael Oppenheimer, Robert H. Boyle. New York : Basic Books, c1990. xii, 268 p. ;
89-018532          363.73/87          0465098045
*Greenhouse effect, Atmospheric. Greenhouse effect, Atmospheric -- Social aspects. Environmental protection -- Economic aspects.*

### QC913.2 Meteorology. Climatology — Temperature and radiation — Atmospheric radioactivity

**QC913.2.R3.E35 1998**
**Edelstein, Michael R.**
Radon's deadly daughters : science, environmental policy, and the politics of risk / Michael R. Edelstein and William J. Makofske. Lanham : Rowman & Littlefield Publishers, c1998. xviii, 361 p.
96-035148          363.17/99          0847683338
*Atmospheric radon -- Government policy -- United States. Environmental policy -- United States.*

### QC921-921.6 Meteorology. Climatology — Aqueous vapor — Clouds

**QC921.S357**
**Scorer, R. S.**
Clouds of the world; a complete color encyclopedia, by Richard Scorer. [Harrisburg, Pa.] Stackpole Books [1972] 176 p.
72-001115          551.5/76          0811719618
*Clouds -- Atlases.*

**QC921.5.F55**
**Fletcher, Neville H.**
The physics of rainclouds. With an introductory chapter by P. Squires. And a foreword by E. G. Bowen. Cambridge [Eng.] University Press, 1962. 386 p.
62005557
*Cloud physics.*

**QC921.6.D95.C67 1989**
**Cotton, William R.,**
Storm and cloud dynamics / William R. Cotton, Richard A. Anthes. San Diego : Academic Press, c1989. xii, 883 p. :
88-008049          551.57/6          0121925307
*Clouds -- Dynamics. Cumulus. Precipitation (Meteorology)*

### QC929 Meteorology. Climatology — Aqueous vapor — Other topics, A-Z

**QC929.A8.M39 1993**
**McClung, David.**
The avalanche handbook / David McClung and Peter Schaerer. Seattle : Mountaineers, c1993. 271 p. :
93-002027          551.57/848          0898863643
*Avalanches -- Handbooks, manuals, etc.*

**QC929.D8.T3**
**Tannehill, Ivan Ray,**
Drought, its causes and effects, by Ivan Ray Tannehill. Princeton, N.J., Princeton University Press, 1947. xii, 264 p.
47002193          551.57
*Droughts. Dust storms.    United States -- Climate.*

**QC929.H1.F4**
**Flora, Snowden Dwight,**
  Hailstorms of the United States. Norman, University of Oklahoma Press [1956] xiii, 201 p.
56-011231          551.573
  *Hailstorms -- United States.*

### QC939 Meteorology. Climatology — Wind — Constant, local, and periodic winds, A-Z

**QC939.L37.S56 1994**
**Simpson, John E.,**
  Sea breeze and local winds / John E. Simpson. Cambridge ; Cambridge University Press, 1994. ix, 234 p. :
93-029979          551.5/185          0521452112
  *Sea breeze.*

### QC943.5-955.5 Meteorology. Climatology — Wind — Storms. Cyclones

**QC943.5.U6.S83 1982**
  Storm data for the United States, 1970-1974 : a quinquennial compilation of the U.S. Environmental Data Service's official monthly reports of storm activity logged by the National Weather Service wi  Detroit, Mich. : Gale Research Co., c1982. 884 p. ;
81013436          551.5/5/0973          0810311402
  *Storms -- United States.*

**QC944.F58 1999**
**Fitzpatrick, Patrick J.**
  Natural disasters, hurricanes : a reference handbook / Patrick J. Fitzpatrick. Santa Barbara, Calif. : ABC-CLIO, c1999. xx, 286 p. ;
99-040280          551.55/2          1576070719
  *Hurricanes.*

**QC944.L66 1998**
**Longshore, David.**
  Encyclopedia of hurricanes, typhoons, and cyclones / David Longshore. New York : Facts on File, c1998. 372 p. :
97-020860          551.55/2          0816033986
  *Hurricanes -- Encyclopedias. Typhoons -- Encyclopedias. Cyclones -- Encyclopedias.*

**QC945.B35 1998**
**Barnes, Jay.**
  Florida's hurricane history / Jay Barnes ; foreword by Neil Frank. Chapel Hill : University of North Carolina Press, c1998. x, 330 p. :
98-013012          551.55/2/09759          0807824437
  *Hurricanes -- Florida -- History.*

**QC945.B37 2001**
**Barnes, Jay,**
  North Carolina's hurricane history / Jay Barnes. 3rd ed. Chapel Hill : University of North Carolina Press, c2001. 319 p. :
          363.34/922/09756 21
*Hurricanes -- North Carolina -- History.*

**QC945.E46 1999**
**Elsner, James B.**
  Hurricanes of the North Atlantic : climate and society / James B. Elsner, A. Birol Kara. New York : Oxford University Press, 1999. xiv, 488 p. :
98-016652          551.55/2/091631          0195125088
  *Hurricanes -- North Atlantic Ocean Region. Hurricanes – United States. Hurricanes -- Social aspects.*

**QC945.P64 1997**
**Pielke, Roger A.,**
  Hurricanes : their nature and impacts on society / Roger A. Pielke, Jr. and Roger A. Pielke, Sr. Chichester ; Wiley, c1997. xviii, 279 p.
97-014116          363.34/922/0973          0471973548
  *Hurricanes -- Government policy -- United States. Hurricanes – Social aspects -- United States.*

**QC945.T82**
**Tannehill, Ivan Ray,**
  Hurricanes, their nature and history, particularly those of the West Indies and the southern coasts of the United States, by Ivan Ray Tannehill. Princeton, Princeton university press; 1938. x, 257 p.
38027260          551.55
  *Hurricanes.*

**QC955.B72 2001**
**Bradford, Marlene.**
  Scanning the skies : a history of tornado forecasting / Marlene Bradford. Norman : University of Oklahoma Press, c2001. xv, 220 p. :
00-059979          551.64/53/0973          0806133023
  *Tornadoes.*

**QC955.G74 2001**
**Grazulis, T. P.**
  The tornado : nature's ultimate windstorm / Thomas P. Grazulis. Norman : University of Oklahoma Press, c2001. xix, 324 p. :
00-032609          551.55/3          0806132582
  *Tornadoes -- United States. Weather forecasting -- United States. Tornado warning systems -- United States.*

**QC955.5.U6.F45 1992**
**Felknor, Peter S.**
  The tri-state tornado : the story of America's greatest tornado disaster / by Peter S. Felknor. Ames : Iowa State University Press, 1992. xvii, 131 p.
91-045860          551.55/3/0977          0813806232
  *Tornadoes -- Missouri -- History -- 20th century. Tornadoes -- Illinois -- History -- 20th century. Tornadoes -- Indiana – History – 20th century.*

## QC961 Meteorology. Climatology — Electrical phenomena in the atmosphere — General works, treatises, and textbooks

**QC961.C73 1982**
CRC handbook of atmospherics / editor, Hans Volland. Boca Raton, Fla. : CRC Press, c1982. 2 v. :
81-000674       551.5/6       0849332265
*Atmospherics.*

**QC961.M18 1998**
**MacGorman, D. R.**
The electrical nature of storms / Donald R. MacGorman, W. David Rust. New York : Oxford University Press, 1998. ix, 422 p. :
96-027498       551.5/6       0195073371
*Atmospheric electricity. Thunderstorms.*

## QC966 Meteorology. Climatology — Electrical phenomena in the atmosphere — Lightning (General)

**QC966.S55**
**Singer, Stanley,**
The nature of ball lightning. New York, Plenum Press, 1971. ix, 169 p.
70-128512       551.5/634       0306304945
*Ball lightning.*

**QC966.U4 1987**
**Uman, Martin A.**
The lightning discharge / Martin A. Uman. Orlando : Academic Press, 1987. xii, 377 p. :
86-025884       551.5/632       0127083502
*Lightning.*

## QC968 Meteorology. Climatology — Electrical phenomena in the atmosphere — Thunderstorms (General)

**QC968.T48 1981**
Thunderstorms--a social, scientific, & technological documentary / Edwin Kessler, editor. [Boulder, Colo.?] : U.S. Dept. of Commerce, National Oceanic and Atm 1981- v. 1 :
82-601021       363.3/492
*Thunderstorms -- United States. Thunderstorms – Social aspects - - United States.*

## QC971 Meteorology. Climatology — Auroras — General works, treatises, and textbooks

**QC971.D38 1992**
**Davis, T. Neil.**
The aurora watcher's handbook / Neil Davis. Fairbanks : University of Alaska Press, 1992. ix, 230 p. :
91-043080       538/.768       0912006595
*Auroras.*

**QC971.S28 1994**
**Savage, Candace Sherk,**
Aurora : the mysterious northern lights / Candace Savage. San Francisco : Sierra Club Books, c1994. 144 p. :
94-001458       538/.768       087156419X
*Auroras.*

## QC975.2 Meteorology. Climatology — Meteorological optics — General works, treatises, and textbooks

**QC975.2.G73**
**Greenler, Robert,**
Rainbows, halos, and glories / Robert Greenler. Cambridge ; Cambridge University Press, 1980. x, 195 p., [1
80-014722       551.5/6       0521236053
*Meteorological optics. Rainbow. Halos (Meteorology)*

## QC976 Meteorology. Climatology — Meteorological optics — Special topics, A-Z

**QC976.H15.T36 1994**
**Tape, Walter.**
Atmospheric halos / by Walter Tape. Washington, D.C. : American Geophysical Union, 1994. 143 p. :
93-029785       551.5/67       0875908349
*Halos (Meteorology)*

## QC981 Meteorology. Climatology — Climatology and weather — General works, treatises, and textbooks

**QC981.B33 1985**
**Battan, Louis J.**
Weather / Louis J. Battan. Englewood Cliffs, N.J. : Prentice-Hall, c1985. 135 p. :
84-017844       551.5       0139476989
*Weather.*

**QC981.C72 1995**
**Cotton, William R.,**
Human impacts on weather and climate / William R. Cotton, Roger A. Pielke. Cambridge ; Cambridge University Press, 1995. viii, 288 p.
94-045988       551.6       0521499291
*Climatology -- Social aspects. Weather -- Social aspects. Nature - - Effect of human beings on.*

**QC981.H3**
**Hare, F. Kenneth**
The restless atmosphere. London, New York, [1953] viii, 192 p.
53011610       551.5
*Climatology.*

**QC981.K4 1961**
**Kendrew, W. G.**
  The climates of the continents. Oxford, Clarendon Press, 1961. 608 p.
61-019753          551.59
  *Climatology.*

**QC981.L27**
**Lamb, H. H.**
  The changing climate: selected papers, by H. H. Lamb. London, Methuen, 1966. iii-xi, 236 p
66-068388          551.6
  *Climatology -- Addresses, essays, lectures.*

**QC981.L277 1995**
**Lamb, H. H.**
  Climate, history, and the modern world / H.H. Lamb. London ; Routledge, 1995. xxiv, 433 p.
94-044666          551.6          0415127343
  *Climatology.*

**QC981.M43**
**Mather, John Russell,**
  Climatology: fundamentals and applications [by] John R. Mather. New York, McGraw-Hill [1974] xiii, 412 p.
73-023082          551.5          0070408912
  *Climatology. Climate. Weather.*

**QC981.P434 1991**
**Peixoto, Jose Pinto.**
  Physics of climate / Jose P. Peixoto and Abraham H. Oort ; foreword by Edward N. Lorenz. New York : American Institute of Physics, c1992. xxxix, 520 p.
91-011565          551.5          0883187116
  *Climatology. Dynamic meteorology. Atmospheric physics.*

**QC981.S5**
**Shapley, Harlow.**
  Climatic change: evidence, causes, and effects. Contributors: Harlow Shapley [and others] Cambridge, Harvard University Press, c1953. xii, 318 p.
53009041          551.59*
  *Climatology.*

**QC981.T65 1980**
**Trewartha, Glenn Thomas,**
  An introduction to climate / Glenn T. Trewartha, Lyle H. Horn ; cartography by Randall D. Sale. New York : McGraw-Hill, c1980. xii, 416 p. :
79-014203          551.5          0070651523
  *Climatology. Weather.*

**QC981.W67 vol. 14**
  Climates of the Polar Regions; edited by S. Orvig. Amsterdam, Elsevier Pub. Co., 1970. x, 370 p.
75-103355          551.6/9/98          0444408282
  *Polar regions -- Climate.*

**QC981.4 Meteorology. Climatology — Climatology and weather — Addresses, essays, lectures**

**QC981.4.L36 1988**
**Lamb, H. H.**
  Weather, climate & human affairs : a book of essays and other papers / Hubert H. Lamb. London ; Routledge, 1988. xiv, 364 p. :
87-015347          551.6          0415006740
  *Climatology. Human beings -- Effect of climate on.*

**QC981.7 Meteorology. Climatology — Climatology and weather — Special types of climatology, A-Z**

**QC981.7.M5.O34 1978**
**Oke, T. R.**
  Boundary layer climates / T. R. Oke. London : Methuen ; 1978. xxi, 372 p. :
77-025266          551.6/6          0470993642.
  *Microclimatology. Boundary layer (Meteorology)*

**QC981.7.U7.L36**
**Landsberg, Helmut Erich,**
  The urban climate / Helmut E. Landsberg. New York : Academic Press, 1981. x, 275 p. :
80-002766          551.5/09173/2          0124359604
  *Urban climatology.*

**QC981.8 Meteorology. Climatology — Climatology and weather — Special topics, A-Z**

**QC981.8.C5.G666 2001**
  The no-nonsense guide to climate change / edited by Dinyar Godrej. London, Eng. : Verso, 2001. 143 p. :
          551.6          1859843352
  *Climatic changes. Global environmental change. Glaciers -- Environmental aspects.*

**QC981.8.C5.B35 1992**
**Balling, Robert C.**
  The heated debate : greenhouse predictions verus climate reality / by Robert C. Balling, Jr. ; introduction by Aaron Wildavsky. San Francisco, Calif. : Pacific Research Institute for Public Policy, c1992. 195 p. :
91-029747          551.6          0936488476
  *Climatic changes. Greenhouse gases -- Environmental aspects.*

**QC981.8.C5.B76 1997**
**Bryant, Edward**
  Climate process & change / Edward Bryant. Cambridge ; Cambridge University Press, 1997. xvi, 209 p. :
97-003764          551.6          0521481899
  *Climatic changes. Climatology.*

**QC981.8.C5.B8313 1982**
**Budyko, M. I.**
The Earth's climate, past and future / M.I. Budyko ; translated by the author. New York : Academic Press, 1982. x, 307 p. :
81-017673          551.6          0121394603
*Climatic changes. Nature -- Effect of human beings on.*

**QC981.8.C5.F45 1998**
**Fleming, James Rodger.**
Historical perspectives on climate change / James Rodger Fleming. New York : Oxford University Press, 1998. xi, 194 p. :
97-022545          306.4/5          0195078705
*Climatic changes -- Europe -- History. Climatic changes – United States -- History. Global environmental change -- History.*

**QC981.8.C5.N35 1990**
**National Research Council (U.S.).**
Confronting climate change : strategies for energy research and development / Committee on Alternative Energy Research and Development Strategies, Energy Engineering Board, Commission on Engineering and Technical Systems, National Research Council. Washington, D.C. : National Academy Press, 1990. xv, 127 p. :
90-062882          363.73/87          0309043476
*Climatic changes -- Government policy -- United States. Greenhouse gases -- Environmental aspects. Greenhouse effect, Atmospheric -- Environmental aspects.*

**QC981.8.C5.N66 1994**
**Nordhaus, William D.**
Managing the global commons : the economics of climate change / William D. Nordhaus. Cambridge, Mass. : MIT Press, c1994. x, 213 p. :
94-003992          363.73/87          0262140551
*Climatic changes -- Economic aspects. Climatic changes -- Mathematical models. Global warming -- Economic aspects.*

**QC981.8.G56.D73 2000**
**Drake, Frances.**
Global warming : the science of climate change / Frances Drake. London : Arnold ; 2000. xii, 273 p. :
00-711952          363.738/74          0340653019
*Greenhouse effect, Atmospheric- -- Dictionaries. English language- -- Dictionaries. Global warming- -- Dictionaries- -- French.*

**QC981.8.G56**
**Victor, David G.**
The collapse of the Kyoto Protocol and the struggle to slow global warming / David G. Victor. Princeton : Princeton University Press, c2001. xiv, 178 p. :
00-051633          363.738/74526          0691088705
*Greenhouse gas mitigation -- Government policy. Global warming -- Government policy.*

**QC981.8.G56.B44 1992**
**Benarde, Melvin A.**
Global warning-- global warming / Melvin A. Benarde. New York : Wiley, c1992. xi, 317 p., [
91-022276          363.73/87          0471513237
*Global warming. Climatic changes.*

**QC981.8.G56.B47 1995**
Biotic feedbacks in the global climatic system : will the warming feed the warming? / edited by George M. Woodwell, Fred T. Mackenzie. New York : Oxford University Press, 1995. xv, 416 p., [
94-007773          551.5          0195086406
*Global warming. Climatic changes. Ecosystem management.*

**QC981.8.G56.C48 1999**
**Christianson, Gale E.**
Greenhouse : the 200-year story of global warming / Gale E. Christianson. New York : Walker and Company, 1999. xiii, 305 p.
98-055251          363.738/74          0802713467
*Global warming -- History.*

**QC981.8.G56.G45 1998**
**Gelbspan, Ross.**
The heat is on : the climate crisis, the cover-up, the prescription / Ross Gelbspan. Reading, Mass. : Perseus Books, c1998. viii, 278 p.
98-086419          363.738/74          0738200255
*Global warming -- Government policy. Energy industries -- Political activity. Greenhouse effect, Atmospheric -- Government policy.*

**QC981.8.G56.G58195 1992**
Global warming : physics and facts : Washington, D.C., 1991 / editors, Barbara Goss Levi, David Hafemeister, Richard Scribner. New York : American Institute of Physics, c1992. xvi, 311 p. :
91-078423          551.5          0883189321
*Global warming.*

**QC981.8.G56.H68 1997**
**Houghton, John Theodore.**
Global warming : the complete briefing / John Houghton. Cambridge ; Cambridge University Press, 1997. xv, 251 p. :
97-016353          363.738/74          0521620899
*Global warming. Climatic changes.*

**QC981.8.G56.P39 1995**
**Parsons, M. L.**
Global warming : the truth behind the myth / Michael L. Parsons. New York : Insight Books, c1995. xvi, 271 p. :
95-024650          363.73/87          0306450836
*Global warming -- Mathematical models. Greenhouse gases – Mathematical models. Climatic changes -- Mathematical models.*

**QC981.8.G56.P48 1998**
**Philander, S. George.**
Is the temperature rising? : the uncertain science of global warming / S. George Philander. Princeton, N.J. : Princeton University Press, c1998. xv, 262 p. :
97-037613          551.5/2          0691057753
*Global warming. Environmental sciences -- Philosophy. Human ecology.*

## QC981.8.G56.S3 1989
**Schneider, Stephen Henry.**

Global warming : are we entering the greenhouse century? / Stephen H. Schneider. San Francisco, : Sierra Club Books, c1989. xiv, 317 p. :

89-006048          363.7/3922          0871566931

*Global warming. Greenhouse effect, Atmospheric. Climatic changes.*

## QC982-993.6 Meteorology. Climatology — Climatology and weather — Geographic divisions

## QC982.P43
**Pearce, E. A.**

The Times Books world weather guide / by E.A. Pearce and Gordon Smith. New York : Times Books/Random House, 1990. p. cm.

90-050319          551.6          0812918819

*Climatology -- Handbooks, manuals, etc. Travel -- Guidebooks.*

## QC983.C56 1985

Climates of the states : National Oceanic and Atmospheric Administration narrative summaries, tables, and maps for each state, with overview of state climatologist programs / new material by James A. Ruffner. Detroit, Mich. : Gale Research Co., c1985. v. 1   :

85-025271          551.6973          0810310422

*United States -- Climate -- Charts, diagrams, etc.*

## QC983.M455 2000
**Meyer, William B.**

Americans and their weather / William B. Meyer. Oxford ; Oxford University Press, 2000. viii, 278 p.

99-033193          304.2/5/0973          0195131827

*Climatology -- Social aspects. Weather -- Social aspects. Nature -- Effect of human beings on. United States -- Climate -- Social aspects.*

## QC983.W38

The Weather almanac. Detroit : Gale Research Co., c1974-
v. :

81-644322          551.6973

*Air quality -- United States -- Handbooks, manuals, etc. United States -- Climate -- Handbooks, manuals, etc.*

## QC983.W393 1987

Weather of U.S. cities / James A. Ruffner and Frank E. Bair, editors. Detroit, Mich. : Gale Research Co., c1987. v. 1-2   ;

87-011869          551.6973          0810321025

*Urban climatology -- United States -- Handbooks, manuals, etc. United States -- Climate -- Handbooks, manuals, etc.*

## QC989.A1
**Fagan, Brian M.**

The Little Ice Age : how climate made history, 1300-1850 / Brian Fagan. New York, NY : Basic Books, c2000. xxi, 246 p. :

00-048627          551.694          0465022715

*Climatic changes -- Europe -- History.*

## QC993.6.W48 2000
**Whiteman, C. D.**

Mountain meteorology : fundamentals and applications / C. David Whiteman. New York : Oxford University Press, 2000. xiii, 355 p.

99-024940          551.6914/3          0195132718

*Mountain climate.*

## QC995 Meteorology. Climatology — Climatology and weather — Weather forecasting

## QC995.F55 1994
**Fishman, Jack,**

The weather revolution : innovations and imminent breakthroughs in accurate forecasting / Jack Fishman and Robert Kalish. New York : Plenum Press, c1994. xiv, 276 p. :

94-025380          551.6/3          0306447649

*Weather forecasting.*

## QC995.I43 1995

Images in weather forecasting : a practical guide for interpreting satellite and radar imagery / edited by M.J. Bader ... [et al.] ; foreword by K.A. Browning. Cambridge ; Cambridge University Press, 1995. xxiii, 499 p.

95-018308          551.6/3          0521451116

*Weather forecasting -- Remote-sensing maps -- Handbooks, manuals, etc. Satellite meterology -- Remote-sensing maps -- Handbooks, manuals, etc. Radar meteorology – Remote-sensing maps -- Handbooks, manuals, etc.*

## QC995.P52
**Petterssen, Sverre,**

Weather analysis and forecasting. New York, McGraw-Hill, 1956. 2 v.

55-011568          551.5

*Meteorology. Weather forecasting.*

# QD Chemistry

# QD1 Societies, congresses, serial collections, yearbooks

## QD1.A355 no. 225

Archaeological wood : properties, chemistry, and preservation / Roger M. Rowell, editor, R. James Barbour, editor. Washington, DC : American Chemical Society, 1990. xii, 472 p. :

89-039451          540 s          0841216231

*Wood -- Chemistry. Wood -- Preservation. Archaeological chemistry.*

## QD1.A355 no. 237
**American Chemical Society.**

Environmental chemistry of lakes and reservoirs / Lawrence A. Baker, editor. Washington, DC : American Chemical Society, 1994. xii, 627 p. :

93-031891          551.48/2          0841225265

*Limnology -- Congresses. Biogeochemical cycles -- Congresses. Environmental chemistry -- Congresses.*

**QD1.A355 no. 241**
**American Chemical Society.**
  Environmental epidemiology : effects of environmental chemicals on human health / William M. Draper, editor. Washington, DC : American Chemical Society, 1994. xii, 266 p. :
94-028456          540 s          0841225176
  *Environmental health -- Congresses. Pollution -- Toxicology – Congresses. Environmentally-induced diseases -- Epidemiology – Congresses.*

**QD1.A355 no. 6, etc.**
**Dow Chemical Company.**
  Azeotropic data, compiled by L. H. Horsley and coworkers at the Dow Chemical Co. Washington, American Chemical Society, 1952-73. 3 v.
52-003085          541.36          0841201668
  *Azeotropes -- Tables.*

## QD4 Encyclopedias

**QD4.A2313 1994**
  Concise encyclopedia chemistry / translated and revised by Mary Eagleson. Berlin ; Walter de Gruyter, 1994. 1201 p. :
93-036813          540/.3          0899254578
  *Chemistry -- Encyclopedias.*

**QD4.M33 1997**
  Macmillan encyclopedia of chemistry / Joseph J. Lagowski, editor in chief. New York : Macmillan Reference USA, c1997. 4 v. (lxxi, 1
97-001824          540/.3          0028972252
  *Chemistry -- Encyclopedias.*

## QD5 Dictionaries

**QD5.C5 1987**
  Hawley's condensed chemical dictionary. New York : Van Nostrand Reinhold, c1987. xv, 1288 p. :
86-023333          540/.3/21          0442280971
  *Chemistry -- Dictionaries.*

**QD5.H34 1982**
**Hampel, Clifford A.**
  Glossary of chemical terms / Clifford A. Hampel and Gessner G. Hawley. New York : Van Nostrand Reinhold, c1982. ix, 306 p. ;
81-011482          540/.3/21          0442238711
  *Chemistry -- Dictionaries. Dictionaries, Chemical.*

**QD5.P3 1991**
**Patterson, Austin M.**
  Patterson's German-English dictionary for chemists / by Austin M. Patterson ; revised by James C. Cox ; edited by George E. Condoyannis. New York : Wiley, c1992. liii, 890 p.
90-045365          540/.3          0471669911
  *Chemistry -- Dictionaries -- German. German language -- Dictionaries -- English.*

## QD7 Nomenclature, terminology, notation, abbreviations

**QD7.C2 1979**
**Cahn, R. S.**
  Introduction to chemical nomenclature / R. S. Cahn, O. C. Dermer. London ; Butterworths, 1979. 200 p. :
79-040303          540/.1/4          0408106085
  *Chemistry -- Nomenclature.*

**QD7.I543**
**International Union of Pure and Applied Chemistry.**
  Rules for I.U.P.A.C. notation for organic compounds. New York, Wiley [1962, c1961] 107 p.
62-004916          547.0148
  *Chemistry -- Notation. Chemistry, Organic.*

## QD8.5 Communications of chemical information — Chemical literature

**QD8.5.A25 1997**
  The ACS style guide : a manual for authors and editors / Janet S. Dodd, editor. 2nd ed. Washington, DC : American Chemical Society, c1997. xii, 460 p. :
          808/.06654 21
*Chemical literature -- Authorship -- Handbooks, manuals, etc. English language -- Style -- Handbooks, manuals, etc.*

**QD8.5.M34 1998**
**Maizell, Robert E.**
  How to find chemical information : a guide for practicing chemists, educators, and students / Robert E. Maizell. New York : Wiley, c1998. xxiii, 515 p.
97-029120          540/.7          0471125792
  *Chemical literature.*

**QD8.5.M44 1982**
**Mellon, M. G.**
  Chemical publications, their nature and use / M.G. Mellon. New York : McGraw-Hill, c1982. xii, 419 p. :
81-020947          540/.72          0070415145
  *Chemical literature. Chemistry -- Study and teaching. Best books.*

**QD8.5.W54 1991**
**Wiggins, Gary,**
  Chemical information sources / Gary Wiggins. New York : McGraw-Hill, c1991. xxiv, 352 p.
90-061663          540/.072
  *Chemical literature.*

## QD9 Communications of chemical information — Abstracting and indexing

**QD9.A43 1994**
**Allan, Barbara**
  How to use Biological abstracts, Chemical abstracts, and Index chemicus / Barbara Allan and Brian Livesey. Aldershot, Hampshire, England ; Gower, c1994. ix, 103 p. :
94-012968          025.06/54          0566075563

## QD11 History — General works

**QD11.A8**
**Asimov, Isaac,**
A short history of chemistry. Garden City, N.Y., Anchor Books, 1965. 263 p.
65-010641        540.9
*Chemistry -- History.*

**QD11.B76 1993**
**Brock, W. H.**
The Norton history of chemistry / William H. Brock. New York : W.W. Norton, 1993. xxvii, 744 p.
93-019054        540/.9        0393035360
*Chemistry -- History.*

**QD11.C59 1995**
**Cobb, Cathy.**
Creations of fire : chemistry's lively history from alchemy to the atomic age / Cathy Cobb and Harold Goldwhite. New York : Plenum Press, c1995. xvi, 475 p. :
95-024804        540/.9        0306450879
*Chemistry -- History.*

**QD11.F34 1969**
**Farber, Eduard,**
The evolution of chemistry; a history of its ideas, methods, and materials. 2nd ed. New York, Ronald Press Co. [1969] vii, 437 p.
69-014669        540/.9
*Chemistry -- History.*

**QD11.H84 1992**
**Hudson, John,**
The history of chemistry / John Hudson. New York : Chapman & Hall, 1992. x, 285 p. :
92-008311        540/.9        041203641X
*Chemistry -- History.*

**QD11.I44 1984**
**Ihde, Aaron John,**
The development of modern chemistry / Aaron J. Ihde. New York : Dover, c1984. xii, 851 p. :
82-018245        540/.9        0486642356
*Chemistry -- History.*

**QD11.K53 1992**
**Knight, David M.**
Ideas in chemistry : a history of the science / David Knight. New Brunswick, N.J. : Rutgers University Press, 1992. 213 p. ;
91-047598        540/.9        0813518350
*Chemistry -- History.*

**QD11.P28**
**Partington, J. R.**
A history of chemistry, by J.R. Partington. London, Macmillan; 1961-70 4 vols. 1, 2, 3, 4
62-001666        540/.9
*Chemistry -- History. Chemists -- Biography.*

**QD11.S23 1990**
**Salzberg, Hugh W.**
From caveman to chemist : circumstances and achievements / by Hugh W. Salzberg. Washington, DC : American Chemical Society, 1991. xix, 294 p. :
90-044612        540/.9        0841217866
*Chemistry -- History.*

**QD11.S84 1960**
**Stillman, John Maxson,**
The story of alchemy and early chemistry (The story of early chemistry) New York, Dover Publications [1960] 566 p.
60-003183        540.1
*Chemistry -- History.*

## QD13 History — History of alchemy

**QD13.D62**
**Doberer, Kurt Karl,**
The goldmakers; 10,000 years of alchemy. Tr. by E.W. Dickes. London, Nicholson & Watson [1948] 301 p.
48-020185        540.1
*Alchemy -- History.*

## QD14 History — Early works through 1800

**QD14.C77**
**Conant, James Bryant,**
The overthrow of the phlogiston theory; the chemical revolution of 1775-1789. Cambridge, Harvard University Press, 1950. 59 p.
50-008087        540.1
*Phlogiston.*

**QD14.M97 1967a**
**Multhauf, Robert P.**
The origins of chemistry [by] Robert P. Multhauf. New York, F. Watts [1967] 412 p.
67-024564        540/.9
*Chemistry -- History.*

## QD15 History — 1801-

**QD15.F45 1948**
**Findlay, Alexander,**
A hundred years of chemistry. London, G. Duckworth [1948] 318 p.
49001070        540.9
*Chemists. Chemistry -- History.*

## QD18 History — By region or country, A-Z

**QD18.E85.L48 1994**
**Levere, Trevor Harvey.**
   Chemists and chemistry in nature and society, 1770-1878 / Trevor H. Levere. Aldershot, Hampshire, Great Britain ; Variorum, 1994. 1 v. (various
94-003122          540/.94/09033          0860784126
*Beddoes, Thomas, -- 1760-1808.    Chemistry -- Europe – History – 19th century.   Chemistry -- Europe -- History -- 18th century. Chemistry -- Philosophy.*

**QD18.G3.J64 1990**
**Johnson, Jeffrey Allan.**
   The Kaiser's chemists : science and modernization in imperial Germany / Jeffrey Allan Johnson. Chapel Hill : University of North Carolina Press, c1990. x, 279 p. :
89-070576          540/.943          0807819026
   *Science and state -- Germany -- History -- 20th century. Chemistry -- Germany -- History -- 20th century.*

## QD21 Biography of chemists — Collective

**QD20.R39 1998**
**Rayner-Canham, Marelene F.**
   Women in chemistry : their changing roles from alchemical times to the mid-twentieth century / Marelene Rayner-Canham, Geoffrey Rayner-Canham. Washington, DC : American Chemical Society : 1998. xiv, 284 p. :
98-003890          540/.82          0841235228
   *Women in chemistry -- History. Women chemists -- Biography.*

**QD21.A43**
   American chemists and chemical engineers / Wyndham D. Miles, editor. Washington : American Chemical Society, 1976-1994 v. 1-2   ;
76-000192          540/.92/2          0841202788
   *Chemists -- United States -- Biography. Chemical engineers – United States -- Biography.*

**QD21.F35**
**Farber, Eduard,**
   Great chemists. New York, Interscience Publishers, 1961. 1642 p.
60-016809          925.4
   *Chemists. Chemistry -- History.*

**QD21.F37 1963**
**Farber, Eduard,**
   Nobel prize winners in chemistry, 1901-1961. London, Abelard-Schuman [1963] 341 p.
62-017263          925.4
   *Chemists. Nobel Prizes.*

**QD21.J3 1976**
**Jaffe, Bernard,**
   Crucibles : the story of chemistry from ancient alchemy to nuclear fission / Bernard Jaffe. New York : Dover Publications, 1976. viii, 368 p.
75-038070          540/.9          0486233421
   *Chemists -- Biography. Chemistry -- History.*

**QD21.N63 1993**
   Nobel laureates in chemistry, 1901-1992 / Laylin K. James, editor. [Washington, D.C.] : American Chemical Society : 1993. xvii, 798 p.
93-017902          540/.92/2          0841224595
   *Chemists -- Biography. Nobel Prizes.*

**QD21.W62 1993**
   Women in chemistry and physics : a biobibliographic sourcebook / edited by Louise S. Grinstein, Rose K. Rose, and Miriam H. Rafailovich ; foreword by Lilli S. Hornig. Westport, Conn. : Greenwood Press, 1993. xix, 721 p. ;
92-040224          540/.92/2          0313273820
   *Women chemists -- Biography. Women physicists -- Biography.*

## QD22 Biography of chemists — Individual, A-Z

**QD22.C4.J86 1999**
**Jungnickel, Christa.**
   Cavendish : the experimental life / by Christa Jungnickel and Russell McCormmach. [Lewisburg, Pa.] : Bucknell, 1999. xvi, 814 p. :
99-060985          540/.92          0838754457
*Cavendish, Henry, -- 1731-1810. Cavendish, Charles, – Lord, – 1692 or 3-1783.    Chemists -- Great Britain -- Biography. Politicians – Great Britain -- Biography. Fathers and sons -- Great Britain.*

**QD22.C8.C85 1937**
**Curie, Eve,**
   Madame Curie, a biography by Eve Curie. Translated by Vincent Sheean ... Garden City, N.Y., Doubleday, Doran & Company, inc., 1937. xi, 393 p.
37028462          925.4
*Curie, Marie, -- 1867-1934. Curie, Marie, -- 1867-1934. Physics – biography Chemists.*

**QD22.C8.Q56 1995**
**Quinn, Susan.**
   Marie Curie : a life / Susan Quinn. New York : Simon & Schuster, c1995. 509 p. :
94-043517          540/.92          0671675427
*Curie, Marie, -- 1867-1934.    Chemists -- Poland -- Biography.*

**QD22.L4.D58 1993**
**Donovan, Arthur,**
   Antoine Lavoisier : science, administration, and revolution / Arthur Donovan. Oxford, UK ; Blackwell, 1993. xv, 351 p. :
93-019063          540/.92          0631178872
*Lavoisier, Antoine Laurent, -- 1743-1794.    Chemists -- France – Biography.*

**QD22.L4.M32 1952**
**McKie, Douglas.**
   Antoine Lavoisier: scientist, economist, social reformer. New York, H. Schuman [1952] 440 p.
52013428          925.4
*Lavoisier, Antoine Laurent, -- 1743-1794.*

**QD22.M43.P67**
**Posin, Daniel Q.**
 Mendeleyev, the story of a great scientist. New York, Whittlesey House [1948] xii, 345 p.
48-009043        925.4
*Mendeleyev, Dmitry Ivanovich, -- 1834-1907.*

**QD22.M43S87 2001**
**Strathern, Paul,**
 Mendeleyev's dream : the quest for the elements / Paul Strathern. 1st U.S. ed. New York : Thomas Dunne Books, c2001. 308 p. :
                    0312262043
*Mendeleyev, Dmitry Ivanovich, 1834-1907. Chemists -- Russia (Federation) -- Biography. Chemical elements. Chemistry – History.*

**QD22.S73.A313**
**Staudinger, Hermann,**
 From organic chemistry to macromolecules; a scientific autobiography based on my original papers. Translated from the German with a foreword by Herman F. Mark. New York, Wiley-Interscience [1970] xvi, 303 p.
67-021664        547/.008        0471820865
*Staudinger, Hermann, -- 1881-1965.    Chemists -- Germany -- Biography. Macromolecules.*

## QD27 Early works through 1761

**QD27.B75**
**Boyle, Robert,**
 The sceptical chymist, by the Hon. Robert Boyle. London, J.M. Dent & Sons, ltd.; [1911] xxii p., 1 .
12000670        540.1
*Chemistry -- Early works to 1800.*

## QD31.2 General works, treatises, and advanced textbooks — 1970-

**QD31.2.B68**
**Bowen, H. J. M.**
 Environmental chemistry of the elements / H. J. M. Bowen. London ; Academic Press, 1979. xv, 333 p. :
79-050305        574.5/2        0121204502
*Environmental chemistry.*

**QD31.2.B75 1997**
**Breslow, Ronald.**
 Chemistry today and tomorrow : the central, useful, and creative science / Ronald Breslow. Washington, DC : American Chemical Society ; c1997. ix, 134 p. :
96-045078        540        0841234604
*Chemistry.*

**QD31.2.C375 1984**
 Chemical principles / Richard E. Dickerson ... [et al.]. Menlo Park, Calif. : Benjamin/Cummings Pub. Co., c1984. xv, 930, 63,
84-000360        540        0805324224
*Chemistry.*

**QD31.2.C682 1995**
**Cox, P. A.**
 The elements on earth : inorganic chemistry in the environment / P.A. Cox. Oxford ; Oxford University Press, 1995. p. cm.
94-042633        546        0198562411
*Environmental chemistry.*

**QD31.2.M35 1994**
**Manahan, Stanley E.**
 Environmental chemistry / Stanley E. Manahan. 6th ed. Boca Raton : Lewis, c1994. xvi, 811 p. :
                628.5/01/54 20        1566700884
*Environmental chemistry.*

**QD31.2.N49 1999**
**Newton, David E.**
 Chemistry / by David E. Newton. Phoenix, Ariz. : Oryx Press, 1999. ix, 294 p. :
98-040880        540        1573561606
 *Chemistry.*

**QD31.2.P38 1975**
**Pauling, Linus,**
 Chemistry / Linus Pauling, Peter Pauling. San Francisco : W. H. Freeman, [1975] xi, 767 p. :
74-034071        540        0716701766
 *Chemistry.*

**QD31.2.T47 1996**
**Thibodeaux, Louis J.**
 Environmental chemodynamics : movement of chemicals in air, water, and soil / Louis J. Thibodeaux. New York : Wiley, c1996. xx, 593 p. :
95-035279        628.5/01/54        0471612952
 *Environmental chemistry.*

## QD33 Elementary textbooks

**QD33.W718 1999**
**Williams, R. J. P.**
 Bringing chemistry to life : from matter to man / R.J.P. Williams and J.J.R. Frausto da Silva. New York : Oxford University Press, 1999. 548 p.
99-024780        540        0198505469
 *Chemistry.*

## QD37 Popular works

**QD37.G64 1995**
**Gray, Harry B.**
 Braving the elements / Harry B. Gray, John D. Simon, William C. Trogler. Sausalito, Calif. : University Science Books, c1995. xiii, 418 p.
94-045685        540        0935702342
 *Chemistry -- Popular works.*

**QD37.H612 1995**
**Hoffmann, Roald.**
    The same and not the same / Roald Hoffmann. New York : Columbia University Press, c1995. xvi, 294 p. :
94039467        540        0231101392
    *Chemistry.*

## QD39 Addresses, essays, lectures

**QD39.N47 2000**
    The new chemistry / edited by Nina Hall. New York : Cambridge University Press, 2000. xi, 493 p.
99-016729        540        0521452244
    *Chemistry.*

## QD39.3 Special topics, A-Z

**QD39.3.E46.U84 1997**
    Using computers in chemistry and chemical education / edited by Theresa Julia Zielinski and Mary L. Swift. Washington, DC : American Chemical Society, c1997. xiii, 385 p.
97-014325        542/.85        0841234655
    *Chemistry -- Data processing. Chemistry -- Computer-assisted instruction.*

**QD39.3.M3.H43 1990**
**Hecht, Harry G.**
    Mathematics in chemistry : an introduction to modern methods / Harry G. Hecht. Englewood Cliffs, N.J. : Prentice Hall, c1990. x, 357 p. :
89-016369        540/.15/1        0135610699
    *Chemistry -- Mathematics.*

**QD39.3.S7.D53 1997**
**Diamond, Dermot.**
    Spreadsheet applications in chemistry using Microsoft Excel / Dermot Diamond, Venita C.A. Hanratty. New York : Wiley, c1997. xii, 244 p. :
96-026223        540/.285/5369        0471140872
    *Electronic spreadsheets. Chemistry -- Statistical methods – Data processing.*

**QD39.3.S7.G73 1993**
**Graham, Richard C.**
    Data analysis for the chemical sciences : a guide to statistical techniques / Richard C. Graham. New York, NY : VCH, c1993. xx, 536 p. :
93-012473        540/.72        1560810483
    *Chemistry -- Statistical methods.*

## QD51 Laboratories — General works

**QD51.A88 1981**
**Assembly of Mathematical and Physical Sciences (U.S.).**
    Prudent practices for handling hazardous chemicals in laboratories / Committee on Hazardous Substances in the Laboratory, Assembly of Mathematical and Physical Sciences, National Research Council. Washington, D.C. : National Academy Press, 1981. xiv, 291 p. :
80-026877        542/.028/9        0309031281
    *Chemical laboratories -- Safety measures.*

**QD51.C73 2000**
**Furr, A. Keith,**
    CRC handbook of laboratory safety / A. Keith Furr. 5th ed. Boca Raton : CRC Press, c2000. xxvii, 774 p. :
        542/.1/0289 21
    *Chemical laboratories -- Safety measures -- Handbooks, manuals, etc.*

## QD53 Laboratories — Instruments and apparatus — General works

**QD53.C69 1992**
**Coyne, Gary S.**
    The laboratory handbook of materials, equipment, and technique / Gary S. Coyne. Englewood Cliffs, N.J. : Prentice Hall, c1992. xviii, 468 p.
91-027821        542        0131262289
    *Chemical apparatus -- Handbooks, manuals, etc. Chemical laboratories -- Handbooks, manuals, etc.*

**QD53.C69 1997**
**Coyne, Gary S.**
    The laboratory companion : a practical guide to materials, equipment, and technique / Gary S. Coyne. New York : Wiley, c1997. xviii, 527 p.
97-016689        542        0471184225
    *Chemical apparatus -- Handbooks, manuals, etc. Chemical laboratories -- Handbooks, manuals, etc.*

**QD53.I57 2000**
    Instruments and experimentation in the history of chemistry / edited by Frederic L. Holmes and Trevor H. Levere. Cambridge, Mass. : MIT Press, c2000. xxi, 415 p. :
99-021064        542        0262082829
    *Chemical apparatus -- History. Chemistry -- Experiments -- History.*

## QD61 Laboratories — Techniques and operations — General works

**QD61.W67 1965**
**Willard, Hobart Hurd,**
    Instrumental methods of analysis [by] Hobart H. Willard, Lynne L. Merritt, Jr. [and] John A. Dean. Princeton, N.J., Van Nostrand [1965] xviii, 784 p.
65-006775        543.08
    *Instrumental analysis.*

## QD63 Laboratories — Techniques and operations — Special, A-Z

**QD63.E88.D43 1998**
**Dean, John R.**
Extraction methods for environmental analysis / John R. Dean. Chichester ; John Wiley, c1998. xiii, 225 p.
97-048744          628.5/01/543          0471982873
*Extraction (Chemistry) Environmental chemistry -- Technique.*

**QD63.E88.T58 1998**
**Thurman, E. M.**
Solid-phase extraction : principles and practice / E.M. Thurman, M.S. Mills. New York : Wiley, c1998. xxvi, 344 p.
97-027535          543/.0892          047161422X
*Extraction (Chemistry)*

**QD63.L3.V36 1998**
**Van Hecke, Gerald R.**
A guide to lasers in chemistry / Gerlad R. Van Hecke, Kerry K. Karukstis. Boston : Jones and Bartlett, c1998. xi, 252 p. :
97-013440          542/.8          0763704121
*Lasers in chemistry. Laser spectroscopy. Laser photochemistry.*

**QD63.5.E38 1998**
Educating for OSHA savvy chemists / Paul J. Utterback, editor, David A. Nelson, editor. Washington DC : American Chemical Society, 1998. ix, 191 p. :
          542/.1/0289 21          0841235694
*Chemical laboratories -- Safety measures -- Study and teaching (Higher) -- United States -- Congresses.*

## QD64 Laboratories — Waste disposal

**QD64.A76 1996**
**Armour, M. A.**
Hazardous laboratory chemicals disposal guide / Margaret-Ann Armour. Boca Raton, FL : CRC Press, c1996. 546 p. :
96-002428          542/.89          1566701082
*Chemical laboratories -- Waste disposal. Hazardous substances.*

# QD65 Handbooks, tables, formulas, etc.

**QD65.B29 1971**
**Bauer, Edward L.**
A statistical manual for chemists [by] Edward L. Bauer. New York, Academic Press, 1971. xiv, 193 p.
73-154404          540/.01/5195          0120827565
*Chemistry -- Tables. Mathematical statistics.*

**QD65.C88 1988**
CRC handbook of chemistry and physics / editor-in-chief, Robert C. Weast. Boca Raton, FL : CRC Press, c1988. 1 v. (various
87-026820          540/.212          0849307406
*Chemistry -- Tables. Physics -- Tables.*

**QD65.S537 1990**
**Shugar, Gershon J.,**
The chemist's ready reference handbook / Gershon J. Shugar, John A. Dean ; consulting editors, Ronald A. Shugar ... [et al.]. New York : McGraw-Hill, c1990. 1 v. (various
89-008166          543          0070571783
*Chemistry -- Handbooks, manuals, etc.*

## QD71 Analytical chemistry — Societies, congresses, serial collections, yearbooks

**QD71.A2**
Advances in analytical chemistry and instrumentation. [New York, Wiley-Interscience, etc.] 1960-1973. 11 v.
60-013119          543.082
*Chemistry, Analytic. Electrodes. Spectrophotometer.*

## QD71.5 Analytical chemistry — Dictionaries and encyclopedias

**QD71.5.E52 2000**
Encyclopedia of analytical chemistry : applications, theory, and instrumentation / editor-in-chief, Robert A. Meyers. New York : Wiley, c2000. 15 vols.
00-042282          543/.003          0471976709
*Chemistry, Analytic -- Encyclopedias.*

## QD75 Analytical chemistry — General works, treatises, and textbooks — Through 1970

**QD75.E9 1960**
**Ewing, Galen Wood,**
Instrumental methods of chemical analysis. New York, McGraw-Hill, 1960. 454 p.
59-014446          544
*Chemistry, Analytic. Chemical apparatus.*

## QD75.2 Analytical chemistry — General works, treatises, and textbooks — 1971-

**QD75.2.K64 1978**
**Kolthoff, I. M.**
Treatise on analytical chemistry / edited by I.M. Kolthoff and Philip J. Elving. New York : Wiley, c1978-c1993 pt. 1, v. 1-2
78-001707          543          047103438X
*Chemistry, Analytic.*

**QD75.2.P49**
Physical methods in modern chemical analysis / edited by Theodore Kuwana. New York : Academic Press, 1978- v. :
77-092242          543          0124308015
*Chemistry, Analytic.*

**QD75.2.V35 2000**
**Valcarcel Cases, Miguel.**
   Principles of analytical chemistry : a textbook / Miguel Valcarcel. Berlin ; Springer, c2000. xv, 371 p. :
00-033829         543         354064007X
   *Chemistry, Analytic.*

## QD75.25 Analytical chemistry — Addresses, essays, lectures

**QD75.25.A5 1983**
   The Analytical approach / edited by Jeanette G. Grasselli. Washington, D.C. : American Chemical Society, 1983. x, 239 p. :
82-022618         543         0841207534
   *Chemistry, Analytic.*

## QD75.4 Analytical chemistry — Special topics, A-Z

**QD75.4.S8**
**De Levie, Robert.**
   How to use Excel in analytical chemistry and in general scientific data analysis / Robert de Levie. Cambridge ; Cambridge University Press, 2001. xiv, 487 p. :
98-050543     543/.00285/5369    0521642825
   *Science -- Statistical methods -- Data processing. Chemistry, Analytic -- Statistical methods -- Data processing. Electronic spreadsheets.*

**QD75.4.S8.O88 1999**
**Otto, Matthias.**
   Chemometrics : statistics and computer application in analytical chemistry / Matthias Otto. Weinheim ; Wiley-VCH, c1999. xvi, 314 p. :
99-186538     543/.007/27     352729628X
   *Chemistry, Analytic -- Statistical methods. Chemistry, Analytic – Mathematics. Chemistry, Analytic -- Data processing.*

## QD77 Analytical chemistry — Reagents, indicators, test papers, etc.

**QD77.A54 2000**
**American Chemical Society.**
   Reagent chemicals : American Chemical Society specifications, official from January 1, 2000. 9th ed. New York : American Chemical Society, 2000. xi, 752 p. :
              543/.01 21
*Chemical tests and reagents.*

**QD77.H37 1999**
   Handbook of reagents for organic synthesis. New York : Wiley, 1999. 4 vols.
98-053088       547/.2     0471979244
   *Chemical tests and reagents. Organic compounds -- Synthesis.*

## QD79 Analytical chemistry — Methods of analysis (Qualitative and quantitative), A-Z

**QD79.C4.C485 1983**
   Chromatography : fundamentals and applications of chromatographic and electrophoretic methods / edited by E. Heftmann. Amsterdam ; Elsevier Scientific Pub. Co. ; 1983. 2 v. :
84-129336     543/.089     0444420452
   *Chromatographic analysis.*

**QD79.C4.M55 1988**
**Miller, James M.,**
   Chromatography : concepts and contrasts / James M. Miller. New York : Wiley, 1988. xii, 297 p. :
87-016084     543/.089     0471848212
   *Chromatographic analysis.*

**QD79.C4.R38 1989**
**Ravindranath, B.**
   Principles and practice of chromatography / B. Ravindranath. Chichester, West Sussex, England : E. Horwood ; 1989. 502 p. :
88-013889     543/.089     0470213280
   *Chromatographic analysis.*

**QD79.C45.M425 1998**
**McNair, Harold Monroe,**
   Basic gas chromatography / Harold M. McNair, James M. Miller. New York : Wiley, c1998. xii, 200 p. :
97-018151     543/.0896    047117260X
   *Gas chromatography.*

**QD79.C453.W35 1990**
**Walton, Harold F.**
   Ion exchange in analytical chemistry / authors, Harold F. Walton and Roy D. Rocklin. Boca Raton, Fla. : CRC Press, c1990. 229 p. :
89-070839     543/.0893    0849361990
   *Ion exchange chromatography.*

**QD79.C453.W4513 1995**
**Weiss, Joachim.**
   Ion chromatography / Joachim Weiss ; [translator, Jorg Monig]. Weinheim ; VCH, c1995. xi, 465 p. :
94-023903     543/.0893    3527286985
   *Ion exchange chromatography.*

**QD79.C454.H63 1997**
   HPLC and CE : principles and practice / [edited by] Andrea Weston, Phyllis R. Brown. San Diego : Academic Press, c1997. xiv, 280 p. :
96-049198     543/.0871    0121366405
   *High performance liquid chromatography. Capillary electrophoresis.*

**QD79.C454.M36 1994**
**McMaster, Marvin C.**
  HPLC, a practical user's guide / Marvin C. McMaster. New York, N.Y. : VCH, c1994. xii, 211 p. :
93-042139          543/.0894          1560816368
  *High performance liquid chromatography.*

**QD79.C4E63 2001**
  Encyclopedia of chromatography / edited by Jack Cazes. New York : Marcel Dekker, c2001. xxx, 927 p. :
          543/.089/03 21          0824705114
*Chromatography -- Encyclopedias. Chromatography – Methodology - - Encyclopedias. Chromatography -- Methods. Electrophoresis, Capillary -- Methods. Fractionation -- Methods.*

**QD79.I5.H36 1997**
  Handbook of instrumental techniques for analytical chemistry / Frank A. Settle, editor. Upper Saddle River, NJ : Prentice Hall PTR, c1997. xxi, 995 p. :
97-010618          543/.07          0131773380
  *Instrumental analysis.*

## QD81 Analytical chemistry — Qualitative analysis — General works, treatises, and advanced textbooks

**QD81.F453 1972**
**Feigl, Fritz,**
  Spot tests in inorganic analysis, by Fritz Feigl, and Vinzenz Anger. Translated by Ralph E. Oesper. Amsterdam, Elsevier Pub. Co., 1972. xxix, 669 p.
76-135494          544/.834          0444409297
  *Chemistry, Analytic -- Qualitative. Spot tests (Chemistry)*

**QD81.V6 1987**
**Vogel, Arthur Israel.**
  Vogel's qualitative inorganic analysis. 6th ed.  Harlow, Essex, England : Longman Scientific & Technical ; 1987. ix, 310 p. :
86-010453          544          0470207108
  *Chemistry, Analytic -- Qualitative. Chemistry, Inorganic.*

## QD95-96 Analytical chemistry — Qualitative analysis — Spectrum analysis (Qualitative and quantitative)

**QD95.B37**
**Barrow, Gordon M.**
  The structure of molecules; an introduction to molecular spectroscopy. New York, W. A. Benjamin, 1963. 156 p.
63-015835          544.6
  *Molecular spectroscopy. Molecular structure.*

**QD95.I486 1999**
  Inorganic electronic structure and spectroscopy / edited by Edward I. Solomon, A.B.P. Lever. New York : Wiley, c1999. 2 v. :
98-038180          543/.0858          0471326836
  *Inorganic compounds -- Analysis. Spectrum analysis.*

**QD95.J24**
**Jaffe, Hans H.**
  Theory and applications of ultraviolet spectroscopy [by] H. H. Jaffe and Milton Orchin. New York, Wiley [1962] 624 p.
62-015181          544.6
  *Ultraviolet spectroscopy.*

**QD95.N28**
**Nachtrieb, Norman Harry,**
  Principles and practice of spectro-chemical analysis.  New York, McGraw-Hill, 1950. x, 324 p.
50009462          544.6
  *Spectrum analysis.*

**QD95.P25 1990**
**Parish, R. V.**
  NMR, NQR, EPR, and Mossbauer spectroscopy in inorganic chemistry / R.V. Parish. New York : E. Horwood, 1990. 223 p. :
90-004873          543/.087          0136255183
  *Spectrum analysis. Chemistry, Inorganic.*

**QD95.S6368 1988**
  Spectroscopy source book / Sybil P. Parker, editor in chief. New York : McGraw-Hill, c1988. 288 p. :
87-035254          543/.0858          0070455058
  *Spectrum analysis -- Encyclopedias.*

**QD95.T57**
**Tobin, Marvin Charles.**
  Laser Raman spectroscopy [by] Marvin C. Tobin. New York, Wiley-Interscience [1971] xi, 171 p.
70-148511          544/.64          0471875503
  *Raman spectroscopy.*

**QD96.I5.N33 1997**
**Nakamoto, Kazuo,**
  Infrared and Raman spectra of inorganic and coordination compounds / Kazuo Nakamoto. New York : Wiley, c1997. 2 v. :
96-033456          543/.08583          0471194069
  *Infrared spectroscopy. Raman spectroscopy.*

**QD96.I5.N96 2001**
**Nyquist, Richard A.**
  Interpreting infrared, Raman, and nuclear magnetic resonance spectra / Richard Allen Nyquist. San Diego : Academic Press, c2001. 2 v. :
00-108478          543/.0858          0125234759
  *Infrared spectroscopy -- Handbooks, manuals, etc. Raman spectroscopy -- Handbooks, manuals, etc. Nuclear magnetic resonance spectroscopy -- Handbooks, manuals, etc.*

**QD96.M3**
**Sparkman, O. David**
  Mass spectrometry desk reference / O. David Sparkman. Pittsburgh, Pa. : Global View Pub., c2000. xvi, 106 p. :
00-100995          543/.0873/014          0966081323
  *Mass spectrometry -- Terminology.*

**QD96.M3.H6413 1996**
**Hoffmann, Edmond de.**
　Mass spectrometry : principles and applications / Edmond de Hoffmann, Jean Charette, Vincent Stroobant ; translated by Julie Trottier and the authors. Chichester ; Wiley ; c1996. xii, 340 p. :
96-006746　　　543/.0873　　　0471966967
　*Mass spectrometry.*

**QD96.M3.S65 1999**
**Smith, R. Martin.**
　Understanding mass spectra : a basic approach / R. Martin Smith ; with Kenneth L. Busch. New York : Wiley, c1999. xvii, 290 p.
98-018136　　　543/.0873　　　0471297046
　*Mass spectrometry.*

**QD96.N8.M3 1998**
**Macomber, Roger S.**
　A complete introduction to modern NMR spectroscopy / Roger S. Macomber. New York : Wiley, c1998. xvii, 382 p.
97-017106　　　543/.0877　　　0471157368
　*Nuclear magnetic resonance spectroscopy.*

**QD96.N8.P68 1983**
**Pouchert, Charles J.**
　The Aldrich library of NMR spectra / Charles J. Pouchert. Milwaukee, Wis. (P.O. Box 355, Milwaukee 53201) Aldrich Chemical Co., c1983. 2 v. :
83-070633　　　538/.362
　*Nuclear magnetic resonance spectroscopy -- Tables.*

**QD96.V53.D54 1993**
**Diem, Max,**
　Introduction to modern vibrational spectroscopy / Max Diem. New York : Wiley, c1993. xiii, 285 p.
93-001036　　　543/.0858　　　0471595845
　*Vibrational spectra.*

### QD98 Analytical chemistry — Qualitative analysis — Other special methods, A-Z

**QD98.C45 1965**
**Cheronis, Nicholas Dimitrius,**
　Semimicro qualitative organic analysis; the systematic identification of organic compounds [by] Nicholas D. Cheronis, John B. Entrikin [and] Ernest M. Hodnett. New York, Interscience Publishers [1965] xi, 1060 p.
64-025892　　　547.348
　*Chemistry, Analytic -- Qualitative. Chemistry, Organic – Tables. Microchemistry.*

### QD101.2 Analytical chemistry — Quantitative analysis — General works, treatises, and textbooks

**QD101.2.F74 1987**
**Fritz, James S. (James Sherwood),**
　Quantitative analytical chemistry / James S. Fritz, George H. Schenk. 5th ed. Boston : Allyn and Bacon, c1987. xiv, 690 p. :
　　　　　　544 19
　*Chemistry, Analytic -- Quantitative.*

**QD101.2.L34 1975**
**Laitinen, Herbert A.**
　Chemical analysis; an advanced text and reference [by] Herbert A. Laitinen [and] Walter E. Harris. 2nd ed. New York, McGraw-Hill [1975] xix, 611 p.
74-011497　　　545　　　0070360863
　*Chemistry, Analytic -- Quantitative. Chemistry, Analytical.*

### QD111 Analytical chemistry — Quantitative analysis — Volumetric analysis

**QD111.K642**
**Kolthoff, I. M.**
　Volumetric analysis, by I.M. Kolthoff [and] V.A. Stenger. New York, Interscience Publishers, 1942-57. 3 v.
42-014617　　　545.5
　*Volumetric analysis.*

### QD115-117 Analytical chemistry — Quantitative analysis — Electrochemical analysis

**QD115.L23 1984**
　Laboratory techniques in electroanalytical chemistry / editors, Peter T. Kissinger, William R. Heineman. New York : Dekker, c1984. xv, 751 p. :
84-004274　　　543/.0871　　　082471864X
　*Electrochemical analysis -- Laboratory manuals.*

**QD115.W33 2000**
**Wang, Joseph,**
　Analytical electrochemistry / Joseph Wang. New York : John Wiley & Sons, 2000. xvi, 209 p. :
99-089637　　　543/.0871　　　0471282723
　*Electrochemical analysis.*

**QD117.M6**
**Morrison, George H.**
　Solvent extraction in analytical chemistry [by] George H. Morrison [and] Henry Freiser. New York, Wiley [1957] 269 p.
57-010810　　　545
　*Chemistry, Analytic -- Quantitative. Solvent extraction. Solvents.*

### QD131 Analytical chemistry — Technical analysis — General works, treatises, and textbooks

**QD131.S68**
　Standard methods of chemical analysis. Princeton, N.J., Van Nostrand [1962-66] 3 v. in 5.
62-002869　　　545
　*Chemistry, Analytic. Chemistry, Technical.*

## QD139 Analytical chemistry — Technical analysis — Other special, A-Z

**QD139.T7.V355 1993**
**Vandecasteele, Carlo.**
Modern methods for trace element determination / C. Vandecasteele and C.B. Block. Chichester ; Wiley, c1993. xi, 330 p. :
93-010292          543          0471940399
*Trace elements -- Analysis.*

## QD142 Analytical chemistry — Water analysis

**QD142.A5**
Standard methods for the examination of water and wastewater : including bottom sediments and sludges / prepared and published jointly by American Public Health Association, American Water Works Association, Water Pollution Control Federation. New York : American Public Health Association, c1960- v. :
55-001979          543.3
*Water -- Analysis. Sewage -- Analysis.*

## QD149 Inorganic chemistry — Nomenclature, terminology, notation, abbreviations

**QD149.B59 1990**
**Block, B. Peter,**
Inorganic chemical nomenclature : principles and practice / B. Peter Block, Warren H. Powell, W. Conard Fernelius. Washington, DC : American Chemical Society, 1990. xiv, 210 p. :
90-000760          546/.014          0841216975
*Chemistry, Inorganic -- Nomenclature.*

## QD151 Inorganic chemistry — General works, treatises, and advanced textbooks — 1801-1969

**QD151.A45**
Advances in inorganic chemistry and radiochemistry. New York, Academic Press. 30 v.
59-007692          546.082
*Chemistry, Inorganic. Radiochemistry.*

**QD151.L3 1951**
**Latimer, Wendell M.**
Reference book of inorganic chemistry, by Wendell M. Latimer and Joel H. Hildebrand. 3rd ed. New York, Macmillan [1951] 625 p.
51-014977          546
*Chemistry, Inorganic.*

**QD151.R443**
**Remy, Heinrich,**
Treatise on inorganic chemistry. Translated by J. S. Anderson, edited by J. Kleinberg. Amsterdam, Elsevier Pub. Co., 1956. 2 v.
57008603
*Chemistry, Inorganic.*

**QD151.S69**
**Sneed, M. Cannon**
Comprehensive inorganic chemistry [edited by] M. Cannon Sneed, J. Lewis Maynard [and] Robert C. Brasted. New York, Van Nostrand [1953- v.
53-008775          546
*Chemistry, Inorganic. Chemistry, Physical and theoretical.*

## QD151.2 Inorganic chemistry — General works, treatises, and advanced textbooks — 1970-

**QD151.2.C68 1999**
Advanced inorganic chemistry. 6th ed. New York : Wiley, c1999. xv, 1355 p. :
98-008020          546          0471199575
*Chemistry, Inorganic.*

**QD151.2.K5 1995**
**King, R. Bruce.**
Inorganic chemistry of main group elements / R. Bruce King. New York : VCH, c1995. xx, 326 p. :
94-035433          546          1560816791
*Chemistry, Inorganic.*

**QD151.2.M37 2000**
**Massey, A.G.**
Main group chemistry / A.G. Massey. 2nd ed. Chichester ; New York : Wiley, c2000. 534 p. :
546 21
*Chemistry, Inorganic.*

**QD151.2.M63 1982**
**Moeller, Therald.**
Inorganic chemistry, a modern introduction / Therald Moeller. New York : Wiley, c1982. viii, 846 p.
81-016455          546          0471612308
*Chemistry, Inorganic.*

**QD151.2.P89 1998**
**Put, Paul J. van der.**
The inorganic chemistry of materials : how to make things out of elements / Paul J. van der Put. New York : Plenum Press, c1998. xiii, 391 p.
98-033993          546          0306457318
*Chemistry, Inorganic. Inorganic compounds -- Synthesis. Materials.*

### QD151.5 Inorganic chemistry — General works, treatises, and advanced textbooks — Elementary textbooks

**QD151.5.S93 1997**
**Swaddle, T. W.**
   Inorganic chemistry : an industrial and environmental perspective / T.W. Swaddle. San Diego : Academic Press, c1997. xvi, 482 p. :
97-001552        546        0126785503
   *Chemistry, Inorganic. Environmental chemistry.*

## QD155.5 Inorganic chemistry — Handbooks, tables, formulas, etc.

**QD155.5.H36 1995**
   Handbook of inorganic compounds / edited by Dale L. Perry, Sidney L. Phillips. Boca Raton : CRC Press, c1995. 1 v. (various
95-015997        546/.0212        0849386713
   *Inorganic compounds -- Handbooks, manuals, etc.*

## QD156 Inorganic chemistry — Inorganic synthesis

**QD156.I56**
   Inorganic syntheses. New York [etc.] Wiley [etc.] 1939- v.
39-023015        541/.39
   *Inorganic compounds -- Synthesis -- Periodicals.*

### QD162 Inorganic chemistry — Nonmetals — Gases

**QD162.H6**
**Holloway, John H.**
   Noble-gas chemistry [by] John H. Holloway. London, Methuen, 1968. viii, 213 p.
78-362932        546/.75
   *Gases, Rare.*

### QD169 Inorganic chemistry — Nonmetals — Other, A-Z

**QD169.W3**
**Franks, Felix.**
   Water / Felix Franks. London : Royal society of chemistry, 1984. 96 p. :
87-017457        553.7        0851864732
   *Water. Water*

### QD171 Inorganic chemistry — Metals — General works, treatises, and textbooks

**QD171.B32 1967**
**Basolo, Fred,**
   Mechanisms of inorganic reactions; a study of metal complexes in solution [by] Fred Basolo and Ralph G. Pearson. New York, Wiley [1967] xi, 701 p.
66-028755        546.3
   *Chemistry, Inorganic. Chemical reactions. Metal complexes.*

**QD171.G65**
**Goodenough, John B.**
   Magnetism and the chemical bond. New York, Interscience Publishers, 1963. xv, 393 p.
62-022257        547.3
   *Transition metals. Magnetism. Chemical bonds.*

### QD172 Inorganic chemistry — Metals — By group, A-Z

**QD172.T6.B48 1996**
**Bersuker, I. B.**
   Electronic structure and properties of transition metal compounds : introduction to the theory / Isaac B. Bersuker. New York : Wiley, c1996. xxiv, 668 p.
95-000461        546/.6        0471130796
   *Transition metal compounds.*

**QD172.T7.S38**
**Seaborg, Glenn Theodore,**
   The transuranium elements. New Haven, Yale University Press, 1958. xx, 328 p.
58-011258        546
   *Transuranium elements.*

**QD172.T7.T69 1992**
   Transuranium elements : a half century / edited by L. R. Morss, J. Fuger. Washington, DC : American Chemical Society, 1992. xxiv, 562 p.
92-007475        546/.44        0841222193
   *Transuranium elements -- Congresses.*

## QD181 Inorganic chemistry — Special elements. By chemical symbol, A-Z

**QD181.B1.B73**
**Brown, Herbert Charles,**
   Boranes in organic chemistry, by Herbert C. Brown. Ithaca [N.Y.] Cornell University Press [1972] xiv, 462 p.
79-165516        547/.05/671        0801406811
   *Borane. Organic compounds -- Synthesis.*

**QD181.C1.A43 1995**
**Aldersey-Williams, Hugh.**
   The most beautiful molecule : the discovery of the buckyball / Hugh Aldersey-Williams. New York : John Wiley, c1995. ix, 340 p. :
95-012422        546/.681        047110938X
   *Buckminsterfullerene.*

## QD181.C1.F85 1992
Fullerenes : synthesis, properties, and chemistry of large carbon clusters / George S. Hammond, editor, Valerie J. Kuck, editor. Washington, DC : American Chemical Society, 1992. xiii, 195 p.
91-040807          546/.681          0841221820
*Fullerenes -- Congresses. Buckminsterfullerene -- Congresses.*

## QD181.O1.S18 1991
**Sawyer, Donald T.**
Oxygen chemistry / Donald T. Sawyer ; foreword by R.J.P. Williams. New York : Oxford University Press, 1991. xii, 223 p. :
91-006766          546/.721          0195057988
*Oxygen.*

## QD181.P1.G67
**Goldwhite, Harold.**
Introduction to phosphorus chemistry / Harold Goldwhite. Cambridge [Eng.] ; Cambridge University Press, 1981. xiv, 113 p. :
79-027141          546/.712          0521229782
*Phosphorus.*

## QD181.S6.L614 1985
**Liebau, Friedrich,**
Structural chemistry of silicates : structure, bonding, and classification / Friedrich Liebau. Berlin ; Springer-Verlag, c1985. xii, 347 p. :
84-023532          546/.68324          0387137475
*Silicates.*

## QD196 Inorganic chemistry — Inorganic polymers

## QD196.M37 1992
**Mark, James E.,**
Inorganic polymers / James E. Mark, Harry R. Allcock, Robert C. West. Englewood Cliffs, N.J. : Prentice Hall, c1992. xiv, 272 p. :
91-009936          546          0134658817
*Inorganic polymers.*

## QD243 Organic chemistry — Yearbooks

## QD243.F5
**Fieser, Louis Frederick,**
Current topics in organic chemistry / Louis F. Fieser, Mary Fieser. New York : Reinhold Pub. Corp., c1964- v. :
64-017547          547/.005
*Chemistry, Organic -- Periodicals.*

## QD245 Organic chemistry — Collected works (nonserial)

## QD245.C65 1979
Comprehensive organic chemistry : the synthesis and reactions of organic compounds / chairman and deputy chairman of the editorial board, Sir Derek Barton and W. David Ollis. Oxford ; Pergamon Press, 1979. 6 v. :
78-040502          547          0080213197
*Chemistry, Organic.*

## QD246 Organic chemistry — Dictionaries and encyclopedias

## QD246.D5 1996
Dictionary of organic compounds. 6th ed. London ; New York : Chapman & Hall, 1996-<1998> v.
          547/.003 21
*Organic compounds -- Dictionaries.*

## QD251 Organic chemistry — General works, treatises, and advanced textbooks — Through 1970

## QD251.F44
**Fieser, Louis Frederick,**
Advanced organic chemistry [by] Louis F. Fieser [and] Mary Fieser. New York, Reinhold Pub. Corp. [1961] 1158 p.
61-014594          547
*Chemistry, Organic.*

## QD251.F5 1956
**Fieser, Louis Frederick,**
Organic chemistry [by] Louis F. Fieser and Mary Fieser. 3rd ed. New York, Reinhold, 1956. 1112 p.
56006691          547
*Chemistry, Organic.*

## QD251.O7
Organic reactions. New York, John Wiley & Sons, 1942- v.
42-020265          547
*Chemistry, Organic.*

## QD251.R6 1964
Rodd's Chemistry of carbon compounds; a modern comprehensive treatise. Amsterdam, Elsevier Pub. Co., 1964-89 v. 1, pts. A-
64-004605          547          0444406646
*Chemistry, Organic. Carbon compounds.*

## QD251.W3683
**Weissberger, Arnold,**
Technique of organic chemistry. New York, Interscience Publishers, 1959-69. 20 v. in 11.
59012438
*Chemistry, Organic.*

## QD251.2 Organic chemistry — General works, treatises, and advanced textbooks — 1971-

**QD251.2.B4813 1996**
**Beyer, Hans,**
Handbook of organic chemistry / [Hans Beyer], Wolfgang Walter ; translated by Douglas Lloyd. London ; New York : 1996. xx, 1037 p. :
93-011632          547          013010356X
*Chemistry, Organic.*

**QD251.2.M37 2001**
**Smith, Michael,**
March's advanced organic chemistry : reactions, mechanisms, and structure. 5th ed. / Michael B. Smith and Jerry March. New York : Wiley, c2001. xviii, 2083 p>
          547 21
*Chemistry, Organic.*

**QD251.2.M53 1992**
**Miller, Audrey.**
Writing reaction mechanisms in organic chemistry / Audrey Miller. San Diego : Academic Press, c1992. x, 488 p. :
91-048080          547.1/39          0124967116
*Organic reaction mechanisms.*

**QD251.2.M67 1992**
**Morrison, Robert Thornton,**
Organic chemistry / Robert Thornton Morrison, Robert Neilson Boyd. 6th ed. Englewood Cliffs, N.J. : Prentice Hall, c1992. xxvi, 1279 p. :
          547 20
*Chemistry, Organic.*

## QD255 Organic chemistry — Addresses, essays, lectures

**QD255.B85**
**Breger, Irving A.**
Organic geochemistry. New York, Macmillan, 1963. x, 658 p.
62009173          547
*Geochemistry. Chemistry, Organic.*

## QD257.7 Organic chemistry — Handbooks, tables, formulas, etc.

**QD257.7.H35 1995**
Handbook of data on common organic compounds / editors, David R. Lide, G.W.A. Milne. Boca Raton : CRC Press, c1995. 3 v. ;
          547/.00212 20          0849304040
*Organic compounds -- Tables.*

**QD257.7.H374 1997**
Handbook of physical properties of organic chemicals / edited by Philip H. Howard and William M. Meylan ; associate editors, Julie Funk ... [et al.]. Boca Raton, Fla. : Lewis Publishers, c1997. 1 v. (various
96-051427          547          1566702275
*Organic compounds -- Handbooks, manuals, etc.*

## QD261 Organic chemistry — Operations in organic chemistry — Laboratory manuals

**QD261.F5 1998**
**Fieser, Louis Frederick,**
Organic experiments / Louis F. Fieser, Kenneth L. Williamson. 8th ed. Boston : Houghton Mifflin Co., c1998. xiii, 644 p.
          547/.0078 21
*Chemistry, Organic -- Laboratory manuals.*

**QD261.V63 1989**
**Vogel, Arthur Israel.**
Vogel's Textbook of practical organic chemistry. 5th ed. / rev. by Brian S. Furniss . . . [et al.]. New York, Longman Scientific & Technical ; Wiley, 1989. xxviii, 1514 p.
          547 19
*Chemistry, Organic -- Laboratory manuals. Chemistry, Analytic – Qualitative.*

## QD262 Organic chemistry — Operations in organic chemistry — Organic synthesis

**QD262.N6 1978**
**Norman, R. O. C.**
Principles of organic synthesis / R. O. C. Norman. London : Chapman and Hall ; 1978. xiii, 800 p.
78-000784          547/.2          0470263172
*Organic compounds -- Synthesis.*

**QD262.O7**
Organic syntheses. New York [etc.] J. Wiley & Sons, inc. [etc.] v.
21-017747          547.058
*Organic compounds -- Synthesis.*

**QD262.S24 1992**
**Sandler, Stanley R.,**
Sourcebook of advanced organic laboratory preparations / Stanley R. Sandler, Wolf Karo. San Diego : Academic Press, c1992. xiv, 332 p. :
92-013631          547.2/078          0126185069
*Organic compounds -- Synthesis.*

## QD271-272 Organic chemistry — Operations in organic chemistry — Organic analysis

**QD271.F3513 1966**
**Feigl, Fritz,**
Spot tests in organic analysis, by Fritz Feigl in collaboration with Vinzenz Anger. Translated by Ralph E. Oesper. Amsterdam, Elsevier Pub. Co., 1966. xxiii, 772 p.
65-013235          547.34834
*Chemistry, Analytic -- Qualitative. Spot tests (Chemistry) Chemistry, Organic.*

**QD271.L95 1990**
**Lyman, Warren J.**
Handbook of chemical property estimation methods : environmental behavior of organic compounds / Warren J. Lyman, William F. Reehl, David H. Rosenblatt. Washington, DC : American Chemical Society, 1990. 1 v. :
          547.3 20
*Organic compounds -- Analysis.*

**QD271.M46**
Methods of biochemical analysis. New York, Wiley [etc., 1954- v.
54-007232          543.8
*Chemistry, Analytic -- Periodicals. Biochemistry -- Periodicals. Biochemistry -- collected works.*

**QD272.S6.C74 1998**
**Crews, Phillip,**
Organic structure analysis / Phillip Crews, Jaime Rodriguez, Marcel Jaspars. New York : Oxford University Press, 1998. xxiv, 552 p.
97-031686          547/.122          0195101022
*Organic compounds -- Analysis. Spectrum analysis.*

**QD272.S6.F45 1995**
**Feinstein, Karen.**
Guide to spectroscopic identification of organic compounds / Karen Feinstein. Boca Raton : CRC Press, c1995. 124 p. :
94-038923          547.3/0858          0849394481
*Organic compounds -- Analysis. Spectrum analysis.*

**QD272.S6.O74 1998**
Organic structural spectroscopy / Joseph B. Lambert ... [et al.]. Upper Saddle River, N.J. : Prentice Hall, c1998. viii, 568 p.
97-040522          547/.122          0132586908
*Organic compounds -- Analysis. Spectrum analysis.*

**QD272.S6S55**
**Silverstein, Robert Milton,**
Spectrometric identification of organic compounds / R.M. Silverstein, G. Clayton Bassler, Terence C. Morrill. 5th ed. New York : Wiley, c1991. x, 419 p. :
          543/.0858 20          0471634042
*Spectrum anaylsis. Organic compounds -- Spectra.*

## QD281 Organic chemistry — Operations in organic chemistry — Other special, A-Z

**QD281.O9.C55**
**Clark, W. Mansfield**
Oxidation-reduction potentials of organic systems. Baltimore, Williams & Wilkins [1960] 584 p.
60-005143          547.23
*Oxidation-reduction reaction. Chemistry, Organic.*

**QD281.O9.H83 1990**
**Hudlicky, Milos,**
Oxidations in organic chemistry / Milos Hudlicky. Washington, DC : American Chemical Society, 1990. xx, 433 p. :
90-034564          547/.23          0841217807
*Oxidation. Chemistry, Organic.*

**QD281.P6.S27**
**Sandler, Stanley R.,**
Polymer syntheses [by] Stanley R. Sandler [and] Wolf Karo. New York, Academic Press, 1974-1980. 3 v.
73-002073          547/.84          0126185013
*Polymerization.*

## QD291 Organic chemistry — Nomenclature, terminology, notation, abbreviations

**QD291.L35 1998**
**Laue, Thomas,**
Named organic reactions / Thomas Laue and Andreas Plagens. Chichester ; Wiley, c1998. x, 288 p. :
          0471971421
*Chemical reactions. Chemistry, Organic -- Nomenclature.*

**QD291.N36 1995**
Names, synonyms, and structures of organic compounds : a CRC reference handbook / editors, David R. Lide, G.W.A. Milne. Boca Raton : CRC Press, c1995. 3 v. (2162, 2
94-025283          547/.00212          0849304059
*Organic compounds -- Nomenclature.*

**QD291.T55**
**Timmermans, Jean,**
Physico-chemical constants of pure organic compounds. New York, Elsevier Pub. Co., 1950-65 2 vols.
50-009668          547
*Chemistry, Organic -- Tables.*

## QD305 Organic chemistry — Aliphatic compounds — Special groups, A-Z

**QD305.A7.G85**
**Greenstein, Jesse P.**
Chemistry of the amino acids [by] Jesse P. Greenstein and Milton Winitz. New York, Wiley [1961] 3 v. (xxi, 28
61-006474          547.75
*Amino acids.*

**QD305.H5.H85 1995**
Hydrocarbon chemistry / George A. Olah, Arpad Molnar. New York : Wiley, c1995. xviii, 632 p.
94-031442          547/.01          047111359X
*Hydrocarbons.*

**QD305.H7.P3**
**Patai, Saul.**
The chemistry of alkenes, edited by Saul Patai. London, Interscience Publishers, 1964-1970. 2 v.
64-025218          547.412
*Alkenes.*

**QD305.H8.C43**
The Chemistry of the carbon-carbon triple bond / edited by Saul Patai. Chichester [Eng.] ; J. Wiley, 1978. 2 v. (xiv, 10
79-300116          547/.413          0471994960
*Acetylene compounds.*

**QD305.I6.P3**
**Patai, Saul.**
The chemistry of the carbon-nitrogen double bond; edited by Saul Patai. London, Interscience Publishers, 1970. xiii, 794 p.
70-104166          547/.044          0471669423
*Organonitrogen compounds. Methylenimine. Schiff bases.*

### QD321 Organic chemistry — Carbohydrates — General works, treatises, and textbooks

**QD321.P6243**
The Carbohydrates : chemistry and biochemistry / edited by Ward Pigman, Derek Horton ; assistant editor, Anthony Herp. 2nd ed. New York : Academic Press, 1970-1980. 2 v. in 4 :
          547/.7.8 19
*Carbohydrates.*

### QD325 Organic chemistry — Carbohydrates — Glycosides

**QD325.C66 1995**
**Collins, P. M.**
Monosaccharides : their chemistry and their roles in natural products / Peter M. Collins, Robert J. Ferrier. Chichester ; Wiley & Sons, c1995. xix, 574 p. :
94-026989          547.7/813          0471953431
*Monosaccharides.*

### QD331 Organic chemistry — Aromatic compounds — General works, treatises, and textbooks

**QD331.B2**
**Badger, G. M.**
The structures & reactions of the aromatic compounds. Cambridge [Eng.] University Press, 1954. 456 p.
54003317          547.25
*Aromatic compounds.*

**QD331.S25 1992**
**Sainsbury, Malcolm.**
Aromatic chemistry / Malcolm Sainsbury. Oxford ; Oxford University Press, 1992. 92 p. :
91-047606          547/.6          0198556756
*Aromatic compounds.*

### QD341 Organic chemistry — Aromatic compounds — Special groups, A-Z

**QD341.A2.W315**
**Watson, James D.,**
The double helix; a personal account of the discovery of the structure of DNA, by James D. Watson. New York, Atheneum, 1968. xvi, 226 p.
68-016217          547/.596
*Watson, James D., -- 1928- Watson, James D., -- 1928- Molecular biologists -- United States -- Biography. DNA.*

### QD381 Organic chemistry — Polymers. Macromolecules — General works, treatises, and textbooks

**QD381.F87 1998**
**Furukawa, Yasu.**
Inventing polymer science : Staudinger, Carothers, and the emergence of macromolecular chemistry / Yasu Furukawa. Philadelphia : University of Pennsylvania Press, c1998. xi, 310 p. :
97-036390          547/.7          0812233360
*Staudinger, Hermann, -- 1881-1965. Carothers, Wallace Hume, – 1896-1937. Macromolecules -- History. Polymers -- History. Polymerization -- History.*

**QD381.G755 1997**
**Grosberg, A. IU.**
Giant molecules : here, and there, and everywhere-- / Alexander Yu. Grosberg and Alexei R. Khokhlov ; [foreword by Pierre-Gilles de Gennes]. San Diego : Academic Press, c1997. xv, 244 p. :
96-027593          547.7          0123041309
*Polymers.*

**QD381.P68**
**Price, Charles C.**
Geometry of molecules [by] Charles C. Price. New York, McGraw-Hill [1971] x, 118 p.
77-159314          547/.84
*Polymers. Stereochemistry. Chemical bonds.*

**QD381.T65 2001**
**Tonelli, Alan E.**
Polymers from the inside out : an introduction to macromolecules / Alan E. Tonelli with Mohan Srinivasarao. New York : Wiley-Interscience, c2001. xxv, 249 p. :
00-047990          547/.7          0471381381
*Polymers. Polymerization.*

## QD381.8 Organic chemistry — Polymers. Macromolecules — Special aspects of the subject as a whole

**QD381.8.S86 1994**
Sun, S. F.,
Physical chemistry of macromolecules : basic principles and issues / S.F. Sun. New York : Wiley, c1994. xviii, 469 p.
93-028871        547.7/045        0471597880
*Macromolecules. Chemistry, Physical organic.*

## QD388 Organic chemistry — Polymers. Macromolecules — Handbooks, tables, formulas, etc.

**QD388.P65 1999**
Polymer handbook / editors, J. Brandrup, E.H. Immergut, and E.A. Grulke ; associate editors, A. Abe, D.R. Bloch. 4th ed. New York : Wiley, c1999. 1 v. :
547/.7 21
*Polymers -- Tables. Polymerization -- Tables.*

## QD400 Organic chemistry — Heterocyclic and macrocyclic chemistry and compounds — General works, treatises, and textbooks

**QD400.B25**
Badger, G. M.
The chemistry of heterocyclic compounds.  New York, Academic Press, 1961. 498 p.
60-014273        547.59
*Heterocyclic chemistry.*

**QD400.P59**
Physical methods in heterocyclic chemistry, edited by A.R. Katritzky. New York, Academic Press, 1963-1974. 6 v.
63-012034        547/.59        0124011039
*Heterocyclic chemistry.*

## QD405 Organic chemistry — Heterocyclic and macrocyclic chemistry and compounds — Cyclic compounds containing O

**QD405.F44**
Fieser, Louis Frederick,
Steroids [by] Louis F. Fieser and Mary Fieser. New York, Reinhold Pub. Corp. [1959] 945 p.
59-012534        547.73
*Steroids.*

## QD411 Organic chemistry — Organometallic chemistry and compounds — General works, treatises, and textbooks

**QD411.D53 1984**
Dictionary of organometallic compounds.   London ; Chapman and Hall, 1984. 3 v. ;
84-019952        547/.05/0321        0412247100
*Organometallic compounds -- Dictionaries.*

## QD411.8 Organic chemistry — Organometallic chemistry and compounds — Special groups of substances, A-Z

**QD411.8.T73**
Crabtree, Robert H.,
The organometallic chemistry of the transition metals / Robert H. Crabtree. 3rd ed. New York : John Wiley, c2001. xv, 534 p. :
00-033009        547/.056        0471184233
*Organotransition metal compounds.*

## QD412 Organic chemistry — Organometallic chemistry and compounds — Special compounds. By chemical symbol of added element, A-Z

**QD412.N1.S5 1966**
Sidgwick, Nevil Vincent,
The organic chemistry of nitrogen, by the late N. V. Sidgwick. Oxford, Clarendon P., 1966 [i.e. 19 xii, 909 p.
67-077211        547/.04
*Organonitrogen compounds.*

**QD412.S6.P37 1989**
Patai, Saul.
The chemistry of organic silicon compounds / edited by Saul Patai and Zvi Rappoport. Chichester [England] ; Wiley, 1989. 2 v. (xvi, 16
87-031709        547/.08        0471919934
*Organosilicon compounds.*

## QD415.A25 Organic chemistry — Biochemistry — Dictionaries and encyclopedias

**QD415.A25.B713 1997**
Concise encyclopedia biochemistry and molecular biology. Berlin ; Walter de Gruyter, 1997. 737 p. :
96-047538        572/.03        3110145359
*Biochemistry -- Dictionaries.*

## QD415.C483-415.F54 Organic chemistry — Biochemistry — General works, treatises, and textbooks

**QD415.C483 1993**
The Chemistry of natural products / edited by R. H. Thomson. 2nd ed. London ; New York : Blackie Academic & Professional, 1993. x, 452 p.:
547.7 20
*Natural products.*

**QD415.F54**
Florkin, Marcel,
Comprehensive biochemistry, edited by Marcel Florkin and Elmer H. Stotz. Amsterdam, Elsevier Pub. Co., 1962- v. in .
62-010359        547.1
*Biochemistry*

## QD421 Organic chemistry — Biochemistry — Alkaloids

**QD421.B45**
**Bentley, K. W.**
The alkaloids. New York, Interscience Publishers, 1957-65
2 v.
57-009154          547.72
*Alkaloids.*

## QD431 Organic chemistry — Biochemistry — Proteins, peptides, amino acids, etc.

**QD431.B28 1998**
**Barrett, G. C.,**
Amino acids and peptides /G.C. Barrett and D.T. Elmore. Cambridge ; Cambridge University Press, 1998. xv, 224 p. :
97-031093          572/.65          0521462924
*Amino acids. Peptides.*

**QD431.N453**
**Neurath, Hans,**
The proteins, edited by Hans Neurath [and] Robert L. Hill. Assisted by Carol-Leigh Boeder. New York, Academic Press, 1975- v.
74-010195          547/.75          0125163010
*Proteins. Proteins.*

## QD433 Organic chemistry — Biochemistry — Nucleic acids

**QD433.B44**
**Bloomfield, Victor A.**
Physical chemistry of nucleic acids [by] Victor A. Bloomfield, Donald M. Crothers [and] Ignacio Tinoco, Jr. New York, Harper & Row [1974] x, 517 p.
73-008373          547/.596          0060407794
*Nucleic acids. Chemistry, Physical. Nucleic acids.*

## QD441 Organic chemistry — Colored compounds

**QD441.M55 1997**
**Milgrom, Lionel R.**
The colours of life : an introduction to the chemistry of porphyrins and related compounds / Lionel R. Milgrom. Oxford ; Oxford University Press, 1997. vi, 249 p. :
96-027452          547/.593          0198553803
*Porphyrins.*

## QD452 Physical and theoretical chemistry — History — General works

**QD452.L35 1993**
**Laidler, Keith James,**
The world of physical chemistry / Keith J. Laidler. Oxford ; Oxford University Press, 1993. xii, 476 p. :
92-041635          541.3          0198555970
*Chemistry, Physical and theoretical -- History.*

## QD452.5 Physical and theoretical chemistry — History — By region or country, A-Z

**QD452.5.U6.S47 1990**
**Servos, John W.**
Physical chemistry from Ostwald to Pauling : the making of a science in America / John W. Servos. Princeton, N.J. : Princeton University Press, c1990. xxiii, 402 p.
89-070256          541.3/0973          0691085668
*Chemistry, Physical and theoretical -- United States -- History.*

## QD453 Physical and theoretical chemistry — General works, treatises, and textbooks — Through 1970

**QD453.E9**
**Eyring, Henry,**
Quantum chemistry, by Henry Eyring ... John Walter ... [and] George E. Kimball ... New York, J. Wiley & Sons, inc.; [1944] vi, 394 p.
44002961          541
*Chemistry. Chemistry, Physical. Quantum theory.*

**QD453.G53 1960**
**Glasstone, Samuel,**
Elements of physical chemistry [by] Samuel Glasstone and David Lewis. 2nd ed. Princeton, N.J., Van Nostrand [1960] 758 p.
60-011063          541
*Chemistry, Physical and theoretical.*

## QD453.2 Physical and theoretical chemistry — General works, treatises, and textbooks — 1971-

**QD453.2.B373**
**Barrow, Gordon M.**
Physical chemistry for the life sciences [by] Gordon M. Barrow. New York, McGraw-Hill [1974] x, 405 p.
73-018289          541./3/024574          0070038554
*Chemistry, Physical and theoretical.*

**QD453.2.M394 1997**
**McQuarrie, Donald A.**
Physical chemistry : a molecular approach / Donald A. McQuarrie, John D. Simon. Sausalito, Calif. : University Science Books, c1997. xxiii, 1360 p.
97-000142          541          0935702997
*Chemistry, Physical and theoretical.*

## QD455.3 Physical and theoretical chemistry — Special topics, A-Z

**QD455.3.C64.H46 1999**
**Hinchliffe, Alan.**
Chemical modeling : from atoms to liquids / Alan Hinchliffe. Chichester ; Wiley, c1999. xviii, 395 p.
99-032077          541/.01/13          0471999040
*Chemistry, Physical and theoretical -- Computer simulation. Chemistry, Physical and theoretical -- Mathematica! models.*

**QD455.3.G75.K56 1999**
**Kim, Shoon Kyung,**
  Group theoretical methods and applications to molecules and crystals / Shoon K. Kim. Cambridge, U.K. ; Cambridge University Press, 1999. xvi, 492 p. :
98-026493        512/.2        0521640628
  *Group theory. Chemistry, Physical and theoretical -- Mathematics. Crystallography, Mathematical.*

**QD455.3.M3M67 1999**
**Mortimer, Robert G.**
  Mathematics for physical chemistry / Robert G. Mortimer. 2nd ed. San Diego, CA : Harcourt/Academic Press, c1999. x, 444 p. :
         510/.24541 21
  *Chemistry, Physical and theoretical -- Mathematics.*

**QD457 Physical and theoretical chemistry — Study and teaching. Research — Laboratory manuals**

**QD457.G37 2002**
**Garland, Carl W.**
  Experiments in physical chemistry. 7th ed. / Carl W. Garland, Joseph W. Nibler, David P. Shoemaker. Dubuque, Iowa : McGraw-Hill, 2002. p. cm.
         541.3/078 21
  *Chemistry, Physical and theoretical -- Laboratory manuals.*

**QD461 Physical and theoretical chemistry — Atomic and molecular theory and structure. Laws of chemical combination and chemical bonds. Molecular dimensions**

**QD461.A85 1987**
**Atkins, P. W.**
  Molecules / P.W. Atkins. New York : Scientific American Library, 1987. viii, 197 p.
87-020681        547.1        0716750198
  *Molecular structure. Molecules.*

**QD461.C422 1992**
  The Chemical bond : structure and dynamics / edited by Ahmed Zewail. Boston : Academic Press, c1992. xv, 313 p. :
91-029643        541.2/24        0127796207
  *Chemical bonds.*

**QD461.C65 1990**
**Cotton, F. Albert**
  Chemical applications of group theory / F. Albert Cotton. 3rd ed. New York : Wiley, c1990. xiv, 461 p. :
89-016434        541/.22/015122        0471510947
  *Molecular theory. Group theory.*

**QD461.G52 2000**
**Gil, Victor M. S.,**
  Orbitals in chemistry : modern guide for students / Victor M.S. Gil. Cambridge ; Cambridge University Press, 2000. xii, 314 p. :
99-461968        541.2/8        0521661676
  *Molecular orbitals. Chemistry, Physical organic.*

**QD461.H263 1995**
**Hanson, Robert M.,**
  Molecular origami : precision scale models from paper / Robert M. Hanson. Sausalito, Calif. : University Science Books, c1995. xiii, 223 p.
94-037451        541.2/2/0228        093570230X
  *Molecules -- Models. Models and modelmaking. Paper work.*

**QD461.J4313 1993**
**Jean, Yves,**
  An introduction to molecular orbitals / by Yves Jean and Francois Volatron ; translated and edited by Jeremy Burdett. New York : Oxford University Press, 1993. xiv, 337 p. :
92-045676        514.2/24        0195069188
  *Molecular orbitals.*

**QD461.J44 1997**
**Jeffrey, George A.,**
  An introduction to hydrogen bonding / George A. Jeffrey. New York : Oxford University Press, 1997. vii, 303 p. :
96-026792        541.2/26        0195095480
  *Hydrogen bonding.*

**QD461.M583 1993**
**Mezey, Paul G.**
  Shape in chemistry : an introduction to molecular shape and topology / Paul G. Mezey. New York, NY : VCH, c1993. xi, 224 p. :
93-015622        541.2/2        0895737272
  *Molecular structure. Topology.*

**QD462 Physical and theoretical chemistry — General works, treatises, and textbooks**

**QD462.A84 1996**
**Atkins, P. W.**
  Molecular quantum mechanics / P.W. Atkins and R.S. Friedman. 3rd ed. New York : Oxford University Press, 1996. p. cm.
96-023892        541.2/8        0198559488
  *Quantum chemistry.*

**QD462.F55 1999**
**Fitts, Donald D.,**
  Principles of quantum mechanics as applied to chemistry and chemical physics / Donald D. Fitts. New York : Cambridge University Press, 1999. ix, 351 p. :
98-039486        541.2/8        0521651247
  *Quantum chemistry.*

**QD462.S53 1997**
**Simons, Jack.**
  Quantum mechanics in chemistry / Jack Simons, Jeff Nichols. New York : Oxford University Press, 1997. xxiii, 612 p.
96-034013        541.2/8        0195082001
  *Quantum chemistry.*

### QD466 Physical and theoretical chemistry — Chemical elements — Nature and properties

**QD466.A845 1995**
**Atkins, P. W.**
The periodic kingdom : a journey into the land of the chemical elements / P.W. Atkins. New York : BasicBooks, c1995. ix, 161 p. :
95-007362          541.2/4          0465072658
*Chemical elements. Periodic law.*

**QD466.C875 1989**
**Cox, P. A.**
The elements : their origin, abundance, and distribution / P.A. Cox. Oxford [England] ; Oxford University Press, 1989. viii, 207 p.
88-037342          546          019855298X
*Chemical elements.*

**QD466.E48 1998**
**Emsley, John.**
The elements / written and compiled by John Emsley. 3rd ed. Oxford University Press ; / 1998. vii, 292 p. :

**QD466.E48 1998**
**Emsley, John.**
The elements / written and compiled by John Emsley. 3rd ed. Oxford ; New York : Oxford University Press ; Clarendon Press, 1998. vii, 292 p. :
          546 21          0198558198
*Chemical elements -- Handbooks, manuals, etc.*

**QD466.G74 1997**
**Greenwood, N.N. (Norman Neill)**
Chemistry of the elements / N.N. Greenwood and A. Earnshaw. 2nd ed. Oxford ; Boston : Butterworth-Heinemann, c1997. xxii, 1341 p. :
          546 21          0750633654
*Chemical elements.*

**QD466.H295**
**Hampel, Clifford A.**
The encyclopedia of the chemical elements, edited by Clifford A. Hampel. New York, Reinhold Book Corp. [1968] viii, 849 p.
68-029938          546/.11/03
*Chemical elements -- Dictionaries.*

**QD466.K69 1998**
**Krebs, Robert E.,**
The history and use of our earth's chemical elements : a reference guide / Robert E. Krebs ; illustrations by Rae Dejur. Westport, Conn. : Greenwood Press, 1998. ix, 346 p. :
96-049735          546          0313301239
*Chemical elements.*

**QD466.L37 1978**
Table of isotopes. New York : Wiley, c1978. 1628 p. in va
78-014938          541/.388          0471041793.
*Isotopes -- Tables.*

### QD467 Physical and theoretical chemistry — Chemical elements — Classification. Periodic law

**QD467.M35 1974**
**Mazurs, Edward G.**
Graphic representations of the periodic system during one hundred years [by] Edward G. Mazurs. University, Ala., University of Alabama Press, c1974. 251 p.
73008051          541/.901          0817332006
*Periodic law. Chemical elements.*

**QD467.S3**
**Sanderson, R. T.**
Chemical periodicity / R.T. Sanderson. New York : Reinhold, c1960. x, 330 p. :
60011081          541.901
*Periodic law.*

### QD469 Physical and theoretical chemistry — Chemical elements — Valence

**QD469.C74 1979**
**Coulson, Charles Alfred,**
Coulson's Valence / Roy McWeeny. 3d ed. Oxford ; New York : Oxford University Press, 1979. x, 434 p. :
          541/.224          0198551444
*Valence (Theoretical chemistry)*

**QD469.P38 1960**
**Pauling, Linus,**
The nature of the chemical bond and the structure of molecules and crystals; an introduction to modern structural chemistry. 3rd ed. Ithaca, N.Y., Cornell University Press, 1960. 644 p.
60-016025          541.396
*Chemical bonds. Quantum chemistry. Molecules.*

### QD471 Physical and theoretical chemistry — Chemical compounds - Structure and formulas

**QD471.B23**
**Bailar, John Christian,**
The chemistry of the coordination compounds. Daryle H. Busch, editorial assistant. New York, Reinhold Pub. Corp., 1956. x, 834 p.
56-006686          541.39
*Coordination compounds. Chemistry, Organic Chemistry, Physical*

**QD471.L5 1993**
**Leffler, John E.**
An introduction to free radicals / John E. Leffler. New York : Wiley, c1993. 287 p. :
92-035288          541.2/24          0471594067
*Free radicals (Chemistry)*

## QD474 Physical and theoretical chemistry — Complex compounds

**QD474.A44 1993**
**American Chemical Society.**
Coordination chemistry : a century of progress : developed from a symposium sponsored by the Divisions of the History of Chemistry, Chemical Education, Inc., and Inorganic Chemistry, Inc., at the 20 George B. Kauffman, editor. Washington, DC : American Chemical Society, 1994. xvi, 464 p. :
94-034445          541.2/242          0841229503
*Coordination compounds -- Congresses.*

## QD475 Physical and theoretical chemistry — Physical inorganic chemistry

**QD475.D65 1983**
**Douglas, Bodie Eugene,**
Concepts and models of inorganic chemistry / Bodie E. Douglas, Darl H. McDaniel, John J. Alexander. 2nd ed. New York : Wiley, c1983. xii, 800 p. :
82-002606          546          0471219843
*Chemistry, Inorganic.*

**QD475.F54 2000**
**Figgis, B. N.**
Ligand field theory and its applications / Brian N. Figgis, Michael A. Hitchman. New York : Wiley-VCH, c2000. xviii, 354 p.
99-028986          541.2/242          0471317764
*Ligand field theory.*

**QD475.W27 2000**
**Warren, Warren S.**
The physical basis of chemistry / Warren S. Warren. San Diego : Academic Press, c2000. xvii, 211 p.
99-068993          541/.01/53          0127358552
*Chemistry, Physical and theoretical. Chemistry, Inorganic.*

## QD476 Physical and theoretical chemistry — Physical organic chemistry

**QD476.A4**
Advances in physical organic chemistry. London, Academic Press. v.
62-022125          547.1082
*Chemistry, Physical organic.*

**QD476.B6713 1993**
**Breitmaier, E.**
Structure elucidation by NMR in organic chemistry : a practical guide / Eberhard Breitmaier ; translated by Julia Wade. Chichester ; Wiley, c1993. xii, 265 p. :
92-018531          547.3/0877          0471937452
*Organic compounds -- Structure. Nuclear magnetic resonance spectroscopy.*

**QD476.H33 1970**
**Hammett, Louis P.**
Physical organic chemistry; reaction rates, equilibria, and mechanisms [by] Louis P. Hammett. New York, McGraw-Hill [1970] 420 p.
73-091680          547/.1/3
*Chemistry, Physical organic.*

**QD476.K53 1995**
**Klessinger, Martin.**
Excited states and photochemistry of organic molecules / Martin Klessinger, Josef Michl. New York : VCH, c1995. xxiv, 537 p.
92-046464          547.1/35          1560815884
*Chemistry, Physical organic. Photochemistry. Excited state chemistry.*

**QD476.L68 1987**
**Lowry, Thomas H.**
Mechanism and theory in organic chemistry / Thomas H. Lowry, Kathleen Schueller Richardson. 3rd ed. New York : Harper & Row, c1987. xii, 1090 p.
86-022851          547.1/3          0060440848
*Chemistry, Physical organic.*

**QD476.M66 1992**
**Moody, Christopher J.**
Reactive intermediates / Christopher J. Moody and Gordon h. Whitham. Oxford ; Oxford University Press, 1992. 89 p. :
92-012267          547.2          019855673X
*Intermediates (Chemistry) Organic compounds -- Synthesis.*

**QD476.P35**
**Pasto, Daniel J.,**
Organic structure determination [by] Daniel J. Pasto [and] Carl R. Johnson. Englewood Cliffs, N.J., Prentice-Hall [1969] xiii, 513 p.
69-015046          547/.1/2          0136408540
*Chemistry, Physical organic.*

**QD476.P755 1995**
**Pross, Addy,**
Theoretical and physical principles of organic reactivity / Addy Pross. New York : Wiley, c1995. xv, 294 p. :
95-021389          547.1          0471555991
*Chemistry, Physical organic.*

## QD477 Physical and theoretical chemistry — Acids and bases (General theory)

**QD477.F56 1982**
**Finston, H. L.**
A new view of current acid-base theories / Harmon L. Finston and Allen C. Rychtman. New York : Wiley, c1982. viii, 216 p.
81-016030          541.3/94          0471084727
*Acid-base chemistry.*

**QD477.J46**
**Jensen, William B.**
 The Lewis acid-base concepts : an overview / William B. Jensen. New York : Wiley, c1980. xi, 364 p. :
79-015561      546/.24      0471039020
 *Acid-base chemistry.*

## QD478 Physical and theoretical chemistry — Solids. Solid state chemistry (Inorganic and organic)

**QD478.S6334 1991**
 Solid state chemistry : compounds / edited by A.K. Cheetham and Peter Day. Oxford [England] : Clarendon Press ; 1992. xii, 304 p. :
91-012173      541/.0421      0198551665
 *Solid state chemistry.*

## QD480 Physical and theoretical chemistry — Models of atoms, molecules, or chemical compounds

**QD480.C66 1995**
**Comba, Peter.**
 Molecular modeling / Peter Comba, Trevor W. Hambley. Weinheim ; VCH, c1995. x, 197 p. ;
95-024487      541.2/2/015118      3527290761
 *Inorganic compounds -- Mathematical models. Chemical models.*

## QD481 Physical and theoretical chemistry — Stereochemistry. Molecular rotation

**QD481.E525 1994**
**Eliel, Ernest Ludwig,**
 Stereochemistry of organic compounds / Ernest L. Eliel, Samuel H. Wilen ; with a chapter on stereoselective synthesis by Lewis N. Mander. New York : Wiley, c1994. xv, 1267 p. :
93-012476      547.1/223      0471016705
 *Stereochemistry. Organic compounds.*

**QD481.W44 1984**
**Wells, A. F.**
 Structural inorganic chemistry / A.F. Wells. 5th ed. Oxford [Oxfordshire] : Clarendon Press ; 1984, c1975. xxxi, 1382 p.
82-018866      546/.252      0198553706
 *Chemical structure. Stereochemistry. Crystallography.*

## QD501 Physical and theoretical chemistry — Conditions and laws of chemical reactions — General works

**QD501.G323**
**Gardiner, William C.**
 Rates and mechanisms of chemical reactions [by] W. C. Gardiner, Jr. New York, W. A. Benjamin, 1969. xiii, 284 p.
76-080660      541/.39      080533100X
 *Chemical kinetics.*

**QD501.K7514 1964b**
**King, Edward Louis,**
 How chemical reactions occur : an introduction to chemical kinetics and reaction mechanisms / Edward L. King. 2nd print., with corrections. New York : W.A. Benjamin, 1964. xi, 148 p.
541.3/9 19
 *Chemical kinetics. Reaction mechanisms (Chemistry)*

**QD501.K7557**
**Klotz, Irving M.**
 Energy changes in biochemical reactions [by] Irving M. Klotz. New York, Academic Press, 1967. x, 108 p.
66-030088      574.1/92
 *Bioenergetics.*

## QD502 Physical and theoretical chemistry — Conditions and laws of chemical reactions — Chemical kinetics and mechanisms

**QD502.D96 1996**
 Dynamics of molecules and chemical reactions / edited by Robert E. Wyatt, John Z.H. Zhang. New York : Marcel Dekker, 1996. ix, 677 p.
96-018104      541.39/4      0824795385
 *Chemical kinetics. Molecular dynamics.*

**QD502.J67 1998**
**Jordan, Robert B.**
 Reaction mechanisms of inorganic and organometallic systems / Robert B. Jordan. New York : Oxford University Press, 1998. viii, 371 p.
97-031222      541.3/9      0195115554
 *Reaction mechanisms (Chemistry) Organometallic compounds. Inorganic compounds.*

**QD502.P54 1995**
**Pilling, M. J.**
 Reaction kinetics / Michael J. Pilling and Paul W. Seakins. Oxford ; Oxford University Press, 1995. xiii, 305 p.
94-046221      541.3/94      0198555288
 *Chemical kinetics.*

## QD503 Physical and theoretical chemistry — Conditions and laws of chemical reactions — Chemical equilibrium. Phase rule, etc.

**QD503.H554 1998**
**Hillert, Mats,**
 Phase equilibria, phase diagrams, and phase transformations : their thermodynamic basis / Mats Hillert. Cambridge, U.K. ; Cambridge University Press, 1998. xv, 538 p. :
97-012280      541.3/63      0521562708
 *Phase rule and equilibrium. Chemical equilibrium. Thermodynamics.*

**QD503.Y68 1991**
**Young, D. A.**
 Phase diagrams of the elements / David A. Young. Berkeley : University of California Press, c1991. xi, 291 p. :
90-025978      541.3/63      0520074831
 *Phase diagrams. High pressure (Science)*

## QD504 Physical and theoretical chemistry — Conditions and laws of chemical reactions — Thermodynamics

**QD504.K55 1994**
**Klotz, Irving Myron,**
  Chemical thermodynamics : basic theory and methods / Irving M. Klotz, Robert M. Rosenberg. 5th ed. New York : Wiley, c1994. xxiii, 533 p. :
            541.3/69 20        0471534390
*Thermodynamics.*

## QD505 Physical and theoretical chemistry — Conditions and laws of chemical reactions — Catalysis

**QD505.C36 1988**
**Campbell, Ian M.**
  Catalysis at surfaces / Ian M. Campbell. London ; Chapman and Hall, 1988. viii, 250 p.
88-004383        660.2/995        0412318806
  *Catalysis. Surface chemistry.*

**QD505.C383x 2000**
  Catalysis from A to Z : a concise encyclopedia / edited by Boy Cornils . . . [et al.] Weinheim ; New York : Wiley-VCH, 2000. xviii, 640 p. :
            541.3/95/03 21        352729855X
*Catalysis -- Encyclopedias.*

**QD505.C57 1994**
**Clark, James H.**
  Catalysis of organic reactions by supported inorganic reagents / James H. Clark. New York : VCH, c1994. xi, 126 p. :
94-002230        547.1/398        1560815078
  *Catalysis. Supported reagents.*

**QD505.G38 1991**
**Gates, Bruce C.**
  Catalytic chemistry / Bruce C. Gates. New York : Wiley, c1992. xxi, 458 p. :
91-004192        541.3/95        0471517615
  *Catalysis.*

## QD506 Physical and theoretical chemistry — Surface chemistry — Societies, congresses, serial collections, yearbooks

**QD506.A3 1997**
**Adamson, Arthur W.**
  Physical chemistry of surfaces / Arthur W. Adamson and Alice P. Gast. 6th ed. New York, Wiley, c1997. xxi, 784 p. :
            541.3/3 21        0471148733
*Surface chemistry. Chemistry, Physical and theoretical.*

**QD506.F39 1986**
**Feldman, Leonard C.**
  Fundamentals of surface and thin film analysis / Leonard C. Feldman, James W. Mayer. New York : North-Holland, c1986. xviii, 352 p.
86-002479        530.4/1        0444009892
  *Surfaces (Technology) -- Analysis. Thin films -- Analysis.*

**QD506.M26 1990**
**MacRitchie, Finlay.**
  Chemistry at interfaces / Finlay MacRitchie. San Diego : Academic Press, c1990. x, 283 p. :
89-032329        541.3/3        0124647855
  *Surface chemistry.*

**QD506.M93 1999**
**Myers, Drew,**
  Surfaces, interfaces, and colloids : principles and applications / Drew Myers. 2nd ed. New York : Wiley-VCH, c1999. xx, 501 p. :
            541.3/3 21        0471330604
*Surface chemistry. Interfaces (Physical sciences) Colloids.*

## QD508 Physical and theoretical chemistry — Surface chemistry — Addresses, essays, lectures

**QD508.H36 1997**
  Handbook of surface and colloid chemistry / edited by K.S. Birdi. Boca Raton, Fla. : CRC Press, c1997. 763 p. :
97-003758        541.3/3        0849394597
  *Surface chemistry. Colloids.*

## QD516 Physical and theoretical chemistry — Thermochemistry — Heat of formation, combustion, flame, explosion

**QD516.B6713 1998**
**Borghi, R.**
  Combustion and flames : chemical and physical principles / Roland Borghi, Michel Destriau ; with the collaboration of Gerard de Soete ; translated from the French by Richard Turner. Paris : Editions Technip, 1998. xv, 371 p. :
99-208655        541.3/61        2710807408
  *Combustion. Flame.*

**QD516.W2813 2001**
**Warnatz, J.**
  Combustion : physical and chemical fundamentals, modeling and simulation, experiments, pollutant formation / J. Warnatz, U. Maas, R.W. Dibble. 3rd ed. Berlin ; New York : Springer, 2001. x, 299 p. :
            541.3/61 21        3540677518
*Combustion.*

## QD541 Physical and theoretical chemistry — Theory of solution — General works, treatises, and textbooks

**QD541.M9 1994**
**Murrell, John Norman**
   Properties of liquids and solutions / J.N. Murrell and A.D. Jenkins. 2nd ed. Chichester [England] ; New York : Wiley & Sons, c1994. x, 303 p. :
            540/.0422 20        0471944181
*Liquids.  Solution (Chemistry)*

## QD543 Physical and theoretical chemistry — Theory of solution — Solubility, osmotic pressure, diffusion, etc.

**QD543.H258 2000**
**Hansen, Charles M.**
   Hansen solubility parameters : a user's handbook / Charles M. Hansen. Boca Raton, Fla. : CRC Press, c2000. 208 p. :
99-026234         547/.70454         0849315255
   *Solution (Chemistry)  Polymers -- Solubility  Thin films.*

## QD547 Physical and theoretical chemistry — Theory of solution — Flocculation, precipitation, adsorption, etc.

**QD547.S63 1992**
**Sohnel, Otakar.**
   Precipitation : basic principles and industrial applications / Otakar Sohnel and John Garside. Oxford [England] ; Butterworth-Heinemann, 1992. xvii, 391 p.
92-022007         541.3/422         0750611073
   *Precipitation (Chemistry)*

## QD549 Physical and theoretical chemistry — Theory of solution — Colloids, sols, gels

**QD549.E93 1999**
**Evans, D. Fennell.**
   The colloidal domain : where physics, chemistry, biology, and technology meet / Fennell Evans and Hakan Wennerstrom. 2nd ed. New York : Wiley-VCH, c1999. xl. 632 p.
            541.3/45 21
*Colloids.  Surface chemistry.*

## QD553 Physical and theoretical chemistry — Electrochemistry. Electrolysis — General works, treatises, and textbooks

**QD553.B37**
**Bard, Allen J.**
   Electrochemical methods : fundamentals and applications / Allen J. Bard, Larry R. Faulkner. New York : Wiley, c1980. xviii, 718 p.
79-024712         541/.37         0471055425
   *Electrochemistry.*

**QD553.H29 1998**
**Hamann, Carl H.**
   Electrochemistry / Carl H. Hamann, Andrew Hamnett, Wolf Vielstich. Weinheim ; Wiley-VCH, c1998. xvii, 423 p.
98-155076         541.3/7         3527290966
   *Electrochemistry.*

**QD553.P48 1995**
   Physical electrochemistry : principles, methods, and applications / edited by Israel Rubinstein. New York : M. Dekker, c1995. viii, 595 p.
94-047122         541.3/7         0824794524
   *Electrochemistry.*

**QD553.S32 1995**
**Sawyer, Donald T.**
   Electrochemistry for chemists / Donald T. Sawyer, Andrzej Sobkowiak, Julian L. Roberts, Jr. 2nd ed. New York : Wiley, c1995. xv, 505 p. :
95-002738         541.3/7         0471594687
   *Electrochemistry.*

## QD555.5 Physical and theoretical chemistry — Electrochemistry. Electrolysis — Special topics, A-Z

**QD555.5.N66 1999**
   Nonaqueous electrochemistry / edited by Doron Aurbach. New York : Marcel Dekker, c1999. viii, 602 p.
99-035915         541.3/7         0824773349
   *Electrochemistry.  Nonaqueous solvents.*

**QD555.5.S65 1995**
   Solid state electrochemistry / edited by Peter G. Bruce. Cambridge ; Cambridge University Press, 1995. xvi, 344 p. :
93-042634         541/.042         0521400074
   *Electrochemistry.  Solid state chemistry.*

## QD561 Physical and theoretical chemistry — Electrochemistry. Electrolysis — Ions and ionization

**QD561.A366 1984**
**Albert, Adrien.**
   The determination of ionization constants : a laboratory manual / Adrien Albert, E.P. Serjeant. 3rd ed. London ; New York : Chapman and Hall, 1984. x, 218 p. :
            541.3/722/028 19         0412242907
*Ionization constants -- Measurement -- Laboratory manuals.*

**QD561.B32 1973**
**Bates, Roger G.**
   Determination of pH; theory and practice [by] Roger G. Bates. New York, Wiley [1973] xv, 479 p.
72-008779         541/.3728         0471056472
   *Hydrogen-ion concentration -- Measurement.  Electrochemistry. Hydrogen-ion concentration.*

**QD561.B9525 1988**
**Burgess, John,**
  Ions in solution : basic principles of chemical interactions / J. Burgess. Chichester, England : E. Horwood ; 1988. 191 p. :
88-000662          541.3/72          0745801722
  *Ionic solutions.  Solution (Chemistry)*

**QD561.B985 1998**
**Butler, James Newton.**
  Ionic equilibrium : solubility and pH calculations / James N. Butler ; with a chapter by David R. Cogley. New York : Wiley, c1998. xi, 559 p. :
97-013435          541.3/723          0471585262
  *Ionic equilibrium.*

**QD561.L35 1952**
**Latimer, Wendell M.**
  The oxidation states of the elements and their potentials in aqueous solutions. New York, Prentice-Hall, 1952. 392 p.
52-010791          541.37
  *Electrolysis. Oxidation. Chemical elements.*

### QD571 Physical and theoretical chemistry — Electrochemistry. Electrolysis — Electrode phenomena. Polarization, etc.

**QD571.M27**
**McClellan, Aubrey Lester,**
  Tables of experimental dipole moments.  San Francisco, W.H. Freeman [1963] 713 p.
63014844          541.377
  *Dipole moments -- Tables.*

### QD601.2 Physical and theoretical chemistry — Radiochemistry. Nuclear chemistry — General works, treatises, and textbooks

**QD601.2.A35 1993**
**Adloff, J. P.**
  Fundamentals of radiochemistry / Jean-Pierre Adloff, Robert Guillaumont. Boca Raton : CRC Press, c1993. 414 p. :
92-029544          541.3/8          0849342449
  *Radiochemistry.*

**QD601.2.C47 1980**
**Choppin, Gregory R.**
  Nuclear chemistry : theory and applications / by Gregory R. Choppin and Jan Rydberg. Oxford [Eng.] ; Pergamon Press, 1980. viii, 667 p.
79-040371          541/.38          0080238262
  *Nuclear chemistry. Radiochemistry. Radiation chemistry.*

### QD636 Physical and theoretical chemistry — Radiation chemistry — General works, treatises, and textbooks

**QD636.M69 1999**
**Mozumder, A.**
  Fundamentals of radiation chemistry / A. Mozumder. San Diego : Academic Press, c1999. xvi, 392 p. :
99-060404          541.3/82          012509390X
  *Radiation chemistry.*

### QD708.2 Physical and theoretical chemistry — Photochemistry — General works, treatises, and textbooks

**QD708.2.C69 1986**
**Coyle, J. D.**
  Introduction to organic photochemistry / J.D. Coyle. Chichester [West Sussex] ; Wiley, c1986. viii, 176 p.
85-029593          547.1/35          0471909742
  *Organic photochemistry.*

**QD708.2.W39 1988**
**Wayne, Richard P.**
  Principles and applications of photochemistry / Richard P. Wayne. Oxford [England] ; Oxford University Press, 1988. xiii, 268 p.
88-005283          541.3/5          0198552335
  *Photochemistry.*

### QD719 Physical and theoretical chemistry — Photochemistry — Handbooks, tables, formulas, etc.

**QD719.C73 1994**
  CRC handbook of organic photochemistry and photobiology / editor, William M. Horspool ; associate editor, Pill-Soon Song. Boca Raton : CRC Press, c1995. 1636 p. :
94-012056          547.1/35          0849386349
  *Photochemistry -- Handbooks, manuals, etc. Photobiology -- Handbooks, manuals, etc.*

### QD801 Physical and theoretical chemistry — Sonochemistry

**QD801.M374 1999**
**Mason, T. J.**
  Sonochemistry / Timothy J. Mason. New York : Oxford University Press, 1999. 92 p.
99-015703          541.3          0198503717
  *Sonochemistry.*

**QD903 Crystallography — History — General works**

**QD903.H57 1990**
Historical atlas of crystallography / edited by J. Lima-de-Faria ; with the collaboration of M.J. Buerger ... [et al.]. Dordrecht ; Published for International Union of Crystallogr 1990. x, 158 p. :
89-071700          549/.09          079230649X
*Crystallography -- History -- Atlases.*

**QD905 Crystallography — General works, treatises, and textbooks — 1801-1969**

**QD905.B96**
**Buerger, Martin Julian,**
Elementary crystallography; an introduction to the fundamental geometrical features of crystals. New York, Wiley [1956] 528 p.
55-009511          548
*Crystallography.*

**QD905.2 Crystallography — General works, treatises, and textbooks — 1970-**

**QD905.2 H355 2001**
**Hammond, C.**
The basics of crystallography and diffraction / Christopher Hammond. New York : Oxford University Press, 2001. xiii, 331 p.
00-053086          548          0198505531
*Crystallography. X-ray crystallography.*

**QD905.2.H36 1990**
**Hammond, C.**
Introduction to crystallography / C. Hammond. Oxford [England] ; Oxford University Press ; 1990. viii, 101 p.
89-022835          548          0198564236
*Crystallography.*

**QD905.2.R6813 1998**
**Rousseau, J.-J.**
Basic crystallography / J.-J. Rousseau ; translated from the French by A. James. Chichester ; J. Wiley, c1998. xii, 414 p. :
97-044185          548/.81          0471970484
*Crystallography.*

**QD921 Crystallography — Crystal structure and growth — General works**

**QD921.H58 1982**
**Holden, Alan.**
Crystals and crystal growing / Alan Holden and Phylis Morrison ; introduction by Philip Morrison. Cambridge, Mass. : MIT Press, 1982. 318 p., [32]
81-023639          548          0262580500
*Crystals. Crystal growth.*

**QD921.K676613 1994**
**Kosuge, Koji,**
Chemistry of non-stoichiometric compounds / Koji Kosuge. Oxford ; Oxford University Press, 1994. x, 262 p. :
93-021864          548/.8          0198555555
*Crystals -- Defects. Inorganic compounds.*

**QD923 Crystallography — Crystal structure and growth — Liquid crystals**

**QD923.C638 2002**
**Collings, Peter J.,**
Liquids crystals : nature's delicate phase of matter / Peter J. Collings. 2nd ed. Princeton, N.J. : Princeton University Press, 2002. p. cm.
          530.4/29 21          0691086729
*Liquid crystals.*

**QD945 Crystallography — Physical properties of crystals — X-ray crystallography**

**QD945.D84 1979**
**Dunitz, Jack D.**
X-ray analysis and the structure of organic molecules / by Jack D. Dunitz. Ithaca : Cornell University Press, c1979. 514 p. :
78-015588          547/.1/22          0801411157
*X-ray crystallography. Molecular structure.*

**QD945.G58 1985**
**Glusker, Jenny Pickworth.**
Crystal structure analysis : a primer / Jenny Pickworth Glusker, Kenneth N. Trueblood. New York : Oxford University Press, 1985. xvii, 269 p.
84-014823          547/.83          0195035313
*X-ray crystallography.*

**QD945.G583 1994**
**Glusker, Jenny Pickworth.**
Crystal structure analysis for chemists and biologists / Jenny P. Glusker with Mitchell Lewis, Miriam Rossi. New York : VCH, c1994. xvii, 854 p.
92-007886          548/.83          0895732734
*X-ray crystallography.*

**QD945.M37713 2000**
**Massa, Werner,**
Crystal structure determination / Werner Massa ; translated into English by Robert O. Gould. Berlin ; Springer, 2000. xi, 206 p. :
99-036317          548/.83          3540659706
*X-ray crystallography.*

**QD945.W59 1995**
**Woolfson, M. M.**
Physical and non-physical methods of solving crystal structures / Michael Woolfson and Fan Hai-fu. Cambridge ; Cambridge University Press, 1995. xii, 276 p. :
94-008254          548/.83          0521412994
*X-ray crystallography -- Technique.*

# QE Geology

## QE5 Dictionaries and Encyclopedias

**QE5.B38 1997**
Glossary of geology. 4th ed. / Julia A. Jackson, editor. Alexandria, Va. : American Geological Institute, 1997. p. cm.
550/.3 21
*Geology -- Dictionaries.*

**QE5.D54 1999**
A dictionary of earth sciences. 2nd ed. /edited by Ailsa Allaby and Michael Allaby. Oxford ; New York : Oxford University Press, 1999. vii, 619 p. :
550/.3 21       0192800795
*Earth sciences -- Dictionaries.*

**QE5.E514 1991**
Encyclopedia of earth system science / William A. Nierenberg, editor-in-chief. San Diego : Academic Press, c1992. 4 v. :
90-029045     550/.3    0122267222
*Earth sciences -- Encyclopedias.*

**QE5.F33**
**Fairbridge, Rhodes Whitmore,**
The encyclopedia of world regional geology /edited by Rhodes W. Fairbridge. Stroudsburg, Pa. : Dowden, Hutchinson & Ross ; [1975- v. :
75-001406     550/.9    047025145X
*Geology -- Dictionaries.*

**QE5.M364 1997**
McGraw-Hill dictionary of earth science / Sybil P. Parker, editor in chief. New York : McGraw-Hill, c1997. xii, 468 p. ;
96-042986     550/.3    0070524270
*Earth sciences -- Dictionaries.*

**QE5.M3654 1997**
McGraw-Hill dictionary of geology and mineralogy / Sybil P. Parker, editor in chief. New York : McGraw-Hill, c1997. xi, 346 p. :
550/.3 21      0070524327
*Geology -- Dictionaries. Mineralogy -- Dictionaries.*

**QE5.O94 2000**
Oxford companion to the earth / editors Paul L. Hancock and Brian J. Skinner ; associate editor David L. Dineley ; subject editor, Alastair G. Dawson, K. Vala Ragnarsdottir, Iain S. Stewart. Oxford ; Oxford University Press, 2000. x, 1174 p. :
01-016311     550/.3    0198540396
*Earth sciences -- Dictionaries.*

**QE5.W5 1968**
**Wilmarth, M. Grace**
Lexicon of geologic names of the United States (including Alaska) Washington, U.S. Govt. Print. Off., 1938. Grosse Pointe, Mich., Scholarly Press, 1968. 2 v. (2396 p.
71-003260     551.7/003
*Geology -- United States -- Nomenclature.*

## QE11 History — General works

**QE11.S38 1998**
Sciences of the earth : an encyclopedia of events, people, and phenomena /edited by Gregory A. Good. New York : Garland Pub., 1998. 2 v. (xlv, 90
97-025163    550/.9    081530062X
*Earth sciences -- History -- Encyclopedias.*

## QE21 Biography — Collective

**QE21.F4 1952**
**Fenton, Carroll Lane,**
Giants of geology, by Carroll Lane Fenton and Mildred Adams Fenton. Garden City, N.Y., Doubleday, 1952. 333 p.
52-005125     925.5
*Geologists. Geology -- History.*

## QE22 Biography — Individual, A-Z

**QE22.H3**
**Cassidy, James G.,**
Ferdinand V. Hayden : entrepreneur of science / James G. Cassidy. Lincoln : University of Nebraska Press, c2000. xxv, 389 p. :
99-058427     338.97306/09/034
080321507X
*Hayden, F. V. -- (Ferdinand Vandeveer), -- 1829-1887. Science and state -- United States -- History -- 19th century. Geologists – United States -- Biography. West (U.S.) -- Discovery and exploration -- History -- 19th century.*

**QE22.H76.D74 1996**
**Drake, Ellen T.**
Restless genius : Robert Hooke and his earthly thoughts / Ellen Tan Drake. New York : Oxford University Press, 1996. xiv, 386 p. :
95-042703     550/.92    0195066952
*Hooke, Robert, -- 1635-1703. Hooke, Robert, -- 1635-1703 -- Contributions in geology. Hooke, Robert, -- 1635-1703 – Influence. Earthquakes. Volcanism. Geologists -- England -- Biography.*

**QE22.L8L94 1998**
Lyell : the past is the key to the present / edited by Derek J. Blundell & Andrew C. Scott. London ; Tulsa, OK : AAPG Bookstore [distributor] ; Geological Society, 1998. viii, 376 p. :
550 s 550/.92 21    1862390185
*Lyell, Charles, Sir, 1797-1875 -- Congresses. Geologists -- Great Britain -- Biography -- Congresses. Geology -- Congresses.*

**QE22.S6W55 2001**
**Winchester, Simon.**
The map that changed the world : William Smith and the birth of modern geology / Simon Winchester ; [illustrations by Soun Vannithone]. 1st ed. New York, N.Y. : HarperCollins, c2001. xix, 329 p. :
550/.92 B 21      0060193611
*Smith, William, 1769-1839. Geology, Stratigraphic -- History. Geologists -- Great Britain -- Biography.*

**QE22.W26.S3913 1986**
**Schwarzbach, Martin,**
Alfred Wegener, the father of continental drift / by Martin Schwarzbach ; with an introduction to the English edition by Anthony Hallam ; and an assessment of the earth science revolution by I. Bernard Cohen. Madison, Wis. : Science Tech, c1986. xx, 241 p. :
86-013760      551.1/36      0910239037
*Wegener, Alfred, -- 1880-1930. Earth scientists -- Germany -- Biography. Continental drift. Earth sciences -- History.*

## QE26 General works, treatises, and advanced textbooks — 1801-1969

**QE26.G5 1968**
**Gilluly, James,**
Principles of geology [by] James Gilluly, Aaron C. Waters [and] A. O. Woodford. San Francisco, W. H. Freeman [1968] 687 p.
68-014228      550
*Geology.*

## QE26.2 General works, treatises, and advanced textbooks — 1970-

**QE26.2.U53 1992**
Understanding the Earth / edited by Geoff Brown, Chris Hawkesworth, and Chris Wilson. Cambridge [England] ; Cambridge University Press, 1992. xii, 551 p. :
91-022281      550      0521370205
*Earth sciences.*

**QE26.2.W9**
**Wyllie, Peter J.,**
The dynamic earth: textbook in geosciences [by] Peter J. Wyllie. New York, Wiley [1971] xiv, 416 p.
73-155909      551      0471968897
*Earth sciences.*

## QE28 Elementary textbooks — General

**QE28.C374 1994**
**Chapman, Richard E.**
Physics for geologists / Richard E. Chapman. London ; UCL Press, 1994. p. cm.
94-032051      550/.1/53      1857282590
*Geology. Physics.*

**QE28.L2 1961**
**Lahee, Frederic H.**
Field geology. New York, McGraw-Hill Book Co., 1961. 926 p.
60-015291      550
*Geology -- Field work.*

## QE28.2 Elementary textbooks — Physical geology

**QE28.2.H35 1998**
**Hamblin, William Kenneth,**
Earth's dynamic systems / W. Kenneth Hamblin, Eric H. Christiansen. 8th ed. Upper Saddle River, NJ : Prentice Hall, c1998. xvii, 740 p. :
550 21      0137453736
*Physical geology.*

## QE28.3 Elementary textbooks — Historical geology

**QE28.3.H57 1996**
The historical atlas of the earth : a visual exploration of the earth's physical past / general editors, Roger Osborne and Donald Tarling ; consultant editor, Stephen Jay Gould ; additional contributions by G.A.L. Johnson. New York : H. Holt, 1996. 192 p. :
95-079328      551.7      080504552X
*Historical geology. Historical geology -- Maps. Paleontology.*

**QE28.3.L48 1996**
**Levin, Harold L. (Harold Leonard),**
The Earth through time / Harold L. Levin. 5th ed. Fort Worth : Saunders College Pub., c1996.
0030051673
*Historical geology.*

**QE28.3.R64 1993**
**Rogers, John James William,**
A history of the earth / John J.W. Rogers. New York, NY, USA : Cambridge University Press, 1993. xiii, 312 p. :
551.7 20      0521394805
*Historical geology.*

## QE31 Popular works

**QE31.A4413 1992**
**Allegre, Claude J.**
From stone to star : a view of modern geology / Claude Allegre ; translated by Deborah Kurmes Van Dam. Cambridge, Mass. : Harvard University Press, 1992. viii, 287 p.
91035773      550      0674838661
*Geology -- Popular works. Earth sciences -- Popular works. Astronomy -- Popular works.*

# QE33 Special aspects of the subject as a whole

**QE33.E28 1942**
**Eardley, A. J.**
Aerial photographs: their use and interpretation, by A. J. Eardley ... New York, Harper & Brothers [1942] xxii p., 1 .,
42024839          526.98
*Geology -- Maps. Aerial photography.*

**QE33.E75 1993**
**Erickson, Jon,**
Rock formations and unusual geologic structures : exploring the earth's surface / Jon Erickson. New York : Facts on File, c1993. x, 196 p. :
92-032097          550          0816025894
*Geology. Geomorphology.*

**QE33.S79 2000**
**Strangeways, Ian,**
Measuring the natural environment / Ian Strangeways. Cambridge ; Cambridge University Press, 2000. viii, 365 p.
99-018381          363.7/063          0521573106
*Earth sciences -- Measurement. Environmental monitoring.*

**QE33.T45 1999**
**Thompson, Graham R.**
Earth science and the environment / Graham R. Thompson, Jonathan Turk. 2nd ed. Fort Worth : Saunders College Pub., c1999. xvi, 589 p. :
          550 21          0030060486
*Earth sciences. Environmental protection.*

# QE33.2 Special topics, A-Z

**QE33.2.M3.I83 1989**
**Isaaks, Edward H.**
Applied geostatistics / Edward H. Isaaks, R. Mohan Srivastava. New York : Oxford University Press, 1989. xix, 561 p. :
89-034891          551/.72          0195050126
*Geology -- Statistical methods.*

**QE33.2.M3.T87 1992**
**Turcotte, Donald Lawson.**
Fractals and chaos in geology and geophysics / Donald L. Turcotte. Cambridge ; Cambridge University Press, 1992. x, 221 p. :
91-027970          550/.1/51474          0521412706
*Geology -- Mathematics. Geophysics -- Mathematics. Fractals.*

**QE33.2.R4.R44**
Remote sensing in geology / edited by Barry S. Siegal, Alan R. Gillespie. New York : Wiley, c1980. xviii, 702 p.
79-017967          550/.28          0471790524
*Geology -- Remote sensing.*

**QE33.2.S82M53 2000**
**Middleton, Gerard V.**
Data analysis in the earth science using Matlab / Gerald V. Middleton. Upper Saddle River, NJ : Prentice Hall, 2000. ix, 260 p. :
          550/.72 21          0133935051
*Earth sciences -- Statistical methods -- Data processing. MATLAB.*

# QE35 Addresses, essays, lectures

**QE35.K97613 1986**
**Kurten, Bjorn.**
How to deep-freeze a mammoth / Bjorn Kurten ; based on a translation by Erik J. Friss of the original work. New York : Columbia University Press, 1986. 121 p. :
85024725          550          0231059787
*Geology. Paleontology. Fossil hominids.*

# QE36 Geological maps

**QE36.B33 1995**
**Barnes, J.W. (John Wykeham),**
Basic geological mapping/ John W. Barnes. 3rd ed. New York : Wiley, c1995. x, 133 p. :
          550/.22/3 20          0471960314
*Geological mapping.*

**QE36.B5**
**Bishop, Margaret S.**
Subsurface mapping. New York, Wiley [1960] 198 p.
60-005736          551
*Geology -- Maps.*

**QE36.B68 1989**
**Boulter, Clive A.**
Four dimensional analysis of geological maps : techniques of interpretation / Clive A. Boulter ; illustrated by Josie Wilkinson. Chichester ; Wiley, c1989. xxiii, 296 p.
88-33369          550/.22          0471921610
*Geology -- Maps.*

**QE36.M67 1979**
**Moseley, F.**
Advanced geological map interpretation / Frank Moseley. New York : Wiley, 1979. 79, [1] p. :
79-011243          550/.2/22          0470267089
*Geology -- Maps. Map reading.*

**QE36.R63 1982**
**Roberts, John L.**
Introduction to geological maps and structures / John L. Roberts. Oxford ; Pergamon Press, 1982. vii, 332 p. :
81-021018          550/.222          008023982X
*Geology -- Maps. Geology, Structural.*

## QE36.S64 2000
**Spencer, Edgar Winston.**
 Geologic maps : a practical guide to the preparation and interpretation of geologic maps : for geologists, geographers, engineers, and planners / Edgar W. Spencer. 2nd ed. Upper Saddle River, N.J. : Prentice Hall, c2000. viii, 148 p. :
 550/.022/3 21        0130115835
*Geology -- Maps. Geological mapping.*

## QE38 Special fields — Environmental geology

## QE38.K45 2000
**Keller, Edward A.,**
 Environmental geology / Edward A. Keller. 8th ed. Upper Saddle River, NJ. : Prentice Hall, c2000. xiii, 562 p. :
 304.2 21        0130224669
*Environmental geology.*

## QE38.R46 2000
 Remote sensing for site characterization / Friedrich Kuehn ... [et al.]. New York : Springer, 2000. p. cm.
 99-053337        550/.28        354063469X
 *Environmental geology -- Remote sensing. Environmental geology -- Remote sensing -- Case studies.*

## QE39 Special fields — Submarine geology

## QE39.B85
**Burk, Creighton A.**
 The geology of continental margins, edited by Creighton A. Burk and Charles L. Drake. New York, Springer-Verlag [1974] xiii, 1009 p.
 74-016250        551.4/608        038706866X
 *Continental margins. Submarine geology.*

## QE39.K46
**Kennett, James P.**
 Marine geology / James P. Kennett. Englewood Cliffs, N.J. : Prentice-Hall, c1982. xv, 813 p. :
 81-010726        551.46/08        0135569362
 *Submarine geology.*

## QE45 Field work

## QE45.C63 1985
**Compton, Robert R.**
 Geology in the field / Robert R. Compton. New York : Wiley, c1985. xi, 398 p. :
 85-002325        551/.0723        0471829021
 *Geology -- Field work.*

## QE45.C65
**Compton, Robert R.**
 Manual of field geology. New York, Wiley [c1961] 378 p.
 61-017357        552
 *Geology -- Field work.*

## QE48.8 Data Processing

## QE48.8.D38 1986
**Davis, John C.**
 Statistics and data analysis in geology / John C. Davis. New York : Wiley, c1986. x, 646 p. :
 85-012331        550/.72        0471080799
 *Geology -- Data processing. Geology -- Statistical methods.*

## QE49.5 Instruments and apparatus

## QE49.5.W64 1974
**Wolff, Edward A.**
 Geoscience instrumentation, edited by Edward A. Wolff [and] Enrico P. Mercanti. New York, Wiley [1974] xxvi, 819 p.
 73-018195        550/.28        0471959529
 *Earth science instruments.*

## QE71-147 Geographical divisions — America — United States

## QE71.E17 1962
**Eardley, A. J.**
 Structural geology of North America. New York, Harper & Row [c1962] xv, 743 p.
 62-017482        551.8
 *Geology, Structural -- North America.*

## QE75.B9 serial
 Bibliography of North American geology. Washington, U.S. Govt. Print. Off.; v.
 09-000427        016.557
 *Geology -- North America -- Bibliography -- Periodicals. Geology -- North America -- Indexes -- Periodicals. Paleontology -- North America -- Bibliography -- Periodicals.*

## QE77.E45 1996
**Ellwood, B. B.**
 Geology and America's national park areas / Brooks B. Ellwood. Upper Saddle River, N.J. : Prentice Hall, c1996. xii, 372 p. :
 95-040818        557.3        0023327537
 *Geology -- United States. National parks and reserves -- United States.*

## QE77.G325 1996
 Geology of the United States' seafloor : the view from GLORIA / edited by James V. Gardner, Michael E. Field, David C. Twichell. New York : Cambridge University Press, 1996. xii, 364 p. :
 95-046492        557.3        052143310X
 *Geology -- United States. Continental margins -- United States. Economic zones (Law of the sea) -- United States.*

**QE77.H36 1997**
**Harris, Ann G.**
 Geology of national parks / Ann G. Harris, Esther Tuttle, Sherwood D. Tuttle. 5th ed. Dubuque, Iowa : Kendall/Hunt Pub Co., c1997. xvi, 758 p. :
          557.3 21          078721065X
*Geology -- United States. National parks and rerserves -- United States.*

**QE77.T5**
**Thornbury, William D.**
 Regional geomorphology of the United States [by] William D. Thornbury. New York, Wiley [1965] viii, 609 p.
65-012698          551.40973
 *Geology -- United States. Physical geography -- United States.*

**QE78.H65**
**Hough, Jack Luin,**
 Geology of the Great Lakes. Urbana, University of Illinois Press, 1958. xviii, 313 p.
58-006995          551.4820977
 *Geology -- Great Lakes.*

**QE79.A46 1995**
**Alt, David D.**
 Northwest exposures : a geologic story of the Northwest / David Alt and Donald W. Hyndman. Missoula, Mont. : Mountain Press Pub., 1995. xi, 443 p. :
95-037140          557.95          0878423230
 *Geology -- Northwest, Pacific.*

**QE79.F54 1986**
**Fiero, Bill,**
 Geology of the Great Basin / by Bill Fiero. Reno : University of Nevada Press, 1986. xi, 198 p. :
85-014001          557.9          0874170834
 *Geology -- Great Basin. Mines and mineral resources -- Great Basin. Hydrology -- Great Basin.*

**QE79.M28 1981**
**McPhee, John A.**
 Basin and range / John McPhee. New York : Farrar, Straus, Giroux, c1981. 215 p. ;
80-028679          557.9          0374109141
 *Geology -- West (U.S.)*

**QE79.5.B285 1995**
**Baars, Donald.**
 Navajo country : a geology and natural history of the Four Corners Region / Donald L. Baars. Albuquerque : University of New Mexico Press, c1995. xii, 255 p.,
95-004344          557.91/3          0826315879
 *Geology -- Colorado Plateau.*

**QE86.G73.G73 1990**
 Grand Canyon geology / edited by Stanley S. Beus and Michael Morales. New York : Oxford University Press ; 1990. x, 518 p. :
90-007163          557.91/32          0195050142
 *Geology -- Arizona -- Grand Canyon.*

**QE89.N67 1990**
**Norris, Robert M.**
 Geology of California / Robert M. Norris, Robert W. Webb. New York : Wiley, c1990. xiii, 541 p.,
89-036302          557.94          0471509809
 *Geology -- California.*

**QE99.G47 1997**
 The Geology of Florida / edited by Anthony F. Randazzo and Douglas S. Jones. Gainesville, Fla. : University Press of Florida, c1997. xviii, 327 p.
96-028022          557.59          0813014964
 *Geology -- Florida.*

**QE111.A582 1998**
**Anderson, Wayne I.,**
 Iowa's geological past : three billion years of earth history / Wayne I. Anderson. Iowa City : University of Iowa Press, c1998. xii, 424 p. :
98-038373          557.77          0877456399
 *Geology -- Iowa.*

**QE131.U54 1992**
**Unklesbay, A. G.**
 Missouri geology : three billion years of volcanoes, seas, sediments, and erosion / A.G. Unklesbay and Jerry D. Vineyard. Columbia : University of Missouri Press, c1992. xii, 189 p. :
92-007561          557.78          0826208363
 *Geology -- Missouri.*

**QE147.G46 1991**
 The Geology of the Carolinas : Carolina Geological Society fiftieth anniversary volume / edited by J. Wright Horton, Jr. and Victor A. Zullo. Knoxville : University of Tennessee Press, c1991. xvii, 406 p.
90-041459          557.56          087049662X
 *Geology -- North Carolina. Geology -- South Carolina.*

### QE230 Geographical divisions — America — Latin America

**QE230.J4**
**Jenks, William Furness,**
 Handbook of South American geology; an explanation of the geologic map of South America, containing papers by A. I. de Oliveira [and others. New York] Geological Society of America, 1956. xix, 378 p.
56058161          558
 *Geology -- South America.*

### QE260-285 Geographical divisions — Europe

**QE260.A37 1980**
**Ager, D. V.**
 The geology of Europe : a regional approach / Derek V. Ager. New York : Halsted Press, c1980. xix, 535 p. :
80-040318          554          0470269901
 *Geology -- Europe.*

**QE260.B723**
**Brinkmann, Roland,**
  Geologic evolution of Europe. Translated from the German by John E. Sanders. Stuttgart, F. Enke; 1960. vi, 161 p.
60-004061          554
  *Geology -- Europe. Geology, Stratigraphic.*

**QE271.H54 1996**
**Higgins, Michael Denis,**
  A geological companion to Greece and the Aegean / Michael Denis Higgins and Reynold Higgins. Ithaca, N.Y. : Cornell University Press, 1996. xvi, 240 p.,
96-018855          554.95    0801433371
  *Geology -- Greece. Geology -- Aegean Sea Region.*

**QE276.N2813 1973b**
**Nalivkin, D. V.**
  Geology of the U.S.S.R. / D.V. Nalivkin ; translated from the Russian by N. Rast ; edited by N. Rast and T.S. Westoll. Toronto ; University of Toronto Press, 1973. xxviii, 855 p
75-317194          554.7     0802019846
  *Geology -- Soviet Union. Mines and mineral resources – Soviet Union.*

**QE285.H7813 1995**
**Hsu, Kenneth J.**
  The geology of Switzerland : an introduction to Tectonic Facies / Kenneth J. Hsu. Princeton, N.J. : Princeton University Press, c1995. xxv, 250 p. :
94-018000          554.94    0691087873
  *Geology -- Switzerland.*

## QE294-319 Geographical divisions — Asia

**QE294.C4834 1991**
  China : stratigraphy, paleogeography, and tectonics / Arthur A. Meyerhoff ... [et al.]. Dordrecht ; Kluwer Academic Publishers, c1991. viii, 188 p.
90-005340          555.1     0792309723
  *Geology -- China. Geology, Stratigraphic. Paleogeography – China.*

**QE319.H5.S56 1989**
**Sinha, Anshu K.**
  Geology of the higher central Himalaya / Anshu K. Sinha. Chichester ; Wiley, c1989. xiv, 219 p.,
86-009169          555.4     0471911224
  *Geology -- Himalaya Mountains.*

## QE320 Geographical divisions — Africa

**QE320.F813**
**Furon, Raymond,**
  Geology of Africa. Translated by A. Hallam and L.A. Stevens. New York, Hafner Pub. Co. [1963] 377 p.
63-002498          556
  *Geology -- Africa. Geology, Stratigraphic.*

## QE340 Geographical divisions — Australia

**QE340.B7 1968**
**Brown, D. A.**
  The geological evolution of Australia & New Zealand, by D. A. Brown, K. S. W. Campbell [and] K. A. W. Crook. Oxford, Pergamon Press [1968] x, 409 p.
66-029583          551.7/00994
  *Geology -- Australia. Geology -- New Zealand. Geology, Stratigraphic.*

**QE349.H3M32 1983**
**Macdonald, Gordon Andrew,**
  Volcanoes in the sea : the geology of Hawaii / Gordon A. Macdonald, Agatin T. Abbott, Frank L. Peterson. 2nd ed. Honolulu : University of Hawaii Press, 1983. x, 517 p. :
          559.69 19          0824808320
*Geology -- Hawaii.*

## QE350 Geographical divisions — Antarctica

**QE350.A49 1999**
**Anderson, John B.,**
  Antarctic marine geology / John B. Anderson. New York : Cambridge University Press, 1999. vii, 289 p. :
98-037219          559.8/9     0521593174
  *Geology -- Antarctica. Submarine geology.*

**QE350.G456 1990**
  The Geology of Antarctica / edited by Robert J. Tingey. Oxford : New York : Clarendon Press ; Oxford University Press, 1991. xxiv, 680 p. :
          559.8/9 20          0198544677
*Geology -- Antarctica.*

## QE355 Mineralogy — Dictionaries and encyclopedias

**QE355.E49**
  The Encyclopedia of mineralogy / edited by Keith Frye. Stroudsburg, Pa. : Hutchinson Ross Pub. Co., c1981. xx, 794 p. :
81-000982          549/.03/21          0879331844
  *Mineralogy -- Dictionaries.*

**QE355.R6 1990**
**Roberts, Willard Lincoln.**
  Encyclopedia of minerals / Willard Lincoln Roberts, Thomas J. Campbell, George Robert Rapp, Jr. ; photo editor, Wendell E. Wilson. New York : Van Nostrand Reinhold, c1990. xxiii, 979 p.
89-005633          549/.03/21          0442276818
  *Mineralogy -- Dictionaries.*

## QE357 Mineralogy — Nomenclature, terminology, notation, abbreviations

**QE357.C53 1993**
**Clark, Andrew,**
 Hey's mineral index : mineral species, varieties, and synonyms / A.M. Clark. 3rd ed. London ; New York : Chapman & Hall, c1993. xi, 848 p. :
      549/.012 20      0412399504
 *Mineralogy -- Nomenclature.*

## QE363.2 Mineralogy — General works, treatises, and textbooks — 1970-

**QE363.2.D52 1990**
**Dietrich, Richard Vincent,**
 Gems, granites, and gravels : knowing and using rocks and minerals / R.V. Dietrich and Brian J. Skinner. Cambridge ; Cambridge University Press, 1990. viii, 173 p.,
90-001506      549      0521344441
 *Mineralogy. Petrology.*

**QE363.2.N48 2000**
**Nesse, William D.**
 Introduction to mineralogy / William D. Nesse. New York : Oxford University Press, 2000. xiii, 442 p.,
98-045279      549      0195106911
 *Mineralogy.*

## QE363.8 Mineralogy — Pictorial works and atlases

**QE363.8.B56 1999**
**Bishop, A. C.**
 Cambridge guide to minerals, rocks, and fossils / A.C. Bishop, A.R. Woolley, W.R. Hamilton. Cambridge, U.K. ; Cambridge University Press, c1999. 336 p. :
00-268194      552      0521778816
 *Minerals -- Pictorial works. Rocks -- Pictorial works. Fossils – Pictorial works.*

## QE365 Mineralogy — Popular works

**QE365.H845 1998**
**Hurlbut, Cornelius Searle,**
 Dana's minerals and how to study them. New York : Wiley, c1998. viii, 328 p.
97-021330      549/.1      0471156779
 *Mineralogy. Crystallography.*

## QE366.2 Mineralogy — Collection and preservation

**QE366.2.C37 1992**
 The care and conservation of geological material : minerals, rocks, meteorites, and lunar finds / edited by Frank M. Howie. Oxford [England] ; Butterworth-Heinemann, 1992. xv, 138 p., [
91-045839      552/.075      0750603712
 *Minerals -- Collection and preservation. Rocks -- Collection and preservation. Meteorites -- Collection and preservation.*

**QE366.2.M6713**
 Simon and Schuster's Guide to rocks and minerals / edited by Martin Prinz, George Harlow, and Joseph Peters. New York : Simon and Schuster, [1978] 607 p. :
78-008610      552/.075      0671243969.
 *Rocks -- Collection and preservation. Minerals -- Collection and preservation.*

## QE366.8 Mineralogy — Handbooks, tables, formulas, etc.

**QE366.8.M55 1995**
 Mineral physics & crystallography : a handbook of physical constants / Thomas J. Ahrens, editor. Washington, DC : American Geophysical Union, c1995. vii, 354 p. :
95-003663      549/.1      0875908527
 *Mineralogy -- Handbooks, manuals, etc. Crystallography -- Handbooks, manuals, etc.*

## QE367.2 Mineralogy — Determinative mineralogy — General works, treatises, and textbooks — 1970-

**QE367.2.P68 1976**
**Pough, Frederick H.**
 A field guide to rocks and minerals / by Frederick H. Pough. Boston : Houghton Mifflin, 1976. xix, 317 p.,
75-022364      549/.1      0395081068.
 *Mineralogy, Determinative. Rocks.*

## QE369 Mineralogy — Determinative mineralogy — Special topics, A-Z

**QE369.O6.G74 1993**
**Gribble, C. D.**
 Optical mineralogy : principles and practice / C.D. Gribble, A.J. Hall. New York : Chapman & Hall, 1993. xv, 303 p., [
92-036265      549/.125      0412040816
 *Optical mineralogy.*

## QE372 Mineralogy — Descriptive mineralogy — General works, treatises, and textbooks

**QE372.K54 1999**
**Klein, Cornelis,**
   Manual of mineralogy : (after James D. Dana) / Cornelis Klein, Cornelius S. Hurlbut, Jr. New York : J. Wiley, c1999. xiv, 681 p. c
98-023230          549          0471312665
   *Mineralogy.*

## QE375 Mineralogy — Descriptive mineralogy — Geographical divisions

**QE375.L6**
**Loomis, Frederic Brewster,**
   Field book of common rocks and minerals; for identifying the rocks and minerals of the United States and interpreting their origins and meanings. New York, Putnam [1948] xviii, 352 p.
50006033
   *Mineralogy -- United States. Petrology -- United States.*

## QE390 Mineralogy — Special groups of minerals — Ore minerals (General)

**QE390.G85 1986**
**Guilbert, John M.**
   The geology of ore deposits / John M. Guilbert, Charles F. Park, Jr. New York : W.H. Freeman, c1986. xiv, 985 p. :
85-010099          553.4          0716714566
   *Ore deposits. Geology.*

## QE390.5 Mineralogy — Special groups of minerals — Hydrothermal deposits. Hydrothermal alteration

**QE390.5.G43 1997**
   Geochemistry of hydrothermal ore deposits. New York : Wiley, c1997. xx, 972 p. :
96-034529          553          047157144X
   *Hydrothermal deposits. Geochemistry.*

## QE391 Mineralogy — Descriptive of special minerals, A-Z

**QE391.A5.G76 1996**
**Grimaldi, David A.**
   Amber : window to the past / David A. Grimaldi. New York : Harry N. Abrams, Publishers, in association with 1996. 216 p. :
95-000651          553.2/9          0810919664
   *Amber. Amber art objects.*

**QE391.Z5.T73 1992**
**Tschernich, Rudy W.**
   Zeolites of the world / Rudy W. Tschernich. Phoenix : Geoscience Press, c1992. 563 p., [16]
91-074048          549/.68          0945005075
   *Zeolites.*

## QE392 Mineralogy — Precious stones

**QE392.H65 1991**
**Holden, Martin.**
   The encyclopedia of gemstones and minerals / Martin Holden ; consulting editor, E.A. Mathez ; principal photography by the British Museum (Natural History), with line drawings from Viktor Goldschmidt's Atlas der Krystallformen. New York : Facts on File, c1991. 303 p. :
91-007782          553.8/03          0816021775
   *Gems -- Encyclopedias. Mineralogy -- Encyclopedias.*

**QE392.M29 2000**
**Manutchehr-Danai, Mohsen,**
   Dictionary of gems and gemology / Mohsen Manutchehr-Danai. Berlin ; Springer, c2000. 565 p. :
00-055699          553.8/03          3540674829
   *Precious stones -- Dictionaries. Gems -- Dictionaries.*

**QE392.W37 1994**
**Webster, Robert.**
   Gems : their sources, descriptions, and identification / Robert Webster. Oxford ; Butterworth-Heinemann, 1994. xxviii, 1026
93-044841          553.8          0750616741
   *Precious stones. Jewelry.*

## QE423 Petrology — Dictionaries and encyclopedias

**QE423.M58 1985**
**Mitchell, Richard Scott,**
   Dictionary of rocks / Richard Scott Mitchell. New York : Van Nostrand Reinhold, c1985. xi, 228 p., [
84-022062          552/.003/21          0442263287
   *Petrology -- Dictionaries.*

## QE431 Petrology — General works, treatises, and textbooks — 1801-1969

**QE431.P68 1947**
**Pirsson, Louis V.**
   Rocks and rock minerals. New York, J. Wiley [1947] vii, 349 p.
47031208          552
   *Petrology.*

## QE431.2 Petrology — General works, treatises, and textbooks — 1970-

**QE431.2.E38**
**Ehlers, Ernest G.**
   Petrology : igneous, sedimentary, and metamorphic / Ernest G. Ehlers, Harvey Blatt. San Francisco : Freeman, c1982. xvi, 732 p. :
81-012517          552          0716712792
   *Petrology.*

## QE431.5 Petrology — Special aspects of the subject as whole

**QE431.5.G8413 1994**
**Gueguen, Yves.**
Introduction to the physics of rocks / Yves Gueguen and Victor Palciauskas. Princeton, N.J. : Princeton University Press, c1994. viii, 294 p.
93-040793        552/.06        0691034524
*Petrology. Rock mechanics.*

## QE431.6 Petrology — Special topics, A-Z

**QE431.6.M3D86 1997**
**Dunlop, David J.**
Rock magnetism : fundamentals and frontiers / by David J. Dunlop, Ozden Ozdemir. Cambridge ; New York : Cambridge University Press, 1997. xxi, 573 p. :
        552/.06 20        0521325145
*Rocks -- Magnetic properties.*

**QE431.6.P5.P73 1989**
Practical handbook of physical properties of rocks and minerals / edited by Robert S. Carmichael. Boca Raton, Fla. : CRC Press, c1989. 741 p. :
88-021004        552        0849337038
*Rocks -- Handbooks, manuals, etc. Mineralogy -- Handbooks, manuals, etc.*

## QE433 Petrology — Laboratory manuals

**QE433.H87**
**Hutchison, Charles S.**
Laboratory handbook of petrographic techniques [by] Charles S. Hutchison. New York, Wiley [1974] xxvii, 527 p.
73-017336        552/.0028        0471425508
*Petrology -- Laboratory manuals.*

## QE433.8 Petrology — Handbooks, tables, formulas, etc.

**QE433.8.R63 1995**
Rock physics & phase relations : a handbook of physical constants / Thomas J. Ahrens, editor. Washington, DC : American Geophysical Union, c1995. vii, 236 p. :
95-003664        552        0875908535
*Petrology -- Handbooks, manuals, etc.*

## QE434 Petrology — Microscopic analysis of rocks. Thin sections

**QE434.M33 1994**
**MacKenzie, W. S.**
A color atlas of rocks and minerals in thin section / W.S. MacKenzie, A.E. Adams. New York : Halsted Press, c1994. 192 p. :
93-006167        552/.06        0470233389
*Rocks -- Pictorial works. Minerals -- Pictorial works. Thin sections (Geology) -- Pictorial works.*

## QE461 Petrology — Igneous rocks, volcanic ash, tuff, etc. — General works

**QE461.B53 1982**
**Best, Myron G.**
Igneous and metamorphic petrology / Myron G. Best. San Francisco : Freeman, c1982. xviii, 630 p.
81-017530        552/.1        0716713357
*Rocks, Igneous. Rocks, Metamorphic.*

**QE461.E56 1990**
The Encyclopedia of igneous and metamorphic petrology / edited by D.R. Bowes. New York : Van Nostrand Reinhold, c1989. xviii, 666 p.
89-030622        552/.1/0321        0442206232
*Rocks, Igneous -- Encyclopedias. Rocks, Metamorphic -- Encyclopedias.*

**QE462.U4A92 1979**
**Augustithis, S.S.**
Atlas of the textural patterns of basic and ultrabasic rocks and their genetic significance / S.S. Augustithis. Berlin ; New York : W. de Gruyter, 1979. x, 393 p. :
        552/.1        3110065711
*Rocks, Ultrabasic. Rocks, Igneous.*

## QE471 Petrology — Sedimentary rocks. Sedimentology — General works

**QE471.F73 1992**
**Friedman, Gerald M.**
Principles of sedimentary deposits : stratigraphy and sedimentology/ Gerald M. Friedman, John E. Sanders, David C. Kopaska-Merkel. New York : Macmillan ; c1992. xiv, 717 p. :
91-027866        551.3        0023393599
*Sedimentology. Geology, Stratigraphic.*

**QE471.P46 1975**
**Pettijohn, F. J.**
Sedimentary rocks [by] F. J. Pettijohn. New York, Harper & Row [1975] xii, 628 p.
74-012043        552/.5        0060451912
*Rocks, Sedimentary. Sedimentation and deposition.*

### QE471.15 Petrology — Sedimentary rocks. Sedimentology — Special, A-Z

**QE471.15.C3A33 1998**
**Adams, A.E.**
A color atlas of carbonate sediments and rocks under the microscope / A.E. Adams, W.S. MacKenzie. New York : Wiley, 1998. 180 p. :
       552/.58 21        0470296224
*Rocks, Carbonate -- Pictorial works. Thin sections (Geology) -- Pictorial works.*

## QE471.2 Petrology — Sediments (Unconsolidated)

**QE471.2.M53 1996**
**Miall, Andrew D.**
The geology of fluvial deposits : sedimentary facies, basin analysis, and petroleum geology / Andrew D. Miall. Berlin ; Springer, c1996. xvi, 582 p. :
96-139242       551.3/5       3540591869
*Alluvium. Sedimentation and deposition.*

**QE471.2.P47 1987**
**Pettijohn, F. J.**
Sand and sandstone / F.J. Pettijohn, P.E. Potter, R. Siever. New York : Springer-Verlag, c1987. xviii, 553 p.
86-017925       552/.5       0387963553
*Sand. Sandstone.*

## QE472 Petrology — Sedimentary structures

**QE472.C64 1982**
**Collinson, J. D.**
Sedimentary structures / J.D. Collinson, D.B. Thompson. London ; Allen & Unwin, 1982. xiv, 194 p. :
81-019110       552/.5       0045520178
*Sedimentary structures.*

### QE475.A2-475.T89 Petrology — Metamorphic rocks. Metamorphism — Special, A-Z

**QE475.A2B84 1994**
**Bucher, Kurt,**
Petrogenesis of metamorphic rocks / K. Bucher, M. Frey. 6th ed. Complete revision of Winkler's textbook. Berlin ; New York : Springer-Verlag, c1994. xiv, 318 p. :
       552/.4 20       3540575677
*Rocks, Metamorphic.*

**QE475.M95.P75 1998**
Fault-related rocks : a photographic atlas / edited by Arthur W. Snoke, Jan Tullis, and Victoria R. Todd. Princeton, N.J. : Princeton University Press, 1998. p. cm.
97-019775       552/.4    0691012202
*Mylonite -- Atlases. Petrofabric analysis -- Atlases.*

**QE475.T89 1981**
**Turner, Francis J.**
Metamorphic petrology : mineralogical, field, and tectonic aspects / Francis J. Turner. Washington : Hemisphere Pub. Corp. ; c1981. xv, 524 p. :
79-027497       552/.4
*Rocks, Metamorphic.*

## QE501 Dynamic and structural geology — General works, treatises, and textbooks

**QE501.C6148 1994**
Continental deformation / edited by Paul L. Hancock. Oxford ; Pergamon Press, 1994. ix, 421 p. :
93-007258       551.8      0080379311
*Geodynamics. Geology, Structural.*

**QE501.J25 1973**
**Jacobs, John Arthur,**
Physics and geology [by] J. A. Jacobs, R. D. Russell [and] J. Tuzo Wilson. New York, McGraw-Hill [1973, c1974] xvi, 622 p.
73-006621       551      0070321485
*Geophysics.*

**QE501.J4 1976**
**Jeffreys, Harold,**
The earth : its origin, history, and physical constitution / Harold Jeffreys. Cambridge [Eng.] ; Cambridge University Press, 1976. xii, 574 p.,
74-019527       551      0521206480
*Earth.*

**QE501.S54 1964**
**Sitter, L. U. de**
Structural geology [by] L.U. de Sitter. New York, McGraw-Hill [1964] xii, 551 p.
63-023533       551.8
*Geology, Structural.*

**QE501.T83 2001**
**Turcotte, Donald Lawson.**
Geodynamics / Donald L. Turcotte, Gerald Schubert. 2nd ed. New York : Cambridge University Press, 2001. p. cm.
           0521661862
*Geodynamics.*

## QE501.3 Dynamic and structural geology — Special aspects of the subject as whole

**QE501.3.S48 1986**
**Sharma, P. Vallabh.**
Geophysical methods in geology / P.V. Sharma. New York : Elsevier, c1986. xviii, 442 p.
85-025360       551/.028      0444008365
*Geophysics. Prospecting -- Geophysical methods. Geology -- Methodology.*

## QE501.4 Dynamic and structural geology — Special topics, A-Z

**QE501.4.N9.F38 1986**
**Faure, Gunter.**
Principles of isotope geology / Gunter Faure. New York : Wiley, c1986. xv, 589 p. :
86-009147      550/.28      0471864129
*Isotope geology.*

**QE501.4.P3.O45 1991**
**Ollier, Cliff.**
Ancient landforms / Cliff Ollier. London ; Belhaven Press, 1991. 233 p. :
91-023692      551.4/1      1852930748
*Paleogeography. Geomorphology.*

**QE501.4.P35.M35 2000**
**McElhinny, M. W.**
Paleomagnetism : continents and oceans / Michael W. McElhinny, Phillip L. McFadden. San Diego : Academic Press, c2000. xii, 386 p. :
99-065104      538/.727      0124833551
*Paleomagnetism. Plate Tectonics.*

**QE501.4.P35.Q38 1999**
Quaternary climates, environments, and magnetism / edited by Barbara A. Maher and Roy Thompson. Cambridge, UK ; Cambridge University Press, 1999. xii, 390 p. :
99-011967      538/.727      0521624177
*Paleomagnetism -- Quaternary. Paleoclimatology – Quaternary. Paleoecology -- Quaternary.*

## QE506 Dynamic and structural geology — Geological cosmogony

**QE506.A34 1993**
**Ager, D. V.**
The new catastrophism : the importance of the rare event in geological history / Derek Ager. Cambridge ; Cambridge University Press, 1993. xx, 231 p. :
93-000178      550      0521420199
*Catastrophes (Geology)*

**QE506.F7313 1999**
**Frankel, Charles.**
The end of the dinosaurs : Chicxulub crater and mass extinctions / Charles Frankel. New York : Cambridge University Press, 1999. xii, 223 p. :
98-049427      551.3/97      0521474477
*Catastrophes (Geology) Extinction (Biology) Cryptoexplosion structures -- Mexico -- Campeche, Bay of, Region. Chicxulub Crater.*

**QE506.P735 1998**
**Powell, James Lawrence,**
Night comes to the Cretaceous : dinosaur extinction and the transformation of modern geology / James Lawrence Powell. New York : W.H. Freeman, c1998. xvi, 250 p. :
98-013192      576.8/4      0716731177
*Catastrophes (Geology) Extinction (Biology) Dinosaurs.*

## QE508 Dynamic and structural geology — Geological time. Age of the earth

**QE508.A35 1998**
**Aitken, M. J.**
An introduction to optical dating : the dating of Quaternary sediments by the use of photon-stimulated luminescence / M.J. Aitken. Oxford ; Oxford University Press, 1998. xi, 267 p. :
98-003904      551.7/01      0198540922
*Thermoluminescence dating.*

**QE508.D28 1991**
**Dalrymple, G. Brent.**
The age of the earth / G. Brent Dalrymple. Stanford, Calif. : Stanford University Press, c1991. xvi, 474 p. :
90-047051      551.1      0804715696
*Geochronometry. Earth -- Age.*

**QE508.G443 1990**
**Geyh, Mebus A.**
Absolute age determination : physical and chemical dating methods and their application / Mebus A. Geyh, Helmut Schleicher ; English by R. Clark Newcomb. Berlin ; Springer-Verlag, c1990. xi, 503 p., [
90-009406      551.7/01      3540512764
*Geochronometry. Radiocarbon dating.*

**QE508.W34 1992**
**Wagner, Gunther A.**
Fission track dating / by Gunther Wagner and Peter Van den Haute. Dordrecht ; Kluwer, c1992. xiii, 285 p.
91-047967      551.7/01      079231624X
*Fission track dating.*

## QE509-509.4 Dynamic and structural geology — Interior of the earth

**QE509.B69 1982**
**Bolt, Bruce A.,**
Inside the earth : evidence from earthquakes / Bruce A. Bolt ; [artist, Eric Hieber]. San Francisco : W.H. Freeman, c1982. xi, 191 p. :
81-017431      551.1/1      0716713594
*Seismology. Earth -- Internal structure.*

**QE509.E234 1998**
The Earth's mantle : composition, structure, and evolution / edited by Ian Jackson. Cambridge, [Eng.] ; Cambridge University Press, 1998. xxv, 566 p. :
97-011995      551.1/16      0521563445
*Earth -- Mantle.*

**QE509.J27 1992**
**Jacobs, J. A.**
Deep interior of the earth / J.A. Jacobs. London ; Chapman & Hall, 1992. x, 167 p. :
91-024856      551.1/12      0442314698
*Geodynamics. Earth -- Mantle. Earth -- Core.*

**QE509.4.D38 1999**
**Davies, Geoffrey F.**
 Dynamic earth : plates, plumes, and mantle convection / Geoffrey F. Davies. Cambridge ; Cambridge University Press, 1999. xi, 458 p. :
98-051722            551.1/16            0521590671
 *Geodynamics.    Earth -- Mantle.*

**QE509.4.S38 2001**
**Schubert, Gerald.**
 Mantle convection in the earth and planets / Gerald Schubert, Donald L. Turcotte, Peter Olson. Cambridge ; New York : Cambridge University Press, 2001. xv, 940 p. :
            551.1/16 21            052135367X
*Earth -- Mantle.  Heat -- Convection.  Geodynamics.*

**QE511.4 Dynamic and structural geology — Plate tectonics — General works**

**QE511.4.K45 1996**
**Keller, Edward A.,**
 Active tectonics : earthquakes, uplift, and landscape / Edward A. Keller, Nicholas Pinter. Upper Saddle River, N.J. : Prentice Hall, c1996. xii, 338 p. :
95-004854            551.8    0023632615
 *Plate tectonics.  Earthquakes.  Geomorphology.*

**QE511.4.P74 2000**
**Price, Neville J.**
 Major impacts and plate tectonics : a model for the Phanerzoic evolution of the earth's lithospehere / Neville Price. New York : Taylor & Francis, 2000. p. cm.
00-037717            551.1/36            0748408509
 *Plate tectonics.  Catastrophes (Geology) Impact.*

**QE511.5 Dynamic and structural geology — Continental drift**

**QE511.5.S93 1991**
**Sullivan, Walter.**
 Continents in motion : the new earth debate / Walter Sullivan. New York : American Institute of Physics, c1991. xi, 430 p. :
90-022116            551.1/36            0883187035
 *Continental drift.*

**QE515 Dynamic and structural geology — Geochemistry — General works, treatises, and textbooks**

**QE515.A53 1995**
**Albarede, Francis.**
 Introduction to geochemical modeling / Francis Albarede. [Cambridge] : Cambridge University Press, 1995. xix, 543 p. :
93-049747            553.9/01/5118            0521454514
 *Geochemical modeling.*

**QE515.E48 1999**
 Encyclopedia of geochemistry / edited by C.P. Marshall and R.W. Fairbridge. Dordrecht ; Boston : Kluwer Academic Publishers, 1999. xxxiv, 712 p. :
            551.9/03 21            0412755009
*Geochemistry -- Encyclopedias.*

**QE515.F28 1991**
**Faure, Gunter.**
 Principles and applications of inorganic geochemistry : a comprehensive textbook for geology students / Gunter Faure. New York, Toronto : Macmillan Pub. Co. ; Collier Macmillan, c1991. xiii, 626 p. :
            551.9 20            0023364416
*Geochemistry.*

**QE515.L385 2000**
**Li, Yuan-Hui,**
 A compendium of geochemistry : from solar nebula to the human brain / Yuan-Hui Li. Princeton, N.J. : Princeton University Press, c2000. xiii, 475 p.
99-089467            551.9            0691009384
 *Geochemistry.*

**QE515.O8813 1997**
**Ottonello, Giulio.**
 Principles of geochemistry / Giulio Ottonello. New York : Columbia University Press, c1997. xii, 894 p. :
96-023987            551.9            0231099843
 *Geochemistry.*

**QE515.W42**
**Wedepohl, Karl Hans.**
 Handbook of geochemistry. Executive editor: K. H. Wedepohl. Editorial board: C. W. Correns [and others] Berlin, Springer, 1969-1978. 2 v. in 6 wit
78-085402            551.9
 *Geochemistry.*

**QE515.5 Dynamic and structural geology — Geochemistry — Special topics, A-Z**

**QE515.5.T46.A53 1996**
**Anderson, G. M.**
 Thermodynamics of natural systems / G.M. Anderson. New York : Wiley, c1996. xi, 382 p. :
95-023040            541.3/69            0471109436
 *Geochemistry.  Thermodynamics.*

**QE515.5.T46.F57 1993**
**Fletcher, Philip.**
 Chemical thermodynamics for earth scientists / Philip Fletcher. Harlow, Essex, England : Longman Scientific & Technical ; 1993. xv, 464 p. :
93-233054            541.3/69/02455            058206435X
 *Thermodynamics.*

### QE516.5 Dynamic and structural geology — Geochemistry — Organic geochemistry

**QE516.5.O7 1993**
Organic geochemistry : principles and applications / edited by Michael H. Engel and Stephen A. Macko. New York : Plenum Press, c1993. xxiii, 861 p.
93-028298      551.9      0306443783
*Organic geochemistry.*

## QE517.5 Dynamic and structural geology — General works, treatises, and textbooks

**QE517.5.F87 1997**
**Furbish, David Jon.**
Fluid physics in geology : an introduction to fluid motions on Earth's surface and within its crust / David Jon Furbish. New York : Oxford University Press, 1997. xx, 476 p. :
95-051658      550/.1/532      0195077016
*Fluid dynamics. Geophysics.*

## QE521 Dynamic and structural geology — Volcanoes and earthquakes — General works, treatises, and textbooks

**QE521.O43 1988**
**Ollier, Cliff.**
Volcanoes / Cliff Ollier. Oxford, UK ; Blackwell, 1988. vii, 228 p. :
87-034132      551.2/1      063115664X
*Volcanism.*

**QE521.R58 1994**
**Ritchie, David,**
The encyclopedia of earthquakes and volcanoes / by David Ritchie. New York : Facts on File, c1994. 232 p. :
93-007670      551.2/03      0816026599
*Earthquakes -- Encyclopedias. Volcanoes -- Encyclopedias.*

## QE522-524 Dynamic and structural geology — Volcanoes and earthquakes — Volcanoes

**QE522.B6 1984**
**Blong, R. J.**
Volcanic hazards : a sourcebook on the effects of eruptions / R.J. Blong. Sydney ; Academic Press, c1984. xvi, 424 p. :
83-073405      363.3/495      0121071804
*Volcanic hazard analysis.*

**QE522.E53 2000**
Encyclopedia of volcanoes / editor-in-chief, Haraldur Sigurdsson ; associate editors, Bruce F. Houghton ... [et al.] ; forword by Robert D. Ballard. San Diego : Academic Press, c2000. xxiv, 1417 p.
99-062781      551.21/03      012643140X
*Volcanoes -- Encyclopedias.*

**QE522.S87 1995**
**Sutherland, Lin.**
The volcanic earth : volcanoes and plate tectonics, past, present & future / Lin Sutherland. Sydney, Australia : University of New South Wales Press, c1995. vi, 248 p. :
96-171407      551.2/1      0868400718
*Volcanoes. Volcanoes -- Australia. Plate tectonics.*

**QE522.V92 1994**
**Simkin, Tom.**
Volcanoes of the world : a regional directory, gazetteer, and chronology of volacanism during the last 10,000 years. 2nd ed. / Tom Simkin & Lee Siebert ; with the collaboration of Russell Blong . . . [et al.]. Tucson, Ariz. : Geoscience Press, 1994. x, 349 p. :
     551.2/1 20      0945005121
*Volcanoes.*

**QE522.W64 1992**
**Wohletz, Kenneth.**
Volcanology and geothermal energy / Kenneth Wohletz, Grant Heiken. Berkeley : University of California Press, c1992. xiv, 432 p. :
91-043707      551.2/1      0520079140
*Volcanism. Geothermal resources.*

**QE523.S23.R67 1982**
**Rosenfeld, Charles.**
Earthfire : the eruption of Mount St. Helens / Charles Rosenfeld and Robert Cooke. Cambridge, Mass. : MIT Press, c1982. 155 p. :
82-009969      551.2/1/0979784      0262181061
*Saint Helens, Mount (Wash.) -- Eruption, 1980.*

**QE523.S27.F65 2000**
**Friedrich, Walter L.**
Fire in the sea : the Santorini volcano : natural history and the legend of Atlantis / Walter L. Freidrich ; translated by Alexander R. McBirney. Cambridge ; Cambridge University Press, 2000. xiv, 258 p. :
99-025753      551.21/09495/85      0521652901
*Geology -- Greece -- Thera Island Region. Volcanism – Greece – Thera Island Region. Minoans -- Greece -- Crete. Santorini Volcano (Greece) -- Eruptions.*

**QE524.V66 1990**
Volcanoes of North America : United States and Canada / compiled and edited by Charles A. Wood and Jurgen Kienle. Cambridge [England] ; Cambridge University Press, 1990. 354 p. :
90-001516      551.2/1/0973      0521364698
*Volcanoes -- United States. Volcanoes -- Canada.*

## QE531-539.2 Dynamic and structural geology — Volcanoes and earthquakes — Earthquakes. Seismology

**QE531.H57 1988**
Historical seismograms and earthquakes of the world / edited by W.H.K. Lee, H. Meyers, K. Shimazaki. San Diego : Academic Press, c1988. xiv, 513 p. :
87-028993          551.2/2          0124408702
*Seismology -- Congresses. Earthquakes -- Congresses. Seismograms -- Congresses.*

**QE534.2.B64 1993**
**Bolt, Bruce A.,**
Earthquakes / Bruce A. Bolt. New York : W.H. Freeman, c1993. xvii, 331 p.
92-018504          551.2/2          0716723581
*Earthquakes.*

**QE534.2.H68 1990**
**Howell, Benjamin F.**
An introduction to seismological research : history and development / Benjamin F. Howell, Jr. Cambridge ; Cambridge University Press, 1990. viii, 193 p.
90-001551          551.2/2          0521385717
*Seismology -- Research.*

**QE534.2.K695 1997**
**Koyama, Junji.**
The complex faulting process of earthquakes / by Junji Koyama. Dordrecht ; Kluwer, c1997. xii, 194 p. :
97-008159          551.2/2          0792344995
*Earthquakes. Faults (Geology)*

**QE534.2.M62 1995**
**Lay, Thorne.**
Modern global seismology / Thorne Lay, Terry C. Wallace. San Diego : Academic Press, c1995. xii, 521 p. :
              551.2/2 20          012732870X
*Seismology.*

**QE534.2.P73 2000**
**Prager, Ellen J.**
Furious earth : the science and nature of earthquakes, volcanoes, and tsunamis / Ellen J. Prager. New York : McGraw-Hill, c2000. xv, 235 p., [
99-048386          551.2     0071351612
*Earthquakes. Volcanoes. Tsunamis.*

**QE534.2.S455 1999**
**Shearer, Peter M.,**
Introduction to seismology / Peter M. Shearer. Cambridge ; Cambridge University Press, 1999. xii, 260 p. :
98-043740     551.22     0521660238
*Seismology.*

**QE535.2.U6**
**Yeats, Robert S.**
Living with earthquakes in California : a survivor's guide / Robert S. Yeats. Corvallis, Or. : Oregon State University Press, 2001. x, 406 p. :
00-011859          551.22/09794          0870714937
*Earthquakes -- California. Earthquakes -- California -- Safety measures.*

**QE535.2.U6.H37 1990**
**Harris, Stephen L.,**
Agents of chaos : earthquakes, volcanoes, and other natural disasters / Stephen L. Harris. Missoula, Mont. : Mountain Press Pub. Co., 1990. vii, 260 p. :
90-006165          551.2/0978          0878422439
*Earthquakes -- West (U.S.) Volcanoes -- West (U.S.) Natural disasters -- West (U.S.)*

**QE537.2.J3.K6 1996**
The Kobe earthquake : geodynamical aspects / editor, C.A. Brebbia. Southampton, UK ; Computational Mechanics Publications, c1996. 145 p. :
95-070470          624.1/762/0952          1853124303
*Kobe Earthquake, Kobe-shi Region, Japan, 1995. Soil dynamics – Japan -- Kobe-shi Region. Building failures -- Japan -- Kobe-shi Region.*

**QE538.8.L66 1994**
**Lomnitz, Cinna.**
Fundamentals of earthquake prediction / Cinna Lomnitz. New York : John Wiley & Sons, c1994. xi, 326 p. :
93-040909          551.2/2          0471574198
*Earthquake prediction.*

**QE539.2.S34D38 1999**
**Dargahi-Noubary, G.R.**
Statistical methods for earthquake hazard assessment and risk analysis / Reza Noubary. Commack, NY : Nova Science Publishers, 1999. p. cm.
              363.34/952 21          1560727705
*Earthquake hazard anaylysis -- Statistical methods. Risk assessment – Statistical methods.*

## QE565 Dynamic and structural geology — Coral islands and reefs. Atolls — General works

**QE565.D2 1962**
**Darwin, Charles,**
The structure and distribution of coral reefs. Foreword by H. W. Menard. Berkeley, University of California Press, 1962. 214 p.
62003186          551.42
*Coral reefs and islands.*

**QE565.G46 1997**
Geology and hydrogeology of carbonate islands / edited by H. Leonard Vacher and Terrence M. Quinn. Amsterdam ; New York : Elsievier, 1997. xvii, 948 p. :
              551.42 21          0444815201
*Coral reefs and islands. Rocks, Carbonate. Hydrogeology.*

**QE565.H57 2001**
The history and sedimentology of ancient reef systems / edited by George D. Stanley, Jr. New York : Kluwer Academic/Plenum, c2001. xviii, 458 p. :
    551.42/4 21    0306464675
*Coral reefs and islands.*

## QE570 Dynamic and structural geology — Weathering

**QE570.B5685 1998**
**Bland, Will,**
Weathering : an introduction to the scientific principles / Will Bland, David Rolls. London ; Arnold, 1998. x, 271 p. :
98-034261    551.3/02    0340677457
*Weathering.*

**QE570.P35 1999**
Palaeoweathering, palaeosurfaces, and related continental deposits / edited by Medard Thiry and Regine Simon-Coincon. Oxford ; Malden, MA : Blackwell Science, c1999. ix, 406 p. :
    551.3/02 21    0632053119
*Paleoweathering. Paleogeography.*

## QE571-581 Dynamic and structural geology — Sedimentation — General works

**QE571.B47**
**Berner, Robert A.,**
Early diagenesis : a theoretical approach / Robert A. Berner. Princeton, N.J. : Princeton University Press, c1980. xii, 241 p. :
80-007510    552/.5    0691082588
*Diagenesis.*

**QE571.C555 1999**
Computerized modeling of sedimentary systems / Jan Harff, Wolfram Lemke, Karl Stattegger, (eds.). Berlin ; New York : Springer, c1999. xv, 452 p. :
    551.3/03 21    3540641092
*Sedimentary basins -- Environmental aspects -- Computer simulation. Sedimentation and deposition -- Environmental aspects –Computer simulation.*

**QE571.E36 1992**
**Einsele, Gerhard.**
Sedimentary basins : evolution, facies, and sediment budget / Gerhard Einsele. Berlin ; Springer-Verlag, c1992. x, 628 p. :
91-041002    551.3    3540547436
*Sedimentary basins. Sedimentation and deposition. Facies (Geology)*

**QE581.A435 1993**
Alluvial sedimentation / edited by M. Marzo and C. Puigdefabregas. Oxford [England] ; Boston : Blackwell Scientific Publications, 1993. xi, 586 p. :
    551.3/53 20    0632035455
*Alluvium. Sediment transport.*

## QE601 Dynamic and structural geology — Structural geology

**QE601.B36 1992**
**Bayly, M. Brian,**
Mechanics in structural geology / Brian Bayly. New York : Springer-Verlag, c1992. xiii, 253 p.
91-017251    551.8/01/531    0387976159
*Geology, Structural. Mechanics, Analytic.*

**QE601.B5 1972**
**Billings, Marland Pratt,**
Structural geology [by] Marland P. Billings. Englewood Cliffs, N.J., Prentice-Hall [1972] xv, 606 p.
73-167628    551.8    0138538468
*Geology, Structural.*

**QE601.E53 1987**
The Encyclopedia of structural geology and plate tectonics / edited by Carl K. Seyfert. New York : Van Nostrand Reinhold, c1987. xii, 876 p. :
87-018879    551.8/03/21    0442281250
*Geology, Structural -- Dictionaries. Plate tectonics -- Dictionaries.*

**QE601.P694 1990**
**Price, Neville J.**
Analysis of geological structures / N.J. Price, J.W. Cosgrove. Cambridge ; Cambridge University Press, 1990. ix, 502 p. :
88-034089    551.8    0521265819
*Geology, Structural.*

## QE615 Dynamic and structural geology — Mountain building. Orogeny

**QE615.M3 2000**
**Miall, Andrew D.**
Principles of sedimentary basin analysis / Andrew D. Miall. 3rd updated and enl. Ed. Berlin ; New York : Springer, c2000. xxi, 616 p. :
    552/.5 21    3540657908
*Sedimentary basins. Stratigraphic correlation.*

## QE621.5 Dynamic and structural geology — Mountain building. Orogeny

**QE621.5.N7.H83 1995**
**Hubler, Clark.**
America's mountains : an exploration of their origins and influences from the Alaska Range to the Appalachians / Clark Hubler. New York, NY : Facts on File, c1995. x, 196 p. :
94-015321    551.8/2/097    0816026610
*Orogeny -- North America.*

## QE651 Stratigraphy — General works, treatises, and textbooks

**QE651.B68 1991**
**Blatt, Harvey.**
  Principles of stratigraphic analysis / Harvey Blatt, William B.N. Berry, Scott Brande. Boston : Blackwell Scientific Publications, c1991. xix, 512 p. :
90-043784          551.7          0865420696
  *Geology, Stratigraphic. Paleontology, Stratigraphic.*

**QE651.B785 1988**
**Brenner, Robert L.,**
  Integrative stratigraphy : concepts and applications / Robert L. Brenner, Timothy R. McHargue. Englewood Cliffs, N.J. : Prentice Hall, c1988. xii, 419 p. :
          551.7 19          0134689844
*Geology, Stratigraphic.*

**QE651.D64 1994**
**Doyle, Peter.**
  The key to earth history : an introduction to stratigraphy / Peter Doyle, Matthew R. Bennett, Alistair N. Baxter. Chichester ; Wiley, c1994. 231 p. :
94-000325          551.7          0471948454
  *Geology, Stratigraphic.*

**QE651.F75 1987**
**Frazier, William J.,**
  Regional stratigraphy of North America / William J. Frazier, David R. Schwimmer. New York : Plenum Press, c1987. xxiv, 719 p.
87-007019          557          0306423243
  *Geology, Stratigraphic. Geology -- North America.*

**QE651.I57 1976**
**International Union of Geological Sciences.**
  International stratigraphic guide : a guide to stratigraphic classification, terminology, and procedure / by International Subcommission on Stratigraphic Classification of IUGS Commission on Stratigraphy ; Hollis D. Hedberg, editor. New York : Wiley, c1976. xvii, 200 p.
75-033086          551.7          0471367435
  *Geology, Stratigraphic.*

## QE653 Stratigraphy — Precambrian — General works

**QE653.P7322 1989**
  The Precambrian-Cambrian boundary / edited by J.W. Cowie, M.D. Brasier. Oxford : Clarendon Press ; 1989. viii, 213 p.,
88-017865          551.7/1          0198544812
  *Geology, Stratigraphic -- Pre-Cambrian. Geology, Stratigraphic -- Cambrian. Paleontology -- Pre-Cambrian.*

## QE654 Stratigraphy — Paleozoic

**QE654.P242 1996**
  Paleozoic sequence stratigraphy : views from the North American craton / edited by Brian J. Witzke, Greg A. Ludvigson, and Jed Day. Boulder, Colo. : Geological Society of America, 1996. v, 446 p. :
96-002879          551.7/2/097          081372306X
  *Geology, Stratigraphic -- Paleozoic. Geology -- North America.*

## QE681 Stratigraphy — Mesozoic — Jurassic

**QE681.A6 1956**
**Arkell, William Joscelyn,**
  Jurassic geology of the world. New York, Hafner Pub. Co. [1956] xv, 806 p.
56-003105          551.76
  *Geology, Stratigraphic -- Jurassic. Geology, Stratigraphic -- Bibliography.*

## QE690 Stratigraphy — Cenozoic — General works

**QE690.G44**
  Geological background to fossil man : recent research in the Gregory Rift Valley, East Africa / edited by Walter W. Bishop. Edinburgh : Scottish Academic Press, 1978. ix, 585 p., [
78-323378          551.7/8/0967          0707301432
  *Geology, Stratigraphic -- Cenozoic -- Congresses. Geology -- Africa, East -- Congresses. Fossil hominids -- Congresses.*

## QE692.8 Stratigraphy — Cenozoic — Tertiary

**QE692.8.P76 1994**
**Prothero, Donald R.**
  The Eocene-Oligocene transition : paradise lost / Donald R. Prothero. New York : Columbia University Press, c1994. xvii, 291 p.
93-044535          560/.178          0231080905
  *Eocene-Oligocene boundary. Extinction (Biology) Paleontology -- Eocene.*

**QE692.8.T47 1996**
  The terrestrial Eocene-Oligocene transition in North America / edited by Donald R. Prothero, Robert J. Emry. Cambridge [Enngland] ; Cambridge University Press, 1996. xiii, 688 p.
95-040903          551.7/84          0521433878
  *Eocene-Oligocene boundary -- North America. Geology, Stratigraphic. Geology -- North America.*

## QE696-698 Stratigraphy — Cenozoic — Quaternary

**QE696.E2813 1996**
**Ehlers, Jurgen.**
  Quaternary and glacial geology / Jurgen Ehlers ; translated from Allgemeine und historische Quartargeologie ; English version by Philip L. Gibbard. Chichester ; J. Wiley & Sons, c1996. ix, 578 p. :
95-052107          551.7/9          0471955760
  *Geology, Stratigraphic -- Quaternary.*

**QE696.F54**
**Flint, Richard Foster,**
  Glacial and Pleistocene geology. New York, Wiley [1957] xiii, 553 p.
57-008884     551.79
  *Geology, Stratigraphic -- Pleistocene. Glaciology.*

**QE696.F553**
**Flint, Richard Foster,**
  Glacial and Quaternary geology. New York, Wiley [1971] xii, 892 p.
74-141198     551.7/9     0471264350
  *Glacial epoch. Geology, Stratigraphic -- Quaternary.*

**QE696.L29 1983**
  Late-Quaternary environments of the United States / H.E. Wright, Jr., editor. Minneapolis : University of Minnesota Press, c1983. 2 v. :
83-005804     551.7/9/0973     0816612528
  *Geology, Stratigraphic -- Quaternary -- Congresses. Geology– United States -- Congresses.*

**QE697.E17 1994**
  Earth's glacial record / edited by M. Deynoux ... [et al.]. Cambridge ; Cambridge University Press, 1994. xvii, 266 p.
93-029826     551.7/92     0521420229
  *Glacial epoch.*

**QE697.G8 1993**
**Grayson, Donald K.**
  The desert's past : a natural prehistory of the Great Basin / Donald K. Grayson. Washington : Smithsonian Institution Press, c1993. xvii, 356 p.
92-025065     979/.01     1560982225
  *Geology, Stratigraphic -- Pleistocene. Geology, Stratigraphic – Holocene. Geology -- Great Basin. Great Basin -- Antiquities.*

**QE697.L2945 1997**
  Late glacial and postglacial environmental changes : Quaternary, Carboniferous-Permian, and Proterozoic / edited by I. Peter Martini. New York : Oxford University Press, 1997. xii, 343 p. :
95-051665     551.7/9     0195085418
  *Glacial epoch. Paleoecology. Glacial climates.*

**QE698.M85 2000**
**Muller, R.**
  Ice ages and astronomical causes : data, spectral analysis, and mechanisms / Richard A. Muller and Gordon J. MacDonald. London ; Springer, c2000. ix, 318 p. :
00-059473     551.79/2     185233634X
  *Glacial epoch. Earth -- Orbit.*

## QE703 Paleontology — Dictionaries and encyclopedias

**QE703.E523 1999**
  Encyclopedia of paleontology / editor, Ronald Singer. Chicago : Fitzroy Dearbon Publishers, 1999. 2 v. :
    560/.3 21
*Paleontology -- Encyclopedias.*

## QE705 Paleontology — History

**QE705.A1.R8 1976**
**Rudwick, M. J. S.**
  The meaning of fossils : episodes in the history of palaeontology / Martin J. S. Rudwick. New York : Science History Publications, 1976. 287 p. :
76-040050     560/.903     088202163X
  *Paleontology -- History.*

**QE705.G8.M39 2000**
**Mayor, Adrienne,**
  The first fossil hunters : paleontology in Greek and Roman times / Adrienne Mayor. Princeton, N.J. : Princeton University Press, c2000. xx, 361 p. :
99-043073     560/.938     0691058636
  *Paleontology -- Greece -- History. Paleontology -- Rome -- History. Science, Ancient.*

### QE707.A2 Paleontology — Biography — Collective

**QE707.A2**
**McGowan, Christopher.**
  The dragon seekers : how an extraordinary circle of fossilists discovered the dinosaurs and paved the way for Darwin / Chris McGowan. Cambridge, Mass. : Persus Pub., c2001. xvi, 254 p. :
    560.92242     0738202827
  *Fossils -- Collection and preservation -- History -- 19th century. Paleontology -- England -- History -- 19th century. Paleontologists– England -- Biography.*

### QE707.C63 Paleontology — Biography — Individual, A-Z

**QE707.C63.J34 2000**
**Jaffe, Mark.**
  The gilded dinosaur : the fossil war between E.D. Cope and O.C. Marsh and the rise of American science / by Mark Jaffe. New York : Crown, c2000. 424 p. :
99-038510     560/.978/09034     0517707608
*Cope, E. D. -- (Edward Drinker), -- 1840-1897. Marsh, Othniel Charles, -- 1831-1899. Paleontologists -- United States –Biography. Fossils -- West (U.S.) -- Collection and preservation -- History –19th century.*

## QE711-711.2 Paleontology — General works, treatises, and textbooks

**QE711.S5**
**Simpson, George Gaylord,**
  Life of the past; an introduction to paleontology. New Haven, Yale University Press, 1953. 198 p.
52-012078     560
  *Paleontology.*

**QE711.2.C68 1995**
**Cowen, Richard,**
   History of life / Richard Cowen. 2nd ed. Boston : Blackwell Scientific Publications, c1995. xviii, 462 p. :
   560 20      0865423547
   *Paleontology.*

**QE711.2.E47 1991**
**Eldredge, Niles.**
   Fossils : the evolution and extinction of species / Niles Eldredge ; photography by Murray Alcosser ; introduction by Stephen Jay Gould. New York : H.N. Abrams, 1991. xx, 220 p. :
   91-000302      560      0810933055
   *Fossils. Evolution.*

**QE711.2.F66 1991**
**Fortey, Richard A.**
   Fossils : the key to the past / Richard Fortey. Cambridge, Mass. : Harvard University Press, 1991. 187 p. :
   90-024760      560      0674311353
   *Fossils. Paleontology.*

**QE711.2.M3913 1992**
**Mayr, Helmut.**
   A guide to fossils / Helmut Mayr ; translated by D. Dineley & G. Windsor. Princeton, N.J. : Princeton University Press, c1992. 256 p. :
   92-015856      560      069108789X
   *Fossils. Paleontology.*

**QE711.2.R37 1978**
**Raup, David M.**
   Principles of paleontology / David M. Raup, Steven M. Stanley. San Francisco : W. H. Freeman, c1978. x, 481 p. :
   77-017443      560      0716700220
   *Paleontology.*

## QE719 Paleontology — Micropaleontology — General works

**QE719.I57**
   Introduction to marine micropaleontology / edited by Bilal U. Haq, Anne Boersma ; contributors, W. A. Berggren ... [et al.]. New York : Elsevier, c1978. 376 p. :
   78-004516      560/.92      0444002677
   *Micropaleontology. Marine sediments.*

## QE720 Paleontology — Paleocology

**QE720.D45 1991**
**Delcourt, Hazel R.**
   Quaternary ecology : a paleoecological perspective / Hazel R. Delcourt and Paul A. Delcourt. London ; Chapman & Hall, 1991. x, 242 p. :
   91-231070      560/.45      0412297809
   *Paleoecology -- Quaternary.*

**QE720.P316 1999**
   Paleocommunities : a case study from the Silurian and Lower Devonian / edited by A.J. Boucot and J.D. Lawson. Cambridge ; Cambridge University Press, 1999. xv, 895 p. :
   96-037795      560/.45      0521363985
   *Paleoecology -- Silurian. Paleoecology -- Devonian. Biotic communities.*

**QE720.P3 1990**
   Packrat middens : the last 40,000 years of biotic change / edited by Julio L. Betancourt, Thomas R. Van Devender, and Paul S. Martin. Tucson : University of Arizona Press, c1990. vii, 467 p. :
   89-038454      560/.45/0978      0816511152
   *Paleoecology -- West (U.S.) Paleoecology -- Mexico. Paleoecology -- Holocene.*

**QE720.T47 1992**
   Terrestrial ecosystems through time : evolutionary paleoecology of terrestrial plants and animals / edited by Anna K. Behrensmeyer ... [et al.]. Chicago : University of Chicago Press, 1992. xix, 568 p. :
   91-044166      560/.45      0226041549
   *Paleoecology. Paleobiology.*

## QE721 Paleontology — Special aspects of the subject as whole

**QE721.E53 1993**
   Palaeobiology : a synthesis / edited by Derek E.G. Briggs and Peter R. Crowther ; on behalf of the Palaeontological Association. Oxford ; Blackwell Scientific Publications, 1993. xiii, 583 p.
   88-035060      560/.3/21      0632025255
   *Paleobiology.*

**QE721.H64 1989**
**Hoffman, Antoni.**
   Arguments on evolution : a paleontologist's perspective / Antoni Hoffman. New York : Oxford University Press, 1989. xiii, 274 p.
   88-009973      560      0195044436
   *Evolutionary paleobiology.*

**QE721.H84 1989**
**Hughes, Norman F.**
   Fossils as information : new recording and stratal correlation techniques / Norman F. Hughes. Cambridge ; Cambridge University Press, 1989. vii, 136 p. :
   89-000475      560/.12      0521366569
   *Fossils -- Classification. Paleontology, Stratigraphic.*

**QE721.P34**
   Patterns of evolution as illustrated by the fossil record / edited by A. Hallam. Amsterdam ; Elsevier Scientific Pub. Co. : distributors for 1977. xiii, 591 p.
   77-002819      575      0444414959
   *Evolutionary paleobiology.*

**QE721.T87 1989**
**Turek, Vojtech.**
　Fossils of the world : a comprehensive practical guide to collecting and studying fossils / V. Turek, J. Marek, J. Benes ; edited by Julian Brown. New York : Arch Cape Press, 1989, c1988. 495 p. :
　　　　　560 10　　0517679043
*Fossils -- Classification.*

## QE721.2 Paleontology — Special topics, A-Z

**QE721.2.E85.N49 1995**
　New approaches to speciation in the fossil record / edited by Douglas H. Erwin and Robert L. Anstey. New York : Columbia University Press, c1995. viii, 342 p.
　95-007117　　　560　　　0231082487
　*Evolutionary paleobiology.*

**QE721.2.E85.N63 1992**
　Early life on earth / Nobel Symposium no. 84 ; Stefan Bengtson, editor. New York : Columbia University Press, 1994. x, 630 p. :
　94-003822　　　560　　　0231080883
　*Evolutionary paleobiology -- Congresses.*

**QE721.2.E85.O75 1992**
　Origin and early evolution of the Metazoa / edited by Jere H. Lipps and Philip W. Signor. New York : Plenum Press, c1992. xiii, 570 p.
　92-016461　　　563　　　0306440679
　*Evolutionary paleobiology. Metazoa. Paleontology – Cambrian.*

**QE721.2.E87**
　Evolutionary paleoecology : the ecological context of macroevolutionary change / edited by Warren D. Allmon, David J. Bottjer. New York : Columbia University Press, c2001. xi, 357 p. :
　00-064522　　　560/.45　　　0231109946
　*Evolutionary paleoecology.*

**QE721.2.E97**
**Ward, Peter Douglas,**
　Rivers in time : the search for clues to earth's mass extinctions / Peter D. Ward. New York : Columbia University Press, c2000. viii, 315 p.
　00-056954　　　576.8/4　　　0231118627
　*Extinction (Biology) Catastrophes (Geology) Biological diversity.*

**QE721.2.E97.M37 1989**
　Mass extinctions : processes and evidence / edited by Stephen K. Donovan. New York : Columbia University Press, c1989. xiv, 266 p. :
　89-000959　　　575/.7　　　023107090X
　*Extinction (Biology)*

**QE721.2.E97.O36 1996**
**Officer, Charles B.**
　The great dinosaur extinction controversy / Charles Officer & Jake Page. Reading, Mass. : Addison-Wesley, c1996. xiii, 209 p.
　96-003809　　　567.9/1　　　020148384X
　*Extinction (Biology) Dinosaurs. Cretaceous-Tertiary boundary.*

**QE721.2.F6.P76 1991**
　The Processes of fossilization / edited by Stephen K. Donovan. New York: Columbia University Press, c1991. p. cm.
　91-016327　　　560　　　0231076746
　*Fossilization. Taphonomy.*

**QE721.2.P24**
**Lieberman, Bruce S.**
　Paleobiogeography / Bruce S. Lieberman. New York : Kluwer Academic/Plenum Publishers, c2000. xvii, 208 p.
　99-055322　　　560　　　030646277X
　*Paleobiogeography.*

**QE721.2.P24.P54 1991**
**Pielou, E. C.,**
　After the Ice Age : the return of life to glaciated North America / E.C. Pielou. Chicago : University of Chicago Press, 1991. ix, 366 p. :
　90-011024　　　560/.1/78　　　0226668118
　*Paleobiogeography -- North America. Paleontology – Holocene. Glacial epoch -- North America.*

**QE721.2.S7.G44 1999**
**Gee, Henry.**
　In search of deep time : beyond the fossil record to a new history of life / Henry Gee. New York : Free Press, 1999. 267 p. :
　99-032137　　　560/.7/2　　　068485421X
　*Cladistic analysis. Paleontology -- Statistical methods.*

## QE724-724.5 Paleontology — Stratigraphic divisions (General and zoological) — Precambrian

**QE724.E27 1983**
　Earth's earliest biosphere : its origin and evolution / edited by J. William Schopf. Princeton, N.J. : Princeton University Press, c1983. xxv, 543 p.,
　82-061383　　　560/.1/71　　　0691083231
　*Paleontology -- Precambrian.*

**QE724.5.P76 1992**
　The Proterozoic biosphere : a multidisciplinary study / edited by J. William Schopf and Cornelis Klein. Cambridge ; Cambridge University Press, 1992. xxiv, 1348 p.
　91-015085　　　560/.171　　　0521366151
　*Paleontology -- Proterozoic.*

**QE734.5 Paleontology — Stratigraphic divisions (General and zoological) — Mesozoic**

**QE734.5.A73 1996**
**Archibald, J. David.**
   Dinosaur extinction and the end of an era : what the fossils say / J. David Archibald. New York : Columbia University Press, c1996. xviii, 237 p.
95-031113          567.9/1            023107624X
   *Cretaceous-Tertiary boundary. Extinction (Biology)*

**QE742 Paleontology — Stratigraphic divisions (General and zoological) — Amber fauna and flora**

**QE742.P65 1992**
**Poinar, George O.**
   Life in amber / George O. Poinar, Jr. Stanford, Calif. : Stanford University Press, 1992. xiii, 350 p.
91-005045          560            0804720010
   *Amber fossils. Amber.*

**QE742.P66 1994**
**Poinar, George O.**
   The quest for life in amber / George and Roberta Poinar. Reading, Mass. : Addison-Wesley, c1994. xiii, 219 p.,
94-003043          560            0201626608
   *Amber fossils. DNA, Fossil. Amber.*

**QE745 Paleontology — Geographical divisions (General and zoological) — North America**

**QE745.S48**
**Shimer, Hervey Woodburn,**
   Index fossils of North America: a new work based on the complete revision and reillustration of Grabau and Shimer's "North American index fossils," by Hervey W. Shimer and Robert R. Shrock. A publication of the Technology press, Massachusetts institute of technology. New York, J. Wiley & Sons, inc.; [1944] ix, 837 p.
44-005139          562
   *Paleontology -- North America. Invertebrates, Fossil -- North America.*

# QE761 Paleozoology — General works, treatises, and textbooks

**QE761.K8413 1986**
**Kuhn-Schnyder, Emil.**
   Handbook of paleozoology / Emil Kuhn-Schnyder, Hans Rieber ; translated by Emil Kucera. Baltimore : Johns Hopkins University Press, c1986. xi, 394 p. :
               560 19      0801828376
*Paleontology.*

**QE770 Paleozoology — Invertebrates — General works, treatises, and textbooks**

**QE770.D69 1996**
**Doyle, Peter.**
   Understanding fossils : an introduction to invertebrate palaeontology / Peter Doyle ; with contributions by Florence M.D. Lowry. Chichester ; Wiley, 1996. 409 p. :
95-049411          562            0471963518
   *Invertebrates, Fossil.*

**QE770.G54 1984**
**Glaessner, Martin F.**
   The dawn of animal life : a biohistorical study / Martin F. Glaessner. Cambridge ; Cambridge University Press, 1984. xi, 244 p. :
83-005188          562            0521235073
   *Invertebrates, Fossil. Marine invertebrates -- Evolution. Paleontology -- Precambrian.*

**QE770.G67 1989**
**Gould, Stephen Jay.**
   Wonderful life : the Burgess Shale and the nature of history / Stephen Jay Gould. New York : W.W. Norton, c1989. 347 p. :
88-037469          560/.9      0393027058
   *Invertebrates, Fossil -- British Columbia -- Yoho National Park. Paleontology -- Cambrian. Paleontology -- British Columbia – Yoho National Park. Burgess Shale (B.C.) Yoho National Park (B.C.)*

**QE770.L485 1999**
**Levin, Harold L.**
   Ancient invertebrates and their living relatives / Harold L. Levin. Upper Saddle River, N.J. : Prentice Hall, c1999. x, 358 p. :
98-002690          562            0137489552
   *Invertebrates, Fossil. Invertebrates.*

**QE770.M6**
**Moore, Raymond Cecil,**
   Invertebrate fossils [by] Raymond C. Moore, Cecil G. Lalicker [and] Alfred G. Fischer. New York, McGraw-Hill, 1952. 766 p.
51012632          562
   *Invertebrates, Fossil.*

**QE772 Paleozoology — Invertebrates — Protozoa**

**QE772.S85 1989**
   Stratigraphical atlas of fossil Foraminifera / editors, D.G. Jenkins and J.W. Murray. Chichester, West Sussex, England : E. Horwood for the British Micropalaeontological 1989. 593 p. :
88-013890          563/.12            085312826X
   *Foraminifera, Fossil -- Atlases.*

### QE821-831 Paleozoology — Invertebrates — Arthropoda

**QE821.F67 2000**
**Fortey, Richard A.**
Trilobite! : eyewitness to evolution / by Richard Fortey. New York : Alfred Knopf, 2000. xiii, 284 p.
00-034908          565/.39          0375406255
*Trilobites.*

**QE821.L46 1993**
**Levi-Setti, Riccardo.**
Trilobites / Riccardo Levi-Setti. Chicago : University of Chicago Press, c1993. x, 342 p. :
92-038716          565/.393          0226474518
*Trilobites -- Pictorial works.*

**QE831.E45 1993**
**Elias, Scott A.**
Quaternary insects and their environments / Scott A. Elias; foreword by G. Russell Coope. Washington, D.C. : Smithsonian Institution Press, c1994. xiii, 284 p.
93-018570          565/.7          1560983035
*Insects, Fossil. Paleontology -- Quaternary.*

### QE841-882 Paleozoology — Chordata — Vertebrates

**QE841.C2538 1997**
**Carroll, Robert Lynn,**
Patterns and processes of vertebrate evolution / Robert L. Carroll. New York : Cambridge University Press, 1997. xvi, 448 p. :
96-044161          596.138          0521472326
*Vertebrates, Fossil -- Evolution. Vertebrates -- Evolution.*

**QE841.E96 2000**
Evolution of herbivory in terrestrial vertebrates : perspectives from the fossil record / edited by Hans-Dieter Sues. Cambridge ; Cambridge University Press, 2000. x, 256 p. :
00-020863          566          0521594499
*Vertebrates, Fossil -- Florida. Animals, Fossil -- Florida.*

**QE841.F86 1995**
Functional morphology in vertebrate paleontology / edited by Jeff Thomason. Cambridge ; Cambridge University Press, 1995. xi, 277 p. :
93-047981          566          0521440955
*Vertebrates, Fossil.*

**QE841.R5 1999**
**Rich, Pat Vickers.**
Wildlife of Gondwana : dinosaurs and other vertebrates from the ancient supercontinent / Patricia Vickers-Rich and Thomas Hewitt-Rich ; principal photography by Francesco Coffa and Steven Morton ; reconstructions by Peter Trusler. Bloomington : Indiana University Press, c1999. 304 p. :
99-036298          566          0253336430
*Vertebrates, Fossil -- Southern Hemisphere. Paleontology -- Southern Hemisphere. Gondwana (Geology)*

**QE845.L625 1995**
**Lockley, M. G.**
Dinosaur tracks : and other fossil footprints of the western United States / Martin Lockley and Adrian P. Hunt ; artwork by Paul Koroshetz. New York : Columbia University Press, c1995. xx, 338 p. :
94-024198          560.978          0231079265
*Footprints, Fossil -- West (U.S.)*

**QE845.L626 1999**
**Lockley, M. G.**
The eternal trail : a tracker looks at evolution / Martin Lockley. Reading, Mass. : Perseus Books, c1999. xvii, 334 p.
99-064158          576.8          0738201650
*Footprints, Fossil. Animal tracks. Tracking and trailing.*

**QE851.F89213 1995**
**Frickhinger, Karl Albert,**
Fossil atlas, fishes / Karl Albert Frickhinger ; translated by R.P.S. Jefferies. Melle, Germany : Mergus ; 1995. 1088 p. :
95-000138          567/.022/3          1564651150
*Fishes, Fossil -- Atlases.*

**QE861.A53 1997**
Ancient marine reptiles / edited by Jack M. Callaway, Elizabeth L. Nicholls. San Diego : Academic Press, c1997. xlvi, 501 p.
96-041835          567.9          0121552101
*Marine reptiles, Fossil.*

**QE862.D5.A33 1989**
**Alexander, R. McNeill.**
Dynamics of dinosaurs and other extinct giants / R. McNeill Alexander. New York : Columbia University Press, c1989. 167 p. :
88-020373          567.9/1          023106666X
*Dinosaurs -- Locomotion. Extinct animals – Locomotion. Animal mechanics.*

**QE862.D5.C235 1999**
**Carpenter, Kenneth,**
Eggs, nests, and baby dinosaurs : a look at dinosaur reproduction / Kenneth Carpenter. Bloomington : Indiana University Press, c1999. xi, 336 p. :
99-042739          567.9          0253334977
*Dinosaurs -- Reproduction. Dinosaur -- Eggs. Dinosaurs -- Infancy.*

**QE862.D5.C697 1997**
The complete dinosaur / edited by James O. Farlow and M.K. Brett-Surman ; art editor, Robert F. Walters. Bloomington : Indiana University Press, c1997. xi, 752 p. :
97-023698          567.9          0253333490
*Dinosaurs.*

**QE862.D5.C862 1997**
**Currie, Philip J.**
Encyclopedia of dinosaurs / edited by Philip J. Currie, Kevin Padian. San Diego : Academic Press, c1997. xxx, 869 p. :
97-023430          567.9/03          0122268105
*Dinosaurs -- Encyclopedias.*

**QE862.D5.F38 1996**
**Fastovsky, David E.**

The evolution and extinction of the dinosaurs / David E. Fastovsky, David B. Weishampel ; with original illustrations by Brian Regal. Cambridge ; Cambridge University Press, 1996. xvi, 460 p.,
95-006002          567.9/7          0521444969
*Dinosaurs -- Evolution. Extinction (Biology)*

**QE862.D5.P38 1988**
**Paul, Gregory S.**

Predatory dinosaurs of the world : a complete illustrated guide / written and drawn by Gregory S. Paul. New York : Simon and Schuster, c1988. 464 p. :
88-023052          567.9/1          0671619462
*Dinosaurs. Predatory animals.*

**QE862.O6.H65 2000**
**Holman, J. Alan,**

Fossil snakes of North America : origin, evolution, distribution, paleoecology / J. Alan Holman. Bloomington : Indiana University Press, c2000. xi, 357 p. :
99-053487          567.9/6/097          0253337216
*Snakes, Fossil -- North America.*

**QE862.O65.D64 1996**
**Dodson, Peter.**

The horned dinosaurs : a natural history / Peter Dodson ; paintings by Wayne D. Barlowe ; additional illustrations and art editing by Robert Walters. Princeton, N.J. : Princeton University Press, c1996. xiv, 346 p. :
96-000105          567.9/7          0691028826
*Ceratopsidae.*

**QE862.S3.F54 2000**
**Fiffer, Steve.**

Tyrannosaurus Sue : the extraordinary saga of the largest, most fought over T. rex ever found / Steve Fiffer ; foreword by Robert T. Bakker. New York : W.H. Freeman, 2000. xvi, 248 p. ;
00-021596          567.912/9/09783          0716735121
*Larson, Peter L.     Paleontology -- South Dakota -- History – 20th century. Tyrannosaurus rex -- South Dakota.*

**QE867.H63 1998**
**Holman, J. Alan,**

Pleistocene amphibians and reptiles in Britain and Europe / J. Alan Holman. New York : Oxford University Press, 1998. vi, 254 p. :
97-030058          567/.8/094          0195112326
*Amphibians, Fossil -- Europe. Reptiles, Fossil -- Europe. Amphibians, Fossil -- Great Britain.*

**QE867.H65 1995**
**Holman, J. Alan,**

Pleistocene amphibians and reptiles in North America / J. Alan Holman. New York : Oxford University Press ; 1995. 243 p. :
94-032144          567/.6          0195086104
*Amphibians, Fossil -- North America. Reptiles, Fossil -- North America. Paleontology -- Pleistocene.*

**QE881.E857 1998**

Evolution of Tertiary mammals of North America / edited by Christine M. Janis, Kathleen M. Scott, Louis L. Jacobs. Cambridge, UK ; Cambridge University Press, 1998- v. 1  :
97-005757          569/.097
*Mammals, Fossil -- North America. Paleontology -- Tertiary. Animals, Fossil -- North America.*

**QE881.K796 1988**
**Kurten, Bjorn.**

On evolution and fossil mammals / Bjorn Kurten. New York : Columbia University Press, 1988. xvii, 301 p.
86-032630          569          0231058683
*Mammals, Fossil. Evolution.*

**QE881.R83 1997**
**Rudwick, M. J. S.**

Georges Cuvier, fossil bones, and geological catastrophes : new translations & interpretations of the primary texts / Martin J.S. Rudwick. Chicago : University of Chicago Press, 1997. xvi, 301 p. :
97-015628          569          0226731065
*Mammals, Fossil. Catastrophes (Geology) Geology – History – 18th century.*

**QE882.P8.H39 1991**
**Haynes, Gary.**

Mammoths, mastodons, and elephants : biology, behavior, and the fossil record / Gary Haynes. Cambridge : Cambridge University Press, 1991. xi, 413 p. :
90-028972          569/.6          0521384354
*Elephants, Fossil. Elephants.*

**QE882.P8.W37 1997**
**Ward, Peter Douglas,**

The call of distant mammoths : why the ice age mammals disappeared / Peter D. Ward. New York : Copernicus, c1997. xviii, 241 p.
96-048690          569/.67          0387949151
*Mastodon. Extinction (Biology)*

**QE882.U6.M27 1992**
**MacFadden, Bruce J.**

Fossil horses : systematics, paleobiology, and evolution of the family Equidae / Bruce J. MacFadden. Cambridge [England] ; Cambridge University Press, 1992. xii, 369 p. :
92-015810          569/.72          0521340411
*Horses, Fossil. Horses -- Evolution. Horses -- Classification.*

## QE905 Paleobotany — General works, treatises, and textbooks

**QE905.A35 1995**
**Agashe, Shripad N.**

Paleobotany : plants of the past, their evolution, paleoenvironment, and application in exploration of fossil fuels / Shripad N. Agashe. New Delhi : Oxford & IBH Pub. Co., c1995. vi, 359 p. :
95-905188                    8120409426
*Paleobotany. Plants, Fossil -- India.*

**QE905.P55 2001**

Plants invade the land : evolutionary and environmental perspectives / editors, Patricia G. Gensel, Dianne Edwards. New York : Columbia University Press, c2001. x, 304 p. :
00-057021          561          0231111606
*Paleobotany. Plants -- Evolution.*

**QE905.S73 1983**
**Stewart, Wilson N.**

Paleobotany and the evolution of plants / Wilson N. Stewart. Cambridge [Cambridgeshire] ; Cambridge University Press, 1983. x, 405 p. :
82-021986          561          0521233151
*Paleobotany. Plants -- Evolution.*

### QE915 Paleobotany — Stratigraphic divisions — Paleozoic

**QE915.P58 1991**

Plant fossils in geological investigation : the palaeozoic / editor, Christopher J. Cleal. New York : Ellis Horwood, 1991. 233 p. :
91-029159          560/.172          0136808778
*Paleobotany -- Paleozoic. Paleontology, Stratigraphic. Paleogeography.*

### QE923 Paleobotany — Stratigraphic divisions — Mesozoic

**QE923.V35 1991**
**Vakhrameev, Vsevolod Andreevich.**

Jurassic and Cretaceous floras and climates of the earth / V.A. Vakhrameev ; translated by Ju. V. Litvinov ; edited by Norman F. Hughes. Cambridge ; Cambridge University Press, 1991. xvii, 318 p.
91-011017          560/.1764          0521402913
*Paleobotany -- Jurassic. Paleobotany -- Cretaceous. Paleoclimatology -- Jurassic.*

### QE948 Paleobotany — Geographical divisions — Australia

**QE948.A1.W47 1990**
**White, M. E.**

The flowering of Gondwana / Mary E. White ; photography of fossils by Jim Frazier. Princeton, N.J. : Princeton University Press, c1990. 256 p. :
90-031732          581.994          0691085927
*Paleobotany -- Australia. Botany -- Australia. Gondwana (Geology)*

### QE993 Paleobotany — Systematic divisions — Palynology

**QE993.S43 1994**

Sedimentation of organic particles / edited by Alfred Traverse. Cambridge, England ; Cambridge University Press, c1994. xii, 544 p. :
92-039221          561/.13          0521384362
*Palynology. Sedimentation and deposition. Micropaleontology.*

# QH11-251 Natural History (General)

## QH11 Voyages and expeditions

**QH11.B43**

The Beagle record : selections from the original pictorial records and written accounts of the voyage of H.M.S. Beagle / edited by Richard Darwin Keynes. Cambridge ; Cambridge University Press, 1979. xiv, 409 p. :
77-082500          500.9/8          0521218225
*Darwin, Charles, -- 1809-1882. Naturalists -- England -- Biography. Naturalists -- England -- Correspondence.*

**QH11.D2 1839a**
**Darwin, Charles,**

Journal of researches into the geology and natural history of the various countries visited by H. M. S. Beagle. New York, Hafner Pub. Co., 1952. xiv, 615 p.
53002985          574
*Natural history. Geology. Voyages around the world. South America -- Description and travel.*

**QH11.V57 1996**

Visions of empire : voyages, botany, and representations of nature / edited by David Philip Miller and Peter Hanns Reill. Cambridge [England] ; Cambridge University Press, 1996. xix, 370 p. :
95-019085          508/.09/033          0521483034
*Natural history. Scientific expeditions. Botany.*

## QH13 Dictionaries and encyclopedias

**QH13.J3 1960**
**Jaeger, Edmund Carroll,**

The biologist's handbook of pronunciations. Illus. by Morris Van Dame and the author. Springfield, Ill., Thomas [1960] 317 p.
59-014924          574.03
*Biology -- Dictionaries.*

**QH13.L56 1987**
**Lincoln, Roger J.**

The Cambridge illustrated dictionary of natural history / R.J. Lincoln and G.A. Boxshall ; illustrations by Roberta Smith. Cambridge ; Cambridge University Press, 1987. 413 p. :
87-008018          508/.03/21          0521305519
*Natural history -- Dictionaries. Biology -- Dictionaries.*

### QH15 History — General works

**QH15.F27 2000**
**Farber, Paul Lawrence,**

Finding order in nature : the naturalist tradition from Linnaeus to E.O. Wilson / Paul Lawrence Farber. Baltimore, Md. : Johns Hopkins University Press, 2000. x, 136 p. :
99-089621          508/.09          0801863899
*Natural history -- History.*

## QH21 History — By region or country, A-Z

**QH21.E853.L37 1994**
**Larson, James L.**
Interpreting nature : the science of living form from Linnaeus to Kant / James L. Larson. Baltimore : Johns Hopkins University Press, c1994. ix, 227 p. :
94-002904        574/.094/09033        0801848407
*Natural history -- Europe, Northern -- History -- 18th century. Physiology -- Europe, Northern -- History -- 18th century.*

## QH26 Biography — Collective

**QH26.B535 1997**
Biographical dictionary of American and Canadian naturalists and environmentalists / edited by Keir B. Sterling ... [et al.]. Westport, Conn. : Greenwood Press, 1997. xix, 937 p. ;
96-000156        508/.092/273        0313230471
*Naturalists -- United States -- Biography. Naturalists – Canada – Biography. Environmentalists -- United States -- Biography.*

**QH26.B66 1991**
**Bonta, Marcia,**
Women in the field : America's pioneering women naturalists / Marcia Myers Bonta. College Station : Texas A & M University Press, c1991. xix, 299 p. :
90-020729        508/.092/2        089096467X
*Women naturalists -- United States -- Biography.*

**QH26.E44**
**Elman, Robert.**
First in the field : America's pioneering naturalists / by Robert Elman ; foreword by Dean Amadon. New York : Mason/Charter, 1977. xx, 231 p., [
77-003437        500.9/2/2        0884054993
*Naturalists -- United States -- Biography.*

**QH26.N68 1996**
Notable women in the life sciences : a biographical dictionary / edited by Benjamin F. Shearer and Barbara S. Shearer. Westport, Conn. : Greenwood Press, 1996. xi, 440 p. :
95-025603        574/.092/2        0313293023
*Women life scientists -- Biography -- Dictionaries.*

## QH31-31.5 Biography — Individual, A-Z

**QH31.A2.L8**
**Lurie, Edward,**
Louis Agassiz: a life in science. [Chicago] University of Chicago Press [1960] xiv, 449 p.
59-011623        925.9
*Agassiz, Louis, -- 1807-1873.*

**QH31.B19.O27 1993**
**O'Brian, Patrick,**
Joseph Banks, a life / Patrick O'Brian. Boston : D.R. Godine, 1993. 328 p. :
92-012180        508.42/092        0879239301
*Banks, Joseph, -- Sir, -- 1743-1820. Naturalists -- England -- Biography. Botanists -- England -- Biography. Explorers – England - - Biography.*

**QH31.B23.A3**
**Bartram, John,**
John and William Bartram's America : selections from the writings of the Philadelphia naturalists / Edited with an introduction by Helen Gere Cruickshank. New York : Devin-Adair Company, 1957. xxii, 418 p.
57008862        574.973
*Bartram, William, -- 1739-1823. Bartram, John, -- 1699-1777. Naturalists -- Correspondence, reminiscences, etc. Natural history – United States. United States -- Description and travel -- To 1783.*

**QH31.B715.A3 1993**
**Bonner, John Tyler.**
Life cycles : reflections of an evolutionary biologist / John Tyler Bonner. Princeton, N.J. : Princeton University Press, c1993. xii, 209 p. :
92-041540        574/.092        0691033196
*Bonner, John Tyler. Biologists -- United States -- Biography. Biology.*

**QH31.B859.A3 1990**
**Brower, David Ross,**
For earth's sake : the life and times of David Brower. Salt Lake City : Peregrine Smith Books, c1990. xvii, 556 p.
89-026605        333.7/2/092        0879050136
*Brower, David Ross, -- 1912- Conservationists -- United States – Biography. Environmentalists -- United States -- Biography.*

**QH31.C33.A4 1995**
**Carson, Rachel,**
Always, Rachel : the letters of Rachel Carson and Dorothy Freeman, 1952-1964 / edited by Martha Freeman. Boston : Beacon Press, c1995. xxx, 567 p. :
94-025849        574/.092        0807070106
*Carson, Rachel, -- 1907-1964 -- Correspondence. Freeman, Dorothy, -- 1898-1978 -- Correspondence. Biologists -- Correspondence. Environmentalists -- Correspondence. Women biologists -- Correspondence.*

**QH31.C33.M34 1993**
**McCay, Mary A.**
Rachel Carson / Mary A. McCay. New York : Twayne Publishers ; c1993. xvii, 122 p.
92-039795        574/.092        0805739882
*Carson, Rachel, -- 1907-1964 -- Literary art. Ecologists – United States -- Biography. Environmentalists -- United States – Biography. Science writers -- United States -- Biography.*

**QH31.C85.A3 1988**
**Crick, Francis,**
What mad pursuit : a personal view of scientific discovery / Francis Crick. New York : Basic Books, c1988. xiii, 182 p.,
88-047693          574.19/1/0924          0465091377
*Crick, Francis, -- 1916-     Molecular biology -- History. Biologists – England -- Biography. Physicists -- England -- Biography.*

**QH31.D2.A16**
**Darwin, Charles,**
Autobiography. With original omissions restored; edited with appendix and notes by his grand-daughter, Nora Barlow. London, Collins, 1958. 253 p.
58-003624          925.9
*Darwin, Charles, -- 1809-1882.     Naturalists -- Great Britain -- Biography.*

**QH31.D2.A37**
**Darwin, Charles,**
The red notebook of Charles Darwin / edited and with an introd. and notes by Sandra Herbert. [London] : British Museum (Natural History) ; 1980. 164 p. :
78-074215          575/.0092/4          0801412269
*Darwin, Charles, -- 1809-1882.     Natural history. Naturalists -- England -- Biography.*

**QH31.D2.A4 1985**
**Darwin, Charles,**
The correspondence of Charles Darwin / [editors, Frederick Burkhardt, Sydney Smith]. Cambridge [England] ; Cambridge University Press, 1985-1997 v. 1-10   :
84-045347          575/.0092          0521255872
*Darwin, Charles, -- 1809-1882.     Naturalists -- England -- Correspondence.*

**QH31.D2.B742 1991**
**Bowlby, John.**
Charles Darwin : a new life / John Bowlby. New York : W.W. Norton, 1991. xiv, 511 p. :
90-007484          575/.0092          0393029409
*Darwin, Charles, -- 1809-1882.     Naturalists -- England -- Biography.*

**QH31.D2.B743 1991**
**Bowler, Peter J.**
Charles Darwin : the man and his influence / Peter J. Bowler. Oxford, UK ; Blackwell, 1990. xii, 250 p. :
90-034922          575/.0092          0631168184
*Darwin, Charles, -- 1809-1882.     Evolution (Biology) -- History. Naturalists -- England -- Biography.*

**QH31.D2.B84 1995**
**Browne, E. J.**
Charles Darwin : a biography / Janet Browne. New York : Knopf : 1995- v. 1   :
94-006598          575/.0092          0394579429
*Darwin, Charles, -- 1809-1882.     Naturalists -- England -- Biography.*

**QH31.D2.C57 1984**
**Clark, Ronald William.**
The survival of Charles Darwin : a biography of a man and an idea / Ronald W. Clark. New York : Random House, c1984. x, 449 p., [1
84-042507          575/.0092/4          039452134X
*Darwin, Charles, -- 1809-1882.     Evolution (Biology) -- History. Naturalists -- England -- Biography.*

**QH31.D2.D4**
**De Beer, Gavin,**
Charles Darwin; evolution by natural selection. London, T. Nelson [1963] xi, 290 p.
63-023628
*Darwin, Charles, -- 1809-1882.*

**QH31.D2.G55**
**Gillespie, Neal C.,**
Charles Darwin and the problem of creation / Neal C. Gillespie. Chicago : University of Chicago Press, c1979. xiii, 201 p.
79-011231          575/.0092/4          0226293742
*Darwin, Charles, -- 1809-1882.     Life -- Origin. Naturalists -- England -- Biography.*

**QH31.D2.I7 1959**
**Irvine, William,**
Apes, angels, and Victorians; Darwin, Huxley, and evolution. New York, Meridian Books [1959, c1955] 399 p.
59012909          575.0162
*Darwin, Charles, -- 1809-1882. Huxley, Thomas Henry, – 1825-1895. Evolution.*

**QH31.D2.M54 1982**
**Miller, Jonathan,**
Darwin for beginners / Jonathan Miller & Borin Van Loon. New York : Pantheon Books, c1982. 176 p. :
82-047888          575/.0092/4          0394748476
*Darwin, Charles, -- 1809-1882.     Naturalists -- England -- Biography.*

**QH31.D2.O74**
**Ospovat, Dov.**
The development of Darwin's theory : natural history, natural theology, and natural selection, 1838-1859 / Dov Ospovat. Cambridge ; Cambridge University Press, 1981. xii, 301 p. :
81-004077          575.01/62          0521238188
*Darwin, Charles, -- 1809-1882.     Natural selection -- History. Natural history -- History. Biology -- History.*

**QH31.D2B745 1980**
**Brackman, Arnold C.**
A delicate arrangement : the strange case of Charles Darwin and Alfred Russel Wallace / Arnold C. Brackman. New York : Times Books, c1980. xi, 370 p. :
          575.01/62/0924          081290883X
*Darwin, Charles, 1809-1913. Wallace, Alfred Russel, 1823-1913. Evolution (Biology) -- History. Naturalists -- England --Biography.*

**QH31.D434.F573 1988**
**Fischer, Ernst Peter,**
 Thinking about science : Max Delbruck and the origins of molecular biology / Ernst Peter Fischer and Carol Lipson. New York : Norton, c1988. 334 p. :
87-016626                574.8/8/0924              039302508X
*Delbruck, Max.     Molecular biologists -- United States – Biography.*

**QH31.H88.J85 1992**
 Julian Huxley, biologist and statesman of science : proceedings of a conference held at Rice University, 25-27 September 1987 / edited by C. Kenneth Waters, Albert Van Helden. Houston, Tex. : Rice University Press, c1992. xii, 344 p. :
92-050136                574/.092              089263314X
*Huxley, Julian, -- 1887-1975 -- Congresses.     Biologists – England -- Biography -- Congresses.*

**QH31.H9.J46 1991**
**Jensen, J. Vernon**
 Thomas Henry Huxley : communicating for science / J. Vernon Jensen. Newark : University of Delaware Press ; c1991. p.
89-040762                574/.092              0874133793
*Huxley, Thomas Henry, -- 1825-1895.     Naturalists – Great Britain -- Biography. Orators -- Great Britain -- Biography. Science -- Philosophy.*

**QH31.H9.L96 1999**
**Lyons, Sherrie Lynne,**
 Thomas Henry Huxley : the evolution of a scientist / Sherrie L. Lyons. Amherst, N.Y. : Prometheus Books, 1999. 347 p. :
99-039254                570/.92              1573927066
*Huxley, Thomas Henry, -- 1825-1895.     Biologists -- England -- Biography. Scientists -- England -- Biography.*

**QH31.L2.B87**
**Burkhardt, Richard W.**
 The spirit of system : Lamarck and evolutionary biology / Richard W. Burkhardt, Jr. Cambridge, Mass. : Harvard University Press, 1977. 285 p. ;
76-053804                575.01/66/0924              0674833171
*Lamarck, Jean Baptiste Pierre Antoine de Monet de, -- 1744-1829. Evolution (Biology) -- History. Biologists -- France -- Biography. Evolution -- History.*

**QH31.L55.S3**
**Schierbeek, Abraham,**
 Measuring the invisible world; the life and works of Antoni van Leeuwenhoek. With a biographical chapter by Maria Rooseboom. London, Abelard-Schuman [c1959] 223 p.
59-013233                925.9
*Leeuwenhoek, Antoni van, -- 1632-1723.*

**QH31.L618.E77 1999**
 The essential Aldo Leopold : quotations and commentaries / edited by Curt Meine & Richard L. Knight. Madison, Wis. : University of Wisconsin Press, c1999. xxii, 362 p.
99-006424                333.7/2              0299165507
*Leopold, Aldo, -- 1886-1948 -- Quotations.     Naturalists – United States -- Biography.*

**QH31.L618.M45 1988**
**Meine, Curt.**
 Aldo Leopold : his life and work / Curt Meine. Madison, Wis. : University of Wisconsin Press, 1988. xv, 638 p. :
87-040367                508.32/4              0299114902
*Leopold, Aldo, -- 1886-1948.     Naturalists -- Wisconsin – Biography.*

**QH31.M45.O67 1994**
**Orel, Vitezslav.**
 Gregor Mendel : the first geneticist / Vitezslav Orel ; translated by Stephen Finn. New York : Oxford University Press, 1996. xii, 363 p. :
94-029077                575.1/092              0198547749
*Mendel, Gregor, -- 1822-1884.     Geneticists -- Austria – Biography. Genetics -- History. Mendel's law -- History.*

**QH31.M78.W54 1995**
**Wilkins, Thurman.**
 John Muir : apostle of nature / by Thurman Wilkins. Norman : University of Oklahoma Press, c1995. xxvii, 302 p.
95-011426                333.7/2/092              0806127120
*Muir, John, -- 1838-1914.     Naturalists -- United States – Biography. Conservationists -- United States -- Biography.*

**QH31.M9.M85 1996**
**Muir, John,**
 John Muir : his Life and letters and other writings / edited and introduced by Terry Gifford. London : Baton Wicks ; 1996. 912 p. :
96-221226                508/.092              1898573077
*Muir, John, -- 1838-1914.     Natural history -- United States. Nature conservation -- United States. Naturalists -- United States -- Biography.*

**QH31.N8.G7**
**Graustein, Jeannette E.**
 Thomas Nuttall, naturalist; explorations in America, 1808-1841 [by] Jeannette E. Graustein. Cambridge, Harvard University Press, 1967. xiii, 481 p.
67-013253                574/.0924
*Nuttall, Thomas, -- 1786-1859.*

**QH31.O27**
**Craige, Betty Jean.**
 Eugene Odum : ecosystem ecologist & environmentalist / Betty Jean Craige. Athens : University of Georgia Press, c2001. xxii, 226 p.
00-056826                577/.092              0820322814
*Odum, Eugene Pleasants, -- 1913-     Ecologists -- United States – Biography. Environmentalists -- United States -- Biography.*

**QH31.O94.R86 1994**
**Rupke, Nicolaas A.**
 Richard Owen : Victorian naturalist / Nicolaas A. Rupke. New Haven, CT : Yale University Press, 1994. xvii, 462 p.
93-005739                508/.092              0300058209
*Owen, Richard, -- 1804-1892.     Naturalists -- Great Britain -- Biography.*

**QH31.T4.A3  1957**
**Teale, Edwin Way,**
 Dune boy : the early years of a naturalist / by Edwin Way Teale ; illustrated by Edward Shenton. New York : Dodd, Mead, 1957. 275 p. :
57014144          925.7
*Teale, Edwin Way, -- 1899-*          *Indiana -- Social life and customs.*

**QH31.T485**
**Botkin, Daniel B.**
 No man's garden : Thoreau and a new vision for civilization and nature / Daniel B. Botkin. Washington, D.C. : Island Press [for] Shearwater Books, c2001. xxii, 310 p.
00-010445          304.2          1559634650
*Thoreau, Henry David, -- 1817-1862 -- Knowledge – Natural history. Naturalists -- United States -- Biography. Authors, American – 19th century -- Biography. Civilization.*

**QH31.W2.B76  1984**
**Brooks, John Langdon,**
 Just before the origin : Alfred Russel Wallace's theory of evolution / John Langdon Brooks. New York : Columbia University Press, 1984. xiii, 284 p.,
83-007710          575.01/62/0924          0231056761
*Wallace, Alfred Russel, -- 1823-1913.     Evolution (Biology) -- History. Naturalists -- England -- Biography.*

**QH31.W64.A3  1994**
**Wilson, Edward Osborne,**
 Naturalist / Edward O. Wilson. Washington, D.C. : Island Press/Shearwater Books, c1994. xii, 380 p.,
94-013111          508/.092          1559632887
*Wilson, Edward Osborne, -- 1929-     Naturalists -- United States – Biography.*

**QH31.5.S48.A36  1978**
**Seton, Ernest Thompson,**
 Trail of an artist-naturalist : the autobiography of Ernest Thompson Seton. New York : Arno Press, 1978, c1940. xii, 412 p.,
77-081134          574/.092/4          040510734X
*Seton, Ernest Thompson, -- 1860-1946.     Naturalists – United States -- Biography.*

# QH41 Pre-Linnaean works (through 1735)

**QH41.P713  1961**
**Pliny,**
 Natural history. With an English translation by H. Rackham. Cambridge, Harvard University Press, 1961- v.iov.
74-015292          500
*Natural history -- Pre-Linnean works.*

**QH41.P78.W4  1937**
**Wethered, Herbert Newton,**
 The mind of the ancient world: a considerations of Pliny's Natural history, by H. N. Wethered. London, New York Longmans, Green. [1937] xv, 301 p.
38013693          878.9
*Pliny, -- the Elder. -- Naturalis historia.*

# QH44 Works about Linnaeus

**QH44.B54**
**Blunt, Wilfrid,**
 The compleat naturalist: a life of Linnaeus, [by] Wilfrid Blunt; with the assistance of William T. Stearn. London, Collins, 1971. 256 p.;
77-857629          581/.0924          000211142X
*Linne, Carl von, -- 1707-1778.*

**QH44.L56  1983**
 Linnaeus, the man and his work / edited by Tore Frangsmyr ; with contributions by Sten Lindroth, Gunnar Eriksson, Gunnar Broberg. Berkeley : University of California Press, c1983. xii, 202 p.,
82-002044          580/.92/4          0520045688
*Linne, Carl von, -- 1707-1778.     Naturalists -- Sweden – Biography.*

## QH45.2 General works, treatises, and advanced textbooks — 1970-

**QH45.2.B32  1999**
**Barnes-Svarney, Patricia L.**
 The oryx guide to natural history : the earth and all its inhabitants / by Patricia Barnes-Svarney and Thomas E. Svarney. Phoenix, Ariz. : Oryx Press, 1999. xi, 252 p. :
99-041783          508          1573561592
*Natural history.*

**QH45.2.B66  1995**
 American women afield : writings by pioneering women naturalists / edited by Marcia Myers Bonta. College Station : Texas A&M University, c1995. xvi, 248 p. :
94-003664          508.73          0890966338
*Natural history -- United States. Women naturalists -- United States -- Biography. Naturalists -- United States -- Biography.*

# QH45.5 Popular works

**QH45.5.G68  1991**
**Gould, Stephen Jay.**
 Bully for brontosaurus : reflections in natural history / Stephen Jay Gould. New York : Norton, c1991. 540 p. :
91-006916          508          0393029611
*Natural history -- Popular works. Evolution -- Popular works.*

**QH45.5.G7  1993**
**Gould, Stephen Jay.**
 Eight little piggies : reflections in natural history / Stephen Jay Gould. New York : Norton, c1993. 479 p. :
92-018737          575/.001          039303416X
*Natural history -- Philosophy -- Popular works. Evolution (Biology) -- Popular works.*

## QH46.5 Natural history illustration

**QH46.5.C54 1991**
**Clewis, Beth.**
Index to illustrations of animals and plants / Beth Clewis.
New York : Neal-Schuman, c1991. xix, 217 p. ;
90-023816          574/.022/2          1555700721
*Natural history illustration -- Indexes.*

## QH75 Nature conservation. Landscape protection. Biological diversity conservation. Endangered species and ecosystems (General). Habitat conservation. Ecosystem management. Conservation biology — Societies, congresses, serial collections, yearbooks

**QH75.A1.E24 1993**
Ecological integrity and the management of ecosystems / edited by Stephen Woodley, James Kay, George Francis. Delray Beach, FL : St. Lucie Press, c1993. viii, 220 p.
93-006949          363.7          096340301X
*Ecosystem management -- Congresses. Ecological integrity -- Congresses. Ecosystem management -- Canada -- Congresses.*

**QH75.A1.L58 1999**
The living planet in crisis : biodiversity science and policy / [edited by] Joel Cracraft and Francesca T. Grifo. New York : Columbia University Press, c1999. xxiv, 311 p.
98-031465          333.95/16          0231108648
*Biological diversity conservation -- Government policy -- Congresses. Endangered species -- Social aspects -- Congresses. Biological diversity -- Congresses.*

**QH75.A32 1995**
**Ackerman, Diane.**
The rarest of the rare : vanishing animals, timeless worlds / Diane Ackerman. New York : Random House, c1995. xxi, 184 p. ;
95-008499          574.5/29          0679403469
*Endangered species. Rare animals. Endangered ecosystems.*

**QH75.A44 2000**
Applied wetlands science and technology / edited by Donald M. Kent. 2nd ed. Boca Raton, FL : Lewis Publishers, c2000. 454 p. :
                   333.91/8 21          156670359X
*Wetland conservation. Ecosystem management. Wetlands. Water quality management.*

**QH75.B43 1994**
**Beatley, Timothy,**
Habitat conservation planning : endangered species and urban growth / Timothy Beatley. Austin : University of Texas Press, 1994. ix, 234 p. ;
93-022810          333.95/416          0292707991
*Habitat conservation -- Planning. City planning – Environmental aspects. Endangered species.*

**QH75.B45 2000**
Behaviour and conservation / edited by L. Morris Gosling and William J. Sutherland. Cambridge, U.K. ; Cambridge University Press ; 2000. xi, 438 p. ;
99-026461          333.95/16          0521662303
*Conservation biology. Animal behavior.*

**QH75.B5228 1997**
Biodiversity II : understanding and protecting our biological resources / Marjorie L. Reaka-Kudla, Don E. Wilson, and Edward O. Wilson, editors. Washington, D.C. : Joseph Henry Press, 1997. v, 551 p. :
96-030851          333.95/16          0309052270
*Biological diversity conservation. Biological diversity.*

**QH75.B823 1995**
**Budiansky, Stephen.**
Nature's keepers : the new science of nature management / Stephen Budiansky. New York : Free Press, c1995. 310 p., [8] p
95-024100          333.7          0029049156
*Nature conservation. Nature -- Effect of human beings on. Philosophy of nature.*

**QH75.C38 1996**
**Caughley, Graeme.**
Conservation biology in theory and practice / Graeme Caughley, Anne Gunn. Cambridge, Mass., USA : Blackwell Science, c1996. xii, 459 p. :
95-001616          333.95/16          0865424314
*Conservation biology.*

**QH75.C66**
Conservation biology : an evolutionary-ecological perspective / edited by Michael E. Soule and Bruce A. Wilcox. Sunderland, Mass. : Sinauer Associates, c1980. xv, 395 p. :
79-026463          333.9/5          0878938001
*Conservation biology -- Congresses.*

**QH75.C664 1986**
Conservation biology : the science of scarcity and diversity / edited by Michael E. Soule. Sunderland, Mass. : Sinauer Associates, c1986. xiii, 584 p.
86-001902          574.5          0878937943
*Conservation biology.*

**QH75.C6819 1996**
Conserving peatlands / edited by L. Parkyn, R.E. Stoneman, and H.A.P. Ingram. New York : CAB International, c1997. xxi, 500 p. :
96-048876          333.91/816
*Peatland conservation. Peatlands.*

**QH75.E58 1998**
**Eldredge, Niles.**
Life in the balance : humanity and the biodiversity crisis / Niles Eldredge ; illustrations by Patricia Wynne. Princeton, N.J. : Princeton University Press, c1998. xv, 224 p. :
97-052087          333.95          0691001251
*Biological diversity conservation. Human ecology.*

**QH75.G645 1991**
**Goulty, George A.**
   A dictionary of landscape : a dictionary of terms used in the description of the world's land surface / George A. Goulty. Aldershot : Avebury Technical ; c1991. vi, 309 p. ;
91-002518          712/.03          1856282147
   *Landscape -- Dictionaries. Landforms -- Dictionaries.*

**QH75.G68**
**Graham, Frank,**
   Since Silent spring. Boston, Houghton-Mifflin, 1970. xvi, 333 p.
77-082948          632/.95
   *Carson, Rachel, -- 1907-1964. -- Silent spring.     Pesticides -- Environmental aspects.*

**QH75.H37 1984**
**Harris, Larry D.**
   The fragmented forest : island biogeography theory and the preservation of biotic diversity / Larry D. Harris ; with a foreword by Kenton R. Miller. Chicago : University of Chicago Press, 1984. xviii, 211 p.
84-000144          639.9          0226317641
   *Nature conservation. Biogeography. Island ecology.*

**QH75.H38 1997**
   Harvesting wild species : implications for biodiversity conservation / edited by Curtis H. Freese. Baltimore : Johns Hopkins University Press, 1997. xii, 703 p. :
96-050972          333.95/16          080185573X
   *Biological diversity conservation. Sustainable development.*

**QH75.M32125 1999**
   Maintaining biodiversity in forest ecosystems / edited by Malcolm L. Hunter, Jr. Cambridge, UK ; Cambridge University Press, 1999. xiv, 698 p. :
98-040458          639.9          0521631041
   *Biological diversity conservation. Forest conservation. Ecosystem management.*

**QH75.M353 1995**
   Managing habitats for conservation / edited by William J. Sutherland and David A. Hill. Cambridge ; Cambridge University Press, 1995. x, 399 p., [8
94-034332          639.9/2          0521442605
   *Habitat conservation.*

**QH75.P7525 2000**
**Primack, Richard B. ,**
   A primer of conservation biology / Richard B. Primack. 2nd ed. Sunderland, Mass. : Sinauer Associates, c2000. xiii, 319 p. :
          333.95/16 21          0878937323
*Conservation biology.*

**QH75.R432 1999**
   Recovering the prairie / edited by Robert F. Sayre. Madison, Wis. : University of Wisconsin Press, c1999. viii, 225 p.
99-025650          333.74/16          0299164608
   *Prairie conservation. Prairies. Prairies -- Pictorial works.*

**QH75.R535 1998**
**Riley, Ann L.**
   Restoring streams in cities : a guide for planners, policy makers, and citizens / Ann L. Riley. Washington, D.C. : Island Press, c1998. xxii, 423 p.
97-042715          333.91/6216          1559630434
   *Stream conservation -- Planning. Stream conservation -- Government policy. Stream conservation -- Citizen participation.*

**QH75.S815 1994**
**Swanson, Timothy M.**
   The international regulation of extinction / Timothy M. Swanson. Washington Square, N.Y. : New York University Press, 1994. xiv, 289 p. :
93-036643          333.95/11          0814779921
   *Biological diversity conservation -- Government policy. Biological diversity conservation -- International cooperation. Economic development -- Environmental aspects.*

**QH75.W43 1997**
**Weeks, W. William.**
   Beyond the Ark : tools for an ecosystem approach to conservation / W. William Weeks ; foreword by Bruce Babbitt. Washington, D.C. : Island Press, c1997. xvi, 172 p. :
96-023724          333.7/2          1559633921
   *Nature conservation. Ecosystem management.*

**QH76-76.5 Nature conservation. Landscape protection. Biological diversity conservation. Endangered species and ecosystems (General). Habitat conservation. Ecosystem management. Conservation biology — By region or country — United States**

**QH76.B65 1994**
**Bolling, David M.**
   How to save a river : a handbook for citizen action / River Network, David M. Bolling. Washington, D.C. : Island Press, c1994. xx, 266 p. :
93-050690          333.91/6216/0973
1559632496
   *Stream conservation -- United States -- Citizen participation.*

**QH76.C73 1999**
**Crawford, Mark,**
   Habitats and ecosystems : an encyclopedia of endangered America / Mark Crawford. Santa Barbara, Calif. : ABC-CLIO, c1999. xvii, 398 p.
00-698072          333.78/0973          0874369975
   *Natural areas -- United States -- States -- Registers. Endangered ecosystems -- United States -- States -- Registers. Biotic communities -- United States -- States -- Registers.*

**QH76.D58 1993**
**DiSilvestro, Roger L.**
   Reclaiming the last wild places : a new agenda for biodiversity / Roger L. DiSilvestro. New York : Wiley, c1993. xvii, 266 p.
92-046457          333.95/16/0973          0471572446
   *Biological diversity conservation -- United States. Wildlife conservation -- United States. Biological diversity conservation -- United States -- Philosophy.*

**QH76.E336 1996**
Ecosystem management in the United States : an assessment of current experience / Steven L. Yaffee ... [et al.]. Washington, D.C. : Island Press, c1996. xvii, 352 p.
96-021825          333.7/0973          1559635029
*Ecosystem management -- United States.*

**QH76.F58 1999**
**Fitzsimmons, Allan K.**
Defending illusions : federal protection of ecosystems / Allan K. Fitzsimmons. Lanham, Md. : Rowman & Littlefield Publishers, c1999. xvi, 331 p. :
99-017318          577/.0973          0847694216
*Ecosystem management -- Government policy -- United States.*

**QH76.F69**
**Fox, Stephen R.**
John Muir and his legacy : the American conservation movement / Stephen Fox. Boston : Little, Brown, c1981. xii, 436 p. :
81-001852          333.95/0973          0316291102
*Muir, John, -- 1838-1914.     Nature conservation -- United States -- History.  Conservationists -- United States -- Biography.  Naturalists -- United States -- Biography.*

**QH76.N67 1994**
**Noss, Reed F.**
Saving nature's legacy : protecting and restoring biodiversity / Reed F. Noss and Allen Y. Cooperrider ; foreword by Rodger Schlickeisen. Washington, D.C. : Island Press, c1994. xxvii, 416 p.
93-048895          333.95/16/0973          155963247X
*Ecosystem management -- United States.  Biological diversity conservation -- United States.  Ecosystem management.*

**QH76.P355 1994**
**Palmer, Tim.**
Lifelines : the case for river conservation / Tim Palmer. Washington, D.C. : Island Press, c1994. xii, 254 p. :
94-008951          333.91/6216          1559632194
*Stream conservation -- United States.  Ecosystem management -- United States.*

**QH76.P36 1993**
**Palmer, Tim.**
The wild and scenic rivers of America / Tim Palmer. Washington, D.C. : Island Press, c1993. 338 p. :
92-032660          333.91/62/0973          1559631457
*Wild and scenic rivers -- United States.  Stream conservation -- United States.*

**QH76.P69 2000**
Precious heritage : the status of biodiversity in the United States / edited by Bruce A. Stein, Lynn S. Kutner, Jonathan S. Adams ; graphics by Nicole S. Rousmaniere. Oxford ; Oxford University Press, c2000. xxv, 399 p. :
99-030213          333.95/16/0973          0195125193
*Biological diversity conservation -- United States.*

**QH76.5.N96**
Wilderness comes home : rewilding the Northeast / edited by Christopher McGrory Klyza. Hanover : University Press of New England, c2001. xv, 320 p. :
00-012160          333.95/0974          1584651016
*Wilderness areas -- Northeastern States.  Nature conservation -- Northeastern States.*

**QH76.5.N97.B37 1993**
**Barker, Rocky.**
Saving all the parts : reconciling economics and the Endangered Species Act / Rocky Barker. Washington, D.C. : Island Press, c1993. xii, 268 p. :
93-004640          333.95/11          155963202X
*Biological diversity conservation -- Law and legislation -- Economic aspects -- Northwest, Pacific.  Biological diversity conservation -- Law and legislation -- Economic aspects -- Rocky Mountains.  Economic development -- Environmental aspects.  United States -- Economic policy.*

**QH76.5.P4.O93 1993**
**Owens, Owen D.**
Living waters : how to save your local stream / Owen D. Owens. New Brunswick, N.J. : Rutgers University Press, c1993. xiv, 245 p. :
93-007641          333.91/6216          0813519977
*Water -- Pollution -- Pennsylvania -- Valley Creek.  Stream conservation -- Pennsylvania -- Valley Creek -- Citizen participation.  Stream conservation -- Handbooks, manuals, etc.  Valley Creek (Pa.)*

**QH76.5.T4.B385 1995**
**Bartlett, Dick,**
Saving the best of Texas : a partnership approach to conservation / Richard C. Bartlett ; photographs by Leroy Williamson. Austin : University of Texas Press, 1995. xviii, 221 p.
94-043734          333.7/2/09764          0292708343
*Environmental protection -- Texas.  Natural history -- Texas.  Nature conservation -- Texas.*

**QH76.5.W34.C65 1999**
Contested landscape : the politics of wilderness in Utah and the West / edited by Doug Goodman and Daniel McCool. Salt Lake City : University of Utah Press, c1999. xvii, 266 p.
99-027465          333.78/2/0978          0874806046
*Wilderness areas -- Political aspects -- West (U.S.)  Wilderness areas -- Political aspects -- Utah.  Wilderness areas -- Government policy -- United States.*

**QH76.5.W34.W55 1992**
Wilderness issues in the arid lands of the western United States / edited by Samuel I. Zeveloff and Cyrus M. McKell. Albuquerque : University of New Mexico Press, c1992. xi, 145 p. :
92-004070          333.78/2/0978          0826313655
*Nature conservation -- Government policy -- West (U.S.)  Arid regions ecology -- Government policy -- West (U.S.)  Environmental policy -- West (U.S.)*

## QH77 Nature conservation. Landscape protection. Biological diversity conservation. Endangered species and ecosystems (General). Habitat conservation. Ecosystem management. Conservation biology — By region or country — Other regions or countries, A-Z

**QH77.A35.G525 1999**
Gibson, Clark C.,
 Politicians and poachers : the political economy of wildlife policy in Africa / Clark C. Gibson. Cambridge, UK ; Cambridge University Press, 1999. xiv, 245 p. :
98-039627          333.95/416/096          0521623855
 *Wildlife conservation -- Government policy -- Africa. Wildlife conservation -- Economic aspects -- Africa.*

**QH77.A53.F67 1991**
Foresta, Ronald A.,
 Amazon conservation in the age of development : the limits of providence / Ronald A. Foresta. Gainesville : University of Florida Press, Center for Latin Am c1991. x, 366 p. :
91-000094          333.7/2/09811          0813010926
 *Biological diversity conservation -- Amazon River Region. Rural development -- Environmental aspects -- Amazon River Region.*

**QH77.A53.G68 1996**
Goulding, Michael.
 Floods of fortune : ecology and economy along the Amazon / Michael Goulding, Nigel J.H. Smith, Dennis J. Mahar. New York : Columbia University Press, c1996. vi, 193 p. :
95-010904          574.5/0981/1          0231104200
 *Endangered ecosystems -- Amazon River Valley. Nature – Effect of human beings on -- Amazon River Valley. Floodplain ecology – Amazon River Valley. Amazon River Valley -- Environmental conditions.*

**QH77.D44.D59 1990**
Dixon, John A.,
 Economics of protected areas : a new look at benefits and costs / John A. Dixon, Paul B. Sherman. Washington, D.C. : Island Press, c1990. xvii, 234 p.
90-033702          333.7/2/091724          1559630337
 *Natural areas -- Developing countries -- Management. Natural areas -- Economic aspects -- Developing countries. Natural areas – Government policy -- Developing countries.*

**QH77.L25.C66 1995**
 A conservation assessment of the terrestrial ecoregions of Latin America and the Caribbean / Eric Dinerstein ... [et al.]. Washington, D.C. : World Bank, 1995. xvii, 129 p.
95-000227          333.9516/098          0821332953
 *Biological diversity conservation -- Latin America -- Evaluation. Biological diversity conservation -- Caribbean Area -- Evaluation. Biotic communities -- Latin America -- Evaluation.*

**QH77.N56**
 Beacham's guide to the endangered species of North America / edited by Walton Beacham, Frank V. Castronova, Suzanne Sessine. Detroit : Gale Group, c2001. 6 v. (viii, 3
00-062297          578.68/0973          0787650285
 *Endangered species -- North America. Nature conservation -- North America.*

**QH77.N56.F69 2000**
 Freshwater ecoregions of North America : a conservation assessment / Robin A. Abell ... [et al.]. Washington, D.C. : Island Press, c2000. xxii, 319 p.
99-016796          577.6          155963734X
 *Biological diversity conservation -- North America. Biotic communities -- North America. Freshwater ecology – North America.*

**QH77.N56.P735 1996**
 Prairie conservation : preserving North America's most endangered ecosystem / edited by Fred B. Samson and Fritz L. Knopf ; foreword by E. Benjamin Nelson. Washington, D.C. : Island Press, 1996. xii, 339 p. :
96-011227          333.74/16/097          1559634278
 *Prairie conservation -- North America. Ecosystem management – North America.*

**QH77.N56.T47 1999**
 Terrestrial ecoregions of North America : a conservation assessment / Taylor H. Ricketts ... [et al.]. Washington, D.C. : Island Press, c1999. xxiv, 485 p.
99-018912          333.95/16/097          1559637226
 *Biological diversity conservation -- North America.*

**QH77.S626.W45 1988**
Weiner, Douglas R.,
 Models of nature : ecology, conservation, and cultural revolution in Soviet Russia / Douglas R. Weiner. Bloomington : Indiana University Press, c1988. xiv, 312 p. :
87-045370          333.95/16/0947          0253338379
 *Nature conservation -- Soviet Union. Nature conservation -- Social aspects -- Soviet Union. Communism and culture -- Soviet Union. Soviet Union -- Social conditions.*

## QH78 Extinction (Biology)

**QH78.E95 1995**
 Extinction rates / edited by John H. Lawton and Robert M. May. Oxford ; Oxford University Press, 1995. xii, 233 p. :
95-169009          575/.7          019854829X
 *Extinction (Biology).*

**QH78.R38 1991**
Raup, David M.
 Extinction : bad genes or bad luck? / David M. Raup. New York : W.W. Norton, c1991. xvii, 210 p.
90-027192          575/.7          0393030083
 *Extinction (Biology)*

## QH81 Addresses, essays, lectures

**QH81.B963 1951**
Burroughs, John,
 John Burroughs' America; selections from the writings of the Hudson River naturalist, edited, with an introd., by Farida A. Wiley. Foreword by Julian Burroughs. Illustrated by Francis Lee Jaques. New York, Devin-Adair, 1951. xv, 304 p.
51-013897          574.081
 *Natural history -- Outdoor books. Natural history – United States.*

## QH81.C3546 1998
**Carson, Rachel,**
Lost woods : the discovered writing of Rachel Carson / edited and with an introduction by Linda Lear. Boston : Beacon Press, c1998. xiv, 267 p. ;
98-020058          570          0807085464
*Nature. Wildlife conservation. Marine ecology.*

## QH81.D56 1974
**Dillard, Annie.**
Pilgrim at Tinker Creek.  New York, Harper's Magazine Press [1974] 271 p.
73-018655          508.755/9          0061219800
*Nature.*

## QH81.E6
**Eiseley, Loren C.,**
The night country [by] Loren Eiseley. Illus. by Leonard Everett Fisher. New York, Scribner [1971] xi, 240 p.
78-162747          500.9/08          0684125684
*Nature -- Addresses, essays, lectures. Natural history -- Addresses, essays, lectures.*

## QH81.G673 1985
**Gould, Stephen Jay.**
The flamingo's smile : reflections in natural history / Stephen Jay Gould. New York : Norton, c1985. 476 p. :
85-004916          508          0393022285
*Natural history.*

## QH81.H898
**Hutchinson, G. Evelyn**
The enchanted voyage, and other studies. New Haven, Yale University Press, 1962. 163 p.
62-016234          574.081
*Biology -- Addresses, essays, lectures.*

## QH81.L56
**Leopold, Aldo,**
A Sand County almanac, and Sketches here and there; illus. by Charles W. Schwartz. New York, Oxford Univ. Press, 1949. xiii, 226 p.
49-011164          574
*Natural history -- Outdoor books. Natural history – United States. Wildlife, conservation.*

## QH81.L563.C66 1987
Companion to A sand county almanac : interpretive & critical essays / edited by J. Baird Callicott. Madison, Wis. : University of Wisconsin Press, 1987. x, 308 p. :
87-010396          508.73          0299112306
*Leopold, Aldo, -- 1886-1948. -- Sand county almanac.*

## QH81.P8613
**Prishvin, Mikhail Mikhailovich,**
The root of life / Mikhail Prishvin ; translated from the Russian by Alice Stone Nakhimovsky and Alexander Nakhimovsky ; ill. by Stefen Bernath. New York : Macmillan ; c1980. 115 p. :
80-010428          891.78/4207
*Nature. Deer -- Anecdotes.*

## QH81.S8725 1996
**Stratton-Porter, Gene,**
Coming through the swamp : the nature writings of Gene Stratton Porter / edited and with an introduction by Sydney Landon Plum. Salt Lake City : University of Utah Press, c1996. xxvii, 172 p.
95-048024          813/.52          0874804973
*Natural history. Nature stories.*

# QH83 Classification. Nomenclature

## QH83.H86 1999
**Humphries, Christopher John,**
Cladistic biogeography : interpreting patterns of plant and animal distributions / Christopher J. Humphries and Lynne R. Parenti. 2nd ed. Oxford ; New York : Oxford University Press, c1999. xi, 187 p. :
          578/.01/2 21          0198548184
*Cladistic analysis. Biogeography.*

## QH83.J43 1977
**Jeffrey, Charles.**
Biological nomenclature / [by] Charles Jeffrey for the Systematics Association ; foreword by V. H. Heywood. London : Edward Arnold, 1977. viii, 72 p. ;
78-301399          574/.01/4          0713126140
*Biology -- Nomenclature.*

## QH83.M36 1998
**Margulis, Lynn,**
Five kingdoms : an illustrated guide to the phyla of life on earth / Lynn Margulis, Karlene V. Schwartz. New York : W.H. Freeman, c1998. xx, 520 p. :
97-021338          570/.1/2          071673026X
*Biology -- Classification.*

## QH83.S89
Synopsis and classification of living organisms / Sybil P. Parker, editor in chief. New York : McGraw-Hill, c1982. 2 v. :
81-013653          574.012          0070790310
*Biology -- Classification. Biology -- Classification.*

## QH83.T77 1999
**Tsur, Samuel A.,**
Elsevier's dictionary of the genera of life / compiled by Samuel A. Tsur (Mansoor). Amsterdam ; Elsevier, 1999. p. cm.
99-017292          570/.3          0444829059
*Biology -- Classification -- Dictionaries.*

## QH83.T84 2000
**Tudge, Colin.**
The variety of life : a survey and a celebration of all the creatures that have ever lived / Colin Tudge. London ; Oxford University Press, 2000. xii, 684 p. :
99-050043          578/.01/2          0198503113
*Biology -- Classification. Biological diversity.*

**QH83.W57 1999**
**Winston, Judith E.**
Describing species : practical taxonomic procedure for biologists / Judith E. Winston. New York : Columbia University Press, c1999. xx, 518 p. :
99-014019          570/.1/2          0231068247
*Biology -- Classification. Species.*

## QH84 Geographical distribution. Biogeography — General works, treatises, and textbooks

**QH84.A95 2000**
**Avise, John C.**
Phylogeography : the history and formation of species / John C. Avise. Cambridge, Mass. : Harvard University Press, 2000. viii, 447 p.
99-019648          578/.09          0674666380
*Phylogeography.*

**QH84.C65 1980**
**Cox, C. Barry**
Biogeography : an ecological and evolutionary approach / C. Barry Cox, Peter D. Moore. New York : Wiley, 1980. xi, 234 p. :
79-022636          574.5/2          047026893X
*Biogeography.*

**QH84.C678 1999**
**Craw, R. C.**
Panbiogeography : tracking the history of life / Robin C. Craw, John R. Grehan, and Michael J. Heads. New York : Oxford University Press, 1999. 229 p. :
97-041638          578/.09          0195074416
*Biogeography. Life -- Origin.*

## QH84.1 Geographical distribution. Biogeography — Arctic regions

**QH84.1.S78 1989**
**Stonehouse, Bernard.**
Polar ecology / B. Stonehouse. Glasgow : Blackie ; 1989. viii, 222 p.
89-015809          574.5/2621          0412017016
*Ecology -- Polar regions.*

**QH84.1.Y68 1990**
**Young, Steven B.**
To the Arctic : an introduction to the far northern world / Steven B. Young. New York : Wiley, c1989. xiii, 354 p.
88-017423          508.311/3          0471620823
*Natural history -- Arctic regions.     Arctic regions -- Description and travel.*

## QH84.2 Geographical distribution. Biogeography — Antarctica

**QH84.2.M67 1988**
**Moss, Sanford A.**
Natural history of the Antarctic Peninsula / text by Sanford Moss ; illustrations by Lucia deLeiris. New York : Columbia University Press, 1988. xii, 208 p. :
87-010971          508.98/9          0231062680
*Natural history -- Antarctica -- Antarctic Peninsula.*

## QH84.5 Geographical distribution. Biogeography — Tropics

**QH84.5.L3613 2000**
**Lambertini, M.**
A naturalist's guide to the tropics / Marco Labertini ; translated by John Venerella ; with illustrations by Kitty Capua. Chicago : University of Chicago Press, c2000. xxiv, 312 p.
99-032802          508.313          0226468283
*Natural history -- Tropics.*

**QH84.5.O82 2000**
**Osborne, Patrick L.**
Tropical ecosystems and ecological concepts / Patrick L. Osborne. Cambridge, U.K. ; Cambridge University Press, 2000. p. cm.
99-047853          577/.0913          0521642515
*Ecology -- Tropics.*

## QH85-88 Geographical distribution. Biogeography — Physiographic divisions — Land

**QH85.M3**
**MacArthur, Robert H.**
The theory of island biogeography [by] Robert H. MacArthur and Edward O. Wilson. Princeton, N.J., Princeton University Press, 1967. xi, 203 p.
67-024102          574.91
*Biogeography.*

**QH87.3.W46 1991**
Wetlands / general editors, Max Finlayson and Michael Moser ; International Waterfowl and Wetlands Research Bureau. Oxford ; Facts on File, c1991. 224 p. :
91-023683          574.5/26325          0816025568
*Wetlands. Wetland ecology. Wetland conservation.*

**QH87.3.W47 1990**
Wetlands : a threatened landscape / edited by Michael Williams. Oxford, UK ; B. Blackwell, 1991. ix, 419 p. :
90-030985          333.91/8          0631166149
*Wetlands. Wetland ecology. Wetlands -- Economic aspects.*

**QH88.F58 1993**
**Flegg, Jim.**
  Deserts : miracle of life / Jim Flegg. New York : Facts on
File, 1993. 160 p. :
92-046603          910/.02154          0816029024
  *Deserts. Desert biology. Desert ecology.*

**QH90.8-98 Geographical distribution. Biogeography
— Physiographic divisions — Water**

**QH90.8.P5.P59 1989**
  Plankton ecology : succession in plankton communities /
Ulrich Sommer (ed.). Berlin ; Springer-Verlag, c1989. x, 369
p. :
89-011455          574/.92          0387513736
  *Plankton -- Ecology. Ecological succession.*

**QH91.C3**
**Carson, Rachel,**
  The edge of the sea. With illus. by Bob Hines. Boston,
Houghton Mifflin, 1955. 276 p.
54-010759          591.921
  *Seashore biology.*

**QH91.C628**
**Cousteau, Jacques Yves.**
  The living sea. With James Dugan. New York, Harper &
Row [1963] 325 p.
62-014525          574.92
  *Deep diving. Underwater photography. Marine biology.*

**QH91.C66**
**Cousteau, Jacques Yves.**
  The silent world, by J. Y. Cousteau, with Frederic Dumas.
New York, Harper [c1953] 266 p.
52-005431          574.92
  *Marine biology. Deep diving. Underwater photography.*

**QH91.L35 1997**
**Lalli, Carol M.**
  Biological oceanography : an introduction / Carol M. Lalli
and Timothy R. Parsons. 2nd ed. Oxford [England] :
Butterworth Heinemann, c1997. xii, 314 p. :
          574.92 20          0750627425
*Marine biology. Marine ecology. Oceanography.*

**QH91.L427 1995**
**Levinton, Jeffrey S.**
  Marine biology : function, biodiversity, ecology / Jeffrey S.
Levinton. New York : Oxford University Press, 1995. x, 420
p., [1
94-037466          574.92          0195085736
  *Marine biology.*

**QH91.N9 2001**
**Nybakken, James Willard.**
  Marine biology : an ecological approach / James W.
Nybakken. 5th ed. San Francisco : Benjamin Cummings,
c2001. xi, 516 p. :
          577.7 21          0321030761
*Marine biology. Marine ecology.*

**QH91.T45 1999**
**Thorne-Miller, Boyce.**
  The living ocean : understanding and protecting marine
biodiversity / Boyce Thorne-Miller ; foreword by Sylvia Earle.
2nd ed. Washington, D.C. : Island Press, c1999. xviii, 214 p. :
          333.95/616 21          1559636777
*Marine biological diversity. Marine biological diversity conservation.*

**QH91.15.C652**
**Cousteau, Jacques Yves.**
  The ocean world / Jacques Cousteau. New York : H. N.
Abrams, 1979. 446 p. :
77-020197          574.92          0810907771
  *Marine biology. Ocean.*

**QH91.57.A1.M3 1997**
  Marine biodiversity : patterns and processes / edited by
Rupert F.G. Ormond, John D. Gage, and Martin V. Angel.
Cambridge, U.K. ; Cambridge University Press, 1997. xxii,
449 p.
96-009334          574.5/2636          0521552222
  *Marine biological diversity.*

**QH91.8.B4.G34 1990**
**Gage, John D.**
  Deep-sea biology : a natural history of organisms at the
deep-sea floor / John D. Gage, Paul A. Tyler. Cambridge ;
Cambridge University Press, 1991. xvi, 504 p. :
90-045683          591.92          0521334314
  *Benthos. Marine animals -- Ecology. Deep-sea biology.*

**QH92.C3 1952**
**Carson, Rachel,**
  Under the sea-wind; a naturalist's picture of ocean life. New
York, Oxford University Press, 1952 [c1941] 314 p.
52-007613          591.921
  *Marine biology -- Atlantic Ocean.*

**QH95.58.K58 1994**
**Knox, G. A.**
  The biology of the southern ocean / George A. Knox.
Cambridge [England] ; Cambridge University Press, 1994. xiv,
444 p. :
93-028273          574.92/4          0521322111
  *Marine ecology -- Antarctic Ocean. Biotic communities --
Antarctic Ocean. Ecosystem management -- Antarctic Ocean.*

**QH95.7.L57 1996**
**Little, Colin,**
  The biology of rocky shores / Colin Little and J.A. Kitching.
Oxford ; Oxford University Press, 1996. ix, 240 p. :
95-042040          574.5/2638          0198549369
  *Seashore biology. Seashore ecology.*

**QH95.8.D38 1998**
**Davidson, Osha Gray.**
  The enchanted braid : coming to terms with nature on the
coral reef / Osha Gray Davidson. New York : Wiley, c1998.
xii, 269 p.,
97-039797          578.77/89          047117727X
  *Coral reef biology. Coral reefs and islands. Human ecology.*

**QH95.9.P47**
**Perkins, Eric John.**
    The biology of estuaries and coastal waters / E. J. Perkins. London ; Academic Press, 1974. ix, 678 p. :
73-009473      574.92      012550750X
    *Estuarine biology. Seashore biology. Coastal zone management.*

**QH96.W47 1983**
**Wetzel, Robert G.**
    Limnology/ Robert G. Wetzel. Philadelphia : Saunders, c1983. xii, 767, 81,
81-053073      551.48/2      0030579139
    *Limnology.*

**QH97.B37**
**Bardach, John E.**
    Downstream: a natural history of the river. New York, Harper & Row [1964] ix, 278 p.
62-014596      574.929
    *Freshwater biology. Rivers. Natural history.*

**QH98.H82**
**Hutchinson, G. Evelyn**
    A treatise on limnology. New York, Wiley [1957]-c1993. 4 v.
57-008888      574.929
    *Limnology.*

## QH102-106 Geographical distribution. Biogeography — Topographical divisions — America

**QH102.B76 1998**
**Brown, David E.**
    A classification of North American biotic communities / David E. Brown, Frank Reichenbacher, Susan E. Franson. Salt Lake City : University of Utah Press, c1998. x, 141 p. :
97-053161      577.8/2/097      0874805627
    *Biotic communities -- North America -- Classification.*

**QH102.C56 2000**
    Nonindigenous freshwater organisms : vectors, biology, and impacts / edited by Renata Claudi and Joseph H. Leach. Boca Raton : Lewis Publishers, c2000. 464 p. :
99-028607      577.6/097      1566704499
    *Freshwater ecology -- North America. Animal introduction -- North America. Nonindigenous aquatic pests -- North America.*

**QH102.F63 2001**
**Flannery, Tim F.**
    The eternal frontier : an ecological history of North America and its peoples / Tim Flannery. New York : Atlantic Monthly Press, 2001. p. cm.
01-018841      508.7      0871137895
    *Desert ecology -- North America.*

**QH102.K75 1988**
**Kricher, John C.**
    A field guide to eastern forests, North America / text and photographs by John C. Kricher ; illustrated by Gordon Morrison. Boston : Houghton Mifflin Co., 1988. xviii, 368 p.
87-035247      574.5/2642/0974      0395353467
    *Forest ecology -- North America. Forest animals – North America -- Identification. Forest plants -- North America -- Identification.*

**QH102.P38**
**Peterson, Roger Tory,**
    Wild America; the record of a 30,000 mile journey around the continent by a distinguished naturalist and his British colleague, by Roger Tory Peterson and James Fisher. Illustrated by Roger Tory Peterson. Boston, Houghton Mifflin, 1955. 434 p.
55-008876      574.97
    *Natural history -- North America.*

**QH102.S69 2001**
**Sowell, John,**
    Desert ecology : an introduction to life in the arid southwest / John Sowell. Salt Lake City : University of Utah Press, c2001. xii, 193 p. :
00-011599      577.54/097      087480678X
    *Desert ecology -- North America.*

**QH104.L95 1993**
**Lyon, J. G.**
    Practical handbook for wetland identification and delineation / John Grimson Lyon. Boca Raton : Lewis Publishers, c1993. 157 p. :
92-043804      574.5/26325      087371590X
    *Wetlands -- United States -- Classification. Land use -- United States -- Planning. Wetland conservation -- United States.*

**QH104.M37 1995**
**Manning, Richard,**
    Grassland : the history, biology, politics, and promise of the American prairie / Richard Manning. New York : Viking, 1995. ix, 306 p. :
95-010073      574.5/2643/0973      0670853429
    *Grassland ecology -- United States. Grasslands -- United States. Grassland conservation -- United States.*

**QH104.M57 2000**
**Mitsch, William J.**
    Wetlands / William J. Mitsch, James G. Gosselink. 3rd ed. New York : John Wiley, c2000. xiii, 920 p. :
     577.68/0973 21      047129232X
    *Wetland ecology -- United States. Weltands -- United States. Wetland management -- United States.*

**QH104.W74**
**Wright, Henry A.**
    Fire ecology, United States and southern Canada / Henry A. Wright and Arthur W. Bailey. New York : Wiley, c1982. xxi, 501 p. :
81-014770      581.5/222      0471090336
    *Fire ecology -- United States. Fire ecology -- Canada. Plant ecology -- United States.*

**QH104.5.A6.C65 1994**
**Constantz, George,**

Hollows, peepers, and highlanders : an Appalachian Mountain ecology / George Constantz. Missoula, Mont. : Mountain Press Pub. Co., c1994. vi, 264 p. :
94-002315        508.74      0878422633
*Natural history -- Appalachian Region. Forest animals -- Adaptation -- Appalachian Region. Forest plants -- Adaptation – Appalachian Region. Appalachian Region.*

**QH104.5.E73.M35 2000**
**McGucken, William.**

Lake Erie rehabilitated : controlling cultural eutrophication, 1960s-1990s / William McGucken. Akron, Ohio : University of Akron Press, 2000. p. cm.
99-053826        363.739/46/097712
1884836577
*Eutrophication -- Control -- Erie, Lake. Detergent pollution of rivers, lakes, etc. -- Erie, Lake. Lake renewal -- Erie, Lake.*

**QH104.5.G68.N38 1994**

Natural history of the Colorado Plateau and Great Basin / Kimball T. Harper ... [et al.], editors. Niwot, Colo. : University Press of Colorado, c1994. viii, 294 p.
94-011604        508.79      0870813358
*Natural history -- Great Basin. Natural history -- Colorado Plateau. Glacial epoch -- Great Basin. Great Basin. Colorado Plateau.*

**QH104.5.G84.C48 1988**
**Chabreck, R. H.**

Coastal marshes : ecology and wildlife management / Robert H. Chabreck. Minneapolis : University of Minnesota Press, c1988. xiii, 138 p.,
88-001168        574.5/2636      0816616620
*Salt marsh ecology -- United States. Salt marsh ecology – Gulf Coast (U.S.) Wildlife management -- United States.*

**QH104.5.N58.M58 1985**
**Mitchell, John Hanson.**

A field guide to your own back yard / John Hanson Mitchell ; illustrations by Laurel Molk. New York : Norton, c1985. 288 p. :
84-014760        574.974      0393019233
*Urban ecology (Biology) -- Northeastern States. Natural history – Northeastern States.*

**QH104.5.P32.R35 1997**

The rain forests of home : profile of a North American bioregion / edited by Peter K. Schoonmaker, Bettina von Hagen, and Edward C. Wolf ; foreword by M. Patricia Marchak and Jerry F. Franklin. Washington, D.C. : Island Press, c1997. xvi, 431 p. :
96-032773        574.5/2642/09795
1559634790
*Rain forest ecology -- Northwest Coast of North America -- Congresses. Rain forests -- Northwest Coast of North America -- Congresses.*

**QH104.5.S58.A39 1993**
**Alcock, John,**

The masked bobwhite rides again / John Alcock. Tucson : University of Arizona Press, c1993. ix, 186 p. ;
93-015416        508.791/7      0816513872
*Natural history -- Sonoran Desert. Desert ecology -- Sonoran Desert. Cattle -- Sonoran Desert -- Ecology. Sonoran Desert.*

**QH104.5.S58.N38 2000**

A natural history of the Sonoran Desert / Arizona-Sonora Desert Museum ; edited by Steven J. Phillips & Patricia Wentworth Comus. Tucson : Arizona-Sonora Desert Museum ; c2000. xi, 628 p.:
99-033675        508.791/7      0520220293
*Natural history -- Sonoran Desert.*

**QH104.5.S59.B565 1993**

Biodiversity of the southeastern United States / edited by William H. Martin, Stephen G. Boyce, Arthur C. Echternacht. New York : Wiley, c1993- v. 1-2    :
92-026503        574.5/0975      0471628832
*Natural history -- Southern States. Biological diversity – Southern States. Ecology -- Southern States.*

**QH104.5.S6.B77 1996**
**Briggs, Mark K.**

Riparian ecosystem recovery in arid lands : strategies and references / Mark K. Briggs. Tucson : University of Arizona Press, 1996. xiv, 159 p. :
96-009957        333.91/8      0816516421
*Riparian ecology -- Southwest, New. Riparian ecology – Mexico. Restoration ecology -- Southwest, New.*

**QH104.5.S6.D47 1995**

The desert grassland / edited by Mitchel P. McClaran and Thomas R. Van Devender. Tucson : University of Arizona Press, c1995. ix, 346 p. :
95-000327        574.5/2652/0979      0816515808
*Deserts -- Southwestern States. Deserts -- Mexico. Grasslands – Southwestern States.*

**QH105.A4.W44 1992**
**Weeden, Robert B.,**

Messages from earth : nature and the human prospect in Alaska / Robert B. Weeden. Fairbanks : University of Alaska Press, 1992. xiv, 189 p. :
91-043178        333.7/09798      0912006560
*Ecology -- Alaska. Human ecology -- Alaska. Natural resources – Alaska.*

**QH105.A65.C38 1991**
**Carothers, Steven W.**

The Colorado River through Grand Canyon : natural history and human change / Steven W. Carothers and Bryan T. Brown. Tucson : University of Arizona Press, c1991. xix, 235 p.,
90-046390        574.5/26323/097913
0816511314
*Stream ecology -- Arizona -- Glen Canyon Dam Region. Stream ecology -- Arizona -- Grand Canyon. Stream ecology -- Colorado River (Colo.-Mexico)*

**QH105.C2**
**Langstroth, Lovell.**
A living bay : the underwater world of Monterey Bay / Lovell Langstroth and Libby Langstroth ; Todd Newberry, editorial associate. Berkeley, Calif. : University of California Press : c2000. xiv, 287 p. :
00-022014          577.7/432          0520216865
*Marine ecology -- California -- Monterey Bay. Marine biology – California -- Monterey Bay.*

**QH105.C2.R86 1990**
**Runte, Alfred,**
Yosemite : the embattled wilderness / Alfred Runte. Lincoln : University of Nebraska Press, c1990. xii, 271 p.,
89-035128          508.794/47          0803238940
*Natural history -- California -- Yosemite National Park. Nature conservation -- California -- Yosemite National Park. Natural resources -- California -- Yosemite National Park. Yosemite National Park (Calif.) -- Management.*

**QH105.C2.V35 1998**
**Vale, Thomas R.,**
Walking with Muir across Yosemite / Thomas R. Vale and Geraldine R. Vale. Madison : University of Wisconsin Press, c1998. x, 166 p. :
97-020321          508.794/47          0299156907
*Muir, John, -- 1838-1914.    Natural history -- California – Yosemite Valley.*

**QH105.F6.E94 1994**
Everglades : the ecosystem and its restoration / editors, Steve M. Davis, John C. Ogden ; associate editor, Winifred A. Park. Delray Beach, FL : St. Lucie Press, c1994. xv, 826 p. :
93-044643          574.5/26325/0975939
0963403028
*Swamp ecology -- Florida -- Everglades. Restoration ecology – Florida -- Everglades.*

**QH105.F6.L37 1995**
**Larson, Ron,**
Swamp song : a natural history of Florida's swamps / Ron Larson. Gainesville : University Press of Florida, 1995. xviii, 214 p.
95-009806          574.5/26325/09759
0813013550
*Swamp ecology -- Florida. Swamp animals -- Florida. Swamp plants -- Florida.*

**QH105.I8.K87 1996**
**Kurtz, Carl.**
Iowa's wild places : an exploration / with Carl Kurtz. Ames, Iowa : Iowa State University Press ; 1996. xii, 236 p. :
96-002422          508.777          0813821614
*Natural history -- Iowa -- Pictorial works. Nature photography – Iowa. Landscape photography -- Iowa.*

**QH105.K3.G73 1998**
Grassland dynamics : long-term ecological research in tallgrass prairie / edited by Alan K. Knapp ... [et al.]. New York : Oxford University Press, 1998. p. cm.
97-008334          577.4/4/09781          0195114868
*Prairie ecology -- Research -- Kansas – Konza Prairie Research Natural Area.    Konza Prairie Research Natural Area (Kan.)*

**QH105.M55.H43 1996**
**Heinselman, Miron L.**
The Boundary Waters Wilderness ecosystem / Miron Heinselman. Minneapolis, Minn. : University of Minnesota Press, c1996. xiii, 334 p.,
95-050347          508.776/7          0816628041
*Natural history -- Minnesota -- Boundary Waters Canoe Area. Ecology -- Minnesota -- Boundary Waters Canoe Area.    Boundary Waters Canoe Area (Minn.)*

**QH105.M55.T47 1995**
**Tester, John R.**
Minnesota's natural heritage : an ecological perspective / John R. Tester ; Mary Keirstead, developmental editor. Minneapolis : University of Minnesota Press, c1995. ix, 332 p. :
94-045153          574.5/247/09776          0816621330
*Biotic communities -- Minnesota. Natural history -- Minnesota.*

**QH105.N2.J64 1995**
**Johnsgard, Paul A.**
This fragile land : a natural history of the Nebraska Sandhills / Paul A. Johnsgard. Lincoln : University of Nebraska Press, c1995. xv, 256 p. :
94-036409          508.782          0803225784
*Natural history -- Nebraska -- Sandhills. Sand dune ecology – Nebraska -- Sandhills.    Sandhills (Neb.)*

**QH105.N4.E3 1985**
An Ecosystem approach to aquatic ecology : Mirror Lake and its environment / edited by Gene E. Likens. New York : Springer-Verlag, c1985. xiv, 516 p. :
84-026686          574.5/26322/097423
0387961062
*Lake ecology -- New Hampshire -- Mirror Lake (Grafton County) Limnology -- New Hampshire -- Mirror Lake (Grafton County) Freshwater ecology -- New Hampshire -- Mirror Lake Watershed (Grafton County)    Mirror Lake (Grafton County, N.H.)*

**QH105.N4.L55 1995**
**Likens, Gene E.,**
Biogeochemistry of a forested ecosystem / Gene E. Likens, F. Herbert Bormann. New York : Springer-Verlag, c1995. xii, 159 p. :
94-041866          574.5/2642/097423
0387945024
*Forest ecology -- New Hampshire -- Hubbard Brook Experimental Forest. Biogeochemistry -- New Hampshire -- Hubbard Brook Experimental Forest.    Hubbard Brook Experimental Forest (N.H.)*

**QH105.O7**
Wildlife-habitat relationships in Oregon and Washington / managing directors, David H. Johnson, Thomas O'Neil. Corvallis : Oregon State University Press, 2001. xix, 736 p. :
00-010729          591.7/09795          0870714880
*Animal ecology -- Oregon. Animal ecology – Washington (State). Habitat (Ecology) -- Oregon.*

**QH105.U8.F58 1999**
**Fleischner, Thomas Lowe,**
Singing stone : a natural history of the Escalante Canyons / Thomas Lowe Fleischner. Salt Lake City : University of Utah Press, c1999. xix, 212 p. :
99-037578          508.792/51          0874806194
*Natural history -- Utah -- Grand Staircase-Escalante National Monument.    Grand Staircase-Escalante National Monument (Utah)*

**QH105.W6.M435 1998**
**Meagher, Margaret Mary.**
Yellowstone and the biology of time : photographs across a century / Mary Meagher & Douglas B. Houston. Norman : University of Oklahoma Press, 1998. xv, 287 p. :
97-040591          508.787/52          0806129964
*Natural history -- Yellowstone National Park. Natural history -- Yellowstone National Park -- Pictorial works.*

**QH105.W8.G75 1991**
The Greater Yellowstone ecosystem : redefining America's wilderness heritage / Robert B. Keiter and Mark S. Boyce, editors ; with a foreword by Luna B. Leopold. New Haven : Yale University Press, c1991. xvii, 428 p.
91-010623          333.95/09787/52          0300049706
*Ecology -- Yellowstone National Park Region -- Congresses. Environmental policy -- Yellowstone National Park Region -- Congresses. Wildlife conservation -- Yellowstone National Park Region -- Congresses.*

**QH105.W8.Y45 1990**
The Yellowstone primer : land and resource management in the greater Yellowstone ecosystem / edited by John A. Baden and Donald Leal. San Francisco, Calif. : Pacific Research Institute for Public Policy, c1990. xii, 226 p. :
88-064201          333.78/3/0978752
0936488239
*Ecology -- Yellowstone National Park. Environmental policy -- Yellowstone National Park.*

**QH106.L283 1989**
**Larsen, James Arthur.**
The northern forest border in Canada and Alaska : biotic communities and ecological relationships / James A. Larsen. New York : Springer-Verlag, c1989. xiii, 255 p.
88-024973          574.5/2642/0971          0387967532
*Forest ecology -- Canada. Forest ecology -- Alaska. Timberline -- Canada.*

**QH106.5-130 Geographical distribution. Biogeography — Topographical divisions — Latin America**

**QH106.5.K75 1997**
**Kricher, John C.**
A neotropical companion : an introduction to the animals, plants, and ecosystems of the New World tropics / John Kricher ; illustrated by William E. Davis, Jr. Princeton, N.J. : Princeton University Press, c1997. xvi, 451 p. :
97-009784          577/.098/0913          0691044333
*Ecology -- Latin America. Natural history -- Latin America.*

**QH109.A1.I83 1991**
The Islands and the sea : five centuries of nature writing from the Caribbean / edited by John A. Murray. New York : Oxford University Press, 1991. xvi, 329 p. :
90-022372          508.729          0195066774
*Natural history -- Caribbean Area. Nature stories.    Caribbean Area -- Discovery and exploration.*

**QH109.P6.F66 1996**
The food web of a tropical rain forest / edited by Douglas P. Reagan and Robert B. Waide. Chicago : University of Chicago Press, 1996. xi, 616 p. :
95-050299          574.5/2642/097295
0226705994
*Food chains (Ecology) -- Puerto Rico -- Luquillo Experimental Forest. Rain forest ecology -- Puerto Rico -- Luquillo Experimental Forest.*

**QH123.B4**
**Beebe, William,**
Galapagos, world's end, by William Beebe ... with 24 coloured illustrations by Isabel Cooper, and 83 photographs, mostly by John Tee-Van. Published under the auspices of the New York zoological society. New York, G.P. Putnam's Sons, 1924. xxi, 443 p.
24004777
*Natural history -- Galapagos Islands.    Galapagos Islands -- Description and travel.*

**QH130.S2713 1984**
**Sarmiento, Guillermo.**
The ecology of neotropical savannas / Guillermo Sarmiento ; translated by Otto Solbrig. Cambridge, Mass. : Harvard University Press, 1984. xii, 235 p. :
83-012904          574.5/2643/098          0674224604
*Savanna ecology -- Venezuela. Savanna ecology.*

**QH135-151 Geographical distribution. Biogeography — Topographical divisions — Europe**

**QH135.E26 1984**
Ecology of European rivers / edited by B.A. Whitton. Oxford ; Blackwell Scientific, 1984. 644 p. :
84-208600          574.5/26323/094          0632008164
*Stream ecology -- Europe.*

**QH137.A85 1992**
**Atherden, Margaret,**
Upland Britain : a natural history / Margaret Atherden. Manchester ; Manchester University Press ; c1992. xv, 224 p. :
92-031788          508.41          0719034930
*Natural history -- Great Britain.*

**QH150.G76 2001**
**Grove, A. T.**
The nature of Mediterranean Europe : an ecological history / A.T. Grove and Oliver Rackham. New Haven : Yale University Press, 2001. 384 p. :
00-109791          577/.09182/2          0300084439
*Ecology -- Mediterranean Region.*

**QH151.D8 1956a**
**Durrell, Gerald Malcolm,**
My family and other animals. New York, Viking Press, 1957 [c1956] 273 p.
57-006436    574.9495
*Natural history -- Greece -- Corfu Island.    Corfu Island (Greece) -- Description and travel.*

## QH186-193 Geographical distribution. Biogeography — Topographical divisions — Asia

**QH186.C83 1992**
**Cubitt, Gerald S.**
Wild Indonesia : the wildlife and scenery of the Indonesian archipelago / photographs by Gerald Cubitt ; text by Tony and Jane Whitten. Cambridge, Mass. : MIT Press, 1992. 208 p. :
92-014891    508.598    0262231654
*Natural history -- Indonesia. National parks and reserves -- Indonesia. Ecology -- Indonesia. Indonesia -- Description and travel.*

**QH193.S59.T48 1997**
**Thapar, Valmik.**
Land of the tiger : a natural history of the Indian subcontinent / Valmik Thapar. Berkeley : University of California Press, 1997. 288 p. :
98-181919    508.54    0520214706
*Natural history -- South Asia. Tigers -- South Asia. Natural history -- South Asia -- Pictorial works.*

**QH193.S6.W47 1984**
**Whitmore, T. C.**
Tropical rain forests of the Far East / T.C. Whitmore ; with a chapter on soils by C.P. Burnham. Oxford [Oxfordshire] : Clarendon Press, 1984. xvi, 352 p. :
83-013441    574.5/2642/0959    0198541368
*Rain forest ecology -- Asia, Southeastern. Rain forests -- Asia, Southeastern. Forests and forestry -- Asia, Southeastern.*

## QH194-195 Geographical distribution. Biogeography — Topographical divisions — Africa

**QH194.A38 2001**
African rain forest ecology and conservation : an interdisciplinary pespective / edited by William Weber ... [et al.]. New Haven : Yale University Press, c2001. xii, 588 p. :
00-043678    577.34/096    0300084331
*Rain forest ecology -- Africa. Rain forest conservation – Africa.*

**QH195.A23.B56 1993**
Biogeography and ecology of the rain forests of eastern Africa / edited by Jon C. Lovett and Samuel K. Wasser. Cambridge [England] ; Cambridge University Press, 1993. ix, 341 p. :
92-036758    574.5/2642/09676
0521430836
*Rain forest ecology -- Africa, Eastern. Rain forest animals -- Africa, Eastern. Rain forest plants -- Africa, Eastern.*

**QH195.M2.P74 1991**
**Preston-Mafham, Ken.**
Madagascar : a natural history / Ken Preston-Mafham ; foreword by Sir David Attenborough. Oxford ; Facts on File, c1991. 224 p. :
91-016787    508.691    0816024030
*Natural history -- Madagascar. Natural history --Madagascar – Pictorial works.*

**QH195.S6.S38 1993**
**Scholes, R. J.**
An African savanna : synthesis of the Nylsvley study / R.J Scholes, B.H. Walker. Cambridge [England] ; Cambridge University Press, 1993. xii, 306 p. :
92-046453    574.5/2643/09682
0521419719
*Savanna ecology -- South Africa -- Nylsvley Nature Reserve.*

## QH197 Geographical distribution. Biogeography — Topographical divisions — Australia

**QH197.B46 1998**
**Berra, Tim M.,**
A natural history of Australia / by Tim M. Berra. San Diego : Academic Press, 1998. p. cm.
97-042820    508.94    0120931559
*Natural history -- Australia.*

**QH197.L68 2001**
**Love, Rosaleen.**
Reefscape : reflections on the Great Barrier Reef / Rosaleen Love. Washington, DC : Joseph Henry Press, 2001. 264 p. 23 cm.
01-024281    508.943    0309072603
*Natural history -- Australia -- Great Barrier Reef (Qld.)    Great Barrier Reef (Qld.) -- History. Great Barrier Reef (Qld.) -- Description and travel.*

**QH197.O34 2001**
Oceanographic processes of coral reefs : physical and biological links in the Great Barrier Reef / edited by Eric Wolanski. Boca Raton : CRC Press, c2001. 356 p. :
00-048569    577.7/89476    084930833X
*Natural history -- Australia -- Great Barrier Reef (Qld.)    Great Barrier Reef (Qld.) -- History. Great Barrier Reef (Qld.) -- Description and travel.*

**QH197.V36 1988**
**Vandenbeld, John.**
Nature of Australia : a portrait of the island continent / John Vandenbeld. New York : Facts On File, c1988. vi, 292 p. :
88-011697    508.94    081602006X
*Natural history -- Australia.*

### QH198 Geographical distribution. Biogeography — Topographical divisions — Pacific Area. Pacific islands

**QH198.A1.M58 1990**
**Mitchell, Andrew W.**
The fragile South Pacific : an ecological odyssey / Andrew Mitchell ; introduction by James A. Michener. Austin : University of Texas Press, 1990. 256 p. :
90-070632     508.95     0292724667
*Natural history -- Oceania. Natural history -- South Pacific Ocean. Marine biology -- Oceania.*

**QH198.G3.S72 1988**
**Steadman, David W.**
Galapagos : discovery on Darwin's islands / David W. Steadman and Steven Zousmer ; color plates by Lee M. Steadman. Washington, D.C. : Smithsonian Institution Press, c1988. 207 p. :
87-062629     508.866/5     0874748828
*Natural history -- Galapagos Islands. Paleontology –Galapagos Islands. Evolution (Biology)*

### QH204 Microscopy — History

**QH204.F65 1985**
**Ford, Brian J.**
Single lens : the story of the simple microscope / Brian J. Ford. New York : Harper & Row, 1985. x, 182 p. :
84-048161     502/.8/22     0060153660
*Leeuwenhoek, Antoni van, -- 1632-1723.     Microscopes –History. Biologists -- Netherlands -- Biography.*

### QH205.2 Microscopy — General works, treatises, and textbooks — 1970-

**QH205.2.S54 1993**
**Slayter, Elizabeth M.**
Light and electron microscopy / Elizabeth M. Slayter, Henry S. Slayter. Cambridge [England] ; Cambridge University Press, 1993. p. cm.
92-007825     578/.4     0521327148
*Microscopy. Compound microscopes. Electron microscopy.*

### QH212 Microscopy — Microscopes — Special microscopes, A-Z

**QH212.N43.P34 1996**
**Paesler, Michael A.**
Near-field optics : theory, instrumentation, and applications / Michael A. Paesler, Patrick J. Moyer. New York : Wiley, c1996. xii, 355 p. :
95-046171     502/.8/2     0471043117
*Near-field microscopy.*

**QH212.S33**
Scanning probe microscopy and spectroscopy : theory, techniques, and applications / edited by Dawn A. Bonnell. New York : Wiley-VCH, c2001. xiv, 493 p. :
00-036821     502/.8/25     047124824X
*Scanning probe microscopy. Tunneling spectroscopy.*

### QH251 Microscopy — Photomicrography

**QH251.B73 1994**
**Breger, Dee.**
Journeys in microspace : the art of the scanning electron microscope / Dee Breger. New York : Columbia University Press, c1994. 201 p. :
94-037829     778.3/1     0231082525
*Photomicrography. Scanning electron microscopy. Photography, Artistic.*

# QH302.5-671 Biology (General)

## QH302.5 Dictionaries and encyclopedias

**QH302.5.A2313 1996**
Concise encyclopedia biology / translated and revised by Thomas A. Scott. Berlin ; Walter de Gruyter, 1996. v, 1287 p. :
95-039080     574/.03     3110106612
*Biology -- Dictionaries.*

**QH302.5.B59 1990**
**Blinderman, Charles,**
Biolexicon : a guide to the language of biology / by Charles Blinderman. Springfield, Ill., U.S.A. : C.C. Thomas, c1990. xv, 363 p. :
90-010765     574/.014     0398056714
*Biology -- Terminology. English language –Etymology. Biology-- terminology.*

**QH302.5.D5 2000**
A dictionary of biology.     Oxford [England] : Oxford University Press, 2000. 641 p. :
00-268817     570/.3     0192801023
*Biology -- Dictionaries.*

**QH302.5.E47 1998**
Elsevier's dictionary of biology / Rauno Tirri ... [et al.]. Amsterdam ; Elsevier, 1998. p. cm.
98-031199     570/.3     0444825258
*Biology -- Dictionaries.*

**QH302.5.M382 1997**
McGraw-Hill dictionary of bioscience / Sybil P. Parker, editor in chief. New York : McGraw-Hill, 1997. p. cm.
96-046183     574/.03     0070524300
*Biology -- Dictionaries. Life sciences -- Dictionaries.*

# QH303 General works, treatises, and textbooks

**QH303.S6 1980**
**Smith, Roger Cletus,**
  Smith's Guide to the literature of the life sciences / Roger C. Smith, W. Malcolm Reid, Arlene E. Luchsinger. Minneapolis, Minn. : Burgess Pub. Co., c1980. xi, 223 p. :
79-055580          574/.07          0808735764
  *Life sciences literature.*

## QH303.6 Communication in biology — Biological literature. Life sciences literature

**QH303.6.C433 2001**
**Ceccarelli, Leah.**
  Shaping science with rhetoric : the cases of Dobzhansky, Schrodinger, and Wilson / Leah Ceccarelli. Chicago : University of Chicago Press, c2001. xi, 204 p. :
00-012179          507.2          0226099067
*Wilson, Edward Osborne, -- 1929- -- Consilience. Dobzhansky, Theodosius Grigorievich, -- 1900-1975 -- Genetics and the origin of species. Schrodinger, Erwin, -- 1887-1961 -- What is life? Life sciences literature. Rhetoric. Interdisciplinary approach to knowledge.*

**QH303.6.D38 2002**
**Schmidt, Diane,**
  Using the biological literature : a practical guide / Diane Schmidt, Elisabeth B. Davis, Pamela F. Jacobs. 3rd ed., rev. and expanded New York : Marcel Dekker, 2002. p. cm.
          570/.7/2 21          0824706676
*Biological literature.*

## QH304 Communication in biology — Authorship

**QH304.C33 1983**
**CBE Style Manual Committee.**
  CBE style manual : a guide for authors, editors, and publishers in the biological sciences / prepared by CBE Style Manual Committee. Bethesda, Md. : Council of Biology Editors, c1983. xx, 324 p. :
83-007172          808/.02          0914340042
  *Biology -- Authorship. Printing -- Style manuals.*

## QH305 History and conditions — General works

**QH305.M26 1982**
**Mayr, Ernst,**
  The growth of biological thought : diversity, evolution, and inheritance / Ernst Mayr. Cambridge, Mass. : Belknap Press, 1982. ix, 974 p. ;
81-013204          574/.09          0674364457
  *Biology -- History. Biology -- Philosophy -- History.*

**QH305.S48 1993**
**Serafini, Anthony.**
  The epic history of biology / Anthony Serafini. New York : Plenum, c1993. xi, 395 p. :
93-027895          574/.09          0306445115
  *Biology -- History. Medicine -- History. Biologists.*

## QH305.2 History and conditions — By region or country, A-Z

**QH305.2.U6**
**Pauly, Philip J.**
  Biologists and the promise of American life : from Meriwether Lewis to Alfred Kinsey / Philip J. Pauly. Princeton, N.J. : Princeton University Press, C2000. xvi, 313 p. :
00-020896          570/.973          0691049777
  *Biology -- United States -- History.    United States – Civilization.*

## QH307 General works and treatises — 1861-1969

**QH307.B32**
**Benton, Allen H.**
  Principles of field biology & ecology [by] Allen H. Benton [and] William E. Werner, Jr. New York, McGraw-Hill, 1958. 341 p.
57-013330          575.3
  *Biology -- Field work. Ecology.*

## QH307.2 General works and treatises — 1970-

**QH307.2.M34 1991**
  Magill's survey of science. edited by Frank N. Magill, consulting editor, Laura L. Mays Hoopes. Pasadena, Calif. : Salem Press, c1991-c1998. 7 v. (liv, 31
90-019102          574          0893566128
  *Life sciences.*

**QH307.2.M47 2000**
**Mertz, Leslie A.**
  Recent advances and issues in biology / by Leslie A. Mertz. Phoenix, Ariz. : Oryx Press, 2000. ix, 282 p. :
00-027080          570          1573562343
  *Biology.*

### QH308.2 Textbooks — Advanced — 1970-

**QH308.2.C34 2000**
**Campbell, Neil A.,**
  Biology : concepts & connections / Neil A. Campbell, Lawrence G. Mitchell, Jane B. Reece. 3rd ed. San Francisco : Benjamin/Cummings, c2000. xxxiii, 809 p.
          570 21          0805365850
*Biology.*

**QH308.2.S35 1994**
**Schlesinger, Allen B.**
Explaining life / Allen B. Schlesinger. New York : McGraw-Hill, c1994. viii, 277 p.
93-023895          574          0070554625
*Biology. Life (Biology)*

# QH309 Popular works

**QH309.S78 2000**
**Stansfield, William D.,**
Death of a rat : understandings and appreciations of science / William D. Stansfield. Amherst, N.Y. : Prometheus Books, 2000. 360 p. :
00-020932          174/.957          1573928143
*Life sciences -- Popular works. Science -- Popular works.*

# QH311 Addresses, essays, lectures

**QH311.C63 1971**
Classics in biology; a course of selected reading by authorities. Introductory reading guide by Sir S. Zuckerman. Port Washington, N.Y., Kennikat Press [1971, c1960] xxix, 351 p.
78-122974          574/.08 s          0804613559
*Biology -- Addresses, essays, lectures.*

**QH311.H9**
**Huxley, Julian,**
The individual in the animal kingdom, by Julian S. Huxley ... Cambridge [Eng.] University press; 1912. ix, [1] p., 1
13-006037
*Individuality. Biology.*

**QH311.H916**
**Huxley, Julian,**
Man in the modern world; an eminent scientist looks at life today. [New York] New American Library [1948] 191 p.
48011349
*Biology.*

**QH311.H918 1957a**
**Huxley, Julian,**
New bottles for new wine, essays. New York, Harper [1957] 318 p.
58006151          574.04
*Biology Humanism -- 20th century.*

**QH311.M37 1997**
**Margulis, Lynn,**
Slanted truths : essays on Gaia, symbiosis, and evolution / Lynn Margulis, Dorion Sagan ; foreword by Philip and Phylis Morrison. New York : Copernicus, c1997. xxiii, 368 p.
97-002160          570          0387949275
*Biology. Gaia hypothesis. Symbiosis.*

# QH313 Special aspects of the subject as whole

**QH313.C74 1991**
**Cockburn, Andrew,**
An introduction to evolutionary ecology / Andrew Cockburn ; illustrated by Karina Hansen. Oxford ; Blackwell Scientific Publications, 1991. xii, 370 p. :
90-027704          574.5          0632027290
*Biological diversity. Ecology. Species.*

**QH313.S585 1993**
**Sigmund, Karl,**
Games of life : explorations in ecology, evolution, and behaviour / Karl Sigmund. Oxford [England] ; Oxford University Press, 1993. vi, 244 p. :
93-019918          574/.011          0198546653
*Life (Biology) -- Simulation games. Life (Biology) -- Computer simulation. Game theory.*

**QH313.W55 1992**
**Wilson, Edward Osborne,**
The diversity of life / Edward O. Wilson. Cambridge, Mass. : Belknap Press of Harvard University Press, 1992. 424 p. :
92-009018          333.95          0674212983
*Biological diversity. Biological diversity conservation.*

## QH318.5 Study and teaching. Research — Fieldwork

**QH318.5.B4 1966**
**Benton, Allen H.**
Field biology and ecology [by] Allen H. Benton [and] William E. Werner, Jr. New York, McGraw-Hill [1966] ix, 499 p.
65-021571          574.50723
*Ecology. Biology -- Field work.*

# QH323.5 Biometry. Biomathematics. Mathematical models

**QH323.5.H325 1996**
**Haefner, James W.**
Modeling biological systems : principles and applications / James W. Haefner. New York : Chapman & Hall, c1996. xvii, 473 p.
96-007085          574/.01/13          0412042010
*Biological systems -- Computer simulation. Biological systems -- Mathematical models.*

**QH323.5.S63 1995**
**Sokal, Robert R.**
Biometry : the principles and practice of statistics in biological research / Robert R. Sokal and F. James Rohlf. 3rd ed. New York : W.H. Freeman, c1995. xix, 887 p. :
          574/.01/5195 20          0716724111
*Biometry.*

**QH323.5.S74 1998**
**Stewart, Ian,**
Life's other secret : the new mathematics of the living world / Ian Stewart. New York : John Wiley, c1998. xiii, 285 p.,
97-018152          570/.1/51          0471158453
*Biomathematics.*

**QH323.5.Z64 1993**
**Zolman, James F.**
Biostatistics : experimental design and statistical inference / James F. Zolman. New York : Oxford University Press, 1993. xv, 343 p. :
92-022605          574/.01/5195          0195078101
*Biometry. Experimental design.*

## QH324.2 Methods of research. Technique — Data processing

**QH324.2.E4613 1994**
**Emmeche, Claus,**
The garden in the machine : the emerging science of artificial life / Claus Emmeche ; translated by Steven Sampson. Princeton, N.J. : Princeton University Press, c1994. xiv, 199 p. :
93-039101          577          0691033307
*Biological systems -- Computer simulation. Biology – Philosophy. Life.*

**QH324.2.H45 1998**
**Helmreich, Stefan,**
Silicon second nature : culturing artificial life in a digital world / Stefan Helmreich. Berkeley : University of California Press, c1998. xii, 314 p. :
98-019393          570/.1/13          0520207998
*Biological systems -- Computer simulation -- Philosophy. Biological systems -- Computer simulation -- Research.*

## QH325 Origin and beginnings of life

**QH325.D345 1999**
**Davies, P. C. W.**
The fifth miracle : the search for the origin and meaning of life / Paul Davies. New York, NY : Simon & Schuster, c1999. 304 p. :
98-033421          576.8/3          0684837994
*Life -- Origin. Life.*

**QH325.D4 1990**
**De Duve, Christian.**
Blueprint for a cell : the nature and origin of life / Christian de Duve. Burlington, N.C. : N. Patterson, c1991. 275 p. :
90-062090          577          0892784105
*Life -- Origin. Cells.*

**QH325.D42 1995**
**De Duve, Christian.**
Vital dust : life as a cosmic imperative / Christian de Duve. New York : Basic Books, c1995. xix, 362 p. :
94-012964          577          0465090443
*Life -- Origin. Life (Biology) Evolution (Biology)*

**QH325.F47 1998**
**Fisher, David E.,**
Strangers in the night : a brief history of life on other worlds / David E. Fisher and Marshall Jon Fisher. Washington, D. C. : Counterpoint, c1998. xii, 348 p. :
98-035513          576.8/39          1887178872
*Life -- Origin. Exobiology. Life on other planets.*

**QH325.F76 2002**
Frontiers of life / advisory board, editorial directors, David Baltimore . . . [et al.]. San Diego ; Rome : Academic ; Treccani, c2002. 4 v. :
                    012077346
*Life (Biology) Life.*

**QH325.F78 2000**
**Fry, Iris.**
The emergence of life on Earth : a historical and scientific overview / Iris Fry. New Brunswick, N.J. : Rutgers University Press, 2000. ix, 327 p. :
99-023153          576.8/3          0813527392
*Life -- Origin.*

**QH325.K388 1995**
**Kauffman, Stuart A.**
At home in the universe : the search for laws of self-organization and complexity / Stuart Kauffman. New York : Oxford University Press, 1995. viii, 321 p.
94-025268          577          0195095995
*Life -- Origin. Self-organizing systems. Molecular evolution.*

**QH325.M298 1995**
**Margulis, Lynn,**
What is life? / Lynn Margulis and Dorion Sagan ; foreword by Niles Eldredge. New York : Simon & Schuster, c1995. 207 p. :
94-044213          577          0684813262
*Life (Biology) Biology -- Philosophy. Biological diversity.*

**QH325.M32 1990**
**Mason, Stephen Finney,**
Chemical evolution : origin of the elements, molecules, and living systems / Stephen F. Mason. Oxford : Clarendon Press ; 1991. xiii, 317 p.
90-007321          577          0198552726
*Molecular evolution.*

**QH325.R57 1991**
**Rosen, Robert,**
Life itself : a comprehensive inquiry into the nature, origin, and fabrication of life / Robert Rosen. New York : Columbia University Press, c1991. xix, 285 p. :
91-003110          574          0231075642
*Life (Biology) Life -- Origin. Biological systems.*

**QH325.S24 1992**
**Sagan, Carl,**
Shadows of forgotten ancestors : a search for who we are / Carl Sagan, Ann Druyan. New York : Random House, c1992. xvi, 505 p. ;
92-050155          304.5          0394534816
*Life -- Origin. Evolution (Biology)*

**QH325.S85 2000**
**Strick, James Edgar,**
   Sparks of life : Darwinism and the Victorian debates over spontaneous generation / James E. Strick. Cambridge, Mass. : Harvard University Press, 2000. xi, 283 p. :
00-031915          576.8/8          067400292X
   *Spontaneous generation -- Great Britain -- History -- Victoria, 1837-1901. Evolution (Biology) -- Great Britain – History – Victoria, 1837-1901.*

**QH325.Z83 2000**
**Zubay, Geoffrey L.**
   Orgins of life on the earth and in the cosmos / Geoffrey Zubay. 2nd ed. San Diego : Academic Press, c2000. xx, 564 p. :
          576.8/3 21          012781910X
*Life -- Origin.*

## QH327 Space biology — General works

**QH327.D37 2001**
**Darling, David J.**
   Life everywhere : the maverick science of astrobiology / by David Darling. New York : Basic Books, 2001. p. cm.
01-025147          576.8/39          0465015638
   *Exobiology. Life -- Origin.*

## QH331 Philosophy of biology

**QH331.B475 2000**
   Biology and epistemology / edited by Richard Creath, Jane Maienschein Cambridge [England] ; Cambridge University Press, 2000. xviii, 295 p.
99-022990          570/.1     0521592909
   *Biology -- Philosophy.*

**QH331.C9**
**Crick, Francis,**
   Of molecules and men, by Francis Crick. Seattle, University of Washington Press [1966] 99 p.
66-026994          574.01
   *Biology -- Philosophy. Life (Biology) Molecular biology.*

**QH331.G624 1998**
**Goodenough, Ursula.**
   The sacred depths of nature / Ursula Goodenough. New York : Oxford University Press, 1998. xxi, 197 p. :
98-006579          574/.01          0195126130
   *Biology -- Philosophy. Biology -- Religious aspects. Naturalism – Religious aspects.*

**QH331.L528 2001**
**Lennox, James G.**
   Aristotle's philosophy of biology : studies in the origins of life science / James G. Lennox. Cambridge, UK ; Cambridge University Press, 2001. xxiii, 321 p.
00-026070          570/.1     0521650275
*Aristotle.     Biology -- History. Biology -- Philosophy.*

**QH331.M59 1993**
**Moore, John Alexander,**
   Science as a way of knowing : the foundations of modern biology / John A. Moore. Cambridge, Mass. : Harvard University Press, 1993. viii, 530 p.
92-046325          574/.09          067479480X
   *Biology -- Philosophy. Biology -- History.*

**QH331.P4682 1998**
   The philosophy of biology / edited by David L. Hull and Michael Ruse. Oxford ; New York : Oxford University Press, 1998. ix, 772 p. :
          570/.1 21          019875213X
*Biology -- Phylosophy.*

**QH331.R425 1995**
   Reinventing biology : respect for life and the creation of knowledge / edited by Lynda Birke and Ruth Hubbard. Bloomington : Indiana University Press, c1995. xvii, 291 ;
95-001443          574/.01          0253329094
   *Biology -- Philosophy. Biology -- Research. Animal experimentation -- Moral and ethical aspects.*

**QH331.S3557**
**Schrodinger, Erwin,**
   What is life? the physical aspect of the living cell & Mind and matter. Cambridge, University P., 1967. 178 p.
68-081857          574/.01
   *Biology -- Philosophy. Molecular biology. Human evolution.*

**QH331.S375 1991**
   Scientists on Gaia / edited by Stephen H. Schneider and Penelope J. Boston. Cambridge, Mass. : MIT Press, c1991. xxii, 433 p.
91-000344          550     0262193108
   *Gaia hypothesis -- Congresses. Geobiology -- Congresses.*

**QH331.S5**
**Sinnott, Edmund Ware,**
   Cell and psyche : the biology of purpose / by Edmund W. Sinnott. Chapel Hill, N.C. : University of North Carolina Press, 1950. 121 p. ;
50010556          570.1
   *Biology -- Philosophy.*

**QH331.S82 1999**
**Sterelny, Kim,**
   Sex and death : an introduction to philosophy of biology / Kim Sterelny and Paul E. Griffiths. Chicago, Ill. : University of Chicago Press, 1999. p. cm.
98-047555          570/.1     0226773035
   *Biology -- Philosophy.*

**QH331.W555 1999**
**Wilson, Jack,**
   Biological individuality : the identity and persistence of living entities / Jack Wilson. Cambridge ; Cambridge University Press, 1999. xii, 137 p. ;
98-032177          570/.1     0521624258
   *Biology -- Philosophy. Individuality.*

## QH332 Bioethics

**QH332.F68 2001**
**Fox, Michael W.,**
   Bringing life to ethics : global bioethics for a humane society / Michael W. Fox ;[foreword by Bernard E. Rollin. Albany : State University of New York Press, c2001. xiii, 251 p.
00-026522          174/.957          0791448010
   *Bioethics. Environmental ethics. Animal rights.*

## QH333 Social aspects of biology

**QH333.V36 1995**
**Vandermeer, John H.**
   Reconstructing biology : genetics and ecology in the new world order / John Vandermeer. New York : Wiley, c1996. xvii, 478 p.
95-012076          304.2          0471109177
   *Biology -- Social aspects. Human ecology. Genetics -- Social aspects.*

## QH343.4 Geobiology. Biosphere

**QH343.4.S36 1999**
**Schwartzman, David**
   Life, temperature, and the earth : the self-organizing biosphere / David Schwartzman. New York : Columbia University Press, c1999. xiii, 241 p.
99-025856          577.2/2          0231102127
   *Biosphere. Bioclimatology. Weathering.*

**QH343.4.S65 1997**
**Smil, Vaclav.**
   Cycles of life : civilization and the biosphere / Vaclav Smil. New York : Scientific American Library : c1997. x, 221 p. :
96-042326          574.5/222          0716750791
   *Biosphere. Biogeochemical cycles. Nature -- Effect of human beings on.*

## QH344 Biogeochemistry — Biogeochemical cycles

**QH344.D43 1992**
**DeAngelis, D. L.**
   Dynamics of nutrient cycling and food webs / D.L. DeAngelis. London ; Chapman & Hall, 1992. xv, 270 p. :
91-003275          574.5/3          0412298309
   *Nutrient cycle. Food chains (Ecology)*

## QH345 General biochemistry of plants and animals

**QH345.H347 1975**
   Handbook of biochemistry and molecular biology / editor, Gerald D. Fasman. Cleveland : CRC Press, c1975-1977. 5 v. in 9 :
75-029514          574.1/92/0212          0878195033
   *Biochemistry -- Handbooks, manuals, etc. Molecular biology – Handbooks, manuals, etc. Nucleic acids -- Tables.*

## QH351 Morphology

**QH351.P58 2000**
   Phylogenetic analysis of morphological data / edited by John J. Wiens. Washington, D.C. : Smithsonian Institution Press , c2000. x, 220 p. :
00-023910          571.3          156098841X
   *Morphology. Phylogeny.*

**QH351.W25 1988**
**Wainwright, Stephen A.,**
   Axis and circumference : the cylindrical shape of plants and animals / Stephen A. Wainwright. Cambridge, Mass. : Harvard University Press, 1988. viii, 132 p.
87-021099          574.4          0674057007
   *Morphology.*

## QH352 Population biology

**QH352.B43 1981**
**Begon, Michael.**
   Population ecology : a unified study of animals and plants / Michael Begon, Martin Mortimer. Sunderland, Mass. : Sinauer Associates, 1981. vii, 200 p. :
81-005641          574.5/248          0878930663
   *Population biology. Ecology.*

**QH352.C36 1993**
**Carey, James R.**
   Applied demography for biologists with special emphasis on insects / James R. Carey. New York : Oxford University Press, 1993. xvi, 206 p. :
91-045843          574.5/248/072          0195066871
   *Population biology. Demography.*

**QH352.G67 1995**
**Gotelli, Nicholas J.,**
   A primer of ecology / Nicholas J. Gotelli. Sunderland, Mass. : Sinauer Associates, c1995. xvii, 206 p.
94-045884          574.5/248/0151          0878932704
   *Population biology -- Mathematical models. Ecology -- Mathematical models.*

**QH352.H39 1997**
**Hayek, Lee-Ann C.**
Surveying natural populations / Lee-Ann C. Hayek and Martin A. Buzas. New York : Columbia University Press, 1997. xvi, 563 p. :
96-022434        574.5/248/072        0231102402
*Population biology -- Statistical methods. Paleoecology -- Statistical methods.*

**QH352.M47 1997**
Metapopulation biology : ecology, genetics, and evolution / edited by Ilkka Hanski, Michael E. Gilpin. San Diego, CA : Academic Press, c1997. xvi, 512 p. :
96-028242        574.5/248        012323445X
*Population biology.*

**QH352.P628 1996**
Population dynamics in ecological space and time / edited by Olin E. Rhodes, Jr., Ronald K. Chesser, and Michael H. Smith. Chicago : University of Chicago Press, 1996. viii, 388 p.
96-003246        574.5/248        0226710572
*Population biology -- Congresses. Ecology -- Congresses.*

## QH353 Biological invasions

**QH353.I59 2000**
Invasive species in a changing world / edited by Harold A. Mooney and Richard J. Hobbs. Washington, D.C. : Island Press, c2000. xv, 457 p. :
00-008791        577/.18        1559637811
*Biological invasions. Nonindigenous pests.*

**QH353.S54 1997**
**Shigesada, Nanako,**
Biological invasions : theory and practice / Nanako Shigesada and Kohkichi Kawasaki. Oxford ; Oxford University Press, 1997. xiii, 205 p.
96-034591        574.5/247        0198548516
*Biological invasions. Biological invasions -- Mathematical models.*

**QH353.V36 2000**
**Van Driesche, Jason.**
Nature out of place : biological invasions in the global age / Jason Van Driesche and Roy Van Driesche. Washington, D.C. : Island Press, c2000. xiv, 363 p. :
00-010477        577/.18        1559637579
*Biological invasions.*

## QH359 Evolution — Societies, congresses, serial collections, yearbooks

**QH359.E92 1983**
Evolution from molecules to men / edited by D.S. Bendall on behalf of Darwin College. Cambridge [Cambridgeshire] ; Cambridge University Press, 1983. xiii, 594 p.
82-022020        575        0521247535
*Evolution (Biology) -- Congresses.*

**QH359.E926 1999**
Evolution! : facts and fallacies / edited by J. William Schopf. San Diego : Academic Press, c1999. xii, 159 p. :
98-084494        576.8        0126288607
*Evolution (Biology) -- Congresses.*

## QH360.5 Evolution — Philosophy

**QH360.5.C38 1997**
**Caudill, Edward.**
Darwinian myths : the legends and misuses of a theory / Edward Caudill. Knoxville : University of Tennessee Press, c1997. xxi, 184 p. ;
97-004691        576.8/2        087049984X
*Darwin, Charles, -- 1809-1882 -- Legends.        Social Darwinism. Evolution (Biology) -- Philosophy.*

**QH360.5.G48 1997**
**Ghiselin, Michael T.,**
Metaphysics and the origin of species / Michael T. Ghiselin. Albany : State University of New York Press, c1997. xi, 377 p. ;
96-038957        576.8/01        0791434672
*Evolution (Biology) -- Philosophy. Species -- Philosophy.*

**QH360.5.H86 2001**
**Hull, David L.**
Science and selection : essays on biological evolution and the philosophy of science / David L. Hull. Cambridge, U.K. ; Cambridge University Press, 2001. x, 267 p. ;
00-027938        576.8/01        0521643392
*Evolution (Biology) -- Philosophy. Animal intelligence.*

**QH360.5.R874 1999**
**Ruse, Michael.**
Mystery of mysteries : is evolution a socal construction? / Michael Ruse. Cambridge, Mass. : Harvard University Press, 1999. viii, 296 p. :
576.8/01 21        067446706X
*Evolution (Biology) -- Philosophy. Science -- Philosophy. Biologists. Scientists.*

## QH360.6 Evolution — Nomenclature, terminology, notation, abbreviations

**QH360.6.K49 1992**
Keywords in evolutionary biology / edited by Evelyn Fox Keller, Elisabeth A. Lloyd. Cambridge, Mass. : Harvard University Press, 1992. xiii, 414 p.
92-008283        575/.0014        0674503120
*Evolution (Biology) -- Terminology.*

## QH361 Evolution — History

**QH361.B685 1996**
**Bowler, Peter J.**
Life's splendid drama : evolutionary biology and the reconstruction of life's ancestry, 1860-1940 / Peter J. Bowler. Chicago : University of Chicago Press, c1996. xiii, 525 p.
95-025394    575/.009    0226069214
*Evolution (Biology) -- History. Biology -- History.*

**QH361.B693 1988**
**Bowler, Peter J.**
The non-Darwinian revolution : reinterpreting a historical myth / Peter J. Bowler. Baltimore : Johns Hopkins University Press, c1988. x, 238 p. :
88-009738    575/.009    0801836786
*Evolution (Biology) -- History.*

**QH361.D46 1995**
**Depew, David J.,**
Darwinism evolving : systems dynamics and the genealogy of natural selection / David J. Depew and Bruce H. Weber. Cambridge, Mass. : MIT Press, c1995. xiii, 588 p.
94-016590    575.01/62    0262041456
*Evolution (Biology) -- Philosophy -- History.*

**QH361.E35**
**Eiseley, Loren C.,**
Darwin's century: evolution and the men who discovered it. Garden City, N.Y., Doubleday, 1958. 378 p.
58-006638    575.09
*Evolution (Biology) -- History.*

**QH361.G55**
**Glass, Bentley,**
Forerunners of Darwin: 1745-1859. Edited by Bentley Glass, Owsei Temkin [and] William L. Straus, Jr., under the auspices of the Johns Hopkins History of Ideas Club. Baltimore, Johns Hopkins Press [1959] 471 p.
59-009978    575.016
*Evolution (Biology) -- History.*

**QH361.G65 1977**
**Gould, Stephen Jay.**
Ever since Darwin : reflections in natural history / Stephen Jay Gould. New York : Norton, c1977. 285 p. :
77-022504    575.01/62    0393064255
*Evolution (Biology) -- History. Natural selection -- History.*

**QH361.G66 1980**
**Gould, Stephen Jay.**
The panda's thumb : more reflections in natural history / Stephen Jay Gould. New York : Norton, c1980. 343 p. :
80-015952    575.01/62    0393013804
*Evolution (Biology) -- History. Natural selection -- History.*

**QH361.R87 1999**
**Ruse, Michael.**
The Darwinian revolution : science red in tooth and claw / Michael Ruse. Chicago : University of Chicago Press, c1999. xv, 346 p. :
99-023377    576.8/2    0226731685
*Darwin, Charles, -- 1809-1882. Darwin, Charles – 1809-1882. – On the origin of species. Evolution (Biology) -- History.*

**QH361.S64 1996**
**Smocovitis, Vassiliki Betty.**
Unifying biology : the evolutionary synthesis and evolutionary biology / Vassiliki Betty Smocovitis. Princeton, N.J. : Princeton University Press, c1996. xxiv, 230 p.
96-005605    575/.009    0691033439
*Evolution (Biology) -- History. Biology -- History.*

**QH361.Z48 2001**
**Zimmer, Carl,**
Evolution : the triumph of an idea / Carl Zimmer ; introduction by Stephen Jay Gould ; foreword by Richard Hutton. 1st ed. New York : HarperCollins, c2001. xx, 364 p. :
576.8/09 21    0060199067
*Evolution (Biology) -- History.*

## QH362 Evolution — Study and teaching. Research

**QH362.E86 1983**
Evolution versus Creationism : the public education controversy / edited by J. Peter Zetterberg. Phoenix, AZ : Oryx Press, 1983. xi, 516 p. ;
82-018795    575/.007    0897740610
*Evolution (Biology) -- Study and teaching. Creationism – Study and teaching.*

## QH363 Evolution — Early works through 1800

**QH363.S4 2000**
**Secord, James A.**
Victorian sensation : the extraordinary publication, reception, and secret authorship of Vestiges of the natural history of creation / James A. Secord. Chicago : University of Chicago Press, c2000. xix, 624 p. :
00-009124    576.8/0941/09034
0226744108
*Chambers, Robert, -- 1802-1871. -- Vestiges of the natural history of creation.*

### QH365.A1 Evolution — Works of Darwin — Collected works. By date

**QH365.A1 1958**
**Darwin, Charles,**
Evolution by natural selection [by] Charles Darwin and Alfred Russel Wallace. Cambridge, Pub. for the XV International Congress of Zoolog 1958. viii, 287 p.
58014868    575.0162
*Evolution. Evolution. Natural selection.*

**QH365.A1 1977**
**Darwin, Charles,**
   The collected papers of Charles Darwin / edited by Paul H. Barrett ; with a foreword by Theodosius Dobzhansky. Chicago : University of Chicago Press, 1977. 2 v. :
76-000606          575/.008          0226136574
*Darwin, Charles, -- 1809-1882.     Natural history.  Naturalists -- England -- Correspondence.*

**QH365.A1 1988**
**Darwin, Charles,**
   Charles Darwin's Beagle diary / edited by Richard Darwin Keynes. Cambridge [Cambridgeshire] ; Cambridge University Press, 1988. xxix, 464 p.
87-031169          508/.92/4          0521235030
   *Natural history.  Geology.*

**QH365.O2-Z9 Evolution — Works of Darwin — Separate works, A-Z**

**QH365.O2**
**Darwin, Charles**
   The origin of species by means of natural selection; or, The preservation of favoured races in the struggle for life. A reprint of the 6th ed. with a pref. by G. R. de Beer. London, Oxford University Press [1951] xxiii, 592 p.
52-007408
   *Evolution.  Evolution  Natural selection.*

**QH365.O2 1859a**
**Darwin, Charles**
   On the origin of species. A facsim. of the 1st ed., with an introd. by Ernst Mayr. Cambridge, Harvard University Press, 1964. xxvii, ix, 50
63-017196          575.0162
   *Evolution (Biology)  Natural selection.*

**QH365.O8.C48 1995**
   Charles Darwin's the origin of species : new interdisciplinary essays / David Amigoni, Jeff Wallace, editors. Manchester ; Manchester University Press ; c1995. xii, 211 p. :
94-026485          575.01/62          0719040248
*Darwin, Charles, -- 1809-1882. -- On the origin of species.  Evolution (Biology)  Natural selection.*

**QH365.O8R87**
**Russett, Cynthia Eagle.**
   Darwin in America : The intellectual response, 1865-1912 / Cynthia Eagle Russett. San Francisco : W. H. Freeman, c1976. ix, 228 p. :
                601.24/3          0716705648
*Darwin, Charles, 1809-1882. On the Origin of Species.*

**QH365.V2.D37 1998**
**Darwin, Charles,**
   The variation of animals and plants under domestication / Charles Darwin ; with a new foreword by Harriet Ritvo. Baltimore, Md. : Johns Hopkins University Press, 1998. 2 v. :
97-040164          576.5/4          0801858666
   *Variation (Biology)  Domestic animals.  Plants, Cultivated.*

**QH365.Z9.D37 1996**
**Darwin, Charles,**
   On evolution : the development of theory of natural selection / Darwin ; edited by Thomas F. Glick and David Kohn. Indianapolis, IN : Hackett Pub., c1996. xvii, 356 p.
96-009388          575.01/62          0872202852
   *Evolution (Biology)  Natural selection.*

**QH366 Evolution — General works, treatises, and textbooks — 1861-1969**

**QH366.D6 1951**
**Dobzhansky, Theodosius Grigorievich,**
   Genetics and the origin of species.  New York, Columbia University Press, 1951. x, 364 p.
51-014816          575
   *Evolution (Biology)*

**QH366.E47**
**Ehrlich, Paul R.**
   The process of evolution [by] Paul R. Ehrlich [and] Richard W. Holm. Illustrated by Anne H. Ehrlich. New York, McGraw-Hill [1963] xvi, 347 p.
63-015891          575
   *Evolution (Biology)  Genetics.*

**QH366.H85 1943**
**Huxley, Julian,**
   Evolution, the modern synthesis, by Julian Huxley. New York, Harper [c1942] 645 p.
43004332          575.01
   *Evolution.  Evolution.*

**QH366.2 Evolution — General works, treatises, and textbooks — 1970-**

**QH366.2.A87 1979b**
**Attenborough, David,**
   Life on Earth : a natural history / David Attenborough. Boston : Little, Brown, c1979. 319 p. :
79-090108          575          0316057452
   *Evolution (Biology)  Zoology -- Miscellanea.*

**QH366.2.A933 1989**
**Avers, Charlotte J.**
   Process and pattern in evolution / Charlotte J. Avers. New York : Oxford University Press, 1989. xvi, 590 p. :
88-005368          575          0195052757
   *Evolution (Biology)*

**QH366.2.C39 1990**
   Causes of evolution : a paleontological perspective / edited by Robert M. Ross and Warren D. Allmon ; with a foreword by Stephen Jay Gould. Chicago : University of Chicago Press, 1990. xiii, 479 p.
90-011049          575          0226728234
   *Evolution (Biology)  Paleontology.*

# Academic Libraries QH366.2.W47 1991

**QH366.2.D67 2000**
**Dover, G. A.**
Dear Mr. Darwin : letters on the evolution of life and human nature / Gabriel Dover. Berkeley : University of California Press, c2000. xvi, 268 p. :
00-042615 576.8 0520227905
*Evolution (Biology) Quantum theory.*

**QH366.2.E52 1989**
**Eldredge, Niles.**
Macroevolutionary dynamics : species, niches, and adaptive peaks / Niles Eldredge. New York : McGraw-Hill, c1989. xii, 226 p. :
88-032585 575 0070194742
*Evolution (Biology)*

**QH366.2.E535 1999**
**Eldredge, Niles.**
The pattern of evolution / Niles Eldredge. New York : W.H. Freeman, c1999. 219 p. :
98-034754 576.8 0716730464
*Evolution (Biology)*

**QH366.2.G655 1994**
**Goodwin, Brian C.**
How the leopard changed its spots : the evolution of complexity / Brian Goodwin. New York : C. Scribner's Sons, c1994. xvi, 252 p. :
94-016891 575 0025447106
*Evolution (Biology) Morphology. Self-organizing systems.*

**QH366.2.G657 1995**
**Gordon, Malcolm S.**
Invasions of the land : the transitions of organisms from aquatic to terrestrial life / Malcolm S. Gordon and Everett C. Olson. New York : Columbia University Press, c1995. xv, 312 p. :
94-020344 575 023106876X
*Evolution (Biology) Adaptation (Biology)*

**QH366.2.G66 1983**
**Gould, Stephen Jay.**
Hen's teeth and horse's toes / Stephen Jay Gould. New York : Norton, c1983. 413 p. :
82-022259 575 0393017168
*Evolution (Biology)*

**QH366.2.G663 2002**
**Gould, Stephen Jay.**
The structure of evolutionary theory / Stephen Jay Gould. Cambridge, Mass. : Belknap Press of Harvard University Press, 2002. xxii, 1433 p. :
576.8 21 0674006135
*Evolution (Biology) Punctuated equilibrium (Evolution)*

**QH366.2.J65 1991**
**Johnson, Phillip E.,**
Darwin on trial / Phillip E. Johnson. Washington, D.C. : Regnery Gateway ; c1991. 195 p. ;
90-026218 575 0895265354
*Evolution (Biology)*

**QH366.2.L375 2001**
**Larson, Edward J.**
Evolution's workshop : God and science on the Galapagos Islands / Edward J. Larson. New York : Basic Books, 2001. p. cm.
00-065159 576.8/09866/5 0465038107
*Evolution (Biology) -- Galapagos Islands. Evolution.*

**QH366.2.M36**
**Margulis, Lynn,**
Symbiosis in cell evolution : life and its environment on the early Earth / Lynn Margulis. San Francisco : W. H. Freeman, c1981. xxii, 419 p.
80-026695 577 0716712555
*Cells -- Evolution. Life -- Origin. Symbiosis.*

**QH366.2.M3933 2001**
**Mayr, Ernst,**
What evolution is / Ernst Mayr. New York : Basic Books, 2001. p. cm.
576.8 21
*Evolution (Biology)*

**QH366.2.M396 2001**
**McFadden, Johnjoe.**
Quantum evolution / Johnjoe McFadden. New York : W. W. Norton, 2001. 338 p. :
00-053320 576.8 0393050416
*Evolution (Biology) Molecular evolution. Natural selection.*

**QH366.2.M683 2001**
**Morris, Richard,**
The evolutionists : the struggle for Darwin's soul / Richard Morris. New York : W.H. Freeman, 2001. p. cm.
00-011832 576.8/2 071674094X
*Evolution (Biology) Quantum theory.*

**QH366.2.P428 1999**
**Pennock, Robert T.**
Tower of Babel : the evidence against the new creationism / Robert T. Pennock. Cambridge, Mass. : MIT Press, c1999. xviii, 429 p.
98-027286 576.8 026216180X
*Evolution (Biology) Evolution (Biology) -- Religious aspects -- Christianity. Creationism.*

**QH366.2.S386 1999**
**Schwartz, Jeffrey H.**
Sudden origins : fossils, genes, and the emergence of species / Jeffrey H. Schwartz. New York : Wiley, c1999. xi, 420 p. :
98-045724 576.8 0471329851
*Evolution (Biology) Homeobox genes. Fossils.*

**QH366.2.W47 1991**
**Wesson, Robert G.**
Beyond natural selection / Robert Wesson. Cambridge, Mass. : MIT Press, c1991. xv, 353 p. :
90-021977 575.01 0262231611
*Evolution. Natural selection. Adaptation (Biology)*

## QH367 Evolution — Popular works

**QH367.B35 2000**
**Barlow, Connie C.**
The ghosts of evolution : nonsensical fruit, missing partners, and other ecological anachronisms / Connie Barlow. New York : Basic Books, c2000. xi, 291 p. :
0465005519
*Evolution (Biology)*

**QH367.H96**
**Huxley, Julian,**
Evolution as a process. [Essays] edited by Julian Huxley, A. C. Hardy [and] H. B. Ford. London, Allen & Unwin [1954] 367 p.
54001781          575.04
*Evolution.*

**QH367.L4 1953**
**Leakey, L. S. B.**
Adam's ancestors ; an up-to-date outline of the old stone age (Palaeolithic) and what is kown about man's origin and evolution. London : Methuen & Co., 1953. 235 p. :
54001955
*Man -- Origin. Stone age. Man, Prehistoric.*

**QH367.L525 1998**
**Liebes, Sidney.**
A walk through time : from stardust to us : the evolution of life on earth / Sidney Liebes, Elisabet Sahtouris & Brian Swimme ; with Hewlett-Packard "Walk" exhibit text by Lois Brynes. New York : Wiley, c1998. 223 P. :
98-034495          576.8          0471317004
*Evolution (Biology) Life -- Origin. Geobiology.*

## QH367.5 Evolution — Phylogenetic relationships

**QH367.5.H66 1994**
Homology : the hierarchical basis of comparative biology / edited by Brian K. Hall. San Diego : Academic Press, c1994. xvi, 483 p. :
93-041646          574          0123189209
*Homology (Biology)*

**QH367.5.N48 1996**
New uses for new phylogenies / edited by Paul H. Harvey ... [et al.]. Oxford ; Oxford University Press, 1996. xi, 349 p. :
96-004800          575          0198549857
*Phylogeny -- Congresses.*

**QH367.5.N53 2001**
**Nielsen, Claus.**
Animal evolution : interrelationships of the living phyla / Claus Nielsen. 2nd ed. Oxford ; New York : Oxford University Press, 2001. x, 563 p. :
591.3/8 21
*Phylogeny. Evolution (Biology)*

## QH368 Evolution — Human evolution

**QH368.D6**
**Dobzhansky, Theodosius Grigorievich,**
Mankind evolving; the evolution of the human species. New Haven, Yale University Press, 1962. 381 p.
62-008243          575
*Human evolution. Human beings -- Origin. Human genetics.*

**QH368.E38**
**Eiseley, Loren C.,**
The immense journey. New York, Random House [1957] 210 p.
57-006657          575
*Human evolution.*

**QH368.H64**
**Howells, W. W.**
Ideas on human evolution, selected essays, 1949-1961. Cambridge, Harvard University Press, 1962. 555 p.
62-011399          573.2082
*Human beings -- Origin.*

## QH368.5 Evolution — Plant evolution (General)

**QH368.5.G7 1981**
**Grant, Verne.**
Plant speciation / Verne Grant. New York : Columbia University Press, 1981. xii, 563 p. :
81-006159          581.3/8          0231051123
*Plants -- Evolution. Plant species.*

## QH371-371.5 Evolution — Special aspects of the subject as whole

**QH371.B47 1990**
**Berra, Tim M.,**
Evolution and the myth of creationism : a basic guide to the facts in the evolution debate / Tim M. Berra. Stanford, Calif. : Stanford University Press, c1990. xvii, 198 p.
89-051484          213          0804715483
*Evolution (Biology) Creationism. Creationism -- Study and teaching -- United States.*

**QH371.B69 1986**
**Brooks, D. R.**
Evolution as entropy : toward a unified theory of biology / Daniel R. Brooks and E.O. Wiley. Chicago : University of Chicago Press, 1986. xiv, 335 p. ;
85-008544          575.01/6          0226075818
*Evolution (Biology) Entropy.*

## QH371.C73 1983

Coevolution / edited by Douglas J. Futuyma and Montgomery Slatkin ; with the assistance of Bruce R. Levin and Jonathan Roughgarden. Sunderland, Mass. : Sinauer Associates, c1983. x, 555 p. :
82-019496          575          0878932283
*Coevolution.*

## QH371.D93 1993

**Dyer, Betsey Dexter.**

Tracing the history of eukaryotic cells : the enigmatic smile / Betsey Dexter Dyer, Robert Alan Obar. New York : Columbia University Press, c1993. p. cm.
93-026798          574.87          0231075928
*Eukaryotic cells -- Evolution. Symbiosis. Evolution (Biology)*

## QH371.E44 1985

**Eldredge, Niles.**

Time frames : the rethinking of Darwinian evolution and the theory of punctuated equilibria / Niles Eldredge. New York : Simon and Schuster, c1985. 240 p. :
84-023632          575.01/62          0671495550
*Evolution (Biology) Punctuated equilibrium (Evolution)*

## QH371.G68

**Gould, Stephen Jay.**

Ontogeny and phylogeny / Stephen Jay Gould. Cambridge, Mass. : Belknap Press of Harvard University Press, 1977. ix, 501 p. :
76-045765          575.01          0674639405
*Phylogeny. Ontogeny.*

## QH371.K53 1983

**Kimura, Motoo,**

The neutral theory of molecular evolution / Motoo Kimura. Cambridge [Cambridgeshire] ; Cambridge University Press, 1983. xv, 367 p. :
82-022225          575.01/6          0521231094
*Molecular evolution.*

## QH371.L58 1990

**Little, Colin,**

The terrestrial invasion : an ecophysiological approach to the origins of land animals / Colin Little. Cambridge ; Cambridge University Press, 1990. ix, 304 p. :
89-017471          560/.45          0521334470
*Evolution (Biology) Adaption (Biology) Animal ecology.*

## QH371.L65 1988

**Loomis, William F.**

Four billion years : an essay on the evolution of genes and organisms / William F. Loomis. Sunderland, Mass. : Sinauer Associates, Inc., c1988. xvi, 286 p. :
88-001848          575          0878934758
*Evolution (Biology) Molecular evolution.*

## QH371.M28 1986

**Margulis, Lynn,**

Microcosmos : four billion years of evolution from our microbial ancestors / Lynn Margulis and Dorion Sagan ; foreword by Lewis Thomas. New York : Summit Books, c1986. 301 p. :
86-004432          575          0671441698
*Evolution (Biology) Microorganisms -- Evolution.*

## QH371.M33

**Mayr, Ernst,**

Animal species and evolution. Cambridge, Belknap Press of Harvard University Press, 1963. xiv, 797 p.
63-009552          575
*Species. Zoology -- Variation. Evolution (Biology)*

## QH371.M336 1991

**Mayr, Ernst,**

One long argument : Charles Darwin and the genesis of modern evolutionary thought / Ernst Mayr. Cambridge, Mass. : Harvard University Press, 1991. xiv, 195 p. :
91-011051          575          0674639057
*Darwin, Charles, -- 1809-1882.      Evolution (Biology) – Philosophy. Evolution (Biology)*

## QH371.M68 1997

**Mitton, Jeffry B.**

Selection in natural populations / Jeffry B. Mitton. Oxford ; Oxford University Press, 1997. xii, 240 p. :
96-049688          572.8/38          019506352X
*Molecular evolution. Natural selection. Enzymes -- Evolution.*

## QH371.P25 2001

**Palumbi, Stephen R.**

The evolution explosion : how humans cause rapid evolutionary change / Stephen R. Palumbi. New York : Norton, c2001. x, 277 p. :
00-067004          576.8          0393020118
*Evolution (Biology) Nature -- Effect of human beings on. Drug resistance in microorganisms.*

## QH371.R77 1986

**Ruse, Michael.**

Taking Darwin seriously : a naturalistic approach to philosophy / Michael Ruse. New York, NY : Blackwell, 1986. xv, 303 p. :
85-015094          128          0631135421
*Evolution (Biology) -- Philosophy.*

## QH371.5.Z55 1998

**Zimmer, Carl,**

At the water's edge : macroevolution and the transformation of life / Carl Zimmer. New York : Free Press, c1998. 290 p. :
97-029331          576.8          0684834901
*Macroevolution.*

## QH375 Evolution — Natural selection

**QH375.D36 2001**
**Davies, Paul Sheldon.**
   Norms of nature : naturalism and the nature of functions / Paul Sheldon Davies. Cambridge, Mass. : MIT Press, c2001. xiv, 234 p. ;
00-055403          570/.1     0262041871
   *Natural selection. Naturalism.*

**QH375.D376 1996**
**Dawkins, Richard,**
   Climbing mount improbable / Richard Dawkins ; original drawings by Lalla Ward. New York : Norton, 1996. xii, 340 p. :
96-019138          575.01/62     0393039307
   *Natural selection. Evolutionary genetics. Morphogenesis.*

**QH375.D38 1982**
**Dawkins, Richard,**
   The extended phenotype : the gene as the unit of selection / Richard Dawkins. Oxford [Oxfordshire] ; Freeman, c1982. viii, 307 p.
81-009889          575     0716713586
   *Natural selection. Gene expression. Genetics.*

**QH375.D38 1999**
**Dawkins, Richard,**
   The extended phenotype : the long reach of the gene / Richard Dawkins ; [with a new afterword by Daniel Dennett]. Rev. ed. Oxford ; New York : Oxford University Press, 1999. viii, 313 p. :
          576.8/2 21          0192880519
*Natural selection. Gene expression. Genetics. Evolution (Biology)*

**QH375.J66 1999**
**Jones, Steve,**
   Darwin's ghost : a radical scientific updating of The origin of species for the 21st century / Steve Jones. New York : Random House, c1999. p. cm.
99-053246          576.8/2          0375501037
   *Natural selection. Evolution (Biology)*

**QH375.W52 1992**
**Williams, George C.**
   Natural selection : domains, levels, and challenges / George C. Williams. New York : Oxford University Press, 1992. x, 208 p. :
91-038938          577.01/62          0195069323
   *Natural selection.*

## QH380 Evolution — Speciation

**QH380.K56 1993**
**King, Max.**
   Species evolution : the role of chromosome change / Max King. Cambridge ; Cambridge University Press, 1993. xxi, 336 p. :
92-033870          575.2          0521353084
   *Species. Variation (Biology) Mutation (Biology)*

## QH390 Evolution — Mutation in evolution. Evolutionary genetics

**QH390.R325 1996**
**Raff, Rudolf A.**
   The shape of life : genes, development, and the evolution of animal form / Rudolf A. Raff. Chicago : University of Chicago Press, 1996. xxiii, 520 p.
95-049224          575.1          0226702650
   *Evolutionary genetics.*

## QH395 Evolution — Heterochrony

**QH395.M36 1997**
**McNamara, Ken.**
   Shapes of time : the evolution of growth and development / Kenneth J. McNamara. Baltimore, Md. : Johns Hopkins University Press, 1997. xii, 342 p. :
96-029775          576.8          0801855713
   *Heterochrony (Biology)*

### QH401 Evolution — Variation — General works

**QH401.K55**
**King, James C.,**
   The biology of race [by] James C. King. New York, Harcourt Brace Jovanovich [1971] viii, 180 p.
70-145650          572/.3          0155054600
   *Variation (Biology) Race. Genetics.*

### QH421 Evolution — Hybridization. Hybrid zones — General works

**QH421.A76 1997**
**Arnold, Michael L.**
   Natural hybridization and evolution / Michael L. Arnold. New York : Oxford University Press, 1997. xiii, 215 p.
96-026496          575.1/32          0195099745
   *Hybridization. Evolution (Biology)*

### QH423 Evolution — Hybridization. Hybrid zones — Plants

**QH423.M5313 1965a**
**Mendel, Gregor,**
   Experiments in plant hybridisation. [Translation made by the Royal Horticultural Society of London] With a foreword by Paul C. Mangelsdorf. Cambridge, Harvard University Press, 1965. vii, 41 p.
67-009611
   *Plant genetics. Hybridization, Vegetable.*

## QH427 Genetics — Dictionaries and encyclopedias

**QH427.E53 1999**
Encyclopedia of genetics / editor, Jeffrey A. Knight ; project editor, Robert McClenaghan. Pasadena, Calif. : Salem Press, c1999. 2 v. (xx, 598
98-031952    576.5/03    089356978X
*Genetics -- Encyclopedias.*

**QH427.R54 1991**
**Rieger, Rigomar.**
Glossary of genetics : classical and molecular / R. Rieger, A. Michaelis, M.M. Green. Berlin ; Springer-Verlag, 1991. 553 p. ;
91-019956    575.1/03    3540520546
*Genetics -- Dictionaries. Molecular genetics -- Dictionaries.*

## QH428 Genetics — History — General works

**QH428.B69 1989**
**Bowler, Peter J.**
The Mendelian revolution : the emergence of hereditarian concepts in modern science and society / Peter J. Bowler. Baltimore : Johns Hopkins University Press, 1989. viii, 207 p.
89-030914    575.1/09    0801838886
*Mendel, Gregor, -- 1822-1884. Genetics -- History. Biology -- History.*

**QH428.B766 2001**
**Brookes, Martin,**
Fly : the unsung hero of twentieth-century science / Martin Brookes, 1st ed. New York : Ecco, c2001. 215 p. :
    576.5/09 21    0066212510
*Genetics -- History. Drosophila melanogaster.*

**QH428.K448 2000**
**Keller, Evelyn Fox,**
The century of the gene / Evelyn Fox Keller. Cambridge, Mass. : Harvard University Press, c2000. 186 p. :
00-038319    576.5    0674003721
*Genetics -- History -- 20th century.*

**QH428.K45 1995**
**Keller, Evelyn Fox,**
Refiguring life : metaphors of twentieth-century biology / Evelyn Fox Keller. New York : Columbia University Press, c1995. xix, 134 p. :
94-044222    575.1/09    0231102046
*Genetics -- History. Biology -- Technological innovations.*

**QH428.W35 1997**
**Wallace, Bruce,**
The study of gene action / Bruce Wallace and Joseph O. Falkinham III. Ithaca, N.Y. : Cornell University Press, 1997. xi, 260 p. :
96-052356    576.5/09    0801432650
*Genetics -- History. Genes -- History.*

## QH429.2 Genetics — Biography — Individual, A-Z

**QH429.2.J33.A313 1988**
**Jacob, Francois,**
The statue within : an autobiography / Francois Jacob ; translated by Franklin Philip. New York : Basic Books, 1988. vi, 326 p. ;
87-047780    575.1/092/4    0465082238
*Jacob, Francois, -- 1920- Geneticists -- France -- Biography. Molecular biologists -- France -- Biography.*

**QH429.2.M38**
**Comfort, Nathaniel C.**
The tangled field : Barbara McClintock's search for the patterns of genetic control / Nathaniel C. Comfort. Cambridge, Mass. : Harvard University Press, 2001. x, 337 p. :
00-069712    576.5/092    0674004566
*McClintock, Barbara, -- 1902- Women geneticists – United States -- Biography.*

## QH430 Genetics — General works, treatises, and textbooks — General works

**QH430.D39 1995**
**Dawkins, Richard,**
River out of eden : a Darwinian view of life / Richard Dawkins ; illustrations by Lalla Ward. New York, NY : Basic Books, c1995. xiii, 172 p.
94-037146    575    0465016065
*Genetics. Evolution.*

**QH430.D96 1992**
The Dynamic genome : Barbara McClintock's ideas in the century of genetics / edited by Nina Fedoroff, David Botstein. [Cold Spring Harbor, N.Y.] : Cold Spring Harbor Laboratory Press, 1992. vii, 422 p. :
92-010074    575.1/092    087969422X
*McClintock, Barbara, -- 1902- Genetics. Women geneticists -- United States -- Biography.*

**QH430.J35 1999**
**Jain, H. K.**
Genetics : principles, concepts, and implications / H.K. Jain. Enfield, NH : Science Publishers, 1999. xv, 438 p. :
99-035445    576.5    1578080541
*Genetics.*

**QH430.L487 2000**
**Lewin, Benjamin.**
Genes VII / Benjamin Lewin. Oxford ; New York : Oxford University Press, 2000. xvii, 990 p. :
    576.5 21    019879276X
*Genetics. Genes.*

**QH430.N46 1995**
**Nelkin, Dorothy.**
The DNA mystique : the gene as a cultural icon / Dorothy Nelkin, M. Susan Lindee. New York : Freeman, c1995. x, 276 p. :
94-048711    304.5    0716727099
*Genetics -- Folklore. DNA -- Folklore. Genes -- Folklore.*

**QH430.W344 1992**
**Wallace, Bruce,**
The search for the gene / Bruce Wallace. Ithaca : Cornell University Press, 1992. ix, 224 p. :
92-004174          575.1          0801426804
*Genetics.*

## QH431 Genetics — General works, treatises, and textbooks — Human genetics

**QH431.A1.A3**
Advances in genetics. New York, Academic Press, 1947- v.
47-030313          575.082
*Genetics. Genetics -- yearbooks.*

**QH431.A72**
**Asimov, Isaac,**
The genetic code. New York, Orion Press 1963, c1962] 187 p.
63-012156          575.12
*Genetics -- Popular works. Genetic code.*

**QH431.B226 2001**
**Barash, David P.**
Revolutionary biology : the new, gene-centered view of life / David P. Barash. New Brunswick, NJ : Transaction Publishers, c2001. vii, 213 p. ;
01-017123          599.93/5          0765800675
*Human genetics -- Popular works. Medical genetics -- Popular works. Genetic engineering -- Popular works.*

**QH431.C395 1994**
**Cavalli-Sforza, L. L.**
The history and geography of human genes / L. Luca Cavalli-Sforza, Paolo Menozzi, Alberto Piazza. Princeton, N.J. : Princeton University Press, c1994. xi, 541, 518
93-019339          573.21/5          0691087504
*Human population genetics -- History. Human evolution. Human geography.*

**QH431.F8765 2000**
From chance to choice : genetics and justice / Allen Buchanan ... [et al.]. Cambridge, U.K. ; Cambridge University Press, c2000. xiv, 398 p. ;
99-024025          174/.25          0521660017
*Genetic engineering -- Moral and ethical aspects. Eugenics -- Moral and ethical aspects. Medical ethics -- Moral and ethical aspects.*

**QH431.H353 1999**
**Hawley, R. Scott.**
The human genome : a user's guide / R. Scott Hawley, Catherine A. Mori. San Diego, Calif. : Academic Press, c1999. xix, 415 p. :
98-085438          611/.01816          0123334608
*Human genome. Human gene mapping. Human genetics.*

**QH431.H837 1994**
The Human Genome Project : deciphering the blueprint of heredity / edited by Necia Grant Cooper ; foreword by Paul Berg. Mill Valley, Calif. : University Science Books, c1994. x, 360 p. :
93-085290          0935702296
*Human gene mapping. Human genetics. Genome, Human – popular works*

**QH431.H8374 1999**
The human inheritance : Genes, language, and evolution / edited by Bryan Sykes. Oxford ; Oxford University Press, 1999. 195 p. 23 cm.
99-015223          599.93/5          0198502745
*Human genetics. Human evolution. Language and languages – Origin.*

**QH431.H89**
**Huxley, Julian,**
Heredity, East and West; Lysenko and world science. New York, H. Schuman [1949] x, 246 p.
49050254          575.1
*Lysenko, Trofim Denisovich, -- 1898-1976.          Genetics.*

**QH431.K54 1996**
**Kitcher, Philip,**
The lives to come : the genetic revolution and human possibilities / Philop Kitcher. New York : Simon & Schuster, c1996. 381 p. :
573.2/1 20          0684800551
*Human genetic -- Popular works. Human Genome Project – Popular works.*

**QH431.M3613**
**Medvedev, Zhores A.,**
The rise and fall of T. D. Lysenko [by] Zhores A. Medvedev. Translated by I. Michael Lerner, with the editorial assistance of Lucy G. Lawrence. New York, Columbia University Press, 1969. xvii, 284 p.
79-077519          575.1/0947
*Lysenko, Trofim Denisovich, -- 1898-          Genetics.*

**QH431.P34 1998**
**Paul, Diane B.,**
The politics of heredity : essays on eugenics, biomedicine, and the nature-nurture debate / Diane B. Paul. Albany : State University of New York Press, c1998. viii, 219 p.
97-045212          174/.25          079143821X
*Human genetics -- Political aspects -- History. Eugenics -- Political aspects -- History. Nature and nurture -- Political aspects – History.*

**QH431.R38 2000**
**Reilly, Philip,**
Abraham Lincoln's DNA and other adventures in genetics / Philip R. Reilly. Cold Spring Harbor, NY : Cold Spring Harbor Laboratory Press, c2000. xx, 339 p. :
00-029467          599.93/5          0879695803
*Human genetics -- Popular works. Medical genetics -- Popular works. Genetic engineering -- Popular works.*

**QH431.R475 1999**
**Ridley, Matt.**
  Genome : the autobiography of a species in 23 chapters / Matt Ridley. 1st U.S. ed. New York : HarperCollins, c1999. 344 p. :
         599.93/5 21        0060194979
*Human genome -- Popular works.  Human genetics – Popular works.*

**QH431.S94**
**Sutton, H. Eldon**
  Genes, enzymes, and inherited diseases.  New York, Holt, Rinehart and Winston [1961] 120 p.
61-007862        575.12
  *Genetics.  Medical genetics.*

**QH431.W368 1970**
**Watson, James D.,**
  Molecular biology of the gene [by] J. D. Watson. With illus. by Keith Roberts. New York, W. A. Benjamin, 1970. xxi, 662 p.
72-134173        575.2/1        0805396039
  *Molecular biology.  Molecular genetics.*

## QH432 Genetics — General works, treatises, and textbooks — Animal genetics (General)

**QH432.S56 1995**
**Silver, Lee M.**
  Mouse genetics : concepts and applications / Lee M. Silver. New York : Oxford University Press, 1995. xiii, 362 p.
94-034127        599.32/33        0195075544
  *Mice -- Genetics.  Mice -- Breeding.  Mice as laboratory animals.*

## QH434 Genetics — General works, treatises, and textbooks — Microbial genetics (General)

**QH434.B57 1988**
**Birge, Edward Asahel**
  Bacterial and bacteriophage genetics :an introduction / Edward A. Birge. 2nd ed. New York : Springer-Verlag, c1988. xvi, 414 p. :
         589.9/015 19        0387966447
*Bacterial genetics.  Bacteriophages -- genetics.  Bacteria -- genetics. Bacteriophages -- genetics.*

**QH434.B76 1990**
**Brock, Thomas D.**
  The emergence of bacterial genetics / by Thomas D. Brock. Cold Spring Harbor, N.Y. : Cold Spring Harbor Laboratory Press, 1990. xix, 346 p. :
90-001828        589.9/015        0879693509
  *Bacterial genetics.*

**QH434.L56 1984**
**Lin, E. C. C.**
  Bacteria, plasmids, and phages : an introduction to molecular biology / E.C.C. Lin, Richard Goldstein, Michael Syvanen. Cambridge, Mass. : Harvard University Press, 1984. ix, 316 p. :
83-022784        576/.139        0674581652
  *Microbial genetics.  Molecular genetics.  Bacteria -- Genetics.*

## QH437 Genetics — Popular works

**QH437.D38 1989**
**Dawkins, Richard,**
  The selfish gene / Richard Dawkins. New ed. Oxford ; New York : Oxford University Press, 1989. xi, 352 p. :
         591.5 20        0192177737
*Genetics.  Evolution (Biology) Sociobiology.*

**QH437.T83 1995**
**Tudge, Colin.**
  The engineer in the garden : genes and genetics : from the idea of heredity to the creation of life / Colin Tudge. New York : Hill and Wang, 1995. xii, 388 p. :
94-006076        575.1        0809042592
  *Genetics -- Popular works.  Genetic engineering – Popular works.*

**QH437.T833 2001**
**Tudge, Colin.**
  The impact of the gene : from Mendel's peas to designer babies / Colin Tudge. 1st American ed. New York : Hill and Wang, 2001. 375 p. :
         576.5 21        0374175233
*Genetics -- Popular works.*

## QH438 Genetics — Addresses, essays, lectures

**QH438.W38 2000**
**Watson, James D.,**
  A passion for DNA : genes, genomes, and society / James D. Watson ; with an introduction, afterword, and annotations by Walter B. Gratzer. Cold Spring Harbor, N.Y. : Cold Spring Harbor Laboratory Press, c2000. xx, 250 p. ;
99-087131        572.8/6        0879695811
  *Genetics.  Medical genetics.  Science -- Research -- Moral and ethical aspects.*

## QH438.4 Genetics — Special aspects of the subject as whole

**QH438.4.B55.A95 1994**
**Avise, John C.**
  Molecular markers, natural history and evolution / John C. Avise. New York : Chapman & Hall, 1994. xiv, 511 p. :
93-020406        574.87/328        0412037718
  *Biochemical markers.  Molecular evolution.*

**QH438.4.M3.C35 1995**
  Calculating the secrets of life : applications of the mathematical sciences in molecular biology / Eric S. Lander and Michael S. Waterman, editors. Washington, D.C. : National Academy Press, 1995. xii, 285 p. :
94-037628        574.8/8/0151        0309048869
  *Genetics -- Mathematical models.  Genetics -- Statistical methods. Molecular biology -- Mathematical models.*

**QH438.4.M33.L36 1997**
**Lange, Kenneth.**
Mathematical and statistical methods for genetic analysis / Kenneth Lange. New York : Springer, 1997. xii, 265 p. :
96-049533        576.5/01/51        0387949097
*Genetics -- Mathematics. Genetics -- Statistical methods.*

## QH438.5 Genetics — Heredity and environment. Nature and nurture

**QH438.5.G68 1992**
**Gottlieb, Gilbert,**
Individual development and evolution : the genesis of novel behavior / Gilbert Gottlieb. New York : Oxford University Press, 1992. xii, 231 p. :
91-006714        575        0195068939
*Nature and nurture. Behavior evolution.*

**QH438.5.M66 2002**
**Moore, David S. (David Scott),**
The dependent gene : the fallacy of nature/nurture/ David Scott Moore. 1st ed. New York : Times Books, 2002. vi, 312 p. :
        576.5/3 21        0716740249
*Nature and nurture. Phenotype.*

## QH438.7 Genetics — Social and moral aspects

**QH438.7.C65 1999**
**Condit, Celeste Michelle,**
The meanings of the gene : public debates about human heredity / Celeste Michelle Condit. Madison : University of Wisconsin Press, c1999. xi, 325 p. ;
99-006274        304.5        0299163601
*Genetics -- Social aspects -- United States -- Hiatory -- 20th century.. Genetics -- Public opinion -- History -- 20th century. Genetics in mass media -- History -- 20th century.*

**QH438.7.P485 2001**
**Peterson, James C.,**
Genetic turning points : the ethics of human genetic intervention / James C. Peterson. Grand Rapids, Mich. : W.B. Eerdmans Pub., 2001. xvi, 364 p. ;
00-067687        174/.28        0802849202
*Human genetics -- Religious aspects -- Christianity. Medical genetics -- Religious aspects -- Christianity. Genetic engineering – Religious aspects -- Christianity.*

**QH438.7.W56 1998**
**Wingerson, Lois.**
Unnatural selection : the promise and the power of human gene research / Lois Wingerson. New York : Bantam Books, c1998. xiii, 399 p.
98-028546        599.93/5        0553097091
*Human genetics -- Social aspects. Human genetics –Moral and ethical aspects. Medical genetics -- Social aspects.*

## QH441.2 Genetics — Data processing

**QH441.2.M55 1996**
**Mitchell, Melanie.**
An introduction to genetic algorithms / Melanie Mitchell. Cambridge, Mass. : MIT Press, c1996. viii, 205 p.
95-024489        575.1/01/13        0262133164
*Genetics -- Computer simulation. Genetics -- Mathematical models.*

**QH441.2.M68 2001**
**Mount, Davi d W.**
Bioinformatics : sequence and genome analysis /David W. Mount. Cold Spring Harbor, N.Y. : Cold Spring Harbor Laboratory Press, c2001. xii, 564 p. :
00-060252        572.8/633        0879695978
*Genetics -- Data processing. Bioinformatics. Nucleotide sequence.*

## QH442 Genetics — Molecular genetics. Genetic engineering — General works

**QH442.A43 1996**
**Aldridge, Susan.**
The thread of life : the story of genes and genetic engineering / Susan Aldridge. Cambridge [England] ; Cambridge University Press, 1996. vii, 258 p. :
95-007354        575.1/0724        0521465427
*Genetic engineering. Genetics. DNA.*

**QH442.A67 1998**
**Appleyard, Bryan.**
Brave new worlds : staying human in the genetic future / Bryan Appleyard. New York : Viking, 1998. 198 p. ;
98-010243        174/.25        0670869899
*Genetic engineering. Genetic engineering -- Moral and ethical aspects.*

**QH442.B355 2001**
**Baldi, Pierre.**
The shattered self : the end of natural evolution /Pierre Baldi. Cambridge, Mass. : MIT Press, c2001. ix, 245 p. :
00-048183        599.93        0262025027
*Genetic engineering. Genetic engineering -- Moral and ethical aspects.*

**QH442.B69 2001**
**Boylan, Michael,**
Genetic engineering : science and ethics on the new frontier / Michael Boylan, Kevin E. Brown. Upper Saddle River, N.J. : Prentice Hall, c2001. xi, 196 p. :
        174/.957 21        0130910856
*Genetic engineering -- Moral and ethical aspects. Medical genetics – Moral and ethical aspects.*

**QH442.M5425 1999**
**Miesfeld, Roger L.**
  Applied molecular genetics / Roger L. Miesfeld. New York :
John Wiley, c1999. xv, 293 p. :
98-029973          572.8          0471156760
  *Molecular genetics -- Methodology. Genetic engineering --*
*Methodology.*

**QH442.O42 1994**
**Old, R. W.**
  Principles of gene manipulation : an introduction to genetic
engineering / R.W. Old, S.B. Primrose. Oxford : Blackwell
Scientific, 1994. vi, 474 p. :
94-000932          575.1/0724          0632037121
  *Genetic engineering. Genetic Engineering. DNA, Recombinant.*

**QH442.R87 1995**
**Russo, V. E. A.**
  Genetic engineering : dreams and nightmares / Enzo Russo
and David Cove. Oxford ; W.H. Freeman/Spektrum, c1995.
xii, 243 p. :
95-016150          174/.25          0716745461
  *Genetic engineering. Genetic engineering -- Social aspects.*
*Genetic engineering -- Moral and ethical aspects.*

**QH442.S476 1999**
**Shannon, Thomas A.**
  Genetic engineering : a documentary history / edited by
Thomas A. Shannon. Westport, Conn. : Greenwood Press,
1999. xxxi, 282 p.
98-046808          660.6/5/09          0313304572
  *Genetic engineering -- History -- Sources.*

**QH442.W37**
**Watson, James D.,**
  The DNA story : a documentary history of gene cloning /
James D. Watson, John Tooze. San Francisco : W.H. Freeman
and Co., c1981. xii, 605 p. :
81-003299          574.87/3282          071671292X
  *Recombinant DNA -- Research -- History -- Addresses, essays,*
*lectures. Cloning -- Research -- History -- Addresses, essays, lectures.*

## QH442.2 Genetics — Molecular genetics. Genetic engineering — Cloning

**QH442.2.C55 1998**
  Clones and clones : facts and fantasies about human cloning
/ edited by Martha C. Nussbaum and Cass R. Sunstein. New
York : Norton, c1998. 351 p. ;
97-051781          174/.25          0393046486
  *Human cloning -- Social aspects. Human cloning -- Moral and*
*ethical aspects.*

**QH442.2.C5678 2001**
  Cloning : responsible science or technomadness? / edited by
Michael Ruse & Aryne Sheppard. Amherst, N.Y. : Prometheus
Books, 2001. 322 p. :
          174/.966 21          1573928364
*Cloning -- Social aspects.*

**QH442.2.D75 1997**
**Drlica, Karl.**
  Understanding DNA and gene cloning : a guide for the
curious / Karl Drlica. New York : Wiley, c1997. xvi, 329 p. :
96-023077          574.87/3282          047113774X
  *Molecular cloning. Recombinant DNA. Genetic engineering.*

**QH442.2.H875 2000**
  Human cloning : science, ethics, and public policy / edited
by Barbara MacKinnon. Urbana : University of Illinois Press,
c2000. 171 p. :
99-050519          174/.25          0252024915
  *Human cloning -- Moral and ethical aspects.*

**QH442.2.K37 1998**
**Kass, Leon.**
  The ethics of human cloning / Leon R. Kass and James Q.
Wilson. Washington, D.C. : AEI Press, 1998. xxi, 101 p. ;
98-018223          174/.25          0844740500
  *Human cloning -- Moral and ethical aspects. Human reproductive*
*technology -- Moral and ethical aspects.*

**QH442.2.L8313 1993**
**Lucotte, Gerard.**
  Introduction to molecular cloning techniques / by Gerard
Lucotte and Francois Baneyx. New York : VCH Publishers,
c1993. xvi, 298 p. :
93-022418          574.87/328/0724          1560816139
  *Molecular cloning -- Laboratory manuals.*

**QH442.2.M32 1985**
**McKinnell, Robert Gilmore.**
  Cloning of frogs, mice, and other animals / Robert Gilmore
McKinnell. Minneapolis : University of Minnesota Press,
c1985. ix, 127 p. :
85-002541          596/.016          0816613605
  *Cloning. Cell nuclei -- Transplantation. Embryology,*
*Experimental.*

**QH442.2.S26 2001**
**Sambrook, Joseph.**
  Molecular cloning : a laboratory manual / Joseph Sambrook,
David W. Russell. 3rd ed. Cold Spring Harbor, N.Y. : Cold
Spring Harbor Laboratory Press, c2001. 3 v. :
          572.8 21          0879695773
*Molecular cloning -- Laboratory manuals. Cloning, Molecular --*
*Laboratory Manuals.*

**QH442.2.W545 1999**
**Wilmut, Ian.**
  The second creation : Dolly and the age of biological control
/ by Ian Wilmut and Keith Campbell and Colin Tudge. New
York : Farrar, Straus and Giroux, 1999. p. cm.
99-050032          174/.957          0374141231
  *Cloning. Cloning -- Moral and ethical aspects. Dolly (Sheep)*

## QH443 Genetics — Recombination mechanisms — General works

**QH443.L43 1996**
**Leach, David**
Genetic recombination / David R.F. Leach. Oxford [England] ; Blackwell Science, 1996. viii, 192 p.
95-021294        575.1/3        0632038616
*Genetic recombination.*

## QH445.2 Genetics — Recombination mechanisms — Crossing over

**QH445.2.C66 1994**
**Cook-Deegan, Robert M.**
The gene wars : science, politics, and the human genome / Robert Cook-Deegan. New York : W.W. Norton & Co., c1994. 416 p. :
93-010762        573.2/12        0393035727
*Human gene mapping.*

**QH445.2.D37 2001**
**Davies, Kevin,**
Cracking the genome : inside the race to unlock human DNA / Kevin Davies. New York : Free Press, c2001. 310 p. :
599.93 21        0743204794
*Human Genome Project -- Popular works. Human genome – Popular works.*

**QH445.2.H866 2001**
The Human Genome Project and minority communities : ethical, social, and political dilemmas / edited by Raymond A. Zilinskas and Peter J. Balint. Westport, Conn. : Praeger, 2001. xiii, 144 p.
00-032390        599.93/5        0275969614
*Minorities -- United States -- Congresses. Genome, Human -- Congresses. Ethics -- Congresses.*

**QH445.2.H87 1996**
The Human Genome Project and the future of health care / edited by Thomas H. Murray, Mark A. Rothstein, and Robert F. Murray, Jr. Bloomington : Indiana University Press, c1996. xii, 248 p. :
96-001718        174/.2        0253332133

## QH447 Genetics — Recombination mechanisms — Genes. Alleles. Genome

**QH447.H45 1996**
**Heller, Jan Cristian.**
Human genome research and the challenge of contingent future persons : toward an impersonal theocentric approach to value / Jan Christian Heller. Omaha, Neb. : Creighton University Press ; c1996. x, 179 p. ;
95083920        1881871207
*Human gene mapping -- Moral and ethical aspects. Human genome -- Research.*

**QH447.M6713 2001**
**Morange, Michel.**
The misunderstood gene / Michel Morange ; translated by Matthew Cobb. Cambridge, MA : Harvard University Press, 2001. ix, 222 p. ;
00-053916        572.8/6        0674003365
*Human genome. Human gene mapping.*

**QH447.Z94 2001**
**Zweiger, Gary.**
Transducing the genome : information, anarchy, and revolution in the biomedical sciences / Gary Zweiger. New York : McGraw-Hill, c2001. xv, 269 p. :
00-049628        599.93/5        0071369805
*Genes -- Popular works. Molecular genetics -- Popular works.*

## QH450.2 Genetics — Recombination mechanisms — Genetic regulation. Gene expression

**QH450.2.K39 2000**
**Kay, Lily E.**
Who wrote the book of life? : a history of the genetic code / Lily E. Kay. Stanford, Calif. : Stanford University Press, c2000. xix, 441 p. :
99-039446        572.8/633        0804733848
*Genetic code -- Research -- History.*

**QH450.2.W37**
**Watson, James D.,**
The double helix : a personal account of the discovery of the structure of DNA / James D. Watson ; edited by Gunther S. Stent. New York : Norton, c1980. xxv, 298 p. :
80-010770        574.87/3282        039301245X
*Watson, James D., -- 1928- . -- Double Helix -- Reviews. Genetic code. DNA. Molecular biology -- History.*

# QH453 Genetics — Developmental genetics

**QH453.B53 2000**
**Bier, Ethan.**
The coiled spring : how life begins / Ethan Bier. Cold Spring Harbor, N.Y. : Cold Spring Harbor Laboratory Press, 2000. p. cm.
00-022975        571.8/5        0879695625
*Developmental genetics.*

# QH455 Genetics — Population genetics

**QH455.G467 1989**
Genetics, speciation, and the Founder principle / edited by Luther Val Giddings, Kenneth Y. Kaneshiro, Wyatt W. Anderson. New York : Oxford University Press, 1989. xviii, 373 p.
88-015249        575.1/5        0195043154
*Population genetics. Population biology. Species.*

## QH455.G56 1991
**Gillespie, John H.**
    The causes of molecular evolution / John H. Gillespie. New York : Oxford University Press, 1991. xiv, 336 p. :
91-016709        575.1/5        0195068831
    *Population genetics. Variation (Biology)*

## QH455.G565 1998
**Gillespie, John H.**
    Population genetics : a concise guide / John H. Gillespie. Baltimore, Md : The Johns Hopkins University Press, c1998. xiv, 174 p. ;
97-019509        576.5/8        0801857546
    *Population genetics.*

## QH455.L48
**Lewontin, Richard C.,**
    The genetic basis of evolutionary change [by] R. C. Lewontin. New York, Columbia University Press, 1974. xiii, 346 p.
73-019786        575.1    0231033923
    *Population genetics. Evolution (Biology) Variation (Biology)*

## QH456 Genetics — Ecological genetics

### QH456.H64 1991
**Hoffmann, Ary A.**
    Evolutionary genetics and environmental stress / Ary A. Hoffmann and Peter A. Parsons. Oxford ; Oxford University Press, 1991. ix, 284 p. :
90-040177        575.1/3       019857732X
    *Ecological genetics. Evolutionary genetics. Population genetics.*

## QH457 Genetics — Behavior genetics

### QH457.M67 1999
**Morrison, Reg.**
    The spirit in the gene : humanity's proud illusion and the laws of nature / Reg Morrison ; with a foreword by Lynn Margulis. Ithaca : Comstock Pub. Associates, a division of Cornell 1999. xviii, 286 p.
99-028205        599.93    0801436516
    *Behavior genetics. Human evolution. Human ecology.*

### QH457.P57 1990
**Plomin, Robert,**
    Nature and nurture : an introduction to human behavioral genetics / Robert Plomin. Pacific Grove, Ca. : Brooks/Cole Pub. Co., c1990. ix, 159 p. :
89-009725        155.42/2    0534107680
    *Behavior genetics. Human genetics. Human behavior.*

## QH467 Genetics — Mutations — Genetic repair mechanisms

### QH467.F748 1997
**Friedberg, Errol C.**
    Correcting the blueprint of life : an historical account of the discovery of DNA repair mechanisms / Errol C. Friedberg. Plainview, N.Y. : Cold Spring Harbor Laboratory Press, c1997. xi, 210 p. :
96-045981        574.87/3282    0879695072
    *DNA repair -- Research -- History.*

## QH470 Genetics — Experimental organisms, A-Z

### QH470.D7.G46
    The Genetics and biology of Drosophila / edited by M. Ashburner and E. Novitski. London ; Academic Press, 1976-c1986 v. 1a-c, 2a-d
75-019614        595.7/74    0120649012
    *Drosophila melanogaster. Drosophila melanogaster – Genetics. Drosophila.*

## QH471 Reproduction — General works, treatises, and textbooks

### QH471.F69 1986
**Forsyth, Adrian.**
    A natural history of sex : the ecology and evolution of sexual behavior / Adrian Forsyth. New York : Scribner's, c1986. xiv, 190 p. ;
86-001826        591.5/6    0684183382
    *Sex (Biology) Sex (Psychology) Behavior evolution.*

## QH481 Reproduction — Sexual — General works, treatises, and textbooks

### QH481.M27 1986
**Margulis, Lynn,**
    Origins of sex : three billion years of genetic recombination / Lynn Margulis, Dorion Sagan. New Haven : Yale University Press, c1986. xiii, 258 p.
85-008385        575.1    0300033400
    *Sex (Biology) Genetic recombination.*

## QH485 Reproduction — Sexual — Fertilization

### QH485.B53 1985
    Biology of fertilization / edited by Charles B. Metz, Alberto Monroy. Orlando : Academic Press, 1985. 3 v. :
84-010982        574.1/66    0124926010
    *Fertilization (Biology) Fertilization.*

## QH491 Development. Morphogenesis

**QH491.B35 1999**
**Ball, Philip,**
The self-made tapestry : pattern formation in nature / Philip Ball. Oxford [England] ; Oxford University Press, 1999. vi, 287 p. :
98-016650          571.3          0198502443
*Pattern formation (Biology) Symmetry.*

**QH491.B595 2001**
**Bonner, John Tyler.**
First signals : the evolution of multicellular development / John Tyler Bonner. Princeton : Princeton University Press, 2000. xi, 146 p. :
00-039976          571.8/35          0691070377
*Developmental biology. Developmental cytology. Cells -- Evolution.*

**QH491.W3**
**Waddington, C. H.**
New patterns in genetics and development. New York, Columbia University Press, 1962. 271 p.
62-012875          575.1081
*Genetics -- Addresses, essays, lectures. Embryology – Addresses, essays, lectures.*

## QH499 Regeneration

**QH499.H57 1991**
A History of regeneration research : milestones in the evolution of a science / edited by Charles E. Dinsmore. Cambridge [England] ; Cambridge University Press, 1991. x, 228 p. :
90-026181          574.3/1/09          0521392713
*Regeneration (Biology) -- History.*

## QH501 Life — General works, treatises, and textbooks

**QH501.A54 1995**
**Angier, Natalie.**
The beauty of the beastly : new views on the nature of life / Natalie Angier. Boston : Houghton Mifflin, 1995. xxii, 278 p.
94-049675          574          0395718163
*Life (Biology)*

**QH501.C33 1997**
**Cairns, John,**
Matters of life and death : perspectives on public health, molecular biology, cancer, and the prospects for the human race / John Cairns. Princeton, N.J. : Princeton University Press, c1997. xi, 257 p. :
96-018026          574.8/8          0691028729
*Life (Biology) Molecular biology. Cancer.*

**QH501.S37 1988**
**Scott, Andrew,**
Vital principles : the molecular mechanisms of life / Andrew Scott. Oxford, OX, UK ; B. Blackwell, 1988. viii, 216 p.
88-006129          574          0631153985
*Life (Biology) Molecular biology.*

**QH501.S54 2000**
**Skutch, Alexander Frank,**
Harmony and conflict in the living world / by Alexander F. Skutch ; illustrated by Dana Gardner. Norman : University of Oklahoma Press, c2000. xii, 216 p. :
99-055168          570/.1          0806132310
*Life (Biology)*

**QH501.S63 2000**
**Sole, Ricard V.,**
Signs of life : how complexity pervades biology / Ricard Sole and Brian Goodwin. New York : Basic Books, c2000. xi, 322 p., 4
00-049825          570          0465019277
*Life (Biology)*

## QH505 Life — Biophysics

**QH505.B397 1990**
**Bergethon, P. R.**
Biophysical chemistry : molecules to membranes / P.R. Bergethon, E.R. Simons. New York : Springer-Verlag, c1990. xiv, 340 p. :
89-026095          574.19          0387970533
*Biophysics. Biochemistry. Thermodynamics.*

**QH505.G5413 2001**
**Glaser, Roland.**
Biophysics / Roland Glaser. Berlin ; Springer, c2001. xvi, 361 p. :
00-030794          571.4          3540670882
*Biophysics.*

**QH505.M62 1991**
**Morowitz, Harold J.**
The thermodynamics of pizza / Harold J. Morowitz. New Brunswick : Rutgers University Press, c1991. vi, 247 p. ;
90-008674          500          0813516358
*Biophysics. Science.*

**QH505.V63 1994**
**Vogel, Steven,**
Life in moving fluids : the physical biology of flow / Steven Vogel. Princeton, N.J. : Princeton University Press, c1994. xiii, 467 p.
93-046149          574.19/1          0691034850
*Fluid mechanics. Biophysics.*

**QH505.Y43 1992**
**Yeargers, Edward K.**
Basic biophysics for biology / Edward K. Yeargers. Boca Raton : CRC Press, c1992. 202 p. :
92-007157          574.19/1          0849344247
*Biophysics.*

## QH506 Life — Molecular biology

**QH506.C74 1999**
**Creighton, Thomas E.,**
Encyclopedia of molecular biology / Thomas E. Creighton. New York : John Wiley, c1999. 4 v. (xix, 28
99-011575          572.8/03          0471153028
*Molecular biology -- Encyclopedias.*

**QH506.E246 2001**
**Echols, Harrison.**
Operators and promoters : the story of molecular biology and its creators / Harrison Echols ; edited by Carol A. Gross. Berkeley: University of California Press, c2001. xx, 466 p. :
00-061523          572.8/09          0520213319
*Molecular biology -- History.*

**QH506.F753 1997**
From genes to cells / Steven R. Bolsover ... [et al.]. New York : Wiley-Liss, c1997. xv, 424 p. :
96-028603          574.87     0471597929
*Molecular biology. Cytology.*

**QH506.I483 1996**
Integrative approaches to molecular biology / edited by Julio Collado-Vides, Boris Magasanik, and Temple F. Smith. Cambridge, Mass. : MIT Press, c1996. x, 345 p. :
95-046156          574.8/8          0262032392
*Molecular biology -- Congresses.*

**QH506.J3313 1998**
**Jacob, Francois,**
Of flies, mice, and men / Francois Jacob ; translated by Giselle Weiss. Cambridge, MA : Harvard University Press, 1998. 158 p. ;
98-007289          572.8/01          0674631110
*Molecular biology.*

**QH506.J83 1996**
**Judson, Horace Freeland.**
The eighth day of creation : makers of the revolution in biology / Horace Freeland Judson. Plainview, N.Y. : CSHL Press, 1996. xxii, 714 p.
95-045151          574.8/8/09          0879694777
*Molecular biology -- History.*

**QH506.L443 2000**
**Lewontin, Richard C.,**
The triple helix : gene, organism, and environment / Richard Lewontin. Cambridge, Mass. : Harvard University Press, 2000. 136 p. :
99-053879          572.8/01          0674001591
*Molecular biology -- Philosophy. Developmental biology -- Philosophy. Ecology -- Philosophy.*

**QH506.M7213 1998**
**Morange, Michel.**
A history of molecular biology / Michel Morange ; translated by Matthew Cobb. Cambridge, Mass. : Harvard University Press, 1998. 336 p. ;
97-047158          572.8/09          0674398556
*Molecular biology -- History.*

## QH507 Life — Information theory in biology

**QH507.O93 2000**
**Oyama, Susan.**
The ontogeny of information : developmental systems and evolution. 2nd ed., rev. and enl. / Susan Oyama ; foreword by Richard C. Lewontin. Durham, N.C. : Duke University Press, 2000. p. cm.
              576.8 21          0822324318
*Information theory in biology. Evolution (Biology)*

## QH510 Life — Bioenergetics

**QH510.H37 1986**
**Harold, Franklin M.**
The vital force : a study of bioenergetics / Franklin M. Harold. New York : W.H. Freeman, c1986. xviii, 577 p.
85-013640          574.19/121          0716717344
*Bioenergetics.*

## QH513 Life — Biomechanics

**QH513.P46 1992**
**Pennycuick, C. J.**
Newton rules biology : a physical approach to biological problems / C.J. Pennycuick. Oxford ; Oxford University Press, 1992. ix, 111 p. :
91-039081          591.1     0198540213
*Biomechanics. Biophysics. Animal mechanics.*

## QH518.5 Life — Anaerobiosis

**QH518.5.F46 1995**
**Fenchel, Tom.**
Ecology and evolution in anoxic worlds / Tom Fenchel, Bland J. Finlay. Oxford ; Oxford University Press, 1995. xii, 276 p. :
94-035058          574.1/28          0198548389
*Anaerobiosis.*

## QH527 Life — Chronobiology. Periodicity. Biorhythms

**QH527.G595 1988**
**Glass, Leon,**
From clocks to chaos : the rhythms of life / Leon Glass and Michael C. Mackey. Princeton, N.J. : Princeton University Press, c1988. xvii, 248 p.
87-032803          574.1/882/0151          0691084963
*Biological rhythms. Biological rhythms -- Mathematics.*

**QH527.W56 1987**
**Winfree, Arthur T.**
The timing of biological clocks / Arthur T. Winfree. New York : Scientific American Library : c1987. xi, 199 p. :
86-015602          574.1/882          071675018X
*Circadian rhythms. Biological rhythms.*

## QH540 Ecology — Societies, congresses, serial collections, yearbooks

**QH540.A23**
Advances in ecological research. London ; Academic Press, v. :
62-021479          574.5082
*Ecology.*

**QH540.B63 1997**
**Bocking, Stephen,**
Ecologists and environmental politics : a history of contemporary ecology / Stephen Bocking. New Haven : Yale University Press, c1997. xiv, 271 p. :
96-034071          574.5/09          0300067631
*Ecology -- History. Environmental policy -- History.*

## QH540.4 Ecology — Dictionaries and encyclopedias

**QH540.4.C66 1998**
A dictionary of ecology / edited by Michael Allaby. 2nd ed. Oxford ; New York : Oxford University Press, 1998. vi, 440 p. :
                    577/.02 21
*Ecology -- Dictionaries. Environmental sciences -- Dictionaries.*

**QH540.4.E52 1995**
Encyclopedia of environmental biology / editor-in-chief, William A. Nierenberg ; executive advisory board, Edward O. Wilson, Peter H. Raven, Isao Karube ; editorial advisory board, F.A. Bazzaz ... [et al.]. San Diego : Academic Press, c1995. 3 v. :
94-024917          574.5/03          0122267303
*Ecology -- Encyclopedias. Environmental sciences -- Encyclopedias.*

**QH540.4.L56 1998**
**Lincoln, Roger J.**
A dictionary of ecology, evolution, and systematics / Roger Lincoln, Geoff Boxshall, Paul Clark. Cambridge ; Cambridge University Press, 1998. ix, 361 p. :
96-051626          570/.3          0521591392
*Ecology -- Dictionaries. Evolution (Biology) -- Dictionaries. Biology -- Classification -- Dictionaries.*

## QH540.7 Ecology — Classification

**QH540.7.B345 1998**
**Bailey, Robert G.,**
Ecoregions : the ecosystem geography of the oceans and continents : with 106 illustraions, with 55 in color / Robert G. Bailey ; illustrations by Lev Ropes. New York : Springer, 1998. ix, 176 p. :
97-026384          577.8/2          0387983058
*Biotic communities -- Classification. Biogeography.*

**QH540.7.B35 1996**
**Bailey, Robert G.,**
Ecosystem geography / Robert G. Bailey ; with a foreword by Jack Ward Thomas ; illustrations by Lev Ropes. New York : Springer, c1996. xii, 204 p. :
95-034178          574.5/012          0387943544
*Biotic communities -- Classification. Natural resources surveys. Ecosystem management.*

### QH540.8 Ecology — History — General works

**QH540.8.G64 1993**
**Golley, Frank B.**
A history of the ecosystem concept in ecology : more than the sum of the parts / Frank Benjamin Golley. New Haven : Yale University Press, c1993. xvi, 254 p. :
93-017577          574.5/09          0300055463
*Ecology -- History. Biotic communities -- History.*

## QH541 Ecology — General works, treatises, and textbooks

**QH541.A524 1984**
**Andrewartha, H. G.**
The ecological web : more on the distribution and abundance of animals / H.G. Andrewartha and L.C. Birch. Chicago : University of Chicago Press, c1984. xiv, 506 p. :
84-000070          591.5          0226020339
*Animal ecology. Zoogeography.*

**QH541.A725 1990**
**Arthur, Wallace.**
The green machine : ecology and the balance of nature / Wallace Arthur. Oxford, UK ; B. Blackwell, 1990. ix, 257 p. :
90-001568          574.5          0631178538
*Biotic communities. Ecology. Nature -- Effect of human beings on.*

**QH541.B415 1990**
**Begon, Michael.**
   Ecology : individuals, populations, and communities / Michael Begon, John L. Harper, Colin R. Townsend. 2nd ed. Boston ; Brookline Village, Mass. : Blackwell Scientific Publications ; 1990. xii, 945 p. :
             574.5 20          0865421110
*Ecology.*

**QH541.B75 1995**
**Brown, James H.,**
   Macroecology / James H. Brown. Chicago : University of Chicago Press, 1995. xiii, 269 p.
94-031250          574.5          0226076148
   *Ecology.*

**QH541.D77 1998**
**Drury, W. H.**
   Chance and change : ecology for conservationists / William Holland Drury Jr. ; edited by John G.T. Anderson ; with a foreword by Ernst Mayr. Berkeley, Calif. : University of California Press, c1998. xxiii, 223 p.
97-014859          577          0520211553
   *Ecology. Evolution (Biology) Natural selection.*

**QH541.E398 2001**
**Elton, Charles S.**
   Animal ecology / Charles Elton ; with new introductory material by Mathew A. Leibold and J. Timothy Wootton. Chicago : University of Chicago Press, 2001. lvi, 209 p. ;
00-069087          591.7          0226206394
   *Animal ecology.*

**QH541.E4 2000**
**Elton, Charles S.**
   The ecology of invasions by animals and plants / by Charles S. Elton ; with a foreword by Daniel Simberloff. Chicago, IL : University of Chicago Press, 2000. p. cm.
99-052582          577/.18          0226206386
   *Ecology. Biogeography. Animal introduction.*

**QH541.F67 1986**
**Forman, Richard T. T.**
   Landscape ecology / Richard T.T. Forman, Michel Godron. New York : Wiley, c1986. xix, 619 p. :
85-012306          712          0471870374
   *Landscape ecology. Landscape protection. Human ecology.*

**QH541.H65 1988**
**Howe, Henry F.**
   Ecological relationships of plants and animals / Henry F. Howe, Lynn C. Westley. New York : Oxford University Press, 1988. xiii, 273 p.
87-005800          574.5          0195044312
   *Ecology.*

**QH541.M225 1995**
**MacNally, Ralph C.**
   Ecological versatility and community ecology / Ralph C. Mac Nally. Cambridge ; Cambridge University Press, 1995. xvii, 435 p.
94-041872          574.5          052140553X
   *Ecology. Biotic communities. Habitat (Ecology)*

**QH541.M384 1999**
**Maurer, Brian A.**
   Untangling ecological complexity : the macroscopic perspective / Brian A. Maurer. Chicago, Ill. : University of Chicago Press, c1999. viii, 251 p.
98-026199          577.8/2          0226511324
   *Biotic communities.*

**QH541.O312 1983**
**Odum, Eugene Pleasants,**
   Basic ecology / Eugene P. Odum. Philadelphia : Saunders College Pub., c1983. x, 613 p. :
82-060633          574.5          0030584140
   *Ecology.*

**QH541.P33 1995**
**Pahl-Wostl, Claudia.**
   The dynamic nature of ecosystems : chaos and order entwined / Claudia Pahl-Wostl. Chichester ; Wiley, c1995. xiii, 267 p.
94-039319          574.5/247          0471955701
   *Biotic communities. Ecology.*

**QH541.P558 1991**
**Pimm, Stuart L.**
   The balance of nature? : ecological issues in the conservation of species and communities / Stuart L. Pimm. Chicago : University of Chicago Press, c1991. xiii, 434 p.
91-003089          574.5/247          0226668290
   *Biotic communities. Ecology. Biological diversity conservation.*

**QH541.S5345 1995**
**Simon, Noel.**
   Nature in danger : threatened habitats and species / Noel Simon in association with the World Conservation Monitoring Centre, Cambridge, England. New York : Oxford University Press, 1995. 240 p. :
94-043391          333.95137          0195211529
   *Habitat (Ecology) Endangered species. Nature conservation.*

**QH541.T819 1991**
**Tudge, Colin.**
   Global ecology / Colin Tudge. New York : Oxford University Press, 1991. ix, 173 p. :
91-002090          304.2          0195209044
   *Ecology.*

**QH541.W638 1985**
**Worster, Donald,**
   Nature's economy : a history of ecological ideas / Donald Worster. Cambridge [Cambridgeshire] ; Cambridge University Press, 1985, c1977. xviii, 404 p.
84-015551          574.5/09          0521267927
   *Ecology -- History.*

## QH541.14 Ecology — Juvenile works

**QH541.14.R556 1998**
**Riley, Peter D.**
Food chains / Peter Riley. New York : Franklin Watts, 1998. 32 p. :
97-050345  577/.16  0531115127
*Food chains (Ecology) -- Juvenile literature. Food chains (Ecology) Food chains (Ecology) -- Experiments.*

## QH541.145 Ecology — Addresses, essays, lectures

**QH541.145.W47**
**Whittaker, Robert Harding,**
Niche : theory and application / edited by Robert H. Whittaker and Simon A. Levin. Stroudsburg, Pa. : Dowden, Hutchinson & Ross ; [1975] xv, 448 p. :
74-023328  574.5/22  0470941170
*Ecology. Species. Biotic communities.*

## QH541.15 Ecology — Special aspects of the subject as whole

**QH541.15.B56**
**Beattie, Andrew J.**
Wild solutions : how biodiversity is money in the bank / Andrew Beattie and Paul Ehrlich ; with illustrations by Christine Turnbull. New Haven : Yale University Press, 2001. xii, 239 p. :
00-043445  333.95/11  0300076363
*Biological diversity. Zoology, Economic.*

**QH541.15.B56.B435 1998**
**Becher, Anne.**
Biodiversity : a reference handbook / Anne Becher. Santa Barbara, Calif. : ABC-CLIO, c1998. xv, 275 p. :
97-042890  333.95  0874369231
*Biological diversity.*

**QH541.15.B56.B574 1998**
Biodiversity dynamics : turnover of populations, taxa, and communities / Michael L. McKinney and James A. Drake, editors. New York : Columbia University Press, c1998. xx, 528 p. :
98-017973  577.8/8  0231104146
*Biological diversity. Evolution (Biology) Population biology.*

**QH541.15.B56.K86 1999**
**Kumar, H. D.,**
Biodiversity and sustainable conservation / Har Darshan Kumar. Enfield, N.H. : Science, c1999. ix, 409 p. :
99-049854  333.95/16  1578080762
*Biological diversity. Biological diversity conservation.*

**QH541.15.B56E53 2001**
Encyclopedia of biodiversity / editor-in-chief, Simon Asher Levin. San Diego : Academic Press, 2001. 5 v. :
  333.95/03 21  0122268652
*Biologica diversity -- Encyclopedias.*

**QH541.15.C44**
**Agosta, William C.**
Thieves, deceivers, and killers : tales of chemistry in nature / William Agosta. Princeton, N.J. : Princeton University Press, c2001. 241 p. :
00-032627  577  0691004889
*Chemical ecology.*

**QH541.15.C44.A38 1996**
**Agosta, William C.**
Bombardier beetles and fever trees : a close-up look at chemical warfare and signals in animals and plants / William Agosta. Reading, Mass. : Addison-Wesley Pub. Co., c1996. vii, 224 p. :
95-009533  574.5  0201626586
*Chemical ecology.*

**QH541.15.C44.C48 1995**
Chemical ecology : the chemistry of biotic interaction / Thomas Eisner and Jerrold Meinwald, editors. Washington, D.C. : National Academy Press, 1995. vii, 214 p.,
95-018685  574.5  0309052815
*Chemical ecology.*

**QH541.15.F73.T76 1997**
Tropical forest remnants : ecology, management, and conservation of fragmented communities / edited by William F. Laurance and Richard O. Bierregaard, Jr. Chicago : University of Chicago Press, c1997. xv, 616 p. :
96-038038  577.34  0226468984
*Fragmented landscapes -- Tropics. Conservation biology -- Tropics. Rain forest ecology.*

**QH541.15.L35.F76 1998**
**Frohn, Robert C.**
Remote sensing for landscape ecology : new metric indicators for monitoring, modeling, and assessment of ecosystems / Robert C. Frohn. Boca Raton : Lewis Publishers, c1998. 99 p. :
97-031769  577/.028  1566702755
*Landscape ecology -- Remote sensing. Geographic information systems.*

**QH541.15.L35.P58 1997**
Placing nature : culture and landscape ecology / edited by Joan Iverson Nassauer. Washington, D.C. : Island Press, c1997. xii, 179 p. :
97-014842  577.5/5  1559635592
*Landscape ecology.*

**QH541.15.M3.S56 1998**
**Shugart, H. H.**
 Terrestrial ecosystems in changing environments / Herman H. Shugart. Cambridge ; Cambridge University Press, 1998. xiv, 537 p. :
97-001235        577.2        0521563429
 *Ecology -- Mathematical models. Global environmental change – Mathematical models.*

**QH541.15.M64.L95 1998**
**Lynch, J. M.**
 Environmental biomonitoring : the biotechnology ecotoxicology interface / James M. Lynch and Alan Wiseman. Cambridge, [Eng.] ; Cambridge University Press, 1998. xiv, 299 p. :
97-014837        571.9/5        0521621410
 *Environmental monitoring. Bioremediation.*

**QH541.15.N84.G67 1996**
**Gotelli, Nicholas J.,**
 Null models in ecology / Nicholas J. Gotelli, Gary R. Graves. Washington : Smithsonian Institution Press, c1996. xvi, 368 p. :
95-026734        574.5/01/5195        1560986573
 *Null models (Ecology) Biotic communities -- Statistical methods. Monte Carlo method.*

**QH541.15.R45.B48 1994**
 Beyond preservation : restoring and inventing landscapes / A. Dwight Baldwin, Jr., Judith De Luce, and Carl Pletsch, editors. Minneapolis : University of Minnesota Press, c1994. vii. 280 p. :
93-004953        333.73/153        0816623465
 *Restoration ecology -- Congresses. Landscape protection -- Congresses. Nature -- Effect of human beings on -- Congresses.*

**QH541.15.R45.M55 1995**
**Mills, Stephanie.**
 In service of the wild : restoring and reinhabiting damaged land / Stephanie Mills. Boston : Beacon Press, c1995. xii, 237 p. ;
94-038094        639.9        0807085340
 *Restoration ecology -- Case studies.*

**QH541.15.R45.R5 1997**
 Restoration ecology and sustainable development / edited by Krystyna M. Urbanska, Nigel R. Webb, and Peter J. Edwards. Cambridge, U.K. ; Cambridge University Press, 1997. xv, 397 p. :
96-052176        333.7/153        0521581605
 *Restoration ecology -- Congresses. Restoration ecology -- Economic aspects -- Congresses. Sustainable development -- Congresses.*

**QH541.15.S5.H36 1996**
 Handbook of environmental and ecological modeling / edited by S.E. Jorgensen, B. Halling-Sorensen, S.N. Nielsen. Boca Raton, FL : Lewis Publishers, c1996. 672 p. ;
95-020624        574.5/01/1
 *Ecology -- Simulation methods. Pollution -- Environmental aspects -- Simulation methods.*

**QH541.15.S64.R67 1995**
**Rosenzweig, Michael L.**
 Species diversity in space and time / Michael L. Rosenzweig. Cambridge ; Cambridge University Press, 1995. xx, 436 p. :
94-043750        574.5/24        0521496187
 *Species diversity. Biogeography.*

**QH541.15.T68.E24 1995**
 Ecological toxicity testing : scale, complexity, and relevance / edited by John Cairns, Jr., B.R. Niederlehner. Boca Raton : Lewis Publishers, c1995. 228 p. :
94-019832        574.2/4        0873715993
 *Toxicity testing. Pollution -- Environmental aspects.*

## QH541.2 Ecology — Study and teaching. Research — General works

**QH541.2.F66 2000**
**Ford, E. D.**
 Scientific method for ecological research / E. David Ford. Cambridge, UK ; Cambridge University Press, 2000. xix, 564 p. :
99-030065        577/.07/2        052166005X
 *Ecology -- Research -- Methodology. Science -- Methodology.*

## QH541.28 Ecology — Technique

**QH541.28.B76 1984**
**Brower, James E.**
 Field & laboratory methods for general ecology / James E. Brower, Jerrold H. Zar. Dubuque, Iowa : W.C. Brown Publishers, c1984. xi, 226 p. :
84-070027        574.5/07/8        0069746575
 *Ecology -- Field work. Ecology -- Laboratory manuals.*

**QH541.28.K74 1985**
**Krebs, Charles J.**
 Ecology : the experimental analysis of distribution and abundance / Charles J. Krebs. New York : Harper & Row, c1985. xi, 800 p. :
84-010845        574.5        0060437782
 *Ecology -- Methodology. Population biology -- Methodology. Biogeography -- Methodology.*

## QH541.5 Ecology — By type of environment, A-Z

**QH541.5.A74.A75 1999**
 Arid lands management : toward ecological sustainability / Thomas W. Hoekstra and Moshe Shachak, technical editors. Urbana : University of Illinois Press, c1999. ix, 279 p. :
98-008908        577.54        0252067177
 *Arid regions ecology. Ecosystem management. Arid regions – Management.*

**QH541.5.C6.A52 1994**
**Adams, Lowell W.**
Urban wildlife habitats : a landscape perspective / Lowell W. Adams. Minneapolis : University of Minnesota Press, c1994. xiii, 186 p.
93-044211          333.95/16/091732
0816622124
*Urban ecology (Biology) Nature conservation. Wildlife management.*

**QH541.5.C62.L27 2000**
**Larson, Douglas W.**
Cliff ecology : pattern and process in cliff ecosystems / Douglas W. Larson, Uta Matthes, Peter E. Kelly. Cambridge, UK ; Cambridge University Press, 2000. xvi, 340 p. :
99-012175          577          0521554896
*Cliff ecology.*

**QH541.5.C65**
**Barnabe, G.**
Ecology and management of coastal waters : the aquatic environment / Gilbert Barnabe and Regine Barnabe-Quet. London; Springer, 2000. xvi, 396 p. :
00-037371          577.7          1852336471
*Coastal ecology. Marine ecology. Coastal zone management.*

**QH541.5.C65**
**Vernberg, F. John,**
The coastal zone : past, present, and future / F. John Vernberg and Winona B. Vernberg. Columbia : University of South Carolina Press, c2001. xiv, 191 p.,
00-011819          577.5/1          1570033943
*Coastal ecology. Marine ecology. Coastal zone management.*

**QH541.5.C7.C613**
**Cousteau, Jacques Yves.**
Life and death in a coral sea [by] Jacques-Yves Cousteau with Philippe Diole. Translated from the French by J. F. Bernard. Garden City, N.Y., Doubleday, 1971. 302 p.
69-013003          574.5/2636
*Coral reef ecology. Underwater exploration.*

**QH541.5.D35.V34 2000**
**Van Dover, Cindy.**
The ecology of deep-sea hydrothermal vents / Cindy Lee Van Dover. Princeton, N.J. : Princeton University Press, c2000. xx, 424 p. :
99-016545          577.7/9          069105780X
*Hydrothermal vent ecology.*

**QH541.5.D4.E28 1991**
The Ecology of desert communities / edited by Gary A. Polis. Tucson : University of Arizona Press, c1991. viii, 456 p.
90-020183          574.5/2652          0816511861
*Desert ecology. Arthropoda -- Ecology.*

**QH541.5.E8.E849 1989**
Estuarine ecology / John W. Day, Jr. ... [et al.]. New York : Wiley, 1989. xiv, 558 p. :
87-027031          574.5/26365          0471062634
*Estuarine ecology.*

**QH541.5.E8.K47 1991**
**Kennish, Michael J.**
Ecology of estuaries : anthropogenic effects / author, Michael J. Kennish. Boca Raton : CRC Press, c1992. 494 p. :
91-029291          574.5/26365          0849380413
*Estuarine ecology. Estuarine pollution -- Environmental aspects. Nature -- Effect of human beings on.*

**QH541.5.F6.F66 1995**
Forest canopies / edited by Margaret D. Lowman, Nalini M. Nadkarni. San Diego : Academic Press, c1995. xix, 624 p. :
94-041251          574.5/2642          0124576508
*Forest canopy ecology. Forest canopies.*

**QH541.5.F6.W34 1998**
**Waring, Richard H.**
Forest ecosystems : analysis at multiple scales / Richard H. Waring, Steven W. Running. San Diego : Academic Press, c1998. xiv, 370 p.,
97-080795          577.3          0127354433
*Forest ecology. Forest management.*

**QH541.5.F7.F86**
The Functioning of freshwater ecosystems / edited by E. D. Le Cren and R. H. Lowe-McConnell. Cambridge [Eng.] ; Cambridge University Press, 1980. xxix, 588 p.
79-050504          574.5/2632          0521225078
*Freshwater productivity. Freshwater ecology.*

**QH541.5.I8.Q35 1996**
**Quammen, David,**
The song of the dodo : island biogeography in an age of extinctions / David Quammen ; maps by Kris Ellingsen. New York : Scribner, c1996. 702 p. :
95-044972          574.9/1          0684800837
*Island ecology. Endangered species. Biogeography.*

**QH541.5.M3**
**Keddy, Paul A.,**
Wetland ecology : principles and conservation / Paul A. Keddy. Cambridge, UK ; Cambridge University Press, 2000. xiv, 614 p. :
99-045443          577.68          0521780012
*Wetland ecology. Wetland conservation.*

**QH541.5.M3.W46 1990**
Wetland creation and restoration : the status of the science / edited by Jon A. Kusler and Mary E. Kentula ; foreword by Senator George J. Mitchell. Washington, D.C. : Island Press, c1990. xxv, 594 p. :
90-004053          333.91/8          1559630450
*Wetland restoration. Wetland conservation.*

**QH541.5.R27.T47 1992**
**Terborgh, John,**
Diversity and the tropical rain forest / John Terborgh. New York : Scientific American Library : c1992. ix, 242 p. :
91-030053          574.5/2642/0913          0716750309
*Rain forest ecology. Biological diversity -- Tropics. Rainforest conservation.*

**QH541.5.R27.T76 1983**

Tropical rain forest ecosystems / edited by F.B. Golley. Amsterdam ; Elsevier Scientific Pub. Co., 1983-1989. 2 v. :
81-007861          574.5/2642          0444418105
*Rain forest ecology.*

**QH541.5.R27G39 2001**
**Gay, Kathlyn.**

Rainforests of the world : a reference handbook / Kathlyn Gay. 2nd ed. Santa Barbara, CA : ABC-CLIO, c2001. xii, 257 p. :
577.34 21          1576074242
*Rain forest ecology. Rain forests. Rain forest conservation. Deforestation -- Environmental aspects -- Tropics.*

**QH541.5.S3.J85 1993**
**Jumars, Peter A.**

Concepts in biological oceanography : an interdisciplinary primer / Peter A. Jumars. New York : Oxford University Press, 1993. vii, 348 p. :
92-039069          574.5/2636          0195067320
*Marine ecology. Oceanography.*

**QH541.5.S3.V34 1995**
**Valiela, Ivan.**

Marine ecological processes / Ivan Valiela. New York : Springer, c1995. xiv, 686 p. :
94-041484          669/.94          0387943218
*Marine ecology.*

**QH541.5.S35**
**Knox, G. A.**

The ecology of seashores / by George A. Knox. Boca Raton, Fla. : CRC Press, c2001. 557 p. :
00-058573          577.69/9          0849300088
*Seashore ecology.*

**QH541.5.S3M254 2001**

Marine chemical ecology / edited by James B. McClintock, Bill J. Baker. Boca Raton, Fla. : CRC Press, c2001. 610 p. :
577.7/14 21          0849390648
*Marine chemical ecology.*

**QH541.5.S6.K54 1994**
**Killham, Ken.**

Soil ecology / Ken Killham ; with electron micrographs by Ralph Foster. Cambridge ; Cambridge University Press, c1994. xviii, 242 p.
93-026150          574.5/26404          052143517X
*Soil ecology. Soil science. Biogeochemical cycles.*

**QH541.5.S7.A435 1995**
**Allan, J. David.**

Stream ecology : structure and function of running waters / J. David Allan. London ; Chapman & Hall, 1995 xii, 388 p. :
94-069372          574.52632          0412294303
*Stream ecology.*

**QH541.5.T8.T86**

Tundra ecosystems : a comparative analysis / edited by L. C. Bliss, O. W. Heal, J. J. Moore. Cambridge [Eng.] ; Cambridge University Press, 1981. xxxvi, 813 p.
79-041580          574.5/2644          0521227763
*Tundra ecology.*

## QH543 Ecology — Bioclimatology. Microclimatology — General works

**QH543.G56 1992**

Global warming and biological diversity / edited by Robert L. Peters & Thomas E. Lovejoy. New Haven : Yale University Press, c1992. xxi, 386 p. :
91-033532          574.5/222          0300050569
*Global warming -- Congresses. Bioclimatology -- Congresses. Biological diversity conservation -- Congresses.*

## QH545.A1-17 Ecology — Influence of special factors in the environment — Congresses

**QH545.A1.B385 1994**

Basic environmental toxicology / edited by Lorris G. Cockerham, Barbara S. Shane. Boca Raton, FL : CRC Press, c1994. 627 p. :
93-007790          574.5/222          0849388511
*Pollution -- Environmental aspects.*

**QH545.A1.E283 1998**

Ecotoxicology : ecological fundamentals, chemical exposure, and biological effects / edited by Gerrit Schuurmann, Bernd Markert. New York : John Wiley ; c1998. xxix, 900 p.
97-028345          571.9/5          0471176443
*Pollution -- Environmental aspects. Environmental chemistry.*

**QH545.A1.F72 1994**
**Francis, Bettina Magnus,**

Toxic substances in the environment / Bettina Magnus Francis. New York : J. Wiley & Sons, c1994. xviii, 360 p.
92-026896          363.73          0471507814
*Pollution -- Environmental aspects. Pollution -- Health aspects. Toxicology.*

**QH545.A1.H36 1995**

Handbook of ecotoxicology / David J. Hoffman ... [et al.]. Boca Raton : Lewis Publishers, c1995. x, 755 p. :
94-019275          574.5/222          0873715853
*Pollution -- Environmental aspects. Environmental toxicology. Environmental risk assessment.*

**QH545.A17.A215 1988**

Acidic deposition and forest soils : context and case studies of the southeastern U.S. / Dan Binkley ... [et al.]. New York : Springer-Verlag, c1988. p. cm.
88-029767          574.5/2642          038796889X
*Acid deposition -- Environmental aspects -- Southern States. Forest soils -- Southern States. Soil acidity -- Southern States.*

**QH545.A17.H69 1988**
**Howells, Gwyneth Parry.**
 Acid rain and acid waters / Gwyneth Howells. New York : E. Horwood, 1990. 215 p. :
88-026889          363.7/386          013004797X
 *Acid rain -- Environmental aspects.*

**QH545.A3-W3 Ecology — Influence of special factors in the environment — General works, treatises, and textbooks**

**QH545.A3.A38 1992**
 Air pollution effects on biodiversity / edited by Jerry R. Barker and David T. Tingey. New York : Van Nostrand Reinhold, [1992] xii, 322 p. :
91-047171          574.5/222          0442007485
 *Air -- Pollution -- Environmental aspects -- Congresses. Biological diversity conservation -- Congresses.*

**QH545.A3.S64 1990**
**Smith, William H.,**
 Air pollution and forests : interactions between air contaminants and forest ecosystems / William H. Smith. New York : Springer-Verlag, c1990. xv, 618 p. :
89-028540          574.5/2642          0387970843
 *Air -- Pollution -- Environmental aspects. Forest ecology. Plants, Effect of air pollution on.*

**QH545.C48**
**Russell, Edmund,**
 War and nature : fighting humans and insects with chemicals from World War I to Silent spring / Edmund Russell. Cambridge ; Cambridge University Press, 2001. xvii, 315 p.
00-040323          577.27          0521790034
 *Chemical warfare -- Environmental aspects -- History. Insect pests -- Control -- Environmental aspects -- History. Chemical warfare -- Effect of technological innovations on -- History.*

**QH545.F5.W48 1995**
**Whelan, Robert J.**
 The ecology of fire / Robert J. Whelan. Cambridge ; Cambridge University Press, 1995. x, 346 p. :
94-034787          574.5/264          0521328721
 *Fire ecology.*

**QH545.N83.S24 1990**
**Sagan, Carl,**
 A path where no man thought : nuclear winter and the end of the arms race / Carl Sagan, Richard Turco. New York : Random House, c1990. xxii, 499 p.,
89-043155          304.2/8          0394583078
 *Nuclear winter. Nuclear warfare -- Environmental aspects.*

**QH545.O5B44 1994**
 Before and after an oil spill : the Arthur Kill / edited by Joanna Burger. New Brunswick, NJ : Rutgers University Press, c1994. xi, 305 p. :
          363.73/82/0916346 20          0813520959
*Oil spills and wildlife -- Arthur Kill (N.J. and N.Y.) Oil spills -- Environmental aspects -- Arthur Kill (N.J. and N.Y.) Oil pollution of rivers, harbors, etc. -- Arthur Kill (N.J. and N.Y.) Exxon Corporation.*

**QH545.P4.C38 1962**
**Carson, Rachel,**
 Silent spring / by Rachel Carson ; drawings by Lois and Louis Darling. Boston : Houghton Mifflin ; 1962. x, 368 p.
60-005148          301.3
 *Pesticides -- Environmental aspects. Pesticides -- Toxicology. Pesticides and wildlife.*

**QH545.P4.D86**
**Dunlap, Thomas R.,**
 DDT : scientists, citizens, and public policy / Thomas R. Dunlap. Princeton, N.J. : Princeton University Press, c1981. 318 p. ;
80-008546          363.7/384          0691046808
 *DDT (Insecticide) -- Environmental aspects -- United States -- History. Pesticides -- Government policy -- United States -- History.*

**QH545.P4.H96 1989**
**Hynes, H. Patricia.**
 The recurring silent spring / H. Patricia Hynes. New York : Pergamon Press, 1989. x, 227 p. ;
88-029049          574/.092/4          0080371175
*Carson, Rachel, -- 1907-1964. -- Silent spring. Carson, Rachel, – 1907-1964.   Ecologists -- United States -- Biography.*

**QH545.P4.V36 1996**
**Van Emden, Helmut Fritz.**
 Beyond silent spring : integrated pest management and chemical safety / Helmut F. van Emden and David B. Peakall. London ; Chapman & Hall, 1996. xviii, 322 p.
95-071377          363.738/4          0412728001
 *Pesticides -- Environmental aspects. Pesticides -- Toxicology. Pests -- Control.*

**QH545.S45.H37 1991**
**Harris, Tom**
 Death in the marsh / Tom Harris. Washington, D.C. : Island Press, c1991. xiv, 245 p. :
91-022602          574.5/26325          1559630701
 *Selenium -- Environmental aspects -- California -- Kesterson National Wildlife Refuge. Selenosis -- California -- Kesterson National Wildlife Refuge. Selenium -- Environmental aspects – West (U.S.) Kesterson National Wildlife Refuge (Calif.)*

**QH545.T4.G38 1993**
**Gates, David Murray,**
 Climate change and its biological consequences / David M. Gates. Sunderland, Mass. : Sinauer Associates, c1993. 280 p. :
92-036886          574.5/222          0878932240
 *Global temperature changes -- Environmental aspects -- North America. Climatic changes -- Environmental aspects -- North America. Global warming -- Environmental aspects – North America.*

**QH545.T4.G56 1991**
 Global climate change and life on earth / Richard L. Wyman, editor ; foreword by Paul R. Ehrlich. New York : Routledge, Chapman and Hall, 1991. xxi, 282 p. :
90-008965          574.5/222          0412028115
 *Global temperature changes -- Environmental aspects -- Congresses. Climatic changes -- Environmental aspects -- United States -- Congresses. Biological diversity conservation -- United States -- Congresses.*

**QH545.W3.A68 1986**
**Ashworth, William,**
The late, Great Lakes : an environmental history / William Ashworth. New York : Knopf : 1986. x, 274 p. :
85-045915          363.7/3942/0977          0394551516
*Water -- Pollution -- Environmental aspects -- Great Lakes -- History. Lake ecology -- Great Lakes -- History. Great Lakes -- History.*

**QH545.W3.N45 2000**
**Neilson, Alasdair H.**
Organic chemicals : an environmental perspective / Alasdair Neilson. Boca Raton, Fla. : Lewis Publishers, c2000. 870 p. :
99-052061          577.6/27          156670376X
*Aquatic organisms -- Effect of water pollution on. Organic water pollutants -- Environmental aspects.*

## QH546 Ecology — Adaptation

**QH546.B55 1993**
Biotic interactions and global change / edited by Peter M. Kareiva, Joel G. Kingsolver, Raymond B. Huey. Sunderland, Mass. : Sinauer Associates, c1993. xii, 559 p. :
92-019162          574.5          0878934294
*Adaptation (Biology) -- Congresses. Nature -- Effect of human beings on -- Congresses. Climatic changes -- Environmental aspects -- Congresses.*

**QH546.G7613 1998**
**Gross, Michael,**
Life on the edge : amazing creatures thriving in extreme environments / Michael Gross. New York : Plenum Trade, c1998. xiii, 200 p.
98-004622          578.4          0306457865
*Adaptation (Biology) Extreme environments. Stress (Physiology)*

**QH546.H63 1997**
**Hoffmann, Ary A.**
Extreme environmental change and evolution / Ary A. Hoffmann, Peter A. Parsons. Cambridge ; Cambridge University Press, 1997. xii, 259 p. :
96-046901          576.8/4          0521441072
*Adaptation (Biology) Extreme environments. Evolutionary genetics.*

**QH546.S36 1998**
**Schlichting, Carl.**
Phenotypic evolution : a reaction norm perspective / Carl D. Schlichting, Massimo Pigliucci. Sunderland, Mass. : Sinauer, 1998. p. cm.
98-007457          576.5/3          0878937994
*Adaptation (Biology) Evolution (Biology) Phenotype.*

## QH546.3 Ecology — Competition. Niche

**QH546.3.A75 1987**
**Arthur, Wallace.**
The niche in competition and evolution / by Wallace Arthur. Chichester [West Sussex] ; New York : Wiley, c1987. xov. 175 p :
574.5 19          0471916153
*Niche (Ecology) Competiion (Biology) Evolution (Biology)*

**QH546.3.P66 1982**
**Pontin, A. J.**
Competition and coexistence of species / A.J. Pontin. Boston : Pitman Advanced Pub. Program, c1982. vii, 102 p. :
81-001654          574.5          0273084895
*Competition (Biology)*

## QH548 Ecology — Symbiosis — General works

**QH548.D68 1994**
**Douglas, A. E.**
Symbiotic interactions / by A.E. Douglas. Oxford ; Oxford University Press, 1994. vi, 148 p. :
93-022183          574.5/2482          0198542860
*Symbiosis.*

**QH548.L46 1999**
**Lembke, Janet.**
Despicable species : on cowbirds, kudzu, hornworms, and other scourges / Janet Lembke ; illustrations by Joe Nutt. New York : Lyons Press, c1999. 216 p. :
99-015220          577.8/5          1558216359
*Symbiosis. Parasitism.*

**QH548.M35 1998**
**Margulis, Lynn,**
Symbiotic planet : a new look at evolution / Lynn Margulis. New York : Basic Books, c1998. vi, 147 p. :
98-038921          576.8/5          0465072712
*Symbiosis. Evolution (Biology) Symbiogenesis.*

**QH548.S26 1994**
**Sapp, Jan.**
Evolution by association : a history of symbiosis / Jan Sapp. New York : Oxford University Press, 1994. xvii, 255 p.
94-006321          574.5/2482/09          0195088212
*Symbiosis -- Research -- History. Symbiogenesis -- Research -- History.*

## QH548.3 Ecology — Symbiosis — Mutualism

**QH548.3.B56 1985**
The Biology of mutualism : ecology and evolution / edited by Douglas H. Boucher. New York : Oxford University Press, 1985. x, 388 p. :
85-007264          574.5/2482          0195204832
*Mutualism (Biology) Evolution (Biology)*

## QH577 Cytology — History — General works

**QH577.H37 1999**
**Harris, Henry,**
  The birth of the cell / Henry Harris. New Haven, Conn. : Yale University Press, c1999. xii, 212 p. :
98-018623          571.6/09          0300073844
  *Cytology -- History.*

## QH581 Cytology — General works, treatises, and textbooks — Through 1969

**QH581.F3**
**Fawcett, Don Wayne,**
  An atlas of fine structure: the cell, its organelles, and inclusions [by] Don W. Fawcett. Philadelphia, W. B. Saunders Co., 1966. vii, 448 p.
66-010500          591.8
  *Cytology -- Atlases.*

## QH581.2 Cytology — General works, treatises, and textbooks — 1970-

**QH581.2.C38 1989**
**Carroll, Mark.**
  Organelles / Mark Carroll. New York : Guilford Press, c1989. xvii, 202 p.
88-024625          574.87/3          0898624037
  *Cell organelles.*

**QH581.2.C66 2000**
**Cooper, Geoffrey M.**
  The cell : a molecular approach / Geoffrey M. Cooper. 2nd ed. Washington, DC ; Sunderland, Mass. : ASM Press ; Sinauer Associates, c2000. xxiv, 689 p. :
          571.6 21          0878931198
*Cytology. Molecular biology.*

**QH581.2.G66 1993**
**Goodsell, David S.**
  The machinery of life / David S. Goodsell. New York : Springer-Verlag, c1993. xiv, 140 p.,
92-002303          574.87          0387978461
  *Cells. Molecular biology. Cells -- Pictorial works.*

**QH581.2.S2 1993**
**Sadava, David E.**
  Cell biology : organelle structure and function / David E. Sadava. Boston : Jones and Bartlett Publishers, c1993. xvii, 698 p.
92-027777          574.87/34          0867202289
  *Cell organelles. Eukaryotic cells.*

## QH583.2 Cytology — Study and teaching. Research — Laboratory manuals

**QH583.2.S64 1998**
**Spector, David L.**
  Cells : a laboratory manual / David L. Spector, Robert D. Goldman, Leslie A. Leinwand. Cold Spring Harbor, NY : Cold Spring Harbor Laboratory Press, c1998. 3 v. :
97-025924          571.6          0879695226
  *Cytology -- Laboratory manuals. Cytology – laboratory manuals.*

## QH585.2 Cytology — Technique — Special techniques, A-Z

**QH585.2.F74 2000**
**Freshney, R. Ian.**
  Culture of animal cells : a manual of basic technique / R. Ian Freshney. New York : Wiley, c2000. xxvi, 577 p.
99-023536          571.6/38          0471348899
  *Tissue culture -- Laboratory manuals. Cell culture – Laboratory manuals.*

**QH585.2.M38 1998**
**Mather, Jennie P.,**
  Introduction to cell and tissue culture : theory and technique / Jennie P. Mather and Penelope E. Roberts. New York : Plenum Press, c1998. xv, 241 p. :
98-027597          571.5/38          0306458594
  *Cell culture. Tissue culture. Tissue Culture -- methods.*

## QH595 Cytology — Nucleus

**QH595.A36 1990**
**Agutter, Paul S.,**
  Between nucleus and cytoplasm / Paul S. Agutter. London ; Chapman and Hall, 1991 x, 148 p. :
89-070876          574.87/5          0412321807
  *Cell nuclei. Cytoplasm. Biological transport.*

## QH601 Cytology — Cell membranes — General works

**QH601.E823 1989**
**Evans, W. Howard.**
  Membrane structure and function / W.H. Evans, J.M. Graham. Oxford, England ; IRL Press at Oxford University Press, 1989. x, 86 p. :
89-002192          574.87/5          0199630046
  *Cell membranes. Cell Membrane -- physiology. Cell Membrane – ultrastructure.*

## QH603 Cytology — Other special, A-Z

**QH603.I54.A33 1996**
**Aidley, David J.**
Ion channels : molecules in action / David J. Aidley, Peter R. Stanfield. Cambridge ; Cambridge University Press, c1996. xii, 307 p. :
96-230439          571.6/4          0521495318
*Ion channels -- Research -- Methodology.*

**QH603.P47.M37 1995**
**Masters, Colin J.**
The peroxisome : a vital organelle / Colin Masters and Denis Crane. Cambridge ; Cambridge University Press, 1995. xvii, 286 p.
94-040110          574.87/4          0521482127
*Peroxisomes.*

## QH604.2 Cytology — Control mechanisms. Cell regulation — Cell interaction

**QH604.2.B37 1991**
**Barritt, Greg J.**
Communication within animal cells / Greg J. Barritt. Oxford ; Oxford University Press, 1992. xiv, 343 p. :
90-026732          591.87/6          0198547277
*Cell interaction. Cellular control mechanisms.*

## QH605 Cytology — Cell division — General works

**QH605.M95 1993**
**Murray, Andrew Wood.**
The cell cycle : an introduction / Andrew Murray, Tim Hunt. New York : W.H. Freeman, c1993. xii, 251 p. :
93-010477          574.87/623          071677044X
*Cell cycle.*

**QH605.R27 1996**
**Rappaport, R.**
Cytokinesis in animal cells / R. Rappaport. Cambridge ; Cambridge University Press, 1996. xii, 386 p. :
95-037443          591.87/62          0521401739
*Cytokinesis.*

## QH607 Cytology — Cell differentiation

**QH607.M87 1990**
**Muramatsu, Takashi,**
Cell surface and differentiation / Takashi Muramatsu. London ; Chapman and Hall, c1990. vii, 159 p. :
91-105654          574.87/612          0412308509
*Cell differentiation. Molecular biology. Cell surface antigens.*

## QH613 Cytology — Physical and chemical properties — Histochemistry

**QH613.H67 1988**
**Horobin, Richard W.**
Understanding histochemistry : selection, evaluation, and design of biological stains / R.W. Horobin. Chichester, West Sussex, England : E. Horwood ; 1988. 172 p. :
88-000763          578/.64          085312678X
*Histochemistry. Staining and stains (Microscopy)*

## QH631 Cytology — Physiological properties — General works

**QH631.C458 2001**
Cell physiology sourcebook : a molecular approach / edited by Nicholas Sperelakis. 3rd ed. San Diego : Academic Press, c2001. xxv, 1235 p. :
          571.6 21
*Cell physiology.*

**QH631.W44 1996**
**Weiss, Thomas Fischer.**
Cellular biophysics / Thomas Fischer Weiss. Cambridge, Mass. : MIT Press, c1996- v. 1   :
95-009801          574.87/6041          0262231832
*Cell physiology. Biophysics. Biological transport.*

## QH647 Cytology — Physiological properties — Motility. Irritability

**QH647.B73 2001**
**Bray, Dennis.**
Cell movements : from molecules to motility / Dennis Bray. New York : Garland Pub., 2001. xiv, 372 p. :
00-055159          571.6/7          0815332823
*Cells -- Motility.*

## QH653 Cytology — Effect of physical and chemical agents on cells — Temperature

**QH653.D38 1991**
**Davenport, J.**
Animal life at low temperature / John Davenport. London ; Chapman & Hall, 1992. xi, 246 p. :
91-027392          591.19/167          0412403501
*Cryobiology.*

## QH671 Cytology — Pathology and death

**QH671.W48 1998**
When cells die : a comprehensive evaluation of apoptosis and programmed cell death / edited by Richard A. Lockshin, Zahra Zakeri, and Jonathan L. Tilly. New York : Wiley-Liss, c1998. xix, 504 p. :
97-023884          571.9/36          0471165697
*Apoptosis. Apoptosis -- physiology.*

# QK Botany

## QK1 Societies, congresses, serial collections, yearbooks

**QK1.A353**
Advances in botanical research. London ; Academic Press, c1963- v. :
62-021144          580.72
*Botany. Botany -- Research. Botanica -- larpcal*

**QK1.A48**
Annual review of plant physiology. Palo Alto, Calif. [etc.] Annual Reviews Inc. 38 v.
51-001660          581.1/05
*Plant physiology -- Periodicals. Plants -- physiology -- periodicals. Biology -- periodicals.*

## QK9 Dictionaries

**QK9.C67 1998**
A dictionary of plant sciences / edited by Michael Allaby. 2nd ed. New York : Oxford University Press, 1998. 508 p. :
580/.3 21
*Botany -- Dictionaries.*

**QK9.H37 1994**
**Harris, James G.,**
Plant identification terminology : an illustrated glossary / James G. Harris, Melinda Woolf Harris. Spring Lake, Utah : Spring Lake Publishing, c1994. ix, 197 p. :
94-065026          581/.01/4          096402215X
*Botany -- Dictionaries. Botany -- Terminology. Plants -- Identification.*

## QK10 Terminology, notation, abbreviations

**QK10.H53 2000**
**Hickey, Michael,**
The Cambridge illustrated glossary of botanical terms / Michael Hickey and Clive King. Cambridge : Cambridge University Press, 2000. xii, 208 p. :
00-1269894          580/.1/4          0521790808
*Botany -- Terminology. Botany -- Pictorial works.*

**QK10.S7 1992**
**Stearn, William T. (William Thomas),**
Botanical Latin : history, grammar, syntax, terminology, and vocabulary / William T. Stearn. 4th ed. Newton Abbot, Devon : David & Charles, 1992. xiv, 546 p. :
581/.014 20
*Botany -- Language. Latin language, Medieval and modern -- Technical Latin.*

## QK11 Indexes of plants

**QK11.M29 1997**
**Mabberley, D. J.**
The plant-book : a portable dictionary of the vascular plants utilizing Kubitzki's The families and genera of vascular plants (1990-), Cronquist's An integrated system of classification of flowering D.J. Mabberley. Cambridge, United Kingdom ; Cambridge University Press, c1997. xvi, 858 p. ;
96-030091          580/.1/4          0521414210
*Botany -- Nomenclature. Plant names, Popular -- Dictionaries. English language -- Dictionaries -- Latin, Medieval and modern.*

## QK13 Popular names

**QK13.E565 2000**
Elsevier's dictionary of plant names and their origin / [compiled] by Donald Watts. Amsterdam ; Elsevier Science B.V., 2000. xxx, 1001 p.
00-042194          580/.1/4          0444503560
*Plant names, Popular -- Dictionaries. Botany -- Nomenclature.*

**QK13.Q38 2000**
**Quattrocchi, Umberto,**
CRC world dictionary of plant names : common names, scientific names, eponyms, synonyms, and etymology / Umberto Quattrocchi. Boca Raton : CRC Press, 2000. 4 v. ;
99-031919          580/.1/4          0849326737
*Plant names, Popular -- Dictionaries. Botany -- Nomenclature.*

## QK26 Biography — Collective

**QK26.I75 1994**
**Isely, Duane,**
One hundred and one botanists / Duane Isely. Ames : Iowa State University, 1994. xiii, 351 p.
94-028380          581/.092/2          0813824982
*Botanists -- Biography.*

## QK31 Biography — Individual

**QK31.B3.B47**
**Berkeley, Edmund.**
The life and travels of John Bartram from Lake Ontario to the River St. John / Edmund Berkeley and Dorothy Smith Berkeley. Tallahassee : University Presses of Florida, c1982. xv, 376 p. :
81-004083          581/.092/4          0813007003
*Bartram, John, -- 1699-1777. Botanists -- Pennsylvania -- Biography. Botany -- United States -- History.*

**QK31.C55.B4**
**Berkeley, Edmund.**
John Clayton, pioneer of American botany, by Edmund Berkeley and Dorothy Smith Berkeley. Chapel Hill, University of North Carolina [1963] 236 p.
63-004274          925.8
*Clayton, John, -- 1686-1773.*

**QK31.G8D8 1988**
**Dupree, A. Hunter,**
Asa Gray, American botanist, friend of Darwin / A. Hunter Dupree. John Hopkins University Press, Baltimore : Johns Hopkins University Press, 1988, c1959. xxii, 503 p. :
581/.092/4 B 19    0801837413
*Gray, Asa, 1810-1888.  Botanists -- United States -- Biography.*

**QK31.S15.S9**
**Sutton, S. B.**
Charles Sprague Sargent and the Arnold Arboretum [by] S. B. Sutton. Cambridge, Harvard University Press, 1970. xvii, 382 p.
73-120322    581/.0924    0674111818
*Sargent, Charles Sprague, -- 1841-1927.*

**QK31.T7.R6**
**Rodgers, Andrew Denny,**
John Torrey; a story of North American botany, by Andrew Denny Rodgers, III. [Princeton] Princeton University Press; 1942. 6 p. ., [3]-3
42019817    925.8
*Torrey, John, -- 1796-1873.*

## QK45.2 General works and treatises — 1970-

**QK45.2.B46 2000**
**Bell, Peter Robert.**
Green plants : their origin and diversity / Peter R. Bell, Alan R. Hemsley. Cambridge, UK ; Cambridge University Press, 2000. vii, 349 p. :
99-047854    581.3/8    0521641098
*Botany. Botany -- Classification. Plants -- Evolution.*

## QK46.5 Special topics, A-Z

**QK46.5.B66.K44 1992**
**Keeney, Elizabeth.**
The botanizers : amateur scientists in nineteenth-century America / Elizabeth B. Keeney. Chapel Hill : University of North Carolina Press, c1992. xii, 206 p. :
92-005022    581/.0973/09034    0807820466
*Botanizers -- United States -- History -- 19th century. Botany — United States -- History -- 19th century.*

**QK46.5.H85**
**Pollan, Michael.**
The botany of desire : a plant's eye view of the world / Michael Pollan. New York : Random House, c2001. xxv, 271 p. ;
00-066479    306.4/5    0375501290
*Human-plant relationships.*

**QK46.5.H85.L48 1996**
**Lewis, Charles A.,**
Green nature/human nature : the meaning of plants in our lives / Charles A. Lewis. Urbana : University of Illinois Press, c1996. xix, 148 p. :
95-017506    304.2/7    0252022130
*Human-plant relationships.*

## QK47 Textbooks

**QK47.B73 1987**
**Bold, Harold Charles,**
The plant kingdom / Harold C. Bold, John W. La Claire II. Englewood Cliffs, N.J. : Prentice-Hall, c1987. x, 309 p. :
86-017009    581    0136803989
*Botany.*

## QK50 Popular works

**QK50.A77 1995**
**Attenborough, David,**
The private life of plants : a natural history of plant behaviour / David Attenborough. Princeton, NJ : Princeton University Press, c1995. 320 p. :
95-017514    581.5    0691006393
*Plants. Botany.*

**QK50.K46 1997**
**King, John,**
Reaching for the sun : how plants work / John King. Cambridge [England] ; New York, NY, USA : 1997. viii, 232 p.
96-045251    571.2    052155148X
*Plants. Botany.*

## QK63 Vegetation mapping

**QK63.D44**
**De Laubenfels, David J.,**
Mapping the world's vegetation : regionalization of formations and flora / David J. de Laubenfels. Syracuse, N.Y. : Syracuse University Press, 1975. xvii, 246 p.
75-025934    581.9    0815621728
*Vegetation mapping. Phytogeography.*

## QK73 Botanical gardens — By region or country, A-Z

**QK73.E85.P73 1981**
**Prest, John M.**
The Garden of Eden : the botanic garden and the re-creation of paradise / John Prest. New Haven : Yale University Press, c1981. 121 p. :
81-011365    712/.5    0300027265
*Botanical gardens -- Europe -- History.*

**QK73.G72R6928 1995**
**Desmond, Ray.**
 Kew : the history of the Royal Botanic Gardens / Ray Desmond ; foreword by Sir Ghillean Prance. London : Harvill Press with the Royal Botanic Gardens, Kew, 1995. xvi, 466 p. :
     580/.7/342195 21       1860460763
*Royal Botanic Gardens, Kew -- History. Botanic gardens History.*

## QK86.A1 Plant conservation. Rare plants. Endangered plants — General works

**QK86.A1.F73 1995**
**Frankel, O. H.**
 The conservation of plant biodiversity / Otto H. Frankel, Anthony H.D. Brown, and Jeremy J. Burdon. Cambridge ; Cambridge University Press, 1995. xiv, 299 p. :
95-006492      639.9/9      0521461650
 *Plant diversity conservation. Germplasm resources, Plant.*

**QK86.A1.G45 1991**
 Genetics and conservation of rare plants / edited by Donald A. Falk, Kent E. Holsinger ; Center for Plant Conservation. New York : Oxford University Press, 1991. xviii, 283 p.
91-010735      631.5/23      0195064291
 *Rare plants -- Genetics. Plant conservation. Plant populations.*

**QK86.A1.G54 1994**
**Given, David R.**
 Principles and practice of plant conservation / David R. Given. Portland, Or. : Timber Press, c1994. viii, 292 p.
93-005240      333.95/316      0881922498
 *Plant conservation. Plant diversity conservation.*

## QK86.U6 Plant conservation. Rare plants. Endangered plants — By region or country, A-Z

**QK86.U6.A93 1978**
**Ayensu, Edward S.**
 Endangered and threatened plants of the United States / Edward S. Ayensu and Robert A. DeFilipps, with the assistance of Sam E. Fowler ... [et al.]. Washington : Smithsonian Institution, 1978. xv, 403 p. ;
77-025138      333.9/5      0874742226
 *Rare plants -- United States. Plant conservation -- United States.*

**QK86.U6.M63 1983**
**Mohlenbrock, Robert H.,**
 Where have all the wildflowers gone? : a region-by-region guide to threatened or endangered U.S. wildflowers / Robert H. Mohlenbrock ; illustrations by Mark Mohlenbrock. New York : Macmillan ; c1983. xiv, 239 p.,
82-023411      581      002585450X
 *Endangered plants -- United States. Wild flowers – United States.*

## QK86.4 Plant conservation. Rare plants. Endangered plants — Plant reintroduction

**QK86.4.R47 1996**
 Restoring diversity : strategies for reintroduction of endangered plants / edited by Donald A. Falk, Constance I. Millar, Margaret Olwell ; foreword by Reed F. Noss. Washington, D.C. : Island Press, c1996. xxii, 505 p.
95-018936      581.5/29      1559632968
 *Plant reintroduction. Endangered plants. Restoration ecology.*

## QK93 Classification — Natural systems — General works, treatises, and textbooks

**QK93.L38**
**Lawrence, George Hill Mathewson,**
 Taxonomy of vascular plants. New York, Macmillan [1951] 823 p.
51007352      580.12
 *Botany -- Classification.*

## QK95 Classification — Systematics and taxonomy. Philosophy and methadology

**QK95.B44**
**Benson, Lyman David,**
 Plant taxonomy: methods and principles.  New York, Ronald Press Co. [1962] 494 p.
62-011646      580.12
 *Botany -- Classification.*

**QK95.J43 1982**
**Jeffrey, Charles.**
 An introduction to plant taxonomy / C. Jeffrey. Cambridge [Cambridgeshire] ; Cambridge University Press, 1982. vii, 154 p. :
81-017090      581/.012      0521245427
 *Botany -- Classification.*

**QK95.J63 1986**
**Jones, Samuel B.,**
 Plant systematics / Samuel B. Jones, Jr., Arlene E. Luchsinger. New York : McGraw-Hill, c1986. xiii, 512 p.
85-023048      581/.01/2      0070327963
 *Botany -- Classification.*

**QK95.P548 1999**
 Plant systematics : a phylogenetic approach / Walter S. Judd . . . [et al.]. Sunderland, Mass. : Sinauer Associates, c1999. xvi, 464 p. :
     580/.1/2 21      0878934049
*Botany -- Classification.*

**QK95.P548 1999**
 Plant systematics : a phylogenetic approach/ Walter S. Judd . . . [et al.]. Sunderland, Mass. : Sinauer Associates, c1999. xvi, 464 p. :
     580/.1/2 21      087893409
*Botany -- Classification.*

## QK95.P6 1967
**Porter, C. L.**
Taxonomy of flowering plants [by] C. L. Porter. San Francisco, W. H. Freeman [1967] 472 p.
66-019914        582.13/01/2
*Angiosperms. Botany -- Classification.*

## QK95.S57 1999
**Singh, Gurcharan.**
Plant systematics / Gurcharan Singh. Enfield, N.H. : Science Publishers, c1999. x, 258 p. :
99-048015        580/.1/2        1578080819
*Botany -- Classification.*

## QK95.S78 1990
**Stuessy, Tod F.**
Plant taxonomy : the systematic evaluation of comparative data / Tod F. Stuessy. New York : Columbia University Press, c1990. xvii, 514 p.
89-017401        581/.012        0231067844
*Botany -- Classification.*

## QK96 Classification — Nomenclature

### QK96.G54 1989
**Gledhill, D.**
The names of plants / D. Gledhill. 2nd ed. Cambridge [England] ; New York : Cambridge University Press, 1989. vi, 202 p. :
          581/.014 19        0521366682
*Botany -- Nomenclature. Botany -- Dictionaires -- Latin (Medieval and modern) Latin language, Medieval and moder -- Dictionaries – English.*

### QK96.P35 1995
**Hyam, R.**
Plants and their names : a concise dictionary / R. Hyam, R. Pankhurst. Oxford [England] ; Oxford University Press ; 1995. x, 545 p. ;
94-005024        581/.014        0198661894
*Botany -- Nomenclature. Plant names, Popular -- Dictionaries. Botany -- Dictionaries.*

### QK96.R4 vol. 111
International code of botanical nomenclature = Code international de la nomenclature botanique = Internationaler Code der botanischen Nomenklatur / adopted by the Thirteenth International Botanical Congress, Sydney, August 1981 ; prepared and edited by E.G. Voss ... [et al.]. Utrecht : Bohn, Scheltema & Holkema ; 1983. xv, 472 p. ;
83-012277        581/.012 s        9031305723
*Botany -- Nomenclature -- Congresses.*

## QK97 Classification — Comprehensive systematic works

### QK97.B45 1979
**Benson, Lyman David,**
Plant classification / Lyman Benson ; principal plant dissections and ill. by Jerome D. Laudermilk. Lexington, Mass. : Heath, c1979. xxiii, 901 p.
78-061856        581/.01/2        0669014893
*Botany -- Classification.*

## QK98 Classification — Pictorial works and atlases (of plants)

### QK98.W7213
**Wit, H. C. D. de**
Plants of the world [by] H. C. D. de Wit. Translated by A. J. Pomerans. New York, Dutton, 1966- v.
66-025815        581
*Botany -- Pictorial works.*

## QK98.5 Edible plants — By region or country, A-Z

### QK98.5.U6.P47
**Peterson, Lee.**
A field guide to edible wild plants of Eastern and Central North America / by Lee Peterson ; line drawings by Lee Peterson and Roger Tory Peterson ; photos. by Lee Peterson. Boston : Houghton Mifflin, 1978, c1977. xiii, 330 p.,
77-027323        581.6/32/0973        0395204453
*Wild plants, Edible -- East (U.S.) -- Identification. Wild plants, Edible -- Middle West -- Identification. Wild plants, Edible – Canada, Eastern -- Identification.*

## QK99 Medical botany — General works, treatises, and textbooks

### QK99.A1
**Sumner, Judith.**
The natural history of medicinal plants / Judith Sumner ; foreword by Mark J. Plotkin. Portland, Or. : Timber Press, c2000. 235 p., [16]
99-076555        581.6/34        0881924830
*Botany, Medical. Medicinal plants.*

### QK99.A1D83 2001
**Duke, James A.,**
Handbook of medicinal herbs / James A. Duke. Boca Raton : CRC Press, c2001. 677 p. :
          615/.321 21        0849329280
*Medicinal plants -- Handbooks, manuals, etc. Herbs -- Handbooks, manuals, etc. Herbals -- Handbooks, manuals, etc. Materia medica, Vegetable -- Handbooks, manuals, etc.*

**QK99.A432.C37 1998**
**Castner, James L.**
A field guide to medicinal and useful plants of the Upper Amazon / by James L. Castner, Stephen L. Timme, James A. Duke. Gainesville, FL : Feline Press, c1998. vi, 154 p. :
97-077509      581.6/3/09811     0962515078
*Medicinal plants -- Amazon River Region. Plants, Useful -- Amazon River Region. Botany, Economic -- Amazon River Region.*

**QK99.N67.E44**
**Elliott, Douglas B.**
Roots : an underground botany and forager's guide / written and illustrated by Douglas B. Elliott. Old Greenwich, Conn. : Chatham Press, c1976. 128 p. :
75-046234      581.6/3     0856991325
*Medicinal plants -- North America -- Identification. Wild plants, Edible -- North America -- Identification. Roots (Botany) -- Identification.*

**QK99.U6.F68 1999**
**Foster, Steven,**
A field guide to medicinal plants and herbs of eastern and central North America / Steven Foster and James A. Duke. Boston : Houghton Mifflin Co., 2000. xiii, 411 p.
99-033189      581.6/34/0973     0395988152
*Medicinal plants -- East (U.S.) -- Identification. Medicinal plants -- Middle West -- Identification. Medicinal plants – Canada, Eastern – Identification.*

## QK100 Poisonous plants — General works, treatises, and textbooks

**QK100.A1.T87 1991**
**Turner, Nancy J.,**
Common poisonous plants and mushrooms of North America / Nancy J. Turner and Adam F. Szczawinski. Portland, Or. : Timber Press, c1991. xv, 311 p. :
90-037574      581.6/9/097     0881921793
*Poisonous plants -- Identification. Poisonous plants – Toxicology. Mushrooms, Poisonous -- Identification.*

**QK100.U6.W43 1998**
**Weathers, Shirley A.**
Field guide to plants poisonous to livestock : Western U.S. / Shirley A. Weathers ; with a foreword by Peter R. Cheeke. Fruitland, UT : Rosebud Press, c1998. xii, 229 p. :
97-075436      636.2/0895952/0978
0966039734
*Livestock poisoning plants -- West (U.S.) -- Identification. Livestock poisoning plants -- West (U.S.) -- Pictorial works.*

## QK101 Geographical distribution. Phytogeography — General works, treatises, and textbooks

**QK101.D26**
**Daubenmire, Rexford F.,**
Plant geography : with special reference to North America / Rexford Daubenmire. New York : Academic Press, 1978. vi, 338 p. :
77-075570      581.9     012204150X
*Phytogeography. Botany -- North America.*

**QK101.S28 1988**
**Sauer, Jonathan D.**
Plant migration : the dynamics of geographic patterning in seed plant species / Jonathan D. Sauer. Berkeley : University of California Press, c1988. xvi, 282 p. :
87-022172      582/.052     0520060032
*Plants -- Migration. Vegetation dynamics. Phytogeography.*

**QK101.S76**
**Stott, Philip Anthony.**
Historical plant geography : an introduction / Philip Stott. London ; Allen & Unwin, 1981. xii, 151 p. :
80-041627      581.9     0045800103
*Phytogeography. Phytogeography -- Methodology.*

**QK101.T313 1986**
**Takhtadzhian, A. L.**
Floristic regions of the world / Armen Takhtajan ; translated by Theodore J. Crovello with the assistance and collaboration of the author and under the editorship of Arthur Cronquist. Berkeley : University of California Press, c1986. xxii, 522 p.
85-008731      582.09     0520040279
*Phytogeography.*

## QK105 Geographical distribution. Phytogeography — Aquatic flora (General) — Freshwater flora (General)

**QK105.F3 1957**
**Fassett, Norman C.**
A manual of aquatic plants. With Revision appendix by Eugene C. Ogden. Madison, University of Wisconsin Press, 1957. 405 p.
57-006593      581.92973
*Aquatic plants -- Northeastern States -- Identification. Aquatic plants -- Maritime Provinces -- Identification.*

## QK110-201 Geographical distribution.
### Phytogeography — Topographical divisions — America

**QK110.B3 1949**
**Bailey, L. H.**
Manual of cultivated plants most commonly grown in the continental United States and Canada, by L. H. Bailey and the staff of the Bailey Hortorium at Cornell University. New York, Macmillan Co., 1949. 1116 p.
49-009666     581.97
   *Botany -- United States. Botany -- Canada. Plants, Cultivated.*

**QK110.C56 1993**
**Coffey, Timothy.**
The history and folklore of North American wildflowers / Timothy Coffey ; foreword by Stephen Foster. New York : Facts on File, c1993. xxiv, 356 p.
92-018392     582.13/097     0816026246
   *Wild flowers -- North America. Wild flowers -- Utilization – North America. Wild flowers -- North America -- Folklore.*

**QK110.F3 1995**
**Farrar, John Laird.**
Trees of the northern United States and Canada / John Laird Farrar. Ames : Iowa State University Press, c1995. x, 502 p. :
95-022678     582.160973     081382740X
   *Trees -- United States -- Identification. Trees -- Canada -- Identification. Trees -- United States -- Pictorial works.*

**QK110.F53 1990**
Fire in North American tallgrass prairies / edited by Scott L. Collins and Linda L. Wallace. Norman [Okla.] : University of Oklahoma Press, c1990. xii, 175 p. :
90-012044     574.5/2643     0806122811
   *Prairie ecology -- North America -- Congresses. Grassland fires – Environmental aspects -- North America -- Congresses. Fire ecology – North America -- Congresses.*

**QK110.F55 1993**
Flora of North America : north of Mexico / edited by Flora of North America Editorial Committee. New York : Oxford University Press, 1993-1997 v. 1-3  :
92-030459     581.97     0195057139
   *Botany -- North America. Botany -- United States. Botany -- Canada.*

**QK110.J64 1992**
**Johnson, Edward A.**
Fire and vegetation dynamics : studies from the North American boreal forest / Edward A. Johnson. Cambridge ; Cambridge University Press, 1992. xiii, 129 p.
91-036693     581.5/2642     0521341515
   *Taiga ecology -- North America. Forest fires -- Environmental aspects -- North America. Fire ecology -- North America.*

**QK110.K37 1994**
**Kartesz, John T.**
A synonymized checklist of the vascular flora of the United States, Canada, and Greenland / John T. Kartesz. Portland, Or. : Timber Press, c1994. 2 v. ;
93-032948     581.97/01/4     0881922048
   *Botany -- United States -- Nomenclature. Botany -- Canada – Nomenclature. Botany -- Greenland -- Nomenclature.*

**QK110.N854 2000**
North American terrestrial vegetation / edited by Michael G. Barbour, William Dwight Billings. Cambridge, U.K. ; Cambridge University Press, 2000. xi, 708 p. :
97-029061     581.7/22/097     0521550270
   *Plant communities -- North America. Plant ecology -- North America. Phytogeography -- North America.*

**QK110.P49 1985**
Physiological ecology of North American plant communities / edited by Brian F. Chabot and Harold A. Mooney. New York : Chapman and Hall, 1985. xiv, 351 p. :
84-009586     581.5/097     0412232405
   *Plant ecophysiology -- North America. Plant communities – North America.*

**QK110.T48 1996**
Textbook of dendrology / William M. Harlow . . . [et al.]. 8th ed. New York : McGraw-Hill, c1996. x, 534 p. :
     582.16097 20     0070265720
*Trees -- United States. Trees -- Canada. Forest plants -- United States. Forest plants -- Canada.*

**QK115.L43 1998**
**Leopold, Donald Joseph,**
Trees of the central hardwood forests of North America : an identification and cultivation guide / Donald J. Leopold, William C. McComb, Robert N. Muller. Portland, Or. : Timber Press, c1998. 469 p., [40]
97-006200     582.16/097     0881924067
   *Trees -- East (U.S.) -- Identification. Trees -- Canada, Eastern – Identification. Hardwoods -- East (U.S.)*

**QK115.R5**
**Rickett, Harold William,**
Wild flowers of the United States. General editor, William C. Steere. Collaborators: Rogers McVaugh [and others. New York, McGraw-Hill [1966-73] 6 v. in 14 pt
66-017920     582.130973
   *Wild flowers -- United States -- Pictorial works.*

**QK115.S38 1999**
Savannas, barrens, and rock outcrop plant communities of North America / edited by Roger C. Anderson, James S. Fralish, Jerry M. Baskin. Cambridge ; Cambridge University Press, 1999. ix, 470 p. :
98025688     581.7/48/0973     052157322X
   *Plant communities -- United States. Plant ecology – United States. Savanna plants -- Canada.*

**QK115.Z65 1994**
**Zomlefer, Wendy B.**
Guide to flowering plant families / Wendy B. Zomlefer. Chapel Hill : University of North Carolina Press, c1994. xiv, 430 p. :
94-005712          582.13     0807821608
*Angiosperms -- United States -- Classification. Angiosperms – Canada -- Classification. Angiosperms -- Classification.*

**QK117.C84 2000**
**Crow, Garrett E.**
Aquatic and wetland plants of northeastern North America : a revised and enlarged edition of Norman C. Fassett's A manual of aquatic plants / Garrett E. Crow and C. Barre Hellquist. Madison, Wis. : University of Wisconsin Press, c2000. 2 v. :
99-019556          581.7/6/0974     029916330X
*Aquatic plants -- Northeastern States -- Identification. Wetland plants -- Northeastern States -- Identification. Aquatic plants -- Atlantic Provinces -- Identification.*

**QK117.G49 1991**
**Gleason, Henry A.**
Manual of vascular plants of northeastern United States and adjacent Canada / Henry A. Gleason and Arthur Cronquist. Bronx, N.Y., USA : New York Botanical Garden, c1991. lxxv, 910 p.
91-023110          582.0974     0893273651
*Botany -- Northeastern States. Botany -- Canada, Eastern. Plants -- Identification.*

**QK117.G75 1950**
**Gray, Asa,**
Manual of botany; a handbook of the flowering plants and ferns of the central and northeastern United States and adjacent Canada.  New York, American Book Company [1950] lxiv, 1632p.
50009007          581.973
*Botany -- United States.*

**QK117.H65 1998**
**Holmgren, Noel H.**
Illustrated companion to Gleason and Cronquist's manual : illustrations of the vascular plants of northeastern United States and adjacent Canada / Noel H. Holmgren ; with the artistic and editorial assistance of Patricia K. Holmgren ... [et al.]. Bronx, N.Y. : New York Botanical Garden, 1998. xvi, 937 p. :
97-047032          581.974     0893273996
*Botany -- Northeastern States. Botany -- Canada, Eastern. Botany -- Northeastern States -- Pictorial works.*

**QK118.N42**
**Newcomb, Lawrence.**
Newcomb's Wildflower guide : an ingenious new key system for quick, positive field identification of the wildflowers, flowering shrubs and vines of Northeastern and North Central North America / Lawrence Newcomb ; illustrated by Gordon Morrison ; foreword by Roland C. Clement. Boston : Little, Brown, c1977. xxii, 490 p.
77-000047          582/.13/0974     0316604410
*Wild flowers -- Northeastern States -- Identification. Shrubs -- Northeastern States -- Identification. Climbing plants – Northeastern States -- Identification.*

**QK121.M34 1999**
**Magee, Dennis W.,**
Flora of the Northeast : a manual of the vascular flora of New England and adjacent New York / Dennis W. Magee and Harry E. Ahles ; drawings by Abigail Rorer. Amherst : University of Massachusetts Press, c1999. xxxi, 1213 p.
98-049300          581.974     1558491899
*Botany -- New England. Botany -- New York (State)  Plants -- Identification.*

**QK122.3.H46 1999**
**Hemmerly, Thomas E.**
Appalachian wildflowers / Thomas E. Hemmerly. Athens, Ga. : University of Georgia Press, 1999. p. cm.
99-029638          582.13/0974     0820321648
*Wild flowers -- Appalachian Region -- Identification. Wildflowers -- Appalachian Region -- Pictorial works.*

**QK125.T55 1993**
**Tiner, Ralph W.**
Field guide to coastal wetland plants of the southeastern United States / Ralph W. Tiner ; drawings by Abigail Rorer. Amherst : University of Massachusetts Press, c1993. xiii, 328 p.
92-036526          582.0975     0870238329
*Wetland plants -- Southern States -- Identification. Coastal plants -- Southern States -- Identification. Wetland plants – Southern States -- Pictorial works.*

**QK133.A5 1982**
Analysis of coniferous forest ecosystems in the Western United States / edited by Robert L. Edmonds. Stroudsburg, Pa. : Hutchinson Ross Pub. Co. ; c1982. xvii, 419 p.
80-026699          581.5/2642/0978     0879333820
*Forest ecology -- West (U.S.)  Conifers -- West (U.S.) -- Ecology. Stream ecology -- West (U.S.)*

**QK135.F55 1986**
Flora of the Great Plains / by the Great Plains Flora Association ; Ronald L. McGregor, coordinator ; T.M. Barkley, editor ; Ralph E. Brooks, associate editor ; Eileen K. Schofield, associate editor. Lawrence, Kan. : University Press of Kansas, c1986. vii, 1392 p.
86-000023          582.0978     070060295X
*Botany -- Great Plains -- Classification.*

**QK141.I58**
Intermountain flora; vascular plants of the Intermountain West, U.S.A., by Arthur Cronquist [and others] New York, Published for the New York Botanical Garden by H 1972-1997 v. 1, 3-6; in
73-134298          581.9/79     0231041209
*Botany -- Great Basin. Plants -- Identification.*

**QK142.T87 1995**
**Turner, R. M.**
Sonoran Desert plants : an ecological atlas / Raymond M. Turner, Janice E. Bowers, Tony L. Burgess. Tucson : University of Arizona Press, c1995. xvi, 504 p. :
94-018723          581.9791/7     0816515328
*Desert plants -- Sonoran Desert -- Geographical distribution. Desert plants -- Sonoran Desert -- Geographical distribution – Maps. Desert plants -- Ecology -- Sonoran Desert.*

## QK149.S73 2001
**Stuart, John David.**
Trees and shrubs of California / John D. Stuart, John O. Sawyer ; illustrated by Andrea J. Pickart. Berkeley : University of California Press, c2001. xii, 467 p. :
00-025834          582.16/09794          0520221095
*Trees -- California -- Identification. Shrubs -- California -- Identification. Trees -- California -- Pictorial works.*

## QK150.V38 1990
**Veblen, Thomas T.,**
The Colorado Front Range : a century of ecological change / Thomas T. Veblen, Diane C. Lorenz. Salt Lake City : University of Utah Press, c1991. 186 p. :
90-031547          581.5/2642/097886
0874803519
*Plant ecology -- Colorado -- History -- Pictorial works. Plant ecology -- Front Range (Colo. and Wyo.) -- History -- Pictorial works. Vegetation dynamics -- Colorado -- History -- Pictorial works. Front Range (Colo. and Wyo.) -- History -- Pictorial works.*

## QK150.N4 2000
**Beidleman, Linda H.**
Plants of Rocky Mountain National Park : a complete revision of Ruth Ashton Nelson's popular manual / Linda H. Beidleman, Richard G. Beidleman, and Beatrice E. Willard. Helena, Mont. : Rocky Mountain Nature Assocation & Falcon Pub., c2000. vi, 266 p. :
00-039044          581.9788/69
*Botany -- Colorado -- Rocky Mountain National Park. Plants -- Identification.*

## QK177.K83 1992
**Kudish, Michael,**
Adirondack upland flora : an ecological perspective / Michael Kudish. Saranac, N.Y. : Chauncy Press, 1992. p. cm.
91-044851          581.9747/5          0918517168
*Botany -- New York (State) -- Adirondack Mountains Region. Botany -- New York (State) -- Adirondack Mountains Region -- Ecology.*

## QK192.B54 2000
**Biek, David.**
Flora of Mount Rainier National Park / by David Biek. Corvallis : Oregon State University Press, 2000. vi, 506 p. :
99-057564          581.9797/782          0870714708
*Botany -- Washington (State) -- Mount Rainier National Park. Plants -- Identification.   Mount Rainier National Park (Wash.)*

## QK192.M68 1987
Mount St. Helens, 1980 : botanical consequences of the explosive eruptions / edited by David E. Bilderback. Berkeley : University of California Press, c1987. vii, 360 p. :
85-024650          581.5/222          0520056086
*Plant ecology -- Washington (State) -- Saint Helens, Mount, Region -- Congresses. Plant communities -- Washington (State) -- Saint Helens, Mount, Region -- Congresses. Vegetation dynamics -- Washington (State) -- Saint Helens, Mount, Region -- Congresses. Saint Helens, Mount -- Eruption, 1980 -- Congresses.*

## QK195.D47 1990
**Despain, Don G.**
Yellowstone vegetation : consequences of environment and history in a natural setting / Don G. Despain. Boulder : Roberts Rinehart, c1990. xiii, 239 p.
90-061588          0911797750
*Vegetation dynamics -- Yellowstone National Park Region. Forest dynamics -- Yellowstone National Park Region. Plant communities -- Yellowstone National Park Region.*

## QK201.S25 1995
**Scott, Geoffrey A. J.**
Canada's vegetation : a world perspective / Geoffrey A.J. Scott. Montreal : McGill-Queen's University Press, 1995. xviii, 361 p.
95-170382          581.971          0773512403
*Phytogeography -- Canada. Plant ecology -- Canada. Phytogeography.*

## QK281-321 Geographical distribution. Phytogeography — Topographical divisions — Europe

## QK281.F59 1993
Flora Europaea / edited by T.G. Tutin ... [et al.] ; assisted by J.R. Akeroyd and M.E. Newton ; appendices edited by R.R. Mills. Cambridge ; Cambridge University Press, 1993- v. 1   :
92-033771          581.94     052141007X
*Botany -- Europe. Botany -- Europe -- Classification.*

## QK306.S78 1997
**Stace, Clive A.**
New flora of the British Isles / Clive Stace ; with illustrations mainly by Hilli Thompson. New York : Cambridge University Press, 1997. xxvii, 1130 p
97-004473          581.941          0521589355
*Botany -- British Isles. Plants -- Identification.*

## QK306.H885 2000
**Humphries, C.J. (Christopher John),**
Guide to trees of Britain and Europe / C.J. Humphries, J.R. Press, D.A. Sutton ; illustrated by I. Garrard, T. Hayward, D. More. London : Hamlyn, 2000. 320 p.
2001347620          582.16/094 21
*Trees -- Great Britain -- Identification. Trees -- Europe -- Identification.*

## QK321.C416 1995
**Cherepanov, Sergei Kirillovich.**
Vascular plants of Russia and adjacent states (the former USSR) / S.K. Czerepanov. Cambridge [England] ; Cambridge University Press, 1995. x, 516 p. :
94-006992          580.947          0521450063
*Botany -- Former Soviet Republics -- Nomenclature.*

## QK358-360 Geographical distribution. Phytogeography — Topographical divisions — Asia

**QK358.C67 1996**
**Cook, Christopher D. K.**
  Aquatic and wetland plants of India : a reference book and identification manual for the vascular plants found in permanent or seasonal fresh water in the subcontinent of India south of the Himalaya Christopher D.K. Cook. Oxford ; Oxford University Press, 1996. 385 p. :
95-035778          581.954/0916/9          0198548214
  *Freshwater plants -- India. Wetland plants -- India. Freshwater plants -- India -- Identification.*

**QK360.Y3513 1997**
**Yamada, Isamu,**
  Tropical rain forests of Southeast Asia : a forest ecologist's view / by Isamu Yamada ; translated by Peter Hawkes. Honolulu : University of Hawai'i Press, c1997. xv, 392 p. :
97-022345          577.34/0959          0824819365
  *Rain forest ecology -- Asia, Southeastern. Rain forest conservation -- Asia, Southeastern.*

## QK394 Geographical distribution. Phytogeography — Topographical divisions — Africa

**QK394.V45 1997**
  Vegetation of southern Africa / edited by R.M. Cowling, D.M. Richardson & S.M. Pierce. Cambridge [England] ; Cambridge University Press, 1997. xxxiv, 615 p.
96-013572          581.5/0968          0521571421
  *Plant ecology -- Africa, Southern. Plant communities -- Africa, Southern. Phytogeography -- Africa, Southern.*

## QK431 Geographical distribution. Phytogeography — Topographical divisions — Australia

**QK431.A9 1994**
  Australian vegetation / edited by R.H. Groves. Cambridge [England] ; Cambridge University Press, 1994. xvii, 562 p.
93-028688          581.994          0521414202
  *Plant ecology -- Australia. Plant communities -- Australia. Phytogeography -- Australia.*

**QK431.B67 2000**
**Bowman, D. M. J. S.**
  Australian rainforests : islands of green in a land of fire / D.M.J.S. Bowman. Cambridge, UK ; Cambridge University Press, 2000. xi, 345 p. :
99-024978          577.34/0994          0521465680
  *Rain forest ecology -- Australia. Fire ecology -- Australia. Fragmented landscapes -- Australia.*

## QK463 Geographical distribution. Phytogeography — Topographical divisions — New Zealand and adjacent islands

**QK463.W385 1991**
**Wardle, Peter.**
  Vegetation of New Zealand / Peter Wardle. Cambridge ; Cambridge University Press, 1991. xx, 672 p. :
91-186520          581.993          0521258731
  *Plant ecology -- New Zealand. Plant communities – New Zealand. Phytogeography -- New Zealand.*

## QK471-473 Geographical distribution. Phytogeography — Topographical divisions — Pacific islands. Oceania

**QK471.E96 1998**
  Evolution and speciation of island plants / edited by Tod F. Stuessy and Mikio Ono. Cambridge ; Cambridge University Press, 1998. xiv, 358 p. :
97-036118          581.3/8          0521496535
  *Island plants -- Islands of the Pacific -- Congresses. Island plants -- Evolution -- Islands of the Pacific -- Congresses. Island plants – Speciation -- Islands of the Pacific -- Congresses.*

**QK473.G2.M37 1999**
**McMullen, Conley K.**
  Flowering plants of the Galapagos / Conley K. McMullen ; with a foreword by Sir Ghillean Prance. Ithaca, N.Y. : Cornell University Press, 1999. xiv, 370 p. :
99-031321          581.9866/5          0801437105
  *Botany -- Galapagos Islands. Plants -- Identification.*

**QK473.H4.W33 1990**
**Wagner, Warren Lambert.**
  Manual of the flowering plants of Hawaii / Warren L. Wagner, Derral R. Herbst, S.H. Sohmer ; Yevonn Wilson-Ramsey, illustrator. [Honolulu] : University of Hawaii Press : c1990. 2 v. (xviii,
88-039649          582.13/09969          0824811526
  *Angiosperms -- Hawaii -- Identification. Botany -- Hawaii.*

## QK475 Spermatophyta. Phanerogams — Trees and shrubs — General works, treatises, and textbooks

**QK475.O93**
  The Oxford encyclopedia of trees of the world / consultant editor, Bayard Hora. Oxford ; Oxford University Press, 1981. 288 p. :
81-129929          582.16          0192177125
  *Trees.*

**QK475.T48 2000**
**Thomas, Peter,**
  Trees : their natural history / Peter Thomas. Cambridge, U.K. ; Cambridge University Press, 2000. ix, 289 p. :
99-015473          582.16          0521453518
  *Trees.*

## QK481-482 Spermatophyta. Phanerogams — Trees and shrubs — Local

### QK481.E38
**Elias, Thomas S.**
The complete trees of North America : field guide and natural history / by Thomas S. Elias ; drawings by Ruth T. Brunstetter, Charles Edward Faxon, Mary W. Gill ; cartography by Delos D. Rowe Associates. New York : Outdoor Life/Nature Books : c1980. xii, 948 p. :
77-012451          582.16097          0442238622
*Trees -- North America -- Identification.*

### QK481.L49 1980
**Little, Elbert Luther,**
The Audubon Society field guide to North American trees / Elbert L. Little ; photos. by Sonja Bullaty and Angelo Lomeo, and others ; visual key by Susan Rayfield and Olivia Buehl. New York : Knopf : distributed by Random House, c1980. 2 v. :
79-003474          582.16097          0394507614
*Trees -- United States -- Identification. Trees -- Canada -- Identification.*

### QK481.S21 1961
**Sargent, Charles Sprague,**
Manual of the trees of North America (exclusive of Mexico) With 783 illus. by Charles Edward Faxon and Mary W. Gill. New York, Dover Publications [1961, c1949] 2 v. (xxvi, 9
61-065275          582.16097
*Trees -- North America.*

### QK482.P43
**Petrides, George A.**
A field guide to trees and shrubs; field marks of all trees, shrubs, and woody vines that grow wild in the Northeastern and North-Central United States and in southeastern and south-central Canada.t Illus. by George A. Petrides (leaf and twig plates) [and] Roger Tory Peterson (flowers, fruits, silhouettes) Boston, Houghton Mifflin, 1958. xxix, 431 p.
57-010783          582.16
*Trees -- North America. Shrubs -- North America. Climbing plants.*

## QK494 Spermatophyta. Phanerogams — Systematic divisions — Gymnosperms

### QK494.N67 1997
**Norstog, Knut,**
The biology of the cycads / Knut J. Norstog, Trevor J. Nicholls. Ithaca, N.Y. : Comstock Pub. Associates, 1997. xi, 363 p. :
96-048889          585/.9          080143033X
*Cycads.*

## QK495 Spermatophyta. Phanerogams — Systematic divisions — Angiosperms

### QK495.A1.C76
**Cronquist, Arthur.**
An integrated system of classification of flowering plants / Arthur Cronquist. New York : Columbia University Press, 1981. xviii, 1262 p
80-039556          582.13/012          0231038801
*Angiosperms -- Classification.*

### QK495.A1.F58 1993
Flowering plants of the world / consultant editor, V.H. Heywood ; advisory editors, D.M. Moore, I.B.K. Richardson, W.T. Stearn ; artists, Victoria Goaman, Judith Dunkley, Christabel King. New York : Oxford University Press, 1993. 335 p. :
93-014014          582.13          0195210379
*Angiosperms.*

### QK495.A1.T35 1991
**Takhtadzhian, A. L.**
Evolutionary trends in flowering plants / Armen Takhtajan. New York : Columbia University Press, c1991. x, 241 p. :
91-007320          582.13/0438          0231073283
*Angiosperms -- Evolution. Plants -- Evolution.*

### QK495.A12M47 1979
**Metcalfe, Charles Russell**
Anatomy of the dicotyledons / by C.R. Metcalfe and L. Chalk ; with contributions from Katherine Esau . . . [et al.]. 2d ed. Oxford : Clarendon Press, 1979-<1998> 4 v. :
          583.044 19          0198543832
*Dicotyledons -- Anatomy. Botany -- Anatomy.*

### QK495.A26.N63 1988
**Nobel, Park S.**
Environmental biology of agaves and cacti / Park S. Nobel. Cambridge ; Cambridge University Press, 1988. x, 270 p. :
87-017314          584/.25          0521343224
*Agaves -- Physiology. Cactus -- Physiology. Agaves – Ecology.*

### QK495.A56.C7
**Cronquist, Arthur.**
The evolution and classification of flowering plants. Boston, Houghton Mifflin [1968] x, 396 p.
68-004883          582.13
*Angiosperms -- Evolution. Angiosperms -- Classification. Plants -- Evolution.*

### QK495.C11
**Anderson, Edward F.,**
The cactus family / Edward F. Anderson ; with a foreword by Wilhelm Barthlott ; and a chapter on cactus cultivation by Roger Brown. Portland, Or. : Timber Press, c2001. 776 p. :
00-060700          583/.56          0881924989
*Cactus. Cactus -- Pictorial works.*

**QK495.C11.B354 1982**
**Benson, Lyman David,**
The cacti of the United States and Canada / Lyman Benson ; with line drawings by Lucretia Breazeale Hamilton. Stanford, Calif. : Stanford University Press, 1982. ix, 1044, [48
73-080617        583/.47/0973        0804708630
*Cactus -- United States. Cactus -- Canada. Botany -- United States.*

**QK495.C11.G5 1986**
**Gibson, Arthur C.**
The cactus primer / Arthur C. Gibson, Park S. Nobel. Cambridge, Mass. : Harvard University Press, 1986. vi, 286 p., [
85-024874        583/.47        0674089901
*Cactus.*

**QK495.C75.D3 1967**
**Dallimore, William.**
A handbook of Coniferae and Ginkgoaccae, by W.Dallimore and A. Bruce Johnson. Rev. by S. G. Harrison. New York, St. Martin's Press, [1967] xix, 729p.
67011838        585.2
*Conifers. Gingkgo.*

**QK495.G74**
**Stanfield, D. P.**
Grasses, by D. P. Stanfield. [Ibadan] Ibadan University Press, 1970. ix, 118 p.
71-014743        548/.9/09669
*Grasses -- Nigeria.*

**QK495.G74.O355 1999**
**Ohrnberger, D.**
The bamboos of the world : annotated nomenclature and literature of the species and the higher and lower taxa / D. Ohrnberger. Amsterdam ; Elsevier, 1999. x, 585 p. :
98-032276        584/.9        0444500200
*Bamboo. Bamboo -- Classification. Bamboo -- Nomenclature.*

**QK495.G9.C5 1966**
**Chamberlain, Charles Joseph,**
Gymnosperms: structure and evolution. New York, Dover Publications [1966] xi, 484 p.
66-020503        585
*Gymnosperms.*

**QK495.O64.A73 1992**
**Arditti, Joseph.**
Fundamentals of orchid biology / Joseph Arditti. New York : Wiley, c1992. xii, 691 p. :
91-032733        584/.15        0471549061
*Orchids.*

**QK495.O64.S49 1994**
**Sheehan, Thomas J.**
An illustrated survey of orchid genera / Tom and Marion Sheehan. Portland, Or. : Timber Press, c1994. 421 p. :
93-049569        584/.15        0881922889
*Orchids. Orchids -- Pictorial works. Orchid culture.*

**QK495.P17.H44 1995**
**Henderson, Andrew,**
Field guide to the palms of the Americas / Andrew Henderson, Gloria Galeano, and Rodrigo Bernal. Princeton, N.J. : Princeton University Press, c1995. viii, 352 p.,
94-030080        584/.5/097        0691085374
*Palms -- America -- Identification.*

## QK505 Cryptogams — General works, treatises, and textbooks

**QK505.N66 1982**
Nonvascular plants : an evolutionary survey / R.F. Scagel ... [et al.]. Belmont, Calif. : Wadsworth Pub. Co., c1982. vi, 570 p. :
81-024066        586        0534010296
*Cryptogams. Cryptogams -- Evolution. Cryptogams – Phylogeny.*

## QK521 Cryptogams — Pteridophyta (Ferns, etc.) — Anatomy, physiology, etc.

**QK521.R34 1989**
**Raghavan, V.**
Developmental biology of fern gametophytes / V. Raghavan. Cambridge [England] ; Cambridge University Press, 1989. xiv, 361 p. :
88-022935        587/.31043        052133022X
*Fern gametophytes -- Development.*

## QK523 Cryptogams — Pteridophyta (Ferns, etc.) — Classification. Systematic works

**QK523.V47 1967**
**Verdoorn, Frans,**
Manual of pteridology; edited by Fr. Verdoorn in collaboration with A. H. G. Alston [and others] foreword by F. O. Bower; with 121 illustrations. Amsterdam, A. Asher, 1967. xx, 640 p.
70-352960        587
*Ferns.*

## QK524.5 Cryptogams — Pteridophyta (Ferns, etc.) — Geographical distribution

**QK524.5.L45 1985**
**Lellinger, David B.**
A field manual of the ferns & fern-allies of the United States & Canada / David B. Lellinger ; with photographs by A. Murray Evans. Washington, D.C. : Smithsonian Institution Press, c1985. ix, 389 p., [
84-022216        587        0874746027
*Ferns -- United States -- Identification. Ferns -- Canada -- Identification. Pteridophyta -- United States -- Identification.*

**QK525.5.I4.M6 1999**
**Mohlenbrock, Robert H.,**
Ferns / Robert H. Mohlenbrock. Carbondale : Southern Illinois University Press, c1999. xiii, 240 p.
99-017308          587/.3/09773          0809322552
*Ferns -- Illinois -- Identification. Ferns -- Illinois -- Pictorial works. Ferns -- Illinois -- Geographical distribution -- Maps.*

## QK533 Cryptogams — Bryophyta. Bryology — General works, treatises, and textbooks

**QK533.B72 1992**
Bryophytes and lichens in a changing environment / edited by Jeffrey W. Bates and Andrew M. Farmer. Oxford [England] : Clarendon Press ; 1992. xii, 404 p. :
91-043550          588/.045          0198542917
*Bryophytes -- Ecology. Lichens -- Ecology.*

## QK533.84 Cryptogams — Bryophyta. Bryology — By region or country

**QK533.84.N67.C66 1979**
**Conard, Henry Shoemaker,**
How to know the mosses and liverworts / Henry S. Conard. Dubuque, Iowa : W. C. Brown Co., c1979. xi, 302 p. :
78-052712          588/.097          0697047687
*Bryophytes -- North America -- Identification. Mosses -- North America -- Identification. Liverworts -- North America -- Identification.*

## QK537 Cryptogams — Bryophyta. Bryology — Musci (Mosses)

**QK537.M35 2000**
**Malcolm, W. M.**
Mosses and other bryophytes : an illustrated glossary / Bill and Nancy Malcolm. Nelson, N.Z. : Micro-Optics Press, 2000. iv, 220 p. :
00-1411832          588/.03          0473067307
*Mosses -- Dictionaries. Bryophytes -- Dictionaries.*

**QK537.R53 1981**
**Richardson, D. H. S.**
The biology of mosses / by D.H.S. Richardson. New York : Wiley, 1981. xii, 220 p. :
81-003029          588/.2          0470271906
*Mosses.*

## QK565-565.2 Cryptogams — Algae. Algology — Anatomy, physiology, etc.

**QK565.L4**
**Lewin, Ralph A.,**
Physiology and biochemistry of algae.    New York, Academic Press, 1962. 929 p.
62-013104          589.3
*Algae -- Physiology. Botanical chemistry.*

**QK565.2.H36**
Handbook of phycological methods. Sponsored by the Phycological Society of America Inc. Cambridge [Eng.] University Press, 1973-1985. 4 v.
73-079496          589.3/028          0521200490
*Algology -- Methodology.*

## QK566 Cryptogams — Algae. Algology — General works, treatises, and textbooks

**QK566.B64 1985**
**Bold, Harold Charles,**
Introduction to the algae : structure and reproduction / Harold C. Bold, Michael J. Wynne. Englewood Cliffs, N.J. : Prentice-Hall, c1985. xvi, 720 p. :
84-004696          589.3          0134777468
*Algology. Algae -- Anatomy. Algae -- Reproduction.*

**QK566.G735 2000**
**Graham, Linda E.,**
Algae / Linda F. Graham, Lee W. Wilcox. Upper Saddler River, NJ : Prentice Hall, c2000. 1 v. (various
99-024517          579.8          0136603335
*Algae. Algology.*

**QK566.L44 1999**
**Lee, Robert Edward,**
Phycology / Robert Edward Lee. Cambridge [England] ; Cambridge University Press, 1999. x, 614 p. :
98-053255          579.8          0521630908
*Algology.*

## QK569 Cryptogams — Algae. Algology — Systematic divisions, A-Z

**QK569.C37.M4513 1999**
**Meinesz, Alexandre.**
Killer algae / Alexandre Meinesz ; translated by Daniel Simberloff ; with a foreword by David Quammen. Chicago : University of Chicago Press, 1999. xvi, 360 p. :
99-032502          579.8/35          0226519228
*Caulerpa taxifolia -- Mediterranean Sea. Toxic marine algae – Mediterranean Sea. Alien plants -- Mediterranean Sea.*

**QK569.C486.H37 1989**
**Harris, Elizabeth H.**
The Chlamydomonas sourcebook : a comprehensive guide to biology and laboratory use / Elizabeth H. Harris. San Diego : Academic Press, c1989. xiv, 780 p. :
88-010453          589.4/7          012326880X
*Chlamydomonas. Chlamydomonas -- Laboratory manuals.*

**QK569.C96.H85**
**Humm, Harold Judson.**
Introduction and guide to the marine bluegreen algae / Harold J. Humm, Susanne R. Wicks. New York : Wiley, c1980. x, 194 p. ;
79-024488          589/.46          0471052175
*Blue-green algae. Marine algae. Cyanobacteria – Identification.*

**QK569.D54.I34 1996**

Identifying marine diatoms and dinoflagellates / editor, Carmelo R. Tomas ; contributors, Grethe R. Hasle ... [et al.]. San Diego : Academic Press, c1996. xiii, 598 p.

95-010871          589.4/3          0126930155

*Diatoms -- Identification. Dinoflagellates -- Identification. Marine phytoplankton -- Identification.*

**QK569.D54.R68 1990**
**Round, F.E.**

The Diatoms : biology & morphology of the genera / F.E. Round, R.M. Crawford, D.G. Mann. Cambridge [England] ; Cambridge University Press, 1990. 747 p. :

88-035276          589.4/81          0521363187

*Diatoms.*

**QK569.L2N67 1971**
**North, Wheeler J.**

The biology of giant kelp beds (Macrocystis) in California, edited by Wheeler J. North. Lehre : J. Cramer, 1971. xiii, 600 p. :

589/.45

*Giant kelp -- California. Giant kelp -- California. Kelp bed ecology – California.*

**QK569.R4.B56 1990**

Biology of the red algae / edited by Kathleen M. Cole, Robert G. Sheath. Cambridge [England] ; Cambridge University Press, 1990. ix, 517 p. :

89-071274          589.4/1          0521343011

*Red algae.*

## QK570.2-571 Cryptogams — Algae. Algology — Geographical distribution

**QK570.2.L64 1994**
**Lobban, Christopher S.**

Seaweed ecology and physiology / Christopher S. Lobban, Paul J. Harrison. Cambridge [England] ; Cambridge University Press, 1994. ix, 366 p. :

93-021306          589.4/5041          0521403340

*Marine algae -- Ecophysiology.*

**QK571.D35 1978**
**Dawson, Elmer Yale,**

How to know the seaweeds / Isabella A. Abbott, E. Yale Dawson. Dubuque, Iowa : W. C. Brown Co., c1978. viii, 141 p.

76-024691          589/.39/214          0697048950.

*Marine algae -- United States -- Identification.*

**QK571.P67 1962**
**Prescott, G. W. (Gerald Webber),**

Algae of the western Great Lakes area, with an illustrated key to the genera of desmids and freshwater diatoms. Rev. ed. Dubuque, Iowa : W. C. Brown Co., [1962] xiii, 977 p. :

589.30977

*Algae -- Lake States. Algae -- Bibliography.*

## QK581 Cryptogams — Lichens — Anatomy, physiology, etc.

**QK581.A35 1993**
**Ahmadjian, Vernon.**

The lichen symbiosis / Vernon Ahmadjian. New York : John Wiley, c1993. xv, 250 p. :

92-042873          589.1          0471578851

*Lichens. Symbiosis.*

## QK583 Cryptogams — Lichens — General works, treatises, and textbooks

**QK583.H35 1983**
**Hale, Mason E.**

The biology of lichens / Mason E. Hale, Jr. London ; E. Arnold, 1983. 190 p. :

85-128739          589.1          0713128674

*Lichens.*

## QK586.5-587 Cryptogams — Lichens — Local

**QK586.5.B76 2001**
**Brodo, Irwin M.**

Lichens of North America / Irwin M. Brodo, Sylvia Duran Sharnoff, Stephen Sharnoff ; with selected drawings by Susan Laurie-Bourque and published in collaboration with the Canadian Museum of Nature. New Haven : Yale University Press, c2001. xxiii, 795 p. :

579.7/097 21          0300082495

*Lichens -- North America -- Identification. Lichens – North America - - Pictorial works.*

**QK587.H25 1979**
**Hale, Mason E.**

How to know the lichens / Mason E. Hale. Dubuque, Iowa : W. C. Brown Co., c1979. viii, 246 p.,

78-055751          589/.1/097          0697047628.

*Lichens -- United States -- Identification. Lichens -- North America -- Identification.*

## QK600.35-601 Cryptogams — Fungi — Anatomy, physiology, etc.

**QK600.35.A35 2001**
**Ainsworth, G. C. (Geoffrey Clough),**

Ainsworth & Bisby's dictionary of the fungi / by P.M. Kirk . . . [et al.] ; with the assistance of A. Aptroot . . . [et al.]. 9th ed / prepared aby CABI Bioscience Wallingford, Oxon, UK ; New York, NY : CABI Publ, 2001. xi, 655 p. :

579.5/03 21          085199377X

*Fungi -- Dictionaires. Mycology -- Dictionaries.*

**QK600.35.U513 2000**
**Ulloa, Miguel,**
   Illustrated dictionary of mycology / by Miguel Ulloa and Richard T. Hanlin ; with the assistance of Samuel Aguila and Elvira Aguirre Acosta. St. Paul, Minn. : APS Press : American Phytopathological Society, c2000. 448 p. :
         579.5/03 21        0890542570
*Mycology -- Dictionaries. Fungi -- Dictionaires.*

**QK601.G27 1984**
**Garraway, Michael O.**
   Fungal nutrition and physiology / Michael O. Garraway, Robert C. Evans. New York : Wiley, c1984. vii, 401 p. :
83-023450        589.2/0413        0471058440
   *Fungi -- Physiology. Fungi -- Nutrition.*

**QK601.J46 1995**
**Jennings, D. H.**
   The physiology of fungal nutrition / D.H. Jennings. Cambridge ; Cambridge University Press, 1995. xv, 622 p. :
93-045578        589.2/0413        0521355249
   *Fungi -- Physiology. Fungi -- Nutrition.*

**QK601.M648 1998**
**Moore, D.**
   Fungal morphogenesis / David Moore. Cambridge ; Cambridge University Press, 1998. xiv, 469 p. :
97-043011        571.8/295        0521552958
   *Fungi -- Morphogenesis.*

## QK603 Cryptogams — Fungi — General works, treatises, and textbooks

**QK603.A55 1979**
**Alexopoulos, Constantine John,**
   Introductory mycology / Constantine J. Alexopoulos, Charles W. Mims ; artwork by Sung-Huang Sun and Raymond W. Scheetz. New York : Wiley, c1979. xvii, 632 p.
79-012514        589/.2        0471022144
   *Mycology.*

**QK603.H79 1998**
**Hudler, George W.**
   Magical mushrooms, mischievous molds / George W. Hudler. Princeton, N.J. : Princeton University Press, c1998. xvi, 248 p. :
98-010163        579.5        0691028737
   *Fungi.*

**QK603.R67**
**Ross, Ian K.**
   Biology of the fungi, their development, regulation, and associations / Ian K. Ross. New York : McGraw-Hill, c1979. xii, 499 p. :
78-023201        589/.2        007053870X
   *Fungi. Mycology.*

**QK603.W4 1980**
**Webster, John,**
   Introduction to fungi / John Webster. Cambridge [Eng.] ; Cambridge University Press, 1980. x, 669 p. :
79-052856        589/.2        0521228883
   *Fungi. Fungi -- Classification.*

## QK604 Cryptogams — Fungi — Special aspects of the subject as whole

**QK604.I73 1991**
**Isaac, Susan,**
   Fungal-plant interactions / Susan Isaac. London ; Chapman & Hall, 1992. xii, 418 p. :
91-027839        589.2/04524        0412364700
   *Plant-fungi relationships.*

## QK604.2 Cryptogams — Fungi — Special topics, A-Z

**QK604.2.E26.D59 1995**
**Dix, Neville J.**
   Fungal ecology / Neville J. Dix and John Webster. London : Chapman & Hall, 1995. viii, 549 p.
94072667        589.24        0412229609
   *Fungal communities. Fungi. Fungi -- Ecology.*

**QK604.2.M64.M665 1999**
   Molecular fungal biology / [edited by] Richard Oliver, Michael Schweizer. Cambridge, U.K. ; Cambridge University Press, c1999. x, 377 p. :
99-010041        572.8/295        0521561167
   *Fungal molecular biology.*

## QK617 Cryptogams — Fungi — Edible and poisonous fungi. Mushrooms (Popular works)

**QK617.B483 1997**
**Bessette, Alan.**
   Mushrooms of northeastern North America / Alan E. Bessette, Arleen R. Bessette, David W. Fischer. Syracuse, N.Y. : Syracuse University Press, 1997. xiv, 582 p. :
96-005729        589.2/22/097485        0815627076
   *Mushrooms -- Northeastern States -- Identification.*

**QK617.L248 1998**
**Laessoe, Thomas.**
   Mushrooms / Thomas Laessoe ; editorial consultant, Gary Lincoff ; photography by Neil Fletcher. New York : DK Pub., 1998. 304 p. :
97044418        579.6        0789432862
   *Mushrooms -- Identification. Mushrooms -- Pictorial works.*

## QK617.M84 1995

Mushrooms of North America in color : a field guide companion to seldom-illustrated fungi / Alan E. Bessette ... [et al.]. Syracuse, N.Y. : Syracuse University Press, 1995. x, 172 p. :
95-011781          589.2/22/097          0815626665
*Mushrooms -- North America -- Identification. Mushrooms -- North America -- Pictorial works.*

## QK617.S56 1980
**Smith, Alexander Hanchett,**

The mushroom hunter's field guide / Alexander H. Smith and Nancy Smith Weber. Ann Arbor : University of Michigan Press, c1980. 316 p. :
80-010514          589.2/097          0472856103
*Mushrooms -- United States -- Identification. Mushrooms -- Canada -- Identification.*

### QK618 Cryptogams — Fungi — Aquatic fungi (General)

## QK618.B56 1986

The Biology of marine fungi / edited by S.T. Moss. Cambridge ; New York : Cambridge University Press, 1986. xii, 382 p. :
                    589.2/092 19          0521308992
*Marine fungi.*

### QK629-635 Cryptogams — Fungi — Systematic divisions

## QK629.B6.B47 2000
**Bessette, Alan.**

North American boletes : a color guide to the fleshy pored mushrooms / Alan E. Bessette, William C. Roody, and Arleen R. Bessette. [Syracuse, N.Y.] : Syracuse University Press, 2000. xiii, 396 p.
99-021065          579.6          0815605889
*Boletaceae -- North America -- Identification. Boletaceae – North America -- Pictorial works.*

## QK629.S77.S735 1996
**Stamets, Paul.**

Psilocybin mushrooms of the world : an identification guide / Paul Stamets ; with a foreword by Andrew Weil. Berkeley, Calif. : Ten Speed Press, c1996. ix, 245 p. :
96-015717          589.2/22          0898158397
*Psilocybe -- Identification. Mushrooms, Hallucinogenic -- Identification.*

## QK635.A1.S73 1994
**Stephenson, Steven L.**

Myxomycetes : a handbook of slime molds / Steven L. Stephenson and Henry Stempen. Portland, Or. : Timber Press, c1994. 183 p.,[16] p
93-031302          589.2/9          0881922773 ;
*Myxomycetes. Myxomycetes -- Handbooks, manuals, etc.*

### QK641-642 Plant anatomy — General works, treatises, and textbooks

## QK641.B45 1990
**Bell, Adrian D.**

Plant form : an illustrated guide to flowering plant morphology / Adrian D. Bell ; with line drawings by Alan Bryan. Oxford ; Oxford University Press, 1991. xiii, 341 p.
90-034783          582.13/044          0198542194
*Angiosperms -- Morphology. Botany --Morphology. Angiosperms -- Morphology -- Atlases.*

## QK641.B596 1987
**Bold, Harold Charles,**

Morphology of plants and fungi / Harold C. Bold, Constantine J. Alexopoulos, Theodore Delevoryas. New York : Harper & Row, c1987. x, 912 p. :
86-014294          581.4          0060408391
*Botany -- Morphology. Plants -- Reproduction.*

## QK641.D53 2000
**Dickison, William C.**

Integrative plant anatomy / William C. dickison. San Diego : Harcourt/Academic Press, c2000. xvii, 533 p. :
                    571.3/2 21          0122151704
*Botany -- Anatomy.*

## QK641.F6 1974
**Foster, Adriance S.**

Comparative morphology of vascular plants [by] Adriance S. Foster [and] Ernest M. Gifford, Jr. San Francisco, W. H. Freeman [1974] viii, 751 p.
73-022459          581.4          0716707128
*Botany -- Morphology. Plants -- Evolution.*

## QK642.B68 1996
**Bowes, Bryan G.**

A color atlas of plant structure / Bryan G. Bowes ; with color drawings by Jo Nicholson. Ames : Iowa State University Press, 1996. 192 p. :
                    581.4/022/2 20          081382687X
*Botany -- Anatomy -- Atlases.*

### QK643 Plant anatomy — Individual plants and groups of plants

## QK643.A5.E2
**Eames, Arthur Johnson,**

Morphology of the angiosperms. New York, McGraw-Hill, 1961. 518 p.
60-015757          582.13
*Angiosperms. Botany -- Morphology.*

## QK643.G99.S65
**Sporne, K. R.**

The morphology of gymnosperms; the structure and evolution of primitive seed-plants [by] K.R. Sporne. London, Hutchinson University Library [1965] 216 p.
66-001105          585
*Gymnosperms. Botany -- Morphology.*

## QK643.M7M4
**Metcalfe, C. R.**
Anatomy of the monocotyledons. Oxford, Clarendon, 1960-1995 v. 1-6, 8
60-052155          584/.14
*Monocotyledones. Botany -- Anatomy.*

## QK648-649 Plant anatomy — Vegetative organs — Shoot

## QK648.S32 1993
**Sandved, Kjell Bloch,**
Bark : the formation, characteristics, and uses of bark around the world / photographs by Kjell B. Sandved ; text by Ghillean Tolmie Prance and Anne E. Prance. Portland, Or. : Timber Press, c1993. 174 p. :
92-019569          582/.047          0881922625
*Bark. Bark -- Composition. Bark -- Utilization.*

## QK649.J44 1994
**Jean, Roger V.**
Phyllotaxis : a systemic study of plant pattern morphogenesis / Roger V. Jean. Cambridge [England] ; Cambridge University Press, 1994. xiv, 386 p. :
93-015285          581.3/32          0521404827
*Phyllotaxis -- Mathematical models. Plant morphogenesis -- Mathematical models.*

## QK649.P7 1985
**Prance, Ghillean T.,**
Leaves, the formation, characteristics, and uses of hundreds of leaes found in all parts of the world / photographs by Kjell B. Sandved; text by Ghillean Tolmie Prance. 1st ed. New York : Crown, c1985. xi, 244 p. :
          582/.01 19          0517551527
*Leaves.*

## QK653-661 Plant anatomy — Reproductive organs of spermatophytes — Flower and inflorescence

## QK653.G75 1994
**Greyson, Richard I.**
The development of flowers / Richard I. Greyson ; with a contribution by Carl N. McDaniel. New York : Oxford University Press, 1994. vi, 314 p. :
93-022316          582.13/043          019506688X
*Flowers. Inflorescences. Angiosperms -- Development.*

## QK661.B37 1998
**Baskin, Carol C.**
Seeds : ecology, biogeography, and evolution of dormancy and germination / Carol C. Baskin, Jerry M. Baskin. San Diego, Calif. : Academic Press, c1998. xiv, 666 p. :
97-080574          575.6/8          0120802600
*Seeds -- Dormancy. Germination.*

## QK665 Plant anatomy — Embryology

## QK665.R34 1997
**Raghavan, V.**
Molecular embryology of flowering plants / V. Raghavan. Cambridge [England] ; Cambridge University Press, 1997. xxi, 690 p. :
96-044410          571.8/62          052155246X
*Botany -- Embryology. Angiosperms -- Embryology.*

## QK671 Plant anatomy — Individual parts

## QK671.E8 1965
**Esau, Katherine,**
Plant anatomy. New York, Wiley [1965] xx, 767 p.
65-012713          581.4
*Botany -- Anatomy. Botany -- Morphology.*

## QK671 M4
**Metcalfe, C. R.**
Anatomy of the dicotyledons; leaves, stem, and wood in relation to taxonomy, with notes on economic uses, by C. R. Metcalfe and L. Chalk, with the assistance of M. M. Chattaway [and others]. Oxford, Clarendon Press, 1950. 2 v. (lxiv, 1
51008940
*Dicotyledons. Botany -- Anatomy.*

## QK710 Plant physiology — Societies, congresses, serial collections, yearbooks

## QK710.A57
Annual review of plant physiology and plant molecular biology. Palo Alto, Calif. : Annual Reviews Inc., c1988- v. :
          581 11     1040-2519
*Plant physiology -- Periodicals. Plant molecular biology -- Periodicals. Plant Physiology. Molecular Physiology.*

## QK710.5-711 Plant physiology — General works, treatises, and textbooks — Through 1969

## QK710.5.U55 1996
Units, symbols, and terminology for plant physiology : a reference for presentation of research results in the plant sciences / sponsored by the International Association for the Plant Physiology ; Frank B. Salisbury, editor. New York : Oxford Univesity Press, 1996. x, 234 p. :
          581.1/014 20          019509445X
*Plant physiology -- Terminology. Botany -- Terminology. Plant physiology -- Authorship.*

## QK711.P58 1959
Plant physiology : a treatise / edited by F.C. Steward. New York : Academic Press, 1959-c1991 v. 1-10; in 1
59-007689          581.1          0126686068
*Plant physiology.*

## QK711.2-717 Plant physiology — General works, treatises, and textbooks — 1970-

**QK711.2.B54 1979**
**Bidwell, R. G. S.**
Plant physiology / R. G. S. Bidwell. New York : Macmillan, c1979. xx, 726 p. :
78-006504          581.1          0023094303
*Plant physiology.*

**QK711.2.K57**
**King, John,**
The genetic basis of plant physiological processes / John King. New York : Oxford University Press, 1991. xiii, 413 p.
91-011129          581.1          0195048571
*Plant physiology -- Genetic aspects -- Case studies. Plant mutation -- Case studies.*

**QK711.2.K72 1997**
**Kozlowski, T. T.**
Physiology of woody plants / Theodore T. Kozlowski, Stephen G. Pallardy. San Diego : Academic Press, c1997. xiv, 411 p. :
96-035505          582.1/5041          012424162X
*Woody plants -- Physiology. Trees -- Physiology.*

**QK711.2.T35 1998**
**Taiz, Lincoln,**
Plant physiology / Lincoln Taiz, Eduardo Zeiger. 2nd ed. Sunderland, Mass : Sinauer Associates, c1998. xxvi, 792 p. :
          571.2 21          0878938311
*Plant physiology.*

**QK717.L35 1998**
**Lambers, H.**
Plant physiological ecology / Hans Lambers, F. Stuart Chapin III, Thijs L. Pons. New York : Springer, c1998. xxvii, 540 p.
97-033273          571.2          0387983260
*Plant ecophysiology.*

## QK731-740 Plant physiology — Physical plant physiology — Growth

**QK731.H68 1998**
**Howell, Stephen H.**
Molecular genetics of plant development / Stephen H. Howell. Cambridge, UK ; Cambridge University Press, 1998. xviii, 365 p.
97-035238          572.8/2          0521582555
*Plants -- Development. Plant molecular genetics.*

**QK731.L4**
**Leopold, A. Carl**
Auxins and plant growth. Berkeley, University of California Press, 1955. 354 p.
55-005386          581.134
*Auxin. Plant growth promoting substances.*

**QK731.L44 1975**
**Leopold, A. Carl**
Plant growth and development / A. Carl Leopold, Paul E. Kriedemann. New York : McGraw-Hill, [1975] xiv, 545 p. :
74-020970          582/.03          0070372004
*Growth (Plants) Plants -- Development. Plant physiology.*

**QK731.R26 2000**
**Raghavan, V.**
Developmental biology of flowering plants / V. Raghavan. New York : Springer, c2000. xxii, 354 p.
99-010027          571.8/2          0387987819
*Angiosperms -- Development. Plants -- Development.*

**QK731.S75 1989**
Spatial components of plant disease epidemics / Michael J. Jeger, editor. Englewood Cliffs, N.J. : Prentice Hall, c1989. xii, 243 p. :
88-013081          581.2/4          013824491X
*Plant diseases -- Epidemiology. Spatial analysis (Statistics) Phytogeography.*

**QK731.W45**
**Wilkins, Malcolm B.**
The physiology of plant growth and development, edited by Malcolm B. Wilkins. New York, McGraw-Hill [1969] xxi, 695 p.
78-006454          581.1/34          0070940886
*Growth (Plants) Plants -- Development.*

**QK740.B73 1988**
**Bradbeer, J. W.**
Seed dormancy and germination / J.W. Bradbeer. Glasgow : Blackie ; 1988. x, 146 p. :
88-004296          582/.0333          0412006111
*Germination. Seeds -- Dormancy. Seeds.*

## QK750-753 Plant physiology — Physical plant physiology — Chemical agents affecting plants

**QK750.E58 2000**
Environmental pollution and plant response / edited by Shashi Bhushan Agarwal, Madhoolika Agarwal. Boca Raton, Fla. : Lewis Publishers, c2000. 393 p. :
99-026504          581.7          1566703417
*Plants, Effect of pollution on.*

**QK751.A36 1984**
Air pollution and plant life / edited by Michael Treshow. Chichester [West Sussex] ; Wiley, c1984. xii, 486 p. :
83-005905          581.5/222          0471901032
*Plants, Effect of air pollution on. Air -- Pollution – Environmental aspects.*

## QK753.C3.E87 1998

European forests and global change : the likely impacts of rising CO2 and temperature / edited by Paul G. Jarvis ; assisted by Anne M. Aitken ... [et al.]. Cambridge, U.K. ; Cambridge University Press, 1998. xviii, 379 p.
97-032152  577.327/094  0521584787
 *Trees -- Effect of atmospheric carbon dioxide -- Europe. Trees – Effect of global warming on -- Europe. Forest microclimatology – Europe.*

## QK753.X45.P58 1994

Plant contamination : modeling and simulation of organic chemical processes / edited by Stefan Trapp and J. Craig McFarlane. Boca Raton : Lewis Publishers, c1995. 254 p. :
94-009734  581.2  1566700787
 *Plants, Effect of xenobiotics on -- Mathematical models.*

## QK754-757 Plant physiology — Physical plant physiology — Physical agents affecting

## QK754.5.G58 1996

Global change and terrestrial ecosystems / edited by Brian Walker, Will Steffen. Cambridge ; Cambridge University Press, 1996. xvi, 619 p. :
96-013050  581.5/264  0521570948
 *Climatic changes. Plant ecophysiology. Crops and climate.*

## QK757.H37 1988
Hart, J. W.

Light and plant growth / J.W. Hart. London ; Unwin Hyman, 1988. xx, 204 p. :
87-014322  581.3/1  0045810222
 *Plants, Effect of light on. Plants -- Photomorphogenesis.*

## QK761 Plant physiology — Physical plant physiology — Periodicity. Dormancy. Photoperiodism Aging. Senescence

## QK761.P58 1996

Plant dormancy : physiology, biochemistry, and molecular biology / edited by G.A. Lang. Wallingford, Oxon, UK : CAB International, c1996. xx, 386 p. :
97-142321  571.7/82  0851989780
 *Dormancy in plants -- Congresses.*

## QK771-793 Plant physiology — Physical plant physiology — Movements. Irritability in plants

## QK771.H36 1990
Hart, J. W.

Plant tropisms and other growth movements / J.W. Hart. London ; Unwin Hyman, 1990. xvii, 208 p.
89-022474  581.1/83  0044453701
 *Plants -- Irritability and movements.*

## QK773.B58 1991

The Biology of vines / edited by Francis E. Putz and Harold A. Mooney. Cambridge ; Cambridge University Press, 1991. xv, 526 p. :
90-023763  582.1/4  0521392500
 *Climbing plants.*

## QK793.N55 1992
Niklas, Karl J.

Plant biomechanics : an engineering approach to plant form and function / Karl J. Niklas. Chicago : University of Chicago Press, c1992. xiii, 607 p.
91-026312  581.19/1  0226586308
 *Plant mechanics.*

## QK826 Plant physiology — Physical plant physiology — Reproduction

## QK826.M64 1992
Mogie, Michael.

The evolution of asexual reproduction in plants / Michael Mogie. London ; Chapman & Hall, 1992. xiv, 276 p. :
91-041024  581.1/65  0412442205
 *Plants -- Reproduction. Plants -- Evolution. Reproduction, Asexual.*

## QK861 Plant physiology — Phytochemistry — General works, treatises, and textbooks

## QK861.B45 2000

Biochemistry & molecular biology of plants / [edited by] Bob B. Buchanan, Wilhelm Gruissem, Russell L. Jones. Rockville, Md. : American Society of Plant Physiologists, c2000. xxxix, 1367 p
00-040591  572.8/2  0943088372
 *Botanical chemistry. Plant molecular biology.*

## QK861.B48

The Biochemistry of plants : a comprehensive treatise / edited by P. K. Stumpf and E. E. Conn. New York : Academic Press, 1980-c1990 v. 1-16 :
80-013168  581.19/2  0126754020
 *Botanical chemistry.*

## QK867-898 Plant physiology — Phytochemistry — Nutrition. Plant food. Assimilation of nitrogen, etc.

## QK867.J64 1998
Jones, J. Benton,

Plant nutrition manual / J. Benton Jones, Jr. Boca Raton : CRC Press, c1998. x, 149 p. :
97-046560  572/.42  188401531X
 *Plants -- Nutrition -- Handbooks, manuals, etc.*

## QK882.H23 1996

Handbook of photosynthesis / edited by Mohammad Pessarakli. New York : Marcel Dekker, c1997. xix, 1027 p. :
  581.1/3342 20  0824797086
*Photosynthesis.*

QK882.E295 1983
**Edwards, Gerry.**
C3, C4 : mechanisms, and cellular and environmental regulation, of photosynthesis / Gerry Edwards, David Walker. Berkeley : University of California Press, c1983. x, 542 p. :
82-049298          581.1/3342
*Photosynthesis -- Regulation. Carbon -- Metabolism. Plants – Assimilation.*

QK882.F64 1984
**Foyer, Christine H.**
Photosynthesis / Christine H. Foyer. New York : Wiley, c1984. xvii, 219 p.
83-021764          581.1/3342          0471864730
*Photosynthesis.*

QK882.H19 1999
**Hall, D. O. (David Oakley)**
Photosynthesis / D.O. hall and K.K. Rao. 6th ed. Cambridge, UK ; New York : Cambridge University Press, 1999. xiv, 214 p. :
572/.46 21          0521642574
*Photosynthesis.*

QK882.K53 1994
**Kirk, John T. O.**
Light and photosynthesis in aquatic ecosystems / John T.O. Kirk. Cambridge [England] ; Cambridge University Press, 1994. xvi, 509 p. :
93-037395          574.5/263          0521453534
*Photosynthesis. Plants, Effect of underwater light on. Aquatic plants -- Ecophysiology.*

QK882.P538 1998
Photosynthesis : a comprehensive treatise / edited by A.S. Raghavendra. Cambridge, U.K. ; Cambridge University Press, 1998. xviii, 376 p.
97-004035          572/.46          052157000X
*Photosynthesis.*

QK891.P483 1984
The Physiology and biochemistry of plant respiration / edited by J.M. Palmer. Cambridge [Cambridgeshire] ; Cambridge University Press, 1984. ix, 195 p. :
83-026279          581.1/2          0521236975
*Plants -- Respiration.*

QK898.N6.D59 1986
**Dixon, R. O. D.**
Nitrogen fixation in plants / R.O.D. Dixon and C.T. Wheeler. Glasgow : Blackie ; 1986. ix, 157 p. :
86-004178          589.9/.504133          0412013819
*Nitrogen -- Fixation. Nitrogen-fixing plants. Nitrogen-fixing microorganisms.*

QK898.P7P43 1988
Plant Pigments / editor, Hans-Peter Kost. Boca Raton, Fla. : CRC Press, c1998. v. <1 > :
581.19/218 19          0849330815
*Plant pigments -- Analysis. Chromatographic analysis.*

## QK901 Plant ecology — Ecological discussion of areas

QK901.G96 2002
**Gurevitch, Jessica.**
The ecology of plants / Jessica Gurevitch, Samuel M. Scheiner, Gordon A. Fox. Sunderland, Mass. : Sinauer Associates, 2002. p. cm.
581.7 21          0878932917
*Plant ecology.*

QK901.L3513 1980
**Larcher, W.**
Physiological plant ecology / W. Larcher ; translated by M. A. Biederman-Thorson. Berlin ; Springer-Verlag, 1980. xvii, 303 p.
79-026396          581.5          0387097953
*Plant ecophysiology.*

QK901.O6 1956
**Oosting, Henry John,**
The study of plant communities; an introduction to plant ecology. San Francisco, W. H. Freeman, 1956. 440 p.
56-011029          581.5
*Plant ecology. Plant communities.*

## QK905 Plant ecology — Plant ecophysiology

QK905.P565 1997
Plant functional types : their relevance to ecosystem properties and global change / edited by T.M. Smith, H.H. Shugart, F.I. Woodward. Cambridge ; Cambridge Unversity Press, 1997. xiv, 369 p. :
96-001582          581.5          0521566436
*Vegetation and climate. Climatic changes. Plant ecophysiology.*

## QK910 Plant ecology — Vegetation dynamics

QK910.S54 1993
**Silvertown, Jonathan W.**
Introduction to plant population biology / Jonathan W. Silvertown and Jonathan Lovett Doust. 3rd ed. Oxford ; Boston : Blackwell Scientific Publications, 1993. xi, 210 p. :
581.5248 20
*Plant populations. Vegetation dynamics.*

QK910.T55 1988
**Tilman, David,**
Plant strategies and the dynamics and structure of plant communities / David Tilman. Princeton, N.J. : Princeton University Press, 1988. xi, 360 p. :
87-025833          581.5/247          0691084882
*Vegetation dynamics. Plant communities.*

## QK910.V42 1993

Vegetation dynamics & global change / edited by Allen M. Solomon and Herman H. Shugart. New York : Chapman & Hall ; 1993. xii, 338 p. :
92-035042        581.5        0412036711
*Vegetation dynamics -- Congresses. Vegetation and climate -- Congresses. Forest ecology -- Congresses.*

## QK911 Plant ecology — Vegetation interrelation. Plant communities. Phytosociology

### QK911.H3

Vegetation mapping / edited by A.W. Kuchler and I.S. Zonneveld. Dordrecht ; Boston : Kluwer Academc Publishers, c1998. ix, 635 p. :
           581.9 19           9061931916
*Vegetation mapping. Phytogeography -- Maps.*

### QK911.H35
Harper, John L.

Population biology of plants / John L. Harper. London ; Academic Press, 1977. xxiv, 892 p.
76-016973        581.5/24        0123258502
*Plant populations. Population biology.*

## QK917-918 Plant ecology — Plant adaptation — Nutritive adaptation

### QK917.S36
Schnell, Donald E.,

Carnivorous plants of the United States and Canada / by Donald E. Schnell. Winston-Salem, N.C. : J. F. Blair, c1976. ix, 125 p. :
76-026883        583/.121/0973        0910244901
*Carnivorous plants -- United States. Carnivorous plants -- Canada.*

### QK918.S64 1991

Soil and plants / edited by Dilip K. Arora ... [et al.]. New York : M. Dekker, c1991. xiii, 720 p.
90-025706        589.2        0824783808
*Mycorrhizas. Phytopathogenic fungi -- Biological control. Wood-decaying fungi.*

## QK922 Plant ecology — Plant adaptation — Protective adaptations

### QK922.L54 1991

Life strategies of succulents in deserts : with special reference to the Namib desert / Dieter J. von Willert ... [et al.]. Cambridge [England] ; Cambridge University Press, 1992. xix, 340 p. :
91-018832        582/.05/2652        0521244684
*Succulent plants. Succulent plants -- Ecophysiology. Succulent plants -- Namibia -- Namib Desert.*

## QK926 Plant ecology — Reproductive interrelation — Pollination

### QK926.B835 1996
Buchmann, Stephen L.

The forgotten pollinators / Stephen L. Buchmann and Gary Paul Nabhan ; with a foreword by Edward O. Wilson ; illustrations by Paul Mirocha. Washington, D.C. : Island Press/Shearwater Books, c1996. xx, 292 p. :
96-000802        574.5/24        1559633522
*Pollinators. Animal-plant relationships. Biological diversity.*

### QK926.M418 1984
Meeuse, Bastiaan.

The sex life of flowers / Bastiaan Meeuse and Sean Morris ; photographs by Oxford Scientific Films ; drawings by Michael Woods. New York : Facts on File, 1984. 152 p. :
84-004044        582.13/04166        0871969076
*Pollination. Plants, Sex in. Flowers.*

### QK926.P75 1996
Proctor, Michael C. F.

The natural history of pollination / Michael Proctor, Peter Yeo, and Andrew Lack. Portland, Or. : Timber Press, 1996. 479 p. :
96-198390        571.8/642        0881923524
*Pollination.*

## QK931-935 Plant ecology — Physiographic regions (General) — Water

### QK931.D38 1998
Dawes, Clinton J.

Marine botany / Clinton J. Dawes. New York : John Wiley, c1998. xiv, 480 p. :
97-010372        579/.177        0471192082
*Marine plants. Plant ecology.*

### QK933.P49

Phytoplankton manual / edited by A. Sournia. Paris : Unesco, 1978. xvi, 337 p. :
79-309840        589/.4        9231015729
*Phytoplankton -- Research. Phytoplankton -- Handbooks, manuals, etc. Marine phytoplankton -- Research.*

### QK934.I44 1997

Identifying marine phytoplankton / edited by Carmelo R. Tomas ; contributors, Grethe R. Hasle ... [et al.]. San Diego : Academic Press, c1997. xv, 858 p. :
97-013861        579.8/1776        012693018X
*Marine phytoplankton -- Identification.*

### QK935.G76 1988

Growth and reproductive strategies of freshwater phytoplankton / edited by Craig D. Sandgren. Cambridge ; Cambridge University Press, 1988. v, 442 p. :
87-030543        589.4        0521327229
*Freshwater phytoplankton -- Growth. Freshwater phytoplankton – Reproduction.*

**QK935.R45 1984**
**Reynolds, Colin S.**
The ecology of freshwater phytoplankton / C. S. Reynolds. Cambridge ; Cambridge University Press, 1984. x, 384 p. :
83-007211        589.4/0916/9        0521237823
*Freshwater phytoplankton -- Ecology.*

### QK936-938 Plant ecology — Physiographic regions (General) — Land

**QK936.L88 1997**
**Luttge, Ulrich.**
Physiological ecology of tropical plants / Ulrich Luttge. Berlin ; Springer, c1997. xii, 384 p. :
96-052359        581.7/0913        3540611614
*Tropical plants -- Ecophysiology. Plant ecophysiology – Tropics.*

**QK937.K67 1999**
**Korner, Christian.**
Alpine plant life : functional plant ecology of high mountain ecosystems / Christian Korner. Berlin ; Springer, c1999. ix, 338 p. :
98-049887        581.7/538        3540650547
*Mountain plants -- Ecology. Mountain plants -- Ecophysiology.*

**QK938.F6.B66 1993**
**Botkin, Daniel B.**
Forest dynamics : an ecological model / Daniel B. Botkin. Oxford ; Oxford University Press, 1993. x, 309 p. :
91-019555        581.5/2642/0113        0195065557
*Forest ecology -- Computer simulation. Trees -- Growth -- Computer simulation.*

**QK938.F6.F674**
Forest succession : concepts and application / edited by Darrell C. West, Herman H. Shugart, Daniel B. Botkin. New York : Springer-Verlag, c1981. xv, 517 p. :
81-016707        581.5/2642        0387905979
*Forest ecology -- Congresses. Plant succession -- Congresses.*

**QK938.F6.P46 1994**
**Perry, David A.**
Forest ecosystems / David A. Perry. Baltimore : Johns Hopkins University Press, c1994. xvi, 649 p. :
94-010796        581.5/2642        0801847605
*Forest ecology.*

**QK938.F6.S68 1980**
**Spurr, Stephen Hopkins.**
Forest ecology / Stephen H. Spurr, Burton V. Barnes. New York : Wiley, c1980. x, 687 p. :
79-010007        574.5/264        0471047325
*Forest ecology.*

**QK938.M3C76 2001**
**Cronk, J.K.**
Wetland plants : biology and ecology / Julie K. Cronk and M. Siobhan Fennessy. Boca Raton, Fla. : Lewis Publishers, c2001. 462 p. :
581.7/68 21        1566703727
*Wetland plants. Wetlands. Wetland ecology.*

**QK938.M45.D35 1998**
**Dallman, Peter R.**
Plant life in the world's mediterranean climates : California, Chile, South Africa, Australia, and the Mediterranean Basin / by Peter R. Dallman ; preface by Robert Ornduff. Sacramento, CA : California Native Plant Society ; c1998. xii, 257 p. :
97-052208        581.4/2        0520208080
*Mediterranean-type plants. Plant communities.*

**QK938.R34.R53 1996**
**Richards, Paul W.**
The tropical rain forest : an ecological study / P.W. Richards ; with contributions by R.P.D. Walsh, I.C. Baillie, and P. Greig-Smith. Cambridge ; Cambridge University Press, 1996. xxiii, 575 p.
93-049019        581.5/2642/0913        0521420547
*Rain forest ecology.*

**QK938.S27.C45 1974**
**Chapman, V. J.**
Salt marshes and salt deserts of the world / by V. J. Chapman. Lehre [Ger.] : J. Cramer, 1974. 102, xvi, 392
77-351046        581.5/2636        3768209274
*Salt marsh plants. Salt marshes. Halophytes.*

### QK980 Plant ecology — Evolution of plants (General) — General works

**QK980.K44 1997**
**Kenrick, Paul.**
The origin and early diversification of land plants : a cladistic study / Paul Kenrick, Peter R. Crane. Washington, DC : Smithsonian Institution Press, c1997. xi, 441 p. :
97-024710        581.3/8        1560987308
*Plants -- Evolution. Plants -- Cladistic analysis. Cladistic analysis.*

### QK981-981.5 Plant ecology — Evolution of plants (General) — Genetics

**QK981.K54 1988**
**Klekowski, Edward J.**
Mutation, developmental selection, and plant evolution / Edward J. Klekowski. New York : Columbia University Press, 1988. xi, 373 p. :
88-002579        581.1/5        0231065280
*Plant genetics. Plant mutation. Plants -- Evolution.*

**QK981.5.W34 1989**
**Walden, R.**
Genetic transformation in plants / R. Walden. Englewood Cliffs, N.J. : Prentice Hall, 1989. xii, 138 p. :
89-003575        581.1/5        0133510409
*Plant genetic transformation. Recombinant DNA.*

## QK982 Plant ecology — Evolution of plants (General) — Hybridization

**QK982.M4613 1993**
**Mendel, Gregor,**
   Gregor Mendel's Experiments on plant hybrids : a guided study / Alain F. Corcos and Floyd V. Monaghan ; original drawings by Maria C. Weber. New Brunswick, N.J. : Rutgers University Press, c1993. xix, 220 p. :
92-030887          581.1/58          0813519209
   *Hybridization, Vegetable. Plant genetics.*

## QK983 Plant ecology — Evolution of plants (General) — Variation

**QK983.B73 1997**
**Briggs, D.**
   Plant variation and evolution / D. Briggs, S.M. Walters. New York : Cambridge University Press, 1997. xxi, 512 p. :
96-039293          581.3/8          0521452953(hb
   *Plants -- Variation. Plants -- Evolution.*

# QL Zoology

# QL1 Societies, congresses, serial collections, yearbooks

**QL1.Z733 no. 71**
   Behaviour and ecology of riparian mammals / edited by Nigel Dunstone and Martyn L. Gorman. Cambridge ; Cambridge University Press, 1998. x, 391 p. :
97-032129          590 s          0521631076
   *Aquatic mammals -- Behavior -- Congresses. Aquatic mammals – Ecology -- Congresses. Riparian animals -- Behavior -- Congresses.*

# QL7 Encyclopedias

**QL7.K56 1992**
   The Kingfisher illustrated encyclopedia of animals : from aardvark to zorille--and 2,000 other animals / consultant editor, Michael Chinery. Rev., enl. Ed. New York : Kingfisher Books, 1992. 379 p. :
                  591/.03 20          185697801X
*Animals -- Encyclopedias, Juvenile. Animals -- Encyclopedias.*

# QL9 Dictionaries

**QL9.G67 1996**
**Gotch, A.F. (Arthur Frederick)**
   Latin names explained : a guide to the scientific classification of reptiles, birds & mammals / A.F. Gotch. New York : Facts on File, 1996. 714 p. :
                  596/.01/4 21          0816033773
*Reptiles -- Nomenclature. Birds -- Nomenclature. Mammals -- Nomenclature.*

## QL26 Biography — Collective

**QL26.M66 1991**
**Montgomery, Sy.**
   Walking with the great apes : Jane Goodall, Dian Fossey, Birute Galdikas / Sy Montgomery. Boston : Houghton Mifflin Co., 1991. xix, 280 p. :
90-048043          599.88/092/2          0395515971
*Goodall, Jane, -- 1934- Fossey, Dian. Galdikas, Birute Marija Filomena. Apes -- Behavior -- Research. Women primatologists – Biography. Primatologists -- Biography.*

## QL31 Biography — Individual, A-Z

**QL31.A9.A2 1960**
**Audubon, John James,**
   Audubon and his journals, by Maria R. Audubon. With zoological and other notes by Elliott Coues. New York, Dover Publications [1960] 2 v.
60-051778          925.9
*Audubon, John James, -- 1785-1851 -- Diaries.     Birds -- North America. Naturalists -- United States -- Diaries.*

**QL31.A9.A35**
**Audubon, John James.**
   Audubon's America : the narratives and experiences of John James Audubon / edited by Donald Culross Peattie ; illustrated with facsimiles of Aududon's prints and paintings. Boston : Houghton Mifflin, 1940. 328 p. :
40032960          917
   *Birds -- United States. Natural history -- North America. North America -- Description and travel.*

**QL31.A9.F63 1988**
**Ford, Alice,**
   John James Audubon : a biography / by Alice Ford. New York : Abbeville Press, c1988. 528 p. :
88-000955          598.092/4          089659744X
*Audubon, John James, -- 1785-1851.   Ornithologists -- United States -- Biography. Artists -- United States -- Biography.*

**QL31.A9.S77 1993**
**Streshinsky, Shirley.**
   Audubon : life and art in the American wilderness / Shirley Streshinsky. New York : Villard Books, 1993. xxiii, 407 p.
93-003665          598/.092          0679408592
*Audubon, John James, -- 1785-1851.   Ornithologists -- United States -- Biography. Animal painters -- United States -- Biography.*

**QL31.B24.K63 1989**
**Kofalk, Harriet,**
   No woman tenderfoot : Florence Merriam Bailey, pioneer naturalist / by Harriet Kofalk. College Station : Texas A&M University Press, c1989. xix, 225 p. :
88-024758          598/.092/4          0890963789
*Bailey, Florence Merriam, -- b. 1863.   Bird watchers -- United States -- Biography. Bird watching -- United States -- History. Birds, Protection of -- United States -- History.*

**QL31.D87.B68 1999**
**Botting, Douglas.**
Gerald Durrell : the authorized biography / Douglas Botting. New York : Carroll & Graf, 1999. xx, 644 p. :
00-268642          590/.92          0786706554
*Durrell, Gerald Malcolm, -- 1925-    Zoologists -- Great Britain – Biography.  Wildlife conservationists -- Great Britain -- Biography.*

**QL31.G58**
**Goodall, Jane,**
Beyond innocence : an autobiography in letters : the later years / Jane Goodall ; edited by Dale Peterson. Boston  : Houghton Mifflin, 2001. xiii, 418 p.
00-054124          590/.92          0618125205
*Goodall, Jane, -- 1934- -- Correspondence.    Primatologists -- Correspondence.*

**QL31.M26.A3 1948**
**Mann, William M.,**
Ant hill odyssey / William M. Mann. Boston : Little, Brown, 1948. 338 p., [3] l
48009280          925.9
*Mann, William M., -- 1886-1960.    Zoologists -- Biography – 20th century.*

**QL31.P57.A3 1994**
**Pianka, Eric R.**
The lizard man speaks / Eric R. Pianka. Austin : University of Texas Press, 1994. 179 p., [8] p
93-038067          597.95/092          0292765525
*Pianka, Eric R.    Zoologists -- United States -- Biography. Lizards.*

**QL31.P68.A3 1996**
**Poole, Joyce,**
Coming of age with elephants : a memoir / by Joyce Poole. New York : Hyperion, c1996. xi, 287 p., [
95-040153          591.5/092          0786860952
*Poole, Joyce, -- 1956-    Ethologists -- Africa -- Biography. Women ethologists -- Africa -- Biography. African elephant -- Behavior – Kenya -- Amboseli National Park.*

**QL31.R67.R63 1983**
**Rothschild, Miriam.**
Dear Lord Rothschild : birds, butterflies, and history / Miriam Rothschild. Philadelphia : Balaban ; c1983. xx, 398 p., [
83-008760          590/.92/4          086689019X
*Rothschild, Lionel Walter Rothschild, -- Baron, -- 1868-1937. Zoologists -- England -- Biography.*

**QL31.T59.A37**
**Tors, Ivan.**
My life in the wild / Ivan Tors. Boston : Houghton Mifflin, 1979. vi, 209 p. :
79-012252          591/.092/4          0395277663
*Tors, Ivan.    Zoologists -- United States -- Biography. Motion picture producers and directors -- United States -- Biography.*

**QL31.W27.A34**
**Wallace, George John,**
My world of birds : memoirs of an ornithologist / by George J. Wallace. Philadelphia : Dorrance, c1979. xii, 345 p. :
78-067257          598.2/092/4          0805925864
*Wallace, George John, -- 1906-    Birds. Ornithologists – Vermont – Biography.  Ornithologists -- Michigan -- Biography.*

## QL41 General works and treatises — Early through 1759

**QL41.A719 1978**
**Aristotle.**
Aristotle's De motu animalium : text with translation, commentary, and interpretive essays / by Martha Craven Nussbaum. Princeton, N.J. : Princeton University Press, 1978. xxiii, 430 p.
77-072132          591          0691072248
*Zoology -- Pre-Linnean works.  Animal locomotion – Early works to 1800.*

**QL41.A7413 1862**
**Aristotle.**
Aristotle's History of animals. In ten books. Tr. by Richard Cresswell ... London, H. G. Bohn, 1862. ix, 326 p.
06-005561          591
*Zoology -- Pre-Linnean works.*

## QL45 General works and treatises — 1760-1969

**QL45.C18 1922**
The Cambridge natural history, ed. by Sir S.F. Harmer ... and Sir A.E. Shipley ... [London, Macmillan and co., limited, 1922-27] 10 v.
30-019238
*Zoology.*

## QL45.2 General works and treatises — 1970-

**QL45.2.K47 1983**
**Kershaw, Diana R.**
Animal diversity / Diana R. Kershaw ; with illustrations by Brian Price Thomas. Slough : University Tutorial Press, 1983. 428 p. :
83-186966          591          0723108471
*Zoology. Anatomy, Comparative. Biological diversity.*

## QL46.5 Zoological illustrating

**QL46.5.B58 1993**
**Blum, Ann Shelby,**
Picturing nature : American nineteenth-century zoological illustration / Ann Shelby Blum. Princeton, N.J. : Princeton University Press, c1993. xxxiv, 403 p.
92-004681          591/.022/2          0691085781
*Zoological illustration -- United States -- History -- 19th century. Animals in art -- History -- 19th century.*

### QL47 Textbooks — Advanced — Through 1969

**QL47.M6**
**Morgan, Ann Haven,**
   Kinships of animals and man; a textbook of animal biology.
New York, McGraw-Hill, 1955. 839 p.
55006859            591.1
   *Physiology, Comparative. Evolution. Physiology, Comparative.*

**QL47.2.V5 1984**
**Villee, Claude Alvin,**
   General zoology / Claude A. Villee, Warren F. Walker, Jr.,
Robert D. Barnes. 6th ed. Philadelphia : Saunders College
Pub., c1984. xvi, 856 p. :
            591 19      0030624517
*Zoology.*

## QL50 Popular works

**QL50.N48 1980**
   The New Larousse encyclopedia of animal life / [based on
La vie des animaux by Leon Bertin with contributions by
Maurice and Robert Burton ... et al. ; foreword to revised
edition by Maurice Burton, to first edition by Robert Cushman
Murphy ; all photographs supplied by Bruce Coleman Ltd.].
New York : Larousse, 1980. 640 p. :
79-091865            591        0883321327
   *Zoology.*

**QL50.T4**
**Terres, John K.,**
   Discovery; great moments in the lives of outstanding
naturalists. With wood engravings by Thomas W. Nason.
Philadelphia, Lippincott [1961] 338 p.
61-008687            590.82
   *Zoology -- Addresses, essays, lectures.  Naturalists.*

**QL50.W82 1982**
**Wood, Gerald L.**
   The Guinness book of animal facts and feats / Gerald L.
Wood. 3rd ed. Enfield, Middlesex : Guinness Superlatives,
1982. 252 p. :
            591/.02 19            0851122353
*Animals -- Miscellanea.*

### QL51 Study and teaching. Research — General works

**QL51.A4813 1989**
   Scientific alternatives to animal experiments / editor, Fred
Lembeck ; translator, Jacqui Welch ; translation editor, John
Francis. Chichester, West Sussex, England : E. Horwood ;
1989. xii, 247 p. :
89-026736            619        0745805892
   *Zoology -- Research. Animal experimentation – Moral and ethical
aspects.  Animal welfare.*

### QL55 Study and teaching. Research — Laboratory animals

**QL55.I44 1992**
   The Inevitable bond : examining scientist-animal
interactions / edited by Hank Davis, Dianne Balfour.
Cambridge ; Cambridge University Press, 1992. xi, 399 p. :
91-027509            591/.0724        0521405106
   *Animal experimentation -- Effect of experimenters on.  Human-
animal relationships.*

### QL61 Collection and preservation — General works, treatises, and textbooks

**QL61.B78 2000**
**Buck, Frank,**
   Bring 'em back alive : the best of Frank Buck / introduced
and edited by Steven Lehrer. Lubbock, Tex. : Texas Tech
University Press, c2000. xxi, 248 p.,
99-086898            591.5        0896724301
   *Wild animal collecting.  Animal behavior.*

### QL76 Zoos. Zoological gardens — General works

**QL76.E53 2001**
   Encyclopedia of the world's zoos / editor, Catharine E. Bell ;
senior advisor, Lester E. Fisher ; photo editor, Catharine E.
Bell ; associate photo editor, Laura Mizicko. Chicago, IL, USA
: Fitzroy Dearborn Publishers, c2001. 3v.(xxix,1577p)
2002265421
*Zoos -- Encyclopedias.  Zoo animals -- Encyclopedias.*

**QL76.H35 2001**
**Hancocks, David.**
   A different nature : the paradoxical world of zoos and their
uncertain future / David Hancocks. Berkeley : University of
California Press, c2001. xxii, 279 p.
00-053209            590/.7/3        0520218795
   *Zoos -- History.*

### QL82 Wildlife conservation. Rare animals. Endangered species — General works

**QL82.B435 1998**
   Beacham's guide to international endangered species / edited
by Walton Beacham, Kirk H. Beetz. Osprey, Fla. : Beacham
Pub., 1998- v. 1-2 (xvi,
97-035751            333.95/42        0933833342
   *Endangered species.  Wildlife conservation.*

**QL82.F58 1989**
**Fitzgerald, Sarah.**
International wildlife trade : whose business is it? / by Sarah Fitzgerald. Washington, D.C. : World Wildlife Fund, c1989. xix, 459 p.,
89-022752          333.95          0942635108
*Wild animal trade. Endangered species. Wild animal trade – Law and legislation.*

**QL82.G73 1993**
**Gray, Gary G.**
Wildlife and people : the human dimensions of wildlife ecology / Gary G. Gray. Urbana : University of Illinois Press, c1993. xii, 260 p. :
92-032828          333.95          0252019474
*Wildlife conservation -- Social aspects. Wildlife conservation – Economic aspects. Human-animal relationships.*

**QL82.S49 1998**
**Sherry, Clifford J.**
Endangered species : a reference handbook / Clifford J. Sherry. Santa Barbara, Calif. : ABC-CLIO, c1998. xiv, 269 p. ;
98-036793          333.95/22          0874368103
*Endangered species. Endangered species -- Law and legislation.*

**QL82.T83 1992**
**Tudge, Colin.**
Last animals at the zoo : how mass extinction can be stopped / Colin Tudge. Washington, D.C. : Island Press, 1992. 266 p. ;
91-039773          639.9          1559631589
*Wildlife conservation. Endangered species -- Breeding. Zoo animals -- Breeding.*

## QL83.4 Wildlife conservation. Rare animals. Endangered species — Wildlife reintroduction

**QL83.4.B49 1991**
Beyond captive breeding : re-introducing endangered mammals to the wild : the proceedings of a symposium held at the Zoological Society of London on 24th and 25th November 1989 / edited by J.H.W. Gipps. Oxford : Published for the Zoological Society of London b 1991. xviii, 284 p.
90-024396          639.9/79          0198540191
*Wildlife reintroduction -- Congresses. Endangered species -- Congresses. Captive mammals -- Breeding -- Congresses.*

### QL84.2-84.24 Wildlife conservation. Rare animals. Endangered species — By region or country — North America

**QL84.2.C47 1996**
**Chadwick, Douglas H.**
The company we keep : America's endangered species / Douglas H. Chadwick and Joel Sartore. [Washington, DC] : National Geographic Society, c1996. 157 p. :
96-018874          591.52/9/0973          0792233107
*Endangered species -- United States. Endangered species -- United States -- Pictorial works. Wildlife conservation -- United States.*

**QL84.2.E55 1994**
Endangered species recovery : finding the lessons, improving the process / edited by Tim W. Clark, Richard P. Reading, Alice L. Clarke. Washington, D.C. : Island Press, c1994. xi, 450 p. :
94-018097          591.52/9/0973          1559632712
*Endangered species -- United States. Wildlife conservation -- United States. Wildlife conservation -- United States -- Case studies.*

**QL84.2.O35 1990**
The Official World Wildlife Fund guide to endangered species of North America / [managing editor, David W. Lowe, editors, John R. Matthews, Charles J. Moseley]. Washington, D.C. : Beacham Pub., c1990-c1994 v. 1-4; (xxii
89-029757          574.5/29/097          0933833172
*Nature conservation -- North America. Endangered species -- North America. Rare animals -- North America.*

**QL84.2.T62 1989**
**Tober, James A.,**
Wildlife and the public interest : nonprofit organizations and federal wildlife policy / James A. Tober. New York, NY : Praeger, 1989. xi, 220 p. ;
88-019045          333.95/16/0973          0275925811
*Wildlife conservation -- Government policy -- United States. Wildlife conservation -- United States -- Societies, etc. Environmental policy -- United States.*

**QL84.2.W53 1999**
**Wilcove, David Samuel.**
The condor's shadow : the loss and recovery of wildlife in America / David S. Wilcove ; foreword by Edward O. Wilson. New York : W.H. Freeman and Co., c1999. xix, 339 p. :
99-012269          333.95/42/0973          0716731150
*Endangered species -- United States. Wildlife conservation -- United States.*

**QL84.2.W54 1991**
Wildlife and habitats in managed landscapes / edited by Jon E. Rodiek and Eric G. Bolen ; foreword by Laurence R. Jahn. Washington, D.C. : Island Press, c1991. xix, 219 p. :
90-041593          639.9/2/0973          1559630531
*Wildlife habitat improvement -- United States. Habitat (Ecology) -- United States. Natural resources -- United States -- Management.*

**QL84.22.G7.M37 1992**
**Matthews, Anne,**
Where the buffalo roam / Anne Matthews. New York : Grove Weidenfeld, 1992. xiii, 193 p.
91-033637          333.95/9          0802114083
*Popper, Frank. Popper, Deborah. Wildlife reintroduction – Great Plains -- Planning. Land use -- Great Plains -- Planning. Wildlife refuges -- Great Plains -- Planning. Great Plains.*

**QL84.24.M69 1984**
**Mowat, Farley.**
Sea of slaughter / Farley Mowat. Boston : Atlantic Monthly Press, c1984. 438 p.
84-072722          333.95/413/097          0871130130
*Extinction (Biology) -- Atlantic Coast (North America) – History. Extinction (Biology) -- North Atlantic Region -- History. Nature – Effect of human beings on -- Atlantic Coast (North America) -- History.*

## QL84.6 Wildlife conservation. Rare animals. Endangered species — By region or country — Africa

**QL84.6.A1.K56 1989**
**Kingdon, Jonathan.**
  Island Africa : the evolution of Africa's rare animals and plants / Jonathan Kingdon. Princeton, N.J. : Princeton University Press, 1989. 287 p. :
89-010579          574.5/29/096          0691085609
  *Rare animals -- Africa -- Ecology. Rare plants -- Africa -- Ecology. Natural history -- Africa.*

**QL84.6.A358.O28 1999**
**Oates, John F.,**
  Myth and reality in the rain forest : how conservation strategies are failing in West Africa / John F. Oates. Berkeley, Calif. : University of California Press, c1999. xxviii, 310 p
99-020220          333.95/416/0966          0520217829
  *Wildlife conservation -- Africa, West. Sustainable development – Africa, West. Rain forest animals -- Africa, West.*

**QL84.6.K4.W47 1997**
**Western, David.**
  In the dust of Kilimanjaro / David Western. Washington, DC : Island Press/Shearwater Books, c1997. xv, 297 p. :
97-014845          333.95/4/096762          1559635339
  *Western, David. Wildlife management -- Kenya. Wildlife conservation -- Kenya. Wildlife conservationists -- Kenya -- Biography. Kenya -- Description and travel.*

# QL85 Animals and civilization. Human-animal relationships

**QL85.L414 1954a**
**Lewinsohn, Richard,**
  Animals, men, and myths; an informative and entertaining history of man and the animals around him. Translated from the German. New York, Harper [1954] 422 p.
53011848          301.24*
  *Animals and civilization.*

**QL85.P44 1989**
  Perceptions of animals in American culture / edited by R.J. Hoage. Washington, D.C. : Smithsonian Institution Press, c1989. xvii, 151 p.
89-600054          591/.0973          0874744938
  *Animals and civilization -- United States. Animals -- Social aspects -- United States.*

**QL85.S22 2001**
**Sabloff, Annabelle,**
  Reordering the natural world : humans and animals in the city / Annabelle Sabloff. Toronto : University of Toronto Press, c2001. xiv, 252 p. :
00-1269539          0802083617
  *Human-animal relationships. Urban ecology. Relations homme-animal.*

# QL86 Animal introduction

**QL86.T64 2001**
**Todd, Kim,**
  Tinkering with Eden : a natural history of exotics in America / Kim Todd ; illustrations by Claire Emery. New York : W.W. Norton, c2001. viii, 302 p.
00-058740          591.6          0393048608
  *Animal introduction.*

## QL88.3 Cryptozoology — General works

**QL88.3.H4813 1995**
**Heuvelmans, Bernard.**
  On the track of unknown animals / by Bernard Heuvelmans ; translated from the French by Richard Garnett ; with 120 drawings by Alika Lindbergh and an introduction by Gerald Durrell. London ; Kegan Paul International ; 1995. xxxv, 677 p.
94-034307          591          0710304986
  *Cryptozoology.*

### QL89.2 Cryptozoology — Alleged animals — By animal, A-Z

**QL89.2.S2.K73 1992**
**Krantz, Grover S.**
  Big foot-prints : a scientific inquiry into the reality of sasquatch / Grover S. Krantz. Boulder : Johnson Books, c1992. 300 p. :
92-025265          001.9/44          1555660991
  *Sasquatch.*

# QL100 Poisonous animals. Dangerous animals

**QL100.C37**
**Caras, Roger A.**
  Venomous animals of the world [by] Roger Caras. Englewood Cliffs, N.J., Prentice-Hall [1974] xix, 362 p.
74-008633          591.6/9          0139415262
  *Poisonous animals. Animals, Poisonous. Behavior, Animal.*

**QL100.G28**
**Gadd, Laurence.**
  Deadly beautiful : the world's most poisonous animals and plants / Laurence Gadd. New York : Macmillan, c1980. 208 p. :
          574.6/5          0025420900
  *Poisonous animals. Poisonous plants.*

**QL100.H3 1995**
**Halstead, Bruce W.**
  Dangerous marine animals : that bite, sting, shock, or are non-edible / Bruce W. Halstead. 3rd ed. Centreville, MD : Cornell Maritime Press, 1995. x, 275 p. :
          591.6/5/09162 20          0870334743
  *Dangerous marine animals.*

## QL101 Geographical distribution — General works, treatises, and textbooks

**QL101.D3**
**Darlington, Philip Jackson,**
   Zoogeography: the geographical distribution of animals. [New York, Wiley, 1957] 675 p.
57-008882          591.9
   *Zoogeography.*

**QL101.W18 1962**
**Wallace, Alfred Russel,**
   The geographical distribution of animals. With a study of the relations of living and extinct faunas as elucidating the past changes of the earth's surface. New York, Hafner Pub. Co., 1962. 2 v.
62015789          591.9
   *Zoogeography. Paleontology.*

## QL114-116 Geographical distribution — Physiographic divisions — Land

**QL114.D34**
**Daiber, Franklin C.**
   Animals of the tidal marsh / Franklin C. Daiber. New York : Van Nostrand Reinhold, c1982. x, 422 p. :
80-026403          591.52/636          0442248547
   *Salt marsh animals.*

**QL116.C58 1991**
**Cloudsley-Thompson, J. L.**
   Ecophysiology of desert arthropods and reptiles / J.L. Cloudsley-Thompson. Berlin ; Springer-Verlag, c1991. x, 203 p. :
90-026981          597.9/0452652          3540520570
   *Desert animals -- Ecology. Arthropoda -- Ecology. Reptiles – Ecology.*

## QL120-138 Geographical distribution — Physiographic divisions — Water

**QL120.I584 1988**
   Introduction to the study of meiofauna / Robert P. Higgins, Hjalmar Thiel, editors. Washington, D.C. : Smithsonian Institution Press, 1988. 488 p. :
88-011336          592.092          0874744881
   *Meiofauna.*

**QL121.G4**
**George, J. David**
   Marine life : an illustrated encyclopedia of invertebrates in the sea / by J. David George and Jennifer J. George ; with a foreword by Sir Eric Smith. New York : Wiley, c1979. 288 p. :
79-010976          592/.09/2          0471056758
   *Marine invertebrates.*

**QL121.N5 1967a**
**Nicol, J. A. Colin**
   The biology of marine animals, by J. A. Colin Nicol. New York, Wiley, Interscience Publishers Division [1967] xi, 699 p.
67-004328          591.9/2
   *Marine fauna. Physiology, Comparative.*

**QL121.P343 1995**
**Palmer, John D.,**
   The biological rhythms and clocks of intertidal animals / John D. Palmer. New York : Oxford University Press, 1995. xiv, 217 p. :
94-025802          574.1/882/09146          0195094352
   *Intertidal fauna. Biological rhythms.*

**QL123.S75 1983**
**Spoel, S. van der.**
   An atlas of comparative zooplankton : biological patterns in the oceans / S. van der Spoel and R.P. Heyman. Berlin ; Springer-Verlag, 1983. p. cm.
83-010440          592          0387125736
   *Marine zooplankton -- Geographical distribution.*

**QL128.B45 1951**
**Beebe, William,**
   Half mile down. New York, Duell, Sloan and Pearce [1951] xxiii, 344 p.
51-010409          591.921
   *Marine animals -- Bermuda Islands. Deep diving. Diving bells – Bermuda Islands. Nonsuch Island (Bermuda Islands)*

**QL138.R5 1985**
**Ricketts, Edward Flanders,**
   Between Pacific tides / Edward F. Ricketts, Jack Calvin, and Joel W. Hedgpeth. 5th ed. Stanford, Calif. : Stanford University Press, 1985. xxvi, 652 p.
83-040620          591.926          0804712298
   *Marine invertebrates -- Pacific Coast (U.S.) Intertidal ecology – Pacific Coast (U.S.) Seashore biology -- Pacific Coast (U.S.)*

## QL151-169 Geographical distribution — Topographical divisions (Faunas) — America

**QL151.E36 2001**
   Ecology and classification of North American freshwater invertebrates / edited by James H. Thorp and Alan P. Covich. 2nd ed. San Diego : Academic Press, c2001. xvi, 1056 p. :
          592.176/097 21
   *Freshwater invertebrates -- North America -- Ecology. Freshwater invertebrates -- North America -- Classification.*

**QL155.B8**
**Burroughs, Raymond Darwin,**
   The natural history of the Lewis and Clark Expedition. [East Lansing] Michigan State University Press [1961] xii, 340 p.
61-008396          591.978
   *Zoology -- West (U.S.)*

## QL169.L39 1989

**Lazell, James D.**

Wildlife of the Florida Keys : a natural history / by James D. Lazell, Jr. Washington, D.C. : Island Press, c1989. xvi, 253 p. :
89-001780     591.9759/41     093328098X
*Island animals -- Florida -- Ecology -- Florida Keys. Island fauna -- Florida -- Florida Keys -- Identification. Nature conservation -- Florida -- Florida Keys.*

## QL336-337 Geographical distribution — Topographical divisions (Faunas) — Africa

## QL336.M6 1960

**Moorehead, Alan,**

No room in the ark. New York, Harper [1960, c1959] 227 p.
59-006315     591.96
*Zoology -- Africa.    Africa -- Description and travel.*

## QL337.M26.A8 1962

**Attenborough, David,**

Bridge to the past; animals and people of Madagascar. New York, Harper [1962, c1961] 160 p.
62014235     591.91691
*Zoology -- Madagascar.    Madagascar -- Description and travel.*

## QL337.T3.S42 1995

Serengeti II : dynamics, management, and conservation of an ecosystem / edited by A.R.E. Sinclair & Peter Arcese. Chicago : University of Chicago Press, c1995. xii, 665 p. :
94-045542     574.5/264     0226760316
*Animal ecology -- Tanzania -- Serengeti National Park Region -- Congresses. Wildlife conservation -- Tanzania -- Serengeti National Park Region -- Congresses. Ecosystem management -- Tanzania -- Serengeti National Park Region -- Congresses.*

## QL337.T3.S43

Serengeti, dynamics of an ecosystem / edited by A. R. E. Sinclair and M. Norton-Griffiths. Chicago : University of Chicago Press, 1979. xii, 389 p.,
79-010146     574.5/264     0226760286
*Animal ecology -- Tanzania -- Serengeti Plain.    Serengeti National Park (Tanzania)*

## QL345 Geographical distribution — Topographical divisions (Faunas) — Pacific islands

## QL345.G2

**Swash, Andy.**

Birds, mammals & reptiles of the Galapagos Islands : an identification guide / Andy Swash and Rob Still ; with illustrations by Ian Lewington. Old Basing, Hampshire : WILDGuides ; 2000. 168 p. :
    1873403828
*Birds -- Galapagos Islands -- Identification. Mammals -- Galapagos Islands -- Identification. Reptiles -- Galapagos Islands -- Identification.*

## QL351 Classification. Systematics and taxonomy — Principles

## QL351.A26 1962

**Agassiz, Louis,**

Essay on classification. Edited by Edward Lurie. Cambridge, Belknap Press of Harvard University Press, 1962. xxxiii, 268 p
62-019211     590.12
*Zoology -- Classification.*

## QL351.M28

**Mayr, Ernst,**

Methods and principles of systematic zoology [by] Ernst Mayr, E. Gorton Linsley [and] Robert L. Usinger. New York, McGraw-Hill, 1953. 336 p.
52010335     590.12
*Zoology -- Classification. Zoology -- Nomenclature. Zoology - classification*

## QL351.M29 1991

**Mayr, Ernst,**

Principles of systematic zoology / Ernst Mayr, Peter D. Ashlock. 2nd ed. New York : McGraw-Hill, c1991. xx, 475 p. :
    591/.012 20     0070411441
*Zoology -- Classification.*

## QL351.S5 1961

**Simpson, George Gaylord,**

Principles of animal taxonomy. New York, Columbia University Press, 1961. 247 p.
60-013939     590.12
*Zoology -- Classification.*

## QL353 Nomenclature — General works. Principles

## QL353.S34 1956

**Schenk, Edward T.**

Procedure in taxonomy, including a reprint in translation of the Regles internationales de la nomenclature zoologique (International code of zoological nomenclature) with titles and notes on the opi By Edward T. Schenk and John H. McMasters. Stanford, Calif., Stanford University Press [1956] vii, 119 p.
56-009336     590.1
*Zoology -- Classification. Zoology -- Nomenclature. Fossils - Classification.*

## QL362 Invertebrates — General works, treatises, and textbooks

## QL362.B27 1987

**Barnes, Robert D.**

Invertebrate zoology / Robert D. Barnes. Philadelphia : Saunders College Pub., c1987. ix, 893 p. :
86-010023     592     003008914X
*Invertebrates.*

## QL362.B924 1990
**Brusca, Richard C.**
Invertebrates / Richard C. Brusca, Gary J. Brusca ; with illustrations by Nancy J. Haver. Sunderland, Mass. : Sinauer Associates, c1990. xviii, 922 p.
90-030061    592    0878930981
*Invertebrates.*

## QL362.B93 1987
**Buchsbaum, Ralph Morris,**
Animals without backbones. Chicago : University of Chicago Press, 1987. x, 572 p. :
86-007046    592    0226078736
*Invertebrates.*

## QL362.B94
**Buchsbaum, Ralph Morris,**
The lower animals; living invertebrates of the world, by Ralph Buchsbaum and Lorus J. Milne. In collaboration with Mildred Buchsbaum and Margery Milne. With photos. by Ralph Buchsbaum, and others. Line drawings by Kenneth Gosner. Garden City, N.Y., Doubleday [1960] 303 p.
60-010650    592
*Invertebrates.*

## QL362.H4 1981
**Engemann, Joseph G.**
Invertebrate zoology / Joseph G. Engemann, Robert W. Hegner. 3rd ed. New York : Macmillan ; c1981. xxi, 746 p. :
80-012063    592    002333780X
*Invertebrates.*

## QL362.H9
**Hyman, Libbie Henrietta,**
The invertebrates. New York, McGraw-Hill, 1940- v.
40-005368    592
*Invertebrates.*

## QL362.R76 1994
**Ruppert, Edward E.**
Invertebrate zoology / Edward E. Ruppert, Robert D. Barnes. 6th ed. Fort Worth : Saunders College Pub., c1994. xii, 1056, 16,
592 20    0030266688
*Invertebrates.*

## QL362.5 Invertebrates — Classification

### QL362.5.W56
**Winsor, Mary P.**
Starfish, jellyfish, and the order of life : issues in nineteenth-century science / Mary P. Winsor. New Haven : Yale University Press, c1976. 228 p. :
74-029739    592/.012    0300016352
*Invertebrates -- Classification -- History -- 19th century.*

## QL362.75 Invertebrates — Evolution

### QL362.75.W55 1990
**Willmer, Pat,**
Invertebrate relationships : patterns in animal evolution / Pat Willmer. Cambridge ; Cambridge University Press, 1990. ix, 400 p. :
87-032019    592/.038    0521330645
*Invertebrates -- Evolution. Invertebrates, Fossil.*

## QL364.2 Invertebrates — Behavior

### QL364.2.P74 1993
**Preston-Mafham, Rod.**
The encyclopedia of land invertebrate behaviour / Rod and Ken Preston-Mafham. Cambridge, Mass. : MIT Press, 1993. 320 p. :
92-047092    595/.20451    0262161370
*Invertebrates -- Behavior.*

## QL365.4 Invertebrates — Animalcules. Early works on infusoria

### QL365.4.A1.I58 1999
Invertebrates in freshwater wetlands of North America : ecology and management / edited by Darold P. Batzer, Russell B. Rader, and Scott A. Wissinger. New York : Wiley, c1999. xviii, 1100 p
98-039322    592.1768/097    0471292583
*Freshwater invertebrates -- Ecology -- North America. Wetland ecology -- North America. Wetlands -- North America.*

## QL366 Invertebrates — Protozoa — General works, treatises, and textbooks

### QL366.H3613 1996
**Hausmann, Klaus.**
Protozoology / Klaus Hausmann, Norbert Hulsmann ; with contributions by Hans Machemar, Maria Mulisch and Gunther Steinbruck ; foreword by John O. Corliss. Stuttgart ; Georg Thieme Verlag ; 1996. viii, 338 p.
95-000643    593.1    3131103019
*Protozoology.*

### QL366.H43 1968
**Hegner, Robert William,**
Big fleas have little fleas; or Who's who among the protozoa. With an new introd. by Reginald D. Manwell. New York, Dover Publications [1968] viii, 285 p.
68-009783    593/.1
*Protozoa. Protozoa, Pathogenic.*

### QL366.M3 1968
**Manwell, Reginald D.**
Introduction to protozoology [by] Reginald D. Manwell. New York, Dover Publications [1968] xii, 642 p.
68-026130    593/.1
*Protozoa.*

## QL368 Invertebrates — Protozoa — Systematic divisions

**QL368.A22.C66 1992**
**Carey, Philip G.**
Marine interstitial ciliates : an illustrated key / Philip G. Carey. London ; Chapman & Hall, 1992. xiii, 351 p.
92-130426          593.1/7          0412406101
*Ciliata -- Identification.*

**QL368.F6.H46 1989**
**Hemleben, Ch.**
Modern planktonic foraminifera / Ch. Hemleben, M. Spindler, O.R. Anderson. New York : Springer-Verlag, c1989. xiii, 363 p.
88-008628          591.1/2          0387968156
*Foraminifera. Marine zooplankton.*

## QL369.2 Invertebrates — Protozoa — Physiology

**QL369.2.L87 1979**
Biochemistry and physiology of protozoa / edited by Michael Levandowsky, S. H. Hutner ; consulting editor, Luigi Provasoli. New York : Academic Press, 1979-1981. 4 v. :
78-020045          593.1/041          0124446019
*Protozoa -- Physiology.*

## QL371 Invertebrates — Porifera (Sponges) — General works, treatises, and textbooks

**QL371.B47 1978**
**Bergquist, Patricia R.**
Sponges / Patricia R. Bergquist. Berkeley : University of California Press, c1978. 268 p., [6] l
77-093466          593/.4          0520036581
*Sponges.*

## QL377 Invertebrates — Coelenterata (Cnidaria) — Geographical distribution

**QL377.C7.S33 1990**
**Shick, J. Malcolm**
A functional biology of sea anemones / J. Malcolm Shick. London ; Chapman & Hall, c1991 xxi, 395 :
90-040757          593.6          0412331500
*Sea anemones.*

## QL384 Invertebrates — Echinodermata — Systematic divisions. By class, A-Z

**QL384.A8.C54 1991**
**Clark, Ailsa McGown.**
Starfishes of the Atlantic / Ailsa M. Clark, Maureen E. Downey. London ; Chapman & Hall, 1992. xxvi, 794 p.
91-015257          593.9/309163          0412432803
*Starfishes -- Atlantic Ocean.*

## QL391 Invertebrates — Worms and other vermiform — Systematic divisions. By phylum, A-Z

**QL391.A6.E25 1998**
Earthworm ecology / edited by Clive A. Edwards. Boca Raton, Fla. : St. Lucie Press, c1998. vi, 389 p. :
98-117270          592/.64          1884015743
*Earthworms -- Ecology -- Congresses. Earthworms -- Habitat – Congresses.*

**QL391.A6.E26 1995**
Earthworm ecology and biogeography in North America / edited by Paul F. Hendrix. Boca Raton : Lewis Publishers, c1995. 244 p. :
94-023801          595.1/46          1566700531
*Earthworms -- Ecology -- North America. Earthworms – North America -- Geographical distribution.*

**QL391.C4.W28 1968**
**Wardle, Robert A.**
The zoology of tapeworms, by Robert A. Wardle and James Archie McLeod. New York, Hafner Pub. Co., 1968 [c1952] xxiv, 780 p.
68-022118          595/.121
*Cestoda.*

**QL391.C6.B56 1991**
The Biology of chaetognaths / edited by Q. Bone, H. Kapp, and A.C. Pierrot-Bults. Oxford ; Oxford University Press, 1991. 173 p. :
90-024016          595.1/86          019857715X
*Chaetognatha.*

**QL391.N4.N5 1984**
**Nicholas, Warwick L.**
The biology of free-living nematodes / by Warwick L. Nicholas. 2nd ed. Oxford : Clarendon Press ; 1984. ix, 251 p. :
83-011437          595.1/82          0198575874
*Nematoda.*

**QL391.P7S58 1983**
**Smyth, James Desmond,**
The physiology of trematodes / J.D. Smyth and D.W. Halton. 2nd ed. Cambridge ; New York : Cambridge University Press, 1983. 446 p. :
          595.1/22 19          0521222834
*Trematoda -- Physiology. Platyhelminthes -- Physiology.*

## QL403 Invertebrates — Mollusca — General works, treatises, and textbooks

**QL403.M67 1967**
**Morton, John Edward.**
Molluscs, [by] J. E. Morton. London, Hutchinson, 1967. 244 p.
67-097532          594
*Mollusks.*

**QL403.V47 1993**
**Vermeij, Geerat J.,**
A natural history of shells / by Geerat J. Vermeij. Princeton, N.J. : Princeton University Press, c1993. viii, 207 p.
92-035371          594/.0471          069108596X
*Shells.*

## QL404 Invertebrates — Mollusca — Pictorial works and atlases

**QL404.W955 1991**
**Wye, Kenneth R.**
The encyclopedia of Shells / Kenneth R. Wye. New York : Facts on File, c1991. 288 p. :
91-012191          594/.0471          0816027021
*Shells -- Pictorial works. Shells -- Identification.*

## QL411 Invertebrates — Mollusca — Geographical distribution

**QL411.A19 1974**
**Abbott, R. Tucker**
American seashells; the marine molluska of the Atlantic and Pacific coasts of North America [by] R. Tucker Abbott. New York, Van Nostrand Reinhold [1974] 663 p.
74-007267          594/.04/7          0442202288
*Mollusks -- North America.*

## QL414-415 Invertebrates — Mollusca — Geographical distribution

**QL414.C68 1998**
Common and scientific names of aquatic invertebrates from the United States and Canada. Mollusks / Donna D. Turgeon, chair ; James F. Quinn, Jr. . . . [et al.]. 2nd ed. Bethesda, MD. : American Fisheries Society, 1998. ix, 526 p. :
                        1888569018
*Mollusks -- United States -- Nomenclature. Mollusks -- Canada -- Nomenclature.*

**QL414.W42**
**Webb, Walter Freeman,**
United States Mollusca; a descriptive manual of many of the marine, land and fresh water shells of North America, north of Mexico. All species covered in the book are fully illustrated. By Walter Freeman Webb. Rochester, N.Y. [New York, Printed by Bookcraft, 1942] 220 p.
42-012164          594.0973
*Mollusks -- United States.*

**QL415.P3K43 1974**
**Keen, A. Myra (Angeline Myra),**
Marine molluscan genera of western North America / an illustrated key [by] A. Myra Keen & Eugene Coan. 2d ed. Stanford, CA : Stanford University Press, 1974. vi, 208 p. :
          594/.09/79          0804708398
*Mollusks -- Pacific Coast (North America) -- Identification.*

**QL415.P3K43 1974**
**Keen, A. Myra (Angeline Myra),**
Marine molluscan genera of western North America / an illustrated key by A. Myra Keen & Eugene Coan. 2d ed. Stanford, Calif., Stanford University Press, 1974. vi, 208 p. :
          594/.09/79          0804708398
*Mollusks -- Pacific Coast (North America) -- Identification.*

## QL430.2-430.6 Invertebrates — Mollusca — Systematic divisions

**QL430.2.H37 1996**
**Hanlon, Roger T.**
Cephalopod behaviour / Roger T. Hanlon, John B. Messenger. Cambridge ; Cambridge University Press, 1996. xvi, 232 p. :
95-010249          594/.50451          0521420830
*Cephalopoda -- Behavior.*

**QL430.4.D55 2000**
**Dillon, Robert T.,**
The ecology of freshwater molluscs / Robert T. Dillon, Jr. Cambridge ; Cambridge University Press, 2000. xii, 509 p. :
99-015476          594.176          052135210X
*Gastropoda -- Ecology. Bivalvia -- Ecology. Freshwater invertebrates -- Ecology.*

**QL430.4.H85 1986**
**Hughes, R. N.**
A functional biology of marine gastropods / Roger N. Hughes. Baltimore, Md. : Johns Hopkins University Press, 1986. 245 p. :
85-045864          594/.3041          0801833396
*Gastropoda. Marine invertebrates.*

**QL430.4.S66 1992**
**South, A.**
Terrestrial slugs : biology, ecology, and control / A. South. London : Chapman & Hall, 1992. x, 428 p. :
92-164043          594/.38          0412368102
*Castropoda. Castropoda -- Control.*

**QL430.6.H43 1986**
**Hedeen, Robert A.,**
The oyster : the life and lore of the celebrated bivalve / Robert A. Hedeen ; drawings by Lynne N. Lockhart. Centreville, Md. : Tidewater Publishers, c1986. xii, 237 p. :
86-005861          594/.11          0870333585
*Oysters -- Chesapeake Bay Region (Md. and Va.) Oyster fisheries -- Chesapeake Bay Region (Md. and Va.) Mollusks – Chesapeake Bay Region (Md. and Va.) Chesapeake Bay Region (Md. and Va.)*

## QL434 Invertebrates — Arthropoda — General works, treatises, and textbooks

**QL434.P85 2000**
**Punzo, Fred,**
  Desert arthropods : life history variations / Fred Punzo. Berlin ; Springer, 2000. xiii, 230p.
99-042825          595/.1754          3540660410
  *Arthropoda -- Life cycles. Desert animals -- Life cycles. Arthropoda -- Adaptation.*

**QL434.S43 1965**
**Snodgrass, R. E.**
  A textbook of arthropod anatomy, by R.E. Snodgrass. New York, Hafner Pub. Co., 1965 [c1952] viii, 363 p.
65025216          595.2
  *Arthropoda.*

## QL434.35 Invertebrates — Arthropoda — Evolution. Speciation

**QL434.35.C55 1988**
**Cloudsley-Thompson, J. L.**
  Evolution and adaptation of terrestrial arthropods / John L. Cloudsley-Thompson. Berlin ; Springer-Verlag, c1988. x, 141 p. :
87-028666          595.2/0438          0387181881
  *Arthropoda -- Evolution. Adaptation (Biology)*

## QL434.8 Invertebrates — Arthropoda — Behavior

**QL434.8.I57 1990**
  Insect defenses : adaptive mechanisms and strategies of prey and predators / edited by David L. Evans and Justin O. Schmidt. Albany : State University of New York Press, c1990. xv, 482 p. :
88-012311          595.7/053          0887068960
  *Arthropoda -- Behavior. Insects -- Behavior. Animal defenses.*

## QL444 Invertebrates — Arthropoda — Systematic divisions. By subclasses and orders, A-Z

**QL444.C58.A53 1994**
**Anderson, D. T.**
  Barnacles : structure, function, development and evolution / D.T. Anderson. London ; Chapman & Hall, 1994. xii, 357 p. :
94-180286          595.3/5          0412444208
  *Barnacles.*

**QL444.M33.B56**
  The Biology and management of lobsters / edited by J. Stanley Cobb, Bruce F. Phillips. New York : Academic Press, 1980. 2 v. :
79-006803          595.3/841          0121774015
  *Lobsters. Lobster fisheries.*

**QL444.M33.B564 1988**
  Biology of the land crabs / edited by Warren W. Burggren, Brian R. McMahon. Cambridge [Cambridgeshire] ; Cambridge University Press, 1988. xii, 479 p. :
87-020734          595.3/842          0521306906
  *Grapsidae. Gecarcinidae. Coenobotidae.*

## QL445 Invertebrates — Arthropoda — Anatomy and morphology

**QL445.G7**
**Green, J.**
  A biology of Crustacea. Chicago, Quadrangle Books [1961] 180 p.
61-006671          595.3
  *Crustacea.*

## QL445.2 Invertebrates — Arthropoda — Physiology

**QL445.2.C78 1990**
  Crustacean sexual biology / edited by Raymond T. Bauer and Joel W. Martin. New York : Columbia University Press, c1991. ix, 355 p. :
90-041006          593.3/0416          0231068808
  *Crustacea -- Reproduction. Sex (Biology)*

## QL449.5-449.6 Invertebrates — Arthropoda — Myriapoda

**QL449.5.L48**
**Lewis, J. G. E.**
  The biology of centipedes / J.G.E. Lewis. Cambridge [Eng.] ; Cambridge University Press, 1981. [vii], 476 p.
80-049958          595.6/2          0521234131
  *Centipedes.*

**QL449.6.H67 1992**
**Hopkin, Stephen P.**
  The biology of millipedes / Stephen P. Hopkin and Helen J. Read. Oxford [England] ; Oxford University Press, 1992. xii, 233 p. :
91-040375          595.6/1          0198576994
  *Millipedes.*

## QL457.1-458.4 Invertebrates — Arthropoda — Arachnida (Scorpions; spiders; mites; etc.)

**QL457.1.C7 1948**
**Comstock, John Henry,**
  The spider book; a manual for the study of the spiders and their near relatives, the scorpions, pseudoscorpions, whip-scorpions, harvestmen, and other members of the class Arachnida, found in Americ Ithaca, N.Y., Comstock Pub. Co., 1948. xi, 729 p.
49-004798          595.4
  *Arachnida -- North America.*

**QL457.1.E53 1961**
**Emerton, J. H.**
The common spiders of the United States. With a new key to common groups of spiders by S. W. Frost. New York, Dover Publications [1961] 227 p.
61-003981                595.440973
*Spiders -- United States.*

**QL458.4.F6313 1996**
**Foelix, Rainer F.,**
Biology of spiders / Rainer F. Foelix. New York : Oxford University Press ; 1996. 330 p. :
95-047791                595.4/4                0195095936
*Spiders.*

**QL458.4.G47 1979**
**Gertsch, Willis John,**
American spiders / Willis J. Gertsch. New York : Van Nostrand Reinhold Co., c1979. xiii, 274 p.,
78-006646                595/.44/097                0442226497
*Spiders -- North America. Arachnida -- North America.*

**QL458.4.S65 1986**
Spiders--webs, behavior, and evolution / edited by William A. Shear. Stanford, Calif. : Stanford University Press, 1986. xiii, 492 p.
83-042833                595.4/4                0804712034
*Spiders -- Congresses.*

**QL458.4.W57 1993**
**Wise, David H.**
Spiders in ecological webs / David H. Wise. Cambridge ; Cambridge University Press, 1993. xii, 328 p. :
92-011137                595.4/405                0521325471
*Spiders -- Ecology. Spider populations. Spiders – Ecophysiology.*

### QL461-596 Invertebrates — Arthropoda — Insects

**QL461.A6**
Annual review of entomology. Palo Alto, Calif. [etc.] Annual Reviews, inc. [etc.] v.
56-005750                595.7
*Insects -- Periodicals.*

**QL461.C54 1956**
Physiology of insect development, edited by Frank L. Campbell. [Chicago] University of Chicago Press [1959] xiv, 167 p.
59-009701                595.7
*Entomology -- Congresses. Insects -- Development. Embryology - - Insects.*

**QL463.C71 1940**
**Comstock, John Henry,**
An introduction to entomology, by John Henry Comstock ... Ithaca, N.Y., Comstock Publishing Company, inc., 1940. 5 p. ., [ix]-
40027640                595.7
*Insects. Entomology.*

**QL463.H89 1993**
**Hubbell, Sue.**
Broadsides from the other orders : a book of bugs / Sue Hubbell ; illustrated by Dimitry Schidlovsky. New York : Random House, c1993. xx, 276 p. :
92-027165                595.7                0679400621
*Insects.*

**QL463.I57 1977**
**Imms, Augustus Daniel,**
Imms' General textbook of entomology. London : Chapman and Hall ; 1977. 2 v. :
76-047011                595.7                0470991224
*Entomology. Insects.*

**QL463.L43 1993**
**Leather, S. R.**
The ecology of insect overwintering / S.R. Leather, K.F.A. Walters, and J.S. Bale. Cambridge [England] ; Cambridge University Press, 1993. x, 255 p. :
91-043260                595.7/0543                0521417589
*Insects -- Ecology. Insects -- Physiology.*

**QL464.A76 1985**
**Arnett, Ross H.**
Insect life : a field entomology manual for the amateur naturalist / Ross H. Arnett, Jr., Richard L. Jacques, Jr. ; illustrated by Adelaide Murphy. Englewood Cliffs, N.J. : Prentice-Hall, c1985. xii, 354 p. :
                595.7/00723 19                0134672593
*Entomology -- Field work.*

**QL467.B47 1989**
**Berenbaum, M.**
Ninety-nine gnats, nits, and nibblers / May R. Berenbaum ; with illustrations by John Parker Sherrod. Urbana : University of Illinois Press, c1989. xxi, 254 p. :
88-015420                595.7                0252015711
*Insects.*

**QL467.B474 1993**
**Berenbaum, M.**
Ninety-nine more maggots, mites, and munchers / May R. Berenbaum ; illustrations by John Parker Sherrod. Urbana : University of Illinois Press, c1993. xix, 285 p. :
92-034639                595.7                0252020162
*Insects -- Popular works. Insect pests -- Popular works.*

**QL467.T23 1944**
**Teale, Edwin Way,**
Grassroot jungles, a book of insects. New York, Dodd, Mead & Company, 1944. xi p., 1 ., 2
44005481                595.7
*Insects.*

**QL468.7.T46 1983**
**Thornhill, Randy.**
The evolution of insect mating systems / Randy Thornhill and John Alcock. Cambridge, Mass. : Harvard University Press, 1983. ix, 547 p. :
82-021351                595.7/056                0674271807
*Insects -- Evolution. Insects -- Reproduction.*

**QL473.A76**
**Arnett, Ross H.**
    Simon and Schuster's guide to insects / by Ross H. Arnett, Jr., and Richard L. Jacques, Jr. New York : Simon and Schuster, c1981. 512 p. :
        595.7097 19      0671250132
*Insects -- North America -- Identification.*

**QL474.A76 2000**
**Arnett, Ross H.**
    American insects : a handbook of the insects of America north of Mexico / Ross H. Arnett, Jr. 2nd ed. Boca Raton, FL. : CRC Press, c2000. xvii, 1003 p. :
        595.7/0973 21      0849302129
*Insects -- United States -- Classification. Insects -- Canada -- Classification.*

**QL476.5.H64 1993**
**Hogue, Charles Leonard.**
    Latin American insects and entomology / Charles L. Hogue. Berkeley : University of California Press, c1993. xiv, 536 p.,
  91-048184      595.7098      0520078497
*Insects -- Latin America.*

**QL487.I5 1991**
    The Insects of Australia : a textbook for students and research workers / Division of Entomology, Commonwealth Scientific and Industrial Research Organisation. Ithaca, N.Y. : Cornell University Press, 1991. 2 v. (1137 p.
  91-009407      595.70994      0801426693
*Insects -- Australia.*

**QL494.L34 1991**
**Lehane, M. J.**
    Biology of blood-sucking insects / M.J. Lehane. London : HarperCollins Academic, 1991. xv, 288 p. :
  90-022268      595.7/05249      0044454090
*Bloodsucking insects -- Anatomy. Bloodsucking insects -- Physiology. Bloodsucking insects -- Digestive organs.*

**QL495.C47 1984**
    Chemical ecology of insects / edited by William J. Bell and Ring T. Carde. Sunderland, Mass. : Sinauer Associates, Inc., 1984-c1995. 2 v. :
  83-020212      595.7/05      0878930698
*Insects -- Ecophysiology. Chemical ecology. Chemical senses.*

**QL495.D4**
**Dethier, V. G.**
    The physiology of insect senses. London, Methuen; [1963] ix, 266 p.
  64-009657      595.701
*Insects -- Physiology. Senses and sensation.*

**QL495.H38 1993**
**Heinrich, Bernd,**
    The hot-blooded insects : strategies and mechanisms of thermoregulation / Bernd Heinrich. Cambridge, Mass. : Harvard University Press, 1993. 601 p. :
  92-013703      595.7/0188      0674408381
*Insects -- Physiology. Body temperature -- Regulation. Insects -- Behavior.*

**QL495.N54 1994**
**Nijhout, H. Frederik.**
    Insect hormones / H. Frederik Nijhout. Princeton, N.J. : Princeton University Press, c1994. xi, 267 p. :
  93-042301      595.7/0142      0691034664
*Insects -- Physiology. Insect hormones. Insects -- Development.*

**QL495.P48 1987**
    Pheromone biochemistry / edited by Glenn D. Prestwich, Gary J. Blomquist. Orlando : Academic Press, 1987. xix, 565 p. :
  86-030224      595.7/0142      012564485X
*Insect hormones. Pheromones. Biochemistry.*

**QL496.D44 1984**
    Defensive mechanisms in social insects / edited by Henry R. Hermann. New York : Praeger, 1984. xii, 259 p. :
  83-024798      595.7/057      0030570026
*Insect societies. Animal defenses.*

**QL496.E94 1997**
    The evolution of mating systems in insects and arachnids / edited by Jae C. Choe and Bernard J. Crespi. Cambridge ; Cambridge University Press, 1997. viii, 387 p.
  96-025108      595.7056      0521580293
*Insects -- Behavior -- Evolution. Arachnida -- Behavior -- Evolution. Sexual behavior in animals.*

**QL496.G59 1994**
**Godfray, H. C. J.,**
    Parasitoids : behavioral and evolutionary ecology / H.C.J. Godfray. Princeton, N.J. : Princeton University Press, c1994. 473 p. :
  93-013158      595.7/053      0691033250
*Parasitic insects -- Behavior. Parasitoids -- Behavior. Insects -- Parasites.*

**QL496.J6**
**Johnson, C. G.**
    Migration and dispersal of insects by flight [by] C. G. Johnson. London, Methuen, 1969. xxii, 763 p.
  70-414616      595.7/05/2
*Insects -- Migration. Insects -- Dispersal. Insects -- Flight.*

**QL496.W57**
**Wheeler, William Morton,**
    The social insects, their origin and evolution, by William Morton Wheeler ... London, K. Paul, Trench, Trubner & co., ltd.; 1928. xviii, 378 p.
  28-016212
*Insects -- Evolution. Insect societies.*

**QL496.W62**
**Wigglesworth, Vincent Brian,**
    The physiology of insect metamorphosis. Cambridge [Eng.] University Press, 1954. vii, 151 p.
  55001618      595.7
*Insects -- Development. Insects -- Physiology.*

**QL496.W64 1966**
**Williams, Carrington Bonsor,**
Insect migration, by C.B. Williams. 2nd ed. London, Collins, 1966. xiii, 237 p. :
595.7/05/2
*Insects -- Migration.*

**QL496.W67 1990**
**Wilson, Edward Osborne,**
Success and dominance in ecosystems : the case of the social insects / Edward O. Wilson ; introduction, Otto Kinne. Oldendorf/Luhe, Federal Republic of Germany : Ecology Institute, c1990. xx, 104 p. :
92-123748        595.7/05248
*Wilson, Edward Osborne, -- 1929-    Insect societies. Biotic communities. Insects -- Ecology.*

**QL496.2.I47 1995**
Insect migration : tracking resources through space and time / edited by V.A. Drake and A.G. Gatehouse. Cambridge ; Cambridge University Press, 1995. xvii, 478 p.
94-049434        595.7052/5        0521440009
*Insects -- Migration. Insect pests -- Migration.*

**QL496.7.B73 1992**
**Brackenbury, John.**
Insects in flight / John Brackenbury. London : Blandford ; 1992. 192 p. :
93-106488        595.7/01852        0713723017
*Insects -- Flight.*

**QL496.7.D83 2000**
**Dudley, Robert,**
The biomechanics of insect flight : form, function, evolution / Robert Dudley. Princeton, N.J. : Princeton University Press, c2000. xii, 476 p. :
99-029653        573.7/98157        0691044309
*Insects -- Flight.*

**QL506.P74 1991**
**Preston-Mafham, Ken.**
Grasshoppers and mantids of the world / Ken Preston-Mafham ; photography by Ken and Rod Preston-Mafham. New York : Facts on File, c1990. 192 p. :
89-039999        595.7/26        0816022984
*Orthoptera.*

**QL508.A2.B55 1990**
Biology of grasshoppers / edited by R.F. Chapman, A. Joern. New York : Wiley, c1990. x, 563 p. :
89-022666        595.7/26        0471609013
*Grasshoppers.*

**QL508.A2.O88**
**Otte, Daniel.**
The North American grasshoppers / Daniel Otte. Cambridge, Mass. : Harvard University Press, 1981-1984 v. 1-2 :
81-006806        595.7/26        0674626605
*Grasshoppers -- North America -- Identification.*

**QL508.B6.A44 1982**
The American cockroach / edited by William J. Bell and K.G. Adiyodi. London ; Chapman and Hall, 1982. xvi, 529 p. :
81-196113        595.7/22        0412161400
*Cockroaches -- United States.*

**QL508.G8.C75 1989**
Cricket behavior and neurobiology / edited by Franz Huber, Thomas E. Moore, Werner Loher. Ithaca : Comstock Pub. Associates, 1989. xiii, 565 p.
88-043256        595.7/26        0801422728
*Crickets -- Behavior. Crickets -- Nervous system. Neurobiology.*

**QL508.M4.P7 1999**
The praying mantids / edited by Frederick R. Prete ... [et al.]. Baltimore : Johns Hopkins University Press, 1999. xiv, 362 p.
99-044360        595.7/27        0801861748
*Mantidae.*

**QL520.C67 1999**
**Corbet, Philip S.**
Dragonflies : behavior and ecology of Odonata / Philip S. Corbet. Ithaca, N.Y. : Comstock Pub. Associates, 1999. xxxii, 829 p.
98-045290        595.7/33        0801425921
*Odonata.*

**QL520.S56 2001**
**Silsby, Jill.**
Dragonflies of the world / Jill Silsby. Washington, D.C. : Smithsonian Institution Press, 2001. vii, 216 p. :
595.7/33 21        1560989599
*Dragonflies.*

**QL521.S38 1995**
**Schuh, Randall T.**
True bugs of the world (Hemiptera:Heteroptera) : classification and natural history / Randall T. Schuh, James A. Slater. Ithaca : Comstock Pub. Associates, 1995. xii, 336 p. :
94-032643        595.7/54        0801420660
*Hemiptera. Hemiptera -- Classification.*

**QL533.D4**
**Dethier, V. G.**
To know a fly. Illustrated by Bill Clark and Vincent Dethier. San Francisco, Holden-Day, 1962. 119 p.
62-021838        595.77
*Flies. Insects -- Behavior.*

**QL537.D75.D4 1965**
**Demerec, M.**
Biology of Drosophila, edited by M. Demerec. New York, Hafner Pub. Co., 1965 [c1950] x, 632 p.
64-066008        595.774
*Drosophila.*

QL563.O53 2001

**QL537.T42.F66 1993**
**Foote, Richard H.**
Handbook of the fruit flies (Diptera: Tephritidae) of America north of Mexico / Richard H. Foote, F.L. Blanc, Allen L. Norrbom. Ithaca : Comstock Pub. Associates, 1993. xii, 571 p. :
92-052844        595.77/4        0801426235
Tephritidae -- United States -- Classification. Tephritidae -- Canada -- Classification.

**QL541.5.F44 1993**
**Feltwell, John.**
The encyclopedia of butterflies / John Feltwell. New York : Prentice Hall General Reference, 1993. 288 p. :
93012184        595.78/9/03        0671868284
Butterflies -- Encyclopedias.

**QL542.K55**
**Klots, Alexander Barrett,**
The world of butterflies and moths / by Alexander Barrett Klots. New York : McGraw-Hill [1958] 207 p. :
58003245        595.78
Butterflies. Moths. Butterflies -- Pictorial works.

**QL542.S2613 1985b**
**Sbordoni, Valerio.**
Butterflies of the world / Valerio Sbordoni, Saverio Forestiero ; [translated from the Italian by Neil Stratton, Hugh Young, and Bruce Penman]. New York, N.Y. : Times Books, c1985. 312 p. :
84-040101        595.78        0812911288
Butterflies.

**QL542.S39 1992**
**Scoble, M. J.**
The lepidoptera : form, function, and diversity / by Malcolm J. Scoble. Oxford ; Oxford University Press, 1992. xi, 404 p. :
92-004297        595.78        0198540310
Lepidoptera. Lepidoptera -- Classification.

**QL548.B8**
The Butterflies of North America / William H. Howe, coordinating editor and illustrator & twenty contributors-- contributors, David L. Bauer ... [et al.]. Garden City, N.Y. : Doubleday, 1975. xiii, 633 p.,
73-015276        595.7/89/097        0385049269
Butterflies -- North America. Insects -- North America.

**QL548.P94 1981**
**Pyle, Robert Michael.**
The Audubon Society field guide to North American butterflies / Robert Michael Pyle ; visual key by Carol Nehring and Jane Opper. New York : Knopf : c1981. 916 p. :
80-084240        595.78/9097        0394519140
Butterflies -- North America -- Identification. Insects -- Identification. Insects -- North America -- Identification.

**QL548.S381986**
**Scott, James A.,**
The butterflies of North America : a natural history and field guide / James A. Scott. Stanford, CA : Stanford University Press, 1986. xii, 583 p. :
595.78/9097 19        0804712050
Butterflies -- North America. Butterflies -- North America -- Identification. Insects -- Identification. Insects -- North America -- Indentification.

**QL555.G7**
**Leverton, Roy.**
Enjoying moths / Roy Leverton ; with line illustrations by Michael Roberts. London : T & A D Poyser Natural History, 2001. xi, 276 p. :
00-107416        595.78/0941        0856611247
Moths -- Great Britain.

**QL561.L3.F58 1995**
**Fitzgerald, Terrence D.**
The tent caterpillars / Terrence D. Fitzgerald. Ithaca, N.Y. : Comstock Pub. Associates, 1995. xiv, 303 p. :
94-048048        595.78/1        0801424569
Tent caterpillars.

**QL561.P2.T82 1994**
**Tyler, Hamilton A.**
Swallowtail butterflies of the Americas : a study in biological dynamics, ecological diversity, biosystematics, and conservation / Hamilton A. Tyler, Keith S. Brown, Jr., Kent H. Wilson. Gainesville, FL : Scientific Publishers, 1994. 376 p. :
92-025090        595.78/9        094541790X
Papilionidae -- America. Papilionidae -- America -- Pictorial works.

**QL562.E28 1988**
**Eaton, John L.,**
Lepidopteran anatomy / John L. Eaton. New York : Wiley, c1988. xiii, 257 p.
87-025226        595.78/044        0471058629
Lepidoptera -- Anatomy. Insects -- Anatomy.

**QL562.4.D46 1993**
**Dennis, Roger L. H.**
Butterflies and climate change / Roger L.H. Dennis. Manchester ; Manchester University Press ; c1993. xv, 302 p. :
93-009186        595.78/9045222        0719035058
Butterflies -- Behavior -- Climatic changes. Climatic changes.

**QL563.O53 2001**
**O'Neill, Kevin M.**
Solitary wasps : behavior and natural history / Kevin M. O'Neill ; with illustrations by Catherine Seibert. Ithaca, N.Y. : Comstock Pub. Associates, 2001. xiii, 406 p.
00-010199        595.79/8        0801437210
Solitary wasps -- Behavior. Solitary wasps.

**QL566.M53 2000**
**Michener, Charles Duncan,**
The bees of the world / Charles D. Michener. Baltimore, Md. : Johns Hopkins University Press, 2000. xiv, 913 p. :
99-030198                595.79/9               0801861330
*Bees -- Classification.*

**QL568.A6.F62 1971**
**Frisch, Karl von,**
Bees: their vision, chemical senses, and language. Ithaca, Cornell University Press [1971] xviii, 157 p.
71-148718                595.79/9               0801406285
*Bees.*

**QL568.A6.F643**
**Frisch, Karl von,**
The dance language and orientation of bees. Translated by Leigh E. Chadwick. Cambridge, Mass., Belknap Press of Harvard University Press, 1967. xiv, 566 p.
67-017321
*Bees -- Behavior. Bees -- Orientation.*

**QL568.F7**
**Taber, Stephen Welton,**
Fire ants / Stephen Welton Taber. College Station, TX: Texas A&M University Press, c2000. xvii, 308 p.
00-026346                595.79/6               0890969450
*Fire ants.*

**QL568.F7.B58 1994**
**Bolton, Barry.**
Identification guide to the ant genera of the world / Barry Bolton. Cambridge, Mass. : Harvard University Press, 1994. 222 p. :
93-041270                595.79/6/012          0674442806
*Ants -- Identification. Ants -- Classification.*

**QL568.F7.G64 1999**
**Gordon, Deborah**
Ants at work : how an insect society is organized / Deborah M. Gordon ; illustrations by Michelle Schwengel. New York, NY : Free Press, c1999. x, 182 p. :
99-035853                595.79/6               0684857332
*Ants -- Behavior. Insect societies.*

**QL568.F7.H57 1990**
**Holldobler, Bert,**
The ants / Bert Holldobler and Edward O. Wilson. Cambridge, Mass. : Belknap Press of Harvard University Press, 1990. xii, 732 p.,
89-030653                595.79/6               0674040759
*Ants.*

**QL568.F7.H575 1994**
**Holldobler, Bert,**
Journey to the ants : a story of scientific exploration / Bert Holldobler and Edward O. Wilson. Cambridge, Mass. : Belknap Press of Harvard University Press, 1994. 228 p. :
94013386                595.79/6               0674485254
*Holldobler, Bert, -- 1936- Wilson, Edward Osborne, – 1929- Insect societies. Ants -- Research. Ants.*

**QL569.M5**
**Michener, Charles Duncan,**
American social insects; a book about bees, ants, wasps, and termites, by Charles D. Michener and Mary H. Michener. New York, Van Nostrand [1951] xiv, 267 p.
51012770                595.79
*Hymenoptera -- United States. Insect societies. Hymenoptera – United States.*

**QL581.W47 1983**
**White, Richard E.**
A field guide to the beetles of North America : text and illustrations / by Richard E. White. Boston : Houghton Mifflin, 1983. xii, 368 p. :
83-000060                595.76/097             0395318084
*Beetles -- North America -- Identification. Insects – Identification. Insects -- North America -- Identification.*

**QL596.C65.D58 2000**
**Dixon, A. F. G.**
Insect predator-prey dynamics : ladybird beetles and biological control / A.F.G. Dixon. Cambridge ; Cambridge University Press, 2000. ix, 257 p. :
99-045440                595.76/9               0521622034
*Ladybugs. Predation (Biology) Insect pests -- Biological control.*

## QL605 Chordates. Vertebrates — Societies, congresses, serial collections, yearbooks

**QL605.R6 1959**
**Romer, Alfred Sherwood,**
The vertebrate story. Chicago] University of Chicago Press [1959] 437 p.
58-011957                596
*Vertebrates. Evolution. Paleontology.*

**QL605.Y68 1981**
**Young, J. Z.**
The life of vertebrates / J.Z. Young. Oxford : Clarendon Press, 1981. xv, 645 p. :
81-206006                596                    0198571720
*Vertebrates. Vertebrates, Fossil.*

## QL607.5 Chordates. Vertebrates — Evolution (General)

**QL607.5.G44 1996**
**Gee, Henry.**
Before the backbone : views on the origin of the vertebrates / Henry Gee. London ; Chapman & Hall, 1996. xx, 346 p. :
95-072203                596.138                0412483009
*Vertebrates -- Evolution. Mammals -- Evolution.*

## QL614.7 Chordates. Vertebrates — Fishes — Dictionaries and encyclopedias

**QL614.7.E535 1995**
Encyclopedia of fishes / consultant editors, John R. Paxton and William N. Eschmeyer ; illustrations by David Kirshner. San Diego : Academic Press, 1995. 240 p. :
94-073232          597/.003          0125476604
*Fishes -- Encyclopedias. Fishes -- encyclopedias*

## QL615 Chordates. Vertebrates — Fishes — General works, treatises, and textbooks

**QL615.M49**
**Migdalski, Edward C.**
The fresh & salt water fishes of the world / by Edward C. Migdalski and George S. Fichter ; ill. by Norman Weaver. New York : Knopf : distributed by Random House, 1976. 316 p. :
76-013704          597          0394492390
*Fishes.*

## QL618 Chordates. Vertebrates — Fishes — Classification. Nomenclature

**QL618.J36 1991**
**Jamieson, Barrie G. M.**
Fish evolution and systematics : evidence from spermatozoa : with a survey of lophophorate, echinoderm, and protochordate sperm and an account of gamete cryopreservation / Barrie G.M. Jamieson with contributions by L. K.-P. Leung. Cambridge ; Cambridge University Press, 1991. xiv, 319 p. :
91-007443          597/.038          0521413044
*Fishes -- Classification. Fishes -- Spermatozoa -- Morphology. Fishes -- Evolution.*

**QL618.N4 1994**
**Nelson, Joseph S.**
Fishes of the world / Joseph S. Nelson. New York : J. Wiley, c1994. xvii, 600 p.
93-037462          597/.0012          0471547131
*Fishes -- Classification.*

## QL618.2 Chordates. Vertebrates — Fishes — Evolution. Speciation

**QL618.2.I59 1996**
Interrelationships of fishes / edited by Melanie L.J. Stiassny, Lynne R. Parenti, G. David Johnson. San Diego : Academic Press, c1996. xiii, 496 p.
96-028224          597/.038          0126709505
*Fishes -- Phylogeny.*

## QL618.55 Chordates. Vertebrates — Fishes — Study and teaching. Research

**QL618.55.Q56 1994**
**Quinn, John R.**
Fishwatching : your complete guide to the underwater world / by John R. Quinn ; foreword by Herbert R. Axelrod. Woodstock, Vt. : Countryman Press, c1994. xv, 231 p., [
93-051025          597          0881502847
*Fish watching. Fishes. Marine animals.*

## QL621.5-627 Chordates. Vertebrates — Fishes — Geographical distribution

**QL621.5.R63 1986**
**Robins, C. Richard.**
A field guide to Atlantic Coast fishes of North America / C. Richard Robins, G. Carleton Ray ; illustrations by John Douglass and Rudolf Freund; sponsored by the National Audubon Society and the National Wildlife Federation. Boston : Houghton Mifflin, 1986. xi, 354 p., [
85-018144          597.092/14          0395318521
*Fishes -- Atlantic coast (North America) -- Identification.*

**QL621.58.L54 1996**
**Lieske, Ewald,**
Coral reef fishes : Caribbean, Indian Ocean, and Pacific Ocean : including the Red Sea / Ewald Lieske and Robert Myers. Princeton, N.J. : Princeton University Press, 1996. 400 p. :
96-010786          597.092          0691026599
*Coral reef fishes -- Caribbean Sea. Coral reef fishes -- Pacific Ocean. Coral reef fishes -- Indian Ocean.*

**QL623.4.E83 1983**
**Eschmeyer, William N.**
A field guide to Pacific Coast fishes of North America : from the Gulf of Alaska to Baja, California / William N. Eschmeyer, Earl S. Herald ; illustrations by Howard Hammann, Katherine P. Smith, associate illustrator. Boston : Houghton Mifflin, 1983. xii, 336 p.,
82-011989          597.0979          0395331889
*Fishes -- Pacific Coast (North America) -- Identification.*

**QL625.A93 1983**
The Audubon Society field guide to North American fishes, whales, and dolphins / Herbert T. Boschung, Jr. ... [et al.]. New York : Knopf : [1983] 848 p. :
83-047962          597.097          0394534050
*Fishes -- North America -- Identification. Cetacea -- North America -- Identification. Mammals -- North America -- Identification.*

**QL625.S87 1992**
Systematics, historical ecology, and North American freshwater fishes / edited by Richard L. Mayden. Stanford, Calif. : Stanford University Press, 1992. xxvi, 969 p.
92-019781          597.092/97          0804721629
*Freshwater fishes -- North America.*

**QL627.P34 1991**
**Page, Lawrence M.**
A field guide to freshwater fishes : North America north of Mexico / Lawrence M. Page, Brooks M. Burr ; illustrations by Eugene C. Beckham III, John Parker Sherrod, Craig W. Ronto. Boston : Houghton Mifflin, 1991. xii, 432 p. :
90-042049          597.092/973          0395353076
*Freshwater fishes -- United States -- Identification. Freshwater fishes -- Canada -- Identification.*

### QL638-638.9 Chordates. Vertebrates — Fishes — Systematic divisions

**QL638.C55**
**Barlow, George W.**
The cichlid fishes : nature's grand experiment in evolution / George W. Barlow. Cambridge, Mass. : Perseus Pub., c2000. xvi, 335 p.,
0738203769
*Cichlids. Fishes -- Evolution.*

**QL638.L26.T46 1991**
**Thomson, Keith Stewart.**
Living fossil : the story of the coelacanth / Keith Stewart Thomson. New York : W.W. Norton, c1991. 252 p. :
90-043053          597/.46          0393029565
*Coelacanth.*

**QL638.9.E44**
**Ellis, Richard,**
The book of sharks / written and illustrated by Richard Ellis. New York : Grosset & Dunlap, c1976. 320 p. :
597/.31          0448124572
*Sharks.*

**QL638.9.M67 1984**
**Moss, Sanford A.**
Sharks : an introduction for the amateur naturalists / Sanford A. Moss. Englewood Cliffs, N.J. : Prentice-Hall, c1984. x, 246 p. :
597/.31 19          0138083126
*Sharks.*

**QL638.9.P437 1999**
**Perrine, Doug.**
Sharks & rays of the world / Doug Perrine. Stillwater, MN : Voyageur Press, c1999. 132 p. :
99-025791          597.3          0896584488
*Sharks -- Juvenile literature. Rays (Fishes) -- Juvenile literature. Sharks.*

### QL639.1 Chordates. Vertebrates — Fishes — Physiology

**QL639.1.P49 1993**
The Physiology of fishes / edited by David H. Evans. Boca Raton : CRC Press, c1993. 592 p. :
93-018071          597/.01          0849380421
*Fishes -- Physiology.*

### QL639.8 Chordates. Vertebrates — Fishes — Ecology

**QL639.8.W66 1992**
**Wootton, R. J.**
Fish ecology / R.J. Wootton. Glasgow : Blackie ; 1992. x, 212 p. :
91-028996          597/.05          0412029219
*Fishes -- Ecology.*

### QL641 Chordates. Vertebrates — Reptiles and amphibians — General works, treatises, and textbooks

**QL641.D6 1933**
**Ditmars, Raymond Lee,**
Reptiles of the world; the crocodilians, lizards, snakes, turtles and tortoises of the eastern and western hemispheres, by Raymond L. Ditmars. New York, The Macmillan company, 1933. xx, 321 p., f
33-032380          598.1
*Reptiles.*

**QL641.H47 1998**
Herpetology / F. Harvey Pough ... [et al.]. Upper Saddle River, NJ : Prentice Hall, c1998. xi, 577 p. :
97-019347          597.9          0138508763
*Herpetology.*

### QL645 Chordates. Vertebrates — Reptiles and amphibians — Classification. Nomenclature

**QL645.F73 1995**
**Frank, Norman.**
A complete guide to scientific and common names of reptiles and amphibians of the world / by Norman Frank and Erica Ramus. Pottsville, PA : N.G. Pub., c1995. 377 p. ;
95-068825          597.9/01/4          0964103230
*Reptiles -- Nomenclature. Amphibians -- Nomenclature. Reptiles -- Nomenclature (Popular)*

### QL645.4 Chordates. Vertebrates — Reptiles and amphibians — Evolution

**QL645.4.M43 1994**
Measuring and monitoring biological diversity. edited by W. Ronald Heyer ... [et al.]. Washington : Smithsonian Institution Press, c1994. xix, 364 p. :
92-044743          597.6/045248/0723
1560982845
*Amphibians -- Speciation -- Research. Biological diversity -- Measurement.*

## QL651-663 Chordates. Vertebrates — Reptiles and amphibians — Geographical distribution

**QL651.D6 1936**
**Ditmars, Raymond Lee,**
  The reptiles of North America; a review of the crocodilians, lizard, snakes, turtles and tortoises inhabiting the United States and northern Mexico, By Raymond L. Ditmars... Eight plates in color and more than four hundred photographs from life. Garden City, N.Y. Doubleday, 1936. xvi, 476 p.,
36027465          596.1097
  *Reptiles -- North America.*

**QL651.S783 1985**
**Stebbins, Robert C.**
  A field guide to western reptiles and amphibians : field marks of all species in western North America, including Baja California / text and illustrations by Robert C. Stebbins ; sponsored by the National Audubon Society and National Wildlife Federation. Boston : Houghton Mifflin, 1985. xiv, 336 p. :
84-025125          597.6/0978          0395382548
  *Reptiles -- North America -- Identification. Reptiles – West (U.S.) -- Identification. Amphibians -- North America -- Identification.*

**QL663.A1.C63 1992**
**Cogger, Harold G.**
  Reptiles & amphibians of Australia / by Harold G. Cogger. Ithaca, N.Y. : Comstock/Cornell, 1992. 775 p. :
91-034103          597.6/0994          0801427398
  *Reptiles -- Australia. Amphibians -- Australia.*

## QL666-668 Chordates. Vertebrates — Reptiles and amphibians — Systematic divisions

**QL666.C5**
  Turtle conservation / edited by Michael W. Klemens. Washington : Smithsonian Institution Press, c2000. xv, 334 p. :
00-030115          333.95/79216          1560983728
  *Turtles. Wildlife conservation.*

**QL666.C5.A43 1988**
**Alderton, David,**
  Turtles & tortoises of the world / David Alderton ; photographs by Tony Tilford. New York, N.Y. : Facts on File, 1988. 191 p. :
88-016240          597.92          0816017336
  *Turtles.*

**QL666.C5.E76 1994**
**Ernst, Carl H.**
  Turtles of the United States and Canada / Carl H. Ernst, Roger W. Barbour, and Jeffrey E. Lovich. Washington : Smithsonian Institution Press, c1994. xxxviii, 578
93-034939          597.92/0973          1560983469
  *Turtles -- United States. Turtles -- Canada.*

**QL666.C5.E77 1989**
**Ernst, Carl H.**
  Turtles of the world / Carl H. Ernst and Roger W. Barbour. Washington : Smithsonian Institution Press, c1989. xii, 313 p.,
88-029727          597.92          0874744148
  *Turtles.*

**QL666.C536.B56 1997**
  The biology of sea turtles / edited by Peter L. Lutz and John A. Musick. Boca Raton, Fla : CRC Press, 1996. 432 p. :
96-036432          597.92          0849384222
  *Sea turtles.*

**QL666.C536.W65 1979**
  Biology and conservation of sea turtles / edited by Karen A. Bjorndal. Washington : Smithsonian Institution Press, c1995. 615 p. :
95-018872          597.92          1560986190
  *Sea turtles -- Congresses. Wildlife conservation -- Congresses.*

**QL666.C9.A33 1991**
**Alderton, David,**
  Crocodiles & alligators of the world / David Alderton ; photography by Bruce Tanner. New York : Facts on File, c1991. 190 p. :
89-039997          597.98          0816022976
  *Crocodilians.*

**QL666.C9.H26 1991**
**Grenard, Steve.**
  Handbook of alligators and crocodiles / Steve Grenard ; illustrated by Wanda Loutsenhizer. Malabar, Fla. : Krieger Pub., 1991. x, 210 p., 8
89-071337          597.98          0894644351
  *Crocodilians.*

**QL666.L2.L57 1994**
  Lizard ecology : historical and experimental perspectives / edited by Laurie J. Vitt and Eric R. Pianka. Princeton, N.J. : Princeton University Press, c1994. xii, 403 p. :
93-046274          597.95/045          0691036497
  *Lizards -- Ecology -- Congresses.*

**QL666.L23.M365 1992**
**Martin, James,**
  Masters of disguise : a natural history of chameleons / text by James Martin ; photographs by Art Wolfe. New York : Facts on File, c1992. xvi, 176 p. :
91-038050          597.95          0816026181
  *Chameleons.*

**QL666.L25.M345 1997**
**Manaster, Jane.**
  Horned lizards / Jane Manaster. Austin : University of Texas Press, 1997. ix, 81 p. :
96-025203          597.95          029275177X
  *Horned toads.*

**QL666.L29.D4 1996**
**De Lisle, Harold F.,**
The natural history of monitor lizards / Harold F. De Lisle. Malabar, Fla. : Krieger, 1996. xiii, 201 p.,
95-003063          597.95          0894648977
*Monitor lizards.*

**QL666.O6.B3295 2000**
**Bartlett, Richard D.,**
Snakes of North America. Western Region Richard D. Bartlett, Alan Tennant ; maps by Patricia Bartlett. Houston, Tex. : Gulf Pub., c2000. xvi, 312 p. :
99-032825          597.96/00978          0877193126
*Snakes -- West (U.S.) -- Identification.*

**QL666.O6.D54**
**Ditmars, Raymond Lee,**
Snakes of the world, by Raymond L. Ditmars, with illustrations from life. New York, The Macmillan company, 1931. xi, 207 p.
31-032044          598.12
*Snakes.*

**QL666.O6.E53 1995**
**Mattison, Christopher.**
The encyclopedia of snakes / Chris Mattison. New York, NY : Facts on File, c1995. 256 p. :
95-002501          597.96          0816030723
*Snakes.*

**QL666.O6.E77 1992**
**Ernst, Carl H.**
Venomous reptiles of North America / Carl H. Ernst. Washington : Smithsonian Institution Press, c1992. ix, 236 p. :
91-003535          597.96/0469/0973
1560981148
*Poisonous snakes -- North America. Gila monster.*

**QL666.O6.M66 1980**
**Minton, Sherman A.**
Venomous reptiles / Sherman A. Minton, Jr., Madge Rutherford Minton. New York : Scribner, c1980. xii, 308 p.,
80-017015          597.96/0469          0684166267
*Poisonous snakes. Poisonous snakes -- Venom.*

**QL666.O6.S65 1993**
Snakes : ecology and behavior / [edited by] Richard A. Seigel, Joseph T. Collins. New York : McGraw-Hill, c1993. xvi, 414 p. :
93-018568          597.96/0451          0070560560
*Snakes -- Ecology. Snakes -- Behavior.*

**QL666.O6.T4565 2000**
**Tennant, Alan,**
Snakes of North America. Eastern and Central Regions. Alan Tennant, R.D. Bartlett ; contributors, Gerard T. Salmon, Richard B. King ; maps by Gerard T. Salmon. Houston, Tex : Gulf, c2000. xxv, 587 p. :
99-035347          597.96/097          087719307X
*Snakes -- North America -- Identification.*

**QL666.O6.W455 1989**
**Williams, Kenneth L.,**
Snakes of the world / by Kenneth L. Williams and V. Wallach. Malabar, Fla. : Krieger Pub. Co., 1989- v. 1   ;
88-000001          597.96          0894642154
*Snakes.*

**QL666.O6.W7**
**Wright, Albert Hazen,**
Handbook of snakes of the United States and Canada, by Albert Hazen Wright and Anna Allen Wright. Ithaca, N.Y., Comstock Pub. Associates, 1957- v.
57001635          598.12          0-8014-0463-0
*Snakes -- North America. Snakes -- United States. Snakes -- Canada.*

**QL666.O63.M87 1997**
**Murphy, John C.,**
Tales of giant snakes : a historical natural history of anacondas and pythons / John C. Murphy and Robert W. Henderson. Malabar, Fla. : Krieger Pub. Co., 1997. ix, 221 p. :
96-054033          597.96          0894649957
*Anaconda. Indian python. Reticulated python.*

**QL666.O636.R67 1996**
**Rossman, Douglas Athon,**
The garter snakes : evolution and ecology / by Douglas A. Rossman, Neil B. Ford, and Richard A. Seigel. Norman : University of Oklahoma Press, c1996. xx, 332 p., [
95-037746          597.96          0806128208
*Garter snakes.*

**QL666.O69.R835 1998**
**Rubio, Manny.**
Rattlesnake : portrait of a predator / Manny Rubio. Washington : Smithsonian Institution Press, c1998. xxvii, 239 p.
98-022935          597.96          1560988088
*Rattlesnakes.*

**QL667.D84 1986**
**Duellman, William Edward,**
Biology of amphibians / William E. Duellman, Linda Trueb ; illustrated by Linda Trueb. New York : McGraw Hill, c1986. xvii, 670 p.
85-014916          597.6          0070179778
*Amphibians.*

**QL667.S84 1995**
**Stebbins, Robert C.**
A natural history of amphibians / Robert C. Stebbins and Nathan W. Cohen ; illustrated by the authors. Princeton, N.J. : Princeton University Press, c1995. xvi, 316 p. :
94-043931          597.6          0691032815
*Amphibians.*

**QL668.E2**
Anuran communication / edited by Michael J. Ryan. Washington, DC : Smithsonian Institution Press, c2001. ix, 252 p. :
00-047006          597.8/159          1560989734
*Anura -- Behavior. Animal communication.*

**QL668.E2.M33 1987**
**Mattison, Christopher.**
Frogs & toads of the world / Chris Mattison. New York, N.Y. : Facts on File, c1987. 191 p. :
87-015615          597.8          081601602X
*Frogs. Toads.*

**QL668.E2.T15 1999**
Tadpoles : the biology of anuran larvae / edited by Roy W. McDiarmid and Ronald Altig. Chicago : University of Chicago Press, 1999. xiv, 444 p. :
99-017655          597.813/9          0226557626
*Tadpoles.*

**QL668.E2.W8 1949**
**Wright, Anna Allen,**
Handbook of frogs and toads of the United States and Canada, by Albert Hazen Wright and Anna Allen Wright. Ithaca, N.Y., Comstock Pub. Co., 1949. xii, 640 p.
49-001510          597.8
*Frogs -- United States. Toads -- United States. Frogs – Canada.*

**QL668.E2S737 2000**
**Souder, William,**
A plague of frogs : the horrifying true story / William Souder. 1st ed. New York : Hyperion, c2000. xv, 299 p. :
          597.8/9 21          0786863609
*Frogs -- Abnormalities. Frogs -- Research. Indicators (Biology)*

## QL672.2 Chordates. Vertebrates — Birds — Dictionaries and encyclopedias

**QL672.2.I45 1991**
The Illustrated encyclopedia of birds : the definitive reference to birds of the world / consultant-in-chief, Christopher M. Perrins. New York : Prentice Hall Editions, c1990. 420 p. :
90-034400          598          0130836354
*Birds -- Encyclopedias.*

## QL673 Chordates. Vertebrates — Birds — General works, treatises, and textbooks

**QL673.E53 1985**
Encyclopedia of birds / edited by Christopher M. Perrins and Alex. L.A. Middleton. New York, N.Y. : Facts on File, 1985. xxxi, 445 p.
84-026024          598          0816011508
*Birds.*

**QL673.H265 1992**
Handbook of the birds of the world / [edited by] Josep del Hoyo, Andrew Elliott, Jordi Sargatal ; Jose Cabot ... [et al.] ; colour plates by Francesc Jutglar ... [et al.]. Barcelona : Lynx Edicions, c1992- v. 1-6
96-171864          598          8487334105
*Birds. Birds -- Classification. Birds -- Identification.*

**QL673.W523 1989**
**Wiens, John A.**
The ecology of bird communities / John A. Wiens. Cambridge [England] ; Cambridge University Press, 1989. 2 v. :
88-038331          598.2/5          0521260302
*Birds -- Ecology.*

## QL674 Chordates. Vertebrates — Birds — Pictorial works and atlases

**QL674.A9 1966**
**Audubon, John James,**
The original water-color paintings by John James Audubon for The birds of America, reproduced in color for the first time from the collection at the New-York Historical Society. Introd. by Marshall B. Davidson. New York, American Heritage Pub. Co.; distributed to books 1966. 2 v.
66-017926          598.2973
*Birds -- North America. Birds -- Pictorial works.*

## QL675 Chordates. Vertebrates — Birds — Birds' eggs and nests

**QL675.H34 2000**
**Hansell, Michael H.**
Bird nests and construction behaviour / Mike Hansell ; pen and ink illustrations, Raith Overhill. New York : Cambridge University Press, 2000. 280 p.
99-087681          598.156/4          0521460387
*Birds -- Nests -- Design and construction. Birds -- Behavior.*

**QL675.W32 1994**
**Walters, Michael.**
Birds' eggs / Michael Walters ; photography by Harry Taylor ; editorial consultant, Mark Robbins. London ; Dorling Kindersley, 1994. 256 p. :
92-053468          598.233          1564581780
*Birds -- Eggs.*

## QL676.55-676.57 Chordates. Vertebrates — Birds — Bird protection. Bird refuges. Bird attracting

**QL676.55.E38 1992**
**Ehrlich, Paul R.**
Birds in jeopardy : the imperiled and extinct birds of the United States and Canada including Hawaii and Puerto Rico / Paul R. Ehrlich, David S. Dobkin, and Darryl Wheye ; illustrations by Darryl Wheye. Stanford, Calif. : Stanford University Press, 1992. x, 259 p. :
91-029555          333.95/8137/097          0804719675
*Rare birds -- United States. Rare birds -- Canada. Rare birds – Puerto Rico.*

## QL676.57.N7.A75 2000
**Askins, Robert.**
Restoring North America's birds : lessons from landscape ecology / Robert A. Askins ; illustrations by Julie Zickefoose. New Haven : Yale University Press, c2000. xiii, 320 p.
99-030205          333.95/816/097          0300079672
*Birds, Protection of -- North America. Landscape ecology – North America.*

## QL677 Chordates. Vertebrates — Birds — Classification. Nomenclature

### QL677.C5 1985
**Choate, Ernest A.**
The dictionary of American bird names / Ernest A. Choate. Boston, Mass. : Harvard Common Press, c1985. xiv, 226 p. ;
84-028975          598/.014          0876450656
*Birds -- Nomenclature -- Dictionaries. Birds -- Nomenclature (Popular) -- Dictionaries. Birds -- United States -- Nomenclature – Dictionaries.*

## QL677.3 Chordates. Vertebrates — Birds — Evolution

### QL677.3.F43 1999
**Feduccia, Alan.**
The origin and evolution of birds / Alan Feduccia. 2nd ed. New Haven : Yale University Press, 1999. x, 466 p. :
          598.138 21          0300078617
*Birds -- Evolution. Birds -- Origin. Birds, Fossil.*

## QL677.4 Chordates. Vertebrates — Birds — Population dynamics

### QL677.4.N48 1998
**Newton, Ian.**
Population limitation in birds / Ian Newton ; drawings by Keith Brockie. San Diego : Academic Press, c1998. x, 597 p. :
          598.1788          0125173652
*Bird populations. Bird populations. Birds -- Ecology.*

## QL677.5 Chordates. Vertebrates — Birds — Study and teaching. Research

### QL677.5.K73
**Kress, Stephen W.**
The Audubon Society handbook for birders / Stephen W. Kress ; drawings by Anne Senechal Faust ; foreword by Olin Sewall Pettingill, Jr. New York : Scribner, c1981. xiii, 322 p.
81-000205          598/.07/234          0684168383
*Bird watching.*

## QL678-695.2 Chordates. Vertebrates — Birds — Geographical distribution

### QL678.S54 1990
**Sibley, Charles Gald,**
Distribution and taxonomy of birds of the world / Charles G. Sibley and Burt L. Monroe, Jr. New Haven : Yale University Press, c1990. xxiv, 1111 p.
90-070494          598.29          0300049692
*Birds -- Geographical distribution. Birds -- Classification.*

### QL681.A97 1990
**Audubon, John James,**
Audubon's birds of America / [edited] by Roger Tory Peterson & Virginia Marie Peterson. New York : Abbeville Press, c1990. [ca.] 200 p.,
90-031607          598.2973          1558591281
*Birds -- North America. Artists -- United States -- Biography. Ornithologists -- United States -- Biography.*

### QL681.B513
**Bent, Arthur Cleveland,**
Life histories of North American birds. Edited and abridged by Henry Hill Collins, Jr. New York, Harper [1960] 2 v.
60005967          598.2973
*Birds -- North America. Birds -- Behavior.*

### QL681.D43 1995
**DeGraaf, Richard M.**
Neotropical migratory birds : natural history, distribution, and population change / Richard M. DeGraaf, John H. Rappole. Ithaca : Comstock Publishing Associates, 1995. ix, 676 p. :
94-037130          598.297          0801482658
*Birds -- North America. Birds -- Wintering -- Latin America. Birds -- Migration -- North America.*

### QL681.E37 1988
**Ehrlich, Paul R.**
The birder's handbook : a field guide to the natural history of North American birds : including all species that regularly breed north of Mexico / Paul R. Ehrlich, David S. Dobkin, Darryl Wheye ; illustrated by Shahid Naeem. New York : Simon & Schuster, c1988. xxx, 785 p. :
87-032404          598.297          0671621335
*Birds -- North America -- Handbooks, manuals, etc. Bird watching -- North America -- Handbooks, manuals, etc.*

### QL681.F53 1983
Field guide to the birds of North America / Thomas B. Allen ... [et al.], writers ; Teresa S. Purvis, index ; contributions by Caroline Hottenstein ... [et al.]. Washington, D.C. : National Geographic Society, c1983. 464 p. :
83-013262          598.297          0870444727
*Birds -- North America -- Identification.*

**QL681.K36 2000**
**Kaufman, Kenn.**
Birds of North America / Kenn Kaufman ; with the collaboration of Rick and Nora Bowers and Lynn Hassler Kaufman. New York : Houghton Mifflin, c2000. 383 p. :
00-056717          598/.097          0395964644
*Birds -- North America -- Identification.*

**QL681.T43 1980**
**Terres, John K.**
The Audubon Society encyclopedia of North American birds / by John K. Terres ; with a foreword by Dean Amadon. New York : Knopf : distributed by Random House, 1980. 1109 p. :
80-007617          598.297/03/21          0394466519
*Birds -- North America -- Dictionaries. Ornithology -- Dictionaries.*

**QL681.S497 2000**
**Sibley, David,**
The Sibley guide to birds / written and illustrated by David Sibley. New York : Alfred A. Knopf, c2000. 544 p. :
00-041239          598/.097          0679451226
*Birds -- North America -- Identification.*

**QL683.R63.D63 1994**
**Dobkin, David S.**
Conservation and management of neotropical migrant landbirds in the Northern Rockies and Great Plains / by David S. Dobkin ; illustrated by Chris Moore. Moscow, Idaho : University of Idaho Press, 1994. xiii, 220 p.
93-011355          333.95/8          0893011681
*Birds -- Migration -- Rocky Mountains. Birds -- Migration -- Great Plains. Birds, Protection of -- Rocky Mountains.*

**QL683.S75**
**Rappole, John H.**
Birds of the Southwest : Arizona, New Mexico, southern California & southern Nevada / John H. Rappole ; with photographs by Barth Schorre ... [et al.]. College Station : Texas A&M University Press, c2000. xiv, 329 p. :
00-044315          598/.0979          0890969574
*Birds -- Southwest, New.*

**QL683.W4.P4 1990**
**Peterson, Roger Tory,**
A field guide to western birds : a completely new guide to field marks of all species found in North America west of the 100th meridian and north of Mexico / text and illustrations by Roger Tory Peterson ; maps by Virginia Marie Peterson. Boston : Houghton Mifflin, 1990. 432 p. ;
89-031517          598.2978          039551424X
*Birds -- West (U.S.) -- Identification. Birds -- Canada, Western -- Identification.*

**QL685.7.N46 1996**
Neotropical birds : ecology and conservation / Douglas F. Stotz ... [et al.] ; with ecological and distributional databases by Theodore A. Parker III, Douglas F. Stotz, John W. Fitzpatrick. Chicago : University of Chicago Press, c1996. xx, 478 p. :
95-031571          598.298          0226776298
*Birds -- Latin America. Birds -- Habitat -- Latin America. Birds -- Ecology -- Latin America.*

**QL685.7.R36 1995**
**Rappole, John H.**
The ecology of migrant birds : a Neotropical perspective / John H. Rappole. Washington : Smithsonian Institution Press, c1995. xvii, 269 p.
95-010214          598.252/5          1560985143
*Birds -- Ecology -- Latin America. Birds -- Wintering -- Latin America. Birds -- Migration -- America.*

**QL687.A1.E39 1998**
**Edwards, Ernest Preston,**
A field guide to the birds of Mexico and adjacent areas : Belize, Guatemala and El Salvador / Ernest Preston Edwards ; principal illustrator, Edward Murrell Butler. Austin : University of Texas Press, 1998. xxi, 209 p.,
97-019414          598/.0972          0292720920
*Birds -- Central America -- Identification.*

**QL689.A1.R53 1989**
**Ridgely, Robert S.,**
The birds of South America / by Robert S. Ridgely and Guy Tudor with the collaboration of William L. Brown in association with World Wildlife Fund. Austin : University of Texas Press, 1989-1994 v. 1-2  :
88-020899          598.298          0292707568
*Birds -- South America.*

**QL690.A1.J6513 1992**
**Jonsson, Lars,**
Birds of Europe : with North Africa and the Middle East / Lars Jonsson ; translated by David Christie ; distribution maps by Magnus Ullman. Princeton, N.J. : Princeton University Press, c1992. 559 p. :
92-041334          598.294          0691033269
*Birds -- Europe -- Identification. Birds -- Africa, North -- Identification. Birds -- Middle East -- Identification.*

**QL690.B65.F47 1992**
**Ferns, P. N.**
Bird life of coasts and estuaries / P.N. Ferns ; with line illustrations by Chris Rose. Cambridge [England] ; Cambridge University Press, 1992. xiv, 336 p. :
92-014095          598.2941/0914/6          0521345693
*Birds -- British Isles. Coastal animals -- British Isles. Estuarine animals -- British Isles.*

**QL693.F54 1996**
The Princeton field guide to the birds of Australia / Simpson and Day. Princeton, N.J. : Princeton University Press, c1996. 400 p. :
95-043361          598.2994          0691025754
*Birds -- Australia -- Identification.*

## QL693.H36 1990

Handbook of Australian, New Zealand & Antarctic birds / S. Marchant and P.J. Higgins (co-ordinators) ; S.J. Ambrose .... [et al.] ; colour illustrations by J.N. Davies. Melbourne ; Oxford University Press, 1990-1999 v. 1, pts. A-
91-209529      598.299      0195530683
*Birds -- Australia -- Handbooks, manuals, etc. Birds -- New Zealand -- Handbooks, manuals, etc. Birds -- Antarctic regions – Handbooks, manuals, etc.*

## QL694.G2.C37 1996
**Castro, Isabel C.**

A guide to the birds of the Galapagos Islands / Isabel Castro and Antonia Phillips ; foreword by Peter R. Grant. Princeton, N.J. : Princeton University Press, c1996. 144 p. :
96-031943      598.29866/5      0691012253
*Birds -- Galapagos Islands -- Identification.*

## QL695.2.P368 1992
**Parmelee, David Freeland,**

Antarctic birds : ecological and behavioral approaches / David Freeland Parmelee ; foreword by Harold F. Mayfield. Minneapolis : University of Minnesota Press, c1992. xviii, 203 p.
91-012378      598.2/5/26210989
0816620008
*Birds -- Ecology -- Antarctica. Birds -- Behavior -- Antarctica.*

## QL696 Chordates. Vertebrates — Birds — Systematic divisions. By order and family, A-Z

## QL696.A52.B335 1994
**Baldassarre, Guy A.**

Waterfowl ecology and management / Guy A. Baldassarre, Eric G. Bolen ; illustrated by D. Andrew Saunders. New York : J. Wiley, c1994. xvii, 609 p.
93-021415      598.4/1045/097      0471597708
*Waterfowl -- North America -- Ecology. Waterfowl management – North America.*

## QL696.A52.M33 1988
**Madge, Steve.**

Waterfowl : an identification guide to the ducks, geese, and swans of the world / Steve Madge and Hilary Burn. Boston : Houghton Mifflin, c1988. 298 p. :
87-026186      598.4/1      0395467276
*Waterfowl -- Identification. Birds -- Identification.*

## QL696.A558.L66 1997
**Long, Kim.**

Hummingbirds : a wildlife handbook / Kim Long. Boulder : Johnson Books, c1997. 182 p. :
96-049302      598.7/64      1555661882
*Hummingbirds.*

## QL696.C42.F85 1999
**Fuller, Errol.**

The great auk / by Errol Fuller. New York : Abrams, 1999. 448 p. :
99-024632      598.3/3      0810963914
*Great auk.*

## QL696.C52.B86 1997
**Butler, Robert William.**

The great blue heron : a natural history and ecology of a seashore sentinel / Robert W. Butler. Vancouver : UBC Press, c1997. xvi, 167 p.,
98-107774      598.3/4      0774806354
*Great blue heron -- British Columbia. Grand heron – Colombie-Britannique.*

## QL696.C63
**Gibbs, David,**

Pigeons and doves : a guide to the pigeons and doves of the world / David Gibbs, Eustace Barnes, and John Cox. New Haven : Yale University Press, 2001. 615 p. :
99-062420      598.6/5      0300078862
*Pigeons. Pigeons -- Identification.*

## QL696.C72.F79 1992
**Fry, C. H.**

Kingfishers, bee-eaters & rollers : a handbook / C. Hilary Fry and Kathie Fry ; illustrated by Alan Harris. Princeton, N.J. : Princeton University Press, c1992. xi, 324 p. :
92-008385      598.8/92      0691087806
*Kingfishers. Bee eaters. Rollers (Birds)*

## QL696.C83
**Davies, N. B.**

Cuckoos, cowbirds and other cheats / N.B. Davies ; illustrated by David Quinn. London : T & A D Poyser, 2000. vi, 310 p. :
                  0856611352
*Cuckoos. Cowbirds. Parasitic birds.*

## QL696.F3
**Weidensaul, Scott.**

Raptors : the birds of prey / Scott Weidensaul. New York : Lyons & Burford, c1996. ix, 382 p. :
95-021839      598.9/1      1558212752
*Birds of prey.*

## QL696.F3.J6 1990
**Johnsgard, Paul A.**

Hawks, eagles & falcons of North America : biology and natural history / Paul A. Johnsgard. Washington : Smithsonian Institution Press, c1990. xvi, 403 p.,
89-048558      598/.916/097      0874746825
*Falconiformes -- North America.*

## QL696.G27.J64 1999
**Johnsgard, Paul A.**

The pheasants of the world : biology and natural history / Paul A. Johnsgard. Washington, DC : Smithsonian Institution Press, c1999. xvii, 398 p.
98-053497      598.6/25      1560988398
*Pheasants.*

**QL696.G27.J65 1988**
Johnsgard, Paul A.
The quails, partridges, and francolins of the world / Paul A. Johnsgard ; colour plates of paintings by Henry Jones from the collection owned by the Zoological Society of London. Oxford ; Oxford University Press, 1988. xix, 264 p.,
87-031366     598/.617     0198571933
*Quails. Partridges. Francolins.*

**QL696.G84.K385 1993**
Katz, Barbara,
So cranes may dance : a rescue from the brink of extinction / Barbara Katz ; [foreword by Roger Tory Peterson]. Chicago, Ill. : Chicago Review Press, c1993. xiv, 279 p.,
92-044904     639.9/7831     1556521715
*Cranes (Birds) Birds, Protection of.*

**QL696.P2.L27 1968**
Lack, David Lambert.
Darwin's finches; an essay on the general biological theory of evolution, by David Lack. Gloucester, Mass., P. Smith, 1968. x, 204 p.
68-004829     598.8/83
*Finches -- Evolution. Birds -- Speciation. Evolution.*

**QL696.P2367.M34 1994**
Madge, Steve.
Crows and jays : a guide to the crows, jays, and magpies of the world / Steve Madge and Hilary Burn. Boston : Houghton Mifflin, 1994. xxiii, 191 p.
93-029832     598.8/64     039567171X
*Crows -- Identification. Jays -- Identification.*

**QL696.P2438.B95 1995**
Byers, Clive.
Sparrows and buntings : a guide to the sparrows and buntings of North America and the world / Clive Byers, Jon Curson, and Urban Olsson. Boston : Houghton Mifflin Company, 1995. 334 p. :
95-004862     598.8/83     0395738733
*Buntings (Birds) -- Identification. Sparrows -- North America – Identification. Emberizidae -- North America -- Identification.*

**QL696.P2438.C87 1994b**
Curson, Jon.
Warblers of the Americas : an identification guide / Jon Curson, David Quinn, and David Beadle. Boston : Houghton Mifflin, 1994. ix, 252 p. :
94-007470     598.8/72/097     0395709989
*Wood warblers -- America -- Identification. Wood warblers -- America -- Pictorial works.*

**QL696.P246.C58 1993**
Clement, Peter.
Finches & sparrows : an identification guide / Peter Clement ; illustrated by Alan Harris and John Davis. Princeton, N.J. : Princeton University Press, c1993. ix, 500 p. :
93-005101     598.8/83     0691034249
*Finches -- Identification. Sparrows -- Identification.*

**QL696.P246.W45 1994**
Weiner, Jonathan.
The beak of the finch : a story of evolution in our time / Jonathan Weiner. New York : Knopf : 1994. x, 332 p. :
93-036755     598.8/830438     0679400036
*Grant, Peter R., -- 1936- Grant, B. Rosemary. Finches – Galapagos Islands -- Evolution. Finches -- Evolution -- Research – Galapagos Islands.*

**QL696.P247.B76 1996**
Brown, Charles Robert,
Coloniality in the cliff swallow : the effect of group size on social behavior / Charles R. Brown and Mary Bomberger Brown. Chicago, IL : University of Chicago Press, c1996. xiii, 566 p.
95-044561     598.8/13     0226076253
*Hirundo pyrrhonota -- Behavior. Social behavior in animals.*

**QL696.P2475.J27 1999**
Jaramillo, Alvaro,
New world blackbirds : the icterids / Alvaro Jaramillo and Peter Burke. Princeton, N.J. : Princeton University Press, 1999. 431 p. :
98-034714     598.8/74     0691006806
*Icteridae. Icteridae -- Identification.*

**QL696.P248.L43 1997**
Lefranc, Norbert.
Shrikes : a guide to the shrikes of the world / Norbert Lefranc ; illustrated by Tim Worfolk. New Haven : Yale University Press, 1997. 192 p. :
97-060716     598.8/62     0300073364
*Shrikes -- Identification.*

**QL696.P2615.S55 1991**
Smith, Susan M.,
The Black-capped chickadee : behavioral ecology and natural history / Susan M. Smith. Ithaca : Comstock Pub. Associates, 1991. ix, 362 p., [
91-055072     598.8/24     0801423821
*Black-capped chickadee. Parus.*

**QL696.P2618.M67 1989**
Morse, Douglass H.,
American warblers : an ecological and behavioral perspective / Douglass H. Morse. Cambridge, Mass. : Harvard University Press, 1989. xii, 406 p. :
89-031622     598.8/72     0674030354
*Wood warblers -- North America.*

**QL696.P4745.J64 1993**
Johnsgard, Paul A.
Cormorants, darters, and pelicans of the world / Paul A. Johnsgard. Washington : Smithsonian Institution Press, c1993. xiv, 445 p.,
92-031997     598.4/3     1560982160
*Cormorants. Pelicans. Anhingidae.*

**QL696.P56.B46 1992**
**Bent, Arthur Cleveland,**
  Life histories of North American woodpeckers / Arthur Cleveland Bent ; with original paintings by William Zimmerman. Bloomington : Indiana University Press, c1992. xii, 262 p. :
91-048014          598/.72          0253311608
  *Woodpeckers -- North America.*

**QL696.P7.J86 1998**
**Juniper, Tony.**
  Parrots : a guide to parrots of the world / Tony Juniper and Mike Parr ; illustrated by Kim Franklin ... [et al.]. New Haven : Yale University Press, 1998. 584 p. :
97-080504          598.7/1          0300074530
  *Parrots.*

**QL696.P7F63 1981**
**Forshaw, Joseph Michael.**
  Parrots of the world / Joseph M. Forshaw ; illustrated by William T. Cooper. 2nd rev. ed., Repr. With corrections. Melbourne ; New York : Lansdowne Editions, 1981. 616 p. :
          598/.71 19          0701806907
  *Parrots.*

**QL696.S473.W55 1995**
**Williams, Tony D.**
  The penguins : Spheniscidae / Tony D. Williams ; with contributions by Rory P. Wilson, P. Dee Boersma, and D.L. Stokes ; colour plates by J.N. Davies ; drawings by John Busby. Oxford ; Oxford University Press, 1995. xiii, 295 p.,
94-028559          598.4/41          019854667X
  *Penguins.*

**QL696.S8.J64 1988**
**Johnsgard, Paul A.**
  North American owls : biology and natural history / Paul A. Johnsgard. Washington : Smithsonian Institution Press, c1988. 295 p., [32]
87-027516          598/.97          0874745608
  *Owls -- North America.*

## QL696.5 Chordates. Vertebrates — Birds — Genetics

**QL696.5.A95 1997**
  Avian molecular evolution and systematics / edited by David P. Mindell. San Diego : Academic Press, c1997. xx, 382 p. :
97-006621          572.8/3818          0124983154
  *Birds -- Molecular genetics. Birds -- Evolution. Birds -- Morphology.*

**QL696.5.S53 1991**
**Sibley, Charles Gald,**
  Phylogeny and classification of birds : a study in molecular evolution / Charles G. Sibley and Jon E. Ahlquist. New Haven : Yale University Press, c1990. xxiii, 976 p.
90-035938          598.23/8          0300040857
  *Birds -- Genetics. Nucleic acid hybridization. Birds -- Classification.*

## QL697 Chordates. Vertebrates — Birds — Anatomy and morphology

**QL697.P76 1993**
**Proctor, Noble S.**
  Manual of ornithology : avian structure & function / Noble S. Proctor, Patrick J. Lynch ; illustrated by Patrick J. Lynch ; foreword by Roger Tory Peterson. New Haven : Yale University Press, c1993. xi, 340 p. :
92-017066          598.2/4/078          0300057466
  *Birds -- Anatomy -- Laboratory manuals.*

## QL698.3 Chordates. Vertebrates — Birds — Behavior

**QL698.3.A88 1998**
**Attenborough, David,**
  The life of birds / David Attenborough. Princeton, NJ : Princeton University Press, 1998. 320 p. :
98-030705          598.15          069101633X
  *Birds -- Behavior.*

**QL698.3.C66 1990**
  Cooperative breeding in birds : long-term studies of ecology and behavior / edited by Peter B. Stacey and Walter D. Koenig. Cambridge ; Cambridge University Press, 1990. xviii, 615 p.
89-009773          598.256          0521372984
  *Birds -- Behavior. Birds -- Ecology. Cooperative breeding in animals.*

**QL698.3.J68 1997**
**Johnsgard, Paul A.**
  The avian brood parasites : deception at the nest / Paul A. Johnsgard. New York : Oxford University Press, 1997. xii, 409 p. :
96-008884          598.2556          0195110420
  *Parasitic birds. Brood parasites.*

**QL698.3.P38 1996**
  Partnerships in birds : the study of monogamy / edited by Jeffrey M. Black ; drawings by Mark Hulme. Oxford ; Oxford University Press, 1996. xi, 420 p. :
95-041167          598.256          0198548613
  *Birds -- Behavior. Sexual selection in animals.*

**QL698.3.S553 1996**
**Skutch, Alexander Frank,**
  The minds of birds / by Alexander F. Skutch ; illustrations by Dana Gardner. College Station : Texas A&M University Press, c1996. xvi, 183 p. :
95-004645          598.251          0890966710
  *Birds -- Psychology. Birds -- Behavior. Animal intelligence.*

## QL698.5 Chordates. Vertebrates — Birds — Song. Vocalization

**QL698.5.E36 1996**
Ecology and evolution of acoustic communication in birds / edited by Donald E. Kroodsma and Edward H. Miller. Ithaca, N.Y. : Comstock Pub., 1996. xx, 587 p. :
95-047777          598.259          0801430496
*Birdsongs. Animal communication. Birds -- Vocalization.*

## QL698.9 Chordates. Vertebrates — Birds — Migration

**QL698.9.A4413 1990**
**Alerstam, Thomas.**
Bird migration / Thomas Alerstam ; translated by David A. Christie. Cambridge [England] ; Cambridge University Press, 1990. vii, 420 p. :
90-031054          598.2/525          0521328659
*Birds -- Migration.*

**QL698.9.A88 1995**
The atlas of bird migration : tracing the great journeys of the world's birds / general editor Jonathan Elphick. New York : Random House, c1995. 180 p. :
94-029378          598.252/5          0679438270
*Birds -- Migration.*

## QL703 Chordates. Vertebrates — Mammals — General works, treatises, and textbooks

**QL703.W222 1999**
**Nowak, Ronald M.**
Walker's mammals of the world. 6th ed. / Ronald M. Nowak. Baltimore : Johns Hopkins University Press, 1999. 2 v.
          599 21          0801857899
*Mammals. Mammals -- Classification.*

## QL708 Chordates. Vertebrates — Mammals — Classification. Nomenclature

**QL708.C67 1991**
**Corbet, G. B.**
A world list of mammalian species / G.B. Corbet & J.E. Hill ; illustrated by Ray Burrows. Oxford ; Oxford University Press, 1991. viii, 243 p.
90-007790          599/.0012          0198540175
*Mammals -- Nomenclature. Mammals -- Classification.*

**QL708.M35 1993**
Mammal species of the world : a taxonomic and geographic reference / edited by Don E. Wilson and DeeAnn M. Reeder. Washington : Smithsonian Institution Press, c1993. xviii, 1206 p
92-022703          599/.0012          1560982179
*Mammals -- Classification. Mammals -- Geographical distribution.*

## QL708.5 Chordates. Vertebrates — Mammals — Evolution

**QL708.5.S28 1986**
**Savage, Robert J. G.**
Mammal evolution : an illustrated guide / text by R.J.G. Savage & ; illustrations by M.R. Long. New York, N.Y. : Facts on File Publications, c1986. 259 p. :
85-029203          599/.03/8          081601194X
*Mammals -- Evolution. Mammals, Fossil.*

## QL713.2-731 Chordates. Vertebrates — Mammals — Geographical distribution

**QL713.2.B47 1999**
**Berta, Annalisa.**
Marine mammals : evolutionary biology / Annalisa Berta, James L. Sumich ; with illustrations by Pieter Arend Folkens, Peter J. Adam. San Diego : Academic Press, c1999. xiii, 494 p.
98-086074          599.5          0120932253
*Marine mammals. Marine mammals -- Evolution.*

**QL715.B8 1976**
**Burt, William Henry,**
A field guide to the mammals : field marks of all North American species found north of Mexico / text and maps by William Henry Burt ; ill. by Richard Philip Grossenheider ; sponsored by the National Audubon Society and National Wildlife Federation. Boston : Houghton Mifflin, 1976. xxv, 289 p.,
75-026885          599/.09/73          0395240824.
*Mammals -- United States -- Identification. Mammals – Canada – Identification.*

**QL715.H15 1981**
**Hall, E. Raymond**
The mammals of North America / E. Raymond Hall. New York : Wiley, 1981. 2 v. :
79-004109          599/.097          0471054437
*Mammals -- North America. Mammals -- West Indies.*

**QL715.W49 1996**
**Whitaker, John O.**
National Audubon Society field guide to North American mammals / John O. Whitaker, Jr. New York : Knopf : c1996. 937 p. :
95-081456          599.0973          0679446311
*Mammals -- North America -- Identification.*

**QL719.E23.W49 1998**
**Whitaker, John O.**
Mammals of the Eastern United States / John O. Whitaker, Jr., and William J. Hamilton, Jr. Ithaca : Comstock Publishing Associates, 1998. xi, 583 p., 2
98-011962          599/.0974          0801434750
*Mammals -- East (U.S.)*

**QL719.R63.W37 1993**
**Wassink, Jan L.**
Mammals of the central Rockies / Jan L. Wassink. Missoula, Mont. : Mountain Press Pub. Co., 1993. x, 161 p. :
92-046268          599.09787          0878422374
   *Mammals -- Rocky Mountains. Wildlife watching -- Rocky Mountains.*

**QL721.B32**
**Banfield, A. W. F.**
The mammals of Canada / A. W. F. Banfield ; ill. by Allan Brooks ... [et al.] ; cartography by Geoffrey Matthews and Jennifer Wilcox. Toronto ; Published for the National Museum of Natural Sci [1974] xxv, 438 p.,
73-092298          599/.09/71          0802021379
   *Mammals -- Canada.*

**QL731.A1.E84 1990**
**Estes, Richard.**
The behavior guide to African mammals : including hoofed mammals, carnivores, primates / Richard Despard Estes ; drawings by Daniel Otte ; foreword by E.O. Wilson. Berkeley : University of California Press, c1991. xxii, 611 p.
89-004877          599/.051/096          0520058313
   *Mammals -- Africa -- Behavior.*

## QL737 Chordates. Vertebrates — Mammals — Systematic divisions. By order and family, A-Z

**QL737.C2.A38 1960**
**Adamson, Joy.**
Born free, a lioness of two worlds. [New York] Pantheon Books [1960] 220 p.
60-006792          599.7442
   *Elsa (Lion) Lions -- Kenya -- Biography. Lions -- Behavior.*

**QL737.C2.A4**
**Adamson, Joy.**
Living free; the story of Elsa and her cubs. Introd. by Julian Huxley. New York, Harcourt, Brace & World [1961] 161 p.
61-015810          599.7442
   *Elsa (Lion) Lions -- Kenya -- Biography. Lions -- Behavior.*

**QL737.C2.C33 1989**
Carnivore behavior, ecology, and evolution / John L. Gittleman, editor. Ithaca : Comstock Pub. Associates, 1989-1996. 2 v. :
88-047725          599.74/045          080142190X
   *Carnivora.*

**QL737.C2.C345 1999**
Carnivores in ecosystems : the Yellowstone experience / edited by Tim W. Clark ... [et al.]. New Haven : Yale University Press, c1999. xii, 429 p. :
99-028229          599.7/09787/52          0300078161
   *Carnivora -- Yellowstone National Park.*

**QL737.C214.S28 1993**
**Schaller, George B.**
The last panda / George B. Schaller. Chicago : University of Chicago Press, 1993. xx, 291 p. :
92-018869          599.74/443          0226736288
   *Giant panda. Endangered species. Wildlife conservation.*

**QL737.C22**
Wolves and human communities : biology, politics, and ethics / edited by Virginia A. Sharpe, Bryan G. Norton, and Strachan Donnelley. Washington, D.C. : Island Press, c2001. xi, 321 p. ;
00-011113          333.95/9773/097475
1559638281
   *Wolves -- Reintroduction -- Northeastern States.*

**QL737.C22.L34 1986**
**Lawrence, R. D.,**
In praise of wolves / by R.D. Lawrence. New York : H. Holt, c1986. viii, 245 p.,
85-021887          599.74/442
   *Wolves -- Behavior. Mammals -- Behavior.*

**QL737.C22.P44 1994**
**Alderton, David,**
Foxes, wolves, and wild dogs of the world / David Alderton ; photographs by Bruce Tanner. New York : Facts on File, c1994. 192 p. :
92-046595          599.74/442          0816029547
   *Foxes. Wolves.*

**QL737.C22.P5 1996**
**Phillips, Michael K.,**
The wolves of Yellowstone / Michael K. Phillips and Douglas W. Smith ; photographs by Barry and Teri O'Neill ; foreword by John D. Varley. Stillwater, MN : Voyageur Press, c1996. 125 p. :
96-014286          599.74/442          0896583309
   *Wolves -- Yellowstone National Park. Wildlife reintroduction – Yellowstone National Park. Wolves -- Yellowstone National Park – Pictorial works. Yellowstone National Park. Yellowstone National Park -- Pictorial works.*

**QL737.C23.B26 1993**
**Bailey, Theodore N.**
The African leopard : ecology and behavior of a solitary felid / Theodore N. Bailey. New York : Columbia University Press, c1993. xviii, 429 p.
93-000828          599.74/428          0231078722
   *Leopard -- Africa -- Behavior. Leopard -- Africa -- Ecology.*

**QL737.C23.K58 1991**
**Kitchener, Andrew.**
The natural history of the wild cats / Andrew Kitchener. Ithaca, N.Y. : Comstock Pub. Associates, 1991. xxi, 280 p. :
90-045833          599.74/428          0801425964
   *Felidae.*

**QL737.C23.S5625 1995**
Sleeper, Barbara.
    Wild cats of the world / text by Barbara Sleeper ; photographs and drawings by Art Wolfe. New York : Crown Publishers, c1995. 216 p. :
94028413          599.74/428          0517799782
    *Wild cats. -- sears Wild cats -- Pictorial works. -- sears*

**QL737.C25.A94 1997**
Clark, Tim W.
    Averting extinction : reconstructing endangered species recovery / Tim W. Clark. New Haven, Conn. : Yale University Press, c1997. ix, 270 p. :
96-037273          333.95/976629          0300068476
    *Black-footed ferret -- Wyoming. Wildlife conservation -- Government Policy -- United States. Endangered species -- Government policy -- United States.*

**QL737.C25.C66 1988**
    The community ecology of sea otters / edited by G.R. VanBlaricom and J.A. Estes. Berlin ; Springer-Verlag, c1988. xv, 247 p. :
87-020553          599.74/47          0387180907
    *Sea otter -- Ecology -- California -- Pacific Coast. Mammal populations -- California -- Pacific Coast. Marine mammals -- Ecology -- California -- Pacific Coast.*

**QL737.C25.L68 1992**
Love, John A.
    Sea otters / John A. Love ; with illustrations by the author. Golden, Colo. : Fulcrum Pub., c1992. xii, 148 p. :
92-053032          599.74/447          1555911234
    *Sea otter.*

**QL737.C27.P425 1995**
Petersen, David,
    Ghost grizzlies / David Petersen. New York : H. Holt, 1995. xx, 296 p. ;
94-039987          599.74/446          0805031170
    *Petersen, David, -- 1946-     Grizzly bear -- San Juan Mountains (Colo. and N.M.) Wildlife reintroduction -- Colorado. Wildlife reintroduction -- San Juan Mountains (Colo. and N.M.)*

**QL737.C27.S726 1988**
Stirling, Ian.
    Polar bears / by Ian Stirling ; photographs by Dan Guravich. Ann Arbor : University of Michigan Press, c1988. viii, 220 p.
88-014244          599.74/446          0472101005
    *Polar bear.*

**QL737.C27.W385 1995**
Ward, Paul,
    Wild bears of the world / Paul Ward & Suzanne Kynaston. New York : Facts On File, 1995. 191 p. :
95-012487          599.74/446          0816032459
    *Bears.*

**QL737.C4.B67 1989**
Bonner, W. Nigel
    Whales of the world / Nigel Bonner. New York : Facts on File, c1989. 191 p. :
88-033315          599.5          0816017344
    *Cetacea.*

**QL737.C4.C28 1995**
Carwardine, Mark.
    Whales, dolphins, and porpoises / Mark Carwardine ; illustrated by Martin Camm ; editorial consultants, Peter Evans, Mason Weinrich. London ; Dorling Kindersley, 1995. 256 p. :
94-033301          599.5          1564586219
    *Cetacea. Cetacea -- Pictorial works. Cetacea -- Identification.*

**QL737.C4.C39 2000**
    Cetacean societies : field studies of dolphins and whales / edited by Janet Mann ... [et al.]. Chicago : University of Chicago Press, 2000. xiv, 433 p. :
99-045607          599.5/156          0226557626
    *Cetacea -- Behavior. Social behavior in animals.*

**QL737.C4.E335 1998**
    The emergence of whales : evolutionary patterns in the origin of Cetacea / edited by J.G.M. Thewissen. New York : Plenum Press, c1998. xii, 477 p. :
98-036333          599.5/138          0306458535
    *Cetacea -- Evolution. Cetacea, Fossil.*

**QL737.C4.M66 1984**
Minasian, Stanley M.,
    The world's whales : the complete illustrated guide / Stanley M. Minasian, Kenneth C. Balcomb III, Larry Foster. Washington, D.C. : Smithsonian Books ; c1984. 224 p. :
84-014142          599.5          0895990148
    *Cetacea.*

**QL737.C432**
Reynolds, John Elliott,
    The bottlenose dolphin : biology and conservation / John E. Reynolds III, Randall S. Wells, Samantha D. Eide. Gainesville : University Press of Florida, c2000. xv, 288 p., [
00-029899          599.53/3          0813017750
    *Killer whale -- British Columbia. Killer whale -- Washington (State)*

**QL737.C432.A92 1993**
Au, Whitlow, W. L.
    The sonar of dolphins / Whitlow W.L. Au. New York : Springer-Verlag, c1993. xi, 277 p. :
92-022696          599.5/3          0387978356
    *Dolphins -- Physiology. Sonar. Echolocation (Physiology)*

**QL737.C432.B67 1990**
    The Bottlenose dolphin / edited by Stephen Leatherwood, Randall R. Reeves. San Diego : Academic Press, c1990. xviii, 653 p.
88-035093          599.5/3          0124402801
    *Bottlenose dolphin.*

**QL737.C5.A4 1996**
**Altringham, John D.**
    Bats : biology and behaviour / John D. Altringham ; drawings by Tom McOwat and Lucy Hammond. Oxford [England] ; Oxford University Press, 1996. ix, 262 p. :
95-049029        599.4        0198540752
    *Bats. Bats -- Behavior.*

**QL737.C5.P65 1989**
**Pollak, G. D.**
    The neural basis of echolocation in bats / G.D. Pollak, J.H. Casseday. Berlin ; Springer-Verlag, c1989. ix, 143 p. :
89-004081        599.4/01852        0387505202
    *Bats -- Physiology. Echolocation (Physiology) Mammals -- Physiology.*

**QL737.C5O58 2000**
    Ontogeny, functional ecology, and evolution of bats / edited by Rick A. Adams and Scott C. Pedersen. London ; New York : Cambridge University Press, 2000. viii, 398 p. :
                599.4/138 21        0521626323
*Bats -- Development. Bats -- Evolution.*

**QL737.I57.G67 1990**
**Gorman, M. L.**
    The natural history of moles / Martyn L. Gorman and R. David Stone. Ithaca, N.Y. : Comstock Pub. Associates, 1990. xiv, 138 p.,
89-025225        599.3/3        0801424666
    *Moles (Animals)*

**QL737.M3.L44 1985**
**Lee, Anthony K.**
    Evolutionary ecology of marsupials / Anthony K. Lee, Andrew Cockburn. Cambridge [Cambridgeshire] ; Cambridge University Press, 1985. viii, 274 p.
84-009440        599.2/0438        052125292X
    *Marsupials -- Ecology. Marsupials -- Evolution.*

**QL737.M35.D39 1995**
**Dawson, Terence J.**
    Kangaroos : biology of the largest marsupials / Terence J. Dawson ; illustrated by Anne Musser and Jillian Hallam. Ithaca, N.Y. : Comstock Pub. Associates, 1995. vi, 162 p. :
94-033542        599.2        0801482623
    *Kangaroos.*

**QL737.P6.R54 1990**
**Riedman, Marianne.**
    The pinnipeds : seals, sea lions, and walruses / Marianne Riedman. Berkeley : University of California Press, c1990. xxiii, 439 p.
89-031542        599.74/5        0520064976
    *Pinnipedia.*

**QL737.P63.G45 1998**
**Gentry, Roger L.**
    Behavior and ecology of the northern fur seal / Roger L. Gentry. Princeton, N.J. : Princeton University Press, c1998. xiii, 392 p.
97-008332        599.79/7315        0691033455
    *Northern fur seal -- Behavior. Sexual behavior in animals. Parental behavior in animals.*

**QL737.P64.B66 1990**
**Bonner, W. Nigel**
    The natural history of seals / W. Nigel Bonner. New York : Facts on File, c1990. xvi, 196 p.,
89-037620        599.74/8        0816023360
    *Seals (Animals) Seals (Animals).*

**QL737.P64.B662 1994**
**Bonner, W. Nigel**
    Seals and sea lions of the world / Nigel Bonner. New York : Facts on File, c1994. 224 p. :
92-046594        599.74/5        0816029555
    *Seals (Animals) Sea lions.*

**QL737.P9.B915**
**Buettner-Janusch, John,**
    Origins of man; physical anthropology. New York, Wiley [1966] xxvii, 674 p.
66-014128        573.2
    *Human evolution. Primates -- Evolution.*

**QL737.P9.C66 1990**
**Conroy, Glenn C.**
    Primate evolution / Glenn C. Conroy. New York : Norton, c1990. xiv, 492 p. :
89-026448        599.8/0438        0393956490
    *Primates -- Evolution. Primates, Fossil.*

**QL737.P9.F57 1999**
**Fleagle, John G.**
    Primate adaptation and evolution / John G. Fleagle. San Diego : Academic Press, c1999. xvii, 596 p.
98-087186        599.8/138        0122603419
    *Primates -- Evolution. Primates -- Adaptation.*

**QL737.P9.M274 1997**
    Machiavellian intelligence II : extensions and evaluations / edited by Andrew W. Whiten and Richard W. Byrne. Cambridge ; Cambridge University Press, 1997. xii, 403 p. :
96-048233        599.8/1513        0521550874
    *Primates -- Behavior. Animal intelligence. Intellect.*

**QL737.P9.M32 1990**
**Martin, R. D.**
    Primate origins and evolution : a phylogenetic reconstruction / R.D. Martin ; animal illustrations by Anne-Elise Martin. Princeton, N.J. : Princeton University Press, c1990. xiv, 804 p. :
89-036955        599/.03        069108565X
    *Primates -- Evolution. Primates, Fossil. Primates -- Phylogeny.*

**QL737.P9.P66 1992**
**Preston-Mafham, Rod.**
   Primates of the world / Rod and Ken Preston-Mafham. New York : Facts on File, c1992. 191 p. :
91-034964          599.8          0816027455
   *Primates.*


**QL737.P9.R48**
**Reynolds, Vernon.**
   The apes: the gorilla, chimpanzee, orangutan, and gibbon; their history and their world. New York, Dutton, 1967. 296 p.
66-021302          599.8/8
   *Apes.*


**QL737.P9.R675 1996**
**Rowe, Noel.**
   The pictorial guide to the living primates / Noel Rowe; foreword by Jane Goodall ; introduction by Russell A. Mittermeier. East Hampton, N.Y. : Pogonias Press, 1996. viii, 263 p.
95-072713          599.8          0964882507
   *Primates. Primates -- Pictorial works.*


**QL737.P9.S595 1993**
**Small, Meredith F.**
   Female choices : sexual behavior of female primates / Meredith F. Small ; drawings by Andrea S. Perkins. Ithaca : Cornell University Press, 1993. xi, 245 p. :
92-056785          599/.80456          0801426545
   *Primates -- Behavior. Females. Sexual behavior in animals.*


**QL737.P9.T65 1997**
**Tomasello, Michael.**
   Primate cognition / Michael Tomasello, Josep Call. New York : Oxford University Press, 1997. ix, 517 p. :
96-041424          599.8/0451          0195106237
   *Primates -- Behavior. Primates -- Psychology. Cognition in animals.*


**QL737.P9.W64 1983**
**Wolfheim, Jaclyn H.**
   Primates of the world : distribution, abundance, and conservation / Jaclyn H. Wolfheim. Seattle : University of Washington Press, c1983. xxiii, 831 p.
82-013464          599.8          0295958995
   *Primates.*


**QL737.P93.O545 2000**
   Old world monkeys / edited by Paul F. Whitehead & Clifford J. Jolly. Cambridge, UK ; Cambridge University Press, 2000. xii, 528 p. :
99-020192          599.8/6          0521571243
   *Cercopithecidae.*


**QL737.P93.S79 1987**
**Strum, Shirley C.**
   Almost human : a journey into the world of baboons / Shirley C. Strum ; drawings by Deborah Ross. New York : Random House, c1987. xvii, 294 p.,
86-029712          599.8/2          0394547241
   *Olive baboon -- Kenya -- Behavior. Mammals -- Behavior. Mammals -- Kenya -- Behavior.*


**QL737.P96.F67 1983**
**Fossey, Dian.**
   Gorillas in the mist / Dian Fossey. Boston, Mass. : Houghton Mifflin, 1983. xviii, 326 p.
82-023332          599.88/460451          0395282179
   *Gorilla -- Behavior. Mammals -- Behavior.*


**QL737.P96.G585 1986**
**Goodall, Jane,**
   The chimpanzees of Gombe : patterns of behavior / Jane Goodall. Cambridge, Mass. : Belknap Press of Harvard University Press, 1986. 673 p., [8] p
85-020030          599.88/440451          0674116496
   *Chimpanzees -- Tanzania -- Gombe Stream Reserve -- Behavior.*


**QL737.P96.K27 1992**
**Kano, Takayoshi,**
   The last ape : pygmy chimpanzee behavior and ecology / Takayoshi Kano ; translated by Evelyn Ono Vineberg. Stanford, Calif. : Stanford University Press, 1992. xxi, 248 p. :
91002147          599.88/44          0804716129
   *Bonobo -- Behavior. Bonobo -- Ecology.*


**QL737.P96.O73 1988**
   Orang-utan biology / edited by Jeffrey H. Schwartz. New York : Oxford University Press, 1988. x, 383 p. :
87-020440          599.88/42          0195043715
   *Orangutan.*


**QL737.P96.P47 1993**
**Peterson, Dale.**
   Visions of Caliban : on chimpanzees and people / Dale Peterson and Jane Goodall. Boston : Houghton Mifflin, 1993. 367 p. :
92-038757          599.88/44          0395537606
   *Chimpanzees. Human-animal relationships.*


**QL737.P96.R424 1996**
   Reaching into thought : the minds of the great apes / edited by Anne E. Russon, Kim A. Bard, Sue Taylor Parker. Cambridge ; Cambridge University Press, 1996. xii, 464 p. :
95-020350          599.88/4/0451          0521471680
   *Apes -- Psychology. Animal intelligence.*


**QL737.P96.S25 1986**
**Savage-Rumbaugh, E. Sue,**
   Ape language : from conditioned response to symbol / E. Sue Savage-Rumbaugh ; foreword by Herbert S. Terrace. New York : Columbia University Press, 1986. xxv, 433 p. :
85-029161          156/.36          0231061986
   *Chimpanzees -- Psychology. Human-animal communication -- Data processing. Animal communication -- Data processing.*


**QL737.P96.W3 1997**
**Waal, F. B. M. de**
   Bonobo : the forgotten ape / Frans de Waal ; photographs, Frans Lanting. Berkeley : University of California Press, c1997. xv, 210 p. :
96-041095          599.88/44          0520205359
   *Bonobo. Bonobo -- Behavior.*

**QL737.P96.W3213 1998**
**Waal, F. B. M. de**
Chimpanzee politics : power and sex among apes / Frans de Waal ; with photographs and drawings by the author. Baltimore : Johns Hopkins University Press, 1998. xv, 235 p. :
97-044284          599.885/156          0801858399
*Chimpanzees -- Behavior. Social behavior in animals. Sexual behavior in animals.*

**QL737.P98.C43 1992**
**Chadwick, Douglas H.**
The fate of the elephant / Douglas H. Chadwick. San Francisco : Sierra Club Books, c1992. xi, 492 p. ;
92-004520          599.6/1          0871566354
*Elephants. Poaching. Wildlife conservation.*

**QL737.P98.S95 1989**
**Sukumar, R.**
The Asian elephant : ecology and management / R. Sukumar. Cambridge ; Cambridge University Press, 1989. xvii, 251 p.
89-009805          599.6/1/095          0521360803
*Asiatic elephant -- Ecology. Wildlife management -- Asia.*

**QL737.P9P67258 2000**
Primate males : causes and consequences of variation in group composition / edited by Peter M. Kappeler. Cambridge, UK ; Cambridge University Press, 2000. xii, 316 p. :
99-015472          599/.15          0521651190
*Primates -- Research. Women primatologists. Human-animal relationships.*

**QL737.R632.M66 1996**
**Moore, Helen H.**
Beavers / by Helen H. Moore ; illustrated by Terri Talas. Greenvale, N.Y. : Mondo, c1996. 32 p. :
95-050295          599.32/32          1572551119
*Beavers -- Juvenile literature. Beavers.*

**QL737.R638.B37 1989**
**Barash, David P.**
Marmots : social behavior and ecology / David P. Barash. Stanford, Calif. : Stanford University Press, 1989. xvii, 360 p.,
89-004284          599.32/32          0804715343
*Marmots -- Behavior. Marmots -- Ecology. Social behavior in animals.*

**QL737.R652.R69 1989**
**Roze, Uldis,**
The North American porcupine / Uldis Roze. Washington, D.C. : Smithsonian Institution Press, c1989. x, 261 p.
89-600055          599.32/34          0874747864
*North American porcupine.*

**QL737.R666.C48 1996**
**Chitty, Dennis.**
Do lemmings commit suicide? : beautiful hypotheses and ugly facts / Dennis Chitty. New York : Oxford University Press, 1996. xxi, 268 p. :
95-022673          599.32/33          0195097866
*Lemmings. Lemmings -- Behavior. Rodent populations.*

**QL737.R68.H65 1995**
**Hoogland, John L.**
The black-tailed prairie dog : social life of a burrowing mammal / John L. Hoogland. Chicago : University of Chicago Press, c1995. xiv, 557 p. :
94-013900          599.32/32          0226351173
*Cynomys ludovicianus -- Behavior. Social behavior in animals. Cynomys ludovicianus -- Reproduction.*

**QL737.R6L48 2000**
Life underground : the biology of subterranean rodents / Eileen A. Lacey, James L. Patton, and Guy N. Cameron, editors. Chicago : University of Chicago Press, 2000. xi, 449 p. :
99-051019          599.35/15648          0226467279
*Rodents. Burrowing animals.*

**QL737.S63.R49 1991**
**Reynolds, John Elliott,**
Manatees and dugongs / John E. Reynolds III and Daniel K. Odell. New York : Facts on File, c1991. xiv, 192 p. :
89-071399          599.5/5          0816024367
*Manatees. Dugong.*

**QL737.S63.Z45 1992**
**Zeiller, Warren,**
Introducing the manatee / Warren Zeiller. Gainesville : University Press of Florida, c1992. ix, 151 p. :
92-009326          599.5/5          0813011523
*Manatees.*

**QL737.U5.A64 2000**
Antelopes, deer, and relatives : fossil record, behavioral ecology, systematics, and conservation / edited by Elisabeth S. Vrba and George B. Schaller. New Haven : Yale University Press, c2000. viii, 341 p.
99-056150          599.63          0300081421
*Artiodactyla. Artiodactyla, Fossil.*

**QL737.U52.B94 1997**
**Byers, John A.**
American pronghorn : social adaptations & the ghosts of predators past / John A. Byers. Chicago : University of Chicago Press, 1997. xviii, 300 p.
97-014726          599.63/915          0226086984
*Pronghorn antelope -- Behavior. Pronghorn antelope -- Adaptation. Pronghorn antelope -- Evolution.*

**QL737.U53R6 1970**
**Roe, Frank Gilbert,**
The North American buffalo; a critical study of the species in its wild state. 2d ed. [Toronto] University of Toronto Press, [1970] xi, 991 p. :
          599.7/358          0802017029
*American bison.*

**QL737.U55.B376 1995**
**Bauer, Erwin A.**
Elk : behavior, ecology, conservation / text by Erwin A. Bauer ; photography by Erwin and Peggy Bauer. Stillwater, MN : Voyageur Press, c1995. 160 p. :
95-024582          599.73/57          0896582752
*Elk -- North America.*

**QL737.U55.B386 1995**
**Bauer, Erwin A.**
Mule deer : behavior, ecology, conservation / text by Erwin A. Bauer ; photographs by Erwin and Peggy Bauer. Stillwater, MN : Voyageur Press, c1995. 159 p. :
94-039531          599.73/57          0896582639
*Mule deer.*

**QL737.U55.H54 1996**
**Hiller, Ilo,**
The white-tailed deer / by Ilo Hiller. College Station : Texas A&M University Press, c1996. xi, 115 p. :
95-047480          599.73/57          0890966974
*White-tailed deer.*

**QL737.U55.P87 1988**
**Putman, Rory.**
The natural history of deer / Rory Putman. Ithaca, N.Y. : Comstock Pub. Associates, c1988. xvi, 191 p.,
88-022856          599.73/57          0801422833
*Deer.*

**QL737.U6.S5**
**Simpson, George Gaylord,**
Horses; the story of the horse family in the modern world and through sixty million years of history. New York, Oxford University Press, 1951. xxiv, 247 p.
51-012082          599.725
*Horses -- History. Horses, Fossil. Mammals -- Evolution.*

## QL739.2 Chordates. Vertebrates — Mammals — Physiology

**QL739.2.B76 1989**
**Bronson, F. H.**
Mammalian reproductive biology / F.H. Bronson. Chicago : University of Chicago Press, 1989. vii, 325 p. :
89-005033          599/.016          0226075583
*Mammals -- Reproduction.*

**QL739.2.Y68 1975**
**Young, J. Z.**
The life of mammals : their anatomy and physiology. Oxford : Clarendon Press, 1975. xv, 528 p. :
76-357378          599/.01          0198571569
*Mammals -- Physiology. Mammals -- Anatomy.*

## QL739.3 Chordates. Vertebrates — Mammals — Behavior

**QL739.3.M34 1990**
Mammalian parenting : biochemical, neurobiological, and behavioral determinants / edited by Norman A. Krasnegor, Robert S. Bridges. New York : Oxford University Press, 1990. xii, 502 p. :
88-037152          599/.056          0195056000
*Mammals -- Behavior -- Congresses. Parental behavior in animals -- Congresses. Parenting -- Congresses.*

## QL739.8 Chordates. Vertebrates — Mammals — Ecology

**QL739.8.D44 1997**
**Degen, A. Allan,**
Ecophysiology of small desert mammals / A. Allan Degen. Berlin ; Springer, c1997. xii, 296 p. :
96-032227          599/.052652          3540592598
*Mammals -- Ecophysiology. Desert animals -- Ecophysiology. Mammals -- Adaptation.*

**QL739.8.E36 2000**
Ecology and management of large mammals in North America / [editors] Stephen Demarais, Paul R. Krausman. Upper Saddle River, NJ : Prentice Hall, c2000. xxi, 778 p. :
99-040881          599.17/097          0137174225
*Mammals -- Ecology -- North America. Wildlife management – North America.*

## QL751 Animal behavior — General works, treatises, and textbooks

**QL751.A77 1990**
**Attenborough, David,**
The trials of life : a natural history of animal behavior / David Attenborough. Boston : Little, Brown, c1990. 320 p. :
90-053592          591.5/1          0316057517
*Animal behavior.*

**QL751.D746 1997**
**Dugatkin, Lee Alan,**
Cooperation among animals : an evolutionary perspective / Lee Alan Dugatkin. New York : Oxford University Press, 1997. xvii, 221 p.
96-018864          591.51          019508621X
*Animal behavior. Cooperativeness.*

**QL751.D7465 2000**
**Dugatkin, Lee Alan,**
The imitation factor : evolution beyond the gene / Lee Alan Dugatkin. New York : Free Press, 2000. xi, 243 p. ;
00-059286          591.5          0684864533
*Animal behavior.*

**QL751.F878 1998**
**Fryxell, John M.,**
   Individual behavior and community dynamics / John M. Fryxell, Per Lundberg. London ; Chapman & Hall, c1998. x, 202 p. :
97-005547          591.5          0412994119
   *Animal behavior -- Evolution. Animal ecology. Animal populations.*

**QL751.L3**
**Lack, David Lambert.**
   The natural regulation of animal numbers.   Oxford, Clarendon Press, 1954. viii, 343 p.
55-004771
   *Animal populations. Bird populations.*

**QL751.L398 1996**
**Lehner, Philip N.,**
   Handbook of ethological methods / Philip N. Lehner. Cambridge ; Cambridge University Press, 1996. xix, 672 p. :
95-042166          591.5/072          0521554055
   *Animal behavior -- Methodology -- Handbooks, manuals, etc.*

**QL751.S616 1999**
**Slater, P. J. B.**
   Essentials of animal behaviour / P.J.B. Slater. Cambridge ; Cambridge University Press, c1999. x, 233 p. :
98-034540          591.5          052162004X
   *Animal behavior.*

## QL751.65 Animal behavior — Special aspects of the subject as whole, A-Z

**QL751.65.M3**
**Clark, Colin Whitcomb,**
   Dynamic state variable models in ecology : methods and applications / Colin W. Clark and Marc Mangel. New York : Oxford University Press, 2000. ix, 289 p. :
99-012265          577/.01/5118          0195122666
   *Animal behavior -- Mathematical models. Animal ecology -- Mathematical models.*

**QL751.65.M3.G25 1998**
   Game theory & animal behavior / edited by Lee Alan Dugatkin and Hudson Kern Reeve. New York : Oxford University Press, 1998. xiv, 320 p. :
96-029891          591.5/015/193          0195096924
   *Animal behavior -- Mathematical models. Game theory.*

## QL752 Animal behavior — Special topics — Animal populations

**QL752.S88 1996**
**Sutherland, William J.**
   From individual behaviour to population ecology / William J. Sutherland. Oxford ; Oxford University Press, 1996. x, 213 p. :
95-030374          596/.05248          0198549113
   *Animal populations. Animal ecology. Animal behavior.*

## QL754 Animal behavior — Special topics — Periodicity. Seasonal habits

**QL754.S77 1976**
**Street, Philip,**
   Animal migration and navigation / Philip Street. New York : Scribner, c1976. 144 p. :
75-030276          591.5/2          0684145162
   *Animal migration. Animal navigation.*

## QL756 Animal behavior — Special topics — Habitations

**QL756.T87 2000**
**Turner, J. Scott,**
   The extended organism : the physiology of animal-built structures / J. Scott Turner. Cambridge, Mass. : Harvard University Press, 2000. x, 235 p. :
99-057571          591.56/4          0674001516
   *Animals -- Habitations. Animals -- Physiology.*

## QL756.5 Animal behavior — Special topics — Food

**QL756.5.V36 1990**
**Vander Wall, Stephen B.**
   Food hoarding in animals / Stephen B. Vander Wall. Chicago : University of Chicago Press, 1990. xii, 445p.
89-020535          591.53          0226847349
   *Animals -- Food. Animal behavior.*

## QL758 Animal behavior — Special topics — Predation. Predatory animals

**QL758.Q513 1989**
   Predators and predation : the struggle for life in the animal world / edited by Pierre Pfeffer ; [translated by Mark Howson]. New York : Facts on File, c1989. viii, 419 p.
88-003880          591.53          0816016186
   *Predation (Biology) -- Encyclopedias.*

**QL758.T38 1984**
**Taylor, Robert J.,**
   Predation / Robert J. Taylor. New York : Chapman and Hall, 1984. 166p.
84-004974          574.5/3          0412250608
   *Predation (Biology)*

## QL758.5 Animal behavior — Special topics — Aggression. Agonistic behavior

**QL758.5.A73 1988**
**Archer, John,**
   The behavioural biology of aggression / John Archer. Cambridge [England] ; Cambridge University Press, 1988. x, 257 p. :
87-021792          591.5/1          0521345588
   *Aggressive behavior in animals. Aggressiveness. Aggression.*

## QL761 Animal behavior — Special topics — Sexual relations

**QL761.B57 2000**
**Birkhead, T. R.**
Promiscuity : an evolutionary history of sperm competition / Tim Birkhead. Cambridge, Mass. : Harvard University Press, 2000. xiii, 272 p.
00-040923          591.56/2          0674004450
*Sexual selection in animals. Sperm competition. Reproduction.*

**QL761.C76 1991**
**Cronin, Helena.**
The ant and the peacock : altruism and sexual selection from Darwin to today / Helena Cronin. Cambridge ; Press Syndicate of the University of Cambridge,o 1991. xiv, 490 p. :
91-007887          575/.5          052132937X
*Sexual selection in animals. Courtship of animals. Altruistic behavior in animals.*

**QL761.G68 1989**
**Gould, James L.,**
Sexual selection / James L. Gould, Carol Grant Gould. New York : Scientific American Library : c1989. viii, 277 p.
89-034588          591.56          0716750538
*Sexual selection in animals. Courtship of animals. Mate selection.*

## QL761.5 Animal behavior — Special topics — Familial behavior. Kin recognition

**QL761.5.K49 1991**
Kin recognition / edited by Peter G. Hepper. Cambridge [England] ; Cambridge University Press, 1991. xii, 457 p. :
90-021776          591.56          0521372674
*Kin recognition in animals. Kin recognition.*

## QL762 Animal behavior — Special topics — Parental behavior

**QL762.C48 1991**
**Clutton-Brock, T. H.**
The evolution of parental care / T.H. Clutton-Brock ; with original drawings by Dafila Scott. Princeton, N.J. : Princeton University Press, c1991. xii, 352 p. :
90-008832          591.56     069108730X
*Parental behavior in animals. Behavior evolution.*

## QL763.5 Animal behavior — Special topics — Play behavior

**QL763.5.A54 1998**
Animal play : evolutionary, comparative, and ecological prespectives / edited by Marc Bekoff and John A. Byers. Cambridge, [England] ; Cambridge University Press, 1998. xvi, 274 p. :
97-022056          591.56/3          0521583837
*Play behavior in animals.*

## QL768 Animal behavior — Special topics — Animal tracks and signs

**QL768.M87 1975**
**Murie, Olaus Johan,**
A field guide to animal tracks. Text and illus. by Olaus J. Murie. Boston, Houghton Mifflin, 1975, c1974. xxi, 375 p. :
74-006294          591.5          0395183235
*Animal tracks. Zoology -- North America. Zoology -- Central America.*

**QL768.R49 1999**
**Rezendes, Paul.**
Tracking & the art of seeing : how to read animal tracks & sign / by Paul Rezendes. 2nd ed. New York : HarperCollins, 1999. 336 p. :
          599 21          0062735241
*Animal tracks. Animal tracks -- Identification.*

## QL775 Animal behavior — Special topics — Social relations. Animal societies

**QL775.D84 1999**
**Dugatkin, Lee Alan,**
Cheating monkeys and citizen bees : the nature of cooperation in animals and humans / Lee Dugatkin. New York : Free Press, 1999. 208p.
98-027768          591.56          0684843412
*Social behavior in animals. Animal behavior -- Evolution. Cooperativeness (Psychology)*

**QL775.O6 2000**
On the move : how and why animals travel in groups / edited by Sue Boinski and Paul A. Garber. Chicago : University of Chicago Press, 2000. xi, 811 p. :
99-013382          591.56          0226063399
*Social behavior in animals. Primates -- Behavior.*

**QL775.W54**
**Wilson, Edward Osborne,**
Sociobiology : the new synthesis / Edward O. Wilson. Cambridge, Mass. : Belknap Press of Harvard University Press, 1975. ix, 697 p. :
74-083910          591.5          0674816218
*Social behavior in animals. Sociobiology.*

## QL776 Animal behavior — Special topics — Communication

**QL776.B73 1998**
**Bradbury, J. W.**
Principles of animal communication / Jack W. Bradbury, Sandra L. Vehrencamp. Sunderland, MA : Sinauer Associates, 1998. xiii, 882 p.
97-044014          591.59          0878931007
*Animal communication.*

**QL776.H38 1996**
**Hauser, Marc D.**
The evolution of communication / Marc D. Hauser. Cambridge, Mass. : MIT Press, c1996. xii, 760 p. :
95-052290        591.59      0262082500
*Animal communication. Communication.*

**QL776.P485 1998**
Pheromone communication in social insects : ants, wasps, bees, and termites / edited by Robert K. Vander Meer ... [et al.]. Boulder, Colo. : Westview Press, 1998. x, 368 p. :
97-029921        595.7159        0813389763
*Animal communication. Pheromones. Insect societies.*

**QL776.R64 2000**
**Rogers, Lesley J.**
Songs, roars, and rituals : communication in birds, mammals, and other animals / Lesley J. Rogers and Gisela Kaplan. Cambridge, Mass. : Harvard University Press, 2000. x, 207 p. :
00-025602        591.59      0674000587
*Animal communication.*

## QL781 Animal behavior — Special topics — Instinct

**QL781.T58 1969**
**Tinbergen, Niko,**
The study of instinct, by N. Tinbergen. Oxford, Clarendon P., 1969. xx, 228 p.
74-452984        591.5/1        019857343X
*Instinct. Animal behavior.*

## QL785-785.25 Animal behavior — Special topics — Psychology. Intelligence. Learning

**QL785.C5 1998**
Cognitive ecology : the evolutionary ecology of information processing and decision making / edited by Reuven Dukas. Chicago : University of Chicago Press, c1998. viii, 420 p.
97-036597        591.5/13        0226169324
*Cognition in animals. Animal ecology. Animal behavior -- Evolution.*

**QL785.G715 2001**
**Griffin, Donald R.**
Animal minds : beyond cognition to consciousness / Donald R. Griffin. Chicago : University of Chicago Press, 2001. xv, 355 p. ;
00-010006        591.5      0226308650
*Cognition in animals. Animal behavior. Animal psychology.*

**QL785.G72 1981**
**Griffin, Donald R.**
The question of animal awareness : evolutionary continuity of mental experience / Donald R. Griffin. New York : Rockefeller University Press, 1981. xi, 209 p. ;
81-051221        156/.3        0874700353
*Animal intelligence. Animal communication. Animals, Habits and behavior of.*

**QL785.H359 2000**
**Hauser, Marc D.**
Wild minds : what animals really think / Marc D. Hauser ; illustrations by Ted Dewan. New York : Henry Holt, 2000. xx, 315p. :
99-036204        591.5/13        0805056696
*Cognition in animals. Animal psychology. Social behavior in animals.*

**QL785.T5 2000**
**Thorndike, Edward L.**
Animal intelligence : experimental studies / Edward L. Thorndike ; with a new introduction by Darryl Bruce. New Brunswick, N.J. : Transaction Publishers, c2000. xx, 297 p. :
99-011926        591.5/13        0765804824
*Animal intelligence.*

**QL785.25.D39 1993**
**Dawkins, Marian Stamp.**
Through our eyes only? : the search for animal consciousness / by Marian Stamp Dawkins. Oxford ; W.H. Freeman : c1993. x, 192 p. :
92-032995        156/.3        0716745011
*Consciousness in animals. Animal behavior.*

## QL799 Morphology — General works, treatises, and textbooks

**QL799.M38 1994**
**McGowan, Christopher.**
Diatoms to dinosaurs : the size and scale of living things / Chris McGowan ; illustrations by Julian Mulock. Washington, D.C. : Island Press/Shearwater Books, c1994. xiii, 288 p.
94-013112        591.4      1559633042
*Morphology (Animals) Body size. Physiology.*

**QL799.S34 1984**
**Schmidt-Nielsen, Knut,**
Scaling, why is animal size so important? / Knut Schmidt-Nielsen. Cambridge ; Cambridge University Press, 1984. xi, 241 p. :
84-005841        596      0521266572
*Body size. Morphology (Animals)*

## QL955 Anatomy — Embryology — General works, treatises, and textbooks

**QL955.E43 1997**
Embryology : constructing the organism / edited by Scott F. Gilbert and Anne M. Raunio ; with illustrations by Nancy J. Haver. Sunderland, MA : Sinauer Associates, c1997. xii, 537 p. :
97-013045        571.8/61        0878932372
*Embryology.*

## QL959 Anatomy — Embryology — Individual orders, genera, species, etc.

**QL959.E33 1991**

Egg incubation : its effects on embryonic development in birds and reptiles / edited by D. Charles Deeming and Mark W.J. Ferguson. Cambridge ; Cambridge University Press, 1991. xiii, 448 p.
92-160144        597.9/04333        0521390710
*Eggs -- Incubation. Embryology -- Birds. Embryology – Reptiles.*

**QL959.H96 1995**
**Hunter, R. H. F.**

Sex determination, differentiation, and intersexuality in placental mammals / R.H.F. Hunter. Cambridge ; Cambridge University Press, 1995. xxi, 310 p. :
94-031834        599/.036        0521462185
*Embryology -- Mammals. Sex differentiation. Sex determination, Genetic.*

# QM Human Anatomy

## QM16 Biography — Individual, A-Z

**QM16.L4.B4**
**Belt, Elmer,**

Leonardo the anatomist. Lawrence, Univ. of Kansas Press, 1955. 76 p.
55006603        611
*Leonardo, -- da Vinci, -- 1452-1519. Leonardo, -- da Vinci, – 1452-1519.*

## QM21 Early works through 1800

**QM21.H313**
**Harvey, William,**

Lectures on the whole of anatomy; an annotated translation of Prelectiones anatomiae universalis, by C.D. O'Malley, F.N.L. Poynter [and] K.F. Russell. Berkeley, University of California Press, 1961. 239 p.
61-016879        611
*Human anatomy -- Early works to 1800.*

**QM21.L49**
**Leonardo da Vinci,**

Leonardo da Vinci on the human body: the anatomical, physiological, and embryological drawings of Leonardo da Vinci; with translations, emendations, and a biographical introd., by Charles D. O'Malley and J. B. de C. M. Saunders. New York, H. Schuman [1952] 506 p.
52004858        611.084
*Anatomy, Human -- Early works to 1800.*

## QM23 General works, treatises, and textbooks — 1801-1969

**QM23.G7 1959**
**Gray, Henry,**

Anatomy of the human body. Philadelphia, Lea & Febiger, 1959. 1458 p.
59-012082        611
*Human anatomy.*

## QM23.2 General works, treatises, and textbooks — 1970-

**QM23.2.B53 1997**
**Biel, Andrew.**

Trail guide to the body : how to locate muscles, bones and more / Andrew Biel ; illustrations by Robin Dorn. Boulder, CO : Andrew Biel, c1997. 297 p. :
97-093767        611        0965853403
*Human anatomy.*

**QM23.2.F68 1984**
**Fowler, Ira.**

Human anatomy / Ira Fowler. Belmont, Calif. : Wadsworth Pub. Co., c1984. xv, 615 p. :
83-016991        611        0534027466
*Human anatomy. Anatomy.*

**QM23.2.G73 1985**
**Gray, Henry,**

Anatomy of the human body / by Henry Gray. Philadelphia : Lea & Febiger, 1985. xvii, 1676 p.
84-005741        611        081210644X
*Human anatomy. Anatomy.*

## QM25 Pictorial works and atlases

**QM25.M23**
**McMinn, R. M. H.**

Color atlas of human anatomy / R. M. H. McMinn, R. T. Hutchings. Chicago : Year Book Medical Publishers, c1977. 352 p. :
76-023581        611/.0022/2        0815158238
*Human anatomy -- Atlases.*

**QM25.V43**
**Vesalius, Andreas,**

The illustrations from the works of Andreas Vesalius of Brussels; with annotations and translations, a discussion of the plates and their background, authorship and influence, and a biographical ske by J. B. de C. M. Saunders and Charles D. O'Malley. Cleveland, World Pub. Co. [1950] 248 p.
50007883        611.084
*Human anatomy -- Atlases. Anatomy, Artistic. Human anatomy.*

## QM28 Special aspects of the subject as whole

**QM28.H23 1989**
**Hall, Judith G.**
Handbook of normal physical measurements / Judith G. Hall, Ursula G. Froster-Iskenius, and Judith E. Allanson. Oxford ; Oxford University Press, 1989. 504 p. :
89-003415          573/.6          019261696X
*Anthropometry -- Handbooks, manuals, etc. Genetic disorders – Diagnosis -- Handbooks, manuals, etc. Growth disorders – Diagnosis -- Handbooks, manuals, etc.*

## QM33.4 Dissection — History

**QM33.4.C3613 1999**
**Carlino, Andrea,**
Books of the body : anatomical ritual and renaissance learning / Andrea Carlino ; translated by John Tedeschi and Anne C. Tedeschi. Chicago : University of Chicago Press, c1999. xiv, 266 p. :
99-025338          611/.009/031          0226092879
*Human dissection -- History -- 16th century. Human anatomy – History -- 16th century. Renaissance.*

## QM34 Dissection — Manuals of practical anatomy. Laboratory manuals

**QM34.A39 1987**
**Allen, B. L.**
Basic anatomy : a laboratory manual : the human skeleton, the cat / B.L. Allen. New York : W.H. Freeman, c1987. xvi, 204 p. :
86-222794          599.74/42          0716717557
*Human anatomy -- Laboratory manuals. Cats -- Anatomy -- Laboratory manuals. Human skeleton -- Laboratory manuals.*

## QM101 Skeleton. Osteology — General works

**QM101.G63 1982**
**Goldberg, Kathy E.**
The skeleton : fantastic framework / by Kathy E. Goldberg and the editors of U.S. News Books. Washington, D.C. : U.S. News Books, c1982. 165 p. :
81-023098          611/.71          089193605X
*Skeleton.*

## QM151 Muscles — General works

**QM151.V4713 1999**
**Vesalius, Andreas,**
On the fabric of the human body. Andreas Vesalius ; [translated] by William Frank Richardson, in collaboration with John Burd Carman. San Francisco : Norman Pub., 1999. xxix, 490 p.
98-034677          611/.73          0930405757
*Muscles -- Anatomy -- Early works to 1800. Ligaments – Anatomy -- Early works to 1800.*

## QM451 Nervous system — General works

**QM451.H18 2000**
**Haines, Duane E.**
Neuroanatomy : an atlas of structures, sections, and systems / Duane E. Haines. 5th ed. Philadelphia : Lippincott Williams & Wilkins, c2000. xi, 256 p. :
611/.8 21          0683306499
*Neuroanatomy -- Atlases. Central Nervous System -- Anatomy & histology -- Atlases.*

## QM455 Nervous system — Brain

**QM455.D49 1988**
**Diamond, Marian Cleeves.**
Enriching heredity : the impact of the environment on the anatomy of the brain / Marian Cleeves Diamond. New York : Free Press ; c1988. xiii, 191 p.
88-007151          599/.048          0029074312
*Brain -- Anatomy. Brain -- Adaptation. Neuroplasticity.*

**QM455.N48 1988**
**Nieuwenhuys, R.,**
The human central nervous system : a synopsis and atlas / R. Nieuwenhuys, J. Voogd, Chr. Van Huijzen. 3rd rev. ed. Berlin ; New York : Springer-Verlag, c1988. xii, 437 p.:
612/.82/0222 19          0387134417
*Central nervous system -- Atlases. Neuroanatomy -- Atlases. Central Nervous System -- Anatomy & histology -- atlases.*

## QM557 Human and comparative histology — Pictorial works and atlases

**QM557.K47 1999**
**Kerr, Jeffrey B.**
Atlas of functional histology / Jeffrey B. Kerr. St. Louis ; Mosby, c1999. p. cm.
98-050142          611/.018/0222          0723430721
*Histology -- Atlases. Histology -- atlases.*

**QM557.K79 1991**
**Krstic, Radivoj V.,**
Human microscopic anatomy : an atlas for students of medicine and biology / Radivoj V. Krstic. Berlin ; Springer-Verlag, c1991. xvi, 616 p. :
91-005012          611/.018          3540536663
*Histology -- Atlases. Histology -- atlases.*

## QM575 Human and comparative histology — Special tissues — Nerve tissues

**QM575.R343 1994**
**Ramon y Cajal, Santiago,**
  Cajal's histology of the nervous system / translated by Neely and Larry W. Swanson. Oxford ; Oxford University Press, 1995. 2 v.
93035437      611/.0188      0195074017
  *Nervous system -- Histology. Nervous System -- anatomy & histology. Nervous System -- ultrastructure.*

## QM601 Human embryology — General works, treatises, and textbooks

**QM601.B553**
**Blechschmidt, Erich,**
  The stages of human development before birth; an introduction to human embryology. Philadelphia, Saunders, 1961. 684 p.
61-010163      612.64
  *Embryology, Human.*

**QM601.L35 1995**
**Langman, Jan.**
  Langman's medical embryology / original illustrations by Jill Leland. 7th / T.W. Sadler ; computer illustration by Kathleen K. Sulik. Baltimore : Williams & Wilkins, c1995. xi, 460 p. :
       612.6/4 20      068307489X
*Embryology. Human. Abnormalities, Human -- Genetic aspects. Abnormalities. Embroyology.*

**QM601.M768 1992**
**Morowitz, Harold J.**
  The facts of life : science and the abortion controversy / Harold J. Morowitz and James S. Trefil. New York : Oxford University Press, 1992. xi, 179 p. :
92-016343      612.6/4      0195079272
  *Embryology, Human. Human reproduction. Abortion.*

## QM602 Human embryology — Pictorial works and atlases

**QM602.G55 1989**
**Gilbert, Stephen G.**
  Pictorial human embryology / illustrations and text by Stephen G. Gilbert. Seattle : University of Washington Press, c1989. xii, 172 p. :
87-034642      611/.013/0222      0295966327
  *Embryology, Human -- Atlases. Embryo – anatomy & histology – atlases.*

## QM603 Human embryology — Popular works

**QM603.W65 1991**
**Wolpert, L.**
  The triumph of the embryo / Lewis Wolpert ; with illustrations drawn by Debra Skinner. Oxford [England] ; Oxford University Press, 1991. vii, 211 p. :
91-007583      612.6/4      0198542437
  *Embryology, Human -- Popular works.*

## QM690 Human embryology — Teratology — Early works through 1800

**QM690.B66 2000**
**Bondeson, Jan.**
  The two-headed boy, and other medical marvels / Jan Bondeson. Ithaca, N.Y. : Cornell University Press, c2000. xxii, 295 p.
00-020902      610      0801437679
  *Abnormalities, Human.*

## QM691 Human embryology — Teratology — 1801-

**QM691.E44 1997**
  Embryos, genes, and birth defects / edited by Peter Thorogood. Chichester ; J. Wiley, c1997. viii, 359 p.
96-046036      616/.043      0471971960
  *Abnormalities, Human. Teratogenesis. Embryology, Human.*

## QM695 Human embryology — Teratology — By region, system, or organ of the body, A-Z

**QM695.F32G37 1999**
**Gartner, Leslie P.,**
  Essentials of oral histology and embryology / Leslie P. Gartner. 3rd ed. Baltimore, Md. : Jen House Pub. Co. : c1999. 163 p. :
       611/.018931 21
*Face. Mouth. Teeth. Embryology, Human. Histology.*

# QP Physiology

## QP1 Societies, congresses, serial collections, yearbooks

**QP1.A535**
  Annual review of physiology. Palo Alto, Calif., Annual Reviews Inc.
39-015404      599.01/05
  *Physiology -- Periodicals. Physiology -- yearbooks.*

## QP11 Dictionaries and encyclopedias

**QP11.E53 1997**

Encyclopedia of human biology / edited by Renato Dulbecco. San Diego : Academic Press, c1997. 9 v. :

97-008627          612/.003          0122269705

*Human biology -- Encyclopedias. Biology -- encyclopedias. Physiology -- encyclopedias.*

## QP21 History

**QP21.D378 2001**
**Des Chene, Dennis.**

Spirits and clocks : machine and organism in Descartes / Dennis Des Chene. Ithaca : Cornell University Press, 2001. xiii, 181 p.

00-009872          571/.01          0801437644

*Descartes, Rene, -- 1596-1650 -- Knowledge -- Physiology. Physiology -- Philosophy.*

**QP21.F76**
**Frank, Robert Gregg,**

Harvey and the Oxford physiologists : a study of scientific ideas / by Robert G. Frank, Jr. Berkeley : University of California Press, c1980. xviii, 368 p.

79-063553          599.01/0942          0520039068

*Harvey, William, -- 1578-1657.     Physiology -- England – History. Physiologists -- England -- Biography. Physiology -- History -- England.*

**QP21.H34 1969**
**Hall, Thomas Steele,**

Ideas of life and matter; studies in the history of general physiology, 600 B.C.-1900 A.D. [by] Thomas S. Hall. Chicago, University of Chicago Press [1969] 2 v.

69-016999          577/.2/09

*Physiology -- History.*

**QP21.I58 1988**

The Investigative enterprise : experimental physiology in nineteenth-century medicine / edited by William Coleman and Frederic L. Holmes. Berkeley : University of California Press, c1988. 342 p. :

87-019207          612/.0072/4          0520060482

*Physiology, Experimental -- History -- 19th century.*

## QP26 Biography — Individual

**QP26.H3.F74 1994**
**French, R. K.**

William Harvey's natural philosophy / Roger French. Cambridge [England] ; Cambridge University Press, 1994. xii, 393 p. :

93-036181          611          0521455359

*Harvey, William, -- 1578-1657.     Blood -- Circulation – Research – History. Human anatomy -- Research -- History.*

**QP26.S33.A3 1998**
**Schmidt-Nielsen, Knut,**

The camel's nose : memoirs of a curious scientist / Knut Schmidt-Nielsen ; illustrations by Kathryn K. Davis. Washington, D.C. : Island Press, c1998. x, 339 p. :

98-005969          571.1/092          1559635126

*Schmidt-Nielsen, Knut, -- 1915-     Physiologists -- Biography.*

## QP31 General works, treatises, and textbooks — 1801-1969

**QP31.F8 1955**
**Fulton, John F.**

A textbook of physiology, edited by John F. Fulton, with the collaboration of Donald H. Barron [and others] Philadelphia, Saunders 1955. 1275 p.

55005200          612

*Physiology. Physiology*

**QP31.P68 1961**
**Prosser, C. Ladd**

Comparative animal physiology [by] C. Ladd Prosser [and] Frank A. Brown, Jr. Philadelphia, Saunders, 1961. 688 p.

61-006735          591.1

*Physiology, Comparative.*

## QP33 Comparative physiology

**QP33.G65 1982**
**Gordon, Malcolm S.**

Animal physiology : principles and adaptations / Malcolm S. Gordon, in collaboration with George A. Bartholomew ... [et al.]. New York : Macmillan ; c1982. xvii, 635 p.

81-008227          591.1          0023453206

*Physiology, Comparative. Adaptation (Physiology) Animal ecology.*

**QP33.H6 1983**
**Hoar, William Stewart,**

General and comparative physiology / William S. Hoar. Englewood Cliffs, N.J. : Prentice-Hall, c1983. xii, 851 p. :

82-024076          591.1          0133493083

*Physiology, Comparative.*

**QP33.W53 1998**
**Widmaier, Eric P.**

Why geese don't get obese (and we do) : how evolution's strategies for survival affect our everyday lives / Eric P. Widmaier. New York : W. H. Freeman, c1998. ix, 213 p. :

98-002698          571.1          0716731479

*Physiology, Comparative -- Popular works.*

## QP33.5 Special aspects of the subject as whole

**QP33.5.C3 1939**
**Cannon, Walter B.**
The wisdom of the body [by] Walter B. Cannon ... New York, W.W. Norton & Company, inc. [c1939] xviii, 19-333
39027360          612
*Physiology  Homeostasis*

**QP33.5.H49 1996**
**Heyward, Vivian H.**
Applied body composition assessment / Vivian H. Heyward, Lisa M. Stolarczyk. Champaign, IL : Human Kinetics, c1996. ix, 221 p. :
95-033160          612          0873226534
*Body composition -- Measurement. Body Composition. Anthropometry.*

**QP33.5.H85 1996**
Human body composition / Alex F. Roche, Steven B. Heymsfield, Timothy G. Lohman, editors. Champaign, IL : Human Kinetics, c1996. x, 366 p. :
95-021397          612          0873226380
*Body composition. Body composition -- Measurement. Anthropometry.*

## QP33.6 Special topics, A-Z

**QP33.6.M36.B87 1994**
**Burton, R. F.**
Physiology by numbers : an encouragement to quantitative thinking / R.F. Burton. Cambridge ; Cambridge University Press, 1994. xv, 185 p. :
93-037134          612/.001/51          0521420679
*Physiology -- Mathematics.*

## QP34 Human physiology — General works, treatises, and advanced textbooks — Through 1969

**QP34.B5 1963**
**Best, Charles Herbert,**
The human body, its anatomy and physiology [by] C. H. Best [and] N. B. Taylor. New York, Holt, Rinehart and Winston [1963] 754 p.
63-007312          612
*Human physiology. Human anatomy.*

**QP34.B54 1966**
**Best, Charles Herbert,**
The physiological basis of medical practice; a text in applied physiology [by] Charles Herbert Best [and] Norman Burke Taylor. With 49 contributors under the general editorship of Norman Burke Taylor. Baltimore, Williams & Wilkins, 1966. xiv, 1793 p.
66-024510          612
*Human physiology.*

**QP34.C25 1961**
**Carlson, Anton J.**
The machinery of the body, by Anton J. Carlson, Victor Johnson [and] H. Mead Cavert. [Chicago] University of Chicago Press [1961] 752 p.
61-014536          612
*Human physiology.*

**QP34.S75 1968**
**Starling, Ernest Henry,**
Principles of human physiology [by] Starling and Lovatt Evans. Philadelphia, Lea & Febiger, 1968. xv, 1668 p.
79-000157          612
*Physiology.*

### QP34.5 Human physiology — General works, treatises, and advanced textbooks — 1970-

**QP34.5.B34 2000**
**Barash, David P.**
The mammal in the mirror : understanding our place in the natural world / David P. Barash, Ilona A. Barash. New York : W.H. Freeman and Co., c2000. x, 384 p. ;
99-038972          599.9          0716733919
*Human biology.*

**QP34.5.B47 1985**
**Best, Charles Herbert,**
Best and Taylor's Physiological basis of medical practice. Baltimore : Williams & Wilkins, c1985. xxvi, 1340 p.
83-006613          612          0683089447
*Human physiology. Physiology.*

**QP34.5.B55 1984**
**Bleier, Ruth,**
Science and gender : a critique of biology and its theories on women / Ruth Bleier. New York : Pergamon Press, c1984. xii, 220 p. :
83-022054          305.4/2          0080309720
*Women -- Physiology -- Philosophy. Human biology -- Philosophy. Sex discrimination against women.*

**QP34.5.T68 1986**
**Tortora, Gerard J.**
Principles of human anatomy / Gerard J. Tortora. New York : Harper & Row, c1986. xxi, 713, 38,
85-008545          612          0060466235
*Human physiology. Human anatomy. Anatomy.*

### QP36 Human physiology — School textbooks of physiology and hygiene

**QP36.M54 2000**
**Cohen, Barbara J.**
The Structure & function of the human body / Barbara Janson Cohen, Dena Lin Wood. 7th ed. Philadelphia : Lippincott Williams & Wilkins, c2000. xxiii, 379 p. :
          612 21          078172113X
*Human physiology. Human anatomy. Anatomy. Physiology.*

## QP38 Human physiology — Popular works

**QP38.N894 1997**
**Nuland, Sherwin B.**
The wisdom of the body / Sherwin B. Nuland. New York : Knopf ; 1997. xxiv, 395 p.
96-045113          612          0679444076
*Human biology -- Popular works. Body, Human – Popular works. Human physiology -- Popular works.*

## QP81.5 Phenomena of animal life (General) — Sex differences

**QP81.5 F38 1992**
**Fausto-Sterling, Anne,**
Myths of gender : biological theories about women and men / Anne Fausto-Sterling. 2nd ed. New York, NY : BasicBooks, 1992. x, 310 p. :
                    155.3/3 20          0465047920
*Sex differences. Feminism. Sexism. Human biology -- Philosophy.*

**QP81.5.G43 1998**
**Geary, David C.**
Male, female : the evolution of human sex differences / David C. Geary. Washington, DC : American Psychological Association, c1998. xii, 397 p. :
98-026961          155.3/3          1557985278
*Sex differences. Human evolution.*

**QP81.5.H83 1990**
**Hubbard, Ruth,**
The politics of women's biology / Ruth Hubbard. New Brunswick, [N.J.] : Rutgers University Press, c1990. viii, 229 p.
89-010242          305.42          0813514894
*Women -- Physiology -- Political aspects. Human biology – Sex differences -- Political aspects. Human reproductive technology – Political aspects.*

**QP81.5.P66 1994**
**Pool, Robert,**
Eve's rib : the biological roots of sex differences / Robert Pool. New York : Crown Publishers, c1994. 308 p. ;
93-039793          612.6          0517592983
*Sex differences. Sex differences (Psychology)*

**QP81.5.R87 1989**
**Russett, Cynthia Eagle.**
Sexual science : the Victorian construction of womanhood / Cynthia Eagle Russett. Cambridge, Mass. : Harvard University Press, 1989. 245 p. ;
88-024521          305.3/09/034          067480290X
*Sex differences. Sex role -- History -- 19th century. Women's studies -- History -- 19th century.*

**QP81.5.S35 1993**
**Schiebinger, Londa L.**
Nature's body : gender in the making of modern science / Londa Schiebinger. Boston : Beacon Press, c1993. viii, 289 p.
92-045026          574/.094/09033          0807089001
*Sex differences -- History -- 18th century. Science -- History – 18th century. Natural history -- History -- 18th century.*

## QP81.6 Phenomena of animal life (General) — Sexual orientation. Homosexuality

**QP81.6.B87 1996**
**Burr, Chandler,**
A separate creation : the search for the biological origins of sexual orientation / Chandler Burr. New York : Hyperion, c1996. viii, 354 p.
95-050776          155.7          0786860812
*Sexual orientation -- Physiological aspects.*

## QP82 Phenomena of animal life (General) — Influence of the environment (General). Animal ecophysiology. Physiological adaptation — General works

**QP82.A75 2000**
**Ashcroft, Frances M.**
Life at the extremes / Frances Ashcroft. Berkeley : University of California Press, c2000. xxi, 326 p. :
00-028672          612/.014          0520222342
*Adaptation (Physiology) Extreme environments.*

**QP82.E59 1976**
Environmental physiology of animals / editors, J. Bligh, J. L. Cloudsley-Thompson, A. G. MacDonald. New York : Wiley : distributed in the United States of Amer 1976. viii, 456 p.
76-025459          591.1          0470989238.
*Adaptation (Physiology). Bioclimatology. Evolution.*

**QP82.H63 1984**
**Hochachka, Peter W.**
Biochemical adaptation / Peter W. Hochachka, George N. Somero. Princeton, N.J. : Princeton University Press, c1984. xx, 537 p. :
83-043076          574.5          0691083436
*Adaptation (Physiology) Biochemistry.*

## QP82.2 Phenomena of animal life (General) — Influence of the environment (General). Animal ecophysiology. Physiological adaptation — Special topics, A-Z

**QP82.2.E43.B418 1990**
**Becker, Robert O.**
Cross currents : the promise of electromedicine, the perils of electropollution / Robert O. Becker. Los Angeles : J.P. Tarcher ; c1990. xv, 336 p. :
89-005067          612/.01427          0874775361
*Electromagnetic waves -- Health aspects. Electrophysiology. Biomagnetism.*

## QP82.2.E43.C73 1996
Handbook of biological effects of electromagnetic fields / edited by Charles Polk, Elliot Postow. Boca Raton : CRC Press, c1996. 618 p. :
95-032947    574.19/17    0849306418
*Electromagnetic fields -- Physiological effect -- Handbooks, manuals, etc.*

## QP82.2.E43.H67 1995
**Horton, William F.**
Power frequency magnetic fields and public health / William F. Horton, Saul Goldberg. Boca Raton : CRC Press, c1995. xi, 276 p. :
95-023092    612/.01442    0849394201
*Electromagnetic fields -- Health aspects. Electic power distribution -- Health aspects.*

## QP82.2.S8
Handbook of stress, coping, and health : implications for nursing research, theory, and practice / Virginia Hill Rice, editor. Thousand Oaks, Calif. : Sage Publications, c2000. xiv, 590 p. :
99-050741    158.7/2/024613    0761918205
*Stress (Physiology) -- Handbooks, manuals, etc. Stress (Psychology) -- Handbooks, manuals, etc. Stress management -- Handbooks, manuals, etc.*

## QP82.2.S8.P79
Psychobiology of stress : a study of coping men / edited by Holger Ursin, Eivind Baade, Seymour Levine. New York : Academic Press, 1978. xv, 236 p. :
78-008119    612/.042    0127092501
*Stress (Physiology) Parachuting -- Physiological aspects. Psychobiology.*

## QP82.2.S8.W45 1992
**Weiner, Herbert.**
Perturbing the organism : the biology of stressful experience / Herbert Weiner. Chicago : University of Chicago Press, 1992. xiii, 357 p.
91-000838    616.9/8    0226890414
*Stress (Physiology) Stress, Psychological -- psychopathology.*

## QP82.2.U45.K66 1989
**Kooyman, Gerald L.**
Diverse divers : physiology and behavior / Gerald L. Kooyman. Berlin ; Springer-Verlag, c1989. v, 200 p. :
88-038507    596/.01    0387502742
*Underwater physiology. Aquatic animals -- Physiology. Deep diving -- Physiological aspects.*

## QP84 Developmental physiology — Growth

### QP84.C26 1998
The Cambridge encyclopedia of human growth and development / edited by Stanley J. Ulijaszek, Francis E. Johnston, and Michael A. Preece. Cambridge, UK ; Cambridge University Press, 1998. xii, 497 p. :
97-014707    612.6/03    0521560462
*Human growth -- Encyclopedias. Developmental psychology -- Encyclopedias. Human Development -- encyclopedias.*

## QP84.C53
**Cloudsley-Thompson, J. L.**
Rhythmic activity in animal physiology and behaviour. New York, Academic Press, 1961. 236 p.
61-010699    591.5
*Biological rhythms. Animal behavior.*

## QP84.R723 1992
**Roche, Alex F.,**
Growth, maturation, and body composition : the Fels Longitudinal Study, 1929-1991 / Alex F. Roche. Cambridge ; Cambridge University Press, 1992. xiii, 282 p.
93-109902    612.6    0521374499
*Human growth -- United States -- Longitudinal studies. Anthropometry -- Longitudinal studies. Body composition -- Longitudinal studies.*

## QP85 Developmental physiology — Longevity. Prolongation of life

### QP85.B45
**Benet, Sula,**
How to live to be 100 : the life-style of the people of the Caucasus / Sula Benet. New York : Dial Press, 1976. xii, 201 p.,
75-040471    612.6/8    080373834X
*Longevity. Caucasus -- Social life and customs.*

### QP85.F47 1990
**Finch, Caleb Ellicott.**
Longevity, senescence, and the genome / Caleb E. Finch. Chicago : University of Chicago Press, 1990. xv, 922 p. :
90-043971    574.3/74    0226248887
*Longevity. Longevity -- Genetic aspects. Aging.*

## QP86 Developmental physiology — Aging. Senescence

### QP86.A97 1997
**Austad, Steven N.,**
Why we age : what science is discovering about the body's journey through life / Steven N. Austad. New York : J. Wiley & Sons, c1997. xii, 244 p. :
97-005542    612.6/7    0471148032
*Aging -- Physiological aspects. Age factors in disease.*

### QP86.B516 1994
Biological anthropology and aging : perspectives on human variation over the life span / edited by Douglas E. Crews, Ralph M. Garruto. New York : Oxford University Press, 1994. xxi, 445 p. :
93-011232    612.6/7    0195068297
*Aging. Physical anthropology.*

**QP86.D54 2000**
**DiGiovanna, Augustine Gaspar.**
Human aging : biological perspectives / Augustine Gaspar DiGiovanna. 2nd ed. Boston, Mass. : WCB/McGraw-Hill, c2000. xiv, 389 p. :
612.6/7 21        0072926910
*Aging -- Physiological aspects.*

**QP86.E47 1988**
Emergent theories of aging / James E. Birren, Vern L. Bengtson, editors ; and Donna E. Deutchman, editorial coordinator. New York : Springer Pub. Co., c1988. xiv, 530 p. :
87-028509     612/.67     0826162509
*Aging.*

**QP86.H65 1995**
**Holliday, R.**
Understanding aging / Robin Holliday. Cambridge ; Cambridge University Press, 1995. xiv, 207 p. :
94-011727     574.3/72     0521417880
*Aging -- Physiological aspects.*

**QP86.I56 1991**
**Institute of Medicine (U.S.).**
Extending life, enhancing life : a national research agenda on aging / Committee on a National Research Agenda on Aging, Division of Health Promotion and Disease Prevention, Institute of Medicine ; Edmund T. Lonergan, editor. Washington, D.C. : National Academy Press, 1991. xii, 152 p. ;
91-002947     362.1/9897/0072073 0309043999
*Aging -- Research. Aging -- Research -- Government policy – United States.*

**QP86.K52 1999**
**Kirkwood, T. B. L.**
Time of our lives : the science of human aging / Tom Kirkwood. Oxford ; Oxford University Press, 1999. x, 277 p. :
98-046932     612.6/7     0195128249
*Aging -- Popular works.*

**QP86.K58 1978**
**Kohn, Robert Rothenberg,**
Principles of mammalian aging / Robert R. Kohn. Englewood Cliffs, N.J. : Prentice-Hall, c1978. xii, 240 p. :
77-020289     599/.03/72     0137093527
*Aging. Mammals -- Aging. Aging.*

**QP86.P3**
**Palmore, Erdman Ballagh,**
Normal aging; reports from the Duke longitudinal study, edited by Erdman Palmore. Durham, N.C., Duke University Press, 1970-74. 2 v.
74-132028     612.6/7     0822302381
*Aging.*

**QP86.R525 1995**
**Ricklefs, Robert E.**
Aging : a natural history / Robert E. Ricklefs, Caleb E. Finch. New York : Scientific American Library : c1995. xi, 209 p. :
95-002334     612.6/7     0716750562
*Aging -- Physiological aspects. Evolution (Biology)*

**QP86.R59 1991**
**Rose, Michael R.**
Evolutionary biology of aging / Michael R. Rose. New York : Oxford University Press, 1991. ix, 221 p. :
90-006787     574.3/72     0195061330
*Aging. Evolution. Aging.*

**QP86.S478 1997**
**Shephard, Roy J.**
Aging, physical activity, and health / Roy J. Shephard. Champaign, IL : Human Kinetics, c1997. viii, 488 p.
96-043852     613.7/0446     0873228898
*Aging. Physical fitness. Age factors in disease.*

**QP86.W287 1999**
**Warshofsky, Fred.**
Stealing time : the new science of aging / Fred Warshofsky. New York : TV Books, c1999. 247 p. :
00-709463     612.6/7     1575000458
*Aging. Longevity.*

**QP86.W45 1988**
**Weindruch, Richard.**
The retardation of aging and disease by dietary restriction / by Richard Weindruch and Roy L. Walford. Springfield, Ill., U.S.A. : C.C. Thomas, c1988. xvii, 436 p.
88-012288     612/.67     0398054967
*Aging -- Nutritional aspects. Low-calorie diet. Rats – Physiology.*

## QP87 Developmental physiology — Death

**QP87.I83 1993**
**Iserson, Kenneth V.**
Death to dust : what happens to dead bodies? / Kenneth V. Iserson. Tucson, AZ : Galen Press, c1993. p. cm.
93-039463     306.9     1883620074
*Death. Death (Biology) Cremation.*

## QP88 Physiology of the tissues (General) — General works

**QP88.B49**
Biochemical responses to environmental stress. Edited by I. A. Bernstein. New York, Plenum Press, 1971. xii, 153 p.
79-151618     612/.405     0306305313
*Homeostasis -- Congresses. Stress (Physiology) -- Congresses.*

**QP88.S63**
**Snively, William Daniel,**
Sea within; the story of our body fluid. Philadelphia, Lippincott [1960] 150 p.
60-012038          612.017
*Body fluids.*

**QP88.W5 1958**
**Willmer, E. N.**
Tissue culture; the growth and differentiation of normal tissues in artificial media. London, Methuen; [1958] 191 p.
58-003834          611.018
*Tissue culture. Cells.*

## QP88.2 Physiology of the tissues (General) — Bone

**QP88.2.S45 1985**
**Shipman, Pat,**
The human skeleton / Pat Shipman, Alan Walker, David Bichell. Cambridge, Mass. : Harvard University Press, 1985. x, 343 p. :
85-005497          612/.75          0674416104
*Bones. Human skeleton. Anthropometry.*

## QP88.5 Physiology of the tissues (General) — Skin

**QP88.5.B62 1993**
Black skin : structure and function / William Montagna, Giuseppe Prota, John A. Kenney, Jr. San Diego : Academic Press, 1993. xiii, 158 p.
93-014784          612.7/927          012505260X
*Skin -- Physiology. Blacks -- Physiology. Human skin color.*

**QP88.5.L37 1996**
**Lappe, Marc.**
The body's edge : our cultural obsession with skin / Marc Lappe. New York : H. Holt, 1996. xi, 242 p. ;
95-045978          612.7/9          0805042083
*Skin -- Physiology. Skin -- Anatomy. Skin -- Social aspects.*

## QP88.6 Physiology of the tissues (General) — Teeth

**QP88.6.D48 2000**
Development, function, and evolution of teeth / edited by Mark F. Teabord, Moya Meredith Smith and Mark W.J. Ferguson. New York, NY : Cambridge University Press, 2000. ix, 314 p. :
99-039565          573.3/56          0521570115
*Teeth -- Physiology. Teeth -- Evolution. Teeth -- Molecular aspects.*

## QP90.2 Regeneration

**QP90.2.T76 1996**
**Tsonis, Panagiotis A.**
Limb regeneration / Panagiotis A. Tsonis. Cambridge [England] ; Cambridge University Press, 1996. xii, 241 p. :
95-022051          596/.031          0521441498
*Extremities (Anatomy) -- Regeneration. Extremities – physiology. Regeneration.*

## QP90.4 Homeostasis

**QP90.4.L48 1996**
**Lewis, Jessica H.**
Comparative hemostasis in vertebrates / Jessica H. Lewis. New York : Plenum Press, c1996. xx, 426 p. :
95-043745          596/.0113          0306448416
*Hemostasis. Blood -- Coagulation. Physiology, Comparative.*

## QP91 Blood — General works

**QP91.H3 1963**
**Harris, John W.**
The red cell: production, metabolism, destruction, normal and abnormal. Cambridge, Mass. Published for the Commonwealth Fund by Harvard U 1963. xix, 482 p.
63-009076          612.111
*Erythrocytes. Blood -- Diseases.*

**QP91.P79 1961**
**Prankerd, T. A. J.**
The red cell; an account of its chemical physiology and pathology. Springfield, Ill., C.C. Thomas [1961] 184 p.
61-004632          612.111
*Erythrocytes.*

### QP93 Blood — Composition and chemistry — Coagulation

**QP93.D38 1974**
**Davenport, Horace Willard,**
The ABC of acid-base chemistry : the elements of physiological blood-gas chemistry for medical students and physicians / Horace W. Davenport. Chicago : University of Chicago Press, 1974. 124 p. :
73-090943          612/.015          0226137058
*Acid-base equilibrium. Blood -- Analysis.*

### QP98 Blood — Blood groups

**QP98.L38 1972**
**Lawler, Sylvia D.**
Human blood groups and inheritance [by] Sylvia D. Lawler and L. J. Lawler. With a foreword by R. R. Race. New York, St. Martin's Press [1972, c1971] x, 107 p.
79-183395          612/.11825
*Blood groups. Heredity.*

**QP98.R3 1975**
**Race, R. R.**
  Blood groups in man / R. R. Race and Ruth Sanger ; with a foreword by Sir Ronald Fisher. Oxford : Blackwell Scientific Publications ; 1975. xix, 659 p. :
75-330416        612/.11825        0632004312
  *Blood groups.*

## QP101.4 Cardiovascular system. Circulation — History of discovery and ideas on circulation. Harvey

**QP101.4.R37 1982**
**Rapson, Helen.**
  The circulation of blood : a history / Helen Rapson. London : F. Muller, 1982. 132 p., [10]
82-216952        612/.1/09        0584110138
  *Blood -- Circulation -- History. Blood.*

### QP105 Cardiovascular system. Circulation — Hemodynamics — General works

**QP105.D38 1991**
**Dawson, Thomas H.**
  Engineering design of the cardiovascular system of mammals / Thomas H. Dawson. Englewood Cliffs, N.J. : Prentice Hall, c1991. xii, 179 p. :
90-024190        599/.011        0132756943
  *Cardiovascular system. Bioengineering. Hemodynamics.*

### QP106.6 Cardiovascular system. Circulation — Systemic system — Microcirculation. Capillaries

**QP106.6.M5**
  Microcirculation / edited by Gabor Kaley and Burton M. Altura. Baltimore : University Park Press, c1977-c1980. 3 v. :
76-053805        596/.01/1        0839109660
  *Microcirculation. Microcirculation.*

## QP109 Cardiovascular system. Circulation — Vasomoter control. Baroreflexes

**QP109.R68 1993**
**Rowell, Loring B.**
  Human cardiovascular control / Loring B. Rowell. New York : Oxford University Press, 1993. xv, 500 p. :
92-016434        612.1/3        0195073622
  *Blood -- Circulation -- Regulation. Blood pressure – Regulation. Adaptation, Physiological.*

**QP121.C26 1989**
**Cameron, James N.**
  The respiratory physiology of animals / James N. Cameron. New York : Oxford University Press, 1989. viii, 353 p.
89-008795        591.1/2        0195060199
  *Respiration. Animals -- Physiology. Physiology, Comparative.*

### QP121 Heart — Respiration. Respiratory organs — General works, treatises, and textbooks

**QP121.D36 1981**
**Dejours, Pierre.**
  Principles of comparative respiratory physiology / Pierre Dejours. Amsterdam ; Elsevier/North-Holland Biomedical Press ; 1981. xvi, 265 p. :
81-004913        596/.012        0444802797
  *Respiration. Physiology, Comparative. Physiology, Comparative.*

**QP121.M378 1996**
**Matthews, L. R.**
  Cardiopulmonary anatomy and physiology / L.R. Matthews. Philadelphia : Lippincott, c1996. p. cm.
96-004884        612.2        0397549547
  *Cardiopulmonary system -- Physiology. Cardiopulmonary system -- Anatomy. Respiratory Mechanics -- physiology.*

**QP121.W395 1984**
**Weibel, Ewald R.**
  The pathway for oxygen : structure and function in the mammalian respiratory system / Ewald R. Weibel. Cambridge, Mass. : Harvard University Press, 1984. xv, 425 p. :
83-018622        612/.2        0674657918
  *Respiration. Oxygen in the body. Respiration.*

## QP135 Heart — Thermoregulation. Animal heat. Body temperature

**QP135.T485 1990**
  Thermoregulation : pathology, pharmacology, and therapy / specialist subject editors, E. Schonbaum and P. Lomax. New York : Pergamon Press, c1991. xxiv, 664 p.
89-037140        612/.01426        0080368530
  *Body temperature -- Regulation. Body temperature -- Effect of drugs on. Fever.*

## QP141 Nutrition — Societies, congresses, serial collections, yearbooks

**QP141.B52 1995**
**Berdanier, Carolyn D.**
  Advanced nutrition / Carolyn D. Berdanier ; illustrations by Toni Kathryn Adkins. Boca Raton : CRC Press, c1995-c1998. 2 v. :
94-011519        612.3/9        0849385008
  *Nutrition. Metabolism. Energy metabolism.*

**QP141.C5 1979**
**Chaney, Margaret Stella,**
  Nutrition / Margaret S. Chaney, Margaret L. Ross, Jelia C. Witschi. Boston : Houghton Mifflin, c1979. xi, 559 p. :
78-069546        613/.2        0395254485
  *Nutrition.*

**QP141.E526 1999**

Encyclopedia of human nutrition / editor-in-chief, Michele Sadler, editors, J.J. Strain, Benjamin Caballero. San Diego : Academic Press, c1999. 3 v. (xlix, 1
97-016267         612.3/03         0122266951
*Nutrition -- Encyclopedias. Dietetics -- Encyclopedias.*

**QP141.N48 1993**
**Newstrom, Harvey.**

Nutrients catalog : vitamins, minerals, amino acids, macronutrients--beneficial use, helpers, inhibitors, food sources, intake recommendations and symptoms of over or under use / by Harvey Newstrom. Jefferson, N.C. : McFarland & Company, c1993. xix, 538 p. ;
92-056671         613.2/8         0899507840
*Nutrition -- Handbooks, manuals, etc. Vitamins in human nutrition -- Handbooks, manuals, etc. Minerals in the body -- Handbooks, manuals, etc.*

**QP141.R535 1987**
**Robinson, David S.,**

Food : biochemistry and nutritional value / David S. Robinson. Harlow, Essex, England : Longman Scientific & Technical ; 1987. xvii, 554 p.
86-021522         641.1         0470207353
*Nutrition. Food -- Composition. Biochemistry.*

**QP141.W485 2000**
**Wildman, Robert E. C.,**

Advanced human nutrition / Robert E.C. Wildman, Denis M. Medeiros. Boca Raton : CRC Press, c2000. xviii, 585 p.
00-501620         612.3         0849385660
*Nutrition.*

**QP141.W513 1990**
**Willett, Walter.**

Nutritional epidemiology / Walter Willett. New York : Oxford University Press, 1990. vii, 396 p. :
89-009317         614.5/939         0195045017
*Nutrition -- Research -- Methodology. Nutrition surveys -- Methodology. Diet in disease -- Research -- Methodology.*

**QP141.B57 1999**

Biochemical and physiological aspects of human nutrition / [edited by] Martha H. Stipanuk. Philadelphia : W.B. Saunders, c2000. xxx, 1007 p.
98-013993         612.3/9         072164452X
*Nutrition. Energy metabolism. Exercise -- Physiological aspects.*

## QP143.4 Nutrition — Study and teaching. Research — Research techniques

**QP143.4.M66 1991**

Monitoring dietary intakes / Ian Macdonald, editor ; preface by Robert Kroes. Berlin ; Springer-Verlag, c1991. p. cm.
90-010410         612.3         0387196455
*Nutrition -- Research -- Methodology. Nutrition surveys -- Methodology. Nutrition.*

## QP144 Nutrition — Other special topics, A-Z

**QP144.R53.J85 1993**
**Juliano, Bienvenido O.**

Rice in human nutrition / prepared in collaboration with FAO by Bienvenido O. Juliano. Rome : Published with the cooperation of the Internatio 1993. vi, 162 p. :
94-219512         613.2/6         9251031495
*Rice in human nutrition.*

## QP171 Nutrition — Metabolism — General works

**QP171.M55 1998**

Molecular biochemical pathways : a comprehensive atlas / edited by Gerhard Michal. New York : John Wiley, 1998. p. cm.
98-033226         572.8/4         0471331309
*Metabolism -- Atlases.*

**QP171.S67 1961**
**Society of General Physiologists.**

Control mechanisms in respiration and fermentation; [papers by] Harlyn O. Halvorson [and others] Edited by Barbara Wright. New York, Ronald Press Co. [1963] vi, 357 p.
63-009287         612.39082
*Respiration -- Addresses, essays, lectures. Fermentation -- Addresses, essays, lectures.*

## QP187 Glands — Endocrinology. Endocrine glands — Societies, congresses, serial collections, yearbooks

**QP187.C5966 1983**

Comparative endocrinology / Aubrey Gorbman ... [et al.]. New York : Wiley, c1983. xvi, 572 p. :
82-013455         596/.0142         0471062669
*Endocrinology, Comparative.*

**QP187.G386**
**Gerontological Society.**

Endocrines and aging; a symposium presented before the Gerontological Society seventeenth annual meeting, Minneapolis, Minnesota. Compiled and edited by Leo Gitman. Springfield, Ill., Thomas [1968, c1967] xvi, 305 p.
66-018931         612/.4
*Endocrinology. Aging.*

**QP187.J4**
**Jenkin, Penelope M.**

Animal hormones; a comparative survey. With a foreword by John E. Harris. Oxford, Pergamon Press, 1962-[70] 2 v.
60-008977         591.1/927         0080156487
*Hormones.*

**QP187.M3458 1995**
**Martin, Constance R.**
   Dictionary of endocrinology and related biomedical sciences / Constance R. Martin. New York : Oxford University Press, 1995. 785 p. :
94-035299          612.4/03          0195060334
   *Endocrinology -- Dictionaries. Endocrinology -- dictionaries. Endocrine Diseases -- dictionaries.*

**QP187.S219**
**Sawin, Clark T.,**
   The hormones; endocrine physiology [by] Clark T. Sawin. Foreword by E. B. Astwood. Illus. by Barry T. O'Neil. Boston, Little, Brown [c1969] xviii, 308 p.
70-082930          612/.405          070000159X
   *Endocrinology.*

### QP249 Urinary and reproductive organs — Urinary organs — Kidneys

**QP249.L67 2000**
**Lote, Christopher J.**
   Principles of renal physiology / Chris Lote. Boston : Kluwer Academic Publishers, c2000. x, 203 p. :
99-052097          612.4/63          0792360745
   *Kidneys -- Physiology.*

**QP249.P57 1974**
**Pitts, Robert Franklin,**
   Physiology of the kidney and body fluids; an introductory text [by] Robert F. Pitts. 3d ed. Chicago, Year Book Medical Publishers [1974] xi, 315 p.
               612/.463          0815167024
*Kidneys. Body fluids.*

### QP251 Urinary and reproductive organs — Reproduction. Physiology of sex — General works, treatises, and textbooks

**QP251.C78 1985**
**Corea, Gena.**
   The mother machine : reproductive technologies from artificial insemination to artificial wombs / Gena Corea. New York : Harper & Row, c1985. x, 374 p. ;
84-048150          306.8/5          0060153903
   *Human reproduction -- Political aspects. Artificial insemination, Human -- Social aspects. Women's rights.*

**QP251.E43 2001**
**Ellison, Peter Thorpe.**
   On fertile ground / Peter T. Ellison. Cambridge, MA : Harvard University Press, 2001. 358 p. :
00-059688          612.6     0674004639
   *Human reproduction. Human evolution. Natural selection.*

**QP251.F7**
**Frazer, John Francis Deryk.**
   The sexual cycles of vertebrates.   London, Hutchinson University Library [1959] 168 p.
60002529          596
   *Vertebrates. Sex (Biology) Reproduction.*

**QP251.J27 1988**
**Jameson, E. W.**
   Vertebrate reproduction / E.W. Jameson, Jr. New York : Wiley, c1988. xi, 526 p. :
88-005891          596/.016          047162635X
   *Vertebrates -- Reproduction.*

**QP251.J636 1991**
**Jones, Richard E.**
   Human reproductive biology / Richard E. Jones. San Diego : Academic Press, c1991. xvii, 585 p.
90-014535          612.6          012389770X
   *Human reproduction. Sex. Reproduction -- physiology.*

**QP251.M35**
**Masters, William H.**
   Human sexual response [by] William H. Masters, research director [and] Virginia E. Johnson, research associate, the Reproductive Biology Research Foundation, St. Louis, Missouri. Boston, Little, Brown [1966] xiii, 366 p.
66018370          612.6          0316549878
   *Sex (Biology) Sex Behavior. Sex (Psychology)*

**QP251.M417 1994**
**Maxwell, Kenneth E.,**
   The sex imperative : an evolutionary tale of sexual survival / Kenneth Maxwell. New York : Plenum, c1994. viii, 324 p.
94-000096          575/.9          0306446499
   *Sex (Biology) -- Evolution.*

**QP251.P467 1999**
**Pfaff, Donald W.,**
   Drive : neurobiological and molecular mechanisms of sexual motivation / Donald W. Pfaff. Cambridge, Mass. : MIT Press, c1999. xvi, 312 p. :
98-043055          573.6          0262161842
   *Sex (Biology) Sexual excitement. Neuropsychology.*

**QP251.R4447 1987**
   Reproductive technologies : gender, motherhood, and medicine / edited by Michelle Stanworth. Minneapolis : University of Minnesota Press, c1987. 227 p. ;
87-019021          303.4/83          0816616450
   *Human reproductive technology -- Social aspects. Feminism. Reproduction.*

**QP251.R626 1988**
**Rosen, Raymond,**
   Patterns of sexual arousal : psychophysiological processes and clinical applications / Raymond C. Rosen and J. Gayle Beck ; foreword by James H. Geer. New York : Guilford Press, c1988. xii, 404 p. :
87-019726          155.3          0898627125
   *Sex (Psychology) Psychophysiology. Psychophysiology.*

**QP251.S485 1988**
**Shannon, Thomas A.**
 Religion and artificial reproduction : an inquiry into the Vatican "Instruction on respect for human life in its origin and on the dignity of human reproduction" / Thomas A. Shannon and Lisa Sowle Cahill. New York : Crossroad, 1988. ix, 201 p. ;
87-030576   241/.66   0824508602
 *Human reproductive technology -- Religious aspects -- Catholic Church.*

## QP259 Urinary and reproductive organs — Reproduction. Physiology of sex — Female sex physiology

**QP259.E45 1988**
**Elia, Irene.**
 The female animal / Irene Elia. New York : H. Holt, c1988. xv, 318 p. :
87-028714   155.6/463   0805007024
 *Reproduction. Females -- Physiology. Females -- Evolution.*

## QP278 Urinary and reproductive organs — Reproduction. Physiology of sex — Sex differentiation

**QP278.M66 1988**
**Money, John,**
 Gay, straight, and in-between : the sexology of erotic orientation / John Money. New York : Oxford University Press, 1988. viii, 267 p.
87-024751   155.3   0195054075
 *Sex differentiation. Sex determination, Genetic. Psychosexual disorders.*

## QP301 Musculoskeletal system. Movements — General works, treatises, and textbooks

**QP301.B48 1982**
 The Body at work : biological ergonomics / edited by W.T. Singleton. Cambridge [Cambridgeshire] ; Cambridge University Press, 1982. x, 430 p. :
81-018096   612/.044   0521240875
 *Work -- Physiological aspects. Kinesiology.*

**QP301.B88 1979**
**Broer, Marion Ruth.**
 Efficiency of human movement / Marion R. Broer, Ronald F. Zernicke. Philadelphia : Saunders, 1979. xi, 427 p. :
79-000125   612/.76   0721620884
 *Human mechanics. Human beings -- Attitude00 and movement. Kinesiology.*

**QP301.E9346 1999**
 Exercise and circulation in health and disease / edited by Bengt Saltin ... [et al.]. Champaign, IL : Human Kinetics, 1999. p. cm.
99-024144   612/.044   0880116323
 *Exercise -- Physiological aspects. Cardiovascular system -- Physiology. Blood -- Circulation.*

**QP301.I65 2000**
 Introduction to exercise science / editors, Terry J. Housh, Dona J. Housh. Boston, MA : Allyn and Bacon, c2000. xii, 290 p. :
99-047827   612/.044   0205291686
 *Exercise -- Physiological aspects. Sports -- Physiological aspects. Sports sciences.*

**QP301.L36 1993**
**Latash, Mark L.,**
 Control of human movement / Mark L. Latash. Chicago, IL : Human Kinetics Publishers, c1993. xi, 380 p. :
92-036991   152.3   0873224558
 *Motor learning. Human locomotion.*

**QP301.L364 1998**
**Latash, Mark L.,**
 Neurophysiological basis of movement / Mark L. Latash. Champaign, IL : Human Kinetics, c1998. x, 269 p. :
97-031920   612.7/6   0880117567
 *Locomotion. Neurophysiology. Motor ability.*

**QP301.L68**
**Lowman, Charles Leroy,**
 Postural fitness; significance and variances. [By] Charles LeRoy Lowman [and] Carl Haven Young. Philadelphia, Lea & Febiger, 1960. 341 p.
60007370   613.78
 *Exercise Therapy. Physical Fitness. Posture.*

**QP301.M1149 2000**
**McArdle, William D.**
 Essentials of exercise physiology / William D. McArdle, Frank I. Katch, Victor L. Katch. Philadelphia : Lippincott Williams & Wilkins, c2000. 679 p. :
99-048195   612/.044   0683305077
 *Human locomotion. Energy metabolism. Human mechanics.*

**QP301.M159 1999**
**Mackinnon, Laurel T.,**
 Advances in exercise immunology / Laurel T. Mackinnon. Champaign, IL : Human Kinetics, c1999. xii, 363 p. :
98-038797   616.07/9   0880115629
 *Exercise -- Immunological aspects. Exercise -- physiology. Immunity.*

**QP301.M38**
 Mechanics and energetics of animal locomotion / edited by R. McN. Alexander and G. Goldspink. London : Chapman and Hall ; 1977. xii, 346 p. :
77-006737   591.1/852   0470991852
 *Animal locomotion. Animal mechanics. Bioenergetics.*

**QP301.M83 1957**
**Muybridge, Eadweard,**
 Animals in motion. Edited by Lewis S. Brown. New York, Dover Publications [1957] 74 p.
57-004552   612.767
 *Human locomotion -- Pictorial works. Animal locomotion -- Pictorial works.*

**QP301.M85 1955**
**Muybridge, Eadweard,**
The human figure in motion. Introd. by Robert Taft. New York, Dover Publications [1955] xvii p., 195
55-013973          612/.76
*Human locomotion -- Pictorial works.*

**QP301.P554 1994**
Physical activity, fitness, and health : international proceedings and consensus statement / Claude Bouchard, Roy J. Shephard, Thomas Stephens editors. Champaign, IL : Human Kinetics Publishers, c1994. xxiv, 1055 p.
93-038996          613.7          0873225228
*Exercise -- Physiological aspects -- Congresses. Physical fitness – Congresses. Health -- Congresses.*

**QP301.P57 1995**
Physiological assessment of human fitness / [edited by] Peter J. Maud, Carl Foster. Champaign, IL : Human Kinetics, c1995. vi, 296 p. :
94-040072          613.7/028/7          087322776X
*Exercise -- Physiological aspects. Physical fitness -- Testing. Exercise tests.*

**QP301.S468 1994**
**Shephard, Roy J.**
Aerobic fitness & health / Roy J. Shephard. Champaign, IL : Human Kinetics Publishers, c1994. x, 358 p. :
93-000457          613.7          0873224175
*Physical fitness. Exercise. Health.*

**QP301.S48 1977**
**Shephard, Roy J.**
Endurance fitness / Roy J. Shephard. Toronto : University of Toronto Press, c1977. xiv, 380 p. :
76-023257          613.7          0802022502
*Physical fitness. Exercise -- Physiological aspects.*

**QP301.S49**
**Shephard, Roy J.**
Human physiological work capacity / R. J. Shephard. Cambridge, [Eng.] ; Cambridge University Press, 1978. xiii, 303 p.
77-080847          612/.042          0521217814
*Work -- Physiological aspects. Human biology.*

**QP301.W34 1999**
**Watkins, James,**
Structure and function of the musculoskeletal system / James Watkins. Champaign, IL : Human Kinetics, c1999. viii, 367 p.
98-027930          612.7          0880116862
*Musculoskeletal system -- Physiology. Musculoskeletal system – Anatomy. Human mechanics.*

## QP303 Musculoskeletal system. Movements — Mechanics. Kinesiology

**QP303.B586 1997**
The biophysical foundations of human movement / Bruce Abernethy ... [et al.]. Champaign, IL : Human Kinetics, c1997. x, 425 p. :
96-050009          612.7/6          088011732X
*Human mechanics. Biophysics.*

**QP303.B87 1998**
**Burton, Allen William,**
Movement skill assessment / Allen W. Burton with Daryl E. Miller. Champaign, IL : Human Kinetics, c1998. vii, 407 p. :
97-021938          612.7/6/0287          0873229754
*Motor ability -- Testing. Movement disorders -- Diagnosis.*

**QP303.D48 1996**
Dexterity and its development / edited by Mark L. Latash, Michael T. Turvey. Mahwah, N.J. : L. Erlbaum Associates, 1996. x, 460 p. :
95-038131          612.7/6          0805816461
*Motor ability.*

**QP303.H389**
**Hay, James G.,**
The anatomical and mechanical bases of human motion / James G. Hay, J. Gavin Reid. Englewood Cliffs, N.J. : Prentice-Hall, c1982. xv, 443 p. :
81-008601          612/.76          0130351393
*Human mechanics. Kinesiology.*

**QP303.K59 1997**
**Knudson, Duane V.,**
Qualitative analysis of human movement / Duane V. Knudson, Craig S. Morrison. Champaign, IL : Human Kinetics, c1997. ix, 204 p. :
96-048347          612.7/6          0880115238
*Kinesiology.*

**QP303.N55 1996**
**Noble, Bruce J.**
Perceived exertion / Bruce J. Noble, Robert J. Robertson. Champaign, IL : Human Kinetics, c1996. xv, 320 p. :
96-000374          612/.044/019          0880115084
*Kinesiology. Muscle contraction -- Regulation. Muscular sense.*

**QP303.Z38 1998**
**Zatsiorsky, Vladimir M.,**
Kinematics of human motion / Vladimir M. Zatsiorsky. Champaign, IL : Human Kinetics, c1998. xi, 419 p. :
97-012025          612.7/6          0880116765
*Human mechanics. Kinematics. Human locomotion.*

**QP303.B56836 2000**
Biomechanics and biology of movement / Benno M. Nigg, Brian R. MacIntosh, Joachim Mester, editors. Champaign, Ill. : Human Kinetics, c2000. xvii, 465 p.
99-059795          612.7/6          0736003312
*Human mechanics. Human locomotion. Exercise – Physiological aspects.*

## QP306 Musculoskeletal system. Movements — Voice and speech. Larynx

**QP306.B28 1999**
Barlow, Steven M.
Handbook of clinical speech physiology / Steven M. Barlow ; with collaborators, Richard D. Andreatta ... [et al.]. San Diego : Singular Pub. Group, c1999. xvii, 384 p.
98-043441        616.85/5        1565932676
*Speech -- Physiological aspects -- Handbooks, manuals, etc. Speech disorders -- Handbooks, manuals, etc. Speech –physiology.*

**QP306.F8 1979**
Fry, Dennis Butler.
The physics of speech / D. B. Fry. Cambridge [Eng.] ; Cambridge University Press, 1979. 148 p. :
78-056752        612/.78        0521221730.
*Speech. Sound-waves.*

**QP306.J83**
Judson, Lyman Spicer.
Voice science, by Lyman Spicer Judson and Andrew Thomas Weaver. New York, Appleton-Century-Crofts [1942] xvii, 377 p.
42004217        612.789
*Voice. Speech. Voice.*

**QP306.K3 1971**
Kaplan, Harold Morris,
Anatomy and physiology of speech [by] Harold M. Kaplan. 2d ed. New York, McGraw-Hill [1971] x, 528 p.
        612/.78        0070332827
*Speech -- Physiological aspects.*

## QP309 Musculoskeletal system. Movements — Work physiology

**QP309.G7313 1997**
Kroemer, K.H.E.,
Fitting the task to the human : a textbook of occupational ergonomics / by K.H.E. Kroemer and E. Grandjean. 5th ed. London ; Bristol, PA : Taylor & Francis, c1997. x, 416 p. :
        612/.042 21        0748406646
*Work -- Physiological aspects. Human mechanics. Human engineering. Industrial hygiene.*

## QP310 Musculoskeletal system. Movements — Other special movements, A-Z

**QP310.D35.L39 1984**
Laws, Kenneth.
The physics of dance / Kenneth Laws ; photographs by Martha Swope. New York : Schirmer Books, c1984. xv, 160 p. :
83-020462        792.8/01        002872030X
*Dance -- Physiological aspects. Ballet dancing -- Physiological aspects. Human mechanics.*

**QP310.F5.W37 1984**
Ward-Smith, A. J.
Biophysical aerodynamics and the natural environment / A.J. Ward-Smith. Chichester [West Sussex] ; Wiley, c1984. x, 172 p. :
84-011870        591.1/852        0471904368
*Animal flight. Biophysics. Aerodynamics.*

**QP310.R85.B56 1990**
Biomechanics of distance running / Peter R. Cavanagh, [editor]. Champaign, IL : Human Kinetics Books, c1990. ix, 362 p. :
89-029302        612/.044        0873222687
*Running -- Physiological aspects. Biomechanics.*

## QP310.5 Musculoskeletal system. Movements — Miscellany and curiosa

**QP310.5.I53 1986**
Inactivity : physiological effects / edited by Harold Sandler, Joan Vernikos. Orlando : Academic Press, 1986. xiv, 205 p. :
86-010937        612        0126185107
*Hypokinesia -- Physiological effect. Stress (Physiology) Exertion.*

## QP321 Musculoskeletal system. Movements — Muscle — General works

**QP321.M3376 1996**
McComas, Alan J.
Skeletal muscle : form and function / Alan J. McComas. Champaign, IL : Human Kinetics, c1996. xiv, 401 p. :
95-024525        612.7/4        0873227808
*Striated muscle -- Physiology. Muscle, Skeletal -- physiology. Neuromuscular Junction -- physiology.*

## QP327 Musculoskeletal system. Movements — By region — Face

**QP327.F75 1994**
Fridlund, Alan J.
Human facial expression : an evolutionary view / Alan J. Fridlund. San Diego : Academic Press, c1994. xiv, 369 p. :
94-002020        153.6/9        0122676300
*Facial expression. Face -- Evolution.*

## QP331 Musculoskeletal system. Movements — By region — Spine

**QP331.E3**
Eccles, John C.
The physiology of nerve cells. Baltimore, Johns Hopkins Press, 1957. 270 p.
57-007108        612.822
*Neurons.*

## QP334 Musculoskeletal system. Movements — By region — Upper extremities

**QP334.H36 1996**
Hand and brain : the neurophysiology and psychology of hand movements / edited by Alan M. Wing, Patrick Haggard, J. Randall Flanagan. San Diego : Academic Press, c1996. xx, 513 p. :
96-005965          612.8          012759440X
*Hand -- Movements. Muscular sense.*

**QP334.W53 1998**
**Wilson, Frank R.**
The hand : how its use shapes the brain, language, and human culture / Frank R. Wilson. New York : Pantheon Books, c1998. xiv, 397 p. :
97-046427          612/.91          0679412492
*Hand -- Physiology.*

# QP341 Electrophysiology

**QP341.P4713 1992**
**Pera, Marcello,**
The ambiguous frog : the Galvani-Volta controversy on animal electricity / Marcello Pera ; translated by Jonathan Mandelbaum. Princeton, N.J. : Princeton University Press, c1992. xxvi, 203 p.
91-003077          591.19/127          0691085129
*Galvani, Luigi, -- 1737-1798. Volta, Alessandro, -- 1745-1827. Elecrophysiology -- History.*

# QP351 Neurophysiology and neuropsychology — Societies, congresses, serial collections, yearbooks

**QP351.C6**
The central nervous system and behavior; transactions. 1st- 1958- [Madison, N.J.] v.
59005052          131.06373
*Behavior Psychophysiology -- Congresses. Central nervous system.*

# QP353 Neurophysiology and neuropsychology — History

**QP353.F548 2000**
**Finger, Stanley.**
Minds behind the brain : a history of the pioneers and their discoveries / Stanley Finger. Oxford ; Oxford University Press, c2000. xii, 364 p. :
99-017110          612.8/2/09          019508571X
*Neurosciences -- History. Brain -- Research -- History.*

**QP353.M367 1998**
**Marshall, Louise H.,**
Discoveries in the human brain : neuroscience prehistory, brain structure, and function / Louise H. Marshall and Horace W. Magoun. Totowa, N.J. : Humana Press, c1998. xi, 322 p. :
97-042118          612.8/09          0896034356
*Neurosciences -- History. Brain. Neurosciences -- history.*

# QP355 Neurophysiology and neuropsychology — General works, treatises, and textbooks — 1801-1969

**QP355.B83 1956**
**Brunswik, Egon,**
Perception and the representative design of psychologicl experiments. Berkeley, University of California Press, 1956. xii, 154 p.
56006984          150.72
*Psychophysiology.*

**QP355.M6 1965**
**Morgan, Clifford Thomas.**
Physiological psychology [by] Clifford T. Morgan. New York, McGraw-Hill [c1965] vii, 627 p.
64-022196          131
*Psychophysiology.*

**QP355.S57**
**Skinner, B. F.**
The behavior of organisms; an experimental analysis, by B. F. Skinner ... New York, D. Appleton-Century Company, incorporated [c1938] ix, 457 p.
38029912          150
*Rats. Psychophysiology.*

**QP355.T45**
**Thompson, Richard F.**
Foundations of physiological psychology [by] Richard F. Thompson. New York, Harper & Row [1967] xxviii, 688 p
67-016705          152
*Psychophysiology.*

# QP355.2 Neurophysiology and neuropsychology — General works, treatises, and textbooks — 1970-

**QP355.2.M33 1990**
**MacKay, Donald MacCrimmon,**
Behind the eye / Donald MacCrimmon MacKay ; edited by Valerie MacKay. Oxford, UK ; B. Blackwell, 1991. xi, 291 p. :
90-000201          612.8/2          0631173323
*Brain. Neurology. Brain -- physiology -- essays.*

**QP355.2.P37 1993**
**Partridge, Lloyd D.,**
The nervous system : its function and its interaction with the world / Lloyd D. Partridge and L. Donald Partridge. Cambridge, Mass. : MIT Press, c1993. x, 579 p. :
92-006225          591.1/88          0262161346
*Neurophysiology. Nervous System -- physiology.*

**QP355.2.U88**
**Uttal, William R.**
 Cellular neurophysiology and integration : an interpretive introduction / William R. Uttal. Hillsdale, N.J. : L. Erlbaum Associates ; 1975. xviii, 310 p.
75-004673      612/.8      0470896558
 *Neurophysiology. Neurons. Neurophysiology.*

## QP356 Neurophysiology and neuropsychology —Special aspects of the subject as whole

**QP356.B345 1997**
**Ballard, Dana Harry.**
 An introduction to natural computation / Dana H. Ballard. Cambridge, Mass. : MIT Press, c1997. xxii, 307 p.
96-044545      573.8/6/011363      0262024209
 *Brain -- Computer simulation.*

**QP356.B35 1961**
**Beach, Frank Ambrose,**
 Hormones and behavior, a survey of interrelationships between endocrine secretions and patterns of overt response. With a foreword by Earl T. Engle. New York, Cooper Square Publishers, 1961 [c1948] 368 p.
61008158      612.405
 *Hormones. Psychophysiology.*

**QP356.C48 1992**
**Churchland, Patricia Smith.**
 The computational brain / Patricia S. Churchland and Terrence J. Sejnowski. Cambridge, Mass. : MIT Press, c1992. xi, 544 p. :
91-028056      612.8/2/0113      0262031884
 *Brain -- Computer simulation. Neural networks (Neurobiology) Brain -- physiology.*

**QP356.F5**
**Fisher, Seymour.**
 Body image and personality, by Seymour Fisher and Sidney E. Cleveland. Princeton, N.J., Van Nostrand [1958] xi, 420 p.
58-008611      616.8
 *Personality. Psychophysiology. Body image.*

**QP356.Y68 1999**
**Simmons, Peter J. (Peter John),**
 Nerve cells and animal behaviour / Peter Simmons and David Young. 2nd ed. Cambridge, U.K.    ; New York Cambridge University Press, 1999. x, 266 p. :
     573.8/6 21      0521622166
*Neurobiology. Neurons. Animal behavior. Neurophysiology.*

## QP356.15 Neurophysiology and neuropsychology — Comparative neurobiology

**QP356.15.N45 1990**
 Neurobiology of comparative cognition / edited by Raymond P. Kesner, David S. Olton. Hillsdale, N.J. : L. Erlbaum Associates, 1990. xii, 476 p. :
89-025908      156/.34      0805801332
 *Comparative neurobiology. Cognitive science.*

## QP356.2 Neurophysiology and neuropsychology — Molecular neurobiology

**QP356.2.R49 1998**
**Revest, Patricia.**
 Molecular neuroscience / P. Revest, A. Longstaff. New York : Springer, 1998. p. cm.
98-017627      612.8      0387915192
 *Molecular neurobiology.*

## QP356.25 Neurophysiology and neuropsychology — Developmental neurophysiology

**QP356.25.P87 1994**
**Purves, Dale.**
 Neural activity and the growth of the brain / Dale Purves. Cambridge [England] ; Cambridge University Press, 1994. xiii, 108 p.,
93-034582      612.8/2      0521454964
 *Brain -- Growth. Neuroplasticity. Neural circuitry.*

**QP356.25.V55 1999**
**Willott, James F.**
 Neurogerontology : aging and the nervous system / James F. Willott. New York, NY : Springer Pub. Co., c1999. xi, 369 p.
98-043500      612.8      0826112595
 *Nervous system -- Aging. Geriatric neurology. Neuropsychology.*

## QP356.3 Neurophysiology and neuropsychology — Neurochemistry. Brain chemistry

**QP356.3.A37 vol. 8**
 Magnetic resonance spectroscopy and imaging in neurochemistry / edited by Herman Bachelard. New York : Plenum Press, c1997. xxii, 413 p.,
97-015443      573.8/419 s      030645520X
 *Brain -- Magnetic resonance imaging. Nuclear magnetic resonance spectroscopy. Brain -- Diseases -- Diagnosis.*

**QP356.3.K3**
**Katz, Bernard,**
Nerve, muscle, and synapse [by] Bernard Katz. New York, McGraw-Hill [1966] ix, 193 p.
66-014815          591.1/8
*Neurochemistry. Electrophysiology. Muscles.*

## QP356.4 Neurophysiology and neuropsychology — Neuroendocrinology

**QP356.4.H685 1993**
Hormonally induced changes in mind and brain / edited by Jay Schulkin. San Diego : Academic Press, c1993. xxi, 407 p. :
93-009947          612.8/22          012631330X
*Neuroendocrinology. Psychoneuroendocrinology. Behavior – physiology.*

## QP356.45 Neurophysiology and neuropsychology — Psychoneuroendocrinology

**QP356.45.H43 1990**
The Healing brain : a scientific reader / edited by Robert Ornstein, Charles Swencionis. New York : Guilford Press, 1990. x, 262 p. :
89-016968          612          0898623944
*Psychoneuroendocrinology. Healing. Mind and body.*

**QP356.45.S38 1999**
**Schulkin, Jay.**
The neuroendocrine regulation of behavior / Jay Schulkin. Cambridge, UK ; Cambridge University Press, 1999. x, 323 p. :
97-041739          612.8          0521453852
*Psychoneuroendocrinology. Steroid hormones -- Physiological effect. Neuropeptides -- Physiological effect.*

## QP356.47 Neurophysiology and neuropsychology — Neuroimmunology

**QP356.47.I46 1997**
Immunology of the nervous system / edited by Robert W. Keane, William F. Hickey. New York : Oxford University Press, 1997. xxii, 824 p.
96-024678          612.8          0195078179
*Neuroimmunology. Nervous system -- Diseases – Immunological aspects. Nervous System -- immunology.*

## QP357.5 Neurophysiology and neuropsychology —Laboratory manuals

**QP357.5.K63 1998**
**Koch, Christof.**
Biophysics of computation : information processing in single neurons / by Christof Koch. New York : Oxford University Press, 1998. p. cm.
97-051390          573.8/536          0195104919
*Computational neuroscience. Neurons. Neural networks (Neurobiology)*

## QP360 Neurophysiology and neuropsychology — Neuropsycology. Physiological psychology. Psychophysiology — General works

**QP360.B577 1996**
The Blackwell dictionary of neuropsychology / edited by J. Graham Beaumont, Pamela M. Kenealy, and Marcus Rogers. Cambridge, Mass. : Blackwell Publishers, 1996. xix, 788 p. :
95-017884          612.8/03          0631178961
*Neuropsychology -- Dictionaries. Neuropsychology -- dictionaries.*

**QP360.C34 1984**
**Camhi, Jeffrey M.,**
Neuroethology : nerve cells and the natural behavior of animals / Jeffrey M. Camhi. Sunderland, Mass. : Sinauer Associates, c1984. xv, 416 p. :
83-014957          591.5/1          0878930752
*Neuropsychology. Animal behavior. Behavior, Animal.*

**QP360.C347 2000**
**Carew, Thomas J.**
Behavioral neurobiology : the cellular organization of natural behavior / Thomas J. Carew. Sunderland, Mass. : Sinauer Associates Publishers, c2000. ix, 435 p. :
00-057348          573.8/6          0878930841
*Neuropsychology -- Popular works. Brain -- Popular works. Neurochemistry -- Popular works.*

**QP360.D52 2001**
Dictionary of biological psychology / edited by Philip Winn. New York : Routledge, 2001. p. cm.
00-059241          612.8/03          0415136067
*Neuropsychology. Brain -- Sex differences. Sex differences (Psychology)*

**QP360.G38**
**Gazzaniga, Michael S.**
Handbook of psychobiology / edited by Michael S. Gazzaniga, Colin Blakemore. New York : Academic Press, 1975. xvi, 639 p. :
74-010193          596/.01/88          0122786564
*Psychobiology.*

**QP360.H34 1993**
**Harth, Erich.**
   The creative loop : how the brain makes a mind / Erich Harth. Reading, Mass. : Addison-Wesley, c1993. xxv, 196 p. :
93-022829                 612.8/2                 0201570793
   *Brain. Mind and body. Mind-brain identity theory.*

**QP360.K454 1995**
**Kelso, J. A. Scott.**
   Dynamic patterns : the self-organization of brain and behavior / J.A. Scott Kelso. Cambridge, Mass. : MIT Press, c1995. xvii, 334 p.,
94-032105                 612.8                 0262112000
   *Neuropsychology. Self-organizing systems.*

**QP360.L4926 1993**
**LeVay, Simon.**
   The sexual brain / Simon LeVay. Cambridge, Mass. : MIT Press, c1993. xvi, 168 p. ;
92-044691                 155.3/3                 0262121786
   *Neuropsychology. Brain -- Sex differences. Sex.*

**QP360.N4958 1994**
   The neuropsychology of individual differences / [edited by] Philip A. Vernon. San Diego : Academic Press, c1994. xiv, 272 p. :
94-007647                 612.8                 0127186700
   *Neuropsychology. Personality -- Physiological aspects. Individual differences -- Physiological aspects.*

**QP360.R37 2001**
**Ratey, John J.,**
   A user's guide to the brain : perception, attention, and the four theaters of the brain / John J. Ratey. New York : Pantheon Books, c2001. 404 p. :
98-027796                 612.8/2                 0679453091
   *Neuropsychology -- Popular works. Brain -- Popular works. Neurochemistry -- Popular works.*

**QP360.R628 2001**
**Rogers, Lesley J.**
   Sexing the brain / Lesley Rogers. New York : Columbia University Press, 2001. p. cm.
00-060255                 612.8/2                 0231120109
   *Psychobiology.*

**QP360.S63 1983**
**Sperry, Roger Wolcott,**
   Science and moral priority : merging mind, brain, and human values / Roger Sperry. New York : Columbia University Press, 1983. xiv, 150 p. ;
81-024206                 174/.95                 0231054068
   *Neuropsychology -- Philosophy. Ethics. Intellect.*

**QP360.T39 1979**
**Taylor, Gordon Rattray.**
   The natural history of the mind / Gordon Rattray Taylor. New York : Dutton, 1979. xii, 370 p. :
79-088891                 152                 0525164243
   *Neuropsychology. Brain. Mind and body.*

**QP360.W64 1997**
**Woodruff-Pak, Diana S.,**
   The neuropsychology of aging / Diana S. Woodruff-Pak. Cambridge, Mass. : Blackwell, 1997. p. cm.
96-037330                 612.8                 1557864543
   *Brain -- Aging. Neuropsychology. Geriatric neurology.*

**QP360.5 Neurophysiology and neuropsychology —
Neuropsycology. Physiological psychology.
Psychophysiology — Cognitive neuroscience**

**QP360.5.C643 1995**
   The new cognitive neurosciences / Michael S. Gazzaniga, editor-in-chief ; section editors, Emilio Bizzi ... [et al.]. Cambridge, Mass. : MIT Press, c1995. xiv, 1447 p.,
93-040288                 153                 0262071576
   *Cognitive neuroscience. Brain -- physiology. Cognition -- physiology.*

**QP360.5.H357 2001**
   The handbook of cognitive neuropsychology : what deficits reveal about the human mind / [edited by] Brenda Rapp. Philadelphia : Psychology Press, c2001. p. cm.
00-042545                 612.8/2                 0863775926
   *Cognitive neuroscience -- Handbooks, manuals, etc. Neuropsychology -- Handbooks, manuals, etc.*

**QP360.5.P56 1997**
**Pinker, Steven,**
   How the mind works / Steven Pinker. New York : Norton, c1997. xii, 660 p. ;
97-001855                 153                 0393045358
   *Cognitive neuroscience. Neuropsychology. Natural selection.*

**QP360.5.P67 1994**
**Posner, Michael I.**
   Images of mind / Michael I. Posner, Marcus E. Raichle. New York : Scientific American Library, c1994. ix, 257 p. :
93-049413                 612.8/2                 0716750457 ;
   *Cognitive neuroscience. Neural networks (Neurobiology) Brain – Localization of functions.*

**QP360.5.S28 2001**
**Satinover, Jeffrey,**
   The quantum brain : the search for freedom and the next generation of man / Jeffrey Satinover. New York : J. Wiley, c2001. xii, 276 p. :
00-033020                 612.8/2                 0471333263
   *Cognitive neuroscience. Quantum theory. Brain -- Philosophy.*

**QP361 Neurophysiology and neuropsychology —
Neuropsycology. Physiological psychology.
Psychophysiology — Nervous system — General
works, treatises, and textbooks**

**QP361.C57**
**Clarke, Edwin.**
The human brain and spinal cord; a historical study
illustrated by writings from antiquity to the twentieth century
[by] Edwin Clarke and C. D. O'Malley. Berkeley, University
of California Press, 1968. xiii, 926 p.
68-011275          612/.82/08
*Central nervous system.*

**QP361.E3**
**Eccles, John C.**
The neurophysiological basis of mind; the principles of
neurophysiology. Oxford, Clarendon Press, 1953. 314 p.
53002728          131.2
*Nervous system. Neurophysiology Psychophysiology*

**QP361.G43**
**Gellhorn, Ernst,**
Physiological foundations of neurology and psychiatry.
Minneapolis, University of Minnesota Press [1953] xiii, 556 p.
53005940          612.8
*Nervous system. Nervous system. Neurophysiology.*

**QP361.N37 1988**
**Nathan, Peter Wilfred.**
The nervous system / Peter Nathan. 3rd ed. Oxford ; New
York : Oxford University Press, 1988. xv, 383 p. :
          612/.8 19          0192821520
*Nervous system.*

**QP361.O874 1983**
**Ottoson, David,**
Physiology of the nervous system / by David Ottoson. New
York : Oxford University Press, 1983. xiv, 527 p. :
82-014171          612/.8          0195204093
*Neurophysiology. Nervous system -- Physiology.*

**QP363 Neuropsycology. Physiological psychology.
Psychophysiology — Nervous system —
Miscellaneous general functions**

**QP363.F35 1999**
**Fain, Gordon L.**
Molecular and cellular physiology of neurons / Gordon L.
Fain. Cambridge, Mass. : Harvard University Press, 1999. x,
693 p. :
98-044886          573.8/536          0674581555
*Neurons. Neurophysiology. Molecular neurobiology.*

**QP363.P87 1988**
**Purves, Dale.**
Body and brain : a trophic theory of neural connections /
Dale Purves. Cambridge, Mass. : Harvard University Press,
1988. 231 p. :
88-000764          599/.0188          0674077156
*Neural networks (Neurobiology) Nervous system -- Growth.
Neuroplasticity.*

**QP363.3 Neurophysiology and neuropsychology —
Nervous system — Neural circuitry. Neural networks**

**QP363.3.A534 1995**
**Anderson, James A.**
An introduction to neural networks / James A. Anderson.
Cambridge, Mass. : MIT Press, c1995. xi, 650 p. :
94-030749          612.8          0262011441
*Neural networks (Neurobiology)*

**QP363.3.H36 1995**
The handbook of brain theory and neural networks / edited
by Michael A. Arbib ; editorial advisory board, George
Adelman ... [et al.] ; editorial assistant, Prudence H. Arbib.
Cambridge, Mass. : MIT Press, c1995. xv, 1118 p. :
94-044408          612.8/2          0262011484
*Neural networks (Neurobiology) -- Handbooks, manuals, etc.
Neural networks (Computer science) -- Handbooks, manuals, etc.*

**QP363.3.H67 1997**
**Hoppensteadt, F. C.**
An introduction to the mathematics of neurons : modeling in
the frequency domain / Frank C. Hoppensteadt. Cambridge,
U.K. ; Cambridge University Press, 1997. xx, 211 p. :
96-036822          573.8/536/0151          0521590752
*Neurons -- Mathematical models. Neural circuitry --
Mathematical models.*

**QP363.3.S55 1999**
**Spitzer, Manfred.**
The mind within the net : models of learning, thinking, and
acting / Manfred Spitzer. Cambridge, Mass : The MIT Press,
c1999. xiv, 359 p. :
98-010911          612.8/2          0262194066
*Neural networks (Neurobiology)*

**QP363.3.V35 1994**
**Valiant, Leslie.**
Circuits of the mind / Leslie G. Valiant. New York : Oxford
University Press, 1994. xiii, 237 p.
94-020869          612.8/2          019508926X
*Neural networks (Neurobiology)*

## QP376-426 Neurophysiology and neuropsychology — Nervous system — Central nervous system

**QP376.A23 1992**
**Ackerman, Sandra.**
   Discovering the brain / Sandra Ackerman for the Institute of Medicine, National Academy of Sciences. Washington, D.C. : National Academy Press, 1992. vii, 180 p. :
92-001231      612.8/2      0309045290
   *Neurology. Neurobiology. Brain.*

**QP376.A423 1999**
**Allman, John Morgan.**
   Evolving brains / John Morgan Allman. New York : Scientifc American Library : c1999. xi, 224 p. :
98-037576      573.8/6      0716750767
   *Brain -- Evolution.*

**QP376.C318 1994**
**Calvin, William H.,**
   Conversations with Neil's brain : the neural nature of thought and language / William H. Calvin, George A. Ojemann. Reading, Mass. : Addison-Wesley Pub. Co., c1994. 343 p. :
93-023661      153      0201632179
   *Brain. Consciousness. Brain -- Surgery.*

**QP376.C496 1995**
**Churchland, Paul M.,**
   The engine of reason, the seat of the soul : a philosophical journey into the brain / Paul M. Churchland. Cambridge, Mass. : MIT Press, c1995. xii, 329 p. :
94-030750      612.8/2/01      0262032244
   *Brain -- Philosophy. Neurosciences -- Philosophy. Cognition.*

**QP376.C59 1988**
**Cohen, Gene D.**
   The brain in human aging / Gene D. Cohen. New York : Springer Pub. Co., c1988. xi, 260 p. :
88-039679      612/.82      0826158307
   *Brain -- Aging. Alzheimer's disease. Aging.*

**QP376.C68 1990**
**Coward, L. Andrew.**
   Pattern thinking / L. Andrew Coward. New York : Praeger, 1990. xi, 180 p. :
89-016377      612.8/2      0275934276
   *Brain -- Physiology. Thought and thinking. Brain -- Computer simulation.*

**QP376.D38 1997**
**Davis, Joel,**
   Mapping the mind : the secrets of the human brain and how it works / Joel Davis. Secaucus, N.J. : Carol Pub. Group, c1997. x, 289 p. :
95-047834      612.8/2      1559723440
   *Brain -- Popular works. Neuropsychology -- Popular works.*

**QP376.E258 1989**
**Eccles, John C.**
   Evolution of the brain : creation of the self / John C. Eccles. London ; Routledge, 1989. xv, 282 p. :
88-024012      152      0415026008
   *Brain -- Evolution. Human evolution. Brain -- physiology.*

**QP376.E265**
**Eccles, John C.**
   The human mystery / John C. Eccles. Berlin ; Springer-Verlag, 1979. xvi, 255 p. :
78-012095      573      0387090169
   *Brain. Life -- Origin. Human evolution.*

**QP376.E27 1977**
**Eccles, John C.**
   The understanding of the brain / John C. Eccles. New York : McGraw-Hill, c1977. xii, 244 p. :
76-014941      612/.82      0070188653
   *Brain. Brain -- Physiology. Neurophysiology.*

**QP376.G69**
**Granit, Ragnar,**
   The purposive brain / Ragnar Granit. Cambridge, Mass. : Mit Press, c1977. x, 244 p. :
77-002347      152.3      0262070693
   *Brain. Neurophysiology. Neurophysiology -- Philosophy.*

**QP376.H292 1990**
**Harth, Erich.**
   Dawn of a millennium : beyond evolution and culture / Erich Harth. Boston : Little, Brown, c1990. 190 p. ;
89-012462      573.2      0316348511
   *Brain -- Evolution. Human evolution. Neurobiology -- Philosophy.*

**QP376.H4 1963**
**Herrick, C. Judson**
   Brains of rats and men; a survey of the origin and biological significance of the cerebral cortex. New York, Hafner Pub. Co., 1963. xviii, 382 p.
63-018168      596.048
   *Cerebral cortex. Rats -- Behavior. Psychology, Comparative.*

**QP376.J36**
**Jastrow, Robert,**
   The enchanted loom : mind in the universe / Robert Jastrow. New York : Simon and Schuster, c1981. 183 p. :
81-013532      153      0671433083
   *Intellect -- Evolution. Brain -- Evolution. Human evolution.*

**QP376.K65**
**Konorski, Jerzy.**
   Integrative activity of the brain; an interdisciplinary approach. Chicago, University of Chicago Press [1967] xii, 531 p.
67-016776      612/.82
   *Brain. Conditioned response.*

**QP376.M28 1963**
**Magoun, Horace Winchell,**
  The waking brain. Springfield, Ill., Thomas [1963] 188 p.
62-021324          612.821
  *Brain.*

**QP376.M525**
**Meltzer, Herbert L.,**
  The chemistry of human behavior / Herbert L. Meltzer ; ill. by Francesca de Majo. Chicago : Nelson-Hall, c1979. viii, 261 p.
77-019195          612/.82          0882291777
  *Brain chemistry. Human behavior.*

**QP376.O76 1984**
**Ornstein, Robert E.**
  The amazing brain / Robert Ornstein and Richard F. Thompson ; illustrated by David Macaulay. Boston : Houghton Mifflin, 1984. 182 p. :
84-012907          612/.82          0395354862
  *Brain.*

**QP376.P39**
**Penfield, Wilder,**
  The mystery of the mind : a critical study of consciousness and the human brain / by Wilder Penfield, with discussions by William Feindel, Charles Hendel, and Charles Symonds. Princeton, N.J. : Princeton University Press, [1975] xxix, 123 p.
74-025626          612/.82          069108159X
  *Brain. Consciousness.*

**QP376.T72 1991**
**Trehub, Arnold.**
  The cognitive brain / Arnold Trehub. Cambridge, Mass. : MIT Press, c1991. viii, 329 p.
91-008800          153          0262200856
  *Brain. Brain -- Computer simulation. Cognition.*

**QP376.W56 1993**
**Wills, Christopher.**
  The runaway brain : the evolution of human uniqueness / Christopher Wills. New York, N.Y. : Basic Books, c1993. xxiv, 358 p.
92-055029          573.2          0465031315
  *Brain -- Evolution. Human evolution.*

**QP381.P4**
**Pavlov, Ivan Petrovich,**
  Lectures on conditioned reflexes, by Ivan Petrovich Pavlov , translated by W. Horsley Gantt. New York, International Publishers [c1928-41] 2 v.
28027883          158.423
  *Brain. Conditioned response. Brain -- Localization of functions.*

**QP382.F7**
**Goldberg, Elkhonon.**
  The executive brain : frontal lobes and the civilized mind / Elkhonon Goldberg. Oxford ; Oxford University Press, 2001. xix, 251 p. :
00-058447          612.8/25          0195140222
  *Frontal lobes. Neuropsychology.*

**QP383.L87 1980**
**Lurieiia, Aleksandr Romanovich,**
  Higher cortical functions in man / Aleksandr Romanovich Luria ; prefaces to the English edition by Hans-Lukas Teuber and Karl H. Pribram ; authorized translation from the Russian by Basil Haigh. 2d ed., rev. and expanded. New York : Consultants Bureau, Basic Books, c1980 xxii, 634 p. :
          612/.825 19          0465029604
*Cerebral cortex. Higher nervous activity. Neuropsychology.*

**QP383.P46 1967**
**Penfield, Wilder,**
  The excitable cortex in conscious man / Wilder Penfield. Liverpool : Liverpool University Press ; 1967, c1958. 42 p. :
86-113920
  *Cerebral cortex. Brain stimulation. Brain -- Localization of functions.*

**QP385.H3**
**Halstead, Ward Campbell,**
  Brain and intelligence; a quantitative study of the frontal lobes. Chicago, University of Chicago Press [c1947] xiii, 206 p.
47002506          612.825261
  *Intelligence -- physiology Frontal Lobe -- physiology Brain -- Localization of functions.*

**QP385.P38**
**Penfield, Wilder,**
  Speech and brain-mechanisms, by Wilder Penfield and Lamar Roberts. Princeton, N.J., Princeton University Press, 1959. 286 p.
59-005602          612.8252
  *Brain -- Localization of functions. Speech. Speech disorders.*

**QP385.5.B695 1993**
**Bradshaw, John L.,**
  The evolution of lateral asymmetries, language, tool use, and intellect / John L. Bradshaw, Lesley J. Rogers. San Diego : Academic Press, c1993. xiii, 463 p.
92-026556          156/.2335          0121245608
  *Laterality. Comparative neurobiology.*

**QP385.5.C67 1991**
**Corballis, Michael C.**
  The lop-sided ape : evolution of the generstive mind / Michael C. Corballis. New York : Oxford University Press, 1991. vii, 366 p. :
90-022905          152.3/35          0195066758
  *Laterality. Human evolution. Brain -- Evolution.*

**QP385.5.H45 1993**
**Hellige, Joseph B.**
  Hemispheric asymmetry : what's right and what's left / Joseph B. Hellige. Cambridge, Mass. : Harvard University Press, 1993. xiii, 396 p.
92-049175          612.8/25          0674387309
  *Cerebral dominance. Brain -- physiology. Dominance, Cerebral.*

**QP385.5.I23 1993**
**Iaccino, James F.**
Left brain--right brain differences : inquiries, evidence, and new approaches / James F. Iaccino. Hillsdale, N.J. : L. Erlbaum Associates, 1993. xi, 284 p. :
92-049108          612.8/25          0805813403
*Cerebral dominance. Dominance, Cerebral.*

**QP385.5.I886 1998**
**Ivry, Richard B.**
The two sides of perception / Richard B. Ivry and Lynn C. Robertson. Cambridge, Mass. : MIT Press, c1998. 315 p. :
96-050975          612.8/25          0262090341
*Cerebral dominance. Laterality. Perception.*

**QP399.D43 1997**
**Deacon, Terrence William.**
The symbolic species : the co-evolution of language and the brain / Terrence W. Deacon. New York : W.W. Norton, c1997. 527 p. :
96-031115          153.6          0393038386
*Neurolinguistics. Brain -- Evolution.*

**QP399.L535 2000**
**Lieberman, Philip.**
Human language and our reptilian brain : the subcortical bases of speech, syntax, and thought / Philip Lieberman. Cambridge, Mass. : Harvard University Press, 2000. 221 p. :
99-086092          612.8/2          0674002261
*Neurolinguistics. Basal ganglia.*

**QP399.P76 1995**
Producing speech : contemporary issues : for Katherine Safford Harris / [edited] by Fredericka Bell-Berti, Lawrence J. Raphael. New York, NY : AIP Press, c1995. xxi, 567 p. :
95-012369          616.7/8          1563962861
*Harris, Katherine S.     Speech -- Physiological aspects.*

**QP401.D3 1965**
**Darwin, Charles,**
The expression of the emotions in man and animals. With a pref. by Konrad Lorenz. Chicago, University of Chicago Press [1965] xiii, 372 p. :
65-017286          157.2
*Emotions. Psychology, Comparative. Instinct.*

**QP401.J3813 1995**
**Jauregui, Jose Antonio.**
The emotional computer : how the individual is manipulated by the emotional strings of his brain / Jose Antonio Jauregui. Oxford, UK : Blackwell Publishers ; c1995. p. cm.
94-044904          152.4          0631198431
*Emotions -- Physiological aspects. Mind-brain identity theory. Human behaviour.*

**QP401.P76 1998**
**Prodger, Phillip.**
An annotated catalogue of the illustrations of human and animal expression from the collection of Charles Darwin : an early case of the use of photography in scientific research / by Phillip Prodger ; with a preface by Paul Ekman. Lewiston, N.Y. : Edwin Mellen Press, c1998. xi, 132 p. :
97-053663          152.4/022/2          0773484671
*Darwin, Charles, -- 1809-1882 -- Art collections -- Catalogs. Expression. Facial expression. Emotions.*

**QP401.T42 1989**
**Thayer, Robert E.**
The biopsychology of mood and arousal / Robert E. Thayer. New York : Oxford University Press, 1989. xi, 234 p. :
89-002914          152.4/54          0195051629
*Mood (Psychology) -- Physiological aspects. Arousal (Physiology) Psychobiology.*

**QP405.L33 1995**
**LaBerge, David.**
Attentional processing : the brain's art of mindfulness / David LaBerge. Cambridge, Mass. : Harvard University Press, 1995. x, 262 p. :
94-038071          153.7/33          0674052684
*Attention. Neuropsychology.*

**QP406.B33 1982**
**Baddeley, Alan D.,**
Your memory, a user's guide / Alan Baddeley. New York : Macmillan, 1982. 222 p. :
82-007226          153.1          0025046608
*Memory.*

**QP406.N48**
Neural mechanisms of learning and memory / Mark R. Rosenzweig and Edward L. Bennett, editors ; prepared with the support of the National Institute of Education. Cambridge, Mass. : MIT Press, c1976. xiii, 637 p.
75-035780          612/.82          0262180766
*Memory -- Congresses. Learning -- Physiological aspects. Information theory in biology -- Congresses.*

**QP406.R677 1994**
**Rowe, Glenn**
Theoretical models in biology : the origin of life, the immune system, and the brain / Glenn Rowe. Oxford ; Clarendon Press ; c1994. xvi, 420 p. :
93-040873          574/.01/13          019859688X
*Memory -- Computer simulation. Immunity -- Computer simulation. Life -- Origin -- Computer simulation.*

**QP409.F73 2001**
**Freeman, Walter J.**
How brains make up their minds / Walter J. Freeman. New York : Columbia University Press, c2000. vii, 171 p. :
00-063864          612.8/2          0231120087
*Intentionality (Philosophy) Neuropsychology. Consciousness.*

## QP411.G69 1995
**Greenfield, Susan.**

Journey to the centers of the mind : toward a science of consciousness / Susan A. Greenfield. New York : W.H. Freeman, c1995. xi, 221 p. :

94-045848　　　　153　　　　0716727234

*Consciousness -- Physiological aspects. Cognitive neuroscience.*

## QP411.H37
**Harth, Erich.**

Windows on the mind : reflections on the physical basis of consciousness / Erich Harth. New York : Morrow, 1982. 285 p. :

81-011158　　　　153　　　　0688007511

*Consciousness. Intellect. Brain.*

## QP411.H63 1994
**Hobson, J. Allan,**

The chemistry of conscious states : how the brain changes its mind / J. Allan Hobson. Boston : Little, Brown, c1994. xiii, 300 p.

94-015538　　　　612.8/2　　　　0316367540

*Consciousness -- Physiological aspects. Neuropsychology. Neurochemistry.*

## QP411.S46 1995
**Scott, Alwyn,**

Stairway to the mind : the controversial new science of consciousness / Alwyn Scott. New York : Copernicus, c1995. xix, 229 p. :

95-005932　　　　153　　　　0387943811

*Consciousness. Neurosciences. Science -- Philosophy.*

## QP425.C62 1996
**Coren, Stanley.**

Sleep thieves : an eye-opening exploration into the science and mysteries of sleep / Stanley Coren. New York, NY : Free Press, c1996. xi, 304 p. ;

95-051549　　　　612.8/21　　　　0684823047

*Sleep -- Physiological aspects. Sleep -- Psychological aspects.*

## QP425.K53 1963
**Kleitman, Nathaniel,**

Sleep and wakefulness. Chicago, University of Chicago Press [1963] x, 552 p.

63-017845　　　　612.8217

*Sleep. Physiology.*

## QP425.L3713 1996
**Lavie, P.**

The enchanted world of sleep / Peretz Lavie ; translated by Anthony Berris. New Haven : Yale University Press, c1996. xii, 270 p. :

95-041304　　　　612.8/21　　　　0300066023

*Sleep -- Popular works. Sleep disorders -- Popular works.*

## QP425.L82
**Luce, Gay Gaer.**

Sleep, by Gay Gaer Luce and Julius Segal. New York, Coward-McCann [1966] 335 p.

66-013124　　　　154.6

*Sleep.*

## QP426.H63 1988
**Hobson, J. Allan,**

The dreaming brain /J. Allan Hobson. New York : Basic Books, c1988. xvi, 319 p. :

87-047774　　　　154.6/3　　　　0465017037

*Dreams. Neuropsychology.*

## QP426.H67 1988
**Horne, James**

Why we sleep : the functions of sleep in humans and other mammals / James Horne. Oxford ; Oxford University Press, 1988. x, 319 p. :

87-022084　　　　599/.0188　　　　019261682X

*Sleep -- Physiological aspects. Sleep -- physiology.*

## QP426.J68313 1999
**Jouvet, Michel.**

The paradox of sleep : the story of dreaming / Michael Jouvet ; translated by Laurence Garey. Cambridge, Mass. : MIT Press, c1999. xiii, 211 p.

98-050198　　　　612.8/21　　　　0262100800

*Dreams. Sleep.*

### QP431 Neurophysiology and neuropsychology — Senses. Sensation. Sense organs — General works, treatises, and textbooks

## QP431.M5
**Milne, Lorus Johnson,**

The senses of animals and men [by] Lorus and Margery Milne. Drawings by Kenneth Gosner. New York, Atheneum, 1962. 305 p.

62-009411　　　　591.18

*Senses and sensation.*

### QP435 Neurophysiology and neuropsychology — Senses. Sensation. Sense organs — General special

## QP435.L34 1997
**Laming, D. R. J.**

The measurement of sensation / Donald Laming. Oxford ; Oxford University Press, 1997. xiii, 262 p.

97-003966　　　　612.8/028/7　　　　0198523424

*Senses and sensation -- Testing. Psychology, Experimental.*

## QP435.S6 1958
**Solomon, Philip,**

Sensory deprivation; a symposium held at Harvard Medical School, edited by Philip Solomon [and others] Foreword by Stanley Cobb. Cambridge, Harvard University Press, 1961. xviii, 262 p.

61-006353　　　　612.8

*Sensory deprivation.*

## QP441 Neurophysiology and neuropsychology — Senses. Sensation. Sense organs — Perceptual process

**QP441.D38 1991**
**Davidoff, Jules B.**
Cognition through color / Jules Davidoff. Cambridge, Mass. : MIT Press, c1991. xiv, 217 p.,
90-013643          152.14/5          0262041154
*Visual perception. Color vision. Cognition.*

## QP455-495 Neurophysiology and neuropsychology — Senses. Sensation. Sense organs — Special senses

**QP455.N47 2000**
The neurobiology of taste and smell / edited by Thomas E. Finger, Wayne L. Silver, Diego Restrepo. New York : Wiley-Liss, c2000. x, 479 p. :
00-020619          573.8/77          0471257214
*Taste. Smell. Neurophysiology.*

**QP458.L4413 1992**
**Le Guerer, Annick.**
Scent, the mysterious and essential powers of smell / Annick Le Guerer ; translated from the French by Richard Miller. New York : Turtle Bay Books, 1992. 260 p. ;
91051049          0394585267
*Smell -- History. Odors -- History.*

**QP458.S77 1990**
**Stoddart, D. Michael**
The scented ape : the biology and culture of human odour / D. Michael Stoddart. Cambridge [England] ; Cambridge University Press, 1990. ix, 286 p. :
89-070840          612.8/6          0521375118
*Smell. Animal behavior. Ethnology.*

**QP458.W38 2000**
**Watson, Lyall.**
Jacobson's organ and the remarkable nature of smell / Lyall Watson. New York : W.W. Norton, 2000. xv, 255 p. :
99-056864          612.8/6          0393049086
*Jacobson's organ. Smell.*

**QP461.B9713 1991**
**Buser, Pierre A.**
Audition / Pierre Buser and Michel Imbert ; translated by R.H. Kay. Cambridge, Mass. : MIT Press, c1992. x, 394 p. :
91-004438          612.8/5          0262023318
*Hearing.*

**QP461.D87 1984**
**Durrant, John D.**
Bases of hearing science / John D. Durrant, Jean H. Lovrinic. Baltimore : Williams & Wilkins, c1984. xxiv, 276 p.
83-021869          612/.85          0683027360
*Hearing. Psychoacoustics.*

**QP461.W27 1999**
**Warren, Richard M.**
Auditory perception : a new analysis and synthesis / Richard M. Warren. Cambridge, UK ; Cambridge University Press, 1999. xiv, 241 p. :
98-015178          152.1/5          0521582563
*Auditory perception. Speech perception.*

**QP469.B5413 1997**
**Blauert, Jens.**
Spatial hearing : the psychophysics of human sound localization / Jens Blauert. Cambridge, Mass. : MIT Press, c1997. xiii, 494 p.
96-012637          152.1/58          0262024136
*Directional hearing.*

**QP474.V44 1991 vol. 8**
Eye movements / edited by R.H.S. Carpenter. Boca Raton : CRC Press, 1991. xii, 339 p. :
90-001887          612.8/4 s          0849375088
*Eye -- Movements. Eye Movements -- physiology.*

**QP475.B8413 1992**
**Buser, Pierre A.**
Vision / Pierre Buser and Michel Imbert ; translated by R.H. Kay. Cambridge, Mass. : MIT Press, c1992. xii, 559 p. :
91-032473          599/.01823          0262023369
*Vision. Retina -- physiology. Vision -- physiology.*

**QP475.O97 1999**
**Oyster, Clyde W.,**
The human eye : structure and function / Clyde W. Oyster. Sunderland, Mass. : Sinauer Associates, c1999. xxviii, 766,
99-025402          612.8/4          0878936459
*Eye -- Physiology. Eye -- Anatomy. Eye -- physiology.*

**QP475.T68 1996**
**Tovee, Martin J.**
An introduction to the visual system / Martin J. Tovee. Cambridge ; Cambridge University Press, 1996. xiv, 202 p. :
95051858          612.8/4          0521482909
*Visual pathways. Vision. Visual perception.*

**QP475.U44 1996**
**Ullman, Shimon.**
High-level vision : object recognition and visual cognition / Shimon Ullman. Cambridge, Mass. : MIT Press, c1996. xviii, 412 p.
95-036691          152.14          0262210134
*Visual perception.*

**QP475.W24 1998**
**Wade, Nicholas.**
A natural history of vision / Nicholas J. Wade. Cambridge, Mass. : MIT Press, c1998. xvi, 466 p. :
97-022697          612.8/4          0262231948
*Vision -- History. Physiological optics -- History. Vision -- physiology.*

**QP481.W58 1995**
**Wolken, Jerome J.**

Light detectors, photoreceptors, and imaging systems in nature / Jerome J. Wolken. New York : Oxford University Press, 1995. xii, 259 p. :
94-014160        591.1/823        0195050029
*Photoreceptors. Visual pigments. Photobiology.*

**QP491.T87 1994**
**Turner, R. Steven**

In the eye's mind : vision and the Helmholtz-Hering controversy / R. Steven Turner. Princeton, N.J. : Princeton University Press, 1994. p. cm.
93-037258        612.8/4        0691033978
*Helmholtz, Hermann von, -- 1821-1894. Hering, Ewald, – 1834-1918. Helmholtz, Hermann von, -- 1821-1894. Visual perception – History - - 19th century. Visual Perception. Vision -- physiology.*

**QP493.B47 2000**
**Berthoz, A.**

The brain's sense of movement / Alain Berthoz ; translated by Giselle Weiss. Cambridge, Mass. : Harvard University Press, 2000. xi, 337 p. :
00-023758        612.8/2        0674801091
*Motion perception (Vision) Orientation (Physiology) Proprioception.*

**QP495.C67**
**Coren, Stanley.**

Seeing is deceiving : the psychology of visual illusions / Stanley Coren, Joan Stern Girgus. Hillsdale, N.J. : Lawrence Erlbaum Associates ; 1978. xiii, 255 p.
78-013509        152.1/48        0470265221
*Optical illusions. Optical illusions -- Psychological aspects.*

**QP495.S73 1994**
**Stafford, Barbara Maria,**

Artful science : enlightenment, entertainment, and the eclipse of visual education / Barbara Maria Stafford. Cambridge, Mass. : MIT Press, c1994. xxix, 350 p.
93-020984        306.4/5        0262193426
*Optical illusions -- History -- 18th century. Scientific recreations - - History -- 18th century. Mathematical recreations -- History – 18th century.*

### QP511 Animal biochemistry — History — General works

**QP511.L44**
**Leicester, Henry Marshall,**

Development of biochemical concepts from ancient to modern times [by] Henry M. Leicester. Cambridge, Mass., Harvard University Press, 1974. 286 p.
73-083965        574.1/92/09        0674200187
*Biochemistry -- History.*

### QP511.8 Animal biochemistry — Biography — Individual, A-Z

**QP511.8.C44.C57 1985**
**Clark, Ronald William.**

The life of Ernst Chain : penicillin and beyond / Ronald W. Clark. New York : St. Martin's Press, 1985. x, 217 p., [8
85-026184        615/.329/0924        0312484194
*Chain, Ernst, -- Sir, -- 1906-    Biochemists – Germany – Biography. Biochemists -- Great Britain -- Biography. Penicillin -- History.*

**QP511.8.H63.A3 1990**
**Hoagland, Mahlon B.**

Toward the habit of truth : a life in science / Mahlon Hoagland. New York : Norton, c1990. xxvii, 206 p.
89-009353        574.19/2/092        0393027546
*Hoagland, Mahlon B.    Biochemists -- United States -- Biography. Molecular biologists -- United States -- Biography.*

**QP511.8.K68.A3 1989**
**Kornberg, Arthur,**

For the love of enzymes : the odyssey of a biochemist / Arthur Kornberg. Cambridge, Mass. : Harvard University Press, 1989. xi, 336 p. :
88-032054        574.19/2/0924        0674307755
*Kornberg, Arthur, -- 1918-    Biochemists -- United States -- Biography.*

**QP511.8.S94.M67 1988**
**Moss, Ralph W.**

Free radical : Albert Szent-Gyorgyi and the battle over vitamin C / Ralph W. Moss ; with a foreword by Studs Terkel. New York : Paragon House, c1988. xviii, 316 p.
87-008865        574.1/92/0924        0913729787
*Szent-Gyorgyi, Albert, -- 1893-    Biochemists -- Biography.*

### QP512 Animal biochemistry — Dictionaries and encyclopedias

**QP512.O94 1997**

Oxford dictionary of biochemistry and molecular biology / A.D. Smith, managing editor ... [et al.]. Oxford ; New York : Oxford University Press, 1997. xi, 738 p. :
97-225841        572/.03        0198547684
*Biochemistry -- Dictionaries. Molecular biology -- Dictionaries.*

### QP514 Animal biochemistry — General works, treatises, and textbooks — 1801-1969

**QP514.C32 1967**
**Cantarow, Abraham,**

Biochemistry [by] Abraham Cantarow [and] Bernard Schepartz. Philadelphia, W. B. Saunders Co., 1967. xvii, 898 p.
67-010134        612/.015
*Biochemistry.*

## QP514.2 Animal biochemistry — General works, treatises, and textbooks — 1970-

**QP514.2.G66 1996**
**Goodsell, David S.**
Our molecular nature / the body's motors, machines, and messages / David S. Goodsell. New York : Copernicus, c1996. x, 183 p. :
95-046846          574.8/8          0387944982
*Biochemistry. Molecular biology. Biomolecules.*

**QP514.2.H86 2002**
**Hunter, Graeme K.**
Vital forces : the discovery of the molecular basis of life / Graeme K. Hunter. San Diego : Academic Press, c2000. xix, 364 p.,
99-067772          572/.09          012361810X
*Biochemistry -- History. Biochemistry -- history. Molecular Biology -- history.*

**QP514.2.O94 1987**
Outlines of biochemistry / Eric E. Conn ... [et al.]. New York : Wiley, c1987. ix, 693 p. :
86-024688          574.19/2          0471052884
*Biochemistry.*

**QP514.2.P374 1998**
**Pasternak, Charles A.**
The molecules within us : our body in health and disease / Charles A. Pasternak. New York : Plenum, c1998. xiv, 336 p. :
98-026173          610          0306459876
*Biochemistry. Molecular biology. Medicine.*

## QP517 Animal biochemistry — Special topics, A-Z

**QP517.B48.K37 1988**
**Katz, Michael Jay,**
Pattern biology and the complex architectures of life / Michael J. Katz. Wolfeboro, NH : Longwood Academic, 1988. vii, 206 p. ;
87-022651          574          0893415219
*Biochemical templates. Morphology -- Philosophy. Biology – Philosophy.*

**QP517.H93.J44 1991**
**Jeffrey, George A.,**
Hydrogen bonding in biological structures / G.A. Jeffrey, W. Saenger. Berlin ; Springer-Verlag, c1991. xiv, 569 p. :
90-026529          574.19/283          0387508392
*Hydrogen bonding. Biomolecules -- Structure. Biopolymers – Structure.*

**QP517.L54.K57 1997**
**Klotz, Irving M.**
Ligand-receptor energetics : a guide for the perplexed / Irving M. Klotz. New York : Wiley, c1997. xi, 170 p. :
96-034518          574.19/283          0471176265
*Ligand binding (Biochemistry) -- Thermodynamics.*

**QP517.T48**
**Haynie, Donald T.**
Biological thermodynamics / Donald T. Haynie. Cambridge ; Cambridge University Press, 2001. xv, 379 p. :
00-031272          572/.436          0521791650
*Thermodynamics. Physical biochemistry. Bioenergetics.*

## QP519.9 Animal biochemistry — Technique. Analytical biochemistry — Special methods, A-Z

**QP519.9.E434.H39  1996**
**Hawcroft, David M.**
Electrophoresis / D.M. Hawcroft. Oxford : IRL Press at Oxford University Press, 1997. 142 p. :
96-023127          574.19/285          0199635633
*Electrophoresis.*

**QP519.9.H53.C86 1998**
**Cunico, Robert L.**
Basic HPLC and CE of biomolecules / Robert L. Cunico, Karen M. Gooding, Tim Wehr. Richmond, CA : Bay Bioanalytical Laboratory, 1998. 388 p. :
98-070600          547/.30894          0966322908
*High performance liquid chromatography. Capillary electrophoresis. Biomolecules -- Analysis.*

**QP519.9.H53.S69 1997**
**Snyder, Lloyd R.**
Practical HPLC method development / Lloyd R. Snyder, Joseph J. Kirkland, Joseph L. Glajch. New York : Wiley, c1997. xxvi, 765 p.
96-034296          543/.0894          047100703X
*High performance liquid chromatography -- Methodology.*

**QP519.9.S6.P37 1983**
**Parker, Frank S.,**
Applications of infrared, raman, and resonance raman spectroscopy in biochemistry / Frank S. Parker. New York : Plenum Press, c1983. xiv, 550 p. :
83-011012          574.19/285          0306412063
*Spectrum analysis. Biochemistry -- Technique. Spectrophotometry, Infrared.*

## QP531-535 Animal biochemistry — Technique. Analytical biochemistry — Special substances

**QP531.C68 1997**
**Cowan, J. A.**
Inorganic biochemistry : an introduction / J.A. Cowan. New York : Wiley-VCH : c1997. xiv, 440 p. :
96-014100          574.19/214          0471188956
*Bioinorganic chemistry. Bioinorganic chemistry.*

**QP535.C2**
**Schulkin, Jay.**
Calcium hunger : behavioral and biological regulation / Jay Schulkin. Cambridge ; Cambridge University Press, 2001. x, 206 p. :
00-034212          612.3/924          0521791707
*Calcium -- Metabolism -- Regulation. Calcium in human nutrition. Appetite.*

QP535.F4
**Mielczarek, Eugenie V.**
Iron, nature's universal element : why people need iron & animals make magnets / Eugenie Vorburger Mielczarek and Sharon Bertsch McGrayne. New Brunswick, N.J. : Rutgers University Press, c2000. xvi, 204 p. :
99-056540          612/.01524          0813528313
*Iron -- Physiological effect. Iron in the body. Biomagnetism.*

QP535.N2.M33 1998
**MacGregor, Graham.**
Salt, diet and health : Neptune's poisoned chalice : the origins of high blood pressure / Graham A. MacGregor and Hugh E. de Wardener. Cambridge ; Cambridge University Press, 1998. xi, 233 p. :
98-017411          612.3/926          0521583527
*Salt in the body. Salt -- Health aspects. Hypertension – Etiology.*

### QP551-801 Animal biochemistry — Technique. Analytical biochemistry — Organic substances

QP551.A693 1991
**Arnstein, H. R. V.**
Protein biosynthesis / H.R.V. Arnstein, R.A. Cox. [Oxford, England] ; IRL Press at Oxford University Press, c1992. xv, 112 p. :
91-003653          574.19/296          0199630402
*Proteins -- Synthesis. Amino Acids. Amino Acyl T RNA Synthetases.*

QP551.B53 1994
**Blackman, David S.**
The logic of biochemical sequencing / David S. Blackman. Boca Raton : CRC Press, c1994. 168 p. :
93-012778          574.87/328          0849344972
*Amino acid sequence -- Philosophy. Logic. Analysis (Philosophy)*

QP551.P42 1998
**Pfeil, W. (Wolfgang),**
Protein stability and folding : a collection of thermodynamic data / W. Pfeil. Berlin ; New York : Springer, c1998. xii, 656 p. :
                    572/.6 21          3540637176
*Proteins -- Stability -- Tables. Protein folding. Proteins -- Biotechnology.*

QP551.P83 1989
**Pugsley, Anthony P.**
Protein targeting / Anthony P. Pugsley. San Diego : Academic Press, c1989. xi, 279 p. :
88-007522          574.19/245          0125667701
*Proteins -- Physiological transport. Proteins -- Secretion.*

QP551.R48 1993
**Rhodes, Gale.**
Crystallography made crystal clear : a guide for users of macromolecular models / Gale Rhodes. San Diego : Academic Press, c1993. xiii, 202 p.
92-043102          547.7/5046          0125870752
*Proteins -- Analysis. X-ray crystallography.*

QP552.E53.B43 1987
**Beck, Deva.**
The pleasure connection : how endorphins affect our health and happiness / Deva Beck & James Beck ; foreword by C. Norman Shealy. San Marcos, Calif. : Synthesis Press, c1987. 235 p. ;
87-060379          612/.822
*Endorphins -- Physiological effect.*

QP552.E53.S68 1989
**Snyder, Solomon H.,**
Brainstorming : the science and politics of opiate research / Solomon H. Snyder. Cambridge, Mass. : Harvard University Press, 1989. 208 p. :
89-011096          612.8/22          0674080483
*Endorphins -- Receptors -- Research. Endorphins –Receptors – Research -- Political aspects -- United States.*

QP572.I5.B58 1982
**Bliss, Michael.**
The discovery of insulin / Michael Bliss. Chicago : University of Chicago Press, 1982. 304 p., [16]
82-050911          615/.365          0226058972
*Insulin -- History. Diabetes -- Research -- History. Medicine – Research -- History.*

QP572.P47.A4 1992
**Agosta, William C.**
Chemical communication : the language of pheromones / William C. Agosta. New York : Scientific American Library : c1992. ix, 179 p. :
92-009412          591.59          0716750368
*Pheromones.*

QP572.S4.O83 1994
**Oudshoorn, Nelly,**
Beyond the natural body : an archaeology of sex hormones / Nelly Oudshoorn. New York ; Routledge, 1994. xi, 195 p. :
94-004945          612.6          041509190X
*Sex hormones -- Research -- History -- 20th century.*

QP601.C738 1998
Comprehensive biological catalysis : a mechanistic reference / edited by Michael Sinnott. San Diego : Academic Press, 1998. 4 v. :
                    572/.7 21          0126468605
*Enzymes.*

QP601.C753 2000
**Copeland, Robert Allen.**
Enzymes : a practical introduction to structure, mechanism, and data analysis / Robert A. Copeland. New York : Wiley, c2000. xvi, 397 p. :
99-050087          572.7          0471359297
*Enzymes. Enzymology.*

QP601.C756
**Cornish-Bowden, Athel.**
Fundamentals of enzyme kinetics / Athel Cornish-Bowden. London ; Butterworths, 1979. xiii, 230 p.
79-040116          574.1/925          0408106174
*Enzyme kinetics. Chemical kinetics.*

**QP601.W734 1995**
**Wong, Dominic W. S.**
Food enzymes : structure and mechanism / Dominic W.S. Wong. New York : Chapman & Hall, c1995. xvi, 390 p. :
94-042926          664/.024          0412056917
*Enzymes. Food -- Composition.*

**QP601.3.G88 1995**
**Gutfreund, H.**
Kinetics for the life sciences : receptors, transmitters, and catalysts / H. Gutfreund. Cambridge ; Cambridge University Press, 1995. xi, 346 p. :
95-000028          574.19/2          0521480272
*Enzyme kinetics. Chemical kinetics. Biophysics.*

**QP601.3.P87 2000**
**Purich, Daniel L.**
Handbook of biochemical kinetics / Daniel L. Purich, R. Donald Allison. San Diego, Ca : Academic Press, c2000. 788 p. :
            572/.744/03 21          0125680481
*Enzyme kinetics -- Handbooks, manuals, etc.*

**QP606.D46.R33 1996**
**Rabinow, Paul.**
Making PCR : a story of biotechnology / Paul Rabinow. Chicago : University of Chicago Press, 1996. vii, 190 p. :
95-049103          574.87/3282          0226701468
*Polymerase chain reaction -- History.*

**QP620.A53 1994**
Ancient DNA : recovery and analysis of genetic material from paleontological, archaeological, museum, medical, and forensic specimens / Bernd Herrmann, Susanne Hummel, editors. New York : Springer-Verlag, c1994. xi, 263 p. :
92-049549          574.87/3282          0387979298
*DNA -- Analysis. Paleobiology. Paleopathology.*

**QP624.C36 1999**
**Cantor, Charles R.,**
Genomics : the science and technology behind the Human Genome Project / Charles R. Cantor, Cassandra L. Smith. New York : Wiley, c1999. xviii, 596 p.
98-040448          572.8/6          0471599085
*DNA -- Analysis. Nucleotide sequence. Gene mapping.*

**QP624.F6913 1993**
**Frank-Kamenetskii, M. D.**
Unraveling DNA / Maxim D. Frank-Kamenetskii ; translated by Lev Liapin. New York : VCH Publishers, c1993. ix, 205 p. :
93-017544          574.87/3282          1560816171
*DNA.*

**QP624.J82**
**Judson, Horace Freeland.**
The eighth day of creation : makers of the revolution in biology / by Horace Freeland Judson. New York : Simon and Schuster, c1979. 686 p., [16]
78-012139          574.8/732          0671225405
*DNA -- History. Molecular biology -- History.*

**QP624.L34 1998**
**Lagerkvist, Ulf.**
DNA pioneers and their legacy / Ulf Lagerkvist. New Haven, CT : Yale University Press, c1998. xi, 156 p. :
97-037281          572.8/6/0072          0300071841
*DNA -- Research -- History. Genetics -- History.*

**QP624.S56 1994**
**Sinden, Richard R.**
DNA structure and function / Richard R. Sinden. San Diego : Academic Press, c1994. xxiii, 398 p.
94-010464          574.87/3282          0126457506
*DNA. Molecular genetics.*

**QP625.N89A45 1997**
**Alphey, Luke.**
DNA sequencing / Luke Alphey. New York : Springer, 1997. p. cm.
            572.8/633 21          0387915095
*Nucleotide sequence.*

**QP701.C2943 2000**
Carbohydrates in chemistry and biology / [edited by] Beat Ernst, Gerald W. Hart, Pierre Sanay. Weinheim ; New York : Wiley-VCH, c2000. 4 v. :
            572/.56 21          3527295119
*Carbohydrates.*

**QP751.P645 1998**
**Pond, Caroline M.**
The fats of life / Caroline M. Pond, with drawings by Mat Cross and Sarah Sutcliffe. Cambridge ; Cambridge University Press, 1998. 337 p. :
97-046515          612.3/97          0521583217
*Fatty acids -- Physiological effect. Lipids in nutrition. Fatty acids in human nutrition.*

**QP771.B44 1992**
**Bender, David A.**
Nutritional biochemistry of the vitamins / David A. Bender. Cambridge ; Cambridge University Press, 1992. xx, 431 p. :
91-034082          612.3/99          0521381444
*Vitamins. Avitaminosis. Nutrition Assessment.*

**QP771.S66 1992**
**Somer, Elizabeth.**
The essential guide to vitamins and minerals / Health Media of America and Elizabeth Somer. New York, NY : HarperPerennial, c1992. xi, 403 p. :
91-055390          612.3/99          006271516X
*Vitamins in human nutrition. Minerals in human nutrition. Minerals.*

**QP772.A8.G66 1991**
**Goodman, Sandra,**
Vitamin C, the master nutrient / Sandra Goodman ; foreword by Richard A. Passwater. New Canaan, Conn. : Keats Pub., c1991. xv, 176 p. :
90-023227          612.3/99          0879835710
*Vitamin C -- Popular works. Vitamin C -- Therapeutic use.*

**QP801.A3.B73 1996**
**Braun, Stephen.**
   Buzz : the science and lore of alcohol and caffeine / Stephen Braun. New York : Oxford University Press, 1996. x, 214 p. :
95-047790          615/.7828          0195092899
   *Alcohol -- Popular works.  Caffeine -- Popular works.*

**QP801.C24**
**Weinberg, Bennett Alan.**
   The world of caffeine : the science and culture of the world's most popular drug / Bennett Alan Weinberg and Bonnie K. Bealer. New York : Routledge, 2001. p. cm.
00-059243          613.8/4          0415927226
   *Caffeine.*

**QP801.C68.C627 1990**
   Cocaine in the brain / edited by Nora D. Volkow and Alan C. Swann. New Brunswick : Rutgers University Press, c1990. xiv, 188 p.,
89-070177          616.86/4707          0813515645
   *Cocaine -- Physiological effect.  Brain -- Effect of chemicals on. Cocaine habit -- Physiological aspects.*

**QP801.C68.K369 1998**
**Karch, Steven B.**
   A brief history of cocaine / Steven B. Karch. Boca Raton, Fla. : CRC Press, c1998. 202 p. :
97-035399          362.29/8/09          0849340195
   *Cocaine -- History.*

**QP801.N48**
   Nicotine and related alkaloids : absorption, distribution, metabolism, and excretion / edited by J.W. Gorrod and J. Wahren. London ; Chapman & Hall, 1993. xvi, 299 p. :
93-025262          615/.785          0412557401
   *Nicotine -- Metabolism.  Alkaloids -- Metabolism.  Nicotine -- pharmacokinetics.*

# QR Microbiology

## QR1 Societies, congresses, serial collections, yearbooks

**QR1.A38**
   Advances in applied microbiology. New York, Academic Press, 1959- v.
59-013823          660.28449
   *Microbiology.  Microbiology -- yearbooks.*

**QR1.A5**
   Annual review of microbiology. Stanford, Calif. : Annual Reviews, Inc., [1947- v. :
49-000432          589.95058
   *Micro-organisms -- Periodicals.  Microbiology -- Periodicals. Microbiology -- yearbooks.*

## QR9 Dictionaries and encyclopedias

**QR9.E53 2000**
   Encyclopedia of microbiology / editor-in-chief, Joshua Lederberg. San Diego : Academic Press, c2000- 4 v. :
99-065283          579/.03          0122268008
   *Microbiology -- Encyclopedias.*

## QR22 History — By region or country, A-Z

**QR22.F8.L3813 1988**
**Latour, Bruno.**
   The pasteurization of France / Bruno Latour ; translated by Alan Sheridan and John Law. Cambridge, Mass. : Harvard University Press, 1988. 273 p. ;
88-002670          306/.45/0944          0674657608
   *Pasteur, Louis, -- 1822-1895.  Microbiology -- France – History – 19th century.  Microbiology -- Social aspects -- France.*

## QR31 Biography — Individual, A-Z

**QR31.A1.D4 1932d**
**De Kruif, Paul,**
   Microbe hunters. Text ed. Edited by Harry G. Grover. New York, Harcourt, Brace and company, 1932. xiii, 368 p.
32010382          925
   *Bacteriology -- History.  Microorganisms.  Scientists.*

**QR31.F5.M353**
**Maurois, Andre,**
   The life of Sir Alexander Fleming, discoverer of penicillin. Translated from the French by Gerard Hopkins and with an introd. by Robert Cruickshank. New York, Dutton [1968, c1959] 293 p.
59005817          926.1
   *Fleming, Alexander, -- Sir, -- 1881-1955.  History of Medicine – biography*

## QR41 General works, treatises, and textbooks — Through 1969

**QR41.F84 1968**
**Frobisher, Martin,**
   Fundamentals of microbiology; an introduction to the microorganisms with special reference to the procaryons. Philadelphia, Saunders, 1968. xiv, 629 p.
68-010401          576
   *Microbiology.*

**QR41.S775 1963**
**Stanier, Roger Y.**
   The microbial world [by] Roger Y. Stanier, Michael Doudoroff [and] Edward A. Adelberg. Englewood Cliffs, N.J., Prentice-Hall, 1963. 753 p.
63-008887          576
   *Microbiology.*

## QR41.2 General works, treatises, and textbooks — 1970-

**QR41.2.H46 1996**
**Heritage, J.**
Introductory microbiology / J. Heritage, E.G.V. Evans and R.A. Killington. Cambridge, [Eng.] ; Cambridge University Press, 1996. xiv, 234 p. :
95-010245          576          0521445167
*Microbiology.*

**QR41.2.P4 1986**
**Pelczar, Michael J.**
Microbiology / Michael J. Pelczar, Jr., E.C.S. Chan, Noel R. Krieg, with the assistance of Merna Foss Pelczar. New York : McGraw-Hill, c1986. ix, 918 p., [
84-028932          576          0070492344
*Microbiology.*

## QR46 By discipline — Medical microbiology

**QR46.B28**
**Baldry, P. E.**
The battle against bacteria; a history of the development of antibacterial drugs, for the general reader, by P. E. Baldry. Cambridge [Eng.] University press, 1965. 102 p.
65-015311          616.0109
*Medical bacteriology -- History.*

## QR56 Popular works

**QR56.D59 1976**
**Dixon, Bernard.**
Magnificent microbes / Bernard Dixon. New York : Atheneum, 1976. 251 p. ;
75-014678          576          0689106777
*Microorganisms.*

**QR56.D594 1994**
**Dixon, Bernard.**
Power unseen : how microbes rule the world / Bernard Dixon. Oxford ; W.H. Freeman, c1994. xvii, 237 p.
93-037697          576          0716745046
*Microbiology -- Popular works.*

## QR63 Study and teaching. Research — Laboratory manuals

**QR63.P455 1990**
**Penn, C. W.**
Handling laboratory microorganisms / Charles Penn. Milton Keynes ; Open University Press, 1990. 160 p. :
90043465          576/.078          0335092047
*Microbiology -- Laboratory manuals.*

## QR66.3 Technique — Culture technique — Culture works

**QR66.3.A85 1997**
**Atlas, Ronald M.,**
Handbook of microbiological media / by Ronald M. Atlas ; edited by Lawrence C. Parks. 2nd ed. Boca Raton : CRC Press, c1997. iv, 1706 p. :
576/.0724 20          0849326389
*Microbiology -- Cultures and culture media -- Handbooks, manuals, etc.*

## QR81 Bacteria — Classification. Nomenclature

**QR81.B46 1984**
Bergey's manual of systematic bacteriology / Noel R. Krieg, editor, volume 1 ; John G. Holt, editor-in-chief. (New ed began in 2001 - Not yet complete) Baltimore : Williams & Wilkins, c1984-c1989. 4 v. (xxvii,
82-021760          589.9/0012          0683041088
*Bacteriology -- Classification. Bacteriology -- Terminology. Bacteria -- Classification.*

## QR82 Systematic divisions. By family or higher taxa, A-Z — Class individual genera under the family.

**QR82.E6.E3 1972**
**Edwards, Philip R.**
Identification of Enterobacteriaceae [by] P. R. Edwards [and] W. H. Ewing. Minneapolis, Burgess Pub. Co. [1972] ix, 362 p.
77-160829          589.9/5          0808705164
*Enterobacteriaceae -- Identification. Diagnostic microbiology.*

**QR89.5.L48 1990**
**Levett, Paul N.**
Anaerobic bacteria : a functional biology / Paul N. Levett. Milton Keynes ; Open University Press, 1990. 122 p. :
90-014155          589.9/0128          0335092055
*Anaerobic bacteria.*

**QR89.7.S67 1990**
**Sprent, Janet I.**
Nitrogen fixing organisms : pure and applied aspects / Janet I. Sprent and Peter Sprent. London ; Chapman and Hall, 1990. viii, 256 p.
90-001434          589.9/0133          041234680X
*Nitrogen-fixing microorganisms. Nitrogen -- Fixation.*

## QR100 Microbial ecology — General works, treatises, and textbooks

**QR100.B325 1997**
  Bacteria as multicellular organisms / edited by James A. Shapiro & Martin Dworkin. New York : Oxford University Press, 1997. xiii, 466 p.
96-004288          589.9/05          0195091590
  *Bacteria -- Ecology. Microbial aggregation.*

**QR100.M516 1992**
  Microbial ecology : principles, methods, and applications / [edited by] Morris A. Levin, Ramon J. Seidler, Marvin Rogul. New York : McGraw-Hill, c1992. xxviii, 945 p
91025208          576/.15          0070375062
  *Microbial ecology.*

### QR100.9 Microbial ecology — By type of environment — Extreme environments (General)

**QR100.9.P67 1994**
**Postgate, J. R.**
  The outer reaches of life / John Postgate. Cambridge [England] ; Cambridge University Press, 1994. ix, 276 p. :
93-011579          576          0521440106
  *Extreme environments -- Microbiology.*

## QR151 Microorganisms of fermentation. Yeasts, etc. — General works

**QR151.C58 1958**
**Cook, A. H.**
  The chemistry and biology of yeasts. New York, Academic Press, 1958. 763 p.
57008374          589.91
  *Yeasts. Yeast.*

## QR181 Immunology — General works, treatises, and textbooks

**QR181.G66 1991**
**Golub, Edward S.,**
  Immunology, a synthesis / Edward S. Golub, Douglas R. Green. 2nd ed. Sunderland, Mass. : Sinauer Associates, c1991. xxviii, 744 p.
          616.07/9 20          0878932631
  *Immunology. Immunity. Immunologic Diseases.*

**QR181.T36 1994**
**Tauber, Alfred I.**
  The immune self : theory or metaphor? / Alfred I. Tauber. Cambridge ; Cambridge University Press, 1994. x, 354 p. :
94-002519          574.2/9/09          052146188X
  *Immunology -- Philosophy. Immunology -- History.*

## QR181.5 Immunology — Addresses, essays, lectures

**QR181.5.M55 1988**
  Milestones in immunology / [edited by] Debra Jan Bibel ; with a foreword by Arthur M. Silverstein. Madison, WI : Science Tech ; c1988. xix, 330 p. :
88-015773          616.07/9          0910239150
  *Immunology. Allergy and Immunology -- history -- collected works.*

## QR181.7 Immunology — Popular works

**QR181.7.C624 1995**
**Clark, William R.,**
  At war within : the double-edged sword of immunity / William R. Clark. New York : Oxford University Press, 1995. xi, 276 p. ;
94-045134          616.07/9          0195092864
  *Immune system -- Popular works. Immunologic diseases -- Popular works.*

**QR181.7.K46 1998**
**Kendall, Marion D.**
  Dying to live : how our bodies fight disease / Marion Kendall. Cambridge ; Cambridge University Press, c1998. xi, 196 p. :
98-003646          616.07/9          0521584795
  *Immune system -- Popular works.*

## QR182 Immunology — Special aspects of the subject as whole

**QR182.M39 1995**
**Mazumdar, Pauline M. H.**
  Species and specificity : an interpretation of the history of immunology / Pauline M.H. Mazumdar. Cambridge ; Cambridge University Press, 1995. xiii, 457 p.
93-031219          574.2/9/09          0521431727
  *Immunology -- History. Allergy and Immunology -- history. Species Specificity.*

## QR182.2 Immunology — Special topics, A-Z

**QR182.2.E94.L36 1989**
**Langman, Rodney E.**
  The immune system : evolutionary principles guide our understanding of this complex biological defense system / Rodney E. Langman ; with a foreword by Melvin Cohn. San Diego : Academic Press, c1989. xlvi, 209 p.
88-007757          616.07/9          012436585X
  *Immune system -- Evolution. Immune System. Immunity.*

## QR184 Immunology — Immunogenetics — General works

**QR184.H54**
**Hildemann, W. H.,**
Comprehensive immunogenetics / W.H. Hildemann, E.A. Clark, R.L. Raison. New York : Elsevier North Holland, c1981. xv, 368 p. :
80-017339      616.07/9      0444003762
*Immunogenetics. Immunogenetics.*

**QR184.S74 1998**
**Steele, E. J.,**
Lamarck's signature : how retrogenes are changing Darwin's natural selection paradigm / Edward J. Steele, Robyn A. Lindley, Robert V. Blanden. Reading, Mass. : Perseus Books, c1998. xix, 286 p. :
98-087900      572.8/38      073820014X
*Lamarck, Jean Baptiste Pierre Antoine de Monet de, -- 1744-1829. Darwin, Charles, -- 1809-1882. Clonal selection theory. Antibody diversity. Immunogenetics.*

## QR189.5 Immunology — Vaccines — By disease or type, A-Z

**QR189.5.A33**
**Cohen, Jon,**
Shots in the dark : the wayward search for an AIDS vaccine / Jon Cohen. New York : Norton, c2001. xvii, 440, [4
00-061635      616.97/9206      0393050270
*AIDS vaccines -- Popular works.*

# QR201 Pathogenic microorganisms. By disease, A-Z

**QR201.A37.M6613 2000**
**Montagnier, Luc.**
Virus : the co-discoverer of HIV tracks its rampage and charts the future / Luc Montagnier ; translated from the French by Stephen Sartarelli. New York : W.W. Norton, c2000. 256 p. :
99-019650      616.97/92      0393039234
*HIV infections -- Etiology -- Research -- History. HIV (Viruses)– Research -- History.*

**QR201.P27.W35 1996**
**Wakelin, Derek.**
Immunity to parasites : how parasitic infections are controlled / Derek Wakelin. Cambridge ; Cambridge University Press, 1996. xvii, 204 p.
95-048213      616.9/6079      0521562457
*Parasitic diseases -- Immunological aspects.*

**QR201.S35.B37 1991**
**Basch, Paul F.,**
Schistosomes : development, reproduction, and host relations / Paul F. Basch. New York : Oxford University Press, 1991. vii, 248 p. :
91-003002      614.5/53      0195058070
*Schistosomiasis. Schistosoma. Host-Parasite Relations.*

## QR359 Virology — History — General works

**QR359.R33 1991**
**Radetsky, Peter.**
The invisible invaders : the story of the emerging age of viruses / Peter Radetsky. Boston : Little, Brown, c1991. xiii, 415 p.,
90-006612      616/.0194      0316732168
*Virology -- History. Viruses -- Research -- History.*

## QR359.72 Virology — History — By region or country, A-Z

**QR359.72.G35.A3 1991**
**Gallo, Robert C.**
Virus hunting : AIDS, cancer, and the human retrovirus : a story of scientific discovery / Robert Gallo. [New York, NY] : BasicBooks, c1991. x, 352 p., [8
90-055600      616/.0194/092      0465098061
*Gallo, Robert C. Virologists -- United States -- Biography. HIV (Viruses) AIDS (Disease)*

## QR360 Virology — General works, treatises, and textbooks

**QR360.A3**
Advances in virus research. New York, Academic Press, 1953- v.
53-011559      576.6
*Virology -- Research. Virology -- yearbooks.*

## QR364 Virology — Popular works

**QR364.C73 2000**
**Crawford, Dorothy H.**
The invisible enemy : a natural history of viruses / Dorothy H. Crawford. Oxford ; Oxford University Press, 2000. x, 275 p. :
00-036756      616/.0194      0198503326
*Viruses -- Popular works. Medical virology -- Popular works. Viruses -- Ecology.*

## QR414.6 Virology — Retroviruses — Special, A-Z

**QR414.6.H58.E95 1999**
The evolution of HIV / edited by Keith A. Crandall. Baltimore, MD : Johns Hopkins University Press, c1999. xii, 504 p. :
98-045736      616.97/92      0801861500
*HIV (Viruses) Viruses -- Evolution.*

# S Agriculture (General)

## S411 Encyclopedias and dictionaries

**S411.D245 1985**
**Dalal-Clayton, D. Barry**
Black's agricultural dictionary / D.B. Dalal-Clayton. 2nd ed.
London : A. & C. Black, 1985. xiii, 432 p. :
            630/.3/21 19
*Agriculture -- Dictionaries.*

**S411.E713 1994**
Encyclopedia of agricultural science / edited by Charles J.
Arntzen, Ellen M. Ritter. San Diego : Academic Press, c1994.
4 v. :
94-003143          630/.3      0122266706
*Agriculture -- Encyclopedias.*

**S411.L39 2002**
**Lewis, Robert Alan**
CRC dictionary of agricultural sciences / Robert A. Lewis.
Boca Raton : CRC Press, c2002. 674 p. :
            630/.3 21        0849323274
*Agriculture -- Dictionaries.*

**S411.L55 1995**
**Lipton, Kathryn L.**
Dictionary of agriculture : from abaca to zoonosis / Kathryn
L. Lipton. Boulder : Lynne Rienner Publishers, 1995. xi, 345
p. ;
94-025260          338.1/03        1555875238
*Agriculture -- Dictionaries. Agriculture -- United States --
Dictionaries.*

**S411.S34 1989**
**Schlebecker, John T.**
The many names of country people : an historical dictionary
from the twelfth century onward / John T. Schlebecker. New
York : Greenwood Press, 1989. xii, 325 p. ;
88-016549          630/.3/21        0313264171
*Agriculture -- Dictionaries. Agriculture -- History – Dictionaries.
Country life -- Dictionaries.*

**S411.W57 2000**
**Womach, Jasper.**
Agriculture : a glossary of terms, programs, laws and
websites / Jasper Womach and Carol Canada. Huntington,
N.Y. : Nova Science Publishers, c2000. 237 p. ;
            1560727993
*Agriculture -- Dictionaries. Agricultural administration – United
States -- Dictionaries. Agricultural laws and legislation -- United
States -- Dictionaries.*

## S417 Biography — Individual, A-Z

**S417.C3.H6 1963**
**Holt, Rackham.**
George Washington Carver, an American biography.
Garden City, N.Y., Doubleday [1963] 360 p.
62-011430          925
*Carver, George Washington, -- 1864?-1943. Agriculturists --
United States -- Biography. Afro-American agriculturists --
Biography.*

**S417.C3.M3**
**McMurry, Linda O.**
George Washington Carver, scientist and symbol / Linda O.
McMurry. New York : Oxford University Press, 1981. x, 367
p. :
81-004896          630/.92/4        0195029712
*Carver, George Washington, -- 1864?-1943. Afro-American
agriculturists -- Biography. Agriculturists -- United States --
Biography.*

**S417.C45.P7**
**Price, Robert,**
Johnny Appleseed : man and myth / by Robert Price.
Bloomington : Indiana University Press, 1954. xv, 320 p., [
54007972          926.3
*Appleseed, Johnny, -- 1774-1845.*

## S419 History and conditions — General

**S419.C82**
**Curwen, E. Cecil**
Plough and pasture, the early history of farming. Pt. 1:
Prehistoric farming of Europe and the Near East, by E. Cecil
Curwen. Pt. 2: Farming of non-European peoples, by
Gudmund Hatt. New York, H. Schuman [1953] xi, 329 p.
53011311          630.9
*Agriculture -- History.*

**S419.G8 1940**
**Gras, Norman Scott Brien,**
A history of agriculture in Europe and America, by Norman
Scott Brien Gras ... New York, F. S. Crofts & co., 1940. xxvii,
496 p.
40027443          630.9
*Agriculture -- Europe -- History. Agriculture -- United States –
History.*

**S419.H9**
**Hyams, Edward Solomon,**
Soil and civilization. London, Thames and Hudson [1952]
312 p.
52007988          631.49
*Agriculture -- History. Soils. Civilization -- History.*

## S421 History and conditions — Antiquity — General works

**S421.S3 1969**
**Sauer, Carl Ortwin,**
  Agricultural origins and dispersals; the domestication of animals and foodstuffs [by] Carl O. Sauer. Cambridge, M.I.T. Press [1969] xi, 175 p.
69-010841          630/.9
  *Agriculture -- Origin. Food crops -- Origin. Domestic animals – Origin.*

## S431 History and conditions — Antiquity — Romans

**S431.W46**
**White, K. D.**
  Roman farming [by] K. D. White. Ithaca, N.Y., Cornell University Press [1970] 536 p.
77-119592          630/.937          0801405750
  *Agriculture -- Rome.*

## S439 History and conditions — General agricultural conditions, world crop zones, etc.

**S439.G788**
**Grigg, David B.**
  The agricultural systems of the world : an evolutionary approach / D. B. Grigg. London ; Cambridge University Press, 1974. ix, 358 p. :
73-082451          630/.9     0521202698
  *Agricultural geography. Agriculture -- History.*

## S441-451 History and conditions — By region or country — United States (and North America)

**S441**
**Beeman, Randal S.,**
  A green and permanent land : ecology and agriculture in the twentieth century / Randal S. Beeman and James A. Pritchard. Lawrence : University Press of Kansas, c2001. ix, 219 p. ;
00-063334          333.76/16/0973     0700610669
  *Agriculture -- United States -- History. Sustainable agriculture – United States -- History. Agricultural ecology -- United States -- History.*

**S441.B5 1941**
**Bidwell, Percy Wells,**
  History of agriculture in the northern United States, 1620-1860, by Percy Wells Bidwell ... and John I. Falconer ... New York, P. Smith, 1941. xii, 512 p.
42036198          630.973
  *Agriculture -- United States.*

**S441.D3**
**Danhof, Clarence H.,**
  Change in agriculture; the northern United States, 1820-1870 [by] Clarence H. Danhof. Cambridge, Harvard University Press, 1969. x, 322 p.
70-075430          530/.973          0674107705
  *Agricultural innovations -- United States -- History. Agriculture -- United States -- History.*

**S441.E23**
**Ebeling, Walter,**
  The fruited plain : the story of American agriculture / Walter Ebeling. Berkeley : University of California Press, c1979. xiii, 433 p.
78-062837          338.1/0973          0520037510
  *Agriculture -- United States.*

**S441.G87 1991**
**Gussow, Joan Dye.**
  Chicken Little, tomato sauce, and agriculture : who will produce tomorrow's food? / Joan Dye Gussow. New York : Bootstrap Press, c1991. viii, 143 p.
91-008899          363.19/2          0942850327
  *Sustainable agriculture -- United States. Agriculture -- United States. Food supply -- United States.*

**S441.H28 2000**
**Hanson, Victor Davis.**
  The land was everything : letters from an American farmer / Victor Davis Hanson. New York : Free Press, c2000. xii, 258 p. ;
99-055317          630/.973          0684845016
  *St. John de Crevecoeur, J. Hector, -- 1735-1813 -- Letters from an American farmer. Agriculture -- Environmental aspects – United States. Nature -- Effect of human beings on -- United States. Agriculture -- United States.*

**S441.H2954 1991**
**Hart, John Fraser.**
  The land that feeds us / John Fraser Hart. New York : W.W. Norton, 1991. p. cm.
90-042720          630/.973          0393029549
  *Agriculture -- United States -- History.*

**S441.H918 1994**
**Hurt, R. Douglas.**
  American agriculture : a brief history / by R. Douglas Hurt. Ames : Iowa State University Press, 1994. xii, 412 p. :
93-039998          338.1/0973          0813823765
  *Agriculture -- United States -- History.*

**S441.H919 1996**
**Hurt, R. Douglas.**
  American farms : exploring their history / R. Douglas Hurt. Malabar, Fla. : Krieger Pub. Co., 1996. xiii, 165 p.
96-011222          630/.973          0894648918
  *Agriculture -- United States -- Historiography. Agriculture -- United States -- History -- Methodology.*

**S441.H92**
**Hurt, R. Douglas.**

The Dust Bowl : an agricultural and social history / R. Douglas Hurt. Chicago : Nelson-Hall, c1981. x, 214 p., [1
81-004031          338.1/0978          0882295411
*Agriculture -- Great Plains -- History -- 20th century. Droughts – Great Plains -- History -- 20th century. Dust storms –Great Plains – History -- 20th century. Great Plains -- Social conditions. Great Plains -- History.*

**S441.K57 1996**
**Knobloch, Frieda.**

The culture of wilderness : agriculture as colonization in the American West / Frieda Knobloch. Chapel Hill : University of North Carolina Press, c1996. xi, 204 p. ;
95-050148          306.3/49/0978          0807822809
*Agriculture -- West (U.S.) -- History.     West (U.S.) –Civilization.*

**S441.P58 1995**

Planting the future : developing an agriculture that sustains land and community / edited by Elizabeth Ann R. Bird, Gordon L. Bultena, John C. Gardner. Ames : Iowa State University Press, 1995. xxiii, 276 p.
94-041959          338.1/0973          0813820723
*Sustainable agriculture -- United States. Agriculture -- United States. Sustainable agriculture -- Research -- United States.*

**S441.S25 1983**
**Sachs, Carolyn E.,**

The invisible farmers : women in agricultural production / Carolyn E. Sachs. Totowa, N.J. : Rowman & Allanheld, 1983. xiv, 153 p. :
82-022824          305.4/33/0973          0865980942
*Women farmers -- United States -- History. Women farmers -- United States.*

**S441.S36**
**Schapsmeier, Edward L.**

Encyclopedia of American agricultural history / Edward L. Schapsmeier, Frederick H. Schapsmeier. Westport, Conn. : Greenwood Press, 1975. xii, 467 p. ;
74-034563          630/.973          0837179580
*Agriculture -- United States -- History -- Encyclopedias. Agriculture -- Encyclopedias.*

**S441.S43**
**Schlebecker, John T.**

Whereby we thrive : a history of American farming, 1607-1972 / John T. Schlebecker. 1st ed. Ames : Iowa State University Press, 1975. x, 342 p. :
          630/.973          0813800900
*Agriculture -- United States -- History.*

**S441.S757 1991**
**Soule, Judith D.**

Farming in nature's image : an ecological approach to agriculture / Judith D. Soule and Jon K. Piper ; foreword by Wes Jackson. Washington, D.C. : Island Press, c1992. xix, 286 p. :
91-021120          630          0933280890
*Sustainable agriculture -- United States. Agricultural ecology – United States.*

**S441.S97 1994**

Sustainable agriculture in the American Midwest : lessons from the past, prospects for the future / edited by Gregory McIsaac and William R. Edwards. Urbana : University of Illinois Press, c1994. x, 291 p. :
93-045671          630/.977          0252021002
*Sustainable agriculture -- Middle West. Agricultural ecology – Middle West.*

**S441.V57 1997**

Visions of American agriculture / edited by William Lockeretz. Ames : Iowa State University, 1997. xii, 243 p. :
97-005083          306.3/49/0973          0813820448
*Agriculture -- United States.*

**S451.N56.V25**
**Van Wagenen, Jared,**

The golden age of homespun. Illus. by Erwin H. Austin. Ithaca, New York, Cornell University Press [1953] 280 p.
53010581          630.9747
*Agriculture -- New York (State) -- History. Farm life – New York (State)*

**S451.V8.J4 1976**
**Jefferson, Thomas,**

Thomas Jefferson's Farm book : with commentary and relevant extracts from other writings / edited by Edwin Morris Betts. [Charlottesville] : University Press of Virginia, 1976, c1953. xxii, 178 [i.
76-151962          630/.9755          0813907055
*Jefferson, Thomas, -- 1743-1826.     Agriculture -- Virginia.*

## S455 History and conditions — By region or country — Europe

**S455.T48 1997**
**Thirsk, Joan.**

Alternative agriculture : a history from the Black Death to the present day / Joan Thirsk. Oxford ; New York : c1997. x, 365 p. :
98-115344          630/.941          0198206623
*Agriculture -- Great Britain. Agriculture -- Great Britain -- History. Agricultural industries -- Great Britain.*

## S470-471 History and conditions — By region or country — Asia

**S470.S64.T73 1986**

Traditional agriculture in Southeast Asia : a human ecology perspective / edited by Gerald G. Marten. Boulder : Westview Press, c1986. xxvi, 358 p.
85-051994          307.7/2          0813370264
*Traditional farming -- Asia, Southeastern. Agricultural ecology – Asia, Southeastern. Agriculture -- Social aspects -- Asia, Southeastern.*

**S471.A35.S5**
**Shantz, Homer Le Roy,**

The vegetation and soils of Africa, by H.L. Shantz and C.F. Marbut ... with a section on the land classification of Africa by the joint authors, and a note on a rainfall map of Africa, by J.B. Kincer. New York, Pub. jointly by the National Research Council an 1923. x, 263 p.
23012087

*Agriculture -- Africa. Deserts. Soils -- Africa.*

## S481 History and conditions — By region or country — Tropics

**S481.N38 1993**
**National Research Council (U.S.).**

Sustainable agriculture and the environment in the humid tropics / Committee on Sustainable Agriculture and the Environment in the Humid Tropics, Board on Agriculture and Board on Science and Technology for International Development, National Research Council. Washington, D.C. : National Academy Press, 1993. xv, 702 p. :
92-036869          333.76/15/0913          0309047498

*Agricultural systems -- Tropics. Sustainable agriculture -- Tropics. Land use, Rural -- Tropics.*

**S481.W45 1993**
**Weischet, Wolfgang.**

The persisting ecological constraints of tropical agriculture / Wolfgang Weischet and Cesar N. Caviedes. Harlow, Essex, England : Longman Scientific & Technical ; 1993. xiv, 319 p. :
92-042133          630/.913          0582056926

*Agricultural ecology -- Tropics. Agriculture -- Tropics. Tropical crops -- Ecology.*

## S493 General works — Comprehensive works (Theory, progress, science)

**S493.S4 1947**
**Sears, Paul Bigelow,**

Deserts on the march. Norman, Univ. of Oklahoma Press, 1947. xi, 178 p.
47027585          630.973

*Agriculture -- Economic aspects -- Economic aspects -- United States. Agriculture -- United States. Natural resources -- United States. United States -- Economic conditions.*

## S494.5 General works — Special aspects of agriculture as a whole, A-Z

**S494.5.A45.T4625 1997**

Temperate agroforestry systems / edited by Andrew M. Gordon and Steven M. Newman. Wallingford, [England] ; CAB International, c1997. xi, 269 p. :
97-022710          634.9/9          0851991475

*Agroforestry systems. Temperate climate.*

**S494.5.A45N69 2000**

North American agroforestry : an integrated science and practice / editors, H.E. (Gene) Garrett, W.J. (Bill) Rietveld, and R.F. (Dick) Fisher. Madison, Wis. : American Society of Agronomy, 2000. xvii, 402 p. :
          634.9/9/0973 21          0891181423

*Agroforestry -- United States. Forest management -- United States.*

**S494.5.A65.A43 1989**

Alternative agriculture / Committee on the Role of Alternative Farming Methods in Modern Production Agriculture, Board on Agriculture, National Research Council. Washington, D.C. : National Academy Press, 1989. xiv, 448 p. :
88-026997          630/.973          0309039878

*Alternative agriculture -- United States. Agricultural systems -- United States -- Case studies.*

**S494.5.A65.H37 1999**
**Hassanein, Neva,**

Changing the way America farms : knowledge and community in the sustainable agriculture movement / Neva Hassanein. Lincoln : University of Nebraska Press, c1999. xii, 216 p. ;
99-018477          338.1/62/0973          0803273215

*Alternative agriculture -- United States. Sustainable agriculture -- United States.*

**S494.5.A65.R63 1991**
**Rodale, Robert.**

Save three lives : a plan for famine prevention / Robert Rodale with Mike McGrath. San Francisco : Sierra Club Books, c1991. xvii, 253 p.
91-015224          338.1/62          0871566214

*Alternative agriculture -- Developing countries. Food supply -- Developing countries. Organic farming -- Developing countries.*

**S494.5.B563**
**Comstock, Gary,**

Vexing nature? : on the ethical case against agricultural biotechnology / by Gary L. Comstock. Boston : Kluwer Academic Publishers, c2000. 297 p. ;
00-064014          631.5/233          079237987X

*Agricultural biotechnology -- Moral and ethical aspects.*

**S494.5.B563.A37 1990**

Agricultural bioethics : implications of agricultural biotechnology / edited by Steven M. Gendel ... [et al.]. Ames : Iowa State University Press, 1990. xxiv, 357 p.
89-015598          174/.963          081380129X

*Agricultural biotechnology -- Moral and ethical aspects.*

**S494.5.B563.H63 1989**
**Hobbelink, Henk.**

Biotechnology and the future of world agriculture / Henk Hobbelink. London ; Zed Books, 1989. p. cm.
89-035866          631          0862328365

*Agricultural biotechnology -- Forecasting.*

**S494.5.B563.K75 1996**
**Krimsky, Sheldon.**
Agricultural biotechnology and the environment : science, policy, and social issues / Sheldon Krimsky and Roger P. Wrubel. Urbana : University of Illinois Press, c1996. 294 p. :
95-032490    338.1/62    0252021649
*Agricultural biotechnology. Agricultural biotechnology – United States.*

**S494.5.C6B56 2000**
**Boone, Kristina.**
Agricultural communications : changes and challenges / Kristina Boone, Terry Meisenbach, Mark Tucker. 1st ed. Ames : Iowa State University Press, 2000. ix, 134 p. :
630/.1/4 21    0813821576
*Communication in agriculture.*

**S494.5.G46.B78 1992**
**Bryant, C. R.,**
Agriculture in the citys countryside / Christopher R. Bryant and Thomas R.R. Johnston. Toronto ; University of Toronto Press, 1992. xiii, 233 p.
92-148686    080202842X
*Agricultural geography. Agriculture -- Economic aspects. Land use.*

**S494.5.I5**
**Paarlberg, Don,**
The agricultural revolution of the 20th century / Don Paarlberg and Philip Paarlberg. Ames : Iowa State University Press, 2000. xvi, 154 p. :
00-057230    338.1/6    0813821983
*Agricultural innovations. Agriculture -- Technology transfer. Agriculture and state.*

**S494.5.I5.F65 1993**
**Fliegel, Frederick C.**
Diffusion research in rural sociology : the record and prospects for the future / Frederick C. Fliegel ; foreword by James J. Zuiches. Westport, Conn. : Greenwood Press, 1993. xv, 132 p. :
92-019426    338.1/6/072    0313264473
*Agriculture -- Technology transfer. Diffusion of innovations. Agricultural innovations.*

**S494.5.I5.R66 1990**
**Roy, Sumit.**
Agriculture and technology in developing countries : India and Nigeria / Sumit Roy. New Delhi ; Sage Publications, 1990. 223 p. :
90-008854    338.1/0954    8170362067
*Agriculture -- Technology transfer -- India. Agriculture -- Technology transfer -- Nigeria. Agricultural innovations -- India.*

**S494.5.S86.S635 1998**
Facilitating sustainable agriculture : particpatory learning and adaptive management in times of environmental uncertainty / [edited by] N.G. Roling and M.A.E. Wagemakers. Cambridge, U.K ; Cambridge University Press, 1998. xxvi, 318 p.
97-011992    630    0521581745
*Sustainable agriculture. Agriculture -- Technology transfer. Agricultural extension work.*

**S494.5.S86.S85 1998**
Sustainability in agricultural and rural development / edited by Gerard E. D'Souza, Tesfa G. Gebremedhin. Aldershot, England ; Ashgate, c1998. xvii, 245 p.
97-051331    307.1/412    1855219778
*Sustainable agriculture. Sustainable development. Rural development.*

**S494.5.S86.S86 1990**
Sustainable agricultural systems / edited by Clive A. Edwards ... [et al.]. Ankeny, Iowa : Soil and Water Conservation Society, c1990. xvi, 696 p. :
89-026370    338.1/62    093573421X
*Sustainable agriculture. Agricultural systems.*

**S494.5.S86.S865 1992**
Sustainable agriculture and the environment : perspectives on growth and constraints / edited by Vernon W. Ruttan. Boulder : Westview Press, 1992. xvi, 189 p. :
91-043184    630    0813385075
*Sustainable agriculture.*

## S521.5 General works — Light literature. Popular works. Country life, etc. — By region or country

**S521.5.C8.T28**
**Taber, Gladys Bagg,**
The best of Stillmeadow : a treasury of country living / Gladys Taber ; edited and with an introd. by Constance Taber Colby ; drawings by Edward Shenton. Philadelphia : Lippincott, c1976. 348 p. :
76-020457    974.6    0397011563
*Taber, Gladys Bagg, -- 1899- Country life -- Connecticut. Connecticut -- Biography.*

## S531 Agricultural education — Schools. Study and teaching — General works

**S531.A57 1991**
Agriculture and natural resources : planning for educational priorities for the twenty-first century / edited by Wava G. Haney and Donald R. Field. Boulder : Westview Press, 1991. xiii, 183 p.
91-014040    630/.71/1    0813383455
*Natural resources -- Study and teaching (Higher) -- Planning. Agriculture -- Study and teaching (Higher) -- Wisconsin – Planning. Natural resources -- Study and teaching (Higher) -- Wisconsin -- Planning.*

## S533 Agricultural education — By region or country — United States

**S533.B17**
**Baker, Gladys L.,**
The county agent ... by Gladys Baker. Chicago, University of Chicago Press, 1939. xxi, 226 p. i
40004932    630.6173
*County agricultural agents.*

## S540.A2 Agricultural education — Research. Experimentation — General works

**S540.A2.L63 1993**
**Lockeretz, William.**
 Agricultural research alternatives / William Lockeretz and Molly D. Anderson. Lincoln : University of Nebraska Press, c1993. x, 239 p. ;
92-047113      630/.72      0803229011
 *Agriculture -- Research.*

**S540.A2.P65 1987**
 Policy for agricultural research / edited by Vernon W. Ruttan and Carl E. Pray. Boulder : Westview Press, 1987. xvii, 558 p.
87-014277      630/.72      0813373697
 *Agriculture -- Research. Agriculture -- Research -- Government policy.*

## S542 Agricultural education — Research. Experimentation — By region or country

**S542.A8.R46 1991**
 Research and productivity in Asian agriculture / [edited by] Robert E. Evenson, Carl E. Pray with the assistance of Zafar Ahmed ... [et al.]. Ithaca : Cornell University Press, 1991. vi, 383 p. :
90055750      338.1/095      0801425352
 *Agriculture -- Research -- Economic aspects -- Asia. Agricultural productivity -- Asia. Farm income -- Asia.*

## S555 Agricultural education — Exhibitions. Fairs — National, state, and local

**S555.V5.F57 1998**
**Fish, Charles.**
 Blue ribbons and burlesque : a book of country fairs / words and pictures by Charles Fish. Woodstock, Vt. : Countryman Press ; c1998. 272 p. :
97-047174      630/.74/743      0881504122
 *Fish, Charles. Fairs -- Vermont. Agricultural exhibitions -- Vermont -- Pictorial works. Fairs -- Vermont -- Pictorial works.*

## S587.73 S95 Agricultural chemistry — Adjuvants — Special adjuvants, A-Z

**S587.73.S95.T33 1995**
**Tadros, Th. F.**
 Surfactants in agrochemicals / Tharwat F. Tadros. New York : M. Dekker, c1995. x, 264 p. :
94-037159      668/.6      0824791002
 *Surface active agents. Agricultural chemicals -- Adjuvants.*

## S589.7 Agricultural ecology (General)

**S589.7.A37 1990**
 Agroecology / [edited by] C. Ronald Carroll, John H. Vandermeer, Peter Rosset. New York : McGraw-Hill, c1990. xiv, 641 p. :
89-012743      333.76      007052923X
 *Agricultural ecology. Agriculture. Agriculture -- Research.*

**S589.7.A38 1990**
 Agroecology : researching the ecological basis for sustainable agriculture / Stephen R. Gliessman, editor. New York : Springer-Verlag, c1990. xiv, 380 p. :
89-027592      630/.2/745      0387970282
 *Agricultural ecology. Sustainable agriculture. Agricultural ecology -- Research.*

**S589.7.E255 1997**
 Ecology in agriculture / edited by Louise E. Jackson. San Diego, Calif. : Academic Press, c1997. xii, 474 p. :
97-025875      630/.1/577      0123782600
 *Agricultural ecology.*

**S589.7. G584 2001**
**Gliessman, Stephen R.**
 Agroecosystem sustainability : developing practical strategies / Stephen R. Gliessman. Boca Raton, Fla. : CRC Press, c2001. 210 p. :
00-056485      630/.2/77      0849308941
 *Agricultural ecology. Sustainable agriculture.*

**S589.7.L66 1992**
**Loomis, R. S.**
 Crop ecology : productivity and management in agricultural systems / R.S. Loomis, D.J. Connor. Cambridge [England] ; Cambridge University Press, 1992. xiv, 538 p. :
91-029201      631      052138379X
 *Agricultural ecology. Agricultural systems.*

**S589.7.S637 1997**
 Soil ecology in sustainable agricultural systems / edited by Lijbert Brussaard, Ronald Ferrera-Cerrato. Boca Raton : CRC/Lewis Publishers, c1997. 168 p. :
96-030093      631.4/22      1566702771
 *Agricultural ecology -- Congresses. Soil ecology -- Congresses. Sustainable agriculture -- Congresses.*

## S590.2 Soils. Soil science — Congresses

**S590.2.M48 1996**
 Methods for assessing soil quality / editors, John W. Doran and Alice J. Jones ; editorial committee, Richard P. Dick ... [et al.] ; editor-in-chief SSSA, Jerry M. Bigham ; managing editor, David M. Kral ; associate editor, Marian K. Viney. Madison, Wis., USA : Soil Science Society of America, 1996. xxvi, 410 p.
96-072332      631.4      0891188266
 *Soils -- Quality -- Congresses. Soils -- Analysis -- Congresses.*

## S590.45 Soils. Soil science — Communication in soil science — Soil science literature

**S590.45.L58 1994**
The Literature of soil science / edited by Peter McDonald. Ithaca : Cornell University Press, 1994. vi, 448 p. :
631.4 20          0801429218
*Soil science literature.*

## S591 Soils. Soil science — General works

**S591.B33 1986**
**Bear, Firman Edward,**
Earth : the stuff of life / by Firman E. Bear. 2nd ed. / revised by H. Wayne Pritchard and Wallace E. Akin. Norman : University of Oklahoma Press, c1986. xviii, 318 p. :
631.4 19
*Soils. Soils -- United States. Soil conservation. Soil conservation – United States.*

**S591.B56**
**Black, C. A.**
Soil-plant relationships.   New York, Wiley [c1957] vi, 332 p.
57010803          631.4
*Plant physiology. Soils.*

**S591.B79 2002**
**Brady, Nyle C.**
The nature and property of soils / Nyle C. Brady, Ray R. Weil. 13th ed. Upper Saddle River, NJ : Prentice Hall, c2002. xvi, 960 p. :
631.4 21
*Soil science. Soils.*

**S591.B886**
**Bunting, Brian T.**
The geography of soil [by] Brian T. Bunting. Chicago, Aldine Pub. Co. [1965] 213 p.
65-020517          553.6012
*Soils -- Classification. Soil formation.*

**S591.B887 1997**
Soil genesis and classification / S.W. Buol . . . [et al.]. 4th ed. Ames : Iowa State University Press, 1997. xvi, 527 p. :
631.4 21
*Soil science. Soil formation. Soils -- Classification.*

**S591.C6 1971**
**Clarke, George Robin.**
The study of soil in the field [by] G. R. Clarke assisted by Philip Beckett. Oxford, Clarendon Press, 1971. xi, 145 p., 7
72-031857          631.4          0198541171
*Soil surveys.*

**S591.F68 1980**
**Foth, H. D.**
Soil geography and land use / Henry D. Foth, John W. Schafer. New York : J. Wiley, c1980. 484 p. :
79-027731          631.4/7          0471017108
*Soil geography. Land use.*

**S591.G44 2000**
**Gerrard, John,**
Fundamentals of soils / John Gerrard. New York : Routledge, 2000. p. cm.
99-054629          631.4          0415170044
*Soils.*

**S591.H23 2000**
Handbook of soil science / editor-in-chief, Malcolm E. Sumner. Boca Raton, Fla : CRC Press, c2000. 1 v. (various
99-029646          631.4          0849331366
*Soil science -- Handbooks, manuals, etc.*

**S591.H28 2001**
**Harpstead, Milo I.,**
Soil science simplified / Milo I. Harpstead, Thomas J. Sauer, William F. Bennett ; illustrated by Mary C. Bratz. 4th ed. Ames : Iowa State University Press, 2001. vii, 225 p. :
631.4 21          0813829429
*Soil science.*

**S591.H62 1991**
**Hillel, Daniel.**
Out of the earth : civilization and the life of the soil / Daniel J. Hillel. New York : Free Press ; c1991. x, 321 p. ;
90-038119          631.4          0029150604
*Soils. Soil and civilization. Water and civilization.*

**S591.J4**
**Jenny, Hans,**
Factors of soil formation; a system of quantitative pedology, by Hans Jenny... New York, McGraw-Hill, 1941. xii,281 p.
41014446          631.4
*Soils.*

**S591.M733 2001**
**Miller, Raymond W.,**
Soils in our environment / Raymond W. Miller, Duane T. Gardiner. 9th ed. Upper Saddle River, N.J. : Prentice Hall, c2001. xiii, 642 p. :
631.4 21          0130200360
*Soil science. Crops and soils. Soil management.*

**S591.P39 1983**
Pedogenesis and soil taxonomy / edited by L.P. Wilding, N.E. Smeck, and G.F. Hall. Amsterdam ; Elsevier ; 1983. 2 v. :
82-024198          631.4/4          0444421009
*Soil science. Soils -- Classification. Soil formation.*

**S591.R68 1994**
**Rowell, David L.,**
Soil science : methods and applications / David L. Rowell. Harlow, Essex : Longman Scientific & Technical ; 1994. 350 p. :
93-012830          631.4          0470221410
*Soil science.*

**S591.R84 1988**
**Russell, Edward J.**
Russell's soil conditions and plant growth. Burnt Mill, Harlow, Essex, Eng. : Longman Scientific & Technical ; 1988. ix, 991 p. :
86-027391          631.4          0470207965
*Soil science. Crops and soils.*

**S591.S555 2002**
**Singer, Michael J. (Michael John),**
Soils : an introduction / Michael J. Singer, Donald N. Munns. 5th ed. Upper Saddle River, N.J. : Prentice Hall, c2002. xv, 429 p. :
          631.4 21          0130278254
*Soil science. Soils. Plant-soil relationships. Soil management.*

**S591.W72 1993**
**Wild, Alan.**
Soils and the environment : an introduction / Alan Wild. Cambridge ; Cambridge University Press, 1993. xix, 287 p. :
92-024680          631.4          0521432804
*Soils -- Environmental aspects.*

**S591.W73 1996**
**Winegardner, Duane L.**
An introduction to soils for environmental professionals / Duane L. Winegardner. Boca Raton : Lewis Publishers, c1996. xvi, 270 p. :
95-035149          631.4          0873719395
*Soil science. Soils.*

## S592 Soils. Soil science — Encyclopedias and dictionaries

**S592.E52**
The Encyclopedia of soil science / edited by Rhodes W. Fairbridge, Charles W. Finkl, Jnr. Stroudsburg, Pa. : Dowden, Hutchinson & Ross : c1979- v. :
78-031233          631.4/03          0879331763
*Soil science -- Encyclopedias.*

**S592.G58 1997**
Glossary of soil science terms. Madison, WI : Soil Science Society of America, c1997. 134 p. :
          631.4/03 21
*Soil science -- Terminology.*

## S592.14 Soils. Soil science — Soil surveys. — General works

**S592.14.O36 1984**
**Olson, Gerald W.**
Field guide to soils and the environment : applications of soil surveys / Gerald W. Olson. New York : Chapman and Hall, 1984. xvii, 219 p.
84-005050          631.4          0412259605
*Soil surveys. Soil science.*

**S592.14.W4 1990**
**Webster, R.**
Statistical methods in soil and land resource survey / R. Webster and M.A. Oliver. Oxford [England] ; Oxford University Press, 1990. 316 p. :
90-035409          631.4/7/072          0198233175
*Soil surveys -- Statistical methods. Soils -- Classification -- Statistical methods.*

## S592.17.A-Z Soils. Soil science — Soil classification — By order, great group, family, etc., A-Z

**S592.17.H93**
Wetland soils : genesis, hydrology, landscapes, and classification / edited by J.L. Richardson and M.J. Vepraskas. Boca Raton, FL : Lewis Publishers, 2000. p. cm.
00-033099          631.4          1566704847
*Hydric soils. Wetlands.*

## S592.2 Soils. Soil science — Soil classification — Soil formation

**S592.2.B57 1984**
**Birkeland, Peter W.**
Soils and geomorphology / Peter W. Birkeland. New York : Oxford University Press, 1984. xiv, 372 p. :
83-013345          551.3/05          0195033981
*Soil formation. Weathering. Soil science.*

**S592.2.P373 1995**
**Paton, T. R.**
Soils : a new global view / T.R. Paton, G.S. Humphreys, P.B. Mitchell. New Haven : Yale University Press, 1995. ix, 213 p., [
95-030335          551.3/05          0300065760
*Soil formation. Soils.*

## S592.3 Soils. Soil science — Soil physics — General works

**S592.3.H53**
**Hillel, Daniel.**
Applications of soil physics / Daniel Hillel. New York : Academic Press, 1980. xiv, 385 p. :
80-000535          631.4/3          0123485800
*Soil physics. Soil moisture. Soil management.*

**S592.3.H535 1998**
**Hillel, Daniel.**
Environmental soil physics / Daniel Hillel. San Diego, CA : Academic Press, 1998. p. cm.
98-023679          631.4          0123485258
*Soil physics. Soil physics -- Environmental aspects.*

**S592.3.H55**
**Hillel, Daniel.**
Introduction to soil physics / Daniel Hillel. New York : Academic Press, 1981. p. cm.
81-010848          631.4/3          0123485207
*Soil physics.*

## S592.5 Soils. Soil science — Soil chemistry — General works

**S592.5.S656 1989**
**Sposito, Garrison,**
　The chemistry of soils / Garrison Sposito. New York : Oxford University Press, 1989. xii, 277 p. :
88-011768　　　631.4/1　　　0195046153
　*Soil chemistry.*

**S592.5.S66 1994**
**Sposito, Garrison,**
　Chemical equilibria and kinetics in soils / Garrison Sposito. New York : Oxford University Press, 1994. x, 268 p. :
93-046714　　　631.4/1　　　0195075641
　*Soil solutions. Thermodynamics. Chemical kinetics.*

## S592.53 Soils. Soil science — Soil chemistry — Soil physical chemistry

**S592.53.S65 1999**
　Soil physical chemistry / edited by Donald L. Sparks. Boca Raton, Fla. : CRC Press, c1999. 409 p. :
98-010571　　　631.4/1　　　0873718836
　*Soil physical chemistry.*

## S592.7 Soils. Soil science — Soil biochemistry — General works

**S592.7.S73 1986**
**Stevenson, F. J.**
　Cycles of soil : carbon, nitrogen, phosphorus, sulfur, micronutrients / F.J. Stevenson. New York : Wiley, c1986. xviii, 380 p.
85-012042　　　631.4/1　　　0471822183
　*Soil biochemistry. Biogeochemical cycles. Soil ecology.*

## S592.8 Soils. Soil science — Soil biochemistry — Humus

**S592.8.M34 1992**
**Magdoff, Fred,**
　Building soils for better crops : organic matter management / Fred Magdoff. Lincoln : University of Nebraska Press, c1992. xii, 176 p. :
92-002362　　　631.4/17　　　0803231601
　*Humus. Soil management.*

## S593 Soils. Soil science — Analysis and experiments

**S593.S7425 1993**
　Soil sampling and methods of analysis / edited by Martin R. Carter. Boca Raton : Lewis Publishers, c1993. 823 p. :
92-038583　　　631.4/028/7　　　0873718615
　*Soils -- Analysis. Soils -- Sampling.*

## S594 Soils. Soil science — Soil moisture

**S594.H563**
**Hillel, Daniel.**
　Soil and water; physical principles and processes. New York, Academic Press [1971] xiv, 288 p.
79-127685　　　631.4/32　　　0123485509
　*Soil moisture. Soil physics.*

**S594.W7 1994**
**Wolt, Jeffrey D.**
　Soil solution chemistry : applications to environmental science and agriculture / Jeffrey D. Wolt. New York : Wiley, 1994. xvii, 345 p.
94-010959　　　631.4/1　　　0471585548
　*Soil solutions -- Research -- Methodology. Soil chemistry -- Methodology.*

## S596 Soils. Soil science — Soils and the environment

**S596.S65 1995**
　Soil management and greenhouse effect / edited by R. Lal ... [et al.]. Boca Raton : Lewis Publishers, c1995. 385 p. :
95-000904　　　574.5/26404　　　1566701171
　*Soils -- Environmental aspects. Greenhouse effect, Atmospheric -- Environmental aspects. Greenhouse gases -- Environmental aspects.*

## S596.7 Soils. Soil science — Soils and crops — General works

**S596.7.B37 1984**
**Barber, Stanley A.**
　Soil nutrient bioavailability : a mechanistic approach / Stanley A. Barber. New York : Wiley, c1984. xiii, 398 p.
83-023331　　　631.4　　　0471090328
　*Crops and soils -- Mathematical models. Crops -- Nutrition -- Mathematical models. Soil fertility -- Mathematical models.*

**S596.7.F68 1997**
**Foth, H.D.**
　Soil fertility / Henry D. Foth and Boyd G. Ellis. 2nd ed. Boca Raton, Fla. : CRC Lewis, c1997. 290 p. :
　　　　　631.4/2 20　　　1566702437
*Soil fertility. Fertilizers.*

**S596.7.R46 1989**
**Rendig, Victor V.**
　Principles of soil-plant interrelationships / Victor V. Rendig, Howard M. Taylor. New York : McGraw-Hill, c1989. xv, 275 p. :
89-002579　　　582/.013　　　0070518793
　*Crops and soils. Plant-soil relationships.*

## S598 Soils. Soil science — Miscellaneous

**S598.S6**
Soil organic matter / edited by M. Schnitzer and S. U. Khan. Amsterdam ; Elsevier Scientific Pub. Co. ; 1978. xiii, 319 p.
78-001906          631.4/17          0444416102
*Humus.*

## S599 Soils. Soil science — Local — United States

**S599.A1.S62 1993**
Soil and water quality : an agenda for agriculture / Committee on Long-Range Soil and Water Conservation, Board on Agriculture, National Research Council. Washington, D.C. : National Academy Press, 1993. xx, 516 p. :
93-035470          333.76/0973          0309049334
*Soil management -- United States. Soils -- United States -- Quality. Water quality management -- United States.*

**S599.A1P76 2002**
Profiles in the history of the U.S. Soil Survey / edited by Douglas Helms, Anne B.W. Elffland, Patricia J. Durana. 1st ed. Ames, Iowa : Iowa State University Press, 2002. xvi, 331 p. :
          631.4/973 21          0813827590
*Soil surveys -- United States -- History. Soil scientists – United States -- History. United States. Division of Soils -- History.*

## S599.9.A-Z Soils. Soil science — Local — Other regions A-Z

**S599.9.T76.S26**
**Sanchez, Pedro A.,**
Properties and management of soils in the tropics / Pedro A. Sanchez. New York : Wiley, c1976. x, 618 p. :
76-022761          631.4/913          0471752002
*Soils -- Tropics. Plant-soil relationships -- Tropics. Soil science.*

**S599.9.T76.W36 1991**
**Wambeke, A. van.**
Soils of the tropics : properties and appraisal / Armand Van Wambeke. New York : McGraw-Hill, c1992. xiii, 343 p.
91-030678          631.4/713          0070679460
*Soils -- Tropics. Land capability for agriculture -- Tropics. Soil management -- Tropics.*

## S600.7.C54 Agricultural meteorology. Crops and climate — Special Topics, A-Z— Climatic changes

**S600.7.C54.R67 1998**
**Rosenzweig, Cynthia.**
Climate change and the global harvest : potential impacts of the greenhouse effect on agriculture / Cynthia Rosenzweig, Daniel Hillel. New York : Oxford University Press, 1998. 324 p. :
97-027058          338.1/4          0195088891
*Climatic changes. Greenhouse effect, Atmospheric. Meteorology, Agricultural.*

## S600.7.T45 Agricultural meteorology. Crops and climate — Special Topics, A-Z— Temperature

**S600.7.T45**
Crop responses and adaptations to temperature stress / Amarjit S. Basra, editor. New York : Food Products Press, c2001. xiv, 302 p. :
00-039305          631.5/233          1560228903
*Crops -- Effect of temperature on. Crops -- Adaptation.*

## S603.5 Methods and systems of culture. Cropping systems — Companion crops

**S603.5.V36 1989**
**Vandermeer, John H.**
The ecology of intercropping / John Vandermeer. Cambridge [England] ; Cambridge University Press, 1989. xi, 237 p. :
87-033830          631.5/8          0521345928
*Intercropping. Agricultural ecology.*

## S603.7 Methods and systems of culture. Cropping systems — Double cropping. Multiple cropping

**S603.7.M85 1986**
Multiple cropping systems / [editor], Charles A. Francis. New York : Macmillan Pub. Co. ; c1986. xiv, 383 p. :
85-019891          631.5/8          0029486106
*Multiple cropping.*

## S604 Methods and systems of culture. Cropping systems — Tillage. Plowing

**S604.N62 1986**
No-tillage and surface-tillage agriculture : the tillage revolution / edited by Milton A. Sprague, Glover B. Triplett. New York : Wiley, c1986. xix, 467 p. :
85-026587          631.5/8          0471884103
*No-tillage. Tillage.*

## S605.5 Melioration: Improvement, reclamation, fertilization, irrigation, etc., of lands — Organic farming. Organiculture

**S605.5.B46 1994**
**Bender, Jim,**
Future harvest : pesticide-free farming / Jim Bender. Lincoln : University of Nebraska Press, c1994. xviii, 159 p.
93-015807          630/.977          080321233X
*Organic farming -- Middle West. Organic farming – Nebraska – Case studies. Sustainable agriculture -- Middle West.*

## S613-618 Melioration: Improvement, reclamation, fertilization, irrigation, etc., of lands — Special classes of lands and reclamation methods — Deserts. Arid lands. Irrigation

**S613.H67 1992**
**Hinman, C. Wiley.**
 The plight and promise of arid land agriculture / C. Wiley Hinman and Jack W. Hinman. New York : Columbia University Press, c1992. 253 p. :
91-043989          630/.9154          0231066120
 *Arid regions agriculture.*

**S616.U6.O65 2000**
**Opie, John,**
 Ogallala : water for a dry land / John Opie. Lincoln : University of Nebraska Press, c2000. xxv, 475 p. :
99-042161          333.91/3/0978          0803286147
 *Irrigation water -- High Plains (U.S.) -- History. Irrigation -- High Plains (U.S.) -- History. Agriculture -- High Plains (U.S.) -- History. Ogallala Aquifer -- History.*

**S618.P67 1999**
**Postel, Sandra.**
 Pillar of sand : can the irrigation miracle last? / Sandra Postel. New York : W.W. Norton & Co., c1999. xv, 313 p. :
00-501134          333.91/3          0393319377
 *Irrigation. Water conservation.*

## S622.2 Soil conservation and protection — Congresses

**S622.2.S65 1985**
 Soil erosion and conservation / edited by S.A. El-Swaify, W.C. Moldenhauer, and Andrew Lo. Ankeny, Iowa : Soil Conservation Society of America, c1985. xxviii, 793 p
85-002507          631.4          0935734112
 *Soil erosion -- Congresses. Soil conservation -- Congresses. Sediment control -- Congresses.*

## S623 Soil conservation and protection — General works

**S623.M435 1998**
 Methods for assessment of soil degradation / edited by R. Lal ... [et al.]. Boca Raton, Fla. : CRC Press, c1998. 558 p. :
97-024696          333.73/137          084937443X
 *Soil degradation.*

**S623.M68**
**Morgan, R. P. C.**
 Soil erosion / R. P. C. Morgan. London ; Longman, 1979. 113 p. :
77-025911          631.4/5          0582486920
 *Soil erosion. Soil conservation. Soil erosion -- Malaysia -- Malaya.*

## S624 Soil conservation and protection — History and conditions — United States

**S624.A1.G58 1995**
**Glanz, James.**
 Saving our soil : solutions for sustaining earth's vital resource / James Glanz. Boulder : Johnson Books, c1995. ix, 182 p. :
95-010257          333.73/16/0973          155566136X
 *Soil conservation -- United States. Agricultural conservation -- United States. Soil conservation.*

**S624.A1.S74 1990**
**Steiner, Frederick R.**
 Soil conservation in the United States : policy and planning / Frederick R. Steiner. Baltimore : Johns Hopkins University Press, c1990. xxii, 249 p.
89-071742          333.76/16/0973          0801839971
 *Soil conservation -- Government policy -- United States. Soil conservation -- United States -- Planning.*

## S625.A-Z Soil conservation and protection — History and conditions — Other regions or countries, A-Z

**S625.T76.L35 1990**
**Lal, R.**
 Soil erosion in the tropics : principles and management / Rattan Lal. New York : McGraw-Hill, c1990. p. cm.
90-030142          631.4/5/0913          0070360871
 *Soil erosion -- Tropics. Soil conservation -- Tropics.*

## S633 Fertilizers and improvement of the soil — General works

**S633.N88 1998**
 Nutrient use in crop production / Zdenko Rengel, editor. New York : Food Products Press, c1998. xiv, 267 p. :
98-039020          631.8          1560220619
 *Fertilizers. Crops -- Nutrition. Soil fertility.*

**S633.P83 1997**
**Prasad, Rajendra,**
 Soil fertility management for sustainable agriculture / Rajendra Prasad, James F. Power. Boca Raton : CRC/Lewis Publishers, c1997. 356 p., [4] p
96-044795          631.4/1          1566702542
 *Soil fertility. Fertilizers. Sustainable agriculture.*

**S633.S715 1993**
 Soil fertility and fertilizers. 5th ed. / Samuel L. Tisdale . . . [et al.] Upper Saddle River, N.J. : Prentice Hall, c1993. xiv, 634 p. :
          631.4/22 20          0024208353
 *Fertilizers. Soil fertility. Crops -- Nutrition.*

## S651 Fertilizers and improvement of the soil — Nitrogen and nitrates — General works

**S651.S56 2001**
**Smil, Vaclav.**
Enriching the earth : Fritz Haber, Carl Bosch, and the transformation of world food production / Vaclav Smil. Cambridge, Mass. : MIT Press, c2001. xvii, 338 p.
00-026291          631.8/4          026219449X
*Nitrogen fertilizers. Ammonia as fertilizer.*

## S674.5 Farm machinery and farm engineering — History (General)

**S674.5.B55 1976**
**Blandford, Percy W.**
Old farm tools and machinery : an illustrated history / by Percy W. Blandford. Fort Lauderdale, Fla. : Gale Research Co., c1976. 188 p. :
75-044376          631.3/09          0810320193
*Agricultural machinery -- History. Agricultural implements -- History. Agricultural machinery -- Pictorial works.*

## S675 Farm machinery and farm engineering — General works

**S675.H83 2001**
**Hunt, Donnell.**
Farm power and machinery management / Donnell Hunt. 10th ed. Ames : Iowa State University Press, 2001. viii, 368 p. :
            631.3 21          0813817560
*Agricultural machinery. Farm mechanization.*

## S676 Farm machinery and farm engineering — Tools and farm devices — General works

**S676.W5**
**White, K. D.**
Agricultural implements of the Roman world [by] K. D. White. London, Cambridge U.P., 1967. xvi, 232 p.
67-010350          631.3/0937          0521069122
*Agricultural implements -- Rome -- History. Agriculture – Rome. Rome -- Antiquities.*

## S926 Conservation of natural resources — Biography

**S926.A2.A94 1993**
**Axelrod, Alan,**
The environmentalists : a biographical dictionary from the 17th century to the present / Alan Axelrod and Charles Phillips. New York : Facts on File, c1993. xiv, 258 p. :
92-038773          363.7/0092/2          0816027153
*Conservationists -- Biography -- Dictionaries. Environmentalists -- Biography -- Dictionaries. Naturalists -- Biography -- Dictionaries.*

## S930-934.A-Z Conservation of natural resources — History and conditions — By region or country

**S930.F57 1990**
**Fitzgerald, Sarah.**
Options for conservation : the different roles of nongovernmental conservation organizations / by Sarah Fitzgerald. Washington, D.C. : World Wildlife Fund ; c1990. xiii, 152 p.
90-024078          333.7/2/0973          0891641238
*Conservation of natural resources -- United States. Conservation of natural resources -- United States -- Societies, etc.*

**S930.R66 1972**
**Roosevelt, Franklin D.**
Franklin D. Roosevelt & conservation, 1911-1945. Compiled and edited by Edgar B. Nixon. New York, Arno Press, 1972. 2 v.
72-002861          333.7/2/0973          0405045255
*Roosevelt, Franklin D. -- (Franklin Delano), -- 1882-1945. Conservation of natural resources -- United States.*

**S930.V65 1991**
Voices from the environmental movement : perspectives for a new era / edited by Donald Snow ; foreword by Patrick F. Noonan. Washington, D.C. : Island Press, c1992. xiv, 237 p. ;
91-039067          333.7/2/0973          1559631333
*Conservation of natural resources -- United States. Conservation leadership -- United States. Conservationists -- United States.*

**S932.W37.W55 1992**
**Wilkinson, Charles F.,**
The eagle bird : mapping a new West / Charles F. Wilkinson. New York : Pantheon Books, c1992. xviii, 203 p.
91-053071          333.95/16/0978          0679408959
*Conservation of natural resources -- West (U.S.) Conservation of natural resources -- Government policy -- West (U.S.) Environmental policy -- West (U.S.)*

**S934.M6.S55 1995**
**Simonian, Lane,**
Defending the land of the jaguar : a history of conservation in Mexico / Lane Simonian. Austin : University of Texas Press, 1995. xiv, 326 p. :
95-001487          333.72/0972          029277690X
*Conservation of natural resources -- Mexico -- History. Environmental protection -- Mexico -- History.*

## S938 Conservation of natural resources — Textbooks

**S938**
Foundations of natural resources policy and management / edited by Tim W. Clark, Andrew R. Willard, and Christina M. Cromley. New Haven : Yale University Press, c2000. xi, 372 p. ;
00-035924          333.7/2          0300083564
*Conservation of natural resources -- Case studies. Nature conservation -- Case studies. Environmental management -- Case studies.*

## S938.O87 1998
**Owen, Oliver S.,**

Natural resource conservation : management for a sustainable future / Oliver S. Owen, Daniel D. Chiras, John P. Reganold. 7th ed. Upper Saddle River, N.J. : Prentice Hall, 1998. xiv, 594 p. :

              333.7/2 21        0138401330

*Conservation of natural resources. Natural resources – Management. Sustainable development. Environmental protection. Conservation of natural resources -- United States. Natural resources -- United States -- Management. Sustainable development -- United States. Environmental protection -- United States.*

### S944.5 Conservation of natural resources — Special topics, A-Z — Leadership

## S944.5.L42.I57 1991

Inside the environmental movement : meeting the leadership challenge / [edited by] Donald Snow ; foreword by Patrick F. Noonan. Washington, D.C. : Island Press, c1992. xxxiv, 295 p. 91-020235       333.7/2/0973      1559630272

*Conservation leadership -- United States. Conservationists -- United States. Environmentalists -- United States.*

# SB Plant culture

# SB45 Encyclopedias and dictionaries

## SB45.B17 1925
**Bailey, L. H.**

The standard cyclopedia of horticulture; a discussion, for the amateur, and the professional and commercial grower, of the kinds, characteristics and methods of cultivation of the species of plants by L. H. Bailey, illustrated with colored plates, four thousand engravings in the text, and ninety-six full-page cuts. New York, The Macmillan company; 1925. 3 v.
25-026333

*Gardening -- Dictionaries.*

## SB45.B22 1976
**Bailey, L. H.**

Hortus third : a concise dictionary of plants cultivated in the United States and Canada / initially compiled by Liberty Hyde Bailey and Ethel Zoe Bailey ;  revised and expanded by the staff of the Liberty Hyde Bailey Hortorium. New York : Macmillan, c1976. xiv, 1290 p.
77-352066      582/.06/1

*Plants, Cultivated -- North America -- Dictionaries. Gardening – North America -- Dictionaries.*

## SB45.G57 1992

Glossary of crop science terms / [Robert F. Barnes and James B. Beard, ed.] Madison, Wisc. : Crop Science Society of America, c1992. 88 p. :

             630/.14 20        0891185356

*Crops -- Terminology. Crops -- Nomenclature. Crop science -- Terminology. Crop science -- Nomenclature.*

### SB45.65 Communication in crop science — Crop science in literature

## SB45.65.L58 1995

The literature of crop science / edited by Wallace C. Olsen. Ithaca : Cornell University Press, 1995. x, 511 p. :

             630 20       0801426774

*Crop science literature.*

### SB63 Biography — Individual, A-Z

## SB63.B3.D6
**Dorf, Philip.**

Liberty Hyde Bailey : an informal biography. Ithaca, NY : Cornell University Press, [1956] 259 p. :
56004695          926.3

*Bailey, L. H. -- (Liberty Hyde), -- 1858-1954.   Horticulturists -- Biography.*

### SB73 History and conditions — Antiquity — General works

## SB73.V3813 1992
**Vavilov, N. I.**

Origin and geography of cultivated plants / N.I. Vavilov ; departmental editor, V.F. Dorofeyev ; translated by Doris Love. Cambridge [England] ; Cambridge University Press, 1992. xxxi, 498 p.
92-025039         630/.9       0521404274

*Plants, Cultivated -- Origin. Plants, Cultivated -- Geographical distribution.*

### SB83 History and conditions — By region or country — United States

## SB83.H4
**Hedrick, Ulysses Prentiss,**

A history of horticulture in America to 1860. New York, Oxford University Press, 1950. xiii, 551 p.
50006898         634

*Horticulture -- United States -- History. Gardening -- United States -- History.*

### SB91 General Works — Comprehensive works

## SB91.P56 2002
**McMahon, Margaret.**

Hartmann's plant science : growth, development, and utilization of cultivated plants / Margaret J. McMahon, Anton M. Kofranek, Vincent E. Rubatzky. 3rd ed. Upper Saddle River, N.J. : Prentice Hall, c2002. xvi, 573 p. :

             631 21      0139554777

*Plants, Cultivated. Botany, Economic.*

**SB91.P78 1998**

Principles of ecology in plant production / edited by T.R. Sinclair and F.P. Gardner. Oxon [England] ; Cab International, c1998. x, 189 p. :

97-033999          630/.2/77          085199220X

*Crops -- Ecology.*

## SB106 Special aspects of crops and plant culture as a whole, A-Z

**SB106.I47C75 2001**

Crop improvement : challenges in the twenty-first century / Manjit S. Kang, editor. New York : Food Products Press, c2002. xix, 389 p. :

631.5/23 21

*Crop improvement.*

**SB106.O74.E93 1993**
**Evans, L. T.**

Crop evolution, adaptation, and yield / L.T. Evans. Cambridge ; Cambridge University Press, 1993. xi, 500 p. :

92-028314          633          052122571X

*Crops -- Evolution. Crops -- Adaptation. Crops yields.*

## SB107 Economic botany — General and comprehensive works

**SB107.M38 2001**

Mansfeld's encyclopedia of agricultural and horticultural crops (except ornamentals) / Peter Hanelt [and] Institute of Plant Genetics and Crop Plant Research, (eds.) ; with contributions by R. Buttner . . . [et al.] ; camera-ready by Norbert Biermann and Jorg Ochsmann ; drawings by Ruth Kilian and Wolfgang Kilian. 1st English ed. Berlin ; New York : Springer, 2001. 6 v. :

630/.3 21          3540410171

*Plants, Cultivated -- Encyclopedias. Botany, Economic -- Encyclopedias.*

**SB107.W485 1999**
**Wiersema, John Harry.**

World economic plants : a standard reference / John H. Wiersema, Blanca Leon. Boca Raton, FL : CRC Press, c1999. xxxv, 749 p. :

581.6 21          0849321190

*Botany, Economic -- Nomenclature. Botany, Economic -- Nomenclature (Popular)*

## SB110 Methods for special areas — Dry farming

**SB110.B685 1982**
**Brengle, K. G.**

Principles and practices of dryland farming / K.G. Brengle. Boulder, Colo. : Colorado Associated University Press, c1982. xii, 178 p. :

80-070691          631.5/86          0870810952

*Dry farming.*

**SB110.H37 1993**
**Hargreaves, Mary W. M.,**

Dry farming in the Northern great plains : years of readjustment, 1920-1990 / Mary W.M. Hargreaves. Lawrence, KS : University Press of Kansas, c1993. xiii, 386 p.

92-008558          338.1/0978/0904          0700605533

*Dry farming -- Great Plains -- History -- 20th century.*

## SB111 Methods for special areas — Tropical agriculture

**SB111.T76 1992**

Tropical forests and their crops / Nigel J.H. Smith ... [et al.]. Ithaca : Comstock Pub. Associates, 1992. xvi, 568 p. :

92-052772          631.5/23          0801427711

*Tropical crops. Tree crops -- Tropics. Forest products – Tropics.*

**SB111.W63**
**Wilson, Charles Morrow,**

New crops for the new world, edited by Charles Morrow Wilson. New York, The Macmillan company, 1945. viii, 295 p.

45000341          630.97

*Agriculture -- Latin America. Agriculture -- Tropics.*

## SB112.5 Physiology

**SB112.5.C76 1999**

Crop yield : physiology and processes / Donald L. Smith, Chantal Hamel (eds.) Berlin ; New York : Springer, 1999. xvi, 504 p. :

631.5/58 21          3540644776

*Crops -- Physiology. Crop yields.*

**SB112.5.E58 1990**

Environmental injury to plants / edited by Frank Katterman. San Diego : Academic Press, c1990. xii, 290 p. :

89-028741          632/.1          0124013503

*Crops -- Effect of stress on. Plants, Effect of stress on. Crops – Physiology.*

**SB112.5.M56 1999**

Mineral nutrition of crops : fundamental mechanisms and implications / Zdenko Rengel, editor. New York : Food Products Press, c1999. xiv, 399 p. :

98-048697          631.8/11          1560228806

*Crops -- Nutrition. Crops -- Effect of minerals on.*

## SB117 Seeds. Seed technology — Seed growing. Seed farms — General works

**SB117.C73 2001**
**Copeland, L.O. (Lawrence O.),**

Principles of seed science and technology / by Lawrence O. Copeland, Miller B. McDonald. 4th ed. Boston : Kluwer Academic Publishers, c2001. xiv, 467 p. :

631.5/21 21          0792373227

*Seeds. Seed technology.*

## SB117.M36 1997
**McDonald, M. B.**

Seed production : principles and practices / Miller B. McDonald and Lawrence O. Copeland. New York : Chapman & Hall, c1997. viii, 749 p.

95-009326        631.5/21        0412075512

*Seed technology.*

### SB117.35.A-Z Seeds. Seed technology — Seed growing. Seed farms — By region or country

## SB117.35.N6.A9 1994
**Ausubel, Ken.**

Seeds of Change : the living treasure : the passionate story of the growing movement to restore biodiversity and revolutionize the way we think about food / Kenny Ausubel. [San Francisco, Calif.] : HarperSanFrancisco, c1994. vii, 232 p. :

92-056185        631.5/21        0062500082

*Food crops -- Seeds. Food crops -- Heirloom varieties. Seed technology.*

## SB118.25 Seeds. Seed technology — Seed quality

## SB118.25.S44 1995

Seed quality : basic mechanisms and agricultural implications / Amarjit S. Basra, editor. New York : Food Products Press, c1995. xiii, 389 p.

93-006092        631.5/21        1560228504

*Seeds -- Quality.*

## SB119 Propogation — General works

## SB119.P55 2002

Plant propagation : principles and practices / Hudson T. Hartmann . . . [et al.] 7th ed. Upper Saddle River, N.J. : Prentice Hall, c2002. xv, 880 p. :

631.5/3 21        0136792359

*Plant propagation.*

### SB123-123.3 Propogation — Special methods — Breeding, crossing, selection, etc.

## SB123.D47 2000

Designing crops for added value / editors C.F. Murphy and D.M. Peterson. Madison, Wisc. American Society of Agronomy, 2000. xvii, 267 p. :

631.5/23 21        089118144X

*Plant breeding.*

## SB123.D75 1990
**Driscoll, C. J.**

Plant sciences : production, genetics, and breeding / Colin J. Driscoll. New York : E. Horwood, 1990. p. cm.

90-035523        633        0136770487

*Plant breeding. Crops -- Genetics. Field crops.*

## SB123.H43 1955
**Hayes, Herbert Kendall,**

Methods of plant breeding [by] Herbert Kendall Hayes, Forrest Rhinehart Immer [and] David Clyde Smith. New York, McGraw-Hill, 1955. 551 p.

54010636        631.522

*Plant breeding. Genetics.*

## SB123.J46 1988
**Jensen, Neal F.**

Plant breeding methodology / Neal F. Jensen. New York : Wiley, c1988. xviii, 676 p.

88-002663        631.5/23        047160190X

*Plant breeding -- Methodology.*

## SB123.S89 1993
**Stoskopf, Neal C.,**

Plant breeding : theory and practice / Neal C. Stoskoph, with Dwight T. Tomes and B.R. Christie. Boulder : Westview Press, 1993. xxi, 531 p. :

92-038294        631.5/23        0813317649

*Plant breeding.*

## SB123.25.U6.R34 1995
**Raeburn, Paul.**

The last harvest : the genetic gamble that threatens to destroy American agriculture / Paul Raeburn. New York : Simon & Schuster, c1995. 269 p. ;

95-007369        338.1/62/0973        0684803658

*Plant breeding -- United States. Crops -- United States -- Germplasm resources. Agricultural innovations -- United States.*

## SB123.3.C58 1990

Climatic change and plant genetic resources / edited by M.T. Jackson, B.V. Ford-Lloyd, M.L. Parry. London ; Belhaven Press, 1990. xii, 190 p. :

90-000330        632/.1        1852931027

*Crops -- Germplasm resources. Crops and climate. Climatic changes.*

## SB123.3.G47 2000

Genes in the field : on-farm conservation of crop diversity / edited by Stephen B. Brush. Rome, Italy : International Plant Genetic Resources Institute c2000. 288 p. :

99-044933        631.5/23        0889368848

*Crops -- Germplasm resources. Germplasm resources, Plant.*

## SB123.3.H65 1993
**Holden, J. H. W.**

Genes, crops, and the environment / John Holden, James Peacock, and Trevor Williams. Cambridge ; Cambridge University Press, 1993. xiii, 162 p.

92-033605        333.95/316        0521431379

*Crops -- Germplasm resources. Germplasm resources, Plant.*

## SB123.3.M34 1995

Making nature, shaping culture : plant biodiversity in global context / Lawrence Busch ... [et al.]. Lincoln : University of Nebraska Press, c1995. xiii, 261 p.

95-010244        306.3/49        0803212569

*Food crops -- Germplasm resources. Germplasm resources, Plant. Plant diversity.*

**SB123.3.P62 1997**

Plant genetic conservation : the in situ approach / edited by N. Maxted, B.V. Ford-Lloyd, and J.G. Hawkes. London ; Chapman & Hall, 1997. xxiv, 446 p.
96-086665          639.9/9          0412634007
*Germplasm resources, Plant.*

**SB123.3.U17 1991**

The U.S. National Plant Germplasm System / Committee on Managing Global Genetic Resources: Agricultural Imperatives. Washington, D.C. : National Academy Press, 1991. xiv, 171 p. :
90-021056          631.5/23/0973          0309043905
*Crops -- United States -- Germplasm resources. Germplasm resources, Plant -- United States -- Management.*

## SB123.57 Propagation — Special methods — Genetic engineering. Transgenic plants

**SB123.57.M37 2001**
**Martineau, Belinda.**

First fruit : the creation of the Flavr savr tomato and the birth of genetically engineered food / Belinda Martineau. New York : McGraw-Hill, c2001. xvi, 269 p. ;
01-018038          635/.642233          0071360565
*Transgenic plants. Plant genetic engineering – Moral and ethical aspects. Crops -- Genetic engineering -- Environmental aspects.*

**SB123.57.R564 1996**
**Rissler, Jane.**

The ecological risks of engineered crops / Jane Rissler and Margaret Mellon. Cambridge, Mass. : MIT Press, c1996. xiv, 168 p. :
95-038926          631.5/23          0262181711
*Transgenic plants. Crops -- Genetic engineering – Environmental aspects. Plant genetic engineering -- Environmental aspects.*

**SB123.57.T69 1998**
**Toyota Conference (12th : 1998 : Shizuoka-shi, Japan)**

Proceedings of the 12th Toyota Conference : challenge of plant and agricultural sciences to the crisis of biosphere on the earth in the 21st century / Kazuo Watanabe and Atsushi Komamine. Georgetown, TX : R.G. Landes Co., c2000. 309 p. :
          631.5/233 21          1570596166
*Crops -- Genetic engineering -- Congresses. Plant biotechnology – Congresses.*

## SB123.6 Propopation — Special methods — Cell and tissue culture

**SB123.6.C65 1998**
**Collin, Hamish A.**

Plant cell culture / Hamish A. Collin, Sue Edwards. New York : Springer, 1998. p. cm.
98-015351          571.6/382          0387915087
*Plant cell culture. plant micropropagation.*

**SB123.6.P4813 1987**
**Pierik, R. L. M.**

In vitro culture of higher plants / by R.L.M. Pierik. Dordrecht ; M. Nijhoff ; 1987. v, 344 p. :
87-011235          582/.00724          9024735300
*Plant micropropagation.*

## SB123.75 Propagation — Special methods — Plant cuttings. Mist propogation

**SB123.75.A38 1988**

Adventitious root formation in cuttings / edited by Tim D. Davis, Bruce E. Haissig, Narendra Sankhla. Portland, Or. : Dioscorides Press, c1988. 315 p. :
88-003711          635/.0435          0931146100
*Plant cuttings -- Rooting. Roots (Botany) -- Formation.*

# SB128 Growth regulators

**SB128.N52**
**Nickell, Louis G.,**

Plant growth regulators : agricultural uses / Louis G. Nickell. Berlin ; Springer-Verlag, 1982. xii, 173 p. :
81-009320          631.8          0387109730
*Plant regulators.*

# SB160 New crops (General)

**SB160.N49 1993**

New crops for temperate regions / edited by K.R.M. Anthony, J. Meadley, G. Robbelen. London ; Chapman & Hall, 1993. xxvii, 247 p.
92-039739          338.1/7/094          0412480204
*New crops -- Congresses. New crops -- Europe -- Congresses.*

## SB170 Tree Crops — General works

**SB170.T723 1995**

Tree management in farmer strategies : responses to agricultural intensification / edited by J.E. Michael Arnold and Peter A. Dewees. Oxford ; Oxford University Press, 1995. xi, 292 p. ;
94-025814          338.1/7499/00954
0198584148
*Tree crops. Woodlots -- Management. Tree crops -- South Asia.*

## SB175 Food crops — General works

**SB175.F332 1998**
**Facciola, Stephen.**

Cornucopia II : a source book of edible plants / by Stephen Facciola. Vista, CA : Kampong Publications, 1998. xiv, 713 p. ;
98-092093          631.5/7          0962808725
*Food crops. Plants, Edible. Food crops -- Varieties.*

**SB175.F68 1990**
**Fowler, Cary.**
 Shattering : food, politics, and the loss of genetic diversity / Cary Fowler and Pat Mooney. Tucson : University of Arizona Press, c1990. xvi, 278 p. :
89-049378          338.1/62          0816511543
 *Food crops -- Breeding -- Economic aspects. Food crops -- Germplasm resources -- Economic aspects. Food crops -- Genetics.*

**SB175.V38 1997**
**Vaughan, J.G. (John Griffith)**
 The new Oxford book of food plants / J.G. Vaughan and C. Geissler ; illustrated by B.E. Nicholson ; with additional illustrations by Elisabeth Dowle and Elizabeth Rice. Oxford ; New York : Oxford University Press, 1997. xx, 239 p. :
          633 21     0198548257
*Food crops.*

## SB176 Food crops — By region or country, A-Z

**SB176.A48.C45 1992**
 Chilies to chocolate : food the Americas gave the world / edited by Nelson Foster & Linda S. Cordell. Tucson : University of Arizona Press, c1992. xvii, 191 p.
92-005243          641.3/097          0816513015
 *Food crops -- America. Food crops -- Origin.*

## SB187 Field crops — By region or country, A-Z

**SB187.U6.S54 1995**
**Smith, C. Wayne.**
 Crop production : evolution, history, and technology / C. Wayne Smith. New York : J. Wiley, c1995. xv, 469 p. :
95-012070          633/.00973          0471079723
 *Field crops -- United States.*

### SB189.73 Field crops — Grain. Cereals — Postharvest technology

**SB189.73.I74 1990**
**Isern, Thomas D.**
 Bull threshers and bindlestiffs : harvesting and threshing on the North American plains / Thomas D. Isern. Lawrence, Kan. : University Press of Kansas, c1990. xiii, 248 p.
90-011967          633.1/045/0978          0700604685
 *Grain -- Harvesting -- Great Plains -- Technological innovations – History. Threshing -- Great Plains -- Technological innovations – History. Grain -- Harvesting -- Machinery -- Great Plains – History.*

### SB191 Field crops — Grain. Cereals — Individual cereals, A-Z

**SB191.B2.B353 1993**
 Barley : chemistry and technology / edited by Alexander W. MacGregor, Rattan S. Bhatty. St. Paul, Minn. : American Association of Cereal Chemists, c1993. 486 p. :
93-072889          664/.725          0913250805
 *Barley.*

**SB191.M2.D685 1996**
**Dowswell, Christopher R.**
 Maize in the Third World / Christopher R. Dowswell, R.L. Paliwal, and Ronald P. Cantrell. Boulder, Colo. : Westview Press, 1996. xiv, 268 p. :
95-048765          338.1/7315/091724
0813389631
 *Corn -- Developing countries. Corn -- Research -- Developing countries. Corn -- Economic aspects -- Developing countries.*

**SB191.M2.M3275 1994**
 The Maize handbook / Michael Freeling, Virginia Walbot, editors. New York : Springer-Verlag, c1994. xxvi, 759 p.
92-032462          633.1/5          0387978267
 *Corn -- Handbooks, manuals, etc. Corn -- Biotechnology -- Handbooks, manuals, etc.*

**SB191.M2.N39 1997**
**Neuffer, M. Gerald,**
 Mutants of maize / M. Gerald Neuffer, Edward H. Coe, Susan R. Wessler. Plainview, N.Y. : Cold Spring Harbor Laboratory Press, 1997. xii, 468 p. :
96-044280          633.1/523          0879694432
 *Corn -- Mutation breeding. Corn -- Varieties.*

**SB191.M2W313 1988**
**Wallace, Henry Agard,**
 Corn and its early fathers / Henry A. Wallace and William L. Brown. Rev. ed. Ames : Iowa State University Press, c1988. xv, 141 p. :
          633.1/523/09 19     0813800129
*Corn -- History. Corn -- Breeding -- History. Corn breeders -- History.*

**SB191.R5**
**Carney, Judith Ann.**
 Black rice : the African origins of rice cultivation in the Americas / Judith A. Carney. Cambridge, Mass. : Harvard University Press, 2001. xiv, 240 p. :
00-053941          633.1/8/0975          0674004523
 *Rice -- Southern States -- History. Rice -- Africa, West – History. Slaves -- Southern States.*

**SB191.R5.G724 1997**
**Greenland, D. J.**
 The sustainability of rice farming / D.J. Greenland. Wallingford, Oxon, UK ; Cab International ; c1997. xi, 273 p. :
96-046785          338.1/7318          0851991637
 *Rice.*

**SB191.R5.L37 1996**
**Lang, James,**
Feeding a hungry planet : rice, research & development in Asia & Latin America / James Lang. Chapel Hill : University of North Carolina Press, c1996. xvi, 185 p. ;
95-050150          338.1/6          0807822841
*Rice -- Asia. Rice -- South America. Rice -- Varieties -- Asia.*

**SB191.R5.R446 2000**
Rice breeding and genetics : research priorities and challenges / editor, Jata S. Nanda. Enfield, N.H. : Science Publishers, c2000. viii, 382 p.
99-053771          633.1/82          157808086X
*Rice -- Breeding. Rice -- Genetics.*

**SB191.S7S648 2000**
Sorghum : origin, history, technology, and production / editors, C. Wayne Smith, Richard A. Frederiksen. New York : Wiley, c2000. xii, 824 p. :
          633.1/74 21          0471242373
*Sorghum.*

**SB191.W5.P42 1997**
**Perkins, John H.**
Geopolitics and the green revolution : wheat, genes, and the cold war / John H. Perkins. New York : Oxford University Press, 1997. xi, 337 p. :
96-008885          338.1/6          0195110137
*Wheat -- Breeding. Wheat -- Breeding -- Government policy. Wheat.*

### SB193.3 Field crops — Forage crops. Feed crops — By region or country, A-Z

**SB193.3.N67.S88 1982**
**Stubbendieck, James L.**
North American range plants / J. Stubbendieck, Stephan L. Hatch, and Kathie J. Kjar. Lincoln : University of Nebraska Press, c1982. xi, 464 p. :
82-008560          582/.06          0803291329
*Range plants -- North America -- Identification. Forage plants -- North America -- Identification. Range plants -- North America.*

### SB198-199 Field crops — Forage crops. Feed crops — Grasses

**SB198**
**Hoffbeck, Steven R.**
The haymakers : a chronicle of five farm families / Steven R. Hoffbeck. St. Paul, Minn. : Minnesota Historical Society Press, c2000. 213 p. :
00-033930          633.2/085/09776          0873513940
*Hay -- Harvesting -- Minnesota -- History. Farmers -- Minnesota -- History.*

**SB199.H84 1997**
**Humphreys, L. R.**
The evolving science of grassland improvement / L.R. Humphreys. Cambridge, U.K. : Cambridge University Press, 1997. xvii, 261 p.
96-009419          633.2/02          0521495679
*Pastures. Forage plants. Grasslands.*

**SB199.P35 1990**
Pastures, their ecology and management / edited by R.H.M. Langer. Auckland ; Oxford University Press, 1990. vii, 499 p. :
90-229118          633.2/02          0195581741
*Pastures. Pastures -- New Zealand. Pastures -- Management.*

### SB203-205 Field crops — Forage crops. Feed crops — Legumes

**SB203.F735 1998**
**Frame, John.**
Temperate forage legumes / J. Frame, J.F.L. Charlton, A.S. Laidlaw. Wallingford, Oxon, UK ; CAB International, c1998. viii, 327 p.
97-022229          633/.3/0912          0851992145
*Legumes. Forage plants.*

**SB205.M4.C48 1996**
**Chatterton, Lynne.**
Sustainable dryland farming : combining farmer innovation and medic pasture in a Mediterranean climate / Lynne Chatterton and Brian Chatterton. Cambridge [England] ; Cambridge University Press, 1996. xvi, 339 p. :
95-013514          633.3/182/096          0521331412
*Medicago -- Africa, North. Medicago -- Middle East. Dry farming -- Africa, North.*

**SB205.S7L585 1997**
**Liu, KeShun,**
Soybeans : chemistry, technology, and utilization / KeShun Liu. New York : Chapman & Hall, c1997. xxvi, 532 p. :
          664/.805655 21          0412081210
*Soybean. Soybean -- Composition. Soyfoods. Soybean products.*

### SB211 Field crops — Root and tuber crops — By plant, A-Z

**SB211.P8.O24 1990**
**Ochoa, Carlos M.**
The potatoes of South America. Carlos M. Ochoa ; translated by Donald Ugent ; color illustrations by Franz Frey. Cambridge [England] ; Cambridge University Press, 1990. xxxii, 512 p.
90-033077          635/.21/0984          0521380243
*Potatoes -- Bolivia. Solanum -- Bolivia. Potatoes -- Germplasm resources -- Bolivia.*

## SB231 Field crops — Sugar plants — Sugar cane

**SB231.B3 1973**
**Barnes, Arthur Chapman,**
The sugar cane [by] A. C. Barnes. New York, Wiley [1974] xviii, 572 p.
72-007590            633/.61            0470053305
*Sugarcane.*

## SB249 Field crops — Textile and fiber plants — Cotton

**SB249.C79375 1999**
Cotton : origin, history, technology, and production / editors, C. Wayne Smith, J. Tom Cothren. New York : Wiley, c1999. xiii, 850 p.
99-022020            633.5/1            0471180459
*Cotton.*

## SB255 Field crops — Textile and fiber plants — Hemp

**SB255.R68 1997**
**Roulac, John,**
Hemp horizons : the comeback of the world's most promising plant / John Roulac and Hemptech. White River Junction, Vt. : Chelsea Green Publishing, 1997. p. cm.
97-018376            338.1/7353            0930031938
*Hemp. Hemp industry.*

## SB268-271 Field crops — Other field crops — Alkaloidal plants

**SB268.C35.Y68 1994**
**Young, Allen M.**
The chocolate tree : a natural history of cacao / Allen M. Young. Washington, D.C. : Smithsonian Institution Press, c1994. xv, 200 p., [
93-044196            633.7/4/0972            1560983574
*Cacao -- Central America. Cacao. Cocoa -- Central America.*

**SB269.W75 1988**
**Wrigley, Gordon.**
Coffee / Gordon Wrigley. Harlow, Essex, England : Longman Scientific & Technical ; 1988. x, 639 p., [8
87-002921            633.7/3            0470208651
*Coffee. Coffee Industry.*

**SB271.T27 1992**
Tea : cultivation to consumption / edited by K.C. Willson and M.N. Clifford. London ; Chapman & Hall, 1992. xviii, 769 p.
91-022774            641.3/372            0412338505
*Tea. Tea trade.*

## SB291.A-Z Field crops — Other field crops — Gum and resin plants. Rubber plants

**SB291.H4.D43 1987**
**Dean, Warren.**
Brazil and the struggle for rubber : a study in environmental history / Warren Dean. Cambridge [Cambridgeshire] ; Cambridge University Press, 1987. xv, 234 p. :
87-005130            338.1/738952/0981
0521334772
*Hevea -- Brazil -- History. Rubber industry and trade – Brazil – History. Hevea -- Diseases and pests -- Brazil -- History.*

## SB293 Field crops — Other field crops — Medicinal plants

**SB293.G9513 1992**
Cultivation and processing of medicinal plants / edited by L. Hornok ; [translated by Katalin Raffalszky]. Budapest : Akademiai Kiado, c1992. xi, 337 p. :
92-223967            633.8/8
*Medicinal plants. Medicinal plants -- Processing.*

## SB298 Field crops — Other field crops — Oil-bearing plants. Wax plants

**SB298.O32 1989**
Oil crops of the world : their breeding and utilization / editors Gerhard Robbelen, R. Keith Downey, Amram Ashri. New York : McGraw-Hill, c1989. xviii, 553 p.
89-002546            633.8/5            0070530815
*Knowles, Paulden F. -- (Paulden Ford), -- 1916-    Oilseed plants – Breeding. Oilseed products. Oilseed plants.*

**SB298.W44 2000**
**Weiss, E.A.**
Oilseed crops / E.A. Weiss ; foreword by Sir Charles Pereira. 2nd ed. Oxford ; Malden, MA, USA : Blackwell Science, 2000. ix, 364 p. :
            633.8/5/0913 21    0632052597
*Oilseed plants. Oilseed plants -- Tropics. Tropical plants.*

## SB305 Field crops — Other field crops — Spice and condiment plants

**SB305.S67**
Spices / J. W. Purseglove ... [et al.]. London ; Longman, 1981. 2 v. (xi, 813
80-040349            633.8/3            0582468116
*Spice plants. Spices. Spice trade.*

## SB317.A-Z Field crops — Other economic plants, A-Z

**SB317.A2.I75 2000**
**Irish, Mary,**
Agaves, yuccas, and related plants : a gardener's guide / Mary & Gary Irish ; illustrated by Karen Bell ; photographs by Gary Irish except where noted. Portland, Or. : Timber Press, 2000. 312 p. :
99-037292          635.9/525          0881924423
*Agaves. Yucca. Agaves -- Identification.*

**SB317.H64.T65 1992**
**Tomlan, Michael A.**
Tinged with gold : hop culture in the United States / Michael A. Tomlan. Athens : University of Georgia Press, c1992. xiv, 273 p. :
90-046389          338.1/7382          0820313130
*Hops -- United States. Hops -- Social aspects -- United States. Hop pickers -- United States.*

**SB317.L43.H36**
Handbook of legumes of world economic importance / [edited by] James A. Duke. New York : Plenum Press, c1981. xi, 345 p. :
80-016421          633.3          0306404060
*Legumes.*

**SB317.N43.N45 1995**
The neem tree : Azadirachta indica A. Juss. and other meliaceous plants : sources of unique natural products for integrated pest management, medicine, industry, and other purposes / edited by H. Schmutterer ; in close cooperation with K.R.S. Ascher ... [et al.]. Weinheim ; VCH, c1995. xxiii, 696 p.
97-173344          583/.77          3527300546
*Neem. Neem products.*

**SB317.P3.J66 1995**
**Jones, David L.**
Palms throughout the world / David L. Jones ; foreword by John Dransfield. Washington, D.C. : Smithsonian Institution Press, c1995. 410 p. :
95-068615          635.9/7745          1560986166
*Palms.*

### SB317.56 Horticulture. Horticulture crops — Directories — By region or country, A-Z

**SB317.56.U6.N67 1991**
North American horticulture : a reference guide / compiled by the American Horticultural Society ; Thomas M. Barrett, editor. New York : Macmillan ; c1992. xvii, 427 p.
90-020435          635/.02573          0028970012
*Horticulture -- United States -- Societies, etc. -- Directories. Gardening -- United States -- Societies, etc. -- Directories. Conservation of natural resources -- United States -- Societies, etc. -- Directories.*

### SB317.58 Horticulture. Horticulture crops — Dictionaries. Encyclopedias. Terminology

**SB317.58.D53 1994**
Dictionary of horticulture / the National Gardening Association ; produced by the Philip Lief Group, Inc. New York, N.Y. : Viking, 1994. xi, 830 p. :
94-184163          635/.03          0670849928
*Horticulture -- Dictionaries.*

**SB317.58.E94**
**Everett, Thomas H.**
The New York Botanical Garden illustrated encyclopedia of horticulture / Thomas H. Everett. New York : Garland Pub., c1980-c1982. 10 v. (xx, 36
80-065941          635.9/03/21
*Horticulture -- Encyclopedias. Gardening -- Encyclopedias. Plants, Ornamental -- Encyclopedias.*

### SB318 Horticulture. Horticulture crops — General works — 1851-

**SB318.A3 1999**
**Acquaah, George.**
Horticulture : principles and practices / George Acquaah. Upper Saddler River, N.J. : Prentice Hall, c1999. xii, 772 p. :
          635 21          0135182751
*Horticulture.*

### SB319.625 Horticulture. Horticulture crops — Plant propogation — Cell and tissue culture

**SB319.625.T67 1989**
**Torres, Kenneth C.,**
Tissue culture techniques for horticultural crops / Kenneth C. Torres. New York : Van Nostrand Reinhold, c1989. vii, 285 p. :
88-005609          582/.00724          0442284659
*Horticultural crops -- Micropropagation. Plant tissue culture.*

### SB320.6 Vegetables — History — By region or country

**SB320.6.T83 1993**
**Tucker, David M.,**
Kitchen gardening in America : a history / by David M. Tucker. Ames : Iowa State University Press, 1993. x, 205 p. :
91-036309          635/.0973          0813818885
*Vegetable gardening -- United States -- History.*

## SB320.9 Vegetables — General works

### SB320.9.H35 1998
Handbook of vegetable science and technology : production, composition, storage, and processing / edited by D.K. Salunkhe, S.S. Kadam. New York : Marcel Dekker, c1998. x, 721 p. :
635 21      0824701054
*Vegetables. Truck farming. Vegetables -- Postharvest technology. Vegetables -- Processing.*

## SB321 Vegetables — General cultural practices — General works

### SB321.L344 1997
**Larkcom, Joy.**
Creative vegetable gardening : accenting your vegetables with flowers / Joy Larkcom. New York : Abbeville Press Publishers, 1997. 208 p. :
97-187471      635      0789203529
*Vegetable gardening. Edible landscaping. Vegetables.*

### SB321.S645 1990
**Splittstoesser, Walter E.**
Vegetable growing handbook / Walter E. Splittstoesser. New York : Van Nostrand Reinhold, 1990. p. cm.
89-028506      635      0442239718
*Vegetable gardening.*

## SB323.A-Z Vegetables — General cultural practices — By region or country

### SB323.C63 1991
**Cleveland, David Arthur.**
Food from dryland gardens : an ecological, nutritional, and social approach to small-scale household food production / by David A. Cleveland and Daniela Soleri ; illustrated by Daniela Soleri. Tucson, Arizona, USA : Center for People, Food, and Environment, c1991. xiii, 387 p.
91-172084      635/.0486/091724
096279970X
*Vegetable gardening -- Developing countries. Truck farming -- Developing countries. Food crops -- Developing countries.*

## SB349 Vegetables — Culture of individual vegetables or types of vegetables — Tomatoes

### SB349.G68 1991
**Gould, Wilbur A.,**
Tomato production, processing & technology / By Wilbur A .Gould. 3rd ed. Baltimore, MD : CTI Publications, c1992. 535 p. :
664/.805642 20      0930027183
*Tomatoes. Tomato products.*

### SB349.J65 1999
**Jones, J. Benton,**
Tomato plant culture : in the field, greenhouse, and home garden / J. Benton Jones, Jr. Boca Raton : CRC Press, c1999. 199 p. :
635/.642 21      0849320259
*Tomatoes.*

## SB351.A-Z Vegetables — Culture of individual vegetables or types of vegetables — Other, A-Z

### SB351.H5.W74 1992
**Wrensch, Ruth D.**
The essence of herbs : an environmental guide to herb gardening / by Ruth D. Wrensch ; photographs by Bernard E. Wrensch ; drawings by Patricia Kozik. Jackson : University Press of Mississippi, c1992. xii, 299 p. :
92-018800      635/.7      0878056041
*Herb gardening. Herb gardening -- Southern States. Herbs.*

### SB351.H5B6464 2001
**Bown, Deni.**
New encyclopedia of herbs & their uses / Deni Bown. 1st American ed. London ; New York : DK Pub. 2001. 448 p. :
581.6/3/03 21      078948031X
*Herbs -- Encyclopedias. Herbs -- Pictorial works. Herb gardening.*

## SB354.8 Fruit and fruit culture — General works

### SB354.8.H35 1995
Handbook of fruit science and technology : production, composition, storage, and processing / edited by D.K. Salunkhe, S.S. Kadam. New York : M. Dekker, c1995. xii, 611 p. :
634 20      0824796438
*Fruit-culture -- Handbooks, manuals, etc. Fruit -- Handbooks, manuals, etc.*

### SB354.8.H43 1997
**Heaton, Donald D.**
A produce reference guide to fruits and vegetables from around the world : nature's harvest / Donald D. Heaton. New York : Food Products Press, c1997. xi, 244 p. :
96-049040      641.3/5      1560228652
*Fruit -- Handbooks, manuals, etc. Vegetables -- Handbooks, manuals, etc. Fruit trade -- Handbooks, manuals, etc.*

## SB355 Fruit and fruit culture — General cultural practices — General works

### SB355.O78 1993
**Otto, Stella,**
The backyard orchardist : a complete guide to growing fruit trees in the home garden / by Stella Otto. Maple City, Mich. : OttoGraphics, c1993. 248 p. :
92-096980      634      0963452029
*Fruit-culture. Fruit trees.*

## SB360 Fruit and fruit culture — Care and preparation for market. Handling — General works

**SB360.P66 1998**

Postharvest : an introduction to the physiology & handling of fruit, vegetables & ornamentals / Ron Wills . . . [et al.]. 4th ed. Sydney, Australia : UNSW Press ; Wallingford. 1998. x, 262 p. :

635/.046 21

*Fruit -- Postharvest physiology. Vegetables -- Postharvest physiology. Plants Ornamental -- Postharvest physiology. Fruit -- Postharvest technology. Vegetables -- Postharvest technology. Plants Ornamental -- Postharvest technology.*

## SB363.3 Fruit and fruit culture — Culture of individual fruits or types of fruit — Apple

**SB363.3.A1.B85 1983**
**Bultitude, John.**

Apples : a guide to the identification of international varieties / John Bultitude. Seattle : University of Washington Press, 1983. 323, [2] p. :

83-232669        634/.117        0295960418

*Apples -- Varieties. Apples -- Identification.*

**SB363.3.A1M36 1995**
**Manhart, Warren.**

Apples for the twenty-first century / by Warren Manhart. Portland, Or. : North American Tree Co., 1995. x, 274 p. :

634/.117/0973 20        0964841703

*Apples -- Varieties. Apples -- United States.*

## SB379 Fruit and fruit culture — Culture of individual fruits or types of fruits — Other fruits not grape nor berry, A-Z

**SB379.C5C455 1996**

Cherries : crop physiology, production and uses / edited by A.D. Webster and N.E. Looney. Wallingford : CAB International. c1996. x, 513 p. :

634/.23 21        0851989365

*Cherry. Fruit.*

## SB381 Fruit and fruit culture — Berries and small fruits — General works

**SB381.B68 2000**
**Bowling, Barbara L.**

The berry grower's companion / Barbara L. Bowling. Portland, Or. : Timber Press, 2000. 284 p.:

634/.7 21        088192489X

*Berries. Ornamental berries.*

## SB385 Fruit and fruit culture — Berries and small fruits — Strawberry

**SB385.H34 1999**
**Hancock, James F.**

Strawberries / James F. Hancock. Oxon, UK ; New York, NY : CABI Pub., c1999. ix, 237 p. :

634/.75 21        0851993397

*Strawberries.*

## SB386 Fruit and fruit culture — Berries and small fruits — Other A-Z

**SB386.B7.E26 1988**
**Eck, Paul,**

Blueberry science / Paul Eck. New Brunswick : Rutgers University Press, c1988. xiv, 284 p. ;

87-016640        634/.737        0813512832

*Blueberries.*

## SB387.7 Fruit and fruit culture — Grapes and grape culture — History and conditions

**SB387.7.U58 1991**
**Unwin, P. T. H.**

Wine and the vine : an historical geography of viticulture and the wine trade / Tim Unwin. London ; Routledge, 1991. xvi, 409 p. :

90-008947        338.1/748/09        0415031206

*Viticulture -- History. Wine industry -- History. Wine and wine making -- History.*

## SB388 Fruit and fruit culture — Grapes and grape culture — General works

**SB388.M85 1991**
**Mullins, Michael G.**

Biology of the grapevine / Michael G. Mullins, Alain Bouquet, and Larry E. Williams. Cambridge ; Cambridge University Press, 1992. xi, 239 p. :

91-028776        634.8        0521305071

*Grapes. Viticulture.*

# SB401 Nuts

**SB401.A4D84 2001**
**Duke, James A.,**

Handbook of nuts / James A. Duke. Boca Raton, Fla. : CRC Press, c2001. 343 p. :

634/.5 21        0849336376

*Nuts -- Handbooks, manuals, etc.*

**SB401.P4.S63 1992**
**Sparks, Darrell.**

Pecan cultivars : the orchard's foundation / Darrell Sparks. Watkinsville, Ga. : Pecan Production Innovations, c1992. xi, 446 p. :

91-068464        635/.527        0963183907

*Pecan -- Varieties.*

## SB403.2 Flowers and flower culture. Ornamental plants — Dictionaries and encyclopedias

**SB403.2.A45 1997**

The American Horticultural Society A-Z encyclopedia of garden plants / Christopher Brickell, Judith D. Zuk editor-in-chief. 1st American ed. New York, N.Y. : DK Pub., 1997. 1092 p. :

635.9/03 21        0789419432

*Plants, Ornamental -- Encyclopedias.*

**SB403.2.G75 1994**
**Griffiths, Mark,**

Index of garden plants / Mark Griffiths. Portland, Oregon : Timber Press, 1994. lxi, 1234 p.

94-187093        0881922463

*Plants, Ornamental -- Dictionaries. Horticulture -- Dictionaries.*

## SB404.5 Flowers and flower culture. Ornamental plants — History — General works

**SB404.5.C63 1970**
**Coats, Alice M.**

The plant hunters; being a history of the horticultural pioneers, their quests, and their discoveries from the Renaissance to the twentieth century [by] Alice M. Coats. New York, McGraw-Hill [1970, c1969] 400 p.

77-101380        581/.0922

*Plants, Ornamental -- Collection and preservation -- History. Plant introduction -- History. Horticulturists.*

## SB405 Flowers and flower culture. Ornamental plants — General cultural practices — General works

**SB405.D58 1999**
**Dole, John M.**

Floriculture : principles and species / John M. Dole, Harold F. Wilkins. Upper Saddle River, N.J. : Prentice Hall, c1999. ix, 613 p. :

635.9 21        0133747034

*Floriculture. Plants, Ornamental.*

## SB406.8 Flowers and flower culture. Ornamental plants —Plant propogation — Breeding

**SB406.8.B74 2000**

Breeding ornamental plants / Dorothy J. Callaway and M. Brett Callaway, editors. Portland, OR : Timber Press, 2000. p. cm.

99-087325        635.9/152        0881924822

*Plants, Ornamental -- Breeding.*

## SB406.93 Flowers and flower culture. Ornamental plants — Identification — By region or country, A-Z

**SB406.93.E85**

The European garden flora : a manual for the identification of plants cultivated in Europe, both out-of-doors and under glass / edited by S.M. Walters ... [et al.]. Cambridge ; Cambridge University Press, 1984-2000 v. 1-6    :

83-007655        635.9        0521248590

*Plants, Ornamental -- Europe -- Identification. Fruit – Europe – Identification. Nuts -- Europe -- Identification.*

**SB406.93.U6.H47 1992**
**Heriteau, Jacqueline.**

The American Horticultural Society flower finder / by Jacqueline Heriteau and Andre Viette ; with the American Horticultural Society staff and consultants. New York : Simon and Schuster, c1992. xvii, 300 p.

91027554        635.9        0671723456

*Flowers -- Identification. Flower gardening -- Dictionaries*

## SB407 Flowers and flower culture. Ornamental plants — Illustrations and descriptions of choice plants — General works

**SB407.G7 1982**
**Graf, Alfred Byrd.**

Exotica, series 4 international : pictorial cyclopedia of exotic plants from tropical and near-tropic regions / by Alfred Byrd Graf. Library ed., 11th ed. East Rutherford, N.J. : Roehrs Co. Publishers, 1982. 2 v. :

635.9/65 19        0911266186

*Plants, Ornamental -- Pictorial works. Tropical plants -- Pictorials works. House plants -- Pictorial works.*

**SB407.G72 1992**
**Graf, Alfred Byrd.**

Hortica : color cyclopedia of garden flora in all climates--worldwide--and exotic plants indoors / Alfred Byrd Graf. 1st ed. East Rutherford, N.J. : Roehrs Co., 1992. 1216 p. :

635/.022/2 20        0911266259

*Plants, Ornamental -- Pictorial works. House plants -- Pictorial works.*

**SB407.H493 1990**
**Heriteau, Jacqueline.**

The National Arboretum book of outstanding garden plants : the authoritative guide to selecting and growing the most beautiful, durable, and care-free garden plants in North America / By Jacqueline Heriteau with H. Marc Cathey and the staff and consultants of the U.S. National Arboretum ; introduction by H. Marc Cathey. New York : Simon and Schuster, c1990. xxvi, 292 p. :

635.9/517 20        0671669575

*Plants, Ornamental. Plants, Ornamental -- North America. Plants, Ornamental -- Pictorial works. Plants, Ornamental – North America -- Pictorial works. Landscape gardening -- North America.*

**SB407.W54 2000**
**Whistler, W. Arthur.**
   Tropical ornamentals : a guide / W. Arthur Whistler. Portland, Or. : Timber Press, 2000. 542 p. :
99-057321          635.9/523          0881924482
   *Plants, Ornamental. Tropical plants.*

## SB407.3 Flowers and flower culture. Ornamental plants — Illustrations and descriptions of choice plants — By region or country

**SB407.3.T73.D45 1998**
**Dehgan, Bijan.**
   Landscape plants for subtropical climates / Bijan Dehgan. Gainesville : University Press of Florida, c1998. xxxii, 638 p.
98-024892          635.9/523          0813016282
   *Landscape plants -- Tropics. Tropical plants.*

## SB408 Flowers and flower culture. Ornamental plants — Lists of ornamental plants — General works

**SB408.H36 1993**
**Harkness, Mabel G.**
   The Bernard E. Harkness seedlist handbook / compiled and updated by Mabel G. Harkness. Portland, Or. : Timber Press, c1993. xii, 506 p. ;
92-021121          635.9/42/0216          0881922269
   *Plants, Ornamental -- Seeds -- Catalogs.*

## SB408.3 Flowers and flower culture. Ornamental plants — Lists of ornamental plants — By region or country

**SB408.3.S645**
**Thompson, Peter,**
   The looking-glass garden : plants and gardens of the Southern Hemisphere / by Peter Thompson. Portland, Or. : Timber Press, 2001. 451 p. :
00-061556          635.9/09181/4          0881924997
   *Plants, Ornamental -- Southern Hemisphere. Gardens – Southern Hemisphere.*

## SB409-409.8 Flowers and flower culture. Ornamental plants — Culture of individual plants — Orchids

**SB409.B25 1991**
**Baker, Margaret L.**
   Orchid species culture. by Margaret L. Baker and Charles O. Baker. Portland, Or. : Timber Press, c1991. 250 p. ;
90-022011          635.9/3415          0881921890
   *Orchid culture. Orchids. Species.*

**SB409.B43313 1991**
**Bechtel, Helmut.**
   The manual of cultivated orchid species / Helmut Bechtel, Phillip Cribb, Edmund Launert. 3rd ed. Cambridge, Mass. : MIT Press, 1992. 585 p. :
          635.9/3415 20
*Orchids. Orchids -- Nomenclature. Orchid culture. Orchids -- Pictorial works.*

**SB409.O65 1992**
   The Orchid book : a guide to the identification of cultivated orchid species / edited by J. Cullen. Cambridge ; Cambridge University Press, 1992. xxvi, 529 p.
91-039794          635.9/3415          0521418569
   *Orchids -- Identification. Orchids -- Europe -- Identification. Orchid culture.*

**SB409.58.A73 1993**
**Arditti, Joseph.**
   Micropropagation of orchids / Joseph Arditti, Robert Ernst. New York : Wiley, c1993. xiii, 682 p.
91-040768          635.9/3415          0471549053
   *Orchids -- Micropropagation.*

**SB409.8.C36.H65 1999**
**Holst, Arthur W.**
   The world of catasetums / Arthur W. Holst. Portland, Or. : Timber Press, 1999. 306 p. :
98-052376          635.9/344          088192430X
   *Catasetums.*

**SB409.8.C95.D8 1988**
**Du Puy, David.**
   The genus Cymbidium / David Du Puy & Phillip Cribb ; [illustrations by Claire Smith ; maps by David Du Puy]. London : C. Helm ; 1988. xx, 236 p., [
88-008581          635.9/3415          088192119X
   *Cymbidium. Cymbidium -- Classification.*

**SB409.8.S65.C37 1991**
**Cash, Catherine.**
   The slipper orchids / Catherine Cash. Portland, Or. : Timber Press, c1991. xi, 228 p. :
90-039595          584/.15          0881921831
   *Slipper orchids.*

**SB409.8.V36.M67 1997**
**Motes, Martin R.**
   Vandas : their botany, history, and culture / by Martin R. Motes ; with photography by Alan L. Hoffman. Portland, Or. : Timber Press, c1997. 140 p. [48] c
96-032199          635.9/3415          0881923761
   *Vanda. Orchid culture.*

## SB411 Flowers and flower culture. Ornamental plants — Culture of individual plants — Roses

### SB411.I45 1992
The illustrated encyclopedia of roses / general editor, Mary Moody ; consulting editor, Peter Harkness. Portland, Or. : Timber Press, 1992. 304 p. :
93-237296      635.9/33734      0881922714
*Roses. Roses -- Varieties. Roses -- Pictorial work.*

### SB411.T4885 1994
**Thomas, Graham Stuart.**
The Graham Stuart Thomas rose book / by Graham Stuart Thomas. Portland, Or. : Sagapress/Timber Press, c1994. xxviii, 385 p.
      635.9/33372 20      0881922803
*Roses. Roses -- Varieties. Rose culture.*

## SB413. A-Z Flowers and flower culture. Ornamental plants — Culture of individual plants — Other plants, A-Z

### SB413.B2.B46 2000
**Bell, Michael,**
The gardener's guide to growing temperate bamboos / Michael Bell. Newton Abbot, Devon : David & Charles ; 2000. 159 p. :
99-089641      635.9/349      0881924458
*Bamboo.*

### SB413.C18.T675 1998
**Trehane, Jennifer.**
Camellias : the complete guide to their cultivation and use / Jennifer Trehane. Portland, OR : Timber Press, c1998. 174 p. :
98-004144      635.9/33624      0881924628
*Camellias.*

### SB413.C2.L48 1998
**Lewis, Peter**
Campanulas : a gardener's guide / Peter Lewis and Margaret Lynch. Portland, Ore. : Timber Press, 1998. 176 p. :
98-017830      635.9/3398      0881924636
*Campanula.*

### SB413.C6.G74 2000
**Grey-Wilson, C.**
Clematis, the genus : a comprehensive guide for gardeners, horticulturists, and botanists / Christopher Grey-Wilson. Portland, Or. : Timber Press, 2000. 219 p. :
99-044853      635.9/3334      0881924288
*Clematis.*

### SB413.C644.F53 1994
**Fiala, John L.**
Flowering crabapples : the genus Malus / by John L. Fiala ; technical editor, Gilbert S. Daniels. Portland, Or. : Timber Press, c1994. 273 p. :
94-000567      635.9/773372      0881922927
*Flowering crabapples.*

### SB413.C88.J65 1993
**Jones, David L.**
Cycads of the world / David L. Jones ; foreword by Dennis Wm. Stevenson. Washington, D.C. : Smithsonian Institution Press, c1993. 312 p. :
93-083068      635.9/359      1560982209
*Cycads. Plants, Ornamental.*

### SB413.D3.E33 1992
**Eddison, Sydney,**
A passion for daylilies : the flowers and the people / by Sydney Eddison. New York, NY : HarperCollins, c1992. xxi, 322 p. :
91-050476      635.9/34324      0060164034
*Daylilies.*

### SB413.G3.K64 1991
**Kohlein, Fritz.**
Gentians / Fritz Kohlein ; translated from the German by David Winstanley ; edited by Jim Jermyn. London : Christopher Helm ; 1991. vi, 183 p. :
92-216436      635.9/3375      071368075X
*Gentians.*

### SB413.H443.A4813 1993
**Ahlburg, Marlene Sophie.**
Hellebores : Christmas rose, lenten rose / Marlene Sophie Ahlburg ; translated by Marlene Sophie Ahlburg and Jennifer Hewitt. London : B.T. Batsford, 1993. 128 p. :
94-138432      635.9/33111      0713470585
*Hellebores.*

### SB413.H7.G34 1997
**Galle, Fred C.**
Hollies : the genus Ilex / Fred C. Galle ; scientific advisor, Theodore R. Dudley ; technical advisor, Gene K. Eisenbeiss. Portland, Or. : Timber Press, c1997. 573 p., [48]
96-031934      635.9/33271      088192380X
*Hollies.*

### SB413.H73.S36 1991
**Schmid, Wolfram George.**
The genus Hosta = Giboshi zoku / Wolfram George Schmid ; technical editor, Gilbert S. Daniels. Portland, Or. : Timber Press, c1991. 428 p., [40]
91-012491      635.9/34324      0881922013
*Hosta.*

### SB413.I84.F43 1991
**Fearnley-Whittingstall, Jane.**
Ivies / Jane Fearnley-Whittingstall. New York : Random House, c1992. 160 p. :
91-051024      635.9/74      067941231X
*Ivy.*

### SB413.I8L39 1998
**Lawton, Barbara Perry.**
Magic of irises / Barbara Perry Lawton. Golden, Colo. : Fulcrum Pub., c1998. x, 206 p. :
      635.9/3438 21      1555912672
*Iris (Plant)*

**SB413.K3.J38 1997**
**Jaynes, Richard A.,**
Kalmia : mountain laurel and related species / Richard A. Jaynes. Portland, Or. : Timber Press, c1997. 295 p., [64]
96-018759        635.9/3362        0881923672
*Kalmia -- North America. Mountain laurel -- North America. Botany -- North America.*

**SB413.L48.D38 2000**
**Davidson, B. LeRoy.**
Lewisias / by B. LeRoy Davidson ; foreword by Sean Hogan ; illustrations by Michael Moshier. Portland, Or. Timber Press, 2000. 236 p. :
99-053481        635.9/3353        0881924474
*Lewisia.*

**SB413.L7.M39 1998**
**McRae, Edward A.**
Lilies : a guide for growers and collectors / Edward Austin McRae ; with a foreword by John Bryan. Portland, Or. : Timber Press, c1998. 392 p. :
97-022341        635.9/343        0881924105
*Lilies.*

**SB413.M34.C34 1994**
**Callaway, Dorothy J.**
The world of magnolias / Dorothy J. Callaway. Portland, Or. : Timber Press, c1994. 260 p., [48]
93-002793        635.9/33114        0881922366
*Magnolias.*

**SB413.M365.G45 1999**
**Gelderen, C. J. van**
Maples for gardens : a color encyclopedia / C.J. van Gelderen and D.M. van Gelderen. Portland, Or. : Timber Press, c1999. 294 p. :
98-044064        635.9/77378        0881924725
*Maple -- Enocuclopedias. Maple -- Pictorial works.*

**SB413.P37.N65 1999**
**Nold, Robert.**
Penstemons / Robert Nold. Portland, Or. : Timber Press, 1999. 259 p. :
98-051574        635.9/3395        0881924296
*Penstemons.*

**SB413.P4.R64 1995**
**Rogers, Allan.**
Peonies / by Allan Rogers ; illustrated and with an essay on landscaping by Linda Engstrom. Portland, Or. : Timber Press. c1995. xi, 296 p., [
94-048535        635.9/33111        0881923176
*Peonies.*

**SB413.P4F425 1999**
**Fearnley-Whittingstall, Jane.**
Peonies / Jane Fearnley-Whittingstall. New York : H.N. Abrams, 1999. 384 p. :
635.9/3362 21        0810943549
*Peonies.*

**SB413.P7.R53 1993**
**Richards, A. J.**
Primula / John Richards ; illustrated by Brigid Edwards. Portland, Or. : Timber Press, 1993. 299 p., [32]
93-201699        583/.672        0881922285
*Primroses. Primroses -- Classification.*

**SB413.R47.C628 1993**
**Cox, Peter Alfred.**
The cultivation of rhododendrons / Peter A. Cox. London : B.T. Batsford, 1993. 288 p. :
94-169831        635.9/3362        0713456302
*Rhododendrons.*

**SB413.R47.D258 1982**
**Davidian, H. H.**
The Rhododendron species / H.H. Davidian. Portland, Ore. : Timber Press, in cooperation with Rhododendron S 1982-c1995. 4 v. :
81-023232        583/.62        0917304713
*Rhododendrons -- Classification.*

**SB413.S22.C58 1997**
**Clebsch, Betsy.**
A book of salvias : sages for every garden / Betsy Clebsch ; drawings by Carol D. Barner. Portland, Or. : Timber Press, c1997. 221 p., [48]
96-022160        635.9/3387        0881923699
*Salvia.*

**SB413.S28.W43 1989**
**Webb, D. A.**
A manual of saxifrages and their cultivation / [D.A. Webb and R.J. Gornall]. Portland, Or. : Timber Press, 1989. viii, 307 p.,
88-020060        635.9/3338        0881921300
*Saxifraga -- Handbooks, manuals, etc.*

**SB413.W57.V34 1995**
**Valder, Peter.**
Wisterias : a comprehensive guide / Peter Valder. Portland, Or. : Timber Press, 1995. 160 p. :
95-175699        635.9/3322        0881923184
*Wisteria.*

## SB419 Flowers and flower culture. Ornamental plants — Indoor gardening and houseplants — General works

**SB419.E795 1994**
**Evans, John.**
The complete book of houseplants : a practical guide to selecting and caring for houseplants / John Evans. New York : Viking Studio Books, 1994. p. cm.
635.9/65 20        0670858684
*House plants. House plants -- Pictorial works. Indoor gardening.*

**SB419.H557413 1985**
**Herwig, Rob,**
   The Good Housekeeping encyclopedia of house plants / Rob Herwig ; [translated from the Dutch by Marian Powell]. 1st U.S. Ed. New York : Hearst Books, 1985, c1984. 288 p. :
   635.9/65 19          0688033210
   *House plants. Indoor gardening.*

**SB419.M32 1988**
**Martin, Tovah.**
   Once upon a windowsill : a history of indoor plants / by Tovah Martin. Portland, Or. : Timber Press, c1988. 303 p. :
   88-031499          635.9/65/0973          0881921203
   *House plants -- United States -- History. Indoor gardening -- United States -- History.*

**SB419.R74**
   Rodale's encyclopedia of indoor gardening / edited by Anne M. Halpin. Emmaus, PA : Rodale Press, c1980. vii, 902 p. :
   80-017019          635.9/65          0878573194
   *Indoor gardening. House plants. Organic gardening.*

## SB421 Flowers and flower culture. Ornamental plants — Classes of plants — Alpine plants. Rock garden plants

**SB421.E3 158**
**Edwards, Alexander,**
   Rock gardens; how to plan and plant them. New York, Abelard-Schuman [1958] 255 p.
   58003848          635.9672
   *Rock gardens.*

**SB421.H34 1992**
**Halliwell, Brian.**
   The propagation of alpine plants and dwarf bulbs / Brian Halliwell. Portland, Or. : Timber Press, 1992. xi, 193 p. :
   92-212107          635.9/6723          0713470194
   *Alpine garden plants -- Propagation. Dwarf bulbs – Propagation.*

**SB421.I56 1995**
**Innes, Clive.**
   Alpines : the illustrated dictionary / Clive Innes. Portland, Or. : Timber Press, 1995. 190, [2] p. :
   95-195327          635.9/6727/03          0881922900
   *Alpine garden plants -- Dictionaries. Rock plants – Dictionaries.*

**SB421.L72 1998**
**Lowry, William R.**
   Preserving public lands for the future : the politics of intergenerational goods / William R. Lowry. Washington, DC : Georgetown University Press, 1998. xvi, 297 p. :
   98-013259          333.78/3          0878407014
   *National parks and reserves -- Management -- Case studies. National parks and reserves -- Government policy -- Case studies. Nature conservation -- Case studies.*

## SB423.7 Flowers and flower culture — Classes of plants — Bedding plants. Beds

**SB423.7.S88 1997**
**Styer, Roger C.,**
   Plug & transplant production : a grower's guide / by Roger C. Styer and David S. Koranski. Batavia, Ill., USA : Ball Pub., c1997. viii, 374 p.,
   96-037957          635/.04531          1883052149
   *Bedding plants -- Propagation. Vegetables -- Propagation. Plant plugs.*

## SB425 Flowers and flower culture — Classes of plants — Bulbs and tuberous plants

**SB425**
**Dash, Mike.**
   Tulipomania : the story of the world's most coveted flower and the extraordinary passions it aroused / Mike Dash. New York : Crown Publishers, c1999. x, 273 p. :
   99-039186          635.9/3432          0609604392
   *Tulip mania, 17th century. Netherlands -- History -- 17th century. Netherlands -- Economic conditions -- 17th century.*

## SB429 Flowers and flower culture — Classes of plants — Ferns and lycopodiums

**SB429**
**Hoshizaki, Barbara Joe.**
   Fern grower's manual / Barbara Joe Hoshizaki and Robbin C. Moran. Portland, Or. : Timber Press, 2001. 604 p. :
   00-059999          635.9/373          0881924954
   *Ferns, Ornamental.*

## SB431.7 Flowers and flower culture — Classes of plants — Grasses, Ornamental

**SB431.7.G74 1992**
**Greenlee, John.**
   The encyclopedia of ornamental grasses : how to grow and use over 250 beautiful and versatile plants / text by John Greenlee ; photography by Derek Fell ; foreword by Wolfgang Oehme. Emmaus, Pa. : Rodale Press ; c1992. vi, 186 p. :
   92-010833          635.9/349          0875961002
   *Ornamental grasses. Ornamental grasses -- Encyclopedias.*

## SB432 Flowers and flower culture — Classes of plants — Ground cover plants

**SB432.M336 1997**
**MacKenzie, David S.**
   Perennial ground covers / David S. MacKenzie. Portland, Or. : Timber Press, c1997. 379 p., [72]
   96-023737          635.9/32          0881923680
   *Ground cover plants.*

## SB433 Flowers and flower culture — Classes of plants — Lawns and turf

**SB433.B64 1993**
**Bormann, F. Herbert,**
Redesigning the American lawn : a search for environmental harmony / F. Herbert Bormann, Diana Balmori, Gordon T. Geballe ; Lisa Vernegaard, editor-researcher. New Haven : Yale University Press, c1993. x, 166 p., [8
92-042918          635.9/647/0973          0300054017
*Lawns -- United States. Lawn ecology -- United States.*

**SB433.E44 2000**
**Emmons, Robert D.,**
Turfgrass science and management / Robert D. Emmons. 3rd ed. Albany, NY : Delmar Publishers, c2000. xvi, 528 p. :
          635.9/642 21          076681551X
*Turfgrasses. Turf management. Turfgrasses industry.*

**SB433.J46 1994**
**Jenkins, Virginia Scott.**
The lawn : a history of an American obsession / Virginia Scott Jenkins. Washington, D.C. : Smithsonian Institution Press, c1994. x, 246 p., [1
93-028003          716          1560984066
*Lawns -- United States -- History.*

## SB433.5 Flowers and flower culture — Classes of plants — Miniature plants. Miniature gardens

**SB433.5.T66 1991**
**Tomlinson, Harry.**
The complete book of bonsai / Harry Tomlinson. New York : Abbeville Press, c1990. 224 p. :
90-048648          635.9/772          1558591184
*Bonsai.*

## SB433.55 Flowers and flower culture — Classes of plants — Mosses. Moss gardening

**SB433.55.S3 1997**
**Schenk, George.**
Moss gardening : including lichens, liverworts, and other miniatures / George Schenk. Portland, Or. : Timber Press, c1997. 261 p. :
96-009357          635.9/36          0881923702
*Moss gardening. Mosses.*

## SB434 Flowers and flower culture — Classes of plants — Perennials

**SB434.H29513 1993**
**Hansen, Richard,**
Perennials and their garden habitats / Richard Hansen and Friedrich Stahl ; translated by Richard Ward. Portland, Or. : Timber Press, 1993. xii, 450 p.,
93-218482          635.9/32          0881922226
*Perennials. Perennials -- Habitat. Landscape gardening.*

**SB434.H56 1999**
**Hinkley, Daniel J.**
The explorer's garden : rare and unusual perennials / Daniel J. Hinkley. Portland, Or. : Timber Press, c1999. 380 p. :
98-048722          635.9/32          0881924261
*Perennials. Rare garden plants.*

**SB434.W66 1992**
**Woods, Christopher.**
Encyclopedia of perennials : a gardener's guide / Christopher Woods. New York : Facts on File, c1992. xviii, 350 p.
91-015280          635.9/32          0816020922
*Perennials -- Encyclopedias. Perennials -- Pictorial works.*

## SB434.3 Flowers and flower culture — Classes of plants — Prairie plants. Prairie gardening

**SB434.3.T35 1997**
The tallgrass restoration handbook : for prairies, savannas, and woodlands / edited by Stephen Packard and Cornelia F. Mutel ; foreword by William R. Jordan III. Washington, D.C. : Island Press, c1997. xxxii, 463 p.
96-009763          639.9/9          1559633190
*Prairie plants -- Middle West -- Handbooks, manuals, etc. Restoration ecology -- Middle West -- Handbooks, manuals, etc.*

## SB434.7 Flowers and flower culture. Ornamental plants — Classes of plants — Shade-tolerant plants. Gardening in the shade

**SB434.7.K45 2001**
**Kellum, Jo.**
Ortho's all about shade gardening / written by Jo Kellum. 1st ed. Des Moines, Iowa : Ortho Books, c2001. 96 p. :
          0897214609
*Gardening in the shade. Shade-tolerant plants.*

## SB435-436 Flowers and flower culture — Classes of plants — Shrubs and ornamental trees

**SB435.B32**
**Bailey, L. H.**
The cultivated conifers in North America, comprising the pine family and the taxads; successor to The cultivated evergreens; by L.H. Bailey. New York, The Macmillan Company, 1933. ix p., 1 ., 4
33011163          585.2
*Conifers. Pinaceae. Taxaceae.*

**SB435.H317 1999**
**Harris, Richard Wilson,**
Arboriculture : integrated management of landscape trees, shrubs, and vines / Richard W. Harris, James R. Clark, Nelda P. Matheny ; illustrations by Vera M. Harris. 3rd ed. Upper Saddle River, N.J. : Prentice Hall, c1999. xvi, 687 p. :
          635.9/77 21          0133866653
*Arboriculture. Ornamental woody plants.*

**SB435.P6 1994**

Plants that merit attention / the Garden Club of America ; Janet Meakin Poor, editor ; Nancy P. Brewster, photographic editor. Portland, Or. : Timber Press, c1984 (1994 p v. 1-2 :
94-007957          635.9          0917304756
*Landscape plants. Plants, Ornamental. Landscape plants -- Pictorial works.*

**SB435.W9 1969**
**Wyman, Donald,**

Shrubs and vines for American gardens. [New York] Macmillan [1969] xviii, 613 p.
69-018249          635.97/6
*Ornamental shrubs -- United States. Ornamental climbing plants -- United States. Ornamental shrubs -- Canada.*

**SB435.W92 1965**
**Wyman, Donald,**

Trees for American gardens. New York, Macmillan [1965] viii, 502 p.
65-016930          635.9770973
*Ornamental trees -- United States. Ornamental trees -- Canada.*

**SB435.5.C26 1999**
**Campana, Richard J.**

Arboriculture : history and development in North America / Richard J. Campana. East Lansing : Michigan State University Press, c1999. xix, 443 p. :
99-006658          635.9/77/097          0870134973
*Arboriculture -- United States -- History. Arboriculture -- Canada -- History.*

**SB435.5.D556 1997**
**Dirr, Michael.**

Dirr's Hardy trees and shrubs : an illustrated encyclopedia / by Michael A. Dirr. Portland, Or. : Timber Press, 1997. 493 p. :
96-054032          635.9/77/097303          0881924040
*Ornamental trees -- United States -- Encyclopedias. Ornamental shrubs -- United States -- Encyclopedias. Ornamental trees -- Encyclopedias.*

**SB435.5.D57 1990**
**Dirr, Michael.**

Manual of woody landscape plants : their identification, ornamental characteristics, culture, propagation and uses / Michael A. Dirr ; illustrations by Margaret Stephan ... [et al.]. Champaign, Ill. : Stipes Pub., c1990. 1007 p. :
90-210541          635.9/76          0875633471
*Landscape plants -- United States -- Handbooks, manuals, etc. Ornamental woody plants -- United States -- Handbooks, manuals, etc. Landscape plants -- Handbooks, manuals, etc.*

**SB435.5.O34 1996**
**Odenwald, Neil G.**

Plants for American landscapes / Neil G. Odenwald, Charles F. Fryling, Jr., and Thomas E. Pope. Baton Rouge : Louisiana State University Press, 1996. p. cm.
96-022844          635.9/0973          0807120936
*Landscape plants -- United States. Landscape plants -- United States -- Pictorial works.*

**SB435.5.P58 2000**
**Plotnik, Arthur.**

The urban tree book : an uncommon field guide for city and town / Arthur Plotnik ; in consultation with the Morton Arboretum ; illustrated by Mary Phelan. New York : Three Rivers Press, c2000. xiv, 432 p. :
99-042452          582.16/0973          0812931033
*Trees in cities -- United States -- Guidebooks. Trees -- United States -- Identification.*

**SB435.65.S66 1990**
**Spongberg, Stephen A.**

A reunion of trees : the discovery of exotic plants and their introduction into North American and European landscapes / Stephen A. Spongberg. Cambridge, Mass. : Harvard University Press, 1990. xiv, 270 p. :
89-071743          635.9/77/097          0674766938
*Tree introduction -- Europe. Ornamental trees -- North America. Ornamental trees -- Europe.*

**SB436.G72 1996**
**Grey, Gene W.,**

The urban forest : comprehensive management / Gene W. Grey. New York : Wiley, 1996. xii, 156 p. :
95-010875          635.9/77/091732          0471122750
*Urban forestry.*

**SB436.M55 1997**
**Miller, Robert W.,**

Urban forestry : planning and managing urban greenspaces / Robert W. Miller. 2nd ed. Upper Saddle River, N.J. : Prentice Hall, c1997. x, 502 p. :
          635.9/77/091732          0134585224
*Urban forestry.*

**SB436.P45 1993**
**Phillips, Leonard E.**

Urban trees : a guide for selection, maintenance, and master planning / Leonard E. Phillips, Jr. New York : McGraw-Hill, c1993. ix, 273 p. :
92-043723          635.9/77/091732          0070498350
*Trees in cities.*

**SB436.U7 1995**

Urban forest landscapes : integrating multidisciplinary perspectives / edited by Gordon A. Bradley. Seattle : University of Washington Press, c1995. ix, 224 p. :
94-023781          333.75/09173/2          0295974389
*Urban forestry. Urban ecology (Biology) Forest landscape design.*

### SB438 Flowers and flower culture — Classes of plants — Succulent plants. Cactus

**SB438.S293 2000**
**Sajeva, Maurizio.**

Succulents II : the new illustrated dictionary / Maurizio Sajeva and Mariangela Costanzo. Portland, Or. : Timber Press, 2000. 234 p. :
00-025160          581.7/54          0881924490
*Succulent plants -- Dictionaries. Succulent plants -- Pictorial works.*

### SB439 Flowers and flower culture — Classes of plants — Wild plants. Wild flowers. Native plants

**SB439.B49 1992**
**Bir, R. E.**
Growing and propagating showy native woody plants / Richard E. Bir ; drawings by Karen Palmer. Chapel Hill : University of North Carolina Press, c1992. viii, 192 p.
91-035993　　　635.9/5175　　　080782027X
*Native plant gardening. Native plants for cultivation -- Propagation. Ornamental woody plants.*

**SB439.L35 1999**
Landscape restoration handbook / by Donald Harker ... [et al.]. Boca Raton : Lewis Publishers, c1999. 1 v. (various
98-046072　　　719/.0973　　　1566701759
*Natural landscaping. Restoration ecology. Natural landscaping – United States.*

**SB439.N43 1997**
Nature and ideology : natural garden design in the twentieth century / edited by Joachim Wolschke-Bulmahn. Washington, D.C. : Dumbarton Oaks Research Library and Collection,t c1997. 278 p. :
96-046176　　　712/.01　　　0884022463
*Natural gardens -- Design -- Congresses.*

### SB439.8 Flowers and flower culture — Classes of plants — Xerophytes. Drought-enduring plants. Dry gardens

**SB439.8.W35 1992**
**Walters, James E.**
Shade and color with water-conserving plants / by James E. Walters and Balbir Backhaus. Portland, Or. : Timber Press, c1992. xiii, 165 p.,
91-026607　　　712　　　0881922145
*Drought-tolerant plants -- Southwest, New. Landscape gardening -- Water conservation -- Southwest, New. Xeriscaping -- Southwest, New.*

## SB450.95 Gardens and gardening — Dictionaries. Encyclopedias

**SB450.95.D53 1992**
Dictionary of gardening / editor in chief, Anthony Huxley ; editor, Mark Griffiths ; managing editor, Margot Levy. London : Macmillan Press ; 1992. 4 v. :
92-003261　　　635/.03　　　0333474945
*Gardening -- Encyclopedias. Horticulture -- Encyclopedias.*

**SB450.95.W96 1986**
**Wyman, Donald,**
Wyman's Gardening encyclopedia / by Donald Wyman. New York : Macmillan ; c1986. xxvi, 1221 p.
86-012509　　　635/.03/21　　　0026320703
*Gardening -- Encyclopedias. Plants, Cultivated – Encyclopedias.*

### SB453 Gardens and gardening — Culture methods — General works

**SB453.C778**
**Crockett, James Underwood.**
Crockett's victory garden / by James Underwood Crockett ; photography by Lee Lockwood/Black Star. Boston : Little, Brown, c1977. 326 p. :
77-002336　　　635/.0973　　　0316161209
*Gardening. Vegetable gardening.*

### SB453.5 Gardens and gardening — Organic gardening — General works

**SB453.5.R633 1992**
Rodale's all-new encyclopedia of organic gardening : the indispensible resource for every gardener / edited by Fern Marshall Bradley and Barbara W. Ellis. Emmaus, Pa. : Rodale Press c1992. xiii, 690 p. :
　　　635.0484 20　　　0878579990
*Organic gardening -- Encyclopedias.*

## SB454.3 Gardens and gardening — Special topics, A-Z

**SB454.3.P45**
**Hirschfeld, Christian Cajus Lorenz,**
Theory of garden art / C.C.L. Hirshfeld ; edited and translated by Linda B. Parshall. Philadelphia : University of Pennsylvania Press, c2001. vii, 496 p. :
00-045574　　　712/.01　　　0812235843
*Gardens -- Philosophy. Landscape gardening.*

## SB455.3 Gardens and gardening — Addresses, essays, lectures

**SB455.3.O53 1999**
The once and future gardener : garden writing from the golden age of magazines, 1900-1940 / edited by Virginia Tuttle Clayton. Boston, Mass. : David R. Godine, 1999. p. cm.
99-025661　　　635.9　　　1567921027
*Gardening. Gardens.*

### SB457 Gardens and gardening — Gardens for special classes and groups of persons — Children's gardens

**SB457.O24 1990**
**Ocone, Lynn.**
The National Gardening Association guide to kids' gardening. New York : Wiley, 1990. p. cm.
89-048993　　　635/.083/4　　　0471520926
*Children's gardens -- Handbooks, manuals, etc. Vegetable gardening -- Handbooks, manuals, etc.*

## SB457.53-458.5 Gardens and gardening — Special styles and types of gardens — Cultural and ethnic garden styles and types

**SB457.53.R44 1995**
Regional garden design in the United States / edited by Therese O'Malley and Marc Treib. Washington, D.C. : Dumbarton Oaks Research Library and Collection,t c1995. vi, 321 p. :
93-023720 712/.0973 0884022234
*Gardens, American -- Congresses. Gardens -- United States – Design -- Congresses. Landscape design -- United States -- Congresses.*

**SB457.55.M66 1983**
**Morris, Edwin T.**
The gardens of China : history, art, and meanings = [Chung-hua yuan lin] / Edwin T. Morris. New York : Scribner, c1983. xii, 273 p.,
83-014181 712/.0951 0684179598
*Gardens, Chinese. Gardens -- China.*

**SB457.6.B76 1989**
**Brown, Jane.**
The art and architecture of English gardens : designs for the garden from the collection of the Royal Institute of British Architects 1609 to the present day / Jane Brown. New York : Rizzoli, 1989. 320 p. :
89-031367 712/.0942 0847810895
*Gardens, English -- History. Gardens, English -- Pictorial works. Gardens -- England -- Design -- History.*

**SB457.6.C64 1994**
**Coffin, David R.**
The English garden : meditation and memorial / David R. Coffin. Princeton, N.J. : Princeton University Press, c1994. xiii, 270 p.
93-034998 712/.0942/09032 069103432X
*Gardens, English -- History -- 17th century. Gardens, English – History -- 18th century. Gardens -- England -- History – 17th century.*

**SB457.6.H865 1992**
**Hunt, John Dixon.**
Gardens and the picturesque : studies in the history of landscape architecture / John Dixon Hunt. Cambridge, Mass. : MIT Press, c1992. xviii, 388 p.
91-036906 712/.2 026208211X
*Gardens, English -- History. Gardens -- Design -- History. Gardens -- History.*

**SB457.6.R67 1998**
**Ross, Stephanie.**
What gardens mean / Stephanie Ross. Chicago : University of Chicago Press, 1998. xiv, 271 p. :
97-022441 712/.2/094209033
0226728226
*Gardens, English -- Philosophy -- 18th century. Gardens, English -- Philosophy. Gardens -- Philosophy.*

**SB457.85.L39 1990**
**Lazzaro, Claudia,**
The Italian Renaissance garden : from the conventions of planting, design, and ornament to the grand gardens of sixteenth-century Central Italy / Claudia Lazzaro ; with photographs by Ralph Lieberman. New Haven : Yale University Press, 1990. ix, 342 p. :
89-078473 712/.0945/09031 0300047657
*Gardens, Italian. Gardens, Renaissance -- Italy. Gardens – Italy, Central -- History -- 16th century.*

**SB458.I833 1984**
**Ito, Teiji,**
The gardens of Japan / text by Teiji Itoh. Tokyo ; Kodansha International ; 1984] 228 p. :
83048882 712/.0952 0870116487
*Gardens, Japanese. Gardens -- Japan.*

**SB458.S66 1987**
**Slawson, David A.,**
Secret teachings in the art of Japanese gardens : design principles, aesthetic values / David A. Slawson. Tokyo ; Kodansha International ; 1987. 220 p. :
86-045723 712/.0952 0870117998
*Gardens, Japanese.*

**SB458.5.K48 19987**
**Khansari, Mehdi.**
The Persian garden : echoes of paradise / Mehdi Khansari, M. Reza Moghtader, Minouch Yavari. Washington, DC : Mage Publishers, 1998. 169 p. :
96-044429 712/.0955 0934211469
*Gardens, Persian -- History. Gardens -- Iran -- History.*

## SB459 Gardens and gardening — Special styles and types of gardens — Special materials and physiographic areas

**SB459**
**Jermyn, Jim.**
The Himalayan garden : growing plants from the roof of the world / Jim Jermyn. Portland, Or. : Timber Press, 2001. 320 p. :
00-064830 635.9/528/095496
0881925004
*Alpine gardens. Alpine garden plants. Alpine gardens -- Himalaya Mountains.*

## SB466.A-Z Gardens and gardening — Illustrations, descriptions, and history of notable gardens — By region or country, A-Z

**SB466.C53**
**Wong, Young-tsu,**
A paradise lost : the imperial garden Yuanming Yuan / Young-tsu Wong. Honolulu : University of Hawai'i Press, c2001. x, 226 p. :
00-036879 712/.6/0951156 0824822269
*Historic gardens -- China -- Beijing. Gardens, Chinese – China – Beijing -- History. Landscape architecture -- China -- Beijing -- History. Yuan Ming Yuan (Beijing, China) -- History.*

**SB466.E9.R68 1997**
**Rothschild, Miriam.**
The Rothschild gardens / Miriam Rothschild, Kate Garton, and Lionel de Rothschild ; photographs by Andrew Lawson and Lionel de Rothschild. New York : H.N. Abrams, 1997. 190 p. :
96-023746          712/.6          0810937905
*Rothschild family -- Homes and haunts -- Europe -- History.*
*Rothschild family.    Gardens -- Europe -- History.*

**SB466.F82.P767 1987**
**Racine, Michel,**
The gardens of Provence and the French Riviera / Michel Racine, Ernest J.-P. Boursier-Mougenot, and Francoise Binet ; translated from French by Alice Parte and Helen Agarathe. Cambridge, Mass. : MIT Press, 1987. 317 p. :
87-016928          712/.0944/9          0262181282
*Gardens -- France -- Provence-Alpes-Cote d'Azur.*

**SB466.F82.V47613 1996**
**Pincas, Stephane.**
Versailles : the history of the gardens and their sculpture / Stephane Pincas ; photographs by Maryvonne Rocher-Gilotte ; [translated from the French by Fiona Cowell]. New York, N.Y. : Thames and Hudson, 1996. 280 p. :
96-060114          712/.5/0944366          0500017018
*Sculpture, French -- France -- Parc de Versailles (Versailles)*
*Landscape architecture -- France -- Parc de Versailles (Versailles)*
*Parc de Versailles (Versailles, France)*

**SB466.G7**
**Bisgrove, Richard.**
The National Trust book of the English garden / Richard Bisgrove. London ; Viking, 1990. viii, 326 p.,
89052084          712.60942          0670809322
*Gardens -- England -- History.*

**SB466.G75.E57**
**Strong, Roy C.**
The Renaissance garden in England / Roy Strong. London : Thames and Hudson, c1979. 240 p. :
78-055191          712/.0942          0500012091
*Gardens, Renaissance -- England -- History. Gardens – England -- History.*

**SB466.G8.R57 1997**
**Roberts, Jane,**
Royal landscape : the gardens and parks of Windsor / Jane Roberts. New Haven : Yale University Press, c1997. xii, 596 p. :
97-015718          942.2/96          0300070799
*Royal gardens -- England -- Berkshire -- History.    Home Park (England) -- History. Windsor Great Park (England) -- History.*

**SB466.I8.A35 1987**
**Agnelli, Marella.**
Gardens of the Italian villas / Marella Agnelli in association with Luca Pietromarchi, Robert Emmett Bright, Federico Forquet. New York : Rizzoli, 1987. 221 p. :
86-031532          712/.6/0945          0847808254
*Gardens -- Italy -- Design -- History. Gardens, Italian – History.*

**SB466.J3.K6 1963**
**Horiguchi, Sutemi,**
Tradition of Japanese garden. Tokyo] Distributed by East West Center Press [Honolulu, 1963, c1962] 185 p.
64002824          712.0952
*Gardens -- Japan. Gardens -- Pictorial works. Landscape gardening -- Japan.*

**SB466.U65.N4825 1996**
**Emmet, Alan.**
So fine a prospect : historic New England gardens / Alan Emmet. Hanover, NH : University Press of New England, c1996. xvi, 238 p. :
95-036320          712/.6/0974          0874517494
*Historic gardens -- New England. Gardens -- New England -- History.*

**SB466.U6J45 1998**
**Jenkins, Mary Zuazua.**
National geographic guide to America's public gardens : 300 of the best gardens to visit in the U.S. and Canada / by Mary Zuazua Jenkins. Washington, DC : National Geographic Society, 1998. 384 p. :
          712/.097 21          0792271521
*Gardens -- United States -- Guidebooks. Gardens -- Canada -- Guidebooks. United States -- Guidebooks. Canada -- Guidebooks.*

## SB469.23 Landscape gardening. Landscape architecture — Congresses

**SB469.23.D46 1991**
Denatured visions : landscape and culture in the twentieth century / edited by Stuart Wrede and William Howard Adams. New York : Museum of Modern Art ; c1991. 143 p. :
91-061459          0870704222
*Landscape architecture -- Congresses. Landscape -- Congresses. Gardens -- Congresses.*

**SB469.23.M64 1993**
Modern landscape architecture : a critical review / edited by Marc Treib. Cambridge, Mass. : MIT Press, c1993. xi, 294 p. :
92-011571          712/.09/04          0262200929
*Landscape architecture -- Congresses.*

### SB470.A-Z Landscape gardening. Landscape architecture — Biography — Individual, A-Z

**SB470.B7.S7 1984**
**Stroud, Dorothy.**
Capability Brown / Dorothy Stroud ; with an introduction by Christopher Hussey. London ; Faber and Faber, 1984. 262 p., [69]
84-013541          712/.092/4          057113405X
*Brown, Lancelot, -- 1716-1783.    Landscape architects – England – Biography.*

**SB470.C33.A78 1997**

Alfred Caldwell : the life and work of a Prairie school landscape architect / edited by Dennis Domer. Baltimore : Johns Hopkins University Press, 1997. xx, 307 p. :
96-049076        712/.092        0801855519
*Caldwell, Alfred, -- 1903-    Landscape architects -- United States -- Biography. Landscape architecture -- United States. Prairie school (Architecture)*

**SB470.E9.J64 1998**

John Evelyn's "Elysium Britannicum" and European gardening / edited by Therese O'Malley and Joachim Wolschke-Bulmann. Washington, D.C. : Dumbarton Oaks Research Library and Collection,P c1998. vii, 310 p. :
97-010072        712        0884022404
*Evelyn, John, -- 1620-1706. -- Elysium Britannicum.    Gardens -- England -- Design -- History -- 17th century. Gardens -- Europe -- Design -- History -- 17th century. Landscape architecture -- England -- History -- 17th century.*

**SB470.F37.B76 1995**
**Brown, Jane.**

Beatrix : the gardening life of Beatrix Jones Farrand, 1872-1959 / Jane Brown. New York : Viking, 1995. xv, 252 p. :
94-001271        712/.092        0670832170
*Farrand, Beatrix, -- 1872-1959.    Landscape architects -- United States -- Biography. Landscape architecture -- United States -- History. Gardens -- United States -- History.*

**SB470.J38.B57 1992**
**Bisgrove, Richard.**

The gardens of Gertrude Jekyll / Richard Bisgrove ; special photography by Andrew Lawson. Boston : Little, Brown, c1992. 192 p. :
92-053850        712/.092        0316096571
*Jekyll, Gertrude, -- 1843-1932.    Gardens -- Design. Landscape gardening.*

**SB470.J4.G74 1992**
**Grese, Robert E.,**

Jens Jensen : maker of natural parks and gardens / Robert E. Grese. Baltimore : Johns Hopkins University Press, c1992. xiv, 304 p. :
91-041190        712/.0973/092        0801842875
*Jensen, Jens, -- 1860-1951.    Landscape architects -- United States -- Biography. Conservationists -- United States -- Biography. Native plant gardening -- United States -- History.*

**SB470.O5.K35 1990**
**Kalfus, Melvin,**

Frederick Law Olmsted : the passion of a public artist / Melvin Kalfus. New York : New York University Press, 1990. xiii, 415 p.
89-013981        712/.092        0814746063
*Olmsted, Frederick Law, -- 1822-1903.    Landscape architects -- United States -- Biography.*

**SB470.R4.D35 1999**
**Daniels, Stephen.**

Humphry Repton : landscape gardening and the geography of Georgian England / Stephen Daniels. New Haven : Published for the Paul Mellon Centre for Studies c1999. ix, 317 p. :
98-052787        712/.092        0300079648
*Repton, Humphry, -- 1752-1818.    Landscape architects -- England -- Biography. Landscape architecture -- England -- History.*

**SB470.S65.K37 1989**
**Karson, Robin S.**

Fletcher Steele, landscape architect : an account of a gardenmaker's life, 1885-1971 / Robin Karson. New York : Abrams/Sagapress, c1989. xxiii, 344 p.
89-000042        712/.092/4        0810915235
*Steele, Fletcher.    Landscape architects -- United States -- Biography.*

### SB470.5 Landscape gardening. Landscape architecture — History and conditions — General works

**SB470.5.C73 1993**
**Crandell, Gina.**

Nature pictorialized : "the view" in landscape history / Gina Crandell. Baltimore : Johns Hopkins University Press, c1993. x, 196 p. :
92-007990        712/.2/09        0801843979
*Landscape architecture -- History. Landscape painting -- Influence. Landscape.*

### SB470.54.A-Z-470.55.A-Z Landscape gardening. Landscape architecture — History and conditions — By region or country

**SB470.54.M54**

Midwestern landscape architecture / edited by William H. Tishler. Urbana : University of Illinois Press, c2000. ix, 256 p. :
99-050980        712/.0977        0252025938
*Landscape architecture -- Middle West -- History. Landscape architects -- Middle West -- History. Landscape architects -- Middle West -- Biography.*

**SB470.55.A9.R68 1995**
**Rotenberg, Robert Louis,**

Landscape and power in Vienna / Robert Rotenberg. Baltimore : Johns Hopkins University Press, c1995. xviii, 385 p.
94-042624        304.2/3        0801849616
*Landscape gardening -- Austria -- Vienna. Gardens -- Austria -- Vienna -- Design.*

**SB470.55.F8.I43 1993**
**Imbert, Dorothee.**

The modernist garden in France / Dorothee Imbert. New Haven : Yale University Press, c1993. xv, 268 p. :
92-030514        712/.0944/0904        0300047169
*Gardens -- France -- Design. Landscape architecture -- France. Architecture, Modern -- 20th century -- France.*

**SB470.55.G7.O44 2000**
**Olin, Laurie.**
Across the open field : essays drawn from English landscapes / Laurie Olin. Philadelphia, Pa. : University of Pennsylvania Press, c2000. xiii, 352 p.
99-015965          712/.0942          0812235312
*Olin, Laurie -- Journeys -- England.     Gardens -- England -- History. Gardens, English -- History.  Landscape architecture -- England -- History.  England -- Description and travel.*

## SB472 Landscape gardening. Landscape architecture — General works — 1876-

**SB472.G73 1986**
Graphic standards for landscape architecture / Richard L. Austin . . . [et al.]. New York : Van Nostrand Reinhold, c1986. 195 p. :
712/.0218 19          0442208340
*Landscape architecture -- Standards.  Landscape architecture -- Standards -- United States.*

**SB472.L375 1998**
**Lassus, Bernard.**
The landscape approach / Bernard Lassus ; introductions by Peter Jacobs and Robert B. Riley ; afterword by Stephen Bann. Philadelphia, Pa. : University of Pennsylvania Press, 1998. p. cm.
98-026259          712.6          0812234502
*Landscape architecture.  Landscape architecture -- Europe. Visual perception.*

**SB472.M64 1988**
**Moore, Charles Willard,**
The poetics of gardens / Charles W. Moore, William J. Mitchell, William Turnbull, Jr. Cambridge, Mass. : MIT Press, c1988. 257 p. :
88-002079          712          0262132311
*Gardens -- Design.  Landscape architecture.*

**SB472.O7 1975**
**Ortloff, H. Stuart (Henry Stuart),**
The book of landscape design / by H. Stuart Ortloff and Henry B. Raymore. New York : Morrow, 1975, c1959. 316 p. :
712
*Landscape architecture.  Landscape design.*

**SB472.S685 1998**
**Spirn, Anne Whiston,**
The language of landscape / Anne Whiston Spirn ; photographs by Anne Whiston Spirn. New Haven, Conn. : Yale University Press, c1998. viii, 326 p.
98-007487          712          0300077459
*Landscape architecture.  Landscape.  Landscape assessment.*

## SB472.3 Landscape gardening. Landscape architecture — Practical works on landscaping. Handbooks, manuals, etc. — General works

**SB472.3.D73 1996**
**Dramstad, Wenche E.**
Landscape ecology principles in landscape architecture and land-use planning / Wenche E. Dramstad, James D. Olson, and Richard T.T. Forman. [Cambridge? Mass.] : Harvard University Graduate School of Design ; c1996. 80 p. :
95-082343          1559635142
*Landscape architecture.  Landscape ecology.  Land use -- Planning.*

## SB472.45 Landscape gardening. Landscape architecture — Landscape design (General). Garden design (General)

**SB472.45.L47 1997**
**Leszczynski, Nancy A.**
Principles of planting design / Nancy A. Leszczynski. New York : Van Nostrand Reinhold, 1997. p. cm.
97-017966          712/.2          0442024290
*Planting design.*

## SB473 Landscape gardening. Landscape architecture — Home grounds. Small estates

**SB473.C52**
**Church, Thomas Dolliver.**
Your private world; a study of intimate gardens, by Thomas Church. San Francisco, Chronicle Books [1969] 202 p.
74-099220          712/.6
*Landscape gardening.  Patios.  Swimming pools.*

## SB475.9.A-Z Landscape gardening. Landscape architecture — Other special topics, A-Z

**SB475.9.F67.L83 1990**
**Lucas, Oliver W. R.**
The design of forest landscapes / Oliver W.R. Lucas. Oxford ; Oxford University Press, 1991. xii, 381 p. :
90-045536          634.9/5          0198542801
*Forest landscape design.*

# SB481 Parks and public reservations

**SB481.A2.W67 1982**

National parks, conservation, and development : the role of protected areas in sustaining society : proceedings of the World Congress on National Parks, Bali, Indonesia, 11-22 October 1982 / edited by Jeffrey A. McNeely and Kenton R. Miller ; International Union for Conservation of Nature and Natural Resources in cooperation with the United Nations Environment Programme ... [et al.]. Washington, D.C. : Smithsonian Institution Press, c1984. xiii, 825 p.
84-600007          333.78/3          0874746639
*National parks and reserves -- Congresses. Natural areas -- Congresses. Nature conservation -- Congresses.*

**SB481.I565 1990**

International handbook of national parks and nature reserves / edited by Craig W. Allin. New York : Greenwood Press, 1990. xvii, 539 p.
89-026039          338.78          0313249024
*National parks and reserves.*

## SB482 Parks and public reservations — By region or country — United States

**SB482.A3 1992**
**United States.**

Science and the national parks / Committee on Improving the Science and Technology Programs of the National Park Service [and] Board on Environmental Studies and Toxicology, Commission on Geosciences, Environment, and Resources, National Research Council. Washington, D.C. : National Academy Press, 1992. xii, 122 p. :
92-026303          333.78/15/0973          0309047811
*National parks and reserves -- United States -- Management. National parks and reserves -- Research -- United States.*

**SB482.A4**

National parks and rural development : practice and policy in the United States / edited by Gary E. Machlis and Donald R. Field. Washington, D.C. : Island Press, c2000. xii, 323 p. :
00-010476          333.78/0973          1559638141
*National parks and reserves -- United States -- Management. Rural development -- United States. Land use, Rural – United States -- Planning.*

**SB482.A4.C37 1998**
**Carr, Ethan,**

Wilderness by design : landscape architecture and the National Park Service / Ethan Carr. Lincoln, Neb. : University of Nebraska Press, c1998. viii, 378 p.
97-022127          712/.5/0973          080321491X
*Landscape architecture -- United States -- History. National parks and reserves -- United States -- Design -- History.*

**SB482.A4.E95 1983**
**Everhart, William C.**

The National Park Service / William C. Everhart ; foreword by Russell E. Dickenson. Boulder, Colo. : Westview Press, 1983. x, 197 p. :
82-010884          353.0086/3          0865311307
*National parks and reserves -- United States.*

**SB482.A4.F76 1991**
**Frome, Michael.**

Regreening the national parks / Michael Frome. Tucson : University of Arizona Press, c1992. x, 289 p. ;
91-017477          333.78/0973          0816509565
*National parks and reserves -- Government policy – United States. National parks and reserves -- United States. National parks and reserves -- United States -- Management.*

**SB482.A4.L68 1994**
**Lowry, William R.**

The capacity for wonder : preserving national parks / William R. Lowry. Washington, D.C. : Brookings Institution, c1994. xii, 280 p. :
94-009122          353.0086/32/09048
0815752989
*National parks and reserves -- Government policy – United States -- History. National parks and reserves -- Government policy -- Canada -- History. Nature conservation -- Government policy -- United States -- History.*

**SB482.A4.R48 1995**
**Rettie, Dwight Fay,**

Our national park system : caring for America's greatest natural and historic treasures / Dwight F. Rettie ; foreword by Stewart L. Udall. Urbana : University of Illinois Press, c1995. xvi, 293 p. :
94-022632          333.78/3/0973          0252021487
*National parks and reserves -- United States -- History.*

**SB482.A4.S35 1996**

Science and ecosystem management in the national parks / William L. Halvorson and Gary E. Davis, editors. Tucson : University of Arizona Press, c1996. xii, 364 p. :
95-032530          333.78/3/0973          0816515662
*Conservation of natural resources -- Government policy – United States. Ecosystem management -- Government policy – United States. Natural resources -- United States -- Management.*

**SB482.A4.W75 1991**
**Wright, R. Gerald.**

Wildlife research and management in the national parks / R. Gerald Wright. Urbana : University of Illinois Press, c1992. viii, 224 p.
91-028602          639.9/0973          0252018249
*Wildlife management -- United States. Wildlife conservation – United States. National parks and reserves -- Government policy – United States. Yellowstone National Park.*

### SB484.A-Z Parks and public reservations — By region or country — By region or country, A-Z

**SB484.C8.W35 1992**
**Wallace, David Rains,**
The Quetzal and the Macaw : the story of Costa Rica's national parks / by David Rains Wallace. San Francisco : Sierra Club Books, c1992. xvi, 222 p. :
91-030500          333.78/097286          0871565854
*National parks and reserves -- Costa Rica -- History. Nature conservation -- Costa Rica -- History.*

**SB484.G7.C59 1991**
**Conway, Hazel.**
People's parks : the design and development of Victorian parks in Britain / Hazel Conway. Cambridge [England] ; Cambridge University Press, 1991. xviii, 287 p.
90-044512          711/.558/094109034
0521390702
*Parks -- Great Britain -- History -- 19th century. Parks – Great Britain -- Design and construction -- History -- 19th century. Architecture, Victorian -- Great Britain.*

**SB484.T3.N48 1998**
**Neumann, Roderick P.,**
Imposing wilderness : struggles over livelihood and nature preservation in Africa / Roderick P. Neumann. Berkeley : University of California Press, c1998. xii, 256 p. :
98-012746          333.78/09678          0520211782
*National parks and reserves -- Social aspects -- Tanzania -- Arusha National Park. Nature conservation -- Social aspects -- Tanzania -- Arusha National Park.    Arusha National Park (Tanzania)*

## SB486.A-Z Parks and public reservations — Special topics, A-Z

**SB486.S65**
**Jacoby, Karl,**
Crimes against nature : squatters, poachers, thieves, and the hidden history of American conservation / Karl Jacoby. Berkeley: University of California Press, c2001. xix, 305 p. :
00-061521          333.78/0973          0520220277
*National parks and reserves -- Social aspects -- United States. Nature conservation -- Social aspects -- United States. National parks and reserves -- History -- United States.*

**SB486.S65.R47 1991**
Resident peoples and national parks : social dilemmas and strategies in international conservation / Patrick C. West and Steven R. Brechin, editors. Tucson : University of Arizona Press, c1991. xxiv, 443 p.
90-011300          333.78/14          0816511284
*National parks and reserves -- Social aspects. Nature conservation -- Social aspects. Eminent domain.*

### SB601 Pests and diseases — General works

**SB601.P57 2002**
Plant pathologist's pocketbook / edited by J.M. Waller, J.M. Lennse and S.J. Waller. 3rd ed. Oxon, UK ; New York : CABI Pub., c2002. x, 516 p. :
632/.3 21          085199458X
*Plant diseases -- Handbooks, manuals, etc. Plant diseases -- Bibliography.*

**SB601.S28 1997**
**Scheffer, Robert P.**
The nature of diseases in plants / Robert P. Scheffer. New York, NY : Cambridge University Press 1997. ix, 325 p. :
632/.3 20          052148247X
*Plant diseases.*

## SB603.5 Pests and diseases — Garden pests and diseases

**SB603.5**
**Capinera, John L.**
Handbook of vegetable pests / John L. Capinera. San Diego, Calif. : Academic Press, c2001. xviii, 729 p.
01-086233          635/.0497          0121588610
*Vegetables -- Diseases and pests -- Handbooks, manuals, etc. Insect pests -- Identification.*

**SB603.5.O78 1994**
The Ortho problem solver / edited by Michael D. Smith. 4th ed. San Ramon, CA : Ortho Information Services, c1994. 960, 64 p. :
635/.049 20          0897212681
*Garden pests -- Control -- Handbooks, manuals, etc. House plants – Diseases and pests -- Control -- Handbooks, manuals, etc.*

**SB603.5.P57 1978**
**Pirone, Pascal Pompey,**
Diseases and pests of ornamental plants / Pascal P. Pirone. New York : Wiley, c1978. x, 566 p. :
77-026893          635.9/2          0471072494
*Plants, Ornamental -- Diseases and pests.*

## SB608.A-Z Pests and diseases — By individual or type of plant or tree, A-Z

**SB608.O7.A44 1995**
**Alford, D. V.**
A color atlas of pests of ornamental trees, shrubs, and flowers / David V. Alford. New York : Halsted Press, 1995. 448 p. :
94-046507          635/.049          0470234946
*Plants, Ornamental -- Diseases and pests -- Atlases. Plants, Ornamental -- Diseases and pests -- Identification.*

**SB608.T87.T86 1994**

Turf weeds and their control / editor, Alfred J. Turgeon ; managing editor, David M. Kral ; associate editor, Marian K. Viney. Madison, Wis., USA : American Society of Agronomy : 1994. xi, 259 p., [
94-004166          635.9/642958          0891181202
*Turfgrasses -- Weed control. Turf management.*

**SB608.T87.V58 1999**
**Vittum, Patricia J.,**

Turfgrass insects of the United States and Canada / Patricia J. Vittum, Michael G. Villani, Haruo Tashiro. Ithaca : Comstock Pub. Associates, 1999. xviii, 422 p.
99-023831          635.9/64297          0801435080
*Turfgrasses -- Diseases and pests -- United States. Turfgrasses – Diseases and pests -- Canada. Insect pests -- United States.*

**SB608.V4.R47 1993**

Resistance to viral diseases of vegetables : genetics & breeding / Molly M. Kyle, editor. Portland, Or. : Timber Press, c1993. 278 p. :
92-008777          635/.0498          0881922560
*Vegetables -- Disease and pest resistance -- Genetic aspects. Virus diseases of plants. Vegetables -- Breeding.*

**SB608.V4.V44 1992**

Vegetable crop pests / edited by Roderick G. McKinlay. Boca Raton : CRC Press, 1992. xv, 406 p. :
91-019954          635.04/96          0849377293
*Vegetables -- Diseases and pests. Vegetables -- Diseases and pests -- Control. Invertebrate pests.*

## SB611 Pests and diseases — Weeds, parasitic plants, etc. — General works

**SB611.C67 1995**
**Cousens, Roger.**

Dynamics of weed populations / Roger Cousens and Martin Mortimer. Cambridge ; Cambridge University Press, 1995. xiii, 332 p.
95-000949          632/.58          0521496497
*Weeds -- Ecology. Vegetation dynamics. Weeds -- Control.*

**SB611.M58 2001**
**Monaco, Thomas J.**

Weed science : principles and practices / Thomas J. Monaco, Stephen C. Weller, Floyd M. Ashton. 4th ed. New York : Wiley, c2002. xi, 671 p. :
                    632/.5 21          0471370517
*Weeds -- Control. Herbicides.*

**SB611.R35 2000**
**Rao, V. S.**

Principles of weed science / V.S. Rao. Enfield, N.H. : Science Publishers, c2000. viii, 555 p.
99-039247          632/.5          157808069X
*Weeds -- Control. Herbicides.*

## SB611.5 Pests and diseases — Weeds, parasitic plants, etc. — Biological control (General)

**SB611.5.L54 2001**
**Liebman, Matt.**

Ecological management of agricultural weeds / written and edited by Matt Liebman, Charles L. Mohler, Charles P. Staver. Cambridge, U.K. ; New York : Cambridge University Press, 2001. xi, 532 p. :
                    632/.5 21          0521560683
*Weeds -- Biological control. Weeds -- Ecology. Agricultural ecology. Tillage. Agricultural systems.*

**SB611.5.R53 1995**
**Rice, Elroy L.**

Biological control of weeds and plant diseases : advances in applied allelopathy / Elroy L. Rice. Norman : University of Oklahoma Press, c1995. viii, 439 p.
94-023242          632/.96          0806126981
*Weeds -- Biological control. Phytopathogenic microorganisms – Biological control. Allelopathy.*

## SB612 Pests and diseases — Weeds, parasitic plants, etc. — By region or country, A-Z

**SB612.A2.C72**
**Crockett, Lawrence J.**

Wildly successful plants : a handbook of North American weeds / by Lawrence J. Crockett ; ill. by Joanne Bradley. New York : Macmillan, c1977. xii, 268 p. :
76-054687          581.6/5          0025288504.
*Weeds -- United States -- Identification. Weeds -- Canada -- Identification.*

## SB614 Pests and diseases — Weeds, parasitic plants, etc. — Aquatic weeds

**SB614.A73 1990**

Aquatic weeds : the ecology and management of nuisance aquatic vegetation / edited by Arnold H. Pieterse and Kevin J. Murphy. Oxford [England] ; Oxford University Press, 1990. xvii, 593 p.
89-003146          628.9/7          0198541813
*Aquatic weeds -- Control. Aquatic weeds -- Ecology.*

## SB617.45.A-Z Pests and diseases — Poisonous plants — By region or country

**S B617.45.W47.N69 1991**

Noxious range weeds / edited by Lynn F. James ... [et al.]. Boulder : Westview Press, 1991. xvi, 466 p. :
91-031637          636.08/4          0813383951
*Livestock poisoning plants -- West (U.S.) Rangelands -- Weed control -- West (U.S.) Livestock poisoning plants -- Control -- West (U.S.)*

### SB728 Pests and diseases — Plant pathology — Dictionaries. Encyclopedias

**SB728.E53 2001**
Encyclopedia of plant pathology / [edited by] Otis C. Maloy, Timothy D. Murray. New York : Wiley, c2001. 2 v. (xv, 134
00-043323          631/.3/03          0471298174
*Plant diseases -- Encyclopedias.*

**SB728.H65 1998**
**Holliday, Paul.**
A dictionary of plant pathology / Paul Holliday. New York : Cambridge University Press, 1998. p. cm.
97-032158          632/.3/03          0521594537
*Plant diseases -- Dictionaries.*

### SB731 Pests and diseases — Plant pathology — General works

**SB731.E58 1997**
Environmentally safe approaches to crop disease control / edited by Nancy A. Rechcigl and Jack E. Rechcigl. Boca Raton : CRC Press, 1997. p. cm.
96-054596          632/.3          0849326273
*Phytopathogenic microorganisms -- Control. Plant diseases. Phytopathogenic microorganisms -- Control -- Environmental aspects.*

**SB731.M364 1993**
**Maloy, Otis C.**
Plant disease control : principles and practice / Otis C. Maloy. New York : J. Wiley, c1993. x, 346 p. :
92-039600          632/.3          0471573175
*Phytopathogenic microorganisms -- Control. Plant diseases.*

**SB731.N94 1999**
**Nyvall, Robert F.**
Field crop diseases / Robert F. Nyvall. 3rd ed. Ames : Iowa State University Press, 1999. xxx, 1021 p. :
                   632 21          0813820790
*Field crops -- Diseases and pests -- Handbooks, manuals, etc. Plant diseases -- Handbooks, manuals, etc. Phytopathogenic microorganisms -- Control -- Handbooks, manuals, etc.*

**SB731.P67 1992**
Plant diseases of international importance / U.S. Singh ... et al.]. Englewood Cliffs, N.J. : Prentice Hall, c1992. 4 v. :
91-022598          632/.3          0136785824
*Plant diseases.*

**SB731.S458 2001**
**Singh, R. S.**
Plant disease management / R.S. Singh. Enfield, NH : Science Publishers, c2001. viii, 238 p.
00-068018          632/.3          1578081580
*Phytopathogenic microorganisms -- Control. Plant diseases.*

**SB731.T48 1991**
**Thurston, H. David**
Sustainable practices for plant disease management in traditional farming systems / H. David Thurston. Boulder : Westview Press ; 1992. xvii, 279 p.
91-015953          632/.9          0813383633
*Phytopathogenic microorganisms -- Control. Plant diseases. Sustainable agriculture.*

**SB731.W47 2001**
**Westcott, Cynthia,**
Westcott's plant disease handbook / revised by R. Kenneth Horst. 6th ed. Boston : Kluwer Academic Publishers, c2001. xx, 1008 p. :
                   632/.3 21          0792386639
*Plant diseases -- Handbooks, manuals, etc. Phytopathogenic microorganisms -- Control -- Handbooks, manuals, etc. Plant diseases -- United States -- Handbooks, manuals, etc. Phytopathogenic microorganisms -- Control -- United States -- Handbooks, manuals, etc.*

### SB732.6 Pests and diseases — Plant pathology — Biological control of phytopathogenic microorganisms (General)

**SB732.6.C33 1989**
**Campbell, R. E.**
Biological control of microbial plant pathogens / R. Campbell. Cambridge ; Cambridge University Press, 1989. x, 218 p. :
88-025812          632/.3          0521340888
*Phytopathogenic microorganisms -- Biological control.*

### SB732.8 Pests and diseases — Plant pathology — Seed pathology. Seed-borne plant diseases (General)

**SB732.8.M38 1996**
**Maude, R. B.**
Seedborne diseases and their control : principles and practice / R.B. Maude. Wallingford, Oxon, UK : CAB International, c1996. xvii, 280 p.
96-214887          632.3          0851989225
*Seed-borne plant diseases.*

### SB734 Pests and diseases — Plant pathology — Bacterial diseases

**SB734.S54 1993**
**Sigee, D. C.**
Bacterial plant pathology : cell and molecular aspects / David C. Sigee. Cambridge ; Cambridge University Press, 1993. xi, 325 p. :
92-018077          632/.32          0521350646
*Bacterial diseases of plants. Phytopathogenic bacteria. Phytopathogenic bacteria -- Control.*

## SB736 Pests and diseases — Plant pathology — Virus diseases

**SB736.S836 1999**
**Sutiac, Dragoljub D.**
  Handbook of plant virus diseases / Dragoljub D. Sutiac, Richard E. Ford, Mali^sa T. To^siac. Boca Raton, FL : CRC Press, c1999. xxiii, 553 p. :
  632/.8 21          0849323029
*Virus diseases of plants -- Diagnosis -- Handbooks, manuals, etc. Plant viruses -- Identification -- Handbooks, manuals, etc.*

## SB741.A-Z Pests and diseases — Plant pathology — Individual and groups of diseases or pathogens, A-Z

**SB741.D68.D68**
  The Downy mildews / edited by D.M. Spencer. London ; Academic Press, 1981. xxi, 636 p. :
  81-066686          632/.452          012656860X
*Downy mildew diseases. Peronosporaceae -- Control.*

**SB741.R8.L39**
**Littlefield, Larry J.**
  Biology of the plant rusts : an introduction / Larry J. Littlefield. Ames : Iowa State University Press, 1981. ix, 103 p., [
  81-003734          632/.425          081381670X
*Rust fungi. Fungous diseases of plants.*

## SB745-745.4 Pests and diseases — Plant pathology — Pollution effects. Crops and pollution

**SB745.A39 1989**
  Air pollution's toll on forests and crops / edited by James J. MacKenzie and Mohamed T. El-Ashry. New Haven : Yale University Press, c1989. ix, 376 p. :
  89-009018          632/.19          0300045697
*Trees -- Effect of air pollution on -- United States. Trees – Effect of air pollution on -- Europe. Crops -- Effect of air pollution on – United States.*

**SB745.A67 1998**
  An Appalachian tragedy : air pollution and tree death in the highland forest of eastern North America / edited by Harvard Ayers, Jenny Hager, and Charles E. Little ; photographs by Jenny Hager. San Francisco, Calif. : Sierra Club Books, 1998. p. cm.
  97-034038          577.3/27/0974          0871569760
*Trees -- Effect of air pollution on -- Appalachian Mountains. Forest declines -- Appalachian Mountains. Forest ecology -- Appalachian Mountains.*

**SB745.4.M43 1990**
  Mechanisms of forest response to acidic deposition / Alan A. Lucier, Sharon G. Haines, editors. New York : Springer-Verlag, c1990. ix, 245 p. :
  89-048303          581.5/2642          0387972056
*Trees -- Effect of acid deposition on. Forest ecology. Trees -- Nutrition.*

## SB761-762 Pests and diseases — Plant pathology — Diseases and pests of trees and shrubs

**SB761.C68 1984**
**Coulson, Robert N.**
  Forest entomology : ecology and management / Robert N. Coulson, John A. Witter. New York : Wiley, c1984. x, 669 p. :
  83-023492          634.9/67          0471025739
*Forest insects. Forest insects -- Control.*

**SB762.L58 1995**
**Little, Charles E.**
  The dying of the trees : the pandemic in America's forests / Charles E. Little. New York, N.Y. : Viking, 1995. xi, 275 p. ;
  94-046136          634.9/61/0973          0670841358
*Forest declines -- United States. Forests and forestry -- United States. Forest ecology -- United States.*

## SB931 Pests and diseases — Economic entomology — General works

**SB931.I58 1994**
  Introduction to insect pest management / edited by Robert L. Metcalf, William H. Luckmann. New York : Wiley, c1994. xiii, 650 p.
  93-044141          632/.7     0471589578
*Insect pests -- Control.*

**SB931.M47 1993**
**Metcalf, Robert Lee,**
  Destructive and useful insects : their habits and control / Robert L. Metcalf, Robert A. Metcalf. New York : McGraw-Hill, c1993. 1 v. (various
  92-018374          632/.7     0070416923
*Insect pests. Beneficial insects. Insect pests -- Control.*

## SB933.3 Pests and diseases — Economic entomology — Biological control

**SB933.3.D43 1991**
**DeBach, Paul.**
  Biological control by natural enemies / Paul DeBach, David Rosen. Cambridge, [England] ; Cambridge University Press, 1991. xiv, 440 p. :
  90-002388          632/.96          0521391911
*Insect pests -- Biological control. Weeds -- Biological control. Agricultural pests -- Biological control.*

**SB933.3.I53 2000**
  Insect pest management : techniques for environmental protection / [edited by] Jack E. Rechcigl and Nancy A. Rechcigl. Boca Raton, Fla. : Lewis Publishers, c2000. 392 p. :
  99-040543          632/.9517          1566704782
*Insect pests -- Biological control.*

**SB933.3.R436 1998**
**Rechcigl, Jack E.**
Biological and biotechnological control of insect pests / Jack E. Rechcigl, Nancy A. Rechcigl. Boca Raton, Fla. : Lewis Publishers, c1998. 374 p. :
99-031226          632/.96          1566704790
*Insect pests -- Biological control. Biological pest control agents. Agricultural biotechnology.*

## SB942 Pests and diseases — Economic entomology — Diseases of insects, mites, etc.

**SB942.T35 1993**
**Tanada, Yoshinori.**
Insect pathology / Yoshinori Tanada, Harry K. Kaya. San Diego : Academic Press, c1993. xii, 666 p. :
92-014551          632/.7          0126832552
*Insects -- Diseases.*

## SB950 Pests and diseases — Pest control and treatment of diseases. Plant protection

**SB950.A2.P467 1993**
Pest control with enhanced environmental safety / Stephen O. Duke, editor, Julius J. Menn, editor, Jack R. Plimmer, editor. Washington, DC : American Chemical Society, 1993. x, 357 p. :
93-012098          632/.9          0841226385
*Agricultural pests -- Control -- Congresses. Agricultural pests -- Control -- Environmental aspects -- Congresses. Pesticides -- Congresses.*

**SB950.E78 1989**
Eradication of exotic pests : analysis with case histories / Donald L. Dahlsten and Richard Garcia, editors ; Hilary Lorraine, associate editor. New Haven : Yale University Press, c1989. vi, 296 p. :
88-037234          628.9/6          0300043325
*Pests -- Control. Pests -- Control -- Case studies.*

**SB950.N68 1995**
Novel approaches to integrated pest management / edited by Reuven Reuveni. Boca Raton, FL : Lewis Publishers, c1995. xiv, 369 p. :
94-029087          632/.9          087371881X
*Agricultural pests -- Integrated control. Plant parasites -- Integrated control.*

**SB950.O35 1991**
**Olkowski, William.**
Common-sense pest control / William Olkowski, Sheila Daar, Helga Olkowski. Newtown, CT : Taunton Press, c1991. xix, 715 p. :
90-026624          635.0496          0942391632
*Pests -- Control.*

## SB951-961 Pests and diseases — Pest control and treatment of diseases. Plant protection — Pesticides

**SB951.A786 2000**
Ashgate handbook of pesticides and agricultural chemicals / edited by G.W.A. Milne. Aldershot, Hampshire ; Ashgate, c2000. xix, 206 p. ;
00-102728          631.8          0566083884
*Pesticides -- Handbooks, manuals, etc. Agricultural chemicals -- Handbooks, manuals, etc. Pesticides -- Handbooks, manuals, etc.*

**SB951.W396 1998**
**Waxman, Michael F.,**
Agrochemical and pesticide safety handbook / Michael F. Waxman. Boca Raton : Lewis Publishers, c1998. 616 p. :
98-005485          632/.95          1566702968
*Pesticides -- Handbooks, manuals, etc. Agricultural chemicals -- Handbooks, manuals, etc. Pesticides -- Safety measures -- Handbooks, manuals, etc.*

**SB951.145.B54.E54 1990**
Enhanced biodegradation of pesticides in the environment / Kenneth D. Racke, editor, Joel R. Coats, editor. Washington, DC : American Chemical Society, 1990. x, 302 p. :
90-034194          632/.95042          084121784X
*Pesticides -- Biodegradation -- Congresses. Microbial metabolism -- Congresses.*

**SB951.145.N37.N38 1991**
Naturally occurring pest bioregulators / Paul A. Hedin, editor. Washington, DC : American Chemical Society, 1991. xii, 456 p. :
90-022914          632/.95          0841218978
*Natural pesticides -- Congresses. Bioactive compounds -- Congresses.*

**SB952.P9.P93 1995**
Pyrethrum flowers : production, chemistry, toxicology, and uses / edited by John E. Casida, Gary B. Quistad. New York : Oxford University Press, 1995. xviii, 356 p.
93-048567          668/.651          0195082109
*Pyrethrum (Insecticide) Pyrethrum (Plant) Pyrethrins.*

**SB961.C49 1995**
CRC handbook of pesticides / editor, G.W.A. Milne. Boca Raton : CRC Press, c1995. vi, 402 p. :
94-039758          615.9/02          0849324475
*Pesticides -- Handbooks, manuals, etc. Pesticides -- Toxicology -- Handbooks, manuals, etc.*

## SB974-975 Pests and diseases — Pest control and treatment of diseases. Plant protection — Organic plant protection

### SB974.E53 1984

The Encyclopedia of natural insect & disease control : the most comprehensive guide to protecting plants--vegetables, fruit, flowers, trees, and lawns--without toxic chemicals / edited by Roger B. Yepsen, Jr. Emmaus, Pa. : Rodale Press, c1984. 490 p. :
83-024643        635/.0494        0878574883
*Plants, Protection of. Organic gardening. Garden pests -- Control.*

### SB975.C66 1998

Conservation biological control / edited by Pedro Barbosa. San Diego : Academic Press, c1998. xxii, 396 p.
97-080315        632/.96        0120781476
*Agricultural pests -- Biological control. Biological pest control agents. Agricultural ecology.*

### SB975.S92
**Swan, Lester A.**

Beneficial insects; nature's alternatives to chemical insecticides: animal predation, parasitism, disease organisms. New York, Harper & Row [1964] xvii, 429 p.
64-012705        632.9
*Insect pests -- Biological control.*

## SB990.5 Pests and diseases — Pest control and treatment of diseases. Plant protection — Pest introduction. Non-indigenous pests

### SB990.5.U6.C68 1999
**Cox, George W.,**

Alien species in North America and Hawaii : impacts on natural ecosystems / George W. Cox. Washington, D.C. : Island Press, c1999. xii, 387 p. ;
99-016652        577/.18        1559636793
*Nonindigenous pests -- United States. Biological invasions -- United States. Biological diversity conservation -- United States.*

## SB993.3 Economic zoology applied to crops. Agricultural zoology — By region or country — United States

### SB993.3.F59 1998
**Flint, Mary Louise,**

Natural enemies handbook : the illustrated guide to biological pest control / Mary Louise Flint and Steve H. Dreistadt ; photographs by Jack Kelly Clark. Oakland, Calif. : UC Division of Agriculture and Natural Sciences c1998. viii, 154 p.
97-062438        1879906414
*Pests -- Biological control -- Handbooks, manuals, etc. Pests -- Integrated control -- Handbooks, manuals, etc.*

# SD Forestry

## SD143-144 History of forestry. Forest conditions — North America — United States

### SD143.A596 1997

American forests : nature, culture, and politics / edited by Char Miller. Lawrence, Kan. : University Press of Kansas, c1997. xiv, 289 p. ;
97-014811        333.75/0973/0904
0700608486
*Forests and forestry -- United States -- History.*

### SD143.B47 1998
**Berger, John J.,**

The Sierra Club guide to understanding forests / John J. Berger. San Francisco, CA : Sierra Club Books, 1998. p. cm.
97-045867        333.75        0871564203
*Forests and forestry -- United States. Forest ecology -- United States.*

### SD143.W285 1999
**Walker, Laurence C.,**

The North American forests : geography, ecology, and silviculture / Laurence C. Walker ; with the collaborating assistance of Brian Oswald ... [et al.]. Boca Raton, Fla. : CRC Press, c1999. 398 p. :
98-003924        634.9/097        1574441760
*Forests and forestry -- United States. Forests and forestry -- Canada. Forest ecology -- United States.*

### SD144.A13C74 1997

Creating a forestry for the 21st century : the science of ecosystem management / edited by Kathryn A. Kohm and Jerry F. Franklin ; foreword by Jack Ward Thomas. Washington, D.C. : Island Press, c1997. xvi, 475 p. :
            634.9 20        1559633980
*Forest management -- Northwest, Pacific. Forest ecology -- Northwest, Pacific. Forests and forestry -- Northwest, Pacific. Ecosystem management -- Northwest, Pacific Forest management. Forest ecology. Forests and forestry. Ecosystem management.*

## SD235 History of forestry. Forest conditions — Other countries

### SD235.A785.K44 1989

Keepers of the forest : land management alternatives in Southeast Asia / editor, Mark Poffenberger. West Hartford, Conn. : Kumarian Press, c1990. xxv, 289 p. :
89-038879        333.75/0959        0931816815
*Forest management -- Asia, Southeastern. Forest management -- Social aspects -- Asia, Southeastern. Agroforestry -- Asia, Southeastern.*

## SD247 History of forestry. Forest conditions — Tropics

**SD247.F66 2001**

Footprints in the jungle : natural resource industries, infrastructure, and biodiversity conservation / edited by Ian A. Bowles, Glenn T. Prickett ; editorial assistance by Amy E. Skoczlas. New York : Oxford University Press, 2001. p. cm.
99-018433          333.95/16/0913          0195125789
*Forest management -- Tropics. Forest products industry -- Environmental aspects -- Tropics. Economic development -- Environmental aspects -- Tropics.*

**SD247.P68 1992**
**Panaiotov, Todor.**

Not by timber alone : economics and ecology for sustaining tropical forests / Theodore Panayotou and Peter S. Ashton. Washington, D.C. : Island Press, c1992. xx, 282 p. ;
92-010222          333.75/0913          1559631953
*Forests and forestry -- Tropics. Forest products – Tropics. Forest products industry -- Tropics.*

## SD373 General works

**SD373.F58 1984**

Forestry handbook / edited for the Society of American Foresters by Karl F. Wenger. New York : Wiley, c1984. xix, 1335 p.
83-017110          634.9          0471062278
*Forests and forestry -- Handbooks, manuals, etc.*

**SD373.F646 2001**

The forests handbook / edited by Julian Evans. Oxford : Malden, MA : Blackwell Science, c2001. 2 v. :
          333.75 21          0632048182
*Forests and forestry.*

**SD373.H65 1997**
**Holland, Israel Irving,**

Forests and forestry / I.I. Holland, G.L. Rolfe. 5th ed. Danville, Ill. : Interstate Publishers, c1997. ix, 558 p. :
          634.9 21          0813430585
*Forests and forestry. Forests and forestry -- United States.*

**SD373.I585 1995**

Introduction to forest and renewable resources / Grant W. Sharpe . . . [et al.]. 6th ed. New York : McGraw-Hill, c1995. xvii, 664 p. :
          634.9 20          0070565678
*Forests and forestry. Forests and forestry -- United States.*

**SD373.L45 1984**
**Leuschner, William A.**

Introduction to forest resource management / William A. Leuschner. New York : Wiley, c1984. vi, 298 p. :
83-021602          634.9/28          0471086681
*Forest management.*

**SD373.M344 1990**
**Mather, Alexander S.**

Global forest resources / Alexander S. Mather. Portland, Or. : Timber Press, 1990. x, 341 p. :
92-139980          333.75/11          0881921785
*Forests and forestry.*

**SD373.N96 1996**
**Nyland, Ralph D.**

Silviculture : concepts and applications / Ralph D. Nyland. New York : McGraw-Hill, c1996. xxii, 633 p. :
          634.9 20          0070569991
*Forests and forestry.*

**SD373.O93 1999**

Our forests, our future : report of the World Commission on Forests and Sustainable Development / Emil Salim and Ola Ullsten, co-chairmen. Cambridge, UK ; New York, NY Cambridge University Press, 1999. xxi, 205 p. :
          333.75 21          0521660211
*Forests and forestry. Forest ecology. Forest management. Sustainable forestry.*

**SD373.S56 1986**
**Sharpe, Grant William.**

Introduction to forestry / Grant W. Sharpe, Clare W. Hendee, Wenonah F. Sharpe. New York : McGraw-Hill, c1986. ix, 629 p. :
85-013318          634.9/0973          0070564825
*Forests and forestry. Forests and forestry -- United States.*

**SD373.S79 1987**
**Stoddard, Charles Hatch,**

Essentials of forestry practice / Charles H. Stoddard, Glenn M. Stoddard. New York : Wiley, c1987. xiv, 407 p. :
86-022408          634.9/0973          0471842370
*Forests and forestry. Forests and forestry -- United States.*

## SD383 Description of remarkable trees, individual and collective — General works

**SD383.L48 1999**
**Lewington, Anna.**

Ancient trees : trees that live for 1000 years / Anna Lewington & Edward Parker. London ; New York : Collins & Brown ; 1999. 185, [7] p. :
          582.16/022/2 21          1855857049
*Trees. Historic trees. Trees -- Pictorial works. Historic trees -- Pictorial works.*

# SD387 Special aspects of forestry, A-Z

**SD387.C58.C53 1994**

Clearcut : the tragedy of industrial forestry / edited by Bill Devall. San Francisco, Calif. : Sierra Club Books : c1993. 291 p. :
93-035989          333.75/137/097          0871564947
*Clearcutting -- Environmental aspects -- United States. Clearcutting -- Environmental aspects -- Canada. Forest ecology – United States.*

**SD387.E58.K57 1992**
**Kimmins, J. P.**

Balancing act : environmental issues in forestry / Hamish Kimmins. Vancouver : UBC Press, c1992. 244 p. :
92-236268          333.75/16          0774804351
*Forests and forestry -- Environmental aspects. Forest ecology.*

**SD387.O43.B66 1994**
**Booth, Douglas E.**

Valuing nature : the decline and preservation of old-growth forests / Douglas E. Booth. Lanham, Md. : Rowman & Littlefield, c1994. xii, 287 p. ;
92-047001          333.75/09795          0847678598
*Old growth forests -- Northwest, Pacific. Old growth forest conservation -- Northwest, Pacific. Old growth forest ecology -- Northwest, Pacific.*

**SD387.S87.D44 1993**

Defining sustainable forestry / edited by Gregory H. Aplet... [et al.] ; the Wilderness Society ; foreword by E.O. Wilson. Washington, D.C. : Island Press, c1993. xiii, 328 p.
93-008389          333.75/16          155963233X
*Sustainable forestry -- Congresses.*

**SD387.S87.R47 1994**

Restoration forestry : an international guide to sustainable forestry practices / Michael Pilarski, editor. Durango, Colo. : Kivaki Press, c1994. 525 p. :
94-076630          634.9/56/09          1882308514
*Sustainable forestry -- Handbooks, manuals, etc. Sustainable forestry -- Directories. Forest protection -- Handbooks, manuals, etc.*

**SD387.S87.S86 1992**

Sustainable harvest and marketing of rain forest products / edited by Mark Plotkin and Lisa Famolare. Washington, D.C. : Island Press, c1992. xv, 325 p. :
91-043278          338.1/74987/0913
1559631694
*Sustainable forestry -- Tropics -- Congresses. Rain forests -- Economic aspects -- Congresses. Forest products -- Tropics -- Congresses.*

# SD390 Forest soils — General works

**SD390.A75**
**Armson, K  A.**

Forest soils : properties and processes / K. A. Armson. Toronto ; University of Toronto Press, c1977. xii, 390 p. :
78-307199          634.9          0802022650
*Forest soils.*

**SD390.P74 1987**
**Pritchett, William L.**

Properties and management of forest soils / William L. Pritchett, Richard F. Fisher. New York : Wiley, c1987. xv, 494 p. :
86-022421          634.9          0471895725
*Forest soils. Soil management. Forest management.*

# SD392 Sylviculture — Sylvicultural systems

**SD392.M38 1989**
**Matthews, John D.**

Silvicultural systems / John D. Matthews. Oxford [England] : Clarendon Press ; 1989. xii, 284 p. :
89-003145          634.9/5          0198594917
*Silvicultural systems.*

# SD397.A-Z Sylviculture — Natural history of forest trees — Description, value, and culture of individual species or groups, A-Z

**SD397.R3.R455 2000**

The redwood forest : history, ecology, and conservation of the coast redwoods / edited by Reed F. Noss. Washington, D.C. : Island Press, c2000. xxvi, 339 p.
99-016799          634.9/758          1559637250
*Coast redwood. Coast redwood -- Ecology. Forest ecology.*

# SD399.5 Sylviculture — Tree breeding and selection. Forest genetics

**SD399.5.N355 1988**
**Namkoong, Gene.**

Tree breeding : principles and strategies / G. Namkoong, H.C. Kang, J.S. Brouard. New York : Springer-Verlag, c1988. viii, 180 p.
88-012352          634.9/56          0387967478
*Trees -- Breeding. Forest genetics.*

# SD399.7 Sylviculture — Forest genetic resources conservation

**SD399.7.F65 2000**

Forest conservation genetics : principles and practice / A. Young, D. Boshier & T. Boyle (editors). Collingwood, VIC, Australia : CSIRO Pub. ; c2000. xiv, 352 p. :
00-057900          333.95/3416          0643062602
*Forest genetic resources conservation.*

## SD411 Conservation and protection — General works

**SD411.W46 1993**
Who will save the forests? : knowledge, power, and environmental destruction / edited by Tariq Banuri and Frederique Apffel Marglin. London ; Zed Books, 1993. 195 p. :
93-002788          333.75/16          1856491595
*Forest conservation. Deforestation. Forest ecology.*

## SD412 Conservation and protection — By region or country — United States

**SD412.J67 1994**
**Jordan, Richard N.,**
Trees and people : forestland, ecosystems, and our future / Richard N. Jordan. Washington, D.C. : Regnery Pub. ; c1994. xx, 276 p. :
94-027423          333.75/16/0973          0895264838
*Forest conservation -- United States. Forest ecology -- United States. Forests and forestry -- Environmental aspects – United States.*

## SD414.A-Z Conservation and protection — By region or country — Other regions or countries, A-Z

**SD414.L29.S68 1998**
**Southgate, Douglas DeWitt,**
Tropical forest conservation : an economic assessment of the alternatives in Latin America / Douglas Southgate. New York : Oxford University Press, 1998. xiii, 175 p.
97-034601          333.75/16/0980913
0195109961
*Rain forest conservation -- Latin America. Deforestation -- Control -- Latin America. Forest ecology -- Latin America.*

**SD414.T76.G73 1988**
**Gradwohl, Judith.**
Saving the tropical forests / by Judith Gradwohl and Russell Greenberg ; preface by Michael Robinson ; illustrated by Lois Sloan. Washington, D.C. : Island Press, 1988. 214 p. :
88-013267          333.75/16/0913          0933280815
*Forest conservation -- Tropics. Deforestation -- Control -- Tropics. Forest reserves -- Tropics.*

**SD414.T76.M55 1991**
**Miller, Kenton.**
Trees of life : saving tropical forests and their biological wealth / Kenton Miller and Laura Tangley. Boston : Beacon Press, c1991. xxi, 218 p. :
90-021623          333.75/16/0913          0807085081
*Forest conservation -- Tropics. Rain forests. Deforestation -- Control -- Tropics.*

## SD418 Conservation and protection — Deforestation — General works

**SD418.P47 1989**
**Perlin, John.**
A forest journey : the role of wood in the development of civilization / John Perlin. New York : W.W. Norton, c1989. 445 p. :
88-025291          333.75          0393026671
*Deforestation -- History. Forests and forestry -- History. Wood – History.*

**SD418.W67 1988**
World deforestation in the twentieth century / edited by John F. Richards and Richard P. Tucker. Durham : Duke University Press, 1988. x, 321 p. :
87-031953          333.75/11/0904          0822307847
*Deforestation -- History -- 20th century -- Congresses.*

## SD418.2-418.3 Conservation and protection — Deforestation — By region or country, A-Z

**SD418.2.T76.T75 1996**
Tropical deforestation : the human dimension / edited by Leslie E. Sponsel, Thomas N. Headland, and Robert C. Bailey ; with a foreword by Jeffrey A. McNeely. New York : Columbia University Press, c1996. xxviii, 365 p
95-047256          304.2/8          0231103182
*Deforestation -- Social aspects -- Tropics. Forest ecology -- Tropics. Forest management -- Tropics.*

**SD418.3.A53.A526 1990**
Alternatives to deforestation : steps toward sustainable use of the Amazon rain forest / Anthony B. Anderson, editor. New York : Columbia University Press, c1990. xiv, 281 p. :
89-024034          333.75/16/09811          0231068921
*Deforestation -- Control -- Amazon River Region -- Congresses. Sustainable forestry -- Amazon River Region -- Congresses. Rain forest ecology -- Amazon River Region -- Congresses.*

**SD418.3.B6.D43 1995**
**Dean, Warren.**
With broadax and firebrand : the destruction of the Brazilian Atlantic forest / Warren Dean. Berkeley : University of California Press, c1995. xx, 482 p. :
94-005681          304.2/8/098109152
0520087755
*Deforestation -- Brazil -- Atlantic Coast -- History. Rainforests – Brazil -- Atlantic Coast -- History. Nature -- Effect of human beings on -- Brazil -- Atlantic Coast -- History. Atlantic Coast (Brazil) -- Environmental conditions -- History.*

## SD421-421.32 Conservation and protection — Damage by elements — Forest fires and wildfires

**SD421.P94 1996**
**Pyne, Stephen J.,**
Introduction to wildland fire / Stephen J. Pyne, Patricia L. Andrews, Richard D. Laven. New York : Wiley, c1996. xxxiii, 769 p
95-044027          363.37/9          0471549134
*Wildfires. Wildfires -- Prevention and control. Wildfires – United States.*

**SD421.3.P96 1982**
**Pyne, Stephen J.,**
Fire in America : a cultural history of wildland and rural fire / Stephen J. Pyne. Princeton, N.J. : Princeton University Press, c1982. xvi, 654 p. :
81-047945          304/.2          0691083002
*Wildfires -- United States -- History. Fires -- United States -- History.*

**SD421.32.M9.M33 1992**
**Maclean, Norman,**
Young men & fire / Norman Maclean. Chicago : University of Chicago Press, 1992. viii, 301 p.,
92-011890          634.9/618/0978664
0226500616
*Smokejumpers -- United States. Forest fires -- Montana – Mann Gulch -- Prevention and control.*

## SD426-428.A-Z Conservation and protection — Forest reserves — United States

**SD426.R63 1988**
**Robinson, Gordon.**
The forest and the trees : a guide to excellent forestry / Gordon Robinson ; foreword by Michael McCloskey. Washington, D.C. : Island Press, c1988. xiv, 257 p. :
88-009011          333.75/15/0973          0933280416
*Forest reserves -- United States -- Management. Forest conservation -- United States. Forest policy -- United States.*

**SD428.T6.D87 1999**
**Durbin, Kathie.**
Tongass : pulp politics and the fight for the Alaska rain forest / by Kathie Durbin. Corvallis : Oregon State University Press, c1999. 328 p. ;
99-040408          333.75/13/097982
087071466X
*Logging -- Environmental aspects -- Alaska -- Tongass National Forest. Wool-pulp industry -- Environmental aspects -- Alaska -- Tongass National Forest. Rain forest conservation -- Alaska -- Tongass National Forest. Tongass National Forest (Alaska) -- Management.*

## SD536 Exploitation and utilization — Sections of woods and descriptive text

**SD536.C67 1979**
**Core, H.A.**
Wood structure and identification / H.A. Core, W.A. Cote, And A.C. Day. 2d ed. Syracuse, N.Y. : Syracuse University Press, 1979. xii, 182 p. :
674/.12
*Wood -- Identification. Wood -- Anatomy -- Atlases.*

## SD538.3 Exploitation and utilization — Logging — By region or country

**SD538.3.M4.B48 1995**
**Bevis, William W.,**
Borneo log : the struggle for Sarawak's forests / William W. Bevis. Seattle : University of Washington Press, c1995. x, 245 p. :
95-018317          959.5/4          0295974168
*Bevis, William W., -- 1941- -- Journeys -- Malaysia -- Sarawak. Deforestation -- Malaysia -- Sarawak. Rain forest conservation -- Malaysia -- Sarawak. Plywood industry -- Japan. Sarawak -- Description and travel.*

## SD555 Exploitation and utilization — Valuation, mensuration, etc. — Mensuration. Scaling

**SD555.H8 1982**
**Husch, Bertram,**
Forest mensuration / Bertram Husch, Charles I. Miller, Thomas W. Beers. New York : J. Wiley, c1982. vii, 402 p. :
82-004811          634.9/285          0471044237
*Forests and forestry -- Mensuration. Forest surveys.*

# SF Animal Culture

## SF22.5 Communication in animal culture — Animal culture literature

**SF22.5.L58 1993**
The Literature of animal science and health / edited by Wallace C. Olsen. Ithaca : Cornell University Press, 1993. v, 404 p. ;
93-007801          636          0801428866
*Animal culture literature. Veterinary literature.*

## SF41 History and conditions — General works

**SF41.C58 1999**
**Clutton-Brock, Juliet.**
A natural history of domesticated mammals / Juliet Clutton-Brock. Cambridge, U.K. ; Cambridge University Press ; 1999. viii, 238 p.
98-037220          636/.009          0521632471
*Domestic animals -- History. Domestication -- History.*

**SF41.H4613 1989**
**Hemmer, Helmut.**
  Domestication : the decline of environmental appreciation / Helmut Hemmer ; translated into English by Neil Beckhaus. Cambridge [England] ; Cambridge University Press, 1990. ix, 208 p. :
89-009993          636          0521341787
  *Domestication. Domestic animals.*

### SF51 History and conditions — By country — United States

**SF51.F69 1996**
**Fox, Michael W.,**
  Agricide : the hidden farm and food crisis that affects us all / Michael W. Fox. 2nd ed. Malabar, FL : Krieger Pub. Co., 1996. xvii, 252 p. :
                338.1/6/0973 20
*Livestock -- United States. Animal industry -- United States. Livestock factories -- United States. Animal welfare -- United States. Agriculture -- United States. Agricultural industries -- United States. Agricultural ecology -- United States. Agricultural pollution – United States. Food industry and trade -- United States.*

## SF61 Comprehensive works. Textbooks

**SF61.A3 2001**
**Cunningham, Merle,**
  Animal science and industry / Merle Cunningham, Duane Acker. 6th ed. Upper Saddle River, N.J. : Prentice Hall, c2001 xix, 746 p .:
          636 21     0130826537
*Livestock. Animal industry.*

**SF61.G5 1995**
**Gillespie, James R.**
  Modern livestock & Poultry production / James R. Gillespie. 5th ed. Albany, NY : Delmar Publications, c1997. xii, 1026 p. :
          636 20     0827367333
*Livestock. Poultry.*

**SF61.P37 1970**
**Park, R. D.**
  Animal husbandry [by] R. D. Park, with the collaboration of L. Coutts, P. J. Hodgkiss and R. Bowers. [London] Oxford University Press, 1970. xiii, 256 p.
79-019201          636.08     0198594224
  *Livestock.*

**SF61.T39 2001**
**Taylor, Robert E. (Robert Ellis),**
  Scientific farm animal science / Robert E. Taylor, Thomas G. Field. 7th ed. Upper Saddle River, NJ : Prentice Hall, c2001. xvii, 744 p. :
          636 21     0130200328
*Livestock.*

### SF65.2 Handbooks, manuals, etc. Practical works — American (United States) — 1976-

**SF65.2.B38 1998**
**Battaglia, Richard A.**
  Handbook of livestock management techniques / Richard A. Battaglia. 2nd ed. Upper Saddle River, N.J. : Prentice Hall, c1998. xviii, 589 p. :
          636 20
*Livestock -- Handbooks, manuals, etc.*

## SF85 Rangelands. Range management. Grazing — General works

**SF85.G73 1991**
  Grazing management : an ecological perspective / edited by Rodney K. Heitschmidt and Jerry W. Stuth. Portland, Or. : Timber Press, c1991. 259 p. :
90-019900          636.01     0881921904
  *Grazing -- Management. Range management. Grazing -- Environmental aspects.*

**SF85.S33**
**Sampson, Arthur William,**
  Range management, principles and practices.  New York, Wiley [1952] xiv, 570 p.
51013123          636.08423
  *Rangelands.*

## SF95 Feeds and feeding. Animal nutrition — General works

**SF95.M35 1979**
  Animal nutrition / Leonard A. Maynard . . . [et al.]. 7th ed. New York : McGraw-Hill, c1979. x, 602 p. :
          636.08/52
*Animal nutrition.*

**SF95.V36 1994**
**Van Soest, Peter J.**
  Nutritional ecology of the ruminant / Peter J. Van Soest. Ithaca : Comstock Pub., 1994. xii, 476 p. :
94-007001          636.2/0852          080142772X
  *Ruminants -- Feeding and feeds. Animal nutrition. Rumen fermentation.*

## SF105 Breeding and breeds — General works

**SF105.B7 1980**
**Briggs, Hilton Marshall,**
  Modern breeds of livestock / Hilton M. Briggs, Dinus M. Briggs. 4th ed. New York : Macmillan, c1980. xiv, 802 p. :
          636
*Livestock breeds.*

## SF105.M34 2002

Mason's world dictionary of livestock breeds, types and varieties / revised by Valerie Porter. 5th ed. New York : CABI Pub., 2002. p. cm.

      636/.003 21      085199430X

*Livestock breeds -- Dictionaries.*

## SF105.275 Breeding and breeds — Rare breeds — By region or country, A-Z

### SF105.275.U6D65 2001
**Dohner, Janet Vorwald,**

The encyclopedia of historic and endangered livestock and poultry breeds / Janet Vorwald Dohner. New Haven : Yale University Press, c2001. xii, 514 p. :

      636/.003 21      0300088809

*Rare breeds -- United States -- Encyclopedias. Livestock breeds -- United States -- Encyclopedias. Rare breeds -- Canada -- Encyclopedias. Livestock breeds -- Canada -- Encyclopedias. Rare breeds -- Great Britain -- Encyclopedias. Livestock breeds -- Great Britain -- Encyclopedias.*

## SF105.3 Breeding and breeds — Germplasm

### SF105.3.L58 1993

Livestock / Committee on Managing Global Genetic Resources: Agricultural Imperatives, Board on Agriculture, National Research Council. Washington, D.C. : National Academy Press, 1993. xiv, 276 p. :

93-016715      636.08/21      0309043948

*Livestock -- Germplasm resources.*

### SF105.3.T34 1994

Taking stock : the North American livestock census / Donald E. Bixby ... [et al.] ; The American Livestock Breeds Conservancy. Blacksburg, Va. : McDonald & Woodward Pub. Co., 1994. vii, 182 p. :

93-047249      636.08/21      0939923351

*Livestock -- Germplasm resources -- United States. Livestock -- Germplasm resources -- Canada. Livestock breeds -- United States.*

## SF140 Other special topics, A-Z

### SF140.L58.J64 1991
**Johnson, Andrew.**

Factory farming / Andrew Johnson. Oxford, UK ; Blackwell, 1991. vi, 272 p. :

90-047620      363.19/2      0631178430

*Livestock factories.*

### SF140.P38.W67 1990

The World of pastoralism : herding systems in comparative perspective / editors, John G. Galaty, Douglas L. Johnson. New York : Guilford Press ; 1990. x, 436 p. :

90-013830      636.08/4      0898627850

*Pastoral systems.*

## SF196 Cattle — History — By region or country, A-Z

### SF196.N7.J67 1993
**Jordan-Bychkov, Terry G.,**

North American cattle-ranching frontiers : origins, diffusion, and differentiation / Terry G. Jordan. Albuquerque : University of New Mexico Press, c1993. xi, 439 p. :

92-036428      636.2/13/097      082631421X

*Cattle -- North America -- History. Ranching -- North America -- History. Cattle -- History. North America -- Historical geography.*

### SF196.U5.S77 1998
**Starrs, Paul F.**

Let the cowboy ride : cattle ranching in the American West / Paul F. Starrs. Baltimore : Johns Hopkins University Press, 1998. xx, 356 p. :

97-021744      636.2/01      0801856841

*Ranching -- West (U.S.)*

## SF197 Cattle — General works

### SF197.R68
**Rouse, John E.**

World cattle, by John E. Rouse. Norman, University of Oklahoma Press [1970] 2 v. (1046 p.

69-010620      636.2      0806108649

*Cattle.*

## SF198 Cattle — Breeds — General works

### SF198.P67 1992
**Porter, Valerie,**

Cattle : a handbook to the breeds of the world / by Valerie Porter ; illustrated by Jake Tebbit. New York : Facts On File, [1992] 400 p. :

90-047367      636.2      0816026408

*Cattle breeds -- Handbooks, manuals, etc.*

## SF203 Cattle — Feeding — General works

### SF203.P45 1995

Beef cattle feeding and nutrition / edited by Tilden Wayne Perry and Michael J. Cecava. 2nd ed. San Diego : Academic Press, c1995. xx, 389 p. :

      636.2/13 20

*Beef cattle -- Feeding and feeds.*

## SF207 Cattle — Beef cattle

### SF207.E5 1997
**Ensminger, M.Eugene.**

Beef cattle science / by M.E. Ensminger and R.C. Perry. 7th ed. Danville, Ill. : Interstate Publishers, 1997. xiii, 1104 p. :

      636.2/13 21      0813430062

*Beef cattle.*

## SF208 Cattle — Dairy cattle

**SF208.D35**
Dairy cattle: principles, practices, problems, profits [by] Richard C. Foley [and others] Philadelphia, Lea & Febiger, 1972. xiii, 693 p.
76-152022        636.2/1/4        0812103092
*Dairy cattle. Dairy farming.*

## SF250.5 Cattle — Dairy processing. Dairy products (General) — General works

**SF250.5.D35 1993**
Dairy science and technology handbook / editor, Y.H. Hui. New York, N.Y. : VCH, c1993. 3 v. :
92-030191        637        1560810785
*Dairy processing. Dairy products.*

## SF271 Cattle — Dairy processing. Dairy products (General) — Cheese

**SF271.M247 1985**
**Marquis, Vivienne.**
The cheese book / Vivienne Marquis and Patricia Haskell with an additional chapter by Laurence Senelick. New York : Simon and Schuster, c1985. 336 p. ;
85-002202        641.3/73        0671531336
*Cheese -- Varieties. Cookery (Cheese)*

## SF283 Horses — History of culture — General works

**SF283.C63 1992**
**Clutton-Brock, Juliet.**
Horse power : a history of the horse and the donkey in human societies / Juliet Clutton-Brock. Cambridge, Mass. : Harvard University Press, 1992. 192 p. :
91-020447        636.1        067440646X
*Horses -- History. Donkeys -- History. Mules -- History.*

## SF285 Horses — General works

**SF285.E345 2000**
**Edwards, Elwyn Hartley.**
The new encyclopedia of the horse / Elwyn Hartley Edwards ; photography by Bob Langrish, Kit Houghton ; foreword by Sharon Ralls Lemon. London ; New York : DK, 2000. 464 p. :
636.1/003 21        0789471817
*Horses -- Encyclopedias. Horse breeds -- Encyclopedias. Horsemanship -- Encyclopedias.*

## SF291 Horses — Breeds and breeding — General works

**SF291.H37 1995**
**Hendricks, Bonnie L.**
International encyclopedia of horse breeds / by Bonnie L. Hendricks ; foreword by Anthony A. Dent. Norman : University of Oklahoma Press, c1995. xx, 486 p., [
95-011430        636.1/003        0806127538
*Horse breeds -- Encyclopedias. Horses -- Encyclopedias. Horses -- Breeding -- Encyclopedias.*

## SF294.2 Horses — Horse sports — General works

**SF294.2.H65 1988**
**Holderness-Roddam, Jane.**
Competitive riding / Jane Holderness-Roddam. New York : Prentice Hall Press, c1988. 208 p. :
88-042985        798.2/4        0131551442
*Horse sports. Dressage. Show jumping.*

## SF363 Horses — Przewalski's horse — General works

**SF363.P78 1994**
Przewalski's horse : the history and biology of an endangered species / edited by Lee Boyd and Katherine A. Houpt. Albany : State University of New York Press, c1994. xvii, 313 p.
93-002363        599.72/5        0791418898
*Przewalski's horse.*

## SF375 Sheep — General works

**SF375.E57 1986**
**Ensminger, M. Eugene.**
Sheep & goat science / By M.E. Ensminger, R.O. Parker. 5th ed. Danville, Ill. : Interstate Printers & Publishers, c1986. 643 p. :
636.3 19
*Sheep. Goats.*

## SF395 Swine — General works

**SF395.P59 1993**
**Porter, Valerie,**
Pigs : a handbook to the breeds of the world / Valerie Porter ; illustrated by Jake Tebbit. Ithaca, N.Y. : Comstock Pub. Associates, c1993. xv, 256 p. :
93-199974        636.4        080142920X
*Swine breeds -- Handbooks, manuals, etc.*

## SF406 Laboratory animals — General breeding and care

**SF406.F69 1986**
**Fox, Michael W.,**
Laboratory animal husbandry : ethology, welfare, and experimental variables / by Michael W. Fox. Albany : State University of New York Press, c1986. xv, 267 p. :
85-009766          636.08/85          0887061370
*Laboratory animals. Laboratory animals -- Behavior. Animal welfare.*

## SF408 Zoo animals. Captive wild animals — Culture and care

**SF408.W55 1996**
Wild mammals in captivity : principles and techniques / editors, Devra G. Kleiman ... [et al.] ; managing editor, Holly Harris. Chicago : University of Chicago Press, 1996. xvi, 639 p. :
95-021376          636.088/9          0226440028
*Captive mammals. Captive mammals -- Housing -- Design and construction.*

## SF408.3 Zoo animals. Captive wild animals — Breeding

**SF408.3.E84 1995**
Ethics on the ark : zoos, animal welfare, and wildlife conservation / edited by Bryan G. Norton ... [et al.] ; with assistance from John Wuichet. Washington : Smithsonian Institution Press, c1995. xxvi, 330 p.
94-037139          639.9/3/01          1560985151
*Captive wild animals -- Breeding -- Moral and ethical aspects -- Congresses. Wildlife conservation -- Congresses. Zoos -- Philosophy -- Congresses.*

## SF411.5 Pets — General works

**SF411.5.S47 1996**
**Serpell, James,**
In the company of animals : a study of human-animal relationships / James Serpell. Cambridge ; New York : Cambridge University Press, 1996. xxii, 283 p. :
304.2/7 20
*Pets -- History. Pets -- Social aspects -- History. Pet owners -- History. Human-animal relationships -- History.*

## SF422 Pets — Dogs — Dictionaries. Encyclopedias

**SF422.D28 1974**
**Dangerfield, Stanley,**
The international encyclopedia of dogs / edited by Stanley Dangerfield and Elsworth Howell ; with special contributions by Maxwell Riddle. New York : Howell Book House, 1974. 479, [1] p. :
74-019842          636.7/003
*Dogs -- Encyclopedias.*

## SF426 Pets — Dogs — General works

**SF426.C66 1997**
The complete dog book. 19th ed. New York : Howell Book House, c1997. viii, 756 p. :
636.7/1 21
*Dog breeds. Dogs. Dogs -- Standards -- United States.*

## SF426.2 Pets — Dogs — Essays and light literature

**SF426.2.L56 1996**
**Limbaugh, Ronald H.**
John Muir's "Stickeen" and the lessons of nature / Ronald H. Limbaugh. Fairbanks, Alaska : University of Alaska Press, c1996. xvi, 185 p. :
96-005172          813/.4          0912006846
*Muir, John, -- 1838-1914. -- Stickeen. Muir, John, -- 1838-1914. Dogs -- Alaska -- Anecdotes.*

## SF433 Pets — Dogs — Behavior

**SF433.C67 1994**
**Coren, Stanley.**
The intelligence of dogs : canine consciousness and capabilities / Stanley Coren. New York : Free Press ; c1994. viii, 271 p.
94-002725          636.7          0029066832
*Dogs -- Psychology. Animal intelligence.*

**SF433.D66 1995**
The domestic dog : its evolution, behaviour, and interactions with people / edited by James Serpell ; pencil drawings by Priscilla Barrett. Cambridge ; Cambridge University Press, 1995. x, 268 p. :
95-013800          599.74/442          0521415292
*Dogs -- Behavior. Dogs. Human-animal relationships.*

## SF442 Pets — Cats — General works

**SF442.B66 1980**
The Book of the cat / edited by Michael Wright and Sally Walters ; designed by Celia Welcomme ; original paintings by Peter Warner ; consulting editors, Barbara S. Stein, Sidney R. Thompson. New York : Summit Books, c1980. 256 p. :
80-023570          636.8          067144753X
*Cats.*

**SF442.N4**
**Necker, Claire.**
The natural history of cats. South Brunswick, A. S. Barnes [1970] 326 p.
73-112775          599.7/4428          0498074854
*Cats.*

## SF446.5 Pets — Cats — Behavior

**SF446.5.D65 2000**
The domestic cat : the biology of its behaviour / edited by Dennis C. Turner, Patrick Bateson. 2nd ed. Cambridge, UK ; Cambridge University Press, 2000. 244 p. :
599.75/215 21
*Cats -- Behavior. Cats -- Social aspects.*

## SF449.A-Z Pets — Cats — By breed or type A-Z

**SF449.C34.G68 1996**
**Gould, Laura L.**
Cats are not peas : a calico history of genetics / Laura Gould. New York, NY : Copernicus, c1996. xvi, 228 p. :
96-018692          636.8/22          0387947965
*Calico cats. Cats -- Genetics. Calico cats -- Anecdotes.*

## SF456.5 Pets — Fishes. Aquariums — Dictionaries. Encyclopedias

**SF456.5.L4913 1983**
The Aquarium encyclopedia / [edited by] Gunther Sterba ; English editor, Dick Mills ; translated by Susan Simpson. Cambridge, Mass. : MIT Press, 1983. 605, [2] p. :
82-000247          639.3/4/0321          0262192071
*Aquariums -- Encyclopedias. Aquarium fishes -- Encyclopedias. Fishes -- Encyclopedias.*

## SF457-457.1 Pets — Fishes. Aquariums — General aquarium culture

**SF457.1.D35 1992**
**Dakin, Nick.**
The Macmillan book of the marine aquarium : a definitive reference to more than 300 marine fish and invertebrate species and how to establish and maintain a reef aquarium / Nick Dakin ; foreword by Julian Sprung. New York : Macmillan ; c1992. 400 p. :
92-045126          639.3/42          0028971086
*Marine aquariums. Marine aquarium fishes. Marine invertebrates as pets.*

**SF457.G648 2000**
**Goldstein, Robert J.**
American aquarium fishes / Robert J. Goldstein, with Rodney W. Harper and Richard Edwards ; photographs by William F. Roston ... [et al.]. College Station, Tex. : Texas A&M University Press, c2000. xiii, 428 p.,
99-043786          639.34     0890968802
*Aquarium fishes. Freshwater fishes -- North America.*

## SF457.5 Pets — Fishes. Aquariums — Environment (Water, temperature, light, etc.)

**SF457.5.A32 1998**
**Adey, Walter H.**
Dynamic aquaria : building living ecosystems / Walter H. Adey, Karen Loveland. 2nd ed. San Diego : Academic Press, c1998. xx, 498 p. :
639.34 21          0120437929
*Aquarium water. Aquariums.*

## SF459.A-Z Pets — Other animals, A-Z

**SF459.L5.R6313 1997**
**Rogner, Manfred.**
Lizards / Manfred Rogner ; translated from the original German by John Hackworth. Malabar, Fla. : Krieger Pub. Co., 1997. 2 v. :
95-031852          639.3/95          0894649728
*Lizards as pets. Lizards.*

## SF473.A-Z Birds. Cage birds — Other pet birds, A-Z

**SF473.M33.A27 1995**
**Abramson, Joanne.**
The large macaws : their care, breeding, and conservation / Joanne Abramson, Brian L. Speer, and Jorgen B. Thomsen ; illustrated by Marsha Mello. Fort Bragg, Calif. : Raintree Publications, c1995. xvii, 534 p.
93-070515          636.6/865          0963596403
*Macaws.*

## SF487 Poultry — General works

**SF487.B182 1979**
**Banks, Stuart.**
The complete handbook of poultry-keeping / Stuart Banks. New York : Van Nostrand Reinhold Co., 1979. 216 p. :
79-014305          636.5/08          0442233825
*Poultry. Chickens.*

**SF487.D27 1996**
**Davis, Karen,**
Prisoned chickens, poisoned eggs : an inside look at the modern poultry industry / Karen Davis. Summertown, Tenn. : Book Pub. Co., c1996. 175 p. ;
96-045937          179/.3          1570670323
*Chickens. Chickens -- Diseases. Eggs -- Production.*

## SF515.5.A-Z Reptiles — Individual, A-Z

**SF515.5.G43.H4613 1995**
**Henkel, Friedrich-Wilhelm.**
  Geckoes : biology, husbandry, and reproduction / Friedrich-Wilhelm Henkel, Wolfgang Schmidt ; translated from the original German by John Hackworth. Melbourne, Fla. : Krieger, 1995. xii, 237 p. :
94-036667          639.3/95          0894649191
  *Captive geckos.*

**SF515.5.S64.R67 1991**
**Rossi, John,**
  Snakes of the United States and Canada : keeping them healthy in captivity / John Rossi. Malabar, Fla. : Krieger Pub. Co., 1992-1995. 2 v. :
91-002199          639.3/96          0894645900
  *Captive snakes. Snakes -- United States. Snakes -- Canada.*

## SF523 Beneficial insects and insect culture — Bee culture — General works

**SF523.C856 1990**
**Crane, Eva.**
  Bees and beekeeping : science, practice, and world resources / Eva Crane. Ithaca, N.Y. : Comstock Pub. Associates, 1990. xvii, 614 p.
89-017477          638/.1     0801424291
  *Bee culture. Honeybee.*

## SF523.3 Beneficial insects and insect culture — Bee culture — Essays and light literature

**SF523.3.W55 1998**
**Winston, Mark L.**
  From where I sit : essays on bees, beekeeping, and science / Mark L. Winston. Ithaca : Comstock Pub. Associates, 1998. x, 171 p. ;
97-041016          638/.1     0801434777
  *Honeybee. Bee culture.*

## SF524 Beneficial insects and insect culture — Bee culture — History and conditions

**SF524.C738 1999**
**Crane, Eva.**
  The world history of beekeeping and honey hunting / Eva Crane. New York : Routledge, 1999. xxii, 682 p.
99-025816          638/.1/09          0415924677
  *Bee culture -- History. Bee hunting -- History.*

## SF538.5.A-Z Beneficial insects and insect culture — Bee culture — Diseases and pests

**SF538.5.A37.A37 1988**
  Africanized honey bees and bee mites / editors, Glen R. Needham ... [et al.]. Chichester, West Sussex, England : E. Horwood ; 1988. xviii, 572 p.
88-011955          638/.15          0745803199
  *Africanized honeybee. Honeybee -- Parasites. Mites.*

**SF538.5.A37.W56 1992**
**Winston, Mark L.**
  Killer bees : the Africanized honey bee in the Americas / Mark L. Winston. Cambridge, Mass. : Harvard University Press, 1992. xiii, 162 p.
91-033113          638/.12          067450352X
  *Africanized honeybee. Africanized honeybee -- America. Africanized honeybee -- Control.*

## SF609 Veterinary medicine — Dictionaries. Encyclopedias

**SF609.M5 1972b**
**Miller, William Christopher,**
  Black's veterinary dictionary, by William C. Miller and Geoffrey P. West. 10th ed. London A. and C. Black, 1972 viii, 1026,
          636/.089/03
*Veterinary medicine -- Dictionaries.*

## SF623 Veterinary medicine — History and conditions — By country

**SF623.S73 1994**
**Stalheim, Ole H. V.**
  The winning of animal health : 100 years of veterinary medicine / O.H.V. Stalheim. Ames, Iowa : Iowa State University Press, 1994. xvi, 251 p. :
94-001629          636.089/0973          081382429X
  *Veterinary medicine -- United States -- History.*

## SF748 Veterinary medicine — Handbooks, manuals, etc.

**SF748.M47 1986**
  The Merck veterinary manual : a handbook of diagnosis, therapy, and disease prevention and control for the veterinarian / Clarence M. Fraser, editor ; Asa Mays, associate editor ; Harold E. Amstutz ... [et al.]. Rahway, N.J., U.S.A. : Merck, 1986. xxvii, 1677 p
85062725          636.089          0911910530
  *Veterinary medicine -- Handbooks, manuals, etc.*

## SF756.7 Veterinary medicine — Veterinary ethology

**SF756.7.B43 1994**
**Beaver, Bonnie V. G.,**
  The veterinarian's encyclopedia of animal behavior / Bonnie V. Beaver. Ames : Iowa State University Press, 1994. xi, 307 p. :
94-027257          599/.051/03          0813821142
  *Domestic animals -- Behavior -- Encyclopedias. Veterinary medicine -- Encyclopedias. Animal behavior -- Encyclopedias.*

**SF756.7.G46 1998**
  Genetics and the behavior of domestic animals / edited by Temple Grandin. San Diego : Academic Press, c1998. x, 356 p. :
97-080382          0122951301
  *Domestic animals -- Behavior. Domestic animals -- Genetics.*

### SF797 Veterinary medicine — Communicable diseases of animals — Special diseases

**SF797.B73 1994**
**Brass, Danny A.**
  Rabies in bats : natural history and public health implications / Danny A. Brass. Ridgefield, Conn. : Livia Press, 1994. xv, 335 p. :
93-078291          614.5/63          0963704516
  *Bats as carriers of disease. Rabies in animals. Vampire bats.*

### SF991 Veterinary medicine — Diseases of special classes of animals — Pets

**SF991.U325 1995**
  UC Davis book of dogs : the complete medical reference guide for dogs and puppies / by the Faculty and Staff, School of Veterinary Medicine, University of California at Davis ; edited by Mordecai Siegal, consulting editor, Jeffrey E. Barlough. 1st ed. New York : HarperCollins Publishers, c1995. xxii, 538 p. :
          636.7/089 20          0062701363
  *Dogs -- Diseases. Dogs -- Health.*

### SF994.2.A-Z Veterinary medicine — Diseases of special classes of animals — Avian diseases

**SF994.2.A1.G47**
**Gerstenfeld, Sheldon L.,**
  The bird care book : everything you need to know to keep any bird healthy and happy / Sheldon L. Gerstenfeld. Reading, Mass. : Addison-Wesley Pub. Co., c1981. 186 p. :
81-004513          636.6/86          0201039087
  *Cage birds -- Diseases. Cage birds. Birds -- Diseases.*

# SH Aquaculture. Fisheries. Angling

## SH20.3 Aquaculture — Dictionaries. Encyclopedias.

**SH20.3.E53 2000**
  Encyclopedia of aquaculture / [edited by] Robert R. Stickney. New York : Wiley, c2000. xiii, 1063 p. :
          639.8/03 21          0471291013
  *Aquaculture -- Encyclopedias.*

## SH135 Aquaculture — General works

**SH135.A25 1994**
**Ackefors, Hans,**
  Introduction to the general principles of aquaculture / Hans Ackefors, Jay V. Huner, Mark Konikoff. New York : Food Products Press, c1994. xviii, 172 p.
93-029833          639.8          1560220120
  *Aquaculture.*

## SH137.4 Aquaculture — Pond Aquaculture

**SH137.4.B69 1995**
**Boyd, Claude E.**
  Bottom soils, sediment, and pond aquaculture / Claude E. Boyd. New York : Chapman & Hall, c1995. xviii, 348 p.
94-044496          639.3/11          0412069415
  *Pond aquaculture. Pond soils. Pond sediments.*

## SH138 Aquaculture — Mariculture

**SH138.I93 1976**
**Iversen, Edwin S.**
  Farming the edge of the sea / E. S. Iversen. Farnham, Eng. : Fishing News Books, c1976. 436 p. :
77-369142          630/.9162          0852380798
  *Mariculture.*

### SH156 Aquaculture — Fish culture — Feeding

**SH156.H47 1988**
**Hepher, Balfour,**
  Nutrition of pond fishes / Balfour Hepher. Cambridge [Cambridgeshire] ; Cambridge University Press, 1988. x, 388 p. :
87-024968          639.3/11          0521341507
  *Fishes -- Feeding and feeds. Fish ponds.*

### SH157.8 Aquaculture — Fish culture — Habitat improvement

**SH157.8.H86 1991**
**Hunter, Chris**
Better trout habitat : a guide to stream restoration and management / Christopher J. Hunter ; edited by Tom Palmer ; illustrated by Ellen Meloy ;foreword by Nick Lyons. Washington, D.C. : Island Press, c1991. xxx, 320 p. :
90-047860          639.3/755          0933280785
*Fish habitat improvement -- Handbooks, manuals, etc. Stream conservation -- Handbooks, manuals, etc. Trout -- Habitat.*

## SH159 Aquaculture — Fish culture — Freshwater culture

**SH159.B38 1983**
**Bennett, George W.**
Management of lakes and ponds / George W. Bennett. Malabar, Fla. : R.E. Krieger Pub. Co., 1983, c1970. xx, 375 p. :
83-006091          639.3/11          0898746264
*Fish-culture. Fishery management. Fish ponds.*

## SH167.A-Z Aquaculture — Fish culture — Individual species, including special classes, A-Z

**SH167.S17.P68 1996**
Principles of salmonid culture / edited by William Pennell, Bruce A. Barton. Amsterdam ; Elsevier, 1996. xxix, 1039 p.
96-031360          639.3/755          044482152X
*Salmon. Fish-culture.*

## SH171-177 Aquaculture — Fish culture — Diseases and adverse factors

**SH171.E4313 1992**
**Egusa, Shuzo,**
Infectious diseases of fish = Sakana no kansensho / Shuzo Egusa. New Delhi : Amerind Pub. Co., 1992. xxiv, 696 p.
96-139044
*Fishes -- Diseases.*

**SH177.B3.B33 1993**
Bacterial diseases of fish / edited by Valerie Inglis, Ronald J. Roberts, Niall R. Bromage. New York : Halsted Press, c1993. xix, 312 p. :
92-032506          639.3          0470221208
*Bacterial diseases in fishes.*

## SH201 Fisheries — Dictionaries. Encyclopedias

**SH201.F56 1969**
**Firth, Frank E.**
The encyclopedia of marine resources. Edited by Frank E. Firth. New York, Van Nostrand Reinhold Co. [1969] xi, 740 p.
70-078014          551.4/6/003
*Fisheries -- Dictionaries. Marine resources -- Dictionaries.*

## SH219.6 Fisheries — By region or country — North America

**SH219.6**
**Bogue, Margaret Beattie,**
Fishing the Great Lakes : an environmental history, 1783-1933 / Margaret Beattie Bogue. Madison, Wis. : University of Wisconsin Press, c2000. xix, 444 p. :
00-008601          333.95/613/0977          0299167607
*Fisheries -- Great Lakes -- History. Fishery policy --Great Lakes -- History. Fisheries -- Environmental aspects -- Great Lakes.*

## SH221.5 Fisheries — By region or country — United States

**SH221.5.M35**
**Dobbs, David,**
The great Gulf : fishermen, scientists, and the struggle to revive the world's greatest fishery / David Dobbs. Washington, D.C. : Island Press, c2000. xv, 206 p. ;
00-010479          333.75/6/0916345
1559636637
*Fisheries -- Maine, Gulf of. Fishery management -- Maine, Gulf of.*

## SH223 Fisheries — By region or country — Canada

**SH223.F586 1999**
Fishing places, fishing people : traditions and issues in Canadian small-scale fisheries / edited by Dianne Newell and Rosemary E. Ommer. Toronto : University of Toronto Press, c1999. vii, 374 p. :
00-500923          338.3/727/0971          0802041167
*Fisheries -- Canada -- History. Fisheries -- Social aspects -- Canada. Fishery management -- Canada -- History.*

## SH281 Fisheries — By region or country — Europe

**SH281.V55**
**Villiers, Alan John,**
The quest of the schooner Argus; a voyage to the banks and Greenland. Illustrated with the author's photos. New York, Scribner, 1951. 348 p.
51006528          639.2756
*Fisheries -- Greenland. Fisheries -- Portugal. Fisheries -- Newfoundland.*

## SH327.5 Fisheries — Fishery resources

**SH327.5.F57 1988**
Fish population dynamics : the implications for management / edited by J.A. Gulland. 2nd ed. Chichester [England] ; New York : Wiley, c1988. xviii, 422 p. :
          333.95/611 19
*Fishery resources. Fishery management. Fish populations.*

## SH327.7 Fisheries — Fishery conservation

**SH327.7.M35 1997**
**Maitland, Peter S.**
Conservation management of freshwater habitats : lakes, rivers, and wetlands / by P.S. Maitland and N.C. Morgan. London ; Chapman & Hall, 1997. x, 233 p. :
96-072121        333.91/6216        0412594102
*Fishery conservation. Wildlife conservation. Conservation of natural resources.*

## SH328 Fisheries — Fishery management. Fishery policy — General works

**SH328.F56**
Fisheries management / edited by Robert T. Lackey and Larry A. Nielsen. New York : Wiley, 1980. x, 422 p. :
80-020028        333.95/6        047027056X
*Fishery management.*

**SH328.M39 1990**
**McGoodwin, James R.**
Crisis in the world's fisheries : people, problems, and policies / James R. McGoodwin. Stanford, Calif. : Stanford University Press, 1990. viii, 235 p.,
90-037484        338.3/727        0804717907
*Fishery management. Fishery policy.*

**SH328.R69 1981**
**Everhart, W. Harry**
Principles of fishery science / W. Harry Everhart, William D. Youngs. Ithaca : Comstock Pub. Associates, 1981. 349 p. :
80-015603        639.3        0801413346
*Fishery management. Fish populations. Fish-culture.*

## SH329 A-Z Fisheries — Fishery management. Fishery policy — Special topics, A-Z

**SH329.A66.D48 1992**
The Development of an aquatic habitat classification system for lakes / edited by W.-Dieter N. Busch, Peter G. Sly. Boca Raton : CRC Press, c1992. 225 p. :
92-006759        639.9/77        0849301483
*Aquatic habitats -- Classification -- Congresses. Fishery management -- Congresses. Lakes -- Classification -- Congresses.*

**SH329.C57.F65 1994**
Folk management in the world's fisheries : lessons for modern fisheries management / Christopher L. Dyer and James R. McGoodwin, editors. Niwot, CO : University Press of Colorado, c1994. xii, 347 p. :
94-001669        333.95/6        0870813250
*Fishery management -- Citizen participation. Fishery management -- Social aspects.*

**SH329.F56.S58 1994**
**Smith, Tim D.**
Scaling fisheries : the science of measuring the effects of fishing, 1855-1955 / Tim D. Smith. Cambridge [England] ; Cambridge University Press, 1994. x, 392 p. :
93-038292        333.95/611/0287        052139032X
*Fish stock assessment -- History.*

## SH331 Fisheries — General works

**SH331.R68 1996**
**Royce, William F.**
Introduction to the practice of fishery science / Rev. ed. San Diego : Academic Press, c1996. xii, 448 p. :
             333.95/6 20
*Fisheries.*

## SH334 Fisheries — Economic aspects. Finance

**SH334.A53 1986**
**Anderson, Lee G.**
The economics of fisheries management / Lee G. Anderson. Baltimore : Johns Hopkins University Press, c1986. xx, 296 p. :
85-024061        338.3/727        0801832535
*Fisheries -- Economic aspects. Fishery management – Economic aspects.*

**SH334.I84 1999**
**Iudicello, Suzanne.**
Fish, markets, and fishermen : the economics of overfishing / Suzanne Iudicello, Michael Weber, and Robert Wieland. Washington, D.C. : Island Press, c1999. xiv, 192 p. :
99-014118        333.95/615        1559636424
*Fisheries -- Economic aspects. Fishery management.*

## SH346-348 Fisheries — Fishery for individual species — Salmon

**SH346.B83 1993**
**Buck, Richard,**
Silver swimmer / Richard Buck. New York, NY : Lyons & Burford, c1993. xvi, 416 p. :
93-041438        333.95/6        1558212515
*Atlantic salmon fisheries -- North Atlantic Ocean -- History. Fishery conservation -- North Atlantic Ocean -- International cooperation -- History. Atlantic salmon.*

**SH346.S54 1992**
**Shearer, W. M.**
The Atlantic salmon : natural history, exploitation, and future management / W.M. Shearer. New York : Halsted Press, c1992. xvii, 244 p.,
92-018941        333.95/6        0470219475
*Atlantic salmon fisheries. Atlantic salmon. Atlantic salmon fisheries -- Great Britain.*

**SH348.L53 1999**
**Lichatowich, Jim.**
 Salmon without rivers : a history of the Pacific salmon crisis / Jim Lichatowich. Washington, D.C. : Island Press, c1999. xvi, 317 p. :
99-016798          333.95/656/09795
1559633603
 *Pacific salmon -- Northwest, Pacific -- History. Fishery conservation -- Northwest, Pacific -- History.*

**SH348.N68 1996**
 The Northwest salmon crisis : a documentary history / edited by Joseph Cone and Sandy Ridlington ; contributors, Bill M. Bakke ... [et al.]. Corvallis, Or. : Oregon State University Press, c1996. v, 374 p. :
96-004604          333.95/6          0870713906
 *Pacific salmon -- Northwest, Pacific -- History -- Sources. Fishery conservation -- Northwest, Pacific -- History -- Sources. Pacific salmon -- Effect of habitat modification on -- Northwest, Pacific -- History -- Sources.*

### SH351.A-Z Fisheries — Fishery for individual species — Other species or groups, A-Z

**SH351.S5.G47 1998**
**Gerstell, Richard.**
 American shad in the Susquehanna River Basin : a three-hundred-year history / Richard Gerstell. University Park, PA : Pennsylvania State University Press, c 1998. 217 p. :
98-019289          333.95/645          0271018054
 *Shad fisheries -- Susquehanna River Watershed. American shad -- Susquehanna River Watershed. Shad fishing -- Susquehanna River Watershed.*

**SH351.T8.N37 1992**
**National Research Council (U.S.).**
 Dolphins and the tuna industry / Committee on Reducing Porpoise Mortality from Tuna Fishing, Board on Biology, Board on Environmental Studies and Toxicology, Commission on Life Sciences, National Research Council. Washington, D.C. : National Academy Press, 1992. xii, 176 p. :
92-010603          333.95/9          0309047358
 *Tuna fisheries -- Environmental aspects. Dolphins -- Mortality. Tuna industry -- Environmental aspects.*

### SH370.A2-Z Fisheries — Shellfish fisheries. Shellfish culture — General works

**SH370.M37 1989**
 Marine invertebrate fisheries : their assessment and management / edited by John F. Caddy. New York : Wiley, c1989. xvi, 752 p. :
87-032436          333.95/5          0471832375
 *Shellfish fisheries.*

### SH380.62.A-Z-380.9 Fisheries — Shellfish fisheries. Shellfish culture — Crustaceans

**SH380.62.U6.I94 1993**
**Iversen, Edwin S.**
 Shrimp capture and culture fisheries of the United States / Edwin S. Iversen, Donald M. Allen, and James B. Higman. New York : Halsted Press, c1993. viii, 247 p.
93-007535          338.3/71543/0973
0470220902
 *Shrimp fisheries -- United States. Shrimp culture -- United States.*

**SH380.62.U6.M37 1996**
**Margavio, Anthony V.,**
 Caught in the net : the conflict between shrimpers and conservationists / by Anthony V. Margavio and Craig J. Forsyth, with Shirley Laska and James Mason. College Station : Texas A & M University Press, c1996. xvi, 156 p. :
95-037565          333.95/7          0890966699
 *Shrimp fisheries -- Environmental aspects -- Southern States. Sea turtles -- Southern States. Wildlife conservation -- Southern States.*

### SH381 Fisheries — Whaling

**SH381.R59**
**Robertson, Robert Blackwood,**
 Of whales and men. New York, Knopf, 1954. 299 p.
53-006858
 *Whaling.*

**SH381.T68 2001**
 Toward a sustainable whaling regime / edited by Robert L. Friedheim. Seattle : University of Washington Press ; c2001. x, 382 p. ;
00-050315          333.95/9517          0295980885
 *Whaling -- Management -- Political aspects. Sustainable fisheries -- International cooperation. Whaling -- Management -- International cooperation.*

### SH383-383.2 Fisheries — Whaling — History and conditions

**SH383.T6413 1982**
**Tonnessen, J. N.**
 The history of modern whaling / J.N. Tonnessen, A.O. Johnsen ; translated from the Norwegian by R.I. Christophersen. Berkeley : University of California Press, c1982. xx, 798 p. :
79-064657          338.3/7295/09          0520039734
 *Whaling -- History.*

**SH383.2.B87 1994**
**Busch, Briton Cooper.**
 Whaling will never do for me : the American whaleman in the nineteenth century / Briton Cooper Busch. Lexington, Ky. : University Press of Kentucky, c1994. xii, 265 p. :
93-010810          305.9/6392          0813118387
 *Whalers (Persons) -- United States -- Social life and customs. Whalers (Persons) -- United States -- Biography. Whaling -- United States -- History -- 19th century.*

### SH390.7 Fisheries — Algae and algae culture — Marine algae. Seaweed

**SH390.7.A44 1988**
Algae and human affairs / edited by Carole A. Lembi, J. Robert Waaland ; sponsored by the Phycological Society of America, Inc. Cambridge [Cambridgeshire] ; Cambridge University Press, 1988. viii, 590 p.
88-011679          589.3/6          0521321158
*Algae -- Utilization.*

## SH411 Angling — Dictionaries. Encyclopedias

**SH411.M18 1974**
**McClane, A. J.**
McClane's new standard fishing encyclopedia and international angling guide, edited by A. J. McClane. Illustrated by Richard E. Younger and Frances Watkins. New York, Holt, Rinehart and Winston [1974] 1156 p.
74-006108          799.1/03          0030603250
*Fishing -- Dictionaries.*

### SH433.A Angling — General works, essays and light literature — Walton. The compleat angler

**SH433.A1983 1983**
**Walton, Izaak,**
The compleat angler, 1653-1676 / Izaak Walton ; edited, with an introduction and commentary by Jonquil Bevan. Oxford ; New York Clarendon Press, Oxford University Press, 1983. vi, 435 p. :
799.1/2 19
*Fishing -- Early works to 1800. Walton, Izaak, 1593-1683. Compleat angler. 1st ed. 1983. Walton, Izaak, 1593-1683. Compleat angler. 5th ed. 1983.*

### SH441 Angling — General works, essays and light literature — 1801-

**SH441.C36 1988**
**Carter, Jimmy,**
An outdoor journal : adventures and reflections / Jimmy Carter. Thorndike, Me. : Thorndike Press, c1988. 443 p. (large
88-026766          799          0896212238
*Carter, Jimmy, -- 1924- -- Views on outdoor life. Presidents -- United States -- Biography. Fishing. Hunting.*

**SH441.F5 1963**
The Fisherman's encyclopedia. Ira N. Gabrielson, editor, Francesca LaMonte, associate editor. Harrisburg, Pa., Stackpole Co. [1963] xxix, 759 p.
63022468          799.1097
*Fishes -- North America. Fishing -- North America.*

### SH456 Angling — Methods of angling — Lure fishing (Fly fishing)

**SH456.M36 1993b**
**McNally, Tom.**
The complete book of fly fishing / Tom McNally. Camden, Me. : Ragged Mountain Press, c1993. xii, 354 p.,
93-009152          799.1/2          0877423458
*Fly fishing.*

### SH462 Angling — Angling in special countries — America

**SH462.M5**
**Migdalski, Edward C.**
Angler's guide to the fresh water sport fishes of North America. New York, Ronald Press Co. [1962] 431 p.
62009760          799.110973
*Freshwater fishes -- North America. Fishing -- North America.*

# SK Hunting sports

## SK14 Philosophy — General works

**SK14.K47 1993**
**Kerasote, Ted.**
Bloodties : nature, culture, and the hunt / Ted Kerasote. New York : Random House, c1993. xxi, 277 p. :
92-056824          799.2/01          0394576098
*Kerasote, Ted -- Journeys. Hunting -- Psychological aspects. Hunting -- Social aspects. Hunting -- Philosophy.*

## SK14.3 Philosophy — Ethical aspects

**SK14.3**
**Petersen, David,**
Heartsblood : hunting, spirituality, and wildness in America / David Petersen. Washington, D.C. : Island Press, c2000. xviii, 269 p.
00-009400          179/.3          1559637617
*Hunting -- Moral and ethical aspects. Hunting -- Philosophy.*

**SK14.3.H86 1994**
**Hummel, Richard**
Hunting and fishing for sport : commerce, controversy, popular culture / Richard Hummel. Bowling Green, OH : Bowling Green State University Popular Press, c1994. ii, 186 p. ;
93-073163          0879726458
*Hunting -- Moral and ethical aspects. Fishing – Moral and ethical aspects. Hunting -- Social aspects.*

## SK17.A-Z Biography — Individual, A-Z

### SK17.B76.A3 1972
**Browning, Meshach,**
"Forty-four years of the life of a hunter," being reminiscences of Meshach Browning, a Maryland hunter, roughly written down by himself. Rev. and illustrated by E. Stabler. Port Washington, N.Y., Kennikat Press [1972] xxiii, 400 p.
70-186088          799.2/924          0804686149
*Browning, Meshach, -- 1781-1859.     Hunting -- Maryland – Garrett County.*

### SK17.K45.A33 1979
**Keith, Elmer,**
Hell, I was there! / By Elmer Keith. Los Angeles, Calif. : Petersen Pub Co., c1979. xi, 308 p. :
79-064610          799.2/92/4          0822730146
*Keith, Elmer, -- 1899-     Hunters -- Biography. Hunting.*

### SK17.M34.A3
**Marshall, Edison,**
The heart of the hunter.  New York, McGraw-Hill [1956] 328 p.
56010323          799.2
*Voyages and travels. Hunting.*

## SK21 History — General works

### SK21.B68
**Brander, Michael.**
Hunting & shooting, from earliest times to the present day. New York, Putnam [1971] 255 p.
71-153992          799.29
*Hunting -- History.*

## SK33 General works, light litereature, etc. — American

### SK33.B36
**Bauer, Erwin A.**
Treasury of big game animals. Text and photos. by Erwin A. Bauer. New York, Outdoor Life [1972] ix, 398 p.
72-090933          799.2/77          0060102438
*Big game hunting. Big game animals. Photography of animals.*

### SK33.H945 1966
The New hunter's encyclopedia. Harrisburg, Pa., Stackpole Books [1966] xx, 1131 p.
66-012713          799.297
*Hunting -- North America. Hunting -- Dictionaries. Game and game-birds -- North America.*

### SK33.R6
**Roosevelt, Theodore,**
Good hunting; in pursuit of big game in the West, by Theodore Roosevelt ... New York, Harper & Brothers, 1907. vi p., 3 ., 1
07-006650
*Hunting -- United States.*

## SK40 By country — North America — General works

### SK40.O28
**O'Connor, Jack,**
The big game animals of North America. With natural histories by George G. Goodwin. Full color paintings and black and white drawings by Douglas Allen, scientific animal portraits by Alexander Seidel. New York, Outdoor life [1961] 264 p.
61-017292          799.297
*Big game hunting -- North America. Big Game animals – North America. Mammals -- North America.*

## SK45 By country — North America — United States

### SK45.R748 1990
**Roosevelt, Theodore,**
Outdoor pastimes of an American hunter / by Theodore Roosevelt ; [with a foreword by Paul Schullery]. Harrisburg, Pa. : Stackpole Books, [1990], c1905 xvii, 369 p.
90-009884          799.2973          0811730336
*Hunting -- West (U.S.)*

### SK45.R75 1970
**Roosevelt, Theodore,**
The wilderness hunter : An account of the Big Game of the United States and Its Chase with Horse, Hound, and Rifle. Upper Saddle River, N.J., Literature House [1970] 2 v.
72-104555          799.26     0839817657
*Hunting -- West (U.S.)*

## SK159 By country — South America — General works

### SK159.N46 1991
Neotropical wildlife use and conservation / edited by John G. Robinson and Kent H. Redford. Chicago : University of Chicago Press, c1991. xvii, 520 p.
90-044430          639.9/098          0226722589
*Hunting -- Latin America. Wild animal collecting -- Latin America. Wildlife conservation -- Latin America.*

## SK183 By country — Europe — General works

### SK183.C86 1988
**Cummins, John G.**
The hound and the hawk : the art of medieval hunting / John Cummins. New York : St. Martin's Press, 1988. x, 306 p., [3
88-027427          799.29/09/02          0312027168
*Hunting -- Europe -- History. Social history -- Medieval, 500-1500. Falconry -- Europe -- History.*

### SK241 By country — Asia — Iran

**SK241.M86 1994**
**Mungall, Elizabeth Cary.**
Exotics on the range : the Texas example / Elizabeth Cary Mungall and William J. Sheffield ; foreword by James G. Teer ; introduction by Charles W. Ramsey. College Station : Texas A & M University Press, c1994. xii, 265 p.,
93-024131          639.9/797/09764     0890963991
*Wildlife management -- Texas. Exotic animals -- Texas. Animal introduction -- Texas.*

### SK252 By country — Africa — Roosevelt expedition, 1909-1910

**SK252.R64 1988**
**Roosevelt, Theodore,**
African game trails : an account of the African wanderings of an American hunter-naturalist / Theodore Roosevelt. New York : St. Martin's Press, c1988. xxiii, 583 p.
88-011533          799.29676           0312021518
*Hunting -- Africa, East.     Africa, East -- Description and travel.*

## SK353 Wildlife management. Game protection — Congresses

**SK353.E513**
**Engelhardt, Wolfgang,**
Survival of the free; the last strongholds of wild animal life. Translated from the German by John Coombs. New York, Putnam [1962] xiv, 257 p.
62014920          799
*Game protection. Wild life, Conservation of. National parks and reserves.*

### SK354.A2-Z Wildlife management. Game protection — Biography — Individual

**SK354.A93.A37 1979**
**Averill, Gerald,**
Ridge runner : the story of a Maine woodsman / Gerald Averill ; illustrated by Peter Stanziale. Thorndike, Me. : Thorndike Press, [1979] c1948. 224 p. :
79-014339          974.1/04/0924       0896210316
*Averill, Gerald, -- 1896-    Game wardens -- Maine -- Biography. Maine -- Description and travel.*

**SK354.H33.R45 1991**
**Reisner, Marc.**
Game wars : the undercover pursuit of wildlife poachers / Marc Reisner. New York, N.Y., U.S.A. : Viking, 1991. 294 p. ;
90-050517          363.2/8             0670814865
*Hall, Dave.    Undercover wildlife agents -- United States -- Biography. Wildlife conservation -- United States.*

## SK355 Wildlife management. Game protection — General works

**SK355.P39 1994**
**Payne, Neil F.**
Techniques for wildlife habitat management of uplands / Neil F. Payne, Fred C. Bryant. New York : McGraw-Hill, c1994. xxv, 840 p. :
93-034866          639.9/2             0070489637
*Wildlife habitat improvement. Forest management. Range management.*

**SK355.W565 1995**
Wildlife in the marketplace / Terry L. Anderson and Peter J. Hill, editors. Lanham, Md. : Rowman & Littlefield, c1995. xv, 191 p. :
95-003095          333.95/417          084768024X
*Wildlife management -- Economic aspects. Wild animal trade.*

### SK361-453 Wildlife management. Game protection — By region or country — United States

**SK361.A66 1962**
**Allen, Durward Leon,**
Our wildlife legacy. New York, Funk & Wagnalls [1962] 422 p.
62-007980          799
*Wildlife conservation -- United States. Wildlife management.*

**SK361.A68 1992**
American fish and wildlife policy : the human dimension / edited by William R. Mangun. Carbondale : Southern Illinois University Press, c1992. viii, 272 p.
91-047741          333.95/0973        0809318210
*Wildlife management -- Government policy -- United States. Fishery management -- Government policy -- United States.*

**SK361.D28 1959**
**Day, Albert M**
North American waterfowl. Sketches by Bob Hines. Harrisburg, Pa., Stackpole Co. [1959] xx, 351 p.
59003953          799.244
*Birds -- North America. Birds, Protection of. Water birds.*

**SK361.L38**
**Leopold, Aldo,**
Game management, by Aldo Leopold ... drawings by Allan Brooks. New York, C. Scribner's Sons, 1933. xxi, 481 p. i
33012580          799.0973
*Wildlife management. Game protection -- United States. Game and game-birds -- United States.*

**SK361.M36**
**Matthiessen, Peter.**
Wildlife in America. Introd. by Richard H. Pough. Drawings by Bob Hines. New York, Viking Press, 1959. 304 p.
59-011635          591.97
*Zoology -- North America. Hunting -- North America. Fishing -- North America.*

**SK367.L4**
**Leopold, A. Starker**
   Wildlife in Alaska, an ecological reconnaissance, by A. Starker Leopold and F. Fraser Darling. Sponsored by the New York Zoological Society and the Conservation Foundation. New York, Ronald Press Co. [1953] 129 p.
53-012201          333.78
   *Wildlife conservation -- Alaska. Game and game-birds – Alaska. Natural resources -- Alaska.*

**SK453.C34 1971**
**Calkins, Frank,**
   Rocky mountain warden.  New York, Knopf, 1971 [c1970] 265 p.
75-123425          799.29/24          0394443187
   *Game wardens -- Biography. Hunting -- Utah.*

### SK473 Wildlife management. Game protection — By region or country — Mexico

**SK473.L4**
**Leopold, A. Starker**
   Wildlife of Mexico; the game birds and mammals. Berkeley, University of California Press, 1959. xiii, 568 p.
59006865          799.20972
   *Zoology -- Mexico. Hunting -- Mexico. Game and game-birds – Mexico.*

### SK571 Wildlife management. Game protection — By region or country — Africa

**SK571.S48 1998**
**Shomon, Joseph James,**
   Wild edens : Africa's premier game parks and their wildlife / Joseph James Shomon. College Station : Texas A&M University Press, c1998. 153 p. :
97-053174          508.676          0890968012
   *Wildlife refuges -- Africa. Endangered species -- Africa.*

# SK601 Camping. Outdoor life

**SK601.B84**
**Brower, David Ross,**
   Going light, with backpack or burro. With contributions by Lewis F. Clark [and others] San Francisco, Sierra Club, [1968, c1951] xiv, 152 p.
51005362
   *Outdoor life. Mountaineering.*

**SK601.B845**
**Brower, David Ross,**
   The Sierra Club wilderness handbook, edited by David Brower. New York, Ballantine Books [1967] xvi, 272 p.
68-000340          796.54
   *Camping.*

# T Technology (General)

## T9 Dictionaries and encyclopedias

**T9.D47**
**De Vries, Louis,**
English-German technical and engineering dictionary. New York, McGraw-Hill, 1954. xv, 997 p.
54-014586          603
*Technology -- Dictionaries. Engineering -- Dictionaries. English language -- Dictionaries -- German.*

## T10 Dictionaries and encyclopedias — Bilingual and polyglot

**T10.R68 1994**
Routledge French technical dictionary = Routledge dictionnaire technique anglais. London ; Routledge, 1994. 2 v. ; 26 cm.
95-149489          603          0415056705
*Technology -- Dictionaries -- French. French language -- Dictionaries -- English. Technology -- Dictionaries.*

**T10.R684 1997**
Routledge Spanish technical dictionary = Diccionario tecnico ingles. London [England] ; Routledge, 1997. 2 v. ;
97-151895                    0415112745
*Technology -- Dictionaries -- Spanish. Spanish language -- Dictionaries -- English. Technology -- Dictionaries.*

# T10.5 Communication of technical information

**T10.5.D66 2000**
**Dombrowski, Paul M.**
Ethics in technical communication / Paul M. Dombrowski. Boston : Allyn & Bacon, c2000. xiii, 258 p. :
174/.96 21          0205274625
*Communication of technical information -- Moral and ethical aspects.*

**T10.5.G64 2000**
Global contexts : case studies in international technical communication / [edited by] Deborah S. Bosley. Boston, MA : Allyn and Bacon, 2001. viii, 216 p. :
601/.4 21          0205286828
*Communication of technical information -- Case studies.*

**T10.5.H39 1995**
**Haydon, Leslie M.**
The complete guide to writing & producing technical manuals / Leslie M. Haydon. New York : Wiley, c1995. xvi, 294 p. :
94-049677          808/.0666          0471122815
*Communication of technical information. Technology -- Documentation. Technical manuals.*

**T10.5.M315 2000**
Managing global communication in science and technology / edited by Peter J. Hager, H.J. Scheiber. New York : Wiley, c2000. xxi, 365 p. :
501.4 21          047124922X
*Communication of technical information.*

**T10.5.M34 2001**
**Markel, Michael H.**
Ethics in technical communication : a critique and synthesis / Mike Markel. Westport, Conn. : Ablex Pub., 2001. ix, 265 p. :
174/.96 21          1567505287
*Communication of technical information -- Moral and ethical aspects.*

**T10.5.R65 2002**
**Roze, Maris.**
Technical communication in the age of the Internet / Maris Roze, Simon Maxwell. 4th ed. Upper Saddle River, NJ : Prentice Hall, 2002. x, 305 p. :
808/.0666 21          0130205745
*Communication of technical information. Technical writing.*

**T10.5.T414 2000**
Technical communication, deliberative rhetoric, and environmental discourse : connections and directions / edited by Nancy W. Coppola and Bill Karis. Stamford, Conn. : Ablex Publishing, c2000. xxviii, 336 p.
601/.4 21          1567504809
*Communication of technical information. Communication in the environmental sciences.*

**T10.5.T53 2000**
**Tidwell, Mike,**
How to produce effective operations and maintenance manuals / Mike Tidwell. Reston, VA : American Society of Civil Engineers, 2000. ix, 85 p. :
808/.0666 21          0784400113
*Communication of technical information. Technology -- Documentation. Technical manuals. Plant maintenance -- Handbooks, manuals, etc.*

## T10.68 Communication of technical information — Risk communication

**T10.68.C64 1990**
Communicating risks to the public : international perspectives / edited by Roger E. Kasperson and Pieter Jan M. Stallen. Dordrecht ; Kluwer Academic Publishers, c1991. vi, 481 p. :
89-048612          363.1/05          0792306015
*Risk communication.*

## T10.7 Communication of technical information — Technical literature

**T10.7.L67 2000**
**Lord, Charles R.**
Guide to information sources in engineering / Charles R. Lord. Englewood, CO : Libraries Unlimited, 2000. xiii, 345 p. :

025.066 21       1563086999
*Technical literature. Technology -- Information services. Engineering -- Bibliography.*

## T11 Communication of technical information — Language. Technical writing

**T11.A515 2001**
**Andrews, Deborah C.**
Technical communication in the global community / Deborah C. Andrews. 2nd ed. Upper Saddle River, N.J. : Prentice Hall, c2001. xvi, 541 p. :
808/.0666 21       0130281522
*Technical writing. Communication of technical information.*

**T11.H28 1998**
**Haramundanis, Katherine,**
The art of technical documentation / Katharine Haramundanis. 2nd ed. Boston : Digital Press, c1998. xiv, 282 p. :
808/.0666 21       155558182X
*Technical writing.*

**T11.R565 2001**
**Rigby, David W.**
Technical document basics for engineering technicians and technologists / David W. Rigby. Upper Saddle River, N.J. : Prentice Hall, c2001. xiv, 536 p. :
808/.0666 21
*Technical writing.*

**T11.S386 1994**
Scientific style and format : the CBE manual for authors, editors, and publishers / Style Manual Committee, Council of Biology Editors. 6th ed. Cambridge ; New York : Cambridge University Press, 1994. xv, 825 p. :
808/.0666 20
*Technical writing -- Handbooks, manuals, etc.*

**T11.V368 2001**
**Van Wicklen, Janet.**
The tech writer's survival guide : a comprehensive handbook for aspiring technical writers / Janet Van Wicklen. New York : Facts on File, 2001. p. cm.
808/.0666 21       0816040389
*Technical writing -- Vocational guidance. Communication of technical information.*

## T11.95 Industrial directories - General works

**T11.95.P58 2000**
Plunkett's engineering and research industry almanac : the only comprehensive guide to research and engineering companies and trends / Jack W. Plunkett [editor] Houston, Tex. : Plunkett Research, Ltd., c2000. xvi, 715 p. ;
01-273402       607/.273       1891775103
*Technology -- Research -- United States -- Directories. Technology -- United States -- Directories. Engineering – Research – United States -- Directories.*

**T12.T6**
Thomas register of American manufacturers. New York, Thomas Pub. Co. v.
06-043937       338.7/6/02573
*Manufactures -- United States -- Directories. Industries – United States -- Directories.*

## T14 Philosophy. Theory. Classification. Methodology

**T14.B36 1970**
**Barbour, Ian G.**
Science & secularity; the ethics of technology [by] Ian G. Barbour. New York, Harper & Row [1970] 151 p.
77-109886       174/.9/6
*Technology -- Philosophy. Ethics.*

**T14.F56**
**Florman, Samuel C.**
The existential pleasures of engineering / Samuel C. Florman. New York : St. Martin's Press, c1976. xi, 160 p. ;
75-009480       601
*Technology -- Philosophy. Engineering.*

**T14.K26 1997**
**Kaufman-Osborn, Timothy V.**
Creatures of Prometheus : gender and the politics of technology / Timothy V. Kaufman-Osborn. Lanham, Md. : Rowman & Littlefield, c1997. xi, 292 p. ;
97-017013       306.4/6/082       0847685640(al
*Technology -- Philosophy. Technology -- Social aspects.*

**T14.M56 1994**
**Mitcham, Carl.**
Thinking through technology : the path between engineering and philosophy / Carl Mitcham. Chicago : University of Chicago Press, 1994. xi, 397 p. :
93-044581       601       0226531961
*Technology -- Philosophy.*

**T14.P28 1999**
**Pacey, Arnold.**
Meaning in technology / Arnold Pacey. Cambridge, Mass. : MIT Press, c1999. viii, 264 p.
98-049287       601       0262161826
*Technology -- Philosophy. Technology -- Social aspects.*

**T14.R599 1990**
**Rosenbrock, H. H.**
Machines with a purpose / Howard Rosenbrock. Oxford [England] ; Oxford University Press, 1990. x, 223 p. :
90-036423      601      0198563469
*Technology -- Philosophy. Human-machine systems. Control theory.*

**T14.S268 1997**
**Sassower, Raphael.**
Technoscientific angst : ethics + responsibility / Raphael Sassower. Minneapolis : University of Minnesota Press, c1997. xv, 140 p. ;
97-020529      174/.96      0816629560
*Technology -- Philosophy. Technology -- Moral and ethical aspects. Science -- Philosophy.*

**T14.T387 1995**
Technology and the politics of knowledge / edited by Andrew Feenberg and Alastair Hannay. Bloomington : Indiana University Press, c1995. x, 288 p. :
94-027789      601      0253321549
*Technology -- Philosophy.*

**T14.W33 2001**
**Wauzzinski, Robert A.,**
Discerning Prometheus : the cry for wisdom in our technological society / Robert A. Wauzzinski. Madison [N.J.] : Fairleigh Dickenson [i.e. Dickinson] University c2001. 214 p. ;
00-049033      303.48/3      083863866X
*Technology -- Philosophy. Pragmatism.*

## T14.5 Social aspects

**T14.5.B54 1995**
**Bijker, Wiebe E.**
Of bicycles, bakelites, and bulbs : toward a theory of sociotechnical change / Wiebe E. Bijker. Cambridge, Mass. : MIT Press, c1995. x, 380 p. :
94-044413      306.4/6      0262023768
*Technology -- Social aspects.*

**T14.5.B69 1984**
**Boyle, Charles.**
People, science, and technology : a guide to advanced industrial society / Charles Boyle, Peter Wheale, Brian Surgess [sic]. Totowa, N.J. : Barnes & Noble Books, 1984. x, 265 p. ;
83-024368      303.4/83      0389204552
*Technology -- Social aspects. Science -- Social aspects.*

**T14.5.C64 1980**
**Collingridge, David.**
The social control of technology / David Collingridge. New York : St. Martin's Press, 1980. 200 p. :
80-021944      303.4/83      031273168X
*Technology -- Social aspects. Technology assessment.*

**T14.5.C645 1998**
**Collins, H. M.**
The golem at large : what you should know about technology / Harry Collins, Trevor Pinch. Cambridge, UK : Cambridge University Press, 1998. xi, 163 p. :
98-029501      303.48/3      0521551412
*Technology -- Social aspects -- Case studies.*

**T14.5.C69 1997**
**Cowan, Ruth Schwartz,**
A social history of American technology / Ruth Schwartz Cowan. New York : Oxford University Press, 1997. x, 342 p. :
96-005505      303.48/3/0973      0195046064
*Technology -- Social aspects -- United States -- History.*

**T14.5.D64 1994**
Does technology drive history? : the dilemma of technological determinism / edited by Merritt Roe Smith and Leo Marx. Cambridge, Mass. : MIT Press, c1994. p. cm.
93-021422      303.48/3      0262193477
*Technology -- Social aspects.*

**T14.5.K57 1990**
**Kipnis, David.**
Technology and power / David Kipnis. New York : Springer-Verlag, c1990. x, 150 p. ;
89-011539      303.48/3      0387970827
*Technology -- Social aspects. Power (Social sciences)*

**T14.5.L52 2000**
**Lienhard, John H.,**
The engines of our ingenuity : an engineer looks at technology and culture / John H. Lienhard. Oxford ; Oxford University Press, 2000. viii, 262 p.
99-037614      303.48/3      0195135830
*Technology -- Social aspects. Creative ability in technology.*

**T14.5.N93 1994**
**Nye, David E.,**
American technological sublime / David E. Nye. Cambridge, Mass. : MIT Press, c1994. xx, 362 p. :
94-019273      303.48/3      026214056X
*Technology -- Social aspects -- United States. Technology -- United States -- History -- 19th century. Technology – United States -- History -- 20th century.*

**T14.5.P87 1995**
**Pursell, Carroll W.**
The machine in America : a social history of technology / Carroll Pursell. Baltimore : Johns Hopkins University Press, 1995. xvi, 358 p. :
94-044114      303.48/3      0801848172
*Technology -- Social aspects -- United States -- History. Industrial revolution -- United States.*

**T14.5.S49 1992**
Shaping technology/building society : studies in sociotechnical change / edited by Wiebe E. Bijker and John Law. Cambridge, Mass. : MIT Press, c1992. vii, 341 p. :
91-048122      303.48/3      0262023385
*Technology -- Social aspects.*

**T14.5.T459 1996**
**Tenner, Edward.**
  Why things bite back : technology and the revenge of unintended consequences / Edward Tenner. New York : Knopf, 1996. xiii, 346 p.
95-038036          303.48/3          0679425632
  *Technology -- Social aspects. Technology -- Economic aspects.*

## T15 History — General works

**T15.A33 1989**
**Adas, Michael,**
  Machines as the measure of men : science, technology, and ideologies of Western dominance / Michael Adas. Ithaca : Cornell University Press, 1989. xii, 430 p. :
89-000845          609          0801423031
  *Technology -- History. Technology -- Philosophy.*

**T15.B684 1997**
**Bruno, Leonard C.**
  Science & technology firsts / Leonard C. Bruno ; Daniel J. Boorstin, guest foreword ; Donna Olendorf, editor. Detroit : Gale Research, c1997. xv, 636 p. :
96-043595          609          0787602566
  *Technology -- History -- Miscellanea. Science -- History -- Miscellanea.*

**T15.B73 1993**
**Bunch, Bryan H.**
  The timetables of technology : a chronology of the most important  people and events in the history of technology / Bryan Bunch and Alexander Hellemans. New York : Simon & Schuster, c1993. v, 490 p.:
          609 20    0671769189
*Technology -- History -- Chronology -- Tables.*

**T15.B76 1995**
**Burke, James,**
  Connections / James Burke ; [with a new introduction by the author]. Rev. ed. Boston : Little, Brown and Company, c1995. ix, 304 p. :
          609 20    0316116726
*Inventions -- History. Technology -- History.*

**T15.B765 1996**
**Burke, James,**
  The pinball effect : how renaissance water gardens made the carburetor possible, and other journeys through knowledge / James Burke. Boston : Little, Brown and Co., c1996. x, 310 p., [1
95-049601          609          0316116025
  *Inventions -- History.*

**T15.D2613**
**Daumas, Maurice,**
  A history of technology & invention; progress through the ages. Edited by Maurice Daumas. Translated by Eileen B. Hennessy. New York, Crown Publishers [1970, c1969- v. 1-3
71-093403          609
  *Technology -- History.*

**T15.D87 2001**
**Dyson, James.**
  A history of great inventions / James Dyson / edited by Robert Uhlig. 1st Carroll & Graf ed. New York : Carroll & Graf Publishers, 2001. 188 p. :
  *Inventions -- History.*

**T15.K7**
**Kranzberg, Melvin,**
  Technology and culture; an anthology. Edited by Melvin Kranzberg and William H. Davenport. New York, Schocken Books [1972] 364 p.
73-185318          301.24/3/08          0805234454
  *Technology -- History -- Addresses, essays, lectures. Technology and civilization -- Addresses, essays, lectures.*

**T15.P353 1990**
**Pacey, Arnold.**
  Technology in world civilization : a thousand-year history / Arnold Pacey. Cambridge, Mass. : MIT Press, 1990. xi, 238 p. :
89-012801          609          0262161176
  *Technology -- History. Technology transfer -- History.*

**T15.W65 1993**
**Wiener, Norbert,**
  Invention : the care and feeding of ideas / Norbert Wiener ; with an introduction by Steve Joshua Heims. Cambridge, Mass. : MIT Press, c1993. xxiv, 159 p.
92-035656          303.48/3          0262231670
  *Inventions -- History. Inventions -- Social aspects – United States -- History.*

## T16 History — Ancient

**T16.J36 1994**
**James, Peter**
  Ancient inventions / Peter James & Nick Thorpe. New York : Ballantine Books, 1994. xxiii, 672 p.
94-007738          609          0345364767
  *Inventions -- History. Technology -- History.*

## T18 History — Modern

**T18.I55 1991**
**Inkster, Ian.**
  Science and technology in history : an approach to industrial development / Ian Inkster. New Brunswick, N.J. : Rutgers University Press, 1991. xvi, 391 p. :
90-024557          609          0813516803
  *Technology -- History. Science -- History. Technology transfer – History.*

### T19 History — 19th-20th centuries

**T19.F75 1994**
**Friedel, Robert D.**
Zipper : an exploration in novelty / Robert Friedel. New York : W.W. Norton, c1994. xiv, 288 p. :
93-027997          609          0393035999
*Inventions -- History -- 20th century. Inventions – History – 19th century. Zippers -- History.*

**T19.H23**
**Habakkuk, H. J.**
American and British technology in the nineteenth century; the search for labour-saving inventions.   Cambridge [Eng.] University Press, 1962. 222 p.
62-003701          609.03
*Technology -- United States -- History -- 19th century. Technology -- Great Britain -- History -- 19th century. Technology -- History.*

**T19.V36 2001**
**Van Dulken, Stephen,**
Inventing the 19th century : 100 inventions that shaped the Victorian Age from aspirin to the Zeppelin / Stephen Van Dulken. New York : New York University Press, 2001. vi, 218 p. :
                   609/.034 21
*Inventions -- History -- 19th century.*

### T20 History — 20th century

**T20.B76 2002**
**Brown, David E.**
Inventing modern America : from the microwave to the mouse / text by David E. Brown ; foreword by Lester C. Thurow ; introductions by James Burke. Cambridge, Mass. : MIT Press, 2002. p. cm.
                   609.73/09/04 21
*Inventions -- United States -- History -- 2oth century. Inventors -- United States -- Biography.*

**T20.C54**
**Clarke, Arthur Charles,**
Profiles of the future; an inquiry into the limits of the possible.  New York, Harper & Row [c1962] 234 p.
62-014563          600
*Inventions. Technology.*

### T21 History — Special regions or countries — America — General works

**T21.B47 1999**
**Berinstein, Paula.**
The statistical handbook on technology / by Paula Berinstein. Phoenix, AZ : Oryx Press, 1999. xxiv, 277 p.
99-041232          609.73/021          1573562084
*Technology -- United States -- Statistics -- Handbooks, manuals, etc.*

**T21.D4713 1990**
**Derian, Jean-Claude.**
America's struggle for leadership in technology / Jean-Claude Derian ; translated by Severen Schaeffer. Cambridge, Mass. : MIT Press, c1990. xii, 309 p. :
89-027972          338.97306          0262041022
*Technology -- United States.*

**T21.G67 1994**
**Gordon, Robert B.**
The texture of industry : an archaeological view of the industrialization of North America / Robert B. Gordon, Patrick M. Malone. New York : Oxford University Press, 1994. xi, 442 p. :
92-017396          609.7          0195058852
*Industrial archaeology -- North America. Industrialization -- North America.*

**T21.H39 1988**
**Hawke, David Freeman.**
Nuts and bolts of the past : a history of American technology, 1776-1860 / David Freeman Hawke. New York : Harper & Row, c1988. x, 308 p. :
87-046145          609/.73          0060159014
*Technology -- United States -- History -- 18th century. Technology -- United States -- History -- 19th century. Inventions – United States -- History -- 18th century.*

**T21.H82 1989**
**Hughes, Thomas Parke.**
American genesis : a century of invention and technological enthusiasm, 1870-1970 / Thomas P. Hughes. New York, N.Y., U.S.A. : Viking, 1989. xii, 529 p. :
88-040275          609.73          0670814784
*Technology -- United States -- History.*

**T21.I76 1993**
**Irwin, Steven M.**
Technology policy and America's future / Steven M. Irwin. New York : St. Martin's Press, 1993. x, 229 p. :
93-000952          338.9/7306          0312099614
*Technology and state -- United States.  High technology industries -- United States.*

**T21.K55 1996**
**Karwatka, Dennis.**
Technology's past / by Dennis Karwatka. Ann Arbor, MI : Prakken Publications, c1996-c1999. 2 v. :
95-072938          609/.2/2          0911168915
*Inventions -- United States -- History -- 19th century. Inventions – United States -- History -- 20th century. Inventors -- United States – History -- 19th century.*

**T21.M372 1999**
**Marcus, Alan I.,**
Technology in America : a brief history / Alan I. Marcus, Howard P. Segal. Fort Worth : Harcourt Brace College Publishers, c1999. xvi, 400 p. :
98-075283          609.73          0155055313
*Technology -- United States -- History.*

**T21.M7 1975**
**Morison, Elting El more.**
From know-how to nowhere; the development of American technology [by] Elting E. Morison. New York, Basic Books [1975, c1974] xiii, 199 p.
74-079279          609/.73          0465025803
*Technology -- United States -- History.*

**T21.S43 1994**
**Segal, Howard P.**
Future imperfect : the mixed blessings of technology in America / Howard P. Segal. Amherst : University of Massachusetts Press, c1994. xviii, 245 p.
93-002265          303.48/3          0870238817
*Technology -- United States -- History -- Case studies. Technology -- Social aspects -- United States -- Case studies.*

**T21.T38 1996**
Technohistory : using the history of American technology in interdisciplinary research / edited by Chris Hables Gray. Malabar, Fla. : Krieger Pub. Co., 1996. xvi, 280 p. :
94-036684          609          0894648535
*Technology -- United States -- History -- Case studies. Technology -- United States -- Historiography -- Case studies.*

**T21.Y68 1998**
**Young, Jeffrey S.,**
Forbes greatest technology stories : inspiring tales of the entrepreneurs and inventors who revolutionized modern business / Jeffrey Young. New York : John Wiley & Sons, c1998. xi, 368 p. :
98-030590          609.73          0471243744
*Inventions -- United States -- History. Inventors – United States – History. High technology -- United States -- History.*

### T27 History — Special regions or countries — Asia

**T27.A3.M67 1994**
**Morris-Suzuki, Tessa.**
The technological transformation of Japan : from the seventeenth to the twenty-first century / Tessa Morris-Suzuki. Cambridge ; Cambridge University Press, 1994. ix, 304 p. :
94-010310          609.52          0521414636
*Technology -- Japan -- History. Technology -- Social aspects – Japan. Technological innovations -- Social aspects -- Japan.*

**T27.C5.M33 1989**
**McDonald, T. David.**
The technological transformation of China / T. David McDonald. Washington, DC : National Defense University Press, 1989. p. cm.
89-012529          338.95107
*Technology -- China -- History -- 20th century.*

## T36 Women in technology

**T36.W64 1994**
Women and technology / editor, Urs E. Gattiker ; managing editor, Rosemarie S. Stollenmaier. Berlin ; W. de Gruyter, 1994. viii, 298 p.
94-015248          331.4/25          3110143070
*Women in technology.*

**T36.Z54 2000**
**Zierdt-Warshaw, Linda.**
American women in technology : an encyclopedia / Linda Zierdt-Warshaw, Alan Winkler, and Leonard Bernstein. Santa Barbara, CA : ABC-CLIO, c2000. xv, 384 p. :
          604/.82/0973 21          1576070727
*Women in technology -- United States -- Encyclopedias.*

## T37 Industrial archaeology

**T37.B55 1992**
The Blackwell encyclopedia of industrial archaeology / edited by Barrie Trinder ; editorial board, Axel Fohl ... [et al.]. Oxford, UK ; Blackwell, 1992. xxii, 964 p.
91-041700          609          0631142169
*Industrial archaeology -- Encyclopedias.*

### T39 Biography — Collective

**T39.B49 1996**
Biographical dictionary of the history of technology / edited by Lance Day and Ian McNeil. London ; Routledge, 1996. xiii, 844 p.
95-026250          609.2/2          0415060427
*Inventors -- Biography -- Dictionaries. Inventions -- History – Dictionaries. Technology -- History -- Dictionaries.*

**T39.W5**
Who's who in technology today. Highland Park, Ill., [etc.] J. Dick [etc.]  4 v.
80-644137          609/.2/2
*Technologists -- United States -- Biography -- Periodicals.*

## T40 Biography — Individual, A-Z

**T40.L46.H49**
**Heydenreich, Ludwig Heinrich,**
Leonardo the inventor / Ludwig H. Heydenreich, Bern Dibner, Ladislao Reti. New York : McGraw-Hill, 1980. 192 p. :
80-010668          620/.0092/4          0070286108
*Leonardo, -- da Vinci, -- 1452-1519. Leonardo, -- da Vinci, – 1452-1519 -- Knowledge -- Engineering. Leonardo, -- da Vinci, – 1452-1519 -- Knowledge -- Military engineering.*

## T45 General works — 19th century and later

**T45.D74 1991**
**Drexler, K. Eric.**
  Unbounding the future : the nanotechnology revolution / K. Eric Drexler and Chris Peterson, with Gayle Pergamit. New York : Morrow, c1991. 304 p. :
91-006341          600          0688091245
  *Nanotechnology.*

**T45.P66 1997**
**Pool, Robert,**
  Beyond engineering : how society shapes technology / Robert Pool. New York : Oxford University Press, 1997. xii, 358 p. ;
96-034364          600          0195107721
  *Technology. Technological innovations. Nuclear energy.*

## T47 General works — Elementary and popular works. Home educators

**T47.V35**
**Van Amerongen, C.**
  The way things work; an illustrated encyclopedia of technology. New York : Simon and Schuster [1967-71] 2 v.
          600 21    0671210866
*Technology -- Popular works.*

**T47.D74 1986**
**Drexler, K. Eric.**
  Engines of creation / K. Eric Drexler ; foreword by Marvin Minsky. Garden City, N.Y. : Anchor Press/Doubleday, 1986. xii, 298 p. ;
85-025362          600          0385199724
  *High technology. Twentieth century -- Forecasts.*

## T49.5 General works — General special

**T49.5.D38 1994**
**Dasgupta, Subrata.**
  Creativity in invention and design : computational and cognitive explorations of technological originality / Subrata Dasgupta. Cambridge [England]; Cambridge University Press, 1994. xvi, 250 p. :
93-028650          608/.019          0521430682
  *Creative ability in technology. Creative thinking. Microprogramming.*

**T49.5.H4 1999**
**Hazeltine, Barrett.**
  Appropriate technology : tools, choices and implications / Barrett Hazeltine, Christopher Bull. San Diego : Academic Press, c1999. p. cm.
98-022150          338.9/27          0123351901
  *Appropriate technology.*

**T49.5.S575 1989**
**Sieden, Lloyd Steven.**
  Buckminster Fuller's universe : an appreciation / Lloyd Steven Sieden ; foreword by Norman Cousins. New York : Plenum Press, c1989. xvii, 511 p.
88-032506          620          0306431785
*Fuller, R. Buckminster -- (Richard Buckminster), -- 1895- Technology. Engineering.*

**T49.5.T4454 1999**
  The technology management handbook / editor-in-chief, Richard C. Dorf. Boca Raton, FL : CRC Press, c1999. 1 v. (various
98-022328          658.5/14          0849385776
  *Technology -- Management -- Handbooks, manuals, etc.*

## T55 Industrial safety. Industrial accident prevention — Periodicals, societies, congresses, etc.

**T55.A35 1995**
**Adams, Edward E.**
  Total quality safety management : an introduction / Edward E. Adams. Des Plaines, IL : American Society of Safety Engineers, c1995. ix, 203 p. :
95-013971          658.4/08          1885581033
  *Industrial safety -- Management. Total quality management.*

**T55.A38 1997**
**Aldrich, Mark.**
  Safety first : technology, labor, and business in the building of American work safety, 1870-1939 / Mark Aldrich. Baltimore, Md. : Johns Hopkins University Press, c1997. xx, 415 p. :
96-028998          363.11/5/097309041
0801854059
  *Industrial safety -- United States -- History -- 19th century. Industrial safety -- United States -- History -- 20th century.*

**T55.L468 2000**
  Lewis' dictionary of occupational and environmental safety and health / [edited by] Jeffrey W. Vincoli. Boca Raton : Lewis Publishers, c2000. 1093 p. :
99-032640          363.11/03          1566703999
  *Industrial safety -- Dictionaries. Environmental health -- Dictionaries.*

**T55.S786 1997**
**Stuart, Ralph.**
  Safety & health on the internet / Ralph Stuart. Rockville, Md. : Government Institutes, c1997. xv, 198 p. :
96-047963          025.06/3631          0865875235
  *Industrial safety -- Computer network resources -- Directories. Internet (Computer network) -- Directories. Computer network resources -- Directories.*

### T55.3.H3 Industrial safety. Industrial accident prevention — Special topics — Hazardous substances

**T55.3.H3.C4857 1995**
**Cheremisinoff, Nicholas P.**
Handbook of emergency response to toxic chemical releases : a guide to compliance / by Nicholas P. Cheremisinoff. Park Ridge, N.J. : Noyes Publications, c1995. x, 315 p. :
94-031268          363.17/6          0815513658
*Hazardous substances -- Safety measures -- Handbooks, manuals, etc. Hazardous substances -- Accidents -- Handbooks, manuals, etc. Chemical spills -- Reporting -- Handbooks, manuals, etc.*

**T55.3.H3.C4859 1996**
**Cheremisinoff, Nicholas P.**
Safety management practices for hazardous materials / Nicholas P. Cheremisinoff, Madelyn Graffia. New York : M. Dekker, c1996. xvi, 350 p. :
95-037548          363.17/6/0973          082479687X
*Hazardous substances -- United States -- Safety measures. Hazardous substances -- United States -- Management. Hazardous substances -- Law and legislation -- United States.*

**T55.3.H3.L494 2000**
**Lewis, Richard J.,**
Sax's dangerous properties of industrial materials / Richard J. Lewis, Sr. New York : Wiley, c2000. 3 v. ;
99-039820          604.7          0471354074
*Hazardous substances -- Handbooks, manuals, etc.*

**T55.3.H3.P64 1996**
**Pohanish, Richard P.**
Hazardous materials handbook / Richard P. Pohanish, Stanley A. Greene. New York : Van Nostrand Reinhold, 1996. xliii, 1792 p
96-005568          604.7          0442022123
*Hazardous substances -- Handbooks, manuals, etc.*

**T55.3.H3.P78 1995**
Prudent practices in the laboratory : handling and disposal of chemicals / Committee on Prudent Practices for Handling, Storage, and Disposal of Chemicals in Laboratories, Board on Chemical Sciences and Technology, Commission on Physical Sciences, Mathematics, and Applications, National Research Council. Washington, D.C. : National Academy Press, 1995. xv, 427 p. :
95-032461          660/.2804          0309052297
*Hazardous substances. Chemicals -- Safety measures. Hazardous wastes.*

**T55.3.H3B73 1999**
**Bretherick, L.**
Bretherick's handbook of reactive chemical hazards : an indexed guide to published data / edited by P.G. Urben ; compiler, M.J. Pitt. 6th ed. Oxford , Boston : Butterworth-Heinemann, 1999. 2 v. :
660/.2804 21          075063605X
*Hazardous substances -- Handbooks, manuals, etc. Chemicals -- Safety measures -- Handbooks, manuals, etc.*

### T55.85 Industrial engineering — Biography

**T55.85.T38.W74 1991**
**Wrege, Charles D.**
Frederick W. Taylor, the father of scientific management : myth and reality / Charles D. Wrege, Ronald G. Greenwood. Homewood, Ill. : Business One Irwin, c1991. xiii, 286 p.
91-008345          670/.92          1556235011
*Taylor, Frederick Winslow, -- 1856-1915.     Industrial engineers – United States -- Biography.*

## T56 Industrial engineering — Treatises

**T56.M3 2001**
Maynard's industrial engineering handbook / edited by Kjell B. Zandin. 5th ed. New York : McGraw-Hill, c2001. 1 v. :
65.5 21          0070411026
*Industrial bibliographical references and index. Industrial engineering -- Handbooks, manuals, etc.*

### T57 Industrial engineering — Applied mathematics. Quantitative methods — General works

**T57.F33 2002**
Facility location : applications and theory / Horst W. Hamacher, Zvi Drezner (editors). New York : Springer, c2002. p. cm.
658.4/034 21          3540421726
*Management science -- Mathematical models. Operations research – Mathematical models. Industrial location -- Mathematical models.*

### T57.37 Industrial engineering — Applied mathematics. Quantitative methods — Experimental design

**T57.37.F75 1997**
**Frigon, Normand L.**
Practical guide to experimental design / Normand L. Frigon, David Mathews. New York : Wiley, c1997. x, 342 p. :
96-023728          658.4/033          047113919X
*Experimental design. Research, Industrial -- Statistical methods.*

### T57.6-T57.62 Industrial engineering — Applied mathematics. Quantitative methods — Operations research

**T57.6.B57 2001**
**Blumenfeld, Dennis.**
Operations research calculations handbook / Dennis Blumenfeld. Boca Raton : CRC Press, 2001. 199 p. :
658.4/034 21          0849321271
*Operations research -- Handbooks, manuals, etc. Mathematical analysis -- Handbooks, manuals, etc.*

**T57.6.C367 2001**
**Carter, Michael W.**
Operations research : a practical introduction / Michael W. Carter, Camille C. Price. Boca Raton : CRC Press, c2001. 394 p. :
    658.4/034 21    0849322561
*Operations research.*

**T57.6.E53 2000**
Encyclopedia of operations research and management science / edited by Saul I. Gass and Carl M. Harris. 2nd ed. Boston : Kluwer Academic, 2000. xxxviii, 917 p.
    658.4/034/03 21    079237827X
*Operations research -- Encyclopedias. Management science -- Encyclopedias.*

**T57.6.H35**
Handbook of operations research / edited by Joseph J. Moder and Salah E. Elmaghraby. New York : Van Nostrand Reinhold, c1978. 2 v. :
77-021580    001.4/24    0442245955
    *Operations research.*

**T57.6.O6455 1998**
Operations research : methods, models, and applications / edited by Jay E. Aronson and Stanley Zionts. Westport, Conn. : Quorum, 1998. xx, 369 p. :
95-042161    658.4/034    1567200273
    *Operations research.*

**T57.6.T3 1992**
**Taha, Hamdy A.**
Operations research : an introduction / Hamdy A. Taha. 5th ed. Toronto ; New York : Macmillan; Maxwell Macmillan Canada, International c1992 xix, 822 p. :
    658.4/034 20    0024189758
*Operations research. Programming (Mathematics)*

**T57.62.S47**
**Shannon, Robert E.,**
Systems simulation : the art and science / Robert E. Shannon. Englewood Cliffs, N.J. : Prentice-Hall, [1975] xii, 387 p. :
75-001174    601/.84    0138818398
    *Simulation methods.*

## T57.74-57.9 Industrial engineering — Programming — General works

**T57.74.B39 1990**
**Bazaraa, M. S.**
Linear programming and network flows / Mokhtar S. Bazaraa, john J. Jarvis, Hanif D. Sherali. 2nd ed. New York : Wiley, c1990. xiv, 684 p. :
    519.7/2 20    0471636819
*Linear programming. Network analysis (Planning)*

**T57.74.K37 1991**
**Karloff, Howard,**
Linear programming / Howard Karloff. Boston : Birkhauser, 1991. viii, 142 p.
91-003387    519.7/2    0817635610
    *Linear programming.*

**T57.74.V36 2001**
**Vanderbei, Robert J.**
Linear programming : foundations and extensions / Robert J. Vanderbei. 2nd ed. Boston : Kluwer Academic, c2001. xviii, 450 p. :
    519.7/2 21    0792373421
*Linear programming. Mathematical optimization.*

**T57.74.V37 2001**
**Vasilyev, F.P.**
In-depth analysis of linear programming / F.P. Vasilyev and A. Yu. Ivanitskiy. Boston : Kluwer Academic Publishers, 2001. p. cm.
    519.7/2 21    1402000855
*Linear programming.*

**T57.9.G76 1998**
**Gross, Donald.**
Fundamentals of queueing theory / Donald Gross, Carl M. Harris. 3rd ed. New York : Wiley, c1998. xi, 439 p. :
    519.8/2 21    0471170836
*Queuing theory.*

## T58.5 Industrial engineering — Information technology. Information systems — General works

**T58.5.B47 1995**
**Bermant, Charles.**
Information technology : new directions for the 21st century / Charles Bermant. Charleston, S.C. : Computer Technology Research Corp., 1995. iv, 178 p. ;
95-008605    658.4/038/09049    1566079500
    *Information technology. Information society. Twenty-first century.*

**T58.5.C655 1996**
Computer networking and scholarly communication in the twenty-first-century university / edited by Teresa M. Harrison and Timothy Stephen. Albany, NY : State University of New York Press, c1996. xii, 468 p. :
95-047786    001.2/0285/46    0791428532
    *Information technology. Scholarly electronic publishing – Data processing. Learning and scholarship -- Data processing.*

**T58.5.J66 1999**
**Jonscher, C.**
The evolution of wired life : from the alphabet to the soul-catcher chip--how information technologies change our world / Charles Jonscher. New York : Wiley, c1999. x, 293 p. :
99-043426    303.48/33    0471357596
    *Information technology -- Social aspects. Information society.*

**T58.5.L48 1995**
**Lesurf, J. C. G.**
Information and measurement / J.C.G. Lesurf. Bristol, Eng. ; Institute of Physics Pub., 1995. xiii, 243 p.
94-046915          003/.54          0750303085
*Information technology.*

## T58.6 Industrial engineering — Information technology. Information systems — Management information systems

**T58.6.B87 1989**
**Burch, John G.**
Information systems : theory and practice / John Burch, Gary Grudnitski. 5th ed. New York : Wiley, c1989. xvii, 921 p. :
          658.4/038 19          0471612936
*Management information systems.*

**T58.6.L45 2000**
**Lerner, Vladimir S.,**
Information systems anaylsis and modeling : an information macrodynamics approach / by Vladimir S. Lerner. Boston : Kluwer Academic, 2000. xxvi, 305 p. :
          003 21          0792386833
*Management information systems. System analysis.*

## T59.5 Industrial engineering — Automation

**T59.5.H27 1995**
**Hall, George M.**
The age of automation : technical genius, social dilemma / George M. Hall. Westport, Conn. : Praeger, 1995. xii, 240 p. :
94-044175          303.48/33          0275951944
*Automation. Automation -- Social aspects.*

## T60.4-T60.8 Industrial engineering — Work measurement. Methods engineering

**T60.4.B39 1980**
**Barnes, Ralph Mosser,**
Motion and time study : design and measurement of work / Ralph M. Barnes. New York : Wiley, c1980. xi, 689 p. :
80-000173          658.5/42          0471059056
*Motion study. Time study.*

**T60.7.N54 1982**
**Niebel, Benjamin W.**
Motion and time study / Benjamin W. Niebel. 7th ed. Homewood, Ill. : R.D. Irwin, 1982. xi, 756 p. :
          658.5/42 19          0256025274
*Motion study. Time study. Wages.*

**T60.8.P39 1998**
**Parker, Sharon.**
Job and work design : organizing work to promote well-being and effectiveness / Sharon Parker, Toby Wall. Thousand Oaks : Sage Publications, c1998. xiv, 169 p. :
98-008932          658.5/4          0761904190
*Work design.*

## T69 Technical education. Technical schools — History

**T69.P45313 2000**
**Pfammatter, Ulrich.**
The making of the modern architect and engineer : the origins and development of a scientific and industrially oriented education / Ulrich Pfammatter. Basel ; Birkhauser-Publishers for Architecture, 2000. 312 p. :
00-267711          607.1          3764362170
*Technical education -- History. Engineering – Study and teaching -- History. Architecture -- Study and teaching -- History.*

## T171 Technical education. Technical schools — Special schools — American schools

**T171.M49.H37 1993**
**Hapgood, Fred.**
Up the infinite corridor : MIT and the technical imagination / Fred Hapgood. Reading, Mass. : Addison-Wesley Pub. Co., c1993. xii, 203 p. ;
92-031683          620/.007207446          0201082934
*Engineering -- United States -- History.*

## T173.8 Technical change — Technical innovations

**T173.8.G3 1970**
**Gabor, Dennis,**
Innovations: scientific, technological, and social. New York, Oxford University Press, 1970. vi, 113 p.
72-176613          301.2/43          0195194128
*Technological innovations.*

## T174.5 Technical change — Technology assessment

**T174.5.L415 1994**
Learning from disaster : risk management after Bhopal / edited by Sheila Jasanoff. Philadelphia : University of Pennsylvania Press, c1994. xiii, 291 p.
93-048100          363.17/91/0954          081223250X
*Technology -- Risk assessment. Technology and state. Technology -- Social aspects.*

**T174.5.R48 1995**
Resistance to new technology : nuclear power, information technology, and biotechnology / edited by Martin Bauer. Cambridge ; Cambridge University Press, 1995. xii, 422 p. :
94-026745          303.48/3          0521455189
*Technology assessment -- Congresses. Technology assessment – Europe -- Congresses. Nuclear energy -- Social aspects – Congresses.*

## T174.7 Nanotechnology

**T174.7.D74 1992**
**Drexler, K. Eric.**
Nanosystems : molecular machinery, manufacturing, and computation / by K. Eric Drexler. New York : Wiley, c1992. xx, 556 p. :
92-030870          620.4          047157547X
*Nanotechnology.*

**T174.7.N375 1996**
Nanotechnology : molecular speculations on global abundance / edited by B.C. Crandall. Cambridge, Mass. : MIT Press, c1996. xi, 214 p., [
96-000149          620          0262032376
*Nanotechnology. Molecular theory.*

**T174.7.R44 1995**
**Regis, Edward,**
Nano : the emerging science of nanotechnology : remaking the world-molecule by molecule / Ed Regis. Boston : Little, Brown, c1995. 325 p. :
94-035378          620.4          0316738581
*Nanotechnology.*

**T174.7.R54 2001**
**Rietman, Ed.**
Molecular engineering of nanosystems / Edward A. Rietman. New York : Springer, 2001. xiii, 258 p. :
          620.5 21          0387989889
*Nanotechnology. Molecular theory.*

## T175 Industrial research. Research and development

**T175.F87 1994**
**Fusfeld, Herbert I.**
Industry's future : changing patterns of industrial research / Herbert I. Fusfeld. Washington, DC : American Chemical Society, 1994. xiv, 369 p. ;
94-025183          607/.2          084122983X
*Research, Industrial.*

## T185 Addresses, essays, lectures

**T185.T76 1983**
The Trouble with technology : explorations in the process of technological change / edited by Stuart Macdonald, D.McL. Lamberton, Thomas Mandeville. New York : St. Martin's Press, 1983. x, 224 p. ;
83-010961          338.4/76          0312819854
*Technology.*

## T210 Patents — Patent literature

**T210.H58 2000**
**Hitchcock, David,**
Paten searching made easy : how to do patent searches on the internet and in the library / by David Hitchcock ; edited by Patricia Gima and Stephen Elias. 2nd ed. Berkeley, C A : Nolo, 2000. 1 v. :
          608.7 21
*Paten searching. Patent literature.*

**T210.S53 2000**
**Sharpe, Charles C.,**
Patent, trademark, and copyright searching on the Internet / by Charles C. Sharpe. Jefferson, N.C. : McFarland, 2000. ix, 229 p. :
          025.06/608 21          0786407573
*Patent searching -- Computer network resources. Internet searching.*

## T212 Patents — Inventors and inventions. How to invent

**T212.P465 1992**
**Petroski, Henry.**
The evolution of useful things / Henry Petroski. New York : Knopf, 1992. xi, 288 p. :
91-039524          609          0679412263
*Inventions. Patents. Design, Industrial.*

**T212.W4 1992**
**Weber, Robert J.**
Forks, phonographs, and hot air balloons : a field guide to inventive thinking / Robert J. Weber. New York : Oxford University Press, 1992. xiv, 277 p. :
92-022785          609          019506402X
*Inventions. Creative thinking.*

## T223 Patents — History of patents

**T223.P2B77 2000**
**Brown, Travis,**
Popular patents : America's first inventions from the airplane to the zipper / Travis Brown. Lanham, MD : Scarecrow Press, 2000. p. cm.
          608.773 21          1578860105
*Patents -- United States -- History.*

**T223.U3L6 2001**
**Lo, Jack.**
How to make patent drawings yourself / by Jack Lo and David Pressman. 3rd ed. Berkeley, CA : Nolo, 2001. 1 v. :
          608/.022/1 21          0873377885
*Patents -- United States -- Drawings.*

**T223.V4.A253**
Trade names dictionary. Detroit, Mich. : Gale Research Co., -1989. v. ;
82-642841          602/.75
*Trademarks -- United States. Business names -- United States.*

## T339 Patents — Inventors' manuals

**T339.G67 2000**
**Gordon, Thomas T.**
Patent fundamentals for scientists and engineers / Thomas T. Gordon, Arthur S. Cookfair. 2nd ed. Boca Raton : Lewis Publishers, c2000. 159 p. :
608.773 21          1566705177
*Patents. Patents -- United States.*

**T339.L38 1990**
**Levy, Richard C.,**
Inventing and patenting sourcebook : how to sell and protect your ideas / Richard C. Levy ; Robert J. Huffman, editor. Detroit : Gale Research, c1990. xxxi, 35, 922
90-100359          608.773          0810348713
*Inventions -- United States -- Handbooks, manuals, etc. Patents -- United States -- Handbooks, manuals, etc.*

## T353 Mechanical drawing. Engineering graphics — General works

**T353.E617 2001**
Engineering drawing and design / David A. Madsen ... [et al]. 3rd ed. Albany, NY : Autodesk Press, 2001. p. cm.
604.2 21
*Mechanical drawing.*

## T385 Mechanical Drawing. Engineering graphics — Computer graphics

**T385.B348 1993**
**Baker, Robin.**
Designing the future : the computer in architecture and design / Robin Baker. New York : Thames and Hudson, 1993. 208 p. :
93-060202          702/.85          0500015783
*Computer graphics. Computer-aided design. Architectural design -- Data processing.*

**T385.C5925 1992**
Computer graphics using object-oriented programming / edited by Steve Cunningham ... [et al.]. New York : J. Wiley, c1992. xii, 302 p.,
91-035774          006.6          0471541990
*Computer graphics. Object-oriented programming (Computer science)*

**T385.F548 2000**
Figuratively speaking in the computer age : techniques for preparing and delivering presentations / authors, David M. Orchard . . . [et al.] ; with a special introductory chapter by Gene Shinn. AAPG Bookstore [distributor], American Association of Petroleum Geologists : c2000. xi, 101 p. :
0891818227
*Computer graphics. Slides (Photography) Lectures and lecturing. Poster presentations. Communication of technical information.*

**T385.F63**
**Foley, James D.,**
Fundamentals of interactive computer graphics / James D. Foley, Andries van Dam. Reading, Mass. : Addison-Wesley Pub. Co., c1982. xx, 664 p. :
80-024311          001.64/43          0201144689
*Computer graphics. Interactive computer systems.*

**T385.G578 1999**
**Glassner, Andrew S.**
Andrew Glassner's notebook : recreational computer graphics / Andrew S. Glassner. San Francisco, Calif. : Morgan Kaufmann, c1999. xviii, 304 p.
99-028111          006.6          1558605983
*Computer graphics.*

**T385.H69613 1993b**
**Hoschek, Josef.**
Fundamentals of computer-aided geometric design / Josef Hoschek, Dieter Lasser ; translated by Larry L. Schumaker. Wellesley, Mass. : A.K. Peters, c1993. xvii, 727 p.
93-016733          516/.6/0285          1568810075
*Computer graphics.*

**T385.K47 1994**
**Kerlow, Isaac Victor,**
Computer graphics for designers & artists / Isaac Victor Kerlow & Judson Rosebush. New York : Van Nostrand Reinhold, c1994. xiii, 306 p.
93-008490          006.6/0247          0442014309
*Computer graphics.*

**T385.M363 1988**
**Mantyla, Martti,**
An introduction to solid modeling / Martti Mantyla. Rockville, Md. : Computer Science Press, c1988. xiv, 401 p. :
87-027852          006.6          0881751081
*Computer graphics. Solids.*

**T385.P376 1995**
The pattern book : fractals, art, and nature / editor, Clifford A. Pickover. Singapore ; World Scientific, c1995. xxix, 427 p.
94-047114          745.4          981021426X
*Computer graphics.*

**T385.W3778 2000**
**Watt, Alan H.,**
3D computer graphics / Alan Watt. 3rd ed. Harlow, England ; Reading, Mass. Addison-Wesley, 2000. xxii, 570 p. :
006.6/93 21          0201398559
*Computer graphics. Three-dimensional display systems.*

**T385.W38 1989**
**Watt, Alan H.,**
Fundamentals of three-dimensional computer graphics / Alan Watt. Wokingham, England ; Addison-Wesley, c1989. xvi, 430 p.,
89-034110          006.6          0201154420
*Computer graphics. Three-dimensional display systems.*

**T385.W6448 2000**
**Wolfe, Rosalee Jean**
  3D graphics : a visual approach / R.J. Wolfe. New York : Oxford University Press, 2000. xvii, 150 p. :
    006.6 21            0195113950
*Computer graphics. Three-dimensional display systems.*

## T395 Exhibitions. Tradeshows — History

**T395.H57 1990**
  Historical dictionary of world's fairs and expositions, 1851-1988 / John E. Findling, editor ; Kimberly D. Pelle, assistant editor. New York : Greenwood Press, 1990. xix, 443 p. :
89-017217        907.4        0313260230
  *Trade shows -- History.*

## T395.5 Exhibitions. Trade shows — History — By region or country, A-Z

**T395.5.U6.R934 2000**
**Rydell, Robert W.**
  Fair America : world's fairs in the United States / Robert W. Rydell, John E. Findling, and Kimberly D. Pelle. Washington, DC : Smithsonian Institution Press, 2000. x, 166 p. :
99-040957        907.4/73        1560983841
  *Trade shows -- United States -- History -- 19th century. Trade shows -- United States -- History -- 20th century.*

# TA Engineering (General). Civil engineering (General).

## TA9 Dictionaries and encyclopedias

**TA9.M36 1993**
  McGraw-Hill encyclopedia of engineering / Sybil P. Parker, editor in chief. New York : McGraw-Hill, c1993. 1414 p. :
92-043106        620/.003        0070513929
  *Engineering -- Encyclopedias.*

**TA9.S35 1993**
**Scott, John S.,**
  The VNR dictionary of civil engineering / John S. Scott. 4th ed. New York : Van Nostrand Reinhold, c1993. xxii, 533 p. :
    624/.03 20
*Civil engineering -- Dictionaries.*

## TA11 Symbols and abbreviations

**TA11.A7**
**Arnell, Alvin.**
  Standard graphical symbols; a comprehensive guide for use in industry, engineering, and science. New York, McGraw-Hill [1963] x, 534 p.
63-018702        620.00148
  *Engineering -- Notation. Technology -- Notation. Science -- Notation.*

**TA11.K45 1994**
**Keller, Harald.**
  Dictionary of engineering acronyms and abbreviations / Harald Keller and Uwe Erb. 2nd ed. New York : Neal-Schuman Publisher, c1994. 878 p. :
    620/.00148 20
*Engineering -- Acronyms. Engineering -- Abbreviations.*

**TA11.K45 1994**
**Keller, Harold.**
  Dictionary of engineering acronyms and abbreviations / Harald Keller and Uwe Erb. 2nd ed. New York : Neal-Schuman Publishers, c1994. 878 p. :
    620/.00148 20        1555701299
*Engineering -- Acronyms. Engineering -- Abbreviations.*

## TA15 History — Modern

**TA15.B42 1998**
**Berlow, Lawrence H.,**
  The reference guide to famous engineering landmarks of the world : bridges, tunnels, dams, roads, and other structures / by Lawrence H. Berlow. Phoenix, Ariz. : Oryx Press, 1998. xiii, 250 p.
97-036051        620/.009        0897749669
  *Engineering -- History.*

**TA15.B53 1996**
**Billington, David P.**
  The innovators : the engineering pioneers who made America modern / David P. Billington. New York : Wiley, c1996. x, 245 p. :
95-043653        620/.00973        0471140260
  *Engineering -- United States -- History. Technological innovations -- United States -- History. Engineers -- United States.*

## TA23-52 Country Divisions (general historical and descriptive literature, reports on public works, etc.)

**TA23.S36 1987**
**Schodek, Daniel L.,**
  Landmarks in American civil engineering / Daniel L. Schodek. Cambridge, Mass. : MIT Press, c1987. xviii, 383 p.
86-020162        624/.0973        026219256X
  *Civil engineering -- United States. Public works -- United States.*

**TA52.W75 2000**
**Wright, Kenneth R.**
  Machu Picchu : a civil engineering marvel / by Kenneth R. Wright and Alfredo Valencia Zegarra ... [et al.]. Reston, VA : American Society of Civil Engineers, c2000. viii, 136 p.
00-024452        624/.0985/37        0784404445
  *Civil engineering -- Peru -- Machu Picchu Site. Hydraulic engineering -- Peru -- Machu Picchu Site. Incas -- Antiquities. Machu Picchu Site (Peru)*

## TA140 A-Z Biography — Individual A-Z

**TA140.F9.B35 1996**
**Baldwin, J.,**
BuckyWorks : Buckminster Fuller's ideas for today / J. Baldwin. New York : John Wiley, c1996. xi, 243 p. :
95-026003          620/.0092          0471129534
*Fuller, R. Buckminster -- (Richard Buckminster), -- 1895- .*
*Engineers -- United States -- Biography. Architects – United States – Biography. Inventors -- United States -- Biography.*

## TA145 General Works. Civil engineering, etc. — 1850-

**TA145.C58 1987**
Civil Engineering Practice / edited by Paul N. Cheremisinoff, Nicholas P. Cheremisinoff, Su Ling Cheng ; in collaboration with C.W. Bert ... [et al.]. Lancaster, Pa. : Technomic Pub. Co., c1987-c1988. 5 v. :
87-050629          624          0877625298
*Civil engineering.*

**TA145.F37 1992**
**Ferguson, Eugene S.**
Engineering and the mind's eye / Eugene S. Ferguson. Cambridge, Mass. : MIT Press, c1992. xiv, 241 p. :
91-042833          620          0262061473
*Engineering. Creative thinking.*

**TA145.M298 1993**
Magill's survey of science. edited by Frank N. Magill ; consulting editor, Martha Riherd Weller. Pasadena, Calif. : Salem Press, c1993-1998. 7 v. (xiv, 32
92-035688          620          0893567051
*Engineering. Science.*

## TA151 Handbooks, manuals, etc.

**TA151.C2 1973**
CRC handbook of tables for applied engineering science. Editors: Ray E. Bolz [and] George L. Tuve. 2nd ed. Engineering -- Tables. [1973] 1166 p. :

**TA151.C57 1995**
The civil engineering handbook / editor-in-chief, W.F. Chen. Boca Raton : CRC Press, c1995. xxvi, 2609 p.
94-045572          624          0849389534
*Civil engineering -- Handbooks, manuals, etc.*

**TA151.E424 1996**
The engineering handbook / editor-in-chief, Richard C. Dorf. Boca Raton : CRC Press ; c1996. xlviii, 2298
95-032292          620          0849383447
*Engineering -- Handbooks, manuals, etc.*

**TA151.M34 1991**
The McGraw-Hill handbook of essential engineering information and data / [edited by] Ejup N. Ganic, Tyler G. Hicks. New York : McGraw-Hill, c1991. 1 v. (various
90-035667          620          0070227640
*Engineering -- Handbooks, manuals, etc.*

**TA151.S8 1995**
Standard handbook for civil engineers / Frederick S. Merritt, editor, M. Kent Loftin, editor, Jonathan T. Ricketts, editor. 4th ed. New York ; McGraw-Hill, c1995. 1 v. :
624 20          0070415978
*Civil engineering -- Handbooks, manuals, etc.*

## TA153 General Special

**TA153.D47 1997**
Design and operation of civil and environmental engineering systems / edited by Charles ReVelle, Arthur E. McGarity. New York : Wiley, c1997. xvi, 752 p. :
97-000052          624          0471128163
*Civil engineering -- Linear programming. Environmental engineering -- Linear programming. Engineering economy – Linear programming.*

## TA157 Engineering as a profession. Including working conditions, ethics, etc. — General Works

**TA157.E673 1997**
Engineering ethics : balancing cost, schedule, and risk-lessons learned from the space shuttle / Rosa Lynn B. Pinkus ... [et al.]. Cambridge ; Cambridge University Press, 1997. xviii, 379 p.
96-012332          174/.962          0521431719
*Engineering ethics. Decision making -- Moral and ethical aspects. Space shuttles -- Propulsion systems -- Design and construction -- Case studies.*

**TA157.F54 1999**
**Fletcher, Joyce K.**
Disappearing acts : gender, power and relational practice at work / Joyce K. Fletcher. Cambridge, Mass. : MIT Press, 1999. xii, 166 p. ;
99-017937          305.43/62          0262062054
*Women engineers. Corporate culture. Women engineers -- Psychological aspects.*

**TA157.F57 1994**
**Florman, Samuel C.**
The existential pleasures of engineering / Samuel C. Florman. 2nd ed. New York : St. Martin's Press, 1994. xviii, 205 p. :
620/.001 20
*Engineering -- Philosphy. Engineering -- Psychological aspects.*

**TA157.P445**

Peterson's job opportunities for engineering and computer science majors. Princeton, N.J. : Peterson's, c1997-c1998. 2 v. :

      620/.0023/73 20    1094-2327

*Engineers -- Employments United States -- Directories. Computer scientists -- Employment -- United States -- Directories. Corporations -- United States -- Directories.*

**TA157.V42 1998**
**Vesilind, P. Aarne.**

Engineering, ethics, and the environment / P. Aarne Vesilind, Alastair S. Gunn. New York : Cambridge University Press, 1998. xvi, 314 p. :

97-000083    179/.1/02462    0521581125

*Engineering ethics. Environmental ethics.*

**TA157.W448 1992**
**Wharton, David E.**

A struggle worthy of note : the engineering and technological education of black Americans / David E. Wharton. Westport, Conn. : Greenwood Press, 1992. xiv, 154 p. ;

92-012524    620/.0089/96073    0313282072

*Afro-American engineers. Afro-Americans – Education (Higher) -- United States. Technical education -- United States.*

# TA159 Technical education. Technical schools, examinations, questions, etc.

**TA159.L3 1984**
**La Londe, William S.**

Professional engineers' examination questions and answers / William S. La Londe, Jr., William J. Stack-Staikidis. New York : McGraw-Hill, c1984. xiii, 539 p.

82-023393    620/.0076    0070360995

*Engineering -- Examinations, questions, etc. Engineers – Licenses -- United States.*

# TA165 Engineering instruments, meters, etc. Industrial instrumentation

**TA165.B38 1993**
**Beckwith, T. G. (Thomas G.)**

Mechanical measurements / Thomas G. Beckwith, Roy D. Marangoni, John H. Lienhard V. 5th ed. Reading, Mass. : Addison-Wesley, c1993. xix, 876 p. :

      681/.2 20

*Engineering instruments. Measuring instruments.*

**TA165.C62 1994**

Concise encyclopedia of measurement & instrumentation / editors, L. Finkelstein, K.T.V. Grattan. Oxford ; Pergamon Press, 1994. xvii, 434 p.

93-010617    681/.2    0080362125

*Engineering instruments -- Encyclopedias. Engineering -- Measurement -- Encyclopedias.*

**TA165.F72 1993**
**Fraden, Jacob.**

AIP handbook of modern sensors : physics, designs, and applications / Jacob Fraden. New York : American Institute of Physics, c1993. xiii, 552 p.

93-000084    681/.2

*Detectors. Interface circuits.*

**TA165.S447 1994**

Semiconductor sensors / edited by S.M. Sze. New York : Wiley, c1994. xii, 550 p. :

94-022271    681/.2    0471546097

*Detectors. Semiconductors.*

# TA166 Human engineering — General works

**TA166.B32 1993**
**Badler, Norman I.**

Simulating humans : computer graphics animation and control / Norman I. Badler, Cary B. Phillips, Bonnie Lynn Webber. New York : Oxford University Press, 1993. xiii, 270 p.

93-012061    620.8/2    0195073592

*Human engineering. Virtual reality. Body, Human – Computer simulation.*

**TA166.H275 1997**

Handbook of human factors and ergonomics / edited by Gavriel Salvendy. 2nd ed. New York : Wiley, c1997. xxii, 2137 p. :

      620.8/5 21

*Human engineering -- Handbooks, manuals, etc.*

**TA166.I556 2001**

International encyclopedia of ergonomics and human factors / edited by Waldemar Karwowski. London ; New York : Taylor & Francis, 2001. 3 v. :

      620.8/2 21    0748408479

*Human engineering -- Encyclopedias.*

# TA168 Systems engineering

**TA168.C42 1996**
**Chapanis, Alphonse.**

Human factors in systems engineering / Alphonse Chapanis. New York : Wiley, c1996. xii, 332 p. :

95-046163    620.8/2    0471137820(cl

*Systems engineering. Human engineering.*

**TA168.E38 1997**
**Eisner, Howard,**

Essentials of project and systems engineering management / Howard Eisner. New York : Wiley, c1997. xii, 358 p. :

96-017691    658.4/06    0471148466

*Systems engineering -- Management. Industrial project management -- Data processing.*

**TA168.H44 1994**
**Hee, Kees Max van,**
Information systems engineering : a formal approach / K.M. van Hee. Cambridge ; Cambridge University Press, 1994. xiii, 421 p.
93-042047          004.2/1          0521455146
*Systems engineering. Information technology.*

**TA168.S15 2000**
**Sage, Andrew P.**
Introduction to systems engineering / Andrew P. Sage, James E. Armstrong, Jr. New York : Wiley, c2000. xiv, 547 p. :
99-033715          620/.001/1          0471027669
*Systems engineering. Large scale systems.*

**TA168.B37 2000**
**Bejan, Adrian,**
Shape and structure, from engineering to nature / Adrian Bejan. New York : Cambridge University Press, 2000. xix, 324 p. :
00-027314          620/.0042          0521790492
*Systems engineering. Large scale systems.*

## TA169 Systems reliability

**TA169.H36 1996**
Handbook of reliability engineering and management / [edited by] W. Grant Ireson, Clyde F. Coombs, Jr., Richard Y. Moss. 2nd ed. New York : McGraw Hill, 1996. 1 v. :
          620/.00452 20
*Reliability (Engineering)*

## TA169.5 System failure

**TA169.5.W44 1994**
When technology fails : significant technological disasters, accidents, and failures of the twentieth century / edited by Neil Schlager ; foreword by Henry Petroski. Detroit : Gale Research, c1994. xxxvi, 659 p.
93-041874          363.1          0810389088
*System failures (Engineering) -- Case studies. Disasters --Case studies.*

**TA171.C5875 2002**
**Condoor, Sridhar S.,**
Mechanical design modeling using ProEngineer / Sridhar S. Condoor. Dubuque, Iowa : McGraw-Hill, 2002. 1 v. :
          620/.0042/02855369 21
*Engineering design -- Data processing. Pro/ENGINEER. Mechanical drawing. Computer-aided design.*

## TA174 Engineering design

**TA174.B756 1994**
**Bucciarelli, Louis L.**
Designing engineers / Louis L. Bucciarelli. Cambridge, Mass. : MIT Press, c1994. x, 220 p. :
94-017348          620/.0042          0262023776
*Engineering design.*

**TA174.E78 1993**
**Ertas, Atila,**
The engineering design process / Atila Ertas, Jesse C. Jones. New York : Wiley, c1993. xiv, 525 p. :
92-034615          620/.0042          0471517968
*Engineering design.*

**TA174.N35 2000**
**Narayanan, R. S.**
Introduction to design for civil engineers / R.S. Narayanan and A.W. Beeby. New York : E & FN Spon, 2000. p. cm.
00-044548          624          0419235507
*Engineering design. Civil engineering.*

**TA174.P473 1994**
**Petroski, Henry.**
Design paradigms : case histories of error and judgment in engineering / Henry Petroski. Cambridge [England] ; Cambridge University Press, 1994. xii, 209 p. :
93-032560          620/.0042          0521461081
*Engineering design -- Case studies. System failures (Engineering) -- Case studies.*

**TA174.S89 1990**
**Suh, Nam P.,**
The principles of design / Nam P. Suh. New York : Oxford University Press, 1990. xiv, 401 p. :
88-019584          620/.00425          0195043456
*Engineering design.*

**TA174.T55 1999**
**Thompson, David E.,**
Design analysis : mathematical modeling of nonlinear systems / David E. Thompson. Cambridge ; Cambridge University Press, 1999. xvi, 275 p. :
98-003588          620/.0042/015118
0521621704
*Engineering design -- Mathematical models. Nonlinear systems – Mathematical models.*

## TA177 Engineering models

**TA177.H36 1995**
Handbook of solid modeling / Donald E. LaCourse, editor in chief. New York : McGraw-Hill, c1995. 1 v. (various
95-004022          658.5/752          0070357889
*Engineering models.*

## TA177.4 Engineering economy

**TA177.4.G7 1990**
**Grant, Eugene Lodewick,**
Principles of engineering economy / Eugene L. Grant, W. Grant Ireson, Richard S. Leavenworth. 8th ed. New York : Wiley, c1990. xiv, 591 p. :
          658.15/5 20
*Engineering economy.*

## TA190 Management of engineering works — General works

**TA190.B36 1996**
**Bennett, F. Lawrence.**
The management of engineering : human, quality, organizational, legal, and ethical aspects of professional practice / F. Lawrence Bennett. New York : Wiley, c1996. xviii, 478 p.
95-034032          620/.0068          047159329X
*Engineering -- Management.*

## TA219 Forensic engineering

**TA219.F67**
**Noon, Randall.**
Forensic engineering investigation / Randall K. Noon. Boca Raton, FL : CRC Press, 2001. xviii, 463 p.
00-044457          620          0849309115
*Forensic engineering.*

## TA330 Engineering mathematics. Engineering analysis — General works

**TA330.C33 1995**
**Cakmak, A. S.**
Applied mathematics for engineers / authors, A.S. Cakamk, J.F. Botha. Southampton, UK ; Computational Mechanics Publications, c1995. 305 p. ;
94-070415          515/.14          1853122750
*Engineering mathematics.*

**TA330.D84 1998**
**Duffy, Dean G.**
Advanced engineering mathematics / Dean G. Duffy. Boca Raton, Fla. : CRC Press, c1998. 634 p. :
97-033991          510          0849378540
*Engineering mathematics.*

**TA330.K64 1998**
**Koenig, Herbert A.**
Modern computational methods / Herbert A. Koenig. Philadelphia : Taylor & Francis, c1998. xv, 300 p. :
98-021966          620/.001/51          1560324686
*Engineering mathematics.*

**TA330.M43 1995**
**Mei, Chiang C.**
Mathematical analysis in engineering : how to use the basic tools / Chiang C. Mei. Cambridge [England] ; Cambridge University press, 1995. xvii, 461 p.
94-030063          620/.00151          0521460530
*Engineering mathematics.*

## TA331 Engineering mathematics. Engineering analysis — General special

**TA331.A62 1993**
Applications of finite fields / by Alfred J. Menezes, editor ; Ian F. Blake ... [et al.]. Boston : Kluwer Academic Publishers, c1993. xi, 218 p. :
92-032895          003.54          0792392825
*Engineering mathematics. Finite fields (Algebra)*

**TA331.S35 1998**
**Santamarina, J. Carlos.**
Introduction to discrete signals and inverse problems in civil engineering / J. Carlos Santamarina and Dante Fratta. Reston, Va. : ASCE Press, c1998. xiii, 327 p.
98-002920          624/.01/51          0784403112
*Civil engineering -- Mathematics. System analysis. Signal processing -- Mathematics.*

## TA332 Engineering mathematics. Engineering analysis — Pocketbooks, tables, etc.

**TA332.K87 1991**
**Kurtz, Max,**
Handbook of applied mathematics for engineers and scientists / Max Kurtz. New York : McGraw-Hill, c1991. 1 v. (various
91-000711          620/.001/51          0070356858
*Engineering mathematics -- Handbooks, manuals, etc.*

**TA332.S73 1995**
Standard handbook of engineering calculations / Tyler G. Hicks, editory ; S. David Hick, coordinating editor; Joseph Leto, assistant editor. 3rd ed. New York : McGraw-Hill, c1995. 1 v. :
          620/.00212 20
*Engineering mathematics -- Handbooks, manuals, etc.*

## TA335 Engineering mathematics. Engineering analysis — Numerical methods. Approximations Schematic and graphic methods

**TA335.F47 1998**
**Ferziger, Joel H.**
Numerical methods for engineering application / Joel H. Ferziger. New York : Wiley, c1998. xvii, 378 p.
97-035864          515/.35          0471116211
*Engineering mathematics. Numerical analysis.*

## TA340 Engineering mathematics. Engineering analysis — Probabilistic and statistical methods

**TA340.B35 1994**
**Barnes, J. Wesley.**
Statistical analysis for engineers and scientists : a computer-based approach / J. Wesley Barnes. New York : McGraw-Hill, c1994. xxvii, 396 p.
93-043834          519.5/02462          0078396085
*Engineering -- Statistical methods -- Data processing.*

**TA340.B87 1999**
**Bury, Karl V.,**
Statistical distributions in engineering / Karl Bury. Cambridge ; Cambridge University Press, 1999. x, 362 p. :
98-022941          620/.0072          0521632323
*Engineering -- Statistical methods. Mathematical statistics.*

**TA340.H34 1998**
Handbook of statistical methods for engineers and scientists / Harrison M. Wadsworth, Jr., editor. New York : McGraw-Hill, c1998. 1 v. in vario
97-038029          519.5          007067678X
*Engineering -- Statistical methods. Science -- Statistical methods.*

**TA340.S35 1996**
**Schiff, Daniel,**
Practical engineering statistics / Daniel Schiff, Ralph B. D'Agostino. New York : Wiley, c1996. xiv, 309 p. :
95-023303          620/.001/5195          0471547689
*Engineering -- Statistical methods.*

## TA342 Engineering mathematics. Engineering analysis — Mathematical models — General works

**TA342.B67 1994**
**Bossel, Hartmut.**
Modeling and simulation / Hartmut Bossel. Wellesley, MA : A.K. Peters ; c1994. xvi, 484 p. :
94-001847          003/.85          1568810334
*Mathematical models. Digital computer simulation.*

**TA342.T78 1997**
**Trujillo, David M.**
Practical inverse analysis in engineering / David M. Trujillo, Henry R. Busby. Boca Raton : CRC Press, c1997. 235 p. :
97-016868          620/.001/519703          084939659X
*Engineering -- Mathematical models -- Data processing. Dynamic programming.*

## TA345 Engineering mathematics. Engineering analysis — Electronic data processing. Computer aided engineering — General works

**TA345.A78 1990**
Artificial intelligence in engineering / edited by Graham Winstanley. Chichester, West Sussex, England ; Wiley, c1991. xxi, 434 p. :
90-031728          620/.00285/63          0471926035
*Engineering -- Data processing. Artificial intelligence. Expert systems (Computer science)*

**TA345.E547 1997**
**Etter, D. M.**
Engineering problem solving with MATLAB / Delores M. Etter. Upper Saddle River, N.J. : Prentice Hall, c1997. xx, 329 p. :
96-022096          620/.001/51          0133976882
*Engineering mathematics -- Data processing.*

**TA345.K63 2000**
**Knight, Andrew**
Basics of MATLAB and beyond / Andrew Knight. Boca Raton, FL : Chapman & Hall/CRC, c2000. 202 p. :
99-031210          620/.001/5118          0849320399
*Engineering mathematics -- Data processing.*

**TA345.K653 1994**
**Kockler, Norbert,**
Numerical methods and scientific computing : using software libraries for problem solving / Norbert Kockler. Oxford : Clarendon Press ; 1994. xviii, 328 p.
94-008064          519.4/0285/51          0198596987
*Engineering mathematics -- Data processing. Numerical analysis -- Data processing.*

## TA347 Engineering mathematics. Engineering analysis — Other specific mathematical aids in the solution of engineering problems A-Z

**TA347.B69.P34 1997**
**Paris, F.**
Boundary element method : fundamentals and applications / Federico Paris and Jose Canas. Oxford ; Oxford University Press, 1997. xv, 392 p. :
96-034311          620/.001/51535          0198565372
*Boundary element methods.*

**TA347.D45.S34 1993**
**Schiesser, W. E.**
Computational mathematics in engineering and applied science : ODEs, DAEs, and PDEs / William E. Schiesser. Boca Raton, FL : CRC Press, 1993. viii, 587 p.
93-017599          515/.35/0285          0849373735
*Engineering mathematics. Differential equations. Mathematical models.*

**TA347.F5.B43 1992**
**Beer, G.**
Introduction to finite and boundary element methods for engineers / G. Beer, J.O. Watson. Chichester ; New York : c1992. xii, 509 p.,
94-107313          620/.001/51535          0471928135
*Finite element method. Boundary element methods.*

**TA347.F5.C665 1995**
**Cook, Robert Davis.**
Finite element modeling for stress analysis / Robert D. Cook. New York : Wiley, c1995. xi, 320 p. :
94-034421          624.1/76          0471107743
*Finite element method -- Data processing. Structural analysis (Engineering) -- Data processing.*

**TA347.F5.H83 1995**
**Huebner, Kenneth H.,**
The finite element method for engineers / Kenneth H. Huebner, Earl A. Thornton, Ted G. Byrom. New York : Wiley, c1995. xxvi, 627 p.
94-014031          620/.001/5153          0471547425
*Finite element method.*

**TA347.F5.M87 1992**
**Mura, Toshio,**
Variational methods in mechanics / Toshio Mura, Tatsuhito Koya. New York : Oxford University Press, 1992. viii, 244 p.
91-018834          620.1          0195068300
*Finite element method. Mechanics, Applied -- Mathematics. Variational principles.*

**TA347.F5.S64 1997**
**Smith, I. M.**
Programming the finite element method / I.M. Smith and D.V. Griffiths. Chichester ; John Wiley & Sons, 1997. xii, 534 p. :
96-054905          620/.001/51535          0471965421
*Finite element method -- Computer programs. Subroutines (Computer programs) Computer-aided engineering.*

**TA347.F5F57 1983**
The Finite element method : abasic introduction / K.C. Rockey ... [et al.]. 2nd ed. New York : Wiley, 1983. x, 239 p. :
624.1/71 19
*Finite element method. Structural analysis (Engineering)*

**TA347.F5G87 2000**
**Gupta, Kajal K.**
Finite element multidisciplinary analysis / Kajal K. Gupta, John L. Meek. Reston, VA : American Institute of Aeronautics and Astronauti c2000. xv, 352 p. :
00-028850          620/.001/51535          1563473933
*Finite element method.*

**TA347.F5K86 2000**
**Kwon, Young W.**
The finite element method using MATLAB / Young W. Kwon, Hyochoong C. Bang. Boca Raton, FL : CRC Press, c2000. 607 p. :
00-044425          620/.001/51535          0849300967
*Finite element method.*

## TA350 Mechanics of engineering — General works

**TA350.B3552 1997**
**Beer, Ferdinand Pierre,**
Vetor mechanics for engineers : statics and dynamics / Ferdinand P. Beer, E. Russell Johnston, Jr., with the collaboration of Elliot R. Eisenber, Robert G. Sarubbi. 6th ed. New York : McGraw-Hill, c1997. xxv, 1280 p. :
620.1/05 20
*Mechanics, Applied. Vector analysis. Statics. Dynamics.*

**TA350.B48 1994**
**Bhavikatti, S. S.**
Engineering mechanics / S.S. Bhavikatti, K.G. Rajashekarappa. New York : J. Wiley, 1994. xiii, 537 p.
92-036073          620.1          0470220546
*Mechanics, Applied.*

**TA350.H48 1998**
**Hibbeler, R. C.**
Engineering mechanics. Statics & dynamics / R.C. Hibbeler. 8th ed. Upper Saddle River, N.J. : Prentice-Hall, c1998. xvi, 672 p. :
620.1 21
*Mechanics, Applied.*

**TA350.R295 2001**
**Reid, David,**
An introduction to engineering mechanics / David Reid. Hampshire ; Palgrave, 2001. xii, 194 p. :
00-050118          620.1          0333949218
*Mechanics, Applied.*

## TA351 Mechanics of engineering — Applied statistics

**TA351.S73 1987**
**Stevens, Karl K.,**
Statics and strength of materials / Karl K. Stevens. Englewood Cliffs, N.J. : Prentice-Hall, c1987. xiii, 572 p.
86-022498          620.1/12          0138446717
*Statics. Strength of materials.*

## TA354-356 Mechanics of engineering — Applied dynamics

**TA354.S77 2000**
**Stronge, W. J.**
Impact mechanics / W.J. Stronge. Cambridge, [England] ; Cambridge University Press, 2000. xix, 280 p. :
99-044947          620.1/125          0521632862
*Impact.*

**TA355.B52 1990**
**Blevins, Robert D.**
  Flow-induced vibration / Robert D. Blevins. New York : Van Nostrand Reinhold, c1990. x, 451 p. :
89-016707          620.3          0442206518
  *Vibration. Fluid dynamics.*

**TA355.D384 2000**
**De Silva, Clarence W.**
  Vibration : fundamentals and practice / Clarence W. de Silva. Boca Raton, FL : CRC Press, 2000. 943 p. :
99-016238          620.3          0849318084
  *Vibration.*

**TA355.I519 2001**
**Inman, D. J.**
  Engineering vibration / Daniel J. Inman. 2nd ed. Upper Saddle River, N.J. : Prentice Hall, c2001. xiv, 621 p. :
          620.3 21
  *Vibration.*

**TA355.S5164 1995**
  Shock and vibration handbook / edited by Cyril M. Harris. New York : McGraw-Hill, 1995. p. cm.
95-038224          620.3          0070269203
  *Vibration -- Handbooks, manuals, etc. Shock (Mechanics) -- Handbooks, manuals, etc.*

**TA356.P47 1990**
**Petyt, M.**
  Introduction to finite element vibration analysis / Maurice Petyt. Cambridge [England] ; Cambridge University Press, 1990. xv, 558 p. :
88-034384          624.1/76          0521266076
  *Vibration. Finite element method.*

## TA357 Mechanics of engineering — Applied fluid mechanics — General works

**TA357.B57 1984**
**Blevins, Robert D.**
  Applied fluid dynamics handbook / Robert D. Blevins. New York, N.Y. : Van Nostrand Reinhold Co., c1984. x, 558 p. :
83-014517          620.1/064          0442212968
  *Fluid dynamics -- Handbooks, manuals, etc.*

**TA357.E53 1986**
  Encyclopedia of fluid mechanics / N.P. Cheremisinoff, editor, in collaboration with G. Akay ... [et al.]. Houston : Gulf Pub. Co., Book Division, c1986-c1990. 10 v. :
85-009742          620.1/06          0872015130
  *Fluid mechanics -- Dictionaries.*

**TA357.M47 1987**
**Merzkirch, Wolfgang.**
  Flow visualization / Wolfgang Merzkirch. Orlando : Academic Press, 1987. x, 260 p. :
86-022279          620.1/064          0124913512
  *Flow visualization.*

**TA357.M67 2000**
**Mott, Robert L.**
  Applied fluid mechanics / Robert L. Mott. 5th ed. Upper Saddle River, N.J. : Prentice Hall, c2000. xvii, 597 p. :
          620.1/06 21
  *Fluid mechanics.*

**TA357.P33 1994**
**Papanastasiou, Tasos C.**
  Applied fluid mechanics / Tasos C. Papanastasiou. Englewood Cliffs, N.J. : P T R Prentice Hall, 1994. xxiii, 520 p.
92-034111          620.1/06          0130607991
  *Fluid mechanics.*

**TA357.R49**
**Reynolds, A. J.**
  Turbulent flows in engineering [by] A. J. Reynolds. London, John Wiley [1974] xvii, 462 p.
73-008464          620.1/064          0471717827
  *Fluid mechanics. Turbulence.*

**TA357.S517 1999**
**Smits, Alexander J.**
  A physical introduction to fluid mechanics / Alexander J. Smits. New York : John Wiley, 1999. p. cm.
99-016027          620.1/06          0471253499
  *Fluid mechanics.*

**TA357. Y68 2000**
**Young, Donald F.**
  A brief introduction to fluid mechanics / Donald F. Young, Bruce R. Munson, Theodore H. Okiishi. 2nd ed. New York : Wiley, 2001. xv, 517 p. :
          620.1/06 21
  *Fluid mechanics.*

## TA357.5 Mechanics of engineering — Applied fluid mechanics — Special topics

**TA357.5.M43.U66 1993**
**Upp, E. L.,**
  Fluid flow measurement : a practical guide to accurate flow measurement / E.L. Upp. Houston : Gulf Pub. Co., c1993. xi, 178 p. :
92-010784          681/.2          0884150178
  *Fluid dynamic measurements. Flow meters.*

## TA365  Acousitcs in engineering. Acoustical engineering — General works

**TA365.N67 1989**
**Norton, M. P.**
  Fundamentals of noise and vibration analysis for engineers / M.P. Norton. Cambridge [England] ; Cambridge University Press, 1989. xix, 619 p. :
88-034385          620.2/3          0521341485
  *Noise. Vibration.*

# TA367.5 Lasers in engineering

**TA367.5.L39 1996**
**Laufer, Gabriel.**

Introduction to optics and lasers in engineering / Gabriel Laufer. Cambridge ; Cambridge University Press, 1996. xvii, 476 p.

95-044046          621.36/6          0521452333

*Lasers in engineering. Optics.*

# TA401 Materials of engineering and construction — Periodicals. Societies. Collections. Yearbooks. Congresses.

**TA401.A653**
**American Society for Testing and Materials.**

Annual book of ASTM standards. Philadelphia, Pa. : ASTM, v. :

83-641658          620.1/1/0218

*Materials -- Standards -- United States -- Periodicals. Materials -- Testing -- Standards -- United States -- Periodicals.*

**TA401.6.A1.H86 1998**
**Hummel, Rolf E.,**

Understanding materials science : history, properties, applications / Rolf E. Hummel. New York : Springer, c1998. xiv, 407 p. :

97-026429          620.1          0387983031

*Materials science.*

# TA403 Materials of engineering and construction — Treatises

**TA403.B2247 1997**
**Ball, Philip,**

Made to measure : new materials for the 21st century / Philip Ball. Princeton, N.J. : Princeton University Press, c1997. 458 p. :

97-004027          620.1/1          0691027331

*Materials -- Technological innovations.*

**TA403.B787 1999**
**Budinski, Kenneth G.**

Engineering materials : properites and selection / Kenneth G. Budinski, Michael K. Budinski. 6th ed. Upper Saddle River, N.J. : Prentice Hall, c1999. xi, 719 p. :

620.1/1 21

*Materials.*

**TA403.J35 1987**
**Jastrzebski, Zbigniew D.**

The nature and properties of engineering materials / Zbigniew D. Jastrzebski. New York : Wiley, c1987. xix, 636 p. :

86-024673          620.1/1          0471818410

*Materials.*

**TA403.M84 1993**
**Murray, G. T.,**

Introduction to engineering materials : behavior, properties, and selection / G.T. Murray. New York : Dekker, c1993. ix, 669 p. :

93-012660          620.1/1          0824789652

*Materials.*

**TA403.S419 1998**

The Science and technology of civil engineering materials / J. Francis Young ... [et al.]. Upper Saddle River, NJ : Prentice Hall, c1998. xiv, 384 p. :

97-031972          624.1/8          0136597491

*Materials.*

**TA403.S515 2000**
**Shackelford, James F.**

Introduction to materials science for engineers / James F. Shackelford. 5th ed. Upper Saddle River, N.J. : Prentice Hall, c2000. xvii, 877 p. :

620.1 21

*Materials.*

**TA403.V35 1989**
**Van Vlack, Lawrence H.**

Elements of materials science and engineering / Lawrence H. Van Vlack. 6th ed. Reading, Mass. : Addison-Wesley, c1989. xxi, 598 p. :

620.1/1 19

*Materials. Solids.*

# TA403.4 Materials of engineering and construction — Pocketbooks, tables, etc.

**TA403.4.C74 2001**

CRC materials science and engineering handbook / [edited by] James F. Shackelford, William Alexander. Boca Raton, FL : CRC Press, c2001. 1949 p. ;

00-048567          620.1/1          0849326966

*Materials -- Handbooks, manuals, etc.*

**TA403.4.E64 1995**

Engineered materials handbook / prepared under the direction of the ASM International Handbook Committee ; Michelle M. Gauthier, volume chair. Materials Park, OH : ASM International, c1995. x, 1317 p. :

95-035405          620.1/1          0871702835

*Materials -- Handbooks, manuals, etc.*

**TA403.4.S482 1995**
**Shackelford, James F.**

CRC practical handbook of materials selection / James F. Shackelford, William Alexander, Jun S. Park. Boca Raton : CRC Press, c1995. xii, 625 p. ;

95-134783          620.1/12          0849337097

*Materials -- Handbooks, manuals, etc.*

## TA403.6 Materials of engineering and construction — General special

**TA403.6.E74 1991**
**Ericksen, J. L.**
 Introduction to the thermodynamics of solids / J.L. Ericksen. London ; Chapman & Hall, 1991. xii, 204 p. :
90-021813          621.402/1          0412398400
 *Materials. Thermodynamics.*

**TA403.6.Q36 1995**
**Kurzydlowski, Krzysztof J.**
 The quantitative description of the microstructure of materials / Krzysztof Jan Kurzydlowski, Brian Ralph. Boca Raton : CRC Press, c1995. 418 p. :
94-041304          620.1/1299          0849389216
 *Materials. Microstructure.*

## TA404.8-418.38 Materials of engineering and construction — Specific characteristics of materials — Mechanical properties

**TA404.8.E53 1994**
 The encyclopedia of advanced materials / editors, David Bloor ... [et al.] ; senior advisory editor, Robert W. Cahn. Oxford, England ; Pergamon, c1994. 4 v. (xxi, 31
94-018013          620.1/1          0080406068
 *Materials.*

**TA405.B39 2002**
**Beer, Ferdinand Pierre,**
 Mechanics of materials / Ferdinand P. Beer, E. Russell Johnston, Jr., John T. DeWolf. 3rd ed. New York : McGraw-Hill, 2002. xix, 788 p. :
          620.1/12 21
*Strength of materials.*

**TA405.C859 2000**
**Courtney, Thomas H.**
 Mechanical behavior of materials / Thomas H. Courtney. 2nd ed. Boston : McGraw-Hill 2000. xviii, 733 p. :
          620.1/1292 21
*Materials -- Mechanical properties.*

**TA405.C89 2000**
**Craig, Roy R.,**
 Mechanics of materials / Roy R. Craig, Jr. 2nd ed. New York : Wiley, c2000. xiv, 752, p. :
          620.1/1292 21
*Strength of materials.*

**TA405.T52 1968**
**Timoshenko, Stephen,**
 Elements of strength of materials [by] S. Timoshenko [and] D. H. Young. 5th ed. Princeton, N.J. : Van Nostrand, [1968] x, 377 p. :
          620.1/12
*Strength of materials.*

**TA407.D32 1991**
**Dally, James W.**
 Experimental stress analysis / James W. Dally, William F. Riley. 3rd ed. New York : McGraw-Hill, c1991. xxii, 639 p. :
          620.1/123 20
*Strains and stresses.  Photoelasticity.*

**TA407.J39 1992**
**Jena, A. K.**
 Phase transformation in materials / A.K. Jena, M.C. Chaturvedi. Englewood Cliffs, N.J. : Prentice Hall, c1992. ix, 482 p. :
91-027752          536/.42          0136630553
 *Materials.  Phase transformations (Statistical physics)*

**TA407.2.P55 1994**
**Pilkey, Walter D.**
 Formulas for stress, strain, and structural matrices / Walter D. Pilkey. New York : J. Wiley, c1994. xvii, 1458 p.
94-001008          624.1/76/0212          0471527467
 *Strains and stresses -- Tables.  Structural analysis (Engineering) – Tables.  Structural analysis (Engineering -- Computer programs.*

**TA409.B76 1986**
**Borek, David.**
 Elementary engineering fracture mechanics / David Broek. 4th rev. ed. Dordrecht ; Boston : Kluwer Academic, 1986. xiv, 501 p. :
          620.1/126 19
*Fracture mechanics.*

**TA409.B773 1988**
**Broek, David.**
 The practical use of fracture mechanics / by David Broek. Dordrecht ; Kluwer Academic Publishers, 1988. xiii, 522 p.
88-009336          620.1/126          9024737079
 *Fracture mechanics.*

**TA409.D96 1995**
 Dynamic fracture mechanics / editor, M.H. Aliabadi. Southampton, UK ; Computational Mechanics Publications, c1995. 311 p. :
94-069711          620.1/126          1562522671
 *Fracture mechanics.*

**TA409.F77 1990**
**Freund, L. B.**
 Dynamic fracture mechanics / L.B. Freund. Cambridge ; New York : Cambridge University Press, 1990. xvii, 563 p. :
          620.1/126 20
*Fracture mechanics.*

**TA417.2.B63 1997**
**Bray, Don E.**
 Nondestructive evaluation : a tool in design, manufacturing, and services / Don E. Bray, Roderic K. Stanley. Rev. ed. Boca Raton : CRC Press, c1997. 586 p. :
          620.1/127 20
*Non-destructive testing.  Engineering inspection.*

**TA417.2.C37 1995**
**Cartz, Louis.**
  Nondestructive testing : radiography, ultrasonics, liquid penetrant, magnetic particle, eddy current / by Louis Cartz. Materials Park, OH : ASM International, c1995. x, 229 p. :
94-073646        620.1/127        0871705176
  *Non-destructive testing. Quality control. Engineering inspection.*

**TA417.2.C56 1995**
**Cloud, Gary L.**
  Optical methods of engineering analysis / Gary L. Cloud. Cambridge ; New York : Cambridge University Press, 1995. xii, 503 p. :
620.1/127 20
  *Non-destructive testing. Holographic interferometry.*

**TA417.6.H46 1996**
**Hertsbert, Richard W.,**
  Deformation and fracture mechanics of engineering materials / Richard W. Hertzberg. 4th ed. New York : J. Wiley & Sons, c1996. xxi, 786 p. :
620.1/123 20
  *Deformations (Mechanics) Fracture mechanics.*

**TA418.S48 1997**
**Shames, Irving Herman,**
  Elastic and inelastic stress analysis / Irving H. Shames, Francis A. Cozzarelli. Washington, DC : Taylor and Francis, c1997. xvi, 722 p. :
620.1/123 21
  *Elasticity. Plasticity. Viscoelasticity.*

**TA418.2.L35 1999**
**Lakes, Roderic S.**
  Viscoelastic solids / Roderic S. Lakes. Boca Raton : CRC Press, c1999. 476 p. :
98-026280        620.1/1232        0849396581
  *Viscoelasticity. Viscoelastic materials.*

**TA418.26.H42 1997**
  Heat-resistant materials / edited by J.R. Davis. Materials Park, Ohio : ASM International, c1997. v, 591 p. :
97-030681        620.1/1217        0871705966
  *Heat resistant materials -- Handbooks, manuals, etc.*

**TA418.38.S87 1998**
**Suresh, S. (Subra)**
  Fatigue of materials / S. Suresh. 2nd ed. Cambridge ; New York : Cambridge University Press, 1998. xxi, 679 p. :
620.1/126 21
  *Materials -- Fatigue. Fracture mechanics.*

**TA418.52 Materials of engineering and construction — Physical properties — Thermal properties and tests**

**TA418.52.R34 1995**
**Ragone, David V.,**
  Thermodynamics of materials / David V. Ragone. New York : Wiley, c1995. 2 v. :
94-025647        536/.7        0471308854
  *Materials -- Thermal properties. Thermodynamics.*

**TA418.74 Materials of engineering and construction — Physical properties — Surface effects and tests**

**TA418.74.C5928 1989**
  Corrosion and corrosion protection handbook / edited by Philip A. Schweitzer. 2nd ed., rev. and expanded. New York : M. Dekker, c1989. xviii, 660 p. :
620.1/1223 19
  *Corrosion and anti-corrosives -- Handbooks, manuals, etc.*

**TA418.74.R63 2000**
**Roberge, Pierre R.**
  Handbook of corrosion engineering / Pierre R. Roberge. New York : McGraw-Hill, c2000. xi, 1139 p. :
99-035898        620.1/1223        0070765162
  *Corrosion and anti-corrosives.*

**TA418.8 Materials of engineering and construction — Physical properties — Surface effects and tests**

**TA418.8.A43 1990**
**Allen, Terence.**
  Particle size measurement / Terence Allen. 4th ed. London ; New York : Chapman and Hall, 1990. xxi, 806 p. :
620/.43 20
  *Particle size determination.*

# TA418.9 Materials of engineering and construction — Materials of special composition or structure, A-Z

**TA418.9.C6.B354 1992**
**Balaguru, Perumalsamy N.**
  Fiber-reinforced cement composites / Perumalsamy N. Balaguru, Surendra P. Shah. New York : McGraw-Hill, c1992. xvii, 530 p.
92-011927        620.1/35        0070564000
  *Fibrous composites. Cement composites. Porland cement -- Additives.*

**TA418.9.C6.H33 1982**
  Handbook of composites / edited by George Lubin. New York : Van Nostrand Reinhold, c1982. x, 786 p. :
81-010341        620.1/18        0442248970
  *Composite materials -- Handbooks, manuals, etc. Fibrous composites -- Handbooks, manuals, etc.*

**TA418.9.C6.H85 1996**
**Hull, Derek.**
An introduction to composite materials / D. Hull and T.W. Clyne. Cambridge ; Cambridge University Press, 1996. xvi, 326 p. :
96-005701          620.1/18          0521381908
*Composite materials.*

**TA418.9.C6.J59 1999**
**Jones, Robert M.**
Mechanics of composite materials / Robert M. Jones. Philadelphia, PA : Taylor & Francis, c1999. xvi, 519 p. :
98-018290          620.1/1892          156032712X
*Composite materials -- Mechanical properties. Laminated materials -- Mechanical properties.*

**TA418.9.C6.K34 1992**
**Kalamkarov, Alexander L.**
Composite and reinforced elements of construction / Alexander L. Kalamkarov. Chichester ; Wiley, c1992. xv, 290 p. :
92-010150          624.1/8          047193593X
*Composite materials -- Mechanical properties. Composite materials -- Thermomechanical properties. Fibrous composites.*

**TA418.9.C6C635 1994**
Concise encyclopedia of composite materials / editor, Anthony Kellly ; exectutive editor Robert W. Cahn ; senior advisory editor, Michael B. Bever. Rev. ed. Oxford, England ; New York : Pergamon, 1994. xxix, 349 p. :
          620.1/18/03 20
*Composite materials -- Encyclopedias.*

**TA418.9.C6E53 1989**
International encyclopedia of composites / Stuart M. Lee, editor. New York : VCH, c1990-c1991. 6 v. :
          620.1/18/03 20          0895732904
*Composite materials -- Dictionaries.*

**TA418.9.N35H37 2001**
Nanostructured materials and nanotechnology / edited by Hari Singh Nalwa. Concise ed. San Diego : Academic Press, 2001. xxiii, 834 p. :
          620/.5 21          0125139209
*Nanostructure materials. Nanotechnology.*

**TA418.9.T45.S65 1995**
**Smith, Donald L.**
Thin-film deposition : principles and practice / Donald L. Smith. New York : McGraw-Hill, c1995. xxiii, 616 p.
94-047002          621.3815/2          0070585024
*Thin films. Vapor-plating. Thin film devices.*

## TA419-455 Materials of engineering and construction — Special materials — Nonmetallic materials

**TA419.C64 1989**
Concise encyclopedia of wood & wood-based materials / editor, Arno P. Schniewind. 1st ed. Oxford, England : Pergamon Press ; MIT Press, 1989. xx, 354 p. :
          620.1/1/0321 19
*Wood -- Encyclopedias.*

**TA439.D39 1999**
**Day, Ken W.**
Concrete mix design, quality control, and specification / Ken W. Day. London ; E & EN Spon, 1999. xxi, 391 p. :
98-051602          620.1/36          0419243305
*Concrete -- Mixing -- Quality control. Concrete -- Specifications.*

**TA450.A55 1997**
**Amstock, Joseph S.**
Handbook of glass in construction / Joseph S. Amstock. New York : McGraw-Hill, c1997. xv, 584 p. :
97-001273          624.1/838          0070016194
*Glass. Glass construction*

**TA455.C43.C66 1990**
Concise encyclopedia of advanced ceramic materials / editor, R.J. Brook ; executive editor, Robert W. Cahn ; senior advisory editor, Michael B. Bever. Oxford ; Pergamon Press ; 1991. xvi, 588 p. :
90-007914          620.1/4/03          0080347207
*Ceramic materials -- Encyclopedias.*

**TA455.C43.G738 1998**
**Green, D. J.**
An introduction to the mechanical properties of ceramics / David J. Green. Cambridge ; Cambridge University Press, 1998. xii, 336 p. :
97-018018          620.1/40423          0521590876
*Ceramic materials -- Mechanical properties.*

**TA455.C43.W38 1996**
**Wachtman, J. B.,**
Mechanical properties of ceramics / John B. Wachtman. New York : Wiley, c1996. xxii, 448 p.
95-036612          620.1/40423          0471133167
*Ceramic materials -- Mechanical properties.*

**TA455.P58**
**Ehrenstein, G. W.**
Polymeric materials / G.W. Ehrenstein, R.P. Theriault. Cincinnati, OH : Hanser Gardner Publications, 2000. p. cm.
00-046239          620.1/92          1569903107
*Polymers -- Testing. Plastics -- Testing.*

**TA455.P58.O68 1996**
**Osswald, Tim A.**
Materials science of polymers for engineers / Tim A. Osswald, Georg Menges. Munich ; Hanser ; c1996. xiv, 475 p. :
95-033357          620.1/92          1569901929
*Polymers. Plastics.*

**TA455.P58.P475 1996**

Physical properties of polymers handbook / editor, James E. Mark. Woodbury, N.Y. : AIP Press, c1996. xv, 723 p. :
95-050256          620.1/92          1563962950
*Polymers.*

**TA455.P58.T5 1997**

Thermal characterization of polymeric materials / edited by Edith A. Turi. San Diego : Academic Press, c1997. 2 v. (xxiv, 2
96-028565          620.1/9204296          0127037837
*Polymers -- Thermal properties.*

**TA459-545 Materials of engineering and construction — Special materials — Metals**

**TA459.A5**

Metals handbook / American Society for Metals. Cleveland, Ohio : The Society, -c1990. v. :
27-012046
*Metals -- Handbooks, manuals, etc. Steel – Handbooks, manuals, etc.*

**TA459.A78 1993**

ASM metals reference book / editor, Michael Bauccio. Materials Park, Ohio : ASM International, 1993. viii, 614 p.
93-028716          620.1/6          0871704781
*Metals -- Handbooks, manuals, etc. Metal-work -- Handbooks, manuals, etc.*

**TA459.N39 1997**
**Nayar, Alok.**

The metals databook / Alok Nayar. New York : McGraw-Hill, c1997. 1 v. (various
97-218568          620.1/6          0070460884
*Metals -- Tables.*

**TA460.C63 1993**
**Collins, J. A.**

Failure of materials in mechanical design : analysis, prediction, prevention / Jack A. Collins. New York : Wiley, 1993. xviii, 654 p.
92-035907          620.1/12          0471558915
*Materials -- Fracture. Machine design. Strains and stresses.*

**TA460.H57 1984**
**Honeycombe, R. W. K.**

The plastic deformation of metals / R.W.K. Honeycombe. London ; E. Arnold, 1984. xiii, 483 p.
85-124042          620.1/633          0713134682
*Metals -- Plastic properties.*

**TA460.M466 1984**
**Meyers, Marc A.**

Mechanical metallurgy : principles and applications / Marc Andre Meyers, Krishan Kumar Chawla. Englewood Cliffs, N.J. : Prentice-Hall, c1984. xxi, 761 p. :
83-000552          620.1/6          0135698634
*Metals -- Mechanical properties. Physical metallurgy.*

**TA460.W85 1999**
**Wulpi, Donald J.**

Understanding how components fail / Donald J. Wulpi. Materials Park, OH : ASM International, 1999. x, 293 p. :
99-040016          620.1/66          0871706318
*Metals -- Fracture.*

**TA461.C66 1997**

Concise metals engineering data book / editor, Joseph R. Davis. Materials Park, Ohio : ASM International, 1997. x, 245 p. :
          620.1/6 21          0871706067
*Metals -- Specifications -- Handbooks, manuals, etc. Metallurgy – Handbooks, manuals, etc.*

**TA462.T26 1998**
**Talbot, David**

Corrosion science and technology / David Talbot, James Talbot. Boca Raton : CRC Press, c1998. 406 p. :
98-104734          620.1/1223          0849382246
*Corrosion and anti-corrosives.*

**TA479.S7.S677 1994**

Stainless steels / edited by J.R. Davis. Materials Park, Ohio : ASM International, c1994. v, 577 p. :
94-023392          620.1/7          0871705036
*Steel, Stainless.*

**TA480.M3.M32 1999**

Magnesium and magnesium alloys / edited by M. Avedesian and Hugh Baker. Materials Park, OH : ASM International, 1999. ix, 314 p. :
99-020208          669/.723          0871706571
*Magnesium -- Handbooks, manuals, etc. Magnesium alloys – Handbooks, manuals, etc.*

**TA480.N6**

Nickel, cobalt, and their alloys / edited by J.R. Davis ; prepared under the direction of the ASM International Handbook Committee. Materials Park, OH : ASM International, c2000. 442 p. :
00-059348          620.1/88          0871706857
*Nickel -- Handbooks, manuals, etc. Nickel alloys -- Handbooks, manuals, etc. Cobalt -- Handbooks, manuals, etc.*

**TA481.F87 1993**

Fundamentals of metal-matrix composites / edited by Subra Suresh, Andreas Mortensen, Alan Needleman. Boston : Butterworth-Heinemann, c1993. ix, 342 p. :
93-004727          620.1/6          0750693215
*Metallic composites.*

**TA483.A78 1997**

ASM ready reference : properties and units for engineering alloys / reviewed by the ASM International Materials Properties Database Committee. Materials Park, Ohio : ASM International, c1997. ix, 168 p. ;
97-013167          620.1/6/021          0871705850
*Alloys.*

**TA545.W77 1994**
**Wolf, Paul R.**
Elementary surveying / Paul R. Wolf, Russell C. Brinker. 9th ed. New York, NY : HarperCollins, c1994. xxiii, 760 p. :
526.9 20
*Surveying.*

## TA555 Surveying — Addresses, essays, lectures

**TA555.S87 1995**
The surveying handbook / edited by Russell C. Brinker and Roy Minnick. 2nd ed. New York : Chapman & Hall, c1995. xxxiii, 967 p.
526.9 20
*Surveying.*

## TA593.25 Surveying — Photography in surveying, aerial surveying, etc. — Handbooks, tables, etc.

**TA593.25.A48 1980**
**American Society of Photogrammetry.**
Manual of photogrammetry / editor-in-chief, Chester C. Slama, associate editors, Charles Theurer, Soren W. Henriksen. Falls Church, Va. : American Society of Photogrammetry, c1980. xv, 1056 p. :
80-021514          526.9/82          0937294012
*Photographic surveying -- Handbooks, manuals, etc. Photogrammetry -- Handbooks, manuals, etc.*

## TA633 Structural engineering (General) — General works — 1850-

**TA633.H36 1997**
Handbook of structural engineering / edited by W.F. Chen. Boca Raton, Fla. : CRC Press, c1997. 1 v. (various
97-000148          624.1          0849326745
*Structural engineering.*

## TA635 Structural engineering (General) — Pocketbooks, tables, etc.

**TA635.G3 1979**
**Gaylord, Edwin Henry.**
Structural engineering handbook / edited by Edwin H. Gaylord, Jr., Charles N. Gaylord. New York : McGraw-Hill, c1979. ca. 600 p. in
78-025705          624/.1
*Structural engineering -- Handbooks, manuals, etc.*

**TA635.S77 1997**
Structural engineering handbook / edited by Edwin H. Gaylord, Jr., Charles N. Gaylord, James E. Stallmeyer. 4th ed. New York : McGraw-Hill, c1997. 1 v. :
624.1 20
*Structural engineering -- Handbooks, manuals, etc.*

## TA645 Structural engineering (General) — Structural analysis. Theory of structures — General works

**TA645.H47 1999**
**Hibbeler, R. C.**
Structural analysis / Russell C. Hibbeler. 4th ed. Upper Saddler River, N.J. : Prentice Hall, c1999. xiv, 600 p. :
624.1/71 21
*Structural analysis (Engineering)*

**TA645.D95 1997**
**Dym, Clive L.**
Structural modeling and analysis / Clive L. Dym. Cambridge, U.K. ; Cambridge University Press, 1997. xviii, 261 p.
96-045567          624.1/7          0521495369
*Structural analysis (Engineering) Structural design.*

**TA645.Y36 1986**
**Yang, T. Y.**
Finite element structural analysis / T.Y. Yang. Englewood Cliffs, N.J. : Prentice-Hall, c1986. xiv, 543 p. :
85-012278          624.1/7          0133171167
*Structural analysis (Engineering) Finite element method.*

## TA646 Structural engineering (General) — Structural analysis. Theory of structures — General special

**TA646.C66 2001**
Concepts and applications of finite element analysis / Robert D. Cook . . . [et al.]. 4th ed. New York : Wiley, c2001. xvi, 719 p. :
624.1/71 21
*Structural analysis (Engineering) Finite element method.*

## TA648 Structural engineering (General) — Structural analysis. Theory of structures — Statistical loading conditions

**TA648.Z35 1998**
**Zalewski, Waclaw.**
Shaping structures : statics / Waclaw Zalewski and Edward Allen ; drawings by Joseph Iano. New York : Wiley, c1998. vii, 408 p. :
96-037609          624.1/71          0471169684
*Structural analysis (Engineering) Statics.*

## TA654-654.6 Structural engineering (General) — Structural analysis. Theory of structures — Dynamic loading conditions

**TA654.G34 1999**
**Gatti, Paolo L.,**
Applied structural and mechanical vibrations : theory, methods, and measuring instrumentation / Paolo L. Gatti and Vittorio Ferrari. New York, NY : E & FN Spon, 1999. xiv, 826 p. :
98-053028          620.3          0419227105
*Structural dynamics. Vibration. Vibration -- Measurement.*

**TA654.J66 1989**
**Jones, Norman,**
Structural impact / Norman Jones. Cambridge ; Cambridge University Press, 1989. xvi, 575 p. :
88-031794          624.1/71          0521301807
*Structural dynamics. Impact. Girders.*

**TA654.5.L58 1991**
**Liu, Henry.**
Wind engineering : a handbook for structural engineers / Henry Liu. Englewood Cliffs, N.J. : Prentice Hall, c1991. xiii, 209 p.
89-048279          624.1/75          0139602798
*Wind-pressure. Buildings -- Aerodynamics. Structural engineering.*

**TA654.5.S55 1996**
**Simiu, Emil.**
Wind effects on structures : fundamentals and applications to design / Emil Simiu, Robert H. Scanlan. New York : John Wiley, 1996. xiv, 688 p. :
96-005238          624.1/76          0471121576
*Wind-pressure. Buildings -- Aerodynamics. Wind resistant design.*

**TA654.6.C466 1995**
**Chopra, Anil K.**
Dynamics of structures : theory and applications to earthquake engineering / Anil K. Chopra. Englewood Cliffs, N.J. : Prentice Hall, c1995. xxviii, 729,
94-046527          624.1/762          0138552142
*Earthquake engineering. Structural dynamics.*

**TA654.6.D39 2002**
**Day, Robert W.**
Geotechnical earthquake engineering handbook / Robert W. Day. New York : McGraw-Hill, 2002. 1 v. :
          624.1/762 21          0071377824
*Earthquake engineering -- Handbooks, manuals, etc. Engineering geology -- Handbooks, manuals, etc.*

## TA656 Structural engineering (General) — Structural analysis. Theory of structures — Stability of structures. Structural failure

**TA656.B39 1991**
**Bazant, Z. P.**
Stability of structures : elastic, inelastic, fracture, and damage theories / Zdenek P. Bazant and Luigi Cedolin. New York : Oxford University Press, c1991. xxiv, 984 p.
90007291          624.1/7          0195055292
*Structural stability. Structural analysis (Engineering)*

## TA658 Structural engineering (General) — Structural design — General works

**TA658.S15 1996**
**Schueller, Wolfgang,**
The design of building structures / Wolfgang Schueller. Upper Saddle River, N.J. : Prentice Hall, c1996. xii, 868 p. :
95-013790          624.1/77          0133465608
*Structural design. Structural analysis (Engineering)*

## TA658.2 Structural engineering (General) — Structural design — General special

**TA658.2.R63 1996**
**Robbin, Tony.**
Engineering a new architecture / Tony Robbins ; foreword by Stuart Wrede. New Haven : Yale University Press, c1996. x, 138 p. :
95-036222          624.1/771          0300061161
*Structural design. Geodesic domes. Shells (Engineering)*

## TA658.44 Structural engineering (General) — Structural design — Structural design for dynamic loads

**TA658.44.A43 1999**
**Ambrose, James E.**
Design for earthquakes / James Ambrose, Dimitry Vergun. New York : John Wiley, c1999. xv, 363 p. :
98-029972          693.8/52          0471241881
*Earthquake resistant design.*

**TA658.44.K75 1993**
**Krinitzsky, E. L.**
Fundamentals of earthquake-resistant construction / Ellis L. Krinitzsky, James P. Gould, Peter H. Edinger. New York : Wiley, c1993. xxiii, 299 p.
92-020059          624.1/762          0471839817
*Earthquake resistant design.*

**TA658.44.P46 1997**
**Penelis, George G.**
Earthquake-resistant concrete structures / George G. Penelis and Andreas J. Kappos ; with a foreword by P.E. Pinto. London ; E & FN Spon, 1997. xx, 572 p. :
96-070571          624.1/762          0419187200
*Earthquake resistant design. Reinforced concrete construction.*

## TA660 Structural engineering (General) — Specific structural forms, analysis, and design, A-Z

**TA660.S5.G644 1999**
**Gould, Phillip L.**
Analysis of shells and plates / Phillip L. Gould. Upper Saddle River, N.J. : Prentice Hall, c1999. xiv, 496 p. :
98-016289          624.1/776          0133749509
*Shells (Engineering) Plates (Engineering)*

**TA660.S5.L457 1998**
**Libai, A.**
The nonlinear theory of elastic shells / A. Libai, J.G. Simmonds. Cambridge ; Cambridge University Press, 1998. xvi, 542 p. :
97-013643          624.1/7762          0521472369
*Shells (Engineering) Elasticity. Nonlinear theories.*

## TA682-683.9 Structural engineering (General) — Design and construction in special materials — Masonry construction

**TA682.H36 1985**
Handbook of concrete engineering / edited by Mark Fintel. New York : Van Nostrand Reinhold, c1985. xiv, 892 p. :
84-007359          624.1/834          0442226233
*Concrete construction -- Handbooks, manuals, etc.*

**TA683.2.W3 1998**
**Wang, Chu-Kia,**
Reinforced concrete design / Chu-Kia Wang, Charles G. Salmon. 6th ed. Menlo Park, Calif. : Addison-Wesley, 1917- xii, 1028 p. :
                   624.1/8341 21
*Reinforced concrete construction.*

**TA683.9.L5 1981**
**Lin, T. Y.**
Design of prestressed concrete structures / T. Y. Lin, Ned H. Burns. New York : Wiley, c1981. vii, 646 p. :
80-020619          693/.542          0471018988
*Prestressed concrete construction.*

## TA684-690 Structural engineering (General) — Design and construction in special materials — Metal construction

**TA684.S79 1999**
Structural steel designer's handbook / roger L. Brockenbrough, editor, Frederick S. Merritt, editor. 3rd ed. New York : McGraw-Hill, c1999. 1 v. :
                   624.1/821 21
*Building, Iron and steel. Steel, Structural.*

**TA690.S44 1993**
**Sharp, Maurice L.**
Behavior and design of aluminum structures / Maurice L. Sharp. New York : McGraw-Hill, c1993. xi, 309 p. :
92-022257          624.1/826          0070564787
*Aluminum construction. Structural design.*

## TA705 Engineering geology — General works

**TA705.B328 1993**
**Bell, F. G.**
Engineering geology / Fred G. Bell. Oxford [England] ; Blackwell Scientific Publications, 1993. vii, 359 p. :
93-007269          624.1/51          0632032146
*Engineering geology.*

**TA705.D3 1996**
**Davis, R. O.**
Elasticity and geomechanics / R.O. Davis, A.P.S. Selvadurai. Cambridge ; Cambridge University Press, 1996. xi, 201 p. :
95-017507          624.1/51          0521495067
*Engineering geology -- Mathematics. Elasticity.*

**TA705.H86 1984**
**Hunt, Roy E.**
Geotechnical engineering investigation manual / Roy E. Hunt. New York : McGraw-Hill, c1984. xiii, 983 p.
82-022886          624.1/51          0070313091
*Engineering geology -- Handbooks, manuals, etc.*

**TA705.L4 1988**
**Legget, Robert Ferguson.**
Geology and engineering / Robert F. Legget, Allen W. Hatheway. 3rd ed. New York : McGraw-Hill, c1988. xviii, 613 p. :
                   624.1/5 19
*Engineering geology.*

**TA705.S515 1997**
**Sharma, P. Vallabh.**
Environmental and engineering geophysics / Prem V. Sharma. Cambridge, U.K. ; Cambridge University Press, 1997. xxiv, 475 p.
96-037797          624.1/51          0521572401
*Engineering geology. Environmental geotechnology.*

## TA705.2 Engineering geology — By region or country

**TA705.2.W47 1990**
**West, Graham.**
The field description of engineering soils and rocks / Graham West. Milton Keynes [England] ; Open University Press, 1991. ix, 129 p. :
91-008598          624.1/51          0335152082
*Engineering geology. Soils -- Classification. Rocks -- Classification.*

# TA706 Rock mechanics

**TA706.G644 1993**
**Goodman, Richard E.**
Engineering geology : rock in engineering construction / Richard E. Goodman. New York : J. Wiley, c1993. xviii, 412 p.
92-026854          624.1/51          0471544248
*Rock mechanics. Engineering geology.*

## TA710 Soil mechanics — General works

**TA710.C393 1995**
**Cernica, John N.**
Geotechnical engineering. Soil Mechanics / John N. Cernica. New York : Wiley, c1995. xv, 453 p. :
          624.1/5136 20
*Soil mechanics.*

**TA710.C5185 2000**
**Chen, F. H.**
Soil engineering : testing, design, and remediation / Fu Hua Chen ; edited by M.D. Morris. Boca Raton : CRC Press, 2000. 288 p. :
99-023653          624.1/51          0849322944
*Soil mechanics. Engineering geology. Foundations.*

**TA710.D264 2002**
**Das, Braja M.,**
Principles of geotechnical engineering / Braja M. Das. 5th ed. Pacific Grove, CA : Brooks Cole/Thompson Learning, c2002. xv, 589 p. :
          624.1/5136 21          053438742X
*Soil mechanics. Engineering geology.*

**TA710.G6286 1996**
**Gray, Donald H.**
Biotechnical and soil bioengineering slope stabilization : a practical guide for erosion control / Donald H. Gray, Robbin B. Sotir. New York : John Wiley & Sons, c1996. xvii, 378 p.
96-010211          624.1/51363          0471049786
*Slopes (Soil mechanics) Soil stabilization. Soil erosion.*

**TA710.H34 1990**
**Hausmann, Manfred R.**
Engineering principles of ground modification / Manfred R. Hausmann. New York : McGraw-Hill, c1990. xxiii, 632 p.
89-002321          624.1/5136          0070272794
*Soil stabilization. Soil mechanics.*

**TA710.I73 1996**
**Ishihara, Kenji.**
Soil behaviour in earthquake geotechnics / Kenji Ishihara. Oxford : Clarendon Press ; 1996. x, 350 p. :
95-042038          624.1/762          0198562241
*Soil dynamics. Earthquake engineering.*

**TA710.T39 1996**
**Terzaghi, Karl,**
Soil mechanics in engineering practice / Karl Terzaghi, Ralph B. Peck, Gholamreza Mesri. New York : Wiley, c1996. xxx, 549 p. :
95-006616          624.1/5136          0471086584
*Soil mechanics.*

## TA710.5 Soil mechanics — Laboratory manuals. Testing of soils. Measurements

**TA710.5.H4 1994**
**Head, K. H.**
Manual of soil laboratory testing / K. H. Head. 2nd ed. London : Pentech Press, 1994. v. 2 :
          624.1/51 20
*Soils -- Testing -- Laboratory manuals.*

## TA711.5 Soil mechanics — Soil dynamics — Soil-structure interaction

**TA711.5.N5 1992**
**Nelson, John D.**
Expansive soils : problems and practice in foundation and pavement engineering / John D. Nelson, Debora J. Miller. New York : J. Wiley, c1992. xxii, 259 p.
91-042720          624.1/5136          0471511862
*Soil-structure interaction. Swelling soils. Foundations.*

## TA730 Earthwork — Excavations — General works

**TA730.C48**
**Church, Horace K.**
Excavation handbook / Horace K. Church. New York : McGraw-Hill, c1981. ca. 1000 p. i
80-019630          624.1/52          0070108404
*Excavation. Engineering geology.*

## TA749 Earthwork — Soil stabilization

**TA749.F67 2001**
**Forrester, Kevin,**
Subsurface drainage for slope stabilization / Kevin Forrester. Reston, Va. : ASCE Press, c2001. xiii, 208 p.
00-048522          624.1/51363          0784400164
*Soil stabilization. Slopes (Soil mechanics) Subsurface drainage.*

## TA775 Foundations — General works

**TA775.B63 1982**
**Bowles, Joseph E.**
Foundation analysis and design / Joseph E. Bowles. New York : McGraw-Hill, c1982. xiv, 816 p. :
81-013649          624.1/5          0070067708
*Foundations. Soil mechanics.*

**TA775.D227 1999**
**Das, Braja M.**
  Principles of foundation engineering Braja M. Das. 4th ed. Pacific Grove, Calif. PWS Pb. c1999. xvii, 862 p.
          624.1/5 21
*Includes bibliographical references and index. Foundations.*

**TA775.F675 1991**
  Foundation engineering handbook / edited by Hsai-Yang Fang 2nd ed. New York : Van Nostrand Reinhold, c1991. xvii, 923 p. :
          324.1/5 20
*Foundations -- Handbooks, manuals, etc. Soil mechanics -- Handbooks, manuals, etc.*

## TA1015 Transportation engineering — Dictionaries and encyclopedias

**TA1015.L39 1992**
**Lay, M. G.**
  Ways of the world : a history of the world's roads and of the vehicles that used them / M.G. Lay. New Brunswick, N.J. : Rutgers University Press, 1992. xix, 401 p. :
91-023148          629.04/9          0813517583
*Transportation -- History. Roads -- History. Vehicles -- History. Bridges -- History.*

## TA1145 Transportation engineering — General works

**TA1145.C58 1991**
  Concise encyclopedia of traffic & transportation systems / editor, Markos Papageorgiou. Oxford, England ; Pergamon Press, 1991. xviii, 658 p.
90-022479          388/.03          0080362036
*Transportation. Transportation engineering. Traffic engineering.*

**TA1145.K48 1990**
**Khisty, C. Jotin,**
  Transportation engineering : an introduction / C. Jotin Khisty. Englewood Cliffs, N.J. : Prentice Hall, c1990. xxi, 673 p. :
89-016323          388          0139292748
*Transportation engineering.*

**TA1145.P34 1982**
**Paquette, Radnor Joseph.**
  Transportation engineering : planning and design / Radnor J. Paquette, Norman J. Ashford, Paul H. Wright. New York : Wiley, c1982. vii, 679 p. :
81-011700          629.04          047104878X
*Transportation engineering. Civil engineering.*

## TA1509 Applied optics. Photonics — Dictionaries and encyclopedias

**TA1509.G76 1998**
**Grotta, Daniel,**
  The illustrated digital imaging dictionary / Daniel Grotta & Sally Wiener Grotta. New York : McGraw Hill, c1998. xii, 364 p. :
          621.36/7/03 21          0070250693
*Image processing -- Digital techniques -- Dictionaries. Computer graphics -- Dictionaries. Photography -- Digital techniques -- Dictionaries. Computer art -- Dictionaries.*

**TA1509.E53 1991**
  Encyclopedia of lasers and optical technology / Robert A. Meyers, editor. San Diego : Academic Press, c1991. xii, 764 p. :
90-039014          621.36/03          0122266935
*Optics -- Encyclopedias. Lasers -- Encyclopedias.*

## TA1540 Applied optics. Photonics — General works

**TA1540.S36 1988**
**Saxby, Graham.**
  Practical holography / Graham Saxby. New York : Prentice Hall, 1988. xix, 488 p.,
87-012649          774          0136937977
*Holography.*

## TA1632 Applied optics. Photonics — Optical data — General special

**TA1632.S33 1993**
**Schreiber, William F.**
  Fundamentals of electronic imaging systems : some aspects of image processing / William F. Schreiber. 3rd ed. Berlin ; New York : Springer-Verlag, c1993.
          621.36/7 20
*Image processing. Imaging systems.*

**TA1632.B35 1991**
**Banks, Stephen P.,**
  Signal processing, image processing, and pattern recognition / Stephen Banks. New York : Prentice Hall, 1990. xiv, 410 p. :
90-007559          621.36/7          0138125872
*Image processing -- Digital techniques. Pattern recognition systems.*

**TA1632.F38 1993**
**Faugeras, Olivier,**
  Three-dimensional computer vision : a geometric viewpoint / Olivier Faugeras. Cambridge, Mass. : MIT Press, c1993. xxxii, 663 p.
93-009126          006.3/7          0262061589
*Computer vision.*

**TA1632.G735 1990**
**Grimson, William Eric Leifur.**
  Object recognition by computer : the role of geometric constraints / W. Eric L Grimson ; with contributions from Tomas Lozano-Perez, Daniel P. Huttenlocher. Cambridge, Mass. : MIT Press, c1990. xv, 512 p. :
90-013547        621.36/7        0262071304
*Image processing -- Digital techniques.*

**TA1632.V28 1992**
**VanderLugt, Anthony,**
  Optical signal processing / Anthony VanderLugt. New York : Wiley, c1992. xxi, 604 p. :
91-023378        621.36/7        0471546828
*Optical data processing. Signal processing.*

## TA1634 Applied optics. Photonics — Optical data — Computer vision

**TA1634.R58 2001**
**Ritter, G. X.**
  Handbook of computer vision algorithms in image algebra / Gerhard X. Ritter, Joseph N. Wilson. 2nd ed. Boca Raton : CRC Press, c2001. 417 p. :
        006.4/2 21
*Computer vision -- Mathematics. Image porcessing -- Mathematics. Computer algorithms.*

**TA1634.G73 1995**
**Granlund, Gosta H.**
  Signal processing for computer vision / by Gosta H. Granlund and Hans Knutsson. Dordrecht ; Kluwer Academic Publishers, c1995. xii, 437 p. :
94-039290        006.4/2        0792395301
*Computer vision. Signal processing -- Digital techniques.*

**TA1634.R58 1996**
**Ritter, G. X.**
  Handbook of computer vision algorithms in image algebra / Gerhard X. Ritter, Joseph N. Wilson. Boca Raton : CRC Press, c1996. xxii, 360 p.
96-015209        006.4/2        0849326362
*Computer vision -- Mathematics. Image processing -- Mathematics. Computer algorithms.*

## TA1637 Applied optics — Optical data processing — Image processing

**TA1637.H36 2000**
  Handbook of image and video processing / editor, Al Bovik. San Diego : Academic Press, c2000. xv, 891 p. :
        621.36/7 21        0121197905
*Image processing -- Digital techniques -- Handbooks, manuals, etc. Video compression -- Handbooks, manuals, etc.*

**TA1637.R87 1999**
**Russ, John C.**
  The image processing handbook / John C. Russ. 3rd ed. Boca Raton, FL : CRC Press, c1999. 771 p. :
        621.36/7 21
*Image procecessing.*

**TA1637.D54 1993**
  Digital images and human vision / edited by Andrew B. Watson. Cambridge, Mass. : MIT Press, c1993. x, 224 p. :
93-019697        621.36/7        0262231719
*Image processing -- Digital techniques. Coding theory. Data compression (Telecommunication)*
*Data compression (Telecommunication)*
*Vision.*

**TA1637.L8 1997**
**Lu, Ning,**
  Fractal imaging / Ning Lu. San Diego : Academic Press, 1997. xix, 412 p. :
97-006616        621.36/7        0124580106
*Image processing -- Digital techniques. Fractals. Image compression.*

## TA1675 Applied optics — Lasers and laser applications — General works

**TA1675.V47 1995**
**Verdeyen, Joseph Thomas**
  Laser electronics / Joseph T. Verdeyen. Englewood Cliffs, N.J. : Prentice Hall, c1995. xxvi, 778 p. :
        621.36/61 20
*Lasers. Semiconductor lasers.*

**TA1675.S5 1986**
**Siegman, A. E.**
  Lasers / Anthony E. Siegman. Mill Valley, Calif. : University Science Books, c1986. xxii, 1283 p.
86-050346        621.36/6        0935702115
*Lasers.*

## TA1677 Applied optics — Lasers and laser applications — General special

**TA1677.R4 1997**
**Ready, John F.**
  Industrial applications of lasers / John F. Ready. 2nd ed. San Diego : Academic Press, c1997. xxi, 599 p. :
        621.36/6 21
*Lasers -- Industrial applications.*

**TA1677.D37 1991**
**Das, Pankaj K.,**
  Lasers and optical engineering / P. Das. New York : Springer-Verlag, c1991. xxii, 470 p.
89-026312        621.36/6        0387971084
*Lasers.*

## TA1683 Applied optics — Lasers and laser applications — Handbooks, tables, etc.

**TA1683.W44 2001**
**Weber, Marvin J.,**
  Handbook of lasers / Marvin J. Weber. Boca Raton : CRC Press, c2001. 1198 p. :
00-057894        621.36/6        0849335094
*Lasers -- Handbooks, manuals, etc.*

**TA1695 Applied optics — Lasers and laser applications — Gas lasers**

**TA1695.D845 1996**
**Duley, W. W.**
UV lasers : effects and applications in materials science / W.W. Duley. Cambridge ; Cambridge University Press, 1996. xi, 407 p. :
96-013553          620.1/1228          0521464986
*Gas lasers -- Industrial applications. Ultraviolet radiation -- Industrial applicaitons. Materials -- Effect of radiation on.*

**TA1705.K63 1999**
**Koechner, Walter**
Solid-state laser engineering / Walter Koechner. 5th rev. and updated ed. Berlin ; New York : Springer, 1999. xi, 746 p. :
          621.36/61 21
*Solid-state lasers.*

**TA1750 Applied optics — Applied electrooptics. Electrooptical devices. — General works**

**TA1750.H63 2000**
**Hobbs, Philip C. D.**
Building electro-optical systems : making it all work / Philip C.D. Hobbs. New York : Wiley, 2000. p. cm.
99-028956          621.381/045          0471246816
*Electrooptical devices -- Design and construction.*

**TA1800 Applied optics — General works**

**TA1800.H42 1999**
**Hecht, Jeff.**
City of light : the story of fiber optics / Jeff Hecht. New York : Oxford University Press, 1999. xii, 316 p. :
98-006135          621.36/92          0195108183

# TC Hydraulic engineering

## TC18 History and description — Modern

**TC18.W38 1990**
Water, engineering, and landscape : water control and landscape transformation in the modern period / edited by Denis Cosgrove and Geoff Petts. London ; Belhaven Press, 1990. xiv, 214 p. :
90-041792          627/.09          1852930691
*Hydraulic engineering -- History. Land use -- History.*

## TC145 General works — 1800-

**TC145.L55 1979**
**Linsley, Ray K.**
Water-resources engineering / Ray K. Linsley, Joseph B. Franzini. New York : McGraw-Hill, c1979. xii, 716 p. :
78-004498          627          0070379653
*Hydraulic engineering. Water resources development.*

**TC160 Technical hydraulics — General works**

**TC160.K38 1998**
**Kay, Melvyn.**
Practical hydraulics / Melvyn Kay. London ; E & FN Spon, 1998. xv, 253 p. :
98-030901          627          0419242309
*Hydraulics.*

**TC172 Technical hydraulics — Hydronamics (Water in motion) — Water waves**

**TC172.S64 1993**
**Sorensen, Robert M.,**
Basic wave mechanics : for coastal and ocean engineers / Robert M. Sorensen. New York : Wiley, c1993. xviii, 284 p.
93-013309          627/.042          0471551651
*Ocean waves. Wave mechanics.*

**TC175.2.C47313 1999**
**Chien, Ning,**
Mechanics of sediment transport / by Ning Chien, Zhaohui Wan ; translated under the guidance of John S. McNown. Reston, Va. : American Society of Civil Engineers, c1999. xix, 913 p. :
98-044496          627/.122          0784404003
*Sediment transport.*

**TC175.2.T87 1993**
Turbulence : perspectives on flow and sediment transport / edited by N.J. Clifford, J.R. French, and J. Hardisty. Chichester ; Wiley, c1993. x, 360 p. :
93-003142          551.3/53          0471939005
*Sediment transport. Boundary layer (Meteorology) Turbulence.*

**TC176 Technical hydraulics — Hydronamics (Water in motion) — Underground flow**

**TC176.C43 2000**
**Charbeneau, Randall J.**
Groundwater hydraulics and pollutant transport / Randall J. Charbeneau. Upper Saddle River, NJ : Prentice Hall, 2000. p. cm.
99-038307          628.1/68          0139756167
*Groundwater flow. Water -- Pollution -- Mathematical models.*

**TC176.H35 1999**
The handbook of groundwater engineering / editor-in chief, Jacques W. Delleur. Boca Raton, Fla. : CRC Press, c1999. 1 v. (various
97-046941          628.1/14          0849326982
*Groundwater flow. Groundwater -- Pollution. Groundwater – Management.*

**TC176.Z55 1993**
**Zijl, Wouter.**
  Natural groundwater flow / Wouter Zijl, Marek Nawalany. Boca Raton : Lewis Publishers, c1993. viii, 321 p.
92-035372         551.49         0873718682
  *Groundwater flow.*

## TC330 Coast protective works — General works

**TC330.H36 1990**
  Handbook of coastal and ocean engineering / John B. Herbich, editor, in collaboration with C.L. Bretschneider ... [et al.]. Houston : Gulf Pub. Co., 1990-c1992. 3 v. :
89-025858         620/.4146         0872014649
  *Coastal engineering -- Handbooks, manuals, etc. Ocean engineering -- Handbooks, manuals, etc.*

## TC409 River, lake, and water-supply engineering (General) — General special

**TC409.H93 1997**
  Hydrology and the management of watersheds / Kenneth N. Brooks ... [et al.]. Ames, Iowa : Iowa State University Press, 1997. xiii, 502 p.
97-000319         627         0813822874
  *Watershed management. Watershed management -- Economic aspects. Watershed management -- Social aspects.*

## TC423.6 River, lake, and water-supply engineering (General) — History and country divisions — United States

**TC423.6.G55 1997**
**Gillilan, David M.,**
  Instream flow protection : seeking a balance in Western water use / David M. Gillilan and Thomas C. Brown. Washington, D.C. : Island Press, c1997. x, 417 p. :
96-052477         333.91/00978         1559635231
  *Rivers -- West (U.S.) -- Regulation. Streamflow -- West (U.S.) Water use -- West (U.S.)*

## TC530 River protective works. Regulation. Flood control. — General works

**TC530.F32 1996**
**Faber, Scott.**
  On borrowed land : public policies for floodplains / by Scott Faber. Cambridge, MA (113 Brattle St., Cambridge 02138-Lincoln Institute of Land Policy, c1996. 32 p. :
97-140776
  *Floodplain management -- Mississippi River Watershed. Flood damage prevention -- Mississippi River Watershed. Floodplain management -- United States.*

**TC540.F45 1992**
**Fell, Robin.**
  Geotechnical engineering of embankment dams.     A.A. Balkema, : Rotterdam : 1992. ix, 675 p.
                  9054101288
  *Earth dams- -- Design and construction. Tailings dams -- Design and construction.*

## TC547 Dams. Barrages — Dam types — Masonry dams

**TC547.E234 1990**
  Earthquake engineering for concrete dams : design, performance, and research needs / Panel on Earthquake Engineering for Concrete Dams, Committee on Earthquake Engineering, Division of Natural Hazard Mitigation, Commission on Engineering and Technical Systems, National Research Council. Washington, D.C. : National Academy Press, 1990. viii, 143 p.
90-062816         627/.8         0309043360
  *Concrete dams -- Earthquake effects. Earthquake engineering. Earthquake hazard analysis.*

## TC557.5 Dams. Barrages — Special countries — By state, A-Z

**TC557.5.H6.S74 1988**
**Stevens, Joseph E.**
  Hoover Dam : an American adventure / Joseph E. Stevens. Norman : University of Oklahoma Press, c1988. ix, 326 p. :
87-040559         627/.82/0979159         0806121157
  *Hoover Dam (Ariz. and Nev.)*

# TC1645-1665 Ocean engineering

**TC1645.G39**
**Gaythwaite, John.**
  The marine environment and structural design / John Gathtwaithe. New York : Van Nostrand Reinhold Co., c1981. xvi, 313 p. :
80-029583         627         0442248342
  *Ocean engineering. Structural design.*

# TD Environmental Technology. Sanitary engineering

# TD9 Dictionaries and encyclopedias

**TD9.E5 1983**
  Encyclopedia of environmental science and engineering / [edited by] J.R. Pfafflin, E.N. Ziegler. New York : Gordon and Breach Science Publishers, c1983. 3 v. (xxiii,
83-016452         628.5         0677064306
  *Environmental engineering -- Dictionaries.*

**TD9.P36 2001**
**Pankratz, Tom M.**
Environmental engineering dictionary and directory / Thomas M. Pankratz. Boca Raton : Lewis, c2001. 328 p. ;
00-044356    628    1566705436
*Environmental engineering -- Dictionaries. Brand name products -- Dictionaries. Trademarks -- Dictionaries.*

## TD145 General works — 1850-

**TD145.E574 1997**
Environmental engineers' handbook / David H.F. Liu, second edition editor ; Bela G. Liptak, handbook editor ; Paul B. Bouis, special consultant. Boca Raton, Fla. : Lewis Publishers, c1997. xxii, 1431 p.
96-046781    628    0849399718
*Environmental engineering.*

**TD145.S72 1990**
Standard handbook of environmental engineering / [edited by] Robert A. Corbitt. New York : McGraw-Hill, c1990. xx, 1281 in v
89-012400    628    0070131589
*Environmental engineering.*

## TD153 General works — General special

**TD153.K44 1993**
Keeping pace with science and engineering : case studies in environmental regulation / Myron F. Uman, editor ; National Academy of Engineering. Washington, D.C. : National Academy Press, 1993. x, 281 p. :
93-005530    363.73/7    0309049385
*Environmental engineering -- Case studies.*

**TD153.V35 2000**
**Valsaraj, K. T.**
Elements of environmental engineering : thermodynamics and kinetics / Kalliat T. Valsaraj. Boca Raton : Lewis Publishers, c2000. 679 p. :
99-053965    628    1566703972
*Environmental engineering. Thermodynamics. Chemical reactions.*

## TD170 Environmental protection — General works

**TD170.C55 1992**
**Chiras, Daniel D.**
Lessons from nature : learning to live sustainably on the earth / Daniel D. Chiras. Washington, D.C. : Island Press, c1992. xiv, 289 p. :
91-039156    304.2    1559631074
*Environmental protection. Human ecology.*

**TD170.D37 2001**
**Darst, Robert G.**
Smokestack diplomacy : cooperation and conflict in East-West environmental politics / Robert G. Darst. Cambridge, Mass. : MIT Press, c2001. xii, 300 p. ;
00-056240    363.7/0526    0262041839
*Environmental protection -- International cooperation -- Case studies. Environmental policy -- International cooperation -- Case studies. Marine pollution -- Baltic Sea -- Case studies.*

**TD170.R83 1992**
**Ryding, Sven-Olof.**
Environmental management handbook / written and edited by Sven-Olof Ryding. Amsterdam : IOS Press ; 1992. xx, 777 p. :
91-043222    363.7    9051990626
*Environmental protection. Environmental management.*

## TD170.2 Environmental protection — General special

**TD170.2.I556 1993**
Institutions for the earth : sources of effective international environmental protection / edited by Peter M. Haas, Robert O. Keohane, and Marc A. Levy. Cambridge, Mass. : MIT Press, c1993. xi, 448 p. ;
92-034908    363.7/0526    0262082187
*Environmental protection -- International cooperation. International agencies.*

## TD171 Environmental protection — Special regions or countries — United States

**TD171.L36 1990**
**Landy, Marc Karnis.**
The Environmental Protection Agency : asking the wrong questions / Marc K. Landy, Marc J. Roberts, Stephen R. Thomas ; foreword by Morris K. Udall. New York : Oxford University Press, 1990. xiv, 309 p. ;
89-025565    363.7/00973    0195050215

## TD171.7 Environmental protection — Special regions or countries —Citizen participation

**TD171.7.G56 1990**
The Global ecology handbook : what you can do about the environmental crisis / the Global Tomorrow Coalition ; edited by Walter H. Corson. Boston : Beacon Press, c1990. xvii, 414 p.
88-043318    363.7/025    0807085006
*Environmental protection -- Citizen participation.*

## TD173 Environmental pollution — Dictionaries and encyclopedias

**TD173.E53 1999**
Encyclopedia of environmental pollution and cleanup / Robert A. Meyers, editor in chief ; Diane Kender Dittrick, editor. New York : Wiley, c1999- 2 v. :
99017884          628.5          0471316121
*Pollution -- Encyclopedias. Environmental protection -- Encyclopedias. Hazardous wastes -- Encyclopedias.*

## TD174 Environmental pollution — General works

**TD174.H55 1997**
**Hill, Marquita K.**
Understanding environmental pollution / Marquita K. Hill. Cambridge ; Cambridge University Press, 1997. xvi, 316 p. :
96-052929          363.73          0521562104
*Pollution. Pollutants.*

## TD180 Environmental pollution — Special countries — United States

**TD180.D39 1998**
**Davies, J. Clarence.**
Pollution control in the United States : evaluating the system / J. Clarence Davies and Jan Mazurek. Washington, DC : Resources for the Future, c1998. xiii, 319 p.
97-049246          091570787X
*Pollution -- United States -- Evaluation. Pollution – Government policy -- United States -- Evaluation. Pollution -- Law and legislation -- United States.*

## TD191.5 Environmental pollution — Special countries — Developing countries

**TD191.5.C48 1993**
**Cheremisinoff, Nicholas P.**
Carbon adsorption for pollution control / Nicholas P. Cheremisinoff, Paul N. Cheremisinoff. Englewood Cliffs, N.J. : PTR Prentice Hall, c1993. xvi, 276 p. :
92-023500          628.5          0133933318
*Pollution. Carbon, Activated.*

**TD191.5.H65 1993**
**Holmes, Gwendolyn,**
Handbook of environmental management and technology / Gwendolyn Holmes, Ben Ramnarine Singh, Louis Theodore. New York : Wiley, c1993. x, 651 p. :
92035451          628          047158584X
*Pollution. Environmental engineering.*

## TD192.5 Environmental pollution — Pollution control methods — Biological treatment

**TD192.5.A43 1994**
**Alexander, Martin,**
Biodegradation and bioremediation / Martin Alexander. San Diego : Academic Press, c1994. xii, 302 p. :
93-037670          628.5/2          012049860X
*Bioremediation.*

**TD192.5.C66 1995**
**Cookson, John T.**
Bioremediation engineering : design and application / John T. Cookson, Jr. New York : McGraw-Hill, c1995. xv, 524 p. :
94-026856          628.5/2          0070126143
*Bioremediation.*

**TD192.5.K56 1998**
**King, R. Barry.**
Practical environmental bioremediation : the field guide / R. Barry King, Gilbert M. Long, John K. Sheldon. Boca Raton : Lewis Publishers, c1998. 184 p. :
97-037142          628.5          1566702089
*Bioremediation -- Handbooks, manuals, etc.*

## TD192.8 Environmental pollution — Pollution control methods — In situ remediation

**TD192.8.I5724 1996**
In situ treatment technology / Evan K. Nyer ... [et al.]. Boca Raton, Fla. : Lewis Publishers, c1996. 329 p. :
95-049907          628.5/2          0873719956
*In situ remediation.*

## TD193 Environmental pollution — Measurement of pollution. Sampling and analysis. Environmental chemistry — General works

**TD193.B37 1997**
**Connell, D. W.**
Basic concepts of environmental chemistry / Des W. Connell. Boca Raton, Fl. : Lewis Pub., 1997. 506 p. :
97007698          628.5          0873719980
*Environmental chemistry.*

**TD193.K45 1991**
**Keith, Lawrence H.,**
Environmental sampling and analysis : a practical guide / by Lawrence H. Keith. Chelsea, Mich. : Lewis Publishers, c1991. 143 p. :
90-026006          628.5/028/7          0873713818
*Environmental monitoring. Environmental chemistry.*

**TD193.P38 1997**
**Patnaik, Pradyot.**
Handbook of environmental analysis : chemical pollutants in air, water, soil, and solid wastes / Pradyot Patnaik. Boca Raton : CRC/Lewis Publishers, c1997. 584 p. :
96-032647          628.5/2          0873719891
*Pollutants -- Analysis.*

**TD193.Y46 1999 vol. B**
**Yen, Teh Fu,**
Chemical principles for environmental processes / Teh Fu Yen. Upper Saddle River, N.J. : Prentice Hall PTR, c1999. xxiv, [763]-1
98-040861          540          0139723250
*Environmental chemistry.*

## TD194 Environmental effects of industries and plants — General works

**TD194.F74 1995**
Industrial pollution prevention handbook / [edited by] Harry M. Freeman. New York : McGraw-Hill, c1995. xxv, 935 p. :
95007979          363.73/1          0070221480
*Industries -- Environmental aspects. Pollution prevention.*

## TD195-195.5 Environmental effects of industries and plants — Special industries, facilities, activities, etc., A-Z

**TD195.B56.B58 1996**
Biomass burning and global change / edited by Joel S. Levine. Cambridge, Mass. : MIT Press, 1996. 2 v. :
96-035030          628.5/3          0262122014
*Burning of land -- Environmental aspects. Fuelwood – Burning – Environmental aspects. Climatic changes.*

**TD195.C5.R36 1997**
**Ramamoorthy, S.**
Chlorinated organic compounds in the environment : regulatory and monitoring assessment / Sub Ramamoorthy, Sita Ramamoorthy. Boca Raton, FL : Lewis Publishers, c1997. 370 p. :
97-006799          363.738/4          1566700418
*Organochlorine compounds -- Environmental aspects -- Handbooks, manuals, etc.*

**TD195.E49.A44 1995**
Alternative fuels and the environment / edited by Frances S. Sterrett. Boca Raton : Lewis Publishers, c1995. 276 p. :
94-025419          621.042          0873719786
*Energy development -- Environmental aspects.*

**TD195.M5.R559 1996**
**Ripley, Earle A.,**
Environmental effects of mining / Earle A. Ripley, Robert E. Redmann, Adele A. Crowder with Tara C. Ariano ... [et al.]. Delray Beach, Fla. : St. Lucie Press, c1996. viii, 356 p.
95-210701          363.73/1          188401576X
*Mineral industries -- Environmental aspects -- Canada. Industrial management -- Environmental aspects.*

**TD195.P26.P335 1993**
Packaging in the environment / edited by Geoffrey M. Levy. London ; Blackie Academic & Professional, 1993. xiv, 273 p. :
93-135423          363.72/88          0751400912
*Packaging waste -- Environmental aspects. Product life cycle. Refuse and refuse disposal.*

**TD195.P4.C63 1991**
**Coates, Peter A.,**
The Trans-Alaska Pipeline controversy : technology, conservation, and the frontier / Peter A. Coates. Bethlehem [Pa.] : Lehigh University Press ; c1991. 447 p. :
89-045420          333.8/2314/09798
0934223106
*Petroleum pipelines -- Environmental aspects -- Alaska. Environmentalists -- United States -- Attitudes. Conservationists – United States -- Attitudes. Trans-Alaska Pipeline (Alaska) Trans-Alaska Pipeline (Alaska) -- Public opinion. Alaska – History – 1867-1959.*

**TD195.R33.C37 1994**
**Carpenter, T. G.**
The environmental impact of railways / T.G. Carpenter. Chichester ; J. Wiley, 1994. viii, 385 p.
93-046722          363.73/1          0471948284
*Railroads -- Environmental aspects. Railroads -- Planning.*

**TD195.5.F67 1993**
**Forster, Bruce A.**
The acid rain debate : science and special interests in policy formation / Bruce A. Forster. Ames : Iowa State University Press, 1993. x, 166 p. :
92-047434          363.73/86          081381684X
*Acid rain -- Environmental aspects -- United States. Acid rain – Government policy -- United States.*

## TD196 A-Z Special environmental pollutants — Other environmental pollutants

**TD196.C45.C483 1994**
Chemical safety : international reference manual / edited by Mervyn Richardson. Weinheim ; VCH, c1994. xvii, 613 p.
94-007950          363.73/8          3527286306
*Pollution -- Environmental aspects. Pollution -- Risk assessment. Chemicals -- Safety measures.*

**TD196.C45.P73 1995**
**Prager, Jan C.**
Environmental contaminant reference databook / Jan C. Prager. New York : Van Nostrand Reinhold, 1995-c1997. 3 v. ;
94-043927          363.73/8          0442019181
*Pollutants -- Handbooks, manuals, etc.*

**TD196.C45E38 2000**
**Eisler, Ronald,**
Handbook of chemical risk assessment / Ronald Eisler. Boca Raton, FL : Lewis Publishers, 2000. 3 v. :
          363.17/9 21          1566705061
*Pollutants -- Handbooks, manuals, etc. Hazardous substances – Risk assessment -- Handbooks, manuals, etc. Environmental chemistry – Handbooks, manuals, etc. Environmental risk assessment -- Handbooks, manuals, etc.*

## TD196.H43.T49 1995
**Thayer, John S.**

Environmental chemistry of the heavy elements : hydrido and organo compounds / John S. Thayer. New York, N.Y. : VCH, c1995. xi, 145 p. :

94-041541      628.5/2      156081540X

*Heavy elements -- Environmental aspects. Hydrides -- Environmental aspects. Organometallic compounds – Environmental aspects.*

## TD196.O73.H35 1996

Handbook of environmental data on organic chemicals / Karel Verschueren. New York : Van Nostrand Reinhold, c1996. vi, 2064 p. :

96-004807      363.73/8      0442019165

*Organic compounds -- Environmental aspects -- Handbooks, manuals, etc.*

## TD196.O73.N49 1995
**Ney, Ronald E.,**

Fate and transport of organic chemicals in the environment : a practical guide / Ronald E. Ney. Rockville, Md. : Government Institutes, c1995. vii, 302 p. :

95-031004      628.5/2      0865874700

*Organic compounds -- Environmental aspects. Pollution – Risk assessment.*

## TD196.P38.P48 1992

Pesticide waste management : technology and regulation / John Bourke, editor ... [et al.]. Washington, DC : American Chemical Society, 1992. xii, 273 p. :

92-032304      363.17/925/0973      0841224803

*Pesticides -- Environmental aspects. Pesticide waste -- Management. Pesticides -- Law and legislation -- United States.*

## TD196.R3.E597 1997
**Eisenbud, Merril.**

Environmental radioactivity : from natural, industrial, and military sources / Merril Eisenbud, Thomas Gesell. San Diego : Academic Press, 1997. xxv, 656 p. :

96-041834      363.1/79      0122351541

*Radioactive pollution.*

## TD196.T45.T43 1998

Thallium in the environment / edited by Jerome O. Nriagu. New York : Wiley, c1998. xiv, 284 p. :

97-014871      363.738      0471177555

*Thallium -- Environmental aspects.*

## TD223-257 Water supply for domestic and industrial purpoases — Country subdivisions including all local or departmental reports

## TD223.G46 1992
**Gilbert, Charles E.**

Regulating drinking water quality / edited by Charles E. Gilbert, Edward J. Calabrese. Boca Raton : Lewis, c1992. xvi, 328 p. :

91-021670      363.6/1      0873715950

*Drinking water -- United States. Water quality management – United States. Drinking water -- United States -- Contamination.*

## TD223.H27 1986

Handbook of public water systems / Culp/Wesner/Culp ; edited by Robert B. Williams, Gordon L. Culp. New York : Van Nostrand Reinhold, c1986. xiv, 1113 p.

85-026458      628.1      0442215975

*Municipal water supply -- United States. Water quality – United States. Water -- Purification -- United States.*

## TD223.M53 1992
**Miller, E. Willard**

Water quality and availability : a reference handbook / E. Willard Miller, Ruby M. Miller. Santa Barbara, Calif. : ABC-CLIO, c1992. xii, 430 p. :

92-033057      333.91/00973      087436647X

*Water quality -- United States. Water-supply -- United States.*

## TD223.T527 1999
**Thompson, Stephen Andrew.**

Water use, management, and planning in the United States / Stephen A. Thompson. San Diego : Academic, c1999. xvii, 371 p.

98-087241      333.91/00973      0126893403

*Water-supply -- United States -- Management. Water use – United States. Water resources development -- United States.*

## TD257.G72 1994
**Gray, N. F.**

Drinking water quality : problems and solutions / N.F. Gray. Chichester ; Wiley, 1994. xx, 315 p. :

93-046719      628.1/0941      0471948179

*Drinking water -- Great Britain. Water quality -- Great Britain. Water -- Pollution -- Great Britain.*

## TD345 Water supply for domestic and industrial purposes — General works — 1800-

## TD345.R44 2001

Reflections on water : new approaches to transboundary conflicts and cooperation / edited by Joachim Blatter and Helen Ingram. Cambridge, Mass. : MIT Press, c2001. xvi, 358 p. :

00-056862      333.91/17      026202487X

*Water-supply -- Management -- International cooperation – Case studies. Water rights -- Case studies. Conflict management -- Case studies.*

**TD345.W2625 2000**

Water for urban areas : challenges and perspectives / edited by Juha I. Uitto and Asit K. Biswas. Tokyo ; United Nations University Press, 2000. p. cm.
99-050477      363.6/1/091732     9280810243
*Municipal water supply -- Congresses. Urbanization -- Congresses. Twenty-first century -- Congresses.*

## TD353 Water supply for domestic and industrial purpoases — General special

**TD353.P7 1994**
**Prasifka, David W.,**
Water supply planning / David W. Prasifka. Malabar, Fla. : Krieger Pub. Co., 1994. xiii, 266 p.
93-028392      333.91/15     0894648381
*Water-supply -- Planning.*

## TD365 Water supply for domestic and industrial purpoases — Water quality management — General works

**TD365.D4897 1997**
**De Zuane, John,**
Handbook of drinking water quality / John De Zuane. New York : Van Nostrand Reinhold, c1997. xi, 575 p. :
96-035504      363.6/1     0442023448
*Water quality management -- Handbooks, manuals, etc. Drinking water -- Standards -- Handbooks, manuals, etc.*

## TD 388 Water supply for domestic and industrial purpoases — Water conservation — Periodicals, societies, congresses, etc.

**TD388.V53 2001**
**Vickers, Amy.**
Handbook of water use and conservation : [homes, landscapes, businesses, industries, farms] / Amy Vickers. Amherst, Mass. : Waterplow Press, c2001. xvii, 446 p.
99-025179      333.91/16     1931579075
*Water conservation -- Handbooks, manuals, etc. Water efficiency -- Handbooks, manuals, etc. Water consumption -- United States -- Handbooks, manuals, etc.*

## TD403 Water supply for domestic and industrial purpoases — Sources of water supply — Groundwater

**TD403.R45 1993**
Regional ground-water quality / edited by William M. Alley. New York : Van Nostrand Reinhold, c1993. xix, 634 p. :
92-036483      628.1/61     0442009372
*Groundwater -- Quality. Groundwater -- Quality -- Case studies.*

## TD420 Water supply for domestic and industrial purpoases — Water pollution — General works

**TD420.N69 1994**
**Novotny, Vladimir,**
Water quality : prevention, identification, and management of diffuse pollution / Vladimir Novotny, Harvey Olem. New York : Van Nostrand Reinhold, c1994. xiii, 1054 p.
93-014571      628.1/68
*Water -- Pollution. Water quality management.*

## TD426 Water supply for domestic and industrial purpoases — Pollution of groundwater — General works

**TD426.B44 1994**
**Bedient, Philip B.,**
Ground water contamination : transport and remediation / Philip B. Bedient, Hanadi S. Rifai, Charles J. Newell. Englewood Cliffs, N.J. : PTR Prentice Hall, c1994. xvi, 541 p. :
94-003073      628.1/68     0133625923
*Groundwater -- Pollution. Groundwater -- Quality -- Management.*

**TD426.G52 1994**
**Gibbons, Robert D.,**
Statistical methods for groundwater monitoring / Robert D. Gibbons. New York : Wiley, c1994. xii, 286 p. :
94-004187      628.1/61     0471587079
*Groundwater -- Pollution -- Measurement -- Statistical methods.*

**TD426.P35 1991**
**Palmer, Christopher M.**
Principles of contaminant hydrogeology / Christopher M. Palmer ; with contributions by Jeffrey L. Peterson, Jerold Behnke. Chelsea, Mich. : Lewis Publishers, c1992. xiv, 211 p. :
91-024703      628.1/68     0873712803
*Groundwater -- Pollution. Hydrogeology.*

## TD427.H3-427.P35 Water supply for domestic and industrial purpoases — Specific pollutants and organizms, A-Z Including presence of naturally occurring substances

**TD427.H3.G76 1992**
Groundwater contamination and analysis at hazardous waste sites / edited by Suzanne Lesage, Richard E. Jackson. New York : M. Dekker, c1992. xv, 545 p. :
92-020758      628.4/2     082478720X
*Hazardous wastes -- Environmental aspects. Groundwater -- Pollution. Groundwater -- Quality -- Measurement.*

**TD427.M44.M45 1993**

Metals in groundwater / edited by Herbert E. Allen, E. Michael Perdue, David S. Brown. Boca Raton : Lewis Publishers, c1993. xviii, 437 p.
93-002362          628.1/683          0873712773
*Metals -- Environmental aspects -- Congresses. Groundwater -- Pollution -- Congresses. Soil pollution -- Congresses.*

**TD427.P35.P447 1995**

Pesticide risk in groundwater / edited by Marco Vighi and Enzo Funari. Boca Raton : Lewis Publishers, c1995. 275 p. :
94-042771          363.73/84          0873714393
*Pesticides -- Environmental aspects. Groundwater -- Pollution.*

## TD430 Water supply for domestic and industrial purpoases — Water purification. Water treatment and conditioning — General works

**TD430.C37 1997**
**Casey, T. J.**

Unit treatment processes in water and wastewater engineering / T.J. Casey. Chichester ; Wiley, c1997. xii, 280 p. :
96-015921          628.1/62          0471966932
*Water -- Purification. Sewage -- Purification.*

**TD430.D764 2001**
**Drinan, Joanne.**

Water & wastewater treatment : a guide for the nonengineering professional / Joanne E. Drinan ; associate editor, Nancy E. Whiting. Lancaster, Pa. : Technomic Pub. Co., c2001. xv, 316 p. :
00-109963          628.1          1587160498
*Water -- Purification. Sewage -- Purification. Water treatment plants -- Management.*

## TD657 Sewage collection and disposal systems. Sewerage — Urban runoff — General works

**TD657.B88 1999**
**Butler, David.**

Urban drainage / David Butler and John W. Davies. New York : E&FN Spon, 1999. p. cm.
99-035421          628/.21          0419223401
*Urban runoff.*

**TD657.F47 1998**
**Ferguson, Bruce K.**

Introduction to stormwater : concept, purpose, design / Bruce K. Ferguson. New York : Wiley, c1998. xi, 255 p. :
97-020304          628/.212          047116528X
*Urban runoff -- Management. City planning -- Environmental aspects.*

## TD745-756.5 Sewage collection and disposal systems. Sewerage — Sewage disposal systems — Treatment, purification, etc.

**TD745.W362 1995**

Wastewater treatment : biological and chemical processes / Mogens Henze ... [et al.]. Berlin ; Springer-Verlag, c1995. 383 p. :
95-010558          628.3          3540588167
*Sewage -- Purification. Sewage disposal plants.*

**TD755.K33 1996**
**Kadlec, Robert H.**

Treatment wetlands / Robert H. Kadlec, Robert L. Knight. Boca Raton : Lewis Publishers, c1996. 893 p. :
95-009492          628.3/5          0873719301
*Sewage -- Purification -- Biological treatment. Wetlands.*

**TD756.5.C35 1999**
**Campbell, Craig S.,**

Constructed wetlands in the sustainable landscape / Craig S. Campbell, Michael Ogden. New York : Wiley, c1999. xiv, 270 p. :
99-024352          628.3/5          0471107204
*Constructed wetlands -- Design and construction. Landscape architecture.*

## TD791 Municipal refuse — General works

**TD791.B5613 1996**
**Bilitewski, Bernd.**

Waste management / Bernd Bilitewski, Georg Hardtle, Kalus Marek ; translated and edited by A. Weissbach, and H. Boeddicker. New York : Springer, c1997. xv, 699 p. :
96-035760          363.72/8/0943          3540592105
*Refuse and refuse disposal. Refuse and refuse disposal -- Germany.*

## TD793 Municipal refuse — General special

**TD793.S43 1994**
**Sharma, Hari D.**

Waste containment systems, waste stabilization, and landfills : design and evaluation / Hari D. Sharma, Sangeeta P. Lewis. New York : J. Wiley, c1994. xv, 585 p. :
94-009078          628.4          0471575364
*Refuse disposal facilities.*

## TD794.5 Municipal refuse — Recycling — General works

**TD794.5.D85 1993**
**Duston, Thomas E.**

Recycling solid waste : the first choice for private and public sector management / Thomas E. Duston. Westport, Conn. : Quorum Books, 1993. xviii, 204 p.
92-031709          363.72/82          089930754X
*Recycling (Waste, etc.) -- Planning. Recycling (Waste, etc.) -- Cost effectiveness.*

### TD794.5.L84 1993
The McGraw-Hill recycling handbook / Herbert F. Lund, editor in chief. New York : McGraw-Hill, c1993. 1 v. (various
92-018267      363.72/82      0070390967
*Recycling (Waste, etc.) Recycling (Waste, etc.) -- United States.*

### TD795.4 Municipal refuse — Special disposal methods — Open dumps

### TD795.4.W47 1995
**Westlake, Kenneth.**
Landfill waste pollution and control / Kenneth Westlake. Chichester, West Sussex, England : Albion Pub., 1995. 144 p. :
96-145417      628.4/4564/068    189856308X
*Sanitary landfills -- Management. Sanitary landfills -- Environmental aspects.*

### TD795.7 Municipal refuse — Special disposal methods — Sanitary landfills

### TD795.7.O93 1990
**Oweis, Issa S.**
Geotechnology of waste management / Issa S. Oweis, Raj P. Khera. London ; Butterworths, 1990. ix, 273 p. :
89-025245      628.4/4564    0408009691
*Sanitary landfills. Waste disposal in the ground. Engineering geology.*

### TD796 Municipal refuse — Special disposal methods — Composting

### TD796.5.E67 1997
**Epstein, Eliot,**
The science of composting / Eliot Epstein. Lancaster, Pa. : Technomic Pub. Co., c1997. xv, 487 p. :
96-061583      631.8/75    1566764785
*Compost. Refuse and refuse disposal -- Biodegradation.*

### TD878 Special types of environment — Soil pollution. Soil remediation — General works

### TD878.B684 1995
**Boulding, Russell.**
Practical handbook of soil, vadose zone, and ground-water contamination : assessment, prevention, and remediation / J. Russell Boulding. Boca Raton : Lewis Publishers, c1995. x, 948 p. :
94-037622      628.5/5    1566700515
*Soil pollution. Soil remediation. Groundwater -- Pollution.*

### TD878.E93 1998
**Evangelou, V. P.**
Environmental soil and water chemistry : principles and applications / V.P. Evangelou. New York : Wiley, c1998. xix, 564 p. :
98-013433      628.5    0471165158
*Soil pollution. Soil chemistry. Water -- Pollution.*

### TD878.P54 2000
**Pierzynski, Gary M.**
Soils and environmental quality / Gary M. Pierzynski, J. Thomas Sims, George F. Vance. Boca Raton : CRC Press, c2000. 459 p. :
99-057039      628.5/5    0849300223
*Soil pollution. Soil remediation. Soils.*

### TD878.W55 1995
**Wilson, David J.**
Modeling of in situ techniques for treatment of contaminated soils : soil vapor extraction, sparging, and bioventing / David J. Wilson ; with contributions by A.N. Clarke ... [et al.] Lancaster, Pa. : Technomic Pub. Co., c1995. xvi, 567 p. :
95-060515      628.5/5    1566762340
*Soil remediation -- Mathematical models. In situ remediation – Mathematical models.*

### TD878.Y65 2001
**Yong, R. N.**
Geoenvironmental engineering : contaminated soils, pollutant fate and mitigation / Raymond N. Yong. Boca Raton, Fla. : CRC Press, c2001. 307 p. :
00-055652      628.5/5    0849382890
*Soil pollution. Soil remediation. Environmental geotechnology.*

### TD879 Special types of environment — Soil pollution. Soil remediation — Particular pollutants, A-Z

### TD879.P4.W65 1997
**Wong, Jimmy.**
Design of remediation systems / Jimmy H.C. Wong, Chin Hong Lim, Greg L. Nolen. Boca Raton, FL : CRC/Lewis Publishers, 1997. 263 p. :
96-043810      628.5/2    1566702178
*Oil pollution of soils. Oil pollution of water. Hazardous waste site remediation.*

### TD881-883.1 Special types of environment — Air pollution and its control

### TD881.M28 1993
Managing hazardous air pollutants : state of the art / edited by Winston Chow, Katherine K. Connor ; contributing editors, Peter Mueller ... [et al.]. Boca Raton : Lewis Publishers, c1993. 582 p. :
92-043825      363.73/92    0873718666
*Air quality management -- Congresses. Hazardous wastes -- Management -- Congresses.*

### TD883.B36313 1996
**Baumbach, Gunter.**
Air quality control : formation and sources, dispersion, characteristics and impact of air pollutants--measuring methods, techniques for reduction of emissions and regulations for air quality contro Gunter Baumbach ; with the assistence [sic] of K. Baumann ... [et al.]. Berlin ; Springer, c1996. xiv, 490 p. :
96-027515      628.5/3    3540579923
*Air quality management. Air -- Pollution.*

**TD883.G564 1993**

Global atmospheric chemical change / edited by C.N. Hewitt and W.T. Sturges. London ; Elsevier Applied Science, c1993. xi, 470 p. :
92-020902          628.5/3          1851668896
*Air -- Pollution. Atmospheric chemistry. Transboundary pollution.*

**TD883.G57 1997**
**Godish, Thad.**
Air quality / Thad Godish. Boca Raton, Fla. : CRC/Lewis Publishers, c1997. 448 p. :
97-010860          363.739/2          1566702313
*Air -- Pollution. Air quality management.*

**TD883.T65 1994**
Toxic air pollution handbook / edited by David R. Patrick. New York : Van Nostrand Reinhold, c1994. xx, 588 p. :
93-021545          363.73/92          0442009038
*Air -- Pollution. Air -- Pollution -- Law and legislation. Air quality management.*

**TD883.1.I476 1993**
Indoor air : quality and control / Anthony L. Hines ... [et al.]. Englewood Cliffs, N.J. : PTR Prentice Hall, c1993. ix, 340 p. :
92-029799          628.5/3          0134639774
*Indoor air pollution. Air quality management.*

### TD883.17 Special types of environment — Air pollution and its control — Indoor air pollution

**TD883.17**
**Godish, Thad.**
Indoor environmental quality / Thad Godish. Boca Raton, Fla. : Lewis Publishers, c2001. 461 p. :
00-057400          628.5/3          1566704022
*Indoor air pollution. Housing and health. Industrial hygiene.*

### TD 885.5-886.5 Special types of environment — Air pollution and its control — Particular pollutants and their control

**TD885.5.G73.T72 1993**
Transportation and global climate change / edited by David L. Greene, Danilo J. Santini. Washington, D.C. : American Council for an Energy-Efficient Economy 1993. xxvi, 357 p.
93-015469          363.73/87          0918249171
*Greenhouse gases -- Environmental aspects -- Congresses. Transportation, Automotive -- Energy conservation -- United States -- Congresses. Transportation, Automotive -- Energy consumption -- United States -- Congresses.*

**TD885.5.R33.W55 1990**
**Wilkening, M.**
Radon in the environment / M. Wilkening. Amsterdam ; Elsevier ; 1990. x, 137 p. :
90-003779          628.5/35          0444881638
*Atmospheric radon -- Environmental aspects. Atmospheric radon. Atmospheric diffusion -- Research.*

**TD886.5.U73 1999**
Urban traffic pollution / edited by Dietrich Schwela and Olivier Zali. London ; E & FN Spon, 1999. ix, 249 p. :
98-042125          363.738/7          0419237208
*Motor vehicles -- Motors -- Exhaust gas -- Environmental aspects. Motor vehicles -- Motors -- Exhaust gas -- Health aspects. Air -- Pollution.*

### TD892 Noise and its control — General works

**TD892.H37 1979**
**Harris, Cyril M.,**
Handbook of noise control / edited by Cyril M. Harris. New York : McGraw-Hill, c1979. ca. 600 p. in
78-006764          620.2/3          0070268142
*Noise control.*

**TD892.T488 1990**
**Thumann, Albert.**
Fundamentals of noise control engineering / by Albert Thumann, Richard K. Miller. Lilburn, GA : Fairmont Press ; c1990. vii, 295 p. :
89-045580          620.2/3          0881730912
*Noise control.*

### TD897.5 Industrial and factory sanitation — Industrial and factory wastes — General special

**TD897.5.P65 1992**
Pollution prevention in industrial processes : the role of process analytical chemistry / Joseph J. Breen, editor, Michael J. Dellarco, editor. Washington, DC : American Chemical Society, 1992. x, 316 p. :
92-030288          628.5          0841224781
*Factory and trade waste -- Analysis -- Congresses. Chemistry, Analytic -- Congresses. Pollution prevention -- Congresses.*

**TD897.5.S74 1998**
**Stephenson, Ralph L.,**
The industrial wastewater systems handbook / Ralph L. Stephenson, James W. Blackburn, Jr. Boca Raton, FL : CRC Press, c1998. P-25, 495 p.
97-024311          628.4/3          1566702097
*Factory and trade waste -- Handbooks, manuals, etc.*

### TD897.845 Industrial and factory sanitation — Industrial and factory wastes — Special topics

**TD897.845.S65 1995**
**Smith, Lawrence A.**
Recycling and reuse of industrial wastes / Lawrence Smith, Jeffrey Means, Edwin Barth. Columbus : Battelle Press, c1995. ix, 102 p. :
95-001591          628.4/458          0935470891
*Factory and trade waste -- Recycling. Hazardous waste site remediation.*

**TD898-898.4 Industrial and factory sanitation — Industrial and factory wastes — Special wastes and their disposal**

**TD898.M87 1994**
**Murray, Raymond LeRoy,**
Understanding radioactive waste / Raymond L. Murray ; edited by Judith A. Powell. Columbus : Batelle Press, c1994. xvi, 212 p. :
94-009995          363.72/89          0935470794
*Radioactive wastes. Radioactive waste disposal.*

**TD898.15.P83 1993**
Public reactions to nuclear waste : citizens' views of repository siting / edited by Riley E. Dunlap, Michael E. Kraft and Eugene A. Rosa. Durham : Duke University Press, 1993. xvi, 332 p. :
93-006980          363.72/89525          0822313553
*Radioactive waste sites -- Location -- Public opinion. Radioactive wastes -- Public opinion. Public opinion -- United States.*

**TD898.4**
**Ringius, Lasse.**
Radioactive waste disposal at sea : public ideas, transnational policy entrepreneurs, and environmental regimes / Lasse Ringius. Cambridge, Mass. : MIT Press, c2001. x, 261 p. :
00-031879          363.72/89          0262182025
*Radioactive waste disposal in the ocean -- International cooperation.*

**TD1030 Rural and farm sanitary engineering — Hazardous substances and their disposal — General works**

**TD1030.O72 2000**
**O'Neill, Kate,**
Waste trading among rich nations : building a new theory of environmental regulation / Kate O'Neill. Cambridge, Mass. : MIT Press, c2000. xix, 298 p. ;
99-088564          363.72/8756          0262150506
*Hazardous wastes -- Management. Hazardous wastes -- Transportation. Environmental policy.*

**TD1030.M66 2000**
**Moore, Emmett Burris,**
An introduction to the management and regulation of hazardous waste / Emmett B. Moore. Columbus : Battelle Press, c2000. xi, 139 p. :
99-057216          363.72/8756          1574770888
*Hazardous wastes -- Management. Hazardous wastes -- Law and legislation -- United States*

**TD1030.W66 1993**
**Woodside, Gayle,**
Hazardous materials and hazardous waste management : a technical guide / Gayle Woodside. New York : Wiley, c1993. xxiii, 383 p.
92-038582          604.7          0471546763
*Hazardous wastes -- Management. Hazardous substances -- Management.*

**TD1040 Rural and farm sanitary engineering — Hazardous substances and their disposal — By region or country**

**TD1040.B53 1992**
**Blackman, William C.**
Basic hazardous waste management / William C. Blackman, Jr. Boca Raton, Fla : Lewis Publishers, c1993. ix, 339 p. :
92-021832          363.72/87          0873717929
*Hazardous wastes -- United States -- Management.*

**TD1050 Rural and farm sanitary engineering — Hazardous substances and their disposal — Special topics, A-Z**

**TD1050.P64.R33 1994**
**Rabe, Barry George,**
Beyond nimby : hazardous waste siting in Canada and the United States / Barry G. Rabe. Washington, D.C. : Brookings Institution, c1994. xvii, 199 p.
94-019039          363.72/87/0971          0815773080
*Hazardous waste sites -- Location -- Political aspects -- Canada. Hazardous waste sites -- Location -- Political aspects – United States.*

**TD1060.H33 1995**
**Haas, Charles N.**
Hazardous and industrial waste treatment / Charles N. Haas, Richard J. Vamos. Englewood Cliffs, N.J. : Prentice Hall, c1995. xii, 363 p. :
94-026977          628.4          0131234722
*Hazardous wastes -- Purification. Factory and trade waste -- Purification. Waste minimization.*

**TD1064.H37 1996**
**Hasan, Syed E.,**
Geology and hazardous waste management / Syed E. Hasan. Upper Saddle River, N.J. : Prentice Hall, c1996. xii, 387 p.,
95-041347          628.4/2          0023516828
*Hazardous wastes -- Management. Waste disposal in the ground – Environmental aspects. Environmental geotechnology.*

# TE Highway engineering. Roads and pavements

**TE23 Country divisions — America — North America**

**TE23.S44 1987**
**Seely, Bruce Edsall,**
Building the American highway system : engineers as policy makers / Bruce E. Seely. Philadelphia : Temple University Press, 1987. xv, 315 p., [
87-001929          388.1/0973          0877224722
*Road construction -- United States -- History -- 19th century. Road construction -- United States -- History -- 20th century.*

## TE145 General works — 1800-

**TE145.G35 2002**
**Garber, Nicholas J.**
 Traffic and highway engineering / Nicholas J. Garber, Lester A. Hoel. 3rd ed. Pacific Grove, CA : Brooks/Cole Pub. Co., 2002. xiii, 1150 p. :
            625.7 21            0534387438
*Highway engineering. Traffic engineering.*

## TE147 General works — Elementary textbooks

**TE147.M28 1998**
**Mannering, Fred L.**
 Principles of highway engineering and traffic analysis / Fred L. Mannering, Walter P. Kilareski. 2nd ed. New York : Wiley, c1998. xii, 340 p. :
            625.7 21            0471130850
*Highway engineering. Traffic engineering.*

# TF Railroad engineering and operation

## TF1 Societies, etc. by language of publication — English

**TF1.J3**
 Jane's world railways. London : Sampson Low, Marston & Co., v. :
98-086778            385.05
 *Railroads -- Periodicals. Railroads -- Statistics -- Periodicals. Railroads -- Directories.*

## TF23-25 Country divisions

**TF23.A48 2000**
**Ambrose, Stephen E.**
 Nothing like it in the world : the men who built the transcontinental railroad, 1863-1869 / Stephen E. Ambrose. New York : Simon & Schuster, 2000. p. cm.
00-041005            385/.0973            0684846098
 *Railroads -- United States -- History -- 19th century. Railroad construction workers -- United States -- History -- 19th centurry.*

**TF23.D67 1992**
**Douglas, George H.,**
 All aboard! : the railroad in American life / George H. Douglas. New York : Paragon House, 1992. xviii, 462 p.
91-011489            385/.0973            1557784868
 *Railroads -- United States -- History.*

**TF23.K54 1994**
**Klein, Maury,**
 Unfinished business : the railroad in American life / Maury Klein. Hanover : University of Rhode Island, University Press of c1994. 226 p. :
93-008112            385/.0973            0874516579
 *Railroads -- United States -- History.*

**TF23.M52 1999**
**Middleton, William D.,**
 Landmarks on the iron road : two centuries of North American railroad engineering / William D. Middleton. Bloomington, IN : Indiana University Press, c1999. x, 194 p. :
            625.1/00973 21            0253335590
 *Railroads -- United States -- History. Railroad engineering – History.*

**TF23.V36 1995**
**Vance, James E.**
 The North American railroad : its origin, evolution, and geography / James E. Vance, Jr. Baltimore : Johns Hopkins University Press, c1995. xvi, 348 p. :
94-016306            0801845734
 *Railroads -- United States. Railroads -- Canada.*

**TF25.U5.K53 1987**
**Klein, Maury,**
 Union Pacific / by Maury Klein. Garden City, N.Y. : Doubleday, 1987. 2 v. :
86-016732            385/.065/78            0385177283
*Union Pacific Railroad Company.*

## TF145 General works — 1850-

**TF145.P76 2000**
**Profillidis, V. A. (Vassilios A.)**
 Railway engineering / V.A. Profillidis. 2nd ed. Aldershot ; Burlington, USA : Ashgate, c2000. xx, 291 p. :
            625.1 21
*Railroad engineering.*

## TF200 Railway construction — General works

**TF200.H38 1982**
**Hay, William Walter,**
 Railroad engineering / William W. Hay. New York : Wiley, c1982. xvi, 758 p.,
81-023117            625.1            0471364002
 *Railroad engineering.*

## TF238 Tunnels and tunneling — Special tunnels, A-Z

**TF238.E5.C47 1994**
 The Channel Tunnel : a geographical perspective / edited by Richard Gibb. Chichester, England ; Wiley, 1994. xvi, 244 p. :
94-007964            385/.312            0471949086
 *Railroad tunnels -- English Channel.*

### TF258 Railway construction — Permanent way. Superstructure. — Details of the permanent way

**TF258.E3713**
Railroad track : theory and practice : material properties, cross-sections, welding, and treatment / edited by Fritz Fastenrath ; translated by Walter Grant. New York : F. Ungar Pub. Co., c1981. xx, 457 p. :
80-005340          625.1/5          0804442312
*Railroads -- Rails.*

## TF302 Railway structures and buildings — Buildings, etc., other than structures enumerated above

**TF302.N7**
**Schlichting, Kurt C.**
Grand Central Terminal : railroads, engineering, and architecture in New York City / Kurt C. Schlichting. Baltimore, Md. : Johns Hopkins University Press, 2001. xiii, 243 p.
00-008641          385.3/14/097471          0801865107
*Railroad terminals -- New York (State) -- New York -- History. Railroad terminals -- Conservation and restoration -- New York (State) -- New York.*

### TF470 Railway equipment and supplies — Varieties of cars — Freight cars

**TF470.W45 1993**
**White, John H.,**
The American railroad freight car : from the wood-car era to the coming of steel / John H. White, Jr. Baltimore : Johns Hopkins University Press, c1993. xi, 644 p. :
92-024255          625.2/4/0973          0801844045
*Railroads -- United States -- Freight cars -- History.*

### TF725 Local and light railways — Municipal and street railways. Interurban railways — Country subdivisions

**TF725.N5.C8**
**Cudahy, Brian J.**
Under the sidewalks of New York : the story of the greatest subway system in the world / by Brian J. Cudahy. Brattleboro, Vt. : S. Greene Press, c1979. 176 p. :
79-015221          388.4/2/097471          0828903522
*Subways -- New York (State) -- New York. Local transit -- New York (State) -- New York.*

### TF847 Local and light railways — Underground railways. Subways — General works

**TF847.N5.H66 1993**
**Hood, Clifton.**
722 miles : the building of the subways and how they transformed New York / Clifton Hood. New York : Simon & Schuster, c1993. 335 p. :
93-011169          388.4/28/097471          067167756X
*Subways -- New York (State) -- New York. Urbanization -- New York (State) -- New York.*

# TG Bridge engineering

### TG23 Country divisions — United States — General works

**TG23.P47 1995**
**Petroski, Henry.**
Engineers of dreams : great bridge builders and the spanning of America / Henry Petroski. New York : Knopf, 1995. xi, 479 p. :
94-048893          624/.2/0973          0679439390
*Bridges -- United States -- History -- 19th century. Bridges -- United States -- History -- 20th century. Civil engineers -- United States -- Biography.*

## TG145 General works — 1800-

**TG145.B85 2000**
Bridge engineering handbook / edited by Wai-Fah Chen, Lian Duan. Boca Raton, FL : CRC Press, c2000. 1 v. (various
99-033175          624/.2          0849374340
*Bridges -- Design and construction.*

### TG260 Structural analysis as applied to bridges — General works

**TG260.M812**
**Morris, Irvine Ernest,**
Handbook of structural design.  New York Reinhold Pub. Corp. [1963] 803 p.
62010728          624.17
*Structural analysis (Engineering) -- Handbooks, manuals, etc.*

### TG300 Bridge design and drafting — General works

**TG300.B76 1993**
**Brown, David J.**
Bridges / David J. Brown. New York : Macmillan ; c1993. 176 p. :
93009747          624/.2          002517455X
*Bridges -- Design and construction.*

**TG300.P64 1996**
**Priestley, M. J. N.**
  Seismic design and retrofit of bridges / M.J.N. Priestley, F. Seible, G.M. Calvi. New York : Wiley, c1996. xvii, 686 p.
95-035406          624/.252          047157998X
  *Bridges -- Design and construction. Earthquake engineering. Bridges -- Remodeling.*

**TG300.T28 1998**
**Taly, Narendra.**
  Design of modern highway bridges / Narenda Taly. New York : McGraw-Hill, c1998. xvi, 1352 p. :
          624/.2 21          0070629986
*Bridges -- Design and construction.*

**TG300.T66 1995**
**Tonias, Demetrios E.**
  Bridge engineering : design, rehabilitation, and maintenance of modern highway bridges / Demetrios E. Tonias. New York : McGraw-Hill, 1995. xxiv, 470 p.
95012958          624.63          007065073X
  *Bridges -- Maintenance and repair. Bridges -- Design and construction.*

**TG300.T76 1994**
**Troitsky, M. S.**
  Planning and design of bridges / M.S. Troitsky. New York : J. Wiley, c1994. xviii, 318 p.
94-006946          624/.25          0471028533
  *Bridges -- Design and construction. Bridges -- Planning.*

**TG300.X36 1994**
**Xanthakos, Petros P.**
  Theory and design of bridges / Petros P. Xanthakos. New York : Wiley, c1994. xix, 1443 p.
92-021520          624/.25          0471570974
  *Bridges -- Design and construction. Load factor design.*

## TG325.6 Floors

**TG325.6.O27 1999**
**O'Brien, Eugene J.,**
  Bridge deck analysis / Eugene J. O'Brien and Damien L. Keogh ; chapter 4 written in collaboration with the authors by Barry M. Lehane. London ; E & FN Spon, 1999. ix, 278 p. :
98-048511          624/.253          0419225005
  *Bridges -- Floors. Structural analysis (Engineering)*

## TG340 Special types of bridges — Arched bridges — Concrete bridges

**TG340.L54 1992**
**Liebenberg, A. C.**
  Concrete bridges : design and construction / A.C. Liebenberg ; advisory editors, F.K. Kong ... [et al.]. Harlow, Essex, England : Longman Scientific & Technical ; 1992. xv, 280 p. :
92-005592          624/.257          058204281X
  *Bridges, Concrete -- Design and construction. Reinforced concrete construction.*

## TG380 Special types of bridges — Trussed bridges — Iron and steel

**TG380.T76 1990**
**Troitsky, M. S.**
  Prestressed steel bridges : theory and design / M.S. Troitsky. New York, N.Y. : Van Nostrand Reinhold, c1990. xx, 386 p. :
89-016479          624/.25          0442319223
  *Bridges, Iron and steel -- Design and construction. Prestressed steel construction.*

## TG405 Special types of bridges — Cable-stayed bridges

**TG405.P6 1986**
**Podolny, Walter.**
  Construction and design of cable-stayed bridges / Walter Podolny, Jr. and John B. Scalzi. New York : Wiley, c1986. xv, 336 p. :
85-026622          624/.55          0471826553
  *Bridges, Cable-stayed -- Design and construction.*

# TH Building construction

# TH9 Dictionaries and encyclopedias

**TH9.E48 1988**
  Encyclopedia of building technology / edited by Henry J. Cowan. Englewood Cliffs, N.J. : Prentice Hall, c1988. xxii, 322 p.
87-002556          690/.03/21          0132755203
  *Building -- Dictionaries. Engineering -- Dictionaries. Architecture -- Dictionaries.*

**TH9.S78 1993**
**Stein, J. Stewart.**
  Construction glossary : an encyclopedic reference and manual / J. Stewart Stein. New York : Wiley, c1993. xx, 1137 p. ;
92-000443          690/.03          047156933X
  *Building -- Dictionaries. Construction industry -- Dictionaries.*

# TH18 History and description — Modern to 1800

**TH18.E45 1992**
**Elliott, Cecil D.**
  Technics and architecture : the development of materials and systems for buildings / Cecil D. Elliott. Cambridge, Mass. : MIT Press, c1992. x, 467 p. :
91-028298          690/.09          0262050455
  *Building -- History. Building materials -- History.*

## TH151 General works — Pocketbooks, tables, etc.

**TH151.B825 1994**
 Building design and construction handbook / Frederick S. Merritt, editor, Jonathan T. Ricketts, editor. New York : McGraw-Hill, 1994. 1 v. (various
94-000777          690          007041596X
 *Building -- Handbooks, manuals, etc.*

## TH153 General special

**TH153.D374 1999**
**Davis, Howard,**
 The culture of building / Howard Davis. New York : Oxford University, 1999. x, 385 p. :
98-019051          720          0195112946
 *Building. Corporate culture. Architecture and society.*

## TH380 The building site — Landscape construction by builders

**TH380.T46 2000**
**Thompson, J. William.**
 Sustainable landscape construction : a guide to green building outdoors / J. William Thompson and Kim Sorvig ; drawings by Craig D. Farnsworth. Washington, D.C. : Island Press, c2000. xxi, 348 p. :
00-008256          712/.01          1559636467
 *Landscape construction. Landscape protection. Green products.*

### TH435 Estimates. Measurements. Quantities and cost — General works — 1890-

**TH435.M42 1990**
 Means estimating handbook. Kingston, MA : R.S. Means Co., c1990. xi, 905 p. :
91-115713          692/.5          0876291779
 *Building -- Estimates -- Handbooks, manuals, etc.*

## TH441 Building failures, errors, defects, etc.

**TH441.F43 1997**
**Feld, Jacob.**
 Construction failure / Jacob Feld and Kenneth L. Carper. New York : Wiley, c1997. xv, 512 p. :
96-033425          624.1/71          0471574775
 *Building failures. Structural engineering.*

**TH441.L48 1992**
**Levy, Matthys.**
 Why buildings fall down : how structures fail / Matthys Levy and Mario Salvadori ; illustrations by Kevin Woest. New York : W.W. Norton, 1992. 334 p. :
91-034954          690/.21          0393033562
 *Building failures. Structural failures.*

## TH443 Building accidents and their prevention

**TH443.R432 2000**
**Reese, Charles D.**
 Annotated dictionary of construction safety and health / Charles D. Reese. Boca Raton : Lewis Publishers, c2000. 256 p. :
99-042159          690/.22/03          1566705142
 *Building -- Safety measures -- Dictionaries.*

## TH845 Architectural engineering. Structural engineering of buildings — Treatises

**TH845.S33 1980**
**Salvadori, Mario George,**
 Why buildings stand up : the strength of architecture / Mario Salvadori ; ill. by Saralinda Hooker and Christopher Ragus. New York : Norton, c1980. 311 p. :
80-016285          624.1/7          0393014010
 *Structural engineering.*

**TH845.T33 1988**
**Taranath, Bungale S.**
 Structural analysis and design of tall buildings / Bungale S. Taranath. New York : McGraw-Hill, c1988. xi, 739 p. :
87-029317          624.1/7          0070628785
 *Tall buildings -- Design and construction.*

## TH900 Construction equipment in building — General works

**TH900.D38 1991**
**Day, David A.,**
 Construction equipment guide / David A. Day, Neal B.H. Benjamin. New York : Wiley, c1991. xxiii, 437 p.
90-029315          624/.028          0471888400
 *Construction equipment.*

### TH1095 Systems of building construction — Earth movements and building. Subsidences, etc. — Earthquakes and building

**TH1095.G76 1984**
 Ground movements and their effects on structures / edited by P.B. Attewell and R.K. Taylor. London : Surrey University Press ; 1984. xviii, 441 p.
84-009428          624.1/5
*Earth movements and building. Mine subsidences. Earthquake engineering.*

## TH1199 Systems of building construction — Masonry building construction

**TH1199.D78 1994**
**Drysdale, Robert G.**
 Masonry structures : behavior and design / Robert G. Drysdale, Ahmad A. Hamid, Lawrie R. Baker. Englewood Cliffs, N.J. : Prentice Hall, c1994. xxvi, 784 p.
92-039538          624.1/832          0135620260
*Masonry.*

## TH1301 Systems of building construction — Masonry building construction — Brick building construction

**TH1301.P55 1993**
**Plumridge, Andrew.**
 Brickwork : architecture and design / Andrew Plumridge & Wim Meulenkamp. New York : Abrams, 1993. 224 p. :
92-024191          693/.21          0810931230
*Building, Brick. Bricks.*

## TH1611 Systems of building construction — Iron and steel building construction — General works

**TH1611.S59 1991**
**Stafford Smith, Bryan,**
 Tall building structures : analysis and design / Bryan Stafford Smith, Alex Coull. New York : Wiley, c1991. xx, 537 p. :
90-013007          690          0471512370
*Tall buildings -- Design and construction. Structural engineering.*

**TH1611.S78 1995**
 Structural systems for tall buildings : systems and concepts / Council on Tall Buildings and Urban Habitat, Committee 3 ; editorial group, Ryszard M. Kowalczyk, Robert Sinn, Max B. Kilmister ; contributors, I.D. Bennetts ... [et al.]. New York : McGraw-Hill, c1995. xvii, 422 p.
94-038031          690          0070125414
*Tall buildings -- Design and construction. Structural engineering.*

## TH2243 Details in building design and construction — Walls — Walls above surface

**TH2243.H46 2000**
**Hendry, A. W.**
 Masonry wall construction / A.W. Hendry and F.M. Khalaf. New York : E&FN Spon, 2000. p. cm.
00-039499          693/.1          0415232821
 *Brick walls -- Design and construction. Stone walls – Design and construction. Masonry.*

## TH4538 Buildings: Construction with reference to use — Factories and mills. Industrial plants — Water treatment plants

**TH4538.K39 1991**
**Kawamura, Susumu.**
 Integrated design of water treatment facilities / Susumu Kawamura. New York : Wiley, c1991. xx, 658 p. :
90-040995          628.1/62          0471615919
*Water treatment plants -- Design and construction.*

## TH6010 Construction by phase of the work (Building trades) — Building fittings and their installation — General works

**TH6010.S74 2000**
**Stein, Benjamin.**
 Mechanical and electrical equipment for buildings / Benjamin Stein, John S. Reynolds. 9th ed. New York : Wiley, c2000. xxxii, 1790 p.:
693 21
*Buildings -- Mechanical equipment. Buildings -- Electric equipment. Buildings -- Environmental engineering.*

## TH7005-7201 Heating and ventilation — Societies, etc.

**TH7005.A83**
 ASHRAE handbook. Atlanta, Ga. : American Society of Heating, Refrigerating and A c1984. 1 v. :
85-644942          697/.005

**TH7011.H36 1990**
 Handbook of HVAC design / editors, Nils R. Grimm, Robert C. Rosaler. New York : McGraw-Hill, c1990. 1 v. (various
89-078110          697          0070248419
*Heating. Ventilation. Air conditioning.*

**TH7201.A8**
 ASHRAE handbook. Fundamentals / Atlanta, CA : Amer. Soc. Of Heating, Refrig, and AC Engineers, c1981. 1 v. :
697
*Heating -- Handbooks, manuals, etc. Refrigeration and refrigerating machinery -- Handbooks, manuals, etc. Air conditioning -- Handbooks, manuals, etc. Ventilation -- Handbooks, manuals, etc.*

## TH7345 Heating and ventilation — Heating of buildings — Equipment and supplies

**TH7345.H85 1994**
 HVAC design data sourcebook / Robert O. Parmley, editor-in-chief. New York : McGraw-Hill, c1994. xxi, 489 p. :
94-004200          697          0070485720
*Heating -- Equipment and supplies -- Design and construction. Ventilation -- Equipment and supplies -- Design and construction. Air conditioning -- Equipment and supplies -- Design and construction.*

## TH7413-7414 Heating and ventilation — Heating of buildings — Heating by special fuels or forms of energy

**TH7413.B4**
**Beckman, William A.**
Solar heating design, by the f-chart method / William A. Beckman, Sanford A. Klein, John A. Duffie. New York : Wiley, c1977. xv, 200 p. :
77-022168        697/.78        0471034061
*Solar heating. FCHART.*

**TH7414.P26 1984**
Passive solar design handbook. New York : Van Nostrand Reinhold Co., c1984. 750 p. :
83-021805        690/.869        0442208103
*Solar houses -- Design and construction. Solar energy -- Passive systems.*

## TH7654 Heating and ventilation — Ventilation of buildings — General works

**TH7654.E84 1996**
**Etheridge, David**
Building ventilation : theory and measurement / David Etheridge, Mats Sandberg. Chichester ; John Wiley & Sons, c1996. xxvi, 724 p.
95-022114        697        047196087X
*Ventilation. Air flow.*

## TH7687.5-7687 Heating and ventilation — Ventilation of buildings — Air conditioning, cooling, etc.

**TH7687.5.G54 1994**
**Givoni, Baruch.**
Passive and low energy cooling of buildings / Baruch Givoni. New York : Van Nostrand Reinhold, c1994. vii, 263 p. :
94-011136        697.9/3        0442010761
*Air conditioning. Ventilation.*

**TH7687.7.L373 1995**
**Langley, Billy C.,**
Fundamentals of air conditioning systems / Billy C. Langley. Lilburn, GA : Fairmont Press ; c1995. viii, 391 p.
94-023108        697.9/3        0881731765
*Air conditioning -- Equipment and supplies.*

**TH7687.W27 2000**
**Wang, Shan K. (Shan Kuo)**
Handbook of air conditioning and refrigeration / Shan K. Wang. 2nd ed. New York : McGraw-Hill, c2000. 1 v. :
697.9/3 21
*Air conditioning. Refrigeration and refrigerating machinery.*

## TH9446 Protection from fire. Fire prevention and extinction — Fire extinction — Fire prevention and extinction in special classes of buildings and facilities, A-Z

**TH9446.H38.D38 1991**
**Davis, Daniel J.,**
Firefighter's hazardous materials reference book / by Daniel J. Davis and Grant T. Christianson. New York : Van Nostrand Reinhold, c1991. xv, 910 p. ;
90-022498        628.9/2        0442003773
*Hazardous substances -- Fires and fire prevention -- Handbooks, manuals, etc.*

**TH9446.H38M48 1989**
**Meyer, Eugene,**
Chemistry of hazardous materials / Eugene Meyer. 2nd ed. Englewood Cliffs, N.J. : Prentice Hall, c1989. xii, 509 p. :
628.9/25 19
*Hazardous substances -- Fires and fire prevention. Hazardous substances.*

# TJ Mechanical engineering and machinery

## TJ151 General works on mechanical engineering — Pocketbooks, rules, tables, etc.

**TJ151.C73 1998**
The CRC handbook of mechanical engineering / editor-in-chief, Frank Kreith. Boca Raton : CRC Press, c1998. 1 v. (various
97-030197        621        084939418X
*Mechanical engineering -- Handbooks, manuals, etc.*

**TJ151.M355 2000**
Machinery's handbook pocket companion : a reference book for the mechanical engineer, designer, manufacturing engineer, draftsman, toolmaker, and machinist / compiled and edited by Richard P. Pohanish New York : Industrial Press, 2000. ix, 317 p. :
00-039669        621.8        083113089X
*Mechanical engineering -- Handbooks, manuals, etc.*

**TJ151.M395 1998**
Mechanical engineers' handbook / edited by Myer Kutz. 2nd ed. New York : Wiley, 1998. xxiii, 2352 p.
621 21
*Mechanical engineering -- Handbooks, manuals, etc.*

## TJ163 Mechanical and electrical engineering combined — General works

### TJ163.G7613 1999
**Gross, Michael,**
Travels to the nanoworld : miniature machinery in nature and technology / Michael Gross. New York : Plenum, 1999. p. cm.
99-013756          620/.5          0306460084
*Microelectromechanical systems. Nanotechnology.*

## TJ163.2 Power resources — General works

### TJ163.2.E46
Energy and man : technical and social aspects of energy / edited by M. Granger Morgan. New York : IEEE Press, c1975. xi, 521 p. :
74-027680          333.9          087942043X.
*Power resources. Energy consumption. Power (Mechanics)*

### TJ163.2.F58 1994
**Flavin, Christopher.**
Power surge : guide to the coming energy revolution / Christopher Flavin, Nicholas Lenssen. New York : W.W. Norton, c1994. 382 p. :
95-109775          333.79          0393036782
*Power resources. Energy consumption. Energy policy.*

### TJ163.2.H53 1995
**Hill, R.**
The future of energy use / Robert Hill, Phil O'Keefe, and Colin Snape. New York : St. Martin's Press, 1995. 197 p. :
95-010927          333.79          0312126565
*Power resources. Energy policy.*

### TJ163.2.M3 1981
McGraw-Hill encyclopedia of energy / Sybil P. Parker, editor in chief. New York : McGraw-Hill Book Co., c1981. viii, 838 p.
80-018078          333.79/03/21          0070452687
*Power resources -- Dictionaries. Power (Mechanics) -- Dictionaries.*

### TJ163.2.M425 1991
**Thumann, Albert.**
Handbook of energy engineering / Albert Thumann, D. Paul Mehta. Lilburn, GA : Fairmont Press ; c1991. 429 p. :
91-002571          621.042          0881731242
*Power resources -- Handbooks, manuals, etc. Power (Mechanics) -- Handbooks, manuals, etc.*

### TJ163.2.R345 1997
**Ramage, Janet,**
Energy, a guidebook / Janet Ramage. Oxford ; Oxford University Press, 1997. xx, 394 p. :
96-052364          333.79          0192880225
*Power resources. Power (Mechanics)*

### TJ163.2.R84 1995
**Rudolph, Joseph R.**
Energy / by Joseph R. Rudolph, Jr. Metuchen, N.J. : Scarecrow Press ; 1995. viii, 177 p.
95-003370          333.79          0810830116
*Power resources.*

### TJ163.2.S618 1999
**Smil, Vaclav.**
Energies : an illustrated guide to the biosphere and civilization / Vaclav Smil. Cambridge, Mass. : MIT Press, c1999. xviii, 210 p.
98-013408          531/.6          0262194104
*Power resources -- Social aspects.*

### TJ163.2.T347 1995
**Tatum, Jesse S.,**
Energy possibilities : rethinking alternatives and the choice-making process / Jesse S. Tatum. Albany : State University of New York Press, c1995. xiii, 159 p.
94-037133          333.79          0791425959
*Power resources. Energy policy.*

### TJ163.2.T87 2001
**Turner, Wayne C.,**
Energy management handbook / by Wayne C. Turner. 4th ed. Lilburn, GA : Fairmont Press, 2001. xvi, 758 p. :
          658.2 21
*Power resources -- Handbooks, manuals, etc. Energy conservation - Handbooks, manuals, etc.*

## TJ163.235  Power resources — Handbooks, tables, etc.

### TJ163.235.E53 1995
Encyclopedia of energy technology and the environment / Attilio Bisio, Sharon Boots, editors. New York : Wiley, 1995. 4 v. (xiii, 2
94-044119          333.79/03          0471544582
*Power resources -- Handbooks, manuals, etc. Environmental protection -- Handbooks, manuals, etc.*

### TJ163.235.L64 1984
**Loftness, Robert L.**
Energy handbook / Robert L. Loftness. New York : Van Nostrand Reinhold, c1984. ix, 763 p. :
83-021834          333.79          0442259921
*Power resources -- Handbooks, manuals, etc. Power (Mechanics) -- Handbooks, manuals, etc.*

### TJ163.235.M55 1993
**Miller, E. Willard**
Energy and American society : a reference handbook / E. Willard Miller, Ruby M. Miller. Santa Barbara, Calif. : ABC/CLIO, c1993. xiv, 418 p. ;
93-030307          333.79/0973          0874366895
*Power resources -- United States -- Handbooks, manuals, etc.*

**TJ163.235.T48 2001**
**Thumann, Albert**
  Handbook of energy engineering / Albert Thumann, D. Paul
Mehta. 5th ed. Lilburn, GA : Fairmont Press, c2001. 479 p. :
          621.042 21
*Power resources -- Handbooks, manuals, etc. Power (Mechanics) –
Handbooks, manuals, etc.*

**TJ163.235.W55 1997**
  The Wiley encyclopedia of energy and the environment /
Attilio Bisio, Sharon Boots, editors. New York : Wiley, c1997.
2 v. (xiii, 1
96-002734              333.79/03              047114827X
  *Power resources -- Handbooks, manuals, etc. Environmental
protection -- Handbooks, manuals, etc.*

## TJ163.25  Power resources — Special regions or countries, A-Z

**TJ163.25.U6.C83 1986**
**Cuff, David J.**
  The United States energy atlas / David J. Cuff, William J.
Young. New York : Macmillan Pub. Co. ; c1986. ix, 387 p. :
85-004867              333.99/0973              0026912406
  *Power resources -- United States.*

## TJ163.27 Energy conservation — Congresses

**TJ163.27.E48 1998**
  Energy & environmental visions for the new millennium /
[compiled and edited by Jana Ricketts]. Lilburn, GA :
Fairmont Press, c1998. xiii, 579 p.
97-077092              333.79      0881732893
  *Energy conservation -- Congresses. Power resources --
Environmental aspects -- Congresses. Power (Mechanics) --
Congresses.*

## TJ163.3 Energy conservation — General works

**TJ163.3.G68 1995**
**Gottschalk, Charles M.**
  Industrial energy conservation / compiled by Charles M.
Gottschalk. Chichester ; John Wiley, c1996. xv, 121 p. :
95-023826              658.2      047196008X
  *Industries -- Energy conservation.*

**TJ163.3.P38 1993**
**Patrick, Steven R.**
  Energy conservation guidebook / by Steven R. Patrick, Dale
R. Patrick, Stephen W. Fardo. Lilburn, GA : Fairmont Press ;
c1993. x, 467 p. :
93-013523              696      0881731544
  *Energy conservation -- Handbooks, manuals, etc.*

**TJ163.3.W85 1999**
**Wulfinghoff, Donald.**
  Energy efficiency manual : for everyone who uses energy,
pays for utilities, controls energy usage, designs and builds, is
interested in energy and environmental preservation / Donald
R. Wulfinghoff. Wheaton, Md. : Energy Institute Press, 1999.
1531 p. :
99-022242              658.2      0965792676
  *Energy conservation -- Handbooks, manuals, etc. Energy
consumption -- Handbooks, manuals, etc.*

## TJ163.4 Energy conservation — Special regions or countries, A-Z

**TJ163.4.U6.C38 1998**
**Casten, Thomas R.**
  Turning off the heat : why America must double energy
efficiency to save money and reduce global warming / Thomas
R. Casten. Amherst, NY : Prometheus Books, c1998. xiii, 269 :
98-028272              333.7916/0973      1573922692
  *Energy conservation -- United States. Fossil fuel power plants –
Environmental aspects -- United States. Global warming.*

## TJ163.5 Energy conservation — Energy conservation or consumption in special industries, facilities, etc., A-Z

**TJ163.5.B84.F86 1996**
  Fundamentals of building energy dynamics / edited by
Bruce D. Hunn. Cambridge, Mass. : MIT Press, c1996. viii,
538 p.
95-046158              696      0262082381
  *Buildings -- Energy conservation. Solar heating.*

**TJ163.5.S623 1994**
**Smil, Vaclav.**
  Energy in world history / Vaclav Smil. Boulder : Westview
Press, 1994. xviii, 300 p.
94-016485              333.79/09      0813319013
  *Power resources -- History.*

## TJ164 Power plants (General)

**TJ164.P64 1986**
  Power plant evaluation and design reference guide / edited
by Tyler G. Hicks. New York : McGraw-Hill, c1986. 1 v.
(various
86-007412              621.31      0070287945
  *Power-plants -- Design and construction -- Handbooks, manuals,
etc. Electric power-plants -- Design and construction -- Handbooks,
manuals, etc.*

# TJ175 Principles of mechanism. Kinematics of machinery

**TJ175.E32 1998**
**Eckhardt, Homer D.**
Kinematic design of machines and mechanisms / Homer D. Eckhardt. New York : McGraw-Hill, c1998. xvii, 621 p.
97-029215          621.8/11          0070189536
*Machinery, Kinematics of. Machine design.*

**TJ175.V56 2000**
**Vinogradov, Oleg**
Fundamentals of kinematics and dynamics of machines and mechanisms / Oleg Vinogradov. Boca Raton : CRC Press, c2000. 290 p. :
00-025151          621.8/11          0849302579
*Machinery, Kinematics of. Machinery, Dynamics of.*

# TJ181 Mechanical movements — General works

**TJ181.S28 2001**
**Sclater, Neil**
Mechanisms and mechanical devices sourcebook / Neil Sclater, Nicholas P. Chironis. 3rd ed. New York : McGraw-Hill, 2001. xv, 495 p. :
                   621.8 21
*Mechanical movements.*

# TJ184-185 Mechanical movements — Special movements and devices — Toothed gears. Gearing

**TJ184.D7 1988**
**Drago, Raymond J.**
Fundamentals of gear design / Raymond J. Drago. Boston : Butterworths, c1988. xiii, 560 p.
87-017850          621.8/33          040990127X
*Gearing.*

**TJ184.D784 1984**
**Dudley, Darle W.**
Handbook of practical gear design / Darle W. Dudley. New York : McGraw-Hill, c1984. 675 p. in var
84-003860          621.8/33          0070179514
*Gearing -- Handbooks, manuals, etc.*

**TJ184.S76 1995**
**South, David W.**
Encyclopedic dictionary of gears and gearing / David W. South, Richard H. Ewert. New York : McGraw-Hill, c1995. xviii, 414 p.
94-010985          621.8/33/03          0070597960
*Gearing -- Dictionaries.*

**TJ185.S74 1992**
**Stokes, Alec.**
Gear handbook : design and calculations / Alec Stokes. Oxford ; Butterworth-Heinemann, 1992. x, 290 p. :
91-036304          621.8/33          0750611499
*Gearing -- Handbooks, manuals, etc.*

# TJ210.4 Mechanical devices and figures. Automata. Ingenuous mechanisms. Robots — Dictionaries and encyclopedias

**TJ210.4.G53 1994**
The McGraw-Hill illustrated encyclopedia of robotics & artificial intelligence / Stan Gibilisco, editor in chief. New York : McGraw-Hill, c1994. ix, 420 p. :
94-014309          629.892/03          0070236135
*Robotics -- Encyclopedias. Artificial intelligence – Encyclopedias.*

# TJ211 Mechanical devices and figures. Automata. Ingenuous mechanisms. Robots — General works

**TJ211.A75 1998**
**Arkin, Ronald C.,**
Behavior-based robotics / Ronald C. Arkin. Cambridge, Mass. : MIT Press, c1998. xiv, 490 p. :
97-018389          629.8/92          0262011654
*Autonomous robots. Intelligent control systems.*

**TJ211.B695 1999**
**Brooks, Rodney Allen.**
Cambrian intelligence : the early history of the new AI / Rodney A. Brooks. Cambridge, Mass. : MIT Press, c1999. xii, 199 p. :
99-017220          629.8/9263          0262522632
*Robotics. Artificial intelligence.*

**TJ211.D84 1996**
**Duffy, Joseph,**
Statics and kinematics with applications to robotics / Joseph Duffy. Cambridge [England] ; Cambridge University Press, 1996. xiii, 174 p.
95-004913          670.42/72          0521482135
*Manipulators (Mechanism) Statics. Machinery, Kinematics of.*

**TJ211.H65 1986**
**Holzbock, Werner G.**
Robotic technology, principles and practice / Werner G. Holzbock ; with a foreword by Jack D. Lane. New York : Van Nostrand Reinhold Co., c1986. xxi, 494 p. :
85-015634          629.8/92          0442231547
*Robotics -- Handbooks, manuals, etc.*

## TJ211.M45 2000
**Menzel, Peter,**

Robo sapiens : evolution of a new species / Peter Menzel and Faith D'Aluisio. Cambridge, Mass. : MIT Press, 2000. 239 p. :

00-033946          629.8/92          0262133822

*Robotics. Artificial intelligence. Intelligent control systems.*

## TJ211.M655 1999
**Moravec, Hans P.**

Robot : mere machine to transcendent mind / by Hans Moravec. New York : Oxford University Press, 1999. ix, 227 p. :

97-047328          303.48/34/0112          0195116305

*Robotics.*

## TJ211.N34 1991
**Nakamura, Yoshihiko.**

Advanced robotics : redundancy and optimization / Yoshihiko Nakamura. Reading, Mass. : Addison-Wesley Pub. Co., c1991. xi, 337 p. :

90-000931          629.8/92          0201151987

*Robotics.*

## TJ211.P65 1989
**Poole, Harry H.**

Fundamentals of robotics engineering / Harry H. Poole. New York : Van Nostrand Reinhold, c1989. x, 436 p. :

88-020861          629.8/92          0442272987

*Robotics.*

## TJ211.R535 1988

Robot design handbook / SRI International ; Gerry B. Andeen, editor-in-chief. New York : McGraw-Hill, c1988. 1 v. (various

87-025360          629.8/92          007060777X

*Robotics. Manipulators (Mechanism) -- Design and construction.*

## TJ211.R54 1982

Robot motion : planning and control / [edited by] Michael Brady ... [et al.]. Cambridge, Mass. : MIT Press, c1982. xv, 585 p. :

82-023929          629.8/92          026202182X

*Robots -- Motion. Manipulators (Mechanism)*

## TJ211.R67 1994
**Rosheim, Mark E.**

Robot evolution : the development of anthrobotics / Mark E. Rosheim. New York, N.Y. : Wiley, c1994. xvi, 423 p. :

94-013687          629.8/92          0471026220

*Robotics.*

## TJ211.Y6713 1990
**Yoshikawa, Tsuneo,**

Foundations of robotics : analysis and control / Tsuneo Yoshikawa. Cambridge, Mass. : MIT Press, c1990. x, 285 p. :

89-029363          629.8/92          0262240289

*Robotics.*

## TJ211.35 Mechanical devices and figures. Automata. Ingenuous mechanisms. Robots — Control systems

### TJ211.35.S26 1990
**Samson, Claude.**

Robot control : the task function approach / Claude Samson, Michel Le Borgne, and Bernard Espiau. Oxford : Clarendon Press : 1991. xvii, 364 p.

90-036440          629.8/92          0198538057

*Robots -- Control systems. Manipulators (Mechanism)*

## TJ211.4 Mechanical devices and figures. Automata. Ingenuous mechanisms. Robots — Robot motion. Robot dynamics

### TJ211.4.P37 1991
**Parkin, Robert E.,**

Applied robotic analysis / Robert E. Parkin. Englewood Cliffs, N.J. : Prentice Hall, c1991. xxii, 421 p.

90-042773          629.8/92

*Robots -- Motion. Machinery, Kinematics of.*

## TJ211.415 Mechanical devices and figures. Automata. Ingenuous mechanisms. Robots — Mobile robots

### TJ211.415.D83 2000
**Dudek, Gregory,**

Computational principles of mobile robotics / Gregory Dudek, Michael Jenkin. New York : Cambridge University Press, 2000. xii, 280 p.

99-018285          629.8/92          0521560217

*Mobile robots.*

### TJ211.415.J65 1999
**Jones, Joseph L.,**

Mobile robots : inspiration to implementation / Joseph L. Jones, Bruce A. Seiger, Anita M. Flynn. 2nd ed. Natick, Mass. : A.K Peters, c1999. xxii, 457 p. :

629.8/92 21

*Mobile robots.*

## TJ213 Control engineering systems. Automatic machinery — General works

### TJ213.B5952 1988
**Bollinger, John G.**

Computer control of machines and processes / John G. Bollinger, Neil A. Duffie. Reading, Mass. : Addison-Wesley, c1988. xxvi, 613 p.

87-014019          629.8/95          0201106450

*Automatic control -- Data processing.*

**TJ213.C293 1990**
**Carstens, James R.**

Automatic control systems and components / James R. Carstens. Englewood Cliffs, N.J. : Prentice Hall, c1990. xix, 441 p. :
89-037977       629.8       0130542970
*Automatic control. Process control.*

**TJ213.F88 1996**

Fuzzy logic : implementation and applications / edited by M.J. Patyra, D.M. Mlynek. Chichester ; Wiley ; c1996. xviii, 317 p.
95-045241       629.8       0471950599
*Automatic control. Fuzzy logic.*

**TJ213.K8354 1995**
**Kuo, Benjamin C.,**

Atuomatic control systems / Benjamin C. Kuo. 7th ed. Englewood Cliffs, N.J. : Prentice Hall, c1995. xxii, 897, 8 p:
      629.8 20
*Automatic control.*

**TJ213.L433 1997**
**Lewis, Harold W.**

The foundations of fuzzy control / Harold W. Lewis III. New York : Plenum Press, c1997. xv, 299 p. :
97-014026       629.8/9       0306454521
*Automatic control. Control theory. Fuzzy systems.*

**TJ213.O28 2001**
**Ogata, Katsuhiko.**

Modern control engineering / Katsuhiko Ogata. 4th ed. Upper Saddle River, NJ : Prentice Hall, 2001. p. cm.
      629.8 21
*Automatic control. Control theory.*

**TJ213.P314 1996**
**Parr, E. A.**

Control engineering / E.A. Parr. Oxford ; Butterworth-Heinemann, 1996. x, 414 p. :
95-042953       629.8       0750624078
*Automatic control.*

**TJ213.R38 1995**
**Raven, Francis H. (Francis Harvey),**

Automatic control engineering / Francis H. Raven. 5th ed. New York : McGraw-Hill, c1995. xv, 619 p. :
      629.8/3 20
*Automatic control.*

**TJ213.S1145 2001**

Perspectives in control engineering : technologies, applications, and new directions / [edited by] Tariq Samad. New York : IEEE Press, c2001. xxv, 503 p. :
00-038854       629.8       0780353560
*Automatic control. Control theory.*

**TJ213.S1157 1999**
**Sandler, B. Z.,**

Robotics : designing the mechanisms for automated machinery / Ben-Zion Sandler. 2nd ed. San Diego : Academic Press, 1999. x, 433 p. :
      670.42/72 21
*Automatic machinery -- Design and construction.*

**TJ213.S474443 1996**
**Siouris, George M.**

An engineering approach to optimal control and estimation theory / George M. Siouris. New York : Wiley, c1996. xvi, 407 p. :
95-006633       629.8       0471121266
*Automatic control. Control theory.*

**TJ213.S47475 1991**
**Skowronski, Janislaw M.**

Control of nonlinear mechanical systems / Janislaw M. Skowronski. New York : Plenum Press, c1991. x, 445 p. :
90-025787       629.8       0306438275
*Automatic control. Nonlinear mechanics.*

## TJ216 Control engineering systems. Automatic machinery — Control systems — Feedback control systems

**TJ216.C55 1996**
**Clark, Robert N.**

Control system dynamics / Robert N. Clark. Cambridge ; Cambridge University Press, 1996. xiii, 509 p.
95-014945       629.8/312       0521472393
*Feedback control systems. Control theory.*

**TJ216.D67 1986**
**Dorf, Richard C.**

Modern control systems / Richard C. Dorf. Reading, Mass. : Addison-Wesley, c1986. xvi, 539 p. :
85-007532       629.8/3       0201053268
*Feedback control systems.*

**TJ216.J29**
**Jacquot, Raymond G.,**

Modern digital control systems / Raymond G. Jacquot. New York : M. Dekker, c1981. xii, 355 p. :
81-007834       629.8/95       0824713222
*Digital control systems.*

**TJ216.K812 1980**
**Kuo, Benjamin C.,**

Digital control systems / Benjamin C. Kuo. New York : Holt, Rinehart and Winston, 1980. xiv, 730 p. :
80-016455       629.8/043       0030575680
*Digital control systems.*

**TJ216.O97 2000**
**Ozbay, Hitay.**

Introduction to feedback control theory / Hitay Ozbay. Boca Raton : CRC Press, c2000. 217 p. :
99-033365       629.8/32       084931867X
*Feedback control systems.*

**TJ216.R67 1986**
**Rowland, James R.**
  Linear control systems : modeling, analysis, and design / James R. Rowland. New York : Wiley, c1986. xii, 511 p. :
85-022612            629.8/3            047103276X
  *Linear control systems. Linear systems.*

## TJ217.5 Control engineering systems. Automatic machinery — Control systems — Intelligent control systems

**TJ217.5.D75 1996**
**Driankov, Dimiter.**
  An introduction to fuzzy control / Dimiter Driankov, Hans Hellendoorn, Michael Reinfrank ; with cooperation from Rainer Palm, Bruce Graham, and Anibal Ollero ; foreword by Lennart Ljung. 2nd, rev. ed. Berlin ; New York : Springer, c1996. xv, 316 p. :
            629.8 20
  *Intelligent control systems. Fuzzy systems.*

## TJ219 Control engineering systems. Automatic machinery — Control systems — Pneumatic control systems

**TJ219.G66 1997**
**Goodman, Robert B.,**
  A primer on pneumatic valves and controls / Robert B. Goodman. Malabar, Fla. : Krieger Pub., 1997. ix, 95, [1] p
96-013242            629.8/045            0894649655
  *Pneumatic control. Pneumatic control valves.*

## TJ223 Control engineering systems. Automatic machinery — Control systems — Special, A-Z

**TJ223.M53F73 1998**
**Franklin, Gene F.**
  Digital control of dynamic systems / Gene F. Franklin, J. David Powell, Michael L. Workman. 3rd ed. Menlo Park, Calif. : Addison-Wesley, c1998. xxiii, 742 p. :
            629.8/9 21
  *Digital control systems. Dynamics.*

**TJ223.M53J34 1995**
**Jacquot, Raymond G.**
  Modern digital control systems / Raymond G. Jacquot. 2nd ed. New York : Marcel Dekker, c1995. xvi, 408 p. :
            629.8 20
  *Digital control systems.*

**TJ223.M56P47 1995**
**Phillips, Charles L.**
  Digital control system analysis and design / Charles L. Phillips, H. Troy Nagle. 3rd ed. Englewood Cliffs, N.J. : Prentice Hall, c1995. xv, 685 p.
            629/895 20
  *Digital control systems. Electric filters, Digital. Intel 8086 (Microprocessor) MATLAB.*

**TJ223.P76**
**Katzen, Sid.**
  The quintessential PIC microcontroller / Sid Katzen. New York : Springer, 2001. ix, 486 p. :
00-066153            629.8/9            185233309X
  *Programmable controllers.*

**TJ223.P76P73 1999**
**Predko, Michael**
  Handbook of microcontrollers / Myke Predko. New York : McGraw-Hill, c1999. xviii, 861 p. :
            629.8/95416 21
*programmable controllers -- Handbooks, manuals, etc.*

## TJ230 Machine design and drawing — General works

**TJ230.J88 2000**
**Juvinall, Robert C.**
  Fundamentals of machine component design / Robert C. Juvinall, Kurt M. Marshek. 3rd ed. New York : John Wiley, c2000. xxiii, 888 p. :
            621.8/15 21
*Machine design.*

**TJ230.M433 1996**
  Mechanical design handbook / Harold A. Rothbart, editor. New York : McGraw-Hill, c1996. p. cm.
95-011164            612.8/15            0070540381
  *Machine design -- Handbooks, manuals, etc.*

**TJ230.N63 1999**
**Norton, Robert L.**
  Design of machinery : an introduction to the synthesis and analysis of mechanisms and machines / Robert L. Norton. Boston : McGraw-Hill, c1999. xxi, 809 p. :
91-007510            621.8/15            0070483957
  *Machine design.*

**TJ230.S5 2001**
**Shigley, Joseph Edward.**
  Mechanical engineering design / Joseph Edward Shigley, Charles R. Mischke. 6th ed. Boston, Mass. : McGraw Hill, 2001. xxxi, 1248 p. :
            621.8/15 21
*Machine design.*

**TJ230.S8235 1996**
  Standard handbook of machine design / [editors in chief,] Joseph E. Shigley, Charles R. Mischke. New York : McGraw-Hill, c1996. 1 v. (various
95-050600            621.8/15            0070569584
  *Machine design -- Handbooks, manuals, etc.*

# TJ243 Machine parts

**TJ243.Z29 1996**
**Zahavi, Eliahu.**
   Fatigue design : life expectancy of machine parts / Eliahu Zahavi with Vladimir Torbilo. Boca Raton : CRC Press, c1996. x, 321 p. :
96-014021          621.8/2          0849389704
   *Machine parts. Materials -- Fatigue.*

# TJ260 Heat engines — Heat in its applications, as a source of power, etc.

**TJ260.H36 1986**
   Handbook of heat and mass transfer / Nicholas P. Cheremisinoff, editor. Houston : Gulf Pub. Co., c1986-c1990 v. 1-4 :
84-025338          621.402/2          0872013383
   *Heat -- Transmission -- Handbooks, manuals, etc. Mass transfer -- Handbooks, manuals, etc.*

**TJ260.I579 1997**
   International encyclopedia of heat & mass transfer / edited by G.F. Hewitt, G.L. Shires, Y.V. Polezhaev. Boca Raton, [Fla.] : CRC Press, c1997. [20], 1312 p.
95-031097          621.402/2/03          0849393566
   *Heat -- Transmission -- Encyclopedias. Mass transfer -- Encyclopedias.*

**TJ260.L59 1994**
**Lock, G. S. H.**
   Latent heat transfer : an introduction to fundamentals / G.S.H. Lock. Oxford ; Oxford University Press, 1994. xxi, 288 p. :
94-011638          621.402/2          0198562853
   *Heat -- Transmission. Fusion, Latent heat of. Evaporation, Latent heat of.*

**TJ260.W217 1997**
**Warhaft, Z.**
   An introduction to thermal-fluid engineering : the engine and the atmosphere / Z. Warhaft. Cambridge ; Cambridge University Press, 1997. xv, 241 p. :
97-000089          621.402          0521581001
   *Heat engineering. Fluid dynamics. Internal combustion engines -- Environmental aspects.*

**TJ260.W48 1984**
**White, Frank M.**
   Heat transfer / Frank M. White. Reading, Mass. : Addison-Wesley, c1984. xvii, 588 p.
82-016404          621.402/2          0201083248
   *Heat -- Transmission.*

# TJ263 Heat engines — Heat exchangers — General works

**TJ263.K25 1998**
**Kakac, S.**
   Heat exchangers : selection, rating, and thermal design / Sadik Kakac, Hongtan Liu. Boca Raton, Fla. : CRC Press, c1998. 432 p. :
97-024314          621.402/5          084931688X
   *Heat exchangers.*

**TJ263.P63 1998**
**Podhorsky, M.**
   Heat exchangers : a practical approach to mechanical construction, design, and calculations / M. Podhorsky, H. Krips ; English edition editors, William Begell, Mike Morris. New York : Begell House, 1998. p. cm.
98-018447          621.402/5          1567001173
   *Heat exchangers -- Design and construction.*

# TJ265 Heat engines — Heat exchangers — Theory of heat engines. Thermodynamics

**TJ265.M317 1994**
**Marquand, C.**
   Thermofluids : an integrated approach to thermodynamics and fluid mechanics / C. Marquand, D. Croft. Chichester ; J. Wiley, c1994. xiv, 403 p. :
93-008776          620.1/06          0471941840
   *Thermodynamics. Fluid mechanics.*

**TJ265.V23 1994**
**Van Wylen, Gord John.**
   Fundamentals of classical thermodynamics / Gordon J. Van Wylen, Richard E. Sonntag, Claus Borgnakke. 4th ed. New York : Wiley, c1994. xii, 852 p. :
                    536/.7 20
*Thermodynamics.*

**TJ265.W39 1992**
**Whalley, P. B.**
   Basic engineering thermodynamics / P.B. Whalley. Oxford ; Oxford University Press, 1992. xi, 230 p. :
92-027653          621.402/1          0198562543
   *Thermodynamics.*

**TJ265.W535 1997**
**Winterbone, D. E.**
   Advanced thermodynamics for engineers / Desmond E. Winterbone. London : Arnold ; c1997. xix, 378 p. :
97-114642          621.402/1          034067699X
   *Thermodynamics.*

## TJ267 Heat engines — Heat exchangers — Theory of turbines. Fluid, aero- and hydrodynamics of turbomachinery

**TJ267.L35 1996**
**Lakshminarayana, B.**
Fluid dynamics and heat transfer of turbomachinery / Budugur Lakshminarayana. New York : Wiley, c1996. xxxii, 809 p.
94-041844          621.406          0471855464
*Turbomachines -- Fluid dynamics. Heat -- Transmission.*

## TJ275 Steam engineering — Steam (Including heated fluids) — Treatises, textbooks, etc.

**TJ275.B827 2000**
**Buecker, Brad.**
Fundamentals of steam generation chemistry / Brad Buecker. Tulsa, OK : PennWell Corp., 2000. xxi, 334 p. :
00-023790          621.1          0878147500
*Steam engineering. Feed-water.*

## TJ280.7 Steam engineering — Geothermal engineering

**TJ280.7.H36 1982**
Handbook of geothermal energy / editors, L.M. Edwards ... [et al.]. Houston : Gulf Pub. Co., c1982. ix, 613 p. :
81-020246          621.44          0872013227
*Geothermal engineering -- Handbooks, manuals, etc. Geothermal resources -- Handbooks, manuals, etc.*

## TJ281 Steam boilers — Societies, etc.

**TJ281.C78 1991**
Boilers, evaporators, and condensers / edited by Sadik Kakac. New York : Wiley, c1991. xxi, 835 p. :
90-022486          621.1/83          0471621706
*Steam-boilers. Evaporators. Condensers (Vapors and gases)*

## TJ288 Steam boilers — General special

**TJ288.T37 1991**
**Taplin, Harry,**
Combustion efficiency tables / by Harry Taplin. Lilburn, Ga ; Englewood Cliffs, NJ : Fairmont Press ; Prentice-Hall, c1991. xvii, 228 p. :
621.1/82 20          0881731439
*Steam-boilers -- Efficiency. Combustion -- Tables.*

## TJ400 Steam powerplants. Boiler plants — Plants for power alone — General works

**TJ400.S73 1999**
Steam power engineering : thermal and hydraulic design principles / edited by Seikan Ishigai. Cambridge, U.K. ; Cambridge University Press, 1999. xiv, 394 p. :
98-015350          621.31/2132          0521626358
*Steam power plants.*

## TJ461 Steam engines — History

**TJ461.H57 1989**
**Hills, Richard Leslie,**
Power from steam : a history of the stationary steam engine / Richard L. Hills. Cambridge [England] ; Cambridge University Press, 1989. xv, 338 p. :
89-007304          621.1/6/09          0521343569
*Steam-engines -- History.*

## TJ755 Miscellaneous motors and engines — General works

**TJ755.H45 1988**
**Heywood, John B.**
Internal combustion engine fundamentals / John B. Heywood. New York : McGraw-Hill, c1988. xxix, 930 p.,
87-015251          621.43          007028637X
*Internal combustion engines.*

**TJ755.L94 1999**
**Lumley, John L.  (John Leask)**
Engines : an introduction / John L. Lumley. Cambridge, UK ; New York : Cambridge University Press, 1999. xvii, 248 p. :
621.43 21
*Internal combustion engines.*

## TJ778 Miscellaneous motors and engines — Gas turbines

**TJ778.B34 1996**
**Bathie, William W.**
Fundamentals of gas turbines / William W. Bathie. 2nd ed. New York : Wiley, 1996. xiv, 453 p. :
621.43/3 20
*Gas-turbines.*

**TJ778.S24 2001**
**Saravanamuttoo, H. I. H.**
Gas turbine theory / H.I.H. Saravanamuttoo, G.F.C. Rogers, H. Cohen. 5th ed. Harlow, England ; New York : Prentice Hall, c2001. xvi, 491 p. :
621.43/3 21
*Gas-turbines.*

## TJ785 Miscellaneous motors and engines — Internal combustion engines, spark ignition — General works

**TJ785.T382 1985**
**Taylor, Charles Fayette,**
   The internal-combustion engine in theory and practice / by Charles Fayette Taylor. Cambridge, Mass. : M.I.T. Press, 1985. 2 v. :
84-028885      621.43      0262200511
   *Internal combustion engines.*

## TJ790 Miscellaneous motors and engines — Internal combustion engines, spark ignition — Special types

**TJ790.B577 1999**
**Blair, Gordon P.**
   Design and simulation of four-stroke engines / Gordon P. Blair. Warrendale, PA : Society of Automotive Engineers, c1999. xxiii, 815 p.
99-027316      621.43      0768004403
   *Four-stroke cycle engines -- Design and construction.*

## TJ795 Miscellaneous motors and engines — Diesel engines

**TJ795.D41355 1984**
   Design and applications in diesel engineering / editor-in-chief, S.D. Haddad ; associate editor, N. Watson. Chichester, West Sussex : E. Horwood ; 1984. 339 p. :
84-004576      621.43/6      047020074X
   *Diesel motor -- Design. Automobiles -- Motors (Diesel)*

## TJ807.9 Renewable energy sources — By region or country, A-Z

**TJ807.9.U6.C37 1993**
**Carless, Jennifer.**
   Renewable energy : a concise guide to green alternatives / Jennifer Carless. New York : Walker, 1993. viii, 168 p.
92-035137      333.79/4      0802782140
   *Renewable energy sources -- United States -- Juvenile literature. Renewable energy sources. Power resources.*

## TJ808 Renewable energy sources — General works

**TJ808.R42 1996**
   Renewable energy : power for a sustainable future / edited by Godfrey Boyle. Oxford : Oxford University Press in association with the 1996. xii, 479 p. :
96-215446      333.79      019856452X
   *Renewable energy sources.*

## TJ808.3 Renewable energy sources — Dictionaries and encyclopedias

**TJ808.3.G65 1993**
**Golob, Richard.**
   The almanac of renewable energy / Richard Golob and Eric Brus. New York : H. Holt, 1993. xiv, 348 p. :
92-013963      333.79/4      0805019480
   *Renewable energy sources -- Handbooks, manuals, etc.*

**TJ808.3.R67 1993**
**Rosenberg, Paul.**
   The alternative energy handbook / by Paul Rosenberg. Lilburn, GA : Fairmont Press ; c1993. x, 266 p. :
92-030937      621.042      0881731404
   *Renewable energy sources -- Handbooks, manuals, etc. Energy development -- Handbooks, manuals, etc.*

## TJ809.95 Renewable energy sources — Solar energy — By region or country

**TJ809.95.S68 1988 vol. 1**
   History and overview of solar heat technologies / edited by Donald A. Beattie. Cambridge, Mass. : MIT Press, c1997. xvii, 278 p.
96-034297      697/.78 s      0262024152
   *Solar energy. Solar energy -- History. Solar heating.*

**TJ809.95.S68 1988 vol. 6**
   Active solar systems / edited by George Lof. Cambridge, Mass. : MIT Press, c1993. xviii, 963 p.
92-025252      697/.78 s      0262121670
   *Solar energy. Solar heating. Solar air conditioning.*

**TJ809.95.S68 1988 vol. 7**
   Passive solar buildings / edited by J. Douglas Balcomb. Cambridge, Mass. : MIT Press, c1992. viii, 534 p.
91-046488      697/.78      0262023415
   *Solar buildings. Solar energy -- Passive systems.*

## TJ810 Renewable energy sources — Solar energy — General works

**TJ810.K73**
**Kreith, Frank.**
   Principles of solar engineering / Frank Kreith, Jan F. Kreider. Washington : Hemisphere Pub. Corp., c1978. xii, 778 p. :
77-027861      621.47      0070354766
   *Solar energy.*

**TJ810.S6244**
   Solar energy handbook / Jan F. Kreider, editor-in-chief, and Frank Kreith. New York : McGraw-Hill, c1981. ca. 1100 p. i
79-022570      621.47      007035474X
   *Solar energy -- Handbooks, manuals, etc.*

## TJ820-825 Renewable energy sources — Wind power

**TJ820.G56 1995**
**Gipe, Paul.**
  Wind energy comes of age / Paul Gipe. New York : Wiley, c1995. xxi, 536 p. :
94-036564          333.792          047110924X
  *Wind power.*

**TJ823.H55 1994**
**Hills, Richard Leslie,**
  Power from wind : a history of windmill technology / Richard L. Hills. Cambridge [England] ; Cambridge University Press, 1994. 324 p. :
93-008858          621.4/53/09          0521413982
  *Windmills -- History.*

**TJ825.W87 1983**
**Wortman, Andrze J.**
  Introduction to wind turbine engineering / by Andrze J. Wortman. Boston : Butterworth Publishers, c1983. xii, 130 p. :
83-071593          621.4/5          0250405628
  *Wind turbines.  Wind power.*

## TJ840 Hydraulic machinery — General works

**TJ840.H44 1993**
**Hehn, Anton H.,**
  Plant engineering magazine's fluid power handbook / Anton H. Hehn. Houston : Gulf Pub. Co., c1993. 2 v. :
92-046504          620.1/06          0884150720
  *Fluid power technology -- Handbooks, manuals, etc.  Plant engineering -- Handbooks, manuals, etc.*

**TJ840.H93 1997**
  Hydraulic design of hydraulic machinery / H.C. Radha Krishna, editor. Aldershot, Hants, England ; Avebury, c1997. xxiv, 570 p.
96-085968          621.2          0291398510
  *Hydraulic machinery -- Design and construction. Fluid dynamics.*

# TJ935 Flow of fluids in pipes. Flowmeters

**TJ935.B46**
**Benedict, Robert P.**
  Fundamentals of pipe flow / Robert P. Benedict. New York : Wiley, c1980. xix, 531 p. :
79-023924          621.8/67          0471033758
  *Pipe -- Fluid dynamics.*

## TJ940 Vacuum technology — General works

**TJ940.O37 1989**
**O'Hanlon, John F.,**
  A user's guide to vacuum technology / John F. O'Hanlon. 2nd ed. New York : Wiley, c1989. xvii, 481 p.:
          621.5/5 19
  *Vacuum technology -- Handbooks, manuals, etc.*

## TJ990 Pneumatic machinery — Compressed air — Air compressors

**TJ990.O815 1993**
**O'Neill, P. A.**
  Industrial compressors : theory and equipment / P.A. O'Neill. Oxford ; Butterworth-Heinemann, 1993. xiii, 591 p.
93-215681          621.5/1          0750608706
  *Compressors.*

## TJ1051 Machinery exclusive of prime movers — Power and power transmission — Power transmission machinery

**TJ1051.P55 1997**
**Phipps, Clarence A.,**
  Variable speed drive fundamentals / Clarence A. Phipps. Liburn, GA : Fairmont Press : c1997. xiii, 212 p.
96-052187          621.8/5          0881732583
  *Variable speed drives.*

## TJ1058 Machinery exclusive of prime movers — Rotors

**TJ1058.H36 1999**
  Handbook of rotordynamics / Fredric F. Ehrich, editor-in-chief. Rev. ed. Malabar, FL : Krieger Pub. Co., 1999. 1 v. :
          621.8 21
  *Rotors -- Dynamics.*

**TJ1058.R673 1992**
  Handbook of rotordynamics / Fredric F. Ehrich, editor-in-chief. New York : McGraw-Hill, c1992. 1 v. (various
91-020752          621.8          0070193304
  *Rotors -- Dynamics.*

## TJ1063 Machinery exclusive of prime movers — Bearings — Plain bearings. Journal bearings

**TJ1063.H35 1994**
**Hamrock, Bernard J.**
  Fundamentals of fluid film lubrication / Bernard J. Hamrock. New York : McGraw-Hill, c1994. xlvi, 690 p.
93-032107          621.8/9          0070259569
  *Fluid-film bearings.*

# Academic Libraries

**TJ1073.5 Machinery exclusive of prime movers — Bearings — Hydrodynamic and hydrostatic lubrication**

**TJ1073.5.S97 1998**
**Szeri, A. Z.**
Fluid film lubrication : theory and design / Andras Z. Szeri. Cambridge ; Cambridge University Press, c1998. xi, 414 p. :
98-011559      621.8/22      0521481007
*Fluid-film bearings.*

**TJ1075 Machinery exclusive of prime movers — Tribology. Lubrication and friction**

**TJ1075.B47 1991**
**Bhushan, Bharat,**
Handbook of tribology : materials, coatings, and surface treatments / Bharat Bhushan, B.K. Gupta. New York : McGraw-Hill, c1991. 1 v. (various
91-007155      621.8/9      0070052492
*Tribology -- Handbooks, manuals, etc.*

**TJ1075.L82 1996**
**Ludema, K. C.**
Friction, wear, lubrication : a textbook in tribology / Kenneth C. Ludema. Boca Raton : CRC Press, c1996. 257 p. :
96-012440      621.8/9      0849326850
*Tribology.*

**TJ1075.T762 1995**
The tribology handbook / edited by M.J. Neale. Oxford ; Butterworth-Heinemann, 1995. 1 v. (various
95-041661      621.8/9      0750611987
*Tribology -- Handbooks, manuals, etc.*

**TJ1185 Machine shops and machine shop practice — Machine tools and machining — General works**

**TJ1185.B8234 1998**
**Brown, James.**
Advanced machining technology handbook / James Brown. New York : McGraw-Hill, c1998. xxvii, 579 p.
97-039192      671.3/5      007008243X
*Machining -- Handbooks, manuals, etc.*

**TJ1185.W35 1994**
**Walsh, Ronald A.**
McGraw-Hill machining and metalworking handbook / Ronald A. Walsh. New York : McGraw-Hill, c1994. xvii, 1518 p.
93-022824      671.3/5      0070679584
*Machining -- Handbooks, manuals, etc. Metal-work -- Handbooks, manuals, etc.*

**TJ1185.W35 1999**
**Walsh, Ronald A.**
McGraw-Hill machining and metalworking handbook / Ronald A. Walsh. 2nd ed. New York : McGraw-Hill, c1999. xxv, 1683 p. :
671.3/5 21
*Machining -- Handbooks, manuals, etc. Metal-work -- Handbooks, manuals, etc.*

**TJ1185.5 Machine shops and machine shop practice — Machine tools and machining — Automatic lines, indexing tables, transfer mahines**

**TJ1185.5.A48 2000**
**Altintas, Yusuf,**
Manufacturing automation : metal cutting mechanics, machine tool vibrations, and CNC design / Yusuf Altintas. New York : Cambridge University Press, 2000. xii, 286 p. :
99-030935      671.3/5      0521650291
*Machining -- Automation. Machine-tools -- Vibration. Machine-tools -- Numerical control.*

**TJ1189 Machine shops and machine shop practice — Machine tools and machining — Numerical control of machine tools**

**TJ1189.E85 2001**
**Evans, Ken (Kenneth W.)**
Programming of computer numerically controlled machines / second edition by Ken Evans ; John Polywka and Stanley Gabrel. 2nd ed. New York : Industrial Press, 2001. p. cm. :
621.9/023/028551 21
*Machine-tools -- Numerical control -- Programming.*

**TJ1280 Machine shops and machine shop practice — Machine tools and machining — Special tools**

**TJ1280.S446 1996**
**Shaw, Milton Clayton,**
Principles of abrasive processing / Milton C. Shaw. Oxford : Clarendon Press ; 1996. xviii, 574 p.
95-038013      621.9/2      0198590210
*Grinding and polishing.*

**TJ1480 Agricultural machinery. Farm machinery — General works**

**TJ1480.K73 1984**
**Krutz, Gary.**
Design of agricultural machinery / Gary Krutz, Lester Thompson, Paul Claar. New York : Wiley, c1984. vii, 472 p. :
83-023251      681/.763      047108672X
*Agricultural machinery -- Design and construction.*

# TK Electrical engineering. Electronics. Nuclear engineering

## TK9 Dictionaries and encyclopedias

**TK9.C47 1996**
**Chambers, Ann.**
Power industry dictionary / by Ann Chambers, Susan D. Kerr. Tulsa, OK : PennWell Books, c1996. v, 388 p. :
621.31/03 20          0878146059
*Electric power systems -- Dictionaries. Electric utilities -- Dictionaries.*

**TK9.D474 1985**
Dictionary of electrical engineering : English, German, French, Dutch, Russian / [Y.N. Luginsky . . . Et al.]. Deventer : Kluwer Technische Boeken ; Paris, 1985. 479 p. :
621.3/03 19          902011909
*Electric engineering -- Dictionaries -- Polyglot. Dictionaries, Polyglot.*

**TK9.I28 2000**
IEEE 100 : the authoritative dictionary of IEEE standards terms. 7th ed.  New York : Standards Information Network, 2000. x, 1352 p. :
621.3/03 21          0738126012
*Electric engineering -- Dictionaries. Electronics -- Dictionaries. Computer engineering -- Dictionaries. Electric engineering -- Acronyms. Electronics -- Acronyms. Computer engineering -- Acronyms.*

**TK9.I35 1996**
**Institute of Electrical and Electronics Engineers.**
The IEEE standard dictionary of electrical and electronics terms / Standards Coordinating Committee 10, Terms and Definitions ; Jane Radatz, chair. 6th ed. [New York, N.Y.] : Institute of Electrical and Electronics Engineers [1996] 1278 p. :
321.3/03 21
*Electric engineering -- Dictionaries. Electronics -- Dictionaires. Computer engineering -- Dictionaries. Electric engineering -- Acronyms. Electronics -- Acronyms Computer engineering -- Acronyms.*

**TK9.K37 1996**
**Kaplan, Steven M.**
English-Spanish, Spanish-English electrical and computer engineering dictionary = Diccionario de ingenieria electrica y de computadoras ingles/espanol, espanol/ingles / Steven M. Kaplan, lexicographer. New York : Wiley, c1996. viii, 792 p.
95-042946          603          0471010375
*Electric engineering -- Dictionaries. Computer engineering -- Dictionaries. English language -- Dictionaries -- Spanish. Electric engineering -- Dictionaries -- Spanish. Computer engineering -- Dictionaries -- Spanish. Spanish language -- Dictionaries – English.*

**TK9.W55 1999**
Wiley encyclopedia of electrical and electronics engineering / John G. Webster, editor. New York : John Wiley, c1999. 24 v. :
98-044761          621.3/03          0471139467
*Electric engineering -- Encyclopedias. Electronics -- Encyclopedias.*

## TK23 Country divisions

**TK23.R9 1984**
**Ryder, John Douglas,**
Engineers & electrons : a century of electrical progress / John D. Ryder, Donald G. Fink. New York : IEEE Press, c1984. xix, 251 p. :
83-022681          621.3/0973          087942172X
*Electric engineering -- United States -- History.*

### TK139 Biography — Collective

**TK139.B73 1995**
**Bray, John,**
The communications miracle : the telecommunication pioneers from Morse to the information superhighway / John Bray. New York : Plenum Press, c1995. xix, 379 p. :
95-024622          621.382/09          0306450429
*Electric engineers -- Biography. Telecommunication -- Biography.*

## TK140 Biography — Individual, A-Z

**TK140.E3.B25 1995**
**Baldwin, Neil,**
Edison, inventing the century / Neil Baldwin. New York : Hyperion, c1995. x, 531 p. :
94-027984          621.3/092          0786860413
*Edison, Thomas A. (Thomas Alva), 1847-1931. Inventors – United States -- Biography. Electric engineering -- United States – History.*

**TK140.T4.S65 1996**
**Seifer, Marc J.**
Wizard : the life and times of Nikola Tesla : biography of a genius / Marc J. Seifer. Secaucus, N.J. : Carol Pub., c1996. xiv, 542 p. :
95-049919          621.3/092          1559723297
*Tesla, Nikola, 1856-1943. Electric engineers -- United States -- Biography. Inventors -- United States -- Biography.*

## TK145 General works — 1870-

**TK145.E354 1997**
The electrical engineering handbook / editor-in-chief, Richard C. Dorf. Boca Raton : CRC Press ; c1997. 2719 p. :
97-035400          621.3          0849385741
*Electric engineering.*

## TK151 Pocketbooks, tables, etc.

**TK151.C468 1998**
**Christoffer, V.F.**
 Handbook of electrical tables and design criteria / V.F. Christoffer. New York : McGraw-Hill, c1998. xiii, 396 p. :
 621.3/02/1 21    0079137229
*Electric engineering -- Tables.*

**TK151.H67 1995**
**Holt, Charles Michael.**
 Electrician's formula and reference book / Michael Holt. New York : Delmar Publishers, c1995. 1 v. (various
 94-018048    621.319/24/0151    0827369611
*Electric engineering -- Mathematics -- Handbooks, manuals, etc. Engineering mathematics -- Formulae -- Handbooks, manuals, etc.*

**TK151.S8**
 Standard handbook for electrical engineers. New York, McGraw-Hill. v.
 56-006964    621.3
*Electric engineering -- Handbooks, manuals, etc.*

## TK152 Safety measures (General)

**TK152.C22 1994**
**Cadick, John.**
 Electrical safety handbook / John Cadick. New York : McGraw-Hill, c1994. 1 v. (various
 94-013347    621.319/028/9    0070095140
*Electric engineering -- Safety measures. Electricity -- Safety measures. Industrial safety.*

## TK153 General special (Including electromechanical transducers)

**TK153.S53 1990**
**Silvester, P. P.**
 Finite elements for electrical engineers / P.P. Silvester, R.L. Ferrari. Cambridge [England] ; Cambridge University Press, 1990, c1989. p. cm.
 89-031655    621.3/01/515353    0521372394
*Electric engineering -- Mathematics. Finite element method.*

## TK260 Insurance requirements

**TK260.G37 1998**
**Garland, J. D.,**
 National Electrical Code reference book / J.D. Garland. 5th ed. Englewood Cliffs, N.J. : Prentice-Hall, c1998. x, 611 p.:
 621.319/24/021 19
*Electric engineering -- Insurance requirements.*

**TK260.N47B**
**National Fire Protection Association.**
 The national electrical code handbook. Boston, Mass. : National Fire Protection Association, v. :
 79-643453    621.319/24/0218
*Electric engineering -- Insurance requirements -- Periodicals. Electric engineering -- Law and legislation -- United States -- Periodicals.*

## TK435 Estimates

**TK435.M415 1998**
 McGraw-Hill's handbook of electrical construction calculations / Joseph F. McPartland ... [et al.]. New York : McGraw-Hill, c1998. 1 v. (various
 97-029144    621.3    0070466416
*Electric engineering -- Estimates -- Handbooks, manuals, etc.*

## TK452 Electric apparatus and materials — General works

**TK452.W55 1996**
**Whitson, Gene.**
 Handbook of electrical construction tools and materials / Gene Whitson. New York : McGraw-Hill, c1996. vi, 478 p. :
 95-042985    621.319/3    0070699208
*Electric apparatus and appliances. Electric engineering – Equipment and supplies.*

## TK453 Electric apparatus and materials — Materials (General)

**TK453.E36 1990**
 Electrical engineering materials reference guide / H. Wayne Beaty, editor. New York : McGraw-Hill, c1990. 1 v. (various
 89-012554    621.3    0070041962
*Electric engineering -- Materials -- Handbooks, manuals, etc.*

## TK454 Electric apparatus and materials — Electric circuits (Electric-power circuits) — General works

**TK454.B48 1997**
**Bird, J. O.**
 Electrical circuit theory and technology / J.O. Bird. Oxford ; Butterworth-Heinemann, 1997. xvi, 939 p. :
 98-134907    621.3    0750635525
 *Electric circuits. Electric engineering.*

**TK454.B68 2000**
**Boylestad, Robert L.**
 Introductory circuit analysis / Robert L. Boylestad. 9th ed. Upper Saddle River, N. J. : Prentice Hall, c2000. xvi, 1200 p. :
 621.319/2 21
*Electric circuits. Electric circuit analysis -- Data processing. Pspice.*

**TK454.D67 2001**
**Dorf, Richard C.**
  Introduction to electric circuits / Richard C. dorf, James A. Svoboda. 5th ed. New York : Wiley, c2001. xxiii, 865 p. :
  621.319/24 2001
*Electric circuits.*

**TK454.H4 2002**
**Hayt, William Hart,**
  Engineering circuit analysis / William H. Hayt, Jr., Jack E. Kemmerly, Steven M. Durbin. 6th ed. Boston : McGraw-Hill, c2002. xviii, 781 p. :
  621.319/2 21
*Electric circuit analysis. Electric network analysis.*

**TK454.M29 1988**
**Markus, John,**
  Essential circuits reference guide / John Markus, Charles Weston. New York : McGraw-Hill, c1988. xv, 531 p. :
  88-000569      621.319/2      0070404623
  *Electric circuits -- Handbooks, manuals, etc. Electronic circuits -- Handbooks, manuals, etc.*

**TK454.M3295 2000**
  Mathematics for circuits and filters / edited by Wai-Kai Chen. Boca Raton, Fla : CRC Press, 2000. 263 p. ;
  99-043798      621.3      0849300525
  *Electric circuits, Linear -- Mathematical models. Electric filters -- Mathematical models. Electric engineering -- Mathematics.*

**TK454.S57 1986**
**Siebert, William McC.**
  Circuits, signals, and systems / William McC. Siebert. Cambridge, Mass. : MIT Press ; c1986. xvi, 651 p. :
  85-004302      621.319/2      0262192292
  *Electric circuits. Discrete-time systems. Linear time invariant systems.*

## TK454.2 Electric apparatus and materials — Electric networks (Electric power networks)

**TK454.2.C4253 1990**
**Chen, Wai-Kai,**
  Linear networks and systems : alogrithms and computer-aided implementations / Wai-Kai Chen. Singapore; Teaneck, N.J. : World Scientific, c1990. 2 v. :
  621.319/2 20
*Electric networks -- Data processing.*

**TK454.2.S65 1994**
**Smith, David L.**
  Introduction to dynamic systems modeling for design / David L. Smith. Englewood Cliffs, N.J. : Prentice Hall, c1994. xv, 472 p. :
  93-003908      620/.0042      013588344X
  *Electric networks -- Mathematical models. System analysis.*

## TK1001 Production of electric energy or power — General works

**TK1001.B44 2000**
**Bergen, Arthur R.**
  Power systems analysis / Arthur R. Bergen, Vijay Vittal. 2nd ed. Upper Saddle River, NJ : Prentice Hall, 2000. xii, 619 p. :
  621.31 21
*Electric power systems. System analysis.*

**TK1001.B275 2000**
**Barnett, Dave.**
  Electric power generation : a nontechnical guide / Dave Barnett & Kirk Bjornsgaard. Tulsa, Okla. : PennWell, c2000. xviii, 337 p.
  99-056998      621.31      0878147535
*Electric power production.*

**TK1001.Y36 1994**
**Yamayee, Zia A.**
  Electromechanical energy devices and power systems / Zia A. Yamayee, Juan L. Bala, Jr. New York : Wiley, c1994. xvi, 503 p. :
  93-005529      621.319      0471572179
*Electric power systems. Electric machinery.*

## TK1005 Production of electric energy or power — General special

**TK1005.K32 1993**
**Kabisama, H. W.**
  Electrical power engineering / H.W. Kabisama. New York : McGraw-Hill, c1993. xii, 292 p. :
  93-009697      621.31      007033157X
*Electric power systems.*

## TK1010 Production of electric energy or power — Electric power system stability

**TK1010.B65 1999**
**Bollen, Math H. J.,**
  Understanding power quality problems : voltage sags and interruptions / Math H.J. Bollen. New York : IEEE Press, 1999. xvii, 543 p.
  99-023546      621.319      0780347137
*Electric power system stability. Electric power failures. Brownouts. Electric power systems -- Quality control.*

### TK1041 Production of electric energy or power — Production from heat. Cogeneration of electric power and heat — General works

**TK1041.C6327 1997**
  Cogeneration management reference guide / F. William Payne, editor. Lilburn, GA : Fairmont Press, c1997. 447 p. :
  96-048537      333.793      0881732486
*Cogeneration of electric power and heat.*

**TK1041.W55 2000**
**Willis, H. Lee,**
  Distributed power generation : planning and evaluation / H. Lee Willis, Walter G. Scott. New York : Marcel Dekker, 2000. xvi, 597 p. :
99-054218          621.31      0824703367
*Total energy systems (On-site electric power production) Electric power-plants -- Planning.*

## TK1056 Production of electric energy or power — Production from heat. Cogeneration of electric power and heat — Production from solar thermal energy

**TK1056.S627 1990**
  Solar power plants : fundamentals, technology, systems, economics / C.-J. Winter, R.L. Sizmann, L.L. Vant-Hull (eds.). Berlin ; Springer-Verlag, c1991. xii, 425 p. :
90-022035          621.31/244      3540188975
*Solar power plants.*

## TK1078 Production of electric energy or power — Production from heat. Cogeneration of electric power and heat — Production from atomic power

**TK1078.D83**
**Duderstadt, James J.,**
  Nuclear power : technology on trial / James J. Duderstadt, Chihiro Kikuchi. Ann Arbor : University of Michigan Press, c1979. x, 228 p. :
79-016455          621.48/3      0472093118
*Nuclear power plants. Nuclear energy.*

**TK1078.M68 1990**
**Mounfield, Peter R.,**
  World nuclear power / Peter R. Mounfield. London ; Routledge, 1991. xxii, 441 p.
90-045131          333.792/4      0415004632
*Nuclear power plants. Nuclear power plants -- Safety measures. Nuclear fuels. Spent reactor fuels.*

## TK1081 Production of electric energy or power — Production from waterpower. Hydroelectric power production — General works

**TK1081.M39**
**McCormick, Michael E.,**
  Ocean wave energy conversion / Michael E. McCormick. New York : Wiley, c1981. xxiv, 233 p.
81-000494          621.31/2134      047108543X
*Ocean wave power.*

## TK1087 Production of electric energy or power — Production from solar energy — Photovoltaic power generation. Photovoltaic power systems

**TK1087.S66 2000**
  Solar electricity / edited by Tomas Markvart. 2nd ed. Chichester ; New York : Wiley, 2000. xiv, 280 p. :
          621.31/244 21
*Photovoltaic power systems. Photovoltaic power generation. Solar cells.*

## TK1191 Production of electric energy or power — Electric power plants — General works

**TK1191.S686 1998**
  Standard handbook of powerplant engineering / [edited by] Thomas C. Elliott, Kao Chen, Robert C. Swanekamp. New York : McGraw Hill, c1998. 1 v. :
          621.31/21 21
*Electric power-plants.*

**TK1191.P6486 1993**
  Power station instrumentation / edited by Max Jervis. Oxford ; Butterworth-Heinemann, 1993. 1 v. (various
92-045003          621.31/21/028      0750611960
*Electric power-plants -- Equipment and supplies. Electric power production -- Instruments.*

## TK1194 Production of electric energy or power — Electric power plants — Directories of electrical industries

**TK1194.N83**
  Nuclear power plants worldwide. Detroit ; Gale Research Inc., c1993- v. :
93-649990          333.792/4/025
*Nuclear power plants -- Directories.*

## TK1343-1541 Production of electric energy or power — Electric power plants — Special

**TK1343.M67 1989**
**Morone, Joseph G.**
  The demise of nuclear energy? : lessons for democratic control of technology / Joseph G. Morone, Edward J. Woodhouse. New Haven : Yale University Press, c1989. xii, 172 p. ;
88-028031          363.1/79      0300044488
*Nuclear power plants -- Risk assessment -- United States. Nuclear energy -- United States -- Decision making.*

**TK1345.H37.T45 1986**
  The Three Mile Island accident : diagnosis and prognosis / L.M. Toth ... [et al.], editors. Washington, D.C. : American Chemical Society, 1986. ix, 301 p. :
85-026852          363.1/79      0841209480
*Three Mile Island Nuclear Power Plant (Pa.) -- Congresses. Nuclear power plants -- Pennsylvania -- Accidents -- Congresses.*

**TK1362.S65.M37 1988**
**Marples, David R.**
   The social impact of the Chernobyl disaster / David R. Marples ; introduction by Victor G. Snell. New York : St. Martin's Press, 1988. xviii, 313 p.
88-018314          363.1/79          0312024320
*Chernobyl Nuclear Accident, Chornobyl§, Ukraine, 1986 -- Social aspects.*

**TK1541.A75 2001**
**Asmus, Peter.**
   Reaping the wind : how mechanical wizards, visionaries, and profiteers helped shape our energy future / Peter Asmus. Washington, D.C. : Island Press, c2001. x, 277 p. ;
00-010901          333.9/2/0973          1559637072
   *Wind power plants.  Electric utilities -- United States.*

**TK1541.H86**
**Hunt, V. Daniel.**
   Windpower : a handbook on wind energy conversion systems / V. Daniel Hunt. New York : Van Nostrand Reinhold Co., c1981. xvii, 610 p.
80-012581          621.4/5          0442273894
*Wind energy conversion systems.*

**TK1541.J64 1985**
**Johnson, Gary L.**
   Wind energy systems / Gary L. Johnson. Englewood Cliffs, N.J. : Prentice-Hall, c1985. viii, 360 p.
83-024779          621.4/5          0139577548
*Wind power.*

## TK2000 Dynamoelectric machinery and auxiliaries (Including motive power, machinery and auxiliaries) — General works

**TK2000.P35 1997**
**Patrick, Dale R.**
   Rotating electrical machines and power systems / Dale R. Patrick, Stephen W. Fardo. Lilburn, GA : Fairmont Press, c1997. xii, 399 p. :
96-009543          621.31/042          0881732397
*Electric machinery.  Electric transformers.*

## TK2181 Dynamoelectric machinery and auxiliaries — Special motive power and driving apparatus for dynamoelectric mahinery — General works

**TK2181.F5 1990**
**Fitzgerald, A. E. (Arthur Eugene),**
   Electric machinery / A.E. Fitzgerald, Charles Kingsley, Jr., Stephen D. Umans. 5th ed. New York : McGraw-Hill, c1990. xiii, 599 p. :
              621.31/042 20
*Electric machinery.*

## TK2411 Dynamoelectric machinery and auxiliaries — Dynamoelectric machinery — Generators

**TK2411.B6 1997**
**Boldea, I.**
   Linear electric actuators and generators / I. Boldea, Syed A. Nasar. Cambridge ; Cambridge University Press, 1997. x, 237 p. :
96-031469          629.8/315          0521480175
*Electric generators.  Actuators.*

## TK2511 Dynamoelectric machinery and auxiliaries — Dynamoelectric machinery — Motors (General)

**TK2511.E423 1988**
   Electric motor handbook / edited by B.J. Chalmers. London ; Butterworths, 1988. 546 p., [4] p
87-020887          621.46/2          0408007079
*Electric motors -- Handbooks, manuals, etc.*

**TK2511.L54 1995**
**Litman, Todd.**
   Efficient electric motor systems handbook / Todd Litman. Lilburn, GA : Fairmont Press ; c1995. xi, 320 p. :
94-043747          621.46          0881731978
*Electric motors -- Handbooks, manuals, etc. Electric driving -- Handbooks, manuals, etc.*

## TK2711-2785 Dynamoelectric machinery and auxiliaries — Dynamoelectric machinery — Alternating-current machinery

**TK2711.S3 1983**
**Say, M. G.**
   Alternating current machines / M.G. Say. New York : Wiley, c1983. xii, 632 p. :
83-010719          621.31/33          0470274514
*Electric machinery -- Alternating current. Electric transformers.*

**TK2785.T75 2001**
**Trzynadlowski, Andrzej.**
   Control of induction motors / Andrzej M. Trzynadlowski. San Diego, Calif. ; Academic Press, c2001. xii, 228 p. :
00-104379          0127015108
   *Electric motors, Induction.  Electric motors -- Electronic control.*

## TK2821 Dynamoelectric machinery and auxiliaries — Apparatus auxiliary to dynamoelectric machinery — General works

**TK2821.S924 1998**
   Switchgear and control handbook / Robert W. Smeaton, editor, William H. Ubert, editor. 3rd ed. New York : McGraw-Hill, c1998. 1 v. :
              621.31/7 21
*Electric switchgear -- Handbooks, manuals, etc. Electric controllers -- Handbooks, manuals, etc. Automatic control --Handbooks, manuals, etc.*

## TK2831 Dynamoelectric machinery and auxiliaries — Apparatus auxiliary to dynamoelectric machinery — Switchboards and accessories

**TK2831.M37 1993**
**Mason, John R.**
 Switch engineering handbook / John R. Mason. New York : McGraw-Hill, c1993. 1 v. (various
92-023508          621.31/7          007040769X
*Electric switchgear -- Handbooks, manuals, etc.*

## TK2896 Devices for production of electricity by direct energy conversion — General works

**TK2896.D43 1997**
**Decher, Reiner.**
 Direct energy conversion : fundamentals of electric power production / Reiner Decher. New York : Oxford University Press, 1997. xiv, 258 p. :
96-004842          621.31/24          0195095723
*Direct energy conversion.*

## TK2901 Devices for production of electricity by direct energy conversion — Production of electricity directly from chemical action — General works

**TK2901.H36 2001**
 Handbook of batteries / David Linden, editor, Thomas B. Reddy, editor. 3rd ed. New York McGraw-Hill, 2002. 1 v. :
          621.31/242 21
*Electric batteries -- Handbooks, manuals, etc.*

## TK2960 Devices for production of electricity by direct energy conversion — Solar batteries. Solar cells

**TK2960.N48 1995**
**Neville, Richard C.**
 Solar energy conversion : the solar cell / Richard C. Neville. Amsterdam ; Elsevier, 1995. xiv, 426 p. :
94-039734          621.31/244          0444898182
*Solar cells. Solar energy.*

**TK2960.Z945 1990**
**Zweibel, Kenneth.**
 Harnessing solar power : the photovoltaics challenge / Ken Zweibel. New York : Plenum Press, c1990. xi, 319 p. :
90-039905          621.31/244          0306435640
*Photovoltaic power generation.*

## TK3001 Distribution or transmission of electric power (Including the electric power circuit) — General works

**TK3001.G73 1994**
**Grainger, John J.**
 Power system analysis / John J. Grainger, William D. Stevenson, Jr. New York : McGraw-Hill, c1994. xix, 787 p. :
93-039219          621.319          0070612935
*Electric power distribution. Electric power systems.*

**TK3001.P37 1999**
**Patrick, Dale R.**
 Electrical distribution systems / Dale R. Patrick, Stephen W. Fardo. Lilburn, GA : Fairmont Press, c1999. ix, 481 p. :
98-036065          621.319          0881732524
*Electric power distribution. Electric power systems.*

## TK3221 Distribution or transmission of electric power — Wiring — The line

**TK3221.K83 1986**
**Kurtz, Edwin Bernard,**
 The lineman's and cableman's handbook / Edwin B. Kurtz, Thomas M. Shoemaker. New York : McGraw-Hill Book, c1986. 1 v. (various
85-017120          621.319/22          0070356866
*Electric lines -- Handbooks, manuals, etc. Electric cables -- Handbooks, manuals, etc.*

## TK3271 Distribution or transmission of electric power — Interior or indoor wiring — General works

**TK3271.M35 1999**
**McPartland, Joseph F.**
 Handbook of practical electrical design / Joseph F. McPartland, Brian J. McPartland. 3rd ed. New York : McGraw-Hill, c1999. vii, 723 p. :
          621.319/24 21
*Electric wiring -- Handbooks, Manuals, etc.*

## TK3284 Distribution or transmission of electric power — Interior or indoor wiring — Commercial building wiring

**TK3284.T75 1996**
**Traister, John E.**
 Electrical wiring design : commercial & institutional / by John E. Traister. Lilburn, GA : Fairmont Press ; c1996. x, 241 p. :
95-040318          621.319/24          0881732141
*Electric wiring, Interior. Commercial buildings -- Electric equipment.*

## TK3301 Distribution or transmission of electric power — Conductors. Wires. Cables — General works

**TK3301.P66 2000**
Power and communication cables : theory and applications / edited by R. Bartnikas, K.D. Srivastava. New York : IEEE Press : c2000. xxi, 858 p. :
99-018442        621.319/34        0780311965
*Electric cables. Telecommunication cables.*

## TK3305 Distribution or transmission of electric power — Conductors. Wires. Cables — Tables of properties and dimensions of wire (Pocketbooks of wiring)

**TK3305.S38 1991**
**Sclater, Neil.**
Wire and cable for electronics : a user's handbook / by Neil Sclater. New York, NY : McGraw Hill, c1991. ix, 237 p. :
91-021811        621.381/044        0830677879
*Electric wire -- Tables. Electric cables -- Tables. Electronics -- Equipment and supplies.*

## TK3307 Distribution or transmission of electric power — Conductors. Wires. Cables — Standards and testing of wire and cable

**TK3307.A69 1997**
**Anders, George J.**
Rating of electric power cables : ampacity computations for transmission, distribution, and industrial applications / George J. Anders. New York : Institute of Electrical and Electronics Engineer c1997. xxxiii, 428 p
96-043345        621.319/34        0780311779
*Electric cables -- Standards. Electric cables -- Mathematical models. Electric currents -- Measurement -- Mathematics. Powerline ampacity.*

## TK3521 Distribution or transmission of electric power — Other details — Connectors

**TK3521.M76 1998**
**Mroczkowski, Robert S.**
Electronic connector handbook : theory and applications / Robert S. Mroczkowski. New York : McGraw-Hill, c1998. 1 v. (various)
98-124562        621.38154        0070414017
*Electric connectors -- Handbooks, manuals, etc. Electronics -- Equipment and supplies. ELECTRIC CONNECTORS nasat ELECTRONIC EQUIPMENT nasat HANDBOOKS nasat*

## TK4035 Applications of electric power — Special applications — Other special, A-Z

**TK4035.F3.P73 1995**
**Prabhakara, F. S.**
Industrial and commercial power system handbook / F.S. Prabhakara, Robert L. Smith, Ray P. Stratford. New York : McGraw-Hill, c1995. p. cm.
95-015990        621.319        0070506248
*Factories -- Power supply. Commercial buildings -- Power supply. Electric power systems.*

## TK4058 Applications of electric power — Mechanical applications of electric power — Use of electric motors

**TK4058.B64 1999**
**Boldea, I.**
Electric drives / Ion Boldea, S.A. Nasar. Boca Raton : CRC Press, c1999. 411 p. :
98-022209        621.46        0849325218
*Electric driving.*

## TK4161 Electric lighting — General works — 1870-

**TK4161.I46 1981**
**Illuminating Engineering Society of North America.**
IES lighting handbook / John E. Kaufman, editor. New York, N.Y. : Illuminating Engineering Society of North Americ c1981 2 v. :
80084964        621.32/2        0879950072
*Electric lighting.*

## TK4399 Electric lighting — Systems of electric lighting — Special uses of electric lighting, A-Z

**TK4399.F2.F74**
**Frier, John P.**
Industrial lighting systems / John P. Frier and Mary E. Gazley Frier. New York : McGraw-Hill, c1980. xii, 322 p. :
79-023138        621.32/25/4        0070224579
*Industrial buildings -- Lighting. Electric discharge lighting.*

## TK5101 Telecommunication — Societies, congresses, etc.

**TK5101C69 2001**
**Couch, Leon W.**
Digital and analog communication systems / Leon W. Couch II. 6th ed. Upper Saddle River, N.J. : Prentice Hall, c2001. xxv, 758 p. :
                        621.382 21
*Telecommunication systems. Digital communications.*

**TK5101.L333 1998**
**Lathi, B. P. (Bhagwandas Pannalal)**
   Modern digital and analog communication systems / B.P. Lathi, 3rd ed. New York : Oxford Univerisity Press, 1998. xii, 781 p. :
   621.382 21
*Telecommunication systems. Digital communications. Statistical communication theory.*

**TK5101.N782 2001**
**Noll, A. Michael.**
   Principles of modern communications technology / A. Michael Noll. Boston, MA : Artech House, 2001. p. cm.
01-022208            621.382            1580532845
   *Telecommunication.*

**TK5101.T625 2001**
**Tomasi, Wayne.**
   Electronic communications systems : fundamentals through advanced / Wayne Tomasi. 4th ed. Upper Saddle River, N.J. : Prentice Hall, c2001. xxv, 947 p. :
   621.382 21
*Telecommunication systems.*

**TK5101.F6595 1999**
**Freeman, Roger L.**
   Fundamentals of telecommunications / Roger L. Freeman. New York : Wiley, c1999. xxii, 676 p.
98-004272            621.382            0471296996
*Telecommunication.*

**TK5101.S13 1994**
**Saadawi, Tarek N.**
   Fundamentals of telecommunication networks / Tarek N. Saadawi, Mostafa H. Ammar with Ahmed El Hakeem. New York : Wiley, c1994. xvii, 485 p.
94-006544            621.382            0471515825
*Telecommunication systems. Computer networks. Data transmission systems.*

**TK5101.T355 2000**
   The telecommunications handbook / editors-in-chief, Kornel Terplan, Patricia Morreale. Boca Raton, Fla. : CRC Press, c2000. 1 v. (various
99-044580            384            0849331374
*Telecommunication -- Handbooks, manuals, etc.*

**TK5101.T79 1990**
**Truxal, John G.**
   The age of electronic messages / John G. Truxal. Cambridge, Mass. : MIT Press, c1990. xvi, 487 p. :
89-012669            621.382            0262200740
*Telecommunication. Electronics.*

**TK5101.W48 1993**
**Winch, Robert G.**
   Telecommunication transmission systems : microwave, fiber optic, mobile cellular radio, data, and digital multiplexing / Robert G. Winch. New York : McGraw-Hill, c1993. xii, 540 p. :
92-026723            621.382            0070709645
*Telecommunication systems.*

## TK5102 Telecommunication — Dictionaries and encyclopedias

**TK5102.H37 2001**
**Hargrave, Frank.**
   Hargrave's communications dictionary / Frank Hargrave. New York : IEEE Press, 2001. ix, 917 p. :
   621.382/03 21            0780360206
*Telecommunication -- Dictionaries.*

**TK5102.M34 1999**
**Mazda, Xerxes.**
   The Focal illustrated dictionary of telecommunications / Xerxes Mazda, Fraidoon Mazda. Oxford ; Boston : Focal, 1999. 685 p. :
   621.382/03 21            0240515447
*Telecommunication -- Dictionaries.*

**TK5102.N49 2001**
**Newton, Harry.**
   Newton's telecom dictionary : the official dictionary of telecommunications networking and Internet / [by Harry Newton]. 17th updated and expanded ed. New York, NY : CMP Books, c2001. viii, 787 p. :
   621.382/03 21
*Telecommunication -- Dictionaries.*

**TK5102.P48 1999**
**Petersen, Julie K.**
   Data & telecommunications dictionary / Julie K. Petersen. Boca Raton : CRC Press, c1999. 820 p. :
98-046077            621.382/03            0849395917
*Telecommunication -- Dictionaries. Data transmission systems -- Dictionaries. Computer networks -- Dictionaries.*

**TK5102.S48 2001**
**Sheldon, Thomas.**
   McGraw-Hill encyclopedia of networking & telecommunications / Tom Sheldon. Berkeley, Calif. : Osborne, c2001. xxxviii, 1447 p
   004.6/03 21            0072120053
*Computer networks -- Encyclopedias. Telecommunication -- Encyclopedias.*

**TK5102.V55 2001**
**Vlietstra, J.**
   Dictionary of acronyms and technical abbreviations : for information and communication technologies and related areas / Jakob Vlietstra. New York : Springer, 2001. vi, 696 p. ;
00-052664            621.382/01/48            1852333979
   *Telecommunication -- Dictionaries. Telecommunication -- Acronyms. Telecommunication -- Abbreviations.*

**TK5102.V55 2001**
**Vlietstra, J.**
Dictionary of acronyms and technical abbreviations : for information and communication technologies and related areas / Jakob Vlietstra. 2nd ed. New York : Springer, 2001. vi, 696 p. :
621.382/01/48 21
*Telecommunication -- Dictionaries. Telecommunication – Acronyms. Telecommunication -- Abbeviations. Information technology -- Acronyms. Information technology -- Abbreviations.*

## TK5102.2 Telecommunication — History

**TK5102.2.J46 2000**
**Jensen, Peter R.**
From the wireless to the web : the evolution of telecommunications, 1901-2001 / Peter R. Jensen. Sydney : University of New South Wales Press, 2000. 306 p. :
384.0904          0868404586
*Telecommunication -- History -- 20th century. Telecommunication – History -- 20th century.*

## TK5102.3 Telecommunication — By region or country, A-Z

**TK5102.3.U6G74 2000**
**Green, James H. (James Harry)**
The Irwin handbook of telecommunications / by James Harry Green. 4th ed. New York : McGraw Hill, 2000. xxxii, 844 p. :
621.382 21
*Telecommunication systems -- United States. Business enterprises – United States -- Communication systems.*

## TK5102.5 Telecommunication — General special

**TK5102.5.C24 1985**
**Cadzow, James A.**
Signals, systems, and transforms / James A. Cadzow, Hugh F. Van Landingham. Englewood Cliff, N.J. : Prentice-Hall, c1985. xi, 348 p. :
84-022841          003          0138095426
*Signal theory (Telecommunication) System analysis. Fourier transformations.*

**TK5102.5.C3 2002**
**Carlson, A. Bruce,**
Communication systems : an introduction to signals and noise in electrical communication / A. Bruce Carlson, Paul B. Crilly, Janet C. Rutledge. 4th ed. Boston : McGraw-Hill, 2002. xiii, 850 p. :
621.382/23 21
*Signal theory (Telecommunication) Modulation (Electronics) Digital communications.*

**TK5102.5.C53 1991**
**Clark, Martin P.**
Networks and telecommunications : design and operation / Martin P. Clark. Chichester, West Sussex, England ; Wiley, c1991. xviii, 635 p.
90-012436          621.382          0471927996
*Telecommunication systems. Data transmission systems. Computer networks.*

**TK5102.5.D55 1994**
**Dixon, Robert C. (Robert Clyde),**
Spread spectrum systems : with commercial applications / Robert C. Dixon. 3rd ed. New York : Wiley, c1994. xv, 573 p. :
621.382 20
*Spread spectrum communications.*

**TK5102.5.F68 2002**
**Freeman, Roger L.**
Reference manual for telecommunications engineering / Roger L. Freeman. 3rd ed. New York Wiley, c2002. 2 v. :
*Telecommunication systems -- Design and construction – Handbooks, manuals, etc.*

**TK5102.5.H318 1993**
Handbook for digital signal processing / edited by Sanjit K. Mitra, James F. Kaiser. New York : Wiley, c1993. xxxi, 1268 p.
92-035700          621.382/2          0471619957
*Signal processing -- Digital techniques.*

**TK5102.5.L83 1986**
**Ludeman, Lonnie C.**
Fundamentals of digital signal processing / Lonnie C. Ludeman. New York : Harper & Row, c1986. xiii, 330 p.
85-021950          621.38/043          0060440937
*Signal processing -- Digital techniques.*

**TK5102.5.M89 1990**
**Myers, Douglas G.**
Digital signal processing : efficient convolution and Fourier transform techniques / Douglas G. Myers. New York : Prentice Hall, c1990. xi, 355 p. ;
90-007840          621.382/2          0132118149
*Signal processing -- Digital techniques.*

**TK5102.5.W67 1988**
**Wood, Harold Baker,**
Mathematics for communications engineering / H.B. Wood. Chichester [England] : New York ; E. Horwood ; Wiley, 1988. 437 p. :
621.38 19          0745805728
*Telecommunication -- Mathematics.*

## TK5102.9 Telecommunication — Signal processing

**TK5102.9.D534 1998**

The digital signal processing handbook / edited by Vijay K. Madisetti, Douglas B. Williams. Boca Raton, Fla. : CRC Press ; c1998. 1 v. (various
97-021848          621.382/2          0849385725
*Signal processing -- Digital techniques -- Handbooks, manuals, etc.*

**TK5102.9.G69 1999**
**Goswami, Jaideva C.**

Fundamentals of wavelets : theory, algorithms, and applications / Jaideva C. Goswami, Andrew K. Chan. New York : Wiley, c1999. xvi, 306 p. :
98-026348          621.3/01/5152433
0471197483
*Signal processing -- Mathematics. Wavelets (Mathematics) Image processing -- Mathematics. Electromagnetic waves -- Scattering – Mathematical models. Boundary value problems.*

**TK5102.9.I545 1997**

Intelligent methods in signal processing and communications / D. Docampo, A.R. Figueiras-Vidal, F. Perez-Gonzalez, editors. Boston : Birkhauser, 1997. xvi, 318 p. :
97-000183          621.382/2/028563
0817639608
*Signal processing. Neural networks (Computer science) Multisensor data fusion.*

**TK5102.9.J34 2000**
**Jaffe, Richard C.**

Random signals for engineers using MATLAB and Mathcad / Richard C. Jaffe. New York : AIP Press ; c2000. xv, 374 p. :
99-053570          621.382/2          0387989560
*Signal processing -- Data processing. MATLAB. MathCAD.*

**TK5102.9.K35 1997**
**Kamen, Edward W.**

Fundamentals of signals and systems using MATLAB / Edward W. Kamen, Bonnie S. Heck. Upper Saddle River, NJ : Prentice Hall, c1997. xiii, 688 p.
96-000330          621.382/23          0023619422
*Signal processing -- Digital techniques System analysis. MATLAB.*

**TK5102.9.M374 1996**
**Mars, P.**

Learning algorithms : theory and applications in signal processing, control, and communications / Phil Mars, J.R. Chen, Raghu Nambiar. Boca Raton : CRC Press, c1996. 230 p. :
96-026721          629.8/95631          0849378966
*Signal processing. Adaptive control systems. Machine learning. Neural networks (Computer science) Genetic algorithms.*

**TK5102.9.M38 1996**
**Marven, Craig.**

A simple approach to digital signal processing / Craig Marven and Gillian Ewers. New York : Wiley, c1996. xi, 236 p. :
96-002518          621.382/2          0471152439
*Signal processing -- Digital techniques.*

**TK5102.9.S745 2000**
**Stein, Jonathan Y.**

Digital signal processing : a computer science perspective / Jonathan (Y) Stein. New York : Wiley, c2000. xx, 859 p. :
00-035905          621.382/2          0471295469
*Signal processing -- Digital techniques.*

## TK5102.94 Telecommunication — Coding theory — Cryptographic techniques

**TK5102.94.S65 1997**
**Smith, Richard E.,**

Internet cryptography / Richard E. Smith. Reading, Mass. : Addison-Wesley, c1997. xx, 356 p. :
97-013773          005.8/2          0201924803
*Internet -- Security measures. Data encryption (Computer science)*

## TK5102.96 Telecommunication — Coding theory — Error correction

**TK5102.96.S35 1997**
**Schlegel, Christian.**

Trellis coding / Christian Schlegel ; contribution by Lance Perez. Piscataway, NJ : IEEE Press, c1997. xv, 274 p. :
96-043184          621.382/2          0780310527
*Error-correcting codes (Information theory) Trellis-coded modulation.*

## TK5103 Telecommunication — Apparatus and supplies — General works

**TK5103.F68 1996**
**Freeman, Roger L.**

Telecommunication system engineering / Roger L. Freeman. New York : Wiley, c1996. xxii, 1023 p.
96-010943          621.382          0471133027
*Telecommunication systems -- Design and construction. Telephone systems -- Design and construction.*

**TK5103.G45 2000**
**Gershenfeld, Neil A.**

The physics of information technology / Neil Gershenfeld. Cambridge ; Cambridge University Press, 2000. xiv, 370 p. :
00-034214          621.38          0521580447
*Telecommunication -- Equipment and supplies -- Evaluation. Physics. Solid state physics.*

## TK5103.12 Telecommunication — Apparatus and supplies — Wiring

**TK5103.12.M39 1995**
**Maybin, Harry B.**
Low voltage wiring handbook : design, installation, and maintenance / Harry B. Maybin. New York : McGraw-Hill, c1995. 1 v. (various
94-035054        621.382/3        0070410836
*Telecommunication wiring. Low voltage systems.*

## TK5103.2 Telecommunication — Wireless communication systems — General works

**TK5103.2.C45 2000**
**Chang, Kai,**
RF and microwave wireless systems / Kai Chang. New York : Wiley, 2000. xvi, 339 p. :
99-089122        621.3845        0471351997
*Wireless communication systems. Mobile communication systems. Microwave communication systems. Radio frequency.*

**TK5103.2.G67 1996**
**Goralski, Walter.**
Wireless communications : a management guide to implementation / Walter Goralski. Charleston, S.C., U.S.A. : Computer Technology Research Corp., 1996. vi, 222 p. :
95-050594        384.5        1566079640
*Wireless communication systems.*

**TK5103.2.P34 1995**
**Pahlavan, Kaveh,**
Wireless information networks / Kaveh Pahlavan, Allen H. Levesque. New York : Wiley, c1995. xx, 572 p. :
94-022900        621.382        0471106070
*Wireless communication systems.*

## TK5103.4 Telecommunication — Wireless communication systems — Broadband communication systems

**TK5103.4.W65 2001**
**Wolf, Jason,**
The last mile : broadband and the next Internet revolution / Jason Wolf, Natalie Zee. New York : McGraw Hill, c2001. xxii, 200 p.
00-055407        384        0071363491
*Broadband communication systems -- Forecasting. Internet -- Forecasting. Electronic commerce -- Forecasting.*

## TK5103.483 Telecommunication — Wireless communication systems — Global system for mobile communications

**TK5103.483.M45 1997**
**Mehrotra, Asha.**
GSM system engineering / Asha Mehrotra. Boston : Artech House, c1997. xvii, 450 p.
97-004029        621.3845/6        0890068607
*Global system for mobile communications.*

## TK5103.59 Telecommunication — Optical communications

**TK5103.59.F85 1992**
Fundamentals of fibre optics in telecommunication and sensor systems / edited by Bishnu P. Pal. New York : Wiley, 1992. xxii, 778 p.
92-036074        621.36/92        0470220511
*Optical communications. Fiber optics. Optical fibers.*

**TK5103.59.H66 1994**
**Hooijmans, Pieter W.**
Coherent optical system design / Pieter W. Hooijmans ; foreword by T.J.B. Swanenburg. Chichester ; J. Wiley, c1994. xxvii, 390 p.
94-004940        621.382/7        0471948365
*Optical communications.*

**TK5103.59.D52 2001**
Fibre optic communication devices / Norbert Grote, Herbert Venghaus, (eds.) Berlin ; Springer, 2001. xxi, 465 p. :
00-039465        621.382/7        3540669779
*Optical communications -- Equipment and supplies. Optoelectronic devices.*

**TK5103.59.R64 2001**
**Rogers, A. J.**
Understanding optical fiber communication / Alan Rogers. Boston, MA : Artech House, 2001. xii, 216 p. :
00-068930        621.382/7        0890064784
*Optical communications. Fiber optics.*

## TK5103.7 Telecommunication — Digital communications — General works

**TK5103.7.B54 1992**
**Bissell, C. C.**
Digital signal transmission / C.C. Bissell, D.A. Chapman. Cambridge ; Cambridge University Press, 1992. x, 321 p. :
91-040848        621.382        0521415373
*Digital communications. Signal processing -- Digital techniques. Integrated services digital networks.*

**TK5103.7.F58 1994**
**Fliege, Norbert.**
Multirate digital signal processing : multirate systems, filter banks, wavelets / N.J. Fliege. Chichester ; Wiley, c1994. xi, 340 p. :
94-010083        621.382/2        0471939765
*Signal processing -- Digital techniques.*

**TK5103.7.N43 1995**
**Negroponte, Nicholas.**
Being digital / Nicholas Negroponte. New York : Knopf, 1995. viii, 243 p.
94-045971        303.48/33        0679439196
*Digital communications -- Social aspects. Technology and civilization. Computer networks -- Social aspects. Interactive multimedia -- Social aspects.*

**TK5103.7.N47 1995**
**Netravali, Arun N.**
  Digital pictures : representation, compression, and standards / Aru N. Netravali and Barry G. Haskell. 2nd ed. New York : Plenum Press, c1995. xix, 686 p. :
  621.36/7/01154 20
*Includes bibliographical references and index. Digital communications. Image processing--Digital techniques.*

## TK5103.75 Telecommunication — Digital communications — Integrated services digital networks

**TK5103.75.H67 1995**
**Hopkins, Gerald.**
  The ISDN literacy book / Gerald L. Hopkins. Reading, Mass. : Addison-Wesley Pub. Co., c1995. xvi, 367 p. ;
  94-041198          004.6/2          0201629798
*Integrated services digital networks.*

## TK5103.8 Telecommunication — Switching systems

**TK5103.8.V36 1998**
**Van Bosse, John G.**
  Signaling in telecommunication networks / John G. van Bosse. New York : Wiley, c1998. xv, 549 p. :
  96-043761          621.382          0471573779
*Telecommunication -- Switching systems. Signaling system 7. Signal theory (Telecommunication)*

## TK5104 Telecommunications — Artifical satellites in telecommunication — General works

**TK5104.R627 2001**
**Roddy, Dennis,**
  Satellite communications / Dennis Roddy. 3rd ed. New York : McGraw-Hill, 2001. xiv, 569 p. :
  621.382/5 21
*Artificial satellites in telecommunication.*

**TK5104.G67 1993**
**Gordon, Gary D.**
  Principles of communications satellites / Gary D. Gordon and Walter L. Morgan. New York : Wiley, c1993. xxxiii, 533 p
  92-029459          621.382/5          047155796X
*Artificial satellites in telecommunication.*

**TK5104.H83 1990**
**Hudson, Heather E.**
  Communication satellites : their development and impact / Heather E. Hudson. New York : Free Press ; c1990. xiii, 338 p.
  89-016918          384.5/1          0029153204
*Artificial satellites in telecommunication.*

## TK5105 Telecommunication — Data transmission systems — General works

**TK5105.A55 1999**
**Anttalainen, Tarmo.**
  Introduction to telecommunications network engineering / Tarmo Anttalainen. Boston : Artech House, c1999. xvii, 297 p.
  98-041082          004.6          0890069840
*Telecommunication systems.*

**TK5105.B358 1995**
**Bartlett, Eugene R.**
  Cable communications : building the information infrastructure / Eugene R. Bartlett. New York : McGraw-Hill, c1995. xi, 319 p. :
  95-031568          621.382          0070053553
*Telecommunication systems -- United States. Information superhighway -- United States.*

**TK5105.G68 1997**
**Gould, Frederick L.**
  Technician's guide to electronic communications / Frederick L. Gould. New York : McGraw-Hill, c1997. xvii, 353 p.
  97-008074          621.382          0070245363
*Telecommunication systems. Electronic circuits.*

**TK5105.H3554 2000**
  Handbook of emerging communications technologies : the next decade / editor, Rafael Osso. Boca Raton, Fla. : CRC Press, c2000. 400 p. :
  99-025427          621.382          0849395941
*Telecommunication -- Technological innovations.*

**TK5105.S73 2000**
**Stallings, William.**
  Data and computer communications / William Stallings. 6th ed. Upper Saddle River, N.J. : Prentice Hall, c2000. xx, 810 p. :
          004.6 21
*Data transmission systems. Computer networks.*

**TK5105.Z54 2002**
**Ziemer, Rodger E.**
  Principles of communication : systems, modulation, and noise / R.E. Ziemer, W.H. Tranter. 5th ed. New York : Wiley, c2002. ix, 637 p. :
          621.382/2 21
*Telecommunication. Signfal theory (Telecommunication)*

## TK5105.5 Telecommunications — Computer networks — General works

**TK5105.5.A7 1988**
**Arazi, Benjamin.**
  A commonsense approach to the theory of error correcting codes / Benjamin Arazi. Cambridge, Mass. : MIT Press, c1988. x, 208 p. :
  87-021889          005.72          0262010984
*Error-correcting codes (Information theory)*

**TK5105.5.B6513 1994**
**Boisseau, M.**
   High speed networks / M. Boisseau, M. Demange et J.-M. Munier ; translated by John C.C. Nelson. Chichester, W. Sussex, Eng. ; Wiley, c1994. xii, 192 p. :
94-010084          004.6          0471951099
*Computer networks.*

**TK5105.5.C5897 1999**
**Comer, Douglas.**
   Computer networks and internets / Douglas E. Comer. Upper Saddler River, NJ : Prentice Hall, 1999. p. cm.
98-047110          004.6          0130836176
*Computer networks. Internetworking (Telecommunication)*

**TK5105.5.G74 1997**
**Grinberg, Arkady.**
   Seamless networks : interoperating wireless and wireline networks / Arkady Grinberg. New York : McGraw-Hill, c1997. ix, 260 p. :
96-034043          004.6          0070248443
*Internetworking (Telecommunication) Wireless communication systems.*

**TK5105.5.H322 1994**
   Handbook of networking & connectivity / edited by Gary R. McClain. Boston : AP Professional, c1994. xv, 415 p. :
94-165473          004.6
*Computer networks.*

**TK5105.5.H865 2001**
**Hura, Gurdeep S.**
   Data and computer communications : networking and internetworking / Gurdeep S. Hura, Mukesh Singhal. Boca Raton, FL : CRC Press, 2001. 1140 p. ;
00-051866          004.6          084930928X
*Computer networks. Internetworking (Telecommunications)*

**TK5105.5.M57 1995**
**Mitchell, William J.**
   City of bits : space, place, and the infobahn / William J. Mitchell. Cambridge, Mass. : MIT Press, c1995. 225 p. :
95-007212          303.48/33          0262133091
*Computer networks. Information technology. Virtual reality.*

**TK5105.5.M85696 1999**
**Muller, Nathan J.**
   Desktop encyclopedia of the Internet / Nathan J. Muller. Boston : Artech House, c1999. xvi, 559 p. :
98-041081          004.67/8/03          0890067295
*Computer networks -- Encyclopedias. Internet -- Encyclopedias. Computers -- Encyclopedias.*

**TK5105.5.N45 1999**
**Nellist, John G.**
   Understanding modern telecommunications and the information superhighway / John G. Nellist, Elliot M. Gilbert. Boston, Mass. : Artech House, c1999. xviii, 285 p.
99-010793          384          0890063222
*Computer networks. Information superhighway.*

**TK5105.5.N4647 1998**
   Network and netplay : virtual groups on the Internet / edited by Fay Sudweeks, Margaret McLaughlin, and Sheizaf Rafaeli ; foreword by Ronald Rice. Menlo Park, CA : AAAI Press ; 1998. xx, 313 p. :
97-043441          302.23          0262692066
*Computer networks. Virtual reality. Computer networks -- Social aspects. Telematics.*

**TK5105.5.R87 1989**
**Russell, D.**
   The principles of computer networking / D. Russell. Cambridge ; Cambridge University Press, 1989. xvii, 513 p.
90-197010          004.6          0521327954
*Computer networks.*

**TK5105.5.T36 1996**
**Tanenbaum, Andrew S.,**
   Computer networks / Andrew S. Tanenbaum. 3rd ed. Upper Saddle River, N.J. : Prentice Hall PTR, c1996. xvii, 813 p. :
          004.6 20
*Computer networks.*

## TK5105.55 Telecommunications — Computer networks — Computer network protocols. Standards

**TK5105.55.S38 1995**
**Sexton, Conor.**
   Beyond the mainframe : a guide to open computer systems / Conor Sexton. Oxford ; Butterworth-Heinemann, 1995. xiii, 305 p.
96-115855                    0750619023
*Computer networks -- Standards. Client/server computing. Computer interfaces.*

## TK5105.7-5105.8 Telecommunications — Computer networks — Local area networks

**TK5105.7.C87 1988**
**Currie, W. Scott**
   LANs explained : a guide to local area networks / W. Scott Currie. Chichester : E. Horwood ; 1988. 208 p. :
87-035284          004.6/8          0745802389
*Local area networks (Computer networks)*

**TK5105.7.F67 1992**
   Handbook of LAN technology / Paul J. Fortier, editor. 2nd ed. New York : Intertext Publications : McGraw-Hill, c1992. xviii, 732 p. :
          004.6/8 20
*Local area networks (Computer networks)*

**TK5105.8.I24.H45 1994**
**Held, Gilbert,**
   Token-ring networks : characteristics, operation, construction, and management / Gilbert Held. Chichester, West Sussex, England ; Wiley, c1994. xvi, 309 p. :
93-013740          004.6/8          0471940410
*IBM Token-Ring Network (Local area network system)*

### TK5105.875–5105.888 Telecommunications — Computer networks — Wide area networks

**TK5105.875.I57**
Internet monthly reports  Los Angeles, Calif. : Internet Research Group, 1984-
96-035870
*Internet. World Wide Web (Information retrieval system) – Software.*

**TK5105.875.I57**
Internet ethics / edited by Duncan Langford. New York : St. Martin's Press, 2000. p. cm.
99-059607        175        0312232799
*Internet -- Moral and ethical aspects.  Computers and civilization. Law and ethics.*

**TK5105.875.I57.A23 1999**
**Abbate, Janet.**
Inventing the Internet / Janet Abbate. Cambridge, Mass : MIT Press, c1999. viii, 264 p.
98-047647        004.67/8/09        0262011727
*Internet -- History.*

**TK5105.875.I57.B64 1999**
**Botto, Francis.**
Dictionary of multimedia and internet applications : a guide for developers and users / Francis Botto. Chichester ; Wiley, c1999. x, 362 p. :
98-029155        004.67/8/03        0471986240
*Internet -- Dictionaries.  Multimedia systems -- Dictionaries.*

**TK5105.875.I57.C658 1999**
**Conner-Sax, Kiersten.**
The whole Internet : the next generation : a completely new edition of the first and best user's guide to the Internet / Kiersten Conner-Sax and Ed Krol. Beijing ; O'Reilly, 1999. xiv, 542 p. :
99-045755        004.67/8        1565924282
*Internet -- Handbooks, manuals, etc.*

**TK5105.875.I57.H58 1999**
History of the Internet : a chronology, 1843 to the present / Christos J.P. Moschovitis ... [et al.]. Santa Barbara, Calif. : ABC-CLIO, c1999. viii, 312 p.
99-013275        004.67/8/09        1576071189
*Internet -- Juvenile literature.  Telecommunication -- History -- Juvenile literature.  Internet.  Telecommunication -- History.*

**TK5105.875.I57.M668 1996**
**Morville, Peter.**
The Internet searcher's handbook : locating information, people & software / Peter Morville, Louis Rosenfeld, Joseph Janes. New York : Neal-Schuman Publishers, c1996. xi, 236 p. :
95-047670        025.04        1555702368
*Internet searching.*

**TK5105.875.I57.P83 1995**
Public access to the Internet / edited by Brian Kahin and James Keller. Cambridge, Mass. : MIT Press, c1995. viii, 390 p.
95-008808        384.3        0262112078
*Internet.*

**TK5105.875.I57.S4 1998**
**Segaller, Stephen.**
Nerds 2.0.1 : a brief history of the Internet / Stephen Segaller. New York : TV Books, c1998. 399 p., [28]
00-710280        004.67/8        1575001063
*Internet -- History.  Computer networks -- History. Telecommunications engineers -- United States.  Information technology -- History -- 20th century.*

**TK5105.875.I57.T48 1996**
**Thomas, Brian J.**
The Internet for scientists and engineers : online tools and resources / Brian J. Thomas. Bellingham, Wash., USA : SPIE Optical Engineering Press ; c1996. xxi, 495 p. :
96-003204        004.6/7        0819421480
*Internet.  Science -- Computer network resources.  Engineering -- Computer network resources.*

**TK5105.875.I57C65 2000**
**Comer, Douglas.**
The Internet book : everything you need to know about computer networking and how the Internet works / Douglas E. comer. 3rd ed. Upper Saddle River, NJ : Prentice Hall, c2000. xxvi, 351 p. :
        004.67/8 21
*Internet.*

**TK5105.884.B47 1999**
**Berry, Michael W.**
Understanding search engines : mathematical modeling and text retrieval / Michael W. Berry, Murray Browne. Philadelphia, PA : Society for Industrial and Applied Mathematics,i c1999. xiii, 116 p.
99-030649        025.04        0898714370
*Web search engines.  Vector spaces.  Text processing (Computer science)*

**TK5105.8865.I57 2001**
Internet telephony / edited by Lee W. McKnight, William Lehr, and David D. Clark. Cambridge, Mass. : MIT Press, c2001. xii, 395 p. :
00-050012        004.6        0262133857
*Internet telephony.*

**TK5105.888.A376 1999**
**Alexander, Janet E.**
Web wisdom : how to evaluate and create information quality on the Web / Janet E. Alexander, Marsha Ann Tate. Mahwah, N.J. : Lawrence Erlbaum Associates, c1999. xv, 156 p. :
99-012314        005.7/2        0805831223
*Web sites.  World Wide Web.*

### TK5105.888.B46 1999
**Berners-Lee, Tim.**
Weaving the Web : the original design and ultimate destiny of the World Wide Web by its inventor / Tim Berners-Lee with Mark Fischetti. San Francisco : HarperSanFrancisco, c1999. xi, 226 p. ;
99-027665          025.04          0062515861
*World Wide Web -- History. Berners-Lee, Tim.*

### TK5105.888.G544 2000
**Gillies, James.**
How the Web was born : the story of the World Wide Web / James Gillies & Robert Cailliau. Oxford : Oxford University Press, 2000. xii, 372 p.,
01-274436                              0192862073
*World Wide Web -- History. European Organization for Nuclear Research. CERN Accelerator School.*

### TK5105.888.L96 1999
**Lynch, Patrick J.,**
Web style guide : basic design principles for creating web sites / Patrick J. Lynch, Sarah Horton. New Haven [Conn.] : Yale University Press, c1999. x, 164 p. :
98-045282          005.7/2          0300076746
*Web sites -- Design.*

### TK5105.888.R67 1998
**Rosenfeld, Louis.**
Information architecture for the World Wide Web / Louis Rosenfeld and Peter Morville. Cambridge ; O'Reilly, 1998. xix, 202 p. :
98-149802                    1565922824
*Web sites -- Design. Information storage and retrieval systems -- Architecture.*

### TK5105.888.U57 2000
Unspun : key concepts for understanding the World Wide Web / edited by Thomas Swiss. New York : New York University Press, 2000. vii, 210 p. :
00-010416          004.67/8          081479758X
*World Wide Web.*

## TK5115 Telegraph — History — General works

### TK5115.C54 1993
**Coe, Lewis,**
The telegraph : a history of Morse's invention and its predecessors in the United States / by Lewis Coe. Jefferson, N.C. : McFarland, c1993. vii, 184 p. :
92-053597          621.383          0899507360
*Telegraph -- United States -- History. Morse, Samuel Finley Breese, 1791-1872. Inventors -- United States -- Biography.*

## TK5981 Electroacoustics. Electroacoustic transucers — General works

### TK5981.B36 1986
**Beranek, Leo Leroy,**
Acoustics / Leo L. Beranek. 1986 ed. New York, N.Y. : American Institute of Physics c1986. xii, 491 p. :
          621.38/028/2 19
*Electro-acoustics. Sound-Recording and reproducing.*

## TK6023 Telephone — Special countries

### TK6023.H57 1975
A History of engineering and science in the Bell System / prepared by members of the technical staff, Bell Telephone Laboratories ; M.D. Fagen, editor. [New York] : The Laboratories, 1975-c1985 v. 1-7   :
75-031499          621.385/0973          0932764002
*Telephone -- United States -- History. Telecommunication – United States -- History. Electronics -- United States -- History. American Telephone and Telegraph Company -- History.*

## TK6143 Telephone — Biography — Individual, A-Z

### TK6143.B4.G76 1997
**Grosvenor, Edwin S.,**
Alexander Graham Bell : the life and times of the man who invented the telephone / Edwin S. Grosvenor and Morgan Wesson ; foreword by Robert V. Bruce. New York : Harry Abrams, 1997. 304 p. :
97-007636          621.385/092          0810940051
*Bell, Alexander Graham, 1847-1922. Inventors -- United States – Biography. Telephone -- United States -- History.*

## TK6397 Telephone — Distribution. Construction. Connections — Switchboards for line connections

### TK6397.F86 1990
Fundamentals of digital switching / edited by John C. McDonald. New York : Plenum Press, c1990. xix, 489 p. :
89-072201          621.3815/37          0306433478
*Telephone switching systems, Electronic. Digital electronics.*

## TK6547 Radio — History

### TK6547.A46
**Aitken, Hugh G. J.**
Syntony and spark : the origins of radio / Hugh G. J. Aitken. New York : Wiley, c1976. xvi, 347 p. :
75-034247          621.3841/09          0471018163
*Radio -- History.*

## TK6550 Radio — General works

**TK6550.N16 2001**
**Nahin, Paul J.**
   The science of radio : with MATLAB and Electronics Workbench demonstrations / Paul J. Nahin. New York : AIP Press, c2001. xliv, 466 p.
00-062062      621.384      0387951504
   *Radio.*

**TK6550.S49795 1998**
**Smith, Albert A.,**
   Radio frequency principles and applications : the generation, propagation, and reception of signals and noise / Albert A. Smith, Jr. New York : IEEE Press, 1998. xiv, 219 p. :
98-006458      621.384/11      0780334310
*Radio waves. Radio -- Transmitters and transmission. Radio -- Receivers and reception. Radio -- Interference.*

## TK6560 Radio — Apparatus — General works

**TK6560.H34 1996**
**Hagen, Jon B.**
   Radio-frequency electronics : circuits and applications / Jon B. Hagen. Cambridge ; Cambridge University Press, 1996. xiii, 358 p.
95-048033      621.384/12      0521553563
*Radio circuits.*

**TK6560.M22 1998**
**Maas, Stephen A.**
   The RF and microwave circuit design cookbook / Stephen A. Maas. Boston : Artech House, c1998. xviii, 267 p.
98-028219      621.381/32      0890069735
*Radio circuits. Microwave circuits.*

## TK6575 Radar — General works

**TK6575.R262 1990**
   Radar handbook / editor in chief, Merrill I. Skolnik. New York : McGraw-Hill, c1990. 1 v. (various
89-035217      621.3848      007057913X
*Radar -- Handbooks, manuals, etc.*

## TK6642 Television — Handbooks, manuals, etc.

**TK6642.T437 1992**
   Television engineering handbook : featuring HDTV systems / K. Blair Benson, editor in chief. Rev. ed. / rev. by Jerry C. Whitaker. New York : McGraw-Hill, c1992. 1 v. :
         621.388/87 20
*Television -- Handbooks, manuals, etc.*

## TK6680.5 Digital video — General works

**TK6680.5.B37 1996**
**Baron, Stanley N.**
   Digital image and audio communications : toward a global information infrastructure / Stanley N. Baron, Mark I. Krivocheev. New York : Van Nostrand Reinhold, 1996. xvi, 288 p. :
95-048897      384.55/2      0442021062
*Digital video. Sound -- Recording and reproducing -- Digital techniques.*

## TK6685 Digital video — Video discs and video disc equipment

**TK6685.I83 1987**
**Isailovic, Jordan,**
   Videodisc systems : theory and applications / Jordan Isailovic. Englewood Cliffs, NJ : Prentice-Hall, c1987. xi, 451 p. :
86003185      621.388/332      0139418652
*Videodiscs.*

## TK7804 Electronics — Dictionaries and encyclopedias

**TK7804.E47 1990**
   Encyclopedia of electronics / Stan Gibilisco, Neil Sclater, co-editors-in-chief. Blue Ridge Summit, PA : TAB Professional and Reference Books, c1990. 960 p. :
89-077660      621.381/03      0830633898
*Electronics -- Dictionaries.*

**TK7804.M354 1994**
**Markus, John,**
   McGraw-Hill electronics dictionary / John Markus, Neil Sclater. New York : McGraw-Hill, c1994. ix, 596 p. :
93039212      621.38/03      0070404348
*Electronics -- Dictionaries.*

## TK7809 Electronics — History

**TK7809.S45 1998**
**Seitz, Frederick,**
   Electronic genie : the tangled history of silicon / Frederick Seitz and Norman G. Einspruch. Urbana : University of Illinois Press, c1998. xvi, 281 p. :
97-021145      621.381/09      0252023838
*Solid state electronics -- History.*

## TK7816 Electronics — Elementary textbooks

**TK7816.D86 2000**
**Dunn, Peter Carroll.**
Gateways into electronics / Peter Carroll Dunn. New York : Wiley, c2000. xiii, 658 p.
98-045207          621.381          0471254487
*Electronics.*

**TK7816.H69 1994**
**Horn, Delton T.**
Basic electronics theory / Delton T. Horn. Blue Ridge Summit, PA : TAB Books, c1994. 692 p. :
93-030749          621.381          0830641998
*Electronics. Electronics -- Experiments.*

**TK7816.K73 2000**
**Krenz, Jerrold H.,**
Electronic concepts : an introduction / Jerrold H. Krenz. Cambridge, UK ; Cambridge University Press, 2000 xiii, 454 p.
99-030407          621.381          0521662826
*Electronics. Solid state electronics. Electronic circuits -- Computer simulation.*

## TK7825 Electronics — Handbooks, pocketbooks, tables, etc.

**TK7825.C63 1989**
**Collins, T. H.**
Analog electronics handbook / T.H. Collins. New York : Prentice-Hall, 1989. xxiv, 460 p.
87-026871          621.381          0130331198
*Analog electronic systems -- Handbooks, manuals, etc.*

## TK7836 Electronics — Electronic plants and equipment. Manufacture of electronic components and apparatus

**TK7836.M65 1995**
**Morrison, Ralph.**
Solving interference problems in electronics / Ralph Morrison. New York : Wiley, c1995. xv, 206 p. :
95-012074          621.382/24          0471127965
*Electronic apparatus and appliances -- Design and construction. Shielding (Electricity) Electromagnetic interference.*

## TK7867 Electronics — Electronic circuits — General works

**TK7867.B66 1999**
**Boyletad, Robert L.**
Electronic devices and circuit theory / Robert Boylestad, Louis Nashelsky. 7th ed. Upper Saddle River, N.J. : Prentice Hall, c1999. xviii, 926 p. :
621.3815 21
*Electronic circuits. Electronic appaatus and appliances.*

**TK7867.C4973 1996**
Circuit, device, and process simulation : mathematical and numerical aspects /G.F. Carey ... [et al.]. Chichester ; J. Wiley, c1996. xiii, 425 p.,
95-049408          621.3815/01/1          0471960195
*Electronic circuit design -- Data processing. Computer-aided design. Semiconductors -- Mathematical models -- Data processing. Numerical analysis -- Data processing.*

**TK7867.E4244 1996**
The electronics handbook / editor-in-chief Jerry C. Whitaker. Boca Raton, Fla. : CRC Press : c1996. xli, 2575 p.
96-003053          621.381          0849383455
*Electronic circuits -- Handbooks, manuals, etc.*

**TK7867.H53 1990**
**Hickman, Ian.**
Analog electronics 2nd ed. /Ian Hickman. Oxford ; Boston Newnes 1999. x, 294 p. : ill
89-070838          621.381          0750644168
*Analog electronic systems. Signal processing.*

**TK7867.M697 2000**
**Mourad, Samiha.**
Principles of testing electronic systems / Samiha Mourad, Yervant Zorian. New York : John Wiley & Sons, 2000. xix, 420 p. :
99-052179          621.3815/48          0471319317
*Electronic circuits -- Testing. Electronic apparatus and appliances -- Testing.*

**TK7867.S39 1998**
**Sedra, Adel S.**
Microelectronic circuits / Adel S. Sedra, Kenneth C. Smith. 4th ed. New York : Oxfor Univerisity Press, c1998. 1 v. :
621.381 21
*Electronic circuits. Integrated circuits.*

## TK7867.5 Electronics — Electronic circuits — Noise

**TK7867.5.F56 1993**
**Fish, Peter J.**
Electronic noise and low noise design / Peter J. Fish. Houndmills, Basingstoke : Macmillan Press, 1993. xiv, 278 p. :
94-109960          621.382/24          0333573099
*Electronic circuits -- Noise.*

## TK7868 Electronics — Electronic circuits — Special circuits

**TK7868.L6R67 1992**
**Roth, Charles H.**
Fundamentals of logic design / Charles H. Roth, Jr. 4th ed. St. Paul : West Pub. Co., c1992. xviii, 770 p. :
621.39/5 20
*Logic circuits. Logic design.*

## TK7868.D5.C68 1985
### Cowan, Sam,
Handbook of digital logic ... with practical applications / Sam Cowan. Englewood Cliffs, N.J. : Prentice-Hall, c1985. x, 309 p. :
84-016049      621.3815      0133771938
*Digital electronics. Logic circuits.*

## TK7868.D5.S65 1990
### Spencer, Charles D.
Digital design for computer data acquisition / Charles D. Spencer. Cambridge [England] ; Cambridge University Press, 1990. xii, 356 p. :
89-071224      621.39/81      0521371996
*Digital electronics. Computer interfaces. Automatic data collection systems.*

## TK7868.L6.S26 1990
### Sandige, Richard S.
Modern digital design / Richard S. Sandige. New York : McGraw-Hill, c1990. xviii, 743 p.
89-012401      621.39/5      0070548579
*Logic circuits -- Design and construction. Logic design.*

## TK7868.P6.L455 1994
### Lenk, John D.
Simplified design of linear power supplies / John D. Lenk. Boston : Butterworth-Heinemann, c1994. xiii, 246 p.
94-016077      621.381/044      0750695064
*Electric power supplies to apparatus -- Design and construction. Electric circuits, Linear -- Design and construction. Power electronics.*

## TK7868.P6.L456 1995
### Lenk, John D.
Simplified design of switching power supplies / John D. Lenk. Boston : Butterworth-Heinemann, c1995. xv, 224 p. :
94-032727      621.381/044      0750695072
*Electronic apparatus and appliances -- Power supply -- Design and construction. Switching power supplies -- Design and construction.*

## TK7868.P7.M65 1999
### Montrose, Mark I.
EMC and the printed circuit board : design, theory, and layout made simple / Mark I. Montrose. New York : IEEE Press, c1999. xviii, 325 p.
98-035408      621.3815/31      078034703X
*Printed circuits -- Design and construction. Electromagnetic compatibility.*

## TK7868.P7.P723 1997
Printed circuit board materials handbook / Martin W. Jawitz, editor in chief. New York : McGraw-Hill, 1997. 1 v. (various
97-200298      621.3815/31      0070324883
*Printed circuits -- Materials -- Handbooks, manuals, etc. Printed circutis -- Design and construction -- Handbooks, manuals, etc.*

## TK7870   Electronics — Apparatus and materials — General works

## TK7870.D496 1997
Digital consumer electronics handbook / Ronald Jurgen, editor in chief. New York : McGraw-Hill, c1997. 1 v. (various
97-001546      621.382      0070341435
*Household electronics. Digital electronics.*

## TK7870.H23 1997
Passive electronic component handbook / Charles A. Harper, editor in chief. New York : McGraw-Hill, c1997. xiv, 786 p. :
97-010743      621.3815/4      0070266980
*Electronic apparatus and appliances -- Handbooks, manuals, etc.*

## TK7870.N66 1997
### Northrop, Robert B.
Introduction to instrumentation and measurements / Robert B. Northrop. Boca Raton, Fla. : CRC Press, c1997. 518 p. :
97-002462      621.3815/48      0849378982
*Electronic instruments. Electronic measurements.*

## TK7870.15.R34 1993
### Rahn, Armin.
The basics of soldering / Armin Rahn. New York : Wiley, c1993. xv, 369 p. :
92-036407      621.381/046      0471584711
*Electronic packaging. Solder and soldering. Surface mount technology.*

## TK7870.2.S96 1986
Systems troubleshooting handbook / Luces M. Faulkenberry, editor ; contributors, Theodore F. Bogart, Jr. ... [et al.]. New York : Wiley, c1986. xvii, 415 p.
85-022527      621.381/1      0471866776
*Electronic systems -- Maintenance and repair. Electronic systems – Testing.*

## TK7871-7871.58 Electronics — Apparatus and materials — Materials (General)

## TK7871.L58 1999
### Livingston, James D.,
Electronic properties of engineering materials / James D. Livingston. New York : Wiley, c1999. xiv, 320 p. :
98-024461      620.1/1297      047131627X
*Electronics -- Materials. Electric conductors. Electric resistors. Capacitors. Semiconductors.*

## TK7871.15.C4.M68 1990
### Moulson, A. J.
Electroceramics : materials, properties, applications / A.J. Moulson and J.M. Herbert. London ; Chapman and Hall, c1990. xii, 464 p. :
89-023841      621.381      0412294907
*Electronic ceramics.*

**TK7871.15.G3.I58 1990**
Introduction to semiconductor technology : GaAs and related compounds / edited by Cheng T. Wang. New York : Wiley, c1990. xxii, 601 p.
89-030939          621.3815/2          0471631191
*Gallium arsenide semiconductors.*

**TK7871.58.O6.N454 1995**
**Nelson, J. C. C.**
Operation amplifier circuits : analysis and design / John C.C. Nelson. Boston : Butterworth-Heinemann, c1995. x, 138 p. :
94-032724          621.39/5          0750694688
*Operational amplifiers -- Design and construction.*

### TK7871.6-7871.67 Electronics — Apparatus and materials — Antennas and waveguides

**TK7871.6.B353 1997**
**Balanis, Constantine A.,**
Antenna theory : analysis and design / Constantine A. Balanis. 2nd ed. New York : Wiley, c1997. xvi, 941 p. :
                    621.382/4 20
*Antennas (Electronics).*

**TK7871.67.M53.H36 1998**
**Hansen, Robert C.**
Phased array antennas / R.C. Hansen. New York : Wiley, c1998. xvi, 486 p. :
97-023708          621.382/4          047153076X
*Microwave antennas. Phased array antennas.*

### TK7871.85-7871.99 Electronics — Apparatus and materials — Semiconductors

**TK7871.85.C25 2001**
**Campbell, Stephen A.,**
The science and engineering of microelectronic fabrication / Stephen A. Campbell. 2nd ed. New York : Oxford University Press, 2001. xiv, 603 p. :
                    621.3815/2 21
*Semiconductors -- Design and construction.*

**TK7871.85.S23 1991**
**Sah, Chih-Tang.**
Fundamentals of solid-state electronics / Chih-Tang Sah. Singapore ; World Scientific, c1991. xxvi, 1010 p.
91-026395          621.381          9810206372
*Solid state electronics.*

**TK7871.85.S77 2000**
**Streetman, Ben G.**
Solid state electronic devices / Ben G. Streetman and Sanjay Banerjee. 5th ed. Upper Saddle River, N.J. : Prentice Hall, c2000. xviii, 558 p. :
                    621.3815/2 21
*Semiconductors.*

**TK7871.85.S988 1981**
**Sze, S. M.,**
Physics of semiconductor devices / S.M. Sze. New York : Wiley, c1981. xii, 868 p. :
81-000213          537.6/22          0471056618
*Semiconductors.*

**TK7871.85.S9883 2002**
**Sze, S. M.,**
Semiconductor devices, physics and technology / S.M. Sze. 2nd ed. New York : Wiley, c2002. vii, 564 p. :
                    621.3815/2 21
*Semiconductors.*

**TK7871.99.M44.M26 1995**
**Marston, R. M.**
Modern CMOS circuits manual / R.M. Marston. Oxford ; Newnes, 1996. viii, 276 p.
95-037490          621.3815          0750625651
*Metal oxide semiconductors, Complementary.*

### TK7872 Electronics — Apparatus and materials — Other, A-Z

**TK7872.F5.C73 1997**
CRC handbook of electrical filters / edited by John T. Taylor, Qiuting Huang. Boca Raton : CRC Press, c1997. 427 p. :
96-026723          621.3815/324          0849389518
*Electric filters.*

**TK7872.F5.H797 1993**
**Huelsman, Lawrence P.**
Active and passive analog filter design : an introduction / Lawrence P. Huelsman. New York : McGraw-Hill, c1993. xx, 480 p. :
92-040111          621.3815/324          0070308608
*Electric filters, Active -- Design. Electric filters, Passive -- Design.*

**TK7872.F73.R62 1997**
**Rohde, Ulrich L.**
Microwave and wireless synthesizers : theory and design / Ulrich L. Rohde. New York : Wiley, c1997. xvii, 638 p.
96-002841          621.3815/486          0471520195
*Frequency synthesizers -- Design and construction. Phase-locked loops. Digital electronics. Microwave circuits -- Design and construction. Radio frequency.*

**TK7872.S4.R6**
**Romanowitz, Harry Alex,**
Fundamentals of semiconductor and tube electronics. New York, Wiley [1965, c1962] xii, 620 p.
62008787          621.3815
*Semiconductors. Electronics. Electron tubes.*

**TK7872.S8.S55 1988**
Simon, Randy.
 Superconductors : conquering technology's new frontier / Randy Simon and Andrew Smith. New York : Plenum Press, c1988. xiii, 326 p.
88-017950         620.1/12973         0306429594
*Superconductors.*

**TK7872.T6.C38 1993**
Carstens, James R.
 Electrical sensors and transducers / James R. Carstens. Englewood Cliffs, N.J. : Regents/Prentice Hall, c1993. xii, 498 p. :
91-043325         681/.2         0132496321
*Transducers. Detectors.*

**TK7872.T6.G37 1994**
Gardner, J. W.
 Microsensors : principles and applications / Julian W. Gardner. Chichester ; Wiley, c1994. xii, 331 p. :
94-010066         681.2         0471941352
*Transducers. Detectors. Microelectronics.*

**TK7872.T74**
Miano, Giovanni.
 Transmission lines and lumped circuits / Giovanni Miano, Antonio Maffucci. San Diego : Academic Press, c2001. xxii, 479 p.
00-108487         621.319         0121897109
*Electric lines. Electric networks. Electronic circuits. Electric circuit analysis -- Mathematics.*

## TK7874 Electronics — Microelectronics. Integrated circuits — General works

**TK7874.A755 1995**
 The art and science of analog circuit design / edited by Jim Williams. Boston : Butterworth-Heinemann, c1995. xv, 398 p. :
95-007364         621.381/5         0750695056
*Linear integrated circuits -- Design and construction. Electronic circuit design.*

**TK7874.D476 1984**
 Designer's handbook of integrated circuits / Arthur B. Williams, editor in chief. New York : McGraw-Hill, c1984. 1 v. (various
82-014955         621.381/73         007070435X
*Integrated circuits -- Handbooks, manuals, etc.*

**TK7874.D53**
 Digital integrated circuits and operational-amplifier and optoelectronic circuit design / edited by Bryan Norris. New York : McGraw-Hill, c1976. 206 p. :
76-043099         621.381/73/042         0070637539
*Digital integrated circuits. Operational amplifiers. Optoelectronic devices.*

**TK7874.E495 1986**
Elliott, David J.
 Microlithography : process technology for IC fabrication / David J. Elliott. New York : McGraw-Hill, c1986. xix, 378 p. :
85-018196         621.381/73         0070193045
*Integrated circuits -- Very large scale integration -- Design and construction. Microlithography. Photoresists.*

**TK7874.F645 1994**
Fonstad, Clifton G.
 Microelectronic devices and circuits / Clifton G. Fonstad. New York : McGraw-Hill, c1994. xviii, 686 p.
93-032500         621.381         0070214964
*Microelectronics. Electric circuit analysis. Electric circuits, Nonlinear.*

**TK7874.G43 1990**
Geiger, Randall L.
 VLSI design techniques for analog and digital circuits / Randall L. Geiger, Phillip E. Allen, Noel R. Strader. New York : McGraw-Hill Pub. Co., c1990. xv, 969 p., [
88-037737         621.381/73         0070232539
*Integrated circuits -- Very large scale integration -- Design and construction.*

**TK7874.H418 1996**
Herbst, L. J.
 Integrated circuit engineering : establishing a foundation / L.J. Herbst. Oxford ; Oxford University Press, 1996. xvi, 472 p. :
97-126840         621.3815         0198562799
*Integrated circuits.*

**TK7874.H675 1996**
Horenstein, Mark N.
 Microelectronic circuits and devices / Mark M. Horenstein. 2nd ed. Englewood Cliffs, N.J. : Prentice Hall, c1996. xxiv, 1126 p. :
         621.3815 20
*Microelectronics.*

**TK7874.L26 1994**
Laker, Kenneth R.,
 Design of analog integrated circuits and systems / Kenneth R. Laker, Willy M.C. Sansen. New York : McGraw-Hill, c1994. xxii, 898 p.
93-049574         621.3815         007036060X
*Linear integrated circuits -- Design and construction.*

**TK7874.L55 1993**
Linsley Hood, John
 The art of linear electronics / John Linsley Hood. Oxford [England] ; Butterworth-Heinemann, 1993. xii, 336 p. :
93019080         621.3815         0750608684
*Linear integrated circuits -- Design. Electronic circuit design.*

**TK7874.P345 1999**
Pallas-Areny, Ramon.
 Analog signal processing / Ramon Pallas-Areny, John G. Webster. New York : Wiley, c1999. xv, 586 p. :
98-007295         621.382/2         0471125288
*Linear integrated cirucits. Signal processing.*

**TK7874.P459 1993**
Peyton, A. J.
Analog electronics with Op Amps : a source book of practical circuits / A.J. Peyton, Y. Walsh. New York, N.Y., U.S.A. : Cambridge University Press, 1993. p. cm.
92-022691      621.3815      0521333059
*Linear integrated circuits. Operational amplifiers. Analog electronic systems.*

**TK7874.V563 1985**
VLSI handbook / Norman G. Einspruch. Orlando, Fla. : Academic Press, 1985. xxvi, 902 p.
84-020373      621.3819/5835      0122341007
*Integrated circuits -- Very large scale integration -- Handbooks, manuals, etc.*

**TK7874.6 Electronics — Microelectronics. Integrated circuits — Application specific integrated circuits**

**TK7874.6.A64 1997**
Application specific processors / edited by Earl E. Swartzlander, Jr. Boston : Kluwer Academic, c1997. xiv, 253 p. :
621.39/5 20      0792397924
*Application specific integrated circuits. Microprocessors.*

**TK7874.6.E54 1992**
Engen, Glenn F.
Microwave circuit theory and foundations of microwave metrology /Glenn F. Engen. London : P. Peregrinus on behalf of the Institution of El c1992. xiii, 240 p.
93-171480      621.381/3/0287      0863412874
*Microwave circuits. Microwaves -- Measurement.*

**TK7874.65 Electronics — Microelectronics. Integrated circuits — Digital integrated circuits**

**TK7874.65.D4 1994**
De Micheli, Giovanni.
Synthesis and optimization of digital circuits / Giovanni De Micheli. New York : McGraw-Hill, c1994. xviii, 579 p.
93-043595      621.39/5/028551      0070163332
*Digital integrated circuits -- Computer-aided design. Digital electronics -- Data processing.*

**TK7874.65.M37 2000**
Martin, Kenneth W.
Digital integrated circuit design / Ken Martin. New York : Oxford University Press, 2000. xv, 543 p. ;
98-053666      621.3815      0195125843
*Digital integrated circuits -- Design and construction.*

**TK7874.65.R33 1996**
Rabaey, Jan M.
Digital integrated circuits : a design perspective / Jan M. Rabaey. Upper Saddle River, N.J. : Prentice Hall, c1996. xviii, 702 p.,
621.39/5 20      0131786091
*Digital integrated circuits -- Design and construction.*

**TK7874.66 Electronics — Microelectronics. Integrated circuits — Low voltage integrated circuits**

**TK7874.66.L69 1999**
Low-voltage/low-power integrated circuits and systems : low-voltage mixed-signal ciruits / edited by Edgar Sanchez-Sinencio, Andreas G. Andreou. New York : IEEE Press, 1999. xxviii, 562 p
98-036702      621.3815      0780334469
*Low voltage integrated circuits.*

**TK7874.8 Electronics — Microelectronics. Integrated circuits — Molecular electronics**

**TK7874.8.I58 1995**
An introduction to molecular electronics / edited by Michael C. Petty, Martin R. Bryce, and David Bloor. New York : Oxford University Press, 1995. xiv, 387 p. :
95-164950      0195211561
*Molecular electronics.*

**TK7876 Electronics — Microelectronics. Integrated circuits — Microwaves**

**TK7876.C44 1994**
Chang, Kai,
Microwave solid-state circuits and applications / Kai Chang. New York : Wiley, c1994. xiv, 442 p. :
93-025582      621.381/3      0471540447
*Microwave devices. Microwave circuits. Semiconductors.*

**TK7876.K35 1997**
Karmel, Paul R.
Introduction to electromagnetic and microwave engineering / Paul R. Karmel, Gabriel D. Colef, Raymond L. Camisa. New York : Wiley, c1997. xvi, 702 p. :
97-016542      621.3      0471177814
*Microwave devices. Microwaves. Microwave transmission lines.*

**TK7876.L436 1994**
Lee, Charles A.,
Microwave devices, circuits and their interaction / Charles A. Lee, G. Conrad Dalman. New York : J. Wiley, c1994. xii, 367 p. :
93-010605      621.381/3      047155216X
*Microwave devices. Microwave circuits.*

**TK7876.R493 2001**
The RF and microwave handbook / editor-in-chief, Mike Golio. Boca Raton, FL : CRC Press, 2001. p. cm.
00-052885      621.381/32      084938592X
*Microwave circuits.*

**TK7876.S36 1993**
Scott, Allan W.
Understanding microwaves / Allan W. Scott. New York : Wiley, c1993. xii, 545 p. :
92-016863      621.381/3      0471575674
*Microwave devices.*

**TK7876.T5313 1991**
**Thuery, Jacques.**
Microwaves : industrial, scientific, and medical applications / Jacques Thuery ; edited by Edward H. Grant. Boston : Artech House, c1992. xviii, 670 p.
91039971          621.381/3          0890064482
*Microwave devices. Microwaves. Microwave devices -- Industrial applications.*

**TK7876.V47 1990**
**Vendelin, George D.**
Microwave circuit design using linear and nonlinear techniques / George D. Vendelin, Anthony M. Pavio, Ulrich L. Rohde. New York : Wiley, c1990. xviii, 757 p.
89-030005          621.381/325          0471602760
*Microwave integrated circuits. Microwave amplifiers. Oscillators, Microwave. Electronic circuit design.*

**TK7876.W42 2001**
**Weber, Robert J.,**
Introduction to microwave circuits : radio frequency and design applications / Robert J. Weber ; IEEE Microwave Theory and Techniques Society, sponsor. New York : IEEE, c2001. xvi, 431 p. :
00-059672          621.381/32          0780347048
*Microwave circuits. Radio circuits. Wireless communication systems.*

### TK7878.4-7878.7 Electronics — Electronic measurements — Electronic instruments

**TK7878.4.O34 1991**
**O'Dell, T. H.**
Circuits for electronic instrumentation / T.H. O'Dell. Cambridge ; Cambridge University Press, 1991. xiii, 218 p.
91-026333          621.381/54          0521404282
*Electronic instruments. Electronic circuits.*

**TK7878.4.V37 1993**
**Vassos, Basil H.**
Analog and computer electronics for scientists / Basil H. Vassos, Galen W. Ewing. New York : Wiley, c1993. xiv, 473 p. :
92-018330          621.3815          0471545597
*Electronic instruments. Analog electronic systems. Digital electronics.*

**TK7878.7.C72 1993**
**Craig, Edwin C.**
Electronics via waveform analysis / Edwin C. Craig. New York : Springer-Verlag, c1993. xi, 420 p. :
92-043410          621.381          0387940154
*Electric circuit analysis. Cathode ray oscillographs. Electric waves – Measurement.*

### TK7881 Electronics — Applications of electronics — Industrial electronics

**TK7881.S52 2001**
**Shanefield, Daniel J.,**
Industrial electronics for engineers, chemists, and technicians / Daniel J. Shanefield. Norwich, NY : William Andrew Pub., 2001. p. cm.
00-052188          621.381          0815514670
*Industrial electronics.*

### TK7881.15 Electronics — Applications of electronics — Power electronics

**TK7881.15.D68 1998**
**Dote, Yasuhiko,**
Intelligent control : power electronic systems / Yasuhiko Dote and Richard G. Hoft. Oxford [England] ; Oxford University Press, 1998. xi, 209 p. :
98-010226          621.31/7          019856466X
*Power electronics. Intelligent control systems.*

**TK7881.15.K84 1999**
**Kularatna, Nihal.**
Modern component families and circuit block design / Nihal Kularatna. Boston : Newnes, c2000. xvii, 452 p.
99-031348          621.31/7          0750699922
*Power electronics -- Design and construction. Low voltage systems – Design and construction. Electronic circuit design.*

**TK7881.15.M37 1997**
**Marston, R. M.**
Power control circuits manual / R.M. Marston. Oxford, [England] ; Newnes, c1997. viii, 220 p.
96-042138          621.31/7          0750630051
*Power electronics. Electronic control.*

**TK7881.15.R37 1993**
**Rashid, M. H.**
Power electronics : circuits, divices, and applications / Muhammad H. Rashid. 2nd ed. Englewood Cliffs, N.J. : Prentice Hall, c1993. xviii, 702 p. :
          621.317. 20
*Power electronics.*

**TK7881.15.T362 1993**
**Tarter, Ralph E.,**
Solid-state power conversion handbook / Ralph E. Tarter. New York : Wiley, c1993. xiv, 719 p. :
92-018179          621.31/7          0471572438
*Power electronics -- Handbooks, manuals, etc. Electric current converters -- Handbooks, manuals, etc. Electromagnetic compatibility -- Handbooks, manuals, etc.*

## TK7881.2-7881.4 Electronics — Applications of electronics — Special applications

**TK7881.2.M68 1998**

Motor control electronic handbook / [edited by] Richard Valentine. New York : McGraw-Hill, c1998. p. cm.
98-005074          621.46          0070668108
*Electronic controllers. Electric motors -- Electronic control.*

**TK7881.4.M47 2001**
**McGee, Marty,**

Encyclopedia of motion picture sound / Marty McGee. Jefferson, N.C. : McFarland, c2001. vii, 292 p. :
00-054803          778.5/344/03          078641023X
*Sound -- Recording and reproducing -- Encyclopedias. Sound motion pictures -- Encyclopedias.*

**TK7881.4.M66 2000**
**Morton, David,**

Off the record : the technology and culture of sound recording in America / David Morton. New Brunswick, N.J. : Rutgers University Press, c2000. xii, 221 p. :
99-027914          621.3899/3/0973          0813527465
*Sound -- Recording and reproducing -- United States – Case studies. Sound recording industry -- United States -- Social aspects.*

**TK7881.4.S72 2002**

Standard handbook of audio and radio engineering / Jerry C. Whitaker and K. Blair Benson, editors. 2nd ed. New York : McGraw-Hill, c2002. 1 v. :
                        0070067171
*Sound -- Recording and reproducing. Radio.*

**TK7881.4.W3834 1994**
**Watkinson, John.**

An introduction to digital audio / John Watkinson. Boston, MA : Focal Press, c1994. ix, 392 p. :
94-014290          621.389/3          0240513789
*Sound -- Recording and reproducing -- Digital techniques.*

**TK7881.4.Z39 1991**
**Zaza, Tony,**

Mechanics of sound recording / Anthony James Zaza. Englewood Cliffs, NJ : Prentice Hall, 1991. p. cm.
90-045899          621.389/3          0135676600
*Sound -- Recording and reproducing.*

## TK7882-7885 Electronics — Applications of electronics — Other, A-Z

**TK7882.E2.L96 1994**
**Lyon, David,**

The electronic eye : the rise of surveillance society / David Lyon. Minneapolis : University of Minnesota Press, 1994. x, 270 p.:
93-035598          303.48/33          0816625131
*Electronic surveillance -- Social aspects. Computers and civilization. Information technology -- Social aspects.*

**TK7882.I6.V445 1988**
**Veith, Richard.**

Visual information systems : the power of graphics and video / Richard H. Veith. Boston, Mass. : G.K. Hall, c1988. xxi, 321 p. :
87-031265          005.74          0816118612
*Information display systems. Information storage and retrieval systems.*

**TK7882.I6.W49 1994**
**Whitaker, Jerry C.**

Electronic displays : technology, design, and applications / Jerry C. Whitaker. New York : McGraw-Hill, c1994. xvii, 393 p.
93-027392          621.39/87          0070696217
*Information display systems. Video display terminals. High definition television.*

**TK7882.P3.P36 1989**
**Pao, Yoh-Han.**

Adaptive pattern recognition and neural networks / Yoh-Han Pao. Reading, Mass. : Addison-Wesley, c1989. xviii, 309 p.
88-007760          006.4          0201125846
*Pattern recognition systems. Neural networks (Computer science)*

**TK7882.S65.B75 1984**
**Bristow, Geoff.**

Electronic speech synthesis : techniques, technology, and applications / Geoff Bristow. New York : McGraw-Hill, c1984. xxi, 346 p. :
84003943          621.3819/5832          0070079129
*Speech synthesis.*

**TK7882.S65.P48 1993**
**Pelton, Gordon E.**

Voice processing / Gordon E. Pelton. New York : McGraw-Hill, c1993. xv, 396 p. :
92-021417          006.4/54          007049309X
*Speech processing systems.*

**TK7882.S65.S29 1996**
**Schindler, Esther,**

The computer speech book / Esther Schindler. Boston : AP Professional, c1996. xvi, 312 p. :
95-047340          006.4/54          0126246602
*Speech processing systems. Automatic speech recognition.*

**TK7885.A5.C67 1993**
**Cortada, James W.**

The computer in the United States : from laboratory to market, 1930 to 1960 / James W. Cortada. Armonk, N.Y. : M.E. Sharpe, c1993. xix, 183 p. :
93-004184          338.4/70040973          1563242346
*Computer engineering -- United States -- History. Computers -- United States -- History. Computer industry -- United States -- History.*

**TK7885.C645 2002**

The computer engineering handbook / edited by Vojin G. Oklobdzija. Boca Raton : CRC Press, c2002. 1 v. :
                        004 21
*Computer engineering. Electronic digital computers.*

## TK7885.4-7895 Electronics — Applications of electronics — Computer engineering. Computer hardware (Including design and construction)

**TK7885.4.K53**
**Kidder, Tracy.**
The soul of a new machine / Tracy Kidder. Boston : Little, Brown, c1981. 293 p. ;
81-006044          621.3819/582          0316491705
*Computer engineering -- Popular works. Data General Corporation.*

**TK7885.7.G46 2000**
**Ghosh, Sumit,**
Hardware description languages : concepts and principles / Sumit Ghosh. New York : IEEE Press, c2000. xxiii, 241 p.
99-027111          621.39/2          0780347447
*Computer hardware description languages.*

**TK7887.5.H668 1995**
**Hordeski, Michael F.**
Personal computer interfaces : macs to pentiums / Michael Hordeski. New York : McGraw-Hill, c1995. xix, 379 p. :
94-024427          004.6/16          007030419X
*Computer interfaces. Microcomputers.*

**TK7887.6.A525 1986**
Analog-digital conversion handbook / by the engineering staff of Analog Devices, Inc. ; edited by Daniel H. Sheingold. 3rd ed. Englewood Cliffs, NJ : Prentice-Hall, c1986. xxi, 672 :
          621.398/14 19          0130328480
*Analog-to-digital converters.*

**TK7887.6.L46 1997**
**Lenk, John D.**
Simplified design of data converters / John D. Lenk. Boston : Newnes, c1997. xiii, 242 p.
96-048397          621.39/814          0750695099
*Analog-to-digital converters -- Design and construction. Digital-to-analog converters -- Design and construction. Electronic circuit design.*

**TK7888.3.H315 2000**
**Hall, Stephen H.**
High speed digital system design : a handbook of interconnect theory and design practices / Stephen H. Hall, Garrett W. Hall, James A. McCall. New York : Wiley, c2000. xiii, 347 p.
00-025717          621.39/8          0471360902
*Electronic digital computers -- Design and construction. Very high speed integrated circuits -- Design and construction. Microcomputers -- Buses. Computer interfaces.*

**TK7888.3.H9**
**Hwang, Kai.**
Computer arithmetic : principles, architecture, and design / Kai Hwang. New York : Wiley, c1979. xiii, 423 p.
78-018922          621.3819/58/2          0471034967
*Electronic digital computers. Computer arithmetic and logic units. Computer arithmetic.*

**TK7888.3.M343 2002**
**Mano, M. Morris,**
Digital design / M. Morris Mano. 3rd ed. Upper Saddle River, NJ : Prentice-Hall, c2002. xii, 516 p. :
*Electonic digital computers -- Circuits. Logic circuits. Logic design. Digital integrated circuits.*

**TK7888.3.P77 1987**
**Prosser, Franklin P.**
The art of digital design : an introduction to top-down design / Franklin P. Prosser, David E. Winkel. Englewood Cliffs, N.J. : Prentice-Hall, c1987. xvii, 525 p.
86-005042          004.2/1          0130467804
*Electronic digital computers -- Design and construction. Minicomputers -- Design and construction.*

**TK7888.3.W46 1998**
**Williams, Colin P.**
Explorations in quantum computing / Colin P. Williams, Scott H. Clearwater. Santa Clara, Calif. : TELOS, c1998. xx, 307 p. :
97-002159          004          038794768X
*Quantum computers.*

**TK7888.4.G74 1998**
**Gregg, John.**
Ones and zeros : understanding Boolean algebra, digital circuits, and the logic of sets / John Gregg. New York : IEEE Press, c1998. xiv, 281 p. :
97-034932          511.3/24          0780334264
*Electronic digital computers -- Circuits -- Design. Logic, Symbolic and mathematical. Algebra, Boolean. Set theory.*

**TK7888.4.W37 1990**
**Ward, Stephen A.**
Computation structures / Stephen A. Ward, Robert H. Halstead, Jr. Cambridge, Mass. : MIT Press ; c1990. xx, 789 p. :
89-012961          621.39/2          0262231395
*Computers -- Circuits. Logic design. Computer architecture.*

**TK7895.E42**
**Ball, Stuart R.,**
Analog inter-facing to embedded microprocessors : real world design / Stuart Ball. Boston, Mass. : Newnes Press, 2001. xi, 271 p. :
00-051961          004.16          0750673397
*Embedded computer systems -- Design and construction. Microprocessors.*

**TK7895.M4.W55 1994**
**Williams, E. W.**
The CD-ROM and optical disc recording systems / E.W. Williams. Oxford ; Oxford University Press, 1994. ix, 166 p. :
94-001194          621.39/767          0198593732
*CD-ROMs.*

**TK7895.S65.A98 1996**
Automatic speech and speaker recognition : advanced topics / edited by Chin-Hui Lee, Frank K. Soong, Kuldip K. Paliwal. Boston : Kluwer Academic Publishers, c1996. xvi, 517 p. :
96-001588      006.4/54      0792397061
*Automatic speech recognition.*

## TK9009 Nuclear engineering. Atomic power — Dictionaries and encyclopedias

**TK9009.C48 1992**
Chambers nuclear energy and radiation dictionary / editor, P.M.B. Walker. Edinburgh ; Chambers, 1992. vii, 260 p. :
93-111539      621.48/03      0550132465
*Nuclear engineering -- Dictionaries. Nuclear energy -- Dictionaries. Radiation -- Dictionaries.*

## TK9145 Nuclear engineering. Atomic power — General works

**TK9145.B54 1996**
**Bodansky, David.**
Nuclear energy : principles, practices, and prospects / David Bodansky. Woodbury, N.Y. : American Institute of Physics, c1996. xvi, 396 p. :
96-000148      333.792/4      1563962446
*Nuclear engineering. Nuclear power plants.*

**TK9145.M87 2001**
**Murray, Raymond LeRoy,**
Nuclear energy : an introduction to the concepts, systems, and applications of nuclear processes / Raymond L. Murray. 5th ed. Boston : Butterworth-Heinemann, c2001. xxv, 490 p. :
621.48 21
*Nuclear engineering. Nuclear energy.*

**TK9145.W59 1993**
**Wolfson, Richard.**
Nuclear choices : a citizen's guide to nuclear technology / Richard Wolfson. Rev. ed. Cambridge, Mass. : MIT Press, c1993. xv, 467 p. :
333.792/4 20
*Nuclear bibliographical references and index.*

## TK9146 Nuclear engineering. Atomic power — Elements. Popular works

**TK9146.H45 2000**
**Henderson, Harry,**
Nuclear power : a reference handbook / Harry Henderson. Santa Barbara, Calif. : ABC-CLIO, c2000. xiii, 250 p.
00-010255      333.792/4/09      1576071286
*Nuclear engineering. Nuclear engineering -- History. Nuclear accidents.*

## TK9152 Nuclear engineering. Atomic power — Radiation environment procedures and equipment — Accidents and their prevention. Nuclear safety

**TK9152.R427 1994**
**Rees, Joseph V.**
Hostages of each other : the transformation of nuclear safety since Three Mile Island / Jospeh V. Rees. Chicago : University of Chicago Press, 1994. xii, 238 p. :
93-035819      363.17/99      0226706877
*Nuclear power plants -- United States -- Safety measures. Nuclear industry -- Safety regulations -- United States.*

**TK9152.W35 2000**
**Walker, J. Samuel.**
Permissible dose : a history of radiation protection in the twentieth century / J. Samuel Walker. Berkeley : University of California Press, 2000. xii, 168 p. :
00-023398      363.17/996/0904      0520223284
*Radiation -- Safety measures -- History. Nuclear energy –Law and legislation -- United States -- History.*

## TK9153 Nuclear engineering. Atomic power — General special

**TK9153.C34 1994**
**Caldicott, Helen.**
Nuclear madness : what you can do / Helen Caldicott. New York : Norton, c1994. 240 p. ;
94-005016      363.7/99      0393310116
*Nuclear energy. Nuclear power plants -- Environmental aspects.*

### TK9360 Nuclear engineering. Atomic power — Reactor fuels. Enrichment. Reprocessing — General works

**TK9360.P38 1984**
**Patterson, Walter C.,**
The plutonium business and the spread of the bomb / Walter C. Patterson for the Nuclear Control Institute. San Francisco : Sierra Club Books, c1984. xvi, 272 p. ;
84-022181      333.79/24      0871568373
*Plutonium industry. Breeder reactors. Nuclear nonproliferation.*

### TK9956 Electricity for amateurs. Amateur constructors' manuals — Radio. Wireless telephone — General works

**TK9956.G467 1994**
Amateur radio encyclopedia / Stan Gibilisco, editor-in-chief. Blue Ridge Summit, PA : TAB Books, c1994. 593 p. :
92-035843      621.3841/6/03      0830640959
*Amateur radio stations -- Encyclopedias.*

# TL Motor vehicles. Aeronautics. Astronautics

## TL9 Motor vehicles — Dictionaries and encyclopedias

**TL9.B43 2000**
The Beaulieu encyclopedia of the automobile / editor in chief, Nick Georgano ; foreword by Lord Montagu of Beaulieu. Chicago : Fitzroy Dearborn Publishers, c2000. 2 v. (xxxii,
01-316285                        1579582931
*Automobiles -- Encyclopedias.*

**TL9.G64 1995**
**Goodsell, Don.**
Dictionary of automotive engineering / Don Goodsell. 2nd ed. Oxford ; Boston : Butterworth-Heinemann, 1995. xiv, 265 p. :
                  629.2/03 20          1560916834
*Automobiles -- Dictionaries.*

**TL9.S64 1997**
**South, David W.**
Delmar's automotive dictionary / [David W.] South, [Boyce H.] Dwiggins. Albany : Delmar Publishers, c1997. 281 p. :
                  629.2/03 21          0827374054
*Automobiles -- Dictionaries.*

## TL23 Motor vehicles — Special countries

**TL23.C593**
**Clymer, Joseph Floyd,**
Treasury of early American automobiles, 1877-1925. New York, McGraw-Hill [1950] 213 p.
50-010680          629.209
*Automobiles -- United States. Automobiles -- United States – History.*

**TL23.C595 1996**
**Coffey, Frank.**
America on wheels : the first 100 years : 1896-1996 / by Frank Coffey and Joseph Layden. Los Angeles : General Pub. Group, c1996. 304 p. :
96-017682          629.222/0973          1881649806
*Automobiles -- United States -- History. Automobile industry and trade -- United States -- History.*

## TL140 Motor vehicles — Biography — Individual, A-Z

**TL140.D83.S33 1993**
**Scharchburg, Richard P.**
Carriages without horses : J. Frank Duryea and the birth of the American automobile industry / Richard P. Scharchburg. Warrendale, PA : Society of Automotive Engineers, c1993. vii, 243 p. :
93-002370                        338.7/629222/0973
1560913800
*Duryea, J. Frank (James Frank), 1869-1967. Automobile engineers– Biography. Duryea automobile -- History. Duryea, Charles E., 1861-1938. Stevens-Duryea Company -- History. Automobile industry and trade -- United States.*

## TL151 Motor vehicles. Aeronautics. Astronautics — Motor vehicles — General works

**TL151.S62**
S.A.E. handbook. New York City : Society of Automotive Engineers, v. :
                            0362-8205
*Automobiles -- Handbooks, manuals, etc.*

## TL152 Motor vehicles — Motor vehicle operation. Automobile operation — Maintenance and repair

**TL152.C692**
**Crouse, William Harry,**
Automotive technician's handbook / William H. Crouse and Donald L. Anglin. New York : McGraw-Hill, c1979. vii, 664 p. :
79-014274          629.28/7          0070147515
*Motor vehicles -- Maintenance and repair.*

## TL154 Motor vehicles — General special

**TL154.A23 1995**
Human-powered vehicles / [edited by] Allan V. Abbott, David Gordon Wilson. Champaign, IL : Human Kinetics Publishers, c1995. viii, 279 p.
95-010636          629.04          0873228278
*Human powered vehicles.*

**TL154.S3913 1991**
**Seiffert, Ulrich.**
Automobile technology of the future / by Ulrich Seiffert and Peter Walzer ; [English translation by Henry R. Jaeckel]. Warrendale, PA : Society of Automotive Engineers, c1991. vi, 251 p. :
90-026193          629.222          1560910801
*Automobiles -- Technological innovations.*

## TL210 Motor vehicles — Special automobile, by power — Gasoline automobiles

**TL210.P637 1994**
**Poulton, M. L.**
  Alternative engines for road vehicles / M.L. Poulton. Southampton, UK ; Computational Mechanics Publications, c1994. 164 p. :
94-070408          629.25          1853123005
*Motor vehicles -- Motors.*

## TL220-221.15 Motor vehicles — Special automobile, by power — Electric vehicles and their batteries, etc.

**TL220.S34 1994**
**Schiffer, Michael B.**
  Taking charge : the electric automobile in America / Michael Brian Schiffer with Tamara C. Butts and Kimberly K. Grimm. Washington : Smithsonian Institution Press, c1994. xiii, 225 p.
93-049483          629.25/02/0973          1560983558
*Automobiles, Electric -- United States.*

**TL220.W343 1994**
**Wakefield, Ernest Henry,**
  History of the electric automobile : battery-only powered cars / Ernest Henry Wakefield. Warrendale, PA : Society of Automotive Engineers, c1994. xxx, 541 p. :
93-032254          629.25/02          1560912995
*Automobiles, Electric -- History. Automobiles, Electric -- Batteries – History.*

**TL220.W343 1998**
**Wakefield, Ernest Henry,**
  History of the electric automobile : hybrid electric vehicles / Ernest Henry Wakefield. Warrendale, Pa. : Society of Automotive Engineers, c1998. xxii, 332 p.
98-003420          629.22/93          0768001250
*Automobiles, Electric -- History. Hybrid electric cars -- History.*

**TL221.15.M68 2000**
**Motavalli, Jim.**
  Forward drive : the race to build "clean" cars for the future / Jim Motavalli. San Francisco : Sierra Club Books, c2000. xxiv, 273 p.
99-032154          629.22/93          1578050359
  *Hybrid electric cars. Fuel cells.*

## TL227 Motor vehicles — Special automobile, by power — Gas turbine automobiles

**TL227.N67 1975**
**Norbye, Jan P.**
  The gas turbine engine : design, development, applications / Jan P. Norbye. Radnor, Pa. : Chilton Book Co., [1975] xvi, 570 p. :
75-006733          629.2/503          0801957532
*Automotive gas turbines. Automobiles, Gas-turbine.*

## TL228 Motor vehicles — Special automobile, by power — Natural gas vehicles

**TL228.I54 1996**
**Ingersoll, John G.,**
  Natural gas vehicles / by John G. Ingersoll. Lilburn, GA : Fairmont Press ; c1996. xiii, 468 p.
95-038382          333.79/68          0881732184
*Natural gas vehicles -- United States. Motor vehicle industry – United States.*

## TL240 Motor vehicles — Design, construction, and equipment

**TL240.G73 1998**
**Graedel, T. E.**
  Industrial ecology and the automobile / Thomas E. Graedel, Braden R. Allenby. Upper Saddle River, NJ : Prentice Hall, c1998. xii, 243 p. :
97-007761          629.2/31          013607409X
*Automobiles -- Design and construction. Industrial ecology. Green technology.*

**TL240.N8597 1998**
**Nunney, M.J. (Malcolm James)**
  Automotive technology / M.J. Nunney. 3rd ed. Warrendale, PA : SAE, 1998. xi, 654 p. :
          629.2/3 21          0768002737
*Motor vehicles -- Design and construction.*

**TL240.W66 2001**
**Wong, Jo Yung**
  Theory of ground vehicles / J.Y. Wong. 3rd ed. New York : John Wiley, c2001. xxxii, 528 p. :
          629.2/3 21          0471354619
*Motor vehicles -- Design and construction. Motor vehicles -- Dynamics. Ground-effect machines -- Design and construction.*

## TL242 Motor vehicles — Design, construction, and equipment — Safety factors. Safety standards. Crashworthiness

**TL242.N3 1972**
**Nader, Ralph.**
  Unsafe at any speed; the designed-in dangers of the American automobile. New York, Grossman, 1972. xciii, 417 p.
79-179071          629.2/3          0670741590
*Automobiles -- Design and Construction. Automobiles -- Safety measures.*

## TL243 Motor vehicles — Design, construction and equipment — Dynamics

**TL243.D85 2000**
**Dukkipati, Rao V.**
  Vehicle dynamics / Rao V. Dukkipati. Boca Raton, FL : CRC Press/Narosa Pub. House, 2000. p. cm.
          629.04/9 21          084930976X
*Motor vehicles -- Dynamics. Railroads -- Trains -- Dynamics.*

**TL243.G548 1992**
**Gillespie, Thomas D.**
  Fundamentals of vehicle dynamics / Thomas D. Gillespie. Warrendale, PA : Society of Automotive Engineers, c1992. xxii, 495 p. :
          629.2 20          1560911999
*Motor vehicles -- Dynamics.*

## TL410 Cycles — Bicycles and tricycles — General works

**TL410.S5 1977**
**Sharp, Archibald,**
  Bicycles and tricycles : an elementary treatise on their design and construction / by Archibald Sharp. Cambridge, Mass. : MIT Press, c1977. xviii, 536 p.
77-004928          629.22/72          0262191563
*Bicycles. Tricycles.*

## TL501 Aeronautics. Aeronautical engineering — Societies, yearbooks, etc. — English language

**TL501.J3**
  Jane's all the world's aircraft, 1909-  London [etc.] S. Low, Marston & company, ltd., 1909- v.
10008268          629.133058
*Aeronautics -- Periodicals.*
          *Airships -- Periodicals. Airplanes -- Periodicals. Rockets (Aeronautics) -- Periodicals.*

## TL506 Aeronautics. Aeronautical engineering — Exhibitions. Museums. Collectors and collecting — General works

**TL506.U6.W37315 1997**
**Chaikin, Andrew,**
  Air and space : the National Air and Space Museum's story of flight / Andrew Chaikin. Boston : Little, Brown and Co., 1997. p. cm.
96-031929          629.1/074753          0821220829
*National Air and Space Museum.*

## TL507 Aeronautics. Aeronautical engineering — Collected works (Nonserial)

**TL507.C34 1999**
  The pioneers of flight : a documentary history / Phil Scott. Princeton, N.J. : Princeton University Press, 1999. p. cm.
98-038412          629.13/09          0691011176
*Aeronautics -- History -- Sources. Aeronautics -- History -- Chronology.*

## TL509-512 Aeronautics. Aeronautical engineering — Dictionaries, encyclopedias, etc. Nomenclature. Symbols. Abbreviations

**TL509.C35 1990**
  Cambridge air and space dictionary / general editor, P.M.B. Walker ; consultant editors, J.E. Allen, D.J. Shapland. Cambridge ; Cambridge University Press, c1990. viii, 216 p.
90-001430          629.13/003          0521394392
*Aeronautics -- Dictionaries. Astronautics -- Dictionaries. Space sciences -- Dictionaries.*

**TL509.C66 1993**
  Concise encyclopedia of aeronautics & space systems / editors, Marc Pelegrin, Walter M. Hollister. Oxford ; Pergamon Press, 1993. xiii, 478 p.
93-010616          629.1/03          0080370497
*Aeronautics -- Systems engineering -- Encyclopedias. Astronautics -- Systems engineering -- Encyclopedias.*

**TL509.C87 1994**
**Cushing, Steven,**
  Fatal words : communication clashes and aircraft crashes / by Steven Cushing. Chicago : University of Chicago Press, c1994. p. cm.
93-024615          363.12/418          0226132005
*Aeronautics -- Terminology. Air traffic control -- Terminology. Airplanes -- Piloting -- Terminology. Aircraft accidents -- Investigation. Communication of technical information.*

**TL509.E55 1977**
  Encyclopedia of aviation.  New York : Scribner, 1977. 218 p. :
77-072699          387.7/03          0684148404
*Aeronautics -- Dictionaries.*

**TL509.S24 1998**
  SAE dictionary of aerospace engineering / Joan L. Tomsic, editor ; with contributions by Charles N. Eastlake. 2nd ed. Warrendale, PA : Society of Automotive Engineers, c1998. x, 748 p. :
          629.1/03 21          0768002451
*Aerospace engineering -- Dictionaries. Aeronautics -- Dictionaries. Astronautics -- Dictionaries.*

**TL509.R44 1990**
**Reithmaier, L. W. (Lawrence W.)**
  The aviation/space dictionary / Larry Reithmaier. 7th ed. Blue Ridge Summit, PA : Aero, c1990. 461 p. :
          629.13/003 20
*Aeronautics -- Dictionaries. Astronautics -- Dictionaries.*

**TL512.M37 1998**
**Merry, John A.**
  Aviation internet directory : a guide to 500 best Aviation Web Sites / by John A. Merry. New York : McGraw-Hill, c2001. 395 :
*Aeronautics -- Computer network resources -- Directories.*

## TL515 Aeronautics. Aeronautical engineering — History — General works

**TL515.B23 1994**
**Baker, David,**
   Flight and flying : a chronology / David Baker. New York : Facts on File, c1994. ix, 549 p. :
92-031491          629.13/009          0816018545
*Aeronautics -- History -- Chronology.*

**TL515.G495 1974**
**Gibbs-Smith, Charles Harvard,**
   Flight through the ages : a complete, illustrated chronology from the dreams of early history to the age of space exploration / by C. H. Gibbs-Smith. New York : Crowell, 1974. 240 p. :
74-008389          629.1/09          0690006071
*Aeronautics -- History.*

**TL515.H455 2001**
**Heppenheimer, T. A.,**
   A brief history of flight : from balloons to Mach 3 and beyond / T.A. Heppenheimer. New York : Wiley, c2001. x, 454 p. :
00-026290          629.13/09          0471346373
   *Aeronautics -- History.*

**TL515.I53 1992**
   From airships to airbus : the history of civil and commercial aviation. Washington : Smithsonian Institution Press, c1995. 2 v. :
94-026006          387.7/09          1560984678
*Aeronautics, Commercial -- History -- Congresses. Private flying – History -- Congresses.*

**TL515.S412 1995**
**Scott, Phil,**
   The shoulders of giants : a history of human flight to 1919 / Phil Scott. Reading, Mass. : Addison-Wesley, c1995. xiv, 337 p.,
94-045977          629.13/09          0201627221
*Aeronautics -- History.*

## TL521-521.312 Aeronautics. Aeronautical engineering — Special regions or countries — America. United States

**TL521.A7183 2000**
   The American aviation experience : a history / edited by Tim Brady. Carbondale, Ill. : Southern Illinois University Press, c2000. vii, 462 p. :
99-088092          629.13/0973          0809323257
   *Aeronautics -- United States -- History.*

**TL521.P38 1998**
**Pattillo, Donald M.,**
   A history in the making : 80 turbulent years in the American general aviation industry / Donald M. Pattillo. New York : McGraw-Hill, c1998. xiv, 216 p. :
98-004213          338.4/762913/00973
0070494487
   *Aeronautics -- United States -- History. Aircraft industry – United States -- History.*

**TL521.312.B76 1999**
**Bromberg, Joan Lisa.**
   NASA and the space industry / Joan Lisa Bromberg. Baltimore : Johns Hopkins University Press, 1999. x, 247 p. :
98-044795          338.4/76291/0973
0801860504
   *Aerospace industries -- Government policy -- United States -- History.*

## TL539 Aeronautics. Aeronautical engineering — Biography — Collective

**TL539.J37 1993**
**Jaros, Dean.**
   Heroes without legacy : American airwomen, 1912-1944 / by Dean Jaros. Niwot, Co. : University Press of Colorado, c1993. x, 265 p. :
93-042989          629.13/092/273          0870813129
   *Women air pilots -- United States -- Biography.*

**TL539.L57 1994**
**Longyard, William H.**
   Who's who in aviation history : 500 biographies / William H. Longyard. Novato, CA : Presidio, 1994. 203 p. :
95-021493          629.13/0092/2          0891415564
   *Aeronautics -- Biography. Aeronautics -- History.*

**TL539.W395 1998**
**Welch, Rosanne.**
   Encyclopedia of women in aviation and space / Rosanne Welch. Santa Barbara, Calif. : ABC-CLIO, c1998. xii, 286 p. :
98-008042          629.13/092/2          0874369584
   *Women air pilots -- Biography. Women astronauts – Biography.*

## TL540 Aeronautics. Aeronautical engineering — Biography — Individual, A-Z

**TL540.C646.R52 1993**
**Rich, Doris L.**
   Queen Bess : daredevil aviator / Doris L. Rich. Washington : Smithsonian Institution Press, c1993. xiv, 153 p.,
93-014785          629.13/092          1560982659
*Coleman, Bessie, 1896-1926. African American women air pilots – Biography. Air pilots -- United States -- Biography.*

**TL540.E3.A3 1977**
**Earhart, Amelia,**
    The fun of it : random records of my own flying and of women in aviation / by Amelia Earhart. Chicago : Academy Press, 1977. 218 p., [15]
77-016052        629.13/092/4        0915864568
*Earhart, Amelia, 1897-1937.*
            *Women in aeronautics. Air pilots. Women in aeronautics.*

**TL540.E3.B88 1997**
**Butler, Susan.**
    East to the dawn : the life of Amelia Earhart / Susan Butler. Reading, Mass. : Addison-Wesley, c1997. xiv, 489 p. :
97-019123        629.13/092        0201311445
*Earhart, Amelia, 1897-1937. Women air pilots -- United States -- Biography.*

**TL540.E3.R53 1989**
**Rich, Doris L.**
    Amelia Earhart : a biography / Doris L. Rich. [Washington, D.C.] : Smithsonian Institution, c1989. xiii, 321 p.,
89-032181        629.13/092
*Earhart, Amelia, 1897-1937. Air pilots -- United States – Biography.*

**TL540.L5.M52 1993**
**Milton, Joyce.**
    Loss of Eden : a biography of Charles and Anne Morrow Lindbergh / Joyce Milton. New York, NY : HarperCollinsPublishers, c1993. vi, 520 p. :
92-053319        629.13/092        0060165030
*Lindbergh, Charles A. (Charles Augustus), 1902-1974. Lindbergh, Anne Morrow, 1906- Air pilots – United States -- Biography. Authors, American -- 20th century -- Biography. Married people -- United States -- Biography.*

**TL540.R38.P57 1997**
**Piszkiewicz, Dennis.**
    From Nazi test pilot to Hitler's bunker : the fantastic flights of Hanna Reitsch / Dennis Piszkiewicz. Westport, Conn. : Praeger, 1997. x, 149 p. :
97-011458        629.13/092        0275954560
*Reitsch, Hanna. Women air pilots -- Germany -- Biography. Air pilots, Military -- Germany -- Biography.*

**TL540.S54.A3 1967**
**Sikorsky, Igor Ivan,**
    The story of the Winged-S; late developments and recent photographs of the helicopter, an autobiography, by Igor I. Sikorsky. New York, Dodd, Mead, 1967. xii, 314 p.
67-008594        629.13/00924
*Airplanes. Helicopters.*

**TL540.V67.A3**
**Von Karman, Theodore,**
    The wind and beyond; Theodore von Karman, pioneer in aviation and pathfinder in space, by Theodore von Karman with Lee Edson. Boston, Little, Brown [1967] 376 p.
67-011227        629.1/0924
*Von Kármán, Theodore, 1881-1963. Aeronautical engineers – United States -- Biography.*

**TL540.W7.A25 2000**
**Wright, Wilbur,**
    The published writings of Wilbur and Orville Wright / edited by Peter L. Jakab and Rick Young. Washington, DC : Smithsonian Institute, 2000. xii, 318 p. :
99-039653        629.13/092/2        1560989386
*Wright, Wilbur, 1867-1912 -- Archives. Aeronautics – United States -- History -- Sources. Wright, Orville, 1871-1948 -- Archives.*

**TL540.Y4A38 1985**
**Yeager, Chuck,**
    Yeager, an autobiography / Chuck Yeager & Leo Janos. Toronto ; New York : Bantam Books, c1985. 342 p. :
            623.74/6048/0924 B 19
*Yeager, Chuck, 1923- Air pilots -- United States -- Biography.*

## TL545 Aeronautics. Aeronautical engineering — General works — 1900-

**TL545.V3 1999**
**Van Sickle, Neil D.**
    Van Sickle's modern airmanship. 8th ed. / edited by John F. Welch, Lewis Bjork, Linda Bjork. New York : McGraw-Hill, 1999. xvi, 991 p. :
            629.132/52 21        0070696330
*Aeronautics. Airplanes -- Piloting.*

## TL551.5 Aeronautics. Aeronautical engineering — High-speed aeronautics

**TL551.5.R68 1994**
**Rotundo, Louis C.**
    Into the unknown : the X-1 story / Louis Rotundo. Washington, D.C. : Smithsonian Institution Press, c1994. xi, 324 p., [
93-015989        629.132/305/0973
1560983051
    *High-speed aeronautics -- History. Bell X-1 (Supersonic planes) Supersonic planes -- Research -- United States -- History.*

## TL553.5 Aeronautics. Aeronautical engineering — Miscellaneous aspects of the general subject — General works

**TL553.5.K73 1996**
**Krause, Shari Stamford.**
    Aircraft safety : accident investigations, analyses, and applications / Shari Stamford Krause. New York : McGraw-Hill, c1996. xvi, 379 p. :
95-047931        363.12/41        007036026X
    *Aeronautics -- Safety measures. Aircraft accidents – Investigation.*

**TL553.5.N25 1994**
**Nader, Ralph.**
    Collision course : the truth about airline safety / Ralph Nader, Wesley J. Smith. Blue Ridge Summit, PA : Tab Books, c1994. xxii, 378 p.
93-008266        363.12/4/0973        0830642714
    *Aeronautics -- United States -- Safety measures.*

# TL559.A86 1999

## TL559 Aeronautics. Aeronautical engineering — Addresses, essays, lectures

**TL559.A86 1999**
Atmospheric flight in the twentieth century / edited by Peter Galison, Alex Roland. Dordrecht : Kluwer, c2000. xvi, 383 p. :
99-058408     629.13     0792360370
*Aeronautics.*

## TL568 Aeronautics. Aeronautical engineering — Special institutions, A-Z (Including research conducted by governments, universities or others)

**TL568.J47.K66 1982**
**Koppes, Clayton R.,**
JPL and the American space program : a history of the Jet Propulsion Laboratory / Clayton R. Koppes. New Haven : Yale University Press, c1982. xiii, 299 p.,
82-040162     629.4/072079493
0300024088
*Jet Propulsion Laboratory (U.S.) -- History. Astronautics -- United States -- History.*

## TL570 Aeronautics. Aeronautical engineering — Mechanics of flight: Aerodynamics — General works

**TL570.A679 1997**
**Anderson, John David.**
A history of aerodynamics and its impact on flying machines / John D. Anderson, Jr. Cambridge ; Cambridge University Press, 1997. xii, 478 p. :
96-045967     629.132/3/09     0521454352
*Aerodynamics -- History.*

**TL570.B42 2002**
**Berin, John J.,**
Aerodynamics for engineers / John J. Bertin. 4th ed. Upper Saddle River, NJ : Prentice Hall, c2002. xvi, 580 p. :
629.132/3 21
*Aerodynamics.*

**TL570.S462 1989**
**Shevell, Richard Shepherd.**
Fundamentals of flight / Richard S. Shevell. 2nd ed. Englewood Cliffs, N.J. : Prentice Hall, c1989. xxv, 438 p. :
629.132/3 19
*Aerodynamics.*

**TL570.W4 1997**
**Wegener, Peter P.,**
What makes airplanes fly? : history, science, and applications of aerodynamics / Peter P. Wegener. New York : Springer, c1997. xii, 260 p. :
96-023154     629.132/3     0387947841
*Aerodynamics.*

**TL570.A69 2001**
**Anderson, David F.**
Understanding flight / David F. Anderson, Scott Eberhardt. New York : McGraw-Hill, c2001. xii, 239 p. :
629.13.21
*Flight. Aerodynamics.*

## TL574 Aeronautics. Aeronautical engineering — Mechanics of flight: Aerodynamics — Special topics, A-Z

**TL574.B6**
**Schlichting, Hermann,**
Boundary-layer theory / Herrmann Schlichting, Klaus Gersten, with contributions from Egon Krause and Herbert Oertel Jr. ; translated by Katherine Mayes. Berlin ; Springer, c2000. xxiii, 799 p.
99-051605     629.132/37     3540662707
*Boundary layer.*

## TL670.3-671.6 Aeronautics. Aeronautical engineering — Aircraft (General) — Heavier-than-air craft

**TL670.3.E52**
Encyclopedia of aircraft / edited by Michael J. H. Taylor & John W. R. Taylor. New York : Putnam, c1978. 253 p. :
78-053408     629.133/34/03
*Airplanes -- History. Airplanes -- Dictionaries.*

**TL670.5.J35 1990**
**Jakab, Peter L.**
Visions of a flying machine : the Wright brothers and the process of invention / Peter L. Jakab. Washington : Smithsonian Institution Press, c1990. xviii, 263 p.
89-039643     629.13/092/2/     0874744563
*Wright, Orville, -- 1871-1948. Wright, Wilbur, -- 1867-1912. Airplanes -- History.*

**TL671.2.C7 1981**
**Crawford, Donald R.**
A practical guide to airplane performance and design / by Donald R. Crawford. Torrance, Ca. : Crawford Aviation, 1981. xiii, 206 p.
81-067801     629.134/1     0960393404
*Airplanes -- Design and construction.*

**TL671.2.I64 1997**
Introduction to aeronautics : a design perspective / Steven A. Brandt . . . [et al.]. Reston, VA : American Institute of Aeronautics and Astronautics 1997. p. cm.
629.134/1 21     1563472503
*Airplanes -- Design and construction. Aeronautics.*

**TL671.2.S77 1998**
**Stinton, Darrol,**
The anatomy of the airplane / Darrol Stinton. 3rd ed. Reston, VA : American Institute of Aeronautics and Astronautics 1998. p. cm.
629.133/34 21
*Airplanes -- Design and construction.*

**TL671.2.S773 1983**
**Stinton, Darrol,**

The design of the aeroplane : which describes common-sense mechanics of design as they affect the flying qualities of aeroplanes needing only one pilot / Darrol Stinton. New York : Van Nostrand Reinhold, 1983. xxix, 642 p.
82-013635          629.134/1          0442282494
   *Airplanes -- Design and construction.*

**TL671.6.C88 1999**
**Cutler, John.**

Understanding aircraft structures / John Cutler. 3rd ed. Malden, Mass. : Blackwell Science, 1999. p. cm.
                   629.134/31 21
*Airframes.*

**TL671.6.D56 1993**
**Donaldson, Bruce K.**

Analysis of aircraft structures : an introduction / Bruce K. Donaldson. New York : McGraw-Hill, c1993. xl, 935 p. :
91-045095          629.134/31          007017539X
   *Airframes. Structural analysis (Engineering) Vehicles – Design and construction.*

## TL716 Aeronautics. Aeronautical engineering — Flying machines other than airplanes — Rotor aircraft

**TL716.F35 1976**
**Fay, John Foster.**

The helicopter : history, piloting, and how it flies / by John Fay ; illustrated by Lucy Raymond, David Gibbings, Dulcie Legg. Newton Abbot ; David & Charles, 1976. xiii, 194 p.,
77-360773          629.133/35          0715372491
*Helicopters.*

**TL716.N39 1994**
**Newman, Simon,**

The foundations of helicopter flight / Simon Newman. New York : Halsted Press, c1994. viii, 303 p.
94-181796          629.133/352          047023394X
*Helicopters -- Aerodynamics -- Mathematics. Helicopters – Piloting.*

## TL725.3 Aeronautics. Aeronautical engineering — Airways (Routes). Airports and landing fields. — Special topics, A-Z

**TL725.3.M16.I58 1998**

Airport facilities : innovations for the next century / edited by Michael T. McNerney. Reston, Va. : American Society of Civil Engineers, 1998. xiii, 602 p.
98-007392          629.136          0784403511
   *Airports -- Maintenance and repair -- Congresses. Airports -- Planning -- Congresses. Military base closures -- United States -- Congresses. Bergstrom Air Force Base (Tex.) -- Congresses.*

**TL725.3.P5.A83 1992**
**Ashford, Norman.**

Airport engineering / Norman Ashford, Paul H. Wright. New York : Wiley, c1992. x, 520 p. :
91-020384          629.136          0471527556
   *Airports -- Planning.*

**TL725.3.P5H6 1994**
**Horonjeff, Robert.**

Planning and design of airports / Robert Horonjeff, Francis X. McKelvey. 4th ed., International ed. New York : McGraw-Hill, c1994. xiii, 829 p. :
                   629.136 20
*Airports -- Planning. Airports -- Design and construction.*

## TL726.6 Aeronautics. Aeronautical engineering — Airways (Routes). Airports and landing fields. — Special countries

**TL726.6.E85.J36**

Jane's airports and handling agents. Coulsdon, Surrey, U.K. ; Jane's Information Group, v. ;
93-650394          387.7/36/02573
   *Airports -- Europe -- Directories. Fixed base operators industry – Europe -- Directories.*

## TL781 Rocket propulsion. Rockets — History — General works

**TL781.B34**
**Baker, David,**

The rocket : the history and development of rocket & missile technology / David Baker. New York : Crown, c1978. 276, [1] p. :
78-000273          358/.17/09          0517534045
   *Rockets (Aeronautics) -- History.*

**TL781.W55 1990**
**Winter, Frank H.**

Rockets into space / Frank H. Winter. Cambridge, Mass. : Harvard University Press, 1990. xii, 165 p. :
89-024551          629.47/52/09          0674776607
   *Rocketry -- History.*

## TL781.85 Rocket propulsion. Rockets — Biography — Individual, A-Z

**TL781.85.G6.A34**
**Goddard, Robert Hutchings,**

The papers of Robert H. Goddard, including the reports to the Smithsonian Institution and the Daniel and Florence Guggenheim Foundation. Esther C. Goddard, editor. G. Edward Pendray, associate editor. New York, McGraw-Hill [1970] 3 v. (xx, 170
68-012660          629.4/0924
*Goddard, Robert Hutchings, -- 1882-1945.*

**TL781.85.V6.P57 1998**
**Piszkiewicz, Dennis.**
   Wernher Von Braun : the man who sold the moon / Dennis Piszkiewicz. Westport, Conn. : Praeger, 1998. x, 240 p. :
98-014481          621.43/56/092          0275962172
*Von Braun, Wernher, -- 1912-1977.     Rocketry -- United States – Biography. Rocketry -- Germany -- Biography.*

**TL781.85.V6.S78 1994**
**Stuhlinger, Ernst,**
   Wernher von Braun, crusader for space : a biographical memoir / Ernst Stuhlinger, Frederick I. Ordway III. Malabar, Fla. : Krieger Pub., 1994. xvi, 375 p. :
93-010677          621.43/56/092          089464842X
*Von Braun, Wernher, -- 1912-1977.     Rocketry -- United States – Biography. Rocketry -- Germany -- Biography.*

## TL788 Astronautics. Space travel — Dictionaries and encyclopedias

**TL788.I44 1981**
   The Illustrated encyclopedia of space technology : a comprehensive history of space exploration / Kenneth Gatland, consultant and chief author ; with a foreword by Arthur C. Clarke. New York : Harmony Books, c1981. 289 p. :
80-028533          629.4/03/21          0517542587
*Astronautics -- Dictionaries.*

**TL788.W54 2001**
**Williamson, Mark.**
   The Cambridge dictionary of space technology / Mark Williamson. New York : Cambridge University Press, 2001. p. cm.
00-059884          629.4/03          0521660777
*Astronautics -- Dictionaries. Aerospace engineering -- Dictionaries. Astronomy -- Dictionaries.*

## TL788.4 Astronautics. Space travel — International cooperation

**TL788.4.I585 1987**
   International space policy : legal, economic, and strategic options for the twentieth century and beyond / edited by Daniel S. Papp and John R. McIntyre. New York : Quorum Books, 1987. xiii, 328 p.
87-002519          341.7/675          0899302157
*Astronautics -- International cooperation -- Congresses. Astronautics and state -- Congresses.*

## TL788.5 Astronautics. Space travel — History — General works

**TL788.5.C37 1999**
**Cassutt, Michael.**
   Who's who in space / Michael Cassutt. New York : Macmillan Library Reference USA, c1999. xxi, 665 p. :
98-035587          629.45/0092/2
*Manned space flight -- History -- Encyclopedias. Astronauts – Biography -- Encyclopedias.*

**TL788.5.L47 1994**
**Levine, Alan J.**
   The missile and space race / Alan J. Levine. Westport, Conn. : Praeger, 1994. viii, 247 p.
93-023673          387.8/0973          0275944514
*Space race -- History. Arms race -- History -- 20th century. Cold War -- History. Outer space -- Exploration -- History.*

## TL789 Astronautics. Space travel — Unidentified flying objects. Flying saucers — General works

**TL789.C555 1998**
**Clark, Jerome.**
   The UFO encyclopedia : the phenomenon from the beginning / by Jerome Clark. Detroit, MI : Omnigraphics, c1998. 2 v. (xix, 11
98-015930          001.942          0780800974
*Unidentified flying objects -- Encyclopedias.*

**TL789.R57 1994**
**Ritchie, David,**
   UFO : the definitive guide to unidentified flying objects and related phenomena / David Ritchie. New York : Facts on File, c1994. vii, 264 p. :
93-031037          001.9/42          081602894X
*Unidentified flying objects -- Encyclopedias.*

## TL789.3 Astronautics. Space travel — Unidentified flying objects. Flying saucers — Personal narratives

**TL789.3.U137 2001**
   The UFO evidence. Volume II, A 30-year report / Richard H. Hall [Editor]. Lanham, MD. : Scarecrow Press, 2001. xiv, 681 p. :
          001.942 21
*Unidentified flying objects.*

**TL789.3.P44 1994**
**Peebles, Curtis.**
   Watch the skies! : a chronicle of the flying saucer myth / Curtis Peebles. Washington : Smithsonian Institution Press, c1994. x, 342 p. ;
93-026819          001.9/42          1560983434
*Unidentified flying objects -- Sightings and encounters – History.*

## TL789.5 Astronautics. Space travel — Unidentified flying objects. Flying saucers — By region or country

**TL789.5.N6.S25 1997**
**Saler, Benson.**
   UFO crash at Roswell : the genesis of a modern myth / Benson Saler, Charles A. Ziegler, and Charles B. Moore. Washington : Smithsonian Institution Press, c1997. xii, 198 p. :
97-008674          001.942/09789/43
1560987510
*Unidentified flying objects -- Sightings and encounters -- New Mexico -- Roswell. Myth -- Miscellanea. Folklore -- Miscellanea.*

## TL789.8 Astronautics. Space travel — By country, region, etc., A-Z

**TL789.8.R9.H37 1996**
**Harvey, Brian,**

The new Russian space programme : from competition to collaboration / Brian Harvey. Chichester ; Wiley, 1996. xvi, 408 p. :
95-039629          387.8/0947          0471960144
*Astronautics -- Russia (Federation) Astronautics – Soviet Union - - History. Astronautics -- International cooperation.*

**TL789.8.S652**
**Hall, Rex,**

The rocket men : Vostok & Voskhod, the first Soviet manned spaceflights / Rex Hall and David J. Shayler. London ; Springer ; c2001. xxxii, 326 p.
01-018373          629.45/00947          185233391X
*Manned space flight -- Soviet Union -- History. World records – Soviet Union.*

**TL789.8.U5.C59 1988**
**Collins, Michael,**

Liftoff : the story of America's adventure in space / Michael Collins ; illustrated by James Dean. New York : Grove Press, 1988. xi, 288 p. :
88-001706          629.4/0973          0802110118
*Astronautics -- United States -- History.*

**TL789.8.U5.D48 1992**
**DeVorkin, David H.,**

Science with a vengeance : how the military created the US space sciences after World War II / David H. DeVorkin. New York : Springer-Verlag, c1992. xxii, 404 p.
91-045040          629.4/0973          0387977708
*Astronautics -- United States -- History. Astronautics, Military – United States -- History. V-2 rocket -- Scientific applications.*

**TL789.8.U5.H49 1997**
**Heppenheimer, T. A.,**

Countdown : a history of space flight / T.A. Heppenheimer. New York : John Wiley & Sons, 1997. x, 398 p. :
96-028245          387.8/09          0471144398
*Space race -- History. Astronautics and state -- United States – History. Astronautics and state -- Soviet Union -- History.*

**TL789.8.U5.M34 1985**
**McDougall, Walter A.,**

The heavens and the earth : a political history of the space age / Walter A. McDougall. New York : Basic Books, c1985. xviii, 555 p.
84-045314          338.4/76294/0973
046502887X
*Astronautics and state -- United States. Astronautics and state – Soviet Union. Astronautics -- United States -- History.*

**TL789.8.U5.R44 1994**
**Reeves, Robert.**

The superpower space race : an explosive rivalry through the solar system / Robert Reeves. New York : Plenum Press, c1994. xiv, 437 p. :
94-028240          327.1          0306447681
*Space race -- United States -- History. Space race – Soviet Union -- History. Space probes. Outer space -- Exploration – Soviet Union - - History. Outer space -- Exploration -- United States -- History.*

**TL789.8.U5M338 1997**
**McCurdy, Howard E.**

Space and the American imagination / Howard E. McCurdy. Washington, D.C. : Smithsonian Institution Press, c1997. x, 294 p. :
          387.8/0973 21          1560987642
*Astronautics -- United States -- Public opinion. Mass media – United States -- Influence. Astronautics and state -- United States.*

**TL789.8.U6**
**Lindsay, Hamish.**

Tracking Apollo to the moon / Hamish Lindsay. London ; Springer, c2001. xiii, 426 p.
00-058348          629.45/4/0973          1852332123

**TL789.8.U6**
**Shayler, David,**

Skylab : America's space station / David J. Shayler. London, Springer, c2001. xxxix, 375 p.
01-020621          629.44/2          185233407X
*X-15 (Rocket aircraft) -- History -- Juvenile literature. Airplanes - - Flight testing -- Juvenile literature. X-15 (Rocket aircraft) – History.*

**TL789.8.U6.M59**

We seven, by the astronauts themselves: M. Scott Carpenter [and others] New York, Simon and Schuster, 1962. 352 p.
62-019074          629.45
*Astronauts -- United States.*

**TL789.8U6A5488 1994**
**Lovell, Jim.**

Lost moon : the perilous voyage of Apollo 13 / Jim Lovell & Jeffrey Kluger. Boston : Houghton Mifflin, c1994. 378 p. :
          629.45/4 20
*Apollo 13 (Spacecraft) -- Accidents. Space vehicle accidents – United States. Lovell, Jim.*

## TL789.85 Astronautics. Space travel — Biography

**TL789.85.A1.H38 1992**
**Hawthorne, Douglas B.**

Men and women of space / by Douglas B. Hawthorne. San Diego, Calif. : Univelt, c1992. xiii, 904 p.
92-213233          091218308X
*Astronautics -- United States -- Biography -- Dictionaries. Astronautics -- Soviet Union -- Biography -- Dictionaries.*

## TL790 Astronautics. Space travel — General works

**TL790.A43 2000**
Allday, Jonathan.
    Apollo in perspective : spaceflight then and now / Jonathan Allday. Bristol, UK : Institute of Physics Pub., c2000. xvi, 320 p. :
99-046328        629.45/4/0973      0750306459
    *Space flight.*

**TL790.W48 1998**
White, Frank,
    The overview effect : space exploration and human evolution / Frank White. Reston, VA : American Institute of Aeronautics and Astronauti c1998. xxii, 314 p.
98-023507        303.48/3        1563472600
    *Astronautics and civilization.     Outer space -- Exploration.*

## TL791 Astronautics. Space travel — Textbooks

**TL791.H35 1994**
Hale, Francis J.
    Introduction to space flight / Francis J. Hale. Englewood Cliffs, N.J. : Prentice Hall, c1994. xiii, 366 p.
93-022436        629.4/1        0134819128
    *Space flight. Orbital mechanics.*

**TL791.S65 1999**
    Space exploration / edited by Christopher Mari. New York : H.W. Wilson Company, 1999. ix, 157 p. :
       919.9/04 21      082420963X
    *Astronautics. Outer Space -- Exploration.*

## TL793 Astronautics. Space travel — Popular works. Juvenile works

**TL793.L3137 1995**
Lee, Wayne.
    To rise from earth : an easy-to-understand guide to space flight / Wayne Lee. New York,NY : Facts on File, c1995. 309 p. :
95-038941        629.4      0816033536
    *Astronautics -- Popular works. Space flight -- Popular works.*

## TL794 Astronautics. Space travel — Handbooks, pocketbooks, tables, etc.

**TL794.B34 1990**
Bali, Mrinal,
    Space exploration : a reference handbook / Mrinal Bali ; introduction by Harrison H. Schmitt. Santa Barbara, Calif. : ABC-CLIO, c1990. xi, 240 p. ;
90-019204        919.9/04      0874365783
    *Astronautics -- Handbooks, manuals, etc.*

## TL795 Astronautics. Space travel — Space vehicles. Space ships — General works

**TL795.K45 2001**
Kelly, Thomas J.,
    Moon lander : how we developed the Apollo lunar module / Thomas J. Kelly. Washington, [D.C.] : Smithsonian Institution Press, c2001. xvii, 283 p.
00-063728        629.44      156098998X
    *Lunar excursion module.*

**TL795.M48 1999**
Meyer, Rudolph X.
    Elements of space technology for aerospace engineers / Rudolf X. Meyer. San Diego : Academic Press, c1999. xi, 329 p. :
       629.4 21      0124929400
*Space vehicles -- Design and construction. Aerospace engineering. Astronautics.*

## TL795.3 Astronautics. Space travel — Space vehicles. Space ships — Space probes

**TL795.3**
Matloff, Gregory L.
    Deep-space probes / Gregory L. Matloff. London : Springer, c2000. xxiv, 184 p. :
00-061255        629.43/5      185233200X
*Kraemer, Robert S. -- Career in space sciences.    Space probes – History. Space sciences -- United States -- History. Planets -- Exploration -- History.*

## TL795.7 Astronautics. Space travel — Space colonies. Space communities

**TL795.7.F64 1995**
Fogg, Martyn J.,
    Terraforming : engineering planetary environments / Martyn J. Fogg. Warrendale, PA, U.S.A. : Society of Automotive Engineers, c1995. xvi, 544 p. :
95-010546        620/.419      1560916095
    *Planets -- Environmental engineering.*

**TL795.7.H37 1991**
Harris, Philip R.
    Living and working in space : human behavior, culture, and organization / Philip R. Harris. New York : Ellis Horwood, c1992. 339 p. :
91-032319        338.0919      0134010507
    *Space colonies. Space industrialization.*

**TL795.7.O53 2000**
O'Neill, Gerard K.
    The high frontier : human colonies in space / Gerard K. O'Neill ; with contributions by David P. Gump ... [et al.] Burlington, Ont : Apogee Books, 2000. 183 p. :
       189652267X
    *Space colonies.*

### TL796 Astronautics. Space travel — Artificial satellights — General works

**TL796.G38 1998**
**Gavaghan, Helen.**
Something new under the sun : satellites and the beginning of the space age / Helen Gavaghan. New York : Copernicus, c1998. xviii, 300 p.
96-048689      629.43/09      0387949143
*Artificial satellites -- History. Astronautics and civilization.*

### TL796.3 Astronautics. Space travel — Artificial satellights — Juvenile works

**TL796.3.B74 2000**
**Bredeson, Carmen.**
NASA planetary spacecraft : Galileo, Magellan, Pathfinder, and Voyager / Carmen Bredeson. Berkeley Heights, NJ : Enslow, c2000. p. cm.
99-050639      629.43/54      0766013030
*Space probes -- Juvenile literature. Planets -- Exploration -- Juvenile literature. Space probes.*

### TL796.6 Astronautics. Space travel — Artificial satellights — By planet, etc., A-Z

**TL796.6.E2.C867 1994**
Space satellite handbook / Anthony R. Curtis, editor. Houston : Gulf Pub. Co., c1994. vi, 346 p. :
93037563      629.46      0884151921
*Artificial satellites -- History. Artificial satellites -- Registers. Artificial satellites -- Handbooks, manuals, etc.*

### TL798 Astronautics. Space travel — Artificial satellights — Special types by use, A-Z

**TL798.M4.H55 1991**
**Hill, Janice,**
Weather from above : America's meteorological satellites / Janice Hill. Washington : Smithsonian Institution Press, c1991. viii, 89 p. :
90-030060      551.5/028      0874744679
*Meteorological satellites.*

## TL799 Astronautics. Space travel — Flights to the special planets, etc. By planet, A-Z

**TL799.M3.O23 1982**
**Oberg, James E.,**
Mission to Mars : plans and concepts for the first manned landing / James E. Oberg. Harrisburg, PA : Stackpole, c1982. 221 p. :
82-005689      629.45/53      0811704327
*Space flight to Mars.*

**TL799.M6**
**Eckart, Peter.**
The lunar base handbook : an introduction to lunar base design, development, and operations / edited by Peter Eckart ; with contributions by Buzz Aldrin ... [et al.]. New York : McGraw-Hill, c1999. xxviii, 850 p
99-068921      629.47      0072401710
*Lunar bases.*

### TL873 Astronautics. Space travel — Systems engineering — Manned space flight

**TL873.F74 2000**
**Freeman, Marsha.**
Challenges of human space exploration / Marsha Freeman. London ; Springer, 2000. xxii, 259 p.
00-020843      629.45      1852332018
*Manned space flight.     Outer space -- Exploration.*

### TL875 Astronautics. Space travel — Specific aspects of space vehicles — Design and construction

**TL875.S68 1995**
Spacecraft systems engineering / edited by Peter Fortescue and John Stark. 2nd ed. Chichester ; New York : Wiley, c1995. xviii, 581 p. :
     629.47/4 20      0471952206
*Space vehicles -- Design and construction. Astronautics -- Systems and engineering.*

### TL1050 Astronautics. Space travel — Astrodynamics. Flight mechanics. Orbital mechanics — General works

**TL1050.P78 1993**
**Prussing, John E.**
Orbital mechanics / John E. Prussing, Bruce A. Conway. New York : Oxford University Press, 1993. xi, 194 p :
92-041505      629.4/1133      0195078349

### TL1489 Astronautics. Space travel — Environmental engineering in space. Space environment — General works

**TL1489.H37 1996**
**Hastings, Daniel.**
Spacecraft--environment interactions / Daniel Hastings, Henry Garrett. Cambridge ; Cambridge University Press, 1996. xxiii, 292 p.
95-047376      629.4/16      0521471281
*Space environment. Space vehicles -- Design and construction.*

**TL1499 Astronautics. Space travel — Environmental engineering in space. Space environment — Space debris**

**TL1499.N38 1995**
**National Research Council (U.S.).**
   Orbital debris : a technical assessment / Committee on Space Debris, Aeronautics and Space Engineering Board, Commission on Engineering and Technical Systems, National Research Council. Washington, D.C. : National Academy Press, 1995. xi, 210 p. :
95-018686            629.4/16            0309051258
*Space debris.*

**TL1500-1550 Astronautics. Space travel — Environmental engineering in space. Space environment — Life support systems. Human engineering. Human environment equipment and testing**

**TL1500.H37 2001**
**Harrison, Albert A.**
   Spacefaring : the human dimension / Albert A. Harrison. Berkeley : University of California Press, c2001. xviii, 324 p.
00-061522            629.45            0520224531
   *Manned space flight. Astronautics -- Human factors. Space colonies.*

**TL1550.K68 1994**
**Kozloski, Lillian D.**
   U.S. space gear : outfitting the astronaut / Lillian D. Kozloski. Washington : Smithsonian Institution Press, c1994. xi, 238 p. :
92-034611            629.47/72            0874744598

**TL4015 Astronautics. Space travel — Ground support systems, operations and equipment — General works**

**TL4015.A15 2001**
   2001 : building for space travel / John Zukowsky, editor. New York : Harry N. Abrams, c2001. 191 p. :
00-058278            629.4/074/77311            0810944901
   *Launch complexes (Astronautics) -- Design and construction -- Exhibitions. Architecture, Postmodern -- Exhibitions. Space vehicles -- Design and construction -- Exhibitions.*

# TN Mining engineering. Metallurgy

## TN9 Dictionaries and encyclopedias — General works

**TN9.D564 1997**
   Dictionary of mining, mineral, and related terms / compiled by the American Geological Institute. 2nd ed. Alexandria, Va.: American Geological Institute c1997. x, 646 p. :
            622/.03 21            0922152365
*Mining engineering -- Dictionaries. Mineral industries -- Dictionaries.*

**TN9.T5**
**Thrush, Paul W.**
   A dictionary of mining, mineral, and related terms, compiled and edited by Paul W. Thrush and the staff of the Bureau of Mines. [Washington, U.S. Bureau of Mines; for sale by the Supt. of D 1968. vii, 1269 p.
68-067091            622/.03
   *Mining engineering -- Dictionaries. Mineral industries -- Dictionaries.*

## TN15 History and description — General works

**TN15.G44 2001**
**Gregory, Cedric Errol.**
   A concise history of mining / Cedric E. Gregory. Rev. ed. Exton, PA : A.A. Balkema, c2001. p. cm.
            622/.09 21            9058093476
*Mining engineering -- History.*

# TN23-115 Special countries (Including government reports on mineral resources and economic geology)

**TN23.C36 1986**
**Cameron, Eugene N.**
   At the crossroads : the mineral problems of the United States / Eugene N. Cameron. New York : Wiley, c1986. xxi, 320 p. :
85-029587            333.8/5/0973            0471839833
   *Mines and mineral resources -- United States.*

**TN23.R56**
**Riley, Charles M.**
   Our mineral resources; an elementary textbook in economic geology. New York, Wiley [1959] 338 p.
59-011807            553.0973
   *Mines and mineral resources -- United States.*

**TN23.U612**

Minerals yearbook / prepared by the staff of the Bureau of Mines. Washington : The Bureau : v. :
33-026551      338.2/0973
*Mineral industries -- United States -- Periodicals. Mines and mineral resources -- United States -- Periodicals. Mineral industries -- Periodicals.*

## TN140 Biography — Individual, A-Z

**TN140.G8.O25**
**O'Connor, Harvey.**
The Guggenheims; the making of an American dynasty, by Harvey O'Connor. New York, Covici, Friede [c1937] 496 p.
37018133      923.373
*Guggenheim family.    Mining industry and finance – United States.*

**TN140.S8.S7**
**Stewart, Robert Ernest.**
Adolph Sutro : a biography.   Howell-North, 1962. 243 p. :
62016167      926.22
*Sutro, Adolph, -- 1830-1898.    Mining engineers.    Comstock Lode (Nev.) San Francisco (Calif.) -- Biography.*

## TN145 General works — 1800-

**TN145.D46 1989**
**Dennen, William H.**
Mineral resources : geology, exploration, and development / William H. Dennen. New York : Taylor & Francis, 1989. x, 255 p. :
88-021672      622      0844815691
*Mines and mineral resources.*

**TN145.U53 2001**
Underground mining methods : engineering fundamentals and international case studies / edited by William A. Hustrulid and Richard L. Bullock. Littleton, Colo. : Society for Mining, c2001. x, 718 p. :
622.2 21      0873351932
*Mining engineering.*

## TN153 General works — General special

**TN153.B58 1985**
**Blunden, John.**
Mineral resources and their management / John Blunden. London ; Longman, 1985. p. cm.
84-010061      333.8/5      0582300584
*Mines and mineral resources. Conservation of natural resources.*

**TN153.I49 1983**
International minerals : a national perspective / edited by Allen F. Agnew. Boulder, Colo. : Published by Westview Press for the American Ass 1983. xv, 164 p. :
83-060538      333.8/5      0865316228
*Mines and mineral resources. Mines and mineral resources -- United States. Strategic materials -- United States.*

## TN260 Economic or applied geology and mineralogy

**TN260.B27 1988**
**Barnes, J. W.**
Ores and minerals : introducing economic geology / J.W. Barnes. Milton Keynes ; Open University Press, 1988. vi, 181 p. :
87-031264      553      0335152163
*Geology, Economic.*

**TN260.B3 1979**
**Jensen, Mead Leroy,**
Economic mineral deposits / Mead L. Jensen, Alan M. Bateman. New York : Wiley, c1979. viii, 593 p.
78-009852      553      0471017698
*Geology, Economic. Mines and mineral resources.*

**TN260.E28**
Economic geology and geotectonics / edited by D. H. Tarling. New York : Wiley, 1981. x, 213 p. :
81-000673      553      0470271450
*Geology, Economic. Geology, Structural.*

**TN260.E93 1997**
**Evans, Anthony M.**
An introduction to economic geology and its environmental impact / Anthony M. Evans. Oxford ; Malden, MA : Blackwell Science, 1997. ix, 364 p. :
553 21      086542876X
*Geology, Economic. Mines and mineral resources -- Environmental aspects.*

**TN260.K8**
**Krynine, Dimitri Pavlovitch,**
Principles of engineering geology and geotechnics; geology, soil and rock mechanics, and other earth sciences as used in civil engineering [by] Dimitri P. Krynine [and] William R. Judd. New York, McGraw-Hill, 1957. 730 p.
56009631      624.151
*Engineering geology. Soil mechanics.*

**TN260.M57 1983**
Mining geology / edited by Willard C. Lacy. Stroudsburg, Pa. : Hutchinson Ross Pub. Co. ; c1983. xiii, 466 p.
82-000968      553      0879334266
*Mining geology.*

## TN263 Mineral deposits. Metallic ore deposits

**TN263.B27**
**Bateman, Alan Mara.**
The formation of mineral deposits.   New York, Wiley [1951] xi, 371 p.
51013033      553.1
*Ore deposits*

**TN263.L7 1933**
Lindgren, Waldemar,
  Mineral deposits, by Waldemar Lindgren ... New York, McGraw-Hill Book Company, inc., 1933. xvii, 930 p.
33024760          553.1
  *Ore deposits.*

## TN264 Marine mineral resources

**TN264.E37 1990**
Earney, Fillmore C. F.
  Marine mineral resources / Fillmore C.F. Earney. London ; Routledge, 1990. xxiv, 387 p.
89-038875          333.8/5/09162          041502255X
  *Marine mineral resources. Ocean mining. Law of the sea.*

## TN265 Metallic ores (General)

**TN265.E33 1986**
Edwards, Richard,
  Ore deposit geology and its influence on mineral exploration / Richard Edwards and Keith Atkinson. London ; Chapman and Hall, 1986. xvi, 466 p. :
85-011713          553/.1          0412246902
  *Ore deposits. Geology. Prospecting.*

## TN269 Geophysical surveying — General works

**TN269.A663**
  Applied geophysics / W. M. Telford ... [et al.]. London ; Cambridge University Press, 1976. xvii, 860 p.
74-016992          622/.15          0521206707
  *Prospecting -- Geophysical methods.*

**TN269.D6 1988**
Dobrin, Milton B. (Milton Burnett)
  Introduction to geophysical prospecting / Milton B. Dobrin, Carl H. Savit ; assisted by Heloise Bloxsom Lynn ; with additional chapters by Norman Neidell, Yoram Shoham, and Ozdogan Yilmaz. 4th ed. New York : McGraw-Hill Book Co., c1988. xix, 867 p. :
          622/.15 19
  *Prospecting -- Geophysical methods.*

**TN269.M53 1996**
Milsom, John,
  Field geophysics / John Milsom. 2nd ed. Chichester ; New York : Wiley, c1996. x, 187 p. :
          622/.15 20
  *Prospecting -- Geophysical methods.*

**TN269.S52417 1989**
Sheriff, Robert E.
  Geophysical methods / Robert E. Sheriff. Englewood Cliffs, N.J. : Prentice Hall, c1989. xviii, 605 p.
88-005798          622/.15          0133525686
  *Prospecting -- Geophysical methods.*

## TN270 Prospecting — General works

**TN270.P4 1973**
Pearl, Richard Maxwell,
  Handbook for prospectors [by] Richard M. Pearl. New York, McGraw-Hill [1973] viii, 472 p.
72-011749          622/.1          0070490252
  *Prospecting.*

## TN271 Prospecting — Special minerals, A-Z

**TN271.P4.P463 1993**
Peters, Kenneth E.
  The biomarker guide : interpreting molecular fossils in petroleum and ancient sediments / Kenneth E. Peters, J. Michael Moldowan. Englewood Cliffs, N.J. : Prentice Hall, c1993. xvi, 363 p. :
91-043815          622/.1828          0130867527
  *Petroleum -- Prospecting. Biogeochemical prospecting. Biochemical markers.*

## TN275 Practical mining operations — General works

**TN275.T33 1998**
  Techniques in underground mining : selections from Underground mining methods handbook / edited by Richard E. Gertsch and Richard L. Bullock.k Littleton, CO : Society for Mining, Metallurgy, and Exploration, c1998. ix, 823 p. :
          622.2 21          0873351630
  *Mining engineering.*

**TN275.T48 1973b**
Thomas, L. J.
  An introduction to mining: exploration, feasibility, extraction, rock mechanics [by] L. J. Thomas. Sydney, Hicks, Smith & Sons, 1973. ix, 436 p.
74-150122          622          0454017308
  *Mining engineering. Prospecting. Rock mechanics.*

## TN343 Electrical engineering and equipment

**TN343.J66 1992**
Jones, Alan V.
  Electrical technology in mining : the dawn of a new age / A.V. Jones and R.P. Tarkenter. London : P. Peregrinus in association with the Science Mu c1992. vii, 207 p. :
93-138419          622          0863411991
  *Electricity in mining -- History. Mining engineering -- Great Britain -- History.*

## TN411 Ore deposits and mining of particular metals — Gold and silver ore deposits and mining. Precious metals — General special

**TN411.G37 1993**
**Gasparrini, Claudia.**
   Gold and other precious metals : from ore to market / Claudia Gasparrini ; with forewords by G.C. Amstutz and P.M.J. Gray. Berlin ; Springer-Verlag, c1993. xxi, 336 p. :
93-007283      669      0387549765
   *Gold ores -- Geology. Precious metals. Ore-dressing.*

## TN413 Ore deposits and mining of particular metals — Gold and silver ore deposits and mining. Precious metals — Special countries

**TN413.N25.W8 1947**
**Wright, William,**
   The big bonanza; an authentic account of the discovery, history, and working of the world-renowned Comstock lode of Nevada, New York, A. A. Knopf, 1947. 4 p. l., [vii
47000970
   *Comstock Lode (Nev.) Nevada -- Description and travel.*

**TN413.N2S55 1998**
**Smith, Grant H. (Grant Horace),**
   The history of the Comstock lode, 1850-1997 / Grant H. Smith ; with new material by Joseph V. Tingley. Reno : Nevada Bureau of Mines and Geology, c1998. 328 p. :
     338.4/76223422/0979356 21
*Comstock Lode (Nev.) -- History. Gold mines and mining – Nevada – Virgina City Region -- History. Mineral industries -- Nevada -- Virgina City Region -- History. Virgina City (Nev.) -- Social life and customs.*

## TN420 Ore deposits and mining of particular metals — Gold ore deposits and mining — General works

**TN420.M7**
**Morrell, William Parker,**
   The gold rushes, by W.P. Morrell ... London, A. and C. Black, 1940. xi, 426, [1]
41003021      622.34
   *Gold mines and mining.*

## TN500 Ore deposits and mining of particular metals — Ore dressing and milling — General works

**TN500.K44 1982**
**Kelly, Errol G.**
   Introduction to mineral processing / Errol G. Kelly, David J. Spottiswood. New York : Wiley, c1982. xxiv, 491 p.
82-002807     622/.7    0471033790
   *Ore-dressing.*

## TN565 Ore deposits and mining of particular metals — Assaying — Metallurgical analysis

**TN565.C43**
**Cameron, Eugene N.**
   Ore microscopy. New York, Wiley [1961] 293 p.
61017355     549.1
   *Ores -- Sampling and estimation. Mineralogy, Determinative. Microscope and microscopy.*

## TN609 Metallurgy — Dictionaries and encyclopedias

**TN609.B76 1998**
**Brown, Colin D.**
   Dictionary of metallurgy / Colin D. Brown. Chichester ; New York : John Wiley Sons, c1998. viii, 308 p. :
     669/.03 21    0471961558
*Metallurgy -- Dictionaries.*

**TN609.M475**
**Merriman, A. D.**
   A dictionary of metallurgy. London, MacDonald & Evans, 1958. xv, 401 p.
59000480     669.03
   *Metallurgy -- Dictionaries.*

**TN609.T68 1984**
**Tottle, C. R.**
   An encyclopaedia of metallurgy and materials / C.R. Tottle. Plymouth : Metals Society ; 1984. ci, 380 p. :
83008099    669/.003/21    0712105719
   *Materials -- Dictionaries. Metallurgy -- Dictionaries.*

## TN615 Metallurgy — History — General works

**TN615.D4 1964**
**Dennis, William Herbert,**
   A hundred years of metallurgy. Chicago, Aldine Pub. Co. [1964, c1963] ix, 342 p.
64012248     669.09
   *Metallurgy -- History.*

**TN615.T94**
**Tylecote, R. F.**
   A history of metallurgy / R. F. Tylecote. London : Metals Society, c1976. ix, 182 p. :
77-361332     669/.009    0904357066
   *Metallurgy -- History.*

## TN617 Metallurgy — History — Medieval

**TN617.A4**
**Agricola, Georg,**
De re metallica. Translated from the first Latin ed. of 1556, with biographical introd., annotations, and appendices upon the development of mining methods, metallurgical processes, geology, mineralogy & mining law from the earliest times to the 16th century, by Herbert New York, Dover Publications, 1950. xxxi, 638 p.
51008994
*Mineral industries -- Early works to 1800. Metallurgy -- Early works to 1800.*

## TN665 Metallurgy — General works — 1800-

**TN665.C69 1967b**
**Cottrell, Alan Howard,**
An introduction to metallurgy [by] A. H. Cottrell. New York, St. Martin's Press, 1967. x, 548 p.
67-023953          669
*Metallurgy.*

**TN665.G48 1989**
**Gilchrist, J. D. (James Duncan)**
Extraction metallurgy / J.D. Gilchrist. 3rd ed. Oxford ; New York : Pergamon Press, 1989. xi, 431 p. :
          669 19
*Metallurgy.*

**TN665.H335 1997**
Handbook of extractive metallurgy / edited by Fathi Habashi. Weinheim ; New York : Wiley-VCH, 1997 v. :
          669 21     3527287922
*Metallurgy -- Handbooks, manuals, etc.*

**TN665.N3 2000**
**Neely, John,**
Practical metallurgy and materials of industry. 5th ed. / John E. Neely, Thomas J. Bertone. Upper Saddle River, N.J. : Prentice Hall, c2000. xiv, 461 p. :
          669 21     0136245528
*Metallurgy. Materials.*

## TN667 Metallurgy — General works — Popular works. Juvenile works

**TN667.C43 1998**
**Chandler, Harry.**
Metallurgy for the non-metallurgist / by Harry Chandler. Materials Park, OH : ASM Int'l., c1998. vii, 284 p. :
98-004664          669     0871706520
*Metallurgy -- Popular works.*

## TN690 Metallurgy — Metallography. Physical metallurgy — General works

**TN690.D47 1983**
**Devereux, Owen F.**
Topics in metallurgical thermodynamics / Owen F. Devereux. New York : Wiley, c1983. xiii, 494 p.
83-001115          669/.9     0471869635
*Physical metallurgy. Thermodynamics.*

**TN690.F59**
**Flemings, Merton C.,**
Solidification processing [by] Merton C. Flemings. New York, McGraw-Hill [1974] x, 364 p.
73-004261          669/.9     007021283X
*Solidification. Alloys.*

**TN690.H95 1963**
**Hume-Rothery, William,**
Electrons, atoms, metals and alloys. New York, Dover Publications [1963] 387 p.
63-017905          669
*Metals. Alloys. Electrons.*

**TN690.P44 1996**
Physical metallurgy / edited by Robert W. Cahn, Peter Haasen. 4th, rev. and enhanced ed. Amsterdam ; New York : North-Holland, 1996. 3 v. :
          669/.9 20
*Physical metallurgy.*

**TN690.S56 1999**
**Smallman, R.E.**
Modern physical metallurgy. 5th ed. /R.E. Smallman, R.J. Bishop. Boston : Butterworth-Heinemann, 1999. p. cm.
          669/.9 21          0750645644
*Physical metallurgy.*

## TN693 Metallurgy — Metallography. Physical metallurgy — Special metals, A-Z

**TN693.I7.H65 1996**
**Honeycombe, R. W. K.**
Steels : microstructure and properties / Robert Honeycombeand H.K.D.H. Bhadeshia. London : Arnold ; 1996. viii, 324 p.
95-023103          669/.96142          0470235683
*Steel. Physical metallurgy.*

**TN693.I7.S485 1989**
**Sinha, Anil Kumar,**
Ferrous physical metallurgy / Anil Kumar Sinha. Boston : Butterworths, c1989. xii, 818 p. :
88-019167          669/.1     0409901393
*Iron -- Metallurgy. Steel -- Metallurgy.*

### TN697 Metallurgy — Powder metallurgy — Special metals, A-Z

**TN697.I7.G47 1998**
**German, Randall M.,**
Powder metallurgy of iron and steel / Randall M. German. New York : Wiley, c1998. xvii, 496 p.
97-031764          672.3/7          0471157392
*Powder metallurgy. Steel -- Metallurgy. Iron -- Metallurgy.*

## TN698 Metallurgy — Mechanical alloying

**TN698.L85 1998**
**Lu, L.**
Mechanical alloying / by L. Lu and M.O. Lai. Boston : Kluwer Academic Publishers, c1998. xv, 276 p. :
97-035207          669/.95          0792380665
*Mechanical alloying.*

### TN703-730 Metallurgy — Metallurgy of ferrous metals — Iron and steel

**TN704.N5.G67 1996**
**Gordon, Robert B.**
American iron, 1607-1900 / Robert B. Gordon. Baltimore, Md. : Johns Hopkins University Press, c1996. xi, 341 p. :
95-044409          669/.141/097          0801851815
*Iron-works -- North America -- History -- 18th century. Iron-works -- North America -- History -- 19th century. Iron – Metallurgy - - History -- 18th century.*

**TN713.P42 1979**
**Peacey, J. G.**
The iron blast furnace : theory and practice / by J. G. Peacey and W. G. Davenport. Oxford ; Pergamon Press, 1979. xiii, 251 p.
78-040823          669/.1413          0080232183
*Blast furnaces.*

**TN730.E77 1994**
**Ethem T. Turkdogan Symposium**
Proceedings of the Ethem T. Turkdogan Symposium : fundamentals and analysis of new and emerging steelmaking technologies, Pittsburgh, PA, May 15-17, 1994 / sponsored by Iron and Steel Society, Inc., the Minerals, Metals and Materials Society, U.S. Steel Group of USX Corporation ; [organizing committee, R.J. Fruehan . . . Et al.]. Warrendale, PA : Iron and Steel Society, c1994. 271 p. :
          669/.142 20          0932897908
*Steel -- Metallurgy -- Congresses.*

**TN730.L53 1998**
**Llewellyn, D. T.**
Steels : metallurgy and applications / D.T. Llewellyn and R.C. Hudd. 3rd ed. Oxford [England] ; Woburn, MA : Butterworth-Heinemann, 1998. x, 389 p. :
          672 21
*Steel -- Metallurgy. Steel alloys -- Metallurgy.*

### TN759-760 Metallurgy — Metallurgy of nonferrous metals — Precious metals

**TN759.B5313 1989**
Handbook of precious metals / editor, E.M. Savitskii ; English editor, A. Prince ; translated by S.N. Gorin ... et al.]. New York : Hemisphere Pub. Corp., c1989. xix, 600 p. :
89-011049          669/.2          0891167099
*Precious metals.*

### TN780 Metallurgy — Metallurgy of nonferrous metals — Copper

**TN780.B57 1994**
**Biswas, A. K.**
Extractive metallurgy of copper / A.K. Biswas and W.G. Davenport. Oxford, OX, England ; Pergamon, 1994. xviii, 500 p.
94-012685          669/.3          0080421245
*Copper -- Metallurgy.*

### TN785 Metallurgy — Metallurgy of nonferrous metals — Lead

**TN785.B63 1990**
**Blaskett, D. R.**
Lead and its alloys / D.R. Blaskett, D. Boxall. New York : Ellis Horwood, 1990. 161 p. :
90-039406          669/.4          0135286964
*Lead. Lead alloys.*

### TN793 Metallurgy — Metallurgy of nonferrous metals — Tin

**TN793.B37 1983**
**Barry, B. T. K.**
Tin and its alloys and compounds / B.T.K. Barry and C.J. Thwaites. Chichester : Ellis Horwood ; 1983. 268 p. :
83-012760          669/.6          0470274808
*Tin. Tin alloys. Tin compounds.*

### TN799-799.5 Metallurgy — Metallurgy of nonferrous metals — Minor metals

**TN799.N6.B45 1984**
**Betteridge, W.**
Nickel and its alloys / W. Betteridge. Chichester, West Sussex, England : Ellis Horwood ; 1984. 211 p. :
84-012796          669/.7332          0853127298
*Nickel. Nickel alloys.*

**TN799.5.A43 1994**
Industrial minerals and rocks / senior editor, Donald D. Carr ; associate editors, A. Frank Alsobrook ... [et al.]. Littleton, Colo. : Society for Mining, Metallurgy, and Exploration, 1994. xvi, 1196 p.
93-084488          553          0873351037
*Industrial minerals. Rocks. Mineralogy.*

## TN802 Nonmetallic minerals — Coal — Mines and mining

**TN802.T49 1992**
**Thomas, Larry.**
   Handbook of practical coal geology / Larry Thomas. Chichester ; Wiley, c1992. xiii, 338 p.
92-005495        553.2/4        0471935573
   *Coal -- Geology -- Handbooks, manuals, etc.*

## TN805 Nonmetallic minerals — Coal — Mines and mining

**TN805.A5.L63 1998**
**Lockard, Duane,**
   Coal : a memoir and critique / Duane Lockard. Charlottesville : University Press of Virginia, 1998. xiv, 225 p. :
98-005196        338.2/724/0973        0813917840
   *Coal mines and mining -- United States. Coal trade -- United States. Social responsibility of business -- United States.*

## TN865-872 Nonmetallic minerals — Other natural carbons and hydrocarbons — Petroleum. Petroleum engineering

**TN865.T83**
**Tver, David F.**
   The petroleum dictionary / David F. Tver, Richard W. Berry. New York : Van Nostrand Reinhold Co., c1980. vi, 374 p. :
79-019346        553/.282/03        0442240465
   *Petroleum -- Dictionaries.*

**TN870.A73 1986**
**Archer, J. S.**
   Petroleum engineering : principles and practice / J.S. Archer and C.G. Wall. London : Graham & Trotman, 1986. xi, 362 p. :
86012125        622/.3382        0860106659
   *Petroleum engineering.*

**TN870.C58 1999**
**Conaway, Charles F.**
   The petroleum industry : a nontechnical guide / Charles F. Conaway. Tulsa, Okla. : PennWell Pub. Co., c1999. xvi, 289 p. :
99-045825        665.5        0878147772
   *Petroleum engineering. Petroleum industry and trade.*

**TN870.L25 1959**
**Landes, Kenneth K.**
   Petroleum geology. New York, Wiley [1959] 443 p.
59014987        553.282
   *Petroleum -- Geology.*

**TN870.R53 1983**
**Riva, Joseph P.**
   World petroleum resources and reserves / Joseph P. Riva, Jr. Boulder, Colo. : Westview Press, 1983. xxiii, 355 p.
82-013625        333.8/23        0865314462
   *Petroleum. Petroleum reserves.*

**TN870.5.G66 1999**
**Gold, Thomas.**
   The deep hot biosphere / Thomas Gold ; foreword by Freeman Dyson. New York : Copernicus, c1999. xiv, 235 p. :
98-042598        576.8/3        0387985468
   *Deep-earth gas theory. Petroleum -- Geology. Hydrocarbons.*

**TN870.5.M493 1989**
**Miles, Jennifer A.**
   Illustrated glossary of petroleum geochemistry / Jennifer A. Miles. Oxford [England] : Clarendon Press ; 1989. ix, 137 p. :
88-035712        553.2/82/0321        0198544928
   *Petroleum -- Geology -- Dictionaries. Geochemical prospecting – Dictionaries.*

**TN870.5.Z56 1995**
**Zimmerle, Winfried.**
   Petroleum sedimentology / by Winfried Zimmerle. Dordrecht ; Kluwer Academic Publishers, c1995. ix, 413 p. :
95-009724        553.2/8        0792334183
   *Petroleum -- Geology. Sedimentology.*

**TN871.15.S9 1987**
   Subsurface geology : petroleum, mining, construction. Golden, Colo. : Colorado School of Mines, 1987. xvii, 1002 p.
86-018806        622/.01/55        0918062683
   *Petroleum -- Geology. Engineering geology. Mining geology.*

**TN872.P4**
**Black, Brian,**
   Petrolia : the landscape of America's first oil boom / Brian Black. Baltimore : Johns Hopkins University Press, c2000. xii, 235 p. :
99-042473        338.4/76223382/0974897        0801863171
   *Petroleum -- Pennsylvania -- Oil Creek Valley (Crawford County and Venango County, Pa.) -- History. Petroleum industry and trade – Pennsylvania -- Oil Creek Valley (Crawford County and Venango County, Pa.) -- History.   Oil Creek Valley (Crawford County and Venango County, Pa.) -- Environmental conditions -- History.*

**TN872.T4**
**Spellman, Paul N.**
   Spindletop boom days / Paul N. Spellman. College Station : Texas A&M University Press, c2001. xii, 266 p. :
00-034398        338.4/76223382/09764145        0890969469
   *Petroleum industry and trade -- Texas -- Beaumont. Gushers – Texas -- Beaumont.   Beaumont (Tex.) -- History.*

## TN880 Nonmetallic minerals — Other natural carbons and hydrocarbons — Natural gas

**TN880.K38 1990**
**Katz, Donald La Verne,**
  Natural gas engineering : production and storage / Donald L. Katz, Robert L. Lee. New York : McGraw-Hill, c1990. xxi, 760 p. :
89-002322          665.7/3          0070333521
  *Natural gas. Natural gas -- Storage.*

## TN919 Nonmetallic minerals — Potassium salts. Potash-bearing rocks and plants.

**TN919.G3 1995**
**Garrett, Donald E.**
  Potash : deposits, processing, properties, and uses / Donald E. Garrett. New York : Chapman & Hall, 1995. p. cm.
94-026047          553.6/36          0412990717
  *Potash mines and mining. Potash industry and trade.*

## TN980 Building and ornamental stones — Ornamental stones. Gems — General works

**TN980.S5 1951**
**Shipley, Robert Morrill,**
  Dictionary of gems and gemology, including ornamental, decorative, and curio stones; a glossary of over 4000 English and foreign words, terms, and abbreviations which may be encountered in English l By Robert M. Shipley, assisted by Anna McConnell Beckley, Edward Wigglesworth, and Robert M. Shipley, Jr. Los Angeles, Gemological Institute of America, 1951. xvii, 261 p.
51005799          549
  *Precious stones -- Dictionaries.*

# TP Chemical technology

## TP9 Dictionaries and encyclopedias

**TP9.A73 1993**
**Ash, Michael.**
  Chemical tradename dictionary / compiled by Michael and Irene Ash. New York : VCH Publishers, c1993. xi, 529 p. ;
92-035154          660/.03          1560816252
  *Chemicals -- Dictionaries. Chemicals -- Trademarks.*

**TP9.E685 1992**
  Encyclopedia of chemical technology / executive editor, Jacqueline I. Kroschwitz ; editor, Mary Howe-Grant. New York : Wiley, c1991-c1998 v. 1-25 :
91-016789          660/.03          047152669X
  *Chemistry, Technical -- Encyclopedias.*

**TP9.G286 1999**
  Gardner's chemical synonyms and trade names / edited by G.W.A. Milne. Brookfield, Vt. : Ashgate, c1999. xvi, 1418 p.
98-051143          660/.03          0566081903
  *Chemicals -- Dictionaries. Chemicals -- Trademarks.*

**TP9.U57 1985**
**Ullmann, Fritz,**
  Ullmann's encyclopedia of industrial chemistry / executive editor, Wolfgang Gerhartz ; senior editor, Y. Stephen Yamamoto ; editors, F. Thomas Campbell, Rudolf Pfefferkorn, James F. Rounsaville. Weinheim, Federal Republic of Germany ; VCH, c1985-c1993 v. A1-A7, A9-
84-025829          660/.03/21          0895731517
  *Chemistry, Technical -- Encyclopedias.*

## TP140 Biography — Individual, A-Z

**TP140.P46**
**Garfield, Simon.**
  Mauve : how one man invented a color that changed the world / Simon Garfield. New York : W.W. Norton & Co., c2001. 222 p. :
00-069533          666/.257          0393020053
  *Perkin, William Henry, -- Sir, -- 1838-1907. Mauve. Dye industry -- Great Britain. Chemists -- England -- Biography.*

## TP145 General works — 1900-

**TP145.R54 1992**
**Riegel, Emil Raymond,**
  Riegel's handbook of industrial chemistry. New York : Van Nostrand Reinhold, c1992. ix, 1288 p. :
92-022660          660          0442001754
  *Chemistry, Technical.*

# TP149-150 General special (Including municipal chemistry, safety measures, etc.)

**TP149.C85 2001**
**Cussler, E. L.**
  Chemical product design / E.L. Cussler, G.D. Moggridge. Cambridge ; Cambridge University Press, 2001. xvii, 229 p.
00-063069          660/.068/5          0521791839
  *Chemical industry.*

**TP149.H285 1994**
  Handbook of chemical engineering calculations / Nicholas P. Chopey, editor. New York : McGraw-Hill, c1994. 1 v. (various
93-025590          660/.212          0070110212
  *Chemical engineering -- Mathematics.*

**TP149.V36 1997**
**Varma, Arvind.**
  Mathematical methods in chemical engineering / Arvind Varma, Massimo Morbidelli. New York : Oxford University Press, 1997. xiv, 690 p. :
  95-026843        515/.14/02466        0195098218
  *Chemical engineering -- Mathematics.*

**TP149.H64 1989**
**Holland, Charles Donald.**
  Fundamentals of chemical reaction engineering / Charles D. Holland, Rayford G. Anthony. 2nd ed. Englewood Cliffs, N.J. : Prentice-Hall, c1989. xiv, 554 p. :
          660.2/99 19
  *Chemical engineering. Chemical reactions.*

**TP150.S24C76 2002**
**Crowl, Daniel A.**
  Chemical process safety : fundamentals with applications / Daniel A. Crowl, Joseph F. Louvar. 2nd ed. Upper Saddle River, J.J. : Prentice Hall PTR, 2002. xox, 625 p. :
          660/.2804 21
  *Chemical plants -- Safety measures.*

# TP151 Tables, pocketbooks, etc.

**TP151.H25**
  Lange's handbook of chemistry. New York : McGraw-Hill, c1973- v. :
  84-643191        540/.5
  *Chemistry, Technical -- Handbooks, manuals, etc. Mathematics -- Handbooks, manuals, etc.*

**TP151.H5 1996**
**Himmelblau, David Mautner,**
  Basic principles and calculations in chemical engineering / David M. Himmelblau. 6th ed. Upper Saddle River, NJ : Prentice Hall PTR, c1996. xvii, 732 p. :
          660/.2 20
  *Chemical engineering -- Tables.*

**TP151.P45 1997**
  Perry's chemical engineers' handbook. New York : McGraw-Hill, c1997. 1 v. (various
  96-051648        660        0070498415
  *Chemical engineering -- Handbooks, manuals, etc.*

**TP151.R85 1998**
  Rules of thumb for chemical engineers : a manual of quick, accurate solutions to everyday process engineering problems / Carl R. Branan, editor. Houston, TX : Gulf Pub. Co., 1998. p. cm.
  98-026530        660        0884157881
  *Chemical engineering -- Handbooks, manuals, etc.*

## TP155 Chemical engineering — General works

**TP155.D74 1998**
**Duncan, T. Michael.**
  Chemical engineering design and analysis : an introduction / T. Michael Duncan and Jeffrey A. Reimer. Cambridge, UK ; Cambridge University Press, 1998. xiv, 380 p. :
  98-016452        660/.2        052163041X
  *Chemical engineering.*

**TP155.G635 1996**
  Green chemistry : designing chemistry for the environment / Paul T. Anastas, Tracy C. Williamson, [editors]. Washington, DC : American Chemical Society, 1996. xii, 251 p. :
  96-000162        660/.281        0841233993
  *Environmental chemistry -- Industrial applications – Congresses. Environmental management -- Congresses.*

**TP155.H58 1998**
**Hocking, M. B.**
  Handbook of chemical technology and pollution control / Martin B. Hocking. San Diego : Academic Press, c1998. xxiv, 777 p.
  97-080796        660        012350810X
  *Chemistry, Technical. Environmental chemistry.*

### TP155.2.M36 Chemical engineering — Special aspects of the subject as a whole, A-Z — Mathematics

**TP155.2.M36**
**Loney, Norman W.**
  Applied mathematical methods for chemical engineers / Norman W. Loney. Boca Raton, Fla. : CRC Press, c2001. 447 p. :
  00-044454        660/.01/51        0849308909
  *Chemical engineering -- Mathematics.*

**TP155.2.T45S58 2001**
**Smith, J. M. (Joseph Mauk),**
  Introduction to chemical engineering thermodynamics. / J. M. Smith, H.C. Van Ness, M.M. Abbott. 6th ed. Boston : McGraw-Hill, c2001. xviii, 789 p. :
          660/32969 21
  *Thermodynamics. Chemical engineering.*

### TP155.5 Chemical engineering — Chemical plants — General works

**TP155.5.C76 1990**
**Crowl, Daniel A.**
  Chemical process safety : fundamentals with applications / Daniel A. Crowl, Joseph F. Louvar. Englewood Cliffs, N.J. : Prentice Hall, c1990. xvii, 426 p.
  89-008766        660/.2804        0131297015
  *Chemical plants -- Safety measures.*

**TP155.5.D28 2001**
**Darby, Ron,**
  Chemical engineering fluid mechanics / Ron Darby. New York : Marcel Dekker, c2001. xvi, 559 p. :
01-017435          660/.284          0824704444
  *Chemical processes. Fluid mechanics.*


## TP155.7 Chemical engineering — Chemical processes — General works

**TP155.7.A53 1998**
  Analysis, synthesis, and design of chemical processes / Richard Turton ... [et al.]. Upper Saddle River, N.J. : Prentice Hall PTR, 1998. p. cm.
97-034025          660/.2812          0135705657
  *Chemical processes.*


**TP155.7.C66 1993**
**Comyns, Alan E.**
  Dictionary of named processes in chemical technology / Alan E. Comyns. Oxford ; New York : Oxford University Press, 1993. xi, 338 p. :
          660/.284/03 20
*Chemical processes -- Dictionaries.*


**TP155.7.C664 1999**
**Comyns, Alan E.**
  Encyclopedia dictionary of named processes in chemical technology / Alan E. Comyns. 2nd ed. Boca Raton : CRC Press c1999. 303 p. :
          660/.281/03 21          0849312051
*Chemical processes -- Dictionaries.*


**TP155.7.M3 2001**
**McCabe, Warren L. (Warren Lee),**
  Unit operations of chemical engineering. 6th ed./ Warren L. McCabe, Julian C. Smith, Peter Harriott. Boston : McGraw Hill, c2001. xvii, 1114 p. :
          660/.2842 21          0070393664
*Chemical processes.*


**TP155.7.W66 1995**
**Woods, Donald R.,**
  Process design and engineering practice / Donald R. Woods. Englewood Cliffs, N.J. : PTR Prentice Hall, c1995. 1 v. (various
93-005526          660/.281          0138057559
  *Chemical processes.*


## TP156 Chemical engineering — Special processes and operations, A-Z

**TP156.A35.R8 1984**
**Ruthven, Douglas M.**
  Principles of adsorption and adsorption processes / Douglas M. Ruthven. New York : Wiley, c1984. xxiv, 433 p.
83-016904          660.2/8423          0471866067
  *Adsorption. Separation (Technology)*


**TP156.C35**
**Bhaduri, Sumit,**
  Homogeneous catalysis : mechanisms and industrial applications / Sumit Bhaduri, Doble Mukesh. New York : Wiley-Interscience, c2000. xiv, 239 p. :
99-045532          660/.2995          0471372218
  *Catalysis. Catalysis -- Industrial applications.*


**TP156.C57P38 1996**
  Surface coatings : science & technology / edited by Swaraj Paul. 2nd ed. Chichester ; New York : J. Wiley, c1996. xv, 931 p. :
          667/.9 20
*Coatings.*


**TP156.D47.C878 1997**
**Cussler, E. L.**
  Diffusion : mass transfer in fluid systems / E.L. Cussler. New York : Cambridge University Press, c1997. xviii, 580 p.
95-047398          660/.28423          0521450780
  *Diffusion. Mass transfer. Fluids.*


**TP156.D5S85 1998**
**Stichlmair, Johann.**
  Distillation : principles and practices / Johann Stichlmair and James R. Fair. New York : Wiley, c1998. xiii, 524 p. :
          660/.28425 21
*Distillation.*


**TP156.E6.E614 1996**
  Emulsions and emulsion stability / edited by Johan Sjoblom. New York : Marcel Dekker, c1996. x, 474 p. :
96-001662          541.3/4514          0824796896
  *Emulsions. Stability.*


**TP156.E6B38 2000**
**Becher, Paul.**
  Emulsions : theory and practice / Paul Becher. 3rd ed. Washington, DC : American Chemical Soc. : Oxford University Press, 2000. p. cm.
          660/.294514 21          0841234965
*Emulsions.*


**TP156.P3.P64 1997**
  Powder technology handbook. New York : Marcel Dekker, c1997. xxiii, 944 p.
97-022484          620/.43          0824700155
  *Powders.*


**TP156.P6.S44 1990**
**Seymour, Raymond Benedict,**
  Engineering polymer sourcebook / Raymond B. Seymour. New York : McGraw-Hill, c1990. xvii, 300 p.
89-035066          668.9          0070563608
  *Polymers.*

**TP156.P83 P47 1996.**
**Armarego, W.L.F.**
Purification of laboratory chemicals / W.L.F. Armarego and D.D. Perrin. 4th ed. Oxford ; Boston : Butterworth Heinemann, c1996. xi, 529 p. :
542 21      0750628391
*Chemicals -- Purification.*

**TP156.S45.H35 1997**
Handbook of separation techniques for chemical engineers / Philip A. Schweitzer, editor-in-chief. New York : McGraw-Hill, c1997. 1 v. (various
96-021065      660/.2842      0070570612
*Separation (Technology) -- Handbooks, manuals, etc.*

**TP156.T7.T48 2000**
**Thomson, William J.**
Introduction to transport phenomena / William J. Thomson. Upper Saddle River, NJ : Prentice Hall, c2000. xv, 509 p. :
99-038330      660/.284      0134548280
*Transport theory. Chemical engineering.*

**TP156.T7S57 1999**
**Slattery, John Charles,**
Advanced transport phenomena / John C. Slattery. New York : Cambridge University Press, 1999. xxii, 709 p. :
660/.2842 21      052163203X
*Transport theory. Chemical engineering.*

## TP159 Apparatus and supplies — Special, A-Z

**TP159.C46C35 1997**
**Cattrall, Robert W.**
Chemical sensors / Robert W. Cattrall. Oxford ; New York : Oxford University Press, 1997. 74 p. :
660/.281 21
*Chemical detectors.*

**TP159.M4M85 1996**
**Mulder, Marcel,**
Basic principles of membrane technology / by Marcel Mulder. 2nd ed. Dordrecht ; Boston : Kluwer Academic, c1996. 564 p. :
660/.2842 21
*Membranes (Technology)*

## TP168 Study and teaching — Problems, exercise, etc.

**TP168.C88 1999**
**Cutlip, Michael B.**
Problem solving in chemical engineering with numerical methods / Michael B. Cutlip, Mordechai Shacham. Upper Saddle River, NJ : Prentice Hall PTR, 1999. p. cm.
98-026056      660/.01/5194      0138625662
*Chemical engineering -- Problems, excercises, etc. Chemical engineering -- Data processing. Problem solving.*

## TP184 Data processing

**TP184.H36 1995**
**Hanna, Owen T.**
Computational methods in chemical engineering / Owen T. Hanna, Orville C. Sandall. Englewood Cliffs, N.J. : Prentice Hall PTR, [1995] p. cm.
94-045872      511/.8/02466      013307398X
*Chemical engineering -- Data processing.*

## TP187 Government and industrial laboratories, etc., General works (Including organization, etc.)

**TP187.H35 1994**
**Hall, Stephen K.**
Chemical safety in the laboratory / Stephen K. Hall. Boca Raton : Lewis Pubishers, c1994. 242 p. :
93-028653      660/.2804      0873718968
*Chemical engineering laboratories -- Safety measures.*

### TP200 Chemicals — General works

**TP200.L49 1999**
**Lewis, Grace Ross.**
1,001 chemicals in everyday products / Grace Ross Lewis. New York : Wiley, c1999. p. cm.
98-006419      363.17/9      0471292125
*Chemicals.*

**TP200.Y35 1999**
**Yaws, Carl L.**
Chemical properties handbook : physical, thermodynamic, environmental, transport, safety, and health related properties for organic and inorganic chemicals / Carl L. Yaws. New York : McGraw-Hill, c1999. vii, 779 p. :
660/.02/1 21      0070734011
*Chemicals -- Handbooks, manuals, etc. Chemicals – Safety measures -- Handbooks, manuals, etc.*

### TP201 Chemicals — General special

**TP201.A84 1998**
**Ash, Michael.**
Handbook of industrial chemical additives / compiled by Michael and Irene Ash. 2nd ed. Endicott, Ny : Synapse Information Resources, c1998. 3 v. :
660/.03 21
*Chemicals -- Dictionaries. Chemical industry -- Directories.*

## TP242 Chemicals — Special inorganic chemicals — Gases

**TP242.P62 2001**
**Poling, Bruce E.**
The properties of gases and liquids / Bruce E. Poling, John M. Prausnitz, John P. O'Connell. New York : McGraw-Hill, c2001. 1 v. (various
00-061622        660/.042        0070116822
*Gases. Liquids.*

## TP247 Chemicals — Organic chemicals and preparations — General works

**TP247.W59 1996**
**Wittcoff, Harold.**
Industrial organic chemicals / Harold A. Wittcoff, Bryan G. Reuben. New York : Wiley, c1996. xxiv, 531 p.
95-035580        661.8        0471540366
*Organic compounds -- Industrial applications.*

## TP247.5 Chemicals — Organic chemicals and preparations — Solvents

**TP247.5.I53 1998**
Industrial solvents handbook / edited by Ernest W. Flick. Westwood, N.J. : Noyes Data Corp., c1998. xxxi, 963 p.
98-005137        661/.807        0815514131
*Solvents -- Handbooks, manuals, etc.*

**TP247.5.L53 1995**
**Lide, David R.,**
Handbook of organic solvents / David R. Lide. Boca Raton : CRC Press, c1995. 565 p. :
94-042775        661.8/07        0849389305
*Organic solvents -- Handbooks, manuals, etc.*

## TP248 Chemicals — Organic chemicals and preparations — Special, A-Z

**TP248.B55.E44 1991**
Emerging technologies for materials and chemicals from biomass / Roger M. Rowell, editor, Tor P. Schultz, editor, Ramani Narayan, editor. Washington, DC : American Chemical Society, 1992. x, 469 p. :
91-036048        661/.8        0841221715
*Biomass chemicals -- Congresses. Biomass energy – Congresses.*

**TP248.E5.U37 1998**
**Uhlig, Helmut.**
Industrial enzymes and their applications / Helmut Uhlig ; translated and updated by Elfriede M. Linsmaier-Bednar. New York : Wiley, c1998. xii, 454 p. :
97-038099        660/.634        0471196606
*Enzymes -- Industrial applications. Enzymes -- Biotechnology. Enzymes.*

**TP248.S7S7 1984**
Starch : chemistry and technology / edited by Roy L. Whistler, James N. BeMiller, Eugene F. Paschall. 2nd ed. Orlando : Academic Press, 1984. xxiii, 718 p. :
            664/.2 19
*Starch.*

## TP248.16 Biotechnology — Dictionaries and encyclopedias

**TP248.16.B33 1998**
**Bains, William,**
Biotechnology from A to Z / by William Bain ; [foreword by G. Kirk Raab]. 2nd ed. Oxford ; New York : Oxford University Press, 1998. vii, 411 p. :
            660.6/03 21
*Biotechnology -- Dictionaries.*

**TP248.16.F54 1998**
**Nill, Kimball R.**
Glossary of biotechnology terms / Kimball R. Nill. Lancaster, Pa. : Technomic Pub. Co., c1998. vi, 264 p. ;
97-062206        660.6/03        1566765803
*Biotechnology -- Dictionaries.*

**TP248.16.S84 2001**
**Seinberg, Mark (Mark L.)**
The Facts on File dictionary of biotechnology and genetic engineering / Mark L. Steinberg, Sharon D. Cosloy. New ed. New York : Facts on File, c2001. x, 228 p. :
            660.6/03 21
*Biotechnology -- Dictionaries. Genetic engineering -- Dictionaries.*

**TP248.16M87 2000**
**Murray, Thomas H.,**
Encyclopedia of ethical, legal, and policy issues in biotechnology /Thomas H. Murray, Maxwell J. Mehlman. New York : John Wiley & Sons, 2000. xiii, 1132 p. :
            174/.96606 21
*Biotechnology -- Moral and ethical aspects -- Encyclopedias.*
*Biotechnology -- Government policy -- United States – Encyclopedias.*

## TP248.2 Biotechnology — General works

**TP248.2.B367 2001**
Basic biotechnology / edited by Colin Ratledge and Bjorn Kristiansen. 2nd ed. Cambridge, U.K. ; New York, NY : Cambridge University Press, 2001. xiii, 568 p. :
            660.6 21        0521770742
*Biotechnology.*

**TP248.2.B5518 1988**
Biotechnology for engineers : biological systems in technological processes / editor, A.H. Scragg. Chichester, West Sussex, England : E. Horwood ; 1988. 390 p. :
88-023081        660/.6        0745802265
*Biotechnology. Chemical engineers.*

**TP248.2.E53 1996**

Enabling the safe use of biotechnology : principles and practice / John J. Doyle, Gabrielle J. Persley, editors. Washington, D.C. : World Bank, c1996. vii, 74 p. :
96-022061          363.1/196606          0821336711
*Biotechnology -- Safety measures.*

**TP248.2.G58 1998**
**Glick, Bernard R.**

Molecular biotechnology : principles and applications of recombinant DNA / Bernard R. Glick and Jack J. Pasternak. 2nd ed. Washington, D.C. : ASM Press, c1998. xxiii, 683 p. :
          660/.65 21          1555811361
*Biotechnology. Genetic engineering. Molecular biology.*

**TP248.2.R54 1998**
**Rifkin, Jeremy.**

The biotech century : harnessing the gene and remaking the world / Jeremy Rifkin. New York : Jeremy P. Tarcher/Putnam, c1998. xvi, 271 p. ;
97-044358          303.48/3          087477909X
*Biotechnology -- Social aspects. Biotechnology -- Moral and ethical aspects. Genetic engineering -- Social aspects.*

**TP248.2.S33 1999**
**Schacter, Bernice Zeldin,**

Issues and dilemmas of biotechnology : a reference guide / Bernice Schacter. Westport, Conn. : Greenwood Press, 1999. xiv, 205 p. :
99-015457          660.6          0313306427
*Biotechnology. Biotechnology -- Social aspects.*

## TP248.215 Biotechnology — Popular works

**TP248.215.B56 2000**

Biotechnology / edited by Lynn Messina. New York : H.W. Wilson, 2000. ix, 186 p. :
          660.6 21          0824209850
*Biotechnology -- Popular works. Genetic engineering -- Popular works.*

## TP248.23 Biotechnology — Processes, operations, and techniques — General works

**TP248.23.Y684 2000**
**Yount, Lisa.**

Biotechnology and genetic engineering / Lisa Yount. New York : Facts on File, c2000. 280 p. ;
99-049532          303.48/3          0816040001
*Biotechnology -- Social aspects. Genetic engineering -- Social aspects.*

**TP248.24.J33 1991**
**Jackson, A. T.**

Process engineering in biotechnology / A.T. Jackson. Englewood Cliffs, N.J. : Prentice Hall, c1991. viii, 147 p.
90-044376          660/.6          0137231989
*Biotechnology. Bioengineering.*

## TP248.25 Biotechnology — Processes, operations, and techniques — Special, A-Z

**TP248.25.S47.R43 1993**

Recovery processes for biological materials / edited by John F. Kennedy and Joaquim M.S. Cabral. Chichester [England] ; Wiley, c1993. viii, 592 p.
92-005624          660/.2842          047193349X
*Biological products -- Separation.*

## TP248.27 Biotechnology — Processes, operations, and techniques — Special biotechnologies, A-Z

**TP248.27.A46.B43 1994**
**Becker, E. W.**

Microalgae : biotechnology and microbiology / E.W. Becker. Cambridge ; Cambridge University Press, 1994. vii, 293 p. :
93-002129          660/.62          0521350204
*Algae -- Biotechnology.*

**TP248.27.A53.B87 1996**
**Butler, M.**

Animal cell culture and technology / Michael Butler. Oxford ; IRL Press at Oxford University Press, 1996. xii, 114 p. :
96-026618          591.87/0724          0199634165
*Animal cell biotechnology. Cell culture.*

**TP248.27.M53.A87 1991**

Assessing ecological risks of biotechnology / edited by Lev R. Ginzburg. Boston : Butterworth-Heinemann, c1991. xvi, 379 p. :
90-001719          660/.62/0289          0409901997
*Microbial biotechnology -- Safety measures. Microbial biotechnology -- Environmental aspects. Genetic engineering – Safety measures.*

**TP248.27.M53.I57 1995**

Introduction to biocatalysis using enzymes and micro-organisms / Stanley M. Roberts ... [et al]. Cambridge ; Cambridge University Press, 1995. xii, 195 p. :
93-048247          660/.63          0521430704
*Microbial biotechnology. Enzymes -- Biotechnology. Biotransformation (Metabolism)*

**TP248.27.P55**
**Chawla, H. S.**

Introduction to plant biotechnology / H.S. Chawla. Enfield, N.H. : Science Publishers, c2000. 368 p. :
00-038797          631.5/233          1578081300
*Plant biotechnology.*

## TP248.3 Biotechnology — Biochemical engineering. Bioprocess engineering

**TP248.3.A853 1983**
**Atkinson, Bernard,**
 Biochemical engineering and biotechnology handbook / Bernard Atkinson, Ferda Mavituna. New York, N.Y. : Nature Press, 1983. 1119 p. :
82-014462          660/.6     0943818028
 *Biochemical engineering. Bioengineering.*

## TP248.6 Biotechnology — Genetic engineering applications

**TP248.6.F687 1999**
**Fox, Michael W.,**
 Beyond evolution : the genetically altered future of plants, animals, the earth--humans / Michael W. Fox. New York, N.Y. : Lyons Press, c1999. 256 p. ;
99-012866          174/.957          1558219013
 *Genetic engineering -- Moral and ethical aspects. Agricultural biotechnology -- Moral and ethical aspects. Genetic engineering – Social aspects.*

**TP248.6.S94 1987**
**Sylvester, Edward J.**
 The gene age : genetic engineering and the next industrial revolution / Edward J. Sylvester and Lynn C. Klotz. Rev. ed. New York : Scribner, c1987. xii, 239 p. :
          660/.6 19          0684188198
*Genetic engineering.*

## TP248.65 Biotechnology — Biotechnological production, modification, and applications of individual compounds or classes of compounds — Special, A-Z

**TP248.65.E59.C48 1990**
**Chaplin, M. F.**
 Enzyme technology / M.F. Chaplin and C. Bucke. Cambridge [England] ; Cambridge University Press, 1990. xvi, 264 p. :
89-007372          660/.634          0521344298
 *Enzymes -- Biotechnology. Immobilized enzymes – Biotechnology.*

**TP248.65.E59F73 2000**
**Faber, K. (Kurt),**
 Biotransformations in organic chemistry : a textbook / Kurt Faber. 4th, completely rev. and extended ed. Berlin ; New York : Springer, c2000. xi, 453 p. :
          660.6/34 21          3540663347
*Enzymes -- Biotechnology. Biotransformation (Metabolism) Organic compounds -- Synthesis.*

**TP248.65.F66**
**McHughen, Alan.**
 Pandora's picnic basket : the potential and hazards of genetically modified foods / Alan McHughen. Oxford ; Oxford University Press, 2000. viii, 277 p.
00-025169          363.19/29          0198507143
 *Genetically modified foods. Food -- Biotechnology. Transgenic plants.*

## TP255 Industrial electrochemistry — General works

**TP255.P74 1991**
**Prentice, Geoffrey.**
 Electrochemical engineering principles / Geoffrey Prentice. Englewood Cliffs, N.J. : Prentice Hall, c1991. xxii, 296 p.
90-035448          660/.297          0132490382
 *Electrochemistry, Industrial.*

## TP256 Industrial electrochemistry — General special

**TP256.B37 1994**
**Bard, Allen J.**
 Integrated chemical systems : a chemical approach to nanotechnology / Allen J. Bard. New York : Wiley, c1994. xv, 324 p. :
93-039694          660/.297          0471007331
 *Electrochemistry, Industrial. Nanotechnology.*

## TP318 Fuel — General works

**TP318.S37 1990**
**Schobert, Harold H.,**
 The chemistry of hydrocarbon fuels / Harold H. Schobert. London ; Butterworths, 1990. viii, 348 p.
90-001311          662/.6          040803825X
 *Fuel. Hydrocarbons.*

## TP339 Fuel — Biomass

**TP339.K54 1998**
**Klass, Donald L.**
 Biomass for renewable energy, fuels, and chemicals / Donald L. Klass. San Diego : Academic Press, c1998. xv, 651 p. ;
98-084422          662/.88          0124109500
 *Biomass energy. Biomass chemicals.*

## TP343 Fuel — Liquid and gaseous fuel — General works

**TP343.B37 1997**
**Bechtold, Richard L.,**
Alternative fuels guidebook : properties, storage, dispensing, and vehicle facility modifications / Richard L. Bechtold. Warrendale, Pa. : Society of Automotive Engineers, c1997. ix, 204 p. :
97-027727          662/.6          0768000521
*Internal combustion engines, Spark ignition -- Alternate fuels.*

**TP343.B38 1997**
**Berkowitz, N.**
Fossil hydrocarbons : chemistry and technology / Norbert Berkowitz. San Diego : Academic Press, c1997. xiii, 351 p.
97-023439          553.2          012091090X
*Hydrocarbons. Fossil fuels.*

**TP343.C54 2000**
Chemistry of diesel fuels / edited by Chunshan Song, Chang S. Hsu, Isao Mochida. New York : Taylor & Francis, 2000. xx, 294 p. :
00-036429          665.5/384          1560328452
*Diesel fuels.*

**TP343.M295 1995**
**Maxwell, T. T.**
Alternative fuels : emissions, economics, and performance / Timothy T. Maxwell, Jesse C. Jones. Warrendale, PA, U.S.A. : Society of Automotive Engineers, c1995. iv, 327 p. :
94-023270          629.25/38          1560915234
*Motor fuels.*

## TP359 Fuel — Liquid and gaseous fuel — Other special, A-Z

**TP359.B48.M48 1988**
Methane from biomass : a systems approach / edited by Wayne H. Smith and James R. Frank ; with foreword by Philip H. Abelson. London ; Elsevier Applied Science, c1988. xxvi, 500 p.
87-009120          665.8/9          1851661026
*Biogas.*

**TP359.H8.W54 1980**
**Williams, L. O.**
Hydrogen power : an introduction to hydrogen energy and its applications / L. O. Williams. Oxford ; Pergamon Press, 1980. ix, 158 p. :
80-040434          665.8/1          0080247830
*Hydrogen as fuel.*

## TP360 Fuel — Other (Including colloidal fuel, mud fuel, artificial fuel)

**TP360.A47 1989**
Alternative transportation fuels : an environmental and energy solution / edited by Daniel Sperling. New York : Quorum Books, 1989. xvi, 326 p. :
89-003759          662/.66
*Synthetic fuels.*

**TP360.H36 1984**
Handbook of synfuels technology / Robert A. Meyers, editor in chief. New York : McGraw-Hill, c1984. 906 p. in var
83-017505          662/.66          0070417628
*Synthetic fuels -- Handbooks, manuals, etc.*

**TP360.L46 1996**
**Lee, Sunggyu.**
Alternative fuels / Sunggyu Lee. Washington, D.C. : Taylor & Francis, c1996. xvi, 485 p. :
96-011367          662/.66          1560323612
*Synthetic fuels.*

**TP360.S9365 1988**
Synthetic fuel technology development in the United States : a retrospective assessment / Michael Crow ... [et al.]. New York : Praeger, 1988. xii, 175 p. :
88-012596          333.79/15/0973          0275930831
*Synthetic fuels -- United States.*

## TP368.2 Food processing and manufacture — Dictionaries and encyclopedias

**TP368.2.E62 2000**
Encyclopedia of food science and technology. New York : Wiley, c2000. 4 v. (xxi, 27
99-029003          664/.003          0471192856
*Food industry and trade -- Encyclopedias.*

## TP369 Food processing and manufacture — By region or country, A-Z

**TP369.H36**
**Hall, Carl W.**
Encyclopedia of food engineering [by] Carl W. Hall, A. W. Farrall [and] A. L. Rippen. Westport, Conn., Avi Pub. Co., 1971. vii, 755 p.
70-137710          664/.003          0870550861
*Food industry and trade -- Dictionaries.*

## TP371.5-371.8 Food processing and manufacture — Special processes — Preservation techniques

**TP371.5.F68 1993**
Food dehydration / Gustavo V. Barbosa-Camovas and Martin R. Okos, Volume editors. New York, N.Y. : American Institute of Chemical Engineers, 1993. 126 p. :
664/.0284 20
*Food -- Drying -- Congresses.*

**TP371.8.S28 1996**
**Satin, Morton.**
Food irradiation : a guidebook / Morton Satin. 2nd ed. Lancaster, PA : Technomic Pub. Co., c1996. xxiii, 211 p. :
664/.0288 20
*Radiation preservation of food.*

## TP372.5 Food processing and manufacture — Chemistry testing. Quality control — General works

**TP372.5.F555 1993**
Flavor science : sensible principles and techniques / Terry E. Acree, editor, Roy Teranishi, editor. Washington, DC : American Chemical Society, 1993. xvi, 351 p. :
93-015928      664/.5      0841225168
*Flavor -- Congresses. Flavoring essences -- Congresses.*

## TP453 Food processing and manufacture — Special foods — Special food constituents, A-Z

**TP453.C65.D53 1992**
**Dickinson, Eric.**
An introduction to food colloids / Eric Dickinson. Oxford ; Oxford University Press, 1992. viii, 207 p.
91-023163      664      0198552246
*Colloids.*

# TP492.7 Refrigeration and icemaking — Miscellaneous special topics

**TP492.7.S87 1996**
**Sweetser, Richard S.,**
The fundamentals of natural gas cooling / by Richard S. Sweetser. Lilburn, GA : Fairmont Press, Inc. ; c1996. xv, 213 p. :
95-033720      621.56      088173232X
*Refrigeraton and refrigerating machinery. Gas appliances.*

## TP546 Fermentation industries. Beverages. Alcohol — Wine and winemaking — Dictionaries and encyclopedias

**TP546.L5 1979**
**Lichine, Alexis,**
Lichine's encyclopedia of wines & spirits / [by Alexis Lichine] in collaboration with William Fifield and with the assistance of ... [others]. London : Cassell, 1979. xv, 716, [1]
79-322909      641.2/22/0321
*Wine and wine making -- Encyclopedias.*

## TP548 Fermentation industries. Beverages. Alcohol — Wine and winemaking — General works

**TP548.A48 1976**
**Amerine, M. A. (Maynard Andrew),**
Wine : an introduction / M. A. Amerine and V. L. Singleton. 2nd rev. ed. Berkeley : University of California Press, c1977. xiv, 373 p. :
663/.2
*Wine and wine making.*

**TP548.J632 1998**
**Johnson, Hugh,**
Hugh Johnson's modern encyclopedia of wine. 4th ed. New York : Simon & Schuster, c1998. 592 p. :
641.2/2/03 21
*Wine and wine making.*

**TP548.L345 1994**
Larousse encyclopedia of wine / general editor, Christopher Foulkes. New York : Larousse, 1994. 608 p. :
94-077220      641.2/2/03      2035070228
*Wine and wine making.*

## TP557 Fermentation industries. Beverages. Alcohol — Wine and winemaking — Special countries

**TP557.F85 1996**
**Fuller, Robert C.,**
Religion and wine : a cultural history of wine drinking in the United States / Robert C. Fuller. Knoxville : University of Tennessee Press, c1996. xii, 140 p. :
95-004379      394.1/3      0870499114
*Wine and wine making -- United States -- History. Wine and wine making -- Religious aspects. Temperance and religion -- United States.*

**TP557.L87 2000**
**Lukacs, Paul**
American vintage : the rise of American wine / Paul Lukacs. Boston : Houghton Mifflin, 2000. xii, 370 p.,
00-040778      641.2/2/0973      0395914787
*Wine and wine making -- United States -- History.*

**TP557.P56 1989**
**Pinney, Thomas.**
A history of wine in America from the beginnings to prohibition / Thomas Pinney. Berkeley : University of California Press, c1989. xvii, 553 p.
88-010798      663/.2/00973      0520062248
*Wine and wine making -- United States -- History.*

### TP568 Fermentation industries. Beverages. Alcohol — Brewing and malting — Dictionaries and encyclopedias

**TP568.D53 1998**
**Rabin, Dan.**
   The dictionary of beer and brewing : 2,500 terms, including 400 new! / compiled by Dan Rabin and Carl Forget. Boulder, Colo. : Brewers Publications, c1998. 306 p. ;
97-047348          641.2/3/03          0937381616
   *Brewing -- Dictionaries.*

### TP640 Nonalcoholic beverages — Chocolate, coffee, tea, etc. — Cacao. Chocolate. Cocoa

**TP640.B43 2000**
**Beckett, S. T.**
   The science of chocolate / Stephen T. Beckett. Cambridge, UK : Royal Society of Chemistry, c2000. xiii, 175 p.
         664.5          0854046003
   *Chocolate.*

### TP670 Oils, fats, and waxes — General works

**TP670.B28 1996**
**Bailey, Alton Edward,**
   Bailey's industrial oil and fat products. 5th ed. / edited by Y.H. Hui. New York : Wiley, c1996. 5 v. :
         665 20          0471594245
*Oils and fats.*

### TP692.3 Oils, fats, and waxes — Mineral oils and waxes — Petroleum refining. Petroleum products

**TP692.3.M38 2001**
**Matar, Sami,**
   Chemistry of petrochemical processes / Sami Matar, Lewis F. Hatch. 2nd ed. Boston : Gulf Professional Pub., c2001 xvi, 382 p. :
         665.5 21
*Petroleum chemicals.*

**TP692.3.W46 1999**
**Wells, G. Margaret,**
   Handbook of petrochemicals and processes / G. Margaret Wells. Aldershot, England ; Gower, c1999. xiv, 494 p. :
98-045655          661/.804          056608046X
   *Petroleum chemicals -- Handbooks, manuals, etc.*

### TP761 Gas industry — Other special kinds, A-Z

**TP761.C65H36 1999**
   Handbook of compressed gases / Compressed Gas Association. 4th ed. Boston : Kluwer Academic Publishers, c1999. xvi, 702 p. :
         665.7 21
*Gases, Compressed.*

### TP788 Clay industries. Ceramics. Glass — Dictionaries and encyclopedias

**TP788.B73 2001**
**Bray, Charles.**
   Dictionary of glass : materials and techniques / Charles Bray. 2nd ed. Philadelphia : University of Pennsylvania Press, 2001. p. cm.
         666/.1/03 21
*Glass -- Dictionaries.*

**TP788.M38 1993**
**McColm, I. J.**
   Dictionary of ceramic science and engineering / Ian J. McColm. 2nd ed. New York : Plenum Press, c1994. x, 384 p. :
         666/.03 20
*Ceramics -- Dictionaries.*

### TP807 Clay industries. Ceramics. Glass — Ceramic technology. Pottery — 1800-

**TP807.B37 1997**
**Barsoum, M. W.**
   Fundamentals of ceramics / Michel W. Barsoum. New York : McGraw Hill, c1997. xvii, 668 p. :
         666 20
*Ceramic engineering.*

**TP807.K52 1975**
**Kingery, W. D.**
   Introduction to ceramics / W. D. Kingery, H. K. Bowen, D. R. Uhlmann. New York : Wiley, c1976. xii, 1032 p.
75-022248          666          0471478601
   *Ceramics.*

**TP807.R28 1995**
**Rahaman, M.N.,**
   Ceramic processing and sintering / M.N. Rahaman. New York : M. Dekker, c1995. xi, 770 p. :
         666 20          0824795733
*Ceramics. Sintering.*

**TP807.S343 1992**
   Handbook of structural ceramics / Mel M. Schwartz, editor in chief. New York : McGraw-Hill, c1992. 1 v. (various
91-028316          666          0070557195
   *Ceramics -- Handbooks, manuals, etc.*

## TP810.5 Clay industries. Ceramics. Glass — Ceramic technology. Pottery — Materials

**TP810.5.G75 1971**
**Grimshaw, Rex W.**
   The chemistry and physics of clays and allied ceramic materials, by Rex W. Grimshaw. New York, Wiley-Interscience [1971] 1024 p.
76-178139      666/.4/2      0471327808
   *Clay. Ceramic materials.*

## TP815 Clay industries. Ceramics. Glass — Ceramic technology. Pottery — General special

**TP815.C47 1999**
   Ceramic innovations in the 20th century / edited by John B. Wachtman, Jr. Westerville, Ohio : The American Ceramic Society, c1999. xiii, 307 p. :
           1574980939
   *Ceramics -- United States -- History -- 20th century.*

## TP857 Clay industries. Ceramics. Glass — Glass and glassmaking — General works

**TP857.D67 1994**
**Doremus, R. H.**
   Glass science / Robert H. Doremus. New York : Wiley, c1994. xi, 339 p. :
93-006343      666/.1      0471891746
   *Glass. Glass manufacture.*

**TP857.V37 1994.**
**Varshneya, Arun K.**
   Fundamentals of inorganic glasses / Arun K. Varshneya. Boston : Academic Press, c1994. xvii, 570 p. :
           620.1/44 20
   *Glass.*

## TP873 Artificial gems — General works

**TP873.5.D5.H39 1999**
**Hazen, Robert M.,**
   The diamond makers / Robert M. Hazen. New York : Cambridge University Press, 1999. xiv, 244 p. :
98-049423      666/.88      0521654742
   *Diamonds, Artificial. High pressure (Technology)*

## TP897 Textile bleaching, dyeing, printing, etc. — Dyeing — General works

**TP897.C523 1990**
   The Chemistry and application of dyes / edited by David R. Waring and Geoffrey Hallas. New York : Plenum Press, c1990. xv, 414 p. :
89-027837      667/.2      0306432781
   *Dyes and dyeing.*

## TP913 Textile bleaching, dyeing, printing, etc. — Dyeing — Dyes

**TP913.V4**
**Venkataraman, K.**
   The chemistry of synthetic dyes. New York, Academic Press, 1952-78. 8 v.
52-005201      667/.25      0127170049
   *Dyes and dyeing -- Chemistry.*

## TP935 Paints, pigments, varnishes, etc. — Nonofficial works

**TP935.P24 1987**
   Paint and surface coatings : theory and practice / editor, R. Lambourne. Chichester : Ellis Horwood ; 1987. 696 p. :
86-027595      667/.6      0470208090
   *Paint. Protective coatings.*

## TP983 Miscellaneous organic chemical industries — Perfumes, cosmetics, and other toilet preparations — Societies, congresses, etc.

**TP983.C33 1994**
**Calkin, Robert R.**
   Perfumery : practice and principles / Robert R. Calkin, J. Stephan Jellinek. New York : John Wiley & Sons, c1994. xiii, 287 p.
93-041844      668/.54      0471589349
   *Perfumes.*

**TP983.T44513 1994**
**Teisseire, Paul Jose.**
   Chemistry of fragrant substances / by Paul Jose Teisseire ; translated by Peter A. Cadby. New York : VCH, c1994. vi, 458 p. :
93-004441      668/.54      1560816104
   *Perfumes.*

## TP994 Miscellaneous organic chemical industries — Surface active agents

**TP994.A85 1993**
**Ash, Michael.**
   Handbook of industrial surfactants : an international guide to more than 16,000 products by tradename, application, composition & manufacturer / compiled by Michael and Irene Ash. Aldershot, Hants, England ; Gower, c1993. xii, 905 p. ;
93-003759      668/.1      0566074575
   *Surface active agents.*

## TP1087 Polymers and polymer manufacture — General works

**TP1087.G75 1995**
**Griskey, Richard G.,**
Polymer process engineering / Richard G. Griskey. New York : Chapman & Hall, c1995. x, 478 p. :
   668.9 20   0412985411
*Polymers.*

**TP1087.C66 1990**
Concise encyclopedia of polymer science and engineering / Jacqueline I. Kroschwitz, executive editor. New York : Wiley, c1990. xxix, 1341 p.
89-070674   668.9/03   0471512532

**TP1087.E46 1985**
Encyclopedia of polymer science and engineering / editorial board, Herman F. Mark ... [et al.] ; editor-in-chief, Jacqueline I. Kroschwitz. New York : Wiley, c1985-c1990 v. 1-17 :
84-019713  668.9 0471895407

**TP1087.R36 1997**
**Ram, Arie.**
Fundamentals of polymer engineering / Arie Ram. New York : Plenum Press, c1997. xxv, 237 p. :
97-041616  668.9 0306457261

## TP1110 Polymers and polymer manufacture — Plastics — Dictionaries and encyclopedias

**TP1110.R66 2000**
**Rosato, Donald V.**
Concise encyclopedia of plastics / Donald V. Rosato, Marlene G. Rosato, Dominick V. Rosato. Boston : Kluwer Academic, c2000. x, 716 p. :
99-029441  668.4/03   0792384962
  *Plastics -- Encyclopedias.*

**TP1110.C66 1998**
Concise polymeric materials encyclopedia / editor-in-chief, Joseph C. Salamone. Boca Raton : CRC Press, 1998. p. cm.
98-006146  668.9/03   084932226X

**TP1110.P65 1996**
Polymeric materials encyclopedia / editor-in-chief, Joseph C. Salamone. Boca Raton : CRC Press, c1996. 12 v. (9218 p
96-012181  668.9/03   084932470X

**TP1110.W46 1993**
Whittington's dictionary of plastics.  Lancaster, Pa. : Technomic Pub. Co., 1993. x, 568 p. ;
93-060943  668.4/03   1566760909

## TP1117 Polymers and polymer manufacture — Plastics — History

**TP1117.M45 1995**
**Meikle, Jeffrey L.,**
American plastic : a cultural history / Jeffrey L. Meikle. New Brunswick, N.J. : Rutgers University Press, c1995. xiv, 403 p. :
95-015187   303.48/3   081352234X

## TP1130 Polymers and polymer manufacture — Plastics — Handbooks, manuals, tables, etc.

**TP1130.H36 1996**
Handbook of plastics, elastomers, and composites / Charles A. Harper, editor-in-chief. 3rd ed. New York : McGraw-Hill, c1996. 1 v. :
   668.4 20   007026693X
*Plastics -- Handbooks, manuals, etc. Elastomers -- Handbooks, manuals, etc.*

**TP1130.S58 1991**
SPI plastics engineering handbook of the Society of the Plastics Industry, Inc. / edited by Michael L. Berins. New York : Van Nostrand Reinhold, c1991. xvi, 845 p. :
90-022784  668.4 0442317999

## TP1175 Polymers and polymer manufacture — Plastics — Technical processes

**TP1175.S6W56 1999**
**Wicks, Zeno W.**
Organic coatings : science and technology / Zeno W. Wicks, Jr., Frank N. Jones, and S. Peter Pappas. 2nd ed. New York : Wiley-Interscience, c1999. xxi, 630 p. :
   667/.9 21
*Plastic coatings.*

## TP1177 Polymers and polymer manufacture — Plastics — General works

**TP1177.M87 1998**
**Murphy, John.**
The reinforced plastics handbook / John Murphy. 2nd ed. Oxford ; New York : Elsevier, c1998. xx, 674 p. :
   668.4/94 21   1856173488
*Plastics, Reinforced.*

**TP1177.C65 1990**
Composite materials technology : processes and properties / P.K. Mallick, S. Newman, eds. ; with contributions from G.B. Chapman ... [et al.]. Munich ; Hanser Publishers ; c1990. 399 p. :
90-038921  620.1/923   3446156844

TP325.B46 1994
**Berkowitz, N. (Norbert),**
An introduction to coal technology / Norbert Berkowitz. 2nd ed. San Diego : Academic Press, c1994. xvi, 398 p. :
662.6/2 20          0120919516
*Coal.*

# TR Photography

## TR6 Exhibitions. Museums —General works

TR6.U6.W18 1999
**Bustard, Bruce I.,**
Picturing the century : one hundred years of photography from the National Archives / by Bruce I. Bustard. Washington, DC : National Archives and Records Adminstration in a c1999. vii, 136 p. :
98-044102          779/.997391/074753
0295977728
*Photograph collections -- Washington (D.C.) -- Exhibitions. Photography -- United States -- History -- 20th century – Exhibitions.*

## TR9 Dictionaries and encyclopedias

TR9.S88
**Stroebel, Leslie D.**
Dictionary of contemporary photography / by Leslie Stroebel & Hollis N. Todd. Dobbs Ferry, N.Y. : Morgan & Morgan, [1974] 217 p. :
73-093536          770/.3     0871000652
*Photography -- Dictionaries.*

## TR12 Directories. Bluebooks

TR12.E85 1996
Index to American photographic collections : compiled at the International Museum of Photography at George Eastman House / Andrew H. Eskind, editor ; Greg Drake, Kirsti Ringger, Lynne Rumney, associate editors. New York : G.K. Hall, c1996. xix, 1058 p.
95-225990          779/.074/73          0783821492
*Photograph collections -- United States -- Directories. Photographers -- United States -- Directories.*

## TR15 History (General)

TR15.C566 1997
**Clarke, Graham,**
The photograph / Graham Clarke. Oxford ; Oxford University Press, 1997. 247 p. :
96-047645          770     019284248X
*Photography -- History.*

TR15.G37 1969
**Gernsheim, Helmut,**
The history of photography from the camera obscura to the beginning of the modern era [by] Helmut Gernsheim, in collaboration with Alison Gernsheim. New York, McGraw-Hill [1969] 599 p.
69-018726          770/.9
*Photography -- History.*

TR15.G37 1982 vol. 2
**Gernsheim, Helmut,**
The rise of photography, 1850-1880 : the age of collodion / [Helmut Gernsheim]. London ; Thames and Hudson, 1988. 285 p. :
87-051303          770/.9 s          0500973490
*Collodion process -- History -- 19th century. Photography -- History -- 19th century.*

TR15.G69 1996
**Green-Lewis, Jennifer.**
Framing the Victorians : photography and the culture of realism / Jennifer Green-Lewis. Ithaca, N.Y. : Cornell University Press, 1996. xii, 255 p. :
96-020784          770/.9/034          0801432766
*Photography -- History -- 19th century. Photography in historiography.*

TR15.H557 2000
**Hirsch, Robert.**
Seizing the light : a history of photography / Robert Hirsch. Boston : McGraw-Hill, c2000. xiii, 530 p.
99-016019          770/.9     0697143619
*Photography -- History.*

TR15.N47 1964
**Newhall, Beaumont,**
The history of photography, from 1839 to the present day. New York, Museum of Modern Art; distributed by Doubleday, [1964] 215 p.
64-015285          770.9
*Photography -- History.*

TR15.R67 1984
**Rosenblum, Naomi.**
A world history of photography / by Naomi Rosenblum. New York : Abbeville Press, c1984. 671 p. :
83-073417          770/.9     0896594386
*Photography -- History.*

## TR23-57 Country divisions

TR23 W55 2000
**Willis, Deborah,**
Reflections in Black : a history of Black photographers, 1840 to the present / Deborah Willis. New York : W.W. Norton, c2000. xviii, 348 p.
99-055185          770/.8996/073          0393048802
*Photography -- United States -- History -- 19th century. Photography -- United States -- History -- 20th century. Afro-American photographers -- History -- 19th century.*

**TR23.B48 1999**
**Bezner, Lili Corbus.**

Photography and politics in America : from the New Deal into the Cold War / Lili Corbus Bezner. Baltimore, Md. : J. Hopkins University Press, 1999. xiv, 307 p. :
99-023281          070.4/9/0973          080186187X
*Photography -- United States -- History -- 20th century. Documentary photography -- United States -- History – 20th century. Photography -- Political aspects -- United States.*

**TR23.D38 1998**
**Davidov, Judith Fryer.**

Women's camera work : self/body/other in American visual culture / Judith Fryer Davidov. Durham : Duke University Press, 1998. xii, 494 p. :
97-034684          770/.82          0822320541
*Photography -- United States -- History. Women photographers – United States -- History.*

**TR23.G68 1988**
**Gover, C. Jane,**

The positive image : women photographers in turn of the century America / C. Jane Gover. Albany : State University of New York Press, c1988. xix, 191 p.,
86-030185          770/.88042          0887065333
*Women photographers -- United States -- History -- 19th century. Women photographers -- United States -- History -- 20th century.*

**TR23.P48 1991**

Photography in nineteenth-century America / edited by Martha A. Sandweiss ; with essays by Alan Trachtenberg ... [et al.]. Fort Worth [Tex.] : Amon Carter Museum ; 1991. xv, 335 p. :
91-000301          770/.973/09034          0883600676
*Photography -- United States -- History -- 19th century.*

**TR57.S32 1992**
**Schaaf, Larry J.**

Out of the shadows : Herschel, Talbot & the invention of photography / Larry J. Schaaf. New Haven : Yale University Press, 1992. xii, 188 p. :
91-051108          770/.9/034          0300057059
*Herschel, John F. W. -- (John Frederick William), – Sir, – 1792-1871. Talbot, William Henry Fox, -- 1800-1877. Photography – England – History -- 19th century.*

## TR139 Biography — Collective

**TR139.A46 1989**

American photographers : an illustrated who's who among leading contemporary Americans / Les Krantz, editor ; foreword by Cornell Capa. New York : Facts on File, c1989. 352 p. :
89-001435          770/.92/273          0816014191
*Photographers -- United States -- Biography.*

**TR139.B767 1983**
**Browne, Turner.**

Macmillan biographical encyclopedia of photographic artists & innovators / Turner Browne, Elaine Partnow. New York : Macmillan ; c1983. xiii, 722 p.,
82-004664          770/.92/2          0025175009
*Photographers -- Biography -- Dictionaries.*

**TR139.C66 1982**

Contemporary photographers / editors, George Walsh, Colin Naylor, Michael Held. New York : St. Martin's Press, [1982] 837 p. :
82-003337          770/.92/2          0312167911
*Photographers -- Biography. Photography, Artistic.*

## TR140 Biography — Individual, A-Z

**TR140.A3.A4 1988**
**Adams, Ansel,**

Ansel Adams : letters and images, 1916-1984 / edited by Mary Street Alinder and Andrea Gray Stillman ; foreword by Wallace Stegner. Boston : Little, Brown, c1988. xii, 401 p.,
88-001245          770/.92/4          0821216910
*Adams, Ansel, -- 1902- -- Correspondence.     Photography, Artistic. Photographers -- United States -- Biography.*

**TR140.B6.A3**
**Bourke-White, Margaret,**

Portrait of myself. New York, Simon and Schuster, 1963. 383 p.
63-011141          770/.92/4
*Bourke-White, Margaret, -- 1904-1971.*

**TR140.C28.A3**
**Capa, Robert,**

Images of war, by Robert Capa, with text from his own writings. New York, Grossman Publishers, 1964. 175 p.
64-004621          908.4
*Military history, Modern -- 20th century -- Pictorial works.*

**TR140.C78.L67 1993**
**Lorenz, Richard.**

Imogen Cunningham : ideas without end : a life in photographs / Richard Lorenz. San Francisco : Chronicle Books, c1993. 180 p. :
93-000067          770/.92          0811803902
*Cunningham, Imogen, -- 1883-1976.     Photographers -- United States -- Biography. Photography, Artistic.*

**TR140.D3.G47 1968**
**Gernsheim, Helmut,**

L. J. M. Daguerre; the history of the diorama and the daguerreotype, by Helmut and Alison Gernsheim. New York, Dover Publications [1968] xxii, 226 p.
68-008044          770/.924          048622290X
*Daguerre, Louis Jacques Mande, -- 1787-1851.*

**TR140.E3.B73 1996**
**Brayer, Elizabeth.**
George Eastman : a biography / Elizabeth Brayer. Baltimore : Johns Hopkins University Press, 1996. xiii, 637 p.
95-009513      338.7/61681418/092
0801852633
*Eastman, George, -- 1854-1932.*

**TR140.E92.R38 1995**
**Rathbone, Belinda.**
Walker Evans : a biography / Belinda Rathbone. Boston : Houghton Mifflin, 1995. xix, 358 p.,
95-003711      770/.92      0395590728
*Evans, Walker, -- 1903-1975.     Photographers -- United States -- Biography.*

**TR140.G35.K38 1991**
**Katz, D. Mark.**
Witness to an era : the life and photographs of Alexander Gardner : the Civil War, Lincoln, and the West / D. Mark Katz. New York, N.Y., U.S.A. : Viking, 1991. xiii, 305 p.
89-040696      770/.92      0670828203
*Gardner, Alexander, -- 1821-1882.     News photographers -- United States -- Biography.*

**TR140.G6.A3**
**Goddard, George W.,**
Overview ; a lifelong adventure in aerial photography [by] George W. Goddard, with DeWitt S. Copp. Garden City, N.Y., Doubleday, 1969. xiii, 415 p.
75-078732      778.3/5

**TR140.H52.G8**
**Gutman, Judith Mara.**
Lewis W. Hine, and the American social conscience. New York, Walker [1967] 156 p.
67-023089      770/.924
*Hine, Lewis Wickes, -- 1874-1940.     United States -- Social conditions -- Pictorial works.*

**TR140.J27.W35 1998**
**Waitley, Douglas.**
William Henry Jackson : framing the frontier / Douglas Waitley. Missoula, Mont. : Mountain Press Pub. Co., 1998. vi, 217 p. :
98-043915      770/.92      0878423818
*Jackson, William Henry, -- 1843-1942.     Photographers -- United States -- Biography. Photography -- United States -- History -- 19th century.     West (U.S.) -- Pictorial works.*

**TR140.J64**
**Berch, Bettina.**
The woman behind the lens : the life and work of Frances Benjamin Johnston, 1864-1952 / Bettina Berch. Charlottesville : University Press of Virginia, 2000. x, 171 p. :
00-022173      770/.92      081391938X
*Johnston, Frances Benjamin, -- 1864-1952.     Women photographers -- United States -- Biography. Photographers -- United States -- Biography.*

**TR140.L3.N4**
**Museum of Modern Art (New York, N.Y.)**
Dorothea Lange. With an introductory essay by George P. Elliott. New York : The Museum ; Distributed by Doubleday, Garden City, N.Y. [1966] 111, [1] p.
66017304      779.0924
*Lange, Dorothea.*

**TR140.M584.H54 1995**
**Hight, Eleanor M.**
Picturing modernism : Moholy-Nagy and photography in Weimar Germany / Eleanor M. Hight. Cambridge, Mass. : MIT Press, c1995. x, 256 p. :
94-021225      770/.92      0262082322
*Moholy-Nagy, Laszlo, -- 1895-1946.     Art and photography -- Germany. Modernism (Art) -- Germany.*

**TR140.S54.A3**
**Siskind, Aaron.**
Aaron Siskind, photographer / Edited, with an introd., by Nathan Lyons. Essays by Henry Holmes Smith and Thomas B. Hess. Statement by Aaron Siskind. George Eastman House; distributed by Horizon Pre 1965. 74 p. :
65020164      770
*Siskind, Aaron.     Photography, Artistic.*

**TR140.S627.H84 1989**
**Hughes, Jim,**
W. Eugene Smith : shadow & substance : the life and work of an American photographer / by Jim Hughes. New York : McGraw-Hill, c1989. xv, 606 p., [
89-012411      770/.92      0070311234
*Smith, W. Eugene, -- 1918-    News photographers -- United States -- Biography.*

**TR140.S68.A25**
**Steichen, Edward,**
A life in photography. Published in collaboration with the Museum of Modern Art. Garden City, N.Y., Doubleday, 1963. 1 v. (unpaged
63-011119      779
*Photography, Artistic.*

**TR140.S7.K53 1991**
**Kiefer, Geraldine W.**
Alfred Stieglitz : scientist, photographer, and avatar of modernism, 1880-1913 / Geraldine Wojno Kiefer. New York : Garland, 1991. xxiii, 648 p.
91-014136      770/.92      0815301146
*Stieglitz, Alfred, -- 1864-1946. Stieglitz, Alfred, -- 1864-1946 -- Aesthetics. Stieglitz, Alfred, -- 1864-1946 -- Criticism and interpretation.*

**TR140.T47.A72 1996**
**Albright, Peggy.**
  Richard Throssel : Crow Indian photographer / Peggy Albright ; with commentaries on the photographs by Crow Tribal members, Barney Old Coyote Jr., Mardell Hogan Plainfeather, and Dean Curtis Bear Claw ; foreword by Joanna Cohan Scherer. Albuquerque : University of New Mexico Press, c1996. p. cm.
96-004498        770/.92        0826317545
*Throssel, Richard, -- d. 1933.    Photographers -- United States -- Biography.  Indians of North America -- Portraits.  Crow Indians -- Portraits.*

**TR140.U426**
**Jacobs, Philip Walker.**
  The life and photography of Doris Ulmann / Philip Walker Jacobs. Lexington : University Press of Kentucky, c2001. xxiii, 325 p.
00-036337        770/.92        0813121752
*Ulmann, Doris, -- d. 1934.    Women photographers -- United States -- Biography.  Portrait photography -- United States.*

**TR140.W45.A3**
**Weston, Edward,**
  Daybooks. Edited by Nancy Newhall. Rochester, N.Y., George Eastman House [1961-66] 2 v.
61-018484        927.7

## TR145 General works — 1850-

**TR145.A42**
**Adams, Ansel,**
  Basic photo [by] Ansel Adams. Hastings-on-Hudson, N.Y., Morgan & Morgan [1970- v.
78-021737        770        0871000563
  *Photography.*

**TR145.L66 1998**
**London, Barbara,**
  Photography / Barbara London and John Upton. 6th ed. New York : Longman, c1998. vii, 399 p. :
            770 21
*Photography.*

**TR145.N4 1977**
**Neblette, C. B.**
  Neblette's Handbook of photography and reprography : materials, processes, and systems.  New York : Van Nostrand Reinhold, c1977. ix, 641 p. :
76-043356        770        0442259484
  *Photography.  Copying processes.*

## TR146 Elementary works. Handbooks, manuals, etc.

**TR146.F43**
**Feininger, Andreas,**
  Successful   photography.     New York, Prentice-Hall [1954]Rev. 1960 249 p.
53-005731        770
  *Photography -- Handbooks, manuals, etc.*

## TR148 Photographic amusements. Trick photography. Special effects

**TR148.D28**
  Darkroom / Wynn Bullock .. [et al]. ; edited by Eleanor Lewis. [New York] : Lustrum Press ; c1977. 183 p. :
76-057201        770/.28        0912810203.
  *Photography -- Special effects.  Photography -- Processing.*

## TR150 Photographers' reference handbooks

**TR150.L364 1982**
**Langford, Michael John,**
  The master guide to photography / Michael Langford. New York : Knopf : 1982. 432 p. :
82-080133        770        0394508734
  *Photography -- Handbooks, manuals, etc.*

## TR179 Composition

**TR179.S56 1998**
**Shore, Stephen,**
  The nature of photographs / Stephen Shore. Baltimore : Johns Hopkins University Press, 1998. xvii, 86 p. :
97-019510        770/.1/1        0801857198
  *Composition (Photography)  Visual perception.  Photographs.*

## TR183 Psychology, aesthetics, etc. (Artistic photography)

**TR183.C33 1997**
**Cadava, Eduardo.**
  Words of light : theses on the photography of history / Eduardo Cadava. Princeton, N.J. : Princeton University Press, c1997. xxx, 173 p. :
96-017708        770/.1        0691034508
*Benjamin, Walter, -- 1892-1940.    Historiography.  Photography -- Philosophy.*

**TR183.S43 1997**
**Shawcross, Nancy M.**
   Roland Barthes on photography : the critical tradition in perspective / Nancy M. Shawcross. Gainesville : University Press of Florida, c1997. xiv, 130 p. :
96-026838        770/.1      0813014697
*Barthes, Roland.    Photographic criticism. Photography -- Philosophy.*

**TR183.S65 1977**
**Sontag, Susan,**
   On photography / Susan Sontag. New York : Farrar, Straus and Giroux, c1977. 207 p. ;
77-011916        770/.1      0374226261
*Photography, Artistic.*

## TR185 Addresses, essays, lectures

**TR185.L9**
**Lyons, Nathan,**
   Photographers on photography; a critical anthology. Englewood Cliffs, N.J., Prentice-Hall [1966] 190 p.
66-022343        770.8
*Photography -- Addresses, essays, lectures.*

**TR185.P487**
   Photography, essays & images : illustrated readings in the history of photography / edited by Beaumont Newhall. New York : Museum of Modern Art ; c1980. 327 p. :
80-083434        770      0870703854
*Photography -- Addresses, essays, lectures.*

## TR187 Photographic criticism

**TR187.M37 1997**
**Marien, Mary Warner.**
   Photography and its critics : a cultural history, 1839-1900 / Mary Warner Marien. Cambridge, U.K. ; Cambridge University Press, 1997. xvi, 222 p.
96-031557        770      0521550432
*Photographic criticism -- United States -- History – 19th century. Photographic criticism -- Europe -- History -- 19th century. Photography -- Philosophy -- History -- 19th century.*

## TR267 Digital photography (Photo CDs)

**TR267.F35 1996**
**Farace, Joe.**
   The digital imaging dictionary / Joe Farace. New York, NY : Allworth Press, c1996. 223 p. :
96-083242            1880559463
*Photography -- Digital techniques -- Dictionaries. Image processing -- Digital techniques -- Dictionaries. Computer graphics – Dictionaries.*

## TR287 Photographic processing. Darkroom technique (General) — General works

**TR287.S48 1983**
**Shaw, Susan,**
   Overexposure : health hazards in photography / Susan Shaw ; edited by David Featherstone. Carmel, Calif. : Friends of Photography, c1983. 329 p. :
83-081548        770/.28/3        093328635X
*Photography -- Processing -- Health aspects.  Photography -- Developing and developers -- Health aspects.*

## TR330 Photographic processing. Darkroom technique — Treatment of positives — Printing

**TR330.C68**
**Crawford, William,**
   The keepers of light : a history & working guide to early photographic processes / William Crawford. Dobbs Ferry, N.Y. : Morgan & Morgan, c1979. 318 p., [12]
79-088815        770/.28        0871001586
*Photography -- Printing processes.  Photography -- Printing processes -- History.*

**TR330.D37**
   Darkroom dynamics : a guide to creative darkroom techniques / Jim Stone, editor. Marblehead, Mass. : Curtin & London, 1979. ix, 199 p. :
78-023902        770/.28/3        0930764072
*Photography -- Printing processes.*

## TR365 Photographic processing. Darkroom technique — Photographic processes — Daguerreotype

**TR365.B37 1991**
**Barger, M. Susan,**
   The daguerreotype : nineteenth-century technology and modern science / M. Susan Barger and William B. White. Washington : Smithsonian Institution Press, c1991. xvi, 252 p. :
90-039533        772/.12        0874743486
*Daguerreotype -- History.*

**TR365.N4 1976**
**Newhall, Beaumont,**
   The daguerreotype in America / by Beaumont Newhall. New York : Dover Publications, 1976. 175 p., [48]
76-000691        772/.12        0486233227
*Daguerreotype -- History. Photography -- United States -- History.*

### TR375 Photographic processing. Darkroom technique — Photographic processes — Ferrotype (Tintype)

**TR375.R56 1999**
**Rinhart, Floyd.**
The American tintype / Floyd Rinhart, Marion Rinhart & Robert W. Wagner. Columbus : Ohio State University Press, c1999. xiii, 258 p.
98-049828          772/.14/097309034
0814208061
*Tintype -- United States -- History -- 19th century. Photography – United States -- History -- 19th century.*

## TR465 Photographic processing. Darkroom technique — Conservation and restoration of photographs

**TR465.W44**
**Weinstein, Robert A.**
Collection, use, and care of historical photographs / Robert A. Weinstein and Larry Booth. Nashville : American Association for State and Local History c1977. 222 p. :
76-027755          770/.28          091005021X
*Photographs -- Conservation and restoration. Photographs – Collectors and collecting.*

### TR591 Lighting — Exposures — General works

**TR591.G73 1997**
**Graves, Carson,**
The zone system for 35mm photographers : a basic guide to exposure control / Carson Graves. 2nd ed. Boston : Focal Press, c1997. xi, 130 p. :
          771 20
*Includes bibliographical references and index.*

### TR593 Lighting — Exposures — Instantaneous

**TR593.E34 1987**
**Edgerton, Harold Eugene,**
Stopping time : the photographs of Harold Edgerton / foreword by Harold Edgerton ; text by Estelle Jussim ; edited by Gus Kayafas. New York : H.N. Abrams, 1987. 167 p. :
87-001064          770/.92/4          0810915146
*Edgerton, Harold Eugene, -- 1903-     Photography, High-speed. Photography -- Scientific applications.*

### TR605 Lighting — Exposures — Flashlight. Flash photography

**TR605.H69 1990**
**Howes, Chris,**
To photograph darkness : the history of underground and flash photography / Chris Howes. Carbondale : Southern Illinois University Press, c1989. xxi, 330 p. :
89-021590          778.7/2          0809316226
*Photography, Flash-light -- History.*

### TR642 Applied photography — Artistic photography — General works

**TR642.P45**
A Photographic vision : pictorial photography, 1889-1923 / edited by Peter C.Bunnell. Santa Barbara : P. Smith, 1980. p. cm.
80-020481          770          0879050594
*Photography, Artistic -- Addresses, essays, lectures.*

### TR645-647 Applied photography — Artistic photography — Exhibitions

**TR645.H8.F673 1998**
Image and memory : photography from Latin America, 1866-1994 : FotoFest / edited by Wendy Watriss, Lois Parkinson Zamora. Austin, Tex. : University of Texas Press, 1998. xi, 450 p. :
94-035532          779/.098          0292791186
*Photography, Artistic -- Exhibitions. Photography -- Latin America -- History -- 19th century -- Exhibitions. Photography -- Latin America -- History -- 20th century -- Exhibitions.*

**TR645.N72.M876 1995**
**Museum of Modern Art (New York, N.Y.)**
American photography, 1890-1965, from the Museum of Modern Art, New York / Peter Galassi ; with an essay by Luc Sante. New York, N.Y. : The Museum : 1995. 256 p. :
94-073385          779/.0973/074
*Photography -- United States -- History -- 19th century -- Exhibitions. Photography -- United States -- History – 20th century – Exhibitions. Photography, Artistic -- Exhibitions.*

**TR646.U6.N484**
**Metropolitan Museum of Art (New York, N.Y.)**
The collection of Alfred Stieglitz : fifty pioneers of modern photography / Weston J. Naef. New York : Metropolitan Museum of Art, 1978. xi, 529 p. :
78-006850          770/.92/2          0670670510
*Stieglitz, Alfred, -- 1864-1946 -- Photograph collections. Photographers.*

**TR646.U6.W378 1989**
The Photography of invention : American pictures of the 1980s, National Museum of American Art, Smithsonian Institution, Washington, D.C. / essay by Joshua P. Smith ; introduction by Merry A. Foresta. Cambridge, Mass. : MIT Press, c1989. 227 p. :
88-029559          779/.0973/0740153
0262192802
*Photography, Artistic -- Exhibitions.*

**TR646.U62.T833 1989**
Decade by decade : twentieth-century American photography from the collection of the Center for Creative Photography / edited by James Enyeart with essays by Estelle Jussim ... [et al.]. Boston : Bulfinch Press, c1989. ix, 245 p. :
88-025798          779/.0973/074019177
0821217216
*Photography, Artistic -- Exhibitions. Photography – United States -- Exhibitions.*

**TR647.C36 1987**
**Galassi, Peter.**
 Henri Cartier-Bresson : the early work / Peter Galassi. New York : Museum of Modern Art ; c1987. 151 p. :
87-061124          779/.092          0870702610
*Cartier-Bresson, Henri, -- 1908- -- Exhibitions. Cartier-Bresson, Henri, -- 1908- -- Criticism and interpretation. Photography, Artistic -- Exhibitions.*

**TR647.E9 2000**
**Evans, Walker,**
 Walker Evans / Maria Morris Hambourg ... [et al.]. New York : Metropolitan Museum of Art in association with P c2000. xiii, 318 p.
99-055746          779/.092          0870999370
*Evans, Walker, -- 1903-1975 -- Exhibitions.    Photography, Artistic -- Exhibitions.*

**TR647.M554.L69 1995**
**Lowe, Sarah M.**
 Tina Modotti : photographs / Sarah M. Lowe. New York, N.Y. : H.N. Abrams in association with the Philadelphia 1995. 160 p. :
95-000889          779/.092          0810942801
*Modotti, Tina, -- 1896-1942 -- Exhibitions.    Photography, Artistic -- Exhibitions.    Mexico -- Social conditions -- Pictorial works.*

**TR647.P512 1997**
**Baldassari, Anne.**
 Picasso and photography : the dark mirror / Anne Baldassari ; translated from the French by Deke Dusinberre. Paris : Flammarion ; c1997. 263 p. :
97-034000          779/.092          2080136461
*Picasso, Pablo, -- 1881-1973 -- Exhibitions.    Photography, Artistic -- Exhibitions.    Art and photography -- Exhibitions.*

**TR647.R3813 1982**
**Ray, Man,**
 Man Ray : photographs / introduction by Jean-Hubert Martin ; with three texts by Man Ray ; [translated from the French, Man Ray, photographe, by Carolyn Breakspear]. New York, N.Y. : Thames and Hudson, 1982. 255 p. :
81-053058          779/.092/4          0500540799
*Ray, Man, -- 1890-1976.    Photography, Artistic -- Exhibitions.*

**TR647.S84 1983**
**Stieglitz, Alfred,**
 Alfred Stieglitz, photographs & writings / Sarah Greenough, Juan Hamilton. Washington : National Gallery of Art, [1983] 246 p. :
82-007925          770/.92/4          0894680277
*Stieglitz, Alfred, -- 1864-1946.    Photography, Artistic -- Exhibitions.*

**TR647.W46.A2 1969**
**White, Minor.**
 Mirrors, messages, manifestations. [New York] Aperture [1969] 242 p. (chief
77-099253          779.0924
 *Photography, Artistic.*

**TR650-654 Applied photography — Artistic photography — Collections**

**TR650.C38**
**Cartier-Bresson, Henri,**
 The world of Henri Cartier Bresson.   New York, Viking Press [1968] [16] p., 210
68-023211          779/.0924
 *Photography, Artistic.*

**TR650.P46**
 Photodiscovery : masterworks of photography, 1840-1940 / [collected] by Bruce Bernard ; with notes on the photographic processes by Valerie Lloyd ; [project director, Robert Morton ; editor, Margaret Donovan]. New York : H. N. Abrams, 1980. 262 p. :
80-012590          779          0810914530
 *Photography, Artistic.  Photography -- History.*

**TR653.B686 1999**
**Brandt, Bill.**
 Brandt : the photography of Bill Brandt / foreword by David Hockney ; introductory essay by Bill Jay ; the career by Nigel Warburton. New York : Henry N. Abrams, 1999. 320 p. :
99-073657          779/.092          0810941090
*Brandt, Bill.    Photojournalism -- Great Britain.    Photography, Artistic.*

**TR653 .S744 2000**
**Steichen, Edward,**
 Steichen's legacy : photographs, 1895-1973 / edited and with text by Joanna Steichen. New York : Alfred A. Knopf, 2000. xxxii, 372 p.
00-020095          770/.92          0679450769
*Stieglitz, Alfred, -- 1864-1946 -- Catalogs.    Photography, Artistic -- Catalogs.    Photograph collections -- New York -- Rochester -- Catalogs.*

**TR654.A34**
**Adams, Ansel,**
 The portfolios of Ansel Adams / introd. by John Szarkowski ; [edited by Tim Hill]. Boston : New York Graphic Society, c1977. xii, 124 p. :
77-071628          779/.092/4          0821207237
*Adams, Ansel, -- 1902-    Photography, Artistic.*

**TR654.E918 1998**
**Evans, Walker,**
 Walker Evans : signs / with an essay by Andrei Codrescu. Los Angeles : J. Paul Getty Museum, c1998. ix, 69 p. :
98-004270          779/.092          0892363762
*Evans, Walker, -- 1903-1975.    Signs and signboards -- Pictorial works.    Photography, Artistic.*

**TR654.W422 1989**
**Welty, Eudora,**
 Eudora Welty : photographs / Eudora Welty ; foreword by Reynolds Price. Jackson : Univerisity Press of Mississippi, c1989. 1 v. :
                   779/.092 20
*Photography, Artistic.    Mississippi -- Pictorial works.*

## TR660-660.5 Applied photography — Artistic photography — Marines. Seashore photography. Water

**TR660.J87 1985**
**Jussim, Estelle.**
  Landscape as photograph / Estelle Jussim, Elizabeth Lindquist-Cock. New Haven : Yale University Press, c1985. xv, 168 p., [
84-040671          778.9/36          0300032218
  *Landscape photography.*

**TR660.5.A33**
**Adams, Ansel,**
  Yosemite and the range of light / Ansel Adams ; introd. by Paul Brooks. Boston : New York Graphic Society, 1979. 28 p., [55] 1
78-072074          779/.36/0979447          0821207504
*Adams, Ansel, -- 1902-     Landscape photography -- California — Yosemite National Park.     Yosemite National Park (Calif.) -- Pictorial works.*

## TR675 Applied photography — Artistic photography — Human figures. Photography of the nude

**TR675.B65 1980**
**Brandt, Bill.**
  Nudes, 1945-1980 : photographs / by Bill Brandt ; introd. by Michael Hiley. Boston : New York Graphic Society, 1980. 12, 100 p. :
80-082724          779/.24/0924          0821210971
*Brandt, Bill.     Photography of the nude.*

## TR680-681 Applied photography — Artistic photography — Portraits

**TR680.D25 1998**
**Daniel, Malcolm R.**
  Edgar Degas, photographer / Malcolm Daniel ; with essays by Eugenia Parry, Theodore Reff. New York : Metropolitan Museum of Art : [1998] 143 p. :
98-029432          779/.092          0870998838
*Degas, Edgar, -- 1834-1917 -- Exhibitions.  Degas, Edgar, –1834-1917 -- Catalogues raisonnes.     Portrait photography – Exhibitions.*

**TR680.K3**
**Karsh, Yousuf,**
  Portraits of greatness. [London, T. Nelson [1959] 207 p.
59065108          779.2
  *Photography, Artistic.  Portraits.*

**TR681.A7.N48**
**Newman, Arnold,**
  Artists, portraits from four decades / by Arnold Newman ; foreword by Henry Geldzahler ; introd. by Arnold Newman. Boston : New York Graphic Society, c1980. 17, 157 p. :
80-023961          779/.2/0924          0821210998
  *Artists -- United States -- Portraits. Artists -- Europe -- Portraits.*

**TR681.W6.L34 1999**
**Leibovitz, Annie,**
  Women / [photographs by] Annie Leibovitz ; [essay by] Susan Sontag. New York : Random House, c1999. 239 p. :
99-024968          779/.24          0375500200
*Leibovitz, Annie, -- 1949-     Photography of women.*

## TR690 Applied photography — Commercial photography — General works

**TR690.M55 1998**
**Miller, Russell.**
  Magnum : fifty years at the front line of history / Russell Miller. New York : Grove Press, c1997. xii, 324 p. :
97-049040          070.4/9          0802116310
  *Commercial photography -- History.*

## TR810 Applied photography — Geographical applications — Aerial photography. Photographic interpretation (Remote sensing in geogrpahy)

**TR810.A9 1985**
**Avery, Thomas Eugene.**
  Interpretation of aerial photographs / Thomas Eugene Avery, Graydon Lennis Berlin. Minneapolis, Minn. : Burgess Pub. Co., c1985. ix, 554 p., 1
84-023249          778.3/5          0808700960
  *Photographic interpretation.  Aerial photography.*

## TR820 Applied photography — Photojournalism

**TR820.C357 1992**
**Carlebach, Michael L.**
  The origins of photojournalism in America / Michael L. Carlebach. Washington : Smithsonian Institution Press, c1992. x, 194 p. :
91-040145          070.4/9/097309034
1560981598
  *Photojournalism -- United States -- History.*

**TR820.F45 1977**
**Weegee,**
  Weegee / edited and with an introd. by Louis Stettner. New York : Knopf, 1977. 183 p. :
77-075356          779/.092/4          0394407709
*Weegee, -- 1899-1968.     Photojournalism.*

## TR820.5 Applied photography — Documentary photography (Photography in historiography)

**TR820.5.C87 1989**
**Curtis, James,**
  Mind's eye, mind's truth : FSA photography reconsidered / James Curtis. Philadelphia : Temple University Press, c1989. x, 139 p. :
89-004375          770/.973          087722627X
  *Documentary photography -- United States.*

**TR820.5.H5 1994**
Heyman, Therese Thau.
   Dorothea Lange : American photographs / Therese Thau Heyman, Sandra S. Phillips, John Szarkowski. San Francisco : San Francisco Museum of Modern Art : c1994. 192 p. :
93-040027          779/.092          0918471303
*Lange, Dorothea -- Exhibitions.     Documentary photography -- Exhibitions.   Photographers -- United States -- Biography -- Exhibitions.*

## TR847 Cinematography. Motion pictures. Video recording — Dictionaries and encyclopedias

**TR847.B43 1994**
Beaver, Frank Eugene.
   Dictionary of film terms : the aesthetic companion to film analysis / Frank E. Beaver. New York : Twayne Publishers ; 1994. xi, 410 p. :
94-006350          791.43/03          0805793283
*Cinematography -- Dictionaries.*

## TR849 Cinematography. Motion pictures. Video recording — Biography — Individual, A-Z

**TR849.C87.H64 1980**
Holm, Bill,
   Edward S. Curtis in the land of the war canoes : a pioneer cinematographer in the Pacific Northwest / Bill Holm and George Irving Quimby. Seattle : University of Washington Press, c1980. 132 p. :
80-012172          778.5/3/0924          0295957085
*Curtis, Edward S., -- 1868-1952.     Cinematographers -- United States -- Biography.*

## TR858 Cinematography. Motion pictures. Video recording — Special photographic process — Trick cinematography. Special effects

**TR858.N48 2000**
Netzley, Patricia D.
   Encyclopedia of movie special effects / by Patricia D. Netzley. Phoenix, Ariz. : Oryx Press, 2000. xi, 291 p. :
99-047733          778.5/345/03          1573561673
*Cinematography -- Special effects -- Encyclopedias.*

## TR893.5 Cinematography. Motion pictures. Video recording — Applied cinematography — Scientific cinematography

**TR893.5.**
Bouse, Derek.
   Wildlife films / Derek Bouse. Philadelphia : University of Pennsylvania Press, c2000. xv, 280 p. :
00-028676          778.5/3859          081223555X
*Wildlife cinematography.*

### TR1045 Photomechanical process — Electrophotography — Electrostatic printing

**TR1045.M67 1989**
Mort, J.
   The anatomy of xerography : its invention and evolution / J. Mort. Jefferson, N.C. : McFarland, c1989. xiii, 226 p.
89-042739          686.4/4          0899504426

# TS Manufacturers

## TS9 Encyclopedias and dictionaries

**TS9.H57 1988**
   A Historical dictionary of American industrial language / edited by William H. Mulligan, Jr. New York : Greenwood Press, c1988. xii, 332 p. ;
87-037544          338/.003/21          0313241716
   *Industries -- United States -- Dictionaries. Industries -- United States -- Terminology -- History. English language – United States – Etymology -- Dictionaries.*

**TS9.M43 1997**
McKenna, Ted.
   Glossary of reliability and maintenance terms / Ted McKenna, Ray Oliverson. Houston, Tex. : Gulf Pub. Co., c1997. x, 141 p. :
97-017097          658.2/02/03          0884153606
   *Plant maintenance -- Dictionaries. Reliability (Engineering) – Dictionaries.*

## TS17.4-23 Country divisions

**TS17.4.B66 2002**
Boothroyd, G. (Geoffrey),
   Product design for manufacture and asssembly / Geoffrey Boothroyd, Peter Dewhurst, Winston Knight. 2nd ed., rev. and expanded. New York : Dekker, c2002. xiii, 698 p. :
          658.5/752 21
*Design, Industrial. Concurrent engineering. Production planning.*

**TS23.P84 1983**
Pulos, Arthur J.
   American design ethic : a history of industrial design to 1940 / Arthur J. Pulos. Cambridge, Mass. : MIT Press, c1983. 441 p. :
82-004625          745.2/0973          0262160854
   *Design, Industrial -- United States -- History.*

## TS140 Biography — Individual, A-Z

**TS140.L63.A34 1979**
Loewy, Raymond,
   Industrial design / Raymond Loewy. Woodstock, N.Y. : Overlook Press, 1979. 250 p. :
79-015104          745.2/092          0879510986
*Loewy, Raymond, -- 1893-1986.   Industrial designers -- United States -- Biography. Design, Industrial -- United States*

## TS146 Juvenile works. Popular works

**TS146.H67**
How products are made : an illustrated guide to product manufacturing. Detroit : Gale Research, c1994- v. :
94-648208          670
*Manufactures -- Popular works. Manufacturing processes -- Popular works.*

## TS149 General special

**TS149.D678 1967**
**Dreyfuss, Henry,**
Designing for people. New York, Paragraphic Books, 1967] 230 p.
67-012937          620.8
*Design, Industrial. Human engineering.*

**TS149.H68 1984**
**Hounshell, David A.**
From the American system to mass production, 1800-1932 : the development of manufacturing technology in the United States / David A. Hounshell. Baltimore : Johns Hopkins University Press, c1984. xxi, 411 p. :
83-016269          338.6/5/0973          0801829755
*Mass production -- United States -- History.*

## TS155 Production management. Operations management (Including factory management) — General works

**TS155.P74 1997**
Production and inventory control handbook / James H. Greene, editor in chief. 3rd ed. New York : McGraw-Hill , c1997. 1 v. :
          658.5 21
*Production management -- Handbooks, manuals, etc. Inventory control -- Handbooks, manuals, etc.*

**TS155.R594 1991**
**Robinson, Stanley L.**
Harnessing technology : the management of technology for the nontechnologist / Stanley L. Robinson. New York : Van Nostrand Reinhold, c1991. x, 143 p. :
90-024733          658.5          0442007531
*Production management. Manufacturing processes – Automation.*

**TS155.S16 1991**
**Samson, Danny.**
Manufacturing and operations strategy / Danny Samson. New York : Prentice Hall, c1991. xvii, 499 p.
91-023350          658.5          0135965780
*Production planning. Strategic planning.*

**TS155.Z39 1988**
**Zembicki, Christine.**
Production and factory management : an information sourcebook / by Christine Zembicki. [Phoenix] : Oryx Press, 1988. viii, 176 p.
88-015415          658.5          0897743407
*Production management. Factory management.*

### TS155.6 Production management. Operations management — Data processing. CAD/CAM system — General works

**TS155.6.M316 1996**
The CAD/CAM handbook / [edited by] Carl Machover. New York : McGraw-Hill, c1996. xxi, 678 p. :
95-025668          670/.285          0070393753
*CAD/CAM systems -- Handbooks, manuals, etc.*

**TS155.6.M45 1991**
**Melnyk, Steven A.**
Computer integrated manufacturing : guidelines and applications from industrial leaders / Steven A. Melnyk, Ram Narasimhan. Homewood, Ill. : Business One Irwin, c1992. xii, 378 p. :
91-024334          670/.285          1556235380
*Computer integrated manufacturing systems.*

### TS155.63 Production management. Operations management — Data processing. CAD/CAM system — Computer integrated manufacturing systems

**TS155.63.S56 1996**
**Singh, Nanua.**
Systems approach to computer-integrated design and manufacturing / Nanua Singh. New York : Wiley, c1996. xx, 643 p. :
94-040012          670/.285          0471585173
*Computer integrated manufacturing systems. CAD/CAM systems.*

## TS155.7 Production management. Operations management — Environmental aspects

**TS155.7.I47 1997**
Implementing ISO 14000 : a practical, comprehensive guide to the ISO 14000 environmental management standards / editd by Tom Tibor and Ira Feldman. Chicago : Irwin Professional Pub., c1997. xxx, 586 p. :
96-043763          658.4/08          0786310146
*ISO 14000 Series Standards. Environmental protection -- Standards.*

## TS155.8 Production management. Operations management — Control of production systems — General works

**TS155.8.O35 1988**
**O'Grady, P. J.**
Putting the just-in-time philosophy into practice / P.J. O'Grady. New York : Nichols Pub. Co., 1988. 138 p. :
88-001415          658.7/87          0893973041
*Production control. Inventory control.*

## TS156 Production management. Operations management — Control of production systems — Quality control

**TS156.B563 1991**
**Bhote, Keki R.,**
World class quality : using design of experiments to make it happen / Keki R. Bhote ; foreword by Dorian Shainin. New York, NY : Amacom, c1991. xvi, 224 p. :
91-019269          658.5/62          0814450539
*Quality control -- Statistical methods. Process control -- Statistical methods. Experimental design.*

**TS156.B563 1999**
**Bhote, Keki R.,**
World class quality : using design of experiments to make it happen / keki R. Bhote, Adi K. Bhote. 2nd ed. New York : American Management Association, 2000. xxiv, 487 p. :
          658.5/62 21
*Quality control -- Statistical methods. Process control -- Statistical methods. Experimental design.*

**TS156.D83 1986**
**Duncan, Acheson J.**
Quality control and industrial statistics / Acheson J. Duncan. Homewood, Ill. : Irwin, 1986. xxii, 1123 p.
85-081998          658.5/62          0256035350
*Quality control -- Statistical methods. Sampling (Statistics)*

**TS156.F44 1991**
**Feigenbaum, A. V. (Armand Vallin)**
Total quality control / A.V. Feigenbaum. 3rd ed., rev. New York : McGraw-Hill, c1991. xxvii, 863 p. :
          658.5/62 20
*Quality control.*

**TS156.M517 1995**
**Miller, Irwin,**
Statistical methods for quality : with applications to engineering and management / Irwin Miller, Marylees Miller. Englewood Cliffs, N.J. : Prentice Hall, c1995. x, 368 p. :
94-004684          658.5/62/015195    0130137499
*Quality control -- Statistical methods.*

## TS156.8-157.4 Production management. Operations management — Control of production systems — Production control

**TS156.8.I5622 1995**
Instrument engineers' handbook : process control / Bela G. Liptak, editor-in-chief. Radnor, Pa. : Chilton Book Co., c1995. xxvii, 1551 p
94-020792          629.8          0801982421
*Process control -- Handbooks, manuals, etc. Measuring instruments -- Handbooks, manuals, etc.*

**TS156.8.P764 1985**
Process instruments and controls handbook / Douglas M. Considine, editor-in-chief ; Glenn D. Considine, managing editor. New York : McGraw-Hill, c1985. 1766 p. in va
84-010044          629.8          0070124361
*Process control -- Handbooks, manuals, etc. Automatic control – Handbooks, manuals, etc. Engineering instruments -- Handbooks, manuals, etc.*

**TS156.8.W455 1990**
**Wetherill, G. Barrie.**
Statistical process control : theory and practice / G. Barrie Wetherill, Don W. Brown. London ; Chapman and Hall, 1991. xiv, 400 p. :
90-002560          670.42          0412357003
*Process control -- Statistical methods.*

**TS157.4.C44 1996**
**Gheng, T. C. E. (T. C. Edwin)**
Just-in-time manufacturing : an introduction / T.C.E. Cheng and S. Podolsky. 2nd ed. / revised and updated by P. Jarvis. London ; New York : Chapman & Hall, 1996. xv, 249 p. :
          658.5/6 21
*Just-in-time systems.*

## TS161 Production management. Operations management — Control of production systems — Inventory control

**TS161.I54 1994**
Industrial ecology and global change / edited by R. Socolow ... [et al.]. Cambridge ; Cambridge University Press, 1994. xxix, 500 p.
94-011814          363.73/1          0521471974
*Industrial ecology.*

**TS161.M353 1999**
**Manahan, Stanley E.**
Industrial ecology : environmental chemistry and hazardous waste / Stanley E. Manahan. Boca Raton, Fla. : Lewis Publishers, c1999. 318 p. :
98-049415          628.4/2          1566703816
*Industrial ecology. Environmental chemistry. Hazardous wastes.*

**TS161.T48**
**Tersine, Richard J.**
   Modern materials management / Richard J. Tersine, John H. Campbell. New York : North-Holland, c1977. xii, 281 p. :
77-002291          658.7          0444002286
   *Materials management.*

### TS165 Production management. Operations management — Control of production systems — Cost control

**TS165.L48 1995**
**Lewis, Ronald J.**
   Activity-based models for cost management systems / Ronald J. Lewis. Westport, Conn. : Quorum Books, 1995. x, 283 p. :
94-037876          658.15/52          0899309658
   *Cost control. Cost accounting.*

### TS170 Production management. Operations management — Product engineering

**TS170 K34 2001**
**Kahn, Kenneth B.**
   Product planning essentials / Kenneth B. Kahn. Thousand Oaks, Calif. : Sage Publications, c2001. viii, 254 p.
00-009514          658.5/75          0761919988
   *New products. Production management. Production planning.*

### TS171-171.4 Production management. Operations management — Product engineering — Product design. Industrial design

**TS171.I26 2000**
   Icons of design! : the 20th century / editorial committee: Volker Albus, Reyer Kras, Jonathan M. Woodham ; with contributions from: Volker Albus ... [et al.] ; with a foreword by Reyer Kras. Munich ; Prestel, c2000. 183 p. :
99-069112          745.2/0904          3791323067
   *Design, Industrial -- History -- 20th century. Industrial designers -- Biography.*

**TS171.M3713 1989**
**Manzini, Ezio.**
   The material of invention / by Ezio Manzini ; with a preface by Francois Dagognet with the contribution of Pasquale Cau, Leonardo Fiore, Giuseppe Gianotti. Cambridge, Mass. : MIT Press, 1989. 255 p. :
88-063574          745.2          0262132427
   *Design, Industrial. Engineering design.*

**TS171.R65 1995**
**Roozenburg, N. F. M.**
   Product design : fundamentals and methods / N.F.M. Roozenburg, J. Eekels. Chichester ; Wiley, c1995. xiii, 408 p.
94-026737          745.2          0471943517
   *Design, Industrial. Production planning.*

**TS171.4.F54 2000**
**Fiell, Charlotte.**
   Industrial design A-Z / Charlotte & Peter Fiell. Koln ; Taschen, c2000. 768 p. :
01-274164          745.2/09          3822863106
   *Design, Industrial -- History.*

**TS171.4.N67 1988**
**Norman, Donald A.**
   The psychology of everyday things / Donald A. Norman. New York : Basic Books, c1988. xi, 257 p. :
87-047782          620.8/2          0465067093
   *Design, Industrial -- Psychological aspects. Human engineering.*

### TS172 Production management. Operations management — Product engineering — Tolerances

**TS172.H46 1995**
**Henzold, G.**
   Handbook of geometrical tolerancing : design, manufacturing, and inspection / G. Henzold. Chichester ; Wiley, c1995. xv, 413 p. :
95-159689          620/.0045          0471948160
   *Tolerance (Engineering)*

### TS173 Production management. Operations management — Product engineering — Reliability of industrial products

**TS173.D48**
**Dhillon, B. S.**
   Engineering reliability : new techniques and applications / B. S. Dhillon, Chanan Singh. New York : Wiley, c1981. xix, 339 p. :
80-018734          620/.00452          0471050148
   *Reliability (Engineering)*

**TS173.H47 1981**
**Henley, Ernest J.**
   Reliability engineering and risk assessment / Ernest J. Henley, Hiromitsu Kumamoto. Englewood Cliffs, N.J. : Prentice-Hall, c1981. xxiv, 568 p.
80-000381          620/.00452          0137722516
   *Reliability (Engineering) Health risk assessment.*

### TS176 Production management. Operations management — Manufacturing engineering. Process engineering (Including manufacturing planning, production planning) — General works

**TS176.M3622 1993**
   Manufacturing engineer's reference book / edited by Dal Koshal ; with specialist contributors. Oxford ; Butterworth-Heinemann, 1993. 1 v. (various
94-121765          670.42          0750611545
   *Production engineering -- handbooks, manuals, etc.*

## TS178 Production management. Operations management — Manufacturing engineering. Process engineering — Plant layout

**TS178.A63 1991**
**Apple, James M.**
Plant layout and material handling / James M. Apple. Malabar, Fla. : Krieger, 1991. vi, 488 p. :
90-048718      658.7      0894645455
*Plant layout. Materials handling.*

**TS178.B54 1996**
**Biggs, Lindy.**
The rational factory : architecture, technology, and work in America's age of mass production / Lindy Biggs. Baltimore : Johns Hopkins University Press, c1996. xiii, 202 p.
96-010947      658.2/3      0801852617
*Plant layout. Mass production -- United States. Production engineering.*

## TS183 Production management. Operations management — Manufacturing engineering. Process engineering — Manufacturing processes

**TS183.B76 1991**
**Brown, James A.**
Modern manufacturing processes / James Brown. New York, N.Y. : Industrial Press, c1991. x, 240 p. :
90-048046      670.42      0831130342
*Manufacturing processes.*

**TS183.H359 1994**
Handbook of design, manufacturing, and automation / edited by Richard C. Dorf and Andrew Kusiak. New York : Wiley, c1994. xvii, 1042 p.
94-007901      670.42/7      0471552186
*Manufacturing processes -- Automation.*

**TS183.T63 1994**
**Todd, Robert H.,**
Manufacturing processes reference guide / by Robert H. Todd, Dell K. Allen, and Leo Alting. New York : Industrial Press, 1994. xxiv, 486 p.
93-031767      671      0831130490
*Manufacturing processes -- Handbooks, manuals, etc.*

**TS183.W38 1996**
**Waters, T. Frederick.**
Fundamentals of manufacturing for engineers / T.F. Waters. London ; UCL Press, 1996. x, 321 p. :
96-149120      670      1857283384
*Manufacturing processes. Production engineering.*

## TS184 Production management. Operations management — Plant engineering — General works

**TS184.M63 1991**
**Moffat, Donald W.,**
Plant engineer's handbook of formulas, charts, and tables / Donald W. Moffat. Englewood Cliffs, N.J. : Prentice-Hall, c1991. xiv, 561 p. :
90-019648      690/.54/0212      0136809014
*Plant engineering -- Handbooks, manuals, etc.*

**TS184.S7 1995**
Standard handbook of plant engineering / Robert C. Rosaler, editor in chief. New York : McGraw-Hill, c1995. 1 v. (various
94-012951      658.2      0070521646
*Plant engineering -- Handbooks, manuals, etc.*

## TS191.8 Production management. Operations management — Plant engineering — Machinery and equipment

**TS191.8.H36 1999**
Handbook of industrial robotics / edited by Shimon Y. Nof. New York : John Wiley, c1999. xxii, 1348 p.
98-008017      670.42/72      0471177830
*Robots, Industrial -- Handbooks, manuals, etc.*

**TS191.8.T63 1986**
**Todd, D. J.**
Fundamentals of robot technology : an introduction to industrial robots, teleoperators, and robot vehicles / D.J. Todd. New York : Wiley, 1986. 244 p. :
86-045039      670.42/7      0470203013
*Robots, Industrial. Manipulators (Mechanism) Automated guided vehicle systems.*

## TS195 Packaging (Shipping of merchandise, containerization of freight) — Dictionaries and encyclopedias

**TS195.A2.W55 1997**
The Wiley encyclopedia of packaging technology / edited by Aaron L. Brody, Kenneth S. Marsh. New York : Wiley, c1997. xii, 1023 p.
96-044725      688.8/03      0471063975
*Packaging -- Dictionaries.*

**TS195.H35 1998**
**Hanlon, Joseph F.**
Handbook of package engineering / Joseph F. Hanlon, Robert J. Kelsey, Hallie E. Forcinio. 3rd ed. Lancaster, Pa. : Technomic Pub. Co., c1998. xvii, 698 p. :
688.8 21
*Packaging -- Handbooks, manuals, etc.*

## TS205 Metal manufactures. Metalworking (Including metal forming and working) — General works

**TS205.B299 1999**
**Beddoes, Jonathan.**
Principles of metal manufacturing processes / J. Beddoes & M. J. Bibby. London : Arnold, 1999. ix, 336 p. :
671 21
*Metal-work. Manufacturing processes. Founding.*

**TS205.M52 1991**
**Mielnik, Edward M.**
Metalworking science and engineering / Edward M. Mielnik. New York : McGraw-Hill, c1991. 976 p. :
90031561        671        0070419043
*Metal-work.*

### TS225 Metal manufactures. Metalworking — Forging. Drop forging — General works

**TS225.F549 1985**
Forging handbook / Thomas G. Byrer, editor ; S.L. Semiatin, associate editor ; Donald C. Vollmer, associate editor. Cleveland, Ohio : Forging Industry Association ; c1985. ix, 296 p. :
85-071789        671.3/32        0871701944
*Forging -- Handbooks, manuals, etc.*

### TS227-227.2 Metal manufactures. Metalworking — Forging. Drop forging — History

**TS227.D22 1992**
**Davies, A. C. (Arthur Cyril)**
The science and practice of welding / A.C. Davies. 10th ed. Cambridge : New York, NY, USA : Cambridge University Press, 1992-c1993. 2 v. :
671.5/2 20
*Welding.*

**TS227.2.S38**
**Schwartz, Mel M.**
Metals joining manual / M. M. Schwartz. New York : McGraw-Hill, c1979. 556 p. in var
78-027886        671.5/02/02        0070557209
*Welding -- Handbooks, manuals, etc. Brazing -- Handbooks, manuals, etc. Solder and soldering -- Handbooks, manuals, etc.*

### TS320 Metal manufactures. Metalworking — Iron and steel — Steelworking. Tool steel

**TS320.B884 1997**
**Bryson, William E.**
Heat treatment, selection, and application of tool steels / by Bill Bryson. Cincinnati, Ohio : Hanser Gardner Publications, c1997. xi, 198 p. :
97-018613        621.9        1569902380
*Tool-steel. Tool-steel -- Heat treatment.*

**TS320.T66 1995**
Tool materials / edited by J.R. Davis. Materials Park, OH : ASM International, c1995. v, 501 p. :
95-003750        621.9        0871705451
*Tool-steel. Metal-cutting tools -- Materials. Dies (Metal-working) -- Materials.*

### TS533.2 Metal manufactures. Metalworking — Firearms. Guns — History

**TS533.2.W37 1975**
**Williamson, Harold Francis.**
Winchester: the gun that won the West / by Harold Francis Williamson. New York : Barnes and Co., c1952. xvi, 494 p. :
52011409        683.4        0498022994
*Winchester firearms.*

### TS533.62 Metal manufactures. Metalworking — Firearms. Guns — Biography

**TS533.62.C65.H67 1996**
**Hosley, William N.**
Colt : the making of an American legend / William Hosley. Amherst : University of Massachusetts Press, c1996. 254 p. :
96-024139        683.4/0092/2        1558490426
*Colt, Samuel, -- 1814-1862. Gunsmiths -- Connecticut – Hartford - - Biography. Colt revolver -- History. Hartford (Connecticut) -- History*

### TS542 Metal manufactures. Metalworking — Watches and clocks — History

**TS542.L24 2000**
**Landes, David S.**
Revolution in time : clocks and the making of the modern world / David S. Landes. Rev. and enl. ed. Cambridge, MA : Harvard University Press, 2000. xxiii, 518 p. :
681.1/13/09 21
*Clocks and watches -- History. Horology -- History.*

### TS610 Metal manufactures. Metalworking — Tinsmithing — Soldering

**TS610.H85 1993**
**Humpston, Giles.**
Principles of soldering and brazing / Giles Humpston, David M. Jacobson. Materials Park, OH : ASM International, c1993. xiii, 281 p.
93-070224        671.5/6        0871704625
*Solder and soldering. Brazing.*

**TS653 Metal manufactures. Metalworking — Metal finishing and surface treatment — General works**

**TS653.B87 1999**
**Burakowski, Tadeusz.**
 Surface engineering of metals : principles, equipment, technologies / Tadeusz Burakowski, Tadeusz Wierzchon. Boca Raton, Fla. : CRC Press, c1999. 592 p. :
98-042176      620.1/6      0849382254
 *Metals -- Surfaces. Surfaces (Technology)*

**TS670 Metal manufactures. Metalworking — Metal finishing and surface treatment — Electroplating. Electrometallurgy**

**TS670.P29 1998**
**Paunovic, Milan.**
 Fundamentals of electrochemical deposition / Milan Paunovic, Mordechay Schlesinger. New York : Wiley, c1998. viii, 301 p.
98-016435      671.7/32      0471168203
 *Electroplating.*

**TS670.M554 2000**
 Moder electroplating / edited by Mordechay Schlesinger, Milan Paunovic. 4th ed. New York : Wiley, 2000. xiv, 868 p. :
      671.7/32 21
*Electroplating.*

**TS695 Metal manufactures. Metalworking — Metal finishing and surface treatment — Vapor-plating. Chemical vapor deposition**

**TS695.G35 1991**
**Galasso, Francis S.**
 Chemical vapor deposited materials / author, Francis S. Galasso. Boca Raton, Fl : CRC Press, 1991. p. cm.
91-018251      671.7/35      0849342198
 *Vapor-plating. Materials.*

**TS722 Metal manufactures. Metalworking — Precious metals. Gold and silver work. Jewelry — Dictionaries and encyclopedias**

**TS722.B3713 1992**
**Bariand, Pierre.**
 The Larousse encyclopedia of precious gems / Pierre Bariand, Jean-Paul Poirot, in collaboration with Michel Duchamp for seals, cylinders, intaglios, and cameos ; photographs by Nelly Bariand ; translated by Emmanuel Fritsch. New York : Van Nostrand Reinhold, 1992. vii, 248 p. :
91-009256      553.8/03      0442302789
 *Precious stones -- Dictionaries.*

**TS752-753 Metal manufactures. Metalworking — Precious metals. Gold and silver work. Jewelry — Jewelry**

**TS752.O3 1988**
**O'Donoghue, Michael.**
 Gemstones / Michael O'Donoghue. London ; Chapman and Hall, 1988. xiv, 372 p. :
87-015746      553.8      041227390X
 *Precious stones.*

**TS752.R44 1998**
**Read, Peter G.**
 Gemmology / P.G. Read. 2nd ed. Oxford ; Boston : Butterworth-Heinemann, 1999. viii, 326 p. :
      553.8 21
*Precious stones.*

**TS752.Z45 1996**
**Zeitner, June Culp.**
 Gem and lapidary materials : for cutters, collectors, and jewelers / June Culp Zeitner. Tucson, Ariz. : Geoscience Press, 1996. ix, 347 p. :
96-075730      0945005180
 *Gems. Gem cutting. Minerals.*

**TS752.5.S56 1981**
**Sinkankas, John.**
 Gemstone & mineral data book : a compilation of data, recipes, formulas, and instructions for the mineralogist, gemologist, lapidary, jeweler, craftsman, and collector / John Sinkankas. New York : Van Nostrand Reinhold Co., 1981, c1972. 352 p. ;
80-052974      736/.2/028      0442247095
 *Gem cutting -- Handbooks, manuals, etc. Mineralogy -- Handbooks, manuals, etc.*

**TS753.T59**
**Tolansky, S.**
 The history and use of diamond. London, Methuen [1962] 166 p.
64001865      736.23
 *Diamonds.*

**TS880 Wood technology. Lumber — Wood products. Furniture — Furniture**

**TS880.E39 1994**
**Edwards, Clive,**
 Twenthieth-century furniture : materials, manufacture, and markets / Clive D. Edwards. Manchester ; Manchester University Press ; c1994. xii, 228 p. :
93-044612      338.4/76841/00904
0719040663
 *Furniture industry and trade -- History -- 20th century.*

## TS1090 Paper manufacture and trade — History — General works

**TS1090.H816 1978**
**Hunter, Dard,**
Papermaking : the history and technique of an ancient craft / by Dard Hunter. New York : Dover Publications, 1978, c1947. xxiv, 611, xx
77-092477      676/.2/09      0486236196
*Papermaking -- History. Watermarks -- History.*

**TS1090.R83 1987**
**Rudin, Bo.**
Making paper : a look into the history of an ancient craft / Bo Rudin. Vallingby, Sweden : Rudins, 1990. 278 p., [16]
            919708882X
*Papermaking -- History. Paper work.*

## TS1105 Paper manufacture and trade — General works — 1800-

**TS1105.K665 1991**
**Kline, James E.**
Paper and paperboard : manufacturing and converting fundamentals / James E. Kline. San Francisco : Miller Freeman Publications, c1991. 245 p. :
91-061732      676      0879301902
*Papermaking. Paperboard.*

**TS1105.S23**
**Saltman, David.**
Paper basics : forestry, manufacture, selection, purchasing, mathematics and metrics, recycling / David Saltman. New York : Van Nostrand Reinhold Co., c1978. xiv, 223 p. :
78-001476      676      0442252211
*Paper.*

## TS1120 Paper manufacture and trade — Chemistry of paper manufacture

**TS1120.P37 1991**
Paper chemistry / edited by J.C. Roberts. Glasgow : Blackie ; 1991. xiii, 234 p.
90-027806      676/.2      0216929091
*Papermaking -- Chemistry.*

## TS1120.5 Paper manufacture and trade — Paper recycling

**TS1120.5.P38 1991**
Paper recycling : strategies, economics, and technology / edited by Ken L. Patrick. San Francisco : Miller Freeman, c1991. vi, 202 p. :
91-061731      363.72/88      0879302313
*Waste paper -- Recycling.*

**TS1120.5.T46 1992**
**Thompson, Claudia G.**
Recycled papers : the essential guide / Claudia G. Thompson. Cambridge, Mass. : MIT Press, c1992. xiii, 162 p.
91-046091      676/.282      0262200899
*Waste paper -- Recycling -- United States.*

## TS1175 Paper manufacture and trade — Woodpulp industry. Pulping processes — General works

**TS1175.B54 1996**
**Biermann, Christopher J.**
Handbook of pulping and papermaking / Christopher J. Biermann. San Diego : Academic Press, c1996. xvi, 754 p.,
96-020451      676      0120973626
*Pulping. Papermaking.*

## TS1309 Textile industries — Dictionaries and encyclopedias

**TS1309.E53 1984**
Encyclopedia of textiles, fibers, and nonwoven fabrics / editor, Martin Grayson. New York : Wiley, c1984. xxvi, 581 p.
84-013213      677/.003/21      047181461X
*Textile fibers -- Dictionaries. Textile fabrics -- Dictionaries. Nonwoven fabrics -- Dictionaries.*

## TS1445 Textile industries — General works — 1800-

**TS1445.A18 1980**
Encyclopedia of textiles / by the editors of American fabrics and fashions magazine. Englewood Cliffs, N.J. : Prentice-Hall, c1980. xvi, 636 p. :
79-026497      677      0132765764
*Textile industry. Textile industry -- Dictionaries. Textile fabrics -- Dictionaries. Textile fabrics.*

**TS1445.A46 1974**
**American Home Economics Association.**
Textile handbook. Washington : American Home Economics Association, [1974] v, 121 p. :
74-031289      677/.002/02      0846116111
*Textile fabrics.*

## TS1449 Textile industries — General special (Including microscopy, testing, safety measures, yarn)

**TS1449.E42 1980**
**Emery, Irene.**
The primary structures of fabrics : an illustrated classification / by Irene Emery. Washington, D.C. : Textile Museum, 1980. xxvi, 341 p.
80-052671      677.6
*Textile fabrics -- Classification.*

**TS1449.P45**
**Peters, Raymond Harry,**
Textile chemistry. Amsterdam, Elsevier Pub. Co., 1963- v.
62016536          547.8
*Textile chemistry.*

## TS1474 Textile industries — Textile chemistry (Bleaching dyeing, printing of textiles)

**TS1474.C48 1995**
Chemistry of the textiles industry / edited by C.M. Carr. London ; Blackie Academic & Professional, 1995. xiii, 361 p.
94-073587          677/.02835          0751400548
*Textile chemistry.*

## TS1540 Textile industries — Textile fibers — General works

**TS1540.C639 1968**
**Cook, James Gordon.**
Handbook of textile fibres, by J. Gordon Cook. Watford (Herts.), Merrow Publishing Co., 1968. 2 v.
72-376353          677/.02
*Textile fibers. Textile fibers, Synthetic.*

## TS1548.5 Textile industries — Textile fibers — Synthetic textile fibers

**TS1548.5.W39 1995**
**Warner, Steven B.**
Fiber science / Steven B. Warner. Englewood Cliffs, NJ : Prentice Hall, c1995. xii, 316 p. :
94-013259          677/.4          0024245410
*Textile fibers, Synthetic.*

## TS1570 Textile industries — Cotton manufactures — Biography

**TS1570.W4.G7**
**Green, Constance McLaughlin,**
Eli Whitney and the birth of American technology. Boston, Little, Brown [1956] 215 p.
56-005930          926
*Whitney, Eli, 1765-1825.*

## TS1625 Textile industries — Woolen manufactures — General works

**TS1625.B9 1969**
**Burnley, James,**
The history of wool & woolcombing. New York, A. M. Kelley, 1969. xvi, 487 p.
68-055497          677/.3          0678005192
*Woolen and worsted manufacture -- History. Wool-combing.*

**TS1767.M66 1984**
**Montgomery, Florence M.**
Textiles in America, 1650-1870 : a dictionary based on original documents : prints and paintings, commercial records, American merchants' papers, shopkeepers' advertisements, and pattern books with Florence M. Montgomery. New York : Norton, 1984. xviii, 412 p.
83-025339          677/.02864/0973          0393017036
*Textile fabrics -- United States -- History. Textile fabrics -- United States -- Dictionaries.*

## TS1890 Rubber industry — General works

**TS1890.H69313 1989**
**Hofmann, Werner,**
Rubber technology handbook / Werner Hofmann ; [translated by Rudolf Bauer and E.A. Meinecke]. Munich ; Hanser Publishers ; c1989. xxv, 611, 15,
88-016251          678          0195207572
*Rubber industry and trade. Rubber, Artificial. Elastomers.*

**TS1890.M68**
**Morton, Maurice.**
Introduction to rubber technology. New York, Reinhold Pub. Corp. [1959] 547 p.
59015496          678.082
*Rubber industry and trade.*

**TS1890.S315 1994**
Science and technology of rubber / edited by James E. Mark, Burak Erman, Frederick R. Eirich. San Diego : Academic Press, c1994. xvi, 751 p.,
93-008796          678/.2          0124725252
*Rubber. Elastomers.*

## TS1925-1928 Rubber industry — Synthetic rubber. Elastomers

**TS1925.T445 1996**
Thermoplastic elastomers / edited by Geoffrey Holden ... [et al.]. Munich ; Hanser Publishers ; 1996. p. cm.
96-014538          678          1569902054
*Elastomers. Thermoplastics.*

**TS1928.H65 2000**
**Holden, G.**
Understanding thermoplastic elastomers / Geoffrey Holden. Munich : Hanser ; 2000. vii, 110 p. :
99-047357          678          1569902895
*Elastomers. Thermoplastics. Copolymers.*

**TS1963 Miscellaneous industries — Animal products
— Special countries**

**TS1963.E37 1997**
**Eisnitz, Gail A.**
   Slaughterhouse : the shocking story of greed, neglect, and inhumane treatment inside the U.S. meat industry / Gail A. Eisnitz. Amherst, NY : Prometheus Books, 1997. 310 p. :
97-027643          664/.9029/0973          1573921661
*Slaughtering and slaughter-houses -- United States. Animal welfare – United States. Meat inspection -- United States. Meat industry and trade -- United States.*

# TT Handicrafts. Arts and crafts

## TT12 Directories

**TT12.B683 1999**
**Boyd, Margaret Ann,**
   Crafts supply sourcebook / Margeret A. Boyd. 5th ed. Cincinnati, Ohio : Betterway Books, c1999. 282 p. :
          745.5/029/473 21
*handicraft -- United States -- Equipment and supplies -- Directories. Handicraft -- Canada -- Equipment and supplies -- Directories.*

## TT23-127 History and country divisions ( General works on the crafts as practiced in particular regions or countries, manuals on how to duplicate craft articles from specific regions or countries)

**TT23.S73 1988**
**Stapleton, Constance,**
   Crafts of America / Constance Stapleton. New York : Harper & Row, c1988. xx, 341 p. :
87-045671          680/.973          0060960795
   *Handicraft -- United States.*

**TT127.G53 2000**
**Gianturco, Paola.**
   In her hands : craftswomen changing the world / Paola Gianturco and Toby Tuttle ; foreword by Alice Walker. Huntington, N.Y. : Monacelli Press, 2000. p. cm.
00-033960          745/.082/091724          1580930689
   *Handicraft -- Developing countries. Women artisans -- Developing countries -- Interviews.*

**TT175 Articles for children — Dolls — General works**

**TT175.L37**
**Lasky, Kathryn.**
   Dollmaker : the eyelight and the shadow / text by Kathryn Lasky ; photographs by Christopher G. Knight. New York : Scribner, [1981] 64 p. :
81-009262          745.592/21          0684171708
   *Dollmaking -- Juvenile literature. Dollmaking.*

**TT180 Articles for children — Woodworking —
General works
— Woodworking — General works**

**TT180.H59 2000**
**Hoadley, R. Bruce.**
   Understanding wood : a craftsman's guide to wook technology / R. Bruce Hoadley. Newtown, CT : Taunton Press, c2000. 280 p. :
          684/.08 21
*Woodwork. Wood.*

## TT185 Woodworking — Elementary works, outline, syllabi, etc. (Including amateurs' manuals)

**TT185.H3915 1972**
**Hayward, Charles Harold,**
   The complete book of woodwork [by] Charles H. Hayward. New York, Drake Publishers [1972, c1959] 344 p.
70-178085          684/.08          0877491623
   *Woodwork -- Amateurs' manuals.*

### TT205 Metal working — General works

**TT205.V35 1996**
**Vandkilde, Helle.**
   From stone to bronze : the metalwork of the late neolithic and earliest bronze age in Denmark / by Helle Vandkilde ; with a contribution by Peter Northover. Moesgard, Aarhus : Jutland Archaeological Society, 1996. 493 p. :
97-101667          8772885823
   *Metal-work -- Denmark. Neolithic period – Denmark. Bronze age -- Denmark. Denmark -- Antiquities.*

### TT267 Metal working — Soldering and brazing

**TT267.M26 1979**
**Manko, Howard H.**
   Solders and soldering : materials, design, production, and analysis for reliable bonding / Howard H. Manko. New York : McGraw-Hill, c1979. xv, 350 p. :
79-009714          671.5/6          0070398976
   *Solder and soldering.*

## TT270 Metal working — Stencil cutting. Stencil work — General works

**TT270.M53 1978**
**Midkiff, Pat.**
The complete book of stenciling : furniture decoration & restoration / Pat Midkiff. New York : Drake Publishers, 1978. 159 p. :
77-088949          745.7/3          0847316688
*Stencil work.*

## TT273 Metal working — Stencil cutting. Stencil work — Screen process work. Silk-screen printing

**TT273.B49**
**Biegeleisen, J. I.**
The complete book of silk screen printing production. With an introd. by Carl S. Auerbach. New York, Dover Publications [1963] xi, 253 p.
63-017898          655.316
*Screen process printing.*

## TT387 Soft home furnishings — Curtain making. Drapes

**TT387.W45 1987**
**Weissman, Judith Reiter.**
Labors of love : America's textiles and needlework, 1650-1930 / Judith Reiter Weissman and Wendy Lavitt ; photographs by Schecter Lee. New York : Knopf : 1987. xiii, 286 p.
87-045133          746/.0973          0394542401
*House furnishings -- United States -- History. Needlework -- United States -- History. Textile crafts -- United States -- History.*

## TT494 Clothing and manufacture (Including the garment industry) — Dictionaries and encyclopedias

**TT494.G56**
**Gioello, Debbie Ann.**
Fashion production terms / Debbie Ann Gioello, Beverly Berke. New York : Fairchild Publications, c1979. xi, 340 p. :
78-062284          687/.01/4          0870052004
*Clothing trade -- Terminology. Fashion -- Terminology.*

## TT497 Clothing and manufacture — General works

**TT497.K44**
**Kidwell, Claudia Brush.**
Suiting everyone: the democratization of clothing in America [by] Claudia B. Kidwell [and] Margaret C. Christman. Washington, Published for the National Museum of History and 1974. 208 p.
74-016239          391/.00973
*Clothing trade -- United States -- History. Costume -- United States -- History.*

## TT503 Clothing and manufacture — Dressmaking and women's tailoring. Fashion — Dictionaries and encyclopedias

**TT503.C34 1998**
**Calasibetta, Charlotte Mankey.**
Fairchild's dictionary of fashion / Charlotte Mankey Calasibetta. 2nd ed., rev. New York : Fairchild Books, c1998. xii, 685 p. :
           391/.003 21
*Fashion -- Dictionaries.  Costume -- Dictionaries.*

## TT504 Clothing and manufacture — Dressmaking and women's tailoring. Fashion — History of dressmaking and tailoring

**TT504.D45**
**De Marly, Diana.**
The history of haute couture, 1850-1950 / Diana de Marly. New York : Holmes and Meier, c1980. 216 p., [4] l
79-022987          391/.07/2          084190586X
*Fashion -- History -- 19th century. Fashion -- History -- 20th century.*

**TT504.W38**
**Waugh, Norah.**
The cut of men's clothes, 1600-1900.  New York, Theatre Arts Books [1964] 160 p.
64021658          391.109          0878300252
*Tailoring -- History.*

## TT505 Clothing and manufacture — Dressmaking and women's tailoring. Fashion — Biography

**TT505.A1.C66 1995**
Contemporary fashion / editor, Richard Martin. New York : St. James Press, c1995. xviii, 575 p.
95-023329          746.9/2/0922          1558621733
*Fashion designers -- Biography -- Encyclopedias. Costume design -- History -- 20th century -- Encyclopedias. Fashion – History – 20th century -- Encyclopedias.*

## TT507 Clothing and manufacture — Dressmaking and women's tailoring. Fashion — Art of dress. Theory. Aesthetics. Costume design

**TT507.I454 2000**
Individuality in clothing selection and personal apearance / Suzanne G. Marshall ... [et al.]. 5th ed. Upper Saddle River, J.J. : Prentice Hall, c2000. xviii, 436 p. :
           646/.3 21
*Clothing and dress -- Psychological aspects. Fashion – Psychological aspects. Costume design.*

**TT507.P84 1985**
The Psychology of fashion / edited by Michael R. Solomon. Lexington, Mass. : Lexington Books, c1985. xii, 428 p. :
84-048079          391/.2/019          0669091286
*Fashion -- Psychological aspects.*

### TT509 Clothing manufacture — Dressmaking and women's tailoring. Fashion — Fashion drawing

**TT509.M33 1997**
**Mackrell, Alice.**
An illustrated history of fashion : 500 years of fashion illustration / Alice Mackrell. New York : Costume & Fashion Press, 1997. p. cm.
        741.6/72 21
*Fashion drawing -- History.*

### TT699 Home arts. Homecrafts — Textile arts and crafts — General works

**TT699.P67 1998**
**Porcella, Yvonne.**
Art & inspirations / Yvonne Porcella. LaFayette, CA : C&T Pub., c1998. 143 p. :
98-004700       746.46     1571200568
*Textile crafts. Quilting. Quilted goods.*

### TT705-715 Home arts. Homecrafts — Textile arts and crafts — Sewing. Needlework

**TT705.C37**
**Carbone, Linda.**
Dictionary of sewing terminology / Linda Carbone. New York : Arco, c1977. 151 p. :
77-002559       646.2/03       0668040394
*Sewing -- Dictionaries.*

**TT715.S9**
**Swan, Susan Burrows.**
Plain & fancy : American women and their needlework, 1700-1850 / Susan Burrows Swan. New York : Holt, Rinehart and Winston, c1977. 240 p. :
77-001627       301.41/2       003015121X
*Needlework -- United States -- History.*

### TT847 Home arts. Homecrafts — Textile arts and crafts — Hand spinning

**TT847.R669 1988**
**Ross, Mabel.**
Encyclopedia of handspinning / Mabel Ross. Loveland, Colo. : Interweave Press, 1988. 224 p., [4] p
87-046354       746.1/4/0321     0934026327
*Hand spinning -- Encyclopedias.*

### TT848 Home arts. Homecrafts — Textile arts and crafts — Hand weaving

**TT848.B5 1980**
**Black, Mary E.**
The key to weaving : a textbook of hand weaving for the beginning weaver / Mary E. Black. New York : Macmillan, c1980. xvii, 698 p.
79-026177       746.1/4       0025111701
*Hand weaving.*

**TT848.H39 1990**
**Hecht, Ann.**
The art of the loom : weaving, spinning, and dyeing across the world / Ann Hecht. New York : Rizzoli, 1990. 208 p. :
89-061382       746.1       0847811476
*Hand weaving. Hand spinning. Dyes and dyeing.*

**TT848.M47 1987**
**Mera, H. P.**
Spanish-American blanketry : its relationship to aboriginal weaving in the Southwest / by H.P. Mera ; with an introduction by Kate Peck Kent ; and a foreword by E. Boyd. Santa Fe, N.M. : School of American Research Press, c1987. ix, 80 p., [1
87-012879       746.9/7/089680789
0933452217
*Hand weaving -- Southwest, New -- History. Blankets -- Southwest, New.*

### TT851 Home arts. Homecrafts — Textile arts and crafts — Textile decoration

**TT851.D79 1993**
**Dryden, Deborah M.**
Fabric painting and dyeing for the theatre / Deborah M. Dryden. Portsmouth, NH : Heinemann, c1993. xiv, 256 p.,
93-031128       746.6       0435086243
*Textile painting. Dyes and dyeing -- Textile fibers. Costume.*

### TT919.5 Home arts. Homecrafts — Decorative crafts — Other special techniques

**TT919.5.H35 1997**
**Hamer, Frank.**
The potter's dictionary of materials and techniques / Frank and Janet Hamer. 4th ed. London ; Philadelphia : A & C Black ; University of Pennsylvania Press, 1997. ix, 406 p. :
        738.1/03 21
*Pottery craft -- Dictionaries. Ceramic materials -- Dictionaries.*

# TX Home economics

### TX15 History and antiquities (Including manners and customs, gastronomy, etc.) — General works

**TX15.D8 1988**
**Du Vall, Nell.**
Domestic technology : a chronology of developments / Nell Du Vall. Boston, Mass. : G.K. Hall, c1988. xi, 535 p. ;
88-021110       640/.9       0816189137
*Home economics -- History. Domestic engineering -- History.*

## TX23 Special countries

**TX23.C64 1983**
**Cowan, Ruth Schwartz,**
   More work for mother : the ironies of household technology from the open hearth to the microwave / Ruth Schwartz Cowan. New York : Basic Books, c1983. xiv, 257 p. :
83-070759          640/.973          0465047319
   *Home economics -- United States -- History. Household appliances -- United States -- History. Housewives -- United States -- History.*

**TX23.S77 1982**
**Strasser, Susan,**
   Never done : a history of American housework / Susan Strasser. New York : Pantheon Books, c1982. xvi, 365 p. :
81-048234          640/.973          0394510240
   *Home economics -- United States -- History. Housewives -- United States -- History.*

## TX158 Pocketbooks, tables, receipts, etc. — 20th century

**TX158.P24 1995**
**Palma, Robert J.,**
   The complete guide to household chemicals / Robert J. Palma, Sr. with Mark Espenscheid. Amherst, N.Y. : Prometheus Books, 1995. 325 p. ;
94-021778          640          0879759836
   *Home economics. Consumer education. Household supplies.*

## TX298 Household apparatus and utensils — General works

**TX298.C58 1982**
**Cohen, Daniel,**
   The last hundred years, household technology / by Daniel Cohen. New York : M. Evans, c1982. 184 p. :
82-015442          683/.8          0871313863
   *Household appliances -- United States -- History -- Juvenile literature. Technology -- United States -- History -- Juvenile literature. Household appliances -- History.*

## TX335 Shopping. Consumer education (Including shopping guides and directories of discount and outlet stores) — General works

**TX335.C669 1993**
   Consumers' guide to product grades and terms : from grade A to VSOP--definitions of 8,000 terms describing food, housewares, and other everyday items / Timothy L. Gall and Susan B. Gall [editors]. Detroit : Gale Research, c1993. xxiii, 603 p.
92-040255          381.3/3/0973          0810388987
   *Consumer goods -- Evaluation. Quality of products. Consumer goods -- Labeling.*

## TX349 Nutrition. Foods and food supply — Dictionaries and encyclopedias (Including dictionaries of cookery)

**TX349.D36 1999**
**Davidson, Alan,**
   The Oxford companion to food / Alan Davidson ; illustrations by Soun Vannithone. Oxford : Oxford University Press, 1999. xviii, 892 p.
00-388324          641.3/003          0192115790
   *Food -- Encyclopedias. Cookery -- Encyclopedias. Food habits -- Encyclopedias.*

**TX349.F575 1994**
   Foods & nutrition encyclopedia / Audrey H. Ensminger ... [et al.]. Boca Raton : CRC Press, c1994. 2 v. (viii, 2
93-036692          641/.03          0849389801
   *Nutrition -- Encyclopedias. Food -- Encyclopedias.*

**TX349.M67 1996**
**Morton, Mark Steven,**
   Cupboard love : a dictionary of culinary curiousities / Mark Morton. Winnipeg : Blizzard Pub., 1996. 399 p. ;
96920067          641.5/03          0921368666
   *Cookery -- Dictionaries.*

**TX349.P353 2000**
**Palmatier, Robert A.**
   Food : a dictionary of literal and nonliteral terms / Robert A. Palmatier. Westport, CT : Greenwood Press, 2000. xix, 461 p. ;
99-088203          641.3/003          0313314365
   *Food -- Dictionaries.*

## TX353 Nutrition. Foods and food supply — General works. Sources, supply, etc.

**TX353.C255 2000**
   The Cambridge world history of food / editors, Kenneth F. Kiple, Kriemhild Conee Ornelas. Cambridge, UK ; Cambridge University Press, 2000. 2 v. (xlii, 2
00-057181          641.3/09          052140214X
   *Food -- History.*

**TX353.C623 2000**
**Cooper, Ann.**
   Bitter harvest : a chef's perspective on the hidden dangers in the foods we eat and what you can do about it / Ann Cooper with Lisa M. Holmes. New York : Routledge, 2000. 278 p. :
          641.3 21
*Food. Food supply.*

**TX353.L23 1994**
**Lacey, Richard**
   Hard to swallow : a brief history of food / Richard W. Lacey. Cambridge [England] ; Cambridge University Press, 1994. xi, 340 p. :
93-020808          641.3          0521440017
   *Food. Food industry and trade. Food contamination.*

## TX354 Nutrition. Foods and food supply — General works. Sources, supply, etc. — Textbooks

**TX354.G8 1983**
**Guthrie, Helen Andrews.**
Introductory nutrition / Helen A. Guthrie. St. Louis : Mosby, 1983. vii, 675 p. :
82-008084            613.2            0801619971
*Nutrition. Nutrition.*

**TX355 Nutrition. Foods and food supply — Popular works. Juvenile works**

**TX355.T72 1995**
**Trager, James.**
The food chronology : a food lover's compendium of events and anecdotes from prehistory to the present / James Trager. 1st ed. New York : Henry Holt, 1995. xiii, 783 p. :
641/.09 20
*Food -- History -- Chronology. Chronology, Historical.*

## TX356 Nutrition. Foods and food supply — Addresses, essays, lectures

**TX356.S74 1995**
**Steinman, David.**
The safe shopper's bible : a consumer's guide to nontoxic household products, cosmetics, and food / David Steinman & Samuel S. Epstein ; [foreword by Ralph Nader]. New York, NY : Macmillan USA, c1995. xvi, 445 p. :
95-002841            640/.73            0020820852
*Grocery shopping. Household supplies -- Toxicology. Consumer goods -- Toxicology.*

## TX357 Nutrition. Foods and food supply — General special (Including dietitians, food economy in war time)

**TX357.A65 1996**
Why we eat what we eat : the psychology of eating / edited by Elizabeth D. Capaldi. Washington, DC : American Psychological Association, c1996. ix, 339 p. :
96-033870            394.1/019            1557983666
*Food habits -- Psychological aspects. Nutrition -- Psychological aspects. Food preferences.*

## TX359 Nutrition. Foods and food supply — Nutrition policy

**TX359.E38 1995**
Eating agendas : food and nutrition as social problems / Donna Maurer and Jeffery Sobal, editors. New York : Aldine de Gruyter, c1995. xiv, 345 p. :
94-049387            363.8            0202305074
*Nutrition policy. Food -- Social aspects. Nutrition -- Social aspects.*

**TX359.R48**
**Reutlinger, Shlomo.**
Malnutrition and poverty : magnitude and policy options / Shlomo Reutlinger, Marcelo Selowsky. Baltimore : Published for the World Bank [by] Johns Hopkins c1976. xii, 82 p. :
76-017240            362.5            0801818680
*Nutrition policy -- Developing countries. Nutrition – Developing countries.*

## TX360 Nutrition. Foods and food supply — Diet, food supply, nutrition policy of special countries by region or country, A-Z

**TX360.U6.P55 1998**
**Pillsbury, Richard.**
No foreign food : the American diet in time and place / Richard Pillsbury. Boulder, Colo. : Westview Press, 1998. x, 262 p. :
97-047342            394.1/0973            0813327385
*Diet -- United States -- History. Food habits -- United States – History.*

**TX360.U6.S58 1998**
**Sims, Laura S.,**
The politics of fat : food and nutrition policy in America / Laura S. Sims. Armonk, N.Y. : M.E. Sharpe, c1998. xiv, 311 p. :
97-026608            363.8/56/0973            0765601931
*Nutrition policy -- United States. Food -- Fat content. Lipids in human nutrition.*

## TX360.5 Nutrition. Foods and food supply —Diet, food supply, nutrition policy of special countries by region or country, A-Z — Developing countries

**TX360.5.B47 1987**
**Berg, Alan.**
Malnutrition : what can be done? : lessons from World Bank experience / Alan Berg. Baltimore : Published for the World Bank [by] Johns Hopkins c1987. x, 139 p. ;
87-045493            363.8/56/091724            0801835534
*Nutrition policy -- Developing countries. Diet -- Developing countries.*

## TX361 Nutrition. Foods and food supply — Diet and nutrition of special classes and groups, A-Z

**TX361.A8.D75 2000**
**Driskell, Judy A.**
Sports nutrition / Judy A. Driskell. Boca Raton, FL : CRC Press, 2000. 280 p. :
99-026360            613.2/024/796            0849381975
*Athletes -- Nutrition. Physical fitness -- Nutritional aspects.*

**TX361.A8.N88 1998**

Nutrition in exercise and sport / edited by Ira Wolinsky. Boca Raton : CRC Press, c1998. 684 p. :
97-008495          613.2/024/796          0849385601
*Athletes -- Nutrition. Exercise -- Physiological aspects.*

**TX361.A8E39 2000**
**Eberle, Suzanne Girard,**

Endurance sports nutrition / Suzanne Girard Eberle. Champaign, IL : Human Kinetics, c2000. viii, 286 p.
00-025081          613.2/024/796          0736001433
*Athletes -- Nutrition.*

**TX361.A8S673 2000**

Sports nutrition : a guide for the professional working with active people / Christine Rosenbloom, editor ; Sports, Cardiovascular, and Wellness Nutritionists Dietetic Practice Group, The American Dietetic Association. Chicago : The American Dietetic Association, c2000. viii, 759 p.
99-052142          613.2/088/796          088091176X
*Athletes -- Nutrition.*

## TX369 Nutrition. Foods and food supply — Natural foods

**TX369.W67 1988**
**Wood, Rebecca Theurer.**

The whole foods encyclopedia : a shopper's guide / Rebecca Wood ; foreword by Michio Kushi. New York : Prentice Hall Press, c1988. xv, 218 p. :
87-043152          641.3/02/0321          0139585540
*Natural foods -- Encyclopedias.*

## TX392 Nutrition. Foods and food supply — Vegetable foods — Vegetarianism

**TX392.H528 1996**
**Hill, John L.**

The case for vegetarianism : philosophy for a small planet / John Lawrence Hill. Lanham, Md. : Rowman & Littlefield Publishers, 1996. xvii, 199 p.
95-026192          613.2/62          0847681378
*Vegetarianism.*

**TX392.S72 1996**
**Spencer, Colin.**

The heretic's feast : a history of vegetarianism / Colin Spencer. Hanover, NH : University Press of New England, 1996. xiii, 402 p.
95-005004          613.2/62/09          0874517605
*Vegetarianism -- History.*

## TX406 Nutrition. Foods and food supply — Condiments, spices, etc. — General works

**TX406.D35 2000**
**Dalby, Andrew,**

Dangerous tastes : the story of spices / Andrew Dalby. Berkeley : University of California Press, 2000. 184 p. :
00-034376          641.3/383          0520227891
*Spices -- History.*

**TX406.S57 1994**
**Skelly, Carole J.,**

Dictionary of herbs, spices, seasonings, and natural flavorings / by Carole J. Skelly. New York : Garland Pub., 1994. xiii, 484 p.
93-028205          641.3/382/03          0815314655
*Spices -- Dictionaries. Herbs -- Dictionaries. Cookery (Herbs) – Dictionaries.*

## TX531 Nutrition. Foods and food supply — Examination and analysis. Composition. Adulteration — General works

**TX531.F685 1999**

Food safety sourcebook : basic comsumer health information about the safe handling of meat ... / edited by Dawn D. Matthews. 1st ed. Detroit, MI : Omnigraphics, c1999. xii, 339 p. :
                    363.19/2 21
*Food adulteration and inspection. Food industry and trade – Safety measures.*

**TX531.R44 2000**
**Redman, Nina.**

Food safety : a reference handbook / Nina E. Redman. Santa Barbara, Calif. : ABC-CLIO, 2000. xiv, 317 p. ;
00-010427          363.19/2          1576071588
*Food adulteration and inspection -- Handbooks, manuals, etc. Food industry and trade -- Safety measures -- Handbooks, manuals, etc.*

## TX545 Nutrition. Foods and food supply — Examination and analysis. Composition. Adulteration — Analysis

**TX545.C44 1997**

Chemical and functional properties of food components / edited by Zdzislaw E. Sikorski. Lancaster, Pa. : Technomic Pub. Co., c1997. xii, 293 p. :
96-061440          664/.07          1566764645
*Food -- Analysis. Food -- Composition.*

## TX551-553 Nutrition. Foods and food supply — Examination and analysis. Composition. Adulteration — Dietary studies, food values, experiments, tests, etc.

**TX551.H264 1982**
Handbook of nutritive value of processed food / Miloslav Rechcigl, Jr., editor. Boca Raton, Fla. : CRC Press, c1982. 2 v. :
80-021652      641.1      0849339510
    *Food -- Composition. Feeds -- Composition. Food industry and trade.*

**TX551.H274 2000**
**Hands, Elizabeth S.**
    Nutrients in food / Elizabeth S. Hands. Philadelphia : Lippincott Williams & Wilkins, c2000. xi, 315 p. ;
99-017028      613.2      0683307053
    *Food -- Composition -- Tables. Food analysis -- Tables.*

**TX551.N38**
**National Research Council (U.S.).**
    Recommended dietary allowances. Washington. v.
63065472
    *Diet.*

**TX553.A3.A84 1995**
    Handbook of food additives : an international guide to more than 7,000 products by trade name, chemical, function, and manufacturer / compiled by Michael and Irene Ash. Aldershot, Hampshire, England ; Gower, c1995. xiv, 1025 p.
94-031149      664/.06      056607592X
    *Food additives. Food additives -- Dictionaries.*

## TX601 Nutrition. Foods and food supply — Preservation and storage of foods in the home. Food handling in the home — General works

**TX601.H54 1991**
**Greene, Janet C.**
    Putting food by / Janet Greene, Ruth Hertzberg, Beatrice Vaughan. 4th ed., newly rev. New York : Dutton, [1991] vi, 420 p. :
     641.4 20
    *Food -- Preservation.*

## TX645 Cookery — History

**TX645.S97 2000**
**Symons, Michael,**
    A history of cooks and cooking / Michael Symons. Urbana, IL : University of Illinois Press, 2000. xii, 388 p. :
99-049876      641.5/09      0252025806
    *Cookery -- History. Cooks.*

## TX649 Cookery — Biography — Individual, A-Z

**TX649.A1**
**McFeely, Mary Drake.**
    Can she bake a cherry pie? : American women and the kitchen in the twentieth century / Mary Drake McFeely. Amherst : University of Massachusetts Press, c2000. x, 194 p. ;
00-023452      641.5973/082      155849250X
    *Women cooks -- United States -- History -- 20th century. Cookery, American -- History -- 20th century.*

## TX651 Cookery — General works — Treatises

**TX651.B37 1977**
**Beard, James,**
    James Beard's theory & practice of good cooking / [James Beard] ; in collaboration with Jose Wilson ; ill. by Karl Stuecklen. New York : Knopf, 1977. ix, 465 p. :
76-047701      641.5
    *Cookery.*

## TX715-725 Cookery — Cookbooks — 1800-

**TX715.G624 1955**
**Good Housekeeping Institute (New York, N.Y.)**
    Good Housekeeping cook book, ed. by Dorothy B. Marsh. New York, Rinehart [1955] 760 p.
54010951      641.5
    *Cookery, American.*

**TX715.H3937 2000**
**Hayes, Joanne Lamb.**
    Grandma's wartime kitchen : World War II and the way we cooked / Joanne Lamb Hayes. 1st ed. New York : St. Martin's Press, 2000. xii, 244 p. :
     641.597./09/044 21
*Cookery, American -- History -- 2oth century. World War, 1939-1945 -- Food Supply -- United States.*

**TX715.R75 1975**
**Rombauer, Irma von Starkloff,**
    Joy of cooking / Irma S. Rombauer, Marion Rombauer Becker ; illustrated by Ginnie Hofmann and Ikki Matsumoto. Indianapolis : Bobbs-Merrill, [1975] xii, 915 p. :
75-010772      641.5973      0672518317
    *Cookery, American.*

**TX715.W874 1955**
**Woman's home companion.**
    Woman's home companion cook book, edited by Dorothy Kirk. New York, Collier, [c1955] 987 p.
55008003
    *Cookery, American.*

**TX715.L822 2000**
**Longacre, Doris Janzen.**
More-with-less cookbook / Doris Janzen Lonacre ; foreword by Mary Emma Showalter Eby ; foreword to Anniversary edition by Mary Beth Lind. 25th anniversary ed. Scottdale, PA : Herald Press, c2000. viii, 328 p. :
641.5/66 21
*Cookery, Mennonite.*

**TX719.B388**
**Beck, Simone.**
Mastering the art of French cooking, by Simone Beck, Louisette Bertholle [and] Julia Child. New York, Knopf, 1961-70. 2 v.
61-012313          641.5944
*Cookery, French.*

**TX725.N4.K43 1969**
**Kerr, Graham.**
The Graham Kerr cookbook, by the Galloping Gourmet. Photography, Hubert Sieben. Garden City, N.Y., Doubleday, 1969. 284 p.
75-095291          641.59931
*Cookery, New Zealand.*

## TX814.5 Cookery — Other, A-Z

**TX814.5.P66.S62 1999**
**Smith, Andrew F.,**
Popped culture : a social history of popcorn in America / Andrew F. Smith. Columbia, S.C. : University of South Carolina Press, c1999. xxi, 264 p. :
98-040193          641.6/5677          1570033005
*Cookery (Popcorn) Popcorn -- History. Popcorn -- Social aspects.*

## TX820 Cookery — Cookery for large numbers. Institutional cookery

**TX820.M57 2001**
**Molt, Mary,**
Food for fifty / Mary Molt. 11th ed. Upper Saddle River, N.J. : Prentice Hall, c2001. xv, 766 p. :
641.5/7 21
*Quantity cookery. Menus.*

**TX820.S355 1990**
**Schmidt, Arno,**
Chef's book of formulas, yields, and sizes / Arno Schmidt. New York, N.Y. : Van Nostrand Reinhold, c1990. vi, 338 p. ;
89-033711          641.5/7          0442318359
*Quantity cookery.*

## TX837 Cookery — Other special varieties of cookery — Vegetarian. Lenten. Fast day

**TX837.R6 1986**
**Robertson, Laurel.**
The new Laurel's kitchen : a handbook for vegetarian cookery & nutrition / Laurel Robertson, Carol flinders & Brian Ruppenthal. Berkeley, Calif. L : Ten Speed Press, c1986. 511 p. :
641.5/636 19
*Vegetarian cookery. Nutrition.*

## TX909 Hospitality industry. Hotels, clubs, restaurants, etc. Food service — History — Special countries

**TX909.J35 1996**
**Jakle, John A.**
The motel in America / John A. Jakle, Keith A. Sculle, Jefferson S. Rogers. Baltimore : Johns Hopkins University Press, 1996. xiv, 387 p. :
96-014762          647.9473/02          0801853834
*Motels -- United States -- History. Architecture, Modern – 20th century -- United States. Roadside architecture -- United States.*

## TX911.3 Hospitality industry. Hotels, clubs, restaurants, etc. Food service — Special topis, A-Z

**TX911.3.M27.Y82 1999**
**Yu, Lawrence.**
The international hospitality business : management and operations / Larry Yu. New York : Haworth Press, c1999. xv, 404 p. :
98-049067          647.94/068          078900559X
*Hospitality industry -- Management. International business enterprises -- Management.*

**TX911.3.S24.H46 1999**
**Hemminger, Jane M.**
Food safety : a guide to what you really need to know / prepared by Jane Hemminger ; approved by the Iowa Dietetic Association ; reviewed for publication by Bonnie Moeller ... [et al.]. Ames, Iowa : Iowa State University Press, 1999. p. cm.
99-045971          647.95/068/4          0813824826
*Food service -- Safety measures -- Handbooks, manuals, etc. Food service -- Sanitation -- Handbooks, manuals, etc.*

## TX945 Hospitality industry. Hotels, clubs, restaurants, etc. Food service — Food service (Including room service) — General works

**TX945.J35 1999**
**Jakle, John A.**
   Fast food : roadside restaurants in the automobile age / John A. Jakle & Keith A. Sculle. Baltimore, Md : Johns Hopkins University Press, 1999. xiii, 394 p.
98-049864            647.9573/0973/0904
0801861098
   *Roadside restaurants -- United States -- History. Fast food restaurants -- United States -- History. Architecture, Modern – 20th century -- United States.*

## TX950.59 Taverns, barrooms, saloons — Societies, etc.

**TX950.59.A8.K57 1997**
**Kirkby, Diane Elizabeth.**
   Barmaids : a history of womens work in pubs / Diane Kirkby. Cambridge ; Cambridge University, 1997. xii, 244 p. :
97-017304            305.43/642            0521560381
   *Cocktail servers -- Australia -- History. Bartenders -- Australia – History. Feminism -- Australia -- History.*

# INDEXES

Berry, Michael W. TK5105.884.B47 1999

Berry, Richard. QB88.B47 2001

Bersuker, I. B. QD172.T6.B48 1996

Berta, Annalisa. QL713.2.B47 1999

Berthoz, A. QP493.B47 2000

Bertin, G. QB858.42.B47 1996

Bessette, Alan. QK617.B483 1997, QK629.B6.B47 2000

Best, Charles Herbert. QP34.B5 1963, QP34.B54 1966, QP34.5.B47 1985

Best, Myron G. QE461.B53 1982

Bethe, Hans Albrecht. QC173.B48 1956

Betounes, David. QA377.B53 1998

Betteridge, W. TN799.N6.B45 1984

Beutelspacher, Albrecht. QA471.B5613 1998

Bevis, William W. SD538.3.M4.B48 1995

Beyer, Hans. QD251.2.B4813 1996

Beyer, William H. QA276.25.B48 1968

Bezner, Lili Corbus. TR23.B48 1999

Bhaduri, Sumit. TP156.C35

Bharath, Ramachandran. QA76.87.B53 1994

Bhavikatti, S. S. TA350.B48 1994

Bhote, Keki R. TS156.B563 1999

Bhushan, Bharat. TJ1075.B47 1991

Bidwell, Percy Wells. S441.B5 1941

Bidwell, R. G. S. QK711.2.B54 1979

Biegeleisen, J. I. TT273.B49

Biek, David. QK192.B54 2000

Biel, Andrew. QM23.2.B53 1997

Bier, Ethan. QH453.B53 2000

Biermann, Alan W. QA76.B495 1997

Biermann, Christopher J. TS1175.B54 1996

Biggs, Lindy. TS178.B54 1996

Biggs, Norman. QA76.73.P2.B54 1989

Bijker, Wiebe E. T14.5.B54 1995

Bilitewski, Bernd. TD791.B5613 1996

Billingham, J. QA927.B25 2000

Billings, Marland Pratt. QE601.B5 1972

Billington, David P. TA15.B53 1996

Bilodeau, Martin. QA278.B55 1999

Biondo, Samuel J. QA76.76.E95.B57 1990

Bir, R. E. SB439.B49 1992

Bird, J. O. TK454.B48 1997

Bird, Marion H. QA135.5.B533 1991

Birge, Edward Asahel. QH434.B57 1988

Birkeland, Peter W. S592.2.B57 1984

Birkhead, T. R. QL761.B57 2000

Birney, D. Scott. QB145.B52 1990

Bisgrove, Richard. SB466.G7, SB470.J38.B57 1992

Bishop, A. C. QE363.8.B56 1999

Bishop, Christopher M. QA76.87.B574 1995

Bishop, Margaret S. QE36.B5

Bishop, O. N. QC39.B57 1984

Bissell, C. C. TK5103.7.B54 1992

Biswas, A. K. TN780.B57 1994

Bittencourt, J. A. QC718.B45 1986

Bjorck, Ake. QA214.B56 1996

Bjorken, James D. QC174.1.B52

Black, Brian. TN872.P4

Black, C. A. S591.B56

Black, Mary E. TT848.B5 1980

Blackburn, James A. Q185.B563 2001

Blackman, David S. QP551.B53 1994

Blackman, William C. TD1040.B53 1992

Blaedel, Niels. QC16.B63.B5713 1988

Blair, Ann. Q125.2.B53 1997

Blair, Gordon P. TJ790.B577 1999

Blaise, Clark. QB223.B58 2000

Blakemore, J. S. QC176.B63 1985

Blakeslee, Ann M. QC5.3.B53 2001

Bland, Will. QE570.B5685 1998

Blandford, Percy W. S674.5.B55 1976

Blaskett, D. R. TN785.B63 1990

Blatner, David. QA484.B55 1997

Blatt, Harvey. QE651.B68 1991

Blatter, Christian. QA403.3.B5713 1998

Blauert, Jens. QP469.B5413 1997

Blay, Michel. QC133.B5313 1998

Blechschmidt, Erich. QM601.B553

Bleier, Ruth. QP34.5.B55 1984

Blevins, Robert D. TA355.B52 1990, TA357.B57 1984

Blinderman, Charles. QH302.5.B59 1990

Bliss, Gilbert Ames. QA315.B5

Bliss, Michael. QP572.I5.B58 1982

Bloch, Felix. QC174.8.B59 1989

Block, B. Peter. QD149.B59 1990

Blong, R. J. QE522.B6 1984

Bloomfield, Louis. QC21.2.B59 1997

Bloomfield, Victor A. QD433.B44

Blum, Ann Shelby. QL46.5.B58 1993

Blum, Bruce I. QA76.758.B78 1992

Blumberg, Stanley A. QC16.T37.B57 1990

Blumenfeld, Dennis. T57.6.B57 2001

Blumenstock, David I. QC863.B55

Blunden, John. TN153.B58 1985

Blunt, Wilfrid. QH44.B54

Boccara, Nino. QA320.B63 1990

Bocking, Stephen. QH540.B63 1997

Bodanis, David. QC73.8.C6

Bodansky, David. TK9145.B54 1996

Bodde, Derk. Q127.C5.B63 1991

Boer, K. W. QC611.B64 1990

Bogue, Margaret Beattie. SH219.6

Bohm, David. QC6.B597 1957a

Bohr, Niels Henrik David. QC3.B584, QC6.B598, QC6.B599 1963, QC173.B535

Bohren, Craig F. QC880.4.T5.B63 1998

Boisseau, M. TK5105.5.B6513 1994

Bok, Bart Jan. QB819.B735 1957, QB857.7.B64 1981

Bold, Harold Charles. QK47.B73 1987, QK566.B64 1985, QK641.B596 1987

Boldea, I. TK2411.B6 1997, TK4058.B64 1999

Bolin, Bert. QC852.B65

Bollen, Math H. J. TK1010.B65 1999

# Author Index

Conard, Henry Shoemaker. QK533.84.N67.C66 1979

Conaway, Charles F. TN870.C58 1999

Condit, Celeste Michelle. QH438.7.C65 1999

Condon, Edward Uhler. QC21.C7 1967, QC174.2.C6, QC454.C64

Condoor, Sridhar S. TA171.C5875 2002

Conlon, Lawrence. QA614.3.C66 1993

Connell, D. W. TD193.B37 1997

Conner-Sax, Kiersten. TK5105.875.I57.C658 1999

Conroy, Glenn C. QL737.P9.C66 1990

Consolmagno, Guy. QB36.C76.A3 2000, QB63.C69 2000

Constantz, George. QH104.5.A6.C65 1994

Conway, Hazel. SB484.G7.C59 1991

Cook, A. H. QR151.C58 1958

Cook, Christopher D. K. QK358.C67 1996

Cook, David B. QC174.26.W28.C657 1988

Cook, James Gordon. TS1540.C639 1968

Cook, James L. QC94.C67 1990

Cook, Robert Davis. TA347.F5.C665 1995

Cook-Deegan, Robert M. QH445.2.C66 1994

Cooke, D. J. QA76.9.M35.C66 1984

Cookson, John T. TD192.5.C66 1995

Coombes, Kevin Robert. QA303.5.C65.C66 1998

Cooper, Alan. QA76.9.H85C673 1999

Cooper, Ann. TX353.C623 2000

Cooper, Geoffrey M. QH581.2.C66 2000

Copeland, L.O. (Lawrence O.). SB117.C73 2001

Copeland, Richard W. QA11.C673

Copeland, Robert Allen. QP601.C753 2000

Copernicus, Nicolaus. QB41.C84 1939a

Corballis, Michael C. QP385.5.C67 1991

Corbet, G. B. QL708.C67 1991

Corbet, Philip S. QL520.C67 1999

Core, H.A. SD536.C67 1979

Corea, Gena. QP251.C78 1985

Coren, Stanley. QP425.C62 1996, QP495.C67, SF433.C67 1994

Cornish-Bowden, Athel. QP601.C756

Cortada, James W. QA76.17.C67 1996, TK7885.A5.C67 1993

Cosslett, V. E. QC447.C63 1950

Cotterill, Rodney. QA76.87.C685 1998, QC173.3.C66 1985

Cotton, F. Albert. QD461.C65 1990

Cotton, William R. QC921.6.D95.C67 1989, QC981.C72 1995

Cottrell, Alan Howard. TN665.C69 1967b

Couch, Leon W. TK5101C69 2001

Coulson, Charles Alfred. QD469.C74 1979

Coulson, Robert N. SB761.C68 1984

Courant, Richard. QA37.C675, QA303.C838, QA303.S845

Courtney, Thomas H. TA405.C859 2000

Cousens, Roger. SB611.C67 1995

Cousineau, Guy. QA76.62.C68 1998

Cousteau, Jacques Yves. QH91.C628, QH91.C66, QH91.15.C652, QH541.5.C7.C613

Coutinho, S. C. QA241.C69513 1999

Cowan, J. A. QP531.C68 1997

Cowan, Ruth Schwartz. T14.5.C69 1997, TX23.C64 1983

Cowan, Sam. TK7868.D5.C68 1985

Coward, L. Andrew. QP376.C68 1990

Cowen, Richard. QE711.2.C68 1995

Cowling, T. G. QC809.M3.C65

Cox, C. Barry. QH84.C65 1980

Cox, C. Philip. QA276.12.C69 1987

Cox, David A. QA564.C688 1992, QA564.C6883 1998

Cox, Earl. QA76.9.S88C72 1999

Cox, George W. SB990.5.U6.C68 1999

Cox, Peter Alfred. QD31.2.C682 1995, QD466.C875 1989, SB413.R47.C628 1993

Coyle, J. D. QD708.2.C69 1986

Coyne, Gary S. QD53.C69 1997

Crabtree, Robert H. QD411.8.T73

Craig, Edwin C. TK7878.7.C72 1993

Craig, Roy R. TA405.C89 2000

Craige, Betty Jean. QH31.O27

Craik, D. J. QC753.2.C73 1995

Cramer, Friedrich. Q172.5.C45.C713 1993

Crandell, Gina. SB470.5.C73 1993

Crane, Eva. SF523.C856 1990, SF524.C738 1999

Cravens, Thomas E. QB529.C7 1997

Craw, R. C. QH84.C678 1999

Crawford, Donald R. TL671.2.C7 1981

Crawford, Dorothy H. QR364.C73 2000

Crawford, Mark. QH76.C73 1999

Crawford, William. TR330.C68

Crease, Robert P. QC789.2.U62.B763 1999

Creese, Mary R. S. Q141.C69 1998

Creighton, Thomas E. QH506.C74 1999

Crevier, Daniel. Q335.C66 1993

Crews, Phillip. QD272.S6.C74 1998

Crick, Francis. QH31.C85.A3 1988, QH331.C9

Crochemore, Maxime. QA76.9.T48.C76 1994

Crockett, James Underwood. SB453.C778

Crockett, Lawrence J. SB612.A2.C72

Crombie, A. C. Q125.C68 1961, Q127.E8.C76 1994

Cromwell, Peter R. QA491.C76 1997

Cronin, Helena. QL761.C76 1991

Cronin, Nigel J. QC661.C76 1995

Cronk, J.K. QK938.M3C76 2001

Cronquist, Arthur. QK495.A1.C76, QK495.A56.C7

Cropper, William H. QC174.1.C7

Croswell, Ken. QB820.C76 1997

Crouse, William Harry. TL152.C692

Crow, Garrett E. QK117.C84 2000

Crowe, Michael J. QB54.C76 1986

Crowl, Daniel A. TP150.S24C76 2002, TP155.5.C76 1990

Crowley, Joseph M. QC571.C76 1986

Cubitt, Gerald S. QH186.C83 1992

588

Lee, Wayne. TL793.L3137 1995
Leedy, Paul D. Q180.55.M4L43 2001
Leffler, John E. QD471.L5 1993
Lefranc, Norbert. QL696.P248.L43 1997
Lefschetz, Solomon. QA371.L36 1977
Legget, Robert Ferguson. TA705.L4 1988
Lehane, M. J. QL494.L34 1991
Lehner, Philip N. QL751.L398 1996
Leibovitz, Annie. TR681.W6.L34 1999
Leicester, Henry Marshall. QP511.L44
Lellinger, David B. QK524.5.L45 1985
Lembke, Janet. QH548.L46 1999
Lemmermeyer, Franz. QA241.L56 2000
Lemon, Harvey Brace. QC23.L4 1946
Lemonick, Michael D. QB981.L36 1993
Lemons, Don S. QC20.7.C3.L46 1997
Lenk, John D. TK7868.P6.L455 1994,
   TK7868.P6.L456 1995, TK7887.6.L46 1997
Lennox, James G. QH331.L528 2001
Leonardo da Vinci. QM21.L49
Leonardo. Q143.L5.A3 1989
Leopold, A. Carl. QK731.L4, QK731.L44 1975
Leopold, A. Starker. SK367.L4, SK473.L4
Leopold, Aldo. QH81.L56, SK361.L38
Leopold, Donald Joseph. QK115.L43 1998
Lerner, Eric J. QB991.B54.L47 1991
Lerner, Marcia. QA39.3.L47 2001
Lerner, Vladimir S. T58.6.L45 2000
Lesurf, J. C. G. T58.5.L48 1995
Leszczynski, Nancy A. SB472.45.L47 1997
Leuschner, William A. SD373.L45 1984
LeVay, Simon. QP360.L4926 1993
Levere, Trevor Harve y. QD18.E85.L48 1994
Leverington, David. QB136.L48 2000
Leverton, Roy. QL555.G7
Levett, Paul N. QR89.5.L48 1990
Levi, Howard. QA681.L4
Levi, Leo. QC371.L48
Levin, Harold L. (Harold Leonard). QE28.3.L48
   1996, QE770.L485 1999
Levine, Alan J. TL788.5.L47 1994
Levinton, Jeffrey S. QH91.L427 1995
Levi-Setti, Riccardo. QC721.L64, QE821.L46 1993
Levy, David H. QB35.L48 2001, QB36.B63.L48
   1993, QB61.L47 1997, QB454.2.S48, QB721.4.L48
   1994, QB723.S56.L48 1995
Levy, Matthys. TH441.L48 1992
Levy, Pierre. QA76.9.H85.L49 1998
Levy, Richard C. T339.L38 1990
Levy, Steven. QA76.6.L469 2001, QA76.8.M3.L487
   1994, QA76.9.A25L49 2001
Lewin, Benjamin. QH430.L487 2000
Lewin, Ralph A. QK565.L4
Lewington, Anna. SD383.L48 1999
Lewinsohn, Richard. QL85.L414 1954a
Lewis, Charles A. QK46.5.H85.L48 1996
Lewis, Gilbert Newton. QC311.L4 1961

Lewis, Grace Ross. TP200.L49 1999
Lewis, Harold W. TJ213.L433 1997
Lewis, Harry R. QA267.L49
Lewis, J. G. E. QL449.5.L48
Lewis, Jessica H. QP90.4.L48 1996
Lewis, John S. QB501.L497 1995, QB721.L419 2000
Lewis, Peter. SB413.C2.L48 1998
Lewis, Richard J. T55.3.H3.L494 2000
Lewis, Robert Alan. S411.L39 2002
Lewis, Ronald J. TS165.L48 1995
Lewontin, Richard C. QH455.L48, QH506.L443
   2000
Ley, Willy. QB15.L4
Li, Yen. QA27.C5.L4713 1987
Li, Yuan-Hui. QE515.L385 2000
Libai, A. TA660.S5.L457 1998
Libby, Willard F. QC798.D3.L5 1955
Lichatowich, Jim. SH348.L53 1999
Lichine, Alexis. TP546.L5 1979
Lickorish, W. B. Raymond. QA612.2.L53 1997
Liddle, Andrew R. QB981.L534 1999
Lide, David R. TP247.5.L53 1995
Lieb, Elliott H. QA300.L54 1997
Liebau, Friedrich. QD181.S6.L614 1985
Liebeck, M. W. QA8.4.L47 2000
Liebenberg, A. C. TG340.L54 1992
Lieberman, Bruce S. QE721.2.P24
Lieberman, Philip. QP399.L535 2000
Liebes, Sidney. QH367.L525 1998
Liebman, Matt. SB611.5.L54 2001
Lienhard, John H. T14.5.L52 2000
Lieske, Ewald. QL621.58.L54 1996
Lightman, Alan P. QB15.L54 1992, QB981.L54
   1990
Likens, Gene E. QH105.N4.L55 1995
Lilja, David J. QA76.9.E94L54 2000
Liller, William. QB63.L55 1985, QB64.L55 1992,
   QB461.L52
Limbaugh, Ronald H. SF426.2.L56 1996
Lin, E. C. C. QH434.L56 1984
Lin, T. Y. TA683.9.L5 1981
Lincoln, Roger J. QH13.L56 1987, QH540.4.L56
   1998
Lind, David. QC26.L56 1997
Lindberg, David C. Q124.95.L55 1992
Lindgren, Waldemar. TN263.L7 1933
Lindley, D. V. QA276.25.L56 1995
Lindley, David. QC794.6.G7.L55 1993
Lindsay, Hamish. TL789.8.U6
Lindsay, Robert Bruce. QC6.L42 1957, QC6.L425,
   QC225.7.L56
Lines, Malcolm E. QA93.L553 1994
Linsley Hood, John. TK7874.L55 1993
Linsley, Ray K. TC145.L55 1979
Lippman, Stanley B. QA76.73.C153L577 2000
Lipton, Kathryn L. S411.L55 1995
Litfin, Karen. QC879.7.L58 1994

Spitzer, Lyman. QC718.S6 1962

Spitzer, Manfred. QP363.3.S55 1999

Splittstoesser, Walter E. SB321.S645 1990

Spoel, S. van der. QL123.S75 1983

Spolter, Pari. QC178.S66 1993

Spongberg, Stephen A. SB435.65.S66 1990

Sporne, K. R. QK643.G99.S65

Sposito, Garrison. S592.5.S656 1989, S592.5.S66 1994

Sprecher, David A. QA331.5.S68

Sprent, Janet I. QR89.7.S67 1990

Sproull, Natalie L. Q180.55.M4S67 1995

Spurr, Stephen Hopkins. QK938.F6.S68 1980

Squires, G. L. QC174.15.S66 1995

Stace, Clive A. QK306.S78 1997

Stacey, F. D. QC806.S65 1977

Staelin, David H. QC661.S74 1994

Stafford Smith, Bryan. TH1611.S59 1991

Stafford, Barbara Maria. QP495.S73 1994

Stahl, Saul. QA162.S73 1997, QA269.S695 1999, QA300.S882 1999, QA685.S79 1993

Stakgold, Ivar. QA379.S72

Stalheim, Ole H. V. SF623.S73 1994

Stallings, William. QA76.76.O63S734 1998, TK5105.S73 2000

Stamets, Paul. QK629.S77.S735 1996

Standage, Tom. QB36.A2

Stanfield, D. P. QK495.G74

Stanier, Roger Y. QR41.S775 1963

Stanley, H. Eugene. QC307.S7 1971b

Stansfield, William D. QH309.S78 2000

Stapleton, Constance. TT23.S73 1988

Stapp, Henry P. QC174.12.S8 1993

Starling, Ernest Henry. QP34.S75 1968

Starrs, Paul F. SF196.U5.S77 1998

Staudinger, Hermann. QD22.S73.A313

Stauffer, Dietrich. QC20.S7413 1990

Stavy, Ruth. Q181.S694 2000

Steadman, David W. QH198.G3.S72 1988

Stearn, William T. (William Thomas). QK10.S7 1992

Stebbins, Robert C. QL651.S783 1985, QL667.S84 1995

Steele, E. J. QR184.S74 1998

Steele, John M. QB175.S83 2000

Stegner, Wallace Earle. Q143.P8.S8

Stehle, Philip. QC7.S78 1994

Steichen, Edward. TR140.S68.A25, TR653 .S744 2000

Stein, Benjamin. TH6010.S74 2000

Stein, J. Stewart. TH9.S78 1993

Stein, Jonathan Y. TK5102.9.S745 2000

Stein, Sherman K. QA22.S85 1999, QA93.S684 1996

Steiner, Frederick R. S624.A1.S74 1990

Steinman, David. TX356.S74 1995

Stephani, Hans. QC178.S8213 1982

Stephenson, Bruce. QB361.S74 1994

Stephenson, G. QA39.2.S745 1990

Stephenson, Ralph L. TD897.5.S74 1998

Stephenson, Steven L. QK635.A1.S73 1994

Sterelny, Kim. QH331.S82 1999

Stern, Alan. QB601.S76 1999

Stern, Judy E. Q180.5.M67S74 1997

Sternglass, Ernest J. QC171.2.S84 1997

Stevens, Charles F. QC21.2.S688 1995

Stevens, Joseph E. TC557.5.H6.S74 1988

Stevens, Karl K. TA351.S73 1987

Stevens, Roger T. QA76.64.S73 1994

Stevenson, F. J. S592.7.S73 1986

Stewart, Ian. QA93.S736 1997, QA93.S737 1995, QH323.5.S74 1998

Stewart, John. QB401.S74 1991

Stewart, Robert Ernest. TN140.S8.S7

Stewart, Wilson N. QE905.S73 1983

Stichlmair, Johann. TP156.D5S85 1998

Stieglitz, Alfred. TR647.S84 1983

Stigler, Stephen M. QA276.15.S755 1999

Stillman, John Maxson. QD11.S84 1960

Stillwell, John. QA39.2.S755 1998, QA155.S75 1994, QA611.S84, QA645.S75 1992

Stinton, Darrol. TL671.2.S77 1998, TL671.2.S773 1983

Stirling, Ian. QL737.C27.S726 1988

Stirzaker, David. QA273.S7534 1994, QA273.S75343 1999

Stoddard, Charles Hatch. SD373.S79 1987

Stoddart, D. Michael. QP458.S77 1990

Stokes, Alec. TJ185.S74 1992

Stoll, Clifford. QA76.9.C66.S88 1995

Stoll, Robert Roth. QA248.S798

Stonehouse, Bernard. QH84.1.S78 1989

Stoskopf, Neal C. SB123.S89 1993

Stott, Philip Anthony. QK101.S76

Straffin, Philip D. QA269.S77 1993

Strahler, Arthur Newell. Q158.5.S73 1992

Strangeways, Ian. QE33.S79 2000

Strasser, Susan. TX23.S77 1982

Strathern, Paul. QD22.M43S87 2001

Stratton-Porter, Gene. QH81.S8725 1996

Strauss, David. QB36.L849

Street, Philip. QL754.S77 1976

Streetman, Ben G. TK7871.85.S77 2000

Streshinsky, Shirley. QL31.A9.S77 1993

Strick, James Edgar. QH325.S85 2000

Stroebel, Leslie D. TR9.S88

Strong, Roy C. SB466.G75.E57

Stronge, W. J. TA354.S77 2000

Stroud, Dorothy. SB470.B7.S7 1984

Stroyan, K. D. QA3.P8 vol. 72, QA303.5.D37.S77 1993

Struik, Dirk Jan. QA21.S87 1967

Strum, Shirley C. QL737.P93.S79 1987

Stuart, John David. QK149.S73 2001

Stuart, Ralph. T55.S786 1997

Stubbendieck, James L. SB193.3.N67.S88 1982

Stueben, Michael. QA11.S83 1998

American fish and wildlife policy : the human dimension / SK361.A68 1992

American forests : nature, culture, and politics / SD143.A596 1997

American genesis : a century of invention and technological enthusiasm, 1870-1970 / T21.H82 1989

American Horticultural Society A-Z encyclopedia of garden plants, The / SB403.2.A45 1997

American Horticultural Society flower finder, The / SB406.93.U6.H47 1992

American insects : a handbook of the insects of America north of Mexico / QL474.A76 2000

American Institute of Physics editorial handbook./QC5.52.A54 1989

American Institute of Physics handbook. / QC61.A5 1963

American iron, 1607-1900 / TN704.N5.G67 1996

American photographers : an illustrated who's who among leading contemporary Americans / TR139.A46 1989

American photography, 1890-1965, from the Museum of Modern Art, New York / TR645.N72.M876 1995

American plastic : a cultural history / TP1117.M45 1995

American pronghorn : social adaptations & the ghosts of predators past / QL737.U52.B94 1997

American railroad freight car : from the wood-car era to the coming of steel, The / TF470.W45 1993

American science in an age of anxiety : scientists, anticommunism, and the cold war / Q127.U6.W36 1999

American seashells; the marine molluska of the Atlantic and Pacific coasts of North America QL411.A19 1974

American shad in the Susquehanna River Basin : a three-hundred-year history / SH351.S5.G47 1998

American social insects; a book about bees, ants, wasps, and termites, QL569.M5

American spiders / QL458.4.G47 1979

American technological sublime / T14.5.N93 1994

American tintype, The / TR375.R56 1999

American vintage : the rise of American wine / TP557.L87 2000

American warblers : an ecological and behavioral perspective / QL696.P2618.M67 1989

American women afield : writings by pioneering women naturalists / QH45.2.B66 1995

American women in science : 1950 to the present : a biographical dictionary / Q141.B254 1998

American women in science : a biographical dictionary / Q141.B25 1994

American women in technology : an encyclopedia / T36.Z54 2000

Americans and their weather / QC983.M455 2000

America's mountains : an exploration of their origins and influences from the Alaska Range to the Appalachians / QE621.5.N7.H83 1995

America's science museums / Q105.U5.D36 1990

America's scientific treasures : a travel companion / Q105.U5.A64 1998

America's struggle for leadership in technology / T21.D4713 1990

Amino acids and peptides / QD431.B28 1998

Anaerobic bacteria : a functional biology / QR89.5.L48 1990

Analog and computer electronics for scientists / TK7878.4.V37 1993

Analog electronics 2nd ed. / TK7867.H53 1990

Analog electronics handbook / TK7825.C63 1989

Analog electronics with Op Amps : a source book of practical circuits / TK7874.P459 1993

Analog inter-facing to embedded microprocessors : real world design / TK7895.E42

Analog signal processing / TK7874.P345 1999

Analog-digital conversion handbook / TK7887.6.A525 1986

Analysis / QA300.L54 1997

Analysis by its history / QA300.H352 1996

Analysis I. / QA300.L27

Analysis II. / QA300.L273

Analysis of aircraft structures : an introduction / TL671.6.D56 1993

Analysis of coniferous forest ecosystems in the Western United States / QK133.A5 1982

Analysis of geological structures / QE601.P694 1990

Analysis of longitudinal data / QA278.D545 1994

Analysis of matter, The. / QC6.R83 1954

Analysis of numerical methods / QA297.I8 1994

Analysis of shells and plates / TA660.S5.G644 1999

Analysis, synthesis, and design of chemical processes / TP155.7.A53 1998

Analytical approach, The / QD75.25.A5 1983

Analytical electrochemistry / QD115.W33 2000

Analytical mechanics : with an introduction to dynamical systems / QA805.T67 2000

Anatomical and mechanical bases of human motion, The / QP303.H389

Anatomy and physiology of speech / QP306.K3 1971

Anatomy of a scientific institution: the Paris Academy of Sciences, 1666-1803, The. / Q46.A15.H33

Anatomy of reality : merging of intuition and reason / Q175.S2326 1983

Anatomy of the airplane, The / TL671.2.S77 1998

Anatomy of the dicotyledons / QK495.A12M47 1979

Anatomy of the dicotyledons; leaves, stem, and wood in relation to taxonomy, with notes on economic uses, / QK671 M4

Anatomy of the human body / QM23.2.G73 1985

Anatomy of the human body. / QM23.G7 1959

Anatomy of the monocotyledons. / QK643.M7M4

Anatomy of xerography : its invention and evolution, The / TR1045.M67 1989

Ancient DNA : recovery and analysis of genetic material from paleontological, archaeological, museum, medical, and forensic specimens / QP620.A53 1994

Ancient Egyptian science : a source book / Q11.P612 vol. 184, etc.

Ancient inventions / T16.J36 1994

Ancient invertebrates and their living relatives / QE770.L485 1999

Ancient Khmer Empire, The. / Q11.P6 n.s., vol.41, pt.1

Ancient landforms / QE501.4.P3.O45 1991

Ancient marine reptiles / QE861.A53 1997

Ancient trees : trees that live for 1000 years / SD383.L48 1999

And yet it moves : strange systems and subtle questions in physics / QC21.2.S47 1993

Andrew Glassner's notebook : recreational computer graphics / T385.G578 1999

Angler's guide to the fresh water sport fishes of North America. / SH462.M5

Animal cell culture and technology / TP248.27.A53.B87 1996

Animal diversity / QL45.2.K47 1983

Animal ecology / QH541.E398 2001

Animal evolution : interrelationships of the living phyla / QH367.5.N53 2001

Animal hormones; a comparative survey. / QP187.J4

Animal husbandry / SF61.P37 1970

Animal intelligence : experimental studies / QL785.T5 2000

Animal life at low temperature / QH653.D38 1991

Animal migration and navigation / QL754.S77 1976

Animal minds : beyond cognition to consciousness / QL785.G715 2001

Animal nutrition / SF95.M35 1979

Animal physiology : principles and adaptations / QP33.G65 1982

Animal play : evolutionary, comparative, and ecological prespectives / QL763.5.A54 1998

Animal science and industry / SF61.A3 2001

Animal species and evolution. / QH371.M33

Animals in motion. QP301.M83 1957

Animals of the tidal marsh / QL114.D34

Animals without backbones. QL362.B93 1987

Animals, men, and myths; an informative and entertaining history of man & the animals around him. / QL85.L414 1954a

Annotated catalogue of the illustrations of human and animal expression from the collection of Charles Darwin : an early case of the use of photography in scientific research / QP401.P76 1998

Ben Franklin stilled the waves : an informal history of pouring oil on water with reflections on the ups and downs of scientific life in general / Q143.F8.T36 1989

Benchmarks for science literacy. / Q183.3.A1.B46 1993

Beneficial insects; nature's alternatives to chemical insecticides: animal predation, parasitism, disease organisms. / SB975.S92

Benjamin Franklin's Experiments; a new edition of Franklin's Experiments and observations on electricity. / QC516.F85 1941

Benjamin Franklin's science / QC16.F68.C64 1990

Benjamin Silliman : a life in the young republic / Q143.S56.B76 1989

Bergey's manual of systematic bacteriology / QR81.B46 1984

Berkeley physics course. / QC21.B4445

Berkeley problems in mathematics / QA43.S695 1998

Bernard E. Harkness seedlist handbook, The / SB408.H36 1993

Berry grower's companion, The / SB381.B68 2000

Best and Taylor's Physiological basis of medical practice. / QP34.5.B47 1985

Best of Stillmeadow : a treasury of country living, The / S521.5.C8.T28

Better trout habitat : a guide to stream restoration and management / SH157.8.H86 1991

Between earth and space. / QC863.O7

Between nucleus and cytoplasm / QH595.A36 1990

Between Pacific tides / QL138.R5 1985

Beyond captive breeding : re-introducing endangered mammals to the wild : the proceedings of a symposium held at the Zoological Society of London on 24th and 25th November 1989 / QL83.4.B49 1991

Beyond contact : a guide to SETI and communicating with alien civilizations / QB54.M23 2001

Beyond engineering : how society shapes technology / T45.P66 1997

Beyond evolution : the genetically altered future of plants, animals, the earth--humans / TP248.6.F687 1999

Beyond formulas in mathematics and teaching : dynamics of the high school algebra classroom / QA159.C48 2000

Beyond innocence : an autobiography in letters : the later years / QL31.G58

Beyond natural selection / QH366.2.W47 1991

Beyond nimby : hazardous waste siting in Canada and the United States / TD1050.P64.R33 1994

Beyond preservation : restoring and inventing landscapes / QH541.15.R45.B48 1994

Beyond silent spring : integrated pest management and chemical safety / QH545.P4.V36 1996

Beyond Star Trek : physics from alien invasions to the end of time / QB500.K64 1997

Beyond the Ark : tools for an ecosystem approach to conservation / QH75.W43 1997

Beyond the hundredth meridian: John Wesley Powell and the second opening of the West. / Q143.P8.S8

Beyond the mainframe : a guide to open computer systems / TK5105.55.S38 1995

Beyond the natural body : an archaeology of sex hormones / QP572.S4.O83 1994

Beyond the science wars : the missing discourse about science and society / Q175.55.B49 2000

Beyond the third dimension : geometry, computer graphics, and higher dimensions / QA691.B26 1990

Bibliography of North American geology. / QE75.B9 serial

Bicycles and tricycles : an elementary treatise on their design and construction / TL410.S5 1977

Bicycles, bakelites, and bulbs : toward a theory of sociotechnical change, Of / T14.5.B54 1995

Big bang never happened, The / QB991.B54.L47 1991

Big bang, The / QB981.S55 2001

Big bonanza; an authentic account of the discovery, history, and working of the world-renowned Comstock lode of Nevada, The / TN413.N25.W8 1947

Big fleas have little fleas; or Who's who among the protozoa. QL366.H43 1968

Big foot-prints : a scientific inquiry into the reality of sasquatch / QL89.2.S2.K73 1992

Big game animals of North America, The / SK40.O28

Billions and billions : thoughts on life and death at the brink of the millennium / Q173.S24 1997

Biochemical adaptation / QP82.H63 1984

Biochemical and physiological aspects of human nutrition / QP141.B57 1999

Biochemical engineering and biotechnology handbook / TP248.3.A853 1983

Biochemical responses to environmental stress. / QP88.B49

Biochemistry / QP514.C32 1967

Biochemistry & molecular biology of plants / QK861.B45 2000

Biochemistry and physiology of protozoa / QL369.2.L87 1979

Biochemistry of plants : a comprehensive treatise, The / QK861.B48

Biodegradation and bioremediation / TD192.5.A43 1994

Biodiversity : a reference handbook / QH541.15.B56.B435 1998

Biodiversity and sustainable conservation / QH541.15.B56.K86 1999

Biodiversity dynamics : turnover of populations, taxa, and communities / QH541.15.B56.B574 1998

Biodiversity II : understanding and protecting our biological resources / QH75.B5228 1997

Biodiversity of the southeastern United States / QH104.5.S59.B565 1993

Biogeochemistry of a forested ecosystem / QH105.N4.L55 1995

Biogeography : an ecological and evolutionary approach / QH84.C65 1980

Biogeography and ecology of the rain forests of eastern Africa / QH195.A23.B56 1993

Biographical dictionary of American and Canadian naturalists and environmentalists / QH26.B535 1997

Biographical dictionary of scientists, The. Q141.B528 2000

Biographical dictionary of scientists, The 3rd ed. / Q141.B528 2000

Biographical dictionary of the history of technology / T39.B49 1996

Biographical dictionary of women in science : pioneering lives from ancient times to the mid-20th century, The / Q141.B5285 2000

Biography of physics. QC7.G26

Bioinformatics : sequence and genome analysis / QH441.2.M68 2001

Biolexicon : a guide to the language of biology / QH302.5.B59 1990

Biological and biotechnological control of insect pests / SB933.3.R436 1998

Biological anthropology and aging : perspectives on human variation over the life span / QP86.B516 1994

Biological control by natural enemies / SB933.3.D43 1991

Biological control of microbial plant pathogens / SB732.6.C33 1989

Biological control of weeds and plant diseases : advances in applied allelopathy / SB611.5.R53 1995

Biological individuality : the identity and persistence of living entities / QH331.W555 1999

Biological invasions : theory and practice / QH353.S54 1997

Biological nomenclature / QH83.J43 1977

Biological oceanography : an introduction / QH91.L35 1997

Biological rhythms and clocks of intertidal animals, The / QL121.P343 1995

Biological thermodynamics / QP517.T48

Biologists and the promise of American life : from Meriwether Lewis to Alfred Kinsey / QH305.2.U6

Biologist's handbook of pronunciations, The. / QH13.J3 1960

Biology : concepts & connections / QH308.2.C34 2000

Biology and conservation of sea turtles / QL666.C536.W65 1979

Biology and epistemology / QH331.B475 2000

Biology and management of lobsters, The / QL444.M33.B56

Biology of amphibians / QL667.D84 1986

Biology of blood-sucking insects / QL494.L34 1991

Biology of centipedes, The / QL449.5.L48

# Title Index

Dust Bowl : an agricultural and social history, The / S441.H92

Dying of the trees : the pandemic in America's forests, The / SB762.L58 1995

Dying to live : how our bodies fight disease / QR181.7.K46 1998

Dynamic aquaria : building living ecosystems / SF457.5.A32 1998

Dynamic earth : plates, plumes, and mantle convection / QE509.4.D38 1999

Dynamic earth: textbook in geosciences, The / QE26.2.W9

Dynamic fracture mechanics / TA409.D96 1995, TA409.F77 1990

Dynamic genome : Barbara McClintock's ideas in the century of genetics, The / QH430.D96 1992

Dynamic modeling / QA76.9.C65.H35 1994

Dynamic nature of ecosystems : chaos and order entwined, The / QH541.P33 1995

Dynamic patterns : the self-organization of brain and behavior / QP360.K454 1995

Dynamic state variable models in ecology : methods and applications / QL751.65.M3

Dynamical theory of gases, The / QC175.J43 1925

Dynamical theory of the electromagnetic field, A / QC665.E4.M38 1982

Dynamics of dinosaurs and other extinct giants / QE862.D5.A33 1989

Dynamics of heat, The / QC311.F83 1996

Dynamics of molecules and chemical reactions / QD502.D96 1996

Dynamics of nutrient cycling and food webs / QH344.D43 1992

Dynamics of structures : theory and applications to earthquake engineering / TA654.6.C466 1995

Dynamics of weed populations / SB611.C67 1995

Dynamics--the geometry of behavior / QA845.A26 1982

e : the story of a number / QA247.5.M33 1994

E=mc2 : a biography of the world's most famous equation / QC73.8.C6

Eagle bird : mapping a new West, The / S932.W37.W55 1992

Early American hurricanes, 1492-1870. / QC857.U6.H56 no.1

Early American tornadoes, 1586-1870 / QC857.U6.H56 no. 4

Early American winters / QC857.U6.H56 no. 2

Early development of the concepts of temperature and heat; the rise and decline of the caloric theory, The. / QC252.R6

Early diagenesis : a theoretical approach / QE571.B47

Early life on earth / QE721.2.E85.N63 1992

Early quantum electrodynamics : a source book / QC680.M55 1994

Early years of radio astronomy : reflections fifty years after Jansky's discovery, The / QB475.A25.E37 1984

Earth : its origin, history, and physical constitution, The / QE501.J4 1976

Earth : the stuff of life / S591.B33 1986

Earth and its atmosphere, The. / QC806.B34 1958

Earth and its gravity field, The / QC815.H4

Earth science and the environment / QE33.T45 1999

Earth through time, The / QE28.3.L48 1996

Earth, moon, and planets / QB601.W6 1968

Earthfire : the eruption of Mount St. Helens / QE523.S23.R67 1982

Earthquake engineering for concrete dams : design, performance, and research needs / TC547.E234 1990

Earthquake-resistant concrete structures / TA658.44.P46 1997

Earthquakes / QE534.2.B64 1993

Earth's climate, past and future, The / QC981.8.C5.B8313 1982

Earth's dynamic systems / QE28.2.H35 1998

Earth's earliest biosphere : its origin and evolution / QE724.E27 1983

Earth's glacial record / QE697.E17 1994

Earth's mantle : composition, structure, and evolution, The / QE509.E234 1998

Earthworm ecology / QL391.A6.E25 1998

Earthworm ecology and biogeography in North America / QL391.A6.E26 1995

East to the dawn : the life of Amelia Earhart / TL540.E3.B88 1997

Eating agendas : food and nutrition as social problems / TX359.E38 1995

Eclipse! : the what, where, when, why, and how guide to watching solar and lunar eclipses / QB541.H35 1997

Ecological integrity and the management of ecosystems / QH75.A1.E24 1993

Ecological management of agricultural weeds / SB611.5.L54 2001

Ecological relationships of plants and animals / QH541.H65 1988

Ecological risks of engineered crops, The / SB123.57.R564 1996

Ecological toxicity testing : scale, complexity, and relevance / QH541.15.T68.E24 1995

Ecological versatility and community ecology / QH541.M225 1995

Ecological web : more on the distribution and abundance of animals, The / QH541.A524 1984

Ecologists and environmental politics : a history of contemporary ecology / QH540.B63 1997

Ecology : individuals, populations, and communities / QH541.B415 1990

Ecology : the experimental analysis of distribution and abundance / QH541.28.K74 1985

Ecology and classification of North American freshwater invertebrates / QL151.E36 2001

Ecology and evolution in anoxic worlds / QH518.5.F46 1995

Ecology and evolution of acoustic communication in birds / QL698.5.E36 1996

Ecology and management of coastal waters : the aquatic environment / QH541.5.C65

Ecology and management of large mammals in North America / QL739.8.E36 2000

Ecology in agriculture / S589.7.E255 1997

Ecology of bird communities, The / QL673.W523 1989

Ecology of deep-sea hydrothermal vents, The / QH541.5.D35.V34 2000

Ecology of desert communities, The / QH541.5.D4.E28 1991

Ecology of estuaries : anthropogenic effects / QH541.5.E8.K47 1991

Ecology of European rivers / QH135.E26 1984

Ecology of fire, The / QH545.F5.W48 1995

Ecology of freshwater molluscs, The / QL430.4.D55 2000

Ecology of freshwater phytoplankton, The / QK935.R45 1984

Ecology of insect overwintering, The / QL463.L43 1993

Ecology of intercropping, The / S603.5.V36 1989

Ecology of invasions by animals and plants / QH541.E4 2000

Ecology of migrant birds : a Neotropical perspective, The / QL685.7.R36 1995

Ecology of neotropical savannas, The / QH130.S2713 1984

Ecology of plants, The / QK901.G96 2002

Ecology of seashores, The / QH541.5.S35

Economic geology and geotectonics / TN260.E28

Economic mineral deposits / TN260.B3 1979

Economics of fisheries management, The / SH334.A53 1986

Economics of protected areas : a new look at benefits and costs / QH77.D44.D59 1990

Ecophysiology of desert arthropods and reptiles / QL116.C58 1991

Ecophysiology of small desert mammals / QL739.8.D44 1997

Ecoregions : the ecosystem geography of the oceans and continents : with 106 illustraions, with 55 in color / QH540.7.B345 1998

Ecosystem approach to aquatic ecology : Mirror Lake and its environment, An / QH105.N4.E3 1985

Ecosystem geography / QH540.7.B35 1996

Ecosystem management in the United States : an assessment of current experience / QH76.E336 1996

Ecotoxicology : ecological fundamentals, chemical exposure, and biological effects / QH545.A1.E283 1998

Edgar Degas, photographer / TR680.D25 1998

Edge of objectivity; an essay in the history of scientific ideas, The. Q125.G49

Edge of the sea, The. QH91.C3

Edison, inventing the century / TK140.E3.B25 1995

Educating for OSHA savvy chemists / QD63.5.E38 1998

Educators guide to free science materials / Q181.A1E3

Edward S. Curtis in the land of the war canoes : a pioneer cinematographer in the Pacific Northwest / TR849.C87.H64 1980

Edward Teller : giant of the golden age of physics : a biography / QC16.T37.B57 1990

Efficiency of human movement / QP301.B88 1979

Efficient electric motor systems handbook / TK2511.L54 1995

Egg incubation : its effects on embryonic development in birds and reptiles / QL959.E33 1991

Eggs, nests, and baby dinosaurs : a look at dinosaur reproduction / QE862.D5.C235 1999

Eight little piggies : reflections in natural history / QH45.5.G7 1993

Eighth day of creation : makers of the revolution in biology, The / QH506.J83 1996

Eighth day of creation : makers of the revolution in biology, The / QP624.J82

Einstein : a life / QC16.E5.B737 1996

Einstein : decoding the Universe / QC16.E5B3513 2001

Einstein and religion : physics and theology / QC16.E5.J36 1999

Einstein dictionary, An  / QC16.E5.K36 1996

Einstein Tower : an intertexture of dynamic construction, relativity theory, and astronomy, The / QB462.65.H4613 1997

Einstein's dream : the search for a unified theory of the universe / QC173.7.P36 1986

Einstein's greatest blunder? : the cosmological constant and other fudge factors in the physics of the Universe / QB981.G594 1995

Einstein's legacy : the unity of space and time / QC173.59.S65.S39 1986

Einstein's miraculous year : five papers that changed the face of physics / QC7.E52 1998

Einstein's theory of relativity. QC6.B66 1962

Elastic and inelastic stress analysis / TA418.S48 1997

Elasticity and geomechanics / TA705.D3 1996

Elasticity, plasticity, and structure of matter. With a chapter on the plasticity of crystals QC171.H75

Electric drives / TK4058.B64 1999

Electric machinery / TK2181.F5 1990

Electric motor handbook / TK2511.E423 1988

Electric power generation : a nontechnical guide / TK1001.B275 2000

Electrical circuit theory and technology / TK454.B48 1997

Electrical distribution systems / TK3001.P37 1999

Electrical engineering handbook, The / TK145.E354 1997

Electrical engineering materials reference guide / TK453.E36 1990

Electrical measurements [by] Forest K. Harris. QC535.H35

Electrical nature of storms, The / QC961.M18 1998

Electrical power engineering / TK1005.K32 1993

Electrical safety handbook / TK152.C22 1994

Electrical sensors and transducers / TK7872.T6.C38 1993

Electrical technology in mining : the dawn of a new age / TN343.J66 1992

Electrical wiring design : commercial & institutional / TK3284.T75 1996

Electrician's formula and reference book / TK151.H67 1995

Electroceramics : materials, properties, applications / TK7871.15.C4.M68 1990

Electrochemical engineering principles / TP255.P74 1991

Electrochemical methods : fundamentals and applications / QD553.B37

Electrochemistry / QD553.H29 1998

Electrochemistry for chemists / QD553.S32 1995

Electrodynamics : a concise introduction / QC631.W47 1997

Electrodynamics and classical theory of fields and particles. QC174.45.B3

Electrodynamics of continuous media, QC518.L313

Electromagnetic fields and interactions. QC670.B42

Electromagnetic fields and waves. QC521.L25

Electromagnetic waves / QC661.S74 1994

Electromagnetism, QC760.S55 1969

Electromechanical energy devices and power systems / TK1001.Y36 1994

Electron paramagnetic resonance : elementary theory and practical applications / QC763.W45 1994

Electron, its isolation and measurement and the determination of some of its properties, The. QC721.M68 1963

Electronic communications systems : fundamentals through advanced / TK5101.T625 2001

Electronic concepts : an introduction / TK7816.K73 2000

Electronic connector handbook : theory and applications / TK3521.M76 1998

Electronic devices and circuit theory / TK7867.B66 1999

Electronic displays : technology, design, and applications / TK7882.I6.W49 1994

Electronic eye : the rise of surveillance society, The / TK7882.E2.L96 1994

Electronic genie : the tangled history of silicon / TK7809.S45 1998

Electronic noise and low noise design / TK7867.5.F56 1993

Electronic properties of engineering materials / TK7871.L58 1999

Electronic speech synthesis : techniques, technology, and applications / TK7882.S65.B75 1984

Electronic structure and properties of transition metal compounds : introduction to the theory / QD172.T6.B48 1996

Electronics handbook, The / TK7867.E4244 1996

Electronics via waveform analysis / TK7878.7.C72 1993

Electrons in metals and semiconductors / QC176.8.E4.C43 1990

Electrons, atoms, metals and alloys. / TN690.H95 1963

Electrophoresis / QP519.9.E434.H39  1996

Electrostatics / QC571.J65 1998

Elegant universe : superstrings, hidden dimensions, and the quest for the ultimate theory, The / QC794.6.S85.G75 1999

Elementary atomic structure / QC173.W66 1980

Elementary crystallography; an introduction to the fundamental geometrical features of crystals. QD905.B96

Elementary differential equations / QA371.R29 1981

Elementary differential equations and boundary value problems / QA371.B773 1986

Elementary engineering fracture mechanics / TA409.B76 1986

Elementary functions : algorithms and implementation / QA331.M866 1997

Elementary geometry / QA453.R66 1993

Elementary geometry of algebraic curves : an undergraduate introduction / QA565.G5 1998

Elementary linear algebra / QA184.K585 1996

Elementary mathematical models : order aplenty and a glimpse of chaos / QA401.K24 1997

Elementary nuclear theory / QC173.B48 1956

Elementary number theory in nine chapters / QA241.T35 1999

Elementary particle physics : concepts and phenomena / QC793.2.N3313 1990

Elementary particle physics. / QC721.G353

Elementary particles and the laws of physics : the 1986 Dirac - memorial lectures / QC793.28.F49 1987

Elementary particles. / QC173.F397

Elementary particles. / QC721.L64

Elementary plasma physics / QC718.A713 1965

Elementary primer for gauge theory, An  / QC793.3.F5.M67 1983

Elementary probability / QA273.S7534 1994

Elementary solid state physics; a short course. QC171.K5 1962

Elementary statistical physics. QC175.K58

Elementary surveying / TA545.W77 1994

Elementary wave mechanics, with applications to quantum chemistry. QC174.2.H4 1956

Elements : their origin, abundance, and distribution, The / QD466.C875 1989

Elements of acoustics / QC243.T46

Elements of advanced quantum theory, QC174.1.Z49

Elements of algebra : geometry, numbers, equations / QA155.S75 1994

Elements of artificial intelligence : an introduction using LISP, The / Q336.T36 1987

Encyclopedia of physical science and technology / Q123.E497 2002

Encyclopedia of plant pathology / SB728.E53 2001

Encyclopedia of polymer science and engineering / TP1087.E46 1985

Encyclopedia of pseudoscience / Q157.E57 2000

Encyclopedia of science and technology / Q121.E53 2001

Encyclopedia of Shells, The / QL404.W955 1991

Encyclopedia of snakes, The / QL666.O6.E53 1995

Encyclopedia of software engineering / QA76.758.E53 1994

Encyclopedia of soil science, The / S592.E52

Encyclopedia of space exploration / QB500.262.A54 2000

Encyclopedia of spectroscopy and spectrometry / QC450.3.E53 2000

Encyclopedia of spectroscopy, The. QC451.E5

Encyclopedia of structural geology and plate tectonics, The / QE601.E53 1987

Encyclopedia of textiles / TS1445.A18 1980

Encyclopedia of textiles, fibers, and nonwoven fabrics / TS1309.E53 1984

Encyclopedia of the chemical elements, The, QD466.H295

Encyclopedia of the scientific revolution : from Copernicus to Newton / Q125.E53 2000

Encyclopedia of the solar system / QB501.E53 1999

Encyclopedia of the world's zoos / QL76.E53 2001

Encyclopedia of time / QB209.E52 1994

Encyclopedia of volcanoes / QE522.E53 2000

Encyclopedia of women in aviation and space / TL539.W395 1998

Encyclopedia of world regional geology, The / QE5.F33

Encyclopedia of world scientists / Q141.O25 2001

Encyclopedia of X-rays and gamma rays, The. QC481.C475

Encyclopedic dictionary of gears and gearing / TJ184.S76 1995

Encyclopedic dictionary of mathematics / QA5.I8313 1987

End of physics : the myth of a unified theory, The / QC794.6.G7.L55 1993

End of science : facing the limits of knowledge in the twilight of the scientific age, The / Q175.H794 1996

End of the dinosaurs : Chicxulub crater and mass extinctions, The / QE506.F7313 1999

End of time : the next revolution in physics, The / QC173.59.S65.B374 2000

Endangered and threatened plants of the United States / QK86.U6.A93 1978

Endangered species : a reference handbook / QL82.S49 1998

Endangered species recovery : finding the lessons, improving the process / QL84.2.E55 1994

Endocrines and aging; a symposium presented before the Gerontological Society seventeenth annual meeting, Minneapolis, Minnesota. QP187.G386

Endurance fitness / QP301.S48 1977

Endurance sports nutrition / TX361.A8E39 2000

Energies : an illustrated guide to the biosphere and civilization / TJ163.2.S618 1999

Energy & environmental visions for the new millennium / TJ163.27.E48 1998

Energy / TJ163.2.R84 1995

Energy and American society : a reference handbook / TJ163.235.M55 1993

Energy and empire : a biographical study of Lord Kelvin / QC16.K3.S65 1989

Energy and man : technical and social aspects of energy / TJ163.2.E46

Energy changes in biochemical reactions QD501.K7557

Energy conservation guidebook / TJ163.3.P38 1993

Energy efficiency manual : for everyone who uses energy, pays for utilities, controls energy usage, designs and builds, is interested in energy and environmental preservation / TJ163.3.W85 1999

Energy handbook / TJ163.235.L64 1984

Energy in world history / TJ163.5.S623 1994

Energy management handbook / TJ163.2.T87 2001

Energy of nature, The/ QC73.P54 2001

Energy possibilities : rethinking alternatives and the choice-making process / TJ163.2.T347 1995

Energy, a guidebook / TJ163.2.R345 1997

Engine of reason, the seat of the soul : a philosophical journey into the brain, The / QP376.C496 1995

Engineer in the garden : genes and genetics : from the idea of heredity to the creation of life, The / QH437.T83 1995

Engineered materials handbook / TA403.4.E64 1995

Engineering a new architecture / TA658.2.R63 1996

Engineering and the mind's eye / TA145.F37 1992

Engineering approach to optimal control and estimation theory, An / TJ213.S474443 1996

Engineering circuit analysis / TK454.H4 2002

Engineering design of the cardiovascular system of mammals / QP105.D38 1991

Engineering design process, The / TA174.E78 1993

Engineering drawing and design / T353.E617 2001

Engineering ethics : balancing cost, schedule, and risk--lessons learned from the space shuttle / TA157.E673 1997

Engineering fluid dynamics : an interdisciplinary systems approach / QA911.K57 1997

Engineering geology / TA705.B328 1993

Engineering geology : rock in engineering construction / TA706.G644 1993

Engineering handbook, The / TA151.E424 1996

Engineering materials : properites and selection / TA403.B787 1999

Engineering mechanics / TA350.B48 1994

Engineering mechanics. Statics & dynamics / TA350.H48 1998

Engineering polymer sourcebook / TP156.P6.S44 1990

Engineering principles of ground modification / TA710.H34 1990

Engineering problem solving with MATLAB / TA345.E547 1997

Engineering reliability : new techniques and applications / TS173.D48

Engineering vibration / TA355.I519 2001

Engineering, ethics, and the environment / TA157.V42 1998

Engineers & electrons : a century of electrical progress / TK23.R9 1984

Engineers of dreams : great bridge builders and the spanning of America / TG23.P47 1995

Engines : an introduction / TJ755.L94 1999

Engines of creation / T47.D74 1986

Engines of our ingenuity : an engineer looks at technology and culture, The / T14.5.L52 2000

English garden : meditation and memorial, The / SB457.6.C64 1994

English-German technical and engineering dictionary. / T9.D47

English-Spanish, Spanish-English electrical and computer engineering dictionary = Diccionario de ingenieria electrica y de computadoras ingles/espanol, espanol/ingles / TK9.K37 1996

Enhanced biodegradation of pesticides in the environment/ SB951.145.B54.E54 1990

Enjoying moths / QL555.G7

Enriching heredity : the impact of the environment on the anatomy of the brain / QM455.D49 1988

Enriching the earth : Fritz Haber, Carl Bosch, and the transformation of world food production / S651.S56 2001

Enrico Fermi, physicist. QC16.F46.S4

Environmental and engineering geophysics / TA705.S515 1997

Environmental biology of agaves and cacti / QK495.A26.N63 1988

Environmental biomonitoring : the biotechnology ecotoxicology interface / QH541.15.M64.L95 1998

Environmental chemistry / QD31.2.M35 1994

Environmental chemistry of lakes and reservoirs / QD1.A355 no. 237

Environmental chemistry of the elements / QD31.2.B68

Environmental chemistry of the heavy elements : hydrido and organo compounds / TD196.H43.T49 1995

Environmental chemodynamics : movement of chemicals in air, water, and soil / QD31.2.T47 1996

Environmental contaminant reference databook / TD196.C45.P73 1995

Fuzzy sets and fuzzy logic : theory and applications / QA248.K487 1995

Fuzzy sets and interactive multiobjective optimization / QA402.5.S25 1993

Fuzzy systems handbook : a practioner's guide to building using, and maintaining fuzzy systems, The / QA76.9.S88C72 1999

Galapagos : discovery on Darwin's islands / QH198.G3.S72 1988

Galapagos, world's end, / QH123.B4

Galaxies in the universe : an introduction / QB857.S63 2000

Galaxies. / QB851.S47 1972

Galileo / QB36.G2.D688

Galileo on the world systems : a new abridged translation and guide / QB41.G173 1997

Galileo's daughter : a historical memoir of science, faith, and love / QB36.G2.S65 1999

Galois theory / QA171.R668 1990

Game management, / SK361.L38

Game theory & animal behavior / QL751.65.M3.G25 1998

Game theory and applications / QA269.G35 1995

Game theory and strategy / by Philip D. Straffin.QA269.S77 1993

Game wars : the undercover pursuit of wildlife poachers / SK354.H33.R45 1991

Games of life : explorations in ecology, evolution, and behaviour / QH313.S585 1993

Games, gods and gambling; the origins and history of probability and statistical ideas from the earliest times to the Newtonian era. QA273.D29 1962

Garden in the machine : the emerging science of artificial life, The / QH324.2.E4613 1994

Garden of Eden : the botanic garden and the re-creation of paradise, The / QK73.E85.P73 1981

Gardener's guide to growing temperate bamboos, The / SB413.B2.B46 2000

Gardens and the picturesque : studies in the history of landscape architecture / SB457.6.H865 1992

Gardens of China : history, art, and meanings = [Chung-hua yuan lin] , The / SB457.55.M66 1983

Gardens of Gertrude Jekyll, The, The / SB470.J38.B57 1992

Gardens of Japan, The, The / SB458.I833 1984

Gardens of Provence and the French Riviera, The / SB466.F82.P767 1987

Gardens of the Italian villas / SB466.I8.A35 1987

Gardner's chemical synonyms and trade names / TP9.G286 1999

Garter snakes : evolution and ecology, The / QL666.O636.R67 1996

Gas turbine engine : design, development, applications, The / TL227.N67 1975

Gas turbine theory / TJ778.S24 2001

Gateways into electronics / TK7816.D86 2000

Gauss : a biographical study / QA29.G3.B83

Gay, straight, and in-between : the sexology of erotic orientation / QP278.M66 1988

Gear handbook : design and calculations / TJ185.S74 1992

Geckoes : biology, husbandry, and reproduction / SF515.5.G43.H4613 1995

Gem and lapidary materials : for cutters, collectors, and jewelers / TS752.Z45 1996

Gemmology / TS752.R44 1998

Gems : their sources, descriptions, and identification / QE392.W37 1994

Gems, granites, and gravels : knowing and using rocks and minerals / QE363.2.D52 1990

Gemstone & mineral data book : a compilation of data, recipes, formulas, and instructions for the mineralogist, gemologist, lapidary, jeweler, craftsman, and collector/TS752.5.S56 1981

Gemstones / TS752.O3 1988

Gender and science reader, The / Q130.G43 2000

Gene age : genetic engineering and the next industrial revolution, The / TP248.6.S94 1987

Gene wars : science, politics, and the human genome, The / QH445.2.C66 1994

General and comparative physiology / QP33.H6 1983

General meteorology. / QC861.B9 1959

General physics; mechanics and molecular physics / QC21.L2713 1967

General relativity : an introduction to the theory of the gravitational field / QC178.S8213 1982

General relativity from A to B / QC173.6.G47

General topology and homotopy theory / QA611.J33 1984

General topology. / QA611.B65813

General zoology / QL47.2.V5 1984

Genes in the field : on-farm conservation of crop diversity / SB123.3.G47 2000

Genes VII / QH430.L487 2000

Genes, crops, and the environment / SB123.3.H65 1993

Genes, enzymes, and inherited diseases. / QH431.S94

Genesis : the origins of man and the universe / QB44.2.G753

Genesis and evolution of time : a critique of interpretation in physics, The / QB209.F7 1982

Genetic basis of evolutionary change, The / QH455.L48

Genetic basis of plant physiological processes, The / QK711.2.K57

Genetic code, The. QH431.A72

Genetic engineering : a documentary history/QH442.S476 1999

Genetic engineering : dreams and nightmares / QH442.R87 1995

Genetic engineering : science and ethics on the new frontier / QH442.B69 2001

Genetic recombination / QH443.L43 1996

Genetic transformation in plants / QK981.5.W34 1989

Genetic turning points : the ethics of human genetic intervention / QH438.7.P485 2001

Genetics : principles, concepts, and implications / QH430.J35 1999

Genetics and biology of Drosophila, The / QH470.D7.G46

Genetics and conservation of rare plants / QK86.A1.G45 1991

Genetics and the behavior of domestic animals / SF756.7.G46 1998

Genetics and the origin of species. QH366.D6 1951

Genetics, speciation, and the Founder principle / QH455.G467 1989

Genius : the life and science of Richard Feynman / QC16.F49.G54 1992

Genius of C. Warren Thornthwaite, climatologist-geographer, The / QC858.T48M38 1996

Genome : the autobiography of a species in 23 chapters / QH431.R475 1999

Genomics : the science and technology behind the Human Genome Project / QP624.C36 1999

Gentians / SB413.G3.K64 1991

Gentle introduction to game theory, A / QA269.S695 1999

Genus Cymbidium, The / SB409.8.C95.D8 1988

Genus Hosta = Giboshi zoku, The / SB413.H73.S36 1991

Geochemistry of hydrothermal ore deposits./QE390.5.G43 1997

Geodynamics / QE501.T83 2001

Geoenvironmental engineering : contaminated soils, pollutant fate and mitigation / TD878.Y65 2001

Geographical distribution of animals. With a study of the relations of living and extinct faunas as elucidating the past changes of the earth's surface, The. / QL101.W18 1962

Geography of science, The / Q125.D65 1991

Geography of soil, The / S591.B886

Geologic evolution of Europe. QE260.B723

Geologic maps : a practical guide to the preparation and interpretation of geologic maps : for geologists, geographers, engineers, and planners / QE36.S64 2000

Geological background to fossil man : recent research in the Gregory Rift Valley, East Africa / QE690.G44

Geological companion to Greece and the Aegean, A / QE271.H54 1996

Geological evolution of Australia & New Zealand, The QE340.B7 1968

Geology and America's national park areas / QE77.E45 1996

Geology and engineering / TA705.L4 1988

Geology and hazardous waste management / TD1064.H37 1996

Geology and hydrogeology of carbonate islands / QE565.G46 1997

# Title Index

Identifying marine diatoms and dinoflagellates / QK569.D54.I34 1996

Identifying marine phytoplankton / QK934.I44 1997

IEEE 100 : the authoritative dictionary of IEEE standards terms. 7th ed. TK9.I28 2000

IEEE standard dictionary of electrical and electronics terms, The / TK9.I35 1996

IES lighting handbook / TK4161.I46 1981

Igneous and metamorphic petrology / QE461.B53 1982

IGY: year of discovery; the story of the International Geophysical Year. QC801.3.C45

Illustrated companion to Gleason and Cronquist's manual : illustrations of the vascular plants of northeastern United States and adjacent Canada / QK117.H65 1998

Illustrated dictionary of mycology / QK600.35.U513 2000

Illustrated digital imaging dictionary, The / TA1509.G76 1998

Illustrated encyclopedia of birds : the definitive reference to birds of the world, The / QL672.2.I45 1991

Illustrated encyclopedia of roses, The / SB411.I45 1992

Illustrated encyclopedia of space technology : a comprehensive history of space exploration, The / TL788.I44 1981

Illustrated encyclopedia of the universe, The / QB14.I588 2001

Illustrated glossary of petroleum geochemistry / TN870.5.M493 1989

Illustrated history of fashion : 500 years of fashion illustration, An / TT509.M33 1997

Illustrated survey of orchid genera, An / QK495.O64.S49 1994

Illustrations from the works of Andreas Vesalius of Brussels, The / QM25.V43

Image and memory : photography from Latin America, 1866-1994 : FotoFest / TR645.H8.F673 1998

Image processing handbook, The / TA1637.R87 1999

Images in weather forecasting : a practical guide for interpreting satellite and radar imagery / QC995.I43 1995

Images of mind / QP360.5.P67 1994

Images of science : a history of scientific illustration / Q222.F67 1993

Images of war, by Robert Capa, with text from his own writings/ TR140.C28.A3

Imaginary tale : the story of [the square root of minus one], An / QA255.N34 1998

Imitation factor : evolution beyond the gene, The / QL751.D7465 2000

Immense journey, The. / QH368.E38

Imms' General textbook of entomology. / QL463.I57 1977

Immune self : theory or metaphor?, The / QR181.T36 1994

Immune system : evolutionary principles guide our understanding of this complex biological defense system, The / QR182.2.E94.L36 1989

Immunity to parasites : how parasitic infections are controlled / QR201.P27.W35 1996

Immunology of the nervous system / QP356.47.I46 1997

Immunology, a synthesis / QR181.G66 1991

Imogen Cunningham : ideas without end : a life in photographs / TR140.C78.L67 1993

Impact Jupiter : the crash of comet Shoemaker-Levy 9 / QB723.S56.L48 1995

Impact mechanics / TA354.S77 2000

Impact of science on society, The. / Q175.R86 1952a

Impact of the gene : from Mendel's peas to designer babies, The / QH437.T833 2001

Impact! : the threat of comets and asteroids / QB721.V48 1996

Implementing ISO 14000 : a practical, comprehensive guide to the ISO 14000 environmental management standards / TS155.7.I47 1997

Importance of being fuzzy : and other insights from the border between math and computers, The / QA76.9.S63.S26 1998

Imposing wilderness : struggles over livelihood and nature preservation in Africa / SB484.T3.N48 1998

Impure science : fraud, compromise, and political influence in scientific research / Q175.37.B45 1992

In at the beginnings : a physicist's life / QC16.M66.A34

In darkness born : the story of star formation / QB806.C64 1988

In Polya's footsteps : miscellaneous problems and essays / QA43.H633 1997

In praise of wolves / QL737.C22.L34 1986

In search of deep time : beyond the fossil record to a new history of life / QE721.2.S7.G44 1999

In search of planet Vulcan : the ghost in Newton's clockwork universe / QB605.2.B38 1997

In search of Schrodinger's cat : quantum physics and reality / QC173.98.G75 1984

In service of the wild : restoring and reinhabiting damaged land / QH541.15.R45.M55 1995

In the dust of Kilimanjaro / QL84.6.K4.W47 1997

In the eye's mind : vision and the Helmholtz-Hering controversy / QP491.T87 1994

In the presence of the Creator : Isaac Newton and his times / QC16.N7.C49 1984

In the shadow of the bomb : Bethe, Oppenheimer, and the moral responsibility of the scientist / QC774.O56.S32 2000

In the shadow of the bomb : physics and arms control / QC773.3.U5.D74 1993

In the wake of Galileo / Q127.I8.S44 1991

Inactivity : physiological effects / QP310.5.I53 1986

In-depth analysis of linear programming / T57.74.V37 2001

Index fossils of North America: a new work based on the complete revision and reillustration of Grabau and Shimer's "North American index fossils," by Hervey W. Shimer and Robert R. Shrock. QE745.S48

Index of garden plants / SB403.2.G75 1994

Index to American photographic collections : compiled at the International Museum of Photography at George Eastman House / TR12.E85 1996

Index to illustrations of animals and plants / QH46.5.C54 1991

Individual behavior and community dynamics / QL751.F878 1998

Individual development and evolution : the genesis of novel behavior / QH438.5.G68 1992

Individual in the animal kingdom, The, / QH311.H9

Individuality in clothing selection and personal apearance / TT507.I454 2000

Indoor air : quality and control / TD883.1.I476 1993

Indoor environmental quality / TD883.17

Inductive logic programming : from machine learning to software engineering / QA76.63.B47 1996

Industrial and commercial power system handbook / TK4035.F3.P73 1995

Industrial applications of lasers / TA1677.R4 1997

Industrial compressors : theory and equipment / TJ990.O815 1993

Industrial design / TS140.L63.A34 1979

Industrial design A-Z / TS171.4.F54 2000

Industrial ecology : environmental chemistry and hazardous waste / TS161.M353 1999

Industrial ecology and global change / TS161.I54 1994

Industrial ecology and the automobile / TL240.G73 1998

Industrial electronics for engineers, chemists, and technicians / TK7881.S52 2001

Industrial energy conservation / TJ163.3.G68 1995

Industrial enzymes and their applications / TP248.E5.U37 1998

Industrial lighting systems / TK4399.F2.F74

Industrial minerals and rocks / TN799.5.A43 1994

Industrial organic chemicals / TP247.W59 1996

Industrial pollution prevention handbook / TD194.F74 1995

Industrial solvents handbook / TP247.5.I53 1994

Industrial wastewater systems handbook, The / TD897.5.S74 1998

Industry's future : changing patterns of industrial research / T175.F87 1994

Inevitable bond : examining scientist-animal interactions, The / QL55.I44 1992

Infamous boundary : seven decades of controversy in quantum physics, The / QC173.98.W53 1995

Infectious diseases of fish = Sakana no kansensho / SH171.E4313 1992

Infinite sequences and series; QA295.K72

# Title Index

Inflationary universe : the quest for a new theory of cosmic origins, The / QB991.I54.G88 1997

Information ages : literacy, numeracy, and the computer revolution / QA76.9.C66.H63 1998

Information and coding theory / Q360.J68 2000

Information and measurement / T58.5.L48 1995

Information architecture for the World Wide Web / TK5105.888.R67 1998

Information seeking in electronic environments / QA76.9.H85.M38 1995

Information systems : theory and practice / T58.6.B87 1989

Information systems anaylsis and modeling : an information macrodynamics approach / T58.6.L45 2000

Information systems engineering : a formal approach / TA168.H44 1994

Information technology : a luddite analysis / QA76.W38 1986

Information technology : new directions for the 21st century / T58.5.B47 1995

Infrared and Raman spectra of inorganic and coordination compounds / QD96.I5.N33 1997

Inmates are running the asylum, The / QA76.9.H85C673 1999

Innovation in Maxwell's electromagnetic theory : molecular vortices, displacement current, and light / QC670.S48 1991

Innovations in science and mathematics education : advanced designs for technologies of learning / Q181.I654 1999

Innovations: scientific, technological, and social / T173.8.G3 1970

Innovators : the engineering pioneers who made America modern, The / TA15.B53 1996

Inorganic biochemistry : an introduction / QP531.C68 1997

Inorganic chemical nomenclature : principles and practice / QD149.B59 1990

Inorganic chemistry : an industrial and environmental perspective / QD151.5.S93 1997

Inorganic chemistry of main group elements / QD151.2.K5 1995

Inorganic chemistry of materials : how to make things out of elements, The / QD151.2.P89 1998

Inorganic chemistry, a modern introduction / QD151.2.M63 1982

Inorganic electronic structure and spectroscopy / QD95.I486 1999

Inorganic polymers / QD196.M37 1992

Inorganic syntheses / QD156.I56

Insanely great : the life and times of Macintosh, the computer that changed everything / QA76.8.M3.L487 1994

Insect defenses : adaptive mechanisms and strategies of prey and predators / QL434.8.I57 1990

Insect hormones / QL495.N54 1994

Insect life : a field entomology manual for the amateur naturalist / QL464.A76 1985

Insect migration : tracking resources through space and time / QL496.2.I47 1995

Insect migration / QL496.W64 1966

Insect pathology / SB942.T35 1993

Insect pest management : techniques for environmental protection / SB933.3.I53 2000

Insect predator-prey dynamics : ladybird beetles and biological control / QL596.C65.D58 2000

Insects in flight / QL496.7.B73 1992

Insects of Australia : a textbook for students and research workers, The / QL487.I5 1991

Inside relativity / QC173.55.M66 1987

Inside the earth : evidence from earthquakes / QE509.B69 1982

Inside the environmental movement : meeting the leadership challenge / S944.5.L42.I57 1991

Insight into optics / QC358.H43 1991

Institutions for the earth : sources of effective international environmental protection / TD170.2.I556 1993

Instream flow protection : seeking a balance in Western water use / TC423.6.G55 1997

Instrument engineers' handbook : process control / TS156.8.I5622 1995

Instrumental methods of analysis QD61.W67 1965

Instrumental methods of chemical analysis. QD75.E9 1960

Instrumentation reference book / QC53.I574 1995

Instruments and experimentation in the history of chemistry / QD53.I57 2000

Instruments of science : an historical encyclopedia / Q184.5.I57 1998

Integral equations : a practical treatment, from spectral theory to applications / QA431.P67 1990

Integrated chemical systems : a chemical approach to nanotechnology / TP256.B37 1994

Integrated circuit engineering : establishing a foundation / TK7874.H418 1996

Integrated design of water treatment facilities / TH4538.K39 1991

Integrated system of classification of flowering plants, An / QK495.A1.C76

Integrative activity of the brain; an interdisciplinary approach. / QP376.K65

Integrative approaches to molecular biology / QH506.I483 1996

Integrative plant anatomy / QK641.D53 2000

Integrative stratigraphy : concepts and applications / QE651.B785 1988

Intellectual mastery of nature : theoretical physics from Ohm to Einstein / QC7.J86 1986

Intelligence of dogs : canine consciousness and capabilities, The / SF433.C67 1994

Intelligent control : power electronic systems / TK7881.15.D68 1998

Intelligent methods in signal processing and communications / TK5102.9.I545 1997

Interacting with audiences : social influences on the production of scientific writing / QC5.3.B53 2001

Interactions : some contacts between the natural sciences and the social sciences / Q175.5.C62 1994

Intermediate mathematical analysis / QA300.T48 1988

Intermountain flora; vascular plants of the Intermountain West, U.S.A., / QK141.I58

Internal combustion engine fundamentals / TJ755.H45 1988

Internal-combustion engine in theory and practice, The / TJ785.T382 1985

International biographical dictionary of computer pioneers / QA76.2.A2.L44 1995

International code of botanical nomenclature QK96.R4 vol. 111

International computer software industry : a comparative study of industry evolution and structure, The / QA76.76.D47.I555 1996

International dictionary of artificial intelligence, The / Q334.2.R39 1999

International dictionary of geophysics; seismology, geomagnetism, aeronomy, oceanography, geodesy, gravity, marine geophysics, meteorology, the earth as a planet and its evolution. QC801.9.I5 1967

International encyclopedia of composites / TA418.9.C6E53 1989

International encyclopedia of dogs, The / SF422.D28 1974

International encyclopedia of ergonomics and human factors / TA166.I556 2001

International encyclopedia of heat & mass transfer / TJ260.I579 1997

International encyclopedia of horse breeds / SF291.H37 1995

International encyclopedia of science and technology, The / Q121.I48 1999

International handbook of national parks and nature reserves / SB481.I565 1990

International hospitality business : management and operations, The / TX911.3.M27.Y82 1999

International minerals : a national perspective / TN153.I49 1983

International regulation of extinction, The / QH75.S815 1994

International space policy : legal, economic, and strategic options for the twentieth century and beyond / TL788.4.I585 1987

International stratigraphic guide : a guide to stratigraphic classification, terminology, and procedure / QE651.I57 1976

International wildlife trade : whose business is it? / QL82.F58 1989

International women in science : a biographical dictionary to 1950 / Q141.H2167 2001

657

Introduction to the visual system, An / QP475.T68 1996

Introduction to theoretical kinematics, An / QA841.M33 1990

Introduction to thermal-fluid engineering : the engine and the atmosphere, An / TJ260.W217 1997

Introduction to thermodynamics and kinetic theory of matter / QC311.B95 1996

Introduction to transport phenomena / TP156.T7.T48 2000

Introduction to turbulent flow, An / QA913.M39 2000

Introduction to wavelets, An / QA403.3.C48 1992

Introduction to wildland fire / SD421.P94 1996

Introduction to wind turbine engineering / TJ825.W87 1983

Introductioncourse in commutative algebra, An / QA251.3.C53 1998

Introductory applications of partial differential equations with emphasis on wave propagation and diffusion / QA374.L32 1995

Introductory astronomy / QB43.2.H65 1999

Introductory circuit analysis / TK454.B68 2000

Introductory functional analysis : with applications to boundary value problems and finite elements / QA320.R433 1998

Introductory microbiology / QR41.2.H46 1996

Introductory modern algebra : a historical approach / QA162.S73 1997

Introductory mycology / QK603.A55 1979

Introductory nutrition / TX354.G8 1983

Invasions of the land : the transitions of organisms from aquatic to terrestrial life / QH366.2.G657 1995

Invasive species in a changing world / QH353.I59 2000

Inventing and patenting sourcebook : how to sell and protect your ideas / T339.L38 1990

Inventing modern America : from the microwave to the mouse / T20.B76 2002

Inventing polymer science : Staudinger, Carothers, and the emergence of macromolecular chemistry / QD381.F87 1998

Inventing the 19th century : 100 inventions that shaped the Victorian Age from aspirin to the Zeppelin / T19.V36 2001

Inventing the Internet / TK5105.875.I57.A23 1999

Invention : the care and feeding of ideas / T15.W65 1993

Inverse problems : activites for undergraduates / QA371.G73 1999

Invertebrate fossils / QE770.M6

Invertebrate relationships : patterns in animal evolution / QL362.75.W55 1990

Invertebrate zoology / QL362.B27 1987, QL362.H4 1981, QL362.R76 1994

Invertebrates / QL362.B924 1990

Invertebrates in freshwater wetlands of North America : ecology and management / QL365.4.A1.I58 1999

Invertebrates, The. / QL362.H9

Investigations on the theory of the Brownian movement. QC183.E53 1956

Investigative enterprise : experimental physiology in nineteenth-century medicine, The / QP21.I58 1988

Invisible enemy : a natural history of viruses, The / QR364.C73 2000

Invisible farmers : women in agricultural production, The / S441.S25 1983

Invisible invaders : the story of the emerging age of viruses, The / QR359.R33 1991

Invitation to algebraic geometry, An / QA564.I62 2000

Ion channels : molecules in action / QH603.I54.A33 1996

Ion chromatography / QD79.C453.W4513 1995

Ion exchange in analytical chemistry / QD79.C453.W35 1990

Ionic equilibrium : solubility and pH calculations / QD561.B985 1998

Ions in solution : basic principles of chemical interactions / QD561.B9525 1988

Iowa's geological past : three billion years of earth history / QE111.A582 1998

Iowa's wild places : an exploration / QH105.I8.K87 1996

Iron blast furnace : theory and practice, The / TN713.P42 1979

Iron, nature's universal element : why people need iron & animals make magnets / QP535.F4

Irwin handbook of telecommunications, The / TK5102.3.U6G74 2000

Is anyone out there? : the scientific search for extraterrestrial intelligence / QB54.D72 1992

Is the temperature rising? : the uncertain science of global warming / QC981.8.G56.P48 1998

Isaac Asimov's guide to earth and space / QB52.A74 1991

Isaac Newton : the last sorcerer / QC16.N7.W45 1997

Isaac Newton, adventurer in thought / QC16.N7.H35 1992

ISDN literacy book, The / TK5103.75.H67 1995

Island Africa : the evolution of Africa's rare animals and plants / QL84.6.A1.K56 1989

Islands and the sea : five centuries of nature writing from the Caribbean, The / QH109.A1.I83 1991

Issues and dilemmas of biotechnology : a reference guide / TP248.2.S33 1999

Italian Renaissance garden : from the conventions of planting, design, and ornament to the grand gardens of sixteenth-century Central Italy, The / SB457.85.L39 1990

Ivies / SB413.I84.F43 1991

iWarp : anatomy of a parallel computing system / QA76.8.I93.G76 1998

J. Robert Oppenheimer : shatterer of worlds / QC16.O62.G66 1981

Jacobson's organ and the remarkable nature of smell / QP458.W38 2000

James Beard's theory & practice of good cooking / TX651.B37 1977

Jane's airports and handling agents. / TL726.6.E85.J36

Jane's all the world's aircraft, 1909- / TL501.J3

Jane's world railways. / TF1.J3

Japanese/English English/Japanese glossary of scientific and technical terms / Q123.T844 1993

Java programming from the beginning / QA76.73.J38

Java programming language, The / QA76.73.J38A76 2000

Jens Jensen : maker of natural parks and gardens / SB470.J4.G74 1992

Job and work design : organizing work to promote well-being and effectiveness / T60.8.P39 1998

John and William Bartram's America : selections from the writings of the Philadelphia naturalists / QH31.B23.A3

John Burroughs' America; selections from the writings of the Hudson River naturalist, QH81.B963 1951

John Clayton, pioneer of American botany, / QK31.C55.B4

John Evelyn's "Elysium Britannicum" and European gardening / SB470.E9.J64 1998

John James Audubon : a biography / QL31.A9.F63 1988

John Muir : apostle of nature / QH31.M78.W54 1995

John Muir : his Life and letters and other writings / QH31.M9.M85 1996

John Muir and his legacy : the American conservation movement / QH76.F69

John Muir's "Stickeen" and the lessons of nature / SF426.2.L56 1996

John Torrey; a story of North American botany, / QK31.T7.R6

John Von Neumann and Norbert Wiener : from mathematics to the technologies of life and death / QA28.H44

Johnny Appleseed : man and myth / S417.C45.P7

Joseph Banks, a life / QH31.B19.O27 1993

Joseph Henry : the rise of an American scientist / QC16.H37.M69 1997

Josiah Willard Gibbs, the history of a great mind. QC16.G5.W45 1962

Journal of researches into the geology and natural history of the various countries visited by H. M. S. Beagle. QH11.D2 1839a

Journal of the American Mathematical Society QA1.J978

Journey into gravity and spacetime, A / QB334.W49 1990

Journey to the ants : a story of scientific exploration / QL568.F7.H575 1994

Journey to the centers of the mind : toward a science of consciousness / QP411.G69 1995

Journeys in microspace : the art of the scanning electron microscope / QH251.B73 1994

Light and plant growth / QK757.H37 1988

Light at the edge of the universe : leading cosmologists on the brink of a scientific revolution, The / QB981.L36 1993

Light detectors, photoreceptors, and imaging systems in nature / QP481.W58 1995

Lighter side of gravity, The / QB331.N37 1982

Lightning discharge, The / QC966.U4 1987

Lilies : a guide for growers and collectors / SB413.L7.M39 1998

Limb regeneration / QP90.2.T76 1996

Limits of science, The / Q175.M433 1984, Q175.R393327 1999

Limnology/ QH96.W47 1983

Linear algebra and differential equations / QA184.B34 1990

Linear algebra done right / QA184.A96 1996

Linear algebra problem book / QA184.5.H35 1995

Linear algebra with applications / QA184.N34 1998

Linear analysis : an introductory course / QA320.B64 1990

Linear control systems : modeling, analysis, and design / TJ216.R67 1986

Linear electric actuators and generators / TK2411.B6 1997

Linear functions and matrix theory / QA184.J333 1995

Linear models in statistics / QA276.R425 2000

Linear networks and systems : alogrithms and computer-aided implementations / TK454.2.C4253 1990

Linear programming / T57.74.K37 1991

Linear programming : foundations and extensions / T57.74.V36 2001

Linear programming and network flows / T57.74.B39 1990

Lineman's and cableman's handbook, The / TK3221.K83 1986

Linnaeus, the man and his work / QH44.L56 1983

Linus Pauling : a life in science and politics / Q143.P25.G64 1995

Linus Pauling : in his own words : selected writings, speeches, and interviews / Q143.P25.A3 1995

Linus Pauling : scientist and peacemaker / Q143.P25

Liquids crystals : nature's delicate phase of matter / QD923.C638 2002

Lise Meitner : a life in physics / QC774.M4.S56 1996

LISP in small pieces / QA76.73.L23.Q4613 1996

Literary structure of scientific argument : historical studies, The / Q126.8.L58 1991

Literature of animal science and health, The / SF22.5.L58 1993

Literature of crop science, The / SB45.65.L58 1995

Literature of soil science, The / S590.45.L58 1994

Little Ice Age : how climate made history, 1300-1850, The / QC989.A1

Lives to come : the genetic revolution and human possibilities, The / QH431.K54 1996

Livestock / SF105.3.L58 1993

Living and working in space : human behavior, culture, and organization / TL795.7.H37 1991

Living bay : the underwater world of Monterey Bay, A / QH105.C2

Living fossil : the story of the coelacanth / QL638.L26.T46 1991

Living free; the story of Elsa and her cubs. QL737.C2.A4

Living ocean : understanding and protecting marine biodiversity, The / QH91.T45 1999

Living planet in crisis : biodiversity science and policy, The / QH75.A1.L58 1999

Living sea, The. QH91.C628

Living waters : how to save your local stream / QH76.5.P4.O93 1993

Living with earthquakes in California : a survivor's guide / QE535.2.U6

Living with radiation : the risk, the promise / QC795.W24 1989

Lizard ecology : historical and experimental perspectives / QL666.L2.L57 1994

Lizard man speaks, The / QL31.P57.A3 1994

Lizards / SF459.L5.R6313 1997

Logic and Boolean algebra. QA266.A7

Logic as algebra / QA9.H293 1998

Logic in computer science : modelling and reasoning about systems / QA76.9.L63.H88 2000

Logic of biochemical sequencing, The / QP551.B53 1994

Logic of scientific discovery, The / Q175.P863

Logical approach to discrete math, A / QA39.2.G7473 1993

Logical construction of systems / QA76.W24513

Logical journey : from Godel to philosophy, A / QA29.G58.W357 1996

Longevity, senescence, and the genome / QP85.F47 1990

Longitude : the true story of a lone genius who solved the greatest scientific problem of his time / QB225.S64 1995

Looking-glass garden : plants and gardens of the Southern Hemisphere, The / SB408.3.S645

Loom of God : mathematical tapestries at the edge of time, The / Q175.P523 1997

Lop-sided ape : evolution of the generstive mind, The / QP385.5.C67 1991

Lord of Uraniborg : a biography of Tycho Brahe, The / QB36.B8.T49 1990

Lords of the fly : Drosophila genetics and the experimental life / Q180.55.M4.K63 1994

Lorentzian wormholes : from Einstein to Hawking / QC173.6.V57 1995

Los Alamos primer : the first lectures on how to build an atomic bomb, The / QC773.A1.S47 1992

Loss of Eden : a biography of Charles and Anne Morrow Lindbergh / TL540.L5.M52 1993

Lost moon : the perilous voyage of Apollo 13 / TL789.8U6A5488 1994

Lost talent : women in the sciences / Q130.H365 1996

Lost woods : the discovered writing of Rachel Carson / QH81.C3546 1998

Louis Agassiz: a life in science / QH31.A2.L8

Louis Pasteur / Q143.P2.D3313 1998

Low temperature physics / QC278.J3 1962

Low temperature solid state physics; some selected topics / QC278.R6

Low voltage wiring handbook : design, installation, and maintenance / TK5103.12.M39 1995

Lower animals; living invertebrates of the world, The / QL362.B94

Low-voltage/low-power integrated circuits and systems : low-voltage mixed-signal ciruits / TK7874.66.L69 1999

Lucifer's legacy : the meaning of asymmetry / QC174.17.S9.C56 2000

Lunar base handbook : an introduction to lunar base design, development, and operations, The / TL799.M6

Lunar sourcebook : a user's guide to the moon / QB581.L766 1991

Lure of the integers / QA141.R63 1992

Lyell : the past is the key to the present / QE22.L8L94 1998

Lysenko and the tragedy of Soviet science / Q127.R9.S65 1994

Machiavellian intelligence II : extensions and evaluations / QL737.P9.M274 1997

Machine in America : a social history of technology, The / T14.5.P87 1995

Machinery of life, The / QH581.2.G66 1993

Machinery of the body, The / QP34.C25 1961

Machinery's handbook pocket companion : a reference book for the mechanical engineer, designer, manufacturing engineer, draftsman, toolmaker, and machinist / TJ151.M355 2000

Machines as the measure of men : science, technology, and ideologies of Western dominance / T15.A33 1989

Machines that learn : based on the principles of empirical control / Q325.5.B76 1994

Machines with a purpose / T14.R599 1990

Machu Picchu : a civil engineering marvel / TA52.W75 2000

Macmillan biographical encyclopedia of photographic artists & innovators / TR139.B767 1983

Macmillan book of the marine aquarium : a definitive reference to more than 300 marine fish and invertebrate species and how to establish and maintain a reef aquarium, The / SF457.1.D35 1992

Macmillan encyclopedia of chemistry / QD4.M33 1997

Macmillan encyclopedia of physics / QC5.M15 1996

Macroecology / QH541.B75 1995

Names, synonyms, and structures of organic compounds : a CRC reference handbook / QD291.N36 1995

Nano : the emerging science of nanotechnology : remaking the world-molecule by molecule / T174.7.R44 1995

Nanostructured materials and nanotechnology / TA418.9.N35H37 2001

Nanosystems : molecular machinery, manufacturing, and computation / T174.7.D74 1992

Nanotechnology : molecular speculations on global abundance / T174.7.N375 1996

NASA and the space industry / TL521.312.B76 1999

NASA planetary spacecraft : Galileo, Magellan, Pathfinder, and Voyager / TL796.3.B74 2000

National Arboretum book of outstanding garden plants : the authoritative guide to selecting and growing the most beautiful, durable, and care-free garden plants in North America, The / SB407.H493 1990

National Audubon Society field guide to North American mammals / QL715.W49 1996

National electrical code handbook, The / TK260.N47B

National Electrical Code reference book / TK260.G37 1998

National Gardening Association guide to kids' gardening, The / SB457.O24 1990

National geographic guide to America's public gardens : 300 of the best gardens to visit in the U.S. and Canada / SB466.U6J45 1998

National Park Service, The / SB482.A4.E95 1983

National parks and rural development : practice and policy in the United States / SB482.A4

National parks, conservation, and development : the role of protected areas in sustaining society : proceedings of the World Congress on National Parks, Bali, Indonesia, 11-22 October 1982 / SB481.A2.W67 1982

National Science Education Standards : observe, interact, change, learn. Q183.3.A1.N364 1996

National Trust book of the English garden, The / SB466.G7

Natural disasters, hurricanes : a reference handbook / QC944.F58 1999

Natural enemies handbook : the illustrated guide to biological pest control / SB993.3.F59 1998

Natural gas engineering : production and storage / TN880.K38 1990

Natural gas vehicles / TL228.I54 1996

Natural groundwater flow / TC176.Z55 1993

Natural history of amphibians, A / QL667.S84 1995

Natural history of Australia, A / QH197.B46 1998

Natural history of cats, The / SF442.N4

Natural history of deer, The / QL737.U55.P87 1988

Natural history of domesticated mammals, A / SF41.C58 1999

Natural history of medicinal plants, The / QK99.A1

Natural history of moles, The / QL737.I57.G67 1990

Natural history of monitor lizards, The / QL666.L29.D4 1996

Natural history of pollination, The / QK926.P75 1996

Natural history of seals, The / QL737.P64.B66 1990

Natural history of sex : the ecology and evolution of sexual behavior, A / QH471.F69 1986

Natural history of shells, A / QL403.V47 1993

Natural history of the Antarctic Peninsula / QH84.2.M67 1988

Natural history of the Colorado Plateau and Great Basin / QH104.5.G68.N38 1994

Natural history of the Lewis and Clark Expedition, The. / QL155.B8

Natural history of the mind, The / QP360.T39 1979

Natural history of the Sonoran Desert, A / QH104.5.S58.N38 2000

Natural history of the wild cats, The / QL737.C23.K58 1991

Natural history of vision, A / QP475.W24 1998

Natural history. / QH41.P713 1961

Natural hybridization and evolution / QH421.A76 1997

Natural regulation of animal numbers, The. / QL751.L3

Natural resource conservation : management for a sustainable future / S938.O87 1998

Natural selection : domains, levels, and challenges / QH375.W52 1992

Naturalist / QH31.W64.A3 1994

Naturalist's guide to the tropics, A / QH84.5.L3613 2000

Naturally intelligent systems / QA76.5.C387 1990

Naturally occurring pest bioregulators / SB951.145.N37.N38 1991

Nature and ideology : natural garden design in the twentieth century / SB439.N43 1997

Nature and nurture : an introduction to human behavioral genetics / QH457.P57 1990

Nature and properties of engineering materials, The / TA403.J35 1987

Nature and property of soils, The / S591.B79 2002

Nature in danger : threatened habitats and species / QH541.S5345 1995

Nature loves to hide : quantum physics and reality, a western perspective / QC174.12.M34 2001

Nature of Australia : a portrait of the island continent / QH197.V36 1988

Nature of ball lightning, The. / QC966.S55

Nature of diseases in plants, The / SB601.S28 1997

Nature of mathematical modeling, The / QA401.G47 1999

Nature of Mediterranean Europe : an ecological history, The / QH150.G76 2001

Nature of photographs, The / TR179.S56 1998

Nature of physical reality; a philosophy of modern physics, The. / QC6.M3514

Nature of physics; a physicist's views on the history and philosophy of his science, The. / QC6.L425

Nature of space and time, The / QC173.59.S65.H4 1996

Nature of the chemical bond and the structure of molecules and crystals; an introduction to modern structural chemistry, The. / QD469.P38 1960

Nature of the universe, The. / QB51.H8 1960

Nature of time, The, / QB209.G56

Nature out of place : biological invasions in the global age / QH353.V36 2000

Nature pictorialized : "the view" in landscape history / SB470.5.C73 1993

Nature's body : gender in the making of modern science / QP81.5.S35 1993

Nature's capacities and their measurement / QC6.4.C3.C37 1989

Nature's economy : a history of ecological ideas / QH541.W638 1985

Nature's keepers : the new science of nature management / QH75.B823 1995

Nature's numbers : the unreal reality of mathematical imagination / QA93.S737 1995

Navajo country : a geology and natural history of the Four Corners Region / QE79.5.B285 1995

Nazi science : myth, truth, and the German atomic bomb / Q127.G3.W35 1995

Nearest star : the surprising science of our sun / QB521.G65 2001

Near-field optics : theory, instrumentation, and applications / QH212.N43.P34 1996

Neblette's Handbook of photography and reprography : materials, processes, and systems. / TR145.N4 1977

Nebulae and interstellar matter. / QB461.N4

Neem tree : Azadirachta indica A. Juss. and other meliaceous plants : sources of unique natural products for integrated pest management, medicine, industry, and other purposes, The / SB317.N43.N45 1995

Nemesis affair : a story of the death of dinosaurs and the ways of science, The / QB631.R38 1986

Neotropical birds : ecology and conservation / QL685.7.N46 1996

Neotropical companion : an introduction to the animals, plants, and ecosystems of the New World tropics, A / QH106.5.K75 1997

Neotropical migratory birds : natural history, distribution, and population change / QL681.D43 1995

Neotropical wildlife use and conservation / SK159.N46 1991

Neptune file : a story of astronomical rivalry and the pioneers of planet hunting, The / QB36.A2

Noble-gas chemistry / QD162.H6

Nonaqueous electrochemistry / QD555.5.N66 1999

Non-Darwinian revolution : reinterpreting a historical myth, The / QH361.B693 1988

Nondestructive evaluation : a tool in design, manufacturing, and services / TA417.2.B63 1997

Nondestructive testing : radiography, ultrasonics, liquid penetrant, magnetic particle, eddy current / TA417.2.C37 1995

Nonindigenous freshwater organisms : vectors, biology, and impacts / QH102.C56 2000

Nonlinear differential equations and dynamical systems / QA372.V47 1990

Nonlinear theory of elastic shells, The / TA660.S5.L457 1998

Non-local universe : the new physics and matters of the mind, The / QC174.12.N32 1999

No-nonsense guide to climate change, The / QC981.8.C5.G666 2001

Nonvascular plants : an evolutionary survey / QK505.N66 1982

Normal aging; reports from the Duke longitudinal study, / QP86.P3

Norms of nature : naturalism and the nature of functions / QH375.D36 2001

North American agroforestry : an integrated science and practice / S494.5.A45N69 2000

North American boletes : a color guide to the fleshy pored mushrooms / QK629.B6.B47 2000

North American buffalo, The; a critical study of the species in its wild state. 2d ed. QL737.U53R6 1970

North American cattle-ranching frontiers : origins, diffusion, and differentiation / SF196.N7.J67 1993

North American forests : geography, ecology, and silviculture, The / SD143.W285 1999

North American grasshoppers, The / QL508.A2.O88

North American horticulture : a reference guide / SB317.56.U6.N67 1991

North American owls : biology and natural history / QL696.S8.J64 1988

North American porcupine, The / QL737.R652.R69 1989

North American railroad : its origin, evolution, and geography, The / TF23.V36 1995

North American range plants / SB193.3.N67.S88 1982

North American terrestrial vegetation / QK110.N854 2000

North American waterfowl. SK361.D28 1959

North Carolina's hurricane history / QC945.B37 2001

Northern forest border in Canada and Alaska : biotic communities and ecological relationships, The / QH106.L283 1989

Northwest exposures : a geologic story of the Northwest / QE79.A46 1995

Northwest salmon crisis : a documentary history, The / SH348.N68 1996

Norton history of chemistry, The / QD11.B76 1993

Norton history of the mathematical sciences : the rainbow of mathematics, The / QA21.G695 1998

Norton's 2000.0 : star atlas and reference handbook (epoch 2000.0) / QB65.N7 1989

Not by timber alone : economics and ecology for sustaining tropical forests / SD247.P68 1992

Notable Black American scientists / Q141.N726 1999

Notable mathematicians : from ancient times to the present / QA28.N66 1998

Notable twentieth century scientists. / Q141.N73 1995 Suppl.

Notable women in mathematics : a biographical dictionary / QA28.N68 1998

Notable women in the life sciences : a biographical dictionary / QH26.N68 1996

Notable women in the physical sciences : a biographical dictionary / Q141.N734 1997

Notable women scientists / Q141.N736 1999

Notes on quantum mechanics; a course given at the University of Chicago. / QC174.F44

Nothing like it in the world : the men who built the transcontinental railroad, 1863-1869 / TF23.A48 2000

Nothing that is : a natural history of zero, The / QA141.K36 2000

Nothingness : the science of empty space / QC6.G35913 1999

No-tillage and surface-tillage agriculture : the tillage revolution / S604.N62 1986

Novel approaches to integrated pest management / SB950.N68 1995

Now it can be told; the story of the Manhattan project. / QC773.A1.G7

Noxious range weeds / SB617.45.W47.N69 1991

Nuclear chemistry : theory and applications / QD601.2.C47 1980

Nuclear choices : a citizen's guide to nuclear technology / TK9145.W59 1991

Nuclear energy : an introduction to the concepts, systems, and applications of nuclear processes / TK9145.M87 2001

Nuclear energy : principles, practices, and prospects / TK9145.B54 1996

Nuclear handbook, The. / QC783.F7

Nuclear madness : what you can do / TK9153.C34 1994

Nuclear muse : literature, physics, and the first atomic bombs, The / QC791.96.C36 2000

Nuclear physics. / QC173.H3854

Nuclear power : a reference handbook / TK9146.H45 2000

Nuclear power : technology on trial / TK1078.D83

Nuclear power plants worldwide. / TK1194.N83

Nuclear structure theory, / QC173.I73

Nuclei and particles; an introduction to nuclear and subnuclear physics. QC721.S4475

Nudes, 1945-1980 : photographs / TR675.B65 1980

Null models in ecology / QH541.15.N84.G67 1996

Number sense : how the mind creates mathematics, The / QA141.D44 1997

Number theory : an approach through history from Hammurapi to Legendre / QA241.W3418 1984

Number theory in science and communication : with applications in cryptography, physics, digital information, computing, and self-similarity / QA241.S318 1997

Numbers and geometry / QA39.2.S755 1998

Numerical algorithms with C / QA297.E56213 1996

Numerical analysis for applied science / QA297.A53 1998

Numerical computation : methods, software, and analysis / QA297.U2413 1997

Numerical computation in science and engineering / QA297.P69 1998

Numerical computation using C / QA76.73.C15.G57 1993

Numerical initial value problems in ordinary differential equations / QA372.G4

Numerical linear algebra / QA184.T74 1997

Numerical methods and scientific computing : using software libraries for problem solving / TA345.K653 1994

Numerical methods for engineering application / TA335.F47 1998

Numerical methods for least squares problems / QA214.B56 1996

Numerical methods of statistics / QA276.4.M65 2001

Numerical recipes example book (C++) / QA76.73.C153N83 2002

Numerical recipes in C : the art of scientific computing / QA76.73.C15N865 1992

Numerical recipes in C++ : the art of scientific computing / QA76.73.C153N85 2002

Numerical recipes in FORTRAN : the art of scientific computing / QA297.N866 1992

Numerical recipes in Pascal : the art of scientific computing / QA76.73.P2.N87 1989

Numerical solution of differential equations. / QA371.M57 1970

Numerical solution of ordinary differential equations / QA372.F69 1987

Numerical techniques in electromagnetics / QC760.S24 2000

Nutrient use in crop production / S633.N88 1998

Nutrients catalog : vitamins, minerals, amino acids, macronutrients--beneficial use, helpers, inhibitors, food sources, intake recommendations and symptoms of over or under use / QP141.N48 1993

Nutrients in food / TX551.H274 2000

Nutrition / QP141.C5 1979

Nutrition in exercise and sport / TX361.A8.N88 1998

Physiological ecology of tropical plants / QK936.L88 1997

Physiological foundations of neurology and psychiatry. / QP361.G43

Physiological plant ecology / QK901.L3513 1980

Physiological psychology QP355.M6 1965

Physiology and biochemistry of algae. / QK565.L4

Physiology and biochemistry of plant respiration, The / QK891.P483 1984

Physiology by numbers : an encouragement to quantitative thinking / QP33.6.M36.B87 1994

Physiology of fishes, The / QL639.1.P49 1993

Physiology of fungal nutrition, The / QK601.J46 1995

Physiology of insect development, QL461.C54 1956

Physiology of insect metamorphosis, The. QL496.W62

Physiology of insect senses, The. QL495.D4

Physiology of nerve cells, The QP331.E3

Physiology of plant growth and development, Th e, QK731.W45

Physiology of the kidney and body fluids; an introductory text QP249.P57 1974

Physiology of the nervous system / QP361.O874 1983

Physiology of trematodes, The / QL391.P7S58 1983

Physiology of woody plants / QK711.2.K72 1997

Phytoplankton manual / QK933.P49

Pi in the sky : counting, thinking, and being / QA36.B37 1992

Picasso and photography : the dark mirror / TR647.P512 1997

Pictorial guide to the living primates, The / QL737.P9.R675 1996

Pictorial human embryology / QM602.G55 1989

Picturing modernism : Moholy-Nagy and photography in Weimar Germany / TR140.M584.H54 1995

Picturing nature : American nineteenth-century zoological illustration / QL46.5.B58 1993

Picturing the century : one hundred years of photography from the National Archives / TR6.U6.W18 1999

Pigeons and doves : a guide to the pigeons and doves of the world / QL696.C63

Pigs : a handbook to the breeds of the world / SF395.P59 1993

Pilgrim at Tinker Creek. / QH81.D56 1974

Pillar of sand : can the irrigation miracle last? / S618.P67 1999

Pinball effect : how renaissance water gardens made the carburetor possible, and other journeys through knowledge, The / T15.B765 1996

Pinnipeds : seals, sea lions, and walruses, The / QL737.P6.R54 1990

Pioneers of flight : a documentary history, The / TL507.C34 1999

Pioneers of science : nobel prize winners in physics / QC15.W4

Placing nature : culture and landscape ecology / QH541.15.L35.P58 1997

Plague of frogs : the horrifying true story, A / QL668.E2S737 2000

Plain & fancy : American women and their needlework, 1700-1850 / TT715.S9

Planet earth : cosmology, geology, and the evolution of life and environment / QB631.E55 1992

Planet Mars : a history of observation & discovery, The / QB641.S484 1996

Planet observer's handbook, The / QB601.P67 2000

Planet quest : the epic discovery of alien solar systems / QB820.C76 1997

Planet Venus, The / QB621.M37 1998, QB621.M6

Planetary astronomy from the Renaissance to the rise of astrophysics / QB15.G38 1984 vol. 2

Planets & perception : telescopic views and interpretations, 1609-1909 / QB601.S54 1988

Planets, The. QB601.M68 1962a

Plankton ecology : succession in plankton communities / QH90.8.P5.P59 1989

Planning and design of airports / TL725.3.P5H6 1994

Planning and design of bridges / TG300.T76 1994

Plant anatomy. QK671.E8 1965

Plant biomechanics : an engineering approach to plant form and function / QK793.N55 1992

Plant breeding : theory and practice / SB123.S89 1993

Plant breeding methodology / SB123.J46 1988

Plant cell culture / SB123.6.C65 1998

Plant classification / QK97.B45 1979

Plant contamination : modeling and simulation of organic chemical processes / QK753.X45.P58 1994

Plant disease control : principles and practice / SB731.M364 1993

Plant disease management / SB731.S458 2001

Plant diseases of international importance / SB731.P67 1992

Plant dormancy : physiology, biochemistry, and molecular biology / QK761.P58 1996

Plant engineering magazine's fluid power handbook / TJ840.H44 1993

Plant engineer's handbook of formulas, charts, and tables / TS184.M63 1991

Plant form : an illustrated guide to flowering plant morphology / QK641.B45 1990

Plant fossils in geological investigation : the palaeozoic / QE915.P58 1991

Plant functional types : their relevance to ecosystem properties and global change / QK905.P565 1997

Plant genetic conservation : the in situ approach / SB123.3.P62 1997

Plant geography : with special reference to North America / QK101.D26

Plant growth and development / QK731.L44 1975

Plant growth regulators : agricultural uses / SB128.N52

Plant hunters; being a history of the horticultural pioneers, their quests, and their discoveries from the Renaissance to the twentieth century, The / SB404.5.C63 1970

Plant identification terminology : an illustrated glossary / QK9.H37 1994

Plant kingdom, The / QK47.B73 1987

Plant layout and material handling / TS178.A63 1991

Plant life in the world's mediterranean climates : California, Chile, South Africa, Australia, and the Mediterranean Basin / QK938.M45.D35 1998

Plant migration : the dynamics of geographic patterning in seed plant species / QK101.S28 1988

Plant nutrition manual / QK867.J64 1998

Plant pathologist's pocketbook / SB601.P57 2002

Plant physiological ecology / QK717.L35 1998

Plant physiology / QK711.2.B54 1979, QK711.2.T35 1998

Plant physiology : a treatise / QK711.P58 1959

Plant Pigments / QK898.P7P43 1988

Plant propagation : principles and practices / SB119.P55 2002

Plant sciences : production, genetics, and breeding / SB123.D75 1990

Plant speciation / QH368.5.G7 1981

Plant strategies and the dynamics and structure of plant communities / QK910.T55 1988

Plant systematics / QK95.J63 1986, QK95.S57 1999

Plant systematics : a phylogenetic approach/ QK95.P548 1999

Plant taxonomy : the systematic evaluation of comparative data / QK95.S78 1990

Plant taxonomy: methods and principles. QK95.B44

Plant tropisms and other growth movements / QK771.H36 1990

Plant variation and evolution / QK983.B73 1997

Plant-book, The : a portable dictionary of the vascular plants QK11.M29 1997

Planting the future : developing an agriculture that sustains land and community / S441.P58 1995

Plants and their names : a concise dictionary / QK96.P35 1995

Plants for American landscapes / SB435.5.O34 1996

Plants invade the land : evolutionary and environmental perspectives / QE905.P55 2001

Plants of Rocky Mountain National Park : a complete revision of Ruth Ashton Nelson's popular manual / QK150.N4 2000

Plants of the world QK98.W7213

Plants that merit attention / SB435.P6 1994

Plasma physics; a course given at the University of Chicago. QC711.C5

Plasma--the fourth state of matter QC718.F713

Plastic deformation of metals, The / TA460.H57 1984

Tales of giant snakes : a historical natural history of anacondas and pythons / QL666.O63.M87 1997

Tales of physicists and mathematicians / QC7.G5613 1988

Tales of the earth : paroxysms and perturbations of the blue planet / QB631.O34 1993

Talking nets : an oral history of neural networks / QA76.87.T37 1998

Tall building structures : analysis and design / TH1611.S59 1991

Tallgrass restoration handbook : for prairies, savannas, and woodlands, The / SB434.3.T35 1997

Tangled field : Barbara McClintock's search for the patterns of genetic control, The / QH429.2.M38

Taxonomy of flowering plants QK95.P6 1967

Taxonomy of vascular plants. QK93.L38

Tea : cultivation to consumption / SB271.T27 1992

Teaching and learning secondary science : contemporary issues and practical approaches / Q181.W4416 2000

Teaching introductory physics / QC30.A78 1997

Teaching mathematics to the new standards : relearning the dance / QA13.H43 2000

Teaching the majority : breaking the gender barrier in science, mathematics, and engineering / Q181.T3538 1995

Tech writer's survival guide : a comprehensive handbook for aspiring technical writers, The / T11.V368 2001

Technical communication in the age of the Internet / T10.5.R65 2002

Technical communication in the global community / T11.A515 2001

Technical communication, deliberative rhetoric, and environmental discourse : connections and directions / T10.5.T414 2000

Technical document basics for engineering technicians and technologists / T11.R565 2001

Technician's guide to electronic communications / TK5105.G68 1997

Technics and architecture : the development of materials and systems for buildings / TH18.E45 1992

Technique of organic chemistry. QD251.W3683

Techniques for wildlife habitat management of uplands / SK355.P39 1994

Techniques in nuclear structure physics QC786.E54

Techniques in underground mining : selections from Underground mining methods handbook / TN275.T33 1998

Techniques of problem solving / QA63.K73 1997

Technobabble / QA76.9.C66.B375 1991

Technohistory : using the history of American technology in ' interdisciplinary research / T21.T38 1996

Technological transformation of China, The / T27.C5.M33 1989

Technological transformation of Japan : from the seventeenth to the twenty-first century, The / T27.A3.M67 1994

Technology 2001 : the future of computing and communications / QA76.9.C66.T34 1991

Technology and culture; an anthology. T15.K7

Technology and power / T14.5.K57 1990

Technology and privacy : the new landscape / QA76.9.A25.T43 1997

Technology and the politics of knowledge / T14.T387 1995

Technology in America : a brief history / T21.M372 1999

Technology in world civilization : a thousand-year history / T15.P353 1990

Technology management handbook, The / T49.5.T4454 1999

Technology policy and America's future / T21.I76 1993

Technology's past / T21.K55 1996

Technoscientific angst : ethics + responsibility / T14.S268 1997

Telecommunication system engineering / TK5103.F68 1996

Telecommunication transmission systems : microwave, fiber optic, mobile cellular radio, data, and digital multiplexing / TK5101.W48 1993

Telecommunications handbook, The / TK5101.T355 2000

Telegraph : a history of Morse's invention and its predecessors in the United States, The / TK5115.C54 1993

Television engineering handbook : featuring HDTV systems / TK6642.T437 1992

Temperate agroforestry systems / S494.5.A45.T4625 1997

Temperate forage legumes / SB203.F735 1998

Temperature measurement / QC271.M483 1991

Tensor analysis, theory and applications to geometry and mechanics of continua. QA433.S64 1964

Tensor calculus / QA433.S9 1969

Tent caterpillars, The / QL561.L3.F58 1995

Terraforming : engineering planetary environments / TL795.7.F64 1995

Terrestrial ecoregions of North America : a conservation assessment / QH77.N56.T47 1999

Terrestrial ecosystems in changing environments / QH541.15.M3.S56 1998

Terrestrial ecosystems through time : evolutionary paleoecology of terrestrial plants and animals / QE720.T47 1992

Terrestrial Eocene-Oligocene transition in North America, The / QE692.8.T47 1996

Terrestrial invasion : an ecophysiological approach to the origins of land animals, The / QH371.L58 1990

Terrestrial slugs : biology, ecology, and control / QL430.4.S66 1992

Text algorithms / QA76.9.T48.C76 1994

Text, ConText, and HyperText : writing with and for the computer / QA76.9.D6.T48 1988

Textbook of arthropod anatomy, A / QL434.S43 1965

Textbook of dendrology / QK110.T48 1996

Textbook of graph theory, A / QA166.B25 2000

Textbook of physiology, A/ QP31.F8 1955

Textile chemistry. / TS1449.P45

Textile handbook. / TS1445.A46 1974

Textiles in America, 1650-1870 : a dictionary based on original documents : prints and paintings, commercial records, American merchants' papers, shopkeepers' advertisements, and pattern books with TS1767.M66 1984

Texture of industry : an archaeological view of the industrialization of North America, The / T21.G67 1994

Thallium in the environment / TD196.T45.T43 1998

Theater of nature : Jean Bodin and Renaissance science, The / Q125.2.B53 1997

Theoretical acoustics QC225.M67 1968

Theoretical and physical principles of organic reactivity / QD476.P755 1995

Theoretical aspects of object-oriented programming : types, semantics, and language design / QA76.64.T49 1994

Theoretical concepts in physics : an alternative view of theoretical reasoning in physics for final-year undergraduates / QC20.L66 1984

Theoretical models in biology : the origin of life, the immune system, and the brain / QP406.R677 1994

Theories of everything : the quest for ultimate explanation / Q175.B225 1991

Theories of light: from Descartes to Newton QC401.S3

Theories of the universe; from Babylonian myth to modern science. / QB981.M9

Theory and applications of partial differential equations / QA377.B295 1997

Theory and applications of ultraviolet spectroscopy/ QD95.J24

Theory and criticism of virtual texts, The : an annotated bibliography, 1988-1999 / QA76.9.H85

Theory and design of bridges / TG300.X36 1994

Theory and evidence : the development of scientific reasoning / Q175.32.R45.K67 1996

Theory of algebraic invariants / QA201.H716 1993

Theory of atomic collisions, The, QC721.M88 1965

Theory of atomic spectra, The, QC454.C64

Theory of computational complexity / QA267.7.D8 2000

Theory of differential equations. QA371.F72

Theory of elasticity / QA931.L283 1986, QA931.T55 1970

Theory of electromagnetism, The. / QC670.J63 1964

Theory of electrons and its applications to the phenomena of light and radiant heat , The; / QC721.L88

Theory of games and economic behavior, QA269.V65 1953

Theory of garden art / SB454.3.P45

War and nature : fighting humans and insects with chemicals from World War I to Silent spring / QH545.C48

Warblers of the Americas : an identification guide / QL696.P2438.C87 1994b

Warm climates in earth history / QC884.W37 2000

Was Einstein right? : putting general relativity to the test / QC173.6.W55 1986

Waste containment systems, waste stabilization, and landfills : design and evaluation / TD793.S43 1994

Waste management / TD791.B5613 1996

Waste trading among rich nations : building a new theory of environmental regulation / TD1030.O72 2000

Wastewater treatment : biological and chemical processes / TD745.W362 1995

Watch the skies! : a chronicle of the flying saucer myth / TL789.3.P44 1994

Watchers of the skies: an informal history of astronomy from Babylon to the space age. QB15.L4

Watching the world's weather / QC879.5.B87 1990

Water & wastewater treatment : a guide for the nonengineering professional / TD430.D764 2001

Water / QD169.W3

Water for urban areas : challenges and perspectives / TD345.W2625 2000

Water quality : prevention, identification, and management of diffuse pollution / TD420.N69 1994

Water quality and availability : a reference handbook / TD223.M53 1992

Water supply planning / TD353.P7 1994

Water use, management, and planning in the United States / TD223.T527 1999

Water, engineering, and landscape : water control and landscape transformation in the modern period / TC18.W38 1990

Waterfields guide to computer software / QA76.754.W377 2000

Waterfowl : an identification guide to the ducks, geese, and swans of the world / QL696.A52.M33 1988

Waterfowl ecology and management / QL696.A52.B335 1994

Water-resources engineering / TC145.L55 1979

Wave motion / QA927.B25 2000

Wave physics : oscillations--solitons--chaos / QC157.N48 1995

Waveforms, QC601.C5

Wavelet methods for time series analysis / QA280.P47 2000

Wavelets : a primer / QA403.3.B5713 1998

Way things work; an illustrated encyclopedia of technology, The / T47.V35

Ways of knowing : a new history of science, technology, and medicine / Q125.P595 2001

Ways of the world : a history of the world's roads and of the vehicles that used them / TA1015.L39 1992

We seven, / TL789.8.U6.M59

Weather / QC981.B33 1985

Weather almanac, The. / QC983.W38

Weather analysis and forecasting. / QC995.P52

Weather cycles : real or imaginary / QC883.2.C5.B87 1992

Weather from above : America's meteorological satellites / TL798.M4.H55 1991

Weather of U.S. cities / QC983.W393 1987

Weather pioneers : the Signal Corps station at Pikes Peak / QC875.U72.P557 1993

Weather revolution : innovations and imminent breakthroughs in accurate forecasting, The / QC995.F55 1994

Weather, climate & human affairs : a book of essays and other papers / QC981.4.L36 1988

Weathering : an introduction to the scientific principles / QE570.B5685 1998

Weaving the Web : the original design and ultimate destiny of the World Wide Web by its inventor / TK5105.888.B46 1999

Web style guide : basic design principles for creating web sites / TK5105.888.L96 1999

Web wisdom : how to evaluate and create information quality on the Web / TK5105.888.A376 1999

Weed science : principles and practices / SB611.M58 2001

Weegee / TR820.F45 1977

Wernher Von Braun : the man who sold the moon / TL781.85.V6.P57 1998

Wernher von Braun, crusader for space : a biographical memoir / TL781.85.V6.S78 1994

Westcott's plant disease handbook / SB731.W47 2001

Wetland creation and restoration : the status of the science / QH541.5.M3.W46 1990

Wetland ecology : principles and conservation / QH541.5.M3

Wetland plants : biology and ecology / QK938.M3C76 2001

Wetland soils : genesis, hydrology, landscapes, and classification / S592.17.H93

Wetlands / QH87.3.W46 1991, QH104.M57 2000

Wetlands : a threatened landscape / QH87.3.W47 1990

Whales and men, Of. SH381.R59

Whales of the world / QL737.C4.B67 1989

Whales, dolphins, and porpoises / QL737.C4.C28 1995

Whaling will never do for me : the American whaleman in the nineteenth century / SH383.2.B87 1994

What are the odds? : chance in everyday life / QA273.15.O75 1999

What computing is all about / QA76.6.S6163 1993

What counts : how every brain is hardwired for math / QA141.5.B786 1999

What do YOU care what other people think? : further adventures of a curious character / QC16.F49.A3 1988

What evolution is / QH366.2.M3933 2001

What gardens mean / SB457.6.R67 1998

What have we learned about science and technology from the Russian experience? / Q175.5.G73 1998

What is life? / QH325.M298 1995

What is life? the physical aspect of the living cell & Mind and matter. QH331.S3557

What is light? QC355.H533 1968

What is mathematics, really? / QA8.4.H47 1997

What is Mathematics? An elementary approach to ideas and methods, QA37.C675

What mad pursuit : a personal view of scientific discovery / QH31.C85.A3 1988

What makes airplanes fly? : history, science, and applications of aerodynamics / TL570.W4 1997

What makes nature tick? / QC21.2.N53 1993

What remains to be discovered : mapping the secrets of the universe, the origins of life, and the future of the human race / Q180.55.D57.M33 1998

What science is and how it works / Q158.5.D47 1999

What to solve? : problems and suggestions for young mathematicians / QA63.C64 1990

When cells die : a comprehensive evaluation of apoptosis and programmed cell death / QH671.W48 1998

When technology fails : significant technological disasters, accidents, and failures of the twentieth century / TA169.5.W44 1994

Where have all the wildflowers gone? : a region-by-region guide to threatened or endangered U.S. wildflowers / QK86.U6.M63 1983

Where is science going? / Q175.P57

Where the buffalo roam / QL84.22.G7.M37 1992

Whereby we thrive : a history of American farming, 1607-1972 / S441.S43

Whitehead's philosophy of science. / Q175.P33

White-tailed deer, The / QL737.U55.H54 1996

Whittington's dictionary of plastics. TP1110.W46 1993

Who succeeds in science? : the gender dimension / Q130.S66 1995

Who will do science? : educating the next generation / Q127.U6.W48 1994

Who will save the forests? : knowledge, power, and environmental destruction / SD411.W46 1993

Who wrote the book of life? : a history of the genetic code / QH450.2.K39 2000

Whole foods encyclopedia : a shopper's guide, The / TX369.W67 1988

# Title Index

Women's camera work : self/body/other in American visual culture / TR23.D38 1998

Wonderful life : the Burgess Shale and the nature of history / QE770.G67 1989

Wonders of numbers : adventures in math, mind, and meaning / QA95.P53 2001

Wood structure and identification / SD536.C67 1979

Words of light : theses on the photography of history / TR183.C33 1997

Words of mathematics : an etymological dictionary of mathematical terms used in English, The / QA5.S375 1994

Works. QA31.A692

World according to wavelets : the story of a mathematical technique in the making, The / QA403.3.H83 1998

World cattle, SF197.R68

World changes : Thomas Kuhn and the nature of science / Q175.3.W67 1993

World class quality : using design of experiments to make it happen / TS156.B563 1999

World deforestation in the twentieth century / SD418.W67 1988

World economic plants : a standard reference / SB107.W485 1999

World enough and space-time : absolute versus relational theories of space and time / QC173.59.S65.E17 1989

World guide to scientific associations = Internationales Verzeichnis wissenschaftlicher Verbande und Gesellschaften / Q10.W67 1982

World history of beekeeping and honey hunting, The / SF524.C738 1999

World history of photography, A / TR15.R67 1984

World list of mammalian species, A / QL708.C67 1991

World nuclear power / TK1078.M68 1990

World of butterflies and moths, The / QL542.K55

World of caffeine : the science and culture of the world's most popular drug, The / QP801.C24

World of catasetums, The / SB409.8.C36.H65 1999

World of Henri Cartier Bresson, The / TR650.C38

World of magnolias, The / SB413.M34.C34 1994

World of mathematics; a small library of the literature of mathematics from Ah-mose the scribe to Albert Einstein, The, QA3.N48

World of measurements : masterpieces, mysteries and muddles of metrology, The / QC88.K58

World of pastoralism : herding systems in comparative perspective, The / SF140.P38.W67 1990

World of physical chemistry, The / QD452.L35 1993

World of physics; readings in the nature, history, and challenge of physics, The. QC3.B4

World of scientific discovery. Q121.W676

World petroleum resources and reserves / TN870.R53 1983

World who's who in science: a biographical dictionary of notable scientists from antiquity to the present. / Q141.W7

World Wide Web for scientists & engineers : a complete reference for navigating, researching & publishing online, The Q179.97.T48 1998

Worlds in the sky : planetary discovery from earliest times through Voyager and Magellan / QB601.S543 1992

Worlds unnumbered : the search for extrasolar planets / QB820.G65 1997

World's whales : the complete illustrated guide, The / QL737.C4.M66 1984

Worlds within worlds : the story of nuclear energy / QC778.A85 1980

Writing reaction mechanisms in organic chemistry / QD251.2.M53 1992

Wyman's Gardening encyclopedia / SB450.95.W96 1986

X-ray analysis and the structure of organic molecules / QD945.D84 1979

X-ray spectroscopy : an introduction / QC482.S6.A34

X-rays : the first hundred years / QC481.X24 1996

Yardsticks of the universe / QC39.B57 1984

Yeager, an autobiography / TL540.Y4A38 1985

Yellowstone and the biology of time : photographs across a century / QH105.W6.M435 1998

Yellowstone primer : land and resource management in the greater Yellowstone ecosystem, The / QH105.W8.Y45 1990

Yellowstone vegetation : consequences of environment and history in a natural setting / QK195.D47 1990

Yes, we have no neutrons : an eye-opening tour through the twists and turns of bad science / Q172.5.E77.B48 1997

Yosemite : the embattled wilderness / QH105.C2.R86 1990

Yosemite and the range of light / TR660.5.A33

You are a mathematician : a wise and witty introduction to the joy of numbers / QA93.W385 1995

Young men & fire / SD421.32.M9.M33 1992

Your memory, a user's guide / QP406.B33 1982

Your private world; a study of intimate gardens, /SB473.C52

Zeolites of the world / QE391.Z5.T73 1992

Zipper : an exploration in novelty / T19.F75 1994

Zone system for 35mm photographers : a basic guide to exposure control, The / TR591.G73 1997

Zoogeography: the geographical distribution of animals. QL101.D3

Zoology of tapeworms, The / QL391.C4.W28 1968